A Companion to World War I

BLACKWELL COMPANIONS TO HISTORY

This series provides sophisticated and authoritative overviews of the scholarship that has shaped our current understanding of the past. Defined by theme, period and/or region, each volume comprises between twenty-five and forty concise essays written by individual scholars within their area of specialization. The aim of each contribution is to synthesize the current state of scholarship from a variety of historical perspectives and to provide a statement on where the field is heading. The essays are written in a clear, provocative, and lively manner, designed for an international audience of scholars, students, and general readers.

BLACKWELL COMPANIONS TO WORLD HISTORY

A Companion to Western Historical Thought
Edited by Lloyd Kramer and Sarah Maza

A Companion to Gender History
Edited by Teresa A. Meade and Merry E. Wiesner-Hanks

A Companion to International History 1900–2001
Edited by Gordon Martel

A Companion to the History of the Middle East
Edited by Youssef M. Choueiri

A Companion to Japanese History
Edited by William M. Tsutsui

A Companion to Latin American History
Edited by Thomas Holloway

A Companion to Russian History
Edited by Abbott Gleason

A Companion to World War I
Edited by John Horne

BLACKWELL COMPANIONS TO BRITISH HISTORY

A Companion to Roman Britain
Edited by Malcolm Todd

A Companion to Britain in the Later Middle Ages
Edited by S. H. Rigby

A Companion to Tudor Britain
Edited by Robert Tittler and Norman Jones

A Companion to Stuart Britain
Edited by Barry Coward

A Companion to Eighteenth-Century Britain
Edited by H. T. Dickinson

A Companion to Nineteenth-Century Britain
Edited by Chris Williams

A Companion to Early Twentieth-Century Britain
Edited by Chris Wrigley

A Companion to Contemporary Britain
Edited by Paul Addison and Harriet Jones

A Companion to the Early Middle Ages: Britain and Ireland c.500-c.1100
Edited by Pauline Stafford

BLACKWELL COMPANIONS TO EUROPEAN HISTORY

A Companion to Europe 1900–1945
Edited by Gordon Martel

A Companion to Eighteenth-Century Europe
Edited by Peter H. Wilson

A Companion to Nineteenth-Century Europe
Edited by Stefan Berger

A Companion to the Worlds of the Renaissance
Edited by Guido Ruggiero

A Companion to the Reformation World
Edited by R. Po-chia Hsia

A Companion to Europe Since 1945
Edited by Klaus Larres

A Companion to the Medieval World
Edited by Carol Lansing and Edward D. English

BLACKWELL COMPANIONS TO AMERICAN HISTORY

A Companion to the American Revolution
Edited by Jack P. Greene and J. R. Pole

A Companion to 19th-Century America
Edited by William L. Barney

A Companion to the American South
Edited by John B. Boles

A Companion to American Indian History
Edited by Philip J. Deloria and Neal Salisbury

A Companion to American Women's History
Edited by Nancy A. Hewitt

A Companion to Post-1945 America
Edited by Jean-Christophe Agnew and Roy Rosenzweig

A Companion to the Vietnam War
Edited by Marilyn B. Young and Robert Buzzanco

A Companion to Colonial America
Edited by Daniel Vickers

A Companion to 20th-Century America
Edited by Stephen J. Whitfield

A Companion to the American West
Edited by William Deverell

A Companion to American Foreign Relations
Edited by Robert D. Schulzinger

A Companion to the Civil War and Reconstruction
Edited by Lacy K. Ford

A Companion to American Technology
Edited by Carroll Pursell

A Companion to African-American History
Edited by Alton Hornsby, Jr

A Companion to American Immigration
Edited by Reed Ueda

A COMPANION TO WORLD WAR I

Edited by

John Horne

A John Wiley & Sons, Ltd., Publication

This edition first published 2010
© 2010 Blackwell Publishing Ltd

Blackwell Publishing was acquired by John Wiley & Sons in February 2007. Blackwell's publishing program has been merged with Wiley's global Scientific, Technical, and Medical business to form Wiley-Blackwell.

Registered Office
John Wiley & Sons Ltd, The Atrium, Southern Gate, Chichester, West Sussex, PO19 8SQ, United Kingdom

Editorial Offices
350 Main Street, Malden, MA 02148-5020, USA
9600 Garsington Road, Oxford, OX4 2DQ, UK
The Atrium, Southern Gate, Chichester, West Sussex, PO19 8SQ, UK

For details of our global editorial offices, for customer services, and for information about how to apply for permission to reuse the copyright material in this book please see our website at www.wiley.com/wiley-blackwell.

The right of John Horne to be identified as the author of the editorial material in this work has been asserted in accordance with the UK Copyright, Designs and Patents Act 1988.

Library of Congress Cataloging-in-Publication Data

A companion to World War I / edited by John Horne.
    p. cm. – (Blackwell companions to world history)
  Includes bibliographical references and index.
  ISBN 978-1-4051-2386-0 (hardcover : alk. paper)   1. World War, 1914–1918.   2. World War, 1914–1918–Social aspects.   I. Horne, John, 1949–
  D521.C5835 2010
  940.3–dc22

                                                        2009042570

A catalogue record for this book is available from the British Library.

Set in 10/12pt Galliard by SPi Publisher Services, Pondicherry, India
Printed and bound in Malaysia by Vivar Printing Sdn Bhd

I   2010

Contents

List of Maps   viii
Notes on Contributors   ix
Editor's Acknowledgments   xv

Introduction   xvi
John Horne

PART I ORIGINS   **1**

1 The War Imagined: 1890–1914   3
    Gerd Krumeich

2 The War Explained: 1914 to the Present   19
    John F. V. Keiger

PART II THE MILITARY CONFLICT   **33**

3 The War Experienced: Command, Strategy, and Tactics, 1914–18   35
    Hew Strachan

4 War in the West, 1914–16   49
    Holger H. Herwig

5 War in the East and Balkans, 1914–18   66
    Dennis Showalter

6 The Italian Front, 1915–18   82
    Giorgio Rochat

7 The Turkish War, 1914–18   97
    Ulrich Trumpener

8 The War in Africa   112
    David Killingray

9   War in the West, 1917–18   127
    Robin Prior and Trevor Wilson

10 The War at Sea   141
    Paul G. Halpern

11 The War in the Air   156
    John H. Morrow, Jr.

PART III FACES OF WAR   **171**

12 Combat   173
    Stéphane Audoin-Rouzeau

13 Combatants and Noncombatants: Atrocities, Massacres, and War Crimes   188
    Alan Kramer

14 War Aims and Neutrality   202
    Jean-Jacques Becker

15 Industrial Mobilization and War Economies   217
    Theo Balderston

16 Faith, Ideologies, and the "Cultures of War"   234
    Annette Becker

17 Demography   248
    Jay Winter

18 Women and Men   263
    Susan R. Grayzel

19 Public Opinion and Politics   279
    John Horne

20 Military Medicine   295
    Sophie Delaporte

21 Science and Technology   307
    Anne Rasmussen

22 Intellectuals and Writers   323
    Christophe Prochasson

23 The Visual Arts   338
    Annette Becker

24 Film and the War   353
    Pierre Sorlin

PART IV STATES, NATIONS, AND EMPIRES   **369**

25 Austria-Hungary and "Yugoslavia"   371
    Mark Cornwall

26 Belgium   386
    Sophie de Schaepdrijver

27 Britain and Ireland   403
    Adrian Gregory

28 France   418
    Leonard V. Smith

29 Germany   432
    Gerhard Hirschfeld

30 German-Occupied Eastern Europe   447
    Vejas Gabriel Liulevicius

31 Italy   464
    Antonio Gibelli

32 Russia   479
    Eric Lohr

33 The Ottoman Empire   494
    Hamit Bozarslan

34 The United States   508
    Jennifer D. Keene

35 The French and British Empires   524
    Robert Aldrich and Christopher Hilliard

PART V LEGACIES   **541**

36 The Peace Settlement, 1919–39   543
    Carole Fink

37 War after the War: Conflicts, 1919–23   558
    Peter Gatrell

38 Mourning and Memory, 1919–45   576
    Laurence Van Ypersele

    Select Primary Sources   591
    Extended Bibliography   601
    Index   634

List of Maps

1 Europe at the outbreak of World War I   4

2 The western front, 1914–18   50

3 The eastern front, 1914–17   67

4 The Austro-Italian front, 1915–18   83

5 The Ottoman Empire, 1914–18   98

6 Africa in World War I   113

7 Occupied Europe, 1914–18   448

8 Europe after World War I   544

Notes on Contributors

Robert Aldrich is Professor of European History at the University of Sydney. Among his works in colonial history are *Greater France: A History of French Overseas Expansion* (1996) and *Vestiges of the Colonial Empire in France: Monuments, Museums and Colonial Memories* (2005). He was guest editor of an issue of *Outre-Mers* in 2006 on "Sites et moments de mémoire," and his edited collection, *Age of Empires*, was published in 2007.

Stéphane Audoin-Rouzeau is Director of Studies at the Ecole des Hautes Etudes en Sciences Sociales and president of the Research Centre at the Historial de la Grande Guerre, Péronne, France. His main area of interest is the history of World War I, and also the historical anthropology of the modern combatant. His publications include *Men at War. National Sentiment and Trench Journalism in France during the First World War* (1992), *Understanding the Great War* (with Annette Becker et al., 2002), *Encyclopédie de la Grande Guerre, 1914–1918* (edited with Jean-Jacques Becker, 2004), *Combattre. Une anthropologie historique de la guerre moderne, XIXe–XXIe siècle* (2008), and *Les armes et la chair. Trois objets de mort en 14–18* (2009).

Theo Balderston was Senior Lecturer in Economic History at the University of Manchester until his retirement in 2008. His publications include *Economics and Politics in the Weimar Republic* (2002) and the edited collection, *The World Economy and National Economies in the Interwar Slump* (Palgrave Macmillan, 2003).

Annette Becker is Professor of Modern History at the University of Paris Ouest Nanterre La Défense, and a member of the Institut Universitaire de France. She shares her activity between the Research Centre at the Historial de la Grande Guerre, Péronne, France and the Memorial de la Shoah, Paris. She has published widely on the history of the two world wars, including studies of intellectuals and artists. Recent publications include *Apollinaire, une biographie de guerre, 1914–1918* (2009), (with Stéphane Audoin-Rouzeau) *Understanding the Great War* (2002), and (with Leonard Smith and Stéphane Audoin-Rouzeau) *France and the Great War, 1914–1918* (2003).

Jean-Jacques Becker, born in 1928 in Paris, is Professor Emeritus of History at the University of Paris Ouest Nanterre La Défense. He has published essentially on World War I and on twentieth century French politics, especially communism. He co-authored (with Gerd

Krumeich) a Franco-German history of World War I (*La Grande Guerre. Une histoire franco-allemande*, 2008). He is Honorary President of the Research Centre of the Historial de la Grande Guerre, Péronne, France.

Hamit Bozarslan, Director of Studies at the Ecole des Hautes Etudes en Sciences Sociales, is currently working on the political and historical sociology of the Middle East. His recent publications include *Conflit kurde* (2009) and *Une histoire de la violence au Moyen-Orient* (2008).

Mark Cornwall is Professor of Modern European History at the University of Southampton and chair of the Forum of British, Czech and Slovak Historians. He specializes in modern East–central Europe, particularly the collapse of the Hapsburg Empire, the creation of Yugoslavia, and the Czech–German relationship in the Bohemian lands. Publications on these themes have included *The Undermining of Austria-Hungary* (2000), *The Last Years of Austria-Hungary* (2002), and (edited with R. J. W. Evans) *Czechoslovakia in a Nationalist and Fascist Europe* (2007).

Sophie Delaporte is Maître de Conférénces in the Faculty of Philosophy and Human and Social Sciences at the Université de Picardie Jules Verne, Amiens. She is the author of *Les Médecins dans la Grande Guerre* (2003) and *Gueules cassées de la Grande Guerre* (2004). She is a member of the Groupe d'Etudes Guerre et Médecine (Study Group on War and Medecine) and editor of the review *Guerre, médecine et trauma* on the website of the Bibliothèque Inter-Universitaire de Médecine. She is currently working on the medical history of wars since the mid-20th century and in particular on Vietnam, the 1973 Arab–Israeli conflict and the wars in the Falkands and Iraq.

Carole Fink, Distinguished Humanities Professor in History at The Ohio State University, and a specialist in European International History, is the author of three monographs, *Defending the Rights of Others: The Great Powers, the Jews, and International Minority Protection, 1878–1938* (2004), *The Genoa Conference: European Diplomacy, 1921–1922* (1984), both of which were awarded the George Louis Beer prize of the American Historical Association, and *Marc Bloch: A Life in History* (1989), which has been translated into five languages. She has edited six volumes and has written some fifty articles and chapters on contemporary European history.

Peter Gatrell is Professor of Economic History at the University of Manchester. He is the author of several books, including *A Whole Empire Walking: Refugees in Russia during World War 1* (1999; paperback 2005) and *Russia's First World War: A Social and Economic History* (2005). He is currently writing a book entitled *The Making of the Modern Refugee* and researching World Refugee Year, 1959–60. He also co-directs a collaborative research project on "Population displacement, state practice and social experience in Russia and Eastern Europe, 1930–1950s," one outcome of which was a special issue of *Contemporary European History* (November 2007). His ongoing interests in Russian economic history include studies of the pre-revolutionary fiscal system and a chapter on "Russia's Age of Economic Extremes, 1900–2000" in R. G. Duny (ed.), *Cambridge History of Russia*, Volume 3, *The Twentieth Century* (2006).

Antonio Gibelli is Professor of Modern History at the University of Genoa and founder of one of the most important centers in Italy for the study of personal writings by ordinary people, including letters of soldiers and prisoners of war during World War I. His publications include: *L'Officina della Guerra: La Grande Guerra e le trasformazioni del* *mondo mentale* (1991, new ed. 2007); *La Grande Guerra degli Italiani* (1998, new ed. 2006); and *Il Popolo bambino: infanzia e nazione dalla Grande Guerra a Salò* (2005). Additionally, he edited *La Prima Guerra Mondiale* (2007), the Italian edition of the *Encyclopédie de la Grande Guerre*, ed. Stéphane Audoin-Rouzeau and Jean-Jacques Becker et al. (2004).

Susan R. Grayzel teaches modern European history at the University of Mississippi. She is the author of two books, *Women's Identities at War: Gender, Motherhood, and Politics in Britain and France during the First World War* (1999), which was awarded the British Council Prize in 2000, and *Women and the First World War* (2002), a global history. Her most recent book project (coedited with Philippa Levine) is *Gender, Labour, War and Empire: Essays on Modern Britain* (2009).

Adrian Gregory is Lecturer in Modern History at Pembroke College, University of Oxford. His previous publications include *The Silence of Memory: Armistice Day, 1919–1946* (1994); as editor, with Senia Paseta, *A War to Unite Us All: Ireland and the Great War* (2002) and most recently, *The Last Great War. British Society and the First World War* (2008).

Paul Halpern is Professor Emeritus at Florida State University, Tallahassee and specializes in twentieth-century naval history. His publications include *The Mediterranean Naval Situation, 1908–1914* (1971), *The Naval War in the Mediterranean, 1914–1918* (1987), *A Naval History of World War I* (1994), *Anton Haus: Österreich-Ungarns Großadmiral* (1998) and *The Battle of the Otranto Straits* (2004). He has edited four volumes for the Navy Records Society, including the *Keyes Papers* (1972–81), and is currently editing two volumes on the Mediterranean Fleet, 1919–39.

Holger H. Herwig is Professor of History and Canada Research Chair in the Centre for Military and Strategic Studies at the University of Calgary. He has published widely on nineteenth- and twentieth-century Germany. His most recent books include *The Marne, 1914*, *War Planning, 1914*, and (with Michael Keren), *War, Memory and Popular Culture* (all 2009).

Christopher Hilliard is a senior lecturer in history at the University of Sydney. He is the author of *To Exercise Our Talents: The Democratization of Writing in Britain* (Harvard, 2006).

Gerhard Hirschfeld is Director of the Bibliothek für Zeitgeschichte/Library of Contemporary History and Professor of Modern European History at the University of Stuttgart. His publications include numerous books and articles on the history of both world wars as well as on the history of the Netherlands in the twentieth century. He coedited (with Gerd Krumeich and Irina Renz) the international *Enzyklopädie Erster Weltkrieg* (2003, revised edition 2009, English edition forthcoming) and *Die Deutschen an der Somme. Krieg, Besatzung, Verbrannte Erde* (2006), which also appeared in Dutch and English.

John Horne is Professor of Modern European History at Trinity College, Dublin, and a member of the Research Centre at the Historial de la Grande Guerre, Péronne, France. He has published widely on the history of World War I and of twentieth-century France, including *Labour at War: France and Britain, 1914–1918* (1991), (ed.) *State, Society and Mobilization in Europe during the First World War* (1997) and (with Alan Kramer), *German Atrocities, 1914: A History of Denial* (2001), which has appeared in French and German.

Jennifer D. Keene is Professor of History and Chair at Chapman University, southern California. She is the author of three books on American involvement in World War I, *Doughboys, the Great War and the Remaking of America* (2001), *The United States and the First World War* (2000), and *World War I* (2006). A recipient of numerous fellowships, including Fulbright awards to Australia and France, she is currently completing a project on African American soldiers' experiences during World War I.

John Keiger is Professor of International History and Director of the European Studies Research Institute at the University of Salford. He is the author of *France and the Origins of the First World War* (1983), *Raymond Poincaré* (1997), *France and the World since 1870* (2001) and editor of 19 volumes of *British Documents on Foreign Affairs: Reports and Papers from the Foreign Office Confidential Print* (1989–91). He has been a Visiting Professor at several foreign universities, including the Institut d'Etudes Politiques in Paris in 2003.

David Killingray is Professor Emeritus at Goldsmiths College, and a Senior Research Fellow at the Institute of Commonwealth Studies, University of London. He is the author of books and articles on aspects of African, Caribbean, imperial, and English local history, and also on the black Diaspora. His most recent book, *Fighting for Britain: African Soldiers in the Second World War*, is forthcoming.

Alan Kramer is Professor of European History at Trinity College Dublin. He has published on the British occupation of Germany, 1945–50, on the West German economy 1945–55, and on the history of World War I. Recent publications include *Dynamic of Destruction. Culture and Mass Killing in the First World War* (2007) and (with John Horne) *German Atrocities 1914: A History of Denial*, 2001 (German translation, 2004; French translation, 2005). He is currently working on the history of Italian prisoners of war during World War I, and a major project on the "International History of Concentration Camps," funded by a grant from the Irish Research Council for the Humanities and Social Sciences.

Gerd Krumeich is Professor of Modern History at the University of Düsseldorf. He was educated at the universities of Innsbruck, Göttingen, Paris, Cologne, and Düsseldorf and was Professor of the History of Western Europe at the University of Freiburg. His publications include *Armaments and Politics in France on the Eve of the First World War* (1980; English ed. 1984) and (with Jean-Jacques Becker), *La Grande Guerre: une histoire franco-allemande* (2008). Together with Gerhard Hirschfeld and Irina Renz, he edited the *Enzyklopädie Erster Weltkrieg* (2003, revised edition 2009, English edition forthcoming), the major German reference work on World War I. He is Vice-president of the Research Centre of the Historial de la Grande Guerre, Péronne, France.

Vejas Gabriel Liulevicius is Associate Professor of Modern European History at the University of Tennessee, Knoxville. He has published *War Land on the Eastern Front: Culture, National Identity, and German Occupation in World War I* (2000), which also appeared in German translation, and *The German Myth of the East: 1800 to the Present* (2009).

Eric Lohr is the author of *Nationalizing the Russian Empire: The Campaign Against Enemy Aliens during World War I* (2003) and *The Papers of Grigorii Nikolaevich Trubetskoi* (2006), and editor (with Marshall Poe) of *Military and Society in Russian History, 1450–1917* (2002). His current book projects include a study of citizenship in imperial and revolutionary Russia and a history of World War I and the end of the

Russian Empire. He is founder and chair of the Washington Russian History Workshop, held monthly at Georgetown University. He received his MA in Russian Studies and PhD in history from Harvard University, then taught there as an assistant professor of history (2000–3). He is currently an assistant professor of history at American University, Washington DC.

John H. Morrow, Jr. is Franklin Professor of History at the University of Georgia. He specializes in the history of modern Europe and of war and society. He is the author of *The Great War: An Imperial History* (2004), *The Great War in the Air: Military Aviation from 1909 to 1921* (1993), *German Air Power in World War I* (1982), and *Building German Air Power, 1909–1914* (1976), and edited *A Yankee Ace in the RAF: The World War I Letters of Captain Bogart Rogers* (1996).

Robin Prior graduated in history at the University of Adelaide and lectured in the Australian Defence Force Academy, before becoming head of the School of Humanities and Social Sciences at ADFA (part of the University of New South Wales). He has published *Churchill's 'World Crisis' as History* (1983) and is currently preparing a book on the Dardanelles conflict, 1915. He has also coauthored four books with Trevor Wilson: *Command on the Western Front* (2004), *Passchendaele: the Untold Story* (1998; new ed. 2002), *The First World War* (1999; new ed. 2006), and *The Somme* (2005).

Christophe Prochasson is Director of Studies in Modern French History at the Ecole des Hautes Études en Sciences Sociales (EHESS), Paris. He has published widely on the cultural and political history of nineteenth- and twentieth-century France. On World War I he has published *Vrai et faux dans la Grande Guerre* (with Anne Rasmussen, 2004) and, more recently, *Sortir de la Grande Guerre: Le monde et l'après 1918* (edited with Stéphane Audoin-Rouzeau, 2008). He has also published *14–18. Retours d'expériences* (2008).

Anne Rasmussen is a historian, Maître de conférences at the University of Strasbourg, and a member of the Research Centre at the Historial de la Grande Guerre, Péronne, France. Her research focuses on the cultural and social history of science in the nineteenth and twentieth centuries. She is the author of articles on the scientific, medical, and intellectual aspects of World War I, and has published (with Christophe Prochasson), *Au nom de la patrie. Les intellectuels et la Première Guerre mondiale, 1910–1919* (1996) and *Vrai et faux dans la Grande Guerre* (2004).

Giorgio Rochat specializes in military, colonial, and political history from Italian unification (1861) to World War II. He was Professor of Modern History and then History of Military Institutions at the University of Milan (1969), Ferrara (1976) and Turin (1980–2005). His most recent works include (with Mario Isnenghi) *La Grande Guerra 1914–1918* (2000, 2008) and *Le guerre italiane 1935–1943* (2005).

Sophie De Schaepdrijver teaches modern European history at Pennsylvania State University. She is a member of the Scientific Councils of the Research Centre of the Historial de la Grande Guerre, Péronne, and of the In Flanders Fields Museum, Ypres, Belgium, and of the editorial board of the journal *First World War Studies*. She has published widely on Belgium in World War I, with specific reference to military occupation (*La Belgique et la Première Guerre Mondiale* (1997, 2004). Her latest book is a study of transnational experiences of occupation, *'We who are so Cosmopolitan': the War Diary of Constance Graeffe, 1914–1915* (2008).

Leonard V. Smith is Frederick B. Artz Professor of History at Oberlin College, Ohio. His books include *Between Mutiny and Obedience: The Case of the French Fifth Infantry Division during World War* I (1994), (with Stéphane Audoin-Rouzeau and Annette Becker) *France and the Great War* (2003), and *The Embattled Self. French Soldiers' Testimonies of the Great War* (2007).

Dennis Showalter is Professor of History at Colorado College and Past President of the Society for Military History. Joint Editor of War in History, he specializes in comparative military history. His recent monographs include *The Wars of Frederick the Great* (1996); *The Wars of German Unification* (2004), and *Patton and Rommel: Men of War in the Twentieth Century* (2005).

Pierre Sorlin is Professor Emeritus of Film Studies at the University of Paris III-Sorbonne Nouvelle and research fellow at the Historical Institute Ferruccio Parri in Bologna. Among his publications on film and history are *European Cinemas, European Societies, 1939–1990* (1991) and *Italian National Cinema, 1896–1996* (1996).

Hew Strachan is Chichele Professor of the History of War at Oxford, and a Fellow of All Souls College. His books include *The First World War: To Arms* (2001), the first volume of a projected trilogy, and *The First World War: a New Illustrated History* (2003) which was linked to the major Channel 4 series on World War I, broadcast in ten parts in 2003.

Ulrich Trumpener is Professor Emeritus of History at the University of Alberta, Edmonton, Canada. Since 1960 he has published extensively on German policies in the Middle East, on the Prussian army, and on various military and naval operations during World War I. His most recent research papers, on Max Hoffmann and Konstantin Schmidt von Knobelsdorf, appeared in *Chief of Staff*, ed. David T. Zabecki (2 vols., 2008).

Trevor Wilson is Professor Emeritus of History at the University of Adelaide. He is a graduate of Auckland University and of Oxford University, and became a lecturer in history in Adelaide in 1960. His books include *The Downfall of the Liberal Party 1914–1935, The Political Diaries of C P Scott 1911–1928*, and *The Myriad Faces of War: Britain and the Great War 1914–1918*. He has also coauthored four books with Robin Prior: *Command on the Western Front* (2004), *Passchendaele: The Untold Story* (1998), *The First World War* (1999), and *The Somme* (2005).

Jay Winter teaches history at Yale University. Educated at Columbia and Cambridge universities, he taught for many years at Pembroke College, Cambridge. He is the author of *Sites of Memory, Sites of Mourning: The Great War in European Cultural History* (1995) and is general editor of the forthcoming *Cambridge History of the First World War*.

Laurence Van Ypersele is Professor of History at the Catholic University of Louvain. Her books include a study of the kingship of Albert I of Belgium, *Le Mythe du roi Albert, 1909–1934* (1995; reedited in 2006), a history of espionage in Belgium during World War I (with Emmanuel Debruyne), *De la Guerre de l'ombre aux ombres de la guerre. L'espionnage de 14–18 en Belgique occupée* (2004) and (ed.), *Imaginaires de guerre: l'histoire entre mythe et réalité* (2003). She is interested in political imagery, national heroes, and collective identities, and the history of World War I in Belgium. She is a member of the Executive Committee of the Research Centre of the Historial de la Grande Guerre, Péronne.

Editor's Acknowledgments

It is perhaps not surprising that a volume with forty contributors has taken a long time to produce. It is even less surprising that as editor, in completing it, I should be acutely aware of just how collaborative such an undertaking is and how much I owe to the many people who have helped me. Christopher Wheeler first proposed the idea. It seemed exciting to me then, as it still does now, and I thank him for it. My thirty-nine fellow authors have been a model of tolerance, good humor, and collegiality. I have been acutely aware of the responsibility of editing and publishing their work, and I hope they feel that the finished volume is adequate reward for their patience. The price of inviting the top scholars in a truly international field to contribute to a book such as this is translation. But the price of translation is skill and fluency so that the reader should have the impression of reading native English. Twelve chapters were translated, nearly a third of the total, from three languages, and I would like to acknowledge the abilities and dedication of my fellow translators, Heather Jones, Mark Jones, Helen McPhail, and Paul O'Brien. I should also like to thank the Grace Lawless Lee Fund of Trinity College Dublin, which helped fund the cost of the translations. Chartwell Illustrators were painstaking in their production of the maps and must be thanked too. I have been fortunate since the outset in my editors at Wiley-Blackwell - Tessa Harvey, Gillian Kane, Helen Lawton, and Hannah Rolls. However, over the last year, my production editor, Tom Bates, and my copy editor, Juanita Bullough, have been truly outstanding. They have thrown me more life-lines than any editor or author has a right to expect and always showed me exemplary courtesy and understanding. If they feel the result is worthwhile, I shall be very gratified. Finally, I would like to thank my wife, Michèle, and my daughters, Alannah and Chloë. Their love and support made the *Companion* possible, as so much else.

John Horne
Dublin, February 2010

Introduction

JOHN HORNE

From the moment it broke out, World War I proved something of an enigma. Few in 1914 doubted that it was an epoch-defining event of a kind not seen since the French Revolution. It was a European War, a "Great War" and even, for the Germans, a "World War," since it promised to make Germany a world power. Yet it was all these things and more in ways that confounded contemporary ideas of what *war* actually was – of how it should be waged and its likely results. The nature of that enigma and its implications for the societies concerned is the subject of this *Companion*. It is what made the Great War the seminal event of twentieth-century history.

In the European tradition, war was a powerful instrument of political change in which military campaigns and climactic battles produced results that bore some relationship to the intentions of those who fought them, endowing commanders with martial glory and giving warfare as an activity both cultural prestige and an aura of heroic masculinity. In the nineteenth century, an entire genre of military painting that drew approving crowds at art exhibitions and graced the pages of the illustrated press testified to this view of war. Even if European general staffs by the early twentieth century knew that industrialization had begun to reshape warfare, from logistics to firepower, they subordinated that knowledge to a view of battle in which the infantry still conducted victorious offensives and wars themselves remained relatively short. But the Great War spread to Africa and the Middle East and was fought across the oceans of the globe. It was ultimately determined by prolonged siege warfare on the western front and it killed between nine and ten million soldiers, the bulk of them Europeans. The shock was profound.

The shock came not only from the transformation of war, with which the industrial age seemed at last to have caught up, and of the place of warfare in European culture, it also arose from the rupture between intention and outcome. The disparity between what caused the war (however this was viewed) and what the war in turn caused was the heart of the matter. In a previous climacteric of the European state system from 1789 to 1815, revolution was the explosive charge that altered war along with so much else. In 1914–18, by contrast, war was the great transformer that reshaped everything in its image, including revolution. In many respects war *was* the revolution, and this helps explain the gulf between intention and outcome. Those who led their states into the conflict were often conservatives who sought to shore up a dynasty and social system – sometimes by defending the diplomatic status quo, sometimes by changing it, but with the aim of preserving the world as they knew it. It is not just that defeat saw them ousted or exiled but that their worlds were shattered. Tsar Nicholas II and his family were shot in a sordid cellar by the Bolsheviks. Kaiser Wilhelm II fled ignominiously to Holland leaving Berlin in the throes of revolution. The young Karl I, last Habsburg emperor, slipped into exile as the Dual Monarchy dissolved into the nation-states it had been designed to avoid. And this time, unlike in 1815, there was no Restoration. The gulf between intention and outcome has rarely been greater.

With hindsight we can identify deeper patterns that connected cause with effect in ways that begin to make sense of the enigma. The process by which nation-states became the organizing unit of European politics culminated in World War I – which is why the current map of Europe looks rather similar to that of the 1920s (with some obvious exceptions). Nation-state formation had accelerated in the wake of the French Revolution and supplied some of the key events (and wars) of nineteenth-century Europe, notably the unification of Italy and Germany and the emergence of successor states to the Ottoman Empire – Greece, Romania, Bulgaria, Serbia. The Great War was triggered by the conflict between a small but expansionist Serbia and the Dual Monarchy of Austria-Hungary, which since 1867 had been organized around the containment of nationalist aspirations within the Habsburg territories. Russia, despite being a multiethnic empire that found it hard to reconcile nationalism and democracy with the Romanov dynasty at home, championed "Slav" nations like Serbia abroad and was drawn into the quarrel. Germany since 1871 had become the most powerful nation-state in Europe. It made the survival of the Dual Monarchy the key to its diplomatic and military plans, and played a pivotal role in July 1914.

At this level World War I enacted the final, doomed defense of the dynastic multinational empires, all of which (Austria-Hungary, Tsarist Russia, and Ottoman Turkey) were defeated and replaced by nation-states. In fact, by an irony of history, the creed of the proletarian revolution, Bolshevism, provided the new bond to maintain the bulk of the Romanov lands in a federation of nations around their Russian core. But as that example shows, the war represented much more than the completion of an essentially nineteenth-century process. The war itself helped redefine the nation where it existed as well as where it was coming into being (as in Ireland and Eastern Europe). One revelation of the conflict was the potency of national identities and national communities. To be sure, this was well known in the longest established nations, such as Britain and France, but even there universal literacy, the mass press, electoral politics, and more inclusive notions of what it meant to be a subject or citizen were relatively recent and evolving processes. Elsewhere, as in Russia, Austria-Hungary, or even Germany, such developments were seen by many in power as potentially subversive. Yet identification with the nation explains why the outbreak of war in 1914 was not met with the protest and obstruction that Socialists and labour militants had long predicted but rather with a surprising degree of cohesion, though this was far removed from the mindless chauvinism of subsequent myth.

National cohesiveness could not be sustained in that form. The war forced societies into unprecedented and largely unanticipated patterns of activity and organization. Prewar opinion had in the main held that the sheer disruption occasioned by a war (as economic production halted and the bulk of adult men left for the armies) was one good reason why it could not last very long. But as it turned out, societies displayed a remarkable capacity to improvise and adapt. Women replaced men in many functions while continuing to sustain the couple and the family through the trials of separation. The mobilization of industry for war production reconstituted the working class (including skilled workers summoned back from the front) and pioneered new relations between the state, organized labor, and business. Food had to be farmed more intensively than ever or substitutes found abroad to sustain both soldiers and civilians, while the essential fuels without which neither war production nor daily life could continue also had to be secured. In World War II, the lessons of the earlier experience were there to be drawn on. But in World War I the need to harness society and the state to war on the scale that became necessary was one more disjuncture between anticipation and reality.

Each of the adaptations in question held major implications for the communities fighting the war since they raised issues of equity and sacrifice and affected relations between different social groups. Conflicts arose along lines of class as workers gained unlooked-for strength, and ethnicity as national groups related variously to the war, especially within the multinational dynastic empires. Gender was also affected as women consciously assumed a role in the national effort while men faced the ultimate sacrifice of death from battle. This multiple effort shaped the nations that fought the war or resulted from it. As a community of experience and as a source of political legitimacy, the nation-state in Europe was transformed by World War I.

Nowhere was this truer than in relation to the core experience of the conflict, industrialized warfare. For the enigma within the enigma was the discrepancy between the requirement of victory and the means of achieving it. Not only was the prewar conception of battle profoundly at odds with the force of modern firepower that resulted in a million dead on all fronts by early 1915, but the warfare that emerged in response to this was marked by the superiority of the defensive over the offensive. Solving the conundrum took the next four years, and the answer that emerged was a matter of trial and error in a thousand different ways rather than one grand plan or a decisive technical transformation. Historians still debate what caused the collapse of the Central Powers (Germany and its Austro-Hungarian, Bulgarian, and Ottoman allies). But the dominance of the defensive proved the distinctive experience of World War I in the sense meant by Carl von Clausewitz in his classic work, *On War*, when he noted that "every age has its own kind of war, its own limiting conditions, and its own peculiar preconceptions."[1]

It is important not to reduce this characteristic of the Great War to the western front as such, and to the all-too familiar images of trench warfare and bloody futility that have provided some of the most enduring stereotypes of the conflict. The war was fought on other fronts, between the Central Powers and Russia in the East (Galicia, Poland, the Baltic states, and the Ukraine), between Russia and Ottoman Turkey in the Caucasus, and between the Western Allies and the Turks in the ill-fated Gallipoli campaign of 1915. The French and British confronted the Bulgarians on an immobile front in Macedonia. Italy entered the conflict against Austria-Hungary in 1915 (precisely to complete the nation forged in the wars of unification) and opened up a front around the rim of the Alps and on the plains of the Veneto that cost 600,000 Italian dead by 1918. Romania joined the Entente in autumn 1916 but was rapidly subdued by the Central Powers. Moreover, as a global and imperial conflict, the war spawned secondary theaters in Africa (where the German colonial empire was eventually liquidated) and in the Ottoman Middle East (Mesopotamia and Palestine). Deep in the background, the maritime war was a relentless struggle for control over international supplies of war materials and food that pitted the British blockade of German-occupied Europe against German efforts to break Allied supply lines by means of the U-boat campaign. Along with the birth of aerial warfare, which provided a "third dimension" to the battlefield and an independent arm as bombing the enemy's homeland became possible, these theaters and forms of combat were all part of the "kind of war" 1914–18 turned out to be.

Yet the deadlock of trench warfare and the costly experimentation with ways to break it constituted the heart of the conflict in military terms. It found its most chronic expression in France and Belgium, where three major powers, Britain, France, and Germany (and the colonial contingents of the former two), suffered the bulk of their casualties. But it was replicated in near-identical forms on the Austro-Italian front and in distant Gallipoli and Macedonia. On the eastern front sparse communications and vast distances made sudden breakthrough more likely (leading to the massive capture of prisoners); but even here, new trench lines restabilized and the decisive battle proved as elusive as elsewhere.[2] More mobile warfare in Africa and the Middle East was a refraction of the deadlock in Europe – either allowed by the latter (as with the conquest of Germany's African colonies) or an attempt to unlock it, as with the efforts to eliminate Turkey and take the Central Powers by the back door.

In the end, the defensive advantage of the enemy could only be resolved in Europe and, after Bolshevik Russia quit the war in 1917, on the western front. While High Commands innovated and learned from each other, the process was hesitant and hampered by the weight of traditional thinking on strategy and tactics. Consequently, the soldiers experienced a mix of growing mastery of the battlefield, continued high casualties in many sectors of the front, and catastrophic episodes when a predicted successful offensive subsided yet again into a brutal logic of attrition. We must be careful not to attribute our own sensitivities to a different age: it is hard to imagine a current western public accepting a daily death-rate of 1,306 for four and a half years, as was the case in Germany, or 881 and 582, respectively, for France and the British Empire. But contemporaries knew that they faced mass death, and even if the exact figures were secret this was both novel and traumatic. As Freud (with two sons and a son-in-law at the front) put it in 1915: "Death will no longer be denied; we are forced to believe in it. People really die; and no longer one by one, but many, often tens of thousands, in a single day."[3]

Making sense of death on this scale was thus a further enigma of the Great War that continued for at least a generation. Both at the time, for soldiers contemplating the losses incurred in proportion to the results gained, and also afterward, when whole societies engaged in the reckoning, this was the most general yet also the most personal measure of the gap between intentions and outcome. Not surprisingly, all the social and cultural resources of the countries concerned were deployed to give the sacrifice meaning and to make the war worthwhile.[4] The focus everywhere was the ordinary soldier and above all the war dead. The sole exception was Russia, swept up in revolution and civil war, where the Bolsheviks rejected the Great War as an "imperialist" conflict.[5]

The Great War was not the first in which soldiers were individually honored by the fatherland for which they died. Already the French inscribed the names of the fallen on the battlefield monuments of the Franco-Prussian War while both sides after the American Civil War devoted considerable effort to identifying bodies and creating suitable monuments for the three-quarters of a million war dead.[6] The idea that the ordinary soldier's death in battle was the crucible of the nation was perhaps born with Lincoln's address on the battlefield of Gettysburg, but as in so many other ways, the American conflict was not widely understood by Europeans as a harbinger of things to come. Hence, the cult of the millions of dead of the Great War was by its scale and import a new experience for European nations. Nothing speaks more eloquently to the way in which the war transformed nationhood than the geography of collective mourning and commemoration that was organized in the decade that followed it, with local monuments complementing the vast cemeteries along the former fronts. The Unknown Soldier emerged as a new embodiment of popular sovereignty, at once anonymous and individual, the democratization of death.

Yet the ability to make sense of the sacrifice also turned on victory or defeat. Whereas the Western Allies (and the "victorious" successor states in Eastern Europe) invented national rituals to sanctify the sacrifice by the result achieved (the defense or creation of the fatherland, the "war for civilization"), this was impossible in the face of defeat or a "mutilated victory," such as that condemned by Italian nationalists. Here "sacrifice" underlined the impossibility of accepting the outcome of the war or of a postwar politics that seemed to do so. The shame of defeat, the burden of an unfulfilled sacrifice, and a political activism that drew on the idealization of the "front soldier" were vital ingredients in the fascism that formed immediately after the war both in Italy, where it began in March 1919, and on the nationalist right in Germany.[7] In both cases paramilitary formations inspired by the war expressed the sense of grievance through violent combat in civil and class war and in frontier conflicts.

Perhaps the ultimate explanation of the discrepancy between anticipation and outcome lies here. The scale of the effort and the size of the sacrifice inclined many who fought in the war to believe while it lasted that such an experience must have a decisive result, a closure that would be worthy of the conflict. That was one reason why it proved impossible to arrange a compromise, negotiated peace in 1916–17. But such a clear-cut diplomatic and political outcome was just as elusive as a decisive battle had been during the war itself. World War I was not an end, but rather a beginning, and the forces and quarrels that it unleashed – and transformed – continued to destabilize the world. The consequences seemed greater and more unmanageable than the origins, and the outcome, in retrospect, ever more disproportionate to the causes.

This was shown by the way peace was made in 1919–20. While the Western Allies dated victory precisely to 11 a.m. on November 11, 1918, the moment when the guns fell silent along the western front, ambiguity surrounded both the timing and the terms of the ending of the war. An expansionist and military-dominated German government had already imposed a harsh treaty on Bolshevik Russia in March 1918 that stripped the former Empire of the bulk of its non-Russian borderlands. Yet in 1919, the new German government (along with much of German opinion) believed that the Armistice was rather less than a defeat and entitled Germany to be part of the peace conference in the tradition of European diplomacy going back to the Congress of Vienna in 1815. The Allies, by contrast, and especially the French, who had borne the worst physical devastation of the war, assumed they were unilaterally imposing peace terms on a defeated and guilty adversary in what had been a war of survival. The gulf was fundamental. In 1945, in reaction against the Treaty of Versailles, the Allies would impose just such a peace on Nazi Germany after insisting on "total surrender." But in 1919–20, peace was transitional in its very form, and the misunderstandings on which it was based accentuated the feelings of dissatisfaction on both sides. Meanwhile, Russia was doubly absent – excluded as a great power and as the source of the revolution spawned by the war – while in a series of aftershocks, the borderlands of the former dynastic empires sank into conflict and civil strife until the early to mid-1920s.

In another sense, too, the war's consequences seemed to bear little relation to its origins. While the ascendancy of the nation-state was a long-term trend, the explosion of an ideological conflict that would reshape national politics and the European balance of power in the interwar period was altogether more unexpected. Of course, the struggle between democracy, communism, and fascism had deep origins in nineteenth-century political thought and movements. But the war itself – not its origins but the internal

dynamics and requirements that both destroyed the multinational empires and transformed the nation-state – produced the ideological contest that was one of its most
profound consequences. The crusading edge imparted to the Allied cause as the United
States replaced Russia in 1917 (summed up by Woodrow Wilson's clarion call to "make
the world safe for democracy"), as well as the desire by British and French politicians in
the interwar period to create a new international order based on the renunciation (or at
least the limitation) of war, helped reformulate democracy as the creed that most clearly
characterized the "victors." Defeat played a pivotal (if contrasting) role in the emergence
of communism and fascism. Not only did the failure of the wartime regimes to secure
victory help both creeds come to power, they both in their different ways internalized
many of the experiences and impulses of the war. The Russian Civil War was a direct
outgrowth of the Great War that profoundly influenced the shape of the new regime,
including its permanent mobilization against internal and external enemies, a command
economy pioneered in the improvisation of "War Communism" and the recourse to
Terror. Fascism was a political remobilization for future war that drew on the "sacrifice"
and military experience of World War I to supply radically new forms of political authority and national community along with aggressive and revisionist foreign policies.

Finally, perhaps the least anticipated outcome of all was the gnawing uncertainty on
the part of many Europeans that they still occupied the central place in the world to
which they were accustomed before 1914. At its outset, the conflict was a world war not
just because Germany, as the strongest European state, aspired to be a "world power,"
but even more because Britain and France were able to bring the resources of the world
(both their colonial empires and their maritime access to the international economy) to
bear on the contest in Europe. Yet if the war in Europe transcended the struggle for
survival of the multinational dynastic states, it did so because it meshed that issue, by
means of the alliance of Germany and Austria-Hungary, with Germany's potential to
exercise hegemony over the Continent. This was only a possibility of German policy
before 1914, not a clear-cut goal. But once again, the process of the war turned it into
reality as Germany's initial failure to defeat the major Entente powers, France and Russia,
left the German army in possession of a sizeable portion of Europe, both east and west,
and in a position to dream of future empire on the Continent. The resultant struggle
over the shape and dominance of Europe concerned the entire world and brought in a
non-European power, the United States, as protagonist and arbiter (a role the Americans
would perform again, and more durably, after 1945). The exhaustion of the European
states in this battle over their own balance of power helped displace them from the center
of worlds affairs and redistribute global influence toward America and Japan.

Paradoxically, this was true also in relation to colonial empires. For if Britain and
France appeared superficially to be at the height of their power at the Paris Peace
Conference as they assigned themselves the German colonies and the provinces of the
Ottoman Middle East in the form of League of Nations mandates, the price they paid for
involving their empires in a democratic crusade was heightened political expectations on
the part of the colonized and a transfer of rhetoric that challenged imperial relations.
After a further world war it would lead to full decolonization.[8] Europeans might still
travel the globe and administer their empires with ingrained assumptions of superiority.
But the emerging theorists of a "European idea," such as the Austrian pacifist, Baron
Richard Coudenhove-Kalergi (inventor of "Pan-Europa"), or the French Foreign
Minister, Aristide Briand, with his 1929 proposal for a European Federal Union, explic-
itly addressed the catastrophe of a war that had divided Europeans and weakened their

place in the world.[9] The poet Paul Valéry wrote in 1919 of this self-destructive legacy for Europe: "We modern civilizations [like the vanished civilizations of antiquity] now know that we too are mortal."[10]

Owing to this enigmatic quality, to the gulf between cause and effect, and to the ways in which it set in motion more than it resolved, World War I has proved particularly difficult to assess historically, despite the libraries of books that have been written about it. Popular perceptions and official memory have likewise reflected the divisive legacies of the conflict.

Most obviously, the nation-states that the war helped consolidate, and their subsequent evolution, shaped how the history was written and the conflict remembered. In Britain and France, alongside the conviction that the war had been both just and justified because it had defeated Germany's bid for continental hegemony, a more pacifist sentiment emerged that emphasized the cost of the victory in human terms (proportion again) and affirmed that such a war should never be repeated.[11] Defeat rendered the war far more divisive in Weimar Germany. It proved impossible to establish a consensus on national commemoration, and while moderate opinion shared the aspiration to reconciliation with the former enemy (though still considering Versailles an unjust settlement), the nationalist right inveighed against the shameful peace and with the help of a state-backed campaign of history-writing declared Germany's "innocence" of the Allied charges of war guilt.[12]

In all three countries, however, the war dominated national memory, a situation that changed fundamentally after 1945. The far greater catastrophe of World War II for Germany, which led to "total defeat" and the subsequent division of the country in the Cold War, effaced the earlier conflict from public memory and marginalized it as a subject of historical inquiry. The major controversy concerning World War I in West Germany arose, significantly, because Fritz Fischer in the 1960s argued on the basis of new evidence that Germany was responsible for war in 1914 and engaged in expansionist policies during the conflict. This suggested continuities with the Third Reich and challenged the prevailing consensus that Nazi Germany was an exception to national history.[13] Although scholarly interest in World War I has grown steadily since the end of the Cold War, public interest remains low as shown by the muted interest in a major exhibition mounted on the subject by the Deutsches Historisches Museum in Berlin in 2004.[14]

Quite different is the situation in Britain and France where World War I has remained a focus of public interest as well as scholarship and attracted increasing attention since the 1990s. While the two countries had different experiences of World War II, the military casualties of both remained lower than in World War I since the land conflict in World War II was fought overwhelmingly in Russia, Eastern Europe and the Pacific.[15] World War I thus remained the great blood sacrifice of the twentieth century, its monuments providing the commemorative framework for subsequent wars. In France, for some, it marks an episode of national cohesion in contrast with the defeat of 1940 while for others it symbolizes the horror and disproportionate suffering entailed by modern warfare.[16] In Britain, since the 1960s, popular understanding of the war has moved decisively in this latter direction (the "pity of war" expressed by the canonical poetry of Wilfred Owen), although military historians emphasize the "learning curve" of the British army which, they suggest, achieved one of its finest performances ever on the western front in the last three months of the war.[17] Variants of the British and French cases obtain in Australia, Canada, and New Zealand, for which the war provided foundation myths of independent nationhood. Especially in Australia, the "legend" of the Anzacs (Australian and New Zealand Army Corps) has been of enduring relevance.[18]

The nation-state provided the frame of reference in Eastern Europe too, albeit more hesitantly. Where the war was a founding moment of national history (Czechoslovakia, Yugoslavia, Romania) or even a national disaster (Austria, Hungary, Bulgaria), the lens through which it was viewed was that of post-war nationhood rather than the multi-national empires of the conflict, although some supporters of the Dual Monarchy attempted to account for the Habsburg defeat and, in the inter-war series of economic and social histories of the war published by the Carnegie Foundation, to deal with the monarchy's war economy.[19] More recently, historians have started to renew the study of Austria-Hungary in World War I in trans-national terms, but the linguistic and archival challenges are daunting.[20]

By contrast, the Bolsheviks' dismissal of what they considered to be an "imperialist" conflict meant that in Russia the war was long ignored, treated as a mere backdrop to the real foundation of the Soviet Union by the Russian Revolution. Only in exile (and in the Russian contributions to the Carnegie series) was the war effort of Tsarist Russia taken seriously, a situation that began to be rectified with the fall of Communism and the opening of the archives.[21] This same ideological dismissal marginalized the war in the memory and historiography of Eastern European countries during the Cold War where, as in Germany, the experience of World War II predominated. This resulted in the paradox of Poland. For in the country that was split between three Empires (Germany, Austria-Hungary, and Russia), in whose opposing armies three and a half million Poles fought (and nearly 400,000 died), and whose territory was the cockpit of the eastern front, World War I, according to a leading Polish historian, remains a "forgotten war."[22]

The predominantly national historiographies of World War I thus reflected wide variations in public and scholarly interest and militated against comparative or transnational approaches to a subject that was intrinsically European and global. They also explain the slow evolution of different approaches to historical research and writing on the war. Down to World War II, the discrepancy between causes and consequences made diplomatic "responsibility" for the outbreak of war in 1914 the primary issue. The "innocentist" campaign of German historians was paralleled by the "revisionism" of British, French, and especially American historians who now pointed to the responsibilities of their own governments for the catastrophe. In the American case this implied retrospective disavowal of US participation in the war and support for renewed isolationism.[23] While the revisionist critique by no means carried the day, especially in Britain and France, the focus on the origins and also on the conduct of the war ensured that political and military history prevailed.

The Carnegie volumes on the economic and social impact of the war remained an exception. However, the books were written by officials and by experts as much as by historians, and the enterprise did not transform the professional historiography of the subject. They are an underused resource to this day. It might be assumed that the place of the ordinary soldier in national commemoration and the significance of the veterans' movements would have guaranteed a flourishing history of combat experience. The soldiers' war was indeed a major subject during the interwar years, but not of historians. The veterans took charge of transmitting their own messages in a flood of memoirs and novels. Works such as the letters of fallen German students published by Philipp Witkop in successive editions in Germany, the "literature of disenchantment" by soldier-writers in Britain, or the attempt by a French literary critic and veteran, Jean Norton Cru, to evaluate the soldiers' literature published in France, testify to the omnipresence of the soldiers' memory in postwar society.[24] But it moved in a different sphere to the historians' concern with high politics as the fulcrum of historical causality.

The diplomatic, political, and military history of the war has remained a preoccupation of historical scholarship, particularly in a national context.[25] However, the opening of the wartime archives in Western Europe in the 1960s and the revival of interest occasioned by the fiftieth anniversary of the war in the same decade shifted the focus to collective experience and to causality understood in economic and social terms. World War I benefited from the primacy of social history and began to be reinterpreted as a conflict determined by economic and social forces as much as by high politics. Class conflicts and the workings of the wartime economy became the relevant issues; social groups, collective movements, strikers, food protestors, and women were the new protagonists.[26] Morale and public opinion became vital for understanding both wartime societies and the legacy of the war.[27] By and large, this was a home-front war. The soldiers' experience remained largely exempt from rigorous study, perhaps tainted for social historians by association with an unfashionable military history.[28]

By far the most fundamental reorientation in the historiography of World War I occurred as part of the larger turn toward cultural history from the 1990s on – though as with political and military history, the social history of the war continued to attract attention.[29] The disintegration of Marxism with the end of the Cold War hastened the search for alternative paradigms. The enlargement of women's studies (already a fertile field of the social history of World War I) to gender and the discursive and symbolic practices that defined the sexes suggested new ways of thinking about experience.[30] Theoretical approaches borrowed from philosophy and sociology (notably the power inherent in intellectual and epistemological categories analyzed by Foucault and others) tended in the same direction. Literary criticism and studies of cinema and the visual arts showed the importance of representations for unlocking the codes of contemporary meaning.

Of course, such developments applied to other fields of history and other disciplines. But they coincided with the historical caesura of the fall of Communism, the reunification of Germany, and the reintegration of Eastern and Western Europe – not to mention the countershock of the brutal wars in the former Yugoslavia with a long artillery siege at (of all places) Sarajevo. The end seemed to reconnect with the beginning, supplying a new measure for the violence unleashed by World War I, which had permeated the interwar period and beyond. The result was a flowering of studies that were less concerned with the origins of the conflict, let alone the responsibility for it, but explored instead its internal processes and legacies.

At the heart of this renewed interest in the war were the people who experienced it and the ways they did so. The gulf between the causes and consequences of the war, between the intention and the outcome, meant that contemporaries between the wars had real difficulty in reconstructing the sense they had given to the conflict while it was going on. This was discounted in retrospect as propaganda and self-delusion, or more subtly transformed into memories compatible with peace and the postwar world – such as the veterans' tendency to cast themselves as victims.[31] When historians since the late 1990s have used a kind of cultural archaeology to disinter the experiences and practices of the war, they have rediscovered the very dynamics that drove its transformative violence and translated its momentum into the postwar period. This does not mean that all contemporaries approved the war – far from it – but rather that they were absorbed by the violence that defined their universe for four and a half years. It is in this sense that some historians have coined the term "cultures of war" to describe that universe.[32]

The result has been studies of heterogeneity and richness – of soldiers in combat and prisoners of war, of women maintaining the home but also engaged as nurses and munitions workers, of children caught up in the conflict, and of civilian victims of violence.[33] As the interwar frameworks of memory were unpicked and the retrospective myths untangled, forgotten categories and untold experiences came to light. These included refugees, civilians under enemy occupation (the bulk of the population in Belgium, Poland, and Serbia), and the victims of atrocities, war crimes – and genocide. For at the heart of the war, in the case of the Young Turk movement, was a negative mobilization against the "enemy within" that turned into the deliberate elimination of the Armenian minority, resulting in the death of about a million people. A subject for so long marginal, if not hidden, in the history of the war, has begun to assume its central place. [34] It is an extreme example of a more general trend.

Although many of these studies have been undertaken in the context of a single nation or state, some have been comparative and transnational, and the historical literature has increasingly become international. In effect, the spaces of World War I have begun to be denationalized, though it is perhaps still not clear what a truly European or global history of the war might consist of.[35] Likewise, the timeframe of the war has been disencumbered of the artificial rigidity of the years 1914 to 1918. The war was the epicenter of a larger cycle of violence that went from 1912 to 1923, from the Balkan Wars in 1912–13 to the end of violence in the collapsed border zones of the former empires in Eastern Europe, the forced exchange of populations between Greece and Turkey, and the stabilization of Bolshevik Russia with Socialism in One Country instead of world revolution. That larger cycle both prepared and prolonged the war itself. Moreover, the powerful and diverse effects of the war on memory and commemoration within and beyond Europe are part of the subject. So too are the myths (the "stab in the back," "Jewish" Bolshevism, cheering crowds in 1914) by which contemporaries addressed the outcomes that no one had predicted. To the extent that much of this new scholarship is the work of a younger, international generation, there is no better place to explore it than through one of its main expressions, the International Society for First World War Studies.[36]

Yet if cultural history has informed the renovation of historical scholarship of World War I, it has by no means displaced the approaches characteristic of earlier and continued history writing. How to reconcile causal explanation (the preoccupation with cause and effect), which has been the forte of political and military history, with the emphasis on experience, representation, and memory that has been the strength of cultural approaches, is a major question in historical scholarship more generally, and the study of World War I would seem particularly well placed to tackle it. Already, the best military history is comparative in approach and takes due note of myth and experience – the "fog of war" that was cultural as well as physical.[37] Likewise, questions of class, social structure, material living standards, and the impact of war on the economy have lost none of their importance.

Such matters will help set the agenda of World War I studies up to and through the centenary reevaluations. It is precisely in order to foster that process, and to bring to a wider readership the richness and mutual dialogue of the different approaches to the subject, that this *Companion to World War I* assembles contributions from some forty leading scholars in the field working in nine countries and four languages. It puts military history in its rightful place at the heart of the war with a set of analytical narratives that give due weight to the western front while restoring to their full importance other fronts in Europe and beyond, including on the sea and in the air. It also provides a set of largely international and comparative chapters on the different "faces of war," those aspects that helped give World War I its distinctive character and that have variously engaged the military, political, economic, social, and more latterly cultural histories of the subject.

The *Companion* recognizes the continued significance of the wartime states as the entities that mobilized and fought the war with profound (and differing) effects on the peoples involved, both at the time and subsequently. Yet it also insists that other spaces mattered because they either contributed to the war and were altered by it (the British and French Empires) or were wartime creations – the German-occupied territories of Northeast Europe and in a way, also, Belgium. The volume addresses the larger time-frame of the war with two opening chapters, one on how the war imagined before 1914 bore little relationship to the event that it helped produce, and a second on how the gulf between prediction and outcome resulted in a debate on "guilt" and "responsibilities" that lasted from 1914 to the present. It concludes with three chapters on the war after the war – the first on peacemaking and its ultimate failure in the interwar period, a second on the conflicts arising from the war, and a third on memory and commemoration.

Readers will use the volume in different ways. Some will want an overview, others a detailed survey of the entire field, and yet others some information or insight on a precise point. Some will simply to wish to browse for pleasure. As well as the individual chapters, which are accompanied by suggestions for further reading in several languages (where relevant), there is an extensive bibliography of secondary literature in English catego-rized under various headings. An annotated bibliography of published primary sources in English gives some indication of the wealth of contemporary material on the war experience that is readily available, much of it translated and relating to the major conti-nental powers. Whatever the purpose the reader has in mind, it is hoped that in every sense of the term, the *Companion* will live up to its name.

Notes

1 Carl von Clausewitz, *On War*, 1832, edited and translated from German by Michael Howard and Peter Paret, Princeton, Princeton University Press, 1976, p. 593.

2 On the predominance of the eastern front among prisoners of war, see Alon Rachamimov, *POWs and the Great War: Captivity on the Eastern Front*, Oxford, Berg, 2002.

3 Sigmund Freud, "Thoughts for the Times on War and Death" (1915), in Penguin Freud Library, vol. 12, *Group Psychology, Civilization and its Discontents and Other Works*, London, Penguin, 1991, pp. 79–80.

4 Jay Winter, *Sites of Memory, Sites of Mourning: European Culture and the Great War*, Cambridge, Cambridge University Press, 1995.

5 Catherine Merridale, *Night of Stone: Death and Memory in Russia*, London, Granta, 2000, pp. 125–7.

6 Drew Gilpin Faust, *This Republic of Suffering: Death and the American Civil War*, New York, Knopf, 2008, pp. 250–65.

7 George Mosse, *Fallen Soldiers: Reshaping the Memory of the World Wars*, Oxford, Oxford University Press, 1990, pp. 159–200.

8 Erez Manela, *The Wilsonian Moment: Self-determination and the International Origins of Anticolonial Nationalism*, Oxford, Oxford University Press, 2007.

9 Richard Coudenhove-Kalergi, *Pan-Europa*, Vienna, Pan-Europa Verlag, 1923; Carl H. Pegg, *The Evolution of the European Idea 1914–1932*, Chapel Hill and London, University of North Carolina Press, 1983, pp. 103–14.

10 Paul Valéry, "Crise de l'esprit" (1919), in *Oeuvres*, vol. 1, Paris, Gallimard, 1957, p. 988.

11 Adrian Gregory, *The Silence of Memory: Armistice Day 1919–1946*, Oxford, Berg, 1994; Antoine Prost, *In the Wake of War. "Les Anciens Combattants" and French Society, 1914–1933*, Oxford, Berg, 1992.

12 Holger Herwig, "Clio Deceived. Patriotic Self-Censorship in Germany after the Great War" in Steven E. Miller, Sean Lynn-Jones and Stephen Van Evera (eds.), *Military Strategy and the Origins of the First World War*, Princeton, Princeton University Press, 1991, pp. 262–301.

13 Fritz Fischer, *Germany's War Aims in the First World War*, 1961; translation from German, London, Chatto and Windus, 1967, and id., *War of Illusions: German Policies from 1911 to 1914*, 1969; translated from German, London, Chatto and Windus, 1975; see also John Keiger, chapter 2 below.

14 Rainer Rother (ed.), *Der Weltkrieg 1914–1918. Ereignis und Erinnerung*, Berlin Deutsches Historisches Museum/Edition Minerva, 2004.

15 Pieter Lagrou, "Les Guerres, les morts et le deuil: bilan chiffré de la Seconde Guerre Mondiale" in Stéphane Audoin-Rouzeau, Annette Becker, Christian Ingrao and Henry Rousso (eds.), *La Violence de guerre, 1914–1945*, Brussels, Editions Complexe, 2002, pp. 313–27.

16 For an insight into this controversy, see Christophe Prochasson, *14–18: Retours d'expériences*, Paris, Tallandier, 2008.

17 On British military history, Brian Bond, *The Unquiet Western Front: Britain's Role in Literature and History*, Cambridge, Cambridge University Press, 2002, and Gary Sheffield, *Forgotten Victory. The First World War: Myth and Realities*, 2001; new ed., London, Review, 2002. On changing public perceptions of the war in Britain, Dan Todman, *The Great War. Myth and Memory*, London, Hambledon Continuum, 2005.

18 Alistair Thomson, *Anzac Memories. Living with the Legend*, Melbourne, Oxford University Press, 1994; Jonathan Vance, *Death So Noble: Memory, Meaning and the First World War*, Vancouver, University of British Columbia Press, 1997.

19 Edmund von Glaise-Horstenau, *The Collapse of the Austro-Hungarian Empire*, 1929, translation from German, London, Dent, 1930; Gustáv Gratz and Richard Schuller, *The Economic Policy of Austria-Hungary during the War*, New Haven, Yale, 1928. The Carnegie series also published separate volumes on Austrian and Hungarian war government.

20 On the military history of Austria-Hungary, see Manfried Rauchensteiner, *Der Tod des Doppeladlers: Österreich-Ungarn und der Erste Weltkrieg*, Graz, Styria Verlag, 1993. Professor Mark Cornwall conducted a research project from 2004 to 2007 on the comparative and transnational study of the legacy of World War I in the former Dual Monarchy, scheduled for future publication as *Sacrifice and Rebirth: the Legacy of the Habsburg Empire's Great War*. See also chapter 25 below.

21 See the summarizing volume on Russia in the Carnegie series, Michael Florinsky, *The End of the Russian Empire*, New Haven, Yale University Press, 1931, and chapter 32 below.

22 Robert Traba, "Der vergessene Krieg 1914–1918" in Andreas Lawaty and Hubert Orlowski (eds.), *Deutsche und Polen. Geschichte-Kultur-Politik*, Munich, Beck, 2003, pp. 53–60. See, however, the volume on Poland in the Carnegie series, Marcel Handelsman (ed.), *La Pologne. Sa vie économique et sociale pendant la Grande Guerre*, Paris, Presses Universitaires de France, 1933. I am indebted to Dr Julia Eichenberg for the first reference.

23 See chapter 2 below.

24 Philipp Witkopp (ed.), *German Students' War Letters*, translated from German, London, Methuen, 1929; new ed., Philadelphia, Pine Street Books, 2002 (foreword by Jay Winter); Paul Fussell, *The Great War and Modern Memory*, Oxford, Oxford University Press, 1975, and Samuel Hynes, *A War Imagined: The First World War and English Culture*, London, Bodley Head, 1990, on the "literature of disenchantment"; Jean Norton Cru, *Témoins*, Paris, Les Etincelles, 1929, new edition, Nancy, Presses Universitaires de Nancy, 2006 (preface by Frédéric Rousseau). Unfortunately, Norton Cru has not been translated into English. On the soldiers' literature in Germany and France, respectively, Wolgang Natter, *Literature at War, 1914–1940: Representing the "Time of Greatness" in Germany*, New Haven, Yale University Press, 1999, and Leonard V. Smith, *The Embattled Self: French Soldiers' Testimony of the Great War*, Ithaca, Cornell University Press, 2007.

25 For the successive phases in the historiography of World War I in what remains the only modern study of this subject, see Antoine Prost and Jay Winter, *The Great War in History: Debates and Controversies 1914 to the Present*, 2004; translated from French, Cambridge, Cambridge University Press, 2005.

26 Two characteristic examples, both relating to Germany, one by an American, the other by a German historian, are: Gerald D. Feldman, *Army, Industry and Labor in Germany, 1914–1918* (1966); new ed., Providence, RI, and Oxford, Berg, 1992; and Jürgen Kocka, *Facing Total War: German Society, 1914–1918* (1973); translation from German, Leamington Spa, Berg, 1984.

27 In France three major examples are Jean-Jacques Becker's study of civilian opinion on the entry into war, *1914: Comment les français sont entrés dans la guerre*, Paris, Presses de la Fondation Nationale des Sciences Politiques, 1977; Antoine Prost's analysis of the postwar veterans, *Les Anciens Combattants et la société française*, 3 vols., Paris, Presses de la Fondation Nationale des Sciences Politiques, 1977, and Jean-Louis Robert's study of the Paris working class and labor movement, *Les Ouvriers, la patrie et la révolution : Paris, 1914–1919*, Besançon, Annales Littéraires de l'Université de Besançon, 1995.

28 A rare exception was Guy Pedroncini's pioneering study of the French mutinies of 1917 based on the military archives, *Les Mutineries de 1917*, Paris, Presses Universitaires de France, 1967.

29 A good example is the first volume of the major collaborative project led by Jay Winter and Jean-Louis Robert that chose three capital cities as a framework for a comparative social history, Jay Winter and Jean-Louis Robert (eds.), *Capital Cities at War: Paris, London, Berlin, 1914–1919*, Cambridge, Cambridge University Press, 1997. This had been preceded by a collective volume on the social and demographic history of the conflict, Richard Wall and Jay Winter (eds.), *The Upheaval of War: Family, Work and Welfare in Europe, 1914–1918*, Cambridge, Cambridge University Press, 1988. Significantly, however, the second volume of the Capital Cities project, published in 2007, was subtitled *A Cultural History*.

30 For an influential early example, see Margaret Higonnet et al. (eds.), *Behind the Lines: Gender and the Two World Wars*, New Haven, Yale University Press, 1987; for a critical assessment from a women's history perspective, see Gail Braybon, "Winners or Losers: Women's Symbolic Role in the War Story," in Braybon (ed.), *Evidence, History and the Great War: Historians and the Impact of 1914–1918*, Oxford, Berghahn, 2003, pp. 86–122.

31 On this point see Smith, *The Embattled Self* pp. 148–94.

32 Among other examples, see Stéphane Audoin-Rouzeau and Annette Becker, *1914–1918: Understanding the Great War*, 2000; translated from French, London, Profile Books, 2002.

33 See sections 6, 7, and 10 of the Extended Bibliography below, on soldiers, gender, and culture, respectively. It is striking how extensive the work on gender and culture now is by comparison with that on economic and social history.

34 See chapters 13 and 33 below. For an attempt to place the genocide in the context of the radicalization of other types of violence by the war in 1914–15, see John Horne (ed.), *Vers la guerre totale: le tournant de 1914–15*, Paris, Tallandier, 2010.

35 See, however, the first volume of the projected trilogy by Hew Strachan, *The First World War. Vol. 1: To Arms*, Oxford, Oxford University Press, 2001, and in a different vein, Alan Kramer, *Dynamic of Destruction. Culture and Mass Killing in the First World War*, Oxford, Oxford University Press, 2007.

36 The International Society for First World War Studies (firstworldwarstudies.org) was established in 2001. Volumes showcasing the work presented at its biennial conferences are: Jenny Macleod and Pierre Purseigle (eds.), *Uncovered Fields. Perspectives in First World War Studies*, Leiden and Boston, Brill, 2004; Pierre Purseigle (ed.), *Warfare and Belligerence: Perspectives in First World War Studies*, Leiden and Boston, Brill, 2005; Heather Jones, Christoph Schmidt-Supprian and Jennifer O'Brien (eds.), *Untold War: New Interpretations of the First World War*, Leiden and Boston, Brill, 2008. The Society's journal, *First World War Studies* (Routledge), was launched in 2010.

37 To take two of the most recent examples, Alex Watson, *Enduring the Great War: Combat, Morale and Collapse in the German and British Armies, 1914–1918*, Cambridge, Cambridge University Press, 2008, and William Philpott, *Bloody Victory: The Sacrifice on the Somme and the Making of the Twentieth Century*, New York, Little, Brown, 2009.

PART I

Origins

CHAPTER ONE

The War Imagined: 1890–1914

GERD KRUMEICH
(translated by Mark Jones)

The years between 1900 and the outbreak of World War I are generally described as the "prewar" period. However, there is no consensus about what the term "prewar" really means or about the period it covers. Some scholars have begun with the Franco-Prussian war of 1870–1, but it is more common to see the years of the "scramble for Africa" and the "imperialist delirium" as the true prewar period.[1] Even here, the precise starting point depends on national perspectives. For Germany, it might be taken as Kaiser Wilhelm's policy of expansion on to the world stage (*Weltpolitik*) in the later 1890s, or the subsequent naval rivalry with Britain. For the French, the military alliance with Russia in 1893, or the First and Second Moroccan Crises of 1905 and 1911, make equally credible starting points. For Russia it is perhaps the recovery from the catastrophe of the Russo-Japanese War of 1904–5 and the 1905 revolution.

I propose to divide the prewar period into a longer phase when enmities were created and a more immediate phase of acute tensions leading to the outbreak of hostilities. The first phase was defined by the gradual increase in international antagonism and the polarization of the European alliance system into two antagonistic blocks. The second phase was marked by an increasingly nervous disposition toward what was seen as the inevitability – and for some the desirability – of a war that would reshape the course of world development. Viewed as a whole, the pattern of events and decisions leading up to July 1914 make World War I seem a logical, and even inevitable, outcome.

Yet what made it so requires an understanding of how contemporaries perceived events and came to decisions. For the murder at Sarajevo, on 28 June 1914, of Archduke Franz Ferdinand, heir apparent to the throne of Austria-Hungary, was an event of relatively minor importance by comparison with its consequences. Various heads of state had been assassinated in the previous 30 years. This outrage only unleashed war because of accumulated preconditions, not the least important of which were the mental dispositions or attitudes of contemporary decision-makers – the "unspoken assumptions," and also the thoroughly pronounced presumptions, that had accumulated in the critical years from around 1900.[2]

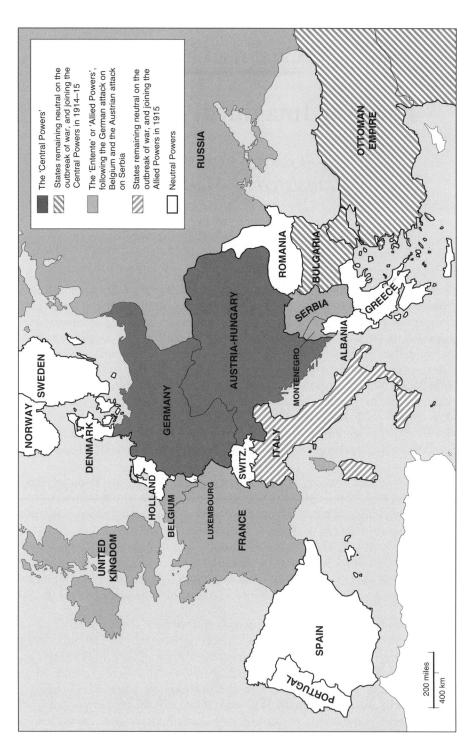

Map 1 Europe at the outbreak of World War I

The 'Central Powers'

States remaining neutral on the outbreak of war, and joining the Central Powers in 1914–15

The 'Entente' or 'Allied Powers', following the German attack on Belgium and the Austrian attack on Serbia

States remaining neutral on the outbreak of war, and joining the Allied Powers in 1915

Neutral Powers

NORWAY

SWEDEN

DENMARK

HOLLAND

UNITED KINGDOM

BELGIUM

LUXEMBOURG

FRANCE

GERMANY

SWITZ.

ITALY

SPAIN

PORTUGAL

RUSSIA

AUSTRIA-HUNGARY

ROMANIA

SERBIA

MONTENEGRO

ALBANIA

BULGARIA

GREECE

OTTOMAN EMPIRE

200 miles

400 km

National Enmities

Notable among these attitudes were deep animosities on the part of the political and military elites of Europe, their readiness to reckon in terms of absolute enmity and their reluctance to set a higher price on resolving conflict than on going to war. This readiness to create and indulge enmities encompassed both hard decisions and the mentalities that helped shape these. Although the phenomenon still requires more investigation, it is worth noting that the great early nineteenth-century Prussian theorist of war, Carl von Clausewitz, wrote in his classic analysis (in which he sought to distil the lessons of the Napoleonic conflicts) that "Even the most civilized of peoples ... can be fired with passionate hatred for each other."[3]

In the introduction to his highly perceptive analysis of the origins and decline of the ideological illusion of communism, François Furet acknowledged that World War I was a decisive turning point in contemporary history. Paradoxically, he insisted that there was no clear causal explanation for the outbreak of the war and that it had not really been necessary. In the end, war had become unavoidable simply because all the key decision-makers had accepted it. But Furet went on to accuse the statesmen of the period of tremendous folly and thoughtlessness when their actions are measured by the enormity of the catastrophe that followed.[4]

In reality the accusation is highly anachronistic, since it presumes a foreknowledge of the consequences of decisions that contemporaries could not possibly have had. To the extent that such a misapprehension results from the involvement of scholars in the events they describe, it is easily forgiven. But today, almost a hundred years after the summer of 1914, we should avoid such anachronism and seek to establish what contemporaries meant by war and how they understood the cumulative events that we know, as they could not, were to produce a devastating European conflict.

Military Misperceptions of Future War

One of the most important elements of the puzzle is why military commanders, those whose function it was to anticipate the next war, so signally failed to predict the reality of warfare in 1914–18. That failure does not mean that no one saw that a future war might be a catastrophe for the societies that waged it. There was a certain vein of pessimistic thinking in this regard even where one might least expect it. Count Helmuth von Moltke the Elder was the victorious German Commander-in-Chief in the Franco-Prussian War and subsequently Chief of the German General Staff, and in one of the best-known examples of such pessimism, he warned the Reichstag in 1899 that:

> If war ... breaks out, its length and end are unforeseeable. The greatest European powers, armed like never before, will go to war against each other. None of these powers can be so completely subjected in one or two campaigns, that they declare themselves defeated ...; it could be a seven year war, it could be a thirty years war – and woe betide him who sets Europe on fire, who first throws the fuse in the powder keg![5]

Even earlier, in the mid-1880s, Friedrich Engels warned of the mass sacrifice entailed by the warfare of the future, a view repeated in the often-quoted speech of the elder statesman of the German Social Democratic Party (SPD), August Bebel, in 1911:

> Both sides are producing arms and will continue to do so ... until the point, at which one or the other one day says: better a horrible end than a horror without end .... Then the

catastrophe will happen. Then in Europe the great mobilization plans will be unleashed, by which sixteen to eighteen million men, the male blood of the different nations, armed with the best instruments of murder, will go to the battlefield against each other .... The damnation of the bourgeois world is approaching.[6]

Yet although these eschatological warnings predicted a long war with enormous casualties, they had nothing to say about the nature of military technology and the form the destruction would take.

The focus upon massive numbers of casualties should come as no surprise. Since the 1880s, new recruiting laws in both France and Germany had made it possible at least in theory to mobilize for the first time the entire male population capable of military service for a future war. The creation of a new kind of army numbering millions of soldiers logically produced a new scale of potential casualties. But few, if any, intellectually mastered the real consequences of such massive armies. Even Engels went in for traditional war games (socialists affectionately nicknamed him "the General"), while Bebel let slip that he would like to fight in a war against the "bloody Tsar."[7] Indeed, despite his description of the destructive power of future wars, Moltke the Elder, along with his successor, Count Alfred von Schlieffen, continued to plan for the next campaign in an entirely conventional manner.

The observations of Colmar von der Goltz, Germany's most popular military writer before the war, are a good example of the persistence of traditional military thinking. In *The Nation in Arms* (1883), which became a kind of Bible for officers and the educated public, Goltz investigated the problem caused by mass conscript armies.[8] He was convinced that no single decisive battle would decide the course of a war. Rather, future wars would consist of numerous battles and might last a long time. Goltz was also one of the first to draw attention to the logistical difficulties of supplying both weapons and food to such massive armies but he was convinced that a well-managed military, such as that of Germany, could overcome such problems and systematically exhaust its enemy during a long war.

The views of the Chief of the German General Staff from 1891 to 1905, Count Alfred von Schlieffen, however, were premised on a short war, and revealed even more clearly than Goltz's writings the ambivalent and limited understanding of the real nature of a future war. Schlieffen's famous war plan (known by his name even after subsequent modifications) was completed in 1904–5. It dealt with the diplomatic situation faced by Germany since the Franco-Russian military agreement of 1893, which exposed Germany to the risk of a war on two fronts. Schlieffen dealt with this by planning to concentrate German forces initially against France, which would mobilize more rapidly than Russia. After a swift invasion, resulting in the encirclement and annihilation of the French armies, the Germans would turn with their Austro-Hungarian ally to eliminate Russia, which it was assumed would mobilize much more slowly. The thinking behind the plan showed a very limited understanding of the dynamics of a war between entire peoples fought with industrialized weaponry. For to reach Paris in six weeks and crush the French assumed that the Belgians would offer no resistance and that the French would behave in the same paralyzed and panic-stricken manner as the armies of Napoleon III had done in the summer and autumn of 1870. How the German armies were meant to handle real resistance when they would be marching over 20 km a day and requiring vast amounts of fodder and munitions from dwindling supply-lines was simply not addressed.

Such intellectual arrogance arose from the belief that Republican France and its army were morally inferior to Germany. It was this that enabled German military and political leaders to discount the "friction" of unforeseeable events that Clausewitz had warned would slow down any military operation.[9] Schlieffen's writings after his retirement betrayed the same fundamental illusions as his Plan. In "War Today," an essay published in the popular *Deutsche Revue* in 1909, he argued that high levels of armaments and general conscription would not make wars longer, as suggested by Moltke the Elder, but would shorten them:

> All the doubts about the horrible cost, the possible high casualties … have emerged from the background. Universal conscription … has dampened the lust for battle. The supposedly impregnable fortresses, behind which one feels warm and safe, appear to have reduced the incentive … to bare one's breasts to combat. The arms factories, the cannon foundries, the steam hammers that harden the steel used in fortresses have produced more friendly faces and more amiable obligingness than all the peace congresses could.[10]

Schlieffen's argument became a commonplace of military thought in the years before the war.[11] As the German army's service regulations of 1 January 1910 stated:

> Today the character of war is defined by the longing for a quick and major decision. The call up of all those capable of military service, the strength of the armies, the difficulty of feeding the army, the cost of the state of war, the disruption of trade and transport, industry and agriculture, as well as the responsiveness of military organization and the ease with which the army can be assembled on a war footing – all mean that war would finish quickly.[12]

Military theory and war planning in France showed many similarities to those in Germany, but also some differences. Like the publications of Goltz, those of Colonel Ardant du Picq shaped opinion in France, although they dated from the 1860s.[13] An authentic hero who had died in the Franco-Prussian War, Ardant du Picq believed that large armies were not suited to long wars. He argued that strategy should focus upon obtaining victory through a small number of major battles determined by the fighting qualities of each nation's soldiers. Over time Ardant du Picq's observations gained such wide acceptance in the French General Staff that they became dogma. This was especially the case in reaction to the 1905 conscription law, which called up every Frenchman who was capable of military service. The resulting specter of the officer corps and military cadres being swamped by citizen soldiers alarmed many French generals, who did not believe that the sheer numbers of the "Nation in Arms" would translate into an effective military force.[14] They preferred to think in terms of an army led by professionals that would be able to show true leadership to its conscripts, instilling in them the fighting spirit that would bring victory. Ardant du Picq's vision of a short but intensive war based on the soldiers' morale matched this outlook perfectly.

Among those who developed this idea was the General Staff officer and artillery specialist, Ferdinand Foch, who in 1918 would become the commander of the Allied armies in France. Foch published two books, *Des principes de la guerre* (The Principles of War, 1903) and *De la conduite de la guerre* (The Conduct of War, 1904), which were reprinted several times before 1914. Foch believed that a future war would be such a massive affair that it must be brought to a conclusion quickly, and that the means to do this was a decisive battle in which the critical edge would be supplied by the fighting qualities and high morale that had been developed in the soldiers. Only this psychological factor could make the Nation in Arms an effective fighting force.[15]

A range of publications disseminated these and similar opinions within the army and to the general public. Perhaps the most notable of these were two lectures delivered in 1911 by Colonel Grandmaison, head of the Bureau of Operations of the French General Staff. Grandmaison conceived of national security solely in terms of the offensive, which in turn he based on the idea that French troops possessed "superior morale" and a more aggressive spirit than their potential enemies. "Let us go to the extreme," he concluded, talking again about the psychological factor, "and perhaps this will still not be enough."[16]

Such views finally became dominant in the French army after the Second Moroccan Crisis when, under the new Commander-in-Chief, Joseph Joffre, the French formally adopted the doctrine of the short, offensive war. A new army regulation for the conduct of battle, the first since 1895, was promulgated on 28 October 1913. It stated:

> The size of the military formations involved, the difficulty of re-supplying them, the disruption of the social and economic life of the country, all this requires as rapid an outcome as possible .... A decisive battle, exploited to the fullest extent, is the only way of bending the enemy to one's will by destroying his armies. This is the central act in war .... Only the offensive leads to positive results. By taking the operational initiative, one makes events happen rather than being at their mercy.[17]

The notorious Plan XVII, which governed the mobilization and deployment of the French armies in the event of war with Germany, shared the same logic. It envisaged an all-out offensive, showing no more understanding than the Schlieffen Plan of the form that a future war would take. Yet it would be unfair to assume that the officers who held such views were naïve in the face of the complex political, strategic and technological realities that they faced. While their projections might seem limited to us and doomed to failure, they were rooted in seemingly valid paradigms of military thought at the time. The military thinkers in question had ample opportunity to observe the technical transformations of weaponry, with enormously expanded firepower, and to observe the emerging conditions of combat on the ground, especially in the Russo-Japanese War and the Balkan Wars of 1912–13. The former war had a profound influence on the French generals, who were greatly impressed by the Japanese use of small assault groups whose attacks culminated in a bayonet charge, despite the devastating impact of field artillery and machine-guns. They believed that this kind of attack generated just the qualities of morale among the attackers that they were looking for and justified the heavy losses incurred. They concluded that despite modern weaponry, offensive war would be successful, especially if the "morale" of the troops was high.[18]

Military observers also drew lessons from the Balkan Wars, which saw the Balkan League of Bulgaria, Greece, Montenegro, and Serbia seize most of Macedonia and Thrace from a declining Ottoman Turkey in 1912–13, before the latter four powers deprived Bulgaria of its share of the spoils in a second war in 1913.[19] It was obvious from these conflicts that machine-guns and rapid-fire field guns would inflict massive losses and that as a result soldiers would have to dig trenches to take cover. Pictures of trenches piled high with corpses were even shown in illustrated magazines and newspapers, for example in the siege by the Bulgarians of Turkish-held Adrianople in the first Balkan War. However, such evidence of the mechanization of warfare did not result in a renunciation or even modification of planning based upon the supremacy of the offensive. On the contrary, the events in the Balkans strengthened the belief that an absolute offensive was necessary precisely in order to avoid the human and material costs that would result from siege and stalemate. The factual observations were not wrong; but they were made to fit prevailing doctrines into which thinking and equipment had been invested, instead of modifying them. The resulting absurdity became clear in the Battle of the Frontiers in August 1914, when both the French and German armies suffered their highest losses of any month throughout the entire war before being forced to go to ground in the siege warfare of the trenches.

Social Darwinism

Calculations of the future nature of combat were an important part of how war was imagined before 1914 because they determined assessments of the cost and likely outcome of going to war. But such evaluations were also part of a broader range of social theories and political values which determined the place assigned to war in moral and political thinking, not just in the military but among the political elites and in public opinion more widely.

Unlike in Britain or France, the discourse of unavoidable war in Germany was paralleled in leading military and conservative circles by a belief that war was also desirable and necessary. The view that war was a natural imperative that drove evolution and revitalized an otherwise decadent society reflected both the traditional values of Prussian militarism and an increasingly popular Social Darwinism. Although Social Darwinism was a wide-ranging influence in Europe and North America in the later nineteenth and early twentieth centuries, it acquired a particular application to the sphere of international relations and foreign and military policy in Germany.[20] General Friedrich von Bernhardi's widely read book, *Germany and the Next War*, offers a good example of how it could be used in support of a doctrine of aggressive military expansion. Published in 1912 at the height of the armaments race that followed the Second Moroccan Crisis, and quickly translated into the main European languages, it quickly obtained a cult following amongst those who supported German *Weltpolitik* and set alarm-bells ringing in Britain and France.

Bernhardi resolutely linked the anthropological necessity of war to Germany's "right to war" in view of its rapidly expanding population. This justified its right to use force to seize what had so far been denied to Germany by jealousy of the established major powers, especially Britain:

> We are compelled to obtain space for our increasing population and markets for our growing industries. But at every step that we take in this direction England will resolutely oppose us. … But if we were involved in a struggle with England, we can be quite sure that France would not neglect the opportunity of attacking our flank. … Since the struggle is … necessary and inevitable, we must fight it out, cost what it may. Indeed, we are carrying it on at the present moment, though not with drawn swords, and only by peaceful means so far.[21]

As a result, Bernhardi declared "that we cannot, under any circumstances, avoid fighting for our position in the world, and that the all-important point is, not to postpone that war as long as possible, but to bring it on under the most favorable conditions possible."[22]

More than almost any other German author, Bernhardi inspired British and French anti-German hate propaganda during World War I, confirming as he did the allied image of the bloodthirsty Hun.[23] But if Bernhardi's book was widely read in Germany, it also aroused considerable controversy and was condemned by the liberal and left-wing press.[24] Even the government of Bethmann Hollweg went to considerable lengths to encourage criticism of it. For example, in his pamphlet *Deutsche Weltpolitik und kein Krieg* (German World Policy and No War), the diplomat Richard von Kühlmann called for German expansion without conflict with Britain, a course that Bethmann Hollweg attempted in 1912.[25] Yet in spite of this, Bernhardi's work achieved cult status. It was highly praised by groups such as the Pan-German League and the German Army League. The latter was an actively belligerent organization founded in 1912 following the Second Moroccan Crisis under the slogan of "national opposition," which immediately found a massive following in conservative and military circles, condemning what it saw as the slack policy of the government.[26]

Germany and the Fear of Encirclement

There was thus no consensus on Social Darwinism amongst the German public before 1914. One slogan, however, rallied almost all shades of opinion and supplied a more direct political link with the idea of a likely, or inevitable, war. This was the specter of the hostile *encirclement* of Germany by the other major powers. This syndrome has remained peripheral to historical research on Germany before World War I. During the 1960s and 1970s, historians were content to show that German isolation simply resulted from its incoherent and aggressive policies. But the decisive factor, as far as the cultural history of political decision-making is concerned, is that most Germans before the war (and indeed long after it) believed that Germany was surrounded by malevolent neighbors and had to defend itself or face extinction. Only by taking into account this view can the willingness of the German leadership to go to war and the national solidarity achieved in August 1914 be explained.

Following the First Moroccan Crisis of 1905, the discourse of encirclement developed with breakneck speed. It appeared that the Kaiser's promised "place in the sun" could not be achieved using the diplomatic instruments of blackmail, threats, and bluff, since these had only stiffened the resistance of France, Russia, and Britain, lending further credence to the sense of encirclement. The Entente Cordiale of 1904, by which France and Britain had resolved their differences in the colonial sphere in order to present a common front to Germany, was viewed by Berlin as a catastrophe. This was compounded by the outcome of the Algeciras conference in 1906, following Germany's challenge in 1905 to French plans for predominance in nominally independent Morocco, at which Britain and Russia backed French claims.

Following Germany's setback at Algeciras, the German Chancellor Bülow expressed the encirclement phobia in a simple and martial fashion to the Reichstag:

> Policies which began with the aim of encircling Germany, of forming a circle of powers around Germany, in order to isolate and paralyze it, would be regrettable for the peace of Europe. The formation of such a ring is impossible without exercising a certain kind of pressure. Pressure gives rise to counter-pressure.[27]

Evidence of just how widespread the encirclement stereotype had become after 1905–6 comes from the celebrated sociologist, Max Weber. Weber was without doubt critical of the Wilhelmine system, yet he was also a convinced "imperialist." He believed that if Germany did not expand it risked suffocation. In an essay on *Russia's Transition to Pseudo-Constitutionalism*, published after the 1905 Revolution, he concluded: "We, for our part, in spite of the need to remain clear-headed in a world of enemies, should not forget that ... the future for "sated" nations is bleak."[28]

Given that the encirclement syndrome was so widespread in Germany, it comes as no surprise that public opinion responded even more intensely to the Second Moroccan Crisis in 1911. It is now clear beyond doubt that German provocation deliberately triggered the crisis as a diplomatic maneuver.[29] However, the fact that once again Britain unambiguously supported France meant that it also seemed to supply definitive proof that the other major powers were encircling Germany, rendering war sooner or later inevitable.

Helmuth von Moltke the Younger, nephew of the victor of 1870–1 and Schlieffen's successor as the chief of the General Staff, wrote in a major strategic reassessment of December 1911 that: "It has become clear, that the tension between Germany and France, which has existed for years and periodically intensified, has resulted in increased military activity in almost all the European States. All are preparing for a major war, which everyone expects sooner or later."[30]

Socialist Views on the Future War

Not everyone was as convinced as Moltke was about war, and there was no shortage of warnings about a looming catastrophe. The speech by Bebel that we have already quoted is perhaps the most relevant example. Indeed, much to the annoyance of the most revolutionary Marxists, the Second Socialist International placed a higher priority on opposing war than on promoting revolution during the decade before 1914. Nevertheless, socialist condemnation of "warmongering imperialism" coexisted with a readiness to defend the nation, especially if faced with enemy aggression.

This may come as a surprise. The resolutions of the Second International continually warned against international politics and the dangers of military folly. The perceptiveness of the International's final resolution at the Basel conference, which was called in November 1912 in response to the First Balkan War, remains striking. After summoning the workers of all countries to oppose capitalist imperialism by international proletarian solidarity, it warned governments not to forget the lesson of the Commune and pointed out that the most likely consequence of war would be revolution. The underlying moral was that: "Proletarians regard it as a crime to shoot at each other for the profits of capitalists, to further the ambitions of dynasties, or for the sake of secret diplomatic treaties."[31]

However, socialists avoided discussing what might happen if the socialists of one or more nations should be convinced of the defensive nature of a future war. Jean Jaurès was an exception in his 1911 book, *L'Armée nouvelle* (The New Army), which recognized that workers did have a *patrie*, which in some circumstances might come under unjustified attack. Jaurès advocated a purely defensive army based to a large extent on citizen reserves to meet such a contingency. But even Jaurès, in the run-up to the war, was more preoccupied by the standard scenario of an "imperialist" war to which the socialist answer would be an international general strike. In fact, the difficulty of organizing such a response, which would disadvantage the best-organized proletariat (namely, the German or British labor movements), paralyzed the Second International in the crucial days preceding the outbreak of war in late July and early August 1914.[32]

French and British Perceptions of Germany

Following the Second Moroccan Crisis, there was increased public belief in both Germany and France that the time for attempts to secure foreign policy gains by diplomatic threat was over. Clemenceau declared to the Senate in November 1911 that France desired peace but, should it prove necessary, would respond to enemy provocation: "If war is imposed on us, we will be ready."[33] Poincaré's speeches as Prime Minister in 1912, and then as President of the Republic from the following year, were similarly firm and popular.[34]

Poincaré's policy of maintaining national security by strengthening existing military agreements with Russia and deepening the "entente" with Britain nonetheless carried increased risks. In particular, France might have to support Russia in a war even if this resulted from conflict between Austria-Hungary and Russia in the Balkans. After the war, and in the light of its catastrophic cost for all the countries concerned, a black myth was forged of *Poincaré-la-guerre* (war-mongering Poincaré), which accused him of plotting with Russia to engineer war with Germany or at least to take an unreasonably hard line that might have the same effect (see chapter 2). This is a huge exaggeration, since the essential French aim was defensive – to limit Germany's threatening behavior and to ensure that Russia stood firm without being provocative. No French government envisaged going to war to recover Alsace-Lorraine; even if the loss of the two provinces remained emotive, it was politically dead. Nonetheless, one can understand why contemporary Germans viewed Poincaré differently. Across the Rhine, he was one of the most hated French leaders, being regarded as an anti-German warmonger interested only in obtaining "revenge" for the defeat of 1871.

The German challenge to British naval superiority (with the "*Dreadnought* race"), following the First Moroccan Crisis, meant that Germany replaced France and Russia as the source of antagonism and possible war for British public opinion. Nonetheless, attempts were made to come to an agreement with Germany on colonial spheres of influence, most notably with the "mission" of Lord Haldane to Berlin in 1912, which sought to transfer Portugal's African colonies to Germany. The mission foundered on German suspicion, and when this resulted in strengthened British relations with France, this too was read in Germany as evidence that Britain had not been serious in the first place.

At the height of the First Balkan War in December 1912, the Kaiser called a "Council of War" of his naval and military chiefs at which he envisaged a European war within 18 months, including "an invasion of England on a grand scale."[35] Historians have failed to agree on the status of this meeting, which seems to have been a response to an immediate crisis rather than a blueprint for future policy. Nonetheless, it painted the imagined scenario of a future conflict embracing the world (through its maritime dimension) as well as Europe. This was reciprocated by the subsequent Anglo-French naval agreement by which the British concentrated their fleet in home waters, including the protection of both shores of the Channel, while the French took over responsibility for security in the Mediterranean.

Rearmament, Eastern Europe, and the Meanings of War

Yet it was events in continental Europe rather than overseas that accentuated the expectation on the part of contemporaries that war had become unavoidable, and supplied the framework of diplomatic confrontation. The realization that *Weltpolitik* had been checked

both by the successful British response to the naval arms race and by the French protectorate in Morocco refocused German attention on the continent in 1912–13. This
occurred at the very moment that nationalist politics were eroding the remains of
Ottoman Turkey's power in the Balkans and, more seriously still, threatening the internal stability and external security of Germany's primary ally since 1879, the multi-ethnic
Dual Monarchy of Austria-Hungary.

A first consequence of this turning point was the decision of the German government
to expand the army after ten years of preference for naval expenditure. The move gained
added urgency from growing fears that Russia was reviving more rapidly than anticipated
from defeat and revolution in 1904–5, and that it was poised to turn Pan-Slav solidarity,
notably with independent Serbia, into an alternative sphere of influence to that of Austria-
Hungary in the Balkans. Any conflict in south-eastern Europe had the potential to set
the two alliance systems against each other, since war between Russia and Austria would
bring in France and Germany on either side, and possibly Britain as well. Perceived failure to face up to a major diplomatic challenge would have equally serious consequences
for the standing and security of the major powers. Hence, a crisis in eastern or south-
eastern Europe would be transmitted to all points of the system of opposed alliances, and
might trigger war, unless there was a countervailing will to use the "concert of Europe"
to prevent a regional conflict engulfing the continent. These were the hardening diplomatic tensions that gave the possibility of war a new actuality.

As early as December 1912, Moltke the Younger, together with Erich Ludendorff, who
was at that time an unknown major on the General Staff, produced a memorandum on the
need for improvements in German military strength. Amongst other demands, they included
an increase of the active German army of some 300,000 men. This demand was criticized
by the civilian government and eventually reduced by around 50 percent.[36] But it triggered
an escalation in military numbers in both countries, as well as a feverish political debate on
army expansion and rearmament. Although still insufficiently studied, such debates were
crucial in bringing contemporaries to accept that war might occur in the near future.

The French discussion of the extension of military service from two to three years may
be used to show how this occurred.[37] The measure, which was debated in the summer of
1913 in direct response to the expansion of the German army, deeply divided French
opinion. Those in favor tended to brand their opponents as traitors or spies. The nationalist poet Charles Péguy, for example, demanded that Jaurès should be "placed against
the wall," and Raoul Villain, the man who actually shot Jaurès on 31 July 1914, claimed
after his arrest that he had done so in order to punish a traitor. Conversely, there was a
minority of hard-core left-wing opinion that rejected any expansion on the simple
grounds of "anti-imperialism."

However, the bulk of opposition to the three-year law by socialists and members of
the all-important Radical Party was more nuanced. Jaurès and others opposed it not
because they rejected national defense, but because they objected to strengthening the
authority of the professional officer corps as opposed to the "Nation in Arms." They
were also not persuaded of the imminence of war. However, enough Radicals felt sufficiently uneasy about the increase in international tensions to ensure that the measure
passed by a two-thirds majority in August 1913. When the issue resurfaced in the general
election in the spring of 1914, over half the deputies who were elected approved of the
Three Year law, despite a swing to the socialists. The debate demonstrates that French
opinion had reached a measure of agreement on the importance of defending France
against a German attack, despite lingering disagreement over the length of military

service. The "Union Sacrée" of August 1914 was the result of this shared acceptance that France was a nation under threat.

The situation in Germany was similar. In the immediate prewar years, the belief that Germany had been encircled by enemy powers was deeply embedded in national discourses. The pace of rearmament by the other major powers, and the dilemma this posed for German strategic planning, made it increasingly urgent to deal with the threat of an apparently resurgent Russia, whose military capacity the German military leadership vastly overrated. The collapsing balance of power in the Balkans seemed to open the glittering prospect of expanded German influence into the declining sphere of Ottoman power, including its Middle Eastern provinces – hence the importance of the Berlin to Baghdad railway as the axis of this one remaining potential colonial domain. Yet the possibility that Austria-Hungary might collapse under the weight of demands from its own Slavic populations, fanned by independent Serbia, opened the opposite prospect of chaos and decline for Germany as well.

This is why the German government firmly supported Austria-Hungary's hard-line approach to the emergent states in the Balkans, and especially Serbia, which pursued a policy of national expansion under the banner of Pan-Serbianism that fed on the inexorable decline of its former overlord, the Ottoman Empire. Austria-Hungary was deeply concerned by the movement for a "Great Serbia" and in order to pre-empt it once and for all, annexed Bosnia-Herzegovina in 1909. Bosnia-Herzegovina was a large multi-ethnic province with a large Serb population over which the Austrians had operated a protectorate since 1878. Germany firmly supported the Austrian coup over Bosnia-Herzegovina, whereas the Russians, still weakened by their defeat in the Russo-Japanese War, were unable to fulfill their traditional role of protector of the Slav peoples.

In the province itself and in Serbia, the Bosnian crisis of 1908–9 left a legacy of hatred and bitterness against Austria-Hungary for what was considered to be a brutal annexation. Meanwhile, Russia found it hard to re-establish its position as protector of the Slav states. For this reason, it tolerated the creation in October 1912 of the Balkan League, an offensive alliance whose aim was to wage war against Ottoman Turkey, which had been further weakened by its military defeat at the hands of Italy in Libya, its sole remaining North African province.

Russia had no choice but to support the alliance of the Balkan states. But in Germany and Austria this fostered the suspicion, and then the certainty, that Russia was promoting "Pan-Slav" objectives whose aim was nothing less than deliberately to overturn the unstable equilibrium between Austria-Hungary and the Balkan states in favor of the latter. In reality, the two Balkan wars of 1912–13 were conducted at the behest of the Balkan powers themselves, the first resulting in the seizure of Thrace and Macedonia from Ottoman Turkey, the second representing an internecine feud in which Greece, Montenegro, and Serbia deprived Bulgaria of its share of the spoils. Only the activation of the "concert" of Europe, by which the great powers prevented the generalization of a regional conflict and imposed a settlement on the participants, prevented a European war though, as we have noted, the socialist Second International at its emergency meeting at Basel and Kaiser Wilhelm II at his hastily-convened Council of War both believed at the end of 1912 that a continental conflict might be nigh. As it happened, the Treaty of London in May 1913 following the first Balkan War appeared to curb Serb ambitions by blocking its access to the Mediterranean with the creation of an Albanian state. But this result was somewhat undermined by the second Balkan War, when Serbia gained most of Macedonia at the expense of Bulgaria, nearly doubling its prewar size.[38]

Following the so-called "Liman von Sanders Affair" in the winter of 1913–14 international suspicions reached new levels. Sanders was a Prussian officer who assumed a high position in the Ottoman army with the goal of both modernizing it and confirming Ottoman Turkey in the German sphere of influence. The Russians were not only opposed to the modernization of the Ottoman military but they also suspected that Germany was using Turkey to gain control over the straits, thus controlling Russian access to the Mediterranean. Consequently, the Russians informed the French that they would do everything necessary to strengthen their army so that, as foreseen in the military convention between the two powers, it could undertake an operation "as simultaneously as possible" against Germany in the event of war.

Because these assurances were made in public and their contents appeared in the press, the Germans were immediately aware of the intensification of Franco-Russian cooperation, which once again appeared to confirm their encirclement. What the public did not know was that the upper echelons of the German military were also concerned at the prospect of quicker Russian mobilization, which might nullify the Schlieffen Plan with its calculation that France could be eliminated before Russia had been fully put on a war footing. This development, which might have suggested greater caution, was taken to mean "better now than later." By the spring of 1914, the stress under which Moltke the Younger labored was palpable, as he combined the belief that action had to be taken with deep fears that it might already be too late.

The July Crisis, 1914

By focusing on how events appeared to contemporaries, it cannot be maintained that the outbreak of war in 1914 came like a bolt from the blue, as is often still said. However, it is important to note the difference between public and press opinion in the major European states and that of their governments. By the summer of 1914 the former were less exercised by the possibility of war than in 1913, during the Second Balkan War and army expansion in Germany and France. In the early summer of 1914, the French public was far more interested in domestic political scandals than in international relations. In Germany the press campaign against Russia, which began in April 1914, achieved little in comparison with the armaments campaign of the previous year.

However, the crucial political and military actors in Germany had a different viewpoint. They immediately understood the murders of Sarajevo as an opportunity to test the strength of the enemy alliances and – if at all possible – to break Germany's "encirclement." Should this not prove successful, they felt that it was better to provoke war in the summer of 1914 than to wait any longer, especially as they feared that within a few years Russia would be more powerful than Germany and the Schlieffen Plan would become inapplicable. These essentially Machiavellian calculations shaped the actions of the key German decision-makers over the course of the July crisis. Whereas the British, in particular, urged the use of the concert mechanism to prevent a general conflict, as had been done the previous year in the case of the two Balkan wars, such an approach now ran counter to the aims of German leaders.

***

It is beyond doubt that the German government bears the most immediate responsibility for the outbreak of the war in August 1914. It issued a blank check for Austria-Hungary to attack Serbia, guaranteeing German support even if it meant war with Russia. This shows that the German military and political leadership intended to challenge the Franco-Russian alliance even at the price of a European war, and that for many (including Moltke the Younger), such a war was precisely the desired goal, as a means of settling the Russian "threat" for good and breaking Germany's "encirclement." The only major unknown factor was whether or not Britain would join in, which explains the outrage in Germany when Britain did so.[39]

Curiously, none of the responsible German politicians appears to have understood that they were opening a Pandora's box. Their conviction that Germany was unjustifiably "encircled" and their view that war was a controlled means of achieving a new freedom of action combined to override any fear that the conflict would turn into a lengthy bloodbath that might transform politics and destroy the social position of those who were waging it, at home and internationally. However, the German and Austrian leaderships were not alone in this. Those who opposed them, while they might have wished for a peaceful resolution to the crisis, were also resolved to embrace war rather than accept a diplomatic coup that would destroy Serbia and diminish Russian power. The illusion that war was still, as Clausewitz had said it should be, "a continuation of policy by other means," remained almost universal.[40] In August 1914, Europe as a whole stood on the brink of a catastrophe that few, if any, understood.

Notes

1 Wolfgang J. Mommsen, *Das Zeitalter des Imperialismus*, Frankfurt am Main, Fischer, 1969, p. 152.
2 Joll, *1914: The Unspoken Assumptions*.
3 Carl von Clausewitz, *On War*, 1832; English translation by Michael Howard and Peter Paret; Princeton, Princeton University Press, 1976; new edition, 1989, p. 76.
4 François Furet, *Le Passé d'une illusion. Essai sur l'idée communiste au XXe siècle*, Paris, Robert Laffont, 1995, p. 49.
5 Quoted in Stig Förster (ed.), *Moltke. Vom Kabinettskrieg zum Volkskrieg*, Bonn, Bouvier, 1992, p. 639.
6 Mommsen, "The Topos of Inevitable War," p. 25.
7 Werner Jung, *August Bebel. Deutscher Patriot und internationaler Sozialist*, Pfaffenweiler, Centaurus Verlag-Gesellschaft, 1988, p. 288 et seq.
8 Goltz, *Nation in Arms*.
9 Clausewitz, *On War*, Book 1, Ch. 7.
10 Alfred von Schlieffen, *Alfred von Schlieffen's Military Writings*, London, Cass, 2003, p. 204.
11 Gerd Krumeich, "Vorstellungen vom Krieg von 1914," in Sönke Neitzel, ed.,*1900: Zukunftsvisionen der Großmächte*, Paderborn, Schönigh, 2004, p. 173 et seq.
12 "Grundzüge der höheren Truppenführung" (1.1.1910), quoted in Jehuda Wallach, *Das Dogma der Vernichtungsschlacht*, Frankfurt am Main, Bernard & Graefe Verlag für Wehrwesen, 1967, p. 119.
13 Ardant du Picq, *Etudes sur le combat*.
14 Richard D. Challener, *The French Theory of the Nation in Arms*, New York, Columbia University Press, 1955; David B. Ralston, *The Army of the Republic*, Cambridge, MA, MIT Press, 1967.
15 Foch, *Principles of War* and *Conduite de la guerre*.
16 Louis de Grandmaison, *Deux Conférences faites aux officiers de l'état-major de l'armée (février 1911)*, Paris, Berger-Levrault, 1911, p. 69.
17 Quoted by Delmas, "La Guerre imaginée," p. 50.
18 Howard, "Men Against Fire."
19 Cosson, "Expériences de guerre du début du 20e siècle"; Hall, *Balkan Wars*.

20 Lindemann, *Les Doctrines darwiniennes et la guerre de 1914.*
21 Friedrich von Bernhardi, *Germany and the Next War*, 1912; translation from German, London, Edward Arnold, 1913, p. 103.
22 Ibid., p. 112.
23 Gerd Krumeich, "Ernest Lavisse und die Kritik an der deutschen 'Kultur', 1914–1918," in Wolfgang J. Mommsen, ed., *Kultur und Krieg. Die Rolle der Intellektuellen, Künstler und Schriftsteller im Ersten Weltkrieg*, Munich, Oldenbourg 1996, pp. 143–54.
24 Mommsen, "The Topos of Inevitable War," p. 24.
25 Ibid., p. 26.
26 Fischer, *War of Illusions*; Chickering, *We Men Who Feel Most German.*
27 Reichstag speech, 14 November 1906. On "encirclement" see Gerd Krumeich, "Einkreisung. Zur Entstehung und Bedeutung eines politischen Schlagwortes," in *Sprache und Literatur in Wissenschaft und Unterricht*, 20, 1989, pp. 99–104.
28 "Russia's Transition to Pseudo-Constitutionalism,' in Max Weber, *The Russian Revolutions* (1906), ed. Gordon C. Wells and Peter Baehr, Cambridge, Polity Press, 1995, p. 233.
29 On the Agadir Crisis, see Geoffrey Barraclough, *From Agadir to Armageddon. Anatomy of a Crisis*, London, Weidenfeld and Nicolson, 1982; Jean-Claude Allain, *Agadir: une crise impérialiste en Europe pour la conquête du Maroc*, Paris, Université de Paris I Panthéon-Sorbonne, 1976.
30 Quoted in Mommsen, "Topos of Inevitable War," p. 205.
31 Haupt, *Socialism and the Great War*, p. 90.
32 Jaurès, *L'Armée nouvelle*; Goldberg, *Jean Jaurès*; Joll, *Second International*, pp. 161–86.
33 Georges Bonnefous, *Histoire politique de la Troisième République*, vol. 1, *L'Avant-guerre (1906–1914)*, Paris, Presses Universitaires de France, 1965, p. 281.
34 Krumeich, *Armaments and Politics*, ch. 1; Weber, *Nationalist Revival*, pp. 129–30; John Keiger, *Raymond Poincaré*, Cambridge, Cambridge University Press, 1997, pp. 145–63.
35 Fischer, *War of Illusions*, p. 163.
36 Cf Stig Förster, *Der doppelte Militarismus. Die deutsche Heeresrüstungspolitik zwischen Status-quo-Sicherung und Aggression 1890–1913*, Stuttgart, Franz Steiner, 1985; Michael Geyer, *Deutsche Rüstungspolitik 1860–1980*, Frankfurt am Main, Suhrkamp, 1984.
37 Krumeich, *Armaments and Politics.*
38 Hall, *Balkan Wars*; Vladimir Dedijer, *The Road to Sarajevo*, London, MacGibbon and Kee, 1967.
39 Stibbe, *German Anglophobia*, pp. 10–47.
40 Clausewitz, *On War*, p. 87.

References and Further Reading

Afflerbach, Holger, and Stevenson, David (eds.), *An Improbable War? The Outbreak of World War I and European Political Culture before 1914*, Oxford and New York, Berghahn, 2007.

Ardant du Picq, Charles, *Etudes sur le combat*, 1880: new edition, Paris, Economica, 2004, with preface by Jacques Frémaux.

Becker, Jean-Jacques, *1914. Comment les Français sont entrés dans la guerre*, Paris, Editions de la Fondation Nationale des Sciences Politiques, 1977.

Becker, Jean-Jacques, *L'Année 14*, Paris, Armand Colin, 2004.

Chickering, Roger, *We Men Who Feel Most German. A Cultural Study of the Pan-German League, 1886–1914*, London, Allen and Unwin, 1984.

Clarke, Ignatius F., *Voices Prophesying War, 1763–1984*, Oxford, Oxford University Press, 1966.

Cooper, Sandi E., *Patriotic Pacifism. Waging War on War in Europe 1815–1914*, New York, Oxford University Press, 1992.

Cosson, Olivier, "Les Expériences de guerre du début du siècle: guerre des Boers, guerre de Mandchourie, guerres des Balkans," in Stéphane Audoin-Rouzeau and Jean-Jacques Becker (eds.), *Encyclopédie de la Grande guerre*, Paris, Bayard, 2006, pp. 97–108.

Delmas, Jean, "La Guerre imaginée par les cinq grands états-majors," in Jean-Jacques Becker et al. (eds.), *Guerre et cultures: 1914–1918*, Paris, Armand Colin 1994, pp. 49–55.

Farrar, Lancelot L., *The Short-War Illusion. German Policy, Strategy and Domestic Affairs, August–December 1914*, London and Santa Barbara, ABC-Clio, 1973.

Fischer, Fritz, *War of Illusions: German Policies from 1911 to 1914*, 1969; English translation, London, Chatto and Windus, 1975.

Foch, Ferdinand, *De la Conduite de la guerre: la manoeuvre pour la bataille*, Paris, Berger-Levrault, 1904.

Foch, Ferdinand, *The Principles of War*, 1903; English translation, London, Chapman and Hall, 1918.

Foley, Robert T., ed., *Alfred von Schlieffen's Military Writings*, London, Frank Cass, 2003.

Geiss, Immanuel, *July 1914: Outbreak of the First World War. Selected Documents*, 1965; translation from German, London, Batsford, 1967.

Goldberg, Harvey, *The Life of Jean Jaurès*, Madison, University of Wisconsin Press, 1968.

Goltz, Colmar von, *The Nation in Arms*, 1883; English translation, London, W. H. Allen, 1887.

Hall, Richard C., *The Balkan Wars, 1912–1913. Prelude to the First World War*, London, Routledge, 2000.

Haupt, Georges, *Socialism and the Great War: the Collapse of the Second International*, 1965; English translation, Oxford, Clarendon Press, 1972.

Herrmann, David G., *The Arming of Europe and the Making of the First World War*, Princeton, Princeton University Press, 1996.

Howard, Michael, "Men Against Fire. Expectations of War in 1914," in Steven Miller, Sean Lynn-Jones, and Stephen Van Evera (eds.), *Military Strategy and the Origins of the First World War. An International Security Reader*, Princeton, Princeton University Press, 1991, pp. 3–19.

Jaurès, Jean, *L'Armée nouvelle*, 1911; new edition, Paris, Imprimerie Nationale, 2003; English, abridged translation, *Democracy and Military Service*, ed. G. G. Coulton, London, Simpkin Marshall, 1916.

Joll, James, *1914: The Unspoken Assumptions*, London, Weidenfeld and Nicolson, 1968 (inaugural lecture), republished in H. W. Koch (ed.), *The Origins of the First World War: Great Power Rivalry and German War Aims*, London, Macmillan, 1984, pp. 307–28.

Joll, James, *The Second International, 1889–1914*, 1955; new edition, London, Routledge and Kegan Paul, 1974.

Krumeich, Gerd, *Armaments and Politics in France on the Eve of the First World War: The Introduction of Three-Year Conscription 1913–1914*, 1980, translated from German, Leamington Spa, Berg, 1984.

Lindemann, Thomas, *Les Doctrines darwiniennes et la guerre de 1914*, Paris, Economica, 2001.

Mombauer, Annika, *Helmuth von Moltke and the Origins of the First World War*, Cambridge, Cambridge University Press, 2001.

Mommsen, Wolfgang J., "The Topos of Inevitable War in Germany in the Decade before 1914," in Volker Berghahn and Martin Kitchen, (eds.), *Germany in the Age of Total War*, London, Croom Helm, 1981, pp. 23–45.

Rueger, Jan, *The Great Naval Game. Britain and Germany in the Age of Empire*, Cambridge, Cambridge University Press, 2007.

Snyder, Jack L., *The Ideology of the Offensive. Military Decision Making and the Disasters of 1914*, Ithaca, Cornell University Press, 1984.

Stibbe, Matthew, *German Anglophobia and the Great War, 1914–1918*, Cambridge, Cambridge University Press, 2001.

Weber, Eugen, *The Nationalist Revival in France, 1905–1914*, Berkeley and Los Angeles, University of California Press, 1968.

Chapter Two

The War Explained:
1914 to the Present

John F. V. Keiger

On Tuesday, June 28, 1983, the British military historian of World War I and Conservative cabinet minister, Alan Clark, recorded in his diary:

> Today is the sixty-ninth anniversary of the assassination of the Archduke Franz Ferdinand at Sarajevo, the date from which the world changed. At the time no one knew what it meant, though I often think of that prize-winning spoof headline in the *New York Daily News* in June 1920: "Archduke found alive, World War a mistake."[1]

How World War I began has long been, and continues to be, a thriving industry, having generated some 25,000 books and articles by 1991.[2] This chapter is not a narration of the events leading up to the outbreak of war in 1914, which can very easily be found elsewhere.[3] Rather, it attempts to explain the context of the historical debate, to show how the causes of the war have been written about, and to see why particular explanations have been developed.

Why Study the Causes?

If the causes of World War I are one of the most written-about subjects in modern history, it is partly because the fierce and polemical debate on the war's causes is almost as old as the war itself. Whole books are now written about how the causes of the war have been written about.[4] Major academic conferences are staged at every conceivable anniversary of the war's outbreak. In all countries, according to the major historian of World War I, Jean-Jacques Becker, the leading contemporary historians, and those of other periods, have never stopped analyzing, first the question of responsibility for the war, and then its origins. Why should that be? He quotes the celebrated French historians Jean-Baptiste Duroselle and François Furet, who at the end of their lives still found World War I respectively "incomprehensible" and "enigmatic" in terms of its outbreak, scale, and destructive power.[5] The American diplomat and historian George Kennan declared in 1979 that World War I was "*the* great seminal catastrophe of this century."[6] A catastrophe, then, whose causes needed to be explained, as a duty to humanity, in order to comprehend the war's momentous consequences: communism, fascism, the gulag, the Holocaust, a further world war and, as the well-known British historian Eric Hobsbawm put it in his *Age of Extremes*, "one of the worst centuries in the history of humanity only brought to a close by the velvet revolutions and the coming down of the Iron Curtain in 1989."[7]

Or is the explanation more prosaic? Is it because for all the research carried out, a strong whiff of doubt continues to surround the origins and causes of the war? This is no mere historical pedantry. There are clear historical and political reasons for the doubt. Historically, there are still areas associated with the immediate causes of the conflict where the archival evidence remains incomplete on important issues such as French President Raymond Poincaré's visit to Russia in July 1914. The question of the causes of the war quickly became embroiled in the politically charged question of responsibility for the war and what became known in the 1920s as the War Guilt Question, to which we shall return later. Viewed as a trend over the almost hundred years since its outbreak it could be argued that responsibility for the conflict has never been firmly fixed and any one country squarely nailed. In almost postmodern fashion the question of causes has mutated through cycles that have reflected international preoccupations of the day, giving rise to a cottage industry in *how* the origins debate has been written about.

History may be written by the victors, but there are different degrees of winning and thus different histories of the war's causes, its conduct, and its conclusion that apply to different states. Take for instance France's role in the origins of the war. The old quip that "the French won the war but lost the peace" is true, but more serious still, the French won the war but lost the history. In other words, the French were not victorious enough on the battlefield to be able to guarantee that the history that was written of the causes of World War I was sufficiently kind to them. The history that predominated was an "Anglo-Saxon" one. And because the Anglo-Americans wanted Germany brought back into the international and trading systems, they were kinder to Germany, consciously or not, and to Germany's role in the causes of World War I, while being harsher to France. This historical trend of harshness on France was true for the 1920s, and did not abate in the light of subsequent extraneous international events, such as French defeat and collaboration in World War II or Gaullist anti-Anglo-Saxon foreign policy in the 1960s, all of which cultivated popular negative images of France that infected serious historical writing on France's role in the outbreak of the war.

The war's outbreak has also found favor with policy makers as a counter-model. As David Stevenson writes: "The decision to halt the war was evaluated much more professionally than had been the decision to start it."[8] Policy and decision-makers have attempted to learn from this so that the outbreak of World War I has become an object lesson in how not to conduct international politics, an example of poor "crisis management." During the 1962 Cuban Missile Crisis, when the world apparently stood on the brink of a third world war between the two nuclear superpowers, American President John F. Kennedy, possessing no textbook of crisis management for presidents, ordered his close decision-making circle to read Barbara Tuchman's *The Guns of August* – which detailed the frenzied and confused international decision-taking process that ended in the outbreak of World War I – so as not to repeat the error.[9] Kennedy's intention in particular was to ensure that the process of decision-making did not run away with itself in the way it seemed to do in 1914 and to ensure that the lines of communication were maintained with the Soviet leadership. Reflecting on the lessons of the Cuban Missile Crisis, American Secretary of Defense Robert McNamara noted soberly: "Today there is no longer any such thing as military strategy; there is only crisis management."[10] Although

an overstatement, before Cuba there was little by way of an explicit theory of crisis management to guide policy makers in international relations. Since then, in the handbooks
of management techniques for decision-makers the unfolding of the 1914 July Crisis is
analyzed in terms of information-processing, decision making under crisis, command
and control, the coordination of diplomatic and military actions and the problems of
communication with an opponent.[11]

Further interest in the "causes" debate has been generated by the changing methodology in studying the war's causes. Analysis has moved a long way from the narrowly
defined "diplomatic history" accounts of international relations prior to 1914 that
focused, in the time-worn phrase, on "what one Foreign Office clerk wrote to another."
Today international historians borrow from a range of disciplines in order to understand
the intricate web of causality.

Structuralist versus Intentionalist Causes

From a methodological point of view, most causality in history involves separating imper-
sonal from personal actions and assessing their relative weight. Social scientists call this
the difference between structural or functional explanations of causality (economic,
social, political, or imperial) and intentionalist (individual decisions) explanations. In
establishing the causes of World War I, structural or big causes and individual or intentionalist ones have vied with each other for primacy. As James Joll noted: "We often feel
that the reasons the politicians themselves were giving are somehow inadequate to
explain what was happening and we are tempted to look for some deeper and more general cause to explain the catastrophe." And Joll quoted the great Italian authority on the
war's origins, Luigi Albertini, who referred to "the disproportion between the intellectual and moral endowments [of the decision makers of 1914] and the gravity of the
problems which faced them, between their acts and the results there-of."[12] This goes to
the heart of the debate about human agency and structural causes in historical causality.
When the German Chancellor, Bethmann Hollweg, remarked on the eve of war on July
30, 1914 that the people were peaceful, "but things are out of control,"[13] does this imply
that individuals could do nothing and that somehow greater forces had taken over? Or
could it be that individual decision-makers can sometimes lose control of events, not
because of greater forces bearing down on them, but for perfectly understandable short-
term reasons – speed of events, lack of communication, error, misinterpretation, incompetence? The actions of politicians and the military can often be a good deal less rational
than conspiracy theorists might have us believe, but absence of rationality does not mean
that historians should immediately reach for structural explanations: human error and
incompetence are legitimate causes in their own right.

Nationalism, militarism, Social Darwinism, public opinion, domestic causes, imperialism, the alliance systems, to name the most prominent, have all at one time or another
jostled for prominence against the activities of individual decision-makers, and James
Joll's *Origins of the First World War* provides a balanced analysis of structural versus individual causes. But what is the nature of these structural causes? While it is not possible
within the constraints of this chapter to outline all of them, it is important to get a flavor
of their nature in order to understand the wider debate on the causes of World War I.

Nationalism's role in causality is usually presented as no longer the positive and liberating nationalism that was said to characterize the French revolutionary armies, but the
subsequent militaristic nationalism that asserted nationhood through conquest. When

combined with philosophers identifying war as positive, such as Friedrich Nietzsche, or modeling the development of society on the discoveries of Charles Darwin's 1859 *Origin of Species*, with its notions of natural selection and survival of the fittest, the resulting Social Darwinism was, it is argued, powerful and pernicious. By the end of the nineteenth century the purely historical concept of Nation began to be fused with the pseudo-biological concept of Race to imply a supposed superiority of certain races and a legitimization of the conquest of the inferior "races." War, then, could be seen as a positive test of the survival of the fittest, as well as a justification for the expansion of armies and the development of a military posture. These underlying trends in European society, it is argued, played a role in the complex matrix of causality.

It is also argued that such abstract theories entered the collective consciousness through the development of national education systems in Europe after 1870, when an increasing number of states adopted free compulsory schooling. In France it was said to have been the Prussian schoolmaster who had won the 1870 Franco-Prussian war; Britain's victories, it was claimed, were won on the playing fields of Eton. Increasingly there were fewer and fewer limits on what the nation could ask of its citizens. The schools of the French Republic, Britain, Germany, Austria-Hungary, and Italy cultivated notions of duty and honor and of serving one's country right down to the supreme sacrifice, so sardonically undermined by the war poet Wilfred Owen in his poem about: "the old lie: *Dulce et decorum est / Pro patria mori*."[14]

The militarization of European societies continued apace in peacetime through compulsory military service on the European continent where an incipient propaganda reinforced notions of the glory and superiority of one's own nation. This was instrumentalized in civil society by the popularity of military bands and tattoos, the romanticism of the soldier, rifle clubs, and paramilitary organizations, such as the Boy Scout movement, founded by Lieutenant-Colonel Baden-Powell, hero of Mafeking, for which the uniform was an exact imitation of Baden-Powell's own, worn in Kashmir in 1907 and whose motto, "Be Prepared," had originally been followed by "to die for your country." By this process the armed forces became the incarnation of the nation.

At the same time the steady democratization of European societies through the extension of the suffrage, participation in state machinery from local government to the payment of taxes, the development of a mass culture through a popular press – with newspapers such as Britain's *Daily Mail* reaching an audience of one million readers by 1896 – meant that citizens increasingly identified with the state, which filled the vacuum left by the decline of religion and the church. Citizens drew direct and tangible benefit from the state, for example through old-age pensions in Germany and Britain in the 1880s and 1909, respectively. Many now had an interest and a stake in the state and were increasingly willing to defend it, even to the death. As a consequence war was no longer the sole prerogative of kings or even political leaders, but was increasingly the focus of the people, and not just the middle classes. The music halls made "jingoism" a source of fun and entertainment for the "man on the Clapham omnibus." His political support could be conjured up for the expansion of armaments programs, as with the well-known cry of "We want eight and we won't wait," which called for the laying-down of more British Dreadnought battleships in 1909 to counter the German naval expansion program.

Even the structuralists would not claim that this made war inevitable, but they would suggest that it helped make the mobilization of the masses easier when a crisis or a conflict came. Public opinion, they would argue, could always be called upon to uphold the values and principles of the Nation. Hence when war came in 1914, all sides, whether the

British, French, or Russians on the one hand, or the Germans and Austro-Hungarians on the other, could claim that they were fighting a just war, a defensive war for the values of their nation which, after all, were superior to those of others. Thus by 1914 war was more than ever a question of life or death, not just for individual citizens, but for states themselves, which believed that if at this moment they did not stand up to their opponents they would disintegrate, become prey to revolution, or at best, have to live in the shadow of their rivals.

This reasoning had long been a stimulant for increased military spending, the development of an arms race and an offensive posture and strategy. It had a direct impact on those who were paid to defend the nation – the military. They increasingly called for the nation to be prepared for any security threat from abroad. This, in conjunction with the underlying trend of technological developments in the nature of armaments (better guns, ships, and equipment), meant that a greater emphasis was placed on having a margin of superiority over one's potential enemy. This in turn meant knowing one's enemy, reflected in the development at the beginning of the twentieth century of modern intelligence agencies seeking to secure that additional information about their potential enemy's strategy, tactics, and equipment, that might give them a margin of superiority in any conflict. This contributed to the European arms race that is also pointed to by some as an underlying cause in the outbreak of war in 1914 – the major powers' total expenditure on defense rising by more than 50 percent in the years 1894–6 alone. The strategic invasion plans of the major powers, from the German Schlieffen Plan to France's Plan XVII, with their emphasis on speed of mobilization, heightened an already febrile international atmosphere with trigger-happy military commands.

One of the oldest structural causes is that of economic rivalry, first made famous by Karl Marx, who claimed that "Wars are inherent in the nature of capitalism: they will only cease when the capitalist economy is abolished."[15] Certainly, economic rivalry between states from the 1890s, epitomized in books such as *Made in Germany* (1896) or *Le Danger allemand* (1896), in which Germany was depicted as stealing British or French markets, was a further source of tension in international relations up to 1914. Also to blame, according to Lenin, was capitalism's offspring – imperialism. In his 1916 pamphlet, *Imperialism, the Highest Stage of Capitalism*, Lenin argued that since the turn of the century capitalism had entered an even more aggressive phase, that placed a premium on new investment opportunities that could only be developed through the control of new colonies and markets leading to imperial rivalry between the powers. Though both economic and imperial rivalries did exist, it should not be overlooked that there was also much economic and imperial cooperation between major powers.

To this list of structural causes could be added certain domestic developments, in which some powers looked to war as a means of overcoming, or defusing, potentially dangerous political situations at home. Equally important was the crystallization of two blocs – the Triple Alliance (Germany, Austria-Hungary, and Italy) and the Triple Entente (France, Russia, and Britain) – which was said to divide the international system into antagonistic camps, rendering it dangerously inflexible when confronted by a crisis. And so the sedimentation of underlying or structural causes can go on being built up until the accumulated strata point to only one conclusion: the inevitability of the war. But such determinism still begs the question as to why the war occurred in 1914 and not before or after. In the end it is not a structural cause that pulls the trigger.

Some historians over the years, notably in Britain, have preferred to concentrate their efforts on the immediate short-term actions of individual decision-makers and the immediate reasons why they took them. They have tended to believe that these "intentionalist" explanations are the only ones that can be supported by documentary evidence and that to reason in terms of structural causes is to impose a pattern on events that cannot be empirically proved. Nevertheless, much of the intentionalist school has taken on board James Joll's pioneering work from the late 1960s on the "unspoken assumptions" that underlie the thought processes of the decision-makers, as well as the constraints on their freedom to choose in particular circumstances. Most would accept that individual leaders and governments were conditioned in their reasoning and perceptions of events by broader societal trends resulting from longer-term cultural, political, social, or educational traditions.

The tension between structural and intentionalist causes has most recently resurfaced in a collection edited by the historian Holger Herwig and the sociologist Richard Hamilton, who criticize the highly deterministic processes that underlie structural causal analysis and the way in which, according to them, this always yields a given outcome whatever the nature or activity of the decision-makers, so that nationalism, for instance, becomes an irresistible force. They also criticize the highly selective way that certain structural explanations are highlighted while others are ignored. Thus nationalism predominates over the forces of internationalism, militarism over pacifism, alliance systems are blamed even though the contents of many of the secret treaties were not known at the time, or public opinion is summoned up when little is known about what mass attitudes represented, given the absence of opinion polling, while the press is analyzed without any explanation of readers' reactions to it.[16] Hamilton and Herwig come down on the side of the intentionalists and call for greater research into the mindsets and actions of what they refer to as the "coterie" of elites among the decision-makers. While one would not disagree with that call for more research, it is to be hoped that in future research the either/or accounts, even antagonism between the two, could be replaced by a more integrated analysis that brings together long-term and immediate causes so that a clearer picture of causality emerges from the given conditions with which governments necessarily live at various moments and the actions that they and individual decision-makers take.

Systemic Causes

Systemic explanations focusing on causality arising from the workings of the international system have a long history. As early as the 1920s the British classicist G. Lowes Dickinson famously described the prevailing state of international relations before 1914 as one of "international anarchy."[17] More recently the end of peace has been explained in terms of the gradual erosion of the old Concert of Europe, whereby the Great Powers, from the end of the Napoleonic Wars a century before, regularly, albeit informally, concerted on problems or adjustments that needed to be made to the international system.[18] Other systemic explanations have found favor with interdisciplinary historians working on the margins of international relations theory, such as Harry Hinsley, who suggested that every general war since 1494 occurred when the international system was undergoing a massive shift in the sources and distribution of international power and that no general wars have occurred outside these shifts in power. Thus World War I resulted from the "international unsettlement" in international relations which began in the 1890s, in part characterized by the rise of Germany.[19]

Other system analysts, such as Paul Schroeder, have suggested that instead of focusing on the causes of war, scholars should analyze the causes of peace and why that peace no longer held. After all, 1914 was the first time that the European Great Powers had been at war with each other for 40 years, and the first conflict involving all the Great Powers for a century. Why should it be that between 1815 and 1914, 23 international wars had been fought on the European continent, of which half had been small wars involving fewer than 10,000 battle fatalities, and that those conflicts had not led to a general conflagration of the Great Powers, even though World War I began as a local war launched by Austria-Hungary against Serbia?[20] Schroeder believes that the break-down of peace requires a deeper understanding of what "realists" in international relations theory would study, such as the nature of the international system, its political culture, its norms, rules, and practices, the existing distribution of power, the constituent states' opportunities for maneuver, their vulnerabilities, the power-political patterns of behavior. Furthermore, less attention should be given to the states in the system whom we now know to have been at greater fault in the war's cause, Austria-Hungary and Germany, and more attention to the dominant powers, France and Britain, whose system it largely was, who regulated it unofficially through the remnants of the Concert of Europe and who held the initiative in world affairs in what was a "zero-sum game."[21]

Reflecting the way that historians write about the present when thinking about the past, models of the war's causality have often expressed contemporary international relations. During the Cold War and the division of the world into two, there was a tendency to view international relations before 1914 as bipolar, and divided between two rigidly separated and rival blocs in which power, prestige, and security were key determinants and in which emphasis was placed on the alliance system in the war's causes. As David Stevenson points out, during the resurgence of superpower tension under Presidents Carter and Reagan in the late 1970s and early 1980s, American political scientists and historians analyzed the pre-1914 system in terms of comparative and thematic studies of war plans, intelligence, and armaments. This analysis turned on how far war was accidental (or system generated) and how far it was willed by governments.[22]

It could be argued that in the post-Cold War era traditional ideological international politics have given way to ethnic nationalism, the primacy of economics, and greater reference to cultural determinants of power politics, from Samuel Huntington's "Clash of Civilizations" to Francis Fukuyama's "End of History," and that this has influenced writing on the causes of World War I. Thus explanations of the war's outbreak have resorted to more ethno-cultural phenomena. Avner Offer has underlined the importance of codes of honor and duty, right down to that of the supreme sacrifice, among the European elites as helping to explain the inflexibility of certain leaders and their inability to back down for fear of dishonoring themselves and their country.[23] Thomas Lindemann has placed the emphasis on the ethno-cultural role of social Darwinism in influencing German decision-makers and their perception of international relations.[24] With the New World Disorder of the opening decade of the second millennium, one might expect historians to begin thinking in terms of earlier causal explanations along the lines of Lowes Dickinson's "international anarchy."

Of growing interest in the writings on the war's causes is the important question of the historiography of the origins debate. This goes to the heart of the question of how and why historians write about certain events and the nature of the evidence they use, which is partly a reflection of contemporary preoccupations in cultural studies with historiography itself.

The Politics of the War Guilt Question

The old adage that history is written by the victors is particularly true of the causes of World War I. The Versailles peace treaty took the unprecedented step of including an article, 231, which laid sole responsibility for the outbreak of the war with Germany – the so-called "war guilt clause." This clause became the justification for the massive war reparations Germany was to pay in the postwar period, principally to France. It followed that if Germany could show that she was not solely to blame for the war, she could challenge the validity of article 231 and, with it, the payment of the reparations. This she set out to do.[25]

The other power with an acute interest in the war guilt debate was the new Soviet regime. For ideological reasons it wished to heap discredit on its Tsarist predecessor in order to bolster its own legitimacy and popularity both internally and externally. If it could show that the autocratic Tsarist regime, in collaboration with the "bourgeois" President of France, Raymond Poincaré, were together responsible through the Franco-Russian alliance for the outbreak of World War I, the Soviets could kill two birds with one stone: discredit Tsarist Russia and justify not repaying to France the massive prewar loans.

The pragmatic Soviet approach found ideological support in Lenin's interpretation of World War I in his 1916 *Imperialism, the Highest Stage of Capitalism*, which resonated with many on the European Left. His description of war as the natural consequence of the Great Powers' competition for colonies and investment markets logically implied that the Central Powers were not alone in shouldering responsibility for the war – a position that many socialists in all countries had adopted during the conflict.

In other countries, even on the side of the victors, the notion of shared responsibility, largely inspired by President Woodrow Wilson's contention that everyone was a victim of the international system and its secret treaties, gained a following. This was music to Germany's ears and a fillip for the revisionists. As the British wartime leader David Lloyd George later put it: "The nations slithered over the brink into the boiling cauldron of war."[26] In 1919 the American Senate refused to ratify the Versailles Treaty and the United States slipped back into isolationism with murmurs of all the powers being somehow at fault. The ground for revisionism was prepared.

The stakes in the *Kriegsschuldfrage*, or war guilt question, were extremely high. France made a most credible scapegoat on to whom the blame could be shifted, given the loss of the provinces of Alsace-Lorraine to Germany in 1871 and the fact that France's effective leader in the two years preceding the war, Raymond Poincaré, had followed resolute policies intent on strengthening France's links with her allies, especially Russia, and was a Lorrainer to boot. It was suggested that Poincaré had plotted a war of *revanche* against Germany to retrieve the lost provinces. The war guilt debate became all the more impassioned in that Poincaré became prime minister again in the 1920s and pursued a strict application of the Treaty of Versailles and the payment of reparations.

Germany began a campaign to undermine article 231. A special office was created in the German Foreign Office to deal with this issue – the War Guilt Section. It organized, financed, and directed two other units: the Working Committee of German Associations for Combating Lies Concerning War Responsibility, which provided the "right" literature and information to organizations such as trade unions and various clubs, and the Centre for the Study of the Causes of the War, created in 1921, which from 1923 published the influential monthly journal *Die Kriegsschuldfrage*, edited by the historian

Alfred von Wegerer. This is where the "serious" historical work was done to demonstrate the inaccuracy of article 231 by "sponsoring" journalists, editors, publicists, and academics in the "cause of patriotic self-censorship." The work of these units provided much of the impetus for the "revisionist school," which in the 1920s dominated historical writing on the war's origins from Europe to the United States, successfully displacing much of the blame from Germany.

Paradoxically, Germany's campaign found support in French domestic politics. The French Left, notably the newly formed French Communist Party, tarred Poincaré with responsibility for the war and depicted him as *Poincaré-la-guerre*. This was fertile ground for German and Soviet propaganda, the former having already financed such initiatives during the war itself, as shown by German documents captured by the allies in 1945 from the German Foreign Ministry and published in the 1960s. The desire to discredit Poincaré was shared by broader currents of opinion on the French left, which wished to thwart or destabilize his return to power. Though the Radical Party would broadly support his firm line against Germany over reparations and vote for it in parliament, they were not averse to exploiting the *Poincaré-la-guerre* myth when politically expedient, as during the 1924 general election campaign. The far left, especially the Communists, were, on the other hand, unswervingly critical of his policy and already in favor of resuming the prewar policy of seeking improved relations with Germany as the solution to what was becoming the German "question." In the 1920s all Poincaré's political opponents were able to draw on the potent myth of *Poincaré-la-guerre* in order to attack him, and did so quite unscrupulously.

The myth was fueled in the postwar period by a mixture of revisionist literature and polemical pamphleteering. It developed in an international intellectual and moral climate which, as a result of the horrors and carnage of the war, tended toward pacifism and antimilitarism and looked to the newly formed League of Nations for the settlement of international disputes. Widespread literature in 1920s France, often supported by Soviet and German propaganda, pointed to Poincaré's alleged guilt and was given greater credence by Poincaré's decision as prime minister to occupy the industrial Ruhr in pursuit of the reparations owed by Germany to France and Belgium.

The only credible counter to this torrent of invective was the serious research by the historian Pierre Renouvin, notably in his 1925 work, *The Immediate Origins of the War,* which showed that the principal responsibility for the war lay with the Central Powers.[27] But this kind of serious scholarly study was more suited to the academic community than the more sensational world of the press where the "revisionist" line prevailed.

Renouvin's work prompted Poincaré in 1928 to commission him to publish the French official diplomatic documents on the origins of the war, the *Documents Diplomatiques Français, 1871–1914 (DDF).*[28] The intention was to counter the biased, often Bolshevik-inspired, documents on the Tsarist period published in the journal *Red Archive* and in *Un Livre Noir* (3 volumes, 1922–3) and the massive Soviet official collection, *International Relations in the Era of Imperialism* (1931–4), which emphasized the responsibility of both the tsar and Poincaré. The *DDF* were also to balance the publication of the 40-volume German collection, *Die Grosse Politik der europäischen Kabinette, 1871–1914,* whose publication from 1922 to 1927 gave Berlin the dual advantage of portraying the German government as apparently wishing to hide nothing, while being the only extensive official collection of documents on which scholars could work.[29] The British official collection began to appear from 1926 under the title *British Documents on the Origins of the War, 1898–1914.*[30] But the delay in publishing the Allied collections was most woefully apparent with the French collection. They eventually appeared between 1929 and 1958, with the important volume on 1914 not appearing until 1936. This partly explains the inability to correct what had become an incipient orthodoxy resulting from nearly two decades of rumor and revisionist literature. The publication of the *Documents Diplomatiques Français* certainly had little effect in balancing the picture by Poincaré's death in 1934, by which time the revisionist cause had the upper hand. The revisionist stance was reinforced abroad by historians who proceeded with greater subtlety and erudition to implicate Poincaré, especially in the United States, where the works of H. E. Barnes and Sidney Bradshaw Fay set the trend for the international domination of the revisionist interpretation.[31]

Much of this revisionist view of Poincaré and France's role continued even after World War II, despite the fact that war made many historians look again at German responsibility for World War I. In Germany revisionism prevailed. In 1951 a committee of French and German historians, doubtless motivated by a spirit of Franco-German reconciliation, concluded that "the documents do not permit attributing [*sic*] a pre-meditated desire for a European war on the part of any government or people in 1914."[32] Following the obvious responsibility of Nazi Germany for World War II, to have cast blame on Germany for the earlier conflict would have confounded the image that leading German historians, supported by the German state, wished to give of Nazism being an aberration in German history. The consequences of Germany also being the aggressor in 1914 were far-reaching. Germany could be viewed by the international community as having a fatal flaw that permanently threatened European peace, thereby justifying the maintenance of her divided status. As David Stevenson points out, this explains the "ferocious reaction" to German Professor Fritz Fischer's challenge to the revisionist thesis by his contention in 1961 (the year the Berlin Wall was built) in *Griff nach der Weltmacht* (*Grasp for World Power*) that Germany willed war.[33] More seriously still, he hinted at parallels between Germany's ambitions in World Wars I and II, thereby implying a continuity in German history. His 1969 sequel volume, translated as *War of Illusions,* pushed the idea of German responsibility further by suggesting that Germany actively sought war by seizing on the Sarajevo assassination as a pretext to launch a continental offensive that had already been designed at the Potsdam War Council of December 8, 1912. According to Stevenson, "'the Fischer controversy' overturned the orthodoxy of the 1950s, without any one view replacing it, and Fischer has rightly claimed that it helped democratize not only the historical profession but German society generally."[34] In the meantime Fischer was blackballed by much of the German patriotic historical community and attacked by certain politicians. The controversy demonstrated once again the high stakes and the political dimensions of the historical debate on the war's causes.

The Fischer controversy stimulated the historical debate, but for similar in-depth historical research to be carried out on the other powers in 1914 it was necessary to wait for the various national archives to be opened to the public. Germany's archives were available because of their capture by the allies in 1945, even if many of the military records had been bombed during the war. Then came the release of the British and Austrian state papers in the 1960s, followed by the French in the early 1970s. These allowed historical research to broaden its focus from the purely diplomatic accounts in the published collections and investigation of documents in the war, finance, colonial, and individual service archives, not to mention cross-referring these with the various private papers of politicians, civil servants, and military personnel that have progressively come into the public domain in most countries since the 1970s. This led to a crop of country-specific studies for the major powers in the Macmillan "Making of the Twentieth Century" series, which looked at the decision-makers and the decision-making process.[35] These studies considered not just the politicians, but also the diplomats and permanent officials, their social and educational backgrounds, their perceptions and "unspoken assumptions," in James Joll's phrase, as well as the "bureaucratic politics" of the foreign ministries and other government agencies. The volume on France assigned a more passive role to France and to Poincaré in the origins of World War I. However, even though this has been done for the major powers and their foreign ministries, little of this methodology has been used to analyze the other ministries which were instrumental in the policy-making and decision-taking process that led to the conflict, notably the war, colonial, and finance ministries.

Such studies have begun to correct much of the literature on the war's origins since 1919 that, according to John Langdon, was influenced by the revisionist thesis of the 1920s and 1930s. He suggests that the origins of the war taught in American classrooms and textbooks, even in the 1990s, were those of the classical revisionist position – as though the debates since the mid-1980s have been reserved for specialists.[36]

***

There is no sign of interest in the causes of World War I abating, and nor is there likely to be as we move toward the centenary of the war's outbreak. The origins of the war have been analyzed dispassionately by some outstanding historians, but also politically and polemically, from varied standpoints and with different objectives in mind, some more honorable than others. Perhaps that is in the nature of historical enquiry into great events. Nevertheless, even in considering the work of serious historians of the causes of World War I we should be alert to the French historian Marc Bloch's words of caution:

> A graduated classification of causes, which is really only an intellectual convenience, cannot safely be elevated to an absolute. Reality offers us a nearly infinite number of lines of force which all converge together upon the same phenomenon. The choice we make among them may well be founded upon characteristics which, in practice, fully merit our attention; but it is always a choice.[37]

Notes

1   Alan Clark, June 28, 1983, *Diaries*, London, Weidenfeld and Nicolson, 1993, p. 19. Clark had written *The Donkey. A History of the BEF in 1915*, London, 1961; new ed., Pimlico, 1991.

2   Langdon, *Long Debate*, p. 51.

3   An excellent starting-point is Joll, *Origins of the First World War*.

4   Droz, *Causes*; Langdon, *July 1914*; Mombauer, *Origins of the First World War*; Andrew Barros and Frédéric Guelton, "Les imprévus de l'histoire instrumentalisée: le Livre jaune de 1914 et les Documents Diplomatiques Français sur les origines de la Grande Guerre, 1914–1918," *Revue d'histoire diplomatique*, 2006, pp. 3–22.

5   Becker, *L'Année 14*, p. 3.

6   George F. Kennan, *The Decline of Bismarck's European Order: Franco-Russian Relations, 1875–1890*, Princeton, Princeton University Press, 1979, p. 3.

7   E. J. Hobsbawm, *Age of Extremes: The Short Twentieth Century, 1914–91*, London, Weidenfeld and Nicolson, 1994.

8   David Stevenson, *1914–18. The History of the First World War*, London, Penguin, 2004, p. 386.

9   Barbara Tuchman, *The Guns of August*, London, Robinson, 2000; originally published as *August 1914*, London, Constable, 1962.

10   Quoted in Gordon A. Craig and Alexander L. George, *Force and Statecraft: Diplomatic Problems of our Time*, New York and Oxford, Oxford University Press, 1983, p. 205.

11   Ibid., pp. 206, 210–11, 214–19, and the bibliography on crisis management p. 219.

12   All quoted by Harry Hearder in original "Editor's Foreword," in James Joll, *The Origins of the First World War*, Harlow, Longman, 1983, pp. vii–viii. For Albertini, see *The Origins of the War of 1914*, 3 vols., 1942–3; trans. from Italian, Oxford, Oxford University Press, 1952–7; new ed., New York, Enigma, 2005.

13   Ibid.

14   *The Collected Poems of Wilfred Owen*, London, 1931: new ed., Chatto and Windus, 1963, ed. C. Day Lewis, p. 55.

15   Quoted in Joll, *Origins*, p. 123.

16   Hamilton and Herwig, "World Wars: Definitions and Causes," in Hamilton and Herwig (eds.), *Origins of World War I*, pp. 15–35.

17   G. Lowes Dickinson, *The International Anarchy: Europe, 1904–1914*, London, George Allen and Unwin, 1926.

18   Langhorne, *The Collapse of the Concert*.

19   Hinsley, "Introduction: The Origins of the First World War," in Wilson (ed.), *Decisions for War*, p. 1; Harry Hinsley, *Power and the Pursuit of Peace: Theory and Practice in the History of Relations between States*, Cambridge, Cambridge University Press, 1963, p. 7.

20   Hamilton, "The European Wars: 1815–1914," in Hamilton and Herwig, *Origins of World War I*, p. 45.

21   Paul W Schroeder, "Embedded Counterfactuals and World War I as an Unavoidable War," http://www.asu.edu/clas/polisci/cqrm/papers/schroedercounterfactual.pdf, 1–53, accessed July 21, 2006.

22   Stevenson, *Outbreak*, p. 41.

23   Avner Offer, "Going to War in 1914: a Matter of Honour," *Politics and Society*, 23, 1995, pp. 213–41.

24   Thomas Lindemann, *Les doctrines darwiniennes et la guerre de 1914*, Paris, Economica, 2001.

25   For what follows see J. F. V. Keiger, *Raymond Poincaré*, Cambridge, Cambridge University Press, 1997, pp. 193–201.

26   David Lloyd George, *War Memoirs*, 6 vols., London, Odhams Press, 1933–6, vol. I, p. 52.

27   Pierre Renouvin, *Immediate Origins of the War* (28th June–4th August 1914), 1925; trans. from French, New Haven, Yale University Press, 1928.

28   *Documents Diplomatiques Français (1871–1914) relatifs à la guerre de 1914*, Paris, Imprimerie Nationale, 41 vols., 1929–59.

29   Johannes Lepsius, Albrecht Mendelssohn Bartholdy and Friedrich Thimme (eds.), *Die Grosse Politik der Europäischen Kabinett, 1871–1914*, Berlin, Deutsche Verlags Gesellschaft für Politik und Geschichte, 41 vols., 1922–7.

30   G. P. Gooch and H. W. V. Temperley (eds.), *British Documents on the Origins of the War, 1898–1914*, 11 vols., London, HMSO, 1926–38.

31   H. E. Barnes, *The Genesis of the World War. An Introduction to the Problem of War Guilt*, New York, Knopf, 1927; S. B. Fay, *The Origins of the World War*, New York, Macmillan, 2 vols., 1928.

32   Quoted in Stevenson, *Outbreak*, p. 9.

33   Translated into English, however, as *Germany's Aims in the First World War* (1967).

34   Ibid., p. 12.

35   Berghahn, *Germany*; Zara S. Steiner, *Britain and the Origins of the First World War*, London, Macmillan, 1977; Lieven, *Russia*; Keiger, *France*; R. J. B Bosworth, *Italy*; Williams, *Austria-Hungary*.

36 Langdon, *Long Debate*, pp. 21–4.
37 Marc Bloch, "Historical Causation," *The Historian's Craft*, Manchester, Manchester University Press, 1976, pp. 192–3, quoted in T. C. W. Blanning, *The Origins of the French Revolutionary Wars*, London, Arnold, 1986, p. 24.

References and Further Reading

Becker, Jean-Jacques, *L'Année 14*, Paris, Armand Colin, 2004.

Berghahn, V. R., *Germany and the Approach of War in 1914*, 2nd ed., London, Macmillan, 1993.

Bosworth, R. J. B., *Italy and the Approach of the First World War*, London, Macmillan, 1983.

Droz, Jacques, *Les causes de la Première Guerre mondiale: Essai d'historiographie*, Paris, Seuil, 1973.

Fischer, Fritz, *Germany's Aims in the First World War*, 1961; English translation, London, Chatto and Windus, 1967.

Fischer, Fritz, *War of Illusions: German Policies from 1911 to 1914*, 1969; English translation, London, Chatto and Windus, 1975.

Hamilton, Richard F., and Herwig Holger, H. (eds.), *The Origins of World War I*, Cambridge, Cambridge University Press, 2003.

Herrmann, David G., *The Arming of Europe and the Making of the First World War*, Princeton, Princeton University Press, 1996.

Herwig, Holger H. (ed.), *The Outbreak of World War I: Causes and Responsibilities*, Boston, Houghton Mifflin, 1997.

Joll, James, 1914: *The Unspoken Assumptions*, London: Weidenfeld and Nicolson, 1968 (inaugural lecture), republished in H. W. Koch (ed.), *The Origins of the First World War: Great Power Rivalry and German War Aims*, London, Macmillan, 1984, pp. 307–28.

Joll, James, *The Origins of the First World War*, 2nd ed., London, Longman, 1992.

Keiger, John, "Patriotism, Politics and Policy in the Foreign Ministry, 1880–1914," in Robert Tombs (ed.), *Nationhood and Nationalism in France from Boulangism to the Great War 1889–1918*, London: HarperCollins, 1991, pp. 255–66.

Keiger, John F. V., *France and the Origins of the First World War*, London, Macmillan, 1983.

Krumeich, Gerd, *Armaments and Politics in France on the Eve of the First World War: The Introduction of Three-Year Conscription 1913–1914*, Leamington Spa, Berg, 1984.

Langdon, J. W., *July 1918–1990: The Long Debate, 1918–1990*, Oxford, Berghahn, 1991.

Langhorne, Richard, *The Collapse of the Concert of Europe: International Politics, 1890–1914*, London, Macmillan, 1981.

Lieven, D. C. B., *Russia and the Origins of the First World War*, London, Macmillan, 1983.

Miller, S. E. (ed.), *Military Strategy and the Origins of the First World War*, revised edition, Princeton, Princeton University Press, 1991.

Mombauer, Annika, *The Origins of the First World War: Controversies and Consensus*, London, Longman, 2002.

Rueger, Jan, *The Great Naval Game: Britain and Germany in the Age of Empire*, Cambridge, Cambridge University Press, 2007.

Steiner, Zara S., and Neilson, Keith, *Britain and the Origins of the First World War*, 2nd ed., London, Macmillan, 2003.

Stevenson, David, *Armaments and the Coming of War, Europe 1904–1914*, Oxford, Clarendon Press, 1996.

Stevenson, David, *The Outbreak of the First World War: 1914 in Perspective*, Basingstoke, Macmillan, 1997.

Williams, Samuel R., *Austria-Hungary and the Origins of the First World War*, London, Macmillan, 1991.

Wilson, Keith (ed.), *Decisions for War*, London, UCL Press, 1995.

PART II

The Military Conflict

The War Experienced: Command, Strategy, and Tactics, 1914–18

HEW STRACHAN

"Grand strategy" is a phrase associated more with World War II than with World War I, and rightly so. It encompasses the direction of war in its widest sense, political as well as military, social as well as economic. After 1941, the Western Allies, in conjunction with Soviet Russia, integrated strategy with policy, and coordinated their military and economic efforts across different theaters of war: they aimed to make the sum even greater than its parts. Grand strategy did not shape the conduct of World War I in the same way, but it was the culmination of an historical process that began in the very different circumstances of 1914. By 1918 the Allies on the western front were beginning to practice grand strategy, even if they did not yet have a name for it. That omission was rectified in 1923 by a veteran of the war, the British military theorist, J. F. C. Fuller: grand strategy, fully and self-consciously applied in World War II, was itself a lesson learned in World War I.

In the nineteenth century, strategy and policy were regarded as distinct. The great military theorist, Carl von Clausewitz, saw the former as an activity engaged in by generals – the use of the battle for the purposes of the war; the latter was the task of politicians, and involved the use of war for the purposes of the state. In strategy the means is battle but the end is the conduct of the war; in policy the means can be war (although in most activities in which the state engages it is not), but the end lies outside the war. This distinction was fundamental to those who directed World War I, and particularly to its generals. When they used the word strategy they meant something more akin to what we today would call operational thought – the movements of an army within a theater of war.

In 1914 the distinction between strategy and policy was more than just theoretical; it was actual. After 30 years' development, grand strategy in World War II was the product of institutional integration: soldiers and statesmen sat round the same tables in order to blend strategy and policy, and where they did not do that (as in Nazi Germany) there was no grand strategy. In 1914 such integration was infrequent, and the relationship between soldiers and statesmen was often adversarial.

The only state with reasonably well-developed machinery for the integration of strategy and policy at the outbreak of World War I was Britain. However, the Committee of

Imperial Defence, created in 1902, had no executive powers: it was an advisory committee of the cabinet, and in August 1914, when the state's principal business became war, the Committee of Imperial Defence lost its *raison d'être* and went into abeyance. During the first year of the war the cabinet made decisions about strategy with no direct input from the professional heads of the armed services. Not only were the First Sea Lord and the Chief of the Imperial General Staff not members, they were also easily challenged in terms of the strategic views they did advance. Sir John (or Jackie) Fisher, recalled as First Sea Lord soon after the war's outbreak, had spent much of his previous tenure of the post, between 1904 and 1909, blocking attempts to create a naval staff. In 1912 Winston Churchill was brought in as First Lord of the Admiralty (the minister for the navy), precisely to remedy this defect, but the naval staff was granted neither the time nor the support to enable it to flourish.

As a result, the Admiralty functioned during the war as both the administrative offices of the Royal Navy and its operational headquarters. The invention of the wireless, while of less significance for the war on land in 1914–18, transformed war at sea, effectively collapsing the distinctions between policy, strategy, and tactics. Churchill was able to bypass his senior professional naval advisers and interfere in the conduct of operations from long distance, with disastrous consequences. At the Battle of Coronel on November 1, 1914, an inferior naval squadron, egged on from Whitehall, quixotically tilted at the German East Asiatic Squadron and was sent to the bottom of the ocean.

The British army's general staff, created in 1904, much later than those of European armies but long enough to bed down, was emasculated for different reasons. The sudden expansion from a diminutive army for colonial war to a mass force for continental conflict required almost all officers with staff training to go to France. Those left in the War Office in London were "dug out" (the phrase used at the time) from retirement and were headed by a Chief of the Imperial General Staff who quailed before his minister. Extraordinarily, in August 1914, the Liberal government had chosen to appoint a general, Britain's most distinguished imperial proconsul, Field Marshal Lord Kitchener, Secretary of State for War. Given the choice to play the soldier or the civilian, Kitchener tended to opt for the former, wearing his uniform and bypassing his staff, as though he still enjoyed the privileges of field command. His appearance in France to remind Sir John French, the commander-in-chief of the British Expeditionary Force, of his obligations to Britain's ally at the crisis of what became the battle of the Marne in September 1914, set the two on a collision course.

These fault-lines in British decision-making, not only the naval and military dimensions but the political too, became evident in the Gallipoli campaign. Churchill was its prime mover and was able to bully the cabinet into backing him. Fisher, having been keen at the outset, turned against it, and then resigned. The army's prewar staff study on the difficulties of an expedition to the Dardanelles was ignored, and it then found itself picking up the campaign just as the navy seemed inclined to let it go. Kitchener had supported the appointment of one of his protégés, Sir Ian Hamilton, to the command, and planned to soft-pedal the campaign in France, but soon found the tensions between himself and Sir John French reaching boiling point. French leaked to the press his view that his failure in the field was due to the War Office's inability to deliver sufficient high explosive shells. Both naval and military crises broke in May, too late to save the Dardanelles expedition from muddled planning and inconsistent execution, but forceful enough to bring down Britain's last Liberal government and to enable Asquith, the British prime minister, to create a coalition.

Between May 1915 and mid-1917 the two services, and particularly the army, dominated the creation of strategy. In December 1915 Sir William Robertson secured the right to present his views directly to the cabinet when he was appointed the Chief of the Imperial General Staff. Kitchener was increasingly sidelined, even before his death on June 5, 1916. But Robertson did not enjoy the status of an Alanbrooke or a Marshall in British and American counsels in World War II. The theater commanders, and particularly Sir Douglas Haig, appointed in succession to French after the failed offensive at Loos in October 1915, had greater political leverage. Moreover, not until the formation of a formal war cabinet with the establishment of Lloyd George's coalition government in December 1916 were soldiers and politicians brought together in an executive committee created for the prosecution of war; here in embryo was the institutional framework for the creation of grand strategy. In the hands of its secretary, Maurice Hankey, the war cabinet's discussions were framed into decisions. However, despite the losses in the battle of the Somme in the second half of 1916, Lloyd George was still unable fully to master the generals. He was a Liberal (and a radical one too) at the head of a government backed by Conservatives, whose inclinations and whose press supported the generals. When Lloyd George tried to subordinate Haig and the British Expeditionary Force to the French high command, he found himself isolated, the army's own outrage mirrored by the king and by many of the cabinet, positions justified when the French offensive of April 1917 miscarried. Moreover, Lloyd George had a personal problem as well. He and Haig had one attribute in common: they were both possessed of unquenchable resolve and a determination to fight through to victory. In the final analysis, albeit with caveats, the prime minister, lured by his need for a great victory, was ready to back the British offensive at Ypres launched in July 1917.

Culminating in the mud of Passchendaele, the Third Battle of Ypres shook public perceptions of Haig. Moreover, it exposed the fault lines between the commander-in-chief and Robertson, his principal support in London. Since late 1915 the latter had become increasingly convinced that limited offensives, designed to wear the enemy down, not big breakthrough battles, were the way ahead for the foreseeable future. In his continuing optimism, Haig believed that a breakthrough was possible and victory achievable in short order, but he was increasingly isolated: he was forced to change his principal staff officers in the winter of 1917–18, and in February 1918 Lloyd George was able to exploit the division between Haig and Robertson and engineer the latter's resignation. Although Haig was not sacked after March 21, 1918, when the Germans launched their most successful offensive in the west since 1914, he had to sacrifice one favored army commander, the youthful cavalryman, Sir Hubert Gough, and accept his own subordination to Ferdinand Foch, appointed allied generalissimo on March 26. The strength of Lloyd George's position in relation to the army was made evident in May 1918, when the director of military operations in London wrote to the press accusing the prime minister of lying to the House of Commons. The army had very little support in parliament and little appetite for a fight outside it. The effect was to make Lloyd George's supremacy all too clear. For the last stages of the war the different components of Britain's national strategy, land operations on all fronts (and not just the principal front in France), the war at sea, and the economic effort that underpinned both elements, were coordinated under overall civilian control.

Developments in France were remarkably similar. The Conseil Supérieur de Guerre was weakened in the aftermath of the Dreyfus affair, itself a symbol of the tensions rather than the cooperation between the army and the Third Republic. Reformed in 1911, it lapsed with the outbreak of the war. The declaration of a state of siege from the outset of the war, the invasion of France, and the evacuation of the government from Paris to Bordeaux meant that the army combined civil and military authority in much of the country. In Germany the promulgation of the Prussian law of siege of 1851 had similar effects, giving corps commanders governmental powers within their districts. Moreover, as in Germany, the chief of the general staff, Joseph Joffre, not only had effective control of all the fronts on which the army was deployed but was also the theater commander on the most important of those fronts, that in France. The union of the Third Republic and the army, after decades of mistrust based on fears that army officers were both Catholic and royalist, was welcomed by both sides and sealed by the "miracle" of the Marne. Joffre had saved Paris, not least in the eyes of a grateful public. But that very popularity, reinforced by the army's real administrative authority within metropolitan France, rekindled another fear, that of Bonapartism. Joffre's star waned in the course of 1915, his offensives doing more harm, it seemed, to the French army than to the German. In December 1915 the prime minister, Aristide Briand, actually extended Joffre's command to theaters outside France, notably Salonika, in order to prevent the British dominating decision making in the eastern Mediterranean.

However, the battle of Verdun, which to all intents and purposes spanned the whole of 1916, and which bonded the army, the nation, and the republic in blood, seriously undermined Joffre. The commanders in the battle itself, first Philippe Pétain, who staved off the German assaults, and then Robert Nivelle, who launched successful counterattacks toward the end of the year, eclipsed their rotund and paternal superior. Parliament went into secret session to discuss Joffre's conduct of the war, and in December, when Joffre was replaced by Nivelle, the posts of commander-in-chief in the field and chief of the general staff were divided.

Although many of his subordinates were (rightly) skeptical when Nivelle said he could break through the enemy's line in 48 hours, the government was still not sufficiently strong politically to call Nivelle's bluff. His failure in April 1917 and his replacement by Pétain left the government in the driving seat, its problem now being its uncertainty as to where to go. With revolution in Russia and war-weariness at home, some favored peace negotiations, but Georges Clemenceau, confronted by a choice of compromise or war to the bitter end, embraced the latter when appointed prime minister in November 1917. The government having fully committed itself to the war effort, the generals now had no other political choice than to back it. Moreover, Clemenceau, like Lloyd George, could master his generals by divide and rule. With Foch's appointment to the allied supreme command and Pétain as commander-in-chief, he had two to choose from; to make sure, he held office as minister of war as well as prime minister. By 1918 both Lloyd George and Clemenceau enjoyed a degree of authority in the formation of policy that also gave them leverage over strategy. After October 1917 and the defeat at Caporetto, the same could be said of their Italian counterpart, Vittorio Orlando, who dismissed the chief of the general staff, Luigi Cadorna.

The same could not be said of either the Kaiser or his chancellors in Germany after 1916. Although the Kaiser in theory embodied supreme civil and military authority, personal rule was probably an impossible task for anybody in an industrialized state fighting a major war in the twentieth century – and was certainly beyond Wilhelm II. Germany was a state caught between autocracy and modernity, its emperor representing Prussian militarism on the one hand and the fastest industrializing state in Europe on the other. To begin with, his status as supreme commander held, in that his decisions both to appoint Helmuth von Moltke the Younger as chief of the general staff in 1905, and to choose as his successor the Prussian minister of war, Erich von Falkenhayn, in September 1914 after the defeat on the Marne, were personal ones.

However, the overrunning of Poland and the conquest of Serbia in 1915 were chalked up not to Falkenhayn's credit but to that of August von Mackensen, the field commander, and even the latter, for all the victories won under his command, found his reputation eclipsed by that of the heroes of Tannenberg, Paul von Hindenburg and Erich Ludendorff. Both the latter, buoyed by their own successes in the Baltic States, argued that Germany's main effort should be on the eastern front, where the opportunities for maneuver seemed greater and where the Tsarist regime looked brittle. Falkenhayn's aim in the east was to secure a separate peace with Russia, but in spite of his massive gains he did not get it. Hindenburg and Ludendorff were not his only problem; so were Germany's ally, Austria-Hungary, and its grandiloquent chief of staff, Franz Conrad von Hötzendorff. The Russians may have been inferior militarily to the Germans, but not to the Austrians, and thus they could offset defeat against one ally with victory against the other.

In October 1915 Germany had to support Austria-Hungary in the Balkans to complete the defeat of Serbia, and thereafter the pull of the Italian front lured Vienna into treating the defense of the Isonzo River as more important than the Russian front. Russia recovered, despite the Tsar taking over the supreme command, and in June 1916 Alexei Brusilov counter-attacked against the Austrians to tremendous effect in Galicia. The Russian success persuaded Romania to throw in its lot with the allies, and Falkenhayn's stock collapsed. Falkenhayn had tried to bring Germany's policy and its strategy into line, but his opponents attacked him at their interface. The chancellor, Theodor von Bethmann-Hollweg, was not prepared to back Falkenhayn's policy without overwhelming military victory, and Hindenburg and Ludendorff sought to resolve their own annexationist ambitions by achieving a victory that was beyond their military powers. The Kaiser knew, when in August 1916 he accepted that his own nominee be replaced as chief of the general staff by Hindenburg, with Ludendorff as his "first quartermaster general," that Germany, not France, would be the war's victim of Bonapartism. His own position as supreme commander had collapsed. The army command, an operational headquarters, stepped into the void.

Hindenburg's and Ludendorff's popularity made them impossible to dismiss, but they too lacked the institutional framework to run the national war effort. Although the army acquired the ability to make and unmake chancellors, it did not have the power to become the government itself. Thus Germany lost the advantages that liberalism and civil subordination of the military ultimately conferred on the Western powers, without gaining any of the benefits of authoritarianism. The most immediate parallel was with Russia, where the Tsar refused to liberalize his government, despite advice from within Russia as well as without that, if he did so, he might be able more effectively to tap Russia's massive resources of men and raw materials. He fell in March 1917 not just because of revolution in Petrograd but also because his generals did not support him. In November 1918 the same fate befell Wilhelm II. The German army's intervention in the running of the national war economy further confused, rather than resolved, its problems. But the army did not begin to forfeit political leverage until it confronted defeat on the western front. What Ludendorff melodramatically called the German army's "black day," its defeat in the battle of Amiens on August 8, 1918, produced a further fragmentation between strategy and policy. Thereafter, until the war's end on November 11, 1918, the army and the government were consistently out of step – with the former first saying its strategy was bankrupt when the latter proposed to continue the war, and then urging the war's continuance when the latter was engaged in seeking an armistice. Even at the very end of the war, however, the army retained sufficient political authority to be responsible for the Kaiser's abdication. Like the Russian generals, it opted to side with the people, or at least its own interpretation of the nation, rather than support the monarchy in countering revolution.

Therefore for much of the war and in most of the belligerents strategy was defined much as it had been before 1914 – in narrow terms. The vocabulary it used was that of operational art, and the supreme embodiment of that art was to be able to maneuver so as to envelop an army's flank and then to cut across its rear, thus dividing it from its base. In Germany Alfred von Schlieffen, the chief of the general staff from 1892 to 1905, and a major contributor to the debate within his own country until his death in 1913, was the most forceful spokesman of envelopment. The historical precedents which he cited were tactical – Hannibal's crushing of the Roman army at Cannae, and Frederick the Great's use of the oblique order at Leuthen. In France the intellectual roots of strategic thought were also historical, if not also tactical: the rediscovery of the origins of Napoleonic strategy, through the work of Hubert Camon and Jean Colin, elevated the emperor's preference for the *manoeuvre sur les derrières* (maneuvering against the enemy's rear).

None of this prewar thought was necessarily predicated on a commitment to the offensive for its own sake. Indeed, all pre-1914 military thinkers recognized that the revolution in firepower wrought by rifling and breech-loading, machine guns and quick-firing artillery made the attack in tactical terms an extraordinarily difficult undertaking. But wariness at the tactical level did not necessarily determine what should happen at the strategic level: the tactical defensive was perfectly compatible with the strategic offensive, as the Germans were to show on the western front for most of 1915 and 1917. The object of strategy, and indeed the focus of staff training, was to maneuver, so as to bring strength to bear on the decisive point. To determine where the decisive point lay depended on an ability to divine the enemy's intentions. French and Russian prewar thought in particular laid much more stress on the use of advance guards, sent out in order to locate the enemy's principal formations. Having found the enemy, advance guards had to engage him in order to fix him. The main body was then free to maneuver. Therefore, a policy that did not involve mounting an attack on a neighboring power could still require a strategy that incorporated the offensive: its advance guard having fixed the enemy, the defending army would then deliver a counter-stroke.

In essence this was the background to the war plan with which France went to war in 1914, Plan XVII. Its aim was efficient and speedy mobilization (which it accomplished), followed by a deployment that would enable the French army to determine the direction of the main weight of the German advance and then deliver a counter-stroke. The fact that this was accomplished on the Marne within the first six weeks of the war helped to confirm maneuver as the key to strategy. Moreover, the pattern was not dissimilar on the eastern front. Both in East Prussia and in Galicia, the opposing armies advanced to contact, and then endeavored to envelop each other. So successful was the German Eighth

Army, which crushed Samsonov's Second Army at Tannenberg at the end of August 1914, that the belief in deep envelopment became dogma for its chief of staff, Erich Ludendorff. Both in Poland later in the same year and again in 1915, Ludendorff conceived schemes that accorded with Schlieffen's teaching but which bore little relationship to the logistical constraints of movement in the more backward part of Europe.

Before the war it had seemed as though railways eased the movements of mass armies. Moreover, their use by the elder Moltke in Prussia's conquest of Austria in 1866 reinvigorated ideas about envelopment and maneuvering against the enemy's rear. But beyond the railhead, the transport of troops was still dependent on horses and wagons. The growth in the size of armies – each of the major belligerents (except Austria-Hungary and Britain) fielded about 2.5 million men on mobilization – therefore worked against mobility, a point which led several professional soldiers after the war to reject conscription and the mass army in favor of an elite, mechanized force. Secondly, railway communications were more secure within one's own territory and thus favored the power of the defense, enabling an army to redeem defeat by rapid reinforcement. Joffre's redeployment from France's eastern frontiers to the areas around Paris at the beginning of September 1914 was a crucial example.

The Marne is remembered as a maneuver battle: the key decisions in the minds of the commanders were shaped by the need to envelop (in the case of Kluck, commanding the First German Army) and the need to defend an exposed flank (in the case of his neighbor, Bülow, commanding the Second German Army). But the railheads of both armies were up to 168 km from their front. Kluck's army had 84,000 horses to bring forward its supplies, but those horses themselves needed 2 million pounds of fodder a day. The further the Germans advanced the more the transport services were meeting their own needs rather than those of the fighting troops. The fact that the German right wing lost five corps, to the demands both of the eastern front and to the security needs of its own rear, was at one level a blessing: it helped delay the impending gridlock. For the Marne was a largely static battle, a point often obscured by the high drama around Paris. It embraced the entire western front, running eastwards to Verdun, and then south toward Switzerland. This southern sector, 280 km long, was already stable when the battle opened on September 6, 1914, and a further 100 km, from Verdun to Mailly, became fixed by September 9. The task that confronted the German armies as a whole was not to envelop the French left with their right, as Kluck hoped to do, but to break through wherever they could. For most French troops the battle was a defensive triumph, the achievement of infantry in trenches, supported by the direct fire of the 75-mm quick-firing field gun.

The battle was decisive. It prevented a quick German victory in the west, and therefore created the conditions for a long war. Britain's entry into the war may have been of only minor military significance in 1914, but it ensured that in a long war the Entente would have the greater resources. However, this did not mean that the result of the war was preordained: its outcome still had to be fought for. Moreover, the first six weeks in the west had bequeathed the Germans advantages of such significance that they continued to operate in their favor until 1918. First, Germany had overrun France's industrial heartland (as well as virtually all Belgium). Although it did not make as much use of this gain as it might have done, the consequence was that France was put on the back foot and had – above all – to attack if it was to regain what it had lost. This task was complicated by the second bonus for Germany that followed from the Marne. The Germans withdrew to positions well adapted to the purposes of the defense, following the heights above the valley of Aisne River. In November Falkenhayn, who had failed in repeated efforts to outflank the British and French to the north after the battle of the Marne, most notably in the first battle of Ypres, resolved to fortify these positions in depth. Now the Entente too would have to break through trenches and their attendant defensive firepower.

Trenches had a clear tactical purpose – essentially to save lives. They may have been smelly, wet, and muddy, but they provided protection. In 1914, however, they also acquired an operational or strategic significance. Men in field fortifications could hold ground with fewer men; commanders could therefore create a mass for maneuver elsewhere. That is how Joffre had used them at the Marne, and that was what Falkenhayn now set out to do in 1915. The establishment of fixed positions in the west enabled the Germans to create a reserve for use in the east. Furthermore, the fact that the front in the east was twice the length of that in the west meant that the force-to-front ratio gave greater opportunities for mobility. The trench stalemate in the west became the means for sweeping victories in the east. But these gains did not win the war. Hindenburg, the German commander in the east until he succeeded Falkenhayn on August 29, 1916, and his chief of staff, Ludendorff, continuously plotted massive envelopment operations that failed to take account of the fact that the railway densities were significantly less than those of Western Europe. They freely criticized Falkenhayn for the lack of ambition in his own conceptions, but by seeking a negotiated settlement with Russia the latter moderated his expectations in the light of operational realities.

The key to Russia's refusal to negotiate, despite the massive defeats it sustained in 1915, was genuinely political, rather than strategic. Rapid strategic outcomes in World War I were prevented because the war was fought by coalitions. Conquered powers were sustained in the field by their allies. The French and British took the heat off Russia in September; they failed to do so in time in the case of Serbia that autumn. Crucial here was Bulgaria's decision to join the Central Powers. Nonetheless, the Serb army was evacuated and redeployed to Salonika, ending up on the winning side at the war's conclusion. By the same token, Austria-Hungary, having essentially lost the Balkan War on which it had embarked in July 1914 by December of the same year, found the outcome reversed a year later. It did not confront the consequences of its defeat until its principal ally, Germany, was also overcome.

Thus trench warfare may have been adopted as a means to another end, but it became an end in itself. It conditioned the soldiers' lives, and became so much the embodiment of the First World War that it also acted as a metaphor for perceptions of its futility. Such a uniform image of the war not only blots out all the other tactical forms it took, particularly in the Middle East and sub-Saharan Africa, it also obscures the diversity within trench warfare itself. The geology of the western front as it snaked its way from the Channel to the Alps ensured that the trench system passed through rich, well-tilled agricultural soil in Flanders, on to chalk in Picardy and the Aisne valley, and then ended in the wooded slopes of the Vosges mountains. In the north the water table was too high for deep excavations, and the labor required to maintain the trench walls was ceaseless. By 1917 German defenders at Ypres used shell holes as points of defense, rather than continuous lines, and constructed pillboxes out of reinforced concrete that provided protection above ground level, not below it. Further south deep dugouts, cut into the chalk as a network of tunnels and underground caverns, provided shelter even from the heaviest of bombardments. By contrast, on the Italian front, trenches could not be cut into the rock, and when shells hit the ground splinters of stone were added to the fragments from the projectiles themselves. Moreover, as the war lengthened, the positions gained in depth horizontally as well as vertically, as successive systems were created behind the initial line, so that the whole position extended several thousand yards to the rear, with the final line possibly well outside the range of the enemy's artillery.

Broadly speaking the initial break-in to a front-line trench was not too difficult, provided it was properly prepared and supported by sufficient artillery. The challenge was to break through, and no strategic outcome seemed possible until this could be achieved. The concentration of the artillery provided the enemy with advance warning of the intention to attack, especially when aerial reconnaissance in the summer months was likely to detect the preparation of artillery positions: this was one important reason why the German attack at Verdun in 1916 began in February. Amassing sufficient ordnance to destroy a position several trench lines thick, particularly in the early stages of the war before industrial mobilization had hit its stride, necessitated attacking on a narrow front, but such attacks proved vulnerable to enfilade fire from enemy positions on the flanks. The British and French, therefore, attacked on the Somme in 1916 on a front over twenty miles long, but – especially on the British sector – that ensured that the artillery was too thinly distributed to be able to destroy the German positions for all that the British Fourth Army was allotted over four million rounds. Too many of these shells were for lighter-caliber field artillery, and about 30 percent failed to explode.

As soon as the attackers left their own trenches they lost direct and real-time communication with their own command chain. The wireless was not yet sufficiently light to be portable. Visual signals, like rockets or flags, were weather-dependent. Runners might report the situation more accurately, but they took time to get back – and by that stage the situation would almost certainly have changed. Thus command and communications systems were insufficiently flexible to enable the rapid reinforcement of success or the redemption of failure. The enemy had time to recover. His own communications were both shorter and more secure. The trench system enabled telephone lines to be buried, and the depth of the positions meant that even if initially defeated he was falling back on his own supports and gun line.

Broadly speaking two sets of tactical solutions emerged as means to the achievement of breakthrough. The first was technical and the second tactical. The technical solutions, largely directed from above, included the procurement of more artillery, particularly larger calibers, and of more high-explosive shell. By the winter of 1914–15 all commanders were blaming their inability to resolve the trench deadlock on the productive capacities of their home industries. But the answer was not just more guns and shells, as became evident by 1916, the date by which most production problems were being resolved. It also lay in their use.

The biggest technical change over the course of the war was the perfection of artillery, which came through its ability to shoot indirectly at an enemy it could not see without any preliminary registration and with shells that exploded on contact (rather than after burying themselves in the ground). These improvements were only partly the result of changes to the guns and their munitions. Just as important were: the surveying of France in sufficient detail and with sufficient accuracy to enable "shooting off the map"; improvements in meteorology to enable allowances for atmospheric pressure; calibration of the guns themselves to incorporate adjustments for such factors as wear to the barrel; and improvements in the identification of enemy batteries through aerial observation, sound-ranging, and flash spotting, so that the artillery could engage the much more lucrative target of the enemy's artillery rather than his infantry positions. Gas, of limited effectiveness when discharged from canisters and reliant on the wind, was far more effective when delivered with precision by artillery shells, especially against enemy gun crews: knocking out the defender's guns was the first step to liberating the infantry for the advance. The artillery was the major killer of the war and the decisive tool at the tactical level.

The domination of artillery had the effect of splitting fire and movement. The artillery fired, and the infantry then advanced, ideally following close behind a creeping barrage. But the barrage was linear and therefore the infantry too advanced in line. The gunners, deprived of real-time communications with the infantry, lifted their fire to a set timetable. Often this resulted in the artillery leaving the infantry behind. The latter, still in line, were increasingly exposed to the fire of the defense, and particularly to the enfilade fire of machine guns. The tank was one solution to this problem. A mobile gun platform which could accompany the infantry, and also crush wire and cross obstacles, both the British and French armies began its development in 1915. However, despite its successful contribution to the fighting of 1917–18, it was not yet a perfected system, proving mechanically unreliable, with its heavier versions confronting problems with their power-to-weight ratios, and its lighter versions (mostly French) lacking sufficient protection. By 1918 the airplane too could provide close support for advancing infantry.

But the real development was in the coordination of all these weapons in combined arms warfare, with the artillery at its heart as it would be also in World War II. Fire became more flexible, more precise, and more instantaneous in its effects. Quantity was also central to quality. In 1918 the allies had enough guns to be able to develop fire plans that reached the whole depth of the enemy position simultaneously. Thus the layers of the defense were unable to provide each other with support. Both science and production had been brought to bear to enable machinery to substitute for manpower.

The second solution to the deadlock was developed from the bottom up. Again it grew from the experiences of 1914–15, and again it sought to reintegrate fire and movement. By giving the infantry its own firepower – grenades, trench mortars, light machine guns, and flame-throwers – it was enabled to dominate the enemy's trenches without being so reliant on artillery. Freed from the linearity of the artillery bombardment, the infantry could deploy in small groups, using such cover as was available and advancing at its own pace. These ideas were best encapsulated in the storm troopers, first organized by the German, Captain Willy Rohr, in 1915. They formed the basis of German tactics on a wider scale in the opening assault at Verdun, when the infantry pressed forward only where the defense was weak; where it was not, the enemy's positions were left to supporting formations and fresh artillery preparation. Ludendorff's efforts to systematize these tactics in 1917–18 were the culmination of a process whose antecedents were to be found long before he and Hindenburg arrived at the German headquarters and were generated from much lower down the command chain. They reflected the realities of leadership on the western front, that generals on the linear battlefield could not know what was happening in real time and therefore had to trust their subordinates to take their own decisions within the framework of their superior's overall intention. In the offensives of early 1918 these principles were applied throughout selected units of the German army. Command and communication problems were resolved through the delegation of tactical control forward, so that the storm troopers led the way, seeking out the soft spots in the enemy's defenses, and sustaining the forward momentum of the attack. The object was to reinforce success, not to redeem failure.

Both solutions had the capacity to achieve breakthrough, but they did so at the expense of what has been called (in a particularly ugly but nonetheless accurate phrase) "the tacticization of strategy."[1] Ludendorff claimed that he had no other ambition than to find a tactical solution in 1917–18: he argued that, if he sorted that out, then the strategy would follow. He did but it did not. He launched five major offensives on the western front between March 21and July 15, 1918, which made considerable territorial gains but failed to use the battle for the purposes of the war. The axes of the attacks followed the line of least resistance, which proved not to be the line of maximum operational impact. Nor did they have reciprocal effects. The Entente countered in a sequence that began on the Marne on July 18, 1918, was carried on with the battle of Amiens on August 8, and was then sustained over the last hundred days of the war. These battles were led by tactics, too, but they had strategic effect because they were coordinated. Foch's appointment as allied generalissimo in the wake of the German offensive of March 21, 1918 provided a command structure within which the cooperation of the Americans was secured, and he was thus able to shift the direction of successive attacks along the length of the western front. No one attack was pushed beyond what Clausewitz would have called "its culminating point of victory," which meant in this case beyond the point where the artillery could provide effective support. The strategic effect of these tactics was the exhaustion of German reserves, as they shuttled from one sector to another. Germany ran out of men.

What this does not mean is that the generals of World War I consciously or deliberately adopted a "strategy of attrition." Before World War I the only theoretical exposition of attrition in relation to land warfare was that of the German historian, Hans Delbrück. He argued that Frederick the Great had adopted an *Ermattungsstrategie* (strategy of exhaustion) in the Seven Years' War. As with Germany in 1914–18, Prussia in 1756 enjoyed a central position surrounded by a coalition. According to Delbrück, Frederick's aim was to exhaust his opponents by maneuver. As in World War I, fighting could only dissipate the resources of the less favored side ahead of the economically stronger. But if historians apply attrition to the events of World War I, they place it in the context of battle, and therefore construe exhaustion in terms of battle casualties. Attrition is applied at the level of tactics, not – as Delbrück was doing in relation to the Seven Years' War – at that of strategy.

By 1915 Joffre realized that he was unlikely to break clean through the enemy positions in a single offensive, and described his attacks as aimed at *grignotage* (nibbling). The result, heavy losses for minimal gains, was what gave World War I generalship a bad name. Some Entente commanders, including Philippe Pétain and Henry Rawlinson, recognized that the best solution to trench warfare might be to adopt methods of fighting which put the weight on the firepower of the artillery and which aimed to maximize the enemy's casualties and minimize one's own. Rawlinson's proposal was to take a "bite" out of the enemy line, to hold it, and thus to force the enemy to incur the costs of attacking. The trouble with this solution was that it assumed that the enemy wanted to regain the ground that he had forfeited. This was only logical if the ground had strategic significance. Some ground on the western front could be lost or gained without major consequences. The Germans abandoned the Somme battlefields when they withdrew to the Siegfried Line in February 1917, and they retook them in March 1918: in neither case was the outcome important for the wider conduct of the war.

Thus true attritional battles, where both sides were prepared to fight, could only take place where the ground mattered. One such sector was Ypres, where the ring of high ground to the east of the town both screened the Channel ports and the British line of communications on the one hand and covered the railway junction at Roulers and German links to the Reich on the other. When Haig planned the third battle of Ypres in May–June 1917 he hoped for breakthrough, but when he failed to achieve it he rationalized his intentions as the attrition of the German army. He had adopted exactly the same device in accounting for the Somme battle in 1916: when he failed to achieve breakthrough he said he was intending to wear down the German army. The most famous instance of such post-hoc explanations is Falkenhayn's so-called Christmas 1915 memorandum, in which he said he planned to bleed the French army white at Verdun. The memorandum first saw the light of day when Falkenhayn published his memoirs in 1919; there is no indication that attrition was his intention in February 1916.[2]

Attrition could never make sense at the level of strategy narrowly defined. The payoff for wearing-out battles had to be eventual breakthrough; otherwise the war could only be concluded by compromise and negotiation as each side became progressively more exhausted. But attrition did work at the level of grand strategy or policy. Here its arms were as much diplomatic, naval, and economic as military. For the Entente the pivot of this sort of thought was Britain. Its contribution on land did not promise to be really effective until 1917. What it could do immediately was be the armorer and financier of the Entente. Indeed, some in Britain reckoned that the more Britain set about the creation of a mass army the more it would disqualify itself from being able to fulfill its economic role. They argued that Britain had to use its international credit to secure the output of the United States, and that it should then provide munitions to arm the Russians.

Not all soldiers were necessarily as opposed to this sort of thinking as their emphasis on the western front suggests. Robertson, as Chief of the Imperial General Staff, was very conscious that Germany and Austria-Hungary could, by virtue of their central position, exploit the advantages of interior lines, shuttling troops from front to front along the chords of a circle. The Entente by contrast had to use the sea to move round the perimeter of that circle. Its difficulty was to get its land operations sufficiently coordinated in time and space. This was the root of the so-called "easterner–westerner" debate, which during the war was far more vituperative in Germany and after the war – in the memoirs of the participants – in Britain. In the winter of 1914–15, Germany debated not just the merits of attacking Russia or France, but also whether to use its alliance with the Ottoman Empire to drive into the Middle East and so threaten both the British Empire and its links with France in North Africa and Russia in Central Asia. The Entente's objective in 1916 and 1917 was coordinated attacks against the Central Powers on exterior lines. The Russian Revolution threatened the strategy, but the fact that Germany maintained annexationist ambitions in the east in 1918, and thus continued to commit troops, there ensured that it had some effect right up until the end of the war. When Ludendorff initiated the armistice negotiations at the end of September he did so because of the surrender of Bulgaria: the collapse of one front could unlock the others.

Sea power was the *sine qua non* for the execution of allied grand strategy. The Royal Navy did not need to destroy the German High Seas Fleet, but it did have to prevent it from escaping out of the North Sea. The battle of Jutland ensured that the status quo in naval terms was maintained. Thus the Entente enjoyed access to the markets of the world. Thus, too, Germany could not carry into effect a global strategy although it was fighting a world war. Its cruisers were sunk or blockaded by the end of 1914, and its colonies overrun or isolated. Its only route out of Europe was through its alliance with the Ottoman Empire, and after 1916 Constantinople, too, was on the defensive. Islam did not prove to be the revolutionary tool within the French, Russian, and British Empires which the declaration of Holy War led the Germans to hope for. The adoption of unrestricted submarine warfare in February 1917 was the nearest Germany came to dealing with war at this level. But significantly, it was not coordinated with the land campaign. If it had been employed in early 1916, as Falkenhayn wished, it would have had a reciprocal effect with the attack at Verdun; instead it was seen as an alternative to action on the western front.

The submarine campaign was justified as retaliation for the allied blockade of Germany. After the war both the British proponents of sea power and the German apologists for their army battened on to the blockade as evidence for their points of view. But the fact that such debates could take place at all showed how rudimentary the public understanding of what would become grand strategy still was. Blockade contributed to the exhaustion of the Central Powers in its broadest sense. However, it did so not in isolation but as part of an integrated package that included land warfare, the wooing of neutrals, the maintenance of morale at home, the use of propaganda to undermine the enemy, and the sustaining of allies abroad. The tendency to see these as alternatives was a reflection of institutional battles for resources as well as national claims for primacy that the Entente powers moderated with increasing effectiveness, especially after 1917. The entry of the United States, the consequent pressure put by the Americans on the allies to coordinate their overseas purchasing, and the shortage of shipping all fostered the creation of allied executives to pool resources. The formation of the allied supreme command in March 1918 was the coping-stone to an increasingly sophisticated edifice. Propagandists in the Clemenceau government coined the phrase "total war" to describe the level of national mobilization that the war required by late 1917. But it was not yet a universal term and it still did not apply to what France planned to do to the enemy. By 1941 "total war" would itself be a strategy.

Notes

1   Herwig, *Germany and Austria-Hungary*, pp. 393–400, and Michael Geyer, "German Strategy in the Age of Machine Warfare, 1914–1945," in Peter Paret (ed.), *Makers of Modern Strategy from Machiavelli to the Nuclear Age*, Oxford, Oxford University Press, 1986, pp. 537–54.

2   Hew Strachan, "German strategy in the First World War," in Wolfgang Elz and Sönke Neitzel (eds.), *Internationale Beziehungen im 19 und 20 Jahrhundert*, Paderborn, Ferdinand Schöningh, 2003, pp. 127–44; Robert Foley takes a different position in *The Path to Verdun*. For the status of the memorandum itself, see Afflerbach, *Falkenhayn*, pp. 543–5.

References and Further Reading

Afflerbach, Holger, *Falkenhayn. Politisches Denken und Handeln im Kaiserreich*, Munich, Oldenbourg, 1994

Cassar, George, *The French and the Dardanelles: a Study of the Failure in the Conduct of War*, London, Allen and Unwin, 1971.

Chickering, Roger, and Förster, Stig (eds.), *Great War, Total War: Combat and Mobilization on the Western Front, 1914–1918*, Cambridge, Cambridge University Press, 2000.

Doughty, Robert A., *Pyrrhic Victory: French Strategy and Operations in the Great War*, Cambridge, MA, Harvard University Press, 2005.

Feldman, Gerald D., *Army, Industry and Labor in Germany 1914–1918*, 1966; new ed., Providence, RI, Berg, 1992.

Foley, Robert T., *German Strategy and the Path to Verdun: Erich von Falkenhayn and the Development of Attrition, 1870–1916*, Cambridge, Cambridge University Press, 2005.

French, David, *British Economic and Strategic Planning 1905–1915*, London, Allen and Unwin, 1982.

French, David, *British Strategy and War Aims 1914–1916*, London, Allen and Unwin, 1986.

French, David, *The Strategy of the Lloyd George Coalition 1916–1918*, Oxford, Clarendon Press, 1995.

Gooch, John, *The Plans of War: the General Staff and British Military Strategy c1900–1916*, London, Routledge and Kegan Paul, 1974.

Greenhalgh, Elizabeth, *Victory through Coalition: Britain and France during the First World War*, Cambridge, 2005.

Halpern, Paul, *A Naval History of World War I*, London, UCL Press, 1994.

Herwig, Holger H., *The First World War: Germany and Austria-Hungary 1914–1918*, London, Edward Arnold, 1997.

Janssen, Karl-Heinz, *Der Kanzler und der General. Die Führungkrise um Bethmann Hollweg und Falkenhayn 1914–1916*, Göttingen, Musterschmidt, 1967.

King, Jere Clemens, *Generals and Politicians: Conflict between France's High Command, Parliament and Government, 1914–1918*, Berkeley, University of California Press, 1951.

Kitchen, Martin, *The Silent Dictatorship: the Politics of the German High Command under Hindenburg and Ludendorff, 1916–1918*, London, Croom Helm, 1976.

Kitchen, Martin, *The German Offensives of 1918*, Stroud, Tempus, 2001.

Millett, Allan, and Williamson, Murray, *Military Effectiveness*, vol. 1, *The First World War*, Boston and London, Unwin Hyman, 1988.

Neilson, Keith, *Strategy and Supply: the Anglo-Russian Alliance, 1914–1917*, London, Allen and Unwin, 1984.

Offer, Avner, *The First World War: An Agrarian Interpretation*, Oxford, Oxford University Press, 1989.

Pedroncini, Guy, *Pétain: général en chef, 1917–1918*, Paris, Presses Universitaires de France, 1974.

Prior, Robin, and Wilson, Trevor, *Command on the Western Front: the Military Career of Sir Henry Rawlinson 1914–1918*, Oxford, Blackwell, 1992.

Rauchensteiner, Manfried, *Der Tod des Doppeladlers. Österreich-Ungarn und der Erste Weltkrieg*, Graz, Styria, 1994.

Ritter, Gerhard, *The Sword and the Sceptre: the Problem of Militarism in Germany*, 4 vols., 1954–68; English translation, London, Allen Lane, 1970–3; esp. vol. 3, *The Tragedy of Statesmanship: Bethmann Hollweg as War Chancellor (1914–1917)*, 1973, and vol. 4, *The Reign of German Militarism and the Disaster of 1918*, 1973.

Shanafelt, Gary W., *The Secret Enemy: Austria-Hungary and the German Alliance, 1914–1918*, Boulder, CO, Eastern European Monographs, 1985.

Sheffield, Gary, *Forgotten Victory: the First World War: Myths and Realities*, London, Headline, 2001.

Soutou, Georges-Henri, *L'Or et le sang: les buts de guerres économiques de la première guerre mondiale*, Paris, Fayard, 1989.

Stone, Norman, *The Eastern Front 1914–1917*, London, Hodder and Stoughton, 1975.

Strachan, Hew, *The First World War*, vol. 1, *To Arms*, Oxford, Oxford University Press, 2001.

Trumpener, Ulrich, *Germany and the Ottoman Empire 1914–1918*, Princeton, Princeton University Press, 1968.

Woodward, David R., *Lloyd George and the Generals*, East Brunswick, NJ, Associated Press, 1983.

CHAPTER FOUR

War in the West, 1914–16

HOLGER H. HERWIG

Western Europe was a beehive of activity in August 1914. France mobilized 78 infantry and 10 cavalry divisions for the heroic charge into the "martyred provinces" of Alsace-Lorraine. These "pioneers in the great war of revenge," as Chief of Staff General Joseph Joffre called them, under Plan XVII were then to sally into central Germany and, hopefully, to link up with the Russians in Berlin. The Germans, for their part, mobilized 76 infantry and 10 cavalry divisions. Under the Schlieffen Plan, in 40 days they were to sweep through Belgium, cut in behind Paris, and drive the enemy onto the "anvil" of the German Sixth and Seventh armies anchored in Alsace-Lorraine. Nearly seven-eighths of the German army was deployed in the West. Neutral Belgium mobilized 117,000 soldiers to make a stand at and behind two of the main fortified cities, Liège (12 forts) and Namur (9 forts). Finally, about 100,000 professionals and reservists of the British Expeditionary Force (BEF) landed on the Continent – and counted on the French to find an area of deployment for them. Planning staffs and field commanders were confident that somewhere in northern France there would take place a great Armageddon, the "cleansing thunderstorm" that they anticipated, after which it would be "business as usual." Europe had seen no major wars in four decades. It was time to sweep away what many leaders called the "foul peace" that Otto von Bismarck had imposed on the Continent after the German Wars of Unification (1864–71).

The War of Maneuver, 1914

Between August 14 and 25, 1914, more than one and a half million French *poilus*, or front-line soldiers, having snatched their trusty Lebel rifles from their regimental depots, were shuttled to the eastern frontiers in 4,300 trains. Their first thrust under General Paul-Marie Pau, a one-armed veteran of the war of 1870–1 now hastily called out of retirement, would come through the "Belfort gap." This newly assembled "Army of Alsace" – in reality mainly the Seventh Army Corps – was to charge the "gap in the Vosges." A second, more serious, offensive from French Lorraine into German Lorraine was launched by the French First and Second armies as part of Plan XVII. Its targets were Sarrebourg and Dieuze-Château-Salins.

Starting on August 14–15, the French mounted four simultaneous operations in what became known as the Battles of the Frontiers. Flags fluttering and bands playing,

Map 2 The western front, 1914–18

some of France's finest soldiers – including cadets from St. Cyr Military Academy in full dress uniform – showed their tenacity and courage. But the lethality of the modern battlefield, with its steel and concrete fortifications, field artillery and howitzers, camouflaged machine-gun nests, and murderous small-arms fire, took a terrible toll on them. Attack after attack in Lorraine foundered. Thereafter, Crown Prince Rupprecht of

Bavaria's Sixth Army and General Josias von Heeringen's Seventh Army – about 328 battalions in all – counterattacked. They, too, were repulsed in bloody charge after bloody charge. The fog of war quickly set in: units became separated from one another by forests and hills and valleys, communications broke down, logistics were uncertain, and sanitation units were ill equipped to deal with the enormous casualties – roughly 200,000 on each side.[1] Only a determined stand by General Ferdinand Foch's XX Corps at Nancy prevented a potentially fatal break in the French lines. By 23 August, Joffre transferred the bulk of the French forces in Lorraine northward to meet the greater threat of the German right wing crashing through Belgium. By September 12, the front had stalemated.

Further to the north, in the Ardennes, Crown Prince Wilhelm's Fifth Army and Duke Albrecht of Württemberg's Fourth Army formed the right flank of the Schlieffen plan's "anchor." For four bloody days, General Pierre-Xavier Ruffey's Third Army and General Fernand de Langle de Cary's Fourth Army – more than 350,000 soldiers – tried to dislodge them. To no avail: the French fell back behind the Meuse, with their right flank based on Verdun. They had sustained more than 200,000 casualties. Lieutenant Charles de Gaulle (later) observed that German firepower had "made nonsense of the current military doctrines. Morally, all the people's illusions, with which they had steeled themselves, went up in smoke." Still, Joffre remained uncertain of where the main German attack would come.

As the initial battles raged in the Ardennes, 2,150 German trains had rattled across the Hohenzollern Bridge spanning the Rhine at Cologne in ten-minute intervals. The spear of the attack-force consisted of General Alexander von Kluck's First Army (320,000 men) and General Karl von Bülow's Second Army (260,000 men). It was an incredible sight: each army corps of more than 30,000 soldiers stretched about 30 km; each munitions train 20 km; and each baggage train another 6 km. This gigantic force of nearly 600,000 men and their horses and equipment had to drive through the narrow defile of Aachen, the Ardennes, and the Maastricht Appendix by August 17–18, and then to fan out to Antwerp, en route to Paris. Immediately, the Germans came hard up against the concrete and steel forts of Liège. The job of storming Europe's greatest defensive barrier fell to General Otto von Emmich's special task force of 39,000 soldiers from the Second Army.

Again, the hard realities of modern industrialized warfare dictated the battlefield. A series of daring night attacks on August 5 and 6 failed to take the main fortress. Cavalry and infantry were useless against concrete and steel. Even Krupp's 28-cm howitzers failed to reduce the forts. Five of the six attacking brigades were forced to retreat to their original positions. The Schlieffen Plan was in danger of falling behind schedule. In desperation, the Germans hauled four batteries of Austrian Škoda 30.5-cm howitzers up to Liège to systematically reduce the steel cupolas of the forts' gun turrets. On August 8 the Supreme Army Command threw 60,000 more soldiers into the fight. General Erich Ludendorff took command of the 14th Brigade and stormed the inner city after a bitter all-night battle. The entire fortress complex surrendered ten days later. Namur fell on August 23. Whereas Alfred von Schlieffen had planned for a single division to take Liège and Namur, in 1914 it took eight divisions to reduce Liège alone. More than 5,400 German casualties attested to the bitter fight for the forts. The First and Second armies thereupon passed through the Liège corridor and headed west and southwest for Mons, Péronne, Compiègne, and Paris. The Schlieffen Plan seemed back on track.

The war now showed its ugly face to civilians. Belgium's roads were clogged as tens of thousands of refugees fled from the advancing armies with whatever they could drag in small carts. Belgian armed forces and special police destroyed the country's rail network, water towers, bridges, and tunnels. The Civic Guard, civilians garbed in semi-military uniforms, took to the streets – and it was immediately attacked by raw German conscripts as saboteurs and assassins. Frightful memories of French *francs-tireurs* in 1870–1 fueled the German harshness: 6,427 Belgian and French civilians were shot.[2] Thousands of buildings were torched – including the church and the university library of Louvain (Leuven). Tens of thousands of Belgian civilians were deported to German work camps. The Allies used these events to show the world that they were fighting "Hun" barbarism.

By August 22, General von Kluck's First Army had reached the industrial town of Mons. There, it battered the two corps of the BEF under Field Marshal Sir John French, a soldier who owed his command to his principled resignation during the army's threatened prewar mutiny at Ulster. Four days later, the BEF was bloodied again, this time in driving rain at Le Cateau. French considered falling back on Le Havre, from whence his forces could be evacuated by the Royal Navy, but Joffre rushed General Charles Lanrezac's Fifth Army (254,000 soldiers) north to stiffen French's resolve. Still, for two weeks, the BEF retreated in sweltering late-summer heat. Anglo-French relations reached their first nadir. The French government abandoned Paris for the safety of Bordeaux.

With French and British armies conducting what was now called the "Great Retreat," General Helmuth von Moltke, the German chief of staff, became seduced by the vision of a classic double envelopment of French forces. He diverted reinforcements for the Sixth and Seventh armies to Lorraine and ordered Generals Rupprecht and Heeringen to press their attacks west from Nancy. Paris would be crushed between two German pincers, one from the north and the other from the east. Moltke was sufficiently optimistic of success that on August 25 he sent two army corps to hold the Russians in East Prussia.

War, as Carl von Clausewitz observed, is never an act of beating on a lifeless body. Thus, as Moltke dreamed of a grand parade down the Champs Elysées, Joffre reacted swiftly to the collapse of Plan XVII. First, he cashiered two army and ten corps commanders as well as nearly half of his 72 infantry division generals. Next, he hurriedly shuttled forces from his right wing to the region around Paris. For on August 30 General Louis Franchet d'Esperey's I Corps had stopped the German Second Army in its tracks near the Aisne and Vesle rivers. Kluck now jettisoned what was left of Schlieffen's grandiose encirclement plans for Paris, and instead ordered the First Army to march southeast to maintain contact with Bülow's Second Army and to roll up the French Fifth Army. Kluck reached the Marne River on September 3. Paris would have to wait.

The battle of the Marne began on September 5, as Joffre hurled his newly constituted Sixth Army under General Michel Maunoury – as well as five battalions of fresh reserves rushed to the front by 600 Parisian taxicabs – against Kluck's exposed right flank. For four days, a million men with 3,000 heavy guns on each side clashed across the entire front stretching from the Ourcq River to Verdun. As Kluck wheeled west to meet the French threat, a 30-km gap developed between his First Army and Bülow's Second Army. British and French forces drove into the gap, threatening to unhinge the German advance. Moltke, ensconced in a girls' school in Luxembourg, grew anxious. Receiving no reports from his two commanders between September 5 and 9, he dispatched one of his staff officers, Richard Hentsch, to reconnoiter the situation. Hentsch found

Bülow's Second Army to be in a state of demoralization and exhaustion – he used the term *Schlacke* (dregs) to describe several of its units – and Kluck's First Army to be on the point of being encircled by the French Sixth and Fifth Armies.[3] Hentsch, a mere lieutenant-colonel but acting in Moltke's name, ordered Kluck and Bülow to retreat to the scrubby heights north of the Aisne River – to positions that the Germans basically were to hold for the next four bloody years. Kluck and Bülow, as well as 31 other generals, were relieved of their commands. Moltke, a "broken man," resigned on September 14. French official figures listed 329,000 casualties for August and September; the Germans registered an equal number.

The so-called "miracle of the Marne" was an operational defeat of the first magnitude for the Germans. Schlieffen's great gamble had failed. The chief of the General Staff had cracked. Two senior field commanders had failed. There would be no 40-day victory over France. There was no fallback plan of operations. Germany was condemned to fight a war on two fronts. By contrast, Joffre's imperturbable calm had carried the day. He had not allowed himself to be trapped by Moltke. He had avoided a catastrophic defeat, which surely would have ended the war. He had kept intact his armies' cohesion and will to win. The Marne was *un miracle mérité*.

What to do? Moltke's successor, former Prussian War Minister Erich von Falkenhayn, decided to "pull victory from the jaws of stalemate" by outflanking the Allied armies, commanded by General Foch, northward through Picardy, Artois, and finally Flanders.[4] On October 17 he mounted the first of what were to become countless assaults against Ypres (Ieper). In what has inaccurately been dubbed "the race to the sea," each of the two opposing armies desperately tried to turn the flank of the other in a symmetrical battle of equals. They slogged some 170 km through the fields of Flanders before halting at the English Channel, bloodied and exhausted. Belgian sappers added to their misery by opening the sluice gates at Nieuport, flooding 35 km of low farmlands. According to official French figures, the spiral movements of this giant leapfrogging (and repeated attacks against German positions along the Aisne) cost the Republic 125,000 soldiers killed in October and November. The German official history of the war lists 66,000 dead and wounded as well as 14,000 missing in action for Fourth and Sixth Armies in Flanders between mid-October and early November, but readily admits that this figure is imprecise because the reports of many units were either lost or incomplete.[5] Most likely, the numbers of Germans killed were close to those of French killed. Notably, at Langemark about 7,000 German volunteers, many of them students under military age and allegedly singing the German national anthem, were mown down by veteran British machine-gunners; Adolf Hitler survived this "Massacre of the Innocents."[6]

Flanders had been laid waste. Churches, homes, and barns had been leveled; horses, hogs, and cows slaughtered by the thousands. Frightened and exhausted men did what came naturally – they dug into the ground for shelter. General Karl von Fasbender, commander of the First Bavarian Reserve Corps, noted in his diary: "Open field warfare has degenerated into a sort of siege warfare – without really being siege warfare."[7] The great Armageddon projected for somewhere in northern France had not materialized.

Falkenhayn was morally shaken by the Flanders debacle. On November 18–19 he informed Chancellor Theobald von Bethmann Hollweg that victory was beyond reach. The Germans, vastly outnumbered by their enemies, ran "the danger of slowly exhausting ourselves." The chief of the General Staff counseled a "decent peace" with Russia, which he hoped would lead to another with France.[8] The chancellor rejected this advice – in part because he had two months earlier drafted an enormous war-aims program designed to turn the Reich into the dominant power in Europe and a global player. Rebuffed, Falkenhayn stabilized the western front by way of building several parallel defensive lines in the form of a shallow "S" about 750 km long from Nieuport on the English Channel to Altkirch on the Swiss border. His order of the day was direct: "Hold on to what you have and never surrender a square foot of that which you have won!"[9]

Yet, apart from Falkenhayn, few soldiers or statesmen thought of peace. France could not give up ten German-occupied departments, one-fifth of its most productive territory. Britain could not leave the Belgian ports in German hands. Germany could not abandon either the Schlieffen Plan's promise of victory or its conquered lands. Popular passions now depicted the war as one of ideologies. In Paris and London, it was turned into a struggle between democracy and the rule of law and "the jackboot of Prussian militarism."[10] In Berlin, it became a defense of German *Kultur* against French decadence and British materialism. For both sides, it had become a struggle of life and death. Sarajevo was but a distant memory.

The butcher's bill for what was to go down as the bloodiest year (in fact, only five months) of the war was horrendous: roughly about 800,000 German and Allied casualties each. Historian Anthony Clayton speaks of "as many as 300,000 French dead" in 1914; later studies claimed 417,000 dead, missing, and captured. The British had sustained 86,237 casualties – out of an original complement of 110,000 combatants. The German official history's figure of 116,000 killed undoubtedly is far too low – historian John Keegan suggests 241,000 dead. Unfortunately, the official German military history mentions only "bloody losses" of 18,000 officers and 800,000 noncommissioned officers and men to the end of 1914; it provides no detailed breakdown.[11]

The war plans had failed to yield the quick victories promised therein. The peacetime cores of the French and German armies had been decimated; the "old British Army was gone past recall."[12] France's industrial northeast was in German hands, Belgium occupied. The warring nations spent the winter of 1914–15 raising new armies of conscripts. And they sought to address what each perceived to be major crises of supply due to shell shortages by mounting massive efforts of industrial mobilization to produce the shells required to break the impasse at the front.

Stalemate 1915

The German Supreme Command decided to stand on the defensive in the West for 1915. Falkenhayn enhanced his haphazard field entrenchments with deep tangles of barbed wire, concrete posts, triple parallel lines of trenches, and connecting communications and resupply trenches running perpendicular to the front – all on grounds of his own choosing. Still shocked by the murderous course of the first five months of the war, he willingly surrendered the initiative to the Allies.

They readily obliged. Joffre refused to abandon the initiative to the enemy. Defensive warfare, he argued, destroyed morale. "Let us attack and attack," he stated; "no peace or rest for the enemy."[13] Thus, 1915 saw escalating efforts on his part to "rupture" the German defensive lines. He devised two strategies to do this: *grignotage*, or attrition attacks, and *la percée*, the major breakthrough offensive. For political reasons – French diplomacy and morale – he chose for his areas of attack several northern regions, first the Champagne (February–March) and then Artois (May–June). The greatest German threat, he calculated, emanated from Noyon in the form of a giant salient stretching from Arras to Craonne and centered on Compiègne, just 90 km from Paris. He was determined to reduce it with a *grande percée*.

Once more, what looked feasible on paper foundered on the hard rock of reality. By firing more than 300,000 shells at German positions in the Champagne over several days, Joffre surrendered the element of surprise. The follow-up frontal assaults, against the salient in the north in the direction of Noyon as well as in the south against the line Reims–Verdun, broke against heavily fortified German defensive positions not destroyed by the French 75-mm flat-trajectory shells. Vicious counterattacks by General Karl von Einem's Third Army repulsed the French assaults with great losses. At the cost of 40,000 casualties, Joffre had reclaimed 3,000 m of devastated land. Nowhere had the salient been ruptured.

Further to the north, Joffre had requested Sir John French to mount a joint Anglo-French attack on La Bassée. French declined and instead ordered General Douglas Haig's First Army to seize the ground around Neuve-Chapelle. Haig planned to deploy the new "bite and hold" tactics developed by General Henry Rawlinson of IV Corps. The idea was for the British to seize a bit of easily defended territory, entice the Germans to counterattack to regain it, and thereby to place the burden of costly attacks on the enemy. At dawn on March 10, after a 35-minute bombardment in which Haig's artillery fired more shells than the British army had fired during the entire Boer War, British and Indian infantry advanced in dense formations against the Germans. After initial gains, Crown Prince Rupprecht's Sixth Army counterattacked late in the afternoon and drove Haig's troops back to almost their original positions. Haig had bought a strip of land 1,000 m deep by 3,000 m long at the cost of 13,000 casualties.

Sir John French blamed the failure at Neuve-Chapelle on British industry and British politicians. The latter had promised to provide six million shells to replace the stocks fired off in 1914; the former had managed to produce but two million. Moreover, many of the shells were still shrapnel rather than high explosive sufficiently heavy to flatten barbed-wire defenses. Charles Repington of the London *Times* took up the call in a sensational front-page "shell crisis" story: "Need for Shells. British Attacks Checked. Limited Supply the Cause."[14] To still the ensuing political storm, on May 9 Prime Minister Asquith formed a coalition government and one month later created a Ministry of Munitions under David Lloyd George. In addition, by then more than a million young men had answered Secretary of State for War Horatio Kitchener's earlier call for New Armies.

The fighting on the western front took on a deadly regularity: attackers stormed enemy trenches in waves, only to be mowed down by hostile artillery and machine-gun fire as they tried to cut the barbed-wire entanglements that protected the earthworks. Every attack evoked a deadly counterattack. Firepower killed, as General Philippe Pétain had caustically but realistically noted before the war. Soldiers spoke of "storms of steel." At Soissons, the German Colonel Hans von Seeckt devised a novel defensive system, using artillery and infantry to pin down the attacking forces, thereby preventing resupply and reinforcement, and morally destroying the attack. Four months later, partly with the help of a captured French document, the Germans developed an "elastic" defense-in-depth consisting of an outpost zone, a battle zone, and a rearward zone. The new defense forced the attacker to expend his forces against several echelons of defenders arranged in depth; counterattack infantry supplied the resiliency, or "elasticity," of the system.

Defensive artillery was deployed on reverse slopes, beyond the view of enemy spotters and thus of counter-battery fire.

The Germans changed over to the attack only once in 1915, at Ypres in April. Falkenhayn, like Joffre at Noyon, hoped to reduce a salient. This one bulged out from Ypres into the German lines like a backward "C." And he was anxious to try out a new weapon – chlorine poison gas, developed by the future Nobel laureates Fritz Haber and Otto Hahn. Late on April 22, after the prevailing westerly winds had become easterlies, the Germans opened 5,500 steel cylinders filled with gas. The surprise was complete. Several thousand French African territorial soldiers panicked at the sight and then the effect of the green clouds, and abandoned an 8,000-m stretch of the front line. But Falkenhayn had not envisaged such a dramatic success and had no reserves ready to exploit the rupture. Three days later, he used gas against the Canadians at St. Julien. They could only respond by holding to their nostrils and mouths rags soaked in whatever liquid was available; respirators, or gas masks, were not yet on hand. The gas-laced action at Ypres ended with 15,000 casualties on each side; overall, the Germans suffered more than 35,000 and the British 59,000 casualties in the second battle of Ypres.[15] The novel green clouds released at Ypres forever changed the "face of battle" on the western front.

Joffre launched his attrition attack in Artois in May and June. His soldiers quickly discovered that they were now charging into a deadly killing ground: entrenchments and barbed wire, protected by enfilading concrete machine-gun posts, and artillery eche-loned in depth. They paid a dear price for Joffre's *grignotage*: "300,000 casualties, of whom 100,000 were men killed" between April and June 1915.[16]

This notwithstanding, "Papa" Joffre in the fall of 1915 decided to launch a series of what historian Michael Neiberg has called "sequenced, concentric attacks," again focused on both the Artois and Champagne regions. Prior diversionary Allied attacks in the north around the mining town of Loos were to be followed up by the main assault by 35 French divisions in the south against the old Noyon salient. By releasing artillery from fortresses (including Verdun) for field service, Joffre was able to muster 660 heavy field guns in Artois and 1,100 in the Champagne. Preliminary barrages were to last four to six days. Ever confident, Joffre promised that his offensive would "compel the Germans to retire to the Meuse and probably end the war."[17] What politician dared dissent?

At Loos on September 25 the British mounted the first large-scale offensive by the New Armies – and the first release of poison gas from cylinders. As with the Germans at Ypres, the gas caused a breach of the enemy front line; and like the Germans at Ypres, the British were caught flatfooted and without the necessary reserves to exploit the breach. Also, fickle winds caused murderous "friendly casualties." The British never released gas from cylinders again, but instead developed projectors able to launch gas shells over great distances. Faulty staff work, confused command, and simple friction resulted in almost 60,000 British casualties, twice those inflicted on the Germans.

In the Champagne, Joffre also used gas and massed his cavalry to exploit the expected gaps in the enemy lines. But the new German "elastic" defenses had removed almost two-thirds of the defenders from the range of French shells and gas. Heavy rains satu-rated the soil, already torn up by French artillery. The offensive quickly became bogged down in mud and blood. French casualties in the Champagne in September and October reached 143,000; German losses were about 82,000.[18] In all, the French in 1915 had suffered 392,000 soldiers dead, wounded, missing, or captured.

The numbing death of the western front demanded changes. In France, Premier René Viviani was deposed in favor of Aristide Briand; War Minister Alexandre Millerand yielded to General Joseph Galliéni, one of the heroes of the first battle of the Marne. On the British side, Sir Douglas Haig used his intimate connections to both government and crown to undermine his field commander, and thus replaced Sir John French. Cold, aloof, arrogant, dour, inarticulate, but iron-willed, "Lucky" Haig, the son of a wealthy Scotch distiller, at once set out to end the war in 1916.

Joseph Joffre escaped the house cleaning of December 1915. Sensing that the new Briand administration was determined to improve Allied cooperation, he had quickly convened a conference of British, French, Russian, Italian, and Serbian commanders at his lavish headquarters in the Château de Chantilly on December 6–8, 1915. Over meals prepared by France's finest chefs and washed down by the best the vineyards of Beaune, Pommard, and Reims had to offer, Joffre forced through his agenda for 1916. There were to be "coordinated offensives" on the "principal fronts": Western, Russian, and Italian. Given that the British New Armies would be ready for large-scale operations in the coming year, that French industry would have removed the bottlenecks in heavy shell production, that the Russians would have recovered from their reverses in 1915, and that "sideshows" such as Gallipoli and Salonika would have been ended or scaled back, Joffre insisted for the decisive western front on synchronized, concentric offensives. The opening attrition operations north of the Somme to wear down the Germans would be commanded by Haig; the French, who had taken the greatest numbers of losses in 1915, would thereupon drive in the decisive breakthrough south of the river. Joffre angrily dismissed suggestions that the Germans might attack at Verdun.

Attrition 1916

Like Joffre, Falkenhayn spent December 1915 pondering his options for the coming year. Also like Joffre, he firmly believed that the western front was the decisive theater. In various meetings with Chancellor von Bethmann Hollweg and Crown Prince Wilhelm – culminating in an audience with Kaiser Wilhelm II on December 21 – the chief of the General Staff dismissed operations in the east as evanescent, and singled out Britain as the "archenemy" that held the hostile coalition together.[19] In his so-called "Christmas Memorandum," Falkenhayn painted his strategy for 1916 with bold brushstrokes. At sea, he demanded that war supplies reaching Britain from the neutral United States ("England's secret ally") be interdicted by a ruthless campaign of unrestricted submarine warfare. On land, he argued that Britain's strength did not yet lie with its New Armies, but rather with the veteran French armies. If Germany could "knock [Britain's] best sword," France, "out of its hands," then the British would be "driven completely from the Continent." The psychological moment was right. France was exhausted, tired of war, drained of reserves, and demoralized. Further carnage would force Paris "to lose any desire to continue the war." Strategic breakthroughs had not worked in 1914. Frontal assaults had failed at Ypres, at Artois, and in the Champagne in 1915. The only recourse was to bludgeon the French into submission, that is, to "bleed" their armies "white" (*Blutapzapfung*).

For historical and psychological reasons, Falkenhayn selected the city of Verdun – "powerful fortress" in Gallic – and its 60 forts and outposts astride the Meuse River as his target. It was not to be stormed and held, but simply used to lure French armies into a deadly artillery fire, "in which not even a mouse could live." The "Meuse mill," as the general termed it, would "bleed to death" Joffre's best forces because of a projected favorable kill ratio of five French to every two German soldiers. He gave the operation the codename *Gericht*, or Court of Justice. He gave command to the Crown Prince's Fifth Army – without, however, telling Wilhelm that attrition rather than capturing the city was his purpose. The assault was set for February 12, 1916. Inclement weather – rain, snow, and hail – forced its postponement for more than a week.

Falkenhayn had correctly appraised the French resolve to hold the historic city at any cost. While Joffre regarded Verdun as strategically unimportant and refused to bolster its defenses, Premier Briand, on the advice of Philippe Berthelot, his political director at the Foreign Ministry, lectured Joffre on "the role of morale in the war and the capital importance of France not giving up Verdun."[20] The politicians, who in August 1914 had given up control to the military and headed for Bordeaux, now began to reassert themselves.

At 8:12 a.m. on the morning of February 21, 1916 more than 1,200 German artillery tubes showered a "storm of steel" down on the French defenders encamped along the 400-m-high escarpment on the east bank of the Meuse. Eight hours later, 10 divisions of infantry charged the French positions in waves. Wilhelm II rushed to Verdun to accept its surrender. Briand visited Joffre at Chantilly in the evening of February 24 and again demanded that Verdun be held.

Verdun would become a synonym for the slaughter of World War I. Between February and December 1916, both sides fired 10 million artillery shells – 1.35 million tons of steel – at each other. In a single day, Crown Prince Wilhelm's Fifth Army expended 17½ railway wagons of shells at Verdun. The rain-soaked hills ringing the city, in the words of a French aviator, looked like "the humid skin of a monstrous toad."[21] For the first time, the Germans attacked wearing 3-lb steel helmets, deploying flamethrowers, firing a new asphyxiating gas (phosgene) by way of artillery shells, and infiltrating French lines with special assault detachments formed by storm-troops. The battlefield became a nightmare of sounds, smells, and sights. Soldiers caught in the barbed wire or hit by shrapnel often lay screaming for hours. Horses lay about with belly wounds, still kicking their legs five or six days after being wounded. The gray and brown and poisonous shell craters sucked in men and animals alike. The fields reeked of decaying flesh. Rats by the tens of thousands ate well and often. The hand-to-hand fighting in the citadel's caverns was especially vicious – and memorable. One German veteran recalled: "The air was suffocating. A mixture of the horribly sweet smell of putrefaction, of phenol and iodoform, the stench of human excrement, explosive gases and dust took our breath away."[22]

The countryside around Verdun took on a deadly pallor. The soil, cultivated, fertilized, and defiled for centuries by the excreta of animals, was laden with pathogenic bacteria. Tetanus infection and gas gangrene led to horrendous rates of amputation. Trench fever, caused by parasites in the fecal matter of lice, produced thousands of casualties. "Billions of flies" caused widespread digestive fever, the so-called "Verdun fever." The corpses were stacked between layers of lime chloride to aid decomposition. The sheer magnitude of the German Fifth Army's medical effort can be appreciated by an analysis of the 10-day casualty reports that it submitted over the seven months of the campaign at Verdun: dressing stations handled 275,770 cases of "light" injuries, while field hospitals treated and then returned 75,000 more "seriously" wounded soldiers to the front. These figures left out the roughly 60,000 cases of venereal disease.

The battle of Verdun reached its climax early in March. On March 4 Crown Prince Wilhelm called on his Fifth Army to take Verdun, "the heart of France." After two days of intensive shelling, his infantry stormed the vital Côte du Poivre guarding the city. They were subjected to withering French artillery fire from the west bank of the Meuse and decimated. By March 9, Wilhelm conceded defeat. But Falkenhayn did not.

He continued the assault for another five months, arguing against all odds that at Verdun Germany would "annihilate France." In the end, he, too, succumbed to Clausewitz's postulate concerning the "diminishing force of the attack." His staff spoke bleakly of a "second Ypres."

Casualty figures for Verdun are legendary: visitors to the battlefield today are told of one million French dead alone, with the bones of 250,000 *poilus* entombed behind the glass windows of the ossuary. Historian Anthony Clayton lists 351,000 French casualties (156,000 dead or missing or captured); and 330,000 German casualties (143,000 dead or missing or captured). In fact, the German Fifth Army reported 81,668 men either killed or missing in action between February and September 1916 – a total that was 300 percent higher than that for the entire Franco-Prussian War of 1870–1, but lower on a monthly basis than that for the battles of 1915.[23] Again, the problem of armies underestimating their own losses may well have played a role in compiling German statistics for Verdun.

Why, then, did the men go on fighting? On the German side, some expressed fear of what they called the "shame of ridicule" of their comrades if they deserted; others feared punishment by their officers. Some stayed at the front "from a simple sense of duty"; others mainly "from habit." Many had the fatalistic feeling that "the terrible must be done." Grenadier Rudolf Koch, injured storming Hill 304 on Easter Sunday, reflected on the issue: "The soldier does his duty and does not question why. It was duty alone that kept us together and held our courage up. At such a place, one cannot speak of enthusiasm; everyone wishes they were a thousand miles away."[24] For the French, the majority of soldiers understood that the battle was defensive in nature and that if they held on, they would win. Their morale thus appears to have remained relatively high.

The German campaign failed in large measure due to excellent French reactions. Joffre, as he had done in the critical first days of September 1914, remained calm and decisive. He dispatched his second in command, General Edouard Noël de Castelnau, to Verdun to assess the situation; de Castelnau ordered a shaken and confused General Frédéric Georges Herr to hold Verdun at any cost. In the meantime, de Castelnau persuaded Joffre to appoint the 60-year-old General Pétain and his Second Army to take command of the citadel. The new commander's slogan – actually coined by one of his subordinates, General Robert Nivelle – was catchy: "*Ils ne passeront pas!*" ("They shall not pass"). He appreciated two things: first, the decisive influence of firepower on the battlefield; and second, the need to keep defenders as fresh as possible. Using excellent counter-battery fire from his 75-mm guns, Pétain systematically destroyed the enemy's 30.5-cm Škoda and 42-cm Krupp howitzers. Artillery eventually accounted for 58 percent of all German deaths. To maintain morale and cohesion, he rotated 66 divisions through the "Meuse mill" up to July 1. He rallied his soldiers with his famous (if colloquial) General Order 94, "*Courage, on les aura*" ("We will get them"). And since the Germans had cut the two rail lines that served Verdun, Pétain deployed a phalanx of 3,500 trucks and 9,000 roadworkers to haul men and supplies along the 47-mile road from Bar-le-Duc to Verdun – the legendary *voie sacrée* (sacred route). At the height of the resupply effort, a vehicle passed every 14 seconds at any given point on the road. Pétain likened the conveyor-belt resupply to a *noria* (chain of buckets).

Falkenhayn's "strategy" had broken before Verdun. The endless slaughter did not force the Parisian politicians to capitulate. The British, as will be discussed next, did not desert their "continental sword." Battlefield casualties were almost even, at 1 German to 1.1 French soldiers. Forty-eight German divisions were heavily bled at Verdun. For the first time, discipline began to break down. Desertions mounted. "Police measures" were required to restore order. The harmonious "spirit of 1914" was crushed. The Fifth Army lost its best noncommissioned officers. The Crown Prince publicly accused Falkenhayn of having destroyed his army at Verdun. "The Meuse mill," Wilhelm later wrote, "ground up the hearts of the soldiers as much as their bodies." German doctors reported countless cases of battlefield fatigue and psychological trauma: "shock, confusion, loss of speech, hysteria, cramps, delirium ... and mental disorientation."[25] Their French counterparts noted much the same, including dramatic increases in shell shock, insanity, acts of indiscipline, and desertion. Some even claimed that the *poilus* arranged "contracts" with their opposite *Landser* not to fire to kill. Pétain caustically noted that the war would be won by the side with the last remaining soldier standing. Shouts of "*à bas la guerre!*" were not uncommon. By December, the two opposing lines were almost exactly where they had been in February. Verdun was spared German occupation for another 24 years.

Not surprisingly, the French looked to their British ally to relieve the pressure on Verdun. General Haig was quite prepared to show the Germans "the fighting will of the British race." Following up on the decisions reached at the Chantilly conference in December 1915, on May 26, 1916 he met Joffre at the French château of Beauquesne, where the two commanders selected the salient from Beaumont-Hamel down to the marshes of the Somme River for a joint Anglo-French assault. Given the bloodletting at Verdun, the original French plan to contribute 40 divisions was scaled back to 16, of which 5 first-line divisions as part of General Marie-Émile Fayolle's Sixth Army were to open the attack. They would be joined by 18 fresh British divisions. It was to be the first large-scale test for the New Armies sent out from Britain. The attack was formalized five days later in President Poincaré's Pullman car south of Amiens. After several cautionary calls for delay by Pétain, newly promoted from Verdun to command Central Army Group, and by Haig, who insisted that all preparations be fully completed, the offensive was set for July 1, 1916.

Never, in the judgment of historian Tim Travers, had an assault been so meticulously prepared. General Henry "Rawly" Rawlinson's Fourth Army and General Edmund ("the Bull") Allenby's Third Army would attack north of the Somme, while General Foch's Northern Army Group would strike south of the river. Between them, they would crush General Fritz von Below's Second Army, with a mere seven divisions in the line. Falkenhayn had simply refused to believe that the French, being "bled white" at Verdun, could mount any kind of a major assault from their position astride the Somme. The Allies enjoyed substantial air superiority (386 versus 129 craft) and virtual heavy artillery superiority (393 to 18 guns). A five-day artillery bombardment rained 1 ½ million shells of 12,000 tons – or 1 ton of steel per square meter – down on the Germans along a front just 16 km wide. All signs pointed to a great and crushing victory. "The wire has never been so well cut," Haig noted on the eve of the attack, "nor artillery preparations so thorough."[26] The soldiers of the New Armies would be able simply to cross no man's land and "relieve" the dead Germans in their positions. Thus, they were to carry mainly 66-lb loads of ammunition, food, entrenching tools, and barbed wire to their new posts.

Zero hour for British infantry came at 7:30 a.m. on July 1, 1916, a beautiful and soon to be hot day. About 66,000 "Tommies" went "over the top" in the first wave, to be followed by 54,000 in a second wave. Slowly they marched uphill across the 200 to 400 meters of no man's land, certain that no one could have survived Haig's massive bombardment. The artillery covered their advance with a mammoth rolling barrage 100 m ahead of the men, advancing the deadly wall of steel every two minutes. As they approached what they believed to be the deserted or destroyed first line of German trenches, they were met by withering machine-gun fire. Many British soldiers compared the effect of the machine guns as being akin to that of a scythe. Casualties were horrendous – 30,000 in the first hour alone. Before the day was over, Haig's New Armies had taken 57,470 casualties, including 19,240 dead. Historian Martin Middlebrook computed that this one-day figure "easily exceeds" the British army's "battle casualties in the Crimean War, the Boer War and the Korean War combined."[27]

To the south, the French had a surprisingly easy time of it, leaving Joffre "beaming." Foch's soldiers of Northern Army Group, in the opinion of historian Michael Neiberg, benefited from more accurate artillery fire, weaker German positions, the advantage of higher ground, the element of surprise, and small group rather than linear tactics. They had learned from Verdun that artillery conquers and that infantry occupies. Thus, they attacked with minimum numbers of infantry and used their excellent counter-battery fire to advantage. They took one-tenth the casualties of the British. Foch's advance toward Péronne was halted mainly because the British attack on their left flank withered under the murderous German machine-gun fire.

What had gone wrong in what British officers called the "Big Push" and their men the "Great Fuck-Up"? First and foremost, Haig and his staff had overestimated the destructive power of artillery and ignored both terrain and weather. The Somme's chalky soil, combined with hot weather, had allowed Below to dig deep dugouts, often 10 m down, and to reinforce them with strong timbers and concrete. He had stretched his "elastic" defense out over seven parallel defensive lines, that is, over a depth of 8 km. He had more than tripled the depth and thickness of his barbed-wire entanglements. He had kept his artillery hidden on reverse slopes. And he had held five divisions in reserve to spring a deadly counterattack on the enemy.

Also, the quality of British shells, hastily produced in the wake of Repington's "shell crisis" scare, left much to be desired: one in four was a dud and two-thirds still contained shrapnel rather than high explosives. Moreover, Haig had ordered the artillery to blanket the German positions to a depth of 2,500 m – the distance he planned to advance on the first day – and thus the artillery support was spread "fatally thin." Little of the German wire had been flattened and few of their hillside bunkers destroyed. Once the German machine-gunners had reemerged from their deep dugouts, resighted their guns, and begun to cut down the advancing and overloaded enemy soldiers, cooperation between British artillery and infantry disintegrated in a veritable fog of war. The end result was a casualty ratio of around 7 to 1 in favor of the German defenders.

Everywhere along the Somme, the battlefield turned into chaos and death. At Beaumont-Hamel, the 1st Newfoundland Battalion in 40 minutes suffered 91 percent losses – 26 officers and 658 men. A soldier of the neighboring 1st King's Own Scottish Borderers bitterly commented: "I cursed the generals for their useless slaughter, they seemed to have no idea what was going on."[28] Opposite Thiepval, Lieutenant-Colonel Percy Crozier of the 36th (Ulster) Division noted: "I see rows upon rows of British soldiers lying dead, dying or wounded, in no man's land … The bursting shells and smoke make visibility poor, but I see … heaped up masses of British corpses suspended on the German wire." At Ovillers, the future novelist Henry Williamson recorded: "I see men … roll and roll, and scream and grip my legs in uttermost fear … my wave melts away, and the second wave comes up, and also melts away, and then the third wave merges into the ruins of the first and second and after a while the fourth blunders into the remnants of the others." Williamson's khaki tunic changed to red from all the blood. "Who could have imagined,' he asked rhetorically, "that the 'Big Push' was going to be like this?"[29]

The "Big Push" continued for another four months – toward Bapaume, Péronne, and Nesle. Haig by now had abandoned his hope for a great breakthrough battle and instead settled on attrition; perhaps he could weaken the Germans sufficiently along the Somme to make a future breakthrough battle possible in Flanders. Artillery pulverized the Somme countryside, turning it, like that at Verdun, into a lunar landscape. Gas killed whoever and whatever it made contact with. To make up for his own losses, Haig called on the Empire: South Africans bled for Britain at Delville Wood, Australians at Pozières, Ulstermen at Thiepval, and Scots and Newfoundlanders at Beaumont-Hamel. At Flers, a British experiment with 49 "tanks" was premature as two-thirds broke down before they ever reached enemy lines.

When it was all done, and the heavy October rains had turned the fields into a veritable quagmire, 53 of Britain's 56 infantry divisions had been in action "athwart the Somme." According to historian Anthony Clayton, roughly 400,000 British soldiers had been killed, wounded, or captured; the French had lost 196,000 men, and the Germans 500,000.[30] Thus, the Somme, especially in view of its shorter duration, was a bloodier battle than Verdun. And while it has been indelibly etched in the British psyche, strangely it hardly figures in French psychology or historiography. The front lines had moved no more than 11 km. The Somme, in the words of military historian B. H. Liddell Hart, "proved both the glory and the graveyard" of Britain's New Armies.[31] It became grist for the mills of "war poets" such as Siegfried Sassoon, Robert Graves, David Jones, and Wilfred Owen. And it secured for the commander of the BEF a lasting sobriquet, "Butcher Haig."

***

The horrendous slaughter at Verdun and the Somme demanded sacrifice also behind the lines. On August 29, 1916, the second anniversary of the battle of Tannenberg, Kaiser Wilhelm II yielded to the demands of a political-military *fronde* headed by Chancellor von Bethmann Hollweg, and replaced Falkenhayn with the duumvirate of Paul von Hindenburg and Erich Ludendorff. In Paris, the Chamber of Deputies met in secret session from November 28 to December 7 and decided to remove Joffre from command. On December 12 he was given the meaningless position of "technical military adviser" to the government and a field marshal's baton – whereupon he resigned with ill grace. His successor, Robert Nivelle, who had succeeded Pétain at Verdun, promised victory for 1917. Briand recalled General Hubert Lyautey from Morocco to serve as war minister. And in Britain, David Lloyd George replaced Prime Minister Asquith and formed a national coalition government on December 7. "Lucky" Haig survived to fight another day, at Passchendaele.

Verdun and the Somme gave rise to new terminology: *Materialschlachten* ("battles of material") and *Ermattungsstrategie* ("strategy of attrition"), in the words of historian Hans Delbrück. War had lost its adventure, its sport, its romance. The future German military historian Gerhard Ritter, a veteran of the Somme, called it "monotonous, mutual mass murder."[32] Another veteran of that campaign, Ernst Jünger, described his fellow warriors as "workers of war." In France, Henri Barbusse coined the phrase "workers of destruction."

Indeed, the very "face of war" had changed dramatically. Gone were the bright blue pants, the red jackets and capes, the lances and sabers of 1914. Cavalry by and large had dismounted, the horses used as draft animals and their riders as trench soldiers. The new troglodyte world of trenches had brought about a new gray everyday: gray steel helmets, gray tunics, gray leggings, and gray mud. At home, civilians wore "greatcoats" and "trench coats." Even French *bleu horizon* uniforms turned grey in the mud. Above all, the incredible body counts dulled the senses. Soon, hardly a family in Britain, France, and Germany did not have a father, son, or some other male relative killed or wounded in the war. Makeshift military cemeteries were packed with the dead. Hospitals bulged with the wounded. Special schools were established to retrain the crippled.

Last but not least, the twin battles of Verdun and the Somme bastardized customary concepts of military strategy, of the "art" of war. In the words of historian Michael Geyer, they "showed the military impasse of World War I, the complete disjuncture between strategy, battle design, and tactics, and the inability to use the modern means of war. But most of all [they] showed, at horrendous costs, the impasse of professional strategies."[33] Yet, throughout the winter of 1916, the new commanders, Nivelle in France as well as Hindenburg and Ludendorff in Germany, set their staffs to planning for the campaigns of 1917. Surely, a breakthrough battle would occur somewhere, at some time, and the troops would at last be home by Christmas.

Notes

1   Casualty figures are notoriously inexact. Most armies understate their own losses and over-state those of their opponent. The records are incomplete: many were not kept in the heat of battle and others often lost in subsequent actions. Moreover, while the German army only included wounded who were evacuated in its 10-day casualty reports, the British army included even the wounded returned to duty after immediate, cursory treatment. I have used the term "casualties" to apply to those killed, wounded, captured, or missing in battle; but not to those affected by disease, mental trauma, psychiatric shock, neuralgia, or battle fatigue. I have used the calculations from the most recent scholarship – fully cognizant that there remains much room for debate. See the entry for "casualties" in R. Holmes (ed.), *The Oxford Companion to Military History*. Oxford, Oxford University Press, 2001, pp. 182–5.
2   See Horne and Kramer, *German Atrocities*, p. 74.
3   Herwig, *First World War*, p. 103.
4   Gray, *Leverage of Sea Power*, p. 195.
5   Reichsarchiv, *Der Weltkrieg 1914 bis 1918*, vol. 5, p. 401.
6   Unruh, *Langemarck*, pp. 151ff.
7   Herwig, *First World War*, p. 115.
8   Reichsarchiv, *Der Weltkrieg 1914 bis 1918*, vol. 6, p. 406.
9   Ibid., vol. 5, p. 585. Dated November 16, 1914.
10 Howard, *First World War*, p. 46.
11 Clayton, *Paths of Glory*, p. 63; Reichsarchiv, *Der Weltkrieg 1914 bis 1918*, vol. 6, pp. 426–7; Keegan, *First World War*, pp. 135–6, lists 306,000 French and 241,000 German dead.
12 Edmonds (ed.), *History of the Great War*, vol. 2, p. 465.
13 Cited in Ferro, *Great War*, p. 75.
14 Herwig, *First World War*, p. 165.
15 Reichsarchiv, *Der Weltkrieg 1914 bis 1918*, vol. 8, pp. 48–9.
16 Clayton, *Paths of Glory*, p. 70.
17 Cited in Howard, *First World War*, pp. 64–5.

18   Reichsarchiv, *Der Weltkrieg 1914 bis 1918*, vol. 9, p. 98.
19   Afflerbach, *Falkenhayn*, pp. 543–5.
20   King, *Generals and Politicians*, pp. 89–100.
21   Horne, *Price of Glory*, p. 173.
22   Werth, *Verdun*, pp. 202–6.
23   Herwig, *First World War*, p. 184; Clayton, *Paths of Glory*, p. 110.
24   Herwig, *First World War*, p. 193.
25   Ibid., pp. 198, 298.
26   Cited in Howard, *First World War*, p. 78.
27   Middlebrook, *First Day on the Somme*, p. 246.
28   Ibid., p. 189.
29   Cited in Travers, "BEF's Darkest Day," p. 29.
30   Clayton, *Paths of Glory*, p. 112.
31   Liddell Hart, *The Real War*, p. 226.
32   Herwig, *First World War*, p. 204.
33   Geyer, "German Strategy," p. 536.

References and Further Reading

Afflerbach, Holger, *Falkenhayn: Politisches Denken und Handeln im Kaiserreich*, Munich, Oldenbourg, 1994.

Asprey, Robert B., *The First Battle of the Marne*, London, Weidenfeld and Nicolson, 1962.

Canini, Gérard (ed.), *Combattre à Verdun. Vie et souffrances quotidiennes du soldat, 1916–1917*, Nancy, Presses Universitaires de Nancy, 1990.

Clayton, Anthony, *Paths of Glory: The French Army 1914–18*, London, Cassell, 2003.

Doughty, Robert, *Pyrrhic Victory. French Strategy and Operations in the Great War*, Cambridge, MA, Belknap Press of Harvard University Press, 2005.

Edmonds, James (ed.), *History of the Great War: Military Operations*, 23 vols., London, Macmillan, 1922–48.

Ferro, Marc, *The Great War 1914–1918*, 1969; trans. from French, London, Routledge and Kegan Paul, 1969.

Foley, Robert T., *German Strategy and the Path to Verdun. Erich von Falkenhayn and the Development of Attrition, 1871–1916*, Cambridge, Cambridge University Press, 2005.

French, David, *British Strategy and War Aims, 1914–1916*, London, Allen and Unwin, 1986.

Geyer, Michael, "German Strategy in the Age of Machine Warfare, 1914–1945," in Peter Paret (ed.), *Makers of Modern Strategy from Machiavelli to the Nuclear Age*, Princeton, Princeton University Press,1986, pp. 527–97.

Gooch, John, *The Plans of War: The General Staff and British Military Strategy, c. 1900–1916*, London, Routledge and Kegan Paul, 1974.

Gray, Colin S., *The Leverage of Sea Power: The Strategic Advantage of Navies in War*, New York, Macmillan, 1992.

Herwig, Holger H.,*The First World War: Germany and Austria-Hungary, 1914–1918*, London, Arnold, 1996.

Hirschfeld, Gerhard, Krumeich, Gerd, and Renz, Irina (eds.), *Scorched Earth: The Germans on the Somme, 1914–18*, 2006, trans. from German, Barnsley, Pen and Sword, 2009.

Horne, Alistair, *The Price of Glory: Verdun 1916*, London, Penguin, 1962.

Horne, John, and Kramer, Alan, *German Atrocities, 1914: A History of Denial*, New Haven, CT, Yale University Press, 2001.

Howard, Michael, *The First World War*, Oxford, Oxford University Press, 2002.

Joffre, Joseph, *The Memoirs of Marshal Joffre*, 2 vols., 1932; trans. from French, London, Geoffrey Bles, 1932.

Jünger, Ernst, *Storm of Steel*, 1920; trans. from German by Michael Hofmann, London, Penguin, 2003.

Keegan, John, *The Face of Battle: A Study of Agincourt, Waterloo and the Somme*, London, Penguin, 1976.

Keegan, John, *The First World War*, London, Pimlico, 1999.

King, Jere Clemens, *Generals & Politicians: Conflict Between France's High Command, Parliament, and Government, 1914–1918*, Berkeley, University of California Press, 1951.

Liddell Hart, Basil Henry, *Reputations: Ten Years After*, London, John Murray, 1928.

Liddell Hart, Basil Henry, *The Real War, 1914–1918*, London, Faber and Faber, 1930.

Middlebrook, Martin, *The First Day on the Somme, 1 July 1916*, London, Allen Lane, 1971.

Mombauer, Annika, *Helmuth von Moltke and the Origins of the First World War*, Cambridge, Cambridge University Press, 2001.

Neiberg, Michael S., *Fighting the Great War: A Global History*, Cambridge, MA, Harvard University Press, 2005.

Pedroncini, Guy, *Pétain: le soldat et la gloire*, Paris, Perrin, 1989.

Porch, Douglas, *The March to the Marne: The French Army 1871–1914*, Cambridge, Cambridge University Press, 1981.

Prior, Robin, and Wilson, Trevor, *The Somme*, New Haven, Yale University Press, 2005.

Reichsarchiv, *Der Weltkrieg 1914 bis 1918. Die militärischen Operationen zu Lande*, 14 vols., Berlin, E. S. Mittler, 1925–44.

Sheffield, Gary, *The Somme*, London, Cassell, 2003.

Strachan, Hew, *The First World War: To Arms*, Oxford, Oxford University Press, 2001.

Travers, Tim, *The Killing Ground: The British Army, the Western Front and the Emergence of Modern Warfare, 1900–1918*, London, Allen and Unwin, 1987.

Travers, Tim, "BEF's Darkest Day," in *Great Battles: Epic Clashes of the 20th Century*, Leesburg, Primedia, 2003, pp. 26–35.

Unruh, Karl, *Langemarck. Legende und Wirklichkeit*, Coblenz, Bernard und Graefe, 1986.

Werth, G., *Verdun: Die Schlacht und der Mythos*, Gladbach, Gustav Lübbe, 1979.

CHAPTER FIVE

War in the East and Balkans, 1914–18

DENNIS SHOWALTER

The eastern front in World War I was a theater of paradoxes. In the Balkans, the initial campaigns were episodic, short, and decisive – at least by World War I standards. Serbia halted Austria-Hungary's attack and mounted a successful counteroffensive: open war at a time when the western front was settling into trenches. The Central Powers later over-ran Serbia, then Romania, in a matter of weeks. But the regional decisions led nowhere in particular. Even the final Allied breakout from the "internment camp" of Salonika in 1918 was more a matter of pushing aside demoralized, overstretched opposition and the collapsing governments behind it than of staging a decisive geo-strategic offensive into the "soft underbelly" of the Central Powers.

In Russia, the *fata morgana* of decisive victory broke the spirits and the spines of three empires. For Germany, in the words of Erich von Falkenhayn, the East gave nothing back beyond ephemeral tactical victories. Even the Treaty of Brest-Litovsk played the role of Faust's Lemures, helping dig Germany's grave as its leaders dreamed of fresh resources and eastern empires. For Austria-Hungary, the Russian front was a vortex, drawing in ever more of a declining system's human and material resources. For Russia, what the Tsarist government initially considered the wrong war at the wrong time proved fatal for a still different reason, by weakening, then fracturing a semi-modern society's "crust of competence", the limited number of people able to make trains run on time, distribute food, and deliver mail.

That last point offers a wedge into understanding the nature of World War I in Russia and the Balkans. In the early years of the twentieth century, northern France and Flanders was the only area of the Eurasian landmass able to support industrial war on a large scale for a significant length of time. Everywhere else the standard pattern was de-moderniza-tion. As forces and doctrines imported from outside overtaxed local infrastructures, war-making regressed to early nineteenth-century paradigms both operationally and administratively. State-of-the-art weapons depended for their ammunition on wagons without springs hauled by oxen along barely marked tracks. Wounds that on the western front were routinely treated successfully, in the East just as routinely turned fatally septic. World War I was the first conflict where deaths in battle exceeded those from disease. The German army in Russia, however, suffered almost four times as many sick as wounded – and its medical services were exponentially superior to anything else in the theater.

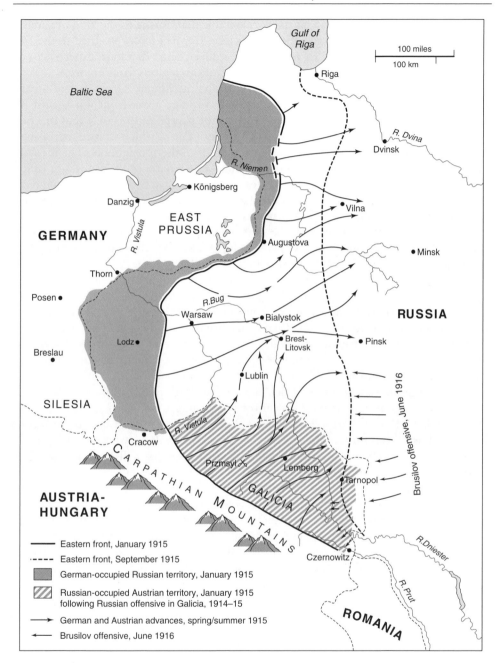

Map 3 The eastern front, 1914–17

The prewar plans of the eastern theater's combatants took at best limited account of its physical and military geography. Germany and Austria, allied since 1872, had long considered the prospects of a joint offensive against the Russian Empire. Well before 1914, however, German strategists dismissed an "eastern deployment" as a serious possibility. The Second Reich lacked the disposable resources to pursue major offensives on

two fronts, and France appeared far more vulnerable than Russia to the kind of paralyzing first strike seen as essential to a German victory. German forces assigned to the East
were correspondingly reduced to a minimum: a dozen or so divisions, expected to do
no more than hold on until reinforced by the victorious legions from France.[1]

Austro-Hungarian planning, by contrast, reflected the Empire's inability and unwillingness to create in peace an army strong enough to wage a two-front war against the
Slavs to the east and Italy or the Balkan states to the south. Yet precisely that prospect
confronted Habsburg strategists as a worst-case contingency, which seemed increasingly
likely as relations deteriorated with their eastern and southern neighbors. The ideology
of Chief of Staff Conrad von Hoetzendorff and the *mentalité* of the Habsburg officer
corps turned to professionalism as a means of bridging the gap between means and ends.
The final Austro-Hungarian mobilization plan divided the army into three parts: 9 divisions directed against Serbia, 27 against Russia, and the remaining 11 held as either a
swing force or a strategic reserve, to be dispatched where needs or opportunities were
greatest. Given merely the distances involved, for this to work the army from privates to
generals would have to be good and also lucky – very lucky.[2]

Russia for its part pursued a strategy shaped more by diplomatic considerations than
by operational ones. Since under no circumstances could Russia stand alone against
Germany and Austria, its most prudent behaviors were to ensure that France was neither overrun nor hopelessly crippled, and that Britain would support an alliance concluded only in 1907. That called for an offensive strategy as proof of good will. The
only question was whether it should be directed against Germany or Austria and the
sweeping military reforms undertaken after the Russo-Japanese War of 1904–5 suggested that Russian strength was sufficient to pursue both options.[3]

Russia's war plan against Germany involved sending two armies against the East
Prussian salient, the First Army advancing west across the Niemen River and the Second
Army southwest from Russian Poland. The intention was to destroy the German army in
the field, occupy the province, and establish conditions for a further advance into
Germany. Initially both halves of the offensives did well against indecisive opposition.
The Russian commanders, however, failed either to coordinate their movements or to
press their advantage. That gave the Germans time to find their feet. A new command
team of Paul von Hindenburg as *chef* and Erich Ludendorff as his Chief of Staff developed plans prepared by staff officers on the spot to concentrate German forces in the
southern sector, against the Second Army. After five days of hard fighting, between
August 26 and 30, 50,000 Russians were casualties, 90,000 more were prisoners, and
Germany had its first heroes of World War I.

Hindenburg and Ludendorff then turned against the First Army, routing it in the
battle of the Masurian Lakes (September 5–13), and driving it across the frontier with
over 100,000 casualties. Like Tannenberg, however, the Masurian Lakes proved a local
victory. Neither opened the way to a strategically or politically significant objective – only
for a further advance into the forests and swamps of eastern Russia. The Germans, moreover, had their attention distracted by the problems of an ally that had marched into
catastrophe.

Austria's decision for war against Serbia was not a product of fatalism, fecklessness, or
incompetence. Whether to preempt any possibility of a solution to the south Slavic question within Habsburg borders, or from murkier motives with domestic roots, Serbia, by
not repudiating the assassination of Archduke Franz Ferdinand, had offered the Dual
Monarchy a mortal challenge.[4] Serbia had also overplayed its military hand. The state

was still assimilating the territories acquired in the Balkan Wars of 1912–13, while the army was recovering from the costs and losses of those conflicts.[5] The Austrians even had the advantage of tactical surprise, putting elements of two armies across the Sava and the Danube Rivers on August 12 and compelling the evacuation of Belgrade without a fight.

At the outbreak of hostilities Serbia's chief of staff, Radomir Putnik, was taking the waters at an Austrian spa, and had taken with him the keys to the safe containing Serbia's war plans. Briefly interned, he was released – policy in 1914 was still implemented by gentlemen – and returned to find his subordinates had blown open the safe and begun mobilization without him. All the advantages, moral and military, seemed to lie with Austria. But Putnik was a shrewd planner and a ruthless fighting man. Willing to sacrifice territory for the sake of position, he drew the invaders deep into a Serbia whose broken terrain and undeveloped road network played havoc with Habsburg logistics and coordination. The Serbs held, then counterattacked, driving the Austrians back to the frontier and reoccupying Belgrade in a week of fighting as heavy as anything experienced in the Balkan Wars.

Conrad's decision to allow the use of his reserve in Serbia only until August 20, when it began disengaging for transportation to Russia, compounded the initial tactical misjudgments of Austrian theater commander Oskar Potiorek. Those in turn were balanced by Putnik's decision to invade Bosnia in the hopes of inspiring revolt among the province's Slavic elements. The revolt failed to materialize, and Potiorek slowly forced the now overextended Serbs back into their central mountains. On both sides disease and privation took a heavy toll of regiments already reduced by casualties as the onset of winter added to the difficulties of supply, maneuver, and combat. Belgrade fell to the Austrians on December 2. The next day Putnik, his army partly re-supplied by France and Britain, counterattacked an enemy trapped by its own advances on the wrong side of the flooded Kolubra River. It took almost two weeks for the Austrians to fight their way out and the Serbs to reoccupy their capital.

Both armies, exhausted, established winter quarters in a countryside so devastated that its recovery arguably required the rest of the twentieth century. On both sides ethnic, cultural, and religious differences were stoked into mutual hatred by the horrors of high-tech battlefields and the privations of devastated rear areas. Combat zones were constantly shifting: civilians could neither run nor hide, nor establish stable relationships with military occupiers. Material damage – burned houses, slaughtered farm animals, devastated fields – was only the tip of the resulting iceberg. A growing climate of "no quarter" on the battlefields spread to an indiscriminate use of firing squads behind the lines. Local infrastructures collapsed as labor forces disappeared and family systems disintegrated. Random violence and brutality became ways of life in an environment of everyone for themselves that had no pity on the weak and the helpless. By 1918, such conditions would encompass most of the Balkans.

Conrad's initial commitment of his reserve against Serbia had no effect on his decision to order a general advance into Russian Poland. The war plan of March 1914, which formed the basis of Habsburg operational planning five months later, provided for an immediate attack northwards from Galicia, aimed at overrunning and destroying a substantial part of the Russian forces in that area before they could complete their concentration. Without a simultaneous German attack across the Narew River toward Warsaw, however, Conrad's initiative invited dismissal as a voyage to nowhere in particular. Habsburg apologists have made much of Germany's alleged failure to mount that attack, even though its general staff had urged an Austrian offensive as recently as May. In fact the initial balance of forces in the Austro-Russian sector made offensive operations imperative by the standards of 1914, no matter what the Germans did. To sacrifice the initiative, to allow Russia to complete its concentration and choose its lines of advance was, according to conventional wisdom, to create a risk approaching certainty of being overrun in the field, trapped in the fortresses of Lemberg and Przemysl, or hammered back against the Carpathian Mountains.

Austria enjoyed an initial marginal superiority in men, and only a slight inferiority in guns. To the officer corps, decisive action seemed the best way to confirm allegiance in a multiethnic, polyglot empire. Colonel Alexander Brosch, commanding a regiment of the elite *Tiroler Kaiserjaeger*, hyperbolically praised the "iron calm, energy, and consequence" with which Austria had gone to war. "Bismarck and Moltke together" could not have managed the affair better: "all at once one could be really proud of his fatherland and its leaders." "Indolence, carelessness, and cowardice" had been banished; Austria had replaced America as "the land of limitless possibilities."[6]

On August 16 four Habsburg armies, almost 800,000 strong, began moving forward – including Colonel Brosch, whose own appointment in Samarra awaited him on September 7. To meet them the Russian high command initially deployed two armies north of Galicia and two more on the southeastern Russo-Austrian frontier, a total of around 700,000 men. As Habsburg forces advanced deeper into Galicia, the Russians sought to counter by driving forward, enveloping their flanks, and threatening or severing their lines of retreat. With cavalry and air reconnaissance providing little useful information to either side, the result was a series of brutal encounter battles. On the Austrian left, the First Army drove the Russians in front of it 20 miles back toward Lublin. The neighboring Fourth Army hammered the Russian Fifth Army at the battle of Komarow.

Determined to exploit these victories, Conrad pressed forward, ignoring his right, where the Third Army was caught in the open and crushed by 20 divisions of the Russian Third and Eighth Armies. The Second Army, Conrad's strategic reserve, was still detraining far from the front lines. Nevertheless Conrad responded by taking the fight to the Russians. Like Adolf Hitler in 1941, he believed any retreat would turn into a rout. Better to go for the throat and hope for the best. As the armies grappled with each other the front was characterized everywhere by mutually vulnerable flanks. Victory, Conrad insisted, would go to the side first able to impose its will on events. But his tool broke in his hands. After three weeks the Austrian soldiers were exhausted and their officers bewildered. Close-order assault tactics had cost thousands of lives. There were too many Russians in too many places. By September 1, his army on the verge of dissolution, even Conrad accepted retreat as the only alternative to annihilation.

Austria's correspondingly desperate appeals to Germany brought the Hindenburg/ Ludendorff team south. Using the superb German railway network, they deployed four corps from Prussia into Poznan, then attacked into the Russian rear, toward Warsaw, on September 28. The Germans were confident that they could easily replicate their earlier victories on a larger scale. This time, however, the Russians traded space for position, retreating, concentrating, and counterattacking as rain, then snow and bitter cold immobilized guns and supply wagons on both sides. A surrounded German corps cut its way back to its own lines, bringing out most of its wounded and 16,000 prisoners. After two months of vicious see-saw fighting the front stabilized, with the Russians holding Warsaw and most of Poland, devastated by mutual policies of scorched earth that left more than 9,000 villages destroyed and over 200,000 homeless.

For a while Austria seemed on the threshold of disaster, despite German intervention. The fortress of Lemberg surrendered without a fight. Przemysl was left to stand a siege, with enough supplies to last until spring. But Conrad was able to match the German initiative with an offensive of his own. Mounted with what remained of the army's pre-war resources, it briefly relieved Przemyśl, sputtered, and then collapsed as a Russian counterattack drove deep into the Carpathians before outrunning its supplies. As the year ended, the combatants paused – but only to regroup.

In Galicia too, a civilian economy barely above subsistence level in peacetime was devastated – and not only by the presence and the demands of the armies. In Austrian Galicia, Russian occupying authorities sought to Russify the province by an early form of ethnic cleansing. Germans, Ukrainians, and Jews were murdered, imprisoned, driven into Russia by hundreds and thousands, their property destroyed, confiscated, or simply allowed to fall into ruin.[7]

The 1915 campaign in the east began on December 3, 1914, when a sharp local counterattack by a mixed Austro-German force checked the Russian advance in the Carpathians and bought time for the German and Austrian high commands to prepare their own offensives. The Austrians struck in January but within days had stuck fast. A quarter-million men were killed or wounded, lost in blizzards, or eaten by wolves. By the end of March the counterattacking Russians were once again considering the prospects of a victory parade through Budapest, while Conrad for the second time in the war sought to cobble a field army together out of what remained of his original forces.

Strategically the main German attack was a study in irrelevance: launched in Masuria, it had no direct objective and was uncoordinated with the Austrian effort. Operationally, however, the offensive inflicted over 200,000 casualties and pushed 70 miles into Russia before grinding to a halt in the face of bad weather and desperate resistance. Its success lent weight to the repeated insistence of Hindenburg and Ludendorff that, given enough of the divisions currently pinned down in France, they could achieve significant results against a Russian army that seemed increasingly vulnerable to an all-out offensive.

Erich von Falkenhayn, who had replaced Helmuth von Moltke the Younger as Chief of the General Staff in the fall of 1914, was less sanguine. With good reason he distrusted Ludendorff as a self-centered careerist. He regarded Britain as Germany's primary enemy, and correspondingly believed the war would be decided in the west. At the same time, Falkenhayn was increasingly convinced that Germany could no longer win that war by direct military action. Russia, however, just might be susceptible to peace offers – especially if given another bloody nose.[8]

Some of Falkenhayn's best subordinates, Wilhelm Groener and Adolph Wild von Hohenborn, lobbied for the operational prospects of sending additional forces eastward. In the aftermath of its Carpathian disaster, moreover, Austria-Hungary needed shoring up, particularly given the increasing likelihood of Italy's entering the war on the Allied side. Weaker partners in a coalition always have an option of collapse. German military and diplomatic reports from both the front lines and the rear echelons indicated the Habsburg Empire was on the verge of disintegration.

Hindenburg and Ludendorff demanded a dozen corps and proposed a strategic double envelopment from the Carpathians and East Prussia: a Cannae that would destroy Russia's armies once and for all (see chapter 3 above). Falkenhayn no longer believed in the prospects of wide-ranging strategic penetration in any theater of war. Large-scale

battles of encirclement might look good on staff maps. In reality they fell victim too easily to "fog and friction." If, moreover, German contributions to the eastern front were
too generous Austria might continue what was becoming an established policy of blackmailing Germany for resources while doing nothing to help itself. The best compromise
seemed to involve inserting German troops into the Austrian sector of the front, where
their presence would be immediately felt, where the offensive would be at least nominally under Austrian command – and where Hindenburg and Ludendorff would not be
able to claim principal credit for any success.

Falkenhayn sent eight divisions eastward as the core of his projected attack. These
were no hastily mobilized civilians, but experienced combat veterans tempered in the
trench warfare of the western front, including two divisions of the elite Prussian Guard.
Their commander was also hand picked. General August von Mackensen is most familiar as a background member of Hitler's entourage in the 1930s: a hawk-faced old man
with fierce mustaches, his eyes deep-set under the fur busby with the skull-and-
crossbones insignia of his former regiment, the 2nd Hussars. But he had fought the
Russians since the start of the war, and was convinced that it was possible to break
through even a fortified sector of any front they occupied.

Giving Mackensen an opportunity to shine might also remove some of the luster from
the overly ambitious duo of Hindenburg and Ludendorff. As an insurance policy
Falkenhayn assigned to Mackensen one of the army's most brilliant young staff officers.
Hans von Seeckt had established his reputation in the positional warfare of the western
front, but had shown unusual skill in planning sector offensives based on surprise and
firepower. He was just the man for the kind of symbiotic relationship between a commander and his chief of staff that the German system sought to generate.

The Russian army meanwhile was seeking to compensate for personnel losses and
material shortcomings. Both were acute. Between January and April 1915 only two million artillery shells reached the front at a time when even limited bombardments on the
western front might absorb a quarter-million rounds. Rifles were in such short supply
that men were sent unarmed into the line, waiting to inherit the weapon of a casualty –
assuming they had enough training to be able to load it and set the sights. By now
Russia's replacement depots were all but empty of men with peacetime service. The
young, the old, and the previously exempted made a poor combination, no matter how
desperate the need to reinforce the surviving veterans of once-proud regiments.

On May 2, 1915, Mackensen's Eleventh Army tore open a 30-mile sector from
Gorlice to Tarnow in Galicia. By the third week of June a quarter-million prisoners
crowded Mackensen's cages. Hundreds of thousands more were dead, wounded, or scattered: total Russian losses in 1915 would approach two million. The Russian army's
material supplies from shells to bandages were virtually exhausted. But the Russian army
remained intact, conducting a fighting retreat out of the Polish salient and shortening its
line by 400 miles as exhaustion, autumn weather, and the demands of other fronts slowed
the Central Powers' advance.

For Falkenhayn and the German chancellor, Theobald von Bethmann Hollweg,
events at the front were a potential step to a negotiated peace with Russia. Bethmann's
initial proposals were relatively moderate, involving frontier rectifications rather than
sweeping annexations. But Russian war aims, like those of all the belligerents, had
grown in proportion to the demands and sacrifices made by the state on its people. The
Western allies raised the stakes. They promised more material assistance. They offered
Constantinople. They guaranteed Russia a large share of the reparations to be exacted

from the Central Powers at war's end. A stronger government might have made peace anyway. Russia, which had entered the war largely from a sense of its own weakness, was in no position to take that risk. Instead, Tsar Nicholas himself assumed supreme command – a step committing Russia to fight to the finish, whatever its outcome.[9]

In the early months of 1915 the Balkans had remained militarily quiet as the Central Powers and the Entente vied for support in those states that were still neutral. The Allied attack on the Gallipoli peninsula in April, however, convinced Falkenhayn of the need to remove the Serbian thorn in the Central Powers' side and open a route down the Danube to their hard-pressed Ottoman ally. Neither Germany nor Austria-Hungary could spare resources for a major operation. They turned to Bulgaria, still smarting from defeat in the Second Balkan War of 1913, still resentful at what it considered Russian abandonment. With the equivalent of 20 divisions, 1,000 guns, and a well-trained officer corps at his disposal, Emperor Ferdinand struck a hard bargain. Bulgaria would receive all of Macedonia, part of Serbia, and territory from Greece and Romania should those states join the Allies. Direct Austro-German contributions included a generous loan, a dozen divisions plus heavy artillery, and a proven command team: Seeckt and Mackensen.

The Central Powers' offensive began on October 7, 1915 against a Serbian army eroded by disease and casualties and low on ammunition and medical supplies. Facing attack from three sides, Serbia called on its allies. As early as December 1914 there had been desultory talk in Paris and London of opening a Balkan front. Cooler heads, however, had correctly observed that such an operation could only be supported through the Greek port of Salonika – which was undeveloped, had no more than a single-track railway connection to Serbia, and was under a resolutely neutral government. Nevertheless, in October, with the Serbs falling back on all fronts, two divisions were transferred from the Dardanelles to Salonika, despite Greek protests.

Merely moving a pawn was unable to prevent Serbia's final defeat or the subsequent retreat of over a quarter-million soldiers and civilians through the Albanian mountains – a three-week nightmare of typhus, dysentery, and frostbite in a Balkan December in which at least 70,000 died.[10] The survivors were initially evacuated to the island of Corfu. Eventually they would be transferred to a front at Salonika, which during 1916 absorbed over a dozen British and French divisions in what was sarcastically described as "the war's largest internment camp." According to the French politician Georges Clemenceau, its occupants contributed nothing to the war effort beyond "cultivating their gardens" in the manner of Voltaire's Candide. Militarily, terrain and logistics combined to frustrate large-scale offensives while the climate was so unhealthy that large numbers of men were disabled by malaria. Politically, nothing significant could be done without the overt support of Greece – which was a long time coming.[11] The Greek premier Eleutherios Venizelos, believed Greece could replace Serbia as the Allies' principal Balkan ally. King Constantine, who was of German descent and sympathetic to the Central Powers, distrusted Venizelos. Their confrontation led in 1917 to a coup that removed Constantine in favor of his son Alexander, who installed a reorganized government headed by Venizelos. Greece entered the war on the allied side on June 29, 1917.

Meanwhile the Russian army was ready – at least at the level of the high command – to try for a conclusion in the field once more. Logistically Russia had made a surprising recovery from the debacles of 1915. Domestic production of small arms, artillery pieces, and above all ammunition had increased to a point where dependence on Allied imports was significantly reduced. By mid-1916 Russian grain reserves were more than twice that of the previous year. Over six million men were under arms, and though most of them

were in garrison or training units a long way from the front they offered at least a possibility of keeping combat units up to strength – an important element of effectiveness in
the war of attrition that had become a general norm.[12]

That the Russian army was still far from top form was demonstrated in March by a
disastrous local offensive at Lake Narocz, where over 100,000 Russians fell before
German artillery and machine guns. Nevertheless the increasingly obvious weakness of
the Austro-Hungarians, the German preoccupation with the attack on Verdun, and
growing French calls for relief in the same campaign convinced the Russian high command to plan in April a series of offensives with their central point a drive on Vilna in the
north.[13]

As a preliminary General Aleksei Brusilov, the newly appointed commander of the
southwestern front, was to mount an attack in his sector to draw enemy reserves south.
Though this was intended as a secondary operation, Brusilov put his considerable intellectual and physical energy into galvanizing his discouraged subordinates to support a
fresh approach. Standard-pattern World War I offensives had involved concentrating on
throwing every available man and round into blasting through enemy defenses in a single
sector. Brusilov understood that this tactic had consistently proven futile. While it was
almost always possible to break *in*, breaking *out* was a much stiffer challenge, and to date
no army had ever broken *through*. Instead the Russian commander proposed to attack
along almost the entire 350 miles of his four-army sector. Each of the southwestern
front's armies would concentrate its efforts in a particular zone where prospects for a
"break-in" seemed favorable. If all went well, the enemy would face four near-simultane-
ous ruptures of the front, with no clear idea of which was the main effort or where the
next blow would fall. While Brusilov's initial intention was to focus on his northern wing
and drive for Lutsk to support the Vilna offensive, he was open to pursuing promising
alternatives that might develop elsewhere.

Strategically, Brusilov argued, this kind of offensive would take advantage of Russia's
space by forcing the Central Powers to disperse their reserves, instead of concentrating
them to contain an attack at one point. Operationally it would shake the morale of
Austrian troops and their commanders by keeping them off balance, wondering where
the next blow would fall. A major Russian initiative near its border, moreover, might
encourage Romania to enter the war on the allied side.

Against the Germans, with their flexible command and administrative systems, the
result might have been immediate disaster. Against an overextended and demoralized
Austro-Hungarian army, the Russians achieved remarkable initial successes. The offensive began on June 4. By June 7, Lutsk had fallen and the Russians in that sector had
advanced between 20 and 25 miles as Austrian resistance virtually collapsed. Brusilov,
however, was hoist on his own petard. With his forces dispersed among four armies, he
lacked the sector reserves to exploit the local victory. The High Command ordered him
to push forward but neither sent him additional troops nor launched its own projected
attack toward Vilna.

Meanwhile the Austrians transferred reinforcements from Italy. The Germans sent ten
divisions and a powerful force of heavy artillery, and for practical purposes took charge
of the fighting. The Russian offensive slowed, then stopped. The reinforcements finally
dispatched by the High Command only swelled the casualty lists. By mid-August, after
several disastrous Russian attacks further north, the front was closing down. Casualties
on both sides totaled over a million. The Austrian army's back was broken; a despairing
Conrad advised his government to accept German terms on war aims and the division of

conquered territory in the east. The Russian army, however, had also spent its last phys-ical and moral reserves in what proved the final military effort of the Tsarist Empire.

Russian military activity and allied diplomacy did persuade Romania to enter the con-flict in August, but the kingdom's army was ill-prepared for the kind of war the Central Powers had learned to wage.[14] It was smashed in a lightning German-Austrian offensive commanded by Falkenhayn who, dismissed as Chief of Staff for his failure at Verdun, demonstrated unexpected competence in field command. The Romanian fragments with-drew to their eastern border. Allied efforts to provide support by an offensive in the Salonika sector were frustrated by the Bulgarians with embarrassing ease.

In the context of the eastern theater, 1916 is best understood as the year of lost illu-sions. Russia's attempts at systematization and belt-tightening increasingly foundered as a semi-modern society proved unable to produce enough competent mid-level officials and administrators to maximize available resources. An overstrained economy depended more and more on human muscle power as opposed to machines that were wearing out and animals conscripted for the war. The men and women who did the work had neither money to spend nor food to buy with it, as inflation soared and distribution systems gridlocked.

Matters were much the same on the other side of the line in Austria-Hungary, where ethnic and nationalist rivalries were fueled by privation and in turn contributed to eco-nomic breakdown. Antagonism between labor and industry flourished as food costs out-stripped an inflation that mocked both wage increases and direct government subsidies. Agricultural production declined as men and animals were drawn into an army that only returned physical and emotional cripples to a civilian life growing increasingly desperate. Attempts to alleviate shortages by exploiting occupied territories in Russia foundered on the shoals of administrative inefficiency and the rocks of a near-subsistence economy that offered correspondingly limited opportunities for levying contributions and forcing sales.

Germany took matters in hand – at least by comparison. The appointment in August 1916 of Paul von Hindenburg as Chief of Staff was more than a military change. Hindenburg, trailing the shadow glory of Tannenberg and the other German triumphs on the Russian front, had become a symbol of national virility, an emotional substitute for a Kaiser who was kept away from any important decisions. With his partner, now Quartermaster-General, Erich Ludendorff, he was expected to bring victory to a sorely tried Fatherland. The 1916 "Hindenburg Program" provided in principle for the com-plete mobilization of German resources under government control. Hindenburg and Ludendorff demanded massive increases in munitions production, and a civilian popula-tion made entirely subject to regulation for the sake of the war effort. They paid no attention to the actual state of the country's resources (see chapter 29 below).

The Hindenburg Plan failed but it drew the occupied east well and truly into Germany's total war effort. Germans of all ranks were frequently, indeed one might say universally, shocked by their first experiences, visual and olfactory, of Poles, Russian, and Jews. As the front stabilized, the German army initiated what it considered a civilizing campaign behind its lines. Wherever the Germans went, they scoured. They cleaned streets, disinfected schools, established public toilets. Whole communities were deloused and bathed, in mass processes more effective than polite (see chapter 30 below).

The Russian defeats and retreats of early 1915 resulted in a near-breakdown of public welfare and utility systems that were none too elaborate to begin with. An already over-worked Tsarist administration was unable to manage the official policy of evacuating civilians when the Russian armies retreated. Masses of dispossessed people were either forcibly deported or drifted more or less aimlessly behind – and across – both front lines. Refugees who were cold and hungry stole food and fuel. Refugees with no access to toilet facilities polluted water. Refugees with no opportunity to wash became lousy.[15]

With lice came disease. Typhoid and cholera were endemic in the eastern theater of war by 1915. They were joined by a typhus epidemic almost medieval in its scope and consequences. The normal coping measures for such plagues were – and remain – the kinds of no-nonsense public health measures that fitted the German army's institutional framework.[16] Refugees under their control were collected and deloused, their possessions disinfected or burned, their persons confined in abandoned buildings or open-air camps. Sanitary and hygiene regulations were at times enforced with persuasion, at others with fines and jail terms, and not infrequently by applications of boots, fists, and rifle butts.

German behavior is easy to describe dismissively as a bourgeois and Freudian obsession, or symbolically, as prefiguring other kinds of "cleansing" in a later war.[17] On the other hand German health officials faced varying degrees of indifference and antagonism from individuals and communities for whom generations of Tsarist rule had made a bad joke of the concept "I'm from the government. I'm here to help you." And while dirt-and-hunger diseases never disappeared from German zones of occupation, they did not explode into pandemics.

At higher levels, German generals and politicians increasingly began playing with the east in a manner inviting comparison with Charlie Chaplin's "Great Dictator" and his balloon. It began soberly enough, with the High Command seeking to develop and exploit the occupied zone's resources with a view to making the eastern theater self-sufficient in routine contexts.[18] Exploitation in the form of taxes and confiscations rapidly took precedent over infrastructure building – not least because the military command in occupied Russia included far more bureaucrats than economists, agronomists, or anyone else capable of building as opposed to administering. Efforts to produce loyal German clients through education similarly unraveled as compulsion replaced resources. As plans failed and goals went unmet, "native" fecklessness and inferiority made handy scapegoats for paper-shufflers.

Across the fighting front, by early 1917 the government of Tsar Nicholas had sacrificed any legitimacy it once might have possessed. A revolution supported by both moderates and radicals overthrew the Empire in March. The new government in part sought to establish its own legitimacy by continuing the war. A major offensive, named after War Minister Alexander Kerensky, began on June 1 and failed in a matter of days. The Germans counterattacked. Russia collapsed into chaos, with the Bolsheviks under Vladimir Lenin seizing power in November by a coup in the war-rechristened capital, Petrograd.

At this stage of the war the German Empire still had the option of seeking a negotiated victory by offering to end the U-boat campaign and withdraw from its conquests in the west. That would put the burden on the Allies of seeking the bargaining table or risking continuation of what by now seemed an endless bloodletting. The failure to consider such a policy had much to do with America's entry into the war in April 1917. Even the massive ad hoc gains of resources and territory accompanying Russia's latest defeat seemed insufficient to assure Germany's future against a developing coalition of the world's two greatest maritime powers. The time had come to consolidate and stabilize Germany's position. The High Command and the German government sought peace negotiations with the Bolsheviks, who had announced their intention to end Russia's participation in the war as soon as possible.

Talks began at Brest-Litovsk on December 21, 1917. To call them negotiations is a misnomer. Austro-Hungarian arguments for a "bread peace," providing vitally needed foodstuffs and raw materials in return for limited territorial annexations, were ignored. German demands reflected a decision at the strategic and policy level to consolidate Central and Eastern Europe into an empire that could serve as a stable base for the expected next round of conflict. A Central European customs union, new thrones in the Baltic states and Poland, German colonization of lands vacated by wartime migrations – these and similar grandiose projects increasingly became the stuff of memoranda and working papers at the highest levels.

When the Bolsheviks declared in February 1918 that they would neither accept German terms nor renew the fighting a Crown Council was summoned to discuss what to do next.[19] Kaiser Wilhelm projected Russia's partition into four lesser empires. Hindenburg asserted that he needed the Baltic States for the maneuvering of his left wing in the next war. Ludendorff suggested annexations ranging as far as the Caspian Sea. Such discourse reflected a developed consciousness of the east as a source of power. It was nevertheless appropriate that the meeting took place at a sanitarium – the dialog at Bad Homburg matched for abstraction anything held on Thomas Mann's *Magic Mountain*.

On February 18 the Central Powers renewed the war unilaterally, occupying the Ukraine and Finland, moving into the Crimea and the Caucasus and meeting no resistance to speak of. On March 3, Lenin accepted the Treaty of Brest-Litovsk. Russia lost three-quarters of its coal and iron resources, half its factories and a third of its population. Just about everything from Narva in the north to Odessa in the south was either declared independent or placed at the disposition of the Central Powers. Similar drastic terms were imposed on Romania in May, with the Central Powers securing a 99-year monopoly on Romanian oilfields.

The Central Powers profited less than anticipated from their victory in the east. The Allies contributed to Austria-Hungary's collapse by playing the nationalist card, especially among dissident Slavic groups. Far more damage was done, however, by Germany increasingly treating the Habsburg monarchy as not merely a client but a supplicant, and disregarding its interests and its complaints with an insouciance that sparked the fury of helplessness. Negotiations for future collaboration between Germany and Austria-Hungary proceeded apace – with Austria's subordinate status plainly and painfully spelled out. But the Habsburg army, finally tried beyond its limits, was on the edge of disintegration. Prisoners returning from a revolutionized Russia spread discontent fueled by hunger.[20] In early 1918 a wave of strikes swept the cities. Disaffection spread to a harbor-bound navy, to the rear echelons of the army, and finally into the front lines.

Germany was able to transfer substantial numbers of divisions to France for the March 1918 offensives that Ludendorff expected to decide the war. Most of those formations, however, had previously been stripped of just about every man who wanted to fight or could be made to fight. What remained was a volatile mixture of the unfit and the unwilling, many of the latter from Alsace-Lorraine. Best suited for static, trench-holding missions, the "East divisions" brought with them levels of disaffection that frequently made them more a liability than an asset once Allied counterattacks began forcing the Germans back toward their own frontier.

The presence of more troops of any quality in the east would have been welcome to occupation and garrison forces stretched thin and under increasing pressure from revolutionaries, nationalists, brigands, and self-demobilized soldiers who brought their rifles home. In particular the Ukraine, projected as the Central Powers' breadbasket, collapsed instead into a state of ongoing turmoil that defied both force and negotiation. Between March and November 1918, the Central Powers learned a painful lesson in the differences between conquest, occupation, and exploitation. By one estimate the Germans saw only a tenth of the grain they anticipated, and much of that was collected virtually at gunpoint.

The eastern occupation was eroded from within as well. The German experience in Russia overwhelmingly involved involuntary participants. Their attitudes to the "east peoples" incorporated amusement and indifference as well as fear and antagonism. The compound was disruptive and destabilizing. It would require reification by *Völkisch* scholars and Nazi ideologues to become the stuff of genocide. Men who prior to 1914 had seldom been beyond the sound of their church bells or factory whistles found Russia alien, foreboding, and dangerous. In German forests the trees seemed to stand to attention. Russian forests were uncultivated, tangles of old trees that seemed impervious to human influence.[21] The *Ostritter* of World War I were conscripted conquerors. If they were racists, they were above all homesick racists. There were few regrets as they boarded trains for Germany in the aftermath of the Armistice.[22]

In a final irony, the Armistice owed more than a little to developments on the Salonika front. The operational stalemate had continued through 1917. Disease debilitated Allied ranks. Morale suffered from a general sense that no one knew what anyone was contributing to the war effort in this backwater. The Serbian government and army spent much of the year purging allegedly disloyal officers. The official entry of Greece into the war, however, encouraged the Serbs to put their house in order more quickly than they might otherwise have done. Serbian divisions, including released prisoners of war from Russia, began taking their place on the line. In the spring of 1918 Greek divisions began joining them. Theater commander Louis Guillaumat and his successor Louis Franchet d'Esperey supervised the introduction of new weapons and improved the administrative infrastructure. By midsummer the French, the Serbs, and the British were convinced that their Central Powers opponents were vulnerable.

It took until August 3, 1918 for the Allied High Command in Paris to agree, and six more weeks to prepare the offensive. On September 15 the Allies struck. By then they confronted primarily a Bulgarian army weakened by casualties and disease and shaken by events in Russia. Within days soviets were forming in the major cities and the government was requesting an armistice. Serb troops reentered their devastated country, fighting their way to Belgrade before collapsing in exhaustion. On October 29, 1918, the Croat Diet in Zagreb declared its allegiance to the new state of Yugoslavia. French divisions thrust up the Danube valley, and Franchet d'Esperey talked of massing an army in Bohemia before marching on Dresden. Instead, on November, 11, 1918, Karl I, the last Habsburg emperor, abdicated as his throne crumbled beneath him.

In four years the Allies and the Central Powers had put enough into the Balkans as a theater of war to destabilize the region, but not enough to facilitate the building of a new order.[23] Following the Armistice, Yugoslavia and Italy clashed over Fiume and the Dalmatian coast. A revived Romania was rewarded with the Judas gift of Hungarian Transylvania. A shrinking British contingent turned toward Constantinople. Greek troops landed in Smyrna, the vanguard of a doomed dream of a Greater Greece in Asia. Treaties signed in the suburbs of Paris did little to avert a descent into chaos tempered by dictatorship (see chapter 37 below).

Events in Russia followed much the same pattern. Brest-Litovsk had produced a fierce reaction among the Allies. Denouncing what they considered the Bolsheviks' betrayal, they sent troops that could ill be spared from other fronts to various remote parts of Russia. They provided financial and material assistance to emerging anti-Bolshevik forces that were strong enough in their own right to contest the Soviet regime from its beginning. For all its subsequent achievements as a revolutionary superpower, the USSR never was fully accepted by the Russian people.[24] Just perhaps, that ambivalence was the ultimate legacy of World War I in the East – a war that continues to define Europe south of the Danube and east of the Vistula to the present.

Notes

1 Showalter, *Tannenberg*.
2 Stone, *The Eastern Front*.
3 Jones, "Imperial Russia's Armed Forces."
4 Kronenbitter, "Krieg im Freiden," p. 528.
5 Lyon, "Serbia and the Balkan Front."
6 Kronenbitter, "Krieg im Frieden," pp. 484–5.
7 Graf, "The Reign of the Generals."
8 Guth, "Der Gegensatz."
9 Linke, *Das zaristische Russland*.
10 Mitrovic, *Serbia's Great War*, p. 152.
11 Leontaritis, *Greece and the First World War*.
12 Stone, *Eastern Front*, pp. 208–11.
13 Feldman, "The Russian General Staff."
14 Torrey, *Romania and World War I*.
15 Gatrell, *A Whole Empire Walking*, pp. 19–31.
16 Cornebise, *Typhus and Doughboys*.
17 Weindling, *Epidemics and Genocide*, pp. 96–108.
18 Strazhas, *Deutsche Ostpolitik*.
19 Herwig, "Tunes of Glory at the Twilight Stage."
20 Rachamimov, *POWs and the Great War*, pp. 151–3.
21 Liulevicius, *War Land*, pp. 27–8.
22 Showalter, "Homesick Revolutionaries."
23 Glenny, *The Balkans*, p. 345.
24 Kennedy-Pike, *Russia and the World*, p. 208.

References and Further Reading

Afflerbach, Holger, *Falkenhayn. Politisches Denken und Handeln im Kaiserreich*, Munich, Oldenbourg, 1984.

Conrad von Hoetzendorff, Franz, *Aus Meiner Dienstzeit*, 5 vols., Vienna, Rikola, 1921–5.

Cornebise, Alfred, *Typhus and Doughboys: The American Polish Typhus Relief Expedition, 1919–21*, Newark, NJ, University of Delaware Press, 1982.

Feldman, Robert S., "The Russian General Staff and the June 1917 Offensive," *Soviet Studies*, 19, 1968, pp. 526–43.

Foley, Robert T., *German Strategy and the Path to Verdun. Erich von Falkenhayn and the Development of Attrition, 1870–1916*, Cambridge, Cambridge University Press, 2005.

Gatrell, Peter, *A Whole Empire Walking: Refugees in Russia during World War I*, Bloomington, University of Indiana Press, 1999.

Glenny, Misha, *The Balkans: Nationalism, War and the Great Powers, 1804–1999,* New York, Viking, 1999.

Golovine, N. M., *The Russian Army in the World War,* New Haven, Yale University Press, 1931.

Graf, Daniel, "The Reign of the Generals: Military Government in Western Russia, 1914–1915," dissertation, University of Nebraska, 1972.

Guth, Ekkehard P., "Der Gegensatz zwischen dem Oberbefehlshaber Ost und dem Chef des Generalstabes des Feldheeres 1914/15," *Militärgeschichtliche Mitteilungen,* 35, 1984, pp. 75–111.

Herwig, Holger, "Tunes of Glory at the Twilight Stage: The Bad Homburg Crown Council and the Evolution of German Statecraft, 1917/18," *German Studies Review,* 6, 1983, pp. 53–63.

Herwig, Holger, "Disjointed Allies: Coalition Warfare in Berlin and Vienna, 1914," *Journal of Military History,* 54, 1990, pp. 265–80.

Herwig, Holger, *The First World War: Germany and Austria-Hungary, 1914–1918.* London, Arnold, 1997.

Hoffman, Max, *War Diaries and Other Papers,* 2 vols., ed. K. Nowak. London, Secker, 1929.

Janssen, Karl-Heinz, *Der Kanzler und der General. Die Führungskrise um Falkenhayn und Bethmann Hollweg, 1914–1916,* Göttingen, Musterschmidt, 1967.

Jones, David R., "Imperial Russia's Armed Forces at War," in A. Millet and W. Murray (eds.), *Military Effectiveness,* Vol. 1, London and Boston, Allen and Unwin,1988, pp. 328–429.

Kennedy-Pike, Claudia, *Russia and the World, 1917–1991,* London, Arnold, 1998.

Knox, A. M., *With the Russian Army, 1914–1917,* 2 vols., London, Hutchinson, 1921.

Kronenbitter, Günther, *"Krieg im Frieden": Die Fuehrung der k.u.k Armee und die Grossmachtpolitik Oesterreich-Ungarns 1908–1914,* Munich, Oldenbourg, 2003.

Leontaritis, George B., *Greece and the First World War: From Neutrality to Intervention, 1917–1918,* Boulder, CO, East European Monographs, 1990.

Lincoln, W. Bruce, *Passage Through Armageddon: The Russians in War and Revolution, 1914–1918,* New York, Simon and Schuster, 1986.

Linke, Horst Gunther, *Das zaristische Russland und der Erste Weltkrieg. Diplomatie und Kriegsziele, 1914–1917,* Munich, Fink, 1982.

Liulevicius, Vejas Gabriel, *War Land on the Eastern Front: Culture, National Identity, and German Occupation in World War I,* Cambridge, Cambridge University Press, 2000.

Lyon, James B., "Serbia and the Balkan Front 1914," dissertation, University of California at Los Angeles, 1995.

Mackenzie, David, *Apis. The Congenial Conspirator: The Life of Colonel Dragutin T. Dimitrijevic,* Boulder, CO, East European Monographs, 1989.

Mitrovic, Andrej, *Serbia's Great War, 1914–18,* London, Hurst, 2007.

Neilson, Keith, *Strategy and Supply: The Anglo-Russian Alliance, 1914–17,* London, Allen and Unwin, 1984.

Rachamimov, Alon, *POWs and the Great War: Captivity on the Eastern Front* Oxford and New York, Berg, 2002.

Rothenberg, Gunther, "The Austro-Hungarian Campaign against Serbia in 1914," *Journal of Military History,* 53, 1989, pp. 127–46.

Schwarzmüller, Theo, *Zwischen Kaiser und "Führer." Generalfeldmarschall August von Mackensen; eine politische Biographie,* 2nd rev. ed., Paderborn, Schoeningh, 1996.

Showalter, Dennis, "The Homesick Revolutionaries: Soldiers' Councils and Newspaper Propaganda in German-Occupied Eastern Europe, 1918–1919," *Canadian Journal of History,* 9, 1976, pp. 69–88.

Showalter, Dennis, "The Eastern Front and German Military Planning, 1871–1914: Some Observations," *East European Quarterly,* 15, 1981, pp. 165–80.

Showalter, Dennis, *Tannenberg: Clash of Empires,* Hamden, CT, Archon, 1991.

Stone, Norman, "Die Mobilmachung der österreichischen-ungarischen Armee 1914," *Militägeschichtliche Mitteilung,* 16, 1974, pp. 64–95.

Stone, Norman, *The Eastern Front, 1914–1917*, New York, Scribner, 1975.

Strazhas, Aba, *Deutsche Ostpolitik im Ersten Weltkrieg: Der Fall Ober Ost, 1915–1917*, Wiesbaden, Harassowitz, 1993.

Torrey, Glen E., *Romania and World War I: A Collection of Studies*, Portland, Center for Romanian Studies, 1999.

Tunstall, Graydon A., "The Schlieffen Plan: The Diplomacy and Military Strategy of the Central Powers in the East, 1905–1914," PhD dissertation, Rutgers University, 1974.

Weindling, Paul, *Epidemics and Genocide in Eastern Europe, 1890–1945*, Oxford, Oxford University Press, 2000.

Wildman, Allan K., *The End of the Russian Imperial Army*, 2 vols., Princeton, Princeton University Press, 1980–7.

CHAPTER SIX

The Italian Front, 1915–18

GIORGIO ROCHAT
(translated by Paul O'Brien)

The Italian army was an extension of the Piedmontese army that had overseen unification. From the 1870s, it was reorganized along German lines as a conscript force based on three years' military service, but with 12 Army Corps and a quarter of a million men, it outstripped its resources in training and equipment.[1] In an attempt to forge a truly national force, regiments were recruited across regions and often changed their urban headquarters, the elite Alpine units being the only exception to this rule.[2] State expenditure on the armed forces was heavy for a country as poor as Italy – some 24 percent of the budget between unification and World War I – but this was still only half the total of French military expenditure and a third that of Germany.[3] The officer corps was small (about 15,000 in 1910) but of good quality.[4]

The prewar army had three essential roles. The first was to complete national unity by expelling the Austro-Hungarian occupant from the Trentino and the Veneto, in the north and northeast. This was the basis of the unsuccessful war fought for the Veneto in 1866 (whose incorporation was achieved by diplomatic, not military means) and of the successful seizure of Rome as the capital during the Franco-Prussian War of 1870. The second role was counter-insurgency in the so-called "war on banditry," against southern resistance to inclusion in the new state, and in other actions against domestic dissidence. Finally, the army pursued Italy's colonial agenda, again unsuccessfully in the case of the humiliating defeat by Ethiopian forces at Adua in 1896, and more successfully (though against stiff opposition) in the war against Turkey for Libya in October 1911.

The Triple Alliance with Germany and Austria-Hungary, which Italy entered in 1882, ended the country's international isolation and offered a counterweight to France, which had seized Tunisia as a colony from under Italy's nose in 1881. However, Italy feared lest the alliance should be turned against Great Britain, soon to become Germany's major rival, with whom Italy had no quarrel. When from the early 1900s it became preoccupied with Austria-Hungary's predicament in the Balkans, Italy became even more uncomfortable. It was enjoying improved relations with France, had its own aspirations in the Balkans, and was under increasing domestic pressure from irredentist claims by Italian nationalists on Trentino and Trieste that were directed openly against Austria-Hungary. In effect, the alliance had entered a state of unspoken crisis. This did not affect military planning. In June 1913, Italy signed a naval convention with Austria and Germany

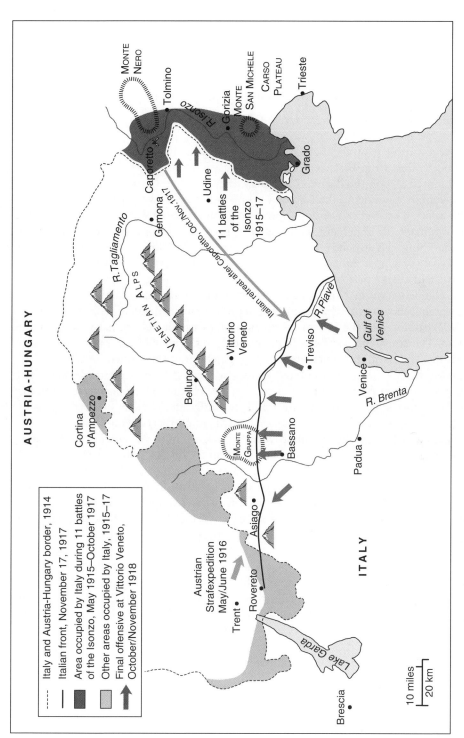

Map 4 The Austro-Italian front, 1915–18

concerning future war in the Mediterranean, and in March 1914 renewed its commitment to send three army corps to the Rhine in case of a French attack on Germany. But such military agreements were subordinate to the political decisions that would be made following the outbreak of war in July 1914.[5]

Italian Intervention and the First Offensives, May–December 1915

Since the Triple Alliance was defensive and Austria-Hungary initiated the war by attacking Serbia, the Italian government was under no obligation to support the Central Powers. In the event it chose neutrality before eventually deciding that intervention on the side of the Entente offered the best chance of pursuing irredentist claims against Austria and rather confused aims in the Balkans.[6] In reality, Italy could not remain outside the conflagration without renouncing the role of a major European power that it had taken such pains to assert. The Pact of London, signed on April 26, 1915 with Britain, France, and Russia, was markedly imperialist in character. It promised major territorial gains, mostly at Austria-Hungary's expense, in the Italian-speaking Trentino and German-speaking South Tyrol (or Upper Adige), Trieste (predominantly Italian), Istria (with an Italian minority), and a large part of South Slav Dalmatia and Albania. The pact also conceded colonial compensation in North Africa if Britain and France expanded in that region.[7] This program is noteworthy for its shortsightedness. Italy demanded poor territories as a basis for expansion into the Balkans, for which in any case it did not have the economic resources. The army command was not consulted on the issue but its opposition on the grounds that the coast of Dalmatia was hard to defend was well known.

Thus on May 24, 1915 Italy entered the war without having been attacked and with the bulk of the country opposed to the venture (see chapter 31). This meant, first, that military operations had to be offensive and, secondly, that Italian soldiers lacked the main motivating belief of their German or French counterparts, namely that they were defending the fatherland against unprovoked attack. Despite this offensive imperative, the war plan of General Luigi Cadorna, commander of the Italian forces since July 1914, was constrained by geography. Mountains dominated much of the front, with peaks fortified by the Austrians rising to between 1,000 and 2,000 meters. An offensive breakthrough was impossible and all the attacks of the summer of 1915 were doomed to fail. Along the lower reaches of the Isonzo, between Tolmino and the sea, the country was less difficult, with a series of hills at low altitude. Here Cadorna placed 22 of his 35 divisions.

The battles in France in October–November 1914 and the Franco-British offensives of 1915 had demonstrated the enormous difficulties of advancing against modern defensive firepower. However, Cadorna paid no heed and was convinced that he could break through to Ljubljana, Trieste, and then Vienna itself.[8] It was an over-optimistic vision for which he has been blamed by history and by historians. In his favor, however, it should be remembered that allied commanders were no closer to accepting the new realities of warfare in 1915, as Joffre's costly offensives of that year showed (see chapter 4). The information that Cadorna received from his military observers with the French and German armies failed to undermine prewar certitudes. It was still believed that while the offensive was more costly than the defensive, it could be made to work if conducted with the necessary energy – and that Cadorna had in abundance.[9] It should also be noted that for much of the war, there was nothing but the most rudimentary coordination with the French, British, and Russian allies.

After an initial, premature operation to the north in May 1915, Cadorna turned this mainly Alpine region into a defensive zone. It was here above all that the army's Alpine battalions were deployed, elite units that fought a "white war" in the snow-clad upper reaches of the mountains, which had little strategic significance but were filled with heroic encounters. However, the bulk of the offensive strength of the army remained concentrated in the northeast, on the lower Isonzo and Carso, which was to remain the principal theater of Italian offensive operations down to the disaster at Caporetto in October 1917.

The Isonzo emerges from the mountains at Tolmino, a well-fortified Austrian position, and flows out to the sea 40 km away as the crow flies. The sector can be divided into three distinct zones from north to south. The first is from the watershed to Plava and is marked by high and steep riverbanks. The Italians crossed these in June 1915 but only managed to cling onto a small bridgehead at Plava at great cost. The second sector faced the city of Gorizia, where the Austrians had created a strong bridgehead on the west bank of the river which they defended from a series of surrounding hills with high peaks. The third sector of the Isonzo was where the river flows out onto the plain. Here the Austrians had pulled their front back by several kilometers as far as the Carso. The latter is an enormous flat and irregular plateau stretching from Gorizia into Slovenia with sparse vegetation, many ravines, and a craggy ridge some 200–300 m high that dominates the Isonzo plain. This ridge and the enemy bridgehead at Gorizia were the main Italian objectives in 1915.

It is impossible to draw up league tables for the many failed offensives of the Great War and the losses and suffering they caused. However, the Italian offensives between June and December 1915 certainly rank amongst the harshest. The army had a total of 300 machine guns, 1,800 light field cannon, 200 guns of medium caliber, and only 132 heavy guns. There was little artillery coordination with the infantry, so that the troops were launched against the Austrian barbed wire and machine guns without adequate support. Once halted, they had to hold onto any terrain gained, however small, from where the offensive was to be relaunched.[10] In the summer, the battles were fought over scorching rock in asphyxiating heat and with unbearable thirst. Autumn brought rain, mud, and the bitter cold. Trenches were improvised and shallow, granting little possibility of rest or protection. To overcome enemy barbed wire, soldiers had little more than tubes of gelatin, which were of dubious efficacy. The High Command could only repeat its orders for hopeless offensives. No heed was paid to officers in the front line who called for a more rational management of the battle, and those who persisted were summarily removed.

By the winter of 1915 the Italian army counted over 200,000 dead and injured, to say nothing of the men who had fallen ill. Infantry regiments had lost up to two-thirds of their men, and all for insignificant gains. In December the troops were already on the verge of collapse, but the Austrians could not take advantage of their plight since their own rigid defense had cost them dearly, with an estimated 165,000 casualties.[11]

The *Strafexpedition* and the Battle of Gorizia, May–August 1916

During the winter of 1915–16, the Italian army was expanded to 1.5 million men and adequately equipped with machine guns and trench mortars (simpler to manufacture than medium artillery, which only came on stream in 1917).[12] Cadorna had prepared a great offensive against Gorizia, but he was preempted by the Austrian commander-in-chief,

Conrad von Hötzendorf. Austria-Hungary had been through a dramatic crisis in the first months of 1915, but by the end of that year the situation had greatly improved. The Russian army had suffered a major defeat and been forced to retreat from Austrian Galicia, while the Serbian army had been driven from its homeland (see chapter 5). Only the Italian army remained intact, and Conrad intended to knock it out of the war with an offensive from the Trentino that would take the bulk of Italian forces massed on the Isonzo from the rear.

Conrad conceived of his ambitious plan as a *Strafexpedition*, or punitive expedition, that would visit due retribution on Italy for its betrayal of the Triple Alliance. However, he lacked sufficient troops and in December 1915 asked the German supreme commander, Erich von Falkenhayn, to contribute eight divisions. Falkenhayn demurred, since he was preparing his own offensive against Verdun and was also convinced that more than eight more divisions would be needed to beat Italy decisively. Unperturbed, Conrad proceeded with his own resources and gathered 14 divisions in the Trentino, some of which were taken from the Russian and Isonzo fronts. A great objective was worth the risk. The *Strafexpedition* was certainly well prepared, with 1,200 cannons, of which 600 were of medium and heavy caliber. Delayed because of the great snowfall that winter, the offensive was finally unleashed from the Altipiano di Asiago on May 15, 1916.[13]

The Italian defense could scarcely have been worse organized. From the start of the war, the First Army had been assigned a strategically defensive role, facing the Trentino. But its troops had been sent forward to precarious positions right under the Austrian lines, and without any defense in depth should this be needed in case of retreat. Cadorna's intelligence services were inefficient and only signaled the Austrian offensive at the last minute.

The Austrians enjoyed an overwhelming initial success but the attack then waned due to the difficulty of the terrain and the arrival of Italian reinforcements, and it was halted when it reached the edge of the plateau of the Asiago. In fact, it could be argued that it was doomed from the start. Conrad had not taken into consideration the expansion of the Italian army and hence the greater quantities of men at Cadorna's disposal. In a brilliant maneuver, the latter used his internal lines to swiftly transport 179,000 men from the Isonzo to the Altipiano. Moreover, on June 4 the Russian army under General Brusilov launched its devastating offensive against the Austrian eastern front, which had been weakened by the removal of the divisions for the *Strafexpedition*. In the middle of June, Conrad took note of the failure of his offensive and withdrew his troops to a more defensive line. The Italian commanders, however, could not resist the temptation to use the numerous troops now stationed in the area to take back the positions that had been lost. With inadequate preparatory bombardments, a series of bloody but unsuccessful attacks dragged on until the end of July. In sum, the Italians won the battle but at a heavy price, with about 150,000 casualties (including 40,000 prisoners taken during the initial phase) against Austria's 80,000 (plus the sick, who are usually forgotten in military casualties).[14]

On August 6 Cadorna moved onto the offensive against Gorizia and on the Carso. At last this was a battle that was well prepared, with 1,200 artillery pieces (450 of them being medium and heavy guns), 800 trench mortars and careful preliminary study of the terrain, including aerial reconnaissance. The Austrian positions were overrun, the decisive factor here being their lack of reserves, since too many divisions had been sent to the Trentino. On August 9 Italian troops entered Gorizia and moved on toward the Carso before their advance was arrested by the arrival of Austrian reinforcements. Gorizia was the first real Italian success in the war (with around 50,000 losses compared to 40,000 for the Austrians). But then the war of attrition set in again. In the autumn, Cadorna launched three limited offensives on the Carso that achieved little but cost nearly 80,000 casualties to the two sides.[15]

One further point should be mentioned about the warfare of 1916. On June 29, the Austrians employed gas in an attack on the Carso, and before long both sides were using the weapon, though in lesser quantities than in France. During the war the Italians produced some 6,000 tonnes of gas compared to 55,000 in Germany, 26,000 in France, and 8,000 in Austria, and suffered perhaps 5,000 deaths by gas, the quality of Italian gas-masks being mediocre.

The Watershed of 1917

In June 1916, Salandra's ministry was replaced by a government of national unity under Boselli that included all the political forces supporting the war. Arms and munitions were now being produced on a vast scale with the full collaboration of industry (and its generous remuneration). All valid men liable for conscription had been called up, and the army on the front numbered 1.5 million soldiers, rising to 2 million in 1917.

Cadorna remained in sole charge of the military effort. There were bitter conflicts between the government and the high command, as in all the countries in the war, but Cadorna was more dominant than commanders in chief elsewhere. He was able to refuse any interference from the government, or even the king, and it is significant in this regard that he chose the name Supreme Command for his office instead of the traditional GHQ. Yet he himself never hesitated to criticize the government for what he saw as its weakness in dealing with internal dissent, to which he attributed the failings of the army. The government tried to remove him early in 1916 but he was able to muster sufficient support, including in the press, to outmaneuver them. Nor did the government have any realistic alternative to his grand offensives.[16]

Trench warfare had its own terrible logic that was independent of Cadorna, as of other major commanders. Nor was he any more to blame for the failure of his offensives than were Joffre and Haig. Cadorna had an unshakeable faith in his own mission and was not without a sense of vision. Like the French and British commanders, he believed that with more men and munitions he would be able to achieve a breakthrough or at least bring about the enemy's collapse by attrition. Two criticisms, however, can legitimately be leveled against him. The first is poor organization. Cadorna over-centralized decision-making and proved unable to incorporate his generals into an effective chain of command. He knew how to impose offensives but not how to direct them or call them off at the right moment. The cult of the offensive was such that Cadorna simply got rid of commanders who hesitated to follow orders, even when they had good reason to do so, but hesitated to stop those who continued attacks with no prospect other than further losses.

The second criticism is that he saw success more in terms of quantity (guns and battalions) than quality, with a better organization of the offensive. In 1917 the Italian troops were still attacking as they had in 1915, with better artillery fire but still in compact formations, with successive waves massacred by the Austrian cannons. Any improvements were due to local commanders in the trenches, and little had been done to disseminate these improvements by training. Cadorna had little concern for his soldiers – a point to which we shall return.

In 1917 Cadorna launched two offensives on the Isonzo, in May and in August–September, which repeated the old story. Numerical superiority of the infantry was offset by a less marked difference in artillery. A prolonged bombardment was followed by an initial tactical success and then a protracted battle of attrition, the only fruits of which were trenches and terrain whose strategic significance was nil. In total, about 300,000 Italian soldiers were killed or wounded compared to Austria's 160,000. In the battles of August–September about 400 of the 600 Italian infantry battalions employed in the assaults lost anything from one-half to two-thirds of their forces. Yet, ironically, there was a significant result. The Austrian army had now used up all its reserves and had to ask Germany for help, since it was no longer capable of holding off another Italian offensive – though Cadorna could not for the moment unleash it due to the exhaustion of his own troops.[17] In fact, help from allies was not limited to the Austrians, since 100 British and French field artillery batteries participated in the second battle. But where Lloyd George, who felt it was time to finish off Austria, had wanted to send a much stronger force, the French and British high commands would only agree to this more limited aid.

Unlike in 1916 with the *Strafexpedition*, Germany now acceded to Austria's request to replace Austrian troops on the eastern front and allow a strategic counterattack against Italy between the Plezzo and Tolmino. The Germans added seven special divisions of their own to the eight Austrian divisions, all of which would form the 14th Austro-German Army under the command of General Otto von Below (though it should be noted that it was Chief of Staff General Konrad Krafft von Dellmensingen who planned and conducted the battle). The Italians were still organized for the offensive and lacked a defense in depth and adequate reserves.

In late 1917, the German army was preparing an offensive battle of a new kind for the western front the following year in the hope of bringing the war to a decisive end (see chapter 9). Histories of the war note that the new tactic (especially the use of elite storm troops) was applied during the offensive against Riga in September 1917, but they often forget the crucial role it also played on the Austro-Italian front in October that same year. The key attack was to proceed through the Isonzo valley via a small provincial capital that played no part in the battle but which nonetheless gave the latter its name – Caporetto (today Kobarid in Slovenia). The Austro-German offensive began with a brief and violent bombardment of the communication lines and trenches from Tolmino at dawn on October 24, 1917. It rapidly overran the Italian lines and achieved deep penetration using agile columns that easily overcame the Italian back-line troops. In the space of two days the Austro-Germans had conquered all of the peaks that dominate the plain of Friulia.

Up to this point the success of the offensive can be compared to those that the Germans would enjoy in France in the spring of 1918, when the British Fifth Army collapsed much like the Italian divisions at Caporetto. But different factors then intervened. In the first place, in France there were no precise strategic objectives, whereas in Italy the progression of the Austro-German troops brought them up behind the bulk of the Italian army stationed on the Isonzo. Then there is the question of reserves. In France, the German offensives were halted by the arrival of new troops, while in Italy there were no reserves. Finally, the high commands responded differently. The British and French generals did not lose their heads or blame their setbacks on the troops. But when the extent of the disaster became apparent to Cadorna, he immediately blamed it on the soldiers, stating on the evening of October 25: "About 10 regiments surrendered *en masse* without fighting. I see a disaster developing." In a bulletin on October 27 he noted a "lack of resistance by units of the Second Army which have vilely retreated without fighting and ignominiously surrendered to the enemy," and he sent a telegram to the government on the same day declaring that: "The army falls under the blows not of the external enemy but of the enemy within." There is no foundation for these accusations, as was shown by the commission of enquiry set up in 1919 to look into the causes of the rout.[18] Abandoning the Isonzo was unavoidable owing to the lack of reserves with which to resist the Austro-German advance. But so convinced was Cadorna of his troops' untrustworthiness, that he abandoned his post as commander without attempting to oversee the withdrawal.

About 1.5 million men (between troops and services) were forced to retreat from the Isonzo in disorder. A virtual torrent of soldiers, some still engaged in sporadic combat, made its chaotic way toward the bridges over the River Tagliamento and then the Piave, accompanied by 400,000 civilian refugees. Since Cadorna had separated the artillery (which suffered few losses) from the infantry, the latter was obliged to retreat without artillery cover while the artillery regiments proceeded without the protection of the infantry. Luckily for the retreating forces, the Austro-Germans were both too few and too tired to be able to block their retreat. On November 4 Cadorna issued the order to fall back on the Piave. The Third Army from the Carso and the Fourth Army from Cadore retreated in good order and secured the defense of the new front. The last units crossed the water on November 10.

The extent of the disaster was still enormous. Overall, the Italian army suffered 40,000 dead and wounded and an enormous 280,000 taken prisoner. The loss of arms and munitions was likewise extremely serious: 3,150 cannons, 1,700 trench mortars, 3,000 machine guns, and huge storehouses of munitions and food.[19] Almost immediately the battle gave rise to potent myths. On the right, it was attributed to defeatism by the home front, with the socialists, Catholics, and liberal Italy bearing the brunt of the blame. This theme was later taken up by the fascist regime, which sought its own legitimization in a vision of the war in which a young Italy triumphed symbolically over old-style generals and the liberal regime. The left oscillated between different interpretations, none of which was entirely satisfactory – a "people's war" versus the dictatorial Cadorna, denunciation of the horrors of the conflict, the defense of the soldiers' "disobedience," and Caporetto as a revolution *manquée*. Abroad, Caporetto became the symbol of Italy's failure in the war.

The first victim of Caporetto was the Boselli government, which fell on October 25. The new prime minister, Vittorio Emanuele Orlando, accepted the post on condition that Cadorna be forced to step down. The king agreed, but the dismissal was to be put off until the end of the battle. Then, at the inter-allied conference of Rapallo on November 6, French Chief of General Staff Ferdinand Foch and British Prime Minister Lloyd George demanded Cadorna's immediate removal as a condition for sending reinforcements to the Italian front. On November 8 Cadorna was replaced by Armando Diaz, a little known general nominated by the king himself (the only moment in the war when Victor Emmanuel III had a decisive role). During November, six French and five British divisions arrived in Italy, totaling 240,000 men. Whereas some British and French commentators consider that they rescued Italy, Italian views have minimized the importance of their help. There is truth in both. The allied troops acted as reserve forces in case of an enemy breakthrough, allowing Diaz to send every last available battalion to the front. However, the battle to block the enemy advance was conducted exclusively by the Italians.[20]

In the north, the new front remained as it had been before Caporetto as far as the Altipiano di Asiago. Then it ran along Mount Grappa, between the rivers Brenta and Piave and, finally, down the Piave to the sea. The Austrians and Germans attacked this front for almost two months, achieving some partial successes but without managing to break through. In a long and furious battle with little use of artillery by either side, the Italian troops held their own, proving (as if this were needed) just how unfounded Cadorna's accusations actually were. The German and Austrian divisions were unable to repeat the success of Caporetto owing to the lack of surprise and adequate preparation. The battle came to a halt at the end of December with complete Italian success, although the final assault on Mount Tomba (on the slopes of Mount Grappa) was in fact conducted by French troops on the 30th of that month. The German divisions called it a day in Italy and left for the western front.

The Last Year: November 1917–November 1918

The new government and army command rose to the challenge. Orlando dealt with dissension on the home front without using excessive force and, with the help of his finance minister, Francesco Saverio Nitti, oversaw an intensification of industrial production that in the space of a few months managed to make good the guns and other material lost at Caporetto.[21] Unlike Cadorna, Diaz and his second-in-command, Pietro Badoglio, had direct combat experience and learned from previous failures.[22] They reorganized the army in three ways. First, they paid attention to the soldiers' well-being in the trenches in terms of food, home leave, and periods of rest. Sensible propaganda was finally promoted in the army with the creation of the *Servizio P* (Propaganda Service), and military intelligence also became more effective. Secondly, Diaz and Badoglio improved troop training and the soldiers' armaments. They also made the unity of divisions sacrosanct, promoting the collaboration of infantry brigades with artillery regiments. Finally, the new commanders established a large reserve force of the kind that had been wholly lacking at Caporetto and also limited costly minor attacks. In the last year of the war the death rate of Italian soldiers fell by three-quarters from that under Cadorna.[23]

The *arditi*, or elite assault troops who had been created in 1917, fitted well with this reform program. They had the best training and a strong esprit de corps and were known for their speed and agility, which made them excellent in surprise attacks, though they were not able to turn these into penetration in depth. The *ardito* was an enthusiastic and highly motivated combatant, different to the infantry bogged down for years in the trenches, and not surprisingly became the stuff of legend, to be exploited after the war by the fascist regime.[24]

Diaz adopted a policy of prudence, with few but well-prepared attacks, because he knew that the Austrians were preparing one last great offensive. In June 1918 the Italian army consisted of 50 divisions (of 4 regiments each), about 700 battalions, 5,650 cannons, and 1,600 trench mortars. There were also three British and two French divisions (the others had been recalled to France, accompanied by two Italian divisions), and one Czechoslovak division made up of volunteer prisoners. The Austrians, for their part, numbered 58 divisions. The attack came on June 15 along the entire front, with partial successes on the Altipiano di Asiago (against the British and French divisions) and on Mount Grappa, though these were immediately pushed back by counterattacks. Austrian penetration was greater on the Piave, but here Diaz disposed of sufficient reserves to retake the lost terrain. The Austrians were back across the water by July 5, and the battle closed with some 87,000 Italian and 118,000 Austrian casualties and the front exactly where it had been before the battle began.[25]

The Allies continued to call on Diaz to attack, but the latter demurred. Following the Austrian June offensive he was more than 85,000 men down, and his last reserves were the young men born in 1900, whom he could use only in 1919. He also noted that compared to the 2 million American soldiers in France, a single American regiment had been sent to Italy (plus some ambulance units in which served Ernest Hemingway and John Dos Passos). Events accelerated in the autumn, however, as the German forces retreated in France and the Dual Monarchy began to crumble. Diaz decided to attack along the entire front on October 24. The first days of the offensive were hard, as the Austrians repulsed the assaults on Mount Grappa, and it took the major Italian advance two days to cross the Piave in the direction of Vittorio Veneto. Here, too, the front-line Austrian troops fought well, but there was nothing behind them now except disorderly soldiers trying to get back to their homelands. From October 29, the Italians found they could advance with little difficulty as far as Trento and Trieste, the latter city being reached on November 3. On the 4th, the armistice took effect, consecrating Italian victory. As if to underline the allied role, Diaz had created two small armies on the eve of the offensive, the Twelfth Army under the French general Jean-César Graziani with one French and three Italian divisions, and the Tenth Army under the British general, Frederick Rudolph Lambert of Cavan, with two British and two Italian divisions. In reality, the victory of Vittorio Veneto was only a semi-victory, consisting as it did of a few days' hard fighting followed by an easy advance. As in France, the victory was due to attrition and the internal collapse of the enemy.[26]

The Italian Soldier

Whether World War I demonstrated the backwardness of Italian civil society or whether it favored the nationalization of the masses and the growth of a unified Italian consciousness remains an open question. Despite nuances of interpretation, most scholars hold that progress was made in this latter sense. There is no doubt that the ruling class did overcome its internal divisions, identified fully with the war and knew how to impose this on the rest of the country with determination, even if it split again over the retrospective significance of the conflict in the postwar period. Nor can there be any doubt as to the conviction of the officers.

Where the question remains open is in relation to the men – though with one firm proviso. In three and a half years of frequently bitter warfare the Italian army demonstrated its solidity and cohesiveness, with no serious breakdown or mutiny. If the army's efficiency can be questioned, the obedience of its soldiers cannot. As we have seen, the idea that Caporetto can be understood in terms of mass indiscipline is a myth, albeit one with contemporary force. Yet we have also seen that the bulk of the infantry, which came from a peasant background, was called on to fight an offensive war in the name of an abstract idea of the fatherland that meant little to many of them.[27] Trento and Trieste were mobilizing myths for the ruling elites and the officer corps, but ordinary soldiers fought in the name of values, such as patriotic honor and glory, that were alien to them, and which in reality meant only military discipline. Why, in these circumstances, they should have served with such resilience continues to attract analysis.[28]

One major factor shaping the soldiers' obedience was the strength of the army as an institution. Military sociologists point to its cohesion, to the role of junior officers, and to the importance of small group solidarity. Also significant was the lack of alternatives. Flight was difficult and costly while internal repression was very harsh. The latter was not the overriding factor that some maintain: no soldiers can be forced to fight at the point of a bayonet. But discipline had an important role.

Cadorna urged firm discipline (and was given a free rein in this regard by weak governments) while caring little for the physical and psychological well-being of the men under his command, who were treated far worse than their French or British counterparts. There was no organized propaganda or pastoral care (except for the reintroduction of chaplains, who had been ousted from the army between 1865 and 1878). Food was mediocre, periods of relief were insufficient, and only one leave period was granted per year – and it was not always guaranteed. Only in 1918, under Diaz, did the soldiers' lot improve. Moreover, Cadorna never understood the need for serious training. Soldiers and junior officers were sent into the trenches with only rudimentary preparation and were called on to obey and to sacrifice themselves.

The harshness of Cadorna's regime is borne out by the statistics. Out of every 12 men sent to the front, one was reported to a military tribunal, amounting to a total of 360,000. The same fate befell 60,000 civilians from the regions declared as war zones. The most striking figure concerns the 100,000 convictions for desertion. It should be remembered that in the Italian army failure to reply to two consecutive roll calls, or an absence of 12 hours, was considered desertion (hence the figures cannot be compared to French statistics). Most "deserters" were men returning from leave a few hours or a few days late, or who were absent for several days. These are "normal" practices in a mass army that has scarce and limited leave. Of course, there were real desertions resulting from a refusal of the war, which took the form of escape toward the rear (almost always blocked by the military police), though it is difficult to say how numerous these were. There were also those who deserted to the enemy – a few thousand, according to the records. But little if any credence should be placed in courts martial that took place in the absence of the accused, since it was hard to establish who surrendered voluntarily and who was taken prisoner by force. In short, it can be argued that the figure of 100,000 convictions for desertion says more about the disciplinary regime than about the soldier's lack of discipline.

According to official figures, 750 soldiers were executed, compared to 600 in a much larger French army, 300 in Britain, and a few dozen in Germany. Unlike in France, condemned Italian soldiers could not plead for mercy from the head of state. Indeed, Cadorna insisted repeatedly that his officers shoot on the spot any man who pulled back during action, though we have little information on the prevalence of such incidents. He also introduced summary execution for acts of disobedience, disbandment, or revolt. This included resort to decimation – that is, the arbitrary extraction and shooting of a certain number of men from a unit in revolt, in particular when it was not possible to identify those responsible. According to recent research, the practice of this form of discipline (which included abuses of power exceeding even Cadorna's ruthless orders) means that we can now add another 300 men to the death toll. Hence there were over 1,000 executions in an army where relatively few units revolted en masse (11 according to official documentation). This shows once more the harshness of the disciplinary regime rather than the lack of cohesion among the men.[29]

One further issue demonstrates the lack of trust in the men by Cadorna, his generals, and the government – prisoners of war. Before Caporetto these numbered about 260,000; another 280,000 were taken during the Caporetto offensive and a further

50,000 were captured in 1918. In comparison with this total of 600,000 Italian prisoners, the Italians took 180,000 Austro-Hungarian prisoners before the battle of Vittorio Veneto. For Cadorna, the figures were excessive and revealed the Italian soldier's poor fighting spirit, cowardice, and tendency to desert. On account of their own increasingly short supplies of food, Austria and Germany had difficulty providing sufficient rations to Italian prisoners, who were engaged in forced labor. The British and French managed to supply their men via Switzerland. The Italian government and Cadorna refused to do likewise, or to facilitate the work of the Red Cross or the sending of food parcels (or even normal mail) to Italian POWs. The latter thus had to pay a high price for their "surrender," and their sad conditions were duly publicized as a warning to the men in the trenches. About 100,000 of them died, effectively abandoned to their fate by the Italian government. By contrast, 20,000 of the 600,000 French prisoners died in captivity, though they were incarcerated on average for a longer period. This was in large part thanks to assistance provided by their government. Only in 1993 was this sad page in the history of the Italian war experience finally rediscovered.[30]

Overall, it remains hard to find a suitable explanation for the cohesion and fighting spirit of the Italian army. The soldiers had different cultural levels and backgrounds; only a minority was patriotically motivated. The great majority had received the traditional education of the peasant and worker – to obey authority. Italian socialists never preached disobedience and revolt in the ranks, and military strikes and agitation were less evident than in Britain or Germany. The political and military elites (and not just Cadorna) were much more concerned with the men's obedience than with their consent. The Italian soldiers deserved better treatment for the extraordinary sacrifices they made, and only received this in part under General Diaz in 1918.

* * *

In the course of the war, 5,903,000 Italian men and 200,000 officers were mobilized. Of this total, 145,000 went into the navy and over 700,000 were employed in war production and essential administration and services. Just over 5 million men put on military uniform, and of these some 4,200,000 went to the front. This was less than the 8 million men mobilized in France, which had only a slightly larger population (39 million compared to 36 million), but the difference is probably accounted for by the size of Italian emigration (though some Italians returned from overseas to join up) and by lower levels of health in a less developed society. As we have seen, the size of the army at the front rose from about a million men in 1915 to two million in 1917–18, with some 186,000 officers in 1918 of whom 84,000 were at the front. By December 1918, the army had lost half a million dead, 80 percent of them to wounds, the remaining 20 percent to illness and disease (the latter figure was only 10 percent in the French case). If to this figure we add the few thousand sailors and 100,000 prisoners of war who died, as well as all those who succumbed to the effects of the war after it was over, it is reasonable to estimate the Italian military dead at 650,000.

The outcome of this effort and sacrifice, after the long peace conference in Paris and the Treaty of Saint-Germain (September 1919), included the main demands of the prewar irredentists – Trentino and the Upper Adige with 200,000 German speakers; the eastern frontier of Venezia-Julia, which incorporated a mixed population of Italians, Slovenes, and Croats; and Trieste, which like the other coastal cities of Istria, had a clear Italian majority, though with a non-urban population of about 600,000 Slovenes and

Croats. Italian claims to Dalmatia were reduced to the annexation of the city of Zara, but the Dodecanese islands, which Italy had taken from Turkey during the 1911–12 Libyan war, were recognized as Italian territories. The city of Fiume (which was "Italian" only if one considered the historical center and ignored the Slovene and Croat suburbs) was not included. In September 1919 the poet Gabriele d'Annunzio, who wanted to stop Fiume becoming part of the new Yugoslavia, occupied the city with paramilitary forces. This remained a burning issue for Italian diplomacy and was only resolved between 1920 and 1924 with the concession of the town, but not its hinterland, to Italy (see chapter 37).

Italy's war closed with the defeat of the democratic left which had seen the conflict as the liberation of Italian minorities under Austrian domination (in the context of respect for all minorities) and with the triumph of the nationalist right with a short-lived imperialism that left a legacy of discord with the new Austria and, above all, with Yugoslavia. The fascist regime exacerbated this disagreement by its brutal policy of forcible nationalization of the Austrian and Yugoslav minorities under Italian control. However, such violence was not the prerogative of the Italian ruling classes. The reorganization of Europe after 1919 presented many similar and indeed more serious cases.

Notes

1   Whittam, *Politics of the Italian Army*, Gooch, *Army, State and Society*.
2   Giorgio Rochat, "Strutture dell'esercito dell'Italia liberale: i reggimenti di fanteria e Bersaglieri," in Rochat, *L'Esercito italiano in pace e in guerra. Studi in storia militare*, Milan, RARA, 1991, pp. 41–73.
3   Giorgio Rochat, "L'Esercito italiano nell'estate 1914," in Rochat, *L'Esercito italiano in pace e in guerra. Studi in storia militare*, Milan, RARA, 1991, pp. 74–112 (75–7).
4   Giorgio Rochat, "La professione militare in Italia dall'ottocento alla seconda Guerra mondiale," and "Gli ufficiali italiani nella prima Guerra mondiale,' both in Rochat, *L'Esercito italiano in pace e in guerra. Studi in storia militare*, Milan, RARA, 1991, pp. 28–40 and 113–30, respectively.
5   Bosworth, *Italy and the Approach of the First World War*.
6   See the memoirs of prime minister Antonio Salandra, *La Neutralità italiana (1914). Ricordi e pensieri*, Milan, Treves, 1928, pp. 173–4, and Luigi Albertini, *Vent'anni di vita politica*, Bologna, Zanichelli, 1951, part 2, vol. 1, pp. 333–45.
7   Leo Valiani, "Italian-Austro-Hungarian Negotiations 1914–1915," *Journal of Contemporary History*, 1, 1966, pp. 113–36, and, for the full text of the Pact of London, René Albrecht-Carrié, *Italy at the Paris Peace Conference*, New York, 1938, pp. 334–9.
8   Pieri, *Prima Guerra mondiale*, pp. 60–3; Schindler, *Isonzo*, ch. 3.
9   Giorgio Rochat, "La Preparazione dell'esercito italiano nell'inverno 1914–1915 in relazione alle informazioni disponibili sulla guerra di posizione," *Risorgimento*, 13, 1961, 10–32; Rocca, *Cadorna*, chs. 2–5.
10 Luigi Cadorna, *Attacco frontale e ammaestramento tattico*, Rome, Ufficio del Capo dello Stato Maggiore, February 25, 1915.
11 Schindler, *Isonzo*, pp. 59, 80, 125.
12 Filippo Cappellano, "Le Bombarde," in Andrea Curami and Alessandro Massignani (eds.), *L'Artigliera italiana nella Grande Guerra*, Vicenza, Rossato, 1998, pp. 195–208.
13 Herwig, *First World War*, pp. 204–7.
14 Luigi Cadorna, *La Guerra alla fronte italiana fino all'arresto sulla linea del Piave e del Grappa (24 May 1915–9 Novembre 1917)*, Milan, Treves, 1921, vol. 1, ch. 5; Isnenghi and Rochat, *Grande Guerra*, pp. 176–83; Herwig, *First World War*, pp. 204–7; Schindler, *Isonzo*, pp. 144–9.

15 Pieri "La Battaglia di Gorizia," in Rochat (ed.), *Storiografia militare italiana*, pp. 119–23; Pieropan, *Grande Guerra sul fronte italiano*, chs. 24, 27, 28, 30; Rocca, *Cadorna*, ch. 8; Isnenghi and Rochat, *Grande Guerra*, pp. 180–90; Schindler, *Isonzo*, chs. 8, 9.

16 Melograni, *Storia politica*, ch. 3; Rocca, *Cadorna*, ch. 6 and pp. 142–5.

17 Pieri, *Prima Guerra mondiale*, pp. 124–40; Mario Silvestri, *Isonzo 1917*, Milan, Mondadori, 1965, chs. 4–5; Pieropan, *Grande Guerra sul fronte italiano*, chs. 37, 42, 43; Rocca, *Cadorna*, pp. 196–203, 239–44; Isnenghi and Rochat, *Grande Guerra*, pp. 195–205; Schindler, *Isonzo*, pp. 205–15 and ch. 11.

18 "Relazione della Commisione d'inchiesta," *Dall'Isonzo al Piave 24 ottobre–9 novembre 1917*, Rome, Stabilimenti tipografici per l'amministrazione della Guerra, 1919.

19 Cadorna, *La Guerra alla fronte italiana*, vol., 2, chs. 10–13; Pieri, *Prima Guerra mondiale*, pp. 141–228; Monticone, Caporetto; Silvestri, *Isonzo, 1917*, ch. 7; Melograni, *Storia politica*, ch. 6; Pieropan, *Grande Guerra sul'fronte italiano*, chs. 46–53; Rocca, *Cadorna*, chs. 13–14; Herwig, *First World War*, pp. 336–44; Isnenghi and Rochat, *Grande Guerra*, pp. 367–85 and 428–42; Labanca, *Caporetto*; Schindler, *Isonzo*, ch. 12; O'Brien, *Mussolini*, pp. 141–4; Morselli, *Caporetto 1917*; Thompson, *White War*, ch. 25.

20 John Wilks and Eileen Wilks, *The British Army in Italy 1917–1918*, Barnsley, Leo Cooper, 1998, p. 178; Cassar, *The Forgotten Front*.

21 Isnenghi and Rochat, *Grande Guerra*, p. 446.

22 Angelo Mangone, *Diaz*, Milan, Frassinelli, 1987; Piero Pieri and Giorgio Rochat, *Pietro Badoglio. Maresciallo d'Italia*, 1974; new ed., Milan, Mondadori, 2002.

23 Melograni, *Storia politica*, pp. 460–61; Pieri and Rochat, *Grande Guerra*, pp. 277–9; Isnenghi, *Giornali di trincea*; Gatti, *Gli Ufficiali P.*

24 Rochat, *Gli Arditi*.

25 Pieri, *Prima Guerra mondiale*, pp. 242–51; Pieropan, *Grande Guerra sul fronte italiano*, chs. 62–68; Isnenghi and Rochat, *Grande Guerrra*, pp. 455–8; Schindler, *Isonzo*, pp. 201–7.

26 Pieropan, *Grande Guerra sul fronte italiano*, chs. 73–74; Pier Paolo Cervone, *Vittorio Veneto: l'ultima battaglia*, Milan, Mursia, 1994, chs. 4–5; Schindler, *Isonzo*, pp. 297–311; O'Brien, *Mussolini*, pp. 154–8; Thompson, *White War*, ch. 26. For the last year of the war in Italy as a whole, Giampietro Berti and Piero Del Negro (eds.), *Al di qua e al di là del Piave. L'ultimo anno della Grande Guerra*, Milan, Angeli, 2001. For the Armistice negotiations, see Giuliano Lenci, *Le Giornate di Villa Gusti. Storia di un armistizio*, Padua, Il Poligrafo, 1998.

27 Precise figures for the social make-up of the Italian army are not available and are still based on Serpieri, *La Guerra e le classe rurali*, pp. 41–2 and 48ff., who suggested that 46 percent of Italy's army in World War I was formed by the peasantry.

28 Giorgio Rochat, "Eserciti di massa e società dalla prima alla seconda guerra mondiale," in Rochat, *L'Esercito italiano in pace e in guerra*, pp. 178–92, and Rochat, "L'Efficienza dell'esercito italiano nella grande guerra," *Italia Contemporanea*, 206, March 1997, pp. 87–105. Further studies on the Italian soldier include Isnenghi, *I Vinti di Caporetto*; Fabi, *Gente di trincea*; Gibelli, *La grande guerra degli italiani*, 1999.

29 Forcella and Monticone, *Plotone di esecuzione*; Pluviano and Guerrini, *Le fucilazioni sommarie*; Wilcox, "Discipline in the Italian Army."

30 Procacci, *Soldati e prigionieri*.

References and Further Reading

Badoglio, Gian Luca, *Il Memoriale di Pietro Badoglio su Caporetto. Le battaglie della ritirata di Caporetto*, Udine, Gaspari, 2000.

Bosworth, Richard, *Italy and the Approach of the First World War*, London, Macmillan, 1983.

Cassar, George H., *The Forgotten Front. The British Campaign in Italy, 1917–1918*, London, Hambledon, 1998.

Fabi, Lucio, *Gente di trincea. La Grande Guerra sul Carso e sul Isonzo*, Milan, Mursia, 1994.

Forcella, Enzo, and Monticone, Alberto, *Plotone d'esecuzione. I processi della prima guerre mondiale*, Bari, Laterza, 1968; new ed., 1998.

Gatti, Luigi Gian, *Dopo Caporetto. Gli ufficiali P nella Grande guerra: propaganda, assistenza, viglianza*, Gorizia, Libreria Editrice Goriziana, 2000.

Gibelli, Antonio, *L'Officina della guerra. La Grande Guerra e le trasformazioni del mondo mentale*, Turin, Bollati-Boringhieri, 1991.

Gibelli, Antonio, *La Grande Guerra degli italiani, 1915–1918*, Milan, Sansoni, 1998.

Gooch, John, *Army, State and Society in Italy, 1870–1915*, Basingstoke, Macmillan, 1989.

Herwig, Holger, *The First World War. Germany and Austria-Hungary 1914–1918*, London, Arnold, 1997.

Isnenghi, Mario, *I Vinti di Caporetto nella letteratura di guerra*, Padua, Marsilio, 1967.

Isnenghi, Mario, *Le Guerre degli italiani fra il 1848 e il 1945*, Rome, Mondadori, 1989.

Isnenghi, Mario, *Il Mito della grande guerra*, 1970; new ed., Bologna, Il Mulino, 1989.

Isnenghi, Mario, and Rochat, Giorgio, *La Grande Guerra, 1914–1918*, Milan, Sansoni, 2000.

Labanca, Nicola, *Caporetto. Storia di una disfatta*, Florence, Giunti, 1997.

Labanca, Nicola, Procacci, Giovanna, and Tomassini, Luigi, *Caporetto. Esercito, stato e società*, Bologna, Il Mulino, 1986.

Leoni, Diego, and Zadra, Camillo (eds.), *La Grande Guerra. Esperienza, memoria, immagini*, Bologna, Il Mulino, 1986.

Lussù, Emilio, *Sardinian Brigade*, 1938; trans. from Italian, New York, 1939; new ed., London, Prion Books, 2000.

Melograni, Piero, *Storia politica della Grande Guerra, 1915–1918*, Milan, Mondadori, 1969.

Monticone, Alberto, *La Battaglia di Caporetto*, 1955; new ed., Udine, Gaspari, 1999.

Morselli, Mario, *Caporetto 1917: Victory or Defeat?*, London, Cassell, 2001.

O'Brien, Paul, *Mussolini in the First World War. The Journalist, the Soldier, the Fascist*, New York and Oxford, Berg, 2005.

O'Brien, Paul, "Summary Executions in Italy during the First World War: Findings and Implications," *Modern Italy*, 11/3, 2006, pp. 353–9.

Omodeo, Adolfo, *Momenti della vita di guerra. Dai diari e dalle lettere dei caduti 1915–1918*, 1933; new ed., Turin, Einaudi, 1968.

Pieri, Piero, *L'Italia nella prima guerra mondiale (1915–1918)*, Turin, Einaudi, 1965.

Pieropan, Gianni, *1914–1918. Storia della Grande Guerra sul fronte italiano*, Milan, Mursia, 1988.

Procacci, Giovanna, *Soldati e prigionieri italiani nella grande guerra*, Rome, Editori Riuniti, 1993.

Rocca, Gianni, *Cadorna*, Milan, Mondodori, 1985.

Rochat, Giorgio, *Gli Arditi nella grande guerra. Origini, battaglie, miti*, Gorizia, La Goriziana, 1990.

Rochat, Giorgio (ed.), *La Storiografia militare italiana negli ultimi vent'anni*, Milan, Angeli, 1985.

Serpieri, Arrigo, *La Guerra e le classe rurali italiane*, Bari, Laterza, 1930.

Thompson, Mark, *The White War. Life and Death on the Italian Front, 1915–1919*, London, Faber, 2008.

Whittam, J., *The Politics of the Italian Army, 1861–1918*, London, Croom Helm, 1977.

Wilcox, Vanda, "Discipline in the Italian Army 1915–1918," in Pierre Purseigle (ed.), *Warfare and Belligerence. Perspectives in First World War Studies*, Boston and Leiden, Brill, 2005, pp. 73–100.

CHAPTER SEVEN

The Turkish War, 1914–18

ULRICH TRUMPENER

Having secretly pledged its support to the Central Powers in a series of written and verbal agreements during the previous three months, the Ottoman (Turkish) Empire openly entered the war on October 29, 1914. On that day, a squadron of German and Ottoman ships, under the command of Rear Admiral Wilhelm Souchon, shelled several points on the Russian Black Sea coast and destroyed some Russian vessels at sea. Four days later, the Tsarist government responded to this provocation with a formal declaration of war, and on November 3 two British battle cruisers and two French battleships subjected the outer defenses of the Dardanelles to a brief but effective bombardment.[1]

During the next four years the Ottoman army, composed primarily of Muslim conscripts (Turks, Arabs, Kurds and others), would engage sizeable Entente forces both in the Middle East and in Europe. As the war progressed, many German staff officers and technical specialists were attached to the Ottoman High Command and to various units in the field. In addition, a growing number of German combat units, particularly artillery batteries, were sent to some of the Middle Eastern fronts where they were sometimes joined by small contingents of Austro-Hungarian troops.[2]

The Sultan's fleet, comprising the recently arrived German battle cruiser *Goeben* (renamed *Yavus Sultan Selim*), three ancient battleships, three small cruisers and two dozen torpedo boats, was likewise honeycombed with German personnel. These ships performed valuable services both in the Black Sea and in the Straits region, but their effectiveness was often severely limited by fuel shortages and equipment failures. Moreover, nearly half of these ships were eventually lost at sea, the last one, the cruiser *Breslau* (renamed *Midilli*), sinking in January 1918. From 1915 on, German submarines became active near the Dardanelles and in the Black Sea, but Allied naval supremacy was firmly maintained everywhere else (see chapter 10).[3]

Before attempting an analysis of the major campaigns in the Middle East, it must be emphasized that the war effort of the Ottoman Empire was severely hampered by its economic backwardness and its underdeveloped transportation system. Constantinople, the capital and industrial center of the empire, was linked to its eastern provinces by a railway line which in 1914 was truncated in several places, particularly in the Taurus and Amanus Mountains, but also between Jerabulus, on the Euphrates River, and the town of Samara. South of the Amanus range, another line extended to Aleppo and Damascus,

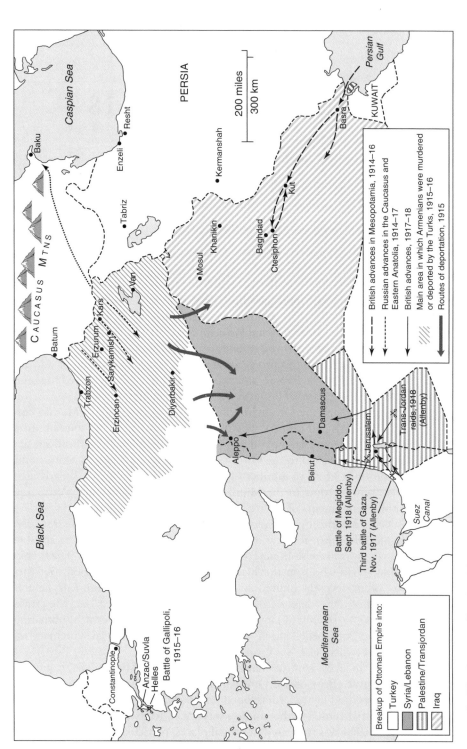

Map 5 The Ottoman Empire, 1914–18

with branch lines to the Mediterranean coast and northern Palestine, and a narrow-gauge track leading down to Medina. Although some parts of the Ottoman rail system were improved during the war years, troops facing the Russians in Transcaucasia and the British in Mesopotamia remained cut off from the nearest railhead by up to four hundred miles of mountains or deserts. As a result, the movement of troops and supplies to those two theaters of war depended on primitive road transport (ox carts, etc.) or the use of even more primitive river craft (rafts constructed of animal hides). Occasionally units of the Ottoman fleet and small coastal vessels were used to ferry troops and supplies to the northern end of the Transcaucasian front, but increasing Russian interference made these operations very hazardous. Both Admiral A. A. Ebergard and his successor in 1916, Aleksandr V. Kolchak, made excellent use of the Russian Black Sea Fleet and conducted highly effective mine-laying operations off the Turkish coast. Their hands were strengthened in 1915, when two new dreadnoughts were put into service.[4]

Finally it should be mentioned that as a result of massive purges in the officer corps, most senior Ottoman commanders during World War I were much younger (and lower in rank) than was the norm in other countries. Divisional commanders were usually men in their early thirties, and most of the field armies were run by brigadier generals only a few years older. The de facto commander of the Ottoman armed forces, Enver Pasha, who was also the Minister of War in the cabinet, was 32 in 1914 and had only recently attained a general's rank (and the title of Pasha) by virtue of a double promotion. For many German officers on wartime service in the Ottoman Empire their subordination to less experienced and much younger Turkish officers presented quite a challenge, but most of them eventually adjusted to the situation.[5]

Transcaucasia

When hostilities began on the Russo-Turkish frontiers, the two sides were fairly evenly matched. The Tsar's Kavkazskaya Army, under the command of Count I. I. Vorontsov-Dashkov and his deputy, A. Z. Myshlayevskii, had about 170,000 men in its ranks while the Sultan's Third Army, headed by Hasan Izzet Pasha, was slightly smaller and included some rather unreliable Kurdish cavalry units. The Russians struck first. Their I Caucasian Corps, under General G. E. Berkhman, advanced in the Aras Valley to the town of Köprüköy, roughly halfway between the border and Erzurum, but then it retreated again. Early in December, Enver Pasha and his deputy in the Ottoman general staff, Colonel Hafiz Hakki Bey, decided that a major Ottoman offensive should be launched against the Kavkazskaya Army. Taking personal command of the Third Army, Enver overruled the chief of the German military mission, General Otto Liman von Sanders, and other critics of the plan, and launched the operation on December 22, 1914. While one Ottoman corps remained in place to pin the Russians down, two others began a difficult flanking movement through snow-covered mountains north of the Aras Valley and eventually reached the town of Sarykamish, which served as the terminus of a railway line running to Kars. After 10 days of inconclusive fighting, massive Russian pressure, supply shortages, and the onset of extremely cold weather forced Enver to order a general retreat (January 4, 1915). During the ensuing days, three Ottoman divisions lost most of their men and all of their equipment. The total cost of the operation exceeded 50,000 men, including 33,000 dead, 10,000 wounded, and 7,000 captured by the Russians. Among the prisoners were one corps commander, Ali Ihsan Bey, and three divisional commanders. Ali Ihsan escaped a few months later and subsequently had a colorful career (see below). One of the divisional commanders, Nazuhi Bey, fled from eastern Siberia in 1916 and likewise made his way back to Turkey. The Russian losses were significantly lower and included 6,000 cases of frostbite.[6]

Under a new commander, Nikolai N. Yudenich, the Kavkazskaya Army spent most of 1915 consolidating its gains and pushing further west in some regions. The town of Van, for instance, changed hands several times during the summer, but more decisive action had to be postponed due to the transfer of several Russian units from the Caucasus to the eastern front.[7]

On January 10, 1916, to the complete surprise of the Turks, Yudenich launched a major offensive in the Aras valley and elsewhere. The Ottoman Third Army, since March 1915 headed by Brigadier General Mahmut Kamil Pasha (but who, like his German chief of staff, was on leave when the Russians struck), fought back bravely for several weeks. In the end, in mid-February, it was forced to abandon Erzurum, losing thousands of men and hundreds of artillery pieces. Although reinforcements, including the highly rated V Corps, were hurriedly dispatched to the front, they did not get there for weeks. As a result, Yudenich (under the watchful eyes of Grand Duke Nikolai Nikolaevich, recently demoted to the vice-regal post in Tiflis), was able to score further gains. On April 18, his troops, with assistance from the fleet, seized the Black Sea port of Trabzon, thereby depriving the Turks of an important logistic base. Under the direction of an energetic new commander, Ferit Vehip Pasha, the Third Army staged some successful counterattacks in the second half of June, but the Russians hit back during the following month, taking the town of Bayburt on July 16 and Erzincan 11 days later. After a painfully slow movement of men and *matériel* from Thrace to the Diyarbakir region, on the southern flank of Yudenich's forces, several corps of Marshal Ahmet Izzet Pasha's Second Army tried to turn the tide in August, but aside from regaining some ground their efforts were in vain. During the following winter, Izzet's troops suffered serious losses from exposure and disease, while Vehip's army had to be rebuilt from scratch.[8]

Fortunately for the Turks, the Russian war effort weakened significantly in 1917, particularly after the overthrow of the Tsarist regime. While Aleksandr Kerensky, the new war minister in the Provisional Government, kept some Russian troops on the eastern front in an offensive mood, the Kavkazskaya Army, by now under the command of General M. A. Przhevalskii, remained quite passive. By the time Lenin seized power in Petrograd, it had also dwindled in size, and on December 18 its staff concluded a formal armistice agreement with the Turks.[9]

Two months later, on February 12, 1918, three Ottoman corps crossed the armistice line and advanced eastward on a broad front. Encountering only sporadic resistance, notably from Armenian units, the Turks reached their prewar border six weeks later and then moved on toward Ardahan, Kars, and Batum, all of which they occupied with relative ease. After a short pause, their advance continued in several directions. In June, a task force made up of an Ottoman division and around ten thousand Azerbaijani militiamen began to fight its way eastward toward the Caspian Sea. Calling itself the "Army of Islam" and commanded by Enver Pasha's younger brother, Major Nuri Bey, the force reached the vicinity of Baku by the end of July. That important Russian oil center was protected by groups of ill-trained local volunteers, who were joined on August 4 by a handful of British troops brought in from northern Persia. After more than a month of skirmishing, Nuri's forces pushed their way into the city (September 15–16, 1918), while many of the defenders escaped by ship.[10] Barely six weeks later, this triumph of Ottoman expansionism was undone by the provisions of the Mudros Armistice, which was signed by Navy Minister Huseyin Rauf Bey on behalf of the new government in Constantinople, headed by Marshal Izzet Pasha.[11]

The Dardanelles

Faced with deadlock on the western front and an appeal from the Russians for additional western help against the Turks, the British government decided in January 1915 that an attempt should be made to force the Dardanelles with an armada of older battleships, which could then threaten Constantinople and thereby, it was hoped, force the Ottoman Empire out of the war. The attack on the Dardanelles by an Anglo-French fleet began on February 19, 1915 with a bombardment of the outer forts. Interrupted occasionally by bad weather, the bombardments continued during the next three weeks, while several attempts were made to clear the minefields inside the Straits. On March 16, Vice-Admiral Sir John de Robeck took over from Sir Sackville Carden, who had to go on sick leave, and two days later the fleet tried to break through. In a lengthy exchange of fire with a variety of Ottoman shore batteries, including mobile howitzer units, several Allied battleships strayed into an undetected minefield. By the end of the day, de Robeck had lost three battleships (including the French *Bouvet*), while at least three more big ships were heavily damaged.[12]

Although both he and some of his superiors in London were initially determined to try again, they soon developed second thoughts. By March 24 it was decided that troops should be landed near the Dardanelles to open them up for further naval action. During the next four weeks, an Anglo-French expeditionary force was assembled under the command of Sir Ian S. Hamilton. The Turks, in turn, created a new field army (the Fifth) at the Dardanelles and appointed General Liman von Sanders to lead it. The permanent fortifications, with their big guns, remained under the control of Brigadier General Cevat Pasha who, in turn, reported to a German coastal defense specialist, Admiral Guido von Usedom. With six infantry divisions at his disposal, General Liman placed two of them on the Asian shore, two in the southern portions of the Gallipoli peninsula, and another two in the Bulair region, the narrow northern neck of the peninsula, between the Gulf of Saros and the Sea of Marmara.[13]

Early on April 25, 1915, Hamilton's expeditionary corps, with supporting fire from the fleet, struck in several places. The British 29th Division, under Lt. Gen. A. G. Hunter-Weston, landed on several beaches at the toe of the peninsula, soon to become known as the Helles sector. A French brigade went ashore on the Asian side, near Kum Kale; the Australian and New Zealand Army Corps (the Anzacs), commanded by Sir W. R. Birdwood, disembarked on a narrow beach north of Gaba Tepe, and the Royal Naval Division participated in a feint near Bulair. Although only small Ottoman units were at most of the landing points, both the 29th Division and the Anzacs incurred heavy losses during the first 36 hours. Rapid countermoves by parts of the Ottoman 19th Division, under the inspired leadership of Lieutenant Colonel Mustafa Kemal (later Atatürk), prevented the Anzacs from seizing an important ridge, and the Ottoman 3rd Division, commanded by Colonel August Nicolai, soon tore into the French troops at Kum Kale and forced them back to their ships. After some hesitation, General Liman moved most of his Bulair forces to the southern region of Gallipoli. Moreover, a few days later, many Ottoman regiments on the Asian side of the Straits were ferried across to reinforce their comrades on Gallipoli.[14]

Hamilton's forces, having failed to reach their objectives during the opening phase of the operation, would henceforth launch periodic attacks both in the Helles sector and in the Ari Burnu region held by the Anzacs, but they usually gained little ground and suffered heavy casualties in the process. Ottoman attempts to push the invaders back into the sea, particularly on May 19, likewise ended in failure and wholesale slaughter. Although a second French division and three additional British divisions were inserted between May and July, they were unable to turn the tide of the battle. On the Ottoman side, too, fresh troops were moved to the peninsula. To simplify matters, General Liman early on had created two group commands: the Ari Burnu area was assigned to a seasoned veteran, Brigadier General Mehmet Esat Pasha, while the Helles sector for the time being was controlled by German officers, initially by Colonel von Sodenstern and then by Colonel Erich Weber. In mid-July, when reinforcements from the Ottoman Second Army were sent to Gallipoli, Weber was replaced by the younger brother of the Ari Burnu commander, Colonel Ferit Vehip Bey.[15]

During the opening battles in the Helles sector, the Ottoman infantry received vital support from several machine-gun detachments made up of German naval personnel. Moreover, the heavy guns of the Asian shore batteries became increasingly effective in harassing the French and British troops at the tip of the peninsula. To make matters worse for the Allies, an Ottoman torpedo boat sank the battleship Goliath in Morto Bay on the night of May 12–13, and about two weeks later two more battleships, the Triumph and Majestic, were sent to the bottom by the torpedoes of the German submarine U-21. The temporary withdrawal of the other Allied capital ships brought welcome relief to the Ottoman troops on Gallipoli. Although British and French submarines repeatedly penetrated the Dardanelles and sank a number of ships in the Sea of Marmara, they were not able to stop the flow of supplies and men to General Liman's army.[16]

Being stymied in the two existing lodgments, the British decided to launch a major operation to the north of the Anzac sector, at Suvla Bay. Starting on the evening of August 6, 1915, several divisions of Lieutenant General Sir Frederick Stopford's IX Corps waded ashore and moved inland. During the next few days, the combined efforts of the Anzacs and additional troops landed at Suvla Bay placed the much weaker Ottoman units in the area under a massive strain. In this crisis, on August 8, Liman placed Colonel Mustafa Kemal in charge of all Ottoman forces in the Suvla sector (soon to be designated as the "Anafarta Group"). Once again Mustafa Kemal distinguished himself by quick and energetic action, personally leading his men into battle and dislodging the enemy from several key mountain ridges. It should be added, though, that the eventual containment of the Allies was equally due to the tenacity of a Bavarian cavalry officer, Major Wilhelm Willmer, who stubbornly held on to some key positions at Kiresh Tepe with a small force of Ottoman soldiers and gendarmes.[17]

While gradually stabilizing the situation in the northern sector, the Turks were also successful in holding their positions at the Helles front, where the crucial Achi Baba heights remained in their possession. In mid-October, the British government relieved General Hamilton of his command. Two weeks later, his replacement, Sir Charles Monro, concluded that the Gallipoli operation should be closed down, and Lord Kitchener eventually recommended to cabinet that all but the Helles sector be evacuated. While some French and British units had already been withdrawn in October for use in the newly established Salonika bridgehead, the bulk of the Allied troops on Gallipoli, now under the local command of General Birdwood, remained in their trenches until December. After the highly skilful evacuation of the northern lodgments on December 18–19, the troops in the Helles sector were gradually thinned out. On January 8–9, 1916, the remaining units were taken out as well, once again with very few casualties, though a lot of equipment had to be left behind.[18] The total cost of the Gallipoli operation on the Allied side was in the neighborhood of 230,000 men, including over 27,000 soldiers of the French Expeditionary Corps. No reliable casualty figures are available for the Ottoman forces, but they probably were close to 300,000 in total. Both sides also lost a sizeable number of generals, either killed or wounded, among them the commander of the French contingent, Henri Gouraud, who lost an arm on June 30.[19]

Egypt, Palestine, and Arabia

As soon as the Ottoman government had agreed to intervene on the side of the Central Powers, the German Supreme Command (OHL) had made it clear to Enver Pasha that it hoped for an early advance of Ottoman troops to the Suez Canal and, if possible, even beyond. Aside from cutting Britain's "lifeline" to India, such an advance by Muslim soldiers might also trigger a popular uprising in Egypt, particularly if some Libyan tribes could be induced to invade Egypt from the west.

Since a march through the Sinai desert required extensive preparations, including the assembly of huge camel caravans, the proposed advance of about twenty thousand troops did not materialize until January 1915. Under the command of Ahmet Cemal Pasha, who combined an important cabinet position in Constantinople with supreme political and military power in Syria and Palestine, a segment of the Ottoman Fourth Army crossed the Egyptian border and slowly moved toward the Suez Canal. The first echelon reached its eastern bank, south of Ismaliya, on February 2, 1915, but even though some men actually crossed the Canal, stiff resistance from British troops eventually persuaded Cemal to disengage his forces and to retreat to the northern edge of the Sinai. The whole operation, micro-managed by a Bavarian staff officer, Lieutenant Colonel Friedrich Baron Kress von Kressenstein, had resulted in the loss of about 1,300 Ottoman soldiers but had also increased British concern over the security of their Egyptian base.[20]

After conducting several smaller raids to the Suez Canal later on in 1915, units of the Ottoman Fourth Army staged a second major advance in July 1916, but once again they were repulsed (on August 4–5, in the battle of Romani). In the meantime the British authorities in Cairo had been able to draw the Sharif of Mekka, Husayn ibn-Ali, into the Allied camp. The Sharif's revolt against his Ottoman overlords in June 1916 mobilized a number of Arab tribes and put the Ottoman regiments in the Hijaz and Asir under considerable pressure. They lost control of Mecca and Jiddah within a week, surrendered Yambo on July 27 and Taif on September 22, but the Ottoman garrison at Medina, under the inspired leadership of Brigadier General Fahrettin Pasha, defied the insurgents and did not surrender until January 1919. Arab troops and irregulars, under the leadership of Husayn's third son, the Amir Faysal, eventually moved northward toward Palestine, with British advisers like Captain T. E. Lawrence, Egyptian artillery units, and a small French colonial force under Colonel Edouard Brémond providing much needed assistance. Aside from capturing Aqaba in July 1917, the Arab insurgents also did serious damage to the Hijaz rail line. While the Turks were able to re-supply their Medina garrison until the spring of 1918, the Ottoman troops stationed in Yemen found themselves almost completely cut off from the rest of the empire throughout the war years. They nevertheless carried out some offensive operations in the region west and north of Aden in 1915, forcing the British to reinforce their garrison there.[21]

From September 1916 on, the British forces in Egypt, including Anzac mounted infantry and Indian cavalry, slowly advanced through the Sinai desert, making good use of a water pipeline and a railway which were constructed behind them. Pushed back with high losses in the first two battles of Gaza (March and April 1917), they successfully broke through the Ottoman defenses seven months later in the third Gaza battle. Advancing on a broad front, the Egyptian Expeditionary Force (EEF), by now under the command of Sir Edmund Allenby, fought its way to the outskirts of Jerusalem, which the Turks evacuated on December 8–9. Although the EEF gained some further ground and seized Jericho in February 1918, the Ottoman forces in Palestine, dubbed Army Group Yildirim (Thunderbolt), eventually stabilized the situation.[22]

Formed originally under General Erich von Falkenhayn (the former chief of the OHL) for an Ottoman counter-offensive in Mesopotamia, the Yildirim Group had subsequently been moved to Palestine. Commanded (since late February 1918) by General Liman von Sanders, the Group was composed of three small field armies, all of them beset by serious supply shortages. Entrenched in a thin line stretching from the coast north of Jaffa through the Judean hills into the high plateaus east of the Jordan River, the Ottoman troops in some areas were interlaced with German infantry and artillery units and a few Austro-Hungarian gun batteries. But it was clear to Liman (and others) that the next British offensive would most likely lead to a major disaster for his forces. When Allenby finally struck, on September 19, the Ottoman Eighth Army in the coastal region crumbled within the first 12 hours. Its commander, Major General Cevat Pasha (of Gallipoli fame), did his best to repair the damage, but eventually he and his staff were sent back to Constantinople. The disintegration of the Eighth Army soon forced the adjacent Seventh Army, headed by Mustafa Kemal Pasha, to pull in its right wing. In the region east of the Jordan, the Fourth Army, under the command of Brigadier General Mersinli Cemal Pasha, likewise soon found its flanks exposed and gradually retreated to the north. General Liman himself barely avoided capture during a cavalry raid on Nazareth.[23]

During the next six weeks, the remnants of the Yildirim army group continued their retreat northward under often chaotic conditions. They were pursued by masses of cavalry, subjected to devastating air attacks, and also harassed by roving Arab bands. On September 30, the Turks evacuated Damascus, which was then occupied by Faysal's Arab warriors and Allenby's cavalry. Among many Ottoman soldiers who surrendered at this time was the wounded commander of VIII Corps, Colonel Yasin al-Hashimi, an Iraqi with close ties to the Arab national movement, who would soon become Faysal's new chief of staff. Another Ottoman corps commander, Colonel Mustafa Ismet Bey, emerged unscathed from the fiasco in Palestine. Later known as Ismet Inönü, he would become a leading figure in Turkey, serving intermittently as its prime minister or president until 1965.[24]

The Ottoman withdrawal from the rest of Syria became somewhat more orderly, especially after some battalions of the Ottoman Second Army entered the fray. While Allenby's troops, including thousands of Arab warriors, reached Aleppo by October 24–25, 1918, they were held back by Ottoman units for several hours. The following day, the revived Ottoman spirit was demonstrated again near Haritan, where a charge by two regiments of Indian lancers was beaten off at considerable cost to them. Five days later, the Mudros Armistice ended the campaign. Allenby's triumph had been achieved with fewer than 6,000 Allied casualties, while his opponents had lost over 73,000 men taken prisoner, plus an unknown number of dead or wounded.[25]

Mesopotamia and Persia

A few days after the Ottoman Empire's entry into the war, an Anglo-Indian brigade disembarked at the mouth of the Shatt-al-Arab and proceeded to the Karun River region for the purpose of protecting the installations of the Anglo-Persian Oil Company. Reinforced in mid-November and placed under the command of Lieutenant General Sir Arthur Barrett, "Force D" then moved on to Basra against ineffectual resistance by a handful of Ottoman battalions and local tribesmen. By December 9, 1914, the Turks had also been dislodged from Qurna, at the confluence of the Tigris and the old channel of the Euphrates. Faced with these setbacks, Enver Pasha sent a senior member of his staff, Lieutenant Colonel Suleyman Askeri Bey, to take command in Mesopotamia. At the same time the 35th Division, in northern Syria, was moved back to its peacetime stations around Baghdad. This made it possible by March 1915 to deploy one division-size force on the Tigris River and in the adjacent Persian region of Arabistan, while a second force guarded the approaches to Nasiriyah on the Euphrates.[26]

During the same winter months "Force D" of the Indian Army was gradually expanded into a corps (with two divisions and a cavalry brigade), and on April 9, 1915 its command was assumed by General Sir John Nixon. A few days later Suleyman Askeri attempted to push the British back to Basra, but the offensive failed and eventually his troops retreated in disorder to Khamisiya, where Suleyman shot himself in disgust. He was promptly replaced by Colonel Yusef Nurettin Bey. A forceful and often ruthless soldier, Nurettin gradually whipped his mostly Arab-speaking troops into shape and eventually created a new division from gendarmes and frontier guards. However, General Nixon did not wait for the Turks to recover. Late in April, he sent the 6th (Poona) Division, under Maj. Gen. Charles Townshend, up the Tigris toward the town of Amara (which was abandoned by the Turks in early June). Seven weeks later, the Turks were also pushed out of Nasiriyah. On September 1, the Poona Division resumed its advance and reached Kut-al-Amara (hereafter Kut) and Aziziya by early October 1915.

Although he was increasingly beset by logistic problems, Nixon authorized Townshend the following month to push on toward Baghdad. By November 21, 1915, Townshend's brigades had reached a strong Turkish position at Ctesiphon and attacked it the next morning. In the ensuing three-day battle, both sides incurred heavy losses. In the end, Nurettin ordered his troops to fall back to the Diyala River, but Townshend was in no position to follow the Turks. Instead, his division began an orderly retreat on November 25, 1915 and arrived at Kut eight days later. Following him there to his fortified camp, Nurettin's troops encircled the Kut peninsula and eventually also established a strong blocking position 20 miles downstream.[27]

After several futile attempts to break into Townshend's camp, the Ottoman Sixth Army, now headed by an elderly German field marshal, Colmar Baron von der Goltz, concentrated on keeping the Kut garrison bottled up and preventing its relief. During the next four months, newly arrived Anglo-Indian troops made several attempts to break open the siege ring, but all of them failed (at a total cost of 23,000 men). Faced with an acute shortage of food, the Poona Division finally surrendered to the new commander of the Ottoman Sixth Army, Brigadier General Halil Pasha, on April 29, 1916. Over 13,000 Indian and British soldiers were captured, many of them soon to die from mal-treatment and disease.[28]

Coming four months after the Allied withdrawal from Gallipoli, the fall of Kut further boosted Ottoman morale and undermined Britain's prestige throughout the Muslim world. The fact that the British had offered £2 million ransom money to Halil Pasha made matters even worse. After much earnest debate in London, the British government decided that the seizure of Baghdad and the rest of Upper Mesopotamia were worth further investments in manpower and material. Aside from the construction of a rail link from Basra to Amara and the augmentation of their already large river fleet during the summer and autumn of 1916, the Anglo-Indian forces in the theater also benefited from massive infusions of personnel. By November, their new commander, Sir Frederick Maude, had a total of 340,000 men at his disposal, with roughly half of them being combat troops. Halil Pasha's army by that time had a total strength of about 42,000. The British offensive began in mid-December 1916, and three months later the Turks were forced to withdraw from Baghdad. During the next eight months, Maude's forces gained further ground, taking Samara on April 24, Ramadi on September 29, and Tikrit on November 5, 1917. Stung by the loss of Baghdad, the Ottoman High Command had meanwhile assembled the Yildirim (Thunderbolt) army group for an eventual counter-offensive in Mesopotamia but in the end the whole project of reconquering Baghdad had to be abandoned because of the deteriorating situation in southern Palestine, where, as we have seen, the Yildirim army group was eventually deployed.[29]

On November 18, 1917, the highly respected commander of the Anglo-Indian troops in Mesopotamia, General Frederick Stanley Maude, succumbed to the cholera. Under his successor, Sir William R. Marshall, both corps of the expeditionary force gradually pushed the Turks further back, taking Hit in March 1918 and Kirkuk eight weeks later. By the time the Mudros Armistice came into effect, some British troops had reached a point roughly 10 miles south of Mosul.[30]

The gradual conquest of what would soon become the Kingdom of Iraq had sucked close to 890,00 Indian and British troops into a theater of war which many people in the Allied camp regarded as a sideshow. Over 92,000 of these troops became casualties. The Ottoman forces deployed in Mesopotamia during the war, including locally raised Arab levies, were only about half that number; however, they lost a much greater proportion of their manpower due to disease, desertion, and enemy action.

Since several regions of "neutral" Persia had become Russian or British "spheres of influence" before 1914, the Turks and their German allies felt no compunction about spreading the war to that country. In December 1914, some Ottoman troops invaded Persian Azerbaijan and eventually occupied Tabriz. Russian units counterattacked in early 1915 and pushed the Turks back to the border. At about the same time, several Ottoman battalions penetrated Persian territory in Arabistan and cut the oil pipeline leading to Abadan. During the remainder of the year and into 1916, small Ottoman units tangled on Persian soil with both British troops and a sizeable Russian force com-manded by Lieutenant General N. N. Baratov. Two months after the fall of Kut, three divisions of the Ottoman XIII Corps began a major operation against the Russians in the Pusht-i-Kuh Mountains and eventually seized the town of Hamadan, roughly 200 miles southwest of Tehran. Though badly weakened by disease, the corps, under the command of Ali Ihsan Bey, held on to its Persian conquest until February 1917, when the growing British threat to Baghdad forced the Ottoman high command to bring all three divisions back to Mesopotamia. Fourteen months later, in June 1918, Ali Ihsan took Halil Pasha's place as commander of the Sixth Army and presided over its continu-ing retreat to the north. Following the cessation of hostilities, he proved quite reluctant in handing over control of Mosul to the British, which earned him the sobriquet "Old Sandbag."[31]

Galicia and the Balkans

Even though the Turks were facing major problems on their Transcaucasian front, Enver Pasha agreed in June 1916 to provide direct assistance to the other Central Powers in several European theaters of war. The first transfer of Ottoman troops got underway the following month, after the Brusilov Offensive had inflicted enormous losses on the Austro-Hungarian armies along the eastern front. Headed by Colonel Yakup Şveki Bey, the Ottoman XV Corps, composed of the 19th and 20th Divisions, was hurriedly brought up to full strength, transported to Hungary, and then sent on to eastern Galicia. There, in late August, the two Ottoman divisions took over 20 miles of front line southeast of Lviv (Lemberg). Flanked by German troops, and with an above-average allotment of artillery behind them, the Ottoman infantry soon proved their mettle, both in repelling massive Russian attacks and in launching counterstrokes. Because of their heavy losses, their sector was gradually narrowed to about six miles of trenches. Headed by a new commander, Brigadier General Cevat Pasha, from mid-November on, the corps continued to hold its positions tenaciously during the next eight months. By the time it returned to Turkey, in the summer of 1917, the corps had lost approximately 25,000 officers and men altogether.[32]

Ottoman help extended to the Balkans as well. As soon as Romania had entered the war (August 27, 1916), three of its armies invaded Hungary and by mid-September had occupied a sizeable slice of Transylvania. In the south, between the Danube and the Black Sea, on the other hand, the Romanians were quickly pushed onto the defensive. On September 2, the Bulgarian Third Army and a handful of German units, under the overall command of Field Marshal August von Mackensen, began an offensive against the Romanian Third Army in the Dobruja. Two weeks later, the 25th Ottoman Division, belonging to Brigadier General Mustafa Hilmi Pasha's VI Corps, joined Mackensen's strike force and gradually fought its way northward. In early October, the second component of Hilmi's corps, the 15th Division, went into action as well. In the ensuing operations of Mackensen's group against six Romanian and three Russian divisions (all under the command of Lieutenant General A. M. Zayonchkovskii) the Turks suffered heavy losses, with the total exceeding 16,000 officers and men by the end of the month. They nevertheless continued their advance and reached the delta of the Danube by late December.[33]

In the meantime, another Ottoman division, the 26th, had reached the Romanian theater of war. It was assigned to the Army of the Danube, a mixed force of German and Bulgarian troops under the command of General Robert Kosch, which crossed the Danube at Sistovo on November 23, 1916 for an advance on Bucharest. Early in 1917, after the conquest of Wallachia had been completed, the 26th Division was formally incorporated into Hilmi's corps and eventually all three of its divisions took up defensive positions along the Sereth (Siret) River. Soon thereafter Colonel Kâzim Bey took command of the VI Corps; he was, in turn, succeeded by Colonel Cafer Tayyar Bey in April 1917. The 25th and 26th Divisions returned to Turkey the same year, but the corps headquarters and the 15th Division remained on Romanian soil until April 1918.

The third European theater of war where Ottoman troops made their appearance in 1916 was Macedonia. In October and November, the 50th and 46th Divisions took over a broad stretch of front line near the Struma River, where they faced the British XVI Corps and some French troops. Having been constituted a brand-new XX Corps, under the command of Brigadier General Abdulkerim Pasha (a veteran of the Transcaucasian front), the two Ottoman divisions saw relatively little action during the ensuing winter and both were withdrawn in April 1917 for redeployment in Palestine and Mesopotamia.[34]

Although General Liman von Sanders and some other people had serious misgivings about the diversion of seven Ottoman divisions to European fronts, arguing that their withdrawal from Turkey undermined its own war effort, it seems clear today that this type of direct military assistance was of great value to the Central Powers, particularly in Galicia and in the campaign against Romania. It might be added that the proffered help also strengthened the political clout of the Ottoman government vis-à-vis its three allies. Moreover, to many patriotic Turks the reappearance of Ottoman troops on Austrian soil and in several regions of the Balkans would also become a matter of some personal satisfaction.

* * *

Although the "Turkish War" has often been depicted as a mere sideshow in World War I, the operations of the Ottoman armed forces actually made a major difference to the war effort of both sides. Campaigning under grave handicaps, often hungry and clad in rags, the Sultan's soldiers tied down large contingents of Russian, British imperial, and French troops throughout the Middle East, troops which might otherwise have been used against Germany or Austria-Hungary on the principal European fronts. Moreover, by their successful defense of the Black Sea Straits, the Turks also blocked an important supply route between Russia and her Western allies.

It is true, of course, that the Germans provided substantial aid to their Ottoman ally, in gold bullion, armaments, technical equipment, and highly trained personnel, particularly after 1915, when the defeat of Serbia opened secure communications through the Balkan peninsula. It is estimated that the Reich delivered over 550 artillery pieces, 1,600 machine guns, 557,000 rifles, 100,000 carbines, almost 300 aircraft, and huge amounts of ammunition to the Turks. The Germans also transferred 120 steam locomotives to the Ottoman railway system and, along with the Habsburg army, hundreds of trucks (with trained drivers) to supplement the primitive road transport in the eastern provinces of the empire. On balance, though, it seems clear that both Germany and Austria-Hungary benefited much more from the co-belligerency of the Ottoman Empire than vice versa, a point which has frequently been ignored by historians of World War I.

Notes

1   Trumpener, *Germany*, ch. 2; Hermann Lorey, *Der Krieg in den türkischen Gewässern*, 2 vols., Berlin, E. S. Mittler, 1928–38, vol. 1, chs. 1–7.

2   Mühlmann, *Waffenbündnis*, passim; Jehüde L. Wallach, *Anatomie einer Miltärhilfe. Die preussisch-deutschen Militärmissionen in der Türkei, 1835–1919*, Düsseldorf, Droste, 1976, chs. 5–8. Trumpener, "Suez"; Hans Werner Neulen, *Feldgrau in Jerusalem: das Levantekorps des kaiserlichen Deutschland*, Munich, Universitas Verlag, 1991, passim; and Erickson, *Ordered to Die*, pp. 231–5.

3   Lorey, *Krieg*, vol. 1, chs. 8–32.

4   On the rail system, see Mühlmann, *Waffenbündnis*, pp. 31–3, 112–16; Trumpener, *Germany*, pp. 285–316; on the Black Sea operations, see Lorey, *Krieg*, vols. 1 and 2, passim; I. I. Rostunov (ed.), *Istoriya pervoi mirovoi voiny*, 2 vols., Moscow, Izdatel'stvo Nauka, 1975, vol. 2, pp. 129–36, 268–80, 387–91; and George Nekrasov, *North of Gallipoli: The Black Sea Fleet at War, 1914–1917*, Boulder, CO, East European Monographs, 1992.

5   Erickson, *Ordered to Die*, ch. 1; Mühlmann, *Waffenbündnis*, passim; Trumpner, "Suez."

6   Rostunov, *Istoriya*, vol 1, pp. 390–8; E. K. Sarkisyan, *Ekspansionistkaya politika Osmanskoi Imperii v Zakavkaze nakanune i v godi pervoi mirovoi voiny*, Yerevan, 1962, pp. 188–99; Erickson, *Ordered to Die*, pp. 46ff., 51–62; Guse, *Kaukasusfront*, pp. 7–55.

7   Rostunov, *Istoriya*, vol. 2, pp. 390–8; Erickson, *Ordered to Die*, pp. 104–8; Guse, *Kaukasusfront*, pp. 55–74. On the Armenian uprising at Van in April 1915 and the ensuing "ethnic cleansing" in the eastern provinces of the Ottoman Empire see chapters 13 and 33 below.

8   Rostunov, *Istoriya*, vol. 2, pp. 221ff.; Sarkisyan, *Ekspansionistkaya*, pp. 214–20; Bihl, *Kaukasuspolitik*, pp. 227–9; Erickson, *Ordered to Die*, pp. 120–37. On Yudenich, later a major figure in the Russian Civil War, see V. P. Mayatskov (ed.), *Pervaya mirovaya v zhizneo-pisanyakh russkikh voenachalnikov*, Moscow, 1994, pp. 209–45.

9   Sarkisyan, *Ekspansionistkaya*, pp. 319–30; Allan K. Wildman, *The End of the Russian Imperial Army*, 2 vols., Princeton, Princeton University Press, 1980–7.

10   Sarkisyan, *Ekspansionistkaya*, pp. 330–420; Trumpener, *Germany*, ch. 6; Gőkay, Bulent, "The Battle for Baku (May-September 1918)," *Middle Eastern Studies*, 34, 1998, pp. 30–50.

11   Trumpener, *Germany*, pp. 352–8; Gwynne Dyer, "The Turkish Armistice of 1918," *Middle Eastern Studies*, 8, 1972, pp. 313–48; Macfie, *End of the Ottoman Empire*, ch. 9.

12   Lorey, *Krieg*, vol. 2, chs. 1–8; Arthur Marder, *From the Dreadnought to Scapa Flow*, vol. 2, London, Oxford University Press, 1965, pp. 199–265; Marder, *From the Dardanelles to Oran*, London, Oxford University Press, 1974, pp. 1–32; Edward J. Erickson, "One More Time: Forcing the Dardanelles in March 1915," *Journal of Strategic Studies*, 24/3, 2001, pp. 158–76.

13   Lorey, *Krieg*, vol. 2, ch. 9; Liman von Sanders, *Fünf Jahre*, pp. 64–83.

14   On the opening days of the Gallipoli Campaign, see Lorey, *Krieg*, vol. 2, pp. 109–25; Winter, *25 April*; Tim Travers, "Liman von Sanders the Capture of Lieutenant Palmer, and Ottoman Anticipation of the Allied Landings at Gallipoli on 25 April 1915," *Journal of Military History*, 65, 2001, pp. 965–79; Erickson, *Ordered to Die*, pp. 83–5.

15   On the Allied operations, see Aspinall-Oglander, *Gallipoli*, vols. 1, 2; Bean, *Anzac*, vols. 1, 2; Pugsley, *Gallipoli. The New Zealand Story*; and *Armées françaises*, vol. 8, pt. 1, chs. 4–8. On the Ottoman side, cf. Mühlmann, *Kampf*; Erickson, *Ordered to Die*, pp. 85–91.

16   Lorey, *Krieg*, vol. 1, chs. 12, 14, 15, 17; vol. 2, pp. 131–59.

17   Erickson, *Ordered to Die*, pp. 90ff.; Liman von Sanders, *Fünf Jahre*, pp. 108–21.

18   Birdwood, later a field marshal and commander of the Indian Army, went out of his way in 1938 to attend Atatürk's funeral in Ankara.

19   For the different legacies of the campaign in Britain and Australia, see Macleod, *Reconsidering Gallipoli*.

20   See MacMunn and Falls, *Egypt*, vol. 1, chs. 1–3; Freidrick Kress von Kressenstein, *Mit den Türken zum Suezkanal*, Berlin, Schlegel, 1938, chs. 2–6; Erickson, *Ordered to Die*, pp. 68–72.

21   See MacMunn and Falls, *Egypt*, vol. 1, chs. 10–14; Busch, *Britain*, chs. 2, 4, 5; Tauber, *Arab*, ch. 107; Wasti, S. Tanvir, "The Defense of Medina, 1916–1919," *Middle Eastern Studies*, 27, 1991, pp. 642–53; Tabachnik, *Puzzle*, pp. 195–201, 204–42.

22   MacMunn and Falls, *Egypt*, vol. 1, chs. 15–19; vol. 2, pts. 1, 2; Gullett, *Australian Imperial Force*, chs. 13ff.; Kress, *Mit den Türken*, chs. 13–20.

23   Falls, *Egypt*, vol. 2, chs. 20–24; Liman von Sanders, *Fünf Jahre*, pp. 247–358; Erickson, *Ordered to Die*, pp. 193–200.

24   Falls, *Egypt*, vol. 2, chs. 25–27; Erickson, *Ordered to Die*, pp. 200ff.; Liman von Sanders, *Fünf Jahre*, pp. 358–99.

25   As soon as the armistice came into effect, Mustafa Kemal (Atatürk) succeeded General Liman as Yildirim group commander, but he too left for Constantinople (the seat of power) only a week later.

26   Moberly, *Mesopotamia*, vol. 1, chs. 6–8; Erickson, *Ordered to Die*, pp. 66ff., 110.

27   Moberly, *Mesopotamia*, vols 1, 2, chs. 9–16; Erickson, *Ordered to Die*, pp. 110–15.

28 Moberly *Mesopotamia*, vol. 2, chs. 17–26; Erickson, *Ordered to Die*, pp. 149ff.
29 Moberly, *Mesopotamia*, vols. 3, 4, chs. 27–39; Erickson, *Ordered to Die*, pp. 165–72.
30 Moberly, *Mesopotamia*, vol. 4, chs. 40, 44–46; Erickson, *Ordered to Die*, p. 203.
31 Moberly, *Mesopotamia*, vol. 1, pp. 221–34; vol. 3, chs. 27–28; vol. 4, chs. 40–43 passim; Moberly, *Persia*; Erickson, *Ordered to Die*, pp. 65, 152f, 192.
32 See *Weltkrieg*, vol. 11, pp. 347–407; vol. 12, pp. 477–512; vol. 13, pp. 148–80; Glaise-Horstenau, *Oesterreich*, vol. 5, pp. 115–220, 359–446; vol. 6, pp. 211–86; Erickson, *Ordered to Die*, pp. 137–42; Stone, *Eastern Front*, ch. 11.
33 Wildman, *End of the Russian Imperial Army*, ch. 10; Erickson, *Ordered to Die*, pp. 142–7; Glaise-Horstenau, *Oesterreich*, vol. 5, pp. 221–358, 447–628; vol. 6, pp. 337–412; *Weltkrieg*, vol. 11, pp. 189–336; vol. 13, pp. 180–8.
34 Erickson, *Ordered to Die*, pp. 147ff.

References and Further Reading

Aspinall-Oglander, Cecil Faber, *Military Operations: Gallipoli*, 2 vols., 1929–32; reprint, London and Nashville, The Battery Press, 1992.

Bean, Charles E. W., *The Story of Anzac*, 2 vols., Sydney, 1921–4, reprint, St Lucia, Queensland University Press, 1981.

Bihl, Wolfdieter, *Die Kaukasus-Politik der Mittelmächte*, part 1, Vienna, Böhlau, 1975.

Busch, Briton C., *Britain, India, and the Arabs, 1914–1921*, Berkeley, University of California Press, 1971.

Erickson, Edward, J., *Ordered to Die: A History of the Ottoman Army in the First World War*, Westport, CT, 2000.

Erickson, Edward J., "The Turkish Official Military Histories of the First World War," *Middle Eastern Studies*, 39, 2003, pp. 190–8.

Erickson, Edward, J., *Ottoman Army Effectiveness in World War One: A Comparative Study*, London, Routledge, 2007.

Falls, Cyril, *Military Operations: Egypt and Palestine*, vol. 2, London, HMSO, 1930.

Glaise-Horstenau, Edmund, et al., *Oesterreich-Ungarns letzter Krieg*, vols. 5–6, Vienna, Verlag der Militärwissenschaftlichen Mitteilungen, 1934–6.

Gullett, H. S., *The Australian Imperial Force in Sinai and Palestine 1914–1918*, Sydney, 1923; reprint, St Lucia, University of Queensland Press, 1984.

Guse, Felix, *Die Kaukasusfront im Weltkrieg bis zum Frieden von Brest*, Leipzig, Koehler und Amelang, 1940.

Liman von Sanders, Otto, *Fünf Jahre Türkei*, Berlin, 1920; *Five Years in Turkey*, 1927; new ed., Nashville, Battery Press, 2000.

Macfie, A. L., *Atatürk*, London, Longman, 1994.

Macfie, A. L., *The End of the Ottoman Empire, 1908–23*, London, Longman, 1998.

Macleod, Jenny, *Reconsidering Gallipoli*, Manchester, Manchester University Press, 2004.

MacMunn, Sir George, and Falls, Cyril, *Military Operations: Egypt and Palestine*, vol. 1, London, HMSO, 1928.

Ministère de la guerre, *Les Armées françaises dans la grande guerre*, vol. 8, part 1, Paris, Minstère de la Guerre, 1923.

Moberly, Frederick James, *The Campaign in Mesopotamia, 1914–1918*, 4 vols., London, HMSO, 1923–7.

Moberly, Frederick James, *Operations in Persia, 1914–1919*, London, HMSO, 1987.

Mühlmann, Carl, *Der Kampf um die Dardanellen, 1915*, Oldenburg, G. Stalling, 1927.

Mühlmann, Carl, *Das deutsch-türkische Waffenbündnis im Weltkriege*, Leipzig, Koehler und Amelang, 1940.

Pugsley, Christopher, *Gallipoli: The New Zealand Story*, Auckland, Reed, 1984.

Reichskriegsministerium, *Der Weltkrieg 1914 bis 1918: Militärische Operationen zu Lande*, vols. 11–13, Berlin, E. S. Mittler, 1938–42.

Stone, Norman, *The Eastern Front 1914–1917*, New York, Scribner, 1975.

Tabachnik, Stephen E. (ed.), *The T. E. Lawrence Puzzle*, Athens, University of Georgia Press, 1984.

Tauber, Eliezer, *The Arab Movement in World War I*, London, Frank Cass, 1993.

Trumpener, Ulrich, *Germany and the Ottoman Empire, 1914–1918*, Princeton, Princeton University Press, 1968.

Trumpener, Ulrich, "Suez, Baku, Gallipoli: The Military Dimensions of the German-Ottoman Coalition, 1914–1918," in Keith Neilson and Ray Prête (eds.), *Coalition Warfare: An Uneasy Accord*, Waterloo, Ont., Wilfrid Laurier University Press, 1983, pp. 31–51.

Winter, Denis, *25 April 1915: The Inevitable Tragedy*, St Lucia, University of Queensland Press, 1994.

Yücel, Yasar, "Türkei: Bibliography of the First World War," in Jürgen Rohwer (ed.), *Neue Forschungen zum Ersten Weltkrieg*, Koblenz, Bernard und Graefe, 1985.

CHAPTER EIGHT

The War in Africa

DAVID KILLINGRAY

By 1914 most of Africa was divided between the Western European imperial powers. Territorial disputes had largely been resolved by 1913 and were not a source of serious contention among the imperial powers. Colonial territories in Africa were drawn into World War I because they were ruled by European powers, and this was global conflict that became total war. In terms of area the French colonial empire was the largest, formed by a contiguous block of colonies that linked North Africa with the sudanic and equatorial regions of west and central Africa. By contrast Britain's African colonial empire was smaller in area, including several non-contiguous colonies, but with a larger population, some 35 million. Germany had four separate colonies: Togo and Kamerun in West Africa, South West Africa, and the more populous territory of German East Africa. Belgium controlled what had formerly been King Leopold's *domaine privé*, the large and harshly exploited tropical region of the Congo basin. Portugal, the oldest colonial power in Africa, had four mainland colonies, the most important being Angola and Mozambique. Most of the colonies in the tropical regions had been recently acquired; the political boundaries drawn on maps belied both possession and control. "Small wars" of conquest and the suppression of rebellion continued and large areas of colonial Africa were only loosely administered by Europeans.

Despite much contemporary talk about the value of empire, African tropical possessions yielded little economic return to Europe. The most valuable colonial possessions were in the subtropical regions of North and South Africa that had well-developed economies and sizeable populations of European settlers. The 700,000 European settlers in Algeria, across the Mediterranean from France, living mainly in coastal towns and farms, dominated the Arabic-speaking majority population and regarded the littoral as an integral part of the metropole. Trade was overwhelmingly with France, the major exports being cereals, wines, other agricultural products, and minerals. The four British colonies in southern Africa had recently been united into the self-governing Union of South Africa, an integration made more possible by a railway network that tied together growing towns and ports. Over one million white people, many being recent settlers, dominated and discriminated against an indigenous population five times that number. White political power was based on control of agricultural and mining production and overseas trade. Of particular value were the gold mines of the Rand, which along with diamonds

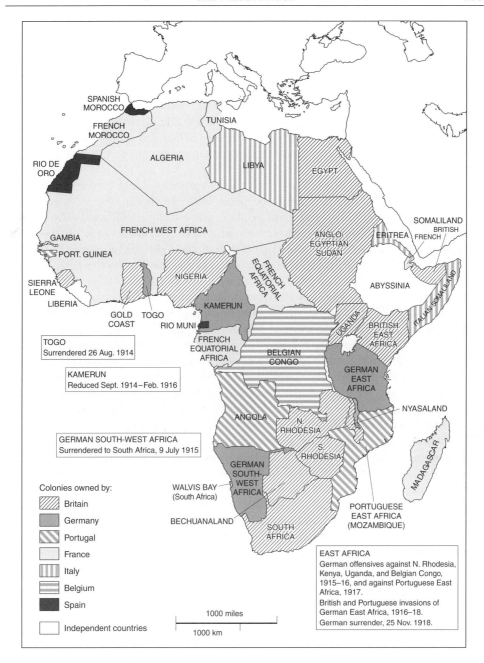

Map 6 Africa in World War I

and coal, provided the base for nascent industrial development during World War I. There was also a small number of white settlers, principally farmers and miners, in German South West Africa, and the British colonies of Southern Rhodesia and the East African Protectorate (Kenya).[1]

Africa provided strategic waterways, ports, and harbors. The most important were the Suez Canal and Cape Town, both controlled by the British, which were key points on the two major sea routes to Asia. Suez ran through Egypt, nominally Ottoman territory, but under British occupation since the 1880s. In November 1914, when the Porte joined the Central Powers, London declared a protectorate over Egypt. The Mediterranean was dominated by the French and British from their naval bases at Oran and Alexandria, while Atlantic waters could be patrolled from the French port of Dakar and the British harbors at Freetown and Simonstown. From the start of the war the British and French were able to dominate the sea-lanes to and from Africa. The submarine telegraph system was also under Allied control. Strategic radio stations in German colonies communicated with commerce raiders, so they became a prime target for the British and French in 1914.

Most European colonies in Africa (with the exception of South Africa and German South West Africa) recruited local military forces, under European officers, used primarily for internal security and to safeguard frontiers. Recruits invariably were enlisted from ethnic groups that Europeans deemed to be martial races. The armies were small infantry forces equipped with older rifles, a few machine guns and light artillery pieces.[2] The largest were those of the French and the Belgians. In the Belgian Congo the *Force publique* numbered around 25,000 men and had a bad reputation for its predatory behavior. The French colonial army in West Africa had been conscripted since 1912 to serve as a garrison force in North Africa and to thus release European troops for the defense of France in event of war with Germany. General Mangin's purpose in creating *la force noire* (or Black Army) was to compensate France for its lower birth rate compared to that of Germany.[3] Initially in the war *tirailleurs sénégalais* (a generic term for soldiers from different parts of French West Africa) were used as garrison troops but from 1915 onward nearly 140,000 served, along with other colonial troops, as combatants in Europe.[4] Contrary to wartime Allied propaganda of German militarism, all of her colonial forces were relatively small and only lightly armed.

Maintaining supply lines posed serious difficulties in tropical campaigns. Roads and bridges were inadequate, railways limited, and many rivers only navigable at certain times of the year. The tsetse fly killed draft horses and cattle and thus military operations relied heavily on large numbers of porters. As the war progressed more lightweight motor trucks were used in the East African campaign, particularly US-produced vehicles, although this required building roads that often became impassable in the rainy season. Recruiting porters, often forcibly, and preventing desertion were vital. Even small military operations required a sizeable number of porters to support supply lines, for example 12,000 were needed to sustain two French columns in Kamerun in 1915. Operations in grasslands were relatively easy; forest and rugged terrain presented much greater difficulties of movement. Porters were often difficult to obtain, and retain, and in those circumstances the average load of 20 kg per man (sometimes women) might be increased. Soldiers could live off the land but large numbers of porters could not. Feeding porters with the right diet was a constant headache. An East African porters' song had the refrain "We are the porters who carry the food to feed the porters who carry the food...." Invariably military columns outpaced the slower-moving lines of porters, and slow delivery of forward stocks hampered front-line military operations. Lengthy supply lines were also vulnerable to attack. On the line of supply porters fell sick, suffered from malnutrition, and their bare feet were attacked by jiggers (tropical fleas that burrow into the skin).[5]

In a continent where the process of military "pacification" continued and rebellion was frequent, colonial powers were anxious not to involve Africa in a global conflict. The idea that Africa could be neutralized in a European conflict that would be solely a "white man's war" misread the changed circumstances of a global contest between imperial powers. In the years immediately before the outbreak of war both the British and Germans had ambitions to take over areas of Portuguese Africa. As the war progressed Allied and German plans were formulated to secure opponents' colonies, the German aim being for a *Mittelafrika* that secured a large part of the tropical region. The French and British sought to wrest from Germany all of her colonies; the later division of the spoils between the victors was highly contested. South Africa also had ambitions to extend northward across the Limpopo and to incorporate German South West Africa and part of Mozambique within the Union. Britain's aim was to realize an all-red route of territory from the Cape to Cairo.

The first British shots of the war were fired by African troops in the short campaign to conquer Togo.[6] Short campaigns could depend mainly on troops from a neighboring colony; more distant operations, for example the long drawn-out war in German East Africa, required troops and labor from all parts of the continent. Thus all the belligerents mobilized their colonial armies and conducted recruitment campaigns to replenish the ranks and to enforce labor for carrying. However, continued demands caused people to flee their villages or cross nearby borders to escape the grasp of military and labor recruiters. The French recruiting drives in West Africa in 1915–16 led to serious revolt.[7] Violent resistance occurred in most colonial territories, opposition to the war feeding off the grievances of recently conquered peoples to the colonial presence.

Colonial armies grew in size, but their numbers were small compared to the large body of labor required to sustain military operations that were spread over a large area. More than 170,000 French *tirailleurs* fought in France, in southeast Europe, and the Levant. British policy was to use African troops only within Africa. However, continuing war and severe manpower crises in 1916 and 1918 led military and political leaders in London to think of employing African soldiers in overseas campaigns. In the event, the main imperial contribution was a 20,000-strong South African Native Labour Contingent sent to the western front from 1916 to 1918, and a few hundred West Africans employed in river work in Mesopotamia.[8]

On the outbreak of war the Allied purpose in Africa was to seize the German colonies in quick campaigns. Germany was at a severe disadvantage compared to France and Britain, who had control of the seas and were able to block access to German colonies. As a continental power Germany's military interests were focused on Europe and not on an overseas empire. Nevertheless the Germans resisted. Togo was quickly captured; Kamerun and South West Africa took longer. The war in East Africa became a long campaign that in the final stages involved irregular warfare, the German force only surrendering after the Armistice of November 1918. A fifth campaign was begun by the British, from Suez on the Sinai front, when the Ottoman Empire entered the war in November 1914. In addition all the combatants had to deal with continued military resistance and rebellions in their African colonies during the war years.

The Conquest of Togo

The small German colony of Togo was surrounded by hostile territory. Attempts by the acting governor, Doering, to gain French and British acceptance that it should remain neutral were unsuccessful. The colony was weakly defended by a local paramilitary force, the *Schutztrüppen*, which consisted of a few hundred men armed with older rifles and only four machine guns. Opposing them were two battalions of the Gold Coast Regiment (GCR) with light artillery, 3,500 *tirailleurs* in the neighboring French colonies, and various small armed forces and locally recruited levies. Troops in the Gold Coast were mobilized on July 31before war was declared in Europe.

The brief campaign was improvised and lacked coordination between the French and the British, both powers being eager to control the German colony. The principal object for the British was to seize the port capital of Lomé, which was just a kilometer within Togo, and to destroy the German wireless station at Kamina, 140 km inland at the end of the central railway line. Local porters were recruited, some by force, and the GCR advanced from the west, supported by the navy. At the same time the French, supported by 1,000 porters, entered Togo from the east and moved along the coast. The Germans abandoned Lomé and retreated northward along the railway line, destroying parts of it as they went, in order to defend Kamina. The capital was taken by the British on August 12. In the following week the GCR moved north along the railway toward Kamina. Resistance was light but in one skirmish the German commander was killed. At the well-defended bridge over the Chra River the GCR was met by fierce German gunfire that killed or wounded nearly one-fifth of the British force. However, with a further French force advancing from Cheti in the east, and a similar British force moving into Togo from Keti Krachi in the west, plus police and irregulars invading the north from three directions, the German position was untenable. Cut off from the coast and surrounded, they destroyed the radio station on August 24–25 and Doering surrendered the next day.

The Kamerun Campaign, 1914–16

Germany's other West African colony, Kamerun, was large and almost surrounded by Allied territory, British Nigeria to the west, French Equatorial Africa to the east and south, and the Belgian Congo in the south east. Kamerun's lengthy frontiers had been extended by the addition of territory ceded by France following the Morocco crisis of 1911. Significant for the subsequent German military campaign was the presence of the small neutral Spanish enclave of Rio Muni to the southwest. The southern part of Kamerun was forested while the northern plateau was mainly upland savanna land. German forces in 1914 consisted of 12 companies of *Schütztruppen*, 205 white officers, and 1,650 African rank and file, although wartime recruitment succeeded in increasing its strength to 6,000 by mid 1915. By contrast the federally organized British West African Frontier Force, with 70 percent of its strength in neighboring Nigeria, numbered 7,550, and the French had 20,000 troops in their West and Equatorial African colonies. In addition the Allies were able to blockade the undefended ports of Duala and Victoria and deny them to German warships. Victoria was served by a railway that in 1914 was being extended north and east.

The strategic plan of Ebermeier, the German governor, was to abandon the coastal ports and to defend the interior of the colony from a base at Ngaundere in the southern central plateau region, his idea being to retain some control of Kamerun until the end of what was expected to be a short and successful European conflict. To defend the colony he established a centralized military administration over the economy with food rationing and the local manufacture of ammunition. However, by early 1915 the shortage of munitions became a serious problem that hampered German military action. The Allies expected that Africans would not support the Germans but although there was some resistance, quickly suppressed, most people stayed loyal, particularly the Beti. In all the colonies there were rebellions and resistance to the recruiting of carriers that tied down troops required for the campaign.[9]

The war in Kamerun began with French independent military assaults from the southeast and south conducted by General Aymerich with the purpose of regaining the territory ceded in 1911. The Belgians, who had failed to keep the Congo neutral, eventually assisted in the assault from the southeast. The newly acquired German territory was very lightly defended and here the French made good progress. However, in the south, to the east of Rio Muni, the Germans were able to repel two French columns. The British had five columns advancing from Nigeria, three in the north, one intent on seizing the German stronghold at Garua, while the Cross River column in the south aimed at the northern railway. The most southerly part of the Nigeria–Kamerun border was river and swamp, difficult terrain for military operations. The German military response in the north even made slight incursions into Nigeria (and the Emir of Yola fled his capital), which put the British on the defensive. In the south the Cross River column was more successful, crossed the border and took the town of Nsamaking on September 6.

Plans for a seaborne attack on Kamerun took time to organize: Togo had to be conquered, and men and ships had to be assembled. By the end of September a joint British and French naval and military expeditionary force, commanded by Brigadier-General Dobell, arrived off Victoria and Duala. Both towns fell without military action. In the north a French force from Chad eventually succeeded in capturing Kusseri. Dobell had achieved the primary British purpose of denying the ports, particularly Duala, to German shipping and destroying the wireless station. He hoped that control over the coastal towns would lead to internal unrest to the disadvantage of the Germans. As the French columns slowly penetrated from the southeast, Dobell's force seized towns along both railway lines in an attempt to eliminate German resistance and strengthen the Allied hold on Duala.

At the end of 1914 the Germans had lost the coastal towns and much of the territory ceded in 1911. But they continued to hold onto the fortified garrisons in the northern plateau region and much of the south of the colony including, importantly, the area along the border with Spanish Rio Muni. Zimmerman, the German commander, was able to recruit additional troops for the *Schütztruppen*, although within a few months he was to face a serious shortage of munitions. Dobell's forces were reduced and, desperately in need of reinforcements, he was forced to retreat to a defensive position. Communications between the French and British and between the different columns was poor, as was local intelligence and knowledge of the area over which they were fighting. Policy required liaison between London and Paris, while French operations lacked sufficient porters and command was "divided over three governments (including the Belgians), four governors-general, six independent commanders-in-chief, and eight column commanders."[10] And for the British in the early stages of the war, both in the Kamerun and East African operations, conflicting views of the Colonial and the Foreign Offices, and Admiralty, hindered the implementation of policy.

It was agreed in early February 1915 that the advance from Duala would join up with the French columns from the south and the southeast. Dobell received additional troops, including an unreliable Indian battalion. By June 1915 the French forward movement in the south had been stalled, although that from the southeast was more successful. Garua and Ngaundere on the northern plateau fell to the British in June 1915. However, lack of French-British cooperation, plus the onset of the rains, allowed the Germans to move their defenses south to Jaunde. The German aim was to keep open access to the border with Rio Muni. That path was threatened when a French column crossed the Ntem River in mid-December. Low on ammunition, the Germans abandoned Jaunde and retreated south as British and French forces met on the Sanaga River in early January 1916. The Allies failed to close the route to Rio Muni and in mid-February a German force of 15,000 soldiers, porters, and followers crossed into neutral Spanish territory. At the same time the isolated German forts in the north surrendered.

South West Africa

German South West Africa lay northwest of the recently formed Union of South Africa and had a northern border with the Portuguese colony of Angola, to the east were British colonies, while on the coast was the small enclave of Walvis Bay. South West Africa had a long Atlantic coastline, much of it desert; large areas of the south and east were also barren, while the north was more fertile. There were 15,000 German settlers, mainly pastoral farmers, miners, and traders, and a relatively small indigenous population, depleted following the harsh suppression of the Herero rising of 1904–5. The colony had a good railway system that ran north–south and linked the interior to the two major ports of Swakopmund and Lüderitz, vital for imports of foodstuffs. German defense forces were small, composed of 2,000 white *Schütztruppen* and 480 police, although wartime enlistment produced a further 3,000 settlers as recruits. Africans were not recruited for the military, and given the recent troubled state of the colony, the defense force was scattered in small units in order to protect settlers. The military had some artillery and machine guns, and three aircraft, but lacked an effective system of central command. For political and strategic reasons German policy in event of war was not to attack South Africa but to defend the colony and await victory in Europe.[11]

The campaign to conquer German South West Africa was undertaken by South African forces with some initial help from the Royal Navy. Unlike the other wartime campaigns in Africa this was largely a "white man's war," although non-European labor was employed. It was also a war of mobility, increased by the German tactic of giving ground rather than fighting, which meant that there were relatively few casualties. By an Act of 1912 South Africa had a white Defence Force of 2,000 men, mainly mounted rifles plus artillery, while a citizen force could be conscripted in event of emergency. However, the army lacked a central staff and command structure, had no war plans, and a poor system of communications. The decision of the South African parliament to support Britain against Germany in August 1914 compounded further the deep antagonism of many Afrikaner republicans toward Britons that had not been resolved by the grant of Union in 1910. In 1914–15 a Boer revolt, involving units of the Defence Force, briefly diverted the authorities from the prosecution of the war against German South West Africa. The other incipient threat from a militant white working class failed to materialize; in 1914 the organized "left," as generally elsewhere, supported the "national" war effort. The spokesmen for the large nonwhite majority that outnumbered Europeans four to one overwhelmingly supported the war effort.[12]

The British primary aim was to seize the German harbors and destroy the wireless stations at Swakopmund and Windhoek. South African initial strategy rested on a three-pronged attack involving forces A, B, and C. Forces A and B, a total of 500 rifles and 14 guns, would cross the Orange River from the Cape and support each other in an invasion of the southern part of the German colony. Meanwhile force C would attack the port of Lüderitz from the sea. The war began badly for South Africa. An advance unit of

300 men from force A crossed the Orange and was totally defeated at Sandfontein on September 26; one week later the Boer commander of force B at Upington rebelled. The rebellion was poorly planned and lacked coordination. It enabled Jan Smuts, the Defense Minister, to declare martial law and to introduce conscription, so that by early 1915 South Africa had 70,000 men under arms, all white, with 43,000 involved in South West Africa. The Germans, handicapped by the death of three commanders, also faced a series of clashes with Portuguese troops on the Angola border. Although Portugal did not formally enter the war on the Allied side until March 1916, Lisbon was highly suspicious of Germany's *Mittelafrika* ambitions that, if successful, would have been at the expense of her East and West African colonies.

In the face of British naval guns the German forces withdrew from Lüderitz on September 19, destroying the railway as they went. On Christmas Day South African forces landed at Walvis Bay, by which time the Germans had built up a western line of defense 80 km inland along the northern railway at Usakos and also concentrated their southern defenses at Aus. In mid-January 1915 the South Africans occupied Swakopmund unopposed, although the Germans destroyed the railway as they retreated inland.

By February 1915 the Afrikaner rebellion had been crushed with the use of Boer troops, and General Botha, the South African premier, set about conciliating the rebels, although there were more South African casualties as a result of the rising than from the war in South West Africa. Botha was also planning coordinated attacks in the north and from the south to end German resistance. He assumed command at Swakopmund and thought that a swift mounted advance on Windhoek would prove decisive by severing German control of the north–south railway. In this he underestimated the transport and supply needs of his column. Water and food were in short supply, and the light railway was only slowly being rebuilt in the standard gauge used in South Africa. The Germans constructed an inadequate defensive line at Jakalswater-Riet, which the South Africans overwhelmed on March 20. Botha's further progress was held up by shortages of water and food for his animals, and he had to withdraw to Swakopmund, thus allowing the Germans a line of retreat to the east and north.

In the south Smuts eventually had command of columns advancing north from Upington and from Lüderitz in the west, although the presence of a defense minister in the field caused problems. The southern campaign was supported by 30,000 African and colored laborers. A third force invaded the German colony from the east, across the Kalahari Desert, a movement intended to split the German forces and confine them to the north of the colony. This plan generally succeeded. German response was hindered by a shortage of oxen and wagons that reduced mobility and the supply of artillery ammunition. They abandoned Aus in late March and South African troops took the rail junction of Kalkfontein on April 5, 1915. The Kalahari force, using motor trucks to transport advance water supplies, crossed the frontier on March 31. German morale was waning and no attempt was made to establish a southern line of defense at the Karas Mountains. The Germans retreated north, abandoning Keetmanshoof on April 19. Although the German commander, von Kleist, underestimated the speed of the South African advance, and was attacked at Gibeon, nevertheless despite losses he was able to elude his pursuers and continue his withdrawal. A new railway line was being built from Prieska in the Cape into South West Africa, but this was not open to traffic until November 1915, and the South African pursuit of the Germans was hindered by shortage of mounts and draft animals as well as of water and food. The German defeat at Gibeon encouraged the Bastard people to revolt, forcing German forces to be diverted to defend isolated settlers.

Von Kleist's weakened army continued to retreat north, avoiding Windhoek and eventually joining up with German forces near Otavi.

In early May 1915 the South Africans entered the railway junction town of Karabib to find its vital water supplies intact. A week later Windhoek, with its wireless station, was occupied and the rebuilt railway to Swakopmund opened. Botha took a breathing space to assemble animals and supplies for what he rightly hoped would be the final operations to defeat the Germans. On June 18 Botha began his advance north with 13,000 men, 30,000 animals, and the help of six aircraft used for reconnaissance. He divided his force into four columns, two following the line of rail and the others flanking to the east and west. The rapidity of Botha's advance surprised the retreating Germans, who had failed to prepare adequate defenses at Otavi. The retreat continued and German morale sank. The aim of the German governor, Theodor Seitz, was to hold onto an area of the colony for as long as possible, not only to tie down South African forces but to secure an armistice and to ensure that Germany maintained a claim to the colony. On July 9, 1915 he succeeded in getting South Africa to agree to an armistice which allowed German reservists to return to their homes and for the civil administration to be maintained. This fitted well with Botha's agenda for the future of South West Africa incorporated into the Union. South African troops had conquered the territory, the railway system had been integrated, and Boers were encouraged to join Germans as settlers in the colony.

The War in East Africa

On November 25, 1918 a long straggling column of German *askari* (indigenous East African soldiers), accompanied by porters and women, surrendered to the British at Abercorn in Northern Rhodesia. The war in East Africa, which seriously affected all the surrounding colonies, had involved mainly colonial troops supplied by Britain, India, Belgium, South Africa, and Portugal. General Lettow-Vorbeck had kept his fighting force intact, but in pursuing a long drawn-out war that served to tie down Allied troops he had harshly exploited Germany's tropical colony by using it "as a mere battlefield."[13] The war brought sustained suffering to the peoples of East and Central Africa.

The Germans had conquered their East African colony by numerous punitive expeditions since 1889. In 1905–6 they had suppressed the serious *Maji Maji* rising in the south. The small German population of 5,500, mainly planters, feared unrest from an indigenous population that outnumbered them a thousand times, yet surprisingly few rebellions against German rule occurred during the war years. Two main railway lines served the colony, from Tanga to Moshi in the north, and the recently completed central line linking the capital Dar es Salaam, on the Indian Ocean, to Kigoma on Lake Tanganyika. Internal security and territorial defense rested with the *Schütztruppen* of 218 Europeans and 2,542 *Askaris*, and 1,600 white reservists, plus a police force of 55 European officers and 2,160 Africans, although police integration with the military was not completed until 1917. Armed with older rifles, machine guns and a few artillery pieces, the *Schütztruppen* had developed skills in bush warfare during punitive campaigns that were to prove useful in the guerrilla campaigns of late 1917–18. It also had a higher ratio of white officers and NCOs than the colonial armies against which it fought. All the colonial powers had gunboats on the large lakes of central Africa. The light cruiser *Königsberg* was stationed at Dar es Salaam but when war was declared it went to sea to avoid a British blockade, briefly raiding shipping and hiding in the Rufiji delta until detected and sunk in July 1915. The Germans salvaged some of the guns and reused them as artillery pieces.

Britain's defense of its East and Central African colonies, with their small settler populations, depended on the locally recruited, three battalion-strong King's African Rifles (KAR) of 62 white officers and 2,319 men. One battalion each was stationed in Kenya, Uganda, and Nyasaland. The Belgian *Force publique*, although engaged in operations in Kamerun, nevertheless in 1914 had 7,000–8,000 men available for an invasion of East Africa. Britain's major concern was to protect shipping in the Indian Ocean and to deprive Germany of its East African ports and wireless stations. Thus the Royal Navy was a vital element in East African defense.

When war was declared the German governor, Heinrich Schnee, attempted to have Dar es Salaam and the port of Tanga declared open towns. Lettow-Vorbeck, the newly arrived German commander, was more bellicose.[14] The British ignored the idea of neutrality and bombarded Dar es Salaam. In accordance with their defense plans the Germans destroyed the wireless station, abandoned the coast, and withdrew inland. Schnee was cautious but Lettow-Vorbeck attacked and captured Taveta just within Kenya on August 15, and then hit at the strategic Uganda railway that cut through the middle of the British colony. The first stage of the war lasted from August 1914 to January 1916. It was marked by Lettow-Vorbeck's view that the campaign could be fought in a conventional way. He moved troops from the central railway to the north in preparation for an offensive against Kenya. They were conveniently placed to repel the landing at Tanga, but used at great cost and with limited purpose in the attack on Jasin in January 1915.[15]

British strategy was to use Indian troops to secure a bridgehead at Tanga, and then to invade from Kenya in order to seize control of the northern railway. An Indian Expeditionary Force was hastily assembled. It was poorly equipped, unfamiliar with bush warfare, and many of the men were seasick when they arrived off Tanga in early November 1914. The attack failed, with British ships and artillery unable to provide adequate protective fire. Lettow-Vorbeck brought reinforcements down from Moshi. His *Schütztruppen* were outnumbered but their Indian opponents were badly led, disorientated, and exhausted, and they were forced to evacuate.[16] The defeat of the Indians at Tanga raised the morale of the German *Askari* whom Lettow now began to use in small units for raids on the Uganda Railway.

At the start of 1915 the Belgians proposed a two-pronged attack on the German colony from the west. Brussels had territorial ambitions, especially in Ruanda and Urundi, and planned to end German domination of Lake Tanganyika. The Belgian plan was for a thrust into Ruanda-Urundi while a second British-Belgian attack came from Northern Rhodesia. Neither occurred as planned due to incomplete supply arrangements, but they posed a threat to the Germans. The British had control of Lake Victoria and, in June 1915, they were able to attack Bukoba and destroy its wireless station before withdrawing. Lettow was defending on many fronts, but in mid-1915 the area that concerned him most was the security of the west of the colony, particularly the wheat-producing area in the southwest highlands, the lake port of Kigoma at the end of the central railway, and navigation on Lake Tanganyika. To meet the threat the Germans attacked into Northern Rhodesia in May and July, both invasions being repelled, but serving to stalemate the Belgians. Toward the end of the year the German position had been strengthened. A relief ship had broken through the Royal Navy's coastal blockade and succeeded in landing much needed ammunition; a year later another ship delivered further supplies.

Careful management of the economy and the currency helped to maintain food supplies and enable troops to be fed and paid. Good military medical services, and successful control of malaria, ensured that the *Schütztruppen* were relatively healthy. Recruiting continued and by December 1915 Lettow's command had over 3,000 Europeans and 12,100 *Askaris*. This ratio of white to black troops, considerably higher than in the opposing colonial armies, made it more effective and also helped to reinforce German control.

To protect his northern front, Lettow, in October 1915, began assembling a force to attack the Belgian supply depots in the northwest. Since May his forces had also been attacking the Uganda railway and the line being built by the British from Voi to Taveta. His objective was to cut the main British rail link from the port of Mombasa to Nairobi. These operations, as Strachan says, indicated that Lettow was pursuing conventional and not guerrilla warfare.[17] The northern plan, involving half of Lettow's total force, was only finally cancelled when news reached the Germans in 1916 that South Africa was sending 25,000 troops to East Africa, Portugal had entered the war, and that South West Africa had fallen. By early 1916 the Germans and British were fighting each other in the Kilimanjaro area.

The British plan, conceived by General Smith-Dorrien for mid-1916, was a main offensive to smash German resistance on the northern railway, accompanied by a Belgian attack from the northwest, a British assault from the southwest, and a landing at Dar es Salaam. Smith-Dorrien fell sick and was replaced by the South African General Smuts. Intellectual ability did not compensate for Smuts's lack of real experience of command. His agenda was partly political, to advance South African expansionism. German East Africa would be conquered, mainly by South African troops, the Union surrendering to Portugal the southern region in exchange for the important port of Delagoa Bay in Mozambique. The use of South African troops conflicted with the views of the War Office, which wanted them for the major European campaigns, and preferred to use Africans to complete the fighting in East Africa.[18]

Smuts reordered his staff, appointing men as inexperienced as himself to positions of command. His strategy in many ways was similar to that of his predecessor. He would strike south from Kenya against the Germans, trying to avoid unnecessary casualties; he would outmaneuver not outfight Lettow, argues Strachan.[19] Smuts's experience led him to underestimate the enormous logistical problems involved: the unmapped terrain, difficult field communications, and lengthy carrier-borne supply lines. In the fierce fighting around Kilimanjaro, the British broke through to take Moshi but failed to envelop and decisively defeat the Germans. Intent on protecting the railway, the Germans retreated southward in two columns during heavy rains, one to take up a defensive position in the Pare Mountains, the other toward Kondoa Irangi. While this was happening the Belgians advanced into Ruanda and Urundi, a British column under Northey invaded the southwest from Northern Rhodesia, and Portugal entered the war. These separate operations were ill-coordinated, lacking a joint command and even effective communications. But Smuts, with his eye on the future of the territory, was determined to try and reach the central railway line before the Belgians.

Van Deventer's force pursued the Germans to Lol Kisali and then on to Tabora, the new German capital. Kondoa Irangi was reached on April 19, 1916. Three weeks later the Germans suffered heavy losses in an attack on the town. Meanwhile, Smuts advanced in three columns along the northern railway and down the Pangani valley to clear the enemy from the Pare Mountains. The Germans staged a fighting retreat to Handeni and the

Nguru Mountains. Smuts took Tanga on July 7. Smuts's purpose now was to advance toward the central railway in two columns and trap the Germans between Morogoro and Dodoma. However, Deventer was held up by problems of supply and health and only reached the railway by the end of July. By mid-August he was moving east along the line to Kilosa. Lettow, damaged at Kondoa Irangi, moved southeast to the Nguru Mountains, which he reached in late June. From there he staged an ordered retreat south across the central railway and toward Mahenge. Lettow used to good advantage the rugged Uluguru Mountains to check the British advance and then crossed the Mgeta River to secure a stronger defensive position. However, the Allied advance had succeeded in separating the Germans from Wahle's 2,000 *Askari* at Tabora. On September 3 Smuts took Dar es Salaam, but believing the war was now almost finished, he failed to use the port's facilities to the best advantage. Other coastal ports were also captured; by November 1916 the central railway was open for light traffic to Morogoro.

In the west, German control of Lake Tanganyika was dented by the British use of two gunboats sent by rail, and hauled, from the Cape. This made it easier for the 12,000-strong Belgian *Force publique* to operate. The Belgians advanced in three columns from Lake Kivu, the Russissi River, and along the western shore of Lake Tanganyika, their progress slowed by lack of porters for their supply lines. African soldiers were expected to live off the land. The movement was largely designed to secure territory rather than to fight. However, the Belgians had to fight to gain Ruanda in May and Urundi by the end of June 1916. A British force crossed Lake Victoria to take Mwanza on July 14, and by the end of August it had taken Shinyanga. The Belgians gained control of the end of the central line and by the end of July Lake Tanganyika was in Allied hands. As the Belgians advanced east along the railway line so the Germans abandoned Tabora and trekked east toward Iringa to join Lettow's forces. From the southwest Northey's column invested Neu Langenburg; he captured Iringa in late August but his troops were stretched and vulnerable, guarding a vast area of the German colony. Wahle with his *Askari* joined Lettow in Mahenge in early November.

In 1916–17 there were several changes of British commander. Smuts had been included in the Imperial War Cabinet and his place taken in January 1917 by Hoskins who, within four months, was relieved of command and replaced by Deventer, another South African. Smuts argued that the war in East Africa was almost ended. White troops were required for other theaters and from mid 1916 the fighting in East Africa was increasingly left to African troops. The KAR was expanded. Recruits took time to train but by the end of the war the regiment numbered over 35,000 men. With the end of the Kamerun campaign, West African troops from the Gold Coast and Nigeria, along with porters, were sent to East Africa.

As Lettow's forces in three columns retreated south they entered an area suffering from famine and where German repression of the *Maji Maji* revolt had deeply scarred the people. Portugal also entered the war, seizing the Kionga triangle. Both Britain and South Africa wanted to exclude Portugal from the East African operations. Besides the political implications, the badly led and ill-disciplined Portuguese army was more hindrance than help, clearly demonstrated by a disastrous incursion into the German colony in October. The British advanced from Kilwa to Liwali and fought a serious battle with the Germans at Kibata on December 21, 1916. One German column, commanded by Wintgens and then Naumann, broke away from the main force, turned north, and from February to October 1917 wove a path through the interior of the German colony that diverted Allied troops. Smuts's plan was to bar German access to Portuguese East

Africa by advancing inland from Kilwa and Lindi. In the second half of 1917 there were frequent engagements fought in the southeast region, including two sizeable battles, at Narangomba in July, and then the final sustained battle of the whole campaign at Mahiwa, in which both sides suffered heavy casualties.

Lettow crossed the Ruvumu River into Portuguese East Africa on November 25, 1917. He left behind the sick and wounded, and many women and children, reducing his force to 300 Europeans and 1,700 *Askaris*. Over the next year his reduced army retreated, pillaged the land, and as far as possible avoided direct contact. The British and South Africans pursued, landing troops at two Mozambique ports. Their Portuguese allies were useless and in any case preoccupied by the Makombe revolt that began in March 1917 and lasted until the end of the year. Lettow continued to believe that his resistance served German interests, although his major opponents were now African, not European, troops. By mid-1918 British columns from the east and from the west joined up, but despite the Allied advantage in men and matériel the Germans were still able occasionally to inflict heavy losses. Lettow moved his column northwest toward the Livingstone Mountains, crossing the Ruvumu on September 28 and advancing to Songea, reaching Ubena in mid-October. British and Belgian forces were too scattered to prevent the Germans crossing the border into Northern Rhodesia. Letttow finally surrendered when he heard of the Armistice in Europe.

During the four and half years of fighting a numerically smaller German colonial army had tied down 160,000 British and Belgian troops and also naval forces. The fighting had been conducted over some appalling terrain that made movement difficult for men, animals, and trucks. Disease killed and disabled both men and animals. For much of the latter part of the war soldiers and especially porters endured meager rations of food. Over one million porters were enlisted or forcibly conscripted from all the colonies of East and Central Africa. Nyasaland alone supplied 200,000 porters, while Northern Rhodesia between April 1915 and March 1917 produced 230,000. The suffering was immense; often neglected, some even died of starvation. Total British loss of troops exceeded 10,000, with twice the number dying of disease as were killed in action. But the harshest imperial exploitation hit the hapless peoples of East Africa. Over 100,000 porters died, belatedly acknowledged in London as a "scandal."[20] Thousands of other civilians suffered from the effects of famine and disease, the high death rate compounded by the influenza pandemic of late 1918.

* * *

To the Allied victors fell the spoils in what has been termed the "second partition of Africa." Possession by military conquest largely determined who kept what, decisions being mainly thrashed out bilaterally between the dominant imperial powers. Control over the conquered colonies was mandated by the newly created League of Nations, thus, for the first time, introducing a limited element of international trusteeship in colonial Africa. Britain's eye was on controlling German East Africa and therefore she was prepared to concede most of Togo and Kamerun to France. South Africa, having conquered German South West Africa, gained control of the territory which was then steadily integrated as a fifth province of the Union. However, there was to be no tradeoff with Portugal, and South Africa's sub-imperial ambitions north of the Limpopo were not realized. Portugal retained her colonies and even gained the Kionga triangle. Britain secured most of Tanganyika, thus completing an all-red route from Cape to Cairo, while the Belgians were granted, as they had planned, the densely populated area of Ruanda-Urundi.

Notes

1 Roberts, *Cambridge History of Africa*, vol. 7, is the best account of colonial Africa.
2 See the essays in Killingray and Omissi, *Guardians of Empire*.
3 Mangin, *La force noire*.
4 Echenberg, *Colonial Conscripts*, ch. 2; Lunn, *Memoirs of the Maelstrom*, pp. 140ff.
5 Hodges, *Carrier Corps*, ch. 9. See also Page, *The Chiwaya* War, and the essays in Page, *Africa and the First World War*.
6 Grove, "First shots of the Great War," pp. 308–23.
7 Michel, *L'Appel à L'Afrique*, ch. 5.
8 Willan, "South African Native Labour Corps."
9 Mentzel, *Die Kampfe in Kamerun*, is the most authoritative account of the campaign.
10 Strachan, *First World War*, p. 528.
11 Hennig, *Deutsch-Sudwest in Weltkriege*, is a well-informed account.
12 Davenport and Saunders, *South Africa*, ch. 10.
13 Iliffe, *Modern History of Tanganyika*, p. 241. See also the comments by Ludwig Deppe, a German doctor who accompanied Lettow's force throughout the campaign, quoted by Strachan, *First World War*, p. 571.
14 See Lettow-Vorbeck, *My Reminiscences of East Africa*, and Schnee, *Deutsch-Ostafrika im Weltkriege*, two important accounts of German policies and campaigns.
15 Anderson, *Forgotten Front*, and Paice, *Tip and Run*, offer the most up-to-date account. See also Boell, *Operationen in Ostafrika* and Miller, *Battle for the Bundu*.
16 Anderson, *Tanga*.
17 Strachan, *First World War*, pp. 597–8; see also pp. 569–70.
18 This is dealt with by Samson, *Britain, South Africa and the East African Campaign*.
19 Strachan, *First World War*, p. 610.
20 National Archives (Kew), CO820/17/22719, May 19, 1934.

References and Further Reading

Anderson, Ross, *The Battle of Tanga 1914*, Stroud, Tempus, 2002.
Anderson, Ross, *The Forgotten Front: the East African Campaign 1914–1918*, Stroud, Tempus, 2004.
Aymerich, Joseph, *La Conquête du Cameroun 1er août 1914–20 février 1916*, Paris, Payot, 1933.
Boell, Ludwig, *Die Operationen in Ostafrika*, Hamburg, Walter Dachert, 1951.
Collyer, J. J., *The Campaign in German South West Africa 1914–1918*, Pretoria, Government Printer, 1937.
Davenport, Thomas R. H., and Saunders, Christopher, *South Africa: A Modern History*, London, Macmillan, new ed., 2004.
Echenberg, Myron, *Colonial Conscripts. The Tirailleurs Sénégalais in French West Africa, 1857–1960*, London, James Currey, 1991.
Fendall, Charles Pears, *The East African Force 1915–1918*, London, Witherby, 1921.
Fogarty, Richard S., *Race & War in France: Colonial Subjects in the French Army, 1914–1918*, Baltimore, Johns Hopkins University Press, 2008.
Frémaux, Jacques, *Les Colonies dans la Grande Guerre. Combats et épreuves des peuples d'outre-mer*, Paris, Soteca, 2006.
Gorges, Edmond Howard, *The Great War in West Africa*, London, Hutchinson, 1930.
Grove, E. J., "The First Shots of the Great War: the Anglo-French Conquest of Togo, 1914," *Army Quarterly*, 106, 1976, pp. 308–23.
Haywood, Austin, and Clarke, Frederick, *The History of the Royal West African Frontier Force*, Aldershot, Gale and Polden, 1964.
Hennig, Richard, *Deutsch-Südwest im Weltkriege*, Berlin, Süsserot, 1920.

Hodges, Geoffrey, *The Carrier Corps. Military Labor in the East African Campaign, 1914–1918*, Westport, CT, Greenwood Press, 1986.

Iliffe, John, *A Modern History of Tanganyika*, Cambridge, Cambridge University Press, 1979.

Journal of African History, 19/1, 1978 (special issue on "World War I and Africa").

Killingray, David, and Matthews, James K., "'Beasts of Burden': British West African Carriers in the First World War," *Canadian Journal of African Studies*, 12, 1979, pp. 5–23.

Killingray, David, and Omissi, David (eds.), *Guardians of Empire*, Manchester, Manchester University Press, 1999.

Lettow-Vorbeck, Paul von, *My Reminiscences of East Africa*, London, Hurst and Blackett, 1920.

Lucas, Charles, *The Empire at War, vol. 4, Africa*, London, Oxford University Press, 1925.

Lunn, Joe, *Memoirs of the Maelstrom: A Senegalese Oral History of the First World War*, Oxford, James Currey, 1999.

Mangin, Charles, *La Force Noire*, Paris, Hachette, 1910.

Mentzel, Heinrich, *Die Kämpfe in Kamerun 1914–1916. Vorebeitung und Verlauf*, Berlin, Junker und Dünnhaupt, 1936.

Michel, Marc, *L'Appel à L'Afrique. Contributions et réactions à l'effort de guerre en A.O.F. 1914–1919*, Paris, Publications de la Sorbonne, 1982; rev. ed., *Les Africains et la Grande Guerre. L'appel à l'Afrique (1914–1918)*, Paris, Editions Karthala, 2003.

Miller, Charles, *Battle for the Bundu. The First World War in East Africa*, London, Macdonald and James, 1974.

Moyse-Bartlett, Hubert, *The King's African Rifles: A Study in the Military History of East and Central Africa, 1890–1945*, Aldershot, Gale and Polden, 1956.

Page, Melvin E. (ed.), *Africa and the First World War*, Basingstoke, Macmillan, 1987.

Page, Melvin E., *The Chiwaya War: Malawians and the First World War*, Boulder, CO, Westview Press, 2000.

Paice, Edward, *Tip and Run: The Untold Tragedy of the Great War in Africa*, London, Weidenfeld and Nicolson, 2007.

Parsons, Timothy H., *The African Rank-and-File. Social Implications of Colonial Military Service in the King's African Rifles, 1902–1964*, Oxford, James Currey, 1999.

Roberts, A. D. (ed.), *Cambridge History of Africa*, vol. 7, *From 1905 to 1940*, Cambridge, Cambridge University Press, 1986.

Samson, Anne, *Britain, South Africa and the East African Campaign: The Union Comes of Age, 1914–1918*, London, I. B. Tauris, 2005.

Schnee, Heinrich, *Deutsch-Ostafrika im Weltkriege: wie wir lebten und kämpften*, Leipzig, Quelle und Meyer, 1919.

Shaw, B. P., "*Force Publique*, Force Unique: the military in the Belgian Congo, 1914–1939," PhD thesis, University of Wisconsin-Madison, 1984.

Strachan, Hew, *The First World War in Africa*, Oxford, Oxford University Press, 2004.

Willan, B. P., "The South African Native Labour Contingent, 1916–1918," *Journal of African History*, 19/1, 1978, pp. 61–86.

Zirkel, K., "Military Power in German Colonial Policy: the *Schutztruppen* and their Leaders in East and South-West Africa, 1888–1918," in Killingray and Omissi (eds.), *Guardians of Empire*, pp. 91–113.

CHAPTER NINE

War in the West, 1917–18

ROBIN PRIOR AND TREVOR WILSON

The years 1917 and 1918 on the western front differ markedly from each other. In 1917, the Germans stood on the defensive in the West and held off first the French assault on the Chemin des Dames and then the British offensive out of the Ypres salient. By and large their endeavors were successful. While sustaining heavy casualties, they inflicted greater losses on their adversaries, reducing the French army to mutiny and profoundly damaging the morale of the British army. And the small areas of French and Belgian territory that they were forced to concede possessed no great significance.[1]

In 1918, the saga was very different.[2] The German command, following the disintegration of Russia, concluded that the moment was at hand to assert supremacy in the West, primarily by driving the forces of Britain across the territory of northern France and into the sea. The capitulation of France, they assumed, would promptly follow. Ultimately, this proved an all-round miscalculation. Despite early successes against the British in March and April, these German endeavors were brought decisively to a standstill. So the German command between May and July was obliged to turn its attentions southward against the French. This initially proved to their advantage, bringing them (as in 1914) across the Marne River and within range of Paris. Yet it did not destroy the French army or capture territory of clear strategic significance.

Then in July–August 1918, first the French and then the British counterattacked. Their purpose was not to accomplish large objectives, such as they had sought after in their great offensives of 1917 (the Chemin des Dames and Third Ypres), nor those for which the German army had striven in the first half of 1918. The only serious objective of first the French and then (yet more compellingly) of the British was to halt the Germans' onrush and push them back from sensitive objectives like the Channel ports and Amiens and Paris. Yet in the very year when confidence in an early victory was at its lowest ebb, the Allied counterattack proved sufficient. The rupture of the German front (which the allies had previously attempted in all their great offensives) was not accomplished, and the forces of Germany still stood exclusively on the territory of their enemies. Yet the experience of constant retreat before unrelenting opponents and unquenchable firepower proved beyond German endurance. With not an Allied troop present on their soil, the leaders of Germany called off the war.

Germany in 1917

These are puzzling events, and have been the subject of many interpretations, some of them complementary, others plainly contradictory. It is necessary to look at each year separately and in detail.

On the western front, Germany spent 1917 in a defensive posture. It had attacked there savagely in 1914 and in the first half of 1916, hoping for a definitive victory, and then again at Verdun in 1916, with the aim of bleeding the French army white and forcing it to sue for peace. Both offensives had failed. Although in 1914 the Germans had overrun fair chunks of Belgium and France, and in 1916 had killed many French soldiers, these were not enough. The western front was the preeminent battlefield of World War I, and only compelling victory there would be decisive. Germany had not accomplished this as 1917 dawned.

In effect, the German military and the German state were now ruled by Hindenburg and Ludendorff.[3] Falkenhayn, their predecessor, had been undermined by his lack of clear success at Verdun, by the pressure of the Allied offensive on the Somme, and by some (briefly threatening) events on the eastern front. In August 1916 the Kaiser, much against his will, had sacked him. Up to that time Hindenburg and Ludendorff had commanded on the eastern front, imposing harsh defeats on the Russians and helping to rescue Germany's enfeebled ally, Austria-Hungary. They had no enthusiasm – at this stage of the war, at least – for Falkenhayn's Western orientation, and during 1917 opted for a defensive posture in the West and an only partially active policy in the East. Their main strategies during this twelve-month period were threefold: a devoted attempt to mobilize the home front for an eventual supreme effort, fierce resistance to first the French at Chemin des Dames and then the British at Third Ypres, and a ruthless attempt to knock Britain out of the war by an all-out assault on merchant shipping – neutral as well as British – that was serving the United Kingdom.

These programs bore decidedly mixed results. Germany suffered heavy casualties holding off the Allied offensives, but it inflicted even heavier losses upon the French and British and it prevented them from amending the strategic situation to their advantage. Mobilization on the German home front helped to find men for the army while still raising German productivity, but with some large, negative consequences (for example the construction of great factories which consumed the metals needed to produce weaponry).[4] Most disappointing for the German command was the effect of the unlimited submarine campaign, which after a few dazzling months was effectively scotched by the British fleet's adoption of convoys.[5] Indeed, the German command's policy of aggression at sea on neutral as well as on British merchant ships proved significantly counterproductive. German attacks on American vessels (intended to cost the British even more than the attack on British vessels) drove the American Congress first to sever diplomatic relations with Germany and then to declare war.

The largest German success in 1917 occurred, almost without intent, in its relations with Russia.[6] In February the Tsarist regime collapsed under the pressure of war and the weight of its own incompetence, and the Liberals in Petrograd who took power proved incapable of generating among the Russian rank and file the military activity appropriate to their combative intentions. By mid-1917 Hindenburg and Ludendorff were moving decisively against Russia's forces, and by year's end the seizure of power in Petrograd by the Bolsheviks placed the German command in an ideal position to impose a brutal peace of annexation and domination.

So by the end of 1917 the German command and people were confronting a war scarcely less baffling than before. Russia was eliminated as a fighting force and its resources beckoned, if Germany had the will and means to gather them. The defeat of Romania was helping to make good Germany's deficiency in oil. But the starvation of Britain was proving an ever-receding prospect, and the intervention of the United States was immediately aiding Germany's enemies by the provision of credit and naval assistance, as well as raising the possibility – sooner or later – of adding hugely to Allied resources of manpower. On the western front Germany had shown enormous capacity to ward off major offensives, yet this was only a device for escaping defeat, not accomplishing victory. So as 1917 drew to a close, the German command still confronted World War I's great question: what to do next?

Britain and France in 1917

For Britain and France, by contrast, 1917 provided no comparable question. On the western front, they were fighting on Belgian and French, not German, territory: that is, on land which proclaimed German aggression and, in a measure, German success. For all the talk of "alternative strategies," of which, anyway, the war presented strikingly few, no other theater represented so directly the war's fundamental purpose. The Western Allies had a quite basic purpose: to drive out the invader and to teach the compelling lesson that aggressors did not and (hopefully) would not prosper.

Already in 1915 the French had launched two great offensives in the West, with limited British assistance. And in 1916 the British, with diminished effort from the heavily burdened French, had launched an assault on the Somme. None of these endeavors had been successful. When, as 1916 ended, Lloyd George took office as the new Prime Minister in Britain, his purpose was certainly to galvanize the nation into a great war-winning enterprise. Yet he also dissented from the prevailing emphasis on the western front, and favored the direction of strategy elsewhere – preferably to an area where Britain might contribute much weaponry but only limited manpower.

This proposal made little sense. It was all too obvious that without a major Anglo-French effort in the West the war would make no progress. So Lloyd George changed tack, endorsing with enthusiasm a proposal by the new French commander-in-chief, General Nivelle. The latter proposed that indeed there should be a great western front offensive but that it should be conducted predominantly by French forces, employing Nivelle's own method of artillery-dominated attack. Lloyd George became so impressed by Nivelle and his proposal that he sought to place the British army, preferably permanently but at the very least during the Nivelle offensive, under French command.[7]

Nivelle's high hopes, which were also those of Lloyd George, failed utterly. In the British sector to the north, into which it was hoped the Germans would be driven by the French assault, the British seized Vimy Ridge dramatically on the opening day but then bogged down. On the Chemin des Dames, where Nivelle was making his own main endeavor, French forces managed to get into the German forward positions, but only because of a calculated withdrawal by the enemy. There followed the familiar slaughter of the French rank and file by well-positioned German artillery.

The disillusionment of the *poilus* was intense. Earlier, after experiencing discontent on account of the bloodbaths of Verdun and the Somme, their waning morale had been raised by Nivelle's promise of enemy slaughter, a quick victory, and a transformed war.

The gross failure that followed produced widespread outbursts of "collective indiscipline," with troops who had briefly been sent to rest in the rear refusing to return to the front. Some 50,000 soldiers actively participated in the mutinies, which became a major factor in the crisis of morale suffered by the country (see chapter 28).[8] Nivelle was promptly sacked by the French government whose doubts about his promises had preceded those of the rank and file. The command went to Pétain, a defensive, pessimistic general who had won eminence in 1916 by directing the resistance at Verdun.

These events placed the ball firmly in the hands of the British. Whatever happened next in 1917 could only be decided in London. Lloyd George's misjudgment over Nivelle had plainly humiliated him, but not in a way that gave Haig the opportunity to impose his strategy on government or politicians. Nor, to all appearances, did Haig have any inclinations to do this. If Lloyd George and the War Cabinet had decided against attempting in the West anything more than small-scale offensives toward accessible objects, then that would have settled the matter. The problem was that in this vital matter, if in few others, Lloyd George and Haig were at one. The Prime Minister, like his Commander-in-Chief, felt only disregard for discrete, limited operations. Both yearned for big offensives against substantial, war-changing objectives. Lloyd George sought diligently outside the western front for such targets. Having failed pretty comprehensively to discover any, he reluctantly concluded that he must go along with Haig.[9]

Haig's strategy was straightforward. He had long hankered after a great, predominantly British offensive out of the Ypres salient. He would strike there with his main force, and drive steadily toward the coast, joining hands in the later stages with his army on the coast and with a further army invading from across the Channel. Thereby Belgium would be cleared of the intruder, its ports and submarine bases would be wrested from German hands, and the German right flank would be turned with potentially large consequences for the entire western front.

There is no sign here, it should be noticed, of Haig's opting for a protracted battle of attrition, situated in just one place and inflicting terrible losses on the British in return for a like number of the enemy. On the contrary, Haig hankered after a major strategic victory, which in its later stages would bring three British armies into coordinated action against an outwitted and outfought opponent. His prime implement for crushing the opposition would be artillery, of which at last the British army appeared to possess ample quantities in terms of both guns and shells. In the first stages his artillery attack would be aided by a powerful set of mines diligently put in place by the British Second Army during the years it had remained motionless before its enemy. Great numbers of infantry would meanwhile be on the ready and would drive home and confirm the victory which the artillery and mines had accomplished. Tanks would be available also, as and when conditions allowed them to be used, and airpower would play a useful part in directing and observing the bombardment and keeping at bay enemy aircraft. Finally, the cavalry would surge into action, converting what otherwise would have been an orderly enemy retreat into a disorganized rout and an unquestionable Allied victory.

As a plan committed to paper, this had the appearance of promising sense. As an actuality, it was unrelieved folly. In spite of Lloyd George, its foolishness did not lie in the alternative notion that the attack should have been undertaken by other nationals, like the Italians, or in another region, such as Palestine. The British had to do the fighting at this stage of the war, as the French collapse during the Nivelle offensive had already shown and the Italian debacle at Caporetto in October 1917 would soon confirm.

And a British operation in Palestine, successful or not, would have suffered under the huge demerit that it was not engaging the only adversary who mattered.

That is, Haig's plan was not nonsense for the reasons that Lloyd George would ultimately pronounce against it. It was also not folly for the reasons alleged by many other critics of the High Command, namely that all Haig was aspiring to was a dreary, murderous battle of attrition in which no ground would change hands and each side would endure huge numbers of casualties.[10] Rather, his plan was highly ambitious, and indeed quite visionary.

These qualities are not usually associated with Douglas Haig. Indeed it is often said that he was no Napoleon, and that herein lay his problem. The truth is quite the opposite. Had Napoleon found himself commanding the battlefield in World War I, and had he sought to apply the methods of his great triumphs of the early 1800s, he would have been ridiculously out of place. Haig's plans were entirely "Napoleonic." They were thereby impossible of accomplishment in the war of 1914–18. The German defenses he was attacking were highly sophisticated, and even if in time and with enough high explosive they could be overwhelmed, this would be a limited and lengthy undertaking. While it was being accomplished, the enemy could establish further defenses to their rear which would require equally painful endeavors for their conquest. This was not remotely the context for rapid advance, breakthrough, and cavalry exploitation. All that could be hoped for was a limited advance, achieved by artillery dominance and the move forward of infantry to the distance that a high-explosive shell could travel. Thereafter the artillery must be brought forward and sighted, and the process repeated.

The difficulty created by Haig's woeful over-ambition was reinforced by the weather. Rain fell throughout the first month of the campaign, turning the battlefield into a quagmire, reducing the accuracy and impact of shellfire, and rendering particularly painful the forward movement of the infantry. With little or nothing achieved in August, Haig shifted command of the operation from General Gough, who shared his eagerness for a swift and commanding victory with his inability to devise a way of achieving it, to the Second Army commander General Plumer. The second month of the battle, September, provided good weather, and Plumer delivered some telling blows in short-objective, well-prepared actions. These have given rise to the notion that Haig–Plumer was a vastly superior combination to Haig–Gough, a notion severely called into question by the concluding six weeks of the operation in October and the first half of November. As drenching rain returned in force, the purpose of maintaining this campaign at all had now totally vanished. Yet Plumer, as much as Haig, insisted on embarking on one fruitless attack after another.[11]

The folly of this large undertaking needs to be stressed. The British and French overall sustained a weightier burden of casualties than their opponents, and the small areas of Belgium overall wrested from the Germans – bearing no relation to the large objectives Haig had earlier proclaimed – simply placed British forces in an unsustainable salient. In the outcome the pitiful gains in territory of Third Ypres had to be abandoned at speed once the Germans, in early 1918, moved to the attack. That an enemy counteroffensive would soon befall the British was evident from what was happening in the East simultaneously with the Third Battle of Ypres. The collapsing morale of the Russian army, followed by the Bolshevik seizure of power, placed it beyond doubt that the Germans would now move powerfully against their only remaining serious adversaries – those on the western front.

Seeking to redeem his melancholy achievement for 1917, Haig late in November made one last attempt to strike an unexpected blow on a quiescent part of the western

front. He employed both his artillery and his tanks – the latter having contributed virtually nothing to his battles of the year so far – against the Germans at Cambrai, which they
had come to regard as virtually a rest area.

Guns and tanks struck without warning, and although the Germans held firm in one
area the British made enough progress on either side of it for their newspapers to
announce a great victory. But it was all short-lived. A week later the Germans counterattacked and overran as much territory – usually the same territory – as they had lost.[12] For
Britons and French, the attempts to transform the war in the West in 1917 had come to
a melancholy conclusion.

The Final German Offensive, 1918

For the German high command, the situation at the end of 1917 was not without hope.
The attempt by means of the U-boat to starve Britain out of the war had plainly failed,
and had brought the United States into the conflict on the Allied side. But Germany's
rulers had warded off a succession of Allied offensives in the West, had carried out a
promising if greatly over-optimistic program of mobilization at home and were totally
victorious on the eastern front.

All this, speculatively, was the precursor to triumph in the West, and so in the war.
Ludendorff, in outlining this possibility in November, made much of the urgency of
a German triumph over the British and French in the West before American intervention could become a reality. Yet it is fair to surmise that his actions in early 1918
would have taken precisely the same form irrespective of US involvement. Other
(hypothetical) Germans might have opted instead for a powerful defensive posture
and an attempt to end the war by negotiation. But if that was an attractive alternative
for some, none of them held power – or the approaches to power – in Germany. For
Hindenburg and Ludendorff, as for all whom they represented, the war was there to
be won, not sweated out. The victory over Russia cleared the way for the next great
step: military victory over Britain and France and a total triumph on the European
continent. The moment for this (irrespective of the Americans) was plainly the
moment when first the French and then the British had drained their armies in unre-
warded endeavors.

Unlike Falkenhayn, who after declaring Britain to be Germany's main enemy had
devoted his 1916 Verdun offensive exclusively to the French, Ludendorff at this moment
was not inclined to shilly-shally. "We must beat the British," he told the crucial conference of military commanders and government dignitaries on November 11, 1917. For
that purpose he would strengthen his army against the British with forces previously
situated in Russia, form a body of exceptional soldiers drawn from his rank and file to
become "storm troopers," and provide his army at the point of attack with a devastating
accumulation of artillery. His purpose was to get his storm troops into and beyond
the British front, in coherent groups if not consistently along the front, and proceed to
the destruction of the British artillery. His target was the Third and Fifth Armies on the
southern sector of the British front to the north of the French, whom Ludendorff wanted
only to hold at bay.

On March 21, 1918, on the far right of the British line, Ludendorff's assault fell dev-
astatingly on Britain's Fifth Army commanded by the hapless General Gough.[13] Gough's
force was occupying ill-prepared territory recently handed over to it by the French, with
its lines gravely overstretched and its artillery woefully inadequate. It had small chance of

withstanding the assault which, although long expected, did not occur where it had been predicted. British morale generally had plainly been dented by 1917's saga of ill-rewarded offensives, but this particular setback was exaggerated by the Fifth Army's consciousness of insufficient artillery, poor trench protection, and general neglect.

As the Fifth Army reeled back, the Third Army on its left did not collapse nearly so decisively, but was rather dragged back by the calamity on its right and by the intensity of the German assault. The Germans in a week advanced some forty miles, a staggering achievement compared with the handful of miles accomplished by the British in the long months of the Somme in 1916 and the Third Battle of Ypres in 1917.

Yet it should be noted that the triumphant German advance in essence achieved little. The territory they captured was less than vital – an advance across the area to the rear of the Somme battlefields of 1916, a region that the Germans had devastated in early 1917 while voluntarily retreating.[14] Furthermore, the Fifth Army's breakdown was drawing Ludendorff's forces in a different direction to that which he had intended – to his army's left, in the direction of Amiens, rather than to its center and right toward the Channel, so as to threaten the whole British presence in France. Still more significantly, the great advance was proving dreadfully costly in German casualties, and particularly in storm troops, and was carrying the infantry well beyond the protection of its artillery.

On March 28 Ludendorff, unwilling to resolve these dilemmas, urged his forces forward against both their diverging objectives. They acted without regard to the limited availability of firepower, which the German infantry had now outrun. Both endeavors failed. Ludendorff, at least for the moment, called off the offensive.

In no time he would be attacking again: first further north against the British in Belgium holding important Channel ports, then southward against the French in a long advance which brought his forces across the Marne River and almost within sight of Paris. But whatever their accomplishments, these attacks did not contribute toward the goal of "beating the British" by a great engulfing movement driving Haig's forces toward the sea, and by mid-1918 they had not achieved any real strategic objective. What they had done was greatly to increase the extent of line that the Germans now occupied, thereby significantly reducing German strength in any given sector.

The Allied Counterattack, 1918

In July–August 1918, the insubstantial nature of Ludendorff's achievements was laid bare. First the French halted their retreat, and then Pétain counterattacked with some success at the second battle of the Marne on July 18, as the French Sixth and Tenth Armies advanced with cover from tanks. Then, on the now largely quiescent British front, Rawlinson's Fourth Army struck out from Amiens on August 8 with compelling initial success.[15] From that moment, the whole nature of the war changed. Despite sometimes stubborn and courageous German resistance (along with some failings of morale), the steady progress of the Allies would not cease until their adversaries abjectly surrendered.[16]

The course of events on the western front in the second half of 1918 is so out of kilter with all that had happened there in the past four years that it has ever since been a source of puzzlement. We do not have a problem up to this point. During 1914–17, the changed technology of warfare had placed so great an advantage in the hands of the defender, and the bemused responses of Joffre and Haig had been so inappropriate, that the events of these years do not appear to require complex explanation. In the first half of 1918, the supposed superiority of Hindenburg and Ludendorff in appreciating and counteracting the predominance of defense is considered sufficient to explain why deadlock gave way to breakout – if not to breakthrough. But the events in the West from mid-1918 do not accord either with the picture of inherent defensibility, or with the notion of the German command's genius in mastering and counteracting this feature.

One contrasting aspect of this last year gives us a clue. The events of the first half of 1918 will always be known as the Ludendorff offensive. That is entirely appropriate. He planned the final German effort, set its objectives, and gave it the go-ahead. By contrast, no one thinks of giving the Allied actions of the second half of 1918 the names of any commander, British or French or American. This also makes good sense. The Allied counterattacks initially took the form not of integrated parts of one person's mighty scheme but of independent actions intended to hold the Germans' assaults, regain some of the territory overrun by them, and push the line of combat further away from key targets such as Amiens. The high commands authorized these actions, overseeing them and providing the manpower and the weaponry, and sometimes they intervened to decree larger objectives and a pretended strategic purpose. But what we are actually observing is a succession of undertakings devised by army commands or corps commands or sometimes even divisional commands. These people were far more conscious of the specificity of, and even limitations upon, what they were trying to do than of any large strategic purpose.

So after initial success followed by diminished rewards at the battle of Amiens, the commander of the Canadian Corps (and others) represented to the Fourth Army commander that the attack had achieved all it could and should be closed down. Rawlinson conveyed this judgment to Haig. The latter, it should be noted, was no longer at the peak of the chain of command. He had to present this judgment to General Foch, who in March had been appointed Supreme Commander of all Allied troops in the West.[17] On a number of occasions since then, Foch had employed his authority beneficially, moving reinforcements and additional weaponry to areas under great threat or where positive action was being planned. But Haig's proposal to call off an assault that had begun so hopefully seemed another matter.

Foch proved unresponsive. He insisted that the morale of the enemy had been so damaged that another good push would entirely shatter it. Haig took this reply back to Rawlinson who inquired, near-mutinously, whether Haig or Foch commanded the British army. Haig decided that it was not Foch. He returned to the Supreme Commander and stated that he would not continue the offensive – even though it was still well short of the objectives which Haig himself, extending those of Rawlinson, had devised. If Foch ordered him to do so he would appeal to the British government. Given Lloyd George's notorious hostility to employing British forces on the western front at all, this settled the matter. Hurt, Foch replied that all he wanted was to be informed what Haig intended to do. Haig thereupon passed the responsibility back to Rawlinson, who acted on the advice of his corps commanders. For the moment, the offensive on this part of the front was called off.

This did not mean that the British army ceased to attack or that the French, Belgian, and American forces desisted from further action either. All along the western front, from Belgium in the north to the Somme (which constituted the British section), through the Aisne and Champagne (held by the French), to the Meuse-Argonne (where the Americans entered the fray alongside the French), the whole line first leaped into life, then lapsed, then became active again. Those in the north had the easier time as the Germans sought to shorten their line and fall back on more secure defenses – retiring so fast that the British were hard put to bring them to battle. But further south, German resistance stiffened and the attempt to limit the Allied advance became more determined. In the Meuse-Argonne region, late in September, the Americans launched a fierce offensive. Although costing more heavily than was needed, in part thanks to inexperienced command, this action yielded good results. Simultaneously, the French also forced the Germans back in this region and at the same time recaptured the Chemin des Dames.

Further north, in the British sector on the Somme, yet more serious progress was being achieved. This made little obvious sense. The French and Americans were striking against the German flank, and so creating the possibility of penetrating toward German lines of communication. The British, attacking the western front in an easterly direction, could accomplish nothing more than to push the Germans back on their lines of communication, with no great strategic objectives near to hand. But it was here that the Germans were determined to stand, and here that the British had to make their cumulative effort.

It was here, also, that the British and Dominion forces won their greatest victory, which was the crowning achievement of Allied troops in World War I. Although Ludendorff later dubbed the German setback at Amiens on August 8 as "the blackest day of the German army," he might well have seen it at the time as a temporary setback occasioned by surprise and poor defenses and the evident inexperience of the German defenders. His army, by a mighty effort, had previously fought its way to this point, and it planned to complete the capture of Amiens in due course. But with other endeavors in immediate demand, the German command had replaced the occupants of the positions outside Amiens by poor-quality troops while taking no action to consolidate their trenches there as a strong defensive position. It was thus not so surprising that on August 8 and the next couple of days, British, Dominion, and French troops there managed a successful advance.

But what happened thereafter was of a different order. In late August and throughout September, the British First, Third, and Fourth Armies, with the French on their right, attacked in steady succession, driving the Germans out of all the conquests of their March offensive and back to their ultimate defensive position established in March 1917, the Hindenburg Line. The first actions, between August 21 and 29, were undertaken first by the Third and Fourth Armies, then by the First. In the course of these days the British armies, although with a steadily declining complement of tanks, employed successfully the methods of August 8. In consequence they took in succession such varied objectives as the city of Albert, from which they had launched the Somme battle two years before, and the town of Bapaume, which had been a main objective of July 1, 1916 and was still in German hands when the first Somme battle had ended after four months. Most strikingly, in between these events they conquered the dominating hill of Monchy-le-Preux, employing no tanks at all but rather an unstoppable combination of massive artillery and Canadian infantry.[18]

By the end of August, the Allied advance had gone as far as Ludendorff was prepared to contemplate. Yet in bleak contrast to this powerful individual's one-time mastery of the battlefield, his diktat now counted for little. In two momentous events of middle to late September, the British carried their advance to the central and most formidable sector of the Hindenburg Line. Action here was fundamental. If successful, it would establish that German reverses were more than just the surrender of recently acquired and thinly held territory but represented a fundamental breach of the most powerful defensive positions that they possessed on the western front.

In keeping with the more realistic, which meant more modest, tactics that the British commanders were now employing, they divided their attack on the central part of the Hindenburg line into two distinct events. The expression "line" to describe this defensive system, it should be noted, is a gross understatement. It consisted of defense-works 10 miles deep, constituting six lines of trenches with acres of supporting wire and concrete strong points equipped with machine guns. Much of it was based on a canal, providing an insuperable barrier to tanks and a formidable obstacle to infantry, and it was all placed behind a ridge providing concealment from direct artillery fire. To counteract this, the British decided in the first instance to confine their efforts to action against the ridge alone. On September 18 they assaulted and captured a significant part of it. By this act they placed the most noteworthy section of the line under direct artillery observation, with canal, trenches, dugouts, artillery positions, and acres of barbed wire subject to their attack.

It was widely assumed that the northernmost sector of the area would be the most vulnerable, as here the canal ran into a tunnel so that it would be possible to employ tanks against the Germans. The Australians, with two American divisions under their command, were concentrated in this area. But the problems they encountered, and the heavy resistance confronting them, severely limited their capacity to advance. Further south, where a less-than-distinguished Midland division was to assail the open canal without tank support, matters went quite differently. The British artillery bombardment was crushing.[19] For the full eight hours of the Midland division's attack, every 500 yards of German trench received, each minute, 126 shells from the field guns alone – that is, 50,000 shells per 500 yards of defense. The Midland soldiers also were well prepared. Equipped with lifebelts and dinghies taken from Channel ferries, and assailing a waterway rendered less of an obstacle by constant bombardment, they first overwhelmed the German trenches on the near side of the canal, then crossed the water barrier, and finally breached the Hindenburg defenses proper to a depth of 6,000 yards, facilitating the Australians to their north in the process. By the time they were done, only some weak German trenches and wire stood between them and open country.

While these dramatic events provided the centerpiece of victory, the whole Allied line in the West, from the Channel coast in the north to Verdun in the south, was on the move. On the far left the Belgian army, some French divisions, and Plumer's Second Army opened on September 28 "the last battle of Ypres," overrunning in a couple of days all the territory which the British had managed to capture in the long agony of the third battle in 1917. After little more than a day, Plumer was once more in control of Messines Ridge and the Belgians had captured Passchendaele. On the far right, the French and Americans, in a district that the Germans by long preparation in a favorable region had rendered ideal for defense, set in motion a painful but ultimately rewarding offensive.

The consequences of the Allied triumph along the western front proved irresistible. There was still no prospect of an advance at such speed as to rupture the enemy's line and surround his forces, if only because of the devastated territory over which the Allies had to transport weapons and reinforcements. But their unrelenting pressure provided the Germans with no opportunity to construct another coherent defense, and forced them stage by stage to surrender one hopeful river position after another. On October 26, in the aftermath of unrelenting defeats, Ludendorff resigned. A fortnight later, without even attempting to take a stand on their last natural obstacle, the Meuse River, the German authorities called off the war and accepted terms scarcely distinguishable from unconditional surrender.

Explanations

What had happened? How had the excruciating slaughters of 1917 been converted to the brisk, onward marching of the second half of 1918? And why did the mighty blows dealt out to the Allies by the Germans in the first half of 1918 bear no permanent consequences, while the far less dramatic Allied advances of the second half proved a prelude to permanent victory?

In attempting to answer these questions, it is not usual to look to the battlefield on the western front. That front is identified with stalemate and futility. Vast offensives launched there, far from transforming the situation, had left the rival armies more or less where they had begun. If Ludendorff, the one commander regarded as possessing strategic insight, proved unable to amend this situation for long, it appeared to follow that no campaign commanded by Foch or Haig or Pétain or Pershing could have made any difference.

So in explaining why the war ended, we are urged to look elsewhere: to the success of convoys in defeating the U-boat; to the tardy entry of the United States into the war; to the grinding down of the German population by the Allied blockade; to the revolutionary tendencies in Central and Eastern Europe which, having taken Russia out of the war, then sapped the will of the German home front. Into all these gripping non-battlefield explanations, only one event on the war front of Western Europe is sometimes admitted. In 1916 the one positive achievement of the British on the western front had been unleashing the tank on their enemies. The numbers were too few, the initial instrument too crude, but at least there was a pointing forward here to how things might in time (that is, by 1918) be done better. Yet, clearly, this is no truly satisfying explanation. After all, Ludendorff had achieved breathtaking successes earlier in 1918 with no tanks at his disposal.

What is so unsatisfying about all these explanations is what is left out. And the one large dimension evidently omitted by this concentration on armored fighting vehicles, blockade-imposed starvation, American doughboys, and the spread of revolutionary influence is the Allied conduct of battle in the last five months of the war. One aspect of this is quantitative. Only in 1917 did British and Allied industry begin to produce weaponry, and especially artillery pieces and high-explosive shells, in the huge numbers required by major battles between great industrial powers.

A second, quite contrary aspect is limitation. This war was never going to produce the master-victory that ruptured enemy lines and took vast numbers of prisoners after which every one of its supposed "attritional" commanders hankered. Their mighty advances could proceed no further than a high-explosive shell would travel; and any attempt to push them further would court catastrophe. Ludendorff, in attacking the British in March 1918, never recognized this, and thereby drove his forces forward beyond the cover of their artillery and so to their destruction. Haig equally did not embrace it, which was why his reinforcement infantry in October 1918 found their way forward cluttered by thousands of useless cavalry awaiting their never-coming moment of glory. But Haig (along with Foch and Pershing) was driven to a form of recognition by the actions of immovable lower-order commanders, by the menace of political masters awaiting one major blunder to move against him, and by the glaring obviousness of what could be achieved by a well-organized infantry and tank advance shielded by overwhelming artillery protection.

Most of all, what is so often forgotten in trying to account for victory in 1918 is what skillfully employed artillery could now do. It is a long-standing myth that what imposed stalemate on the western front was the machine gun, and that what at last drove it to defeat was the tank. Both machine guns and tanks served a powerful purpose, but neither ruled. What imposed stalemate above all was the high-explosive shell, fatal alike to brave infantrymen and lumbering tanks once they left their shelters in the attempt to conquer enemy trenches. Only one thing could checkmate big guns and big shells, and that was an identical set of weaponry from the other side, fired counter-battery with a degree of accuracy and knowledge of their targets by artillerymen of huge skill and dedication. It was this combination of weaponry and skill and knowledge that, step by step, conveyed the armies of Britain, France, and their allies irresistibly forward.

The achievements of the gunners need illustration. Guns were adjusted for wear prior to each battle, so enabling them to fire on specific targets without regard to their age. Shells were sorted into separate batches according to weight, and the guns adjusted to these variations, so that all shells would descend in the same area. Gunners also made adjustments prior to battle in accord with information from the meteorologists about wind speed and temperature, so safeguarding the accuracy of their weapons against the fickleness of weather. But most crucial of all were the devices that enabled a bombardment to crash down upon the big guns of the enemy, without having first to engage in preliminary firing to establish the range. Among these devices were aerial photography, survey, flash spotting, and sound ranging.[20] With the aid of these devices, gunners who had first established their own positions could bring down fiercely accurate fire upon enemy guns whose whereabouts had already been established.

One graphic event illustrates the point. It concerns the Fourth Army's chief of artillery, who on the late afternoon of the first day of the battle of Amiens walked around a battlefield from which the enemy had fled. He knew in advance where each set of hostile guns would be situated, and took distinct satisfaction in viewing the devastation that his gunners had inflicted upon these weapons and – even more – upon the enemy personnel who had sought to employ them.

This, then, is the crux of the matter. In asking why the last half of 1918 was so unlike the second half of 1917, it is doubtless appropriate to give some attention to events beyond the battlefield, like the Allied blockade and the prospect of ultimate American intervention. But at all costs we must not disregard events on the battlefield. In circumstances where the British and French on the one side, and the Germans on the other, were desperately short of manpower (whatever may have been true of the Americans), the part played by the scale and appropriate use of weaponry was fundamental. When the Allies abandoned the attempt to win decisive victories and concentrated on conquering specific objectives lying within artillery range, they opened up the road to a steady and ongoing success. Multiple factors may have contributed to converting specific success into total victory. But without the employment of huge amounts of weaponry in magically appropriate positions, the initial step toward first limited, and then larger, victory could not have been undertaken.

Notes

1 Prior and Wilson, *Passchendaele*, pp. 25–30, 195–200; Wolff, *In Flanders Fields*, pp. 73–88, 269–87.
2 Middlebrook, *The Kaiser's Battle*, pp. 308–58; Terraine, *To Win a War*, passim.
3 Asprey, *German High Command*, pp. 253–94.
4 Gerald Feldman, *Army Industry and Labor in Germany 1914–1918*, 1966; new ed., Providence and Oxford, Berg, pt. 3, sect. 5.
5 Wilson, *Myriad Faces of War*, ch. 39.
6 Asprey, *German High Command*, pp. 355–62.
7 A. J. P. Taylor (ed.), *Lloyd George: a Diary by Frances Stevenson*, London, Hutchinson, 1971, pp. 139–50; E. L. Spears, *Prelude to Victory*, London, Cape, 1939, pp. 143ff.; Woodward, *Lloyd George and the Generals*, ch. 7.
8 Pedroncini, *Les Mutineries*, p. 63; Smith, *Between Mutiny and Obedience*, pp. 175–214.
9 Prior and Wilson, *Passchendaele*, pp. 31–42.
10 Arthur Bryant, *English Saga (1840–1940)*, London, Collins, 1940, ch. 8 ("Battle in the Mud").
11 Prior and Wilson, *Passchendaele*, pp. 159–61.
12 See Jackson Hughes, "The Monstrous Anger of the Guns," PhD thesis, University of Adelaide, 1992, pp. 217–49.
13 Middlebrook, *The Kaiser's Battle*, pp. 308–43.
14 On the establishment of the Hindenburg Line (the Siegfried Line to the Germans), see Michael Geyer, "Rückzug und Zerstörung, 1917," in Hirschfeld et al. (eds.), *Die Deutschen an der Somme*, pp. 163–78.
15 Terraine, *Western Front*, pp. 179–202.
16 Deist, "German Army, Authoritarian Nation-State," pp. 170–1.
17 For Foch's role in 1918, see Greenhalgh, *Victory through Coalition*, pp. 186–264.
18 For the decided limitation on tanks as contributors to the Allies' post-Amiens successes, see Hughes, "The Monstrous Anger of the Guns," pp. 262–4, and John Terraine, *The Smoke and the Fire*, London, Sidgwick and Jackson, 1980, pp. 148–60.
19 The best account of these dramatic events is in Hughes, "The Monstrous Anger of the Guns," ch. 8.
20 See John Innes (compiler), *Flash Spotters and Sound Rangers*, London, Allen and Unwin, 1935, pp. 15, 129ff.

References and Further Reading

Asprey, Robert, B., *The German High Command at War*, London, Warner Books, 1994.
Bourne, John, and Sheffield, Gary (eds.), *Douglas Haig: War Diaries and Letters, 1914–1918*, London, Weidenfeld and Nicolson, 2005.
Bruce, Robert B., *A Fraternity of Arms: America and France in the Great War*, Lawrence, University of Kansas Press, 2003.
Deist, Wilhelm, "Verdeckter Militär-streik im Kriegsjahr 1918," in Wolfram Wette (ed.), *Der Krieg des kleines Männes. Eine Militärgeschichte von unten*, Munich, Piper, 1992, pp. 146–67.
Deist, Wilhelm, "The German Army, the Authoritarian Nation-State and Total War," in John Horne (ed.), *State, Society and Mobilization in Europe during the First World War*, Cambridge, Cambridge University Press, 1997, pp. 160–72.
Doughty, Robert, *Pyrrhic Victory. French Strategy and Operations in the Great War*, Cambridge, MA, Harvard University Press, 2005.
Foch, Ferdinand, *The Memoirs of Marshal Foch*, 1931; translation from French, New York, Doubleday, Doran and Co., 1931.

Greenhalgh, Elizabeth, *Victory through Coalition. Politics, Command and Supply in Britain and France, 1914–1918*, Cambridge, Cambridge University Press, 2005.

Herwig, Holger, H., *The First World War: Germany and Austria-Hungary 1914–1918*, London, Arnold, 1997.

Hirschfeld, Gerhard, Krumeich, Gerd, and Renz, Irina (eds.), *Die Deutschen an der Somme, 1914– 1918. Krieg, Besatzung, Verbrannte Erde*, Essen, Klartext, 2006.

King, Jere C., *Generals and Politicians. Conflict between France's High Command, Parliament and Government 1914–1918*, Berkeley, University of California Press, 1951.

Kitchen, Martin, *The Silent Dictatorship. The Politics of the German High Command under Hindenburg and Ludendorff, 1916–1918*, London, Croom Helm, 1976.

Ludendorff, Erich, *Concise Ludendorff Memoirs*, London, Hutchinson, 1933.

Lupfer, Timothy T., *The Dynamics of Doctrine: the Changes in German Tactical Doctrine during the First World War*, Fort Leavenworth, Leavenworth Paper no. 4, 1981.

Macdonald, Lynn, *They Called it Passchendaele*, London, Macmillan, 1978.

Middlebrook, Martin, *The Kaiser's Battle*, London, Allen Lane, 1978.

Pedroncini, Guy, *Les Mutineries de 1917*, Paris, Presses Universitaires de France, 1967.

Pedroncini, Guy, *Pétain: Général en chef, 1917–1918*, Paris, Presses Universitaires de France, 1974.

Prior, Robin, and Wilson, Trevor, *Command on the Western Front. The Military Career of Sir Henry Rawlinson 1914–18*, Oxford, Blackwell, 1992.

Prior, Robin, and Wilson, Trevor, *Passchendaele: the Untold Story*, New Haven, Yale University Press, 1996.

Sheffield, Gary, *Forgotten Victory. The First World War: Myths and Realities*, London, Headline Publishing, 2001.

Smith, Leonard V., *Between Mutiny and Obedience: The Case of the French Fifth Infantry Division during World War I*, Princeton, Princeton University Press, 1994.

Smythe, Donald, *Pershing: General of the Armies*, Bloomington: Indiana University Press, 1986.

Terraine, John, *Douglas Haig: The Educated Soldier*, London, 1963; new ed., Cassell, 2000.

Terraine, John, *The Western Front 1914–18*, London, Arrow Books, 1970.

Terraine, John, *To Win a War*, London, Sidgwick and Jackson, 1978.

Travers, Tim, *How the War was Won: Command and Technology in the British Army on the Western Front 1917–1918*, London, Routledge, 1992.

Wilson, Trevor, *The Myriad Faces of War: Britain and the Great War, 1914–1918*, Cambridge, Polity Press, 1986.

Wolff, Leon, *In Flanders Fields*, London, Pan Books, 1961.

Woodward, David, R., *Lloyd George and the Generals*, East Brunswick, Associated University Presses, 1983.

CHAPTER TEN

The War at Sea

PAUL G. HALPERN

In the two decades preceding World War I rapid advance in naval technology had been a subject of major interest to many people in the great and medium powers of the world. Naval actions had played an important role in two conflicts, the Spanish-American War of 1898 and the Russo-Japanese War of 1904–5. The battles in those conflicts seem to indicate the unfortunate fate of those who did not keep up with the latest technology and fell behind in training and tactics. In the new century warships and naval weapons such as torpedoes and mines seemed to constantly grow in size and effectiveness. Naval competition between nations appeared to be one of the important factors in international relations. The Anglo-German naval competition following the German naval laws of 1898 and 1900 had been only the most striking example of this competition.[1] There were other rivalries as well with nations like Austria-Hungary, not previously associated with "bluewater" operations, joining in.[2] The Russians were in the process of rebuilding their naval strength after the disasters of 1904–5 and the United States, with perhaps an eye on Japan, joined in the construction of powerful warships. The "ABC" powers of South America – Argentina, Brazil, and Chile – all ordered dreadnoughts. The Italians and Austrians built against each other although they were nominal allies in the Triple Alliance.[3] The French, their navy retarded by technological and ideological controversies, sought to conserve a now-threatened margin of superiority over the two latter powers who were theoretically Germany's allies in the Mediterranean.[4] In the first half of 1914 a potentially explosive naval race also developed between Turkey and Greece, recent foes in the Balkan Wars of 1912–13.[5]

Changing Anticipations of Naval Warfare

The dreadnought-type battleship, with its powerful armament, relatively high speed, and extensive armor protection, seemed at the cutting edge of this competition. It appeared to be the yardstick by which navies might be measured. There were numerous periodicals and newspapers to provide accounts of the latest warship, with appropriate drawings and diagrams combined with comparative tables that seemed to be keeping score. These warships seemed to increase in size and power and by 1914 would be referred to as "super-dreadnoughts," with 15-inch instead of the original 12-inch guns and relative increases in potential speed. The public anticipated that in the event of war there would be classic battles with lines of dreadnoughts ranged against each other. Victory would go to the side with the most accurate gunnery and longest-range guns able to throw the heaviest weight of metal.

The reality behind these general perceptions was rather different. By 1914 things were not what they seemed. The naval staffs were not blind to the implications of the new technology. The devastating effects of mines during the Russo-Japanese War, the steady improvement in self-propelled torpedoes and, perhaps most important of all, the development of submarines implied that the large warship was potentially vulnerable to smaller enemies. The first submarines entered service in the Royal Navy in 1902 and by the end of the year the Admiralty had decided to order 10 per year for the next four years.[6] In the years before the war submarines participated in naval maneuvers and their potential was recognized, although at first there had been a tendency to regard them as "defensive" weapons, a type of living minefield lurking in ambush. These technological developments had major consequences. The British quietly abandoned the old concept that the front line for the navy was off the enemy coast. This was now far too dangerous, and by the outbreak of war the Royal Navy planned in the event of war with Germany to conduct a "distant blockade" rather than risking warships as large attractive targets in proximity to the German coast.[7]

There were even more important potential results from this altered strategy. Recent research has suggested that in the plans for the budgetary year 1914–15 the First Lord of the Admiralty, Winston Churchill, was even ready with the approval of the Board of Admiralty to reduce the number of planned dreadnoughts in favor of building a large flotilla of submarines. It would in effect be a new standard of naval strength.[8] This was a reflection of the former First Sea Lord Admiral Sir John Fisher's concept of "flotilla defense." That is, the defense of the British Isles from invasion would be left to torpedo boats and submarines. These torpedo flotillas would pose a grave threat to enemy transports and deter or repulse an invasion. Fisher, though out of office, was in contact with Churchill. Fisher's idea of flotilla defense was coupled with his plan to use large armored cruisers – battle cruisers – to safeguard the empire's lines of communication. The war broke out before Churchill's plans could be presented to Parliament.[9] One can only speculate what the effects would have been. The political and public outcry was likely to be great over an apparent abandonment or at least downgrading of the dreadnought, a weapon the public had been conditioned to believe in as the standard of naval strength. Would Churchill have been able to implement his plans? How would the major rival, Germany have responded? These are intriguing questions that can never be answered.

The German challenge at sea had been conceived by the dynamic State Secretary of the Imperial Naval Office, Admiral Alfred von Tirpitz, as a "risk fleet." This was designed to alter British action by making a clash with Germany potentially too expensive for the British to risk. It was not an attempt to outbuild the British which, given Germany's obligation to maintain a powerful army, was too expensive.[10] The German Navy, as a relatively new institution, seemed handicapped in its competition for funds with the German army, but the Kaiser's enthusiasm for the fleet was evident. One German naval officer habitually used a phrase in English to describe it: "Wilhelm's mechanical toy."[11] The fleet, however, was expensive, and as Germany faced growing challenges on land from potential rivals, Tirpitz found there were limits on what he could extract from the government. In 1913 his proposal for yet another increase in the naval building program was turned down. The money would go to expansion of the army.[12] The German navy also seems to have been hardly taken into account in the army's war plans.[13]

The British decision to abandon a close blockade also had strategic implications for the Germans. Their general idea was to take advantage of what they believed to be their superiority in technique, protection of individual ships, and large destroyer flotillas to whittle down the British naval forces when they operated deep in the Heligoland Bight, in close proximity to the German coast. There was also the chance that once the British forces had been reduced to a certain level a major naval encounter could be sought in German waters, where the Germans would have the advantage. This strategy was, however, predicated on the British being obliging enough to put their heads into the noose. Tirpitz himself is reported to have discerned the fallacy in the strategy before the war when he inquired in May 1914: "But what will you do if the British do not appear in the German Bight?" The German navy was never to find a satisfactory answer.[14]

The British were more far-seeing and innovative than formerly believed. They had not only the world's largest navy but also the largest empire and merchant marine. These were potential vulnerabilities, but the British had apparently exploited the potential of wireless and cable transmission and the far-flung network of consuls to establish a "War Room" with a centralized plot of their own and potential enemy shipping. The War Room was designed to exploit signals intelligence and control the movements of British naval forces throughout the world in the defense of the Empire. Consequently, historians must now reevaluate the role of intelligence in operations by the Royal Navy during the war.[15]

Opening Campaigns, 1914–15

The War Room added to the British geographical advantage whereby the British Isles formed a breakwater around which German shipping or naval vessels would have to move to reach the open sea. Consequently it is not surprising that the German flag disappeared from the seas within a few months. The German merchant marine was second – admittedly a distant second – to the British, but well before the end of 1914 its ships had been captured, were sheltering in neutral harbors or blockaded in German ports and free only to trade in a closed sea like the Baltic. This is not to say, however, that all went smoothly. The Germans had a powerful cruiser squadron in Asiatic waters, based on the German colony at Tsingtau on the Shantung peninsula. The East Asiatic Squadron under Rear Admiral Maximilian von Spee was in an unenviable position, and once Japan entered the war on the side of the Entente Tsingtau itself was doomed. Spee did not wait to be trapped. He sailed westward across the Pacific after detaching one of his cruisers, the *Emden*, to raid in the Indian Ocean. The *Emden* achieved considerable success before it was caught and driven ashore by the Australian cruiser *Sydney* in the Cocos Islands. Spee, who feinted at Apia, Samoa and bombarded Papeete in Tahiti, seemed to disappear into the vastness of the Pacific. In case he was headed for the west coast of South America a weaker squadron under Rear Admiral Christopher Cradock, which had been in South American waters, was ordered around Cape Horn to the coast of Chile. Cradock, who realized his squadron was likely to be inferior to his potential adversary, especially when he elected not to be tied to his only slow pre-dreadnought, did not flinch. Perhaps he was mindful of the court martial of Rear Admiral Troubridge for failure to engage the *Mittelmeerdivision* (Mediterranean squadron), a German force superior to his own that subsequently escaped to the Dardanelles and would later have a role in Turkey's entry into the war on the side of the Central Powers.[16] Cradock and Spee met off the Chilean coast on November 1. The result was not surprising: two British cruisers were sunk, Cradock going down with his ship. The battle of Coronel was a sharp defeat for the Royal Navy, the first in living memory.

The British now had the problem of where Spee would go next. Would he double back across the Pacific to Asiatic waters or would he head for South Africa to support an anti-British rising? Would he make for the Caribbean through the Panama Canal, or attack British shipping on the east side of South America and then try to break through to Germany? The mobility of sea power raised great difficulties for the British but Fisher, recalled as First Sea Lord in October 1914, took a calculated risk. The Grand Fleet had but a scant margin of superiority in battle cruisers over the Germans. Nevertheless he detached three to the other side of the Atlantic, one to the Caribbean in case Spee tried to come through the newly opened Panama Canal, and two to the South Atlantic. Here the British force had just arrived at the Falklands when Spee appeared, having decided to raid the wireless station at Port Stanley. The British had been lucky, and after a long chase Spee and his squadron were destroyed save for one cruiser, which, when discovered, eventually scuttled herself at the remote island of Mas a Tierra.

There had also been much discussion before the war about the use of auxiliary cruisers, that is, ocean liners with strengthened decks that could be outfitted with guns and then operate against trade. The Germans had a number of them and they achieved a certain amount of success. However, modern ships consumed large quantities of coal and the Germans were hampered by a lack of overseas bases. Their presence in neutral ports could also be quickly signaled by wireless or cable. In the end most were sunk or interned in neutral ports. The Germans would later employ surface raiders such as the *Möwe* and *Wolfe*, disguised as merchant ships. They also achieved a certain success and most, in some cases after incredibly long voyages, successfully returned to German ports. In an age before radar, with observation still largely dependent on what a human eyeball could see from a crow's nest, the British blockade was anything but airtight. The exploits of these raiders were colorful and they certainly caused concern, but given the volume of Allied trade their depredations were pinpricks. They could neither win the war nor even seriously influence events.

The main German battle fleet, the High Seas Fleet, probably stood its best chance of success in the first half-year of the war. At this time, the ratio of strength would be closer than it would be for the remainder of the war. Chance played a role. One British dreadnought sank after hitting a mine, another pair was out of action following a collision and condenser problems laid up others. Furthermore, the fact that Scapa Flow, the Grand Fleet's anchorage in Orkney, lacked sufficient protection from submarines in the early months of the war, added to the Germans' chance of success. Prior to the twentieth century the traditional British naval bases had been in the south, remnants of an age when Holland and France had been the principal enemies. They were far less suited for a war against Germany, but infrastructure seemed mundane compared to the excitement of naval building, and before the war the subject had been neglected. For a time the commander of the Grand Fleet, Admiral John Jellicoe, actually preferred to keep his fleet at sea and used temporary anchorages on the west coast of Scotland or the north coast of Ireland. The High Seas Fleet was, however, restrained by higher orders. At first, in the heady expectation of victory on land, the Kaiser did not want to risk the fleet which, if nothing else, might be a bargaining chip at a peace conference. It was after all, "Wilhelm's mechanical toy." This attitude was bitterly resented by many of the German naval commanders, anxious to prove themselves. Furthermore, it was realized that if the war ended without the navy doing anything it could not expect much in the future in the competition for scarce funds with the army.[17]

The attitude benefited the British. The deployment of the British Expeditionary Force to the Continent took place without any interference. The Germans could never seriously threaten the short supply routes to the Continent during the war. The restrained attitude also meant that over the early months of the war the so-called "Imperial" convoys brought large numbers of men from the British Empire to the Continent without interference. An aggressive attitude on the part of the British contributed to the reluctance of the German high command to take risks. On August 28, 1914, the light cruisers and destroyers of the Harwich force led by Commodore Reginald Tyrwhitt, combined with the submarines shepherded by Roger Keyes, then Commodore (S), staged an operation to "sweep up" the German light forces that had been noted on patrol in the Heligoland Bight. The action turned into a hot if somewhat confused encounter in which the Germans came out from their bases to support their patrols. Tyrwhitt's forces were for a time hard-pressed, but Admiral Jellicoe had wisely decided to send reinforcements from the Grand Fleet led by Rear Admiral David Beatty and the battle cruiser squadron. British staff work was terrible. No one had informed Tyrwhitt or Keyes that other British forces were involved and there was nearly an incident of what is today called "blue on blue," when a British submarine was preparing to attack a cruiser only to discover at the last moment it was one of their own. Beatty's battle cruisers intervened with devastating effect and three German light cruisers and a destroyer were sunk. The Heligoland battle took place right off the German coast and its psychological implications were important. It confirmed the German decision not to risk the fleet.

The Germans quickly stumbled on an alternate weapon: the submarine. They had been trying to employ submarines against the Grand Fleet ever since the beginning of the war without success until September 5, when the scout cruiser *Pathfinder* was sunk by *U.21*, the first British warship to be sunk by a submarine. On September 22 the Germans achieved a spectacular success when *U.9* sank three cruisers in succession off the Dutch coast. The ships were old and had been employed in a foolish fashion – even before the incident they had been dubbed the "live bait" squadron. The implications of the disaster were clear. Nevertheless, although the British lost other generally older ships to submarines in the following months it was usually because they had been poorly handled. The important point to note is that of the main force, the Grand Fleet, no capital ships were lost. Here the intense precautions of Jellicoe might be given credit. However, the Grand Fleet paid a penalty for this. The battle squadrons could not go to sea without the screen of large numbers of destroyers. This might prevent losses to submarines but it also had the effect of tying the movements of the Grand Fleet to the endurance of its destroyers. In an age before replenishment at sea became practical it meant that the time the Grand Fleet could spend on operations at sea or in relative proximity to the enemy coast was limited. Jellicoe would have been delighted for the opportunity to catch the High Seas Fleet at sea and inflict heavy losses, but only under the proper circumstances and with care not to be led into a submarine or mine ambush. The Germans, in turn, would try to lure a portion of the Grand Fleet to sea in order to catch it with the whole of the High Seas Fleet. But they too would only give battle under favorable circumstances in their portion of the North Sea. Given these restraints, it is hardly surprising that the long-anticipated great naval battle did not take place. This produced a strain on both the British and German navies, for they keenly felt the pressure of public opinion and the inevitable question of "What is the navy doing?" The fleets had cost enormous amounts of money. How could they justify their existence? This question became all the more acute when the heavy losses of the armies in fighting on land became known.

The Germans turned to "tip-and-run raids" to lure a portion of the Grand Fleet into an encounter with the bulk of the High Seas Fleet. In these operations German battle cruisers took advantage of their high speed and heavy gun power to bombard points along the eastern coast of Great Britain. The High Seas Fleet came out midway across the North Sea in support and, hopefully, a smaller British squadron would fall into a trap. The operations were difficult to counter, especially since the Grand Fleet's bases were far to the north. To offset this, the battle cruisers were moved further south to the Cromarty Firth. This presented the Germans with a potentially divided enemy force and on December 16 an encounter of the sort the Germans desired nearly took place.[18] However, the Germans also came close to disaster that day because the British had acquired a precious asset. In the autumn of 1914 the British managed to gain access by diverse means to substantial portions of the German naval codes.[19] This included material passed on by the Russians after it had been salvaged from the wreck of the cruiser *Magdeburg*, which ran ashore off the Estonian coast. The organization that exploited intelligence derived from wireless intercepts came to be known as "Room 40" from its location at the Admiralty. It was not enough, however, to possess the codes. The information derived from them had to be properly interpreted and disseminated without revealing the source of that information. This was not always successfully done and the organization suffered at first from excessive centralization and secrecy. Nevertheless it was an invaluable tool and the number of wireless-interception stations created during the war grew significantly. However, all this advantage was dependent on the Germans using their wireless before a raid and in practice it was impossible to actually stop the German raids. They could do no significant damage to the war effort and in the overall scheme of the war were a minor annoyance. This was not an easy thing to explain to the suffering residents of the east-coast towns and it certainly did not help the navy's prestige.

The intelligence derived from wireless intercepts gave the Admiralty an opportunity to intercept the German raid of January 24, 1915. The Germans, convinced that the British were using trawlers in the Dogger Bank fishing area for intelligence purposes, planned a raid to sweep them up along with any British light forces in support. The British hoped to set a trap, and Beatty's battle-cruiser squadron intercepted the Germans commanded by Rear Admiral Franz von Hipper. The results were not all they should have been. Beatty's flagship the *Lion* was damaged and fell behind and Beatty had to turn direction of the pursuit over to his second in command. The latter misinterpreted Beatty's signals and the British concentrated their attention on the rearmost German ship, the armored cruiser *Blücher*. The latter was inferior to the other ships in the German squadron and should never have been on the raid. The *Blücher* was sunk but the remainder of the German squadron got away. Beatty's sentiment was that they ought to have bagged "the lot."[20] The problems with communication based on signal flags, a method that would have been familiar to Nelson, would recur and indicated that the techniques of command and control had not kept up with the conditions of modern warfare. Nevertheless the Dogger Bank action confirmed the Kaiser and naval high command in their decision not to risk the High Seas Fleet in a major encounter.

Submarine Warfare: the First Round

Under these circumstances, the use of submarines became increasingly attractive. Save for a few visionaries before the war like Fisher, the idea that submarines would be used primarily against merchant shipping rather than warships was largely disregarded. The notion that they would sink ships without regard for the safety of passengers and crew was also abhorrent. However, the logic of submarines led in this direction. A submarine's greatest asset was its invisibility and this was sacrificed once it surfaced to stop and examine a ship. Furthermore, submarines were too small to take more than an occasional prisoner aboard and did not have the manpower to provide prize crews. The situation was further complicated by the British tactic of using so-called Q-ships. These were ships with concealed armaments, designed to look like merchantmen. The objective was to lure a submarine close enough for it to be destroyed. Q-ships enjoyed a limited success at first, but once the secret was out the wariness of submarine commanders reduced their effectiveness. They also provided the Germans with at least some justification for sinking ships without warning. The Germans had to consider, however, the diplomatic complications of sinking neutrals or British ships carrying neutrals. The major consideration was the United States, although it should be pointed out that significant maritime nations like Norway and the Netherlands also suffered severely during the war. The actions of submarines led to celebrated incidents like the sinking of the *Lusitania*, and after sharp American protests the Germans drew back. There was another consideration – the number of submarines actually available for operations in the earlier stages of the war was too limited to achieve decisive results.

The rules under which German submarine commanders conducted submarine warfare changed often, a reflection of the diplomatic situation and the balance of power between the adherents of unrestricted submarine warfare and its opponents within the German government. The quarrels were bitter; the German Navy during World War I was far from a "band of brothers." The pressure for unrestricted submarine warfare grew, until finally in February 1917 the German government succumbed to the pressure to begin it regardless of the effects on the United States. The decision was a fatal one.

The Battle of Jutland, May–June 1916

Before reverting to unrestricted submarine warfare, the High Seas Fleet, under the aggressive leadership of its new commander Admiral Reinhard Scheer, made another attempt to lure a portion of the Grand Fleet into the grasp of the main German force. The result was the battle of Jutland on May 31, 1916. Owing to a misinterpretation of intelligence the British did not realize the main German force was at sea. The Germans, in turn, also did not realize the Grand Fleet was at sea. The initial encounter took place between Beatty's battle cruisers, supported by the fast battleships of Vice Admiral Evan-Thomas's Fifth Battle Squadron and Hipper's battle cruisers. Hipper drew the British toward Scheer and the High Seas Fleet, and in this phase of the battle the British lost two battle cruisers to catastrophic explosions. Beatty, when he realized he faced the entire German force, turned away. Now Beatty drew the Germans toward Jellicoe and the Grand Fleet. Jellicoe, hampered by incomplete reports from Beatty as to the latter's position, nevertheless made the correct decision to deploy to port, which put him in an advantageous position when the Germans appeared. Scheer took heavy punishment and turned away, covered by an attack by destroyers who also laid a smokescreen. However, for reasons never adequately explained, he turned back and again blundered into the same potentially disastrous situation. Once more Scheer's turn away was covered by a massed destroyer attack with torpedoes. Jellicoe acted as he had planned, by turning away rather than toward the direction of the torpedoes to minimize the exposure of his ships. The decision would become the source of much later controversy, for the battle had begun late in the day and the Germans disappeared into the gathering darkness. Jellicoe lost contact with the Germans, although during the night he was actually between the Germans and their bases. The High Seas Fleet cut across the tail of the British fleet during the night. There were a few sharp encounters in the darkness and again a failure of initiative on the part of some British commanders to report what was happening. There was also another failure to correctly interpret intelligence gathered from wireless interceptions as to the path the Germans would take through their minefields. The result was Scheer's escape and, since the Germans had inflicted heavier losses than they suffered, a German claim for victory. The claim could be justified only on tactical grounds. The strategic situation, however, remained unchanged. The Grand Fleet had repaired its damage and was ready for action sooner than its German opponents. The pithy statement attributed to an American journalist was true: "The German fleet has attacked its jailors and is back in jail."

The battle of Jutland, because of its inconclusive nature, has been a source of endless discussion. The more recent research has centered on a detailed tactical examination of the gunnery, lighting conditions, and damage inflicted.[21] There has also been reexamination of how Jellicoe intended to use his fleet, and this has been linked to the subject of fire control. The fact that battles were fought at higher speeds and with longer range created gunnery problems that, in terms of mathematics, were difficult to solve without a modern computer. The British had faced the problem before the war but adopted a fire-control method that was a compromise and less effective than it might have been. It has been suggested that Jellicoe realized the limitations of his fire-control devices at long range and had planned to fight at medium range, relying on rapid pulses of fire combined with a turn away before the anticipated torpedoes could arrive.[22] The limitations of fire control and the apparent large expenditure of ammunition, compared to the results obtained in the previous encounters, had led to an emphasis on rapid fire. This in turn led to cutting corners on the safe handling of ammunition, with disastrous results for the battle cruisers at Jutland.[23] There has also been a close examination of what it took to arrive at the top in the Royal Navy, and one historian has pointed out that what he terms the "regulators," or people adept at following the rules, were the ones who succeeded in the peacetime navy. However, it was really the so-called "rat-catchers," who could be unorthodox and break the rules, who had the instinct and initiative necessary for success in war.[24] These concepts have been related to the harmful inertia shown by some commanders at crucial moments. The defects of handling intelligence in the pre-Jutland period have also been examined.[25] The German side of the battle has not yet been examined to the same degree and, given the relatively large amount of underutilized material in the German archives, there is ample opportunity for historians to pursue these subjects.[26]

Jutland was the greatest naval battle of the war and also the last purely between surface ships. Any future large-scale naval engagement would likely have to contend with submarines and air power, both of which developed rapidly in the second half of the war. Shortly after the battle Scheer himself concluded that decisive results could not be obtained by surface action.[27] While the German fleet sortied again on August 16 without serious consequences, the pressure for unrestricted submarine warfare grew. The naval staff argued that adequate results could not be obtained following the rules of "cruiser warfare." The justification was based on a complex calculation by the German naval staff on the anticipated extent of that year's world harvests, available shipping, and anticipated losses. It seemed as if statisticians and economists had become a part of naval warfare alongside gunnery and torpedo experts.[28] In retrospect those calculations were wrong, for they underestimated the amount of shipping that would be available to the Entente and the effects of Allied counter-measures, and they vastly discounted the effects of American intervention. In addition, according to recent research, the Germans tended to neglect the opportunities that possession of bases in occupied Belgium gave them for submarine and surface attacks on British lines of communication to France.[29]

Submarine Warfare: the Second Round

In the opening stages of the submarine campaign the losses inflicted by German submarines were huge, culminating in April 1917. The Germans were initially assisted by the fact that British and Allied anti-submarine measures were based on the wrong concepts, notably that the use of convoys to guard merchant shipping – a technique that had worked well in the Napoleonic Wars – had been invalidated by the development of steam.[30] The British may also have inadvertently helped the German campaign by concentrating too many resources on warship construction and not enough on construction or repair of merchant shipping.[31] The Admiralty at first also vastly overestimated the number of escorts that would have been necessary for a more effective system of defense. Eventually proponents of the convoy system made their point and the system was introduced and progressively extended. It worked, losses fell, and the number of submarines sunk increased. The use of wireless intercepts helped the Admiralty plot the areas where submarines were working and route convoys around them. The submarine commanders who had once only to wait along shipping routes or near focal points for a stream of targets now found the seas empty. If they located a convoy and attacked it, they came within range of escorts and could be attacked themselves. This was far more effective than previous British efforts to "hunt" submarines. The Germans eventually tried to counter by moving their submarines closer to shore to take advantage of convoy dispersal points. This, however, brought submarines within range of aircraft or airships. Aircraft during World War I generally lacked the hitting power to destroy a submarine, but they could keep a submarine down and prevent it from reaching a favorable firing position.[32] The anti-submarine campaign required an immense effort of plotting, control of shipping, routing, and dispersal. It succeeded in reducing losses to acceptable proportions, although losses were never eliminated and could still at times be painful. In the long run, however, the German gamble did not succeed, and this was particularly evident in the summer of 1918 when huge numbers of American troops and supplies were brought across the Atlantic while American shipyards began to turn out large numbers of standardized ships.

One of the first tangible benefits of the entry of the United States into the war was the arrival of American destroyers at Queenstown in southern Ireland to take part in the campaign against submarines. It also involved a little-recognized sacrifice on the part of the American naval leaders for it meant the American battle fleet would be deprived of much of its necessary flotilla craft in any fleet action. An American fleet action was not likely, however, although a squadron of coal-burning American battleships crossed the Atlantic to work with the Grand Fleet. This added to the British margin of superiority, although different methods and levels of experience caused considerable problems in integrating this force with the British. The American leaders were rightly convinced that the decision would be reached on the other side of the Atlantic, and did not succumb to the politically expedient temptation of withdrawing anti-submarine forces from European waters after German submarines began briefly to operate off the American coast in the spring and summer of 1918. The Germans also did not find it profitable to operate on the other side of the Atlantic, given the limitations of 1918 submarine technology. Consequently, the Americans were not to be diverted from the center of gravity of the naval war.

Other Theaters: the Baltic Sea and the Black Sea

The fact that the largest naval battles during World War I took place between the British and the Germans in the North Sea area should not obscure the fact that naval operations took place in other areas. In the Baltic the resurgent Russian fleet could have been in a position of superiority over those German naval forces, generally consisting of older or obsolescent ships, that the Germans left in the Baltic while they concentrated against the British in the North Sea. However, the ability of the Germans to shift forces from the North Sea to the Baltic by means of the Kiel Canal made it possible for the naval balance to swing rapidly in favor of the Germans. The Russians initially were content to remain on the defensive behind extensive minefields in the Gulf of Finland sheltering the capital, Petrograd, and taking advantage of powerful shore batteries to coordinate defense of those minefields. The situation was complicated by the fact that during the winter months the Gulf of Finland was frozen, thereby limiting operations. The Russians did conduct raids into the western Baltic in the first two years of the war and laid a large number of mines. The Baltic in fact eventually became saturated with minefields, both Russian and German. The Germans managed to keep open their essential lines of communication to Sweden, a source of iron ore, although British submarines, a handful of which managed to get into the Baltic, proved a threat. The Swedes tacitly cooperated with the Germans by escorting ships within Swedish territorial waters. With the onset of the Russian revolution in 1917 discipline in the Russian Baltic fleet collapsed and Russian operations wound down. In October 1917 the Germans undertook a large amphibious operation, Operation "Albion," to capture the island of Ösel and clear the Gulf of Riga. The operation was in support of the German army on land. The remnants of the Russian navy fought surprisingly hard and the Germans suffered far from negligible damage from mines. At least some of the German naval officers, such as Rear Admiral Hopman, commander of the scouting forces in the Baltic, considered that the operation was unnecessary and exposed the best of the German fleet to risks in excess of the possible gains, especially since the Russians were by then on the verge of collapse. He thought, if the operation was necessary, it might have been accomplished with far less force. Operation "Albion," however, was undertaken as much for reasons of morale and politics as from purely military motives. It gave the underemployed High Seas Fleet, which had already suffered its first incidents of unrest in the summer of 1917, something to do.[33] Historians have paid relatively little attention to Baltic naval operations, but with the current interest in asymmetric warfare and the possible availability of Russian archives they are worthy of further study.[34]

The Russian navy did not do badly in the Black Sea after its new dreadnoughts and large destroyers began to enter service in 1915.[35] This more than offset the initial Turkish advantage of having the modern German-manned but Turkish-flagged battle cruiser *Goeben*. The Russians tried to implement a blockade of the Bosporus with destroyers and submarines and, in the course of 1916, conducted amphibious operations in the southeastern part of the Black Sea in support of the Russian army's advance on Trabzon. The advantage disappeared after the revolution, and following the Peace of Brest-Litovsk in 1918 German armies entered the major Russian naval base of Sebastopol in the Crimea. The bulk of the Russian Black Sea Fleet got away. While some ships were scuttled, there were real fears that the Germans and their allies might eventually get their hands on the remainder and put them into service. The fears were exaggerated given the state of the ships, conditions in the dockyards, and the difficulties the Germans would have had in manning them.[36]

Other Theaters: the Mediterranean

In the Mediterranean the defection of Italy from the Triple Alliance ended any possibility that a combined Austrian–Italian–German fleet might provide a serious challenge to French and whatever British naval forces were left in the Mediterranean. The Austrian fleet was now in a position of considerable inferiority compared to the French, with a potential Italian enemy only a few hours' steaming distance away on the other side of the Adriatic. The Austrian commander Admiral Anton Haus declined impractical suggestions on the part of his German ally – and some of the Austrian military – that he take the fleet to the Dardanelles for potential operations against the Russians in the Black Sea.[37] The Austrians remained on the defensive in the Adriatic and the French had difficulty getting at them. Operations in the northern part of the Adriatic were considered too risky and the handful of submarines available to the Austrian navy also demonstrated the hazards of employing large ships in the Adriatic when one of them torpedoed but did not sink the French flagship *Jean Bart* in December 1914. The French had the obligation of supplying their Serbian and Montenegrin allies through the undeveloped Montenegrin port of Antivari, but this was only about 35 miles away from the Austrian naval base in the Gulf of Cattaro. The attempt to assist the Montenegrins by means of French batteries on Mount Lovcen, overlooking the gulf, failed when Austrian warships returned effective counter-battery fire. The possibility of an expedition against Cattaro was also vetoed by the French high command.

The situation in the Adriatic was not changed by the entry of Italy into the war and the Italians soon suffered losses to Austrian submarines when they unwisely attempted to use large warships in proximity to the Austrian coast. The war in the Adriatic developed into a singular struggle between light forces, destroyers, torpedo boats, and submarines. The major battle fleets remained secure in their bases, the Austrians at Pola and the Italians at Taranto. The big ships would only have been employed in the unlikely event the Austrian fleet attempted to come out of the Adriatic. The French fleet eventually settled at Corfu near the entrance to the Adriatic. The large French ships were relatively underemployed but rivalry between the French and Italians over who would command curtailed the prospect of joint operations and in 1918 frustrated the appointment of Jellicoe as Mediterranean *admiralissimo*.[38]

The Dardanelles expedition, which showed the limitations of warships operating against concealed batteries on land sheltered behind minefields, also had the unintended consequence of bringing German submarines to the Mediterranean. The Germans came at first in response to Turkish appeals for help and the inability of the Austrians to supply it.

The Austrian bases of Pola and Cattaro proved excellent points for conducting submarine warfare in the Mediterranean and the Germans eventually employed two flotillas. They had great success, especially since anti-submarine operations were hampered initially by the Mediterranean being divided into separate zones of national responsibility. The Mediterranean had another advantage for the Germans in that they were less likely to meet American ships there and so the diplomatic complications were less serious. The lack of unity among the allies, relative scarcity of suitable French and Italian anti-submarine craft, better weather conditions in comparison to the North Sea, and geographical choke points all contributed to the German success. The British had at first been content to let the French have command in the Mediterranean while they concentrated in the north, but when the submarine campaign became too serious in 1917 they were forced to take more and more of a role, especially since they had the numbers of small craft suitable for anti-submarine warfare and their allies did not. A British commander-in-chief for the Mediterranean was appointed and a central direction for anti-submarine warfare was established at Malta with the British playing a leading role.

The geographical configuration of the Adriatic also encouraged the idea that subma-rines could be shut in by means of a "barrage" in the Strait of Otranto. This was at first attempted by British drifters setting nets with indicator buoys to signal the presence of any submarine that fouled the net. The idea was and remained seductive, although suc-cess was extremely limited. The French and Italians pushed the idea of a "fixed" barrage with nets and minefields and proceeded to lay one in the last year of the war. The Americans, after they entered the war, made their own contribution. This consisted of 110-ft wooden craft, dubbed "submarine chasers," that operated in groups of three in an attempt to fix the position of a submarine by triangulation through hydrophones. They achieved no success. The drifters were also vulnerable and subject to Austrian raids. The most damaging came in May 1917 when Austrian cruisers sank 14 drifters and man-aged to return safely to Cattaro.[39] In June 1918 the new and aggressive Austrian com-mander Admiral Horthy attempted to repeat the raid, with Austrian dreadnoughts backing up the cruisers to provide a nasty surprise to the Allied light forces when they intervened. However, one of the Austrian echelons encountered Italian *MAS* (motor torpedo) boats during the night and the dreadnought *Szent István* was sunk. The Italians had developed these fast *MAS* boats as a weapon well suited for Adriatic conditions.

The Austrian battle fleet at Pola, despite its relative inactivity, performed a valuable service as a "fleet-in-being." The big ships, by their mere existence, meant that any Allied naval force operating in the Adriatic faced the possibility of meeting them. This in turn required the presence of comparable large ships and the latter would be equally exposed to the dangers of mines and torpedoes in those waters, thereby raising the stakes for any Allied landing in the vulnerable portions of the Habsburg monarchy along the Dalmatian coast. The Italian and French military high commands always had better uses for their troops along their respective fronts and the possible gains never quite equaled the poten-tial risks. The Americans actually had serious plans for a landing by US Marines on the Sabbioncello peninsula in 1918, but the operation was canceled when Ludendorff's offensive in March 1918 diverted the Marines to the western front.[40]

It would be wrong to think of the naval aspects of World War I solely in terms of actions and battles. Much of the naval war was carried on in what could be described as routine operations. The history of a successful naval campaign should be boring. A navy often succeeds when nothing happens because it and its country are able to use the sea for their own purposes and when circumstances deprive the enemy of similar use. Many operations during World War I were also conducted by ships that had not initially been designed as warships. A prime example of this was the 10th cruiser squadron, the so-called "Northern Patrol," which enforced the blockade on the northern approaches to Germany. After the older cruisers initially employed proved inadequate in the punishing seas, the British used converted liners crammed with coal but with their high freeboard able to withstand the weather conditions and keep at sea for relatively long periods. They could easily have been mopped up by any of the German cruisers or battle cruisers, but the presence of the Grand Fleet, ready to sortie from its anchorages when necessary, kept the Germans in check. There were also large numbers of British trawlers and drifters absorbed into the auxiliary patrol and minesweeping flotillas, later supplemented by purpose-built craft. On the German side similar ships were constantly engaged in laying, maintaining, and clearing the extensive minefields in the North Sea. It was vital for the Germans that certain paths or *wegs* remain open for submarines. The subject of mine warfare has not yet received justice from historians. In the summer of 1918 the Americans were also the driving force behind the creation of the so-called Northern Barrage, a minefield extending across the North Sea from Orkney to Norwegian territorial waters. These diverse efforts were largely unseen and certainly unappreciated by the public and could readily have answered the question: "What is the Navy doing?" In any final reckoning of the war, navies and sea power played an important role in the Allied victory.

Notes

1   Kennedy, *Rise of the Anglo-German Antagonism*, pp. 415–31.
2   Sondhaus, *Naval Policy of Austria-Hungary*, pp. 191–204.
3   Mariano Gabriele and Giuliano Friz, *La Politica Navale Italiana dal 1885 al 1915*, Rome, Gaeta, 1982, pp. 161–70.
4   Masson, "La marine française de 1871 à 1914," in Guy Pedroncini (ed.), *Histoire militaire de la France*, vol. 3, *De 1870 à 1940*, Paris, Presses Universitaires de France, 1992, pp. 147–59.
5   Paul Halpern, *The Mediterranean Naval Situation, 1908–1914*, Cambridge, MA, Harvard University Press, 1971, pp. 330–54.
6   Lambert, *Fisher's Naval Revolution*, pp. 54–5.
7   Ibid., pp. 272–3.
8   Ibid., pp. 296–303.
9   Ibid., pp. 121–6. On the battle cruiser, which Fisher had originally advocated as an economy measure substituting one class of warship for two or three, see also Sumida, *In Defence of Naval Supremacy*, pp. 51–61.
10 Berghahn, *Germany and the Approach of War in 1914*, Basingstoke, Macmillan, 1973, pp. 32–42.
11 Epkenhans (ed.), *Hopman*, pp. 245, 317.
12 Berghahn, *Germany and the Approach of War*, pp.126–8.
13 Lambi, *Navy and German Power Politics*, pp. 422–3.
14 Ibid., p.423. See also further discussion in Epkenhans, *Hopman*, p. 369, n. 60.
15 Lambert, "Strategic Command," pp. 408–10.
16 On the episode see Geoffrey Miller, *Superior Force. The Conspiracy behind the Escape of the Goeben and Breslau*, Hull, University of Hull Press, 1996, pp. 291–7.
17 Tirpitz, *Memoirs*, vol. 1, pp. 95–6.
18 Goldrick, *The King's Ships*, ch. 7.
19 Beesly, *Room 40*, pp. 14–20.
20 Roskill, *Beatty*, p. 114.

21   Exhaustive detail on these subjects can be found in N. J. M. Campbell, *Jutland: An Analysis of the Fighting*, London, Conway Classics, 1998.
22   Sumida, "Matter of Timing."
23   Lambert, "Our bloody ships."
24   Gordon, *Rules of the Game*.
25   Beesly, *Room 40*, ch. 10.
26   Good beginnings are in Tobias R. Philbin, *Admiral von Hipper: the Inconvenient Hero*, Amsterdam, Gruner, 1982, and V. E. Tarrant, *Jutland: the German Perspective*, London, Cassell, 2001.
27   Tarrant, *Jutland*, pp. 250–1.
28   Avner Offer, *The First World War: An Agrarian Interpretation*, Oxford, Clarendon Press, 1989, p. 362. See also Dirk Steffen, "The Holtzendorff Memorandum of 22 December 1916 and Germany's Declaration of Unrestricted U-boat Warfare," *Journal of Military History*, 68/1, January 2004, pp. 215–24.
29   Mark D. Karau, *"Wielding the Dagger": the MarineKorps Flandern and the German War Effort*, Westport, CT, Greenwood, 2003.
30   See survey in John Winton, *Convoy: The Defence of Sea Trade, 1890–1990*, London, Michael Joseph, 1983, ch. 2.
31   Sumida, "Forging the Trident," pp. 225–9.
32   R. D. Layman, *Naval Aviation in the First World War: Its Impact and Influence*, Annapolis, Naval Institute Press, 1996, pp. 83–9.
33   Epkenhans, *Hopman*, pp. 1014–21, 1023–37.
34   Studies in English are Wilson, *Baltic Assignment*, Nekrasov, *Expendable Glory*, and Michael B. Barrett, *Operation Albion: The German Conquest of the Baltic Islands*, Bloomington, Indiana University Press, 2008.
35   Nekrasov, *North of Gallipoli*.
36   Halpern, *Mediterranean 1914–1918*, pp. 542–55.
37   Ibid., pp. 19–22, 37–9.
38   On Adriatic operations see essays in Rastelli and Massignani, *Guerra navale* and Koburger, *Adriatic*; on the *admiralissimo* question see Halpern, *Mediterranean, 1914–1918*, pp. 522–34.
39   The barrage and raid are examined in Paul Halpern, *The Battle of the Otranto Straits: Controlling the Gateway to the Adriatic in World War I*, Bloomington, Indiana University Press, 2004.
40   Trask, *Captains & Cabinets*, pp. 242–8.

References and Further Reading

Beesly, Patrick, *Room 40: British Naval Intelligence 1914–1918*, London, Hamish Hamilton, 1982.
Corbett, Sir Julian S., *History of the Great War: Naval Operations*. Volume 1: *To the Battle of the Falklands, December 1914*, London, Longmans, Green, 1920.
Epkenhans, Michael (ed.), *Albert Hopman: Das ereignisreiche Lebens eines "Wilhelminers,"* Munich, Oldenbourg, 2004.
Goldrick, James, *The King's Ships Were at Sea: The War in the North Sea August 1914–February 1915*, Annapolis, Naval Institute Press, 1984.
Gordon, Andrew, *The Rules of the Game: Jutland and British Naval Command*, Annapolis, Naval Institute Press, 1996.
Grant, Robert M., *U-Boat Hunters: Code Breakers, Divers and the Defeat of the U-Boats, 1914–1918*, Annapolis, Naval Institute Press, 2003.
Halpern, Paul G., *The Naval War in the Mediterranean, 1914–1918*, London and Annapolis, George Allen and Unwin and Naval Institute Press, 1987.
Halpern, Paul G., *A Naval History of World War I*, Annapolis, Naval Institute Press, 1994.

Herwig, Holger H., *"Luxury Fleet": The Imperial German Navy, 1888–1918,* London, George Allen and Unwin, 1980.

Kennedy, Paul, *The Rise of the Anglo-German Naval Antagonism, 1860–1914,* London, Allen and Unwin, 1982.

Koburger, Charles W., *The Central Powers in the Adriatic, 1914–1918: War in a Narrow Sea,* Westport, CT, Praeger, 2001.

Lambert, Nicholas, A. " 'Our Bloody Ships' or 'Our Bloody System'? Jutland and the Loss of the Battle Cruisers, 1916," *Journal of Military History,* 62/1, January 1998, pp. 29–55.

Lambert, Nicholas A., *Sir John Fisher's Naval Revolution,* Columbia, University of South Carolina Press, 1999.

Lambert, Nicholas A., "Strategic Command and Control for Maneuver Warfare: Creation of the Royal Navy's 'War Room' System, 1905–1915," *Journal of Military History,* 69/2, April 2005, pp. 361–410.

Marder, Arthur J., *From the Dreadnought to Scapa Flow: The Royal Navy in the Fisher Era, 1904–1919,* 5 vols., London, Oxford University Press, 1961–1970.

Nekrasov, George, M., *North of Gallipoli: The Black Sea Fleet at War, 1914–1917,* Boulder, CO, East European Monographs, 1992.

Nekrasov, George M., *A Russian Battleship in the Baltic, 1915–1917,* Boulder, CO, East European Monographs, 2004.

Rastelli, Achille, and Massignani, Alessandro, *La Guerra navale, 1914–18. Un contributo internazionale alle operazioni in Mediterraneo,* Novale, Rossato, 2002.

Roskill, Stephen, *Admiral of the Fleet Earl Beatty: The Last Naval Hero,* London, Collins, 1980.

Rueger, Jan, *The Great Naval Game: Britain and Germany in the Age of Empire,* Cambridge, Cambridge University Press, 2007.

Sondhaus, Lawrence, *The Naval Policy of Austria-Hungary, 1867–1918: Navalism, Industrial Development and the Politics of Dualism,* West Lafayette, IN, Purdue University Press, 1994.

Still, William N., *Crisis at Sea: The United States Navy in European Waters in World War I,* Gainesville, University of Florida Press, 2006.

Sumida, Jon Tetsuro, *In Defence of Naval Supremacy: Finance, Technology, and British Naval Policy, 1889–1914,* Boston, Unwin Hyman, 1989.

Sumida, Jon Tetsuro, "Forging the Trident: British Naval Industrial Logistics, 1914–1918," in John A. Lynn (ed.), *Feeding Mars: Logistics in Western Warfare from the Middle Ages to the Present,* Boulder, CO, Westview Press, 1993, pp. 217–43.

Sumida, Jon Tetsuro, "A Matter of Timing: The Royal Navy and the Tactics of Decisive Battle, 1912–1916," *Journal of Military History,* 67/1, January 2003, pp. 85–136.

Tirpitz, Alfred Von, *My Memoirs,* 2 vols., London, Hurst and Blackett, 1919.

Trask, David F., *Captains and Cabinets: Anglo-American Naval Relations, 1917–1918,* Columbia, University of Missouri Press, 1972.

Wilson, Michael, *Baltic Assignment: British Submarines in Russia, 1914–1919,* London, Leo Cooper, 1985.

CHAPTER ELEVEN

The War in the Air

JOHN H. MORROW, JR.

The late nineteenth and early twentieth centuries witnessed an explosion of technology and industry, from cars and chemicals to dynamos and dynamite. The era of powered flight dawned with the invention of the dirigible in France in 1884 and of the airplane in the United States in 1903. Dreams of flight expressed in the myths of Daedalus and Icarus long antedated powered flight, and visions of aerial warfare preceded World War I in the air. Aviation quickly captured the rapt attention of civilians, and aerial achievements measured the greatness of nations.

Such popular attitudes encouraged the militarization of aviation and formed the context for its development in Europe down to 1914. The United States, lacking this military impetus, rapidly fell behind Europe in the development of land planes, although Glenn Curtiss excelled in the development of seaplanes and flying boats. By the end of 1909, France and Germany were forming military air services, and in Germany the press and public actually helped to prod the army to accept the Zeppelin (or airship) before it met military performance stipulations.

After the Moroccan crisis of 1911, Europe expected war. Finally responding to continental progress and warnings of Zeppelin attacks from the Aerial League of the British Empire and the British Aero Club, in 1912 the British government formed a Royal Flying Corps (RFC) with military and naval divisions. The German army, playing upon chauvinistic notions of cultural supremacy to bolster military aviation, effectively controlled civilian aviation through its pervasive influence in German society. In 1912 government and industry organized a National Aviation Fund that bought airplanes for the army, trained military pilots, and funded airfield construction and an aviation research institute.

Other European countries also established such funds. Sport aviation languished as the era of great races and tournaments ended and accidents cooled public enthusiasm for air transport. In the absence of substantial sport or commercial markets, the supporters of military aviation molded popular attitudes to benefit their cause. Aircraft manufacturers, who were indissolubly tied to the military through contracts by 1912, sponsored civilian aviators, whom the press lionized as defenders of national honor. Designers and manufacturers like the Farman and Voisin brothers, Louis Breguet, and Louis Béchereau of SPAD in France; Anthony Fokker, Robert Thelen, and Ernst Heinkel in Germany;

Geoffrey De Havilland and T. O. M. Sopwith in Britain; and engine firms like Gnome and Renault in France and Daimler in Germany would form the nucleus of the wartime aviation industry.

The competition for national superiority in aviation had cultural and imperial overtones. Germans believed that the Zeppelin symbolized their presumed cultural supremacy, while the French imagined that the initiative necessary to use airplanes accorded with traditional Gallic audacity. British aerial advocates like Rudyard Kipling viewed the airplane as a tool to unify the Empire and to impress white superiority and control on non-white, colonial populations. While the British contemplated using aircraft to police the Empire, the French and Italians actually used airplanes in campaigns in North Africa in 1911 and 1912. Flight thus assumed nationalist, imperialist, and militarist characteristics by 1914.

The Zeppelin generated unrealistic expectations in the German General Staff that its minuscule fleet of some ten airships could deliver a telling first strike against enemies. With its substantial range and apparent potential as a bomber, the giant dirigible did prompt some German aviation magazines to threaten a preemptive strike,[1] thereby heightening prewar tensions.[1] The airplane had generally inspired much popular excitement but not such apocalyptic expectations, since mass destruction clearly lay beyond the capabilities of the fragile craft of the day. Yet by 1914, designers Gianni Caproni in Italy and Igor Sikorsky in Russia were creating multi-engined craft capable of bombing.

The literature of the prewar era foretold nearly every role that aircraft would play in World War I, including the potentially devastating impact on national morale of bombing civilian targets. Such attitudes anticipated Italian aerial theorist Giulio Douhet's postwar advocacy of the bombing of civilian populations to force nations to defeat. The intimate connections between the civilian and military arenas in aviation provided an appropriate context for a weapon that would both galvanize and directly threaten civilians in the coming war. Moreover, where the public of the prewar era already considered aviators to be heroes and masters of technology in the conquest of the heavens, a new warrior elite arose in the air services of Europe, exemplified by the dashing and audacious "Lieutenant Daedalus Icarus Brown," a prewar pilot in the RFC whose "fame and renown" were proclaimed in British doggerel.[2]

Most armies (and navies) emphasized the development of slow, stable aircraft for reconnaissance. Ironically the coming war would catapult the prewar sport aviator's small, speedy and maneuverable airplane, now armed, back into the forefront of public imagination as the vehicle of the war's greatest individual heroes, the air aces, the heirs of prewar daredevil aviators. Before the war, civilian and military experiments had practically ignored the realm of aerial combat in favor of reconnaissance and bombing. Ironically wartime air combat would reintroduce aspects of sport aviation that the prewar military had sought to eradicate – the emphasis on individual exploits and the high-performance airplane that was occasionally dangerous even to its own pilots.

Wartime: the Cult of the Aces

The air war of World War I has become one of the most highly romanticized and mythic subjects of military history. Popular imagination invariably conjures up the aces, the high-scoring fighter pilots, as the ultimate heroes of World War I. Despite the attempts of recent scholarship to "de-romanticize" it, this popular notion possesses enduring strength that reaches back to opinion during the war itself. For airmen, immortalized through their exploits, became *the* heroes of World War I. In Europe, public fascination with these new warriors converged on a single image of individual combat, deadly but chivalrous. In the trenches, mass slaughter on an unprecedented scale rendered individuals insignificant. Aerial heroes provided a much-needed affirmation of the importance of the individual and of youth – despite (or because of) the slaughter of both.

The fliers of World War I were worshiped by the public, particularly in France and Germany. Oswald Boelcke, one of Germany's first and most famous aces, won the highest award for valor, the Pour le Mérite, early in 1916. Photographs of the handsome youth and jaunty verses about his victories flooded the press. When he visited Frankfurt in the spring, crowds stared at him in the streets. During intermission at the opera, the audience flocked around him, and at the finale, instead of singing an encore, the lead tenor sang a verse in Boelcke's honor. The audience went mad, clapping, shouting, and stamping their feet. Boelcke, imperturbable in aerial combat, was so startled that he fled the theater. He crashed to his death in October 1916, the victim of a collision in combat after 40 victories. A German nation in mourning commemorated Boelcke in two elaborate funerals, sent condolences to his family, and composed eulogies to inspire German youth to protect the fatherland as their hero had done.[3] Manfred von Richthofen, Boelcke's pupil and heir, elicited the same worship during 1917 and 1918. The first two editions of his wartime memoirs, *Der Rote Kampfflieger* (The Red War Ace), which appeared in 1918, sold half a million copies. His funeral service in Berlin in May 1918 was even more spectacular than Boelcke's, as the Hohenzollern royal family joined the Richthofens in the pew.[4]

The legendary Georges Guynemer was France's greatest hero, and on his death in the fall of 1917 after scoring 53 victories, teachers instructed schoolchildren that he had flown so high that he could not descend. In October the government enshrined "Captain Guynemer, symbol of the aspirations and enthusiasm of the army of the nation," in France's memorial to its national heroes, the Panthéon, "whose cupola alone has sufficient span to shelter such wings." The frail youth embodied the victory of the spirit over the flesh, of France's will to endure despite her grave wounds.[5]

In Britain, the RFC (more than the now separate Royal Naval Air Service) characterized air combat as a sport, a notion that stemmed from the corps' composition early in the war with commissioned officers recruited mainly from the ranks of public-school sportsmen attracted to military aviation for the adventure. The image of the air war passed down to us in most of their memoirs and histories is one of a clean and glorious struggle, far above the squalor of the western front below. In the most literary British memoirs, such as Cecil Lewis's *Sagittarius Rising*, the war assumed the characteristics of sport and medieval tournament, a joust between heroes who bore only the utmost respect for one another, as, bound together in the brotherhood of the air, they rose daily to do battle.[6] They fought and lived by unwritten codes. In the squadron at the end of the day, for example, they were never to dwell on their losses except in absolute privacy. Instead, maintenance of a "stiff upper lip" was mandatory; these young aviators consequently released nerves, rage, and fears together in "rags," or brawls, in the mess, or bruising football games. Mess bills for broken furniture were common, and although no intrepid historian has yet studied the casualty rates for these "friendly" terrestrial struggles, at least one top British aviator, 40-victory ace Philip Fullard, suffered a seriously broken leg in 1917. Fullard, a tremendously gifted flier and shot, was scoring at such a rapid rate that he seemed destined to become Britain's greatest ace. Yet he never returned to combat, as his nerves gave way when he was finally scheduled to rejoin his squadron at the front after a long and difficult recovery, his sense of invincibility apparently as shattered as his limb.[7]

British aviation magazines such as *Flight* and *The Aeroplane* romanticized the RFC and the sporting, chivalric, heroic, and sacrificial images of the air war. From RFC headquarters Philip Gibbs's *Daily Chronicle* column depicted the RFC as "Knights-Errant of the Air," recalling the Black Prince in Flanders during the Hundred Years War. In a war with precious little romance, Gibbs found this in the "daily tourneys" in the air, as fearless British fliers fought with the ardor of schoolboys flinging themselves into a football scrimmage.[8] And why not? They were, in fact, like their counterparts in all countries, overwhelmingly youthful in their late teens and early twenties, primarily volunteers from the middle class lured to aviation by the adventure, excitement, and risk, schoolboys transformed into warriors by the greatest war humankind had witnessed to that date. *The Aeroplane* of May 30 carried a poem, "The Lament of the Broken Pilot," who bid farewell to France, "the land of adventure and knightly deeds, / where the pilot faces the foe / in single combat as was of yore / giving him blow for blow." No longer among the "throng of chivalry, youth, and pride," where his comrades entered the "airy lists in the name of Freedom and Right," our broken pilot would now keep his "armour bright." Exclusive London stores advertised aviation clothing intended to dress the wealthy young sportsman-knight stylishly and appropriately for the airy lists.[9]

What a glorious way to fight a war that otherwise epitomized brutal and senseless mass slaughter! One discerns the origin of the romantic images immortalized in postwar movies like *Hells Angels*, *Wings*, and the *Dawn Patrol*, where aviators pursue one another in individual combat, fight tenaciously, win gallantly, or die heroically, their flaming craft plunging to earth like meteoric funeral pyres, extinguishing their equally meteoric careers with scorching finality. The greatest of these warriors – Ball, Baracca, Boelcke, Bishop, Fonck, Guynemer, Mannock, Richthofen – were legendary, their exploits, the material of myth. Yet their lives were often terribly short. It is sobering to reflect that of those eight men cited, six died in 1916, 1917, and 1918, waging an aerial conflict that became a mass war of attrition just like the struggle on the ground, thereby seriously eroding any notions of chivalry or sport that still lurked in the breasts of aerial combatants.

The Growth of Air Forces

If the aces undoubtedly have their importance in the cultural history of the war, to focus on them exclusively would be to rob World War I airpower of its genuine military and industrial significance. The air arms did more than provide the warring nations with individual heroes, for their individual exploits occurred within the context of an increasingly mass aerial effort in a war of the masses.

During World War I aviation evolved from an instrument of reconnaissance used singly in 1914 by tiny air arms into an arm with up to 300,000 men in service. Aviation played a significant role, first in rendering ground forces more effective through reconnaissance or artillery observation. Later, its effectiveness as a weapon for fighting, bombing, and strafing required its deployment en masse against the enemy. Air services that had begun the war with some two hundred frontline airplanes had 2,000 to 3,000 airplanes at the front in 1918. National aviation industries that had a few thousand workers to deliver a hundred planes a month in 1914 employed hundreds of thousands of workers to deliver thousands of planes and engines monthly in 1918. French, German, and British wartime aircraft manufacture was 52,000, 48,000, and 43,000, respectively, and the French produced some 88,000 engines to English and German totals of 41,000 each. By the last year of the war, the great powers were producing 2,000–3,000 planes and 2,000–4,000 engines a month.

The French responded most rapidly to the challenge of the unexpectedly high attrition of men and machines by standardizing types and placing priority on aircraft and particularly engine production in the autumn of 1914. The Germans followed suit in the winter. British production remained small scale, more comparable to that of Russia or Austria-Hungary, though the two eastern empires lacked Britain's industrial potential. In October 1914, a French artilleryman, pointing to a German plane near Albert, commented to a British reporter: "There is that wretched bird which haunts us." The bird of war had spread its wings, casting its shadow over the battlefields of Europe. In 1915 it would transmogrify into a bird of prey with fierce talons, transforming the skies, like the earth and seas below, into an arena of mortal combat. In 1915 air arms became more sophisticated, adapting types of aircraft to perform specialized functions at the front and requiring greater technological and industrial mobilization to meet the demand for new and improved *matériel*. Bombardment and pursuit, the air arm's new roles, necessitated the adaptation of the most suitable aircraft types available – light planes such as Moranes, Nieuports, and Fokkers for fighting and heavier ones, such as Voisins and Aviatiks, for bombing. Russia, Italy, and Germany had a few operational large planes – Sikorskiis, Capronis, and Gothas – whose range and load indicated their potential for development as strategic bombers with more powerful engines.

Yet in 1915 only the German Zeppelin airships could carry enough bombs and climb fast and high enough to evade aerial interception, thus making strategic raids possible. England consequently experienced its first air attacks. The giant Zeppelins were still vulnerable to ground fire and weather, however, and they failed to deliver a telling blow, similar to the failure of an inadequate submarine fleet to drive Britain from the war in 1917. The German army removed the costly monsters – irresistible targets for enemy artillery – from the western front and relegated them to the less populous skies over the broader eastern front. The German navy continued to use airships successfully as scouts for the fleet. All powers, including Italy, employed seaplanes or flying boats over the North, Black, and Adriatic seas to scout for their fleets.

The major aerial development of 1915 was the beginning of fighter aviation, heralded first by Frenchman Roland Garros's use of a fixed forward-firing machine gun with only a deflector to protect his propeller, and then Fokker's adaptation of a synchronizing gear to mount a gun on his monoplane. By the end of the year an effective fighter required speed and maneuverability as well as fixed forward-firing machine guns. The early pursuit pilots – Max Immelmann, Oswald Boelcke, Georges Guynemer, and Lanoe Hawker – though varied in temperament, displayed tenacity, determination, courage, and aggressiveness. This new breed of technological warrior evolved new fighting tactics and recommended improvements for pursuit planes. Their efforts would make the skies over Europe's battlefields far more dangerous in the coming year.

Historians have considered 1916 a watershed in World War I, as the battles of Verdun and the Somme finally dashed both sides' hopes for imminent victory. These battles also marked the true beginning of aerial warfare, as both sides committed to develop larger air arms to attain aerial superiority. Aerial warfare in 1916 was as much a technological and industrial as a military affair. Although political and administrative friction marred the aviation mobilization of all the powers, France was winning the race for industrial mobilization. Its aero engine production far outdistanced all other powers because of its early and extensive mobilization of the automotive industry to build a diversity of engines, in particular the revolutionary Hispano-Suiza V8. Germany, strapped by material and manpower shortages, could not match the Entente's industrial superiority in general and its engine production in particular. It could only hope to counter them through superior aircraft technology, such as Hugo Junkers's all metal airplane with cantilever wing and the gigantic airplanes (*Riesenflugzeug* or R-planes), both in 1915, and the Albatros fighter of 1916.

The thinking of the major powers about air power on the western front reflected these industrial realities as well as differences in basic military strategy. British and French air policy was offensive, and RFC commander General Hugh "Boom" Trenchard pursued the air offensive more unrelentingly and inflexibly than the French. The Germans husbanded their resources, fought defensively, and concentrated their aviation forces to seek an aerial mastery limited in time and space. Nineteen sixteen was the golden age of the individual aces whose hero cults have already been discussed. Yet already the aces were in contrast with the increasingly collective nature of air power, and by 1917, industrial mobilization would become even more critical for aviation as the airplane became indispensable to the conduct of the war. In the desperate search to economize men by replacing them with technology and material, aviation offered obvious attractions. Both Philippe Pétain, French commander-in-chief from May 1917, and Winston Churchill, British Minister of Munitions in that year, recognized the capital importance of aviation when deployed in mass, with Churchill aspiring to replace the attrition of men with a war of machines using "masses of guns, mountains of shells, clouds of aeroplanes."[10] Thus, rather than being the domain of the individual warrior, aviation proved the most advanced and innovative technological arm of warfare, the one that epitomized the new total warfare in its requirement of meshing the military, political, technological, and industrial aspects of war – the front and the rear, the military and civilian.

Aircraft Production

Military and political leaders had to make crucial decisions to expand the tiny air arms of 1914 and mobilize the embryonic supporting industries, for in airpower technological and industrial superiority essentially determined the outcome of the struggle. The race for aerial superiority had to be won first in design offices and then on factory floors, as the airplane evolved from an experimental vehicle into a weapon. Aircraft manufacturers like Albatros, SPAD, and Sopwith, engine manufacturers like Daimler, Hispano Suiza, and Rolls Royce (along with their designers and skilled workers) were the essential backbone of their countries' aerial effort.

The aircraft companies evolved into large-scale enterprises during the war, as they expanded their plant to meet the demands for aircraft of the armies and navies of the fighting powers. As the struggle for aerial supremacy developed after 1915, the manufacturers had not only to build more airplanes, but also to develop more specialized aircraft types endowed with steadily improving performance. The aircraft manufacturers themselves evolved with the industry, or were left behind by aviation progress. The rapid progress of aeronautics left the Wright brothers in its wake, and by 1917 their most significant participation in aviation was a patent suit against Glenn Curtiss over aircraft control that may well have delayed the progress of the American aircraft industry.

Louis Blériot's talents as designer were also no longer equal to the pace of aviation development, but his entrepreneurial talents enabled him to direct aircraft manufacture throughout the war. Gabriel Voisin, whose early wartime aircraft proved highly serviceable if mediocre in performance, by the end of the war had been driven from aviation to automobile manufacture, hounded by his lack of success in the former and the rude nickname *Bébé Grillard*, or "Baby Grillmaster," that aircrew had given him due to the tendency of his aircraft to burst into flame when hit.

In contrast, some manufacturers proved themselves capable of continuing to fly and design while directing the wartime expansion of their firms. French designer and manufacturer Louis Breguet had been flying his own airplane as a volunteer military aviator as the German forces approached Paris at the end of August 1914. On 2 September Corporal Breguet returned from a mission to report that the German Army was turning to the east of Paris, information that later reconnaissance flights confirmed and that ultimately led to the Battle of the Marne, where the French Army halted the German advance.[11] Breguet's design and manufacture of bombers for the duration of the war would culminate in the superb Breguet 14 single-engine reconnaissance bomber of 1918.

Probably more widely known is the experience of the "Flying Dutchman," Anthony Fokker, prewar manufacturer of small, light, and maneuverable monoplanes. Fokker's fighter plane designs, from the first *Eindecker*, or monoplane, with a fixed forward firing machine gun, through the Dr1 *Dreidecker*, or triplane, of 1917–18, to the Fokker D7 of 1918, often considered the best production fighter of World War I, and his last parasol winged monoplane fighter, the D8, probably merit his selection as the best fighter plane designer of the war. A key to the success of the young manufacturer was his superb ability as a pilot. His youth and skills enabled him to demonstrate his aircraft to frontline pilots and establish an immediate rapport with Germany's greatest fighter pilots, from Oswald Boelcke and Max Immelmann to Manfred von Richthofen. This rapport in turn enabled him to design his aircraft with intimate knowledge of their requirements in mind, while his talent as a pilot and designer meant that in test flying his own designs he could both ascertain their flaws and make modifications to correct the problem, as he did in the case of the D7.[12]

The airplane and its engine exemplified the harsh demands and enormous waste of modern industrial warfare, as the intensifying air war necessitated increased production to replace destroyed craft. They had to be simple enough to lend themselves to serial production yet of sufficient reliability and performance to remain effective under rapidly changing frontline conditions despite their limited combat life. Planes and engines demanded much higher standards of precision and reliability than the automobile, and their rapid obsolescence in wartime rendered them unlike small arms or artillery, which were of standard types that changed infrequently and could be produced by state-run arsenals.

Strategy, Tactics, and Losses

The sheer numbers of airplanes on the western front by 1918, more than 8,000 on all sides, indicate that the air war in general, and aerial combat in particular, was no longer an individual affair but a matter of collective, coordinated tactics. As the war had expanded in scope, the basic tactical unit, the French escadrille of 6 planes, the German Flieger-Abteilung of 6, and the British squadron of 12 planes expanded in size to 12, 9, and 18 planes respectively. These units were subsumed under increasingly larger ones, like the German fighter circuses of 60 planes, as the attempt to achieve aerial superiority led to concentration of forces. Under these circumstances, only a few exceptional aviators, epitomized by the Frenchman René Fonck, could fly alone and survive in 1918. The ultimate unit was the French aerial division of 1918, with more than 700 bombers and fighters intended for tactical air raids over German lines. Furthermore, wherever the war had spread – to East Africa, Gallipoli, the deserts of the Middle East – aircraft flew to observe, bomb, and fight for aerial superiority.

An aerial war of attrition over the western front meant high casualties for aviators, as illustrated by the most accurate figures available. Some 39 percent of the more than 18,000 aircrew trained in France in the five years from 1914 to 1919 became casualties, as did over 50 percent in Britain. In the absence of figures for aircrew trained in Germany, one can assume that their percentage of casualties was at least as high as that of the French and may have been higher than that of the British, because their force was smaller while their total number of casualties nearly equaled those of the British. While it is hard to compare these loss rates with those in the infantry, we do know that in the first six months of 1918, French infantry losses amounted to 51 percent of effectives, while the losses of French pilots at the front reached seventy-one percent.[13]

The Royal Air Force was sufficiently concerned about fragmentary evidence of casualties to trace the careers to 31 October 1918 of nearly 1,500 pilots sent to France from July to December 1917. The results: 18 percent had been killed; 26 percent had been hospitalized sick or wounded; 20 percent were missing over the lines; 25 percent had been transferred home; and 11 percent were still in France. Overall, then, 64 percent of those nearly 1,500 pilots were killed, wounded (or sick), or missing, and of the surviving 36 percent, about a quarter returned to England early in their tour. Only about a fourth of all pilots completed a tour of duty of nine months, a chastening thought should one be tempted to minimize the toll of flying in World War I.[14]

A further examination of casualties also indicates another reason why aviation was the reverse of heroic. Accidents, termed by an American medical officer "the most important medical problem of aviation," were the greatest source of fatalities. In the US Air Service, of 681 fatalities in flight personnel, 25 percent fell in combat and 75 percent in accidents, most of which occurred in flying school.[15] As slightly more than 2,000 American flying personnel arrived at the front during the war, for every four who survived to fight, one had not, that one symbolized by the short-lived Gary Cooper character in the movie *Wings*. In 1918 five Italian aviators were killed in accidents for every one in combat. But these were relatively small forces.

Among the major combatants, just over thirty-six percent of French fliers dead, or missing and presumed dead, perished in accidents in the rear areas. Of German losses, more than half were not attributable to enemy action. It is impossible to determine similar breakdowns of British losses, but training casualties were high. Admiral Mark Kerr, who commanded the southwest training area in England in 1918, lamented that nearly 300 pilots were killed in his region in a three-month period.[16]

It is certainly safe to say that aviators in all countries were more likely to die in accidents than in combat. The youthful volunteers knew that. Initially their irrepressibility and the callousness of wartime enabled them to cope with the situation. French wartime pilot and aviation artist Marcel Jeanjean recalled one exchange on the training school flight line while watching a crash: "Those poor fellows, they are going to kill themselves." "Too bad! That's war."[17] A British pilot recalled that fatal crashes on Sopwith Camels in training were so frequent that they stopped bothering to look up when they heard a Camel go into a spin and took for granted that they had lost another trainee pilot.

In most popular accounts of the demise of aviators there is a near total absence of blood and gore, giving death in the air a certain cleanliness. Yet the following account from Bernard Lafont's *Au Ciel de Verdun* dispels that romantic illusion. Two aviators have fallen from their Farman when attacked during the battle of Verdun:

> The first of the two men is impaled on the iron gate. There is the pierced body, a bloody rag. The wounds are enormous. Purple streams flow onto the clothes; drops hang and then fall one by one in a large puddle on the ground below. The second fell on the roof of the house. I clearly heard the dull sound of the body when it was crushed in a heap. Flouc! The body was recovered from the roof, entirely broken, shattered, shapeless and without rigidity like a heap of slime. They filled a coffin with it.

Contrary to the myth of Guynemer's death, that he had flown so high he could not descend, Lafont's account graphically reminds us that all aviators returned to earth, one way or another.[18]

This was no sport, no game. It was a deadly, ruthless, and capricious business, where a man's life depended not solely on his individual skills but on a combination of those skills, luck and machines that were very far from perfect. The widespread incidence of occupational hazards such as nerves indicated the stress involved in war flying. Compare photographs of Boelcke and Richthofen taken at the start of their careers to those taken a year or two later; they have aged greatly and no longer look like youths in their mid-twenties. Many men fell victim to flying fatigue, which caused sleeplessness, irritability, exhaustion and shakiness after landing, and most dangerous, carelessness in combat. Guynemer may have suffered from tuberculosis, which, exacerbated by his refusal to rest, meant that he was not only sick but increasingly nervous and irritable in the period before his death in combat in 1917. An American pilot complained that his nerves were shot; he knew that he would die sooner or later, but waiting for the moment was killing him.

Even for the survivors, nerves did not necessarily end with the war. Elliott White Springs, South Carolinian, Princetonian, and postwar textile magnate, spent seven months in combat with Royal Air Force (RAF) Squadron 85 and American squadron 148 attached to the British air arm. He survived to write *The Diary of an Unknown Aviator*, published in book form under the title *War Birds* in 1927, a brawling, boozing, yet grim and moving novel of the American aviators who flew with the British. The persistent postwar anxiety and depression that gripped Springs culminated in a "nervous breakdown" in 1942, from which he never completely recovered. Its roots lay in his poor relationship with his father and "a genuine war neurosis after 1918," which he managed for a time with writing and drink. Springs had written in 1918 that the "best part of me will always remain" at the front.[19] In a sense, he was correct.

American Edwin Parsons attributed the consumption of liquor to the need for a sedative for strained nerves. Opinions varied on the value of liquor, as German ace Max Immelmann, a physical fitness fanatic and teetotaler, believed that liquor led to overstretched nerves. If this was the case, the accounts of some Americans suggest that they must have suffered a surfeit of nerves, and one British author humorously conceded that if the British and Americans had drunk as much as some memoirs declared, they would not have lasted very long at the front.

Perhaps the most graphic account of one pilot's struggle with nerves is contained in the diary of Edward "Mick" Mannock, the Irishman who was Britain's highest-scoring ace. According to his biographer, Frederick Oughton, Mannock had two temporary nervous collapses and was often sick before patrols, much of his tension occasioned by the repeated breakdowns of his airplane, or "bus," as he called it. His diary recounts constant engine failures and gun jams; once during target practice his right bottom wing fell off. By the summer of 1918 the nervous strain was so great that his hands shook and he would burst into tears. He knew that he would die, but he feared burning to death, a hell to which he had gloatingly consigned many of the "Huns" that he passionately hated, so he carried a pistol to shoot himself. Shot down in flames from groundfire, Mannock's remains were never found, thus no one will ever know whether he had time to use the pistol.[20]

Beneath the veneer of glamor and chivalry, aerial combat was undeniably exhilarating and intoxicating for many of its participants, but also nerve-racking and frightening as well. Mannock's tearful outbursts after mechanical failures and witnessing the deaths of friends seem anomalous. Yet an incident cited in a recent edited work, *A Yankee Ace in the RAF. The World War I Letters of Captain Bogart Rogers*, indicates that the unwritten code of the prohibition of mourning in common actually led to the suppression of recollections of incidents that violated the code. Rogers published an article in 1930 describing how 32 Squadron disintegrated into hysterical tears, rage, and mourning in the "mess" the evening of the death of its favorite pilot. The next day the dead flier's best friend took off, shot down a German in revenge, and collapsed upon his return to the field, to be invalided out of the service with nerves from which he had still not recovered nearly a year later. Some of Rogers' former squadron mates reproached him for disclosing such an event; others accused him of exaggerating it. The essential point was that Rogers had compounded their violation of the unwritten code by writing about it twelve years later.[21]

Other Forms of Air War: Ground Attack, Reconnaissance, and Bombing

As grim and dangerous as it was, aerial fighting was only one aspect of air warfare. Ground attack, reconnaissance, and bombing were significant roles that directly affected the course of the war on the ground. One of the most difficult, and important tasks of aviation as the war continued was ground attack, for which the Germans evolved special units of battle or storm fliers equipped with light, maneuverable two-seat biplanes. These infantry fliers became an effective offensive and defensive weapon in 1917, attacking enemy batteries, strong points and infantry reserves with machine guns, grenades, and light fragmentation bombs. They suffered high losses in their dangerous work, as they ranged in squadron or group strength over the front at 2,000 feet, buffeted by the drafts of passing shells, and then descended to strafe troops from 300 feet above the trenches in the dead zone between the artillery fire from both sides. In these German ground attack units, only the commander was a commissioned officer; the crews were almost entirely NCOs and soldiers. Their fighting spirit was high, as they protected their infantry brothers below by flying above the *rue de merde*, or "shit street," as they called the front, on days when heavy rain and low cloud grounded other units. This was the air war at its grittiest, and at the battle of Messines in June and then at Cambrai in November and December 1917, they effectively controlled British breakthroughs and led attacks with demoralizing battlefield strafes of the enemy.[22]

British counterparts to these storm fliers in 1918 flew Sopwith Camels, which had won praise as the war's preeminent dogfighter in 1917, but whose essential task in 1918 was ground attack in high-risk assault squadrons. V. M. Yeates, author of the novel

Winged Victory and survivor of 248 hours and four crashes in Camels during 1918 before being discharged with tuberculosis in the summer, termed ground strafing "the last occupation on earth for longevity" and "the great casualty maker." Yeates considered it the most dangerous and valuable work that fighter pilots performed, though they received little credit for it.[23] From March to November 1918, RAF Assault Squadron 80, with a strength of 22 officers, suffered 168 casualties from all causes, or about 75 percent monthly, with almost half killed.[24] In *War Birds*, an American pilot who flew with the British, after surviving training in which three pilots practicing on Camels were killed in one day, commented that fighting Fokker D7s in Camels during the summer was exhausting and caused high losses. He concluded that it was "only a matter of time until we all get it."[25] As another American explained facetiously: "A Camel pilot had to shoot down every German plane in the sky in order to get home himself, as the Camel could neither out-climb nor outrun a Fokker."[26]

Perhaps the most essential task of all for aviation throughout the war was reconnaissance, and in the French and German air army cooperation planes were the preponderant types. The crews of the two-seater aircraft who routinely carried out these missions often flew in machines that left much to be desired. British BE2 biplanes, already obsolete in 1915, remained in service into 1917 – cannon fodder for German fighters – in part to complete production runs but also because many RFC pilots were not sufficiently well trained to fly higher performance planes. The "Quirks," as fighter pilots named these two-seater crews, flew straight to their target and back at low altitude. An awed fighter pilot presumed that they were so accustomed to being "ruthlessly archied" (shot at by ground fire) at low altitude that they had become fatalistic, like infantrymen. It never occurred to him that inadequate training may also have limited their ability to perform intricate maneuvers. In French aviation many army corps crews similarly struggled in the AR biplane, which was intended only as a stopgap when it appeared in 1916 but which served into 1918. The crews who manned these aircraft provided many of the victories for opposing fighter pilots.

At least the Germans tended to equip some of their reconnaissance crews with better planes in order to husband their dwindling manpower. They sent expert crews alone and at elevated altitude in high performance machines, using their skill and the planes' ability to evade the enemy. By the end of 1917 their Rumpler biplanes were capable of 20,000 foot ceilings on these missions, thanks to their high compression engines. British aces had a healthy respect for these crews, some of whom were formidable. In British ace James McCudden's accounts of separate combats with four two-seaters at high altitude in December 1917, three of them escaped. Canadian ace Billy Bishop's patrol of six once jumped a lone German two-seater, who turned in a flash, attacked them head-on, hitting Bishop's plane and another member of his squadron, and escaped, earning Bishop's accolade: "a very fine pilot and a very brave man."[27] Two-seat crews were usually the prey of fighter pilots, but occasionally the prey became the predator.

The final task of wartime aviation was bombing. On the Italian front by 1917, waves of 30 to 40 Caproni tri-motored biplanes supported infantry attacks by bombing Austro-Hungarian troops. The Capronis also staged long-distance raids across the Adriatic to bomb targets, sometimes flying as low as forty feet above the waves in their effort to strike by surprise and avoid anti-aircraft defenses. Over the western front in 1918 the French aerial division, whose nucleus was the superlative Breguet 14, a fast, sturdy single-engine two-seat biplane carrying twenty-four 22-pound bombs and defended by gunners armed with twin Lewis guns, aggressively raided across the lines in massed formations. Pétain sought clear aerial superiority in 1918 and methodically attacked enemy lines of communi-cation. The culmination of these massed tactical raids was the aerial support of the American Expeditionary Force's attack on St Mihiel in September 1918. There Colonel Billy Mitchell commanded nearly 1,500 airplanes, half American and half French, the largest concentra-tion of allied air forces during the war. The US Air Service had been trained and equipped primarily by the French, and, in the case of a few squadrons, by the British. This armada gained aerial control as the fighters penetrated over German airfields and the bombers struck targets on the battlefield and in the rear.

Tactical bombardment of enemy forces was one thing; the strategic bombing of enemy cities and civilians represented a major transgression of the accepted norms and provisions of international law on the conduct of war. The German government launched Zeppelins in 1915 and 1916, and then large bombers in 1917 and 1918 to bomb England in an attempt to drive Britain from the war. The attempt failed, but the campaign indicated a willingness to strike at civilian morale. The French had waged an unsuccessful strategic campaign against west German industrial towns in 1915. The British, unable to retaliate against German civilians until 1918, wanted to start, in the words of Secretary of State for Air Lord William Weir, "a really big fire" in a German town, assuming that such attacks would undermine German morale.[28] The war ended with the British poised to begin bombing Berlin, and with the value of strategic bombing unproven, but with the notion firmly established that the bombing of civilians could undermine their morale.

* * *

The postwar demobilization was so rapid that air forces and aviation industries shrank within two or three years to mere shadows of their wartime selves. The defeated of the war, such as Germany, were forced to disarm and forbidden to possess an air force, but even the victors, confronting huge wartime debts, dismantled their air forces so rapidly that in some cases they did not give the industry sufficient time to convert to the civil aviation field and many aircraft firms disappeared. The myths of the wartime aces none-theless endured; but the strategic bombing campaigns, however ineffective, remind us that the air weapon of World War I was truly the spawn of the era of total war, which conflated civilian and military targets and deemed the bombing of civilians, women and children included, an acceptable means of winning. These two powerful images – the romantic idealization of individual aerial combat rooted in the past and the brutal vision of massive civilian destruction foreshadowing the future – constituted World War I's dual legacy for military airpower.

Notes

1   KAdL, *Militärluftfahrt*, 2, p. 86. Jürgen Eichler, "Die Militärluftschiffahrt in Deutschland 1911–1914 und ihre Rolle in den Kriegsplänen des deutschen Imperialismus," *Zeitschrift für Militärgeschichte* 24, 4, 1985, pp. 350–60; ibid., 24, 5, 1985, pp. 403–12.

2   *The Aeroplane*, 3, 14 (October 2, 1913), p. 374.

3   Johannes Werner, *Knight of Germany. Oswald Boelcke. German Ace*, 1932; translation from the German, New York, 1972, pp. 145, 164, 172, 233–6.

4   Kennet, *First Air War, 1914–1918*, p. 160; Kilduff, *Richthofen*, pp. 165, 183–4, 219–20.

5   "Guynemer et les Cicognes," *Icare, revue de l'aviation française*, 122, 1987, pp. 27, 74, 87.

6   Cecil Lewis, *Sagittarius Rising*, 1936; new ed., London, Greenhill, 2003.

7   Liddle, *Airman's War*, pp. 64–9.
8   *Flight* 8, no. 5 (February 3, 1916), p. 97; ibid., no. 33 (August 17, 1916), pp. 705–6.
9   *Flight* 9, no. 16 (April 19, 1917); *Aeroplane* 12, no. 22 (May 30, 1917).
10 Randolph S. Churchill and Martin Gilbert, *Winston S. Churchill*, vol. 4, *1916–1922*, London, Heinemann, 1975, p. 61.
11 Christienne and Lissarrague, *Histoire*, pp. 83–7.
12 Morrow, *German Air Power* pp. 41–2, 73–120.
13 *Statistisches Jahrbuch für das Deutschen Reich 1924–1925*, p. 30. Raleigh and Jones, *War in the Air*, app. vol., app. 35. "Statistics regarding French Aviation during the War"; U.S. Naval Attaché to Office of Naval Intelligence, January 14, 1920, National Archives.
14 Folio 5, AIR 9/3, National Archives, London.
15 *Aviation Medicine in the AEF*, Washington, DC, Government Printing Office,1920, pp. 205, 217.
16 Mark Kerr, *Land, Sea, and Air. Reminiscences of Mark Kerr*, London, Longmans, Green, 1927, p. 280.
17 Marcel JeanJean, *Des Ronds dans l'Air: Souvenirs illustrés*, Aurillac: Imprimerie Moderne, 1967; *Sous les Cocardes. Scènes de l'aviation militaire*, 1919; new ed., Paris, Editions Serma, 1964.
18 Bernard Lafont, *Au ciel de Verdun: notes d'un aviateur*, Paris, H. Frémont, 1918, pp. 28–9.
19 Burke Davis, *War Bird: The Life and Times of Elliot White Springs*, Chapel Hill, University of North Carolina Press, 1987, passim.
20 Oughton and Smyth, *Ace with One Eye*.
21 John H. Morrow, Jr. & Earl Rogers, *A Yankee Ace in the RAF. The World War I Letters of Captain Bogart Rogers*, Lawrence, Kansas, University Press of Kansas, 1996.
22 Georg P. Neumann (ed.), *In der Luft unbesiegt: Erlebnisse im Weltkrieg*, Munich, Lehmanns, 1923, pp. 79–91, 166–75. J. C. Nerney, "The Battle of Cambrai," AIR 1/678/21/13/1942, National Archives, London.
23 V. M. Yeates,*Winged Victory*, 1934; new edition, London, Ashford, Buchan and Enright, 1985.
24 John C. Slessor, *Air Power and Armies*, London: Oxford University Press, 1936, p. 100.
25 John M. Grider, *War Birds: Diary of an Unknown Aviator*. Elliot W. Springs ed., Garden City, NY, The Sundial Press, 1938, pp. 221, 233–7.
26 Quoted in James J. Hudson, *Hostile Skies. A Combat History of the American Air Service in World War I*, Syracuse: Syracuse University Press, 1998, p. 202.
27 William A. Bishop, *Winged Warfare, 1918*; new ed., London, Crécy Publishing, 2007, p. 133.
28 Weir to Trenchard, September 10, 1918, MFC 76/1/94, Royal Air Force Museum.

References and Further Reading

Christienne, Charles, and Lissarrague, Pierre, *A History of French Military Aviation*, 1980: translation from the French, Washington, DC, Smithsonian Institution Press, 1980.

Cooper, Malcolm, *The Birth of Independent Airpower: British Air Policy in the First World War*, London, Unwin Hyman, 1986.

Fritzsche, Peter, *A Nation of Fliers: German Aviation and the Popular Imagination*, Cambridge, MA, Harvard University Press, 1992.

Grosz, Peter, et al., *Austro-Hungarian Army Aircraft of World War I*, Mountain View, CA, Flying Machines Press, 1993.

Higham, Robin, and Kipp, Jacob (eds.), *Soviet Aviation and Air Power: A Historical View*, London, Brassey's, 1978.

Kennett, Lee, *The First Air War, 1914–1918*, New York, Free Press, 1991.

Kilduff, Peter, *Richthofen: Beyond the Legend of the Red Baron*, London, John Wiley, 1994.

Liddle, Peter H., *The Airman's War 1914–18*, Poole, Blandford Press, 1987.

Maurer, Maurer (ed.), *The U.S. Air Service in World War I*, 4 vols., Washington, DC, Office of Air Force History, 1978–9.

Morrow, John H., Jr., *German Airpower in World War I*, Lincoln, University of Nebraska Press, 1982.

Morrow, John H., Jr., *The Great War in the Air: Military Aviation from 1909 to 1921*, Washington, DC, Smithsonian Institution Press, 1993.

Orton, Frederick, and Smyth, Vernon, *Ace with One Eye: the Life and Combats of Major Edward Mannock, V.C., D.S.O*, London, Muller, 1963.

Paris, Michael, *Winged Warfare: The Literature of Aerial Warfare in Britain, 1859–1917*, Manchester, Manchester University Press, 1992.

Raleigh, Walter, and Jones, H. A., *The War in the Air: Being the Story of the Part Played in the Great War by the Royal Air Force*, 6 vols, London, Oxford University Press, 1922–37.

Vergnano, Piero, *Origins of Aviation in Italy, 1783–1918*, Genoa, Edizioni Intyprint, 1964.

Winter, Denis, *The First of the Few: Fighter Pilots of the First World War*, London, Allen Lane, 1982.

Wise, S.F., *Canadian Airmen and the First World War: The Official History of the Royal Canadian Air Force*, vol. 1, Toronto, University of Toronto Press, 1980.

Wohl, Robert, *A Passion for Wings: Aviation and the Western Imagination*, New Haven, Yale University Press, 1994.

PART III

Faces of War

CHAPTER TWELVE

Combat

STÉPHANE AUDOIN-ROUZEAU
(translated by Heather Jones)

During the course of World War I combat methods changed radically in ways that would permanently alter how war was waged in the twentieth century and, indeed, how the West related to warfare as an activity. Hence the question of combat and the ways in which it evolved in 1914–18 is a crucial aspect of the war, and one that is inseparable from how the conflict was perceived both at the time and after the armistice on November 11, 1918.

From Imagined Combat to Trench Warfare

Before war became reality for millions of Europeans in August 1914, combat was primarily an *imagined* practice. Anticipating war was naturally a major priority for the chiefs of staff of the different armies of the Western powers. However, imagining war was not restricted to the military. In the prewar period it also concerned public opinion more generally. The kinds of combat the prewar public imagined were largely based upon the experience of previous conflicts. For many the war of 1870–1 provided the most recent example of combat between major European powers. For this reason, there was a shared expectation in Europe that any future war would be a short war of movement in which the offensive would be crucial. The belief was that the combat experience of the individual soldier in battle would be intense but relatively brief. The general perception of war remained deeply marked by a traditional ethos that surrounded combat violence. This ethos was integral to strategic and tactical thinking, and was a central part of the instruction of recruits within early twentieth-century mass armies. It also informed the whole military body, its uniform, equipment, armament, and logistics, as well as greatly influencing the representation of both commanders and combatants.

The massive military engagements in August and September 1914 on the eastern and western fronts occurred within the context of this prewar understanding of war and of the combat experience. The failure to accurately estimate the devastating impact of modern firepower was a determining characteristic of this opening phase of the war. This was the reason for the horrific losses during the first weeks of combat. Yet the military conflicts around the turn of the century had provided many lessons on the transformation of combat that resulted from the use of modern armaments: the Boer War (1899–1902), the Russo-Japanese War (1904–5), and the two Balkan Wars (1912–13) had been closely watched by military observers from the major European powers who had plenty of opportunity to note the new, terrifying effect of firepower upon the armies concerned. But what was missing in 1914 was less the observation of recent developments in warfare than an inability to draw any conclusions from observations that contradicted existing shared beliefs of what a future war *ought* to be like.

Thus there was a belief that because firepower made the battlefield more lethal any future war would of necessity be short, requiring offensive strategies and tactics that demanded the maximum moral exertion by the combatant. This astonishing process of self-deception, that marked prewar expectations of war and of combat, was brutally exposed by the realities of the battlefield experience in 1914. These battlefield realities would profoundly change the use of violence in combat over the course of the following four years in both scale and form.

The "Great War" rapidly became a "trench war" to the extent that the two terms became almost synonymous in the historical memory of westerners. Yet in 1914 trenches were not a new invention. They had been used in siege warfare since antiquity and in the conflicts which directly preceded World War I trenches had played an important role, indicating that this form of combat was about to enjoy something of a renaissance. At the battle of Mukden in February–March 1905 during the Russo-Japanese War, trenches had proved crucial. However, it was during World War I that deploying the infantry in trenches developed into a system that was unprecedented in its extent and sophistication, though at the cost of totally transforming the nature of warfare itself.

Trench warfare originated with the improvised defenses put in place by the infantry immediately after the battle of the Marne in September 1914, and with the "race to the sea" that lasted until the autumn. Exhausted by the enormous efforts they had made during the opening period, soldiers spontaneously dug "foxholes" to protect themselves from shells. These individual holes were progressively linked together and became the basis for the first trench lines. The German infantry, which was better trained at building field defenses, appears to have taken the lead in instigating a systematic trench network, earning the opprobrium of the Allies who accused them of degrading the traditional forms of combat. On the western front consolidation of front-line positions took place during the fall of 1914, creating a strategic impasse that would last for four years. Trenches developed on practically all fronts during the war. In the east, however, they only began to appear in December 1914 and remained relatively rudimentary. These positions, which were shallower and less organized than those on the western front, were more easily abandoned according to the movement of the different armies. Thus on the eastern front mobile warfare continued until the massive Russian retreat in spring and summer 1915, following which a static trench war emerged that was similar to that in the west.

Firepower

World War I thus contributed to a definitive transformation of the *techniques du corps* (or bodily techniques) of the Western combatant.[1] The trench system ensured the superiority of the defensive over the offensive. This was one of the main characteristics of World War I and it helps to explain the new intensity of the use of firepower on the battlefield that the conflict witnessed.

The repeating rifle used by Western armies at the beginning of the twentieth century could fire over ten projectiles a minute in the form of fast, spinning, conical bullets across a target distance of around 600 m. These bullets caused extreme injuries, silently killing and wounding on a battlefield that appeared empty. Alongside the rifle, which was often awkward to handle in the trenches, the grenade came to play an increasingly important role in the soldier's personal weaponry. Originally used in siege warfare, the first modern grenades were employed during the Russo-Japanese war, and this innovation aroused the interest of the German General Staff with the result that the German army had access to a large number of grenades at the opening of World War I. On the western front their use developed rapidly. Grenades required careful handling and armies soon developed grenadiers who were placed in the vanguard of attacks. They were a major element of infantry attacks in 1918, as revealed in the writings of Ernst Jünger, who described the massive use of grenades by assault troops.[2] In this regard the German hand grenades proved a highly effective weapon. However, the grenade, which was originally a weapon of attack, was also frequently used as a defensive weapon in close combat, by night patrols in no man's land, for example, or as a means of "cleaning out" all enemy dugouts after the capture of a trench.

As well as more efficient personal weaponry carried by the individual soldier, World War I was characterized by the machine gun, a weapon that epitomized industrial warfare, and which could fire a hail of bullets, some 400–600 a minute. "Machine-gunning is without parallel as a method of slaughter, since it literally spares no one," wrote the French historian Marc Bloch in his book *Strange Defeat*, referring directly to his experience in World War I.[3] The phrase is revealing, highlighting the terrible memories of the machine gun which former combatants shared. In 1914 the machine gun was a relatively new weapon and its use in actual warfare even more so. The Russo-Japanese War of 1904–5 and the Balkan Wars in 1912–13 were the first to see them deployed, but on too small a scale to play any significant role. In contrast, during World War I, the range of the machine gun was sufficient to prevent attackers from crossing no man's land unless their artillery had first destroyed enemy machine-gun emplacements. The effectiveness of the machine gun was all the greater where the enemy line of attack was predictable and machine-gun emplacements had been set up to cover it: this was the case during the British offensive at the Somme on July 1, 1916, during which machine-gun fire paralyzed the waves of attacking troops the moment they left the shelter of their trenches. The characteristic noise of the machine gun was instantly recognizable. Once they heard it ahead of them, attacking infantry knew that in all likelihood they were marching to their deaths.

Despite the effectiveness of the machine gun, however, throughout the war it was the artillery that offered the main means of dominating the battlefield, especially once gunnery development reached its zenith in 1916. The predominance of the artillery owed its origins to major technical innovations during the final 30 years of the nineteenth century, such as the steel barrel, internal rifling, hydraulic recoil mechanism, and new types of ammunition, including smokeless explosives. Between 1800 and 1914, artillery performance had increased tenfold.

At the start of the war, artillery was basically made up of rapid-fire field guns that were intended to support armies engaged in a war of movement. They were designed to fire shells at high speed against visible targets and operated with a low trajectory. Thus the French 75-mm gun, which was the best field gun at the time, was light and mobile with a firing range of 9 km. It was deployed in small batteries intended to provide immediate support for infantry advances and was capable of firing at the very rapid rate of 30 shells a minute for short periods. Other armies used comparable weapons, such as the German

77-mm Krupp field gun, which was also used by the Austro-Hungarian army, the British 18-pounder, and the 3-in. Russian and American field guns. The same field-gun models were also to be found among smaller armies that had bought them from the larger powers.

Paradoxically, the role that heavy artillery would play in the war became obvious in the very first weeks of the conflict during the period of mobile warfare. The effective use of German and Austrian howitzers to destroy the forts at Liège and Namur in August–September 1914 rapidly convinced army general staffs on both the eastern and western fronts of the value of heavy artillery. The development of trench warfare, which quickly followed, meant that heavy artillery became crucial as it was needed to attack well-entrenched dugouts and underground shelters, to destroy enemy trenches, and to hit enemy rear positions. Mass bombardment was the principal tactical response to the continuation of the strategic impasse and heavy artillery, which until this point had been used to defend permanent defensive positions, now took the place of field artillery. Trench warfare also meant it was necessary to develop new types of heavy guns able to destroy underground positions, something that was beyond the capability of guns designed to fire at a low angle. The result was the howitzer, which was capable of firing shells at a high angle over a relatively short distance against entrenched targets. Here again the demands of the war led to the development of increasingly heavy howitzers.

Overall, heavy artillery came to dominate the many different forms of firepower on the field of battle. Firepower varied widely according to the tactical objectives of any given operation and could be used in multiple ways: barrage fire; reprisal fire; demonstration fire; controlling fire; harassing fire; encircling fire; concentrated fire; destructive or annihilating fire. In addition, firing poison-gas shells became increasingly common over the course of the conflict, and by the armistice a quarter of all shells contained toxic gas. While heavy artillery evolved along the lines of ancient siege weaponry for the modern era, mobile artillery with a high trajectory was also being developed with the aim of carrying out bombardments at short range.

A major shortage of shells provoked a crisis in the Russian army in late summer 1914 and a similar shortage of munitions hit the German and French armies in the fall of the same year, with the British following in the spring of 1915. Once these supply problems had been resolved, the new role of the artillery became strikingly evident. There was a spectacular increase in munitions production and in the number of shells fired. During the seven day Allied bombardment on the Somme that preceded the offensive on July 1, 1916, 1,500,000 shells were fired by 50,000 British gunners, requiring an unimaginable physical effort by these artillery teams. This was an average of 30 shell explosions per 1,000 sq. m. In 1918, the Allied offensives on the western or Italian fronts were regularly supported by 5,000–8,000 guns. This dramatic increase in artillery use had multiple consequences. Armies became increasingly dependent on different forms of aerial observation, which in turn meant it was necessary to camouflage military positions. Forms of traction also evolved as a result of the increasing mechanization of the battlefield. In this regard the tank was seen as a kind of artillery that could move by itself, hence the French description of it as "assault artillery."

Nevertheless it remained impossible to move artillery across battlefields that had already been pulverized by shellfire, hampering the effective use of artillery fire to support infantry assaults once they moved beyond the enemy's front-line trenches. In this way the violence of bombardments in 1914–18 acted as an internal limitation upon the effective use of artillery during major attempts to break through trench lines. In addition, even the most powerful artillery used during the war was never able to destroy deep dugouts. This was illustrated at the Somme in 1916 and at the Chemin des Dames in 1917, where German underground positions remained intact despite the heavy artillery bombardments that preceded these offensives.

Artillery played an absolutely central role in combat in 1914–18. From 70 to 80 percent of all war wounds were caused by shellfire. Shell explosions produced numerous fragments of shrapnel that were extremely dangerous. Those wounded by shellfire often suffered from multiple wounds, with their bodies lacerated by numerous pieces of steel fragments. The largest shell fragments projected at high velocity were capable of slicing through any part of the human body. In the case of a direct hit by a shell human bodies could literally be vaporized. The sensory experience of shellfire was also highly traumatic. In 1917, one soldier wrote somberly in his unit's trench newspaper: "there is nothing worse in war than being bombarded."[4]

Although violence at a distance was one of the key characteristics of World War I, this does not mean that fighting at close quarters did not take place, such as during assaults on enemy trenches. The demands of this kind of fighting, which was particularly terrifying, led to the development of weapons for hand-to-hand combat using such weapons as daggers and maces. It is difficult to know on what scale or in what ways these arms were used. A variety of types of trench club developed, as seen in the many different models that have survived. These appear to have been used for the capture of prisoners in no man's land or as a defensive weapon when fighting an enemy incursion at close quarters. In the German army the spontaneous use of the trench shovel with a sharpened edge as an effective weapon by combatants led to it being recognized as an official weapon for hand-to-hand fighting in tactical regulations issued after 1916.

The experience of combat not only changed soldiers' weaponry, it also radically altered their attire. Bright colors and shiny objects disappeared from uniforms during 1915, including the insignia of rank that officers wore. At the same time armies researched the types of clothing that would better withstand bad weather and prolonged periods living in trenches. The French army was seen as particularly slow to adapt its military clothing to trench warfare, and all kinds of expedients were tried during the first months of the war before it finally settled on the new horizon-blue uniform, definitively adopted during the second half of 1915. The main innovation in the matter of uniforms, however, was the introduction of the steel helmet, which offered protection for the head and neck. From 1915 on the helmet came to be seen as essential in practically all the belligerent armies, with the notable exception of the Russian forces. Although the helmet could do nothing against a direct hit, it offered protection from the impact of shell fragments. It also spared its wearer the injuries caused by falling stones during a shell explosion and could deflect a projectile in certain circumstances.

As the amount and diversity of armaments and equipment increased, soldiers became increasingly weighed down. They were laden with weapons, changes of clothing, drinking flasks, cutlery, a blanket, tent canvas, camping tools, trench tools, reserve rations, leather straps, belts and ammunition pouches, gas masks, dressings, and all manner of personal objects, such as letters, photographs, books, religious objects, medicines, food sent from home, walking sticks, etc. All of this not only weighed down their kitbags but also filled their satchels and pockets. It was not unusual for a World War I soldier to carry 30 kg or more. This helps to explain the exhausting ordeal that the march to the front or a journey to rest positions in the rear across a maze of communication trenches represented for infantrymen, especially in hot or wet weather.

Drawing upon his experience in World War I, the historian Marc Bloch described how the evolution of soldiers' equipment and the accelerated transformation of the modes of combat interacted over the four years of the conflict:

> Early in 1918 General Gouraud, an enthusiastic and ingenious educator, paraded two companies of infantry before a mixed class of officers, of whom I was one. The first of these two companies was equipped with the weapons, and performed the evolutions, of 1914. The other was of an entirely new type, armed, organized and handled in accordance with the latest theories. The contrast was startling.[5]

Technical Expertise in Trench Warfare

On the western front trench warfare gradually reached a high degree of sophistication and the techniques developed there were copied in the secondary theaters of the war such as the Austro-Italian and Balkan fronts, where living conditions and combat were much more difficult because of the mountainous terrain. They were also implemented at the Dardanelles where the Turkish control of the high ground made life particularly difficult for their British adversaries, mainly troops from Australia and New Zealand who held the trenches below them.

In trench warfare opposing soldiers were separated from each other by an extremely dangerous zone known as no man's land. Its size varied from several hundred meters in low-lying areas to just tens of meters in wooded or mountainous terrain. The view across no man's land was obstructed by immense networks of barbed wire placed in position by nocturnal working parties of soldiers.

From one end of no man's land to the other, the trenches appeared as a successive series of lines of defense, lying more or less parallel to each other but never built in a straight line in order to avoid enfilade fire and to limit the impact of shell explosions. The front-line trench was designed for combat with a raised parapet made up of earth-filled sacks, slits, and a fire step from which soldiers could shoot. Beyond the front-line trench there were advanced observation positions or "listening" posts in no man's land, manned by lookouts. Before an attack secret assembly trenches or saps were dug out into no man's land. These provided an advanced "jumping-off" line where troops could assemble before launching an assault on enemy positions.

The front and support lines of trenches were linked by communication trenches that were built at right angles to the front-line positions. The support trenches made up the second line of defense, generally built against a gradient to avoid observation and enemy fire. These support trenches were protected by a second layer of barbed wire. The support trenches in turn were linked to a reserve trench from which other communication trenches led off to the rear where the soldiers' rest billets were located. This extended defense complex corresponded with subtly changing degrees of danger.

In mountainous sectors such as Italy, the Balkans, or the Vosges in eastern France, trenches were dug into the rock at the cost of unimaginable physical effort. Cold and snow were the main problems in these environments. Trenches built in flat sectors faced drainage problems caused by a combination of impermeable soil and a climate that was humid for most of the year. Massive amounts of material were required to maintain the trench lines in working condition and to repair damage caused by bad weather. Timberwork and fascines were used to support the wall of the trench and the walls and roofs of shelters. In the front line shelters were often little more than a hole dug into the wall of the trench. Deeper shelters or dugouts were located underground, with steps leading to them. They were larger, with roofs made of logs to protect their inhabitants. Duckboards were laid on the floor of the trench in an attempt to create a walkway above the stagnant water that gathered on the ground. However, bombardments and bad weather soon illustrated the limits of these different aspects of trench construction. Shellfire rapidly destroyed carefully organized trench positions and in bad weather the trenches became waterlogged, often flooding up to the knee. From the winter of 1914–15 a new illness known as "trench foot" appeared that could turn into gangrene. Trench foot was the result of the atrocious living conditions combatants endured in the trenches. In contrast, on other fronts such as the Dardanelles, illnesses associated with a hot climate and appalling hygiene conditions produced a very high death rate.

The Germans pioneered the use of concrete blocks in the construction of deep, secure underground shelters. These were sometimes linked to form a network and were often heated and lit by electricity. The way that combatants envisaged the trenches differed between the opposing sides. For the Germans who occupied Belgium and large parts of northern and eastern France, as well as vast territories seized from Russia, trench warfare could seem a kind of acceptable provisional situation that was a precursor to the enemy eventually becoming totally exhausted and surrendering. For their opponents, however, to settle in the trenches and accept the prospect of a long period of subterranean existence was to abandon all hope of reconquering the land seized by Germany. This was the reason for the Allies' rudimentary trench building, as they saw trench warfare as a temporary situation. This was also the reason for the large number of useless, bloody attacks against enemy positions and the continual obsession with bringing about a "breakthrough." It also explains the constant counterattacks to retake front-line trenches after any temporary setback.

The Germans were also behind the systematic development of the principle of "in-depth defense." From 1916, successive lines of German trenches were built on the western front separated by 2–3 km and supported by concrete pillboxes with machine-gun emplacements. These allowed defenders to withdraw to secure positions during an attack, letting the enemy take a certain amount of front territory, while the defenders regrouped and then counterattacked.

At the Somme in 1916 and later at the Chemin des Dames in 1917 this defensive structure proved lethally effective against British and French attacks. Begun in September 1916, the Hindenburg Line, composed of fortified zones (*Stellung*) built to the rear of the front across an area of 15 km epitomized this new German system of defense established between the North Sea and Verdun. In 1918, this defensive system considerably slowed down the Allies' advance before its main strongholds finally surrendered during the fall. The British, for their part, adopted in-depth defense only gradually from the end of 1916. The French took even longer, only establishing in-depth defenses from 1917. In 1918, anticipating a German attack, Pétain still found it difficult to convince the French army to abandon the systematic defense of every front-line position.

The trench system posed major logistical problems caused by the lack of troop mobility, the difficulty of transporting *matériel*, and the problems of supplying provisions. The rail networks that were generally used could only run on a straight track and could not provide transport to the front lines for infantry working parties or supplies. Collecting food was often an exhausting chore for front-line troops. The field telephone was used to transmit most information but its wires were fragile and had to be constantly repaired during offensives and bombardments. As a result flares and liaison agents were often used as a replacement means of communication. Above all troop movements were tortuous for the soldiers, who had to pass along a maze of winding communication trenches that tripled the number of kilometers they traveled compared to the same journey as the crow flies. The deliberate narrowness of trench pathways, the obstacles and tunnels, the state of the soil and the trench bulwarks, the weight each individual had to carry, the encounters between columns of troops moving in opposite directions, all contributed to the infantry's state of exhaustion. At night the journey became even more difficult. In spite of their guides troops easily became lost for hours in the labyrinth of trenches. The wounded in particular suffered terribly, slung in a tent canvas or lying on stretchers which were difficult to move through the communication trenches, or forced to make their own way to the first-aid posts.

However, the rudimentary appearance of the trench system was deceptive. The development of new forms of observation such as periscopes, aerial balloons or airplanes using aerial photography, and the novel use of camouflage and decoys were all proof of an increasing sophistication. The modes of combat used in trench warfare, such as elite snipers and nocturnal raiding patrols in no man's land with the objective of taking prisoners, were also not without an element of subtlety. Regular firing on enemy positions maintained a climate of danger that required constant vigilance.

Detailed knowledge of a whole trench sector was very important in combat, something which helps to explain the high losses suffered by novice soldiers or those who had only recently been moved into a new sector they did not know. However, within the trenches combat was not a permanent activity. In fact, it was often an exceptional occurrence. Actual fraternization between adversaries was very rare. The Christmas truce of 1914, where British and French troops met up with Germans, remained an isolated occurrence. However, tacit truces or agreements were far more widespread. These made life in the trenches less dangerous and exhausting for both sides.[6]

Surviving in the trenches required a certain specialized combat "know-how," which explains why it was so difficult for French and British troops to switch to offensive mobile warfare during the summer of 1918. Trained to fight trench warfare and knowing all its potential pitfalls, it was hard for these troops to relate to combat on open ground. In contrast, the Americans experienced far less difficulty adapting to the change.

The New Siege Warfare and the Attack:
the End of the Battle?

Ultimately, the establishment of a trench system turned World War I into an immense, long siege. The trenches were the equivalent of inverted walls that stretched across flat countryside for hundreds of kilometers. Attacking techniques evolved in the face of such an effective system of defense. Initial attempts at a breakthrough occurred without a preliminary artillery bombardment and involved infantrymen running at barbed wire which had not been destroyed by shelling, making it impossible to cross. As the war went on long artillery bombardments were used to destroy enemy defenses so that the attacking infantry could advance more easily. However, these advance bombardments also alerted the enemy that an attack was about to take place. The rolling barrage, which was adopted as a general tactic from 1916 on, was a refined version of the preliminary artillery bombardment. Following meticulous planning, the rolling barrage allowed the attacking infantry to move forward in stages behind a wave of artillery shelling that progressively targeted the areas ahead of them, keeping pace with their advance. However, although this innovation reduced casualty rates among attacking troops, it did not lead to any definitive breakthrough. In contrast, the infiltration tactics, which were developed by the German army in fall 1917, were very successful. Infiltration tactics involved attacks led by elite storm-trooper units who were trained to push as far forward as possible through the enemy's defensive lines.[7] The effectiveness of this approach can be seen in the breakthrough at Caporetto in October 1917, the German counter-offensive at Cambrai in December 1917 and the German breakthrough in Picardy in March 1918.

While the Allied general staffs reacted to the strategic impasse caused by in-depth defense by planning attacks in ever greater detail (prior to attacks officers synchronized their watches), the German tactic of infiltration was more effective. It was facilitated by the greater autonomy allowed to lower-level units backed up by a command structure that was capable of adapting rapidly in response to the lessons learned from battle experience.

However, the German tactic did not prove decisive. In trench warfare the further each offensive pushed through the enemy's defenses, the more its momentum diminished. The exhaustion of the waves of attacking troops, the inability to move artillery forward over terrain that had been destroyed by bombardment, and the enemy's capacity to bring in reinforcements by lorry or train all contributed to the failure of every major attempt to break through the defensive trench systems on the western front. Each such attempt rapidly collapsed into unending, costly clashes, often drawn out over many months. The strategic impasse was only broken in the second half of 1918 owing to the combined effect of the exhaustion of all German manpower reserves, the new effective coordinated use of the tank and the airplane, and the demographic advantage that the Allies gained from the arrival of American troops.

The trenches of 1914–18 had a major effect upon the Western tradition of combat, which was centered upon a form of very violent, but brief, confrontations that took place within a limited area: in other words the battle.[8] The "battles" of World War I pushed the definition of battle to the point of absurdity. The predominance of the defensive over the offensive meant that these were battles in name only. In reality, they were far closer to sieges in open country which used modernized versions of all the techniques that had been used in traditional siege warfare: lines of trenches which in a way acted as hollow ramparts, mines dug underneath enemy positions, grenades, artillery fired at a high angle with a steeply curved trajectory, etc. As with traditional sieges, the process took a very long time. This helps to explain why the "battle" of Verdun lasted 10 months, the Somme five months and Ypres saw two periods of prolonged action lasting a month in 1915 and five months in 1917.

Innovations: Gas, Airplanes, and Tanks

Combat methods changed radically during World War I, leading to the introduction of new technologies that would permanently transform the face of Western warfare.

The use of gas was without doubt one of the most dramatic innovations. At Ypres in April 1915 the Germans became the first army to employ gas in combat on a significant scale. At Ypres, chlorine gas was used. The development of gas warfare proceeded rapidly: new types of gas were introduced, such as mustard gas in 1917, and the release of indiscriminate clouds of gas from canisters was replaced by poison-gas shells which were far more effective, secure, and flexible to use.

Once the initial surprise at the use of gas had passed, however, it proved a rather inefficient weapon. Countermeasures, in particular protective masks, developed more quickly than the different methods of gas attack: once again defensive techniques were more effective than offensive methods. Moreover, gas casualties were only a tiny percentage of total losses in World War I, reaching a maximum of between 3 and 4 percent on the western front. However, the use of gas left an enduring memory of terror. This was probably linked to the anthropological transgression which death by suffocation in battle represented, as those killed by gas died without receiving any battle wound.

In contrast to poison gas, the airplane was developed before the war. Yet it was only during the conflict that it became established as a major new structural development in warfare, adding a third dimension to combat: war in the air (see chapter 11). The military potential of airplanes and balloons was recognized by armies long before 1914. However, the idea of an air force was still in its infancy at the outbreak of the conflict. Aviation proceeded to develop rapidly, especially on the western front, which was the most important theater of operations for air power as for so much else. At the end of the war each belligerent had amassed several thousands of aircraft. However, it was the dramatic improvement in the quality of airplanes available that had the greatest impact on the battlefield.

In 1914, airplanes were not powerful enough to carry heavy loads or to fly against prevailing winds or at night. The role of aviation was limited to reconnaissance missions, such as those that took place before the battle of the Marne, liaison work, and providing information on artillery targets. The advent of trench warfare increased the role of airpower. Long-distance reconnaissance missions were instigated and airplanes carried out low-range aerial photography and target-spotting assignments, which gathered information used to guide artillery fire onto enemy positions. Such operations were extremely costly. The majority of aircraft shot down over the western front between 1914 and 1918 were reconnaissance planes. In response to the development of aerial reconnaissance, anti-aircraft defenses evolved, as well as fighter planes, which were intended to prevent the enemy from entering its adversary's airspace.

There was fierce technological competition between the belligerents in the air war. Over the course of the conflict, technological supremacy shifted several times from one side to the other. By fall 1918 however, Allied planes predominated. They were now deployed in large groups, often consisting of several dozen aircraft, which engaged in aerial combat or dogfights, as well as strategic bombing. Airplanes were also now used to provide major aerial support for infantry during offensives on the ground. Between March and November 1918, attacking the enemy's trenches became the principal tactical role of military aviation. As a result airpower played a major part in all the battles of the last year of the war. Losses remained very heavy largely because of the development of anti-aircraft defenses such as arc lights, anti-aircraft netting, balloon barrages, incendiary ammunition, and fighter planes.

In addition, from 1917, air operations were increasingly closely linked with tank actions. This occurred in direct response to the strategic impasse on the western front. After the British navy had established the first basic specifications for tank models, prototypes were built, followed by the construction of experimental models. This led in turn to the production of the first Mark I tanks in April 1916, which were codenamed "water tanks." From this codename the new weapon soon became known simply as tanks. Tanks were first used by the British at the Somme on September 15, 1916. British progress in tank development encouraged French research into "assault tanks." In late 1915 the first experimental trials took place, followed by the first tank production at the start of 1916 at the Schneider and Creusot factories. These vehicles were used for the first time during the Nivelle Offensive in April 1917.

However, the effectiveness of British tanks in combat proved disappointing. In September 1916 the tanks used at the Somme had not been adequately tested and they were driven by teams that had been insufficiently trained. This led to losses of approximately 50 percent and no tactical advantage whatsoever. Tanks once again failed to produce conclusive results when they were deployed in small groups during the attack at Arras in April 1917. The new models that were used at Messines in June 1917 and Ypres during the following summer became bogged down by the muddy conditions. The French tanks did not enjoy any greater success. In April 1917, tanks were deployed in terrain that had been too heavily bombarded for them to advance, resulting in losses of 60 percent. It was not until the French offensive at Malmaison in October 1917 that tanks were successful for the first time. This was followed by the British attack at Cambrai on November 20, 1917 where 380 tanks led the assault on the German trenches, successfully breaking through the two first lines of German defenses before German fire caused major losses to the Tank Corps.

The Germans were slow to recognize the potential of tanks.[9] Following the British tank attack at Cambrai in November 1917, which the Germans finally repulsed, Ludendorff believed that "the best weapons against tanks were steady nerves, discipline, and initiative." In fact, the Germans had developed many tactics for dealing with tanks such as anti-tank ditches, camouflaged pits, minefields made up of buried mortars, and anti-tank guns. They also used blocking fire from artillery or machine guns and strongholds protected by one or two field guns to combat tanks.

The British army did not abandon heavy tanks although it continued its research to develop lighter variants. The medium-weight Whippet tank was introduced in the British army at the end of 1917 and played an increasingly important role in British armored-vehicle operations in 1918. With the support of 1,000 French planes, a large number of heavy tanks were used in the British offensive in Picardy on August 8, 1918, which met with very little resistance. For its part, the French army had switched its tank production to focus on lighter models. Renault was entrusted with this task in October 1917. Close to five hundred light tanks were used to successfully break through the forest at Villers-Cotterêts during the French counter-offensive at the Aisne on July 18, 1918. They were deployed close to the infantry as a support weapon and used in conjunction with hundreds of airplanes. Tanks were also used during the final offensives of 1918, notably during the joint Franco-American Meuse-Argonne attack on September 26.

In an anthropological sense, heavy tanks first appeared as a land version of the naval warship. In contrast, light tanks can be regarded as the battlefield successors of the horse. From the beginning of the war the cavalry had lost its age-old role as a force used to break through enemy lines. In fact, this cavalry role had been in decline since 1870. Light tanks in many ways offered a second chance to cavalrymen, who were strongly represented among the new tank units. The body language and vocabulary of the Renault tank teams reveals a strong link with cavalry culture. Cavalrymen also entered aviation units, where there was a similar preponderance of terms borrowed from the cavalry.

The link made between the fighter plane and the racehorse was based upon the unstable nature and agility of the plane engines, the importance of balance for both flying and riding, the command of the plane using a joystick and wires akin to controlling a horse using reins, and the use of a vocabulary which was directly borrowed from the cavalry. In the French case pilots "mounted" their plane (*monter*) and the verb used for nosing a plane up in the air was the same as that used to describe a rearing horse (*cabrer*). The ethos of aerial combat was also a direct product of cavalry traditions. Baron von

Richthofen, one of the most famous German flying aces, stated that "one could compare dogfights to the ancient duels of knights." Ultimately, the tank and the plane, which from this point on were indelibly associated with each other, marked a new departure in wartime combat methods that would have long-lasting effects.

The Cost of Combat

The high casualty rates during World War I were historically unprecedented. The number of military dead among the Western belligerents amounted to approximately 9 million (see chapter 17, table 17.1). The average war losses for the years 1914–18 equaled approximately 900 deaths *per day* for France, over 1,300 deaths per day for Germany, and 1,450 for Russia. The French and British records for the highest death toll in battle during the twentieth century belong to World War I, and not World War II. Between August 20 and 23, 1914, the French army counted 40,000 dead, of whom 27,000 were killed on August 22 alone. On July 1, 1916, the British army endured enormous casualties, with 20,000 dead and 40,000 wounded.

Medical services continually struggled in vain to keep up with the evolving methods of killing that the war unleashed (see chapter 20). If death from disease in war had dropped dramatically after the turn of the century, largely due to the introduction of vaccinations against tetanus and typhus, the number of deaths that resulted from combat rose starkly. Comparative studies into survival rates for British soldiers wounded at Waterloo in 1815 and those injured at the Somme in 1916 appear to show that the chances of a wounded soldier surviving were higher during the Napoleonic Wars.[10] During World War I, 70 percent of the wounded treated by the medical services were injured in the legs and arms. This was not because limb injuries were more common than injuries to the rest of the body. Rather it was because head, throat, and stomach wounds were usually the cause of immediate death, before any medical care was possible.

The new combat methods greatly increased physical trauma injuries. The modern bullet propelled by smokeless gunpowder appeared at the end of the nineteenth century. It was able to inflict serious injuries without precedent because of its penetrative force and the blast energy it released on impact. The explosion of a shell resulted in small shell fragments being projected at high speed with enough force to slice through the body, ripping through any part of the human organism. The combatant's sense of his own physical vulnerability was greatly increased by the development of such powerful and diverse arms.

During the interwar period the presence of large numbers of disabled war veterans in towns and villages was a poignant reminder for European society of the cost of the war. At the start of World War I wounded limbs were frequently amputated. This was because of the problems caused by gangrene, which were exacerbated by the delays in evacuating and treating the wounded, as the medical services were overwhelmed by the sheer numbers of injured. Swifter evacuation times and more efficient techniques for cleaning wounds led to a reduction in the number of amputations. As the war continued there was also an increase in the number of medical interventions involving casualties suffering from serious throat or stomach wounds, injuries that previously had almost always proved fatal. World War I also saw the first use of skin grafts to reduce the effects of the terrible facial injuries caused by the new forms of warfare. Such pioneering reconstructive surgery involved multiple operations and extremely long periods in hospital, and was often only able to partially improve the patient's facial wounds. In France, those suffering from facial injuries became known as the *gueules cassées* (smashed faces). Their victimhood came to symbolize the horrors of modern warfare. Thus a delegation of French veterans whose faces were horrifically mutilated attended the signing of the Treaty of Versailles in June 1919 and in Germany, from the mid-1920s on, the painter Otto Dix took those with facial wounds as the main subject of his engraving work and his later paintings.[11]

By the beginning of the nineteenth century military doctors were aware that combat could cause serious psychological trauma, although they described this misunderstood aspect of war using terms that are very different to those used today. For example, they called it "nostalgia" or *vent du boulet* (meaning the shock created by a near-miss from a cannonball – which is close to the original sense of "shell shock"). Modern warfare considerably increased the number of casualties suffering from psychological trauma, forcing military medical services to deal with them and to put therapeutic procedures in place.

Medical care for combatants suffering from psychiatric illnesses was first developed during the Russo-Japanese War in 1904–5. However, once again, it was World War I that marked a major turning point in the development of care for psychiatric patients. This was because of the high level of psychological trauma combatants experienced. On the French side up to 14 percent of troops reported sick were suffering from mental illness. The misleading vocabulary used to describe psychiatric trauma reveals the confusion that surrounded this issue at the time. French doctors called it *commotion* (concussion) whereas their British counterparts termed it "shell shock." Both terms inferred a direct physical link between combatant mental illness and neurological damage caused by violent explosions. In contrast, German doctors had developed the idea of *Kriegsneurosen* (war neurosis) in 1907 and had also studied what they termed *Kriegshysterie* (war hysteria). As a result they were quicker to realize that the mental illnesses from which combatants were suffering were due to psychological trauma rather than neurological disorders. Despite the tentative nature of most of the treatments available for psychological trauma at the time, during World War I the Allied armies established the main therapeutic principles of modern psychiatry, the basis for all psychiatric study up to the present day.[12]

* * *

World War I fundamentally altered Western forms of combat. A new type of combatant emerged during the war, an exhausted, traumatized fighter covered in dirt and mud who crept on the ground trying to remain invisible, powerless before intense bombardment and machine-gun fire. The meaning of psychological terror was all too clear to these men who knew at first hand the humiliating nature of fear. Survival was still linked to a soldier's personal abilities, based upon his training, experience, stamina, and physical courage. However, these attributes often counted for little when faced with the anonymous, brutal efficiency of modern firepower, which killed indiscriminately.

Given this reality, the twentieth-century battlefield inevitably became unrecognizable in comparison to its nineteenth-century precursor, the *champ d'honneur* (field of glory) described by French veterans of the First Empire in their memoirs. Combat was now an experience of total horror, frequently described by French soldiers in their writing in terms of *boucherie* (butchery) or *abattoir* (slaughter). Such descriptions illustrated the dehumanization experienced by combatants, who felt reduced to the status of butchered meat.

Such realities meant that combat rapidly lost all meaning and war itself came to be seen as something disgusting and absurd. This new representation of combat became increasingly powerful during the interwar years, although it never dominated totally.

Whereas prior to the war combat was seen as enhancing self-esteem and as a positive experience, following the conflict it was perceived by soldiers in a negative light. The methods of warfare that emerged between 1914 and 1918 permanently undermined the previous idealizations of combat. It was this devaluation that ultimately led to the many forms of twentieth-century pacifism.

Notes

1   This is an adaptation of the famous phrase by Marcel Mauss, "Les techniques du corps," *Journal de psychologie*, 32, 3–4, March 15–April 15, 1936. Reproduced in Marcel Mauss, *Sociologie et anthropologie*, Paris, Presses Universitaires de France, 1989, pp. 365–86.
2   Ernst Jünger, *Storm of Steel*, 1920; new translation from German, London, Allen Lane, 2003, pp. 184–9.
3   Marc Bloch, *Strange Defeat. A Statement of Evidence Written in 1940,* 1946; translation from French, 1948; new ed., New York and London, Norton, 1968, p. 56. While writing about 1940, Marc Bloch also drew frequently on his experience of 1914–18.
4   *La Saucisse*, April 1917, quoted in Audoin-Rouzeau, *Men at War*, p. 72.
5   Bloch, *Strange Defeat*, p. 120.
6   Ashworth, *Trench Warfare*, pp. 24–47.
7   Gudmundsson, *Stormtroop Tactics.*
8   Victor Davis Hanson, *The Western Way of War. Infantry Battle in Classical Greece*, New York, Alfred Knopf, 1989.
9   The *A7V Panzerkampferwagen* was the only tank produced in Germany. It was the heaviest of the tank models built during World War I, making it an easy target. During 1918, the Germans only had a very small number of these tanks, and despite their appropriation of British tanks captured during the fighting, their use of the tank remained marginal.
10   Keegan, *The Face of Battle.*
11   On the question of facial mutilation see Delaporte, *Les Gueules Cassées,* and Delaporte, *Les Médecins dans la Grande Guerre.*
12   Jay Winter, "Shell-shock and the Cultural History of the Great War," *Journal of Contemporary History*, 35/1, 2000, pp. 7–12 (special issue on "Shell-shock").

References and Further Reading

Ashworth, Tony, *Trench Warfare, 1914–1918. The Live and Let Live System*, London, Macmillan, 1980.

Audoin-Rouzeau, Stéphane, *Men at War. National Sentiment and Trench Journalism in France during the First World War*, 1986; translation from French, Oxford and Providence, RI, Berg, 1992.

Audoin-Rouzeau, Stéphane, *Combattre. Une anthropologie historique de la guerre moderne (XIXe–XXe siècle)*, Paris, Seuil, 2007.

Audoin-Rouzeau, Stéphane, and Becker, Annette, *1914–1918. Understanding the Great War,* 2000; translation from French, London, Profile, 2002.

Bourke, Joanna, *Dismembering the Male. Men's Bodies, Britain and the Great War*, London, Reaktion Books, 1996.

Delaporte, Sophie, *Les Gueules cassées. Les Blessés de la face de la Grande Guerre*, Paris, Noêsis, 1996.

Delaporte, Sophie, *Les Médecins dans la Grande Guerre, 1914–1918*, Paris, Bayard, 2003.

Ellis, John, *The Social History of the Machine Gun*, London, 1976; new ed., Pimlico, 1993.

Fuller, John G., *Troop Morale and Popular Culture in the British and Dominion Armies 1914–1918*, Oxford, Oxford University Press, 1990.

Gibelli, Antonio, *L'Officina della guerra. La Grande Guerra e le trasformzioni del mondo mentale*, Turin, Bollati Boringhiere, 1991; new ed. 1998.

Gudmundsson, Bruce I., *Stormtroop Tactics: Innovation in the German Army, 1914–1918*, London, Praeger, 1989.

Haber, Ludwig F., *The Poisonous Cloud. Chemical Warfare in the First World War*, Oxford, Clarendon Press, 1986.

Hirschfeld, Gerhard, Krumeich, Gerd, and Renz, Irina (eds.), *Keiner fühlt sich hier mehr als Mensch … Erlebnis und Wirkung des Ersten Weltkriegs*, Essen, Klartext, 1993.

Hirschfeld, Gerhard, Krumeich, Gerd, and Renz, Irina (eds.), *Die Deutschen an der Somme, 1914–1918. Krieg, Besatzung, Verbrannte Erde*, Essen, Klartext, 2006.

Keegan, John, *The Face of Battle. A Study of Agincourt, Waterloo and the Somme*, London, Cape, 1976.

Leed, Eric, J., *No Man's Land: Combat and Identity in World War I*, Cambridge, Cambridge University Press, 1979.

Lepick, Olivier, *La Grande Guerre chimique 1914–1918*, Paris, Presses Universitaires de France, 1998.

Smith, Leonard V., *Between Mutiny and Obedience: the Case of the French Fifth Infantry Division during World War I*, Princeton, Princeton University Press, 1994.

Smith, Leonard V., Stéphane Audoin-Rouzeau and Annette Becker, *France and the Great War 1914–1918*, Cambridge, Cambridge University Press, 2003.

Travers, Tim, *The Killing Ground. The British Army, the Western Front and the Emergence of Modern Warfare, 1900–1918*, London, Unwin Hyman, 1987.

Winter, Denis, *Death's Men. Soldiers of the Great War*, London, Allen Lane, 1978.

Winter, Jay, "Shell-shock," special issue of *Journal of Contemporary History*, 35/1, 2000.

CHAPTER THIRTEEN

Combatants and Noncombatants: Atrocities, Massacres, and War Crimes

ALAN KRAMER

The notion that the civilized nations of Europe had enjoyed 100 years of peace when war broke out in 1914 is not entirely misplaced. Wars in the nineteenth century had on the whole been limited in scope and duration. The assumptions of peace had even affected ideas on war itself. For this self-conscious age of progress was marked by attempts to apply the rule of law to war in order to "humanize" conflict and, if possible, to prevent it occurring by means of the rational and peaceful settlement of disputes. By 1914 a substantial body of international law had come into being that sought to regulate and limit the violence of warfare both between soldiers on opposing sides and between soldiers and civilians. While such law covered a range of issues, two central strands stand out, both of which focused on the plight of the noncombatant in the face of the armed might of national armies. The first concerned the soldier once he was made noncombatant by virtue of being wounded or taken prisoner in battle. The second dealt with the civilian who, though a member of the enemy society, was not engaged in battle and thus exempt from military violence. The plight of the wounded and captured soldier had been the subject of the Geneva conferences of 1864 and 1906. The protection of the civilian preoccupied the Hague conferences and resulting conventions of 1899 and 1907, though it should be noted that under strict conditions these did allow civilians to take up arms and resist invasion.[1]

Potentially, the existence of this body of international law converted the traditional terminology of "atrocities" and "massacres," which implied violence toward defenseless victims in defiance of prevailing moral norms, into war crimes that might be the subject of legal proceedings.[2] But there was no precedent or case law to translate this body of new international law into war crimes trials. The great hope was that such international agreement was normative, and would avoid the kind of brutality that it described.

Of course, there was a huge exception to this right-minded thinking – Europe's wars of colonial conquest. For it was assumed that in wars against "uncivilized" natives, other norms applied. Yet even here, the flagrant breach of elementary precepts of humanity produced criticism within and between European nations about their colonial behavior and thus heightened awareness of "atrocities," "massacres," and the inhumane treatment of noncombatants. While German mass murder in the suppression of indigenous rebellion in East Africa (1905–7) passed largely unnoticed, the "war of annihilation" conducted against the Herero people in South West Africa (1904–7), in which almost 80 percent of the latter perished, outraged public opinion and resulted in an improvement in German colonial policies.[3] Likewise, the brutality of Belgian rule in the Congo aroused international opinion and forced the Belgian state to take over what had been a private venture of the monarchy. British concentration camps during the South African War (1899–1902), in which almost 28,000 Boer civilians and at least 20,000 Africans perished, also generated a campaign in Britain and abroad against military "atrocities" which modified policy toward enemy civilians.

Just how much the brutality of the colonial sphere had reinforced norms of civilized behavior became evident in the response to the Balkan Wars of 1912–13. Liberal public opinion in Europe and the United States condemned the atrocities and massacres committed by all sides on defenseless civilians and captured prisoners alike. The implicit assumption of newspapers from the *Frankfurter Zeitung* to the *Manchester Guardian*, and even of the impressive investigation published by the American Carnegie Foundation, was that these were the deeds of backward, barbaric peoples. War between modern civilized nations would be different.

Violence against Enemy Civilians

Yet charges of atrocities, massacres, and war crimes accompanied World War I from beginning to end. The German chancellor Theobald von Bethmann Hollweg freely admitted that the invasion of neutral Belgium broke international law. The invasion of Belgium and France was followed within days by the news of the commission of widespread atrocities against civilians. This not only confirmed the moral justification of the Allied cause, but also lent the Allies a propaganda weapon to mobilize home and neutral opinion.

Although troubled by the charges, the German authorities misled the public at home and abroad, claiming that enemy civilians had risen up in armed resistance to the invasion; the German interpretation of military law rejected international law on the legitimacy of civilian participation in resisting invasion, and the German army prescribed ruthless suppression wherever such resistance occurred. The story told at the time, and partly believed in the army too, was that victims of the executions were *francs-tireurs*, or illegal civilian combatants. That remained the official German line throughout the war, and indeed throughout the rest of the twentieth century. Between the Allied accusations of brutal German "atrocities" and the German counter-charge of justified punishment for illegal fighting lay an unbridgeable gulf, deepened by wartime hatred and lurid propaganda on both sides.

The truth was not somewhere in the middle. Some (privately produced) Allied atrocity propaganda notoriously exaggerated and invented stories (e.g., that German soldiers had severed children's hands, raped nuns, and crucified a Canadian soldier), but the reality was bad enough: from August to October 1914 the German army intentionally killed 5,521 civilians in Belgium and 906 in France. Most reports published by the official commissions of investigation set up by the Belgian, French, and British governments gave a correct picture of the nature and approximate extent of the violence: the victims were virtually all unarmed civilians; many were women and children; civilians were used as human shields before enemy fire; there were instances of torture and widespread arson; and, most damaging for the reputation of Germany as a cultured nation, the university library of Louvain was deliberately burned.[4]

Dry statistics and abstract categories obscure the nature of the killing. The perpetrators were soldiers who were almost always under the command of combat officers; in many cases it is clear that their actions were covered by or expressly ordered by instructions issued by senior officers at the level of brigade, division, and army corps commanders. Nevertheless, both formalized executions and frenzied bouts of killing were accompanied by feelings of rage and hatred. German soldiers had been trained to expect *franc-tireur* resistance from civilians, to regard it as illegal, and punish alleged civilian fighters ruthlessly. They interpreted any shooting by unidentified assailants or by hidden soldiers as "illegal" fighting by civilians. In fact, there was virtually no shooting by civilians; properly constituted civilian volunteer units, the *garde civique*, participated in the defense of a few localities in Belgium, but their activity was not widespread and did not correlate with the broad pattern of German violence against civilians across the invasion zone.

This dynamic of violence is illustrated by the mass killings at Dinant, where a total of 674 civilians were killed, one-tenth of the population. The first German soldiers to enter the suburb of Les Rivages to the south of the town arrested a large group of inhabitants, apparently without harming them. When French troops on the opposite bank of the river began firing, a battalion commander, Major Schlick, "his face contorted with rage," gave the order to kill the civilians. The troops knew the captive civilians, who included many women and children, could not have been firing, for they had been with them from the start.[5] The majority of the 77 civilians killed in this incident were women and children. Right across the invasion zone, orders were issued in similar wording: "All men capable of bearing arms were to be executed on the spot." There was a causal connection between such orders and the mass killing of civilians, including women and children. As one soldier told his French captors, investigating the massacre at Dinant, "We were given the order to kill all civilians shooting at us, but in reality the men of my regiment and I myself fired at all civilians we found in the houses from which we suspected there had been shots fired; in that way we killed women and even children."[6]

Yet Germany was not the only perpetrator. The Russian army committed many acts of violence during the invasion of East Prussia in August–September 1914. Germany denounced the Russian troops for having devastated 39 towns and 1,900 villages and killed almost 1,500 civilians. Newspapers, picture postcards, and pamphlets depicted streams of refugees and ruined towns – "Cossack atrocities." The propaganda not only diverted attention away from the Allied allegations in relation to the western front, but also underlined the notion that Germany was fighting a war of defense. However, internal German investigations showed such incidents were exceptions to the general rule that the Russian troops behaved correctly toward civilians. Even the German foreign ministry's report published in March 1915, which charged the Russians with "indisputably barbarous" methods of warfare and hinted at thousands of executions, could only arrive at a total of 101 German civilians killed.[7]

Across the far larger zone of Austro-Hungarian territory invaded by Russia in 1914–15 there was widespread violence against civilians, above all against Jews. Throughout occupied Galicia and the Bukovina especially Jews, but also notables among the German and Polish population groups, and thousands of Ukrainians, were targeted, with many deportations. The Tsarist commanders attempted to instigate peasants to pillage the property of their Jewish neighbors, and their troops set the example: they unleashed pogroms, for example in November 1914 in Lemberg, injuring 30 and killing 20 Jews, and burning Jewish-owned houses and all the synagogues in Horodenka.[8] It is impossible to provide an exact death toll; from official, but incomplete, Austro-Hungarian figures it seems that the total by the end of 1915 was below 100. There were no mass executions, but rather widespread brutality and pillage, and policies of ethno-nationalism to divide local populations by ethnicity. The greatest impact on civilian life was perhaps made by the policy of widespread deportations.

The Austro-Hungarian invasions of Serbia in 1914 and 1915 were accompanied by atrocities against the population, the extent of which has not yet been properly researched. The estimate of the Swiss observer, Rodolphe A. Reiss, who sympathized with Serbia, that 3,500–4,000 civilians were killed, has never been corroborated, so the true figure may be lower; nevertheless, the Habsburg army leadership later admitted there had been widespread violence and "pointless reprisals."[9] In 1917, there were once again "reprisals" against civilians to suppress guerrilla resistance.

War Crimes during Occupation

As Germany established its occupation in Belgium and northeastern France in 1914, and a great swathe of territory in Eastern Europe in 1915, civilians everywhere were subject to exploitation and arbitrary rule; to prevent escape, a lethal electrified fence was erected on the border between Belgium and the Netherlands. Civilians were deported as forced labor, including 120,000 Belgians and several thousand women and girls from Lille in April 1916. In Eastern Europe the German army imposed a brutal occupation regime with extensive forced labor and deportations; it ruled by the use of public corporal punishment, also of women, and a rigorous pass system to restrict movement. The exploitation of human and natural resources and the disruption of war led to impoverishment, famine, and epidemics in which thousands died in the winter of 1917–18.[10]

During Russia's short-lived occupation of German territory, a large number of East Prussians, perhaps as many as 13,600, including 6,500 women and children, were deported to Russia. Transported in overcrowded cattle wagons on long train journeys with insufficient sanitation and food, they ended up thousands of kilometers away in southern Russia or Siberia. The authorities were unclear on whether to treat them as refugees, exiles, civilian internees, or prisoners of war; many were treated as prisoners of war and were subject to forced labor in mines and railway construction. Only 8,300 of the East Prussian civilian deportees survived the harsh conditions to return home.[11]

Violence against Civilians on Home Territory

Violence was also practiced by some states against their own populations. The most significant case was the massacre of the Armenians by the Ottoman Turkish state. Although the term was not coined until 1944, this amounted to a genocide that is traditionally held to have started on April 24, 1915, when thousands of Armenian political leaders and intellectuals were arrested and deported, 2,345 in Istanbul alone.[12] In fact, this represented the culmination of an explicit policy of "Turkification," as the Ottoman Empire came to grips with Turkish nationalism and thus with the position of subordinate "nationalities" within the state. There had been intense persecution of Armenians in the

1890s when at least 100,000 were killed, which resumed in early 1914 when Turkish terror bands expelled 130,000 people (Greeks and Armenians) from the Izmir (Smyrna) region, Thrace, and the Aegean coastline into Greece.

Yet this violence was overshadowed by the wartime genocide launched against the Armenians. Following deportation from their towns and villages their property was confiscated and auctioned off. Deportation, as the American ambassador in Turkey Henry Morgenthau recognized, was a prelude to massacre; the Ottoman authorities freely admitted to him their intention to issue "the death warrant to a whole race."[13] Armenian men in the Ottoman army were disarmed as from February 25, and Armenian members of labor battalions were being executed probably as from March.[14] Ambassador Morgenthau received troubling reports of Armenian soldiers being taken in groups of 50 to 100, forced to dig their own graves, bound together in groups of four, and shot in summary executions.[15]

From May 1915 civilian Armenians were deported to the deserts of Syria. Some were killed on the spot – burned in their houses or drowned in the Black Sea. During the forced marches many more were shot or hacked to death, and others died from exhaustion, starvation, or disease. Plentiful testimony was provided by Armenian survivors, American and German diplomats, and by Turkish witnesses at the Istanbul trials held after the war.[16] The perpetrators were the regular army, supported by units of the secret "Special Organization," consisting partly of Turkish refugees from the Balkan Wars and convicted criminals released from prison by dispensation.[17] Estimates of the number of deaths vary widely, according to political standpoint, but in March 1919 the Turkish minister of the interior produced the figure of 800,000.[18] At least one million (out of the Ottoman Armenian population of 1.8 million) is the consensus among international scholars.

The fate of the Armenians soon became known abroad, and the Allies condemned the "massacres" as an attempt to "exterminate" an entire people. The moral (though not yet the legal) category of "crimes against humanity" was coined in May 1915 to condemn the actions of the Ottoman state and the Allies promised to hold personally responsible "all members of the Ottoman government and those of their agents who are implicated in such massacres."[19]

Deportations were also used by the Tsarist government in Russia, which conducted a ruthless system of population resettlement from 1915 to 1917. Although without genocidal intent, the result was a vast extent of misery and mortality. The Tsarist army had adopted a policy of scorched earth in its retreat in 1915, destroying supplies and buildings and deporting civilians. At least 300,000 Lithuanians, 250,000 Latvians, at least 500,000 Jews, and 743,000 Poles were driven east into Russia for fear they would assist the enemy.[20]

By the beginning of 1917 there were, according to careful calculation, no fewer than six million refugees in the Russian interior and the Caucasus.[21] Many, naturally, had fled the war zone from fear of the enemy, fear of the fighting, or to follow the men who had been conscripted into the army, but many, especially Jews and Germans, were the victims of forced resettlement. Contemporaries estimated in 1915 that four-fifths of the refugees were the victims of forced displacement.[22] Some 200,000 Germans from Russian Poland alone were deported to Siberia, their lands sold off to ethnic Russians.[23] Estimates of the numbers of deported ethnic Germans vary from around 115,000 from all western regions of the empire to 520,000 from the Polish provinces alone.[24] In line with the higher estimate is the report that 115,889 had been deported from Volhynia province alone by June 1916.[25] Muslims in eastern Anatolia were expelled from Kars and Batum provinces (part of the Russian Empire since 1878), in order to make their land available for Armenian refugees; Crimean Tatars, suspected of sympathy with Turkey, were also deported.[26] However, deportation was not exclusively directed against national minorities suspected of treason: at least 1.1 million Russians, Ukrainians, and White Russians were also evacuated from the war zone.[27] The fate of the deported people, who were usually bereft of all economic resources and left dependent on the meager charity of the poverty-stricken Russian provinces, and how many died in consequence, is a topic that has not yet been systematically researched.

The Russian army's policy, ostensibly based on the fear that the non-Russian populations might conduct espionage and betray secrets to the enemy, was a part of the historic shift in the nature of warfare between the French Revolution and World War I from war between small professional armies to war between mobilized nations, in which some ethnic groups were defined as the nation while others were stigmatized as the "enemy within." This contributed to the development of a Russian ethno-nationalism and to the emergence of violent anti-semitism in Eastern Europe.[28]

One of the least known aspects of violence against civilians on home territory during World War I was the ruthless crushing by the Tsarist army of the revolt in central Asia in 1916. Mainly Kazakh, but also Kirgiz and Uzbek radicals opposed to labor conscription attacked Russian settlers and state officials. The Tsarist army, suspecting the revolt had been instigated by German, Jewish, or Turkish agents, responded brutally, deporting thousands of Kazakhs under harsh conditions; many were executed, and between a quarter and a half million people fled across the border to China. Over three thousand Russian settlers were killed, and at least twice that number of indigenous people.[29]

Crimes against Prisoners of War

The received wisdom that captured enemy soldiers during the war were treated humanely in World War I, at least in comparison with World War II, has been increasingly called into question in recent research. It is no longer possible to generalize for all prisoners: although the great majority of prisoners in Britain, France, Germany, and Italy survived their captivity, there were many exceptions to the rule. The first variable was nationality: British and French prisoners in Germany and German prisoners in Britain and France were most likely to survive their captivity, with mortality rates of not more than around 3 percent. However, the death rate for Russian prisoners in Germany was substantially higher, at 5 percent, and for Serbs it was 6 percent. No fewer than 28.9 percent of the Romanian prisoners died in German captivity.

Such pronounced variations can only be explained by differences in policy. The German authorities repeatedly pointed to the "illegal Allied hunger blockade," which stopped the import of food, causing not only the German civilian population to suffer hunger, but also the prisoners of war. British and French prisoners received food supplies from home, without which they would have been reliant on the ever-worsening German food supply. The other nationalities, mainly because of food shortages in their home countries and sometimes owing to deliberate policy, received far fewer parcels and other supplies. However, that explains neither the vast difference in death rate between the Russians and the Romanians, nor the difference between the mortality of German civilians of about one percent or less (which can be attributed to malnutrition) and that of the prisoners of war, who were supposed under international law to receive the same standard of food as the host country's soldiers.[30] In general, the Russians were more ruthlessly exploited than prisoners from France and Britain by the German authorities.[31] Recent research has revealed that the Romanians, regarded as "traitors" by the German government for entering the war on the side of the Allies in 1916, were deliberately treated harshly and forced to do hard physical labor with insufficient food; despite warnings by neutral observers about the declining health of the Romanians the military authorities refused to improve their rations.[32] Germans and German Austrians were more harshly treated in Russia than captives of other nationalities.[33]

The second variable was differences in conditions within the captor nation. Prisoners in Russia were treated relatively well in some camps, but administrative incompetence and neglect led to mass death in others, such as the typhus epidemic in Tockoe in 1915–16. Similar callous neglect and incompetence led to the outbreak of typhus among French prisoners in the German camp Kassel-Niederzwehren in 1915; 18,000 men fell ill, and 1,300 died. German and Magyar prisoners selected to work on the construction of the Murmansk railway on the Kola peninsula, in the far north, were particularly unfortunate. Owing to the inhospitable environment and the lack of suitable accommodation, food, water, and medical treatment, some 25,000 out of 70,000 members of the labor battalions perished.[34] The conduct of individual camp administrators and medical personnel was no doubt execrable, but neither in Germany nor in Russia was there a systematic policy to kill off enemy prisoners. Nevertheless, widespread epidemics in Russian captivity and bleak conditions led to a high death rate of about 14.5 percent.[35] A combination of intentionally poor nutrition, exhausting hard physical labor, and inadequate fuel and shelter, accounts for the mass death of Italian prisoners in Austro-Hungarian captivity: out of 468,000 men at least 92,451 (19.8 percent on Italian figures) died.[36]

The third variable was the circumstances of capture and transfer into regular captivity. The most dangerous time was the moment of capture. International law (in particular Hague Convention IV of 1907) prohibited the killing of a surrendering or defenseless soldier. Undisciplined elements on all sides carried out such killings, although it was not in their armies' self-interest to do so. Most cases probably went unrecorded, being perpetrated in the heat of the battle. However, there were several cases of senior officers issuing such orders. In August 1914 the German Major-General Karl Stenger gave an order to kill captured French soldiers, including the wounded, on the battlefield at Thiaville, in Lorraine. Despite protests from several German soldiers, about twenty captured French men were killed. During the battle of the Somme, some British officers also issued such illegal orders, and several German soldiers were killed while trying to surrender. Joanna Bourke argues that such practices were an "important part of military expediency."[37] In the absence of any systematic investigation, however, this remains an open question. Conditions immediately after capture could be equally lethal, and equally hidden from public view. Captured men were often put to work on the battlefield or behind the lines, in dangerous work such as clearing unexploded ordnance or digging trenches within range of enemy fire. This, too, contravened international law. The vast extent of such prisoner labor under dangerous conditions, on the German side of the western front, on the Austro-Hungarian front in Italy, and in retaliation on the Allied fronts, indicates that the noncombatant status of the prisoner of war had collapsed by 1916.[38]

Naval Blockade

Another aspect of relations between the military effort and civilians that was contentious at the time and remains so is the naval blockade. Did the Allied blockade of Germany and Austria constitute a war crime? The dominant scholarly (and popular) view today is that the blockade was illegal and led to serious food shortages, causing the mass starvation of German civilians. It is well established that in the last two years of the war, average rations for civilians often dropped below 1,000 calories per day (half of minimum requirements), and that on average adults lost 20 percent of their body weight. According to postwar German estimates, 700,000 civilians died as a result. For German nationalist politicians and scholars in the 1920s it was self-evident that the "English hunger blockade" was a war crime. Historians of the British Navy (Arthur Marder, A. C. Bell) defended its legality, avidly supporting the thesis that the blockade caused hunger and demoralization. Avner Offer, by contrast, has argued that while the blockade caused a reduction in food supplies, Germany did not starve.[39] The legal situation in 1914 was apparently straightforward: blockade and the confiscation of enemy goods or ships on the high seas were allowed under the Declaration of Paris of 1856. The Declaration of London of 1909 extended the rights of neutral shipping and restricted the type of goods liable to seizure as contraband, but Britain, aware of the advantage it afforded an enemy to transfer its imports to neutral shipping, had not ratified it when war began.

Certainly, one of the Allied intentions was to target the civilian population (the other main intention being to prevent the import of military supplies), and the blockade thus represented a step on the road to total warfare. It was not against the letter of the law (the only violations of law being the interference with the rights of neutral shipping), but it was contrary to the spirit of international law, which sought to protect civilians. However, it was not the cause of mass death. Germany imported only about 10 percent of its food before the war. Yet there were 478,500 "excess civilian war-related deaths," according to a modern scholarly calculation,[40] and civilians in Germany's industrial cities suffered real hunger, malnutrition, and disease. If the "excess mortality" of civilians during the war was a war crime, then German war policy bore the heaviest responsibility. The army took 70 percent of all officially available food.[41] Then came armaments industry workers, who were given special rations, followed by various categories of "normal" civilians who needed extra food, and then civilians who had to make do with official rations. The worst treated were the patients in psychiatric hospitals, 70,000 of whom were allowed to die of malnutrition, disease, or neglect, in excess of normal peacetime mortality. At the end of the list came the populations of the German-occupied Europe, who were deprived of their own resources in order to feed Germany (see chapters 26 and 30).

German U-boat warfare against Allied merchant ships was also not as such a war crime. The manner in which it was conducted, however, flouted the laws of war and customary international law, because law and common humanity held that the crew and passengers of a sinking merchant ship had to be rescued. U-boats did not have the space to do so. To signal the intention to attack and allow the passengers and crew the time to get into the lifeboats would have increased the risk that U-boats, which were vulnerable on the surface, might be attacked by warships. As part of the "totalizing" dynamic of the war, the German government, frustrated at the lack of progress in the land war and under pressure from radical nationalists, declared in February 1915 that the waters around the British Isles were a "war zone" in which all ships would be sunk without warning. The first spectacular result of the new policy came on May 7, when the *Lusitania,* a large British luxury liner, was torpedoed off the coast of Ireland en route from New York to Liverpool; it sank quickly, and 1,198 lives were lost, including 127 Americans.[42] Germany suspended unrestricted submarine warfare in the Atlantic after American protests in August 1915, but the army and the navy clamored for its return. They finally had their way in February 1917, when Germany resumed all-out submarine warfare. The government believed the navy's promise to sink so many ships that Britain would starve and be forced to sue for peace by August 1, but it was conscious it was a last, desperate gamble, because this flagrant breach of international law would provoke the United States to enter the war. American entry in the war in April 1917 was thus prompted by what was recognized on all sides as a war crime. Germany's attempt to starve Britain cost the lives of 14,722 merchant (i.e. civilian) seamen. President Woodrow Wilson, in declaring war on Germany, condemned the U-Boats as "outlaws"; "submarine warfare against commerce is a warfare against mankind."[43]

Legal Consequences and Memory

At the Paris Peace Conference in 1919, in a novel departure from the history of warfare that still looks modern today, the European nations that considered themselves the victims of German aggression drew up 32 categories of war crimes (starting with massacre of civilians and the killing of hostages, and including gender-specific crimes of rape and forced prostitution), with the intention of prosecuting suspects before international courts. Against US objections, the European nations thus created a historic precedent in demanding the extradition of suspects for international war crimes trials.

Because the genocide of the Armenians was carried out by a state against its own subjects and was not a "war crime" on a narrow definition of international law, the European Allies at the Paris Peace Conference attempted to prosecute the perpetrators before an international tribunal under the new term of "crimes against humanity." This was rejected, however, by the US delegation, which thought the concept lacked precision and was morally arbitrary. Trials carried out by the Turkish authorities, under British pressure, in Istanbul in 1919 resulted in the prosecution of a few minor officials, three of whom were sentenced to death and executed. A nationalist remobilization based in Ankara soon gained the initiative over the Istanbul government, which was seen as collaborating with the Allies.[44] All the major perpetrators were allowed to escape or tipped off before arrest, and most of the accused were released without trial.[45]

To this day, the Armenian genocide remains politically divisive. The Turkish government and the Turkish historical profession steadfastly deny there was a policy of genocide. Two books published in 2002 and 2004 by the Turkish Historical Society maintained there was no intention to exterminate the Armenians; rather, Armenian "treason," "wickedness," and "rebellion" had made deportations a military necessity.[46] On the other hand, an international campaign by exiled Armenians and their sympathizers since the late 1980s has forced the issue onto the agenda of the public sphere. The UN Commission on Human Rights and several major states worldwide have officially recognized the genocide as historical fact, and some have made its denial a criminal act. Whatever historians may think of the efficacy or propriety of legislating for the spread of historical knowledge, the process has served to wrest the issue from oblivion.[47]

In the Treaty of Versailles, the Allies forced Germany to agree to the extradition of alleged perpetrators (Articles 228 to 230) and furnish evidence for prosecutions. In 1920 the Allies presented the German government with a list of 862 suspects (including nine leading Turkish perpetrators of the Armenian genocide who had fled to Germany). The atrocities of 1914 committed on the civilians of France and Belgium were at the top of the Allied agenda, and represented with 18 percent of the charges the largest category, followed by crimes against prisoners of war (14 percent), and deportation of civilians. Well-orchestrated nationalist protests in Germany, coupled with the claim by the government that its stability would be at risk if it handed over the culprits, made the Allies relent and allow the German Supreme Court at Leipzig instead to conduct war-crimes trials. Leipzig proved to be a failure; a handful of junior officers were convicted in 1921 and sentenced to relatively short prison terms, and senior officers were acquitted without trials or exonerated, although there was often ample German testimony to convict. Among those acquitted was General Stenger, although the French and German evidence showing he had issued illegal orders was overwhelming.[48] If no other legal argument could be found, it was stated that the accused "lacked awareness of illegality."[49]

The legacy of Istanbul and Leipzig was a memory of failure that made the Allies resolve in World War II not to leave the prosecution of war criminals to the states that had perpetrated them. It also resulted in the creation of important judicial concepts, such as crimes against humanity, the justification of international intervention, and the limitation on the absolute sovereignty of states.

***

At this point we should reflect on the nature of atrocities, massacres, and war crimes. For many people opposed to war, both today and at the time, war itself is an atrocity. The present author shares this abhorrence of violence and war; however, the pacifist identification of war with atrocity in effect places all military violence on the same moral plane. Soldiers employing violence to defend their country against invading enemy soldiers act legally; soldiers employing violence against noncombatants act (in general) illegally, and this is justly regarded in the victim societies as atrocity. The German sociologist of violence, Wolfgang Sofsky, argues that the essence of the massacre is face-to-face killing, using a pistol or a knife. The perpetrator, Sofsky writes, "wants to see the body bleed and look into the eyes of mortal fear … He takes pleasure in sharpening his knife before his terrified victim … He wants to wade in blood, he wants to feel with his own hand, with his fingertips, what he does."[50] This is "intimate killing," of the kind described also by Joanna Bourke.

This may have been true of some of the perpetrators during World War I, but we have little evidence to demonstrate it. It is more likely that perpetrators had a range of motivations and emotions. Some were ordinary soldiers, instructed by respected officers and caught in a group dynamic of peer pressure, who obediently formed firing squads to execute suspects. They used rifles, and sometimes machine guns; pistols and knives were seldom the weapons of choice in the atrocities of 1914. We know that one officer, Captain von Loeben, ordered by a commander in August 1914 to shoot a large group of suspect civilians in Dinant, acted without rage, separated and exempted women and children from the killing, and later expressed doubt as to the grounds for the execution. Some soldiers, by contrast, evidently took pleasure in beating and humiliating their victims before killing them; others refused to participate, shot high, or even acted to prevent arbitrary killings.

In massacres, Sofsky argues further, the actors are taken over by a self-perpetuating dynamic that only ends when the ammunition runs out or all potential victims have been killed.[51] Again, however, this was not true of most cases of massacre during the invasions of 1914, or even in the mass murder of the Armenians in 1915. Many of the witnesses to the killings in 1914 were precisely survivors: women and children were usually (although not always) separated from the men; often they were forced to watch the executions. In other words, perpetrators of such massacres followed a system, admittedly a perverse one, in which the perceived security threat in the form of the adult male population was targeted first. Above all, massacres did not take place according to the rules of anthropological theory, but in a concrete historical situation, in which commanders were almost invariably in charge and in a position to stop as well as unleash the killing. The study of atrocities, massacres, and more broadly war crimes reveals a pattern in World War I that shows both a historic shift toward ever more "total" forms of war that involved ever greater sections of society, and conscious decisions taken in the context of specific military cultures.

Notes

1   The most convenient source for the Hague Convention of 1907 is now the Yale University Law School Avalon Project: http://www.yale.edu/lawweb/avalon/lawofwar/lawwar.htm
2   Will Coster, "The English Civil War," in Mark Levene and Penny Roberts (eds.), *The Massacre in History*, New York and Oxford, Berghahn, 1999, pp. 89–106 (p. 90). The term "massacre" originated in sixteenth-century France, when it evolved from meaning a butcher's chopping block to the mass killing of the Waldensians in Provence in 1545. Mark Greengrass, "Hidden Transcripts. Secret Histories and Personal Testimonies of Religious Violence in the French Wars of Religion," in ibid., pp. 69–88.
3   Hull, *Absolute Destruction*, pp. 155–7.
4   Horne and Kramer, *German Atrocities 1914*, chs 1–4.
5   Ibid., p. 51.
6   Ibid., pp. 162–4.
7   Auswärtiges Amt, *Greueltaten russischer Truppen gegen deutsche Zivilpersonen und deutsche Kriegsgefangene*, Berlin, 1915; English-language summary, *Memorial on Atrocities Committed by Russian Troops upon German Inhabitants and Prisoners of War*, Berlin, 1915. For the report of an investigation commission in the Reich Office for Internal Affairs, see Imanuel Geiss, "Die Kosaken kommen! Ostpreußen im August 1914," in Geiss, *Das deutsche Reich und der Erste Weltkrieg*, Munich, Hanser, 1978, pp. 62–3.
8   K.U.K. Ministerium des Äußern: *Sammlung von Nachweisen für die Verletzungen des Völkerrechtes durch die mit Österreich-Ungarn kriegführenden Staaten. II. Nachtrag. Abgeschlossen mit 30. November 1915*, Vienna, 1916, pp. 93–5, 105–6. See the other reports in this series for instances of violence against civilians in the Habsburg territories occupied by the Russian army.
9   "Serbien," in Gerhard Hirschfeld et al. (eds.), *Enzyklopädie Erster Weltkrieg*, Paderborn, Schöningh, 2003, p. 834.
10 Liulevicius, *War Land*.
11 Tiepolato, "La deportazione di civili prussiani." The figures are from Fritz Gause, *Die Russen in Ostpreußen 1914//15*, Königsberg, Gräfe und Unzer, 1931, p. 246, 282, cited in ibid., pp. 108–9. Another contemporary, Elsa Brändström, estimated the number of deportees to be 11,100. Ibid., p. 109.
12 Dadrian, "Genocide," p. 266. The German theologian, Johannes Lepsius, an observer and sympathizer with the plight of the Armenians, estimated that 600 were arrested in Istanbul, all but eight of whom were deported, to disappear without trace. Lepsius, *Deutschland und Armenien*, pp. xix–x.
13 Henry Morgenthau, *Ambassador Morgenthau's Story*, New York, Doubleday, Page, and Co., 1918; new ed., London, Taderon, 2003, p. 309, cited in Dadrian, "Genocide," p. 272.
14 Akçam, *Armenien und der Völkermord*, p. 63.

15 Morgenthau, *Ambassador Morgenthau's Story*, pp. 302–3, cited in Dadrian, "Genocide," p. 272.

16 Naimark, *Fires of Hatred*, pp. 29–34; Akcam, *Armenien und der Völkermord*.

17 On the "Special Organization" see Dadrian, "Genocide," pp. 274–8.

18 "Armenien," in Hirschfeld et al. (eds.), *Enzyklopädie Erster Weltkrieg*, p. 344.

19 Cited in Dadrian, "Genocide," p. 262.

20 Conze, *Polnische Nation*, pp. 83–90; "Judentum," in Hirschfeld et al. (eds.), *Enzyklopädie Erster Weltkrieg*, p. 599.

21 Gatrell, *A Whole Empire Walking*, p. 3.

22 Ibid., pp. 31, 211. The true figure may have been far higher still. Ibid., p. 212.

23 Gatrell, *Russia's First World War. A Social and Economic History*, Harlow, Pearson Longman, 2005, p. 179.

24 The higher estimate is from Lohr, *Nationalizing the Russian Empire*, p. 130; however, he states that the 520,000 "faced deportation," and does not specify whether they were actually deported. The lower estimate is pieced together from apparently incomplete figures given by Fleischhauer, *Die Deutschen im Zarenreich*, pp. 508–10.

25 Lohr, *Nationalizing the Russian Empire*, p. 135.

26 Gatrell, *Russia's First World War*, pp. 182–3.

27 Fleischhauer, *Die Deutschen im Zarenreich*, p. 511.

28 Cf. Lohr, "The Russian army and the Jews," pp. 2–3.

29 Gatrell, *Russia's First World War*, pp. 188–90.

30 On the excess mortality of German civilians see Jay Winter, "Surviving the War: Life Expectation, Illness and Mortality Rates in Paris, London and Berlin, 1914–1919," in Jay Winter and Jean-Louis Robert (eds.), *Capital Cities at War. Paris, London, Berlin 1914–1919*, Cambridge, Cambridge University Press, 1997, pp. 487–523 (p. 517, fn. 34).

31 Nachtigal, *Kriegsgefangenschaft an der Ostfront*, p. 22.

32 Hinz, *Gefangen im Großen Krieg*, pp. 220–47.

33 Nachtigal, *Kriegsgefangenschaft an der Ostfront*, p. 27.

34 Nachtigal, *Die Murmanbahn*.

35 Hinz, *Gefangen im Großen Krieg*, p. 235, n. 421, citing Wurzer, "Die Kriegsgefangenen der Mittelmächte in Rußland," PhD thesis, University of Tübingen, 2000, who stresses that there are no reliable mortality rates for Russia, and estimates range from 10 to 20 percent.

36 Kramer, "Italienische Kriegsgefangene im Ersten Weltkrieg."

37 Bourke, *An Intimate History of Killing*, p. 182; for an example of such "expediency" in 1917, see p. 189.

38 On prisoners of war, see the forthcoming monograph by Heather Jones, based on her PhD thesis, "The Enemy Disarmed. Prisoners of War and the Violence of Wartime: Britain, France and Germany, 1914–1920," University of Dublin, 2006. There is no space in this chapter to discuss the civilians interned by the belligerents during the war, although there is no doubt that such internment was a breach of international law, and a new development in the history of warfare. See Garner, *International Law*, vol. 1, pp. 56–76; Rousseau, *Le Droit de Conflits Armés*, pp. 43–4. Cf. the contrary view put forward by Liszt, *Das Völkerrecht*, p. 461, who depicts the internment of British civilians in Germany as from the end of 1914 as retaliation, since the enemies had interned or deported all German civilians, "including women and children." On the state of research see Jahr, "Zivilisten als Kriegsgefangene," pp. 287–321; Stibbe, "The Internment of Civilians."

39 Archibald Colquhoun Bell, *A History of the Blockade of Germany and of the Countries Associated with Her in the Great War, Austria-Hungary, Bulgaria, and Turkey, 1914–1918*, London, HMSO, 1937; 2nd ed., 1961; Arthur Marder, *From the Dreadnought to Scapa Flow: The Royal Navy in the Fisher Era, 1904–1919*, 5 vols., London, Oxford University Press, 1961–70; Avner Offer, *The First World War: An Agrarian Interpretation*, Oxford, Clarendon Press, 1989.

40 Winter, "Surviving the war," p. 517, fn. 34. It is not altogether clear that the death rate was higher than in France: over the period 1914–18, the standardized death rate for females in Berlin was 15.08 per 1,000; in Paris it was 16.09. Ibid., pp. 494–7, especially Table 16.2. A full comparison can only be made by including the mortality rate among civilians in the occupied zone of France.

41 Ziemann, *Front und Heimat*, p. 142, fn. 496.

42 Patrick O'Sullivan, *The Lusitania. Unravelling the Mysteries*, Cork, Collins, 1999; Colin Simpson, *Lusitania*, London, Longman, 1972. Other estimates speak of 1,201 lives lost, including 128 Americans.

43 Woodrow Wilson, *War Messages*, 65th Cong., 1st Sess. Senate Doc. No. 5, Serial No. 7264, Washington, DC, 1917, pp. 3–8, April 2, 1917.

44 Cf. Bloxham, *The Great Game*, pp. 147–51.

45 Kramer, "The First Wave of International War Crimes Trials," pp. 441–55.

46 Hans-Lukas Kieser, review of Halaçoglu, Yusuf, *Facts on the Relocation of Armenians 1914–1918 [Ermeni tehciri ve gerçekler (1914–1918)]*, Ankara 2002, and Halaçoglu, Yusuf, Çalik, Ramazan, Çiçek, Kemal, Özdemir, Hikmet, Turan, Ömer (Hrsg.), *The Armenians: Banishment and Migration [Ermeniler: Sürgün ve göç]*, Ankara 2004. Both in H-Soz-u-Kult, 21.07.2005, http://hsozkult.geschichte.hu-berlin.de/rezensionen/2005-3-048.

47 Horne and Kramer, *German Atrocities 1914*, ch. 9.

48 Hankel, *Die Leipziger Prozesse*, pp. 248–58.

49 Sofsky, *Traktat über die Gewalt*, pp. 181–2.

50 Ibid., p. 185.

References and Further Reading

Akçam, Taner, *Armenien und der Völkermord. Die Istanbuler Prozesse und die türkische Nationalbewegung*, Hamburg, Hamburger Edition, 1996.

Becker, Annette, *Oubliés de la Grande Guerre. Humanitaire et culture de guerre*, Paris, Noësis, 1998.

Bloxham, Donald, *The Great Game of Genocide. Imperialism, Nationalism, and the Destruction of the Ottoman Armenians*, Oxford, Oxford University Press, 2005.

Bourke, Joanna, *An Intimate History of Killing. Face-to-Face Killing in Twentieth-Century Warfare*, London, Granta, 1999.

Conze, Werner, *Polnische Nation und deutsche Politik im Ersten Weltkrieg*, Cologne and Graz, Böhlau, 1958.

Dadrian, Vahakn N., "Genocide as a Problem of National and International Law: The World War I Armenian Case and its Contemporary Legal Ramifications," *Yale Journal of International Law*, 14/2, 1989, pp. 221–334.

De Schaepdrijver, Sophie, *La Belgique et la Première Guerre mondiale*, 1997; translation from Dutch, Brussels and Berne, Peter Lang, 2004.

Fleischhauer, Ingeborg, *Die Deutschen im Zarenreich. Zwei Jahrhunderte deutsch-russische Kulturgemeinschaft*, Stuttgart, Deutsche Verlags-Anstalt, 1986.

Garner, James Wilford, *International Law and the World War*, 2 vols., London, Longmans, 1920.

Gatrell, Peter, *A Whole Empire Walking. Refugees in Russia in World War I*, Bloomington and Indianapolis, Indiana University Press, 1999.

Geiss, Imanuel, *Das deutsche Reich und der Erste Weltkrieg*, 1978; 2nd ed., Munich, Piper, 1985.

Hankel, Gerd, *Die Leipziger Prozesse. Deutsche Kriegsverbrechen und ihre strafrechtliche Verfolgung nach dem Ersten Weltkrieg*, Hamburg, Hamburger Edition, 2003.

Hinz, Uta, *Gefangen im Großen Krieg. Kriegsgefangenschaft in Deutschland 1914–1921*, Essen, Klartext, 2006.

Hirschfeld, Gerhard, et al. (eds.), *Die Deutschen an der Somme 1914–1918*, Paderborn, etc, Schöningh, 2006.

Horne, John, and Kramer, Alan, *German Atrocities 1914. A History of Denial*, London and New Haven, Yale University Press, 2001.

Hull, Isabel V., *Absolute Destruction. Military Culture and the Practices of War in Imperial Germany*, Ithaca and London, Cornell University Press, 2005.

Jahr, Christoph, "Zivilisten als Kriegsgefangene. Die Internierung von 'Feindstaaten-Ausländern' in Deutschland während des Ersten Weltkrieges am Beispiel des 'Engländerlagers' Ruhleben," in Rüdiger Overmans (ed.), *In der Hand des Feindes. Kriegsgefangenschaft von der Antike bis zum Zweiten Weltkrieg*, Cologne, etc., Böhlau, 1999, pp. 287–321.

Kramer, Alan, "Italienische Kriegsgefangene im Ersten Weltkrieg," in Hermann J. W. Kuprian and Oswald Überegger (eds.), *Der Erste Weltkrieg im Alpenraum. Erfahrung, Deutung, Erinnerung. La Grande Guerra nell'arco alpino. Esperienze e memoria*, Innsbruck, Universitätsverlag Wagner, 2006, pp. 247–58.

Kramer, Alan, *Dynamic of Destruction. Culture and Mass Killing in the First World War*, Oxford, Oxford University Press, 2007.

Kramer, Alan, "The First Wave of International War Crimes Trials: Istanbul and Leipzig," *European Review*, 14, 2006, pp. 441–55.

Lammasch, Heinrich, *Das Völkerrecht nach dem Kriege*, Kristiania, Aschehoug, 1917.

Lepsius, Johannes, *Deutschland und Armenien 1914–1918. Sammlung Diplomatischer Aktenstücke*, Potsdam, Tempelverlag, 1919.

Liszt, Franz von, *Das Völkerrecht. Systematisch dargestellt von F v. L.*, zwölfte Auflage, ed. Max Fleischmann, Berlin, Julius Springer, 1925.

Liulevicius, Vejas Gabriel, *War Land on the Eastern Front. Culture, National Identity, and German Occupation in World War I*, Cambridge, Cambridge University Press, 2000.

Lohr, Eric, "The Russian Army and the Jews: Mass Deportation, Hostage, and Violence during World War I," *Russian Review*, 60, 2001, pp. 2–24.

Lohr, Eric, *Nationalizing the Russian Empire. The Campaign against Enemy Aliens during World War I*, Cambridge, MA and London, Harvard University Press, 2003.

Nachtigal, Reinhard, *Die Murmanbahn: die Verkehrsanbindung eines kriegswichtigen Hafens und das Arbeitspotential der Kriegsgefangenen (1915 bis 1918)*, Remshalden, BAG-Verlag, 2007; 1st ed. 2001.

Nachtigal, Reinhard, *Kriegsgefangenschaft an der Ostfront 1914 bis 1918. Literaturbericht zu einem neuen Forschungsfeld*, Frankfurt, Peter Lang, 2005.

Naimark, Norman, *Fires of Hatred. Ethnic Cleansing in Twentieth-Century Europe*, Cambridge, MA, Harvard University Press, 2001.

Sofsky, Wolfgang, *Traktat über die Gewalt*, Frankfurt, S. Fischer, 1996.

Stibbe, Matthew, *British Civilian Internees in Germany: the Ruhleben Camp 1914–1918*, Manchester, Manchester University Press, 2008.

Tiepolato, Serena, "La deportazione di civili prussiani in Russia (1914–1920)," in Bruna Bianchi, ed., *La violenza contro la popolazione civile nelle Grande Guerra. Deportati, profughi, internati*, Milan, Edizioni Unicopli, 2006, pp. 107–25.

Ziemann, Benjamin, *Front und Heimat. Ländliche Kriegserfahrungen im südlichen Bayern 1914–1923*, Essen, Klartext, 1997; English translation: *War Experiences in Rural Germany, 1914–1923*, Oxford and New York, Berg, 2007.

CHAPTER FOURTEEN

War Aims and Neutrality

JEAN-JACQUES BECKER
(translated by Heather Jones)

In the words of Carl von Clausewitz, "war is merely the pursuit of politics by other means." However, was this the case during World War I? Did European states take up arms in 1914 because they believed they could not obtain their political objectives any other way? Does this mean that diplomacy had no role once the war started? Does it also mean that each state entered the war for well-defined objectives?

The Outbreak of War

In reality, it is doubtful whether Clausewitz's definition applies to World War I. For virtually all the belligerent countries believed that they were fighting a war of defense but that their opponents were guilty of aggressive actions, or at least intentions. Thus for many years it was widely held in France that Austria had declared a general mobilization before Russia, whereas in reality Russia declared a general mobilization against Austria-Hungary's partial mobilization, and opening of hostilities, against Serbia.[1] This error persisted because it conveniently obscured the enormous impact that the news of Russian mobilization had in Germany, where it convinced the population that their survival was threatened by the Russian masses. Russian mobilization in support of Serbia thus played a very large part in triggering war and gave Germany a primary reason for entering the conflict.

To acknowledge this fact is not to absolve Austria-Hungary of its part in the outbreak of war. For in many ways Austria-Hungary was the only country to enter the conflict with a clearly defined war aim, that of attacking Serbia in order to eliminate the continual threat of Serb irredentism. This was in spite of the fact that the assassination of the Archduke Franz Ferdinand and his wife Sophie at Sarajevo on June 28, 1914 had been carried out by young Bosnian-Serb nationalists who were Austro-Hungarian subjects, acting without the support of the Serbian government. Germany greatly increased the likelihood of conflict by offering unconditional support to Austria-Hungary and made no real attempt to limit the Austro-Hungarian reaction against Serbia. Unwilling to weaken its only real European ally, Germany was reluctant to try to restrain the Austro-Hungarians. War between France and Germany was an inevitable consequence of the German Schlieffen Plan that envisaged an initial swift victory over France, Russia's ally in the west, before Germany turned to deal with Russia. Neutral Belgium found itself part of a defensive war, invaded in the context of a conflict that did not originally concern it, and Britain went to war because it believed the German invasion of Belgium endangered its own national interests.

The war aims that existed in Europe in 1914 can thus be seen as largely negative, apart from Austria-Hungary's desire to deal once and for all with Serbia. A haphazard chain of events resulted in an immense escalation of the conflict. Within a few days millions of men were mobilized, an event unprecedented in history. This was a war without any specific cause, other than the idea that the defense of the nation was an absolute priority, a basic principle of the European nation-state that was increasingly the norm by the start of the twentieth century. Therefore, it is clear that war aims were not defined before the outbreak of the war, but afterwards.

War Aims

Defining war aims was a risky process for states that claimed they were only engaged in a war of defense. Germany was the first country clearly to set out what it hoped to gain from the conflict in the September Program.[2] In the short term this was a secret document. Had it been published, Germany would have been seen as the main party responsible for the war. However, throughout the conflict its secret contents continued to filter through into the public domain in one form or another. When the document was drafted, Germany's military leaders were confident of victory and wanted to plan how the country was to profit from the spoils. However, by an irony of history, Chancellor Bethmann Hollweg outlined the September Program in a letter to General Headquarters on September 9, 1914, at the exact moment that the German army was in the process of losing the battle of the Marne. From the very outset there was a gap between the aims of the September Program and the reality on the battlefield.

The basic purpose of the program was to ensure the security of the German Empire in the east and in the west. In the west, France was to disappear as a world power. It would lose new territory: Belfort, the western Vosges, the region of Briey-Longwy, and the coastline from Dunkirk to Boulogne. To a certain extent, these territorial losses represented what Germany had been unable to annex in 1871. In addition, France was to be forced to dismantle its fortresses, to pay a large indemnity, and to sign a commercial treaty that would make it economically dependent upon Germany. Belgium and Luxembourg were to disappear as independent states. Having lost Liège, Verviers, and Antwerp, Belgium would become a rump vassal state, occupied by the German military and integrated into the German economic sphere. As for Luxembourg, it would become a new state (*Bund*) within Germany.

In this context, the case of Belgium is particularly illustrative. King Albert I has traditionally been portrayed as a warrior-prince who constantly fought to regain the independence of his country. In fact, although he wished to restore Belgian independence, Albert intended to do this through negotiation rather than force of arms. His diaries show that he had no sympathy for the French democratic government, nor any respect for the French or British military leaders.[3] Albert's primary concern was to preserve the Belgian army and to keep Belgian territory out of the main battles of the war. He believed he could negotiate a compromise deal with Germany, a country for which he had far more admiration than he felt for the Entente. Between fall 1914 and 1916 he maintained contacts with German representatives, but contrary to what he believed, Germany had no intention of restoring Belgian independence. As the September Program revealed, Germany wished to integrate the country into a German super-state. The fact that King Albert kept all knowledge of his negotiations with German representatives from his own government clearly illustrates his disdain for the Belgian political leadership.

In the east, the September Program envisaged pushing Russia back as far as possible from Germany by removing from Russian control all the non-Russian territories which it governed, such as Finland, the Baltic States, Poland, the Ukraine, and so on. At the heart of this plan was an enormous customs union stretching from France as far as Poland, constituting a German *Mitteleuropa*. Similarly, in Africa, the acquisition of the Belgian Congo would allow for the development of a German *Mittelafrica*.

The September Program was obviously unrealistic. It was drafted by the German military in conjunction with senior representatives of the civil service and heavy industry, and even the Chancellor who transmitted it did not believe in it. Moreover, particular sections of the German population were in favor of focusing upon different aspects of the program over others. Many members of the liberal bourgeoisie, of which the German Chancellor was relatively representative, were interested in the economic advantages the program offered, rather than the annexation of territory that it proposed, and were keen to use it to limit British influence. The Junkers, who were the owners of vast tracts of agricultural land, wanted Germany to annex territory to the east of its existing borders in order to increase the proportion of agricultural land in Germany and thereby reestablish the power balance between agriculture and industry. The Junkers wielded enormous influence over Germany's military leaders who often came from this same background.

The individual details of the September Program were not as important as its message, which was that Germany now intended to profit from a war that it continued to claim it had never wanted. It is significant that Germany made such a rapid transition from depicting itself as a "peace-loving" country to accepting a future role as an "annexationist" state. The September Program was extended as the war continued, to incorporate further gains for Germany according to German perceptions of the sacrifices that their country was making. A fixed idea developed that Germany had to obtain significant gains from the conflict and harshly punish its enemies, France, Britain, and Russia. This notion lasted until the very end of the war and even if some were more moderate in their conception of what Germany should gain from the conflict, the idea was generally widespread that any peace had to bring about German annexations.

By contrast, the French government avoided defining its war aims and generally instructed the press not to broach the subject. For a long time the mistaken belief persisted that the French had gone to war in 1914 to take revenge for 1870 and to recover Alsace-Lorraine. In reality, such ideas only played a minor role in motivating those mobilized in 1914.[4] The real motivation was the widespread sense that Germany had acted as a dangerous aggressor, which emerged following the German invasion of Luxembourg.

Yet once it became clear that the conflict was not going to end in a matter of weeks, it became inevitable that people would begin to question why France was at war and what the results of the conflict would be, beyond the defense of the nation. As Pierre Renouvin pointed out, "the essential war aim, and the only one that was supported by a large majority of the population in all sections of society from the extreme right to the extreme left, was the restitution of Alsace-Lorraine. Even those who supported a compromise peace often stated that negotiations would bring about the return of the lost provinces."[5]

This did not prevent other more discreet war aims developing alongside the public consensus supporting the return of Alsace-Lorraine. These other aspirations were also important, even if they remained relatively undefined. There was a strong sense that it was necessary to reduce the power of Germany in order to protect France in the future. In a speech to the Chamber of Deputies on December 22, 1914, René Viviani announced that France intended to continue the war until victory was achieved, in order to restore "the rights that had been desecrated" (an allusion to the violation of Belgian neutrality), to return to "the French nation those provinces torn from her by force," and to crush "Prussian militarism." This last phrase was not merely rhetorical. As Jacques Bainville immediately noted in his diary: "this agenda could greatly change the Republic, really change it, but no one seems to understand this."[6]

Viviani's phrase caused alarm because of what it implied. When Aristide Briand became Prime Minister and was asked about French war aims on November 3, 1915, he was careful to avoid any further mention of crushing "Prussian militarism." Other ideas also circulated, contributing to the further development of French war aims. Robert Pinot, General-Secretary of the Comité des Forges, claimed that France needed to acquire the coal-producing Saar basin, which would serve as a profitable counterpart to the French iron-ore industry in Lorraine. Maurice Barrès published articles in *L'Echo de Paris* in February, March, and April 1915 calling for France to seize the left bank of the Rhine.

Although Russia had also entered the war against its will, it was not without ambitions. Tsar Nicolas II expected that Russia would profit from the situation in order to bring about one of the traditional objectives of his foreign policy, the conquest of Constantinople and the Straits. Moreover, he told the French ambassador on March 3, 1915 that he was not opposed to French annexations if they were at the expense of Germany. Thus among the main belligerent countries only Great Britain clearly stated that it did not have any national ambitions at stake in the conflict.

The Role of Neutrals during the War

War aims, regardless of whether they were openly stated or not, continually changed according to events on the battlefield and the entry of new countries into the conflict. The belligerent states constantly tried to bring other countries into the war on their side and many neutral countries underwent interminable discussions on the consequences of possible intervention.

Nonetheless, a certain number of neutral countries never entered the war. This was partly because neutral states were needed to keep financial and diplomatic contacts open between the warring parties, partly because their population had divided loyalties to the opposed belligerents, and partly because participation would be more of a burden than an advantage. These factors were often combined. Norway leaned toward the Entente, whereas Sweden was sympathetic toward Germany, but the populations in both countries were deeply divided. Switzerland experienced the most extreme internal tensions in its history between its German-speaking population, which supported the Central Powers, and its French-speaking population, which favored a French victory. Certain neutrals such as Spain were convinced that they could play a role in negotiating peace when the war ended. King Alfonso XIII strongly believed in this outcome. In the event, after the war the victors ignored those who had offered to act as go-betweens at the peace negotiations, shunning the services of both Spain and the papacy.

In contrast, many other neutral states entered the war at different stages. However, they did so for very different motives. Japan was the first to do so, even though it seemed remote from war in Europe and had declared its neutrality. However, Britain informed Japan that it had no choice: under the terms of its alliance with the United Kingdom, Japan could not remain neutral. In addition, the Japanese military saw the war as an opportunity to force the Germans out of the Pacific region. On August 23, 1914, Japan declared war on Germany and seized the German-leased territory of Qingdao in China, as well as the German archipelagos of the North Pacific (the Caroline, Mariana, and Marshall islands). The Allies were not satisfied with this limited contribution. In particular, the French Minister for Foreign Affairs, Delcassé, continually urged his Japanese counterpart to send troops to fight in Europe. On November 19, 1914, the Japanese government, irritated by this behavior, made clear that it declined the French request, stating: "Japan has an army thanks to compulsory military service. Its troops are not mercenaries; their purpose is to defend Japanese national territory."[7] No Japanese soldier ever fought in the West.

The Ottoman Empire was the second state to abandon a policy of neutrality.[8] Germany was particularly interested in it entering the war: Turkey's control of the Straits between the Black Sea and the Mediterranean (the Bosporus and Dardanelles) made it difficult for the Allies to communicate with each other and allowed the Turks to open a new front against Russia in the Caucasus. For the Ottomans, however, the advantages of entering the war were less clear. After their defeats in the Balkan wars and against Italy, it would have made sense for them to avoid any major military campaigns and take time to rebuild their forces. However, this is to reckon without the Young Turks, who had recently come to power in the Empire. The movement, and especially Enver Pasha, was greatly influenced by Germany. Their initial program had focused upon the renewal and modernization of the state, combined with a form of violent nationalism. But following the loss of the Balkan territories, this nationalism was no longer of an imperial "Ottoman" variety, but rather purely Turkish, despite the continued Ottoman possession of vast Arab territories. There were also many Turks who lived outside the borders of the Empire in parts of the Caucasus and Central Asia largely belonging to Russia. Adopting an old word that they brought back into fashion, the Young Turks championed a "Panturanian" or Pan-Turkic nationalism. War with the Russian empire for control of its Turkish populations was the inevitable consequence of this policy, and many Turkish leaders feared the risks such a war posed. However, Enver Pasha sidestepped this difficulty by signing a secret treaty with Germany as early as August 2, 1914, and obtaining significant German financial assistance. Pasha then provoked Russia by bombarding Russian ports on the Black Sea, using two large German naval vessels that had taken refuge in the Straits and had been fictionally "acquired" by Turkey. On November 2, 1914, Russia declared war on the Ottoman Empire. On November 5 France and Britain followed suit. The Turkish government's error was to have overestimated its military capabilities and to have overlooked the importance of the Arab territories within the Empire. It was only at the cost of the Turkish leadership's "Turanian" objectives that the Turkish army under German command was able to resist the Allied attack at the Dardanelles that was intended to reach Constantinople. Following a series of defeats at the hands of the Russians in the Caucasus and faced with an uprising by the Arabs, Turkish nationalism could only express itself through the extermination of the Armenians (see chapters 13 and 33).[9]

Turkish entry into the war led to the Allies' plans to carve up the Ottoman Empire: the British and the French divided the Arab territories between themselves under the terms of the Sykes-Picot Accords of March 1916, while at Saint-Jean-de-Maurienne in April 1917 southern Anatolia and the region of Smyrna were promised to Italy, despite the fact that Greece also laid claim to Smyrna with its largely Greek population.

The third neutral state to enter the war was Italy, which had declared its neutrality on August 4, 1914, despite being a member of the Triple Alliance. The belligerent states made multiple diplomatic and propaganda efforts to try to convince Italy to enter the war on their side or at the very least, to ensure that it did not enter on the side of their enemy. Although the irredentist desire to regain Italian-speaking territories from Austria-Hungary had died down in Italy, the country still considered the war as an opportunity to recover them. Austria-Hungary was prepared to discuss the issue but it was not prepared to cede lands that, among other things, provided it with access to the sea. At the same time, Italian public opinion was not enthusiastic about entering the war. The peasantry was indifferent and Italian Catholics, influenced by the papacy, were staunchly against it. However, sizeable parts of the urban population were gradually won over to the idea that a war against Austria-Hungary would enable Italy to regain Italian territory along the Austrian border. In May 1915, which became known as "radiant May," major nationalist pro-war demonstrations took place. At the same time the government had signed a secret deal with the Allies in London on April 26, 1915 that Italy would be given the irredentist territories in exchange for entering the conflict. On the same day, Italy declared war solely against Austria-Hungary.

With Russia, Serbia, Austria-Hungary, Italy, and Turkey now at war there was extreme pressure upon the Balkan states to take sides. However, given that these states had just been involved in two local wars in 1912 and 1913, the most sensible course for them to pursue was to remain out of the new conflict, which ultimately did not really concern them. However, diplomats acting on behalf of the belligerent countries redoubled their efforts to get the Balkan states to enter the war.

Bringing Bulgaria into the war on the side of the Central Powers was extremely important for Germany, as this would protect its lines of communication with Turkey. Likewise keeping Bulgaria from allying with Germany was as much of a priority for the Entente. Bulgaria had emerged bruised and defeated after the Balkan wars of 1912 and 1913, with significant scores to settle with its neighbors, in particular Serbia and Greece. Delcassé, who according to Jean-Baptiste Duroselle "was growing old and confusing everything,"[10] persisted in negotiating with Bulgaria and trying to win over the country by offering it Serb or Greek territory, lands which the Serbians and Greeks had no intention of ever ceding. By contrast, Germany was able, without too much soul-searching, to offer Bulgaria Macedonia if Bulgaria entered the war on the side of the Central Powers. In return for this promise and a large financial subvention, Bulgaria signed an agreement with Germany on September 16, 1915.[11]

The Entente had hoped that it would prove easy to convince Greece to enter the war on its side.[12] However, the situation was more complicated than it at first appeared. King Constantine of Greece was the brother-in-law of Kaiser Wilhelm II and was completely pro-German. He believed that the only role open to Greece was to stay out of the war. In contrast, the Greek Prime Minister Venizelos was favorable to the Entente. He believed that Greece should see the war as an opportunity to bring about a "magnificent idea" – the reconstitution of the Byzantine Empire through the conquest of Constantinople and those parts of Anatolia that had Greek populations. He was unaware that the Allies had already promised Constantinople to Russia in March 1915. The situation was suddenly dramatically altered when Germany decided to quash Serbia in a combined offensive by Germany,

Austria, and Bulgaria that began in late September 1915. Allied troops, mainly French, were diverted from the Dardanelles to assist Serbia, but to no avail. In the absence of any agreement with Greece, the Allied troops disembarked in Salonika, where they found that not only were they unable to help the Serbs but they had placed themselves in a dangerous situation. Serbia was wiped off the map. Despite this crushing defeat it was still possible to transport the remnants of the Serbian army to Corfu and from there to Salonika, where they remained with the Allied troops who made up the "Army of the Orient." After considerable ups and downs, Greece finally officially entered the war on June 29, 1917.

Romania too had scores to settle with its neighbors. It resented Austria-Hungary's control of Transylvania, where ethnic Romanians were more numerous than Hungarians. Romania also harbored ambitions to seize Bessarabia, a part of the Russian Empire which Romania considered was ethnically Romanian. Everything pointed to Romania staying out of the war, given that the King of Romania, Carol I, was pro-German while the Liberals who were in power, led by Bratianu, favored neutrality and the intellectual bourgeoisie generally supported the Entente. However, the balance of power changed in October 1914, following the accession of a new monarch, Ferdinand, who did not share his uncle Carol I's predilection for the Central Powers. Pressure from French diplomats in particular promoted the belief in Romania that obtaining Transylvania was a national priority. It was simply a matter of choosing the most advantageous moment, and in August 1916 Romania went to war on the side of the Allies.[13]

Portugal was the last of the European belligerents to turn to war. The majority of the Portuguese population at the time could not understand why their country should become embroiled in the conflict. It remains difficult to see what reasons Portugal had for going to war, apart from the fact that it was an old ally of Britain. However, Britain never encouraged Portugal to become involved. It was the Portuguese Republicans, who had just taken power from the monarch, who wished to affirm the legitimacy of the new Republic by engaging the nation in a war.[14] In the end Germany declared war on Portugal first on March 9, 1916, accusing the Portuguese of not respecting the laws of neutrality.

The entry into the conflict of the majority of previously neutral European states profoundly changed the political climate. The war that broke out in 1914, largely without any particular war aims or objectives, had now given rise to national aspirations that clashed at an international level and also often produced contradictory ambitions within countries. In other words it had become increasingly difficult for any belligerent to resist the pressure to establish specific war aims. As we have seen, some countries, such as Germany, had already defined their war aims very early on in the conflict, but war aims could not be separated from the war itself and they evolved with the events of the conflict. There was thus a complex interplay between aspirations and reality, an interplay that was all the more complicated because a large part of this process remained secret. Moreover, the duration of the war, its horrors, the shocks it brought, and the increasing number of dead, which rapidly jumped from hundreds of thousands to millions, all led the remaining neutrals to put pressure on the belligerents to find a solution and to state what their war objectives actually were.

Benedict XV and Wilson

Two neutral figures, the Pope and the President of the United States of America, played a particular role as mediators during the conflict. The papal incumbent at the outbreak of war was Pius X. However, he died in late August 1914 when, according to the Vatican, his death was brought on by his despair at having been unable to prevent a war between Christian countries. It was left to his successor, Benedict XV, to determine the Vatican's response to the conflict.[15] Benedict condemned the war in the strongest terms, considering it an outrage. As the war dragged on his denunciations of the conflict became increasingly vehement. This alienated the Vatican from French Catholics, the vast majority of whom were extremely patriotic. Benedict XV never ceased to hope that he could act as a mediator between the belligerents and tried to use the contacts established with the leaders of the Central Powers by Mgr Pacelli, the future Pius XII, who was already a renowned diplomat. Pacelli was Secretary of the Congregation of Extraordinary Religious Affairs and in May 1917 became Papal Nuncio at Munich which meant, in effect, to the German Empire. Pacelli believed the moment had come for the Pope to intervene to end the war. The Holy See sent a note to the German government on August 1, 1917 and, when it did not receive a reply, published it on August 14. In this note the Pope sought to define the "basis for a just and lasting peace." He set out general principles for peace negotiations such as the need for belligerents to recognize "the moral force of law," which seemed to imply future arbitration measures and armament reduction. In the short term, Pope Benedict XV also called for the freedom of the seas, "the complete, reciprocal renunciation" of war indemnities, the evacuation of all territory that had been conquered, the return of Belgium to full independence, and a compromise resolution of French and Italian demands.

The note did not mention Serbia, an indication perhaps that Austria-Hungary was to be allowed to deal with it as it wished. Nor did it discuss Poland, which seems to suggest that, given the turbulent situation in Russia, the papacy was responding to German requests to hold on to its newly conquered Polish territory. Despite the fact that it avoided discussing the future of either Serbia or Poland, the pontifical note had no chance of being accepted by either of the warring sides.

The Pope's offer represented a return to the *status quo ante* in the West, something that appeared impossible after three years of costly war. With Benedict XV viewed as a *boche* pope by Clemenceau and a "French" pope by Ludendorff, the papal initiative had little hope of success. Its failure only served to reinforce Benedict XV's antiwar position.

The American President, Woodrow Wilson, was reelected in 1916 on the promise that he would keep the United States out of the war, a policy that matched the attitude of the vast majority of Americans, who did not wish to become embroiled in European disputes. However, the American government was unable to ignore the war, given the fact that American industry was a major supplier of the Entente powers. Moreover, the conflict impinged upon the United States because of the nature of the war at sea, involving blockades and submarine warfare. These factors help explain why President Wilson offered to act as a mediator between the belligerents on December 18, 1916. He suggested that they inform him of their war aims and he would then chair a conference at which they would meet to resolve the conflict.

The belligerents reacted in various ways to this suggestion. Germany judged that the moment had come to make peace in 1916, as long as it was made according to their conditions. Germany held a very strong position territorially. However, it had become clear to all the belligerents that winning the war through a crushing victory on the battlefield looked increasingly unlikely. On the western front the German army had resisted the Allies' attack on the Somme but had failed to break through at Verdun. Such enormous battles without any decisive outcome led Germany to reason that it was worth stopping the war at this point, which explains the German peace proposal on December 12, 1916, several days before the American offer of mediation. It was all a long way from the September Program of September 1914. What the Central Powers now proposed was a return to the *status quo ante* in the West and modifications to the old borders in the East, with Poland and the Baltic States removed from Russian control.

Ostensibly the German proposals were unacceptable to the Entente because Alsace-Lorraine was to remain German. However, in reality, any proposal that came from the adversary, whether its terms were acceptable or not, was viewed with suspicion by France. French governments rejected such offers, believing they were set as traps. In fact, the German peace proposal was not an empty gesture. The German government really believed that it was necessary to make peace at this point. However, Germany rejected the American offer of mediation because it had just made its own peace offer. In any case a "victorious" Germany had no need of a mediator.

Given the role which American bank loans and supplies played in their war efforts, it was much more difficult for France or Britain to ignore the American proposal. Germany did not face such constraints, as for geographical reasons it was not possible for it to source supplies in the United States. Until 1916, the French government had remained silent regarding its war aims. It was only at the end of the year that it became less reticent about the subject, a shift that was partly due to a prevailing belief that there was about to be a French victory. This optimism might appear surprising with hindsight, but at the time the entry of Romania into the war, the belief that Germany was running out of resources, Nivelle's success in the Verdun region, and Joffre's plans to coordinate an all-out offensive on the Russian, French, and Italian fronts all gave rise to the belief that the conflict was turning in the Allies' favor. The French government, led by Aristide Briand, allowed the press a little more freedom. It was above all nationalist opinion that was heard. It called for France to seize the left bank of the Rhine and for Germany to be dismembered.

At a government level, the question of war aims was discussed in order to reply to Wilson's peace initiative and the Allies issued a collective reply on January 10, 1917. It demanded "the evacuation and restoration of the invaded territories" and insisted "that nationality be respected." It also called for the "restitution of any provinces or territories which in the past had been taken from the Allies by force or against the wishes of the population" and for the "liberation of nationalities living under the control of the Austro-Hungarian Empire." This reply was so vague and wide-ranging in its aspirations that it was not suited to serve as a basis for peace discussions at this point in the war. Wilson's offer of mediation never went any further.

However, this did not prevent the French government from defining its war aims in greater detail. The Ministerial Declaration made by Alexander Ribot, when he succeeded Briand's government, illustrates the two different points of view that coexisted. He confirmed that France desired "the return of Alsace-Lorraine ... with the necessary reparations and guarantees," but he rejected any spirit of "conquest."[16] This choice of words was highly significant. The President of the Republic, Poincaré, had asked the Prime Minister not to make this announcement, and in doing so Poincaré implicitly spoke for those who believed that any final victory had to be expressed in territorial acquisition. In addition, confused negotiations had only recently taken place between France and Russia, which left the latter at liberty to fix its western borders as it wished. This was on top of the existing agreement that Russia would gain the Straits. The French hoped that this would stop Russia opting for a separate peace with Germany. However, these events proved to be of little consequence, as revolution broke out in Russia soon thereafter.

In fact, all the hopes of a victorious peace that had developed at the end of 1916 crumbled within weeks. Romania was defeated and the coordinated offensives of the different allies did not yield the expected results. In particular, the disastrous offensive at the Chemin des Dames and the outbreak of revolution in Russia were two major setbacks. From this point on, according to Pierre Renouvin, "the question of French war aims was dominated by the consequences of the Russian revolution."[17]

The New Diplomatic Reality

The international situation was determined by three factors: how Germany decided to behave toward revolutionary Russia, the ability of Austria-Hungary to remain in the war and, above all, the entry of the United States into the conflict. Although America entered the war before the final Russian collapse, the effects of American involvement were only felt after Russia had exited the conflict.[18]

In Germany, as elsewhere in 1917, those who believed it was time to end the war, through compromise if necessary, became increasingly prominent.[19] At the same time the public swiftly realized that the launch of unrestricted submarine warfare on January 31 had not improved their daily lives. However, this was not the opinion of the German High Command. During a meeting on April 23, 1917 at Bad Kreuznach, Hindenburg, Ludendorff, and Chancellor Bethmann Hollweg agreed upon an immense program of annexations in Eastern Europe and the Balkans to the benefit of the Central Powers. To placate France, a small part of southern Alsace to the south of Mulhouse was to be returned to her in exchange for the region of Briey-Thionville. Once this plan was established an attempt was made to sound out French reaction. A senior German functionary, Baron von der Lancken, tried to get in contact with Aristide Briand who was no longer in power in France. A meeting was even arranged in Switzerland on September 22, 1917 but Briand was advised not to attend, as it was perceived as a German "ploy."[20]

As was so often the case, the German Chancellor had agreed to a plan he did not support. In reality, he favored a compromise peace as well as internal reforms within Germany. It was these attitudes that had led the Kaiser, under pressure from the generals, to demand Bethmann Hollweg's resignation on July 13, 1917. Despite this, a majority of the Reichstag (Social Democrats, progressives and Centre Party deputies) voted for a "peace resolution" on July 19, 1917, which reiterated that Germany had taken up arms to defend its freedom and independence and that it did not have any need of conquests. However, the last phrase was ambiguous as, although the resolution rejected all conquest, it also stated that the German people were fighting for their "development."[21]

The Reichstag's position was far removed from that of the German Right, the High Command and, it appears, from many sections of the German population. The Fatherland Party, which was profoundly annexationist, was founded at this time and was extremely successful. The situation in Germany was paradoxical: there was a movement in favor of a compromise peace that had gained ground to the extent that it had a majority in the Reichstag, just at the same time that the Russian Revolution opened the way to a victorious peace. In fact, had the German leadership known about the revolution earlier it is likely that they would not have decided that unrestricted submarine warfare was an absolute necessity, especially as Kaiser Wilhelm II and the Chancellor Bethmann Hollweg had unsuccessfully opposed this decision. On the other hand, however, the February revolution did not necessarily mean the collapse of Russia. Indeed, among Russia's Western allies there were rumors that a more democratic state would inject renewed vigor into the Russian war effort. However, by the autumn it was obvious that the Russian army was no longer capable of continuing the war, although it was not until the Bolshevik Revolution in November and the beginning of the negotiations at Brest-Litovsk between newly Soviet Russia and the Germans that the consequences of the Russian collapse became clearly visible.[22]

Viewed with the benefit of hindsight, it was in the German interest to end the war in the East as quickly as possible in order to defeat the Allies in the West before the arrival of American troops. The German generals at the time, however, did not see the situation in this way. Their position was a contradictory one which epitomized the behavior of German military leaders throughout the conflict: they showed the greatest initiative at a military level but were continually unable to abandon earlier grand schemes for Germany's future. Thus General Hoffmann, Commander-in-Chief on the eastern front, was in favor of marching on St Petersburg and destroying Russia, which was no longer able to defend itself. Hindenburg and Ludendorff, however, opposed this, as they feared it would provoke an upsurge in Russian patriotism and would require large numbers of troops to occupy the additional conquered territory, although they were still firmly in favor of an annexationist peace. Yet opting for an annexationist peace meant longer negotiations and leaving German troops in the East that were needed in the West. This was effectively what happened.

For the Bolshevik delegates such as Trotsky there was no question of just accepting any demand the Germans made. Their objective was to play for time by delaying the negotiations as much as possible in the expectation that revolution would break out in Germany. A series of incidents and major disputes occurred between the Bolshevik leaders – Lenin felt that it was necessary to make peace at any price, while the Left Communists, grouped around Bukharin, wanted to appeal to Russian patriotism. Lenin's position won out once the German troops resumed their offensive, and a peace treaty was signed at Brest-Litovsk on March 3, 1918. Soviet Russia lost Finland, the Baltic States, Poland, and the Ukraine, and in the Caucasus Batoum and Kars were given over to Turkey. The irony was that because they had been unable to limit their eastern ambitions, the German generals had actually missed their chance to win the war, owing to the time lost in the lengthy negotiations as well as to the number of divisions that had to be maintained in the east.

The Austro-Hungarian negotiators resented the German hesitation in the negotiations as their sole preoccupation was obtaining food supplies as quickly as possible. Austria-Hungary was at the end of its reserves of strength. In 1916, Emperor Franz-Joseph had died and his great nephew Karl succeeded him on the Austro-Hungarian throne. Among the various leaders of Europe it was Karl, along with King Albert, who most desired peace. However, Karl was caught in a vicious circle. On the one hand it was impossible for him to conclude a separate peace, for this would give the impression of betraying Austria-Hungary's ally, Germany. On the other hand, Karl supported the French desire to regain Alsace-Lorraine, something that he could not admit to the German government and German military leaders. In addition, Karl refused to give Italy the irredentist lands that it coveted. In spite of all these difficulties, he still hoped to be able to negotiate. Most European nobility were related to a greater or lesser degree, and Karl's wife, the Empress Zita, had two brothers, the Princes Sixtus and Xavier of Bourbon-Parma, one of whom was serving in the Belgian army.[23] With the agreement of the French government they agreed to travel to Vienna via Switzerland, where they met with Emperor Karl in March 1917. However, it was obvious that this attempt at negotiation would not succeed.

By the autumn, following the massive Italian defeat at Caporetto and the Bolshevik Revolution, Karl became less convinced of the need for an immediate peace deal.

The diplomatic situation fundamentally changed as a result of America's entry into the war. In early January 1917 President Wilson was still convinced that he could keep America out of the conflict. However, at precisely this moment Germany secretly decided at the Pless conference to launch another campaign of unrestricted submarine warfare. When this was made public on January 31, 1917, the American government found itself in an unprecedented situation. During the preceding months America had mainly clashed with Britain over British enforcement of the blockade of Germany. However, America was unlikely to tolerate Germany torpedoing American ships, as indicated by its angry reaction in 1915 to the German sinking of the British liner *Lusitania* with American citizens on board. In reaction to the German resumption of unrestricted submarine warfare the American government broke off diplomatic relations with Germany on February 5, 1917, before finally declaring war on April 6, 1917.[24]

The rather foolish diplomatic overture to Mexico on January 16, 1917 by the German Minister for Foreign Affairs Arthur Zimmerman also played a significant part in damaging American–German relations. Zimmerman promised the American states of Texas, New Mexico, and Arizona would be restored to Mexico after a German victory in exchange for Mexican entry into the war on the German side. Understandably, this did little to endear Germany to the United States.

From a military point of view the entry of the United States made little immediate difference to the war, as America had practically no army. However, it did significantly change the diplomatic context of the conflict. Prior to America's entry all belligerents on both sides were allied to each other. In contrast, the American President insisted that his country merely be termed an associate of its partners. The United States could not accept the Allies' war aims, which not only included the right to self-defense but also anticipated carving up the Ottoman Empire.

From this point on America would determine the purpose of the war in terms of a crusade: "the battle of good against evil." In a message on January 8, 1918, President Wilson outlined America's war aims in a text that became known as Wilson's 14 points. The details of the 14 points mattered less than the principles they embodied: the right of peoples to self-determination and the establishment of world peace and security through the foundation of a "league" of all nations. It is evident that Wilson had moved beyond his earlier idea of a "peace without victory," which he had developed on January 22, 1917. However, Wilson's shift in position was not as great as it at first appeared. The powers associated with America had to accept Wilson's program in every aspect, though privately they reserved their positions until the end of the conflict. In this regard the German leadership was quicker than America's own associates to recognize who would take charge of future developments: once they were forced to request an armistice they addressed their demands to the President of the United States.

***

Diplomacy never ceased to matter during World War I. The different belligerents continually searched for a way to end the conflict. Yet despite this all the attempts to make peace failed. There were two explanations as to why belligerents who endured unbelievable losses and were incapable of winning the war outright on the battlefield did not opt for a compromise solution. First, the very nature of the immense sacrifices they had already made meant compromise was impossible. After so many dead a return to the prewar status quo was unthinkable. Second, this war was fought differently to previous conflicts, which had mostly been "dynastic" wars, settled by diplomats after the belligerents had achieved a military conclusion with what, for the most part, were professional armies. In these previous conflicts diplomats were given considerable amounts of time to find a solution that was acceptable to all sides. In contrast, World War I was not a dynastic conflict but a war between nations. Thus it followed a different logic to that pursued by diplomats. How could the German nation, after its series of spectacular victories, accept a peace that brought it no reward and forced it to abandon the lands it had conquered? How could the French nation give up its demand for the restoration of its lost territories after experiencing so many disappointments and enduring such material and human losses? In a similar way it was impossible for the British, having lost millions of tons of shipping, to agree to any peace that simply re-created the insecurities of the prewar period. Even though the majority of Italians did not really know why their country had entered the war, Italy as a nation was unable to accept any peace that did not restore those lands it considered rightfully Italian.

National feeling created its own logic, resulting in attitudes that were completely inflexible. Compromise was impossible and, consequently, peace could only result from military victory. This was also the reason why peace conditions could not be discussed with the enemy. Although it was difficult to invite defeated enemies to the peace conference because the victors did not agree on many questions, this was not the real reason why they were not allowed to negotiate. Only a truly dictated peace could end a war of this nature. In a number of important spheres the world of 1918 was no longer that of 1914, even if contemporaries believed that it was possible to return to the past. Diplomacy was one area where any resumption of prewar practices was no longer feasible, because diplomacy was no longer the domain of diplomats but of entire peoples. Contrary to popular assumptions, this was not necessarily a change for the better.

The United States had entered the conflict almost by chance, following a miscalculation by the German generals. America believed that it could leave the war as easily as it had entered it. In reality this was an illusion, even if another 20 years would be necessary before it became clear to all that the Great War had heralded the transition from a European-dominated world to a truly global one.

Notes

1   Jules Isaac, *Un Débat historique. 1914, le problème des origines de la guerre*, Paris, Editions Rieder, 1933.
2   Fischer, *Germany's Aims in the First World War*, translation from German, pp. 103–6. See also Pierre Guillen, *L'Empire allemande (1871–1918)*, Paris, Hatier, 1970, p. 180, and Raymond Poidevin, *L'Allemagne de Guillaume II à Hindenburg*, p. 194.
3   Albert I, *Carnets et correspondance de guerre, 1914–1918*, ed. Marie-Rose Thielemans, Paris and Louvain-la-Neuve, Duculot, 1991, passim.
4   Jean-Jacques Becker, *1914. Comment les Français sont entrés dans la guerre*, Paris, Presses de la Fondation Nationale des Sciences Politiques, 1977, pp. 259–363.
5   Renouvin, "Les buts de guerre du gouvernement français," p. 3.
6   Jacques Bainville, *La Guerre démocratique. Journal 1914–1915*, ed. Dominique Decherf, Paris, Bartillat, 2000, p. 216 (December 22, 1914). See also Renouvin, "Buts de guerre," p. 6.
7   Albert Pingaud, "Les Projets d'intervention japonaise," *Revue des Deux Mondes*, September 1, 1930; Jean-Jacques Becker, "Delcassé pendant la guerre de 1914," in L. Claeys, C. Pailhès,

and R. Pech (eds.), *Delcassé et l'Europe à la veille de la Grande Guerre*, Foix, Archives Départementales de l'Ariège, 2001; Dickinson, *War and National Reinvention. Japan in the Great War 1914–1919*, 1999.

8   See chapter 33 below.

9   See chapter 13 above.

10 Jean-Baptiste Duroselle, *Histoire de la Grande Guerre*, Paris, Editions Richelieu, 1972, p. 114.

11 Jean-Claude Allain, "La Course aux alliances," in Paul-Marie de la Gorce (ed.), *La Première guerre mondiale*, Paris, Flammarion, 1991; Jean-Jacques Becker, "La Guerre dans les Balkans, 1912–1919," in *Matériaux pour l'histoire de notre temps*, July–September 2003, Bibliothèque de Documentation Internationale Contemporaine, Université de Paris X-Nanterre.

12 Ibid.

13 Ibid.

14 Ribeiro de Meneses, *Portugal 1914–1926*, pp. 1–31.

15 Becker, *Le Pape et la Grande Guerre*.

16 Renouvin, "Buts de guerre," p. 23.

17 Ibid., p. 20.

18 Mayer, *Political Origins of the New Diplomacy*.

19 Gunter Mai, *Das Ende des Kaiserreichs. Politik und Kriegsführung im ersten Weltkrieg*, Munich, Deutsche Taschenbuch Verlag, 1987.

20 Pedroncini, *Négociations secrètes*, pp. 68–73.

21 Mai, *Das Ende des Kaiserreichs*, pp. 121–32.

22 Wheeler-Bennett, *Brest-Litovsk: The Forgotten Peace, March 1918*, Fischer, *Germany's Aims in the First World War*, pp. 475–509.

23 Pedroncini, *Négociations secrètes*, pp. 58–67.

24 Fischer, *Germany's War Aims*, pp. 280–324.

References and Further Reading

Becker, Jean-Jacques, *Le Pape et la Grande Guerre*, Paris, Bayard, 2006.

Dickinson, Frederick, *War and National Reinvention. Japan in the Great War, 1914–1919*, Cambridge, MA, Harvard University Press, 1999.

Fischer, Fritz, *Germany's War Aims in the First World War*, 1961; translation from German, London, Chatto and Windus, 1967.

French, David, *British Strategy and War Aims 1914–16*, London, Allen and Unwin, 1986.

Guoqui, Xu, *China and the Great War. China's Pursuit of a New National Identity and Internationalization*, Cambridge, Cambridge University Press, 2005.

Mayer, Arno J., *Political Origins of the New Diplomacy, 1917–1918*, New Haven, Yale University Press, 1959.

Pedroncini, Guy, *Les Négociations secrètes pendant la grande guerre*, Paris, Flammarion, 1969.

Poidevin, Raymond, *L'Allemagne de Guillaume II à Hindenburg: un Empire, une défaite*, Paris, Editions Richelieu, 1972.

Renouvin, Pierre, "Les buts de guerre du gouvernement français, 1914–1918," *Revue historique*, 235, Jan.–March 1966, pp. 1–38.

Ribeiro de Meneses, Filipe, *Portugal 1914–1926*, Bristol, Hispanic, Portuguese and Latin American Monographs, 2004.

Romero Salvadó, Francisco J., *Spain, 1914–1918. Between War and Revolution*, London, Routledge, 2000.

Rothwell, V. H., *British War Aims and Peace Diplomacy, 1914–1918*, Oxford, Oxford University Press, 1971.

Schwabe, Klaus, *Woodrow Wilson, Revolutionary Germany, and Peacemaking, 1918–1919. Missionary Diplomacy and the Realities of Power*, 1971; translation from German Chapel Hill and London, University of North Carolina Press, 1985.

Soutou, Georges-Henri, *L'Or et le sang. Les buts de guerre économiques de la première guerre mondiale*, Paris, Fayard, 1989.

Stevenson, David, *French War Aims against Germany, 1914–1919*, Oxford, Clarendon Press, 1982.

Stevenson, David, *The First World War and International Politics*, Oxford, Oxford University Press, 1988.

Trumpener, Ulrich, *Germany and the Ottoman Empire, 1914–1918*, Princeton, Princeton University Press, 1968.

Wheeler-Bennett, John W., *Brest-Litovsk: The Forgotten Peace, March 1918*, London, 1938; new ed., Macmillan, 1963.

CHAPTER FIFTEEN

Industrial Mobilization and War Economies

THEO BALDERSTON

Few before 1914 anticipated a long war, and even those who did rarely thought of it in economic terms. In the event, the ease with which war matériel could be delivered, and the voracity with which it was consumed, tested to the limits the economic supply that the belligerents could command. It made access to the global economy matter as never before, so that not just US economic might but also Britain's place at the heart of the global economic web became critical advantages for the Allies. It also made "morale" in the civilian economy vital to military success, so that reconciling civilian and military demands became a priority for a successful war effort.

Logistics and Economic Mobilization

As the German First Army pressed into northeastern France in August 1914, it outran its own supply lines and its horses began to sicken. Its human members could live quite well off the rich supplies of the productive northern French agriculture at harvest time, but its 84,000 equine members, consuming about 900 tons of fodder per day, had often to eat local green corn, with significantly disruptive effects on the advance of the cavalry and artillery.[1]

At this extreme end of Schlieffen's great offensive "wheel," therefore, the problems of food and fodder supply, and their solution, were little different from what they had been for thousands of years. But from the battle of the Marne the situation changed. Early modern armies had been small enough to "live off the land" and set out carrying all the ammunition they would need for a campaign. Besieging armies had often faced the hardest time, since they risked exhausting local food supplies and being forced to raise the siege. But railways, delivering the massive supplies needed by vast armies using industrialized means of destruction, inverted that advantage. The advancing German armies both in summer 1914 and in spring 1918 were crippled once they got more than 30 or 50 miles in front of their railheads. One reason why Foch granted an armistice on November 11, 1918 was that logistical problems were hampering his advance.[2]

This was a major reason why the western front in World War I became static. By 1917 the British had perfected a system of delivering seaborne supplies to French Channel ports and transferring them to supply trains that took them to numerous railheads, usually some seven or eight miles behind the front. A vast system of light railways then carried the supplies forward, in some cases right to artillery batteries, in others, to horse transport for the last short distance. Intersecting this transport network was a double set of light railways parallel to the trenches and running the entire length of the western front at 3,000 and 6,000 yards, respectively, behind it. This enabled the redistribution of material among sectors.[3] The whole system carried almost unimaginable quantities of supplies. On a 12-mile sector of the active front during the Somme offensive the *daily* delivery of all supplies peaked at 20,000 tons, and weekly expenditure of ammunition averaged 26,000 tons, delivered over rail links that a year later looked rather rudimentary.[4]

The same ease of delivery to static fronts arrested the impetus of offensives. The supply problems of advancing armies were compounded by the destruction wrought by their own artillery bombardment, not to mention the destructive zeal of retreating armies. This contrasted with the relative ease with which defensive operations could be refueled along intact supply lines. The defensive bias of transport technology, as well as of military technology,[5] thus produced a "field of forces" on the western front that tended to restore fronts after they had been breached. This was a "logistician's dream,"[6] for it resulted in stable conditions for supplying the western front and thus allowed the major industrialized economies to plug directly into the conflict.[7] The eastern front, by contrast, was logistically highly unstable. Static fronts were rapidly displaced even hundreds of miles by short mobile campaigns before solidifying again. Stone argues that a major reason for this was that the far thinner transportation network and greater length of front relative to military forces prevented the rapid redeployment of troops to plug gaps in a defensive line.[8] However, more general and traditional supply problems eventually weakened the impetus of an advance in the east, as the Germans found in 1915 (see chapter 5), so that defensive lines could ultimately be held at least until the aggressor could consolidate his supply lines. Even in the east, of course, railways vastly increased ammunition consumption.

This, then, goes far to explaining the unprecedented economic mobilization within the warring states. Certainly, foreign supplies played an important role. In 1915–18 half of the French steel supply was imported from Britain and the United States (France had been a small steel exporter in 1913), to make good the loss of her northern heavy industrial districts.[9] Especially in 1917–18 Britain also supplied France with ammunition and small arms; however France became the Allies' leading arms producer and provided most of the equipment for the American Expeditionary Force in 1918.[10] Britain was dependent on the United States, for iron and steel, shells, and propellants; at their peak in 1916 about 40 percent of all British munitions came from the United States.[11] Difficulties in overseas transportation and finance made Russia proportionately less dependent on foreign procurement, but about 40 percent of Russian shells were imported in 1916.[12] Inter-allied economic cooperation was at a lower level between Germany and Austria-Hungary; the latter could add only about 12 percent to her limited pig-iron and steel output from German imports, little coal, and little ammunition.[13] However in all the belligerent states, Turkey apart, the preference was for *domestic* supply; military mobilization for the front meant economic mobilization at home.

Supplying the War Effort

Calculating the impact of the war on production in the belligerent countries is no easy matter. It means estimating war-related production as a proportion of the total supply of goods and services available to each belligerent country, and in a consistent manner across countries, if international comparisons are to be attempted. As can be seen from Table 15.1, which estimates Gross Domestic Product (GDP) for the main belligerent states, different ways of calculating this give rather different results.[14] The British and French examples show that if GDP is estimated in terms of expenditure it is higher than if estimated as physical output.[15] This suggests that the available estimates for German, Russian, and Austro-Hungarian GDP, which are calculated on the latter basis, may show too severe a relative fall if compared with British and French measurements in terms of expenditure. Despite these problems, Table 15.1 shows that the war caused a decline of production in all the European belligerents with the possible exception of the United Kingdom. This decline, affecting both industry (a few munitions-related sectors apart) and agriculture, was caused by supply shortages, not demand deficiency. The conscription of adult males resulted in acute labor shortages (after a brief period of unemployment), the prewar organization of production was disrupted, and the necessary material inputs for production became scarce.

However in addition to their own production, all of the major European belligerents could increase supply by reducing exports relative to imports. Table 15.2 transforms Table 15.1 into an index of the change in the supply of goods and services during the war, by adding to the GDP data estimates of the real surplus of imports of goods and services.

This indicates that unlike Germany, Austria-Hungary, and Russia, Britain and France (in 1916 and 1917) were able to make good, or more than make good, the shortfalls from peacetime domestic output by increased net imports. The Central Powers were prevented from doing this by the British blockade, which limited their trade to that with nearby neutrals. Russia was similarly affected by the German and Turkish blockade of the Baltic and Black Seas.

In addition to blockade, foreign borrowing was also a severe constraint on increased net importing. British official pressure on New York issuing houses, supported by the powerful and Anglophile J. P. Morgan bank, prevented the Central Powers from raising more than minuscule loans in the United States. German net importing was limited by the appetite of neutral suppliers for German trade credit, though this was appreciable enough to exceed Germany's loans to her allies.[16] Britain lent lavishly to the Entente, and France also lent to Russia and Italy, but since much of this lending was to finance spending in the United States, the balance of payments with the United States was the real pinch-point.[17] Despite Britain's unimpeachable prewar credit rating, her own loan-raising powers in the United States were limited, and her relations with US financial markets (which determined those of the other Allies) teetered on the brink of bankruptcy throughout the period of American neutrality. Acquisition of dollars through the sale of British-owned US securities did not solve the problem. But Hew Strachan argues that even if the United States had remained neutral, ways would have been found of staving off a British bankruptcy, so as to avert a US slump.[18] As it was, American entry into the war brought significant, though not generous, US governmental lending to the Allies. But what contributed most to Britain's increased powers of importing was an amazingly buoyant *export* – shipping services, due to the tenfold increase of freight rates.[19] In this way, among others, Britain's centrality to the global economy eased her war effort.

Table 15.3 shows what proportion of the overall supply indicated in Table 15.2 was appropriated by governments as outlays on goods and services for war purposes. For Germany and Austria-Hungary the measure of these outlays is direct "expenditure due to the war."[20] For the other three nations, the measure is the increase in central government spending over 1913, excluding loans to allies (all at 1913 prices).

Table 15.1 Estimates of the wartime gross domestic product of major European belligerents at constant prices (1913 = 100)

Year	UK "Expenditure" method	UK "Output" method	France "Expenditure" method	France "Output" method	Germany "Output" method	Austria–Hungary "Output" method	Russia "Output" method
1913	100	100	100	100	100	100	100
1914	98	97	89	84	92	90	95
1915	103	98	75	72	85	89	96
1916	101	94	87	81	81	80	80
1917	101	89	87	79	79	70	68
1918	99	87	74	66	76	62	
1919	95	92	80	72	68		
1920	100	101	88	77	77		

Sources: UK/**Expenditure**: Feinstein, Table 5, col. 12, deducting the excess over 1913 of armed forces' pay in cash and kind, obtaining the former by multiplying number of service personnel by average 1938 pay (Feinstein, Tables 4.4, 33, 57, with p. 79); the latter by deflating estimates in A. R. Prest and A. A. Adams, *Consumers' Expenditure in the United Kingdom 1900–1919* (Cambridge, 1954), p. 168 via Feinstein, Table 62, cols. (1) and (5).

UK/**Output**: Own calculation, combining, like the method of Ritschl and Spoerer as cited under Germany, indexes of real output in industry, agriculture, and transportation. Details available from the author.

France/**Expenditure**: Hautcoeur, "Watershed," p. 189. **France/Output**: ibid., p. 171. **Germany**: Ritschl and Spoerer, *Bruttosozialprodukt*, p. 41. **Austria–Hungary**: Schulze, "Austria–Hungary," p. 83. **Russia**: Gatrell, "Poor Russia," p. 241.

Table 15.2 Estimates of real supply of the belligerents, 1913–20 (1913 prices)

	UK	UK	France	France	Germany	Russia	Austria–Hungary
	"Expenditure" method	"Output" method	"Expenditure" method	"Output" method			
	£ (million)	£ (million)	Francs (billion)	Francs (billion)	Marks (billion)	Crowns (billion)	Crowns (billion)
1913	2636	2636	52.37	52.37	57.32	27.85	20.27
	1913=100	1913=00	1913=100	1913=00	1913=00	1913=100	1913=100
1914	102	101	89	84	94	96	90
1915	111	107	84	82	90	100	91
1916	104	98	106	99	86	84	80
1917	106	96	107	100	82	69	69
1918	107	98	88	80	78		
1919	102	100	91	83			
1920	107	108	91				

Sources: Sources to Table 15.1, plus **UK**: C. H. Feinstein, *National Income, Expenditure and Output of the United Kingdom 1855–1965*, Cambridge, 1972, Table 5, cols. (5) and (7). **France**: Hautcoeur, "Watershed," p. 182. **Germany**: Schulze, "Austria-Hungary," pp. 100, 103. **Russia**: Gatrell, "Poor Russia," pp. 249, 270. **Austria-Hungary**: Schulze, "Austria-Hungary," p. 33. **Russia**: Hardach, *First World War*, p. 33.

Table 15.3   Estimates of government war spending as % of aggregate supply

	UK	France	Germany	Austria-Hungary	Russia
1913	0	0	0	0	0
1914	4	9		25	5
1915	25	25	27	22	24
1916	32	23	33	18	28
1917	35	25	45	13	17
1918	32	27	37		

Note: Austrian data run from July to June.

Method: Estimates of spending on war goods and services, as explained in the text, and from the following sources, reduced to constant prices, and expressed as % of the data underlying Table 15.2. For Britain and France, "expenditure-based" estimates of aggregate supply are used as the denominator.

Sources: **UK**: Feinstein, *National Income*, Table 5, col. (2), plus Table 39, cols. (9) and (10) deflated by Table 63, col. (3), as % of data underlying Table 15.2 of this chapter, col. 1. **France**: Hautcoeur, "Watershed," p. 184, deflated by the GDP deflator, p. 186; and reduced by the estimate of French foreign lending at 1913 prices from H. E. Fisk, *The Inter-Ally Debts. An Analysis of War and Post-War Public Finance 1914–1923* (New York, 1924), p. 28, converted to francs at the peacetime rate of 6 Fr. fr. = $1 (Hautcoeur, "Watershed," p. 190). **Germany**: K. Roesler, *Die Finanzpolitik des Deutschen Reiches im Ersten Weltkrieg*, Berlin, 1967, p. 200, deflated by the wholesale price index from Holtfrerich, *Inflation*, p. 17. **Austria-Hungary**: Schulze, "Austria-Hungary," p. 84. **Russia**: Gatrell, "Poor Russia," p. 247, deflated by the average of price indexes in cols. 2, 3, 4, 6 on p. 270; missing data in cols. 2 and 3 interpolated.

Table 15.4   Estimate of total appropriation of aggregate supply for war purposes by home and foreign governments, 1913–18

	UK	France	Germany
1913	0	0	
1914	10	10	
1915	32	26	29
1916	37	25	34
1917	37	26	46
1918	33	28	39

Sources: Table 3 amended thus: **UK**: British government spending increased by 2/3 of its lending to foreign governments per E. Victor Morgan, *British Financial Policy 1914–1925*, (London, 1952, p. 341) (deflated by the GDP deflator from Feinstein, Table 54), as a percentage of aggregate supply (Table 15.2) plus the whole of this foreign lending. **France**: Hautcoeur, "Watershed," p. 184, deflated by the GDP deflator, p. 186; aggregate supply supplemented by French foreign lending calculated as described for Table 15.3 col. 2. **Germany**: Government war spending and aggregate supply both increased by the global estimate for government foreign lending in Fisk, *Inter-Ally Debts*, p. 37, col. 2, allocated among the years thus: 1914, one-ninth; 1915–18, two-ninths each. All converted to 1913 marks at 4.2 M to the $.

However, it makes sense to include exports of war goods to allied governments in calculating total war outlays affecting each belligerent, and to add the sums which each loaned to its allies as part of its aggregate supply (on the grounds that these sums could in principle have been used to command resources for the use of the domestic economy). Table 15.4 roughly modifies Table 15.3 on these lines to show the proportion of the potential supply at the command of each of the lending belligerents that was appropriated to its own and its allies' war efforts.[21]

What emerges from Tables 15.3 and 15.4 is that the proportion of overall supply devoted to the war was smaller in the less industrialized states. In France, it amounted to just over a quarter in the last two years of the war; in Russia it reached a similar level in 1916 before the onset of the Revolution; and in Austria-Hungary it started at a quarter in 1914 before tailing off sharply to well under a fifth in 1916 and 1917.[22] This was perhaps inevitable, in that importing could not be a perfect substitute for deficient home production: the Russians discovered how unsatisfactory foreign ordering of munitions was.[23] This picture is confirmed by the case of the Ottoman Empire (not shown in the tables), where the additional state spending during the war seems to have peaked at about 10 percent of 1913 national income in 1914/15 and 1915/16, much of this spent on German munitions paid for by German loans.[24]

By contrast, the proportion of supply allocated to the war in the two more industrialized states, the United Kingdom and Germany, was considerably higher and roughly comparable at one third or more in the last three war years.[25] While further transfer of resources to war production might have been possible in Britain, mounting domestic discontent in Germany indicates that a fuller degree of economic mobilization there would have been politically impossible.

Funding the War

In each country, what determined the actual proportion of aggregate supply appropriated to its own war effort was partly the state's powers of requisitioning and partly the real purchasing power at the state's disposal for overcoming competing private claims for goods, services, and labor. Assuming all states were equally capable of requisitioning economic resources, real state purchasing power depended first on taxation and secondly on borrowing. Since in all the belligerents less than 30 percent of revenue was raised by taxation (far less in the cases of France, Austria-Hungary, and Russia), borrowing was crucial. Here I focus on domestic borrowing, which accounted for more than 70 percent of wartime state revenue.

If all taxpayers and lenders to the government had abstained from purchasing equivalent amounts of domestic goods and services, war financing could have proceeded without inflation. If none had so abstained at the initial rates of interest, interest rates could have been allowed to rise to induce them to raise the money from income, instead of finding it from borrowing or from selling assets; this too would have limited inflation. Alternatively, governments, balking at the debt charges that this would entail, could have borrowed from their central banks (in effect printing money), and, armed with this purchasing power, have muscled private competitors out of the relevant markets by higher bids. However, if this inflation-creating strategy was to be effective in diverting goods and services to government use, it had somehow to induce private abstinence. This would occur as inflation induced recipients of the newly printed money to add some of it to their cash balances rather than spend it.

In reality, all governments printed money on a significant scale and inflation became a problem, though in varying degrees. In Britain, France, and Germany prices little more than doubled during the war, even allowing for the black market. But in Austria-Hungary prices had already multiplied sixfold by the end of 1916 and in Russia three- or fourfold.[26] The stock of money at least expanded to match the rise in prices, and in

Germany exceeded the rise of prices until the war's end, owing to hoarding.[27] Even so, it is also clear that in the three Western belligerent societies, citizens and business abstained to a surprising extent from consumption in order to pay taxes and invest in war stock and, buoyed by hopes of victory and foreign indemnities, expected such investment to be profitable.[28] Lending and hoarding were also buoyed by the strong belief that wartime inflation was a temporary aberration, and that the restoration of the prewar gold standard after the war would bring the price level down again.[29] Belief in the restoration of the gold standard was an engine of war (especially for the Entente), but the collapse of this belief after the war precipitated the far more serious postwar inflations.

Organizing and Controlling the War Economy

There were two dimensions to the organization of the war economy. First was the management of the supply of actual munitions – guns, ammunition, warships, military clothing – which were needed in colossal quantities. The second was the management of the intersecting and conflicting demands of the munitions and civilian industries for labor, raw materials, and intermediate goods.

Focusing first on munitions, the European great powers other than Britain, having large standing armies, also had well-developed state arsenals, which in Germany supplied 40 percent, in France 75 percent, and in Russia almost all of munitions at the outbreak of war.[30] They also had large private arms firms such as Krupps (Germany), Schneider (France), and Skoda (Austria-Hungary) and Putilov (Russia). Certainly the huge demand for heavy-gun ammunition, due to the nature of trench warfare, caught all the belligerents out. But the munitions crisis in Germany and Austria-Hungary in fall 1914 could be met by large increases in munitions output over the following two years without a revolution in the supply system.[31] The variety of war products was small compared with peacetime products; the problem was one of huge enlargement of these relatively standard lines of supply. In Germany new munitions producers could be found from the rich array of civilian engineering firms, whilst France's European preeminence in vehicle manufacture provided a similar nucleus of know-how. A huge expansion of French munitions production was managed by the development of a system of production consortiums, each led by an established munitions firm.[32]

Classical liberal-market economics could never have delivered the required volume of armaments, as even its most ardent contemporary theorists realized.[33] U. F. Wintour of the British War Office observed that competitive tendering would never keep down prices when every realistic proposal had to be accepted owing to acute demand.[34] This was compounded by competition among the procurement agencies. Even the British never managed to harmonize army and navy purchasing, while the federal nature of the German army was a recipe for proliferation, despite an attempt to create an overarching Weapons and Munitions Procurement Agency in 1916.[35]

The other side of the price problem was that munitions suppliers justified high prices by the risks entailed in enlarging capacity which peace could render redundant overnight. This market logic ran counter to the criticisms from socialists and others who condemned armaments manufacturers as profiteers. But talk of a reciprocal "conscription of capital" was unrealistic, given the dependence of the state on private enterprise know-how and organization. Hence, in all countries, the state took over much of the risk for enlargement of plant while allowing high profits as a necessary premium for eliciting the desperately needed supplies. However, profiteering jeopardized the domestic pro-war consensus, which included organized labor. In Germany officials were increasingly conscious of the tightrope they walked on this matter in the second half of the war; but they lacked the means, and probably the will, to check the costs of their diverse suppliers. The result was a corresponding inability to control labor. The "Patriotic Auxiliary Service Law" of December 1916 tightened military controls on the deployment of certain classes of civilian labor, but also ended up enshrining their right to change jobs for better conditions, because of inability to control profits.[36] In Germany the Reichstag was a rather toothless watchdog on profiteering until 1918, but even in France, where parliamentary control was far closer, negotiation rather than compulsion was the basis of munitions production, and although the authorities increasingly controlled prices and monitored costs, the profit incentive remained the basis of the system. The French case is the more remarkable for the Socialist, Albert Thomas, being the government minister principally responsible.[37]

In Russia, the state was more suspicious toward private enterprise. An outburst of self-organization by medium and smaller industry in response to the shell shortage in early 1915 met with a reticent reaction from the autocracy, which treated any action on the part of civil society as a threat to its position. Nevertheless a huge increase in Russian munitions production occurred by 1916.[38]

It was in Britain, where the expansion from a small peacetime army was much the greatest, that the most revolutionary changes were needed in army (though not navy) procurement. Various initial arrangements were superseded by Lloyd George's innovation of national factories, state financed and managed, as the best way of economizing on know-how and inspection whilst controlling profits. But the state was reliant on coopted businessmen to do the managing, and the voluntary support and initiatives tapped through the "Area Boards" of the new Ministry of Munitions were indispensable.[39] Strict accounting checks on the costs of private firms doing war work were complemented by quite severe taxation of profits above a prewar norm. These measures were a quid pro quo for trade union concessions, under the Munitions of War Act, regarding customs and arrangements that protected skilled workers.[40] Excess profits taxes of varying severity were introduced by all belligerents.[41]

State planning arguably went furthest in the second layer of management of the war economy, which concerned labor (discussed in chapter 19), raw materials, and intermediate goods. The origins of state intervention in respect of the last two lay in the dependence of war production on the global economy. In Germany, fear of key raw materials shortages due to the British blockade led to the establishment in August 1914 of a War Raw Materials Section of the Prussian War Ministry, under Walther Rathenau, head of the giant electro-engineering firm AEG.[42] This office took over strategic stocks in Germany and German-occupied Europe in order to distribute them according to need. Rathenau used the threat of requisition to force civilian users of war-related raw materials to set up collaborative War Raw Materials Corporations that allocated scarce stocks non-competitively. The armaments firms were not required to work through the Corporations, however. Germany insisted that Austro-Hungarian purchasers of raw materials from Germany be organized into similar *Zentralen*, which often also organized their internal distribution.[43] Germany also responded to the blockade by developing domestic substitutes for vital war commodities – such as aluminum instead of copper, and synthetic nitrates for making explosives (see chapter 21). The War Raw Materials Corporations assisted in this.[44]

A second wave of interventionism in munitions-related sectors in Germany came in 1916–17, when shock at the extent of Allied firepower at the Somme resulted in the Hindenburg Program in August 1916.[45] This dramatically increased steel and other output targets and introduced state control of steel distribution. However, in practice steel firms continued to be able to divert output into the export market with its higher prices, and even home prices were quite lightly regulated, as were profits.[46] The Program also extended state powers to rationalize production between plants and allocate labor. But in practice, the rhythm of production was increasingly governed by allocations of coal, which became scarce at the end of 1916, while the power of trade unions limited state control over the labor supply.[47] The ambitious steel targets could not be realized.

Along with food and rent controls, these measures add up to an allocation system in Germany far removed from the market economy by the turn of 1916–17. However Germany did not achieve an effective, centralized, rational system of deciding priorities in the use of war raw materials as the British did, and the German system depended fundamentally on traditional powers of requisitioning, with or without compensation.[48]

In Britain, state intervention in the war economy had commenced in respect of the railways with the outbreak of war. It spread to all steel production by mid-1916, but with tighter price controls than in Germany. The financial management of coal mines and distribution of coal were taken under state control from February 1917, largely owing to labor concerns, with household rationing of coal being introduced in August, about the same time as it was also introduced in France. To limit coal consumption Lloyd George extended state control even to time itself, with the Daylight Saving Act of 1917.[49] But the revolutionary element of the British management of munitions inputs lay not in controlling domestic supplies through virtual requisitioning but in using its maritime and financial preeminence to negotiate the purchase of most of the world supply of commodities that were vital for the war effort. This policy, which meant defeating private competition, began with the purchase of the Australian wool clip (along with the British and that of the rest of the Empire) in 1916. It extended to major items of mass food consumption and armaments as the "Ministry [of Munitions] became the largest buying and selling concern in the world, with a turnover amounting to hundreds of millions yearly."[50]

In order to avoid unnecessary competition and to rationalize the use of shipping, this policy became inter-allied. Coordination of allied procurement in the United States commenced in August 1914 with the Anglo-French Commission Internationale de Ravitaillement and embraced other Allies and more products from 1915. In spring 1915 the leading US banking house of J. P. Morgan was appointed joint Allied purchasing agent in the United States.[51] In a comparable manner to the Austro-Hungarian case, French iron and steel imports were organized at British insistence under the iron and steel cartel, the Comité des Forges, in November 1915, with similar arrangements for coal imports from June 1916.[52] From the entry of the United States into the war, commodity purchase schemes quickly turned into Inter-Allied Control Boards. By 1918, this control of key internationally traded commodities by the Allies had produced a fleeting revolution in the global economic system of 1913, which, though it would not long outlive the end of the war, was vital to Allied success.[53]

One drawback of all such planning is that it is hard to police and creates profitable incentives for evasion. But for the Allies this was simplified by the absence of notable competitive industrial markets outside their control to which raw materials suppliers could have sold their products, and by the strategic role played by British domination of international shipping. More than 60 percent of world steamship capacity had been British-owned in 1913, and Britain used her control of far-flung coal-bunkering stations to pressure neutral shipping.[54] The fact that all imports had to be landed at a few ports greatly reduced the problems of policing the arrangements inside Britain. This was aided by the coopting of industry associations into running the controls, and by the localization of industrial production (boots and shoes in Leicestershire and Northamptonshire, wool textiles in the West Riding of Yorkshire, etc.), which made evasion difficult since it was in the interest of other producers to prevent it. Controlling trade was thus not as hard for the Allies as for the Central Powers.[55]

Food Supply

Assuring food supplies is one of the most important traditional functions of government, and this is particularly the case with urban populations that have no independent means of subsistence. In 1913 the British population imported three-quarters of its food supplies in calorie terms. The figure for Germany was about ten percent; Austria-Hungary, France and Italy had a rough balance between import and exports; and Rumania and Russia were large grain exporters.[56] But although home food supplies were relatively more abundant in Eastern than Western Europe before the conflict, wartime supplies were much greater in the west. As with industrial output, access to world supplies explains the difference.

Food supply did not begin to be perceived as a problem in the United Kingdom until 1916; but in 1917–18 the calorific value of average food consumption was about 3 percent lower than just before the war, with meat consumption about 20 percent lower and milk and butter about 25 percent lower, but flour products 10 percent higher and margarine more than100 percent higher.[57] These were the worst years, owing to the effect of the U-boat campaign on shipping tonnage (see chapter 10). As a result, under the price incentives and "cropping orders" of the Corn Production Act of 1917, much British grassland was returned to grain production. Equitable distribution was achieved through rationing, culminating in the issue of ration cards for many products from January 1918, plus government purchase at source of all major food types and control of distribution, largely through the established commercial networks. Public confidence in the system is evidenced by the disappearance of queues with the advent of ration cards.[58]

The worst food shortages occurred in urban Germany, Austria-Hungary, and Russia. The statement that Germany was 90 percent self-sufficient in food conceals the indirect globalization of German agriculture through its marked dependence on imported livestock feeds and fertilizers.[59] In addition, the draft of manpower and horsepower to the colors, a burden falling disproportionately on agriculture, reduced wartime agricultural output, as did the loss of about one million seasonal immigrant estate laborers, mainly Polish (though offset by more intense women's labor and eventually by about one million prisoners of war). The simple price controls introduced from the start of the war could not elicit extra supplies, and widened powers of requisitioning were deputed to local-authority associations, with national agencies such as the Reich Cereals Agency supervising redistribution between regions. A Reich Food Office was established to unify controls in May 1916, but with limited powers. Bread was already rationed from January 1915. Price maxima discouraged off-farm sales, and encouraged diversion to non-controlled products. Thus the measures tended to reduce rather than increase supply, and this, coupled with the globally poor harvest of 1916, led to the "turnip winter" of 1916/17. By 1917 the calorific value of typical urban German food consumption was 20 percent below that of 1913. The centrality of *imports* to the British food system made it easier to police than the German, with its innumerable lines of distribution from farm to consumer. In Germany, prosecutions for infringements of rationing were about ten times the British; and the rationing system fell into disrepute as about one-third of all food came to be purchased on the black market, much by large firms on behalf of their workers.[60]

In prewar Austria-Hungary there had been distinct grain-surplus and grain-deficit regions. Declining food production for similar reasons to Germany was compounded by the loss of production in the northern war zones, an internal transport crisis, and regional grain hoarding. Requisitioning at fixed prices diverted supplies to black markets, and advantaged some areas over others, while unreliable statistics misled policy-makers. All this led to such a serious urban food crisis in Austria that in April 1918 the authorities seized grain trains bound from Romania to Germany to relieve the hunger in Vienna.[61] Hungary fared rather better as a rich agricultural country, but used its autonomous status within the Dual Monarchy to keep food supplies from the Austrian lands (see chapter 25). Ironically, it may be that if, in the blockaded countries, urban populations had been willing to be worse off by accepting higher real food prices, they might have ended up better off owing to more adequate food supplies. As it was, the peasantry ended up economically less disadvantaged but feeling politically discriminated against by price controls.

Russia's large grain surplus of prewar years did not save her cities from the same fate as Austria. The large grain exporting estates suffered disproportionately from call-up of manpower and horsepower. The rail-transport crisis across Russia's huge distances deprived cities of supplies. Loss of export markets and difficulties of access to domestic ones reduced the price of agricultural relative to industrial goods; and whilst to some extent peasants banked their earnings in hopes of lower postwar industrial prices, they also reduced their marketable supplies, perhaps in favor of self-consumption.[62]

It is hard to compare the decline in food production in France with that in Germany because of the division between the occupied and unoccupied areas, and because of the size of the refugee population and the change in the size of the migrant-worker population in unoccupied France.[63] French agricultural output fell for similar reasons to Germany: the difference was food imports. Foreign wheat represented 43 percent of domestic production in 1916 and more in subsequent years. Frozen imports buttressed both the military and civilian meat supply. Whereas wheat and bread prices were controlled from late 1915, the meat supply did not begin to pinch until 1917, when "meatless days" were introduced, followed by meat-price controls in 1918. There was food rationing from 1917 and a black market, but not on the German scale. Unlike Berlin, neither Paris nor London experienced a nutritional crisis.[64] The Italian food supply suffered from the Central Powers' blockade of Russian exports through the Dardanelles, but per capita food consumption is said even to have risen during the war, due to North American supplies, though inefficient domestic administration eroded faith in the distribution system, encouraged a black market, and resulted in some food riots.[65] The Allies were concerned enough about the food supply to Britain, France, and Italy during and after the U-boat campaign to cut back on transatlantic munitions and steel imports so as to protect it.[66] It seems clear that what made the decisive difference to living standards (apart from housing) between the belligerents was access to overseas supplies.

***

There is a consensus among economic historians that the productive superiority of the Allies made their victory inevitable.[67] This may have been a necessary condition, but it was not sufficient. Also necessary was power over the international economy, owing to the globalization of the preceding half-century. This chapter has shown how Britain's multiple centrality to the world economy gave her critical leverage in moving resources toward the Allies and away from the Central Powers, and that this was as important as the United States' awesome productive capacity. This leverage operated through imperial politics (e.g., the support of the Dominions for London's policies[68]), finance (in denying dollars to the Central Powers), and transport. Prewar expectations by some observers that international interdependence made prolonged war impossible were confounded by the amazing adaptability in the short term of the economies of Russia and the Central Powers, above all of Germany, which were cut off from the world economy. But the longer the war lasted, the greater the advantage conferred on the Allies by their power to harness the world economy to their own efforts.

Notes

The author gratefully acknowledges his indebtedness to Professor Pierre Villa, CEPII, Paris, Dr Christopher Godden, and Dr Pierre Purseigle for generous replies to his questions.

1   Martin Van Creveld, *Supplying War. Logistics from Wallenstein to Patton*, Cambridge, 1977, pp. 123–5; J. A. Huston, *The Sinews of War: Army Logistics 1775–1953*, Washington, DC, 1966, p. 356.

2   Van Crefeld, *Supplying War*, pp. 5–39, 75–108; Holger Herwig, *The First World War: Germany and Austria-Hungary 1914–1918*, London, 1977, p. 410; Sir James Edmonds, "Introduction," in Henniker, *Transportation*, pp. vii–ix; Huston, *Sinews of War*, p. 386; Edwin Pratt, *The Rise of Rail-Power in War and Conquest 1833–1914*, London, 1916, p. 65. For nineteenth-century antecedents, see Huston, *Sinews of War*, pp. 198–238, 356.

3   For similar developments on the German side, see Wilhelm Groener, *Lebenserinnerungen: Jugend, Generalstab. Weltkrieg*, Göttingen, 1957, e.g., p. 286.

4   Henniker, *Transportation*, p. 161; *Ministry of Munitions*, vol. 2, pt. I, p. 44; cf. pp. 186ff.

5   Cf. John Terraine, *White Heat. The New Warfare 1914–8*, London, 1982, p. 142.

6   Huston, *Sinews of War*, p. 356.

7   Van Crefeld, "World War I and the revolution in logistics," in R. Chickering and S. Förster (eds.), *Great War, Total War. Combat and Mobilization on the Western Front 1914–1918*, Cambridge, 2000, pp, 57–72 (here pp. 67–9).

8   Stone, *Eastern Front*, esp. p. 92.

9   Hardach, "Industrial mobilization," pp. 62–3, 75–6; *Ministry of Munitions*, vol. 2, pt. 7, pp. 88–99.

10 Huston, *Sinews of War*, p. 335.

11 Burk, *Sinews*, p. 81; *Ministry of Munitions*, vol. 2, pt. 3.

12 N. N. Golovine, *The Russian Army in the World War*, New Haven, Yale University Press, 1931, pp. 140, 147.

13 Wegs, *Österreichische Kriegswirtschaft*, pp. 54, 63; Max-Stephan Schulze, "Austria-Hungary's Economy in World War I," in Broadberry and Harrison (eds.), *Economics of World War I*, p. 88; Gustav Gratz and Richard Schüller, *Der Wirtschaftliche Zusammenbruch Österreich-Ungarns. Die Tragödie der Erschöpfung*, Vienna, 1930, pp. 92–7, 116–23.

14 For Italian wartime GDP see Broadberry's note in Broadberry and Harrison (eds.), *Economics*, pp. 305–7.

15 For Britain, the standard "expenditure side" estimates of GDP have been modified to exclude from government expenditure the excess over 1913 of pay in cash and kind of the armed

forces. In this version the excess of forces' pay over 1913 is treated as a "transfer payment" which renders the British estimates more comparable with those for the other countries.

16 Strachan, *Financing*, pp. 164–7; Hardach, *First World War*, pp. 32–4.

17 *Ministry of Munitions*, vol. 2, pt. 7, pp. 47–8.

18 Burk, *Sinews*, pp. 54–95; Strachan, *Financing*, pp. 221–3.

19 Stephen Broadberry and Peter Howlett, "The United Kingdom during World War I," in Broadberry and Harrison (eds.), *Economics*, pp. 206–34 (here p. 220); cf. B. R. Mitchell, *British Historical Statistics* (Cambridge, 1988), p. 540.

20 For Austria-Hungary, measured by increase in military spending over 1913/14. For Germany, the subdivisions of "Expenditure on account of the War" seem to exclude lending to allies, though it is hard to see where this occurs in the overall accounts as reported by Roesler, *Finanzpolitik*, pp. 195–200.

21 These are overlapping estimates: e.g., French munitions imports appear both in the British and French columns. It is assumed that two-thirds of the sums lent by Britain were spent by recipients on British war goods, and that the entire sums lent by France and Germany were so spent.

22 Cf. Stephen Broadberry and Mark Harrison, "The Economics of World War I: an Overview," in Broadberry and Harrison (eds.), *Economics*, pp. 14–17. Even if French war spending is expressed as a percentage of estimates of aggregate supply based on the (lower) output-side estimates of GDP, it peaks at 28–29 percent in 1915–18.

23 Stone, *Eastern Front*, pp. 150–4.

24 S. Pamuk, "The Ottoman Empire in World War I," in Broadberry and Harrison (eds.), *Economics*, pp. 115, 117–18, 127, 129 (government expenditure deflated by the gold exchange rate); Strachan, *Financing*, pp. 171–6.

25 Given uncertainties in the British and German cases over the calculation of GDP, not too much should be made of the differences between Britain and Germany in Tables 15.3 and 15.4.

26 P.-C. Hautcoeur, "Was the Great War a Watershed? The Economics of World War I in France," in Broadberry and Harrison (eds.), *Economics*, pp. 169–234 (here p. 187); Albrecht Ritschl, "The Pity of Peace: Germany's Economy at War 1914–1918 and Beyond," in Broadberry and Harrison (eds.), *Economics*, pp. 41–76 (here p. 66); Holtfrerich, *German Inflation*, pp. 30–1; Broadberry and Howlett, "United Kingdom," p. 219; Schulze, "Austria-Hungary," p. 100; Peter Gatrell, "Poor Russia, Poor Show: Mobilising a Backward Economy," in Broadberry and Harrison (eds.), *Economics of World War I*, pp. 235–75 (here p. 270).

27 Holtfrerich, *German Inflation*, p. 189.

28 Though perhaps least so in Germany: Strachan, *Financing*, pp. 123–5.

29 Cf. Bordo and Kydland, "Gold standard."

30 Feldman, *Army*, p. 58; Hardach, "Industrial mobilization," pp. 59, 77; Gatrell, *Russia's First World War*, p. 23.

31 Feldman, *Army*, p. 52; Gratz and Schüller, *Wirtschaftliche Zusammenbruch Österreich-Ungarns*, pp. 109–19; David French, "The military background to the 'shell crisis' of May, 1915," *Journal of Strategic Studies*, 2 (1979), pp. 192–205.

32 Hardach, "Industrial mobilization," pp. 64–8; Feldman, "The Political and Social Foundations of Germany's Economic Mobilization, 1914–1916," *Armed Forces and Society*, 3, 1976, esp. pp. 126–7.

33 Arthur C. Pigou, *The Political Economy of War*, London, 1921, pp. 67–70, 234–7. I am indebted to Dr. Christopher Godden for this reference.

34 *Ministry of Munitions*, vol. 1, pt. 1, p. 54.

35 Roth, *Staat und Wirtschaft*, pp. 40–75; Feldman, *Army*, pp. 149–96.

36 Feldman, *Army*, pp. 197–249; Roth, *Staat und Wirtschaft*, pp. 275–366.

37 Feldman, *Army*, pp. 480–1; Hardach, "Industrial mobilization"; A. Hennebicque, "Albert Thomas and the War Industries," in Fridenson (ed.), *The French Home Front*, pp. 89–132.

38 Gatrell, *Russia's First World War*, pp. 23–5, 117–24; Gatrell, *Government*, pp. 215ff.; R. Claus, *Die Kriegswirtschaft Russlands bis zur bolshewistischen Revolution*, Bonn, 1922, pp. 70–4; Golovine, *Russian Army*, pp. 126–59, 176–8; Stone, *Eastern Front*, pp. 144–63.

39 *Ministry of Munitions*, vol. 1; vol. 2, pt. 1.

40 *Ministry of Munitions*, vol. 1, pt. 4; vol. 2, pts. 1, 2.

41 Strachan, *Financing*, pp. 65–105.

42 Pogge von Strandmann, *Rathenau*, pp. 186–9.

43 Wegs, *Österreichische Kriegswirtschaft*, pp. 26–33.

44 Roth, *Staat und Wirtschaft*, pp. 78–82, 102–46, 232–56, 295.

45 Feldman, *Army*, pp. 152ff.

46 Feldman, "Political and Social Foundations"; Roth, *Staat und Wirtschaft*, pp. 80, 236–7, 254–75.

47 Feldman, *Army*, pp. 198, 210–11, 273–82.

48 *Ministry of Munitions*, vol. 7, pt. 1, pp. 1, 44–61; Roth, *Staat und Wirtschaft*, pp. 174ff.

49 *Ministry of Munitions*, vol. 7, pt. 2, pp. 5–18, 90ff.; Redmayne, *British Coal-Mining Industry*, pp. 57, 77, 92, 110ff.; Leonard V. Smith, Stéphane Audoin-Rouzeau, Annette Becker, *France and the Great War*, Cambridge, 2003, p. 67.

50 Lloyd, *State Control*, pp. 112–54, 299–315; *Ministry of Munitions*, vol. 7, pt.1, p. 16.

51 *Ministry of Munitions*, vol. 2, pt. 5, pp. 5–25; Burk, *Sinews*, pp. 13–27.

52 Hardach, "Industrial mobilization," pp. 75–6; Redmayne, *British Coal-Mining Industry*, pp. 73, 84–6.

53 *Ministry of Munitions*, vol. 2, pt. 8.

54 C. E. Fayle, *The War and the Shipping Industry*, London, 1927; Redmayne, *British Coal-Mining Industry*, p. 75.

55 Ferguson, *Pity*, p. 266; Lloyd, *State Control*, p. 331.

56 Hardach, *First World War*, pp. 110–11; Augé-Laribé and Pinot, *Food Supply in France*, p. 19.

57 Beveridge, *British Food Control*, p. 313.

58 Whetham, *Agrarian History*, pp. 70–123; Lloyd, *State Control*, pp. 155–200, 231–58; Jose Harris, "Bureaucrats and Businessmen in British Food Control," in Burk (ed.), *War and the State*, pp. 135–56.

59 Augé-Laribé and Pinot, *Food Supply in France*, pp. 24–6.

60 A. Skalweit, *Die Deutsche Kriegsernährungswirtschaft*, Stuttgart, 1927, pp. 82–98, 114–229; Hardach, *First World War*, pp. 112–20; Offer, *Agrarian Interpretation*, p. 47; Beveridge, *British Food Control*, pp. 234–46; Lloyd, *State Control*, p. 331.

61 Schulze, "Austria-Hungary," pp. 91–7; Gratz and Schüller, *Wirtschaftliche Zusammenbruch Österreich-Ungarns*, pp. 42–91.

62 Gatrell, *Russia's First World War*, pp. 73, 154–75; Gatrell, "Poor Russia," pp. 256–9.

63 Hautcoeur's series (p. 170) on French real agricultural output in the post-1918 territory falls less than the German data of A. Ritschl and M. Spoerer, "Das Bruttosozialprodukt in Deutschland nach den amtlichen Volkseinkommens- und Sozialproduktstatistiken 1901–55," *Jahrbuch für Wirtschaftsgeschichte*, 1997, pp. 11–37 (here p. 41), whilst that of Augé-Laribé and Pinot, *Food Supply in France*, p.150, giving agricultural output in unoccupied France compared with the France of 1913, falls comparably. I am indebted to Dr. Pierre Purseigle for his unpublished estimate that the refugee population in France outside the war zone was some 1.5 million; wartime migrant-worker population was about 250,000 (John Horne, "Immigrant Workers in France during World War I," *French Historical Studies*, 14/1, 1985, pp. 58–60).

64 Thierry Bonzon and Belinda Davis, "Feeding the Cities," in Winter and Roberts (eds.), *Capital Cities*, pp. 305–41; Jay Winter, "Surviving the War: Life Expectation, Illness and Mortality Rates in Paris, London and Berlin, 1914–1919," in ibid., pp. 487–523.

65 Francesco Galassi and Mark Harrison, "Italy at War, 1915–1918," in Broadberry and Harrison (eds.), *Economics*, pp. 290–1.

66   Augé-Laribé and Pinot, *Food Supply in France*, pp. 39–54, 62–8, 82, 94–8, 178–97; Burk, *Sinews*, p.186; *Ministry of Munitions*, vol. 2, pt. 1, p. 96.
67   Ferguson, *Pity*, pp. 248–75; Broadberry and Harrison, "Overview," pp. 9–17.
68   Offer, *Agrarian Interpretation*, pp. 402–8.

References and Further Reading

Augé-Laribé, M., and Pinot, P., *Agriculture and Food Supply in France during the War*, New Haven, Yale University Press, 1927.

Beveridge, W. H., *British Food Control*, London, Oxford University Press, 1928.

Bordo, Michael D., and Kydland, Fynn, "The gold standard as a rule," reprinted in Barry Eichengreen and Marc Flandreau (eds.), *The Gold Standard in Theory and History*, London, Routledge, 2nd ed., 1997, pp. 99–128.

Broadberry, Stephen, and Harrison, Mark (eds.), *The Economics of World War I*, Cambridge, Cambridge University Press, 2005.

Burke, Kathleen (ed.), *War and the State*, London, Allen and Unwin, 1982.

Burke, Kathleen, *Britain, America and the Sinews of War, 1914–1918*, Boston, Allen and Unwin, 1985.

Feldman, Gerald D., *Army, Industry and Labor in Germany 1914–1918*, Providence, RI, Berg, 2nd ed., 1992 (1st ed. 1966).

Ferguson, Niall, *The Pity of War*, 2nd ed., London, Penguin, 1999.

Fridenson, Patrick (ed.), *The French Home Front 1914–1918*, Providence, RI, Berg, 1992.

Gatrell, Peter, *Government, Industry and Rearmament in Russia, 1900–1914: the Last Argument of Tsarism*, Cambridge, Cambridge University Press, 1994.

Gatrell, Peter, *Russia's First World War: a Social and Economic History*, Harlow, Pearson, 2005.

Godfrey, John F., *Capitalism at War. Industrial Policy and Bureaucracy in France 1914–1918*, Leamington Spa, Berg, 1987.

Golovine, N. N., *The Russian Army in the World War*, New Haven, Yale University Press, 1931.

Hardach, Gerd, *The First World War 1914–1918*, London and Harmondsworth, 2nd ed., Pelican, 1987; German original 1973.

Hardach, Gerd, "Industrial mobilization in 1914–1918: production, planning and ideology," in Fridenson (ed.), *The French Home Front*, pp. 57–88.

Henniker, A. M., *Transportation on the Western Front 1914–1918. History of the Great War. Based on Official Documents*, London, HMSO, 1937.

History of the Ministry of Munitions, 10 vols., London, 1922.

Holtfrerich, Carl-Ludwig, *The German Inflation 1914–1923. Causes and Effects in International Perspective*, Berlin, De Gruyter, 1986; German original 1980.

Horn, Martin, *Britain, France and the Financing of the First World War*, Montréal, McGill-Queen's University Press, 2002.

Lloyd, E. M. H., *Experiments in State Control at the War Office and the Ministry of Food*, Oxford, Clarendon Press, 1924.

Offer, Avner, *The First World War: An Agrarian Interpretation*, Oxford, Clarendon Press, 1989.

Pogge von Strandmann, H., *Walther Rathenau: Industrialist, Banker, Intellectual and Politician. Notes and Diaries 1907–1922*, Oxford, Oxford University Press, 1985.

Redmayne, Sir R. A. S., *The British Coal-Mining Industry During the War*, Oxford, Clarendon Press, 1923.

Roth, Regina, *Staat und Wirtschaft im Ersten Weltkrieg. Kriegsgesellschaften als kriegswirtschaftliche Steuerungsinstrumente*, Berlin, Duncker und Humblot, 1997.

Stone, Norman, *The Eastern Front 1914–1917*, London, Penguin, 2nd ed., 1998; 1st ed. 1975.

Strachan, Hew, *Financing the First World War*, Oxford, Oxford University Press, 2004.

Wegs, Robert J., *Die österreichische Kriegswirtschaft 1914–1918. Deutsche Bearbeitung von Heinrich Mejzlik*, Vienna, A. Schendl, 1979.

Whetham, Edith H., *The Agrarian History of England and Wales*. Vol. 8, *1914–1939*, Cambridge, Cambridge University Press, 1978.

Winter, Jay, and Robert, J.-L. (eds.), *Capital Cities at War. Paris, London, Berlin 1914–1918*, Cambridge, Cambridge University Press, 1997.

Wrigley, Chris (ed.), *The First World War and the International Economy*, Cheltenham, Edward Elgar, 2000.

Chapter Sixteen

Faith, Ideologies, and the "Cultures of War"

Annette Becker
(translated by John Horne)

All cognition of the All originates in death and in the fear of death. Philosophy takes it upon itself to throw off the fear of things earthly, to rob death of its poisonous sting, and Hades of its pestilential breath [… But] let man creep like a worm into the folds of the naked earth before the fast-approaching volleys of a blind death from which there is no appeal; let him sense there, forcibly, inexorably, what he otherwise never senses: that his I would be but an It if it died; let him therefore cry his very I out with every cry that is still in his throat against Him from whom there is no appeal, from whom such unthinkable annihilation threatens – for all this dire necessity philosophy has only its vacuous smile. With an index finger outstretched, it directs the creature, whose limbs are quivering with terror for its this-worldly existence, to a Beyond of which it doesn't care to know anything at all.[1]

When Franz Rosenzweig began his book *The Star of Redemption* with this reflection on death, he was a German soldier in the Balkans. The experience of World War I showed him that the tradition of philosophical rationality was dead and that he needed to look to the religious sphere for a new kind of thought. The "inexorable violence" that he revisited through eschatological thinking allowed him to find the closing words of his book: "Into Life."[2]

Like millions of other combatants, Rosenzweig defined himself in terms of the search for a meaning in the disaster of war.[3] This meaning could only be grasped in paradoxes such as the way war was embraced in order to achieve peace, or civilization was destroyed so that it might be better rebuilt. Messianic beliefs, hope, despair, the apocalypse, redemption, suffering, sacrifice, crusade, punishment – these were the words that contemporaries uttered, wrote, prayed, wept, and turned into images. Religion was doubly important for the culture of war, since consent to fight the war combined the causes of God and the fatherland, while rejection of the war was often in the name of the religious belief as well.

If modernity really contradicted the very idea of religion, if it had really resulted in secularization, as taught by the founding fathers of religious sociology (Durkheim, Weber, Mauss, and Halbwachs), then modern war should have been a world away from religious ideas.[4] For in this perspective, it was the most extreme and absolute form of the disenchantment of the universe. Yet World War I was by no means a moment when religion was "expelled" from society, to use Durkheim's term, or "absorbed" by it, to use

Max Weber's. A friend and pupil of Durkheim's, the ethnologist Robert Hertz, stated the diametrically opposite view from the trenches in October 1914: "How can one fail to recognize in the war those mysterious forces that sometimes crush us and sometimes save us? I would never have imagined how much war, even this modern war based on science and industry, is full of religion."[5] Many others testified to the force of the sacred in the conflict, including artists who left much visual evidence of it.

What was this wartime "spirituality"? What nourished it and how did it differ from what we more ordinarily call religion? Hertz distinguished what he termed a "religion of the war" or "veritable sacrament," based on a sense of sacrifice and the constant possibility of death, from a common religiosity which he despised as "the religion of the terrified," and which others derided as "lightning-conductor religion." Numerous soldiers and civilians testified to the force of the spiritual in the conflict. How can we understand what they meant by it?

During World War I, it was widely believed that fundamental values were being defended – fatherland, region, religion, family – and tested by suffering, fear, injury, and death. Each contemporary was part of a series of emotional and political relationships, which stretched from their loved ones right up to the state. As members of families, parishes, professions, neighborhoods, and villages, they embodied an individual destiny but they were also part of a collective destiny through their faith and fatherland. Such a double investment lay at the heart of the process of total cultural mobilization for the war and the complexity of the war cultures. Wartime spirituality can only be grasped in the context of the flux that made up the experiences of war – the fighting and home fronts, munitions and food supplies, propaganda and love, religious and patriotic fervor, hope and discouragement, death and mourning, the different roles of women and men. In all these domains, the war hampered some developments but made others possible. Spiritual and political fervor are very good examples of how the religious dimension was refashioned to fit the new experience of the war – as if the "primitive" (Durkheim's formula) had reemerged in this time of hope and despair and the "irrational" (Weber's formula) had destroyed the fine schemes of the men of science at the same time that it destroyed their lives. In the case of Durkheim, who died in 1917 from grief at the loss of his son in the war, the destruction was quite literal; it was more indirect in that of Weber, who succumbed in 1920 from the strain of serving Germany during the conflict, the peace negotiations, and the founding of the Weimar Republic.

Sacred Unions

The central paradox of the war cultures that characterized the conflict is that from the outset, and even more so with the moments of discouragement that appeared later in the war, everyone had the impression of waging war in order to make a radiant, better world, one purified because war itself would have been eliminated. Well before Woodrow Wilson's celebrated formula as the United States entered the conflict, "the war to end all wars," well before the retrospective catch-cry of the French veterans, "*la der des der*" (last of the last), or the Bolsheviks' slogan, "land rather than war," an eschatological view of the conflict had become widespread which counted on the future peace to triumph over the forces of evil and redeem humanity. War could only be waged if it was certain it would never have to be waged again. As the French dramatist Jacques Copeau put it as early as 1914: "This is the really admirable thing [about the French war effort]: a peaceful and pacifist nation being victorious over a formidable militarism, waging war formidably, destroying war with war!"[6] All the belligerents in one way or another believed in this mystical side of the war with its messianic promise. In order to understand the fervor of this belief, we should not read history in reverse, starting with the French mutinies of 1917 or the Bolshevik Revolution. Thus, Henri Barbusse, the French soldier-novelist who wrote the celebrated novel *Le Feu* (Under Fire) in 1916, should not be seen in terms of the "great ray of light from the east" with which he subsequently identified. *Le Feu* was a popular success at home and at the front and won the Prix Goncourt in December 1916 because it conveyed the horror of the fighting, the dying, and the over-all brutality of the war. But it was above all because its final chapter, "The Dawn," both accepted the war and refused the idea that it should continue since its suffering and dehumanization were too great. Consent, in Barbusse's novel, is based on the desire to destroy the "Prussian" militarism that a messianic French Republicanism opposes. In 1914 the Russian poet Vladimir Mayakovsky combined Russian patriotism and human universalism in his opposition to Germanic "cruelty." The same apocalyptic hatred can be found in the American revivalist preacher, Billy Sunday, in 1917, as he preached: "Hey Jesus, you've gotta send a country like that to damnation ... If hell could be turned upside down you would find stamped on its bottom 'Made in Germany'."[7]

Wartime societies were swept by waves of a religious-style faith. Belief in God and the *patrie* was often the same thing, and God was on the side of all the belligerent peoples: "God with us!," "*Dieu est de notre côté!*," "*Gott mit uns!*"[8] True, not everyone was a reli-gious believer, still less a practicing member of a Church, but spiritual values (good, evil) and a religious vocabulary shaped how the war was experienced as a veritable crusade. For during the nineteenth century, nations had been made sacred as much as religion had become nationalized. It was as if various "chosen peoples" all fought for the triumph of their cultures. On August 4, 1914, the German court chaplain, Ernst Dryander, preached a sermon at a historic session of the Reichstag in the Kaiser's presence:

> We are going into battle for our culture (*Kultur*) against the uncultured, for German civili-zation against barbarism, for the free German personality bound to God against the instincts of the undisciplined masses. And God will be with our just weapons! For German faith and German piety are ultimately bound up with German faith and civilization.[9]

Even such an antireligious figure as H. G. Wells conflated the desire to fight barbarism with a holy war when he coined the term "The Great War for Civilization." In this sense the war was portrayed as a two-paneled religious diptych. The warrior-knights, seen as saints and especially as suffering female saints, were arrayed against the enemy. The war was holy because it was "great," and was accepted as a test because it seemed to last for-ever. Yet the war was also eschatological, leading to a third panel, the final judgment. Depending on the religious affiliations of the person concerned, this took the form of an Imitation of the life of Christ, of the Virgin and saints, or of the fatherland. The eschato-logical certainty that a "just peace" would triumph over the evil of war itself as well as the enemy turned the diptych into a triptych.

The *Dictionnaire de théologie catholique*, compiled in France during the conflict, typi-fies this view. Having attacked the Germans at length for their war crimes, allegedly linked to Lutheranism, the author of the article on "War" concluded:

> In spite of the heavy responsibilities of those who declared war, it is certain that war only broke out at the moment decreed by Providence ... . God sometimes punishes with each

other those nations that have dared to live without Him or which trample upon his inalien-
able rights ... That which escapes human understanding, even that of the most perspicacious
and penetrating minds, is in the hands of the God of arms, who foresees all, knows all and
disposes of all things in accordance with His justice and His compassionate goodness ...
Nothing comes to pass as it is predicted. This is particularly true of the Great European War,
whose intensity shows no sign of letting up yet ... . Who could believe that the innumerable
victims of this frightful drama have spilt their blood in vain? Does not the blood spilt on the
field of battle weigh heavily in the scales of divine justice for the expiation of so many crimes
of which so many nations are guilty? Will not these killing fields re-establish the balance
between crimes and atonement? Let us hope that God who normally punishes the nations
not to destroy them but to purify them, will accomplish yet again, with the decrees of His
redoubtable justice, works of compassionate goodness.[10]

All the belligerent peoples were persuaded of the absolute truth of their cause. They
fought for their local homeland (region, village, pals) and for the fatherland, mingling
love of their near ones and love of their native soil. The latter was represented by numerous symbols, from flags and songs to poems learned at school or on military service. In
countries without conscription, such as Britain until 1916 or Australia throughout the
war, volunteering relied on such sentiments.[11] Faced with apparent aggression and encirclement, it was natural to feel loyalty to immediate kinsmen and community as well as to
a broader "culture" or "civilization," which together generated powerful feelings of
unity.[12] This fusion of religious and patriotic sentiments was not confined to the early
months of the war but continued throughout the conflict. There were numerous cultural
mobilizations and remobilizations, and the various "sacred unions" can be understood
as the continuous interaction of the political and the spiritual. In France, the nationalist
and Catholic (but non-practicing) intellectual, Maurice Barrès, pinpointed the exceptional character of this investment in the war:

> We shall always remember the extraordinary nature of this union. It was not a simple ques-
> tion of excitement or expediency on the part of a people surprised by the War. Let nobody
> try to tell us that for a certain period we put our various faiths in the corner of a wardrobe
> like some useless object. The soldiers will tell future generations, to their astonishment, that
> never did they live their faith more fully, that never were they more uplifted by it, than in the
> period when they joined together in unison. The Catholics will say: "We saved Catholicism"
> [and] the Socialists will say: "We saved Socialism". All are right. It was by each defending his
> own faith, his own religion, that we defended the common fatherland which embodies all
> our religions.[13]

Conversely, to condemn the war as evil was to identify it with the evil enemy and thus
to say that only victory could bring the truth of peace and the possibility of life. The
Bishop of London, A. F. Winnington-Ingram, went so far as to call for the extermination
of all Germans in 1915. Such an appeal to mass murder must be understood in the context of the apocalyptic response to the atrocities in 1914–15, when thresholds of violence and cruelty against civilians were crossed on land and sea, on all fronts and against
the Armenians in the Ottoman Empire (see chapter 13).

> Everyone that loves freedom and honour ... are banded in a great crusade – we cannot deny
> it – to kill Germans: to kill them, not for the sake of killing, but to save the world; to kill the
> good as well as the bad, to kill the young men as well as the old, to kill those who have
> shown kindness to our wounded as well as those fiends who crucified the Canadian sergeant,

who superintended the Armenian massacres, who sank the *Lusitania*, and who turned the machine-guns on the civilians of Aerschott and Louvain – and to kill them lest the civilisation of the world itself be killed.[14]

The hatred presupposed by this eschatology was so widespread among all the belligerent peoples that sermons inviting respect for the enemy were extremely rare and inevitably seen as a form of treason, even in Britain, which was generally more tolerant. Hatred of the enemy became the strongest expression of a sacred love of God and the fatherland and was virtually obligatory once the war had been agreed to. "Our Father which art in heaven, enlarge my heart so that it may contain more hatred," cried the very Catholic Jacques Péricard. In Germany, protestant theology contributed strongly to the militarization of public opinion: history became God's judgment, and it is not surprising if the code name given by Falkenhayn to the battle of Verdun should also have been *Gericht* (Judgment).

The impossibility of recognizing the enemy who was held responsible for invasion and atrocities as a Christian, still less a Catholic, explains in large measure the incomprehension of most belligerents, whether Catholic or not, toward the Pope. From the moment of his election in September 1914, Benedict XV was profoundly troubled by the tragedy of the war and had only one goal, the restoration of peace. He exhorted the warring peoples to conclude a just peace and offered to mediate in the pursuit of a general pacification. Despite the failure of these initiatives, he never abandoned his efforts. But with a striking symmetry his attempts at neutrality or even better, at "impartiality," were condemned by both camps as hypocrisy. Where Clemenceau evoked the "*boche* Pope," Ludendorff dismissed the "French Pope." Hatred was central to the crusade, and logically the Pope, who had children on both sides, could not endorse it. The resultant marginalization of the papacy continued until the death of Benedict XV in 1922, especially in his total exclusion from the peacemaking process.[15]

Sacrifice

The Jesuit philosopher and stretcher-bearer, Pierre Teilhard de Chardin, gave poignant expression to the wave of spirituality born of the disaster of the war, and to the fascination with suffering and its sublimation into something greater that seemed to announce a return to the binary nature of man as formulated by Pascal, marked at once by his wretchedness and his greatness. Teilhard de Chardin wrote:

> The war tore through the crust of conventions and the triviality [of ordinary life]. It threw open a window onto the secret mechanisms and profound depths of mankind's evolution. A place opened up in which men could breathe the air charged with the sky … Happy, perhaps, were those taken by death in the very act and atmosphere of the war, when they were animated by a responsibility, a conscience, and a freedom that were greater than themselves, when, exalted, they went to the very edge of the world, close to God![16]

Reading such texts, one understands why the philosopher Jan Patocka, thinking precisely about Teilhard de Chardin and the German veteran and writer, Ernst Jünger, argued that the twentieth century never completely divested itself of World War I. For Patocka, the war illustrated the precept of Heraclitus of Ephesus that "War (*Polemos*) is the father of everything," and he saw it as an archetype of war in history – negative, by its power of destruction, but positive, by the forces that it liberated. "The shock of the front comes not from a momentary trauma but from a fundamental modification of human existence: war, in the shape of the front, leaves a permanent mark."[17]

Early in the war, a certain number of stories celebrated the patriotic and spiritual example of the clergy and believers of different religions. Faith and charitable devotion appeared to be the cement of what the French aptly called the Sacred Union. In all the armies, the military chaplains of the minority faiths (Catholics and Jews in Britain and Germany, Protestants and Jews in France) exercised a greater influence than their numbers suggested, while the rapprochement between faiths resulted in a kind of wartime ecumenism. For the men of religion, whether Catholics, Protestants, or Jews, practiced the same profession: they consoled, encouraged, and assisted.

The phenomenon is particularly interesting in the case of the different Jewish communities, communities that were in a minority if not actually marginalized. French Jews, who had just emerged from the Dreyfus Affair, embraced the war passionately because it allowed them to fight for the Republic that embodied the values of the French Revolution and had given them their citizenship and identity. From this perspective, a French victory would emancipate the oppressed Jews of central Europe.[18] In the same way there appear to have been high levels of military service amongst established Anglo-Jewry, who were concerned to demonstrate the compatibility of Jewishness and British patriotism. The war likewise fostered a sense of integration into the nation on the part of German Jews. Despite a malicious census carried out by the army in November 1916 to check on the accusation that mobilized Jews were avoiding duty and danger, the reverse proved to be the case. German Jews made the same patriotic choice as elsewhere, and 12,000 of them died at the front.[19]

Militants of the faith, whether lay or clerical, acquired real influence during the war. By his exemplary life and death, the Catholic convert and novelist Ernest Psichari, who was killed in Belgium in August 1914, symbolized the mysticism of sacrifice, a mysticism rediscovered in the course of the war by certain Catholic intellectuals, such as Henri Massis. In his book, *Sacrifice*, published in 1917, Massis wrote:

> We will have lived in an incomparable grace during this war ... such is the meditation that is taking place in the cloisters of the trenches. No solitary hermit was ever more intense than this. What cell could offer a more bare and abandoned vista, a deeper and more real vision of death, a more severe solitude, a more fraternal spiritual company, or such ardent support? The holocaust is complete. Whether choosing the pickaxe that breaks up the earth or the spade that heaves it away, everyone digs his own grave there.[20]

This tragic vein of thought was reinforced by the dolorous school of Catholicism, in which the imitation of the life of Jesus takes place above all through the suffering of the Passion. The war from this perspective became an immense Good Friday, and the front a new Golgotha: "To think that He suffered a hundredfold what I see my brothers suffer here all around me: one crushed under sacks of earth, another whipped and torn to shreds by shells, yet another thirsting for water in a shell-hole and calling in vain to his mother."[21] Or as Joyce Kilmer, a New York Irish-American Catholic and volunteer, put it in his *Prayer of a Soldier in France*: "My shoulders ache beneath my pack /(Lie easier cross upon His back) /My rifle hand is stiff and numb /(From Thy pierced palm rivers come)."[22] And some of the products that soldiers fashioned by hand in the trenches from the bric-a-brac of war took the form of sacred objects, such as crucifixes.

The religious ardor born of the war was confirmed by a number of conversions. These exemplified the dolorous tenor of wartime, for the militants of faith were convinced that God is known above all through suffering. Conversions to Catholicism were the most numerous and best known. In countries such as France they were favored by Catholicism's status as the majority religion, but they also benefited from the particular prominence in Catholicism of miracles. The conversions were a response to the miracles of God and in their turn were seen as miracles. For as a collective imitation of the life of Christ, the war meant that those who were newly awoken to their faith imitated Christ personally. Loss of faith was less frequently mentioned. This certainly occurred, but contemporaries less often confided moments of despair and emptiness in their diaries than moments of exaltation. If the conversion tale is a well-known literary genre, the same is not true of the loss of faith. Even more important than the question "How could one believe after Tannenberg or Verdun?" is that of how people actually managed to do so.[23]

From Death to Memory

Faced with a war that killed millions of young men in their prime, recognition of such sacrifice was a fundamental feature of the war experience from the start. On every front, efforts were made to render makeshift tombs as visible as possible. The intention was perhaps to oppose the invisible anonymity of the "great slaughter," and certainly to restore to these countless individuals, of whom little often remained but scattered fragments, their humanity: hence the emergence after the war of the commemorative cult par excellence of World War I – the unknown soldier. Improvised wooden crosses were placed on the tombs. They became the symbol not just of death but also of death in World War I, and soon of the war itself, as demonstrated by the best-selling novel of the French soldier-author, Roland Dorgelès, *Les Croix de bois* (The Wooden Crosses, 1919), which was made into a film with the same name in 1932.

The cross, then, united all combatants, friends and enemies, Christians and non-Christians. Given the predominantly Christian inflection of the cultures of almost all the warring countries, it was not only the sign of Christ that lined the battlefields but also Christ himself. The organized commemoration of the war dead sought to acknowledge life and death with a message about the hope and purpose invested in the soldiers' sacrifice that had a deeply Christian resonance – sacrifice and resurrection. Memory, after all, stands at the heart of Christian sacrifice in the "Do this in memory of me" reported by Paul (1 Corinthians 11: 24–5). All the belligerent states also sought to respect the Judaism and Islam of a minority of their soldiers with appropriate inscriptions on their tombs. But in every case, death was linked to the idea of resurrection, thanks to the holy nature of the war itself as the combined resurrection of the fatherland and of the individuals who composed it. Faced with the long list of Jews who had died for France, André Vervoort exclaimed: "They died so that the fatherland could arise again even more beautiful, greater, more honored and noble and better. They died for the great traditions of France: justice and liberty."[24]

Not only did the soldiers while alive imitate Christ on the battlefields, the dead were re-crucified. If the French were convinced that the "Lutheran barbarians" could not know the *Imitatio Christi*, George Mosse has shown that for the Germans, a tradition born in the nineteenth century drew an analogy between death for the fatherland and the Passion of Christ. For the hugely popular wartime poet, Walter Flex, the war was a "Last Supper" where "Christ's wine is the blood of the Germans."[25] The Germans, too, expected to be buried under a cross, and this was even the case for certain Jewish soldiers, whose probable death in the war led them to participate in a form of Christianity that they accepted not as a religion but as a symbolic "Imitation of Germany," at once spiritual and political and entirely typical of the patriotic engagement of German Jews in the war.

The anguish of temporary separation from home and horror at the definitive separation of death (which carried off young men before their parents, and so inverted the succession of generations) revived ancient devotional practices and with them the "superstitions" of peoples still close to their rural origins. Traditional religious services and spiritualism, prayers and amulets, the suffering of Christ and the intercession of the saints, ordinary piety and extraordinary revelations all contributed to the religion of wartime. Yet it is hard to reconstitute prayers, fears, and suffering when they leave few archival traces. Some observers, both at the time and since, ascribed the religious dimension of the war solely to fear or the omnipresence of death. But this is much too reductive. When reading soldiers' diaries or examining the traces of their presence at the front – such as the graffiti on the walls of the quarries, tunnels, and other shelters where they lived – a clear spirituality appears, that of the man of faith who inhabited the front.

The war elicited two religious attitudes: it was seen as punishment for sinfulness but it also aroused a great need for consolation, and whatever the soldiers and their families may have felt to be their own guilt and dereliction, they sought consolation through the intercession of those who could comfort them in the trials of the war. Here they encountered Christianity with its core message of sacrifice and resurrection. The proliferation of religious devotion was entirely compatible with the revival of superstitious practices, for in the exceptional circumstances of war, extraordinary practices became an everyday occurrence. Devotion and superstition together wove new links between the home and the fighting fronts, between men and women. The former were on the whole less actively religious than the latter, and they were frequently astonished by their own religious practice, even if it was simply being present at the funeral service of comrades. Thus the Jewish and deeply Republican French historian and soldier, Marc Bloch, noted in his memoirs: "I never remember the church at La Neuville without emotion. More than once, on returning from the trenches, I went there to attend services being held for the men of the 272nd Infantry Regiment who had just fallen … I have always believed it a pious duty to remember our dead. But what did the rituals mean to me?"[26]

At the front, men also discovered religious practices that had hitherto been mainly the domain of women. They were accompanied by prayers, religious medallions, and holy images, while medals and votive plaques offered up in recognition of favors were proof of the intercession of the saints and thus formed part of the holy war. There were particularly strong cults in honor of the Virgin and, in France, of two heroines of the faith – Joan of Arc and the more recent Thérèse of Lisieux – the canonization of both of whom in the 1920s owed a good deal to their popularity during the war. Belief in the reversibility of suffering was the basis of these cults. From the drama of Mary confronted with the crucifixion, the martyrdom of Joan in fifteenth-century Rouen, and the long dialog sustained by Thérèse with the invisible God before her death at age 24, contemporaries drew the lesson that great joy is born of great suffering.

Yet for the most fervent, experiencing the pain of the war as divine grace was heightened by an acute sense of personal loss. The "fine death" of the French naval lieutenant, Pierre Dupouey, which was worthy of a medieval knight, was also a terrible drama for his wife and family. Mireille Dupouey kept a notebook in which she mingled intimate notes and letters that she continued to write to her lost husband. She pursued a dialog of love and faith with the man from whom, she felt, the war had separated her only in appearance:

> Lord Jesus, I asked for the cross in order to receive love, and now You lead me to Calvary, thank you; … If You break my heart, my broken heart will adore You … I gave my love to France, and it was abandoned to God's keeping … How could my heart bear to be thus torn? We must love God with a terrible love to accept such a sacrifice. Love Him enough to give Him my loved one? Love Him more than my love? You are not dead and I am not widowed … This mourning is infinitely dear to me because its deep and unvarying darkness is also the image of my grave and unshakeable faithfulness [to he whom I have lost …].[27]

The Dupouey couple had passed from the sacrificed generation to the lost generation.

In order to survive in the midst of death it was necessary to have many kinds of reassurance – from one's family, one's fatherland, one's faith and spirituality – and from superstition too. Rather than canceling each other out, these all reinforced each other. Some children who had not been baptized at birth were so now, with the explicit goal of keeping their fathers safe at the front. Numerous soldiers recounted how they had been protected, whether by a wallet stuffed with a fiancée's letters which had stopped a piece of shrapnel or by the intervention of the Virgin, the saints, a lucky charm, or a copied-out prayer. The immense majority of soldiers in the war were culturally Christian, whether practicing or not. Protestants carried a Bible in their packs. Some read it, most did not, but they were reassured by its physical presence as much as its spiritual content. The Bible as such became a charm. Faced with the modernity of the conflict – rational but with a rationality that was impossible to internalize – the irrational made a dramatic comeback and won over both believers and nonbelievers, including those who opposed the war.

For it was only with hindsight, in the wave of postwar pacifism, that the irrationality of the war seemed an anachronism. At the time, only a tiny minority campaigned for a total rejection of the conflict. In 1915, the celebrated novelist and liberal humanitarian, Romain Rolland, who had chosen to spend the war in exile in Switzerland, wrote to a fellow pacifist, Jeanne Halbwachs in France:

> The tragic thing about our situation is that we are only a handful of independent minds, isolated from the bulk of the army and our people, who are buried alive in the depths of the trenches. We need to speak to them but we can't …. And if we could speak to them, we wouldn't dare to tell them all we really think, for that would risk weakening their strength in the struggle, and we still wouldn't be able to free them. It would be one more act of cruelty. I know of so many who cling to a faith that they no longer really have, who shut their eyes so as to be able to carry out their task to the end … What can we do? … As we did in the past and will in the future, so now we must keep faithful in our hearts to the justice, love, fraternal compassion and inner peace that are the purest treasures of humanity. And from one nation to another, let's try to understand each other and join together. Let's try to create sacred islands in the midst of the torrent, like those that were established in the darkest days of the early middle ages in monasteries such as Saint Gall, which offered a refuge against the rising tide of universal barbarism …. And when the storm is over, we shall restore the Gods whom we will have saved to the broken peoples … I am ready to do all that I can to join your hands to those which are seeking you out in the night.[28]

This religious and prophetic tone is entirely typical of a war culture that integral pacifists were convinced they did not share, and indeed did not share, but whose terms, semantics, and rhetoric they inverted in their crusade against the crusade of war. For them, war was utter folly and they found themselves in a pacifist exile where they constructed a City on the Hill, like the first Puritans exiled to Massachusetts. It was said of Ernest Psichari that he seemed at every moment "ready to receive communion or die." But this imitation of Christ's passion on the part of a young nationalist officer was also that of militant pacifists like Michel Alexandre:

> A flood of blood is inundating the earth, beating against our houses, splattering them higher and higher as the massacre adds victim upon victim ... . Must we see them drowned in the blood of the cross, like the mother of Christ, like his apostles, martyrs for the fatherland whose hearts are pierced with the seven swords of superhuman pain? ... Have we agreed to the devil's pact, a death for a death? Let my son, husband, brother die to ensure, to purchase the death of the hated enemy ... "Cain, Cain, what hast thou done to thy brother?"[29]

Cultural Demobilization: between Fervor and Politics

In the years that followed the war, the nature and fervor of wartime faith were denied and opposed by an upsurge of militant pacifism. Especially in the victor countries, there was a tendency to adopt a creed of peace that overturned the wartime sense of what was involved in the conflict. In literature, memoirs, and the cinema, a new conceptual screen was created, which denied that the experience of the tragedy had been one of consent, especially spiritual consent. It was no longer possible to believe in the "war to end all wars" and the mysticism of peace. In France, a man like the lay Catholic activist, Marc Sangnier, founded his hopes for a Christian world on peace, as did many former army chaplains. Even the most antireligious campaigners incorporated religion into their proposals, if only to reject it. Ernst Friedrich, the German Communist pacifist, presented a poem in the pacifist museum that he opened in Berlin in 1924, which declared that "we have no father in heaven" and argued that the horrors of the war proved the nonexistence of the deity. And the Dada movement, starting with George Grosz, portrayed Christ on atrocious crosses to illustrate the pain of the soldiers misled by their own illusions.

Yet away from the literary and political avant-gardes, there was a good deal of continuity of wartime faith in how the war dead were commemorated, with memorials in stone and bronze in military cemeteries and in stained glass in church windows, where soldiers continued to imitate Christ on the cross. These were places of commemorative mysticism, of mourning, but henceforth without any crusade. The violent intensity of the crusade seemed to belong to a past that was now hard to comprehend, and even rejected. Henceforth it would be replaced by the mysticism of the "new man" promised by communism and fascism, though this time without God. In the 1920s and 1930s, the cultural demobilization of the war would also be accompanied by a remobilization for other wars. The confrontation between messianic beliefs would continue.

In Germany, denial of defeat found expression in the feeling that the war had not ended with the Armistice. "The war against the German people continues. The First World War was only its bloody beginning," declared Freikorps officer Oberlindober, who would become the head of the war veterans' association in Nazi Germany. Numerous veterans transferred the war's brutality to the home front along with their apocalyptic fears. Distance in time does not appear to have modified the denial of defeat and continuation of the war in these circles: the "iron man" of the trenches became the "new man" of the SS who embarked on the path of the Reich that would last 1,000 years, with Nazi millenarianism founded on the triptych of race, violence, and the apocalypse.

The victors exited the war in part through the opposite set of ideological values. Cultural demobilization was accompanied by a powerful belief in the benefits of the peace brought by victory, but over time this was marked by disappointment and disillusionment. Hovering between cynicism and despair, opinion in both the victorious and vanquished nations came to see the peace as stillborn. The treaties of 1919 aimed to de-legitimize the enemy, who was held to be solely responsible for the war as well as for the kind of war he had waged. The result was to re-legitimize the war in the eyes of the former enemy, who felt entirely justified in seeking to renegotiate the peace, if not to renew the war. And on the nationalist right in Germany, it was this bellicosity re-legitimized by another eschatological belief, triumphant racism, which overcame.

The violence of World War I was first channeled into new ideologies in Russia. The atrocities of the November revolution and the Civil War (see chapters 32 and 37) cannot be understood without reference to the world war. The brutality of the conflict that opened in 1914 was refracted and focused on the radical experience of a civil war fought on class lines and on Bolshevik political oppression. The disintegration of the immense peasant army that had been brutalized by three years of fighting on the eastern and Caucasian fronts, and which then deserted en masse toward the interior, provides one of the keys to understanding the Revolution and the state in which it resulted. The fundamental text of the new regime regarding political repression was that issued by Feliks Dzerzhinsky as early as December 20, 1917. Behind its utter cynicism, it expressed the remorseless cruelty deemed necessary to achieve the revolutionary goal which, in its disregard for human life and even its language, drew on the precedent of World War I:

> We must send to this ... most dangerous and cruel of fronts [political repression], comrades who are committed, tough and reliable, who are not temperamental and who are ready to sacrifice themselves to safeguard the Revolution. Comrades, don't think that I'm after some kind of revolutionary justice. We have more to do than carry out "Justice"! We are at war on the cruellest front because the enemy advances under cover, and it is a fight to the death! I propose, I demand the creation of an organism that will settle the fate of the counter-revolutionaries in a manner that is revolutionary, that is distinctively Bolshevik.[30]

Hostage-taking, concentration camps, assassinations, poisonous gas, deportations, and forced labor would all follow rapidly once the *Cheka* had been established: and all these methods had been "tested" against civilians or soldiers by one or other of the armies during World War I.

For the Nazis, and to a lesser extent for the Italian fascists, political violence was the precondition of a new degree of violence in war that would be more systematic and effective than in the previous conflict. The Nazis believed that it was first necessary to purge the nation of anything that might hinder a new energy for war. The biological racism that World War I had helped to produce radicalized the process of ideological mobilization that followed. And the new forms of violence that World War I generated also opened the way to the far greater violence of the totalitarian regimes and World War II. Whereas in the trenches, victims and heroes had been interchangeable since any combatant could be wounded, taken prisoner, or die, this was not the case with the one-sided violence unleashed during World War I against civilians. This type of violence transgressed the moral and legal norms for the conduct of war that were enshrined in the Hague

Conventions on Warfare (see chapter 13). Those who exercised military domination over civilian populations were able to utilize terror against the latter without any constraint. It was particularly in the hinterlands of the eastern fronts (the Baltic states, Poland, Galicia, Lithuania, the Ukraine, Russia, and the Caucasus) that violence against civilians was most brutal. As the four multinational empires of Germany, Russia, Austria-Hungary, and the Ottomans disintegrated during and immediately after the war, an explosion of messianic faiths (nationalist, Bolshevik) targeted the communities and classes that had no place in their vision, singling out the Jews in particular from Romania to Estonia and the Armenians in Ottoman Turkey.

When the Turkish French-language newspaper *Hilal* sought in 1918 to deny the reality of the extermination of the Armenians, it demonstrated the extent to which the apocalyptic hatred that was present in all the faiths and ideologies of wartime had gone beyond mere rhetoric and had become a pathogen in the body politic.

> The Armenian organizations systematically applied their plan to destroy the Turkish race ... One day history will surely deliver its judgment on these civilized criminals. As for the present, these insane people must know that their crimes will cost them dear. It is not given to a handful of Armenians ... to exterminate the Turkish race; the latter is so strong that it is guaranteed by God and by nature against destruction. All that these crimes and atrocities will achieve is to provoke an unforgettable outcry around the world ... and since the Armenians are precisely condemned by God to live in the midst of this world [in exile], wherever they find themselves will become a hell for them. That is the only outcome of all their crimes![31]

In Eastern and Western Europe, in the Italy of the 1920s and the Germany of the 1930s, in the young Soviet Union, the memory of the brutalities of World War I was not lost. Since the great hopes invested in the conflict had failed to materialize, they were recuperated by different forms of totalitarianism and by an accentuated brutality and violence. Of course, there were profound ideological differences between communism and the different types of fascism; but they had in common a capacity to attract the ideological and spiritual fervor of the "new men" born of World War I. In his poem *War and the World* (1916), the Russian avant-garde writer, Vladimir Mayakovsky, offered himself up as a new Christ to save humanity:

> Men!
> beloved
> non-beloved
> known
> unknown
> flow through this gateway in broad procession.
> And he
> the man
> free
> whose annunciation I cry
> he will come
> believe me
> believe him!

After the war, the poet believed in the revolution – until it devoured him, as it did so many of its children.

Notes

1   Franz Rosenzweig, *The Star of Redemption*, 1921, trans. from German, London, Routledge and Kegan Paul, 1971, p. 3.
2   Ibid., p. 424.
3   Pierre Bouretz, "De la nuit du monde aux éclats de la Rédemption: l'étoile de Franz Rosenzweig," in *Témoins du futur. Philosophie et messianisme*, Paris, Gallimard, 2003, p. 164.
4   Annette Becker, "Memory Gaps: Maurice Halbwachs, Memory and the Great War," *Journal of European Studies*, 35/1, March 2005, pp. 102–14.
5   Robert Hertz, *Un Ethnologue dans les tranchées, août 1914 – avril 1915. Lettres de Robert Hertz à sa femme Alice*, Paris, Editions du CNRS, 2002, p. 70.
6   Jacques Copeau, *Journal, 1901–1948*, vol. 1, *1901–1915*, ed. Claude Sicard, Paris, Seghers, 1991, p. 624 (entry for November 13, 1914).
7   Billy Sunday sermon in *New York Herald*, June 6, 1917; Becker, *War and Faith*, pp. 105–11.
8   Krumeich, "Gott mit uns."
9   Quoted in Adrian Gregory and Annette Becker, "Religious Sites and Practices," in Jean-Louis Robert and Jay Winter (eds.), *Capital Cities at War 1914–1918*, Cambridge, Cambridge University Press, 2007, p. 390.
10 T. Ortolan, "Guerre," in *Dictionnaire de théologie catholique*, vol. 6, Paris, Le Touzey, 3rd ed., 1930, pp. 1952–4, 1958–9.
11 Wilkinson, *The Church of England*.
12 Hew Strachan, "Training, Morale and Modern War," *Journal of Contemporary History*, 41/2, 2006, pp. 211–27; Edgar Jones, "The Psychology of Killing: The Combatant Experience of the British Soldiers during the First World War," in ibid., pp. 229–46; and Alex Watson, "Self-deception and Survival: Mental Coping Strategies on the Western Front, 1914–18," in ibid., pp. 247–60.
13 Maurice Barrès, *Mes Cahiers, 1896–1923*, Paris, Plon, 1993, p. 756.
14 A. F. Winnington-Ingram, "Missionary Work the Only Final Cure for War," reproduced in Winnington-Ingram, *The Potter and the Clay*, London, Wells, Gardner, Darton, 1917, p. 40.
15 Annette Becker, "Die Trauer des Papstes," in Gerd Krumeich (ed.), *Versailles 1919. Ziele – Wirkung – Wahrnehmung*, Essen, Klartext, 2001, pp. 288–301.
16 Pierre Teilhard de Chardin, *Ecrits du temps de guerre*, Paris, Grasset, 1965, pp. 212–13.
17 Jan Patocka, "Les Guerres du XXe siècle et le XXe siècle en tant que guerre," *Essais hérétiques. Sur la philosophie de l'histoire*, 1975, translated from Czech, Paris, Verdier, 1981, p. 135.
18 Annette Becker, "Du Philosémitisme d'Union sacrée à l'antisémitisme ordinaire: l'effet de la Grande Guerre," in Marie-Anne Matard-Bonucci (ed.), *Antisemythes. L'image des juifs en culture et politique (1848–1939)*, Paris, Nouveau-Monde Editions, 2005, pp. 149–62.
19 Hoffmann, "Between Integration and Rejection."
20 Henri Massis, *Le Sacrifice*, Paris, Plon, 1917, pp. 204–6.
21 Henry Ghéon, *L'Homme né de la guerre. Témoignage d'un converti*, Paris, Nouvelle Revue Française, 1919 (written on the Yser and in the Artois, 1915).
22 Joyce Kilmer, *Poems, Essays and Letters*, New York, George H. Doran, 1918.
23 Fouilloux, "Première Guerre mondiale et changements religieux," p. 440.
24 André Vervoort, *Les Juifs et la guerre*, première partie, Paris, pub. by author, 1915, p. 9.
25 Mosse, "The Jews and the German War Experience," p. 6.
26 Marc Bloch, *Memoirs of War*, trans. and intro. Carole Fink, Ithaca and London, Cornell University Press, 1980, p. 105.
27 Mireille Dupouey, *Cahiers*, 1915–1919, Paris, Le Cerf, 1944, pp. 36, 96, 117 (September 4 and December 31, 1915; March 20, 1917).
28 Romain Rolland to Jeanne Halbwachs, May 1915, letter in the BDIC, GF Δ Res. 99–103, dossier 333.

29 Municipal library, Nîmes, Michel Alexandre papers, no. 801, dossier 4, notes late 1916 – early 1917.

30 Quoted by Nicolas Werth in Stéphane Courtois (ed.), *The Black Book of Communism: Crimes, Terror, Repression*, 1997; translation from French, Cambridge, MA, Harvard University Press, 1999, p. 74.

31 *Hilal*, March 14, 1918; in Vatican Archives, Secretary of State, Guerra 14–18, 244, fascicule 112.

References and Further Reading

Barry, Gearóid, "Marc Sangnier's War, 1914–1919: Portrait of a Soldier, Catholic and Social Activist," in Pierre Purseigle (ed.), *Warfare and Belligerence. Perspectives in First World War Studies*, Leiden and Boston, Brill, 2005, pp. 163–88.

Becker, Annette, "Tortured and Exalted by War: French Catholic Women, 1914–1915," in Nicole Dombrowski (ed.), *Enlisted With or Without Consent: Women and War in the Twentieth Century*, Princeton, Princeton University Press, 1998, pp. 42–55.

Becker, Annette, *War and Faith. The Religious Imagination in France, 1914–1930*, 1994; translation from French, Oxford and New York, Berg, 1998.

Becker, Annette, "Messianismes et héritage de la violence, de 1914 aux années trente," in Jean-Philippe Schreiber (ed.), *Théologies de la guerre*, Brussels, Editions de l'Université de Bruxelles, 2006, pp. 59–71.

Fouilloux, Etienne, "Première Guerre mondiale et changements religieux en Europe," in Jean-Jacques Becker and Stéphane Audoin-Rouzeau (eds.), *Les Sociétés européennes et la guerre de 1914–1918*, Paris, Université de Paris X-Nanterre, 1990.

Gambarotto, Laurent, *Foi et patrie. La prédication du protestantisme français pendant la première guerre mondiale*, Geneva, Labor et Fides, 1996.

Gregory, Adrian, *The Last Great War: British Society and the First World War*, Cambridge, Cambridge University Press, 2009, pp. 152–86 ("Redemption through War: Religion and the Languages of Sacrifice").

Hoffmann, Christhard, "Between Integration and Rejection: the Jewish Community in Germany, 1914–1918," in John Horne (ed.), *State, Society and Mobilization in Europe during the First World War*, Cambridge, Cambridge University Press, 1997, pp. 89–104.

Jenkins, Julian, *Christian Pacifism Confronts German Nationalism: The Ecumenical Movement and the Cause of Peace in Germany, 1914–1933*, Lampeter, Edwin Mellen Press, 2002.

Krumeich, Gerd, " 'Gott mit uns'; la Grande Guerre fut-elle une guerre de religion?," in Anne Dumenil, Nicolas Beaupré, and Christian Ingrao (eds.), *1914–1945. L'ère de la guerre; violence, mobilisation, deuil*, 2 vols., Paris, Noêsis, 2004, vol. 1, pp. 117–30.

Landau, Philippe, *Les Juifs de France et la Grande Guerre. Un patriotisme républicain*, Paris, Editions CNRS, 1999.

Mosse, George, "The Jews and the German War Experience, 1914–1918," *Leo Baeck Memorial Lecture*, no. 21, New York, 1977.

Porter, Peter, "Beyond Comfort: German and English Military Chaplains and the Memory of the Great War, 1919–1929," *Journal of Religious History*, 29/3, October 2005, pp. 258–89.

'Pour une histoire religieuse de la guerre', *14–18 Aujourd'hui-Heute – Today*, 1, Paris, Noêsis, 1998.

Wilkinson, Alan, *The Church of England and the First World War*, London, SPCK, 1978.

Chapter Seventeen

Demography

Jay Winter

Contemporaries saw World War I as a demographic disaster. Freud noted in 1915 that it overthrew the by then prevalent assumption that death was an individual rather than a collective eventuality and that, in general, parents died before their children. "People really die," he wrote, "and no longer one by one but many, often tens of thousands in a single day."[1] In the interwar years, this gave rise to the myth of the "front generation" and, more poignantly, to that of the "lost generation." The realities were more complex. There were important variations by age, place, and social class. Moreover, while the military dead dominated the memory of World War I, in contrast to the civilian victims of genocide, mass bombing, and nuclear annihilation who epitomized along with military casualties the slaughter of World War II, World War I had major implications for the health and mortality of civilians as well.

Military Participation and Military Losses

Owing to the nature of the conflict, military casualties nonetheless remained numerically superior to civilian casualties, so the first question that the demographic history of World War I must address is that of military participation and military losses. We begin, therefore, with an analysis of military statistics. The rough outline of the story of the war period can be gauged in several ways from the data in Table 17.1. What we cannot see here are the rhythms of military participation and military losses over time. For that story, we need to look at the history of particular campaigns, to which we refer after an examination of aggregate statistics.

The first point about these overall statistics is their unprecedented nature. Given population growth all over Europe in the nineteenth century, the combatant countries engaged in World War I were able to draw on the largest cohort of men of military age in history. While fertility levels had been falling since before the 1870s in France, from the 1870s in Britain and Germany, and from the end of the century in Eastern Europe and Russia, these trends still left a surge of young cohorts to arrive at military age just in time for the war of 1914. Given the legal status of conscription, requiring men of military age to do basic military training and service around the age of 20 for two or three years, this meant that mass armies of a size never seen before could be mobilized and

Table 17.1 Military participation and military losses in World War I (mobilized, killed, wounded, missing, and % casualties of all who served)

Casualties in World War I
Allied Powers

Country	Mobilized	Dead	Wounded	POW/Missing	Total	% Casualties
Russia	15,798,000	1,800,000	4,950,000	2,500,000	9,250,000	59
France	7,891,000	1,375,800	4,266,000	537,000	6,178,800	78
GB, Emp. and Dom.	8,904,467	908,371	2,090,212	191,652	3,190,235	36
Italy	5,615,000	578,000	947,000	600,000	2,125,000	38
USA	4,273,000	114,000	234,000	4,526	352,526	8
Japan	800,000	300	907	3	1,210	0
Romania	1,000,000	250,706	120,000	80,000	450,706	45
Serbia	750,000	278,000	133,148	15,958	427,106	57
Belgium	365,000	38,716	44,686	34,659	118,061	32
Greece	353,000	26,000	21,000	1,000	48,000	14
Portugal	100,000	7,222	13,751	12,318	33,291	33
Montenegro	50,000	3,000	10,000	7,000	20,000	40
Total	45,899,467	5,380,115	12,830,704	3,984,116	22,194,935	46
Central Powers						
Germany	13,200,000	2,037,000	4,216,058	1,152,800	7,405,858	56
Austria-Hungary	9,000,000	1,100,000	3,620,000	2,200,000	6,920,000	77
Turkey	2,998,000	804,000	400,000	250,000	1,454,000	48
Bulgaria	400,000	87,500	152,390	27,029	266,919	67
Total	25,598,000	4,028,500	8,388,448	3,629,829	16,046,777	63
Grand total	71,497,467	9,408,615	21,219,152	7,613,945	38,241,712	53

Sources: J. M. Winter, *The Great War and the British People*, London, Macmillan, 1985, Ch. 3; Spencer C. Tucker (ed.), *The European Powers in the First World War. An Encyclopedia*, New York, Garland, 1996, p. 173.

could be replenished after the initial clash of arms. In the late summer and autumn of 1914, over seven million men took part in the initial German invasion of France and Belgium, in the Russian invasion of Eastern Prussia, and in the Austrian invasion of Serbia and of Russian Poland. By Christmas of 1914 one million of those men were dead.

Such staggering casualties describe the lethality of the war of movement in 1914 (see chapter 12). Those four months saw a bloodbath on both the eastern and western fronts, caused in large part by artillery and machine-gun fire on masses of men on the move. In previous wars, the loss of such substantial numbers of front-line soldiers would have ground offensive operations to a halt. The Battle of Borodino in 1812 was fought by approximately 200,000 men on both sides; twice that number fell in the French army alone in the five months separating August and December 1914. Late nineteenth-century demographic growth made possible the war of position which followed in 1915–18.

The other cause of the survival of armies facing casualties on a level without precedent is medical care. On the western front, and in the cities supplying the armies, advances in medical care over the nineteenth century meant that the time-honored link between war and epidemic disease was broken in 1914. On the eastern front, this was not so, and the sanitary conditions in what is now Poland ensured that cholera, dysentery, typhus, and typhoid fever added to the death toll in the military. Later in the war, epidemic disease spread everywhere. What was termed "Spanish flu" was a mutant influenza virus, which targeted with particular ferocity young men and women between the ages of 15 and 40. The only time the war came to a virtual stop was during the late summer of 1918, when all armies were hit by the flu epidemic. By then the outcome of the conflict was no longer in doubt. Had the epidemic come earlier, it is not unreasonable to suppose that a tacit truce, or even an armistice, would have been necessary in armies devastated by illness. The "Spanish flu" came too late to stop the war, but it added substantially to the death toll of armies in the field. No one has accurate figures for soldiers' deaths from this disease, but it may not be far from the truth to suggest that perhaps half a million soldiers died from it, alongside 20 million civilians around the world.

Before discussing the relative level of casualties suffered during World War I, it is necessary to issue a cautionary warning about the data presented in Table 17.1. Military statistics are always inaccurate owing to one of the following two reasons. First come lies. Military statisticians were subject to informal instructions to play down the losses of their side and play up the losses of the other side. Then comes confusion. The accumulation of accurate data on what was termed "wastage" in battle took time and it was rarely systematic. The fog of war occluded the fate of individuals and at times of entire units. Officers' reports were vague, and understandably inaccurate. Moving up from the platoon all the way to the divisional level, such reports always multiplied inaccuracies. No one in command had accurate statistics on numbers wounded, taken prisoner, or killed, with the consequence that this has also been true for later scholars.

Once this caveat is made, we can still reach several general conclusions about the incidence of casualties in World War I. The first is that roughly half of all those who served became casualties of war at some time during the conflict. The second is that the Central Powers suffered significantly higher casualties than did the Allies. This difference must be qualified owing to the very high numbers of men mobilized by Russia, the United States, and parts of the British Empire, such as India, who never reached the front. If we take a very conservative approach, and examine the data on the other Allied countries, we must leave aside the 20 million men who served either from Russia or the United States, and the nearly three million people who served from British dominions or Imperial holdings. Doing so enables us to see that of the 25 million men who served in other Allied countries, about 12 million became casualties of war. That percentage – 48 – brings the Allied total closer to that of the Central Powers, though the difference is still there. Those who lost the war suffered the highest casualties.

In aggregate, 12 percent, or one out of every eight men who served died in World War I. Roughly 30 percent more were wounded, and 10 percent were taken prisoner. Within the two camps there were real differences in the incidence of loss. The country suffering the highest losses among the Allies was France, where 77 percent of all those who served were either killed, wounded, or taken prisoner. Serbia's casualties were also extremely high, in particular in terms of the proportion killed of those who served. Fully three out of every eight Serbian soldiers died on active service.

Among the Central Powers, Austria-Hungary suffered the highest casualty rates, but in terms of numbers killed, Germany was the hardest hit. Over two million German soldiers died in World War I, the highest total among all combatant countries. The estimates of war losses on the losing side are probably too low, since throughout Eastern Europe and in Turkey, hostilities did not cease on November 11, 1918. This is also true in Russia. The repercussions of the conflict in Eastern Europe were so destabilizing as to swell the totals of those who died from war-related causes. Famine, pillage, rape, and ethnic cleansing in the Balkans and the former Ottoman Empire were aftershocks of World War I, and the victims of these disasters were as much victims of the conflict as were the soldiers who marched off to war in 1914 (see chapter 37). A rough rule of thumb can be established, however, that the further east you went in the European and Ottoman theaters of operation, the higher the casualty rates, and the longer the war and its related conflicts dragged on.

The incidence of military losses varied by age and by social situation. The armies of all combatants were composed overwhelmingly of young men. Fully 80 percent of the British army was under 30 years of age. The longer the war went on, the broader the age spectrum of men serving in it. Some youngsters lied about their age to serve; there are records of 13- and 14-year-olds who joined up in the early years of the war. At the other end, men in their sixties, and even one or two in their seventies, are listed among war casualties.

The bias toward youth was clearly expressed in casualty figures. The most severely affected age cohort was 20–24, where perhaps 70 percent of all deaths occurred. The same concentration on the youngest-serving groups can be seen in the statistics on those wounded. There was a broader age breakdown of men who died of illness and when taken prisoner. Here we enter a difficult area, since most armies described a physical illness as a disabling wound. To be sure, millions of men suffered both, especially when the Spanish flu epidemic hit all armies in late 1918; demobilizing forces were hit again by a second wave of the disease six months later in 1919. Those who died of the flu during the war, like the French poet Guillaume Apollinaire, were as much casualties of war as anyone. Apollinaire reached the rank of sergeant before being hit in the head by a shell fragment, but while recovering he succumbed to influenza. He is listed as both wounded and having died in the war. His case shows the difficulty of using these statistics, since double counting was inevitable. The number of men wounded more than once is also unknown. It is therefore essential that we consider these figures to be indicators rather than accurate estimates of the social incidence of war losses.

With that qualification, we can also claim that there was a social structure of war losses in most combatant countries. The vast majority of those who suffered injury or death in

war were men from the countryside, peasants or rural laborers. The needs of war industry kept many urban workers out of the army for long periods of the war, further enhancing the rural character of manpower in uniform. The rural bias in casualties increases the
further east in Europe we look. It is virtually nonexistent in Britain, and overwhelmingly
evident in Italy, Russia, and Turkey.

But if we turn from aggregates to the proportions of different social groups who were
injured or died in the war, we reach a different conclusion. When we consider those who
served and who lived in urban or suburban areas – the majority in Britain, and large
minorities in Germany, Belgium, France, and Austria-Hungary – then a distinctive social
profile of war losses emerged. The rough generalization substantiated by all available
military statistics is that the higher up in the social scale was a man, the greater were his
chances of becoming a war casualty and of dying in the war.

The primary cause of this social distribution of war losses was that the social selection
of the officer corps mirrored prewar patterns of social inequality. That is, officers were
selected from men from the middle and upper classes deemed to be officer material.
Such men joined up early in the war, passed their medical examinations, and served in
the officer corps throughout the conflict. The stalemate on both fronts placed junior
officers at the front lines and with their men for long periods of time. Offensive operations were led by officers, and consequently, casualty rates among officers, and in particular among lieutenants and captains in the infantry, were twice those of men in the
ranks.

Regular soldiers suffered high casualties as well, but many of the social groups supplying the men in the ranks provided disproportionately fewer soldiers than did their social
superiors. Why? First, poor men failed the rudimentary medical examinations of the day
more regularly than did the better-off. Even when they passed such examinations, more
of those coming from the working class served either on the home front or behind the
lines. They were fit enough to serve, though not fit enough to fight. Secondly, working-
class men served in other ways. When we recall that these armies had lines of supply
stretching for hundreds of miles in all directions, we should not be surprised that manual
labor in uniform occupied hundreds of thousands of soldiers who were not in the front
lines. The war machine required increasing stores of arms, weapons, and matériel; war
industry was concentrated in the heavy metals, engineering, and chemical sectors. Skilled
men were more valuable running the railways, or in war factories than at the front. Many
were kept out of the army, or seconded to war industry for that reason. Consequently
working-class military participation and war losses were proportionately lower than
middle-class war losses, especially in Britain, France, and Germany.

As the war dragged on and the social groups providing officers began to be drained
of young recruits, the officer corps were forced to recruit shopkeepers, businessmen, and
other lower-middle-class men into their ranks. It was still rare in the world of 1914–18
for a working-class man to be promoted from the ranks to the officer corps, though in
exceptional cases, such battlefield promotions did take place. There are some exceptions
to the rule that officers were drawn from socially prosperous groups; the Australian
Imperial Force was more egalitarian than others. But on balance, higher casualties
among officers meant that social elites paid for their privileges by the shedding of blood
in World War I.

Turning to casualties in different battles, Table 17.2 provides approximate statistics
on losses suffered in some of the major encounters of the war. There are three points that
emerge clearly from this table. The first point is that fewer than one-ninth of the total of

Table 17.2 Battle casualties in major encounters, 1914–18

Battle	Total casualties	By army	By year
Tannenberg (1914)	**48,000**		
of which	12,960	German	
	35,040	Russian	
1st Marne (1914)	**550,000**		
of which	297,000	Allies	
	253,000	German	
Total for 1914			**598,000**
Gallipoli (1915)	**500,000**		
of which	315,000	Allies	
	185,000	Turkish	
2nd Ypres (1915)	**95,000**		
of which	35,000	German	
	60,000	British	
Total for 1915			**595,000**
Verdun (1916)	**720,000**		
of which	338,000	German	
	382,000	French	
Somme (1916)	**1,070,000**		
of which	652,700	Allies	
	417,300	German	
Total for 1916			**1,790,000**
Chemin des Dames (1917)	**160,000**		
of which	120,000	French	
	40,000	German	
3rd Ypres (1917)	**470,000**		
of which	268,000	British	
	202,000	German	
Total for 1917			**630,000**
Michael (March 1918)	**270,000**		
of which	118,800	German	
	151,200	Allies	
2nd Marne (July–Aug. 1918)	**288,000**		
of which	168,000	German	
	120,000	Allies	
Total for 1918			**558,000**
Total casualties in major encounters			**4,171,000**
Total casualties in the war			**38,241,712**

Source: J. M. Winter, *The Experience of World War I*, London, Macmillan, 1988.

those casualties in the war fell in the major military encounters on the western front. We include in these statistics the German victory at Tannenberg on the eastern front in 1914, but when we consider only the western front battles, we still reach the conclusion that casualties in the war were greater outside these landmark encounters than in them. Once again, the danger of centering our attention solely on the western front and on the major battles is evident. The war killed men throughout the world and in minor skirmishes as much as in the vast operations summarized here.

The second striking point that emerges from Table 17.2 is the quantitative leap in lethality that took place in 1916. The two battles of Verdun and the Somme dwarf the other major encounters before and after in the human toll they took. It is not at all surprising, therefore, that these two battles have taken on iconic status in the history of the war in Germany, France, and Britain.

The third point is that, with some exceptions, those launching a battle were likely to pay a higher price for it than those defending. In the first battle of the Marne, British, French, and Belgian defenders paid a higher price than did the Germans. But the rule that the attacker suffers more is true in the case of the Russian invasion of East Prussia in 1914, which came to an abrupt end at Tannenberg; it is true at Gallipoli in 1915, on the Somme in 1916, at the Chemin des Dames, and at 3rd Ypres (or Passchendaele) in 1917, and in the German offensives of 1918, when taken together. Failed offensives kept the stalemate going before 1918. In that year, the failure of Germany's offensive on the western front led to a successful Allied counter-offensive which forced German capitulation. That victory was registered at a time when virtually everyone on the German side saw that the war could not be won. The Allies had reserves unavailable to the Central Powers, including millions of American troops still in training. Manpower was finally the arbiter of victory and defeat in World War I.

Civilian Health

Once again, we must separate those combatants who occupied the eastern front from those in the west in order to appreciate the impact of the war on patterns of civilian health and welfare. In Russia, Romania, Austria-Hungary, and Italy, the war was a disaster for the civilian population. This was not at all unprecedented. Sanitary conditions in military encampments and the rudimentary state of military medicine in the nineteenth century meant that war inflicted upward death rates due to epidemic and endemic diseases. There were some improvements evident by 1914, but in the following four years on the eastern front, time and again, pollution of the water supply and requisitioning of livestock and food supplies brought illness to noncombatants and spread it among populations in the penumbra of theaters of military operation. Consequently death rates among civilians on the eastern, Balkan, and Italian fronts soared during the war. Loss of life among civilians was also a direct result of military tactics, as in the German invasion of Belgium and northern France in 1914, the Russian retreat of 1915, or in the intermittent German bombardment of London and Paris, and the increasingly lethal submarine warfare waged by the German navy from 1915 on.

Where World War I broke new ground was in the way in which the targeting of civilians within the boundaries of one combatant country prepared the way for genocide. All the major combatants were imperial powers, with substantial ethnic minorities within them. All tried to subvert the other side by stimulating breakaway movements among subordinate populations. On the Russo-Turkish front, there were Armenians fighting in

Russian forces. The overwhelming majority of the 2 million Armenians in Turkey lived in the south and east of the country, in Anatolia and Celicia. The ruling triumvirate in Turkey decided to ethnically cleanse this part of the country, and issued orders to police, army, and paramilitary groups to deport all Armenians from these eastern provinces. From March 1915 to the summer of 1916, this deportation, accompanied by rape, pillage, and murder, resulted in the deaths of around one million people. Not all Armenians in Turkey were murdered, but the Armenian presence in Turkey was wiped out. Genocide, or the liquidation of the collective life of a people, succeeded (see chapter 13). We shall refer to this set of events below as a form of biological warfare, the logical and criminal outcome of the targeting of enemy civilians by blockade, bombardment, or deportation that were endemic during the war.

In Western Europe, the impact of the war on civilian health was mixed. In Britain, one of the unintended consequences of the creation of a war economy – with full employment, a rise in real wages, the extension of health insurance, and the expansion of infant and maternal welfare – was an increase in the life expectancy of the working class, and in particular of the worst-off sectors within it. Given the fact that 80 percent of the population was working-class, it is hardly surprising that in a number of ways, the war was the occasion for an improvement in the health and welfare of the population as a whole. Infant mortality dropped in wartime, and death rates for many endemic diseases related to malnutrition or poor living conditions went down. These improvements were countered by a rise in death rates owing to respiratory infections. In part this countermovement arose from more deleterious aspects of the war economy – the way rent control led to deterioration in the housing stock, overwork in war factories, and the migration of men and women from rural to urban areas. This brought to the cities thousands of people without the antibodies city dwellers had developed over years of coping with urban conditions and pollution. Deprived of this protection, the newcomers succumbed to respiratory infections, even before the Spanish flu hit with especial severity young men and women in cities and countryside alike.

A modest improvement in civilian health was also registered in France. In both Britain and France these gains were in no way a reflection of better medical care. The majority of general practitioners and specialists served in the army; whatever gains in life expectancy civilians registered came out of material improvements in their conditions.

The story in Germany is different. In the first two years of the war, conditions in Germany as a whole and in German cities in particular were as good as or better than those in France or Britain. But starting in 1916, the situation in Germany began to deteriorate. Over the next two years, the imbalances in the war economy and runaway inflation meant that German civilians faced severe shortages in essential supplies. Bottlenecks in transport and a rampant black market further blocked the distribution of goods to an increasingly hungry and tired civilian population. By the summer of 1918, there were no potatoes in Berlin. The hardships faced by civilians became unbearable, and began to appear unnecessary when, after the failure of the German March 1918 offensive, soldiers came home to tell them that the war was unwinnable. This mixture of disillusionment among the military and severe hardship at home undermined the legitimacy of the war effort and, indeed, the legitimacy of the regime which had launched this doomed war in the first place. The result was a search for a negotiated peace, a revolution at home, and the Armistice on November 11.

Just as was the case further east, the Armistice did not stop the killing in Germany. Over the six months separating the Armistice from the peace settlement, forced on

Germany on June 28, 1919, approximately 10,000 Germans lost their lives in street-fighting and internecine guerrilla warfare. Total war meant not only that the line separating combatants from noncombatants had been blurred, but also the line between war and peace. Armed conflict continued within the defeated countries of the Central Powers and Russia, the one defeated Allied power, long after the armies formally ceased fighting.

Migration

In the history of international migration, World War I is a major divide. In the 30 years before the war, there was a wave of migration larger than any the continent had ever seen. Perhaps 30 million Europeans moved west and either settled in other European cities or continued their journeys across the North and South Atlantic to different parts of the Americas. The war closed this phase of demographic history. In part this was because of the needs of the combatant armies. There was a net inflow of nationals who lived in other parts of the world and who returned to Europe to help their country at the outset of the war. In part it was because the war had spawned revolution, and particularly in the United States, "nativist" politics grew sufficiently powerful to be able to place obstacles in the way of mass immigration. American legislation in 1924 and 1929 meant that the days of the open door were over. Other destinations were hit by economic difficulties after the war. The receiver states for European migrants blocked their path. Before 1914, most people who traveled internationally did not need passports; after the war, passports were necessary, as indicators that an individual arriving in a new destination did not intend to stay.

Within each combatant country, the war was a high-water mark in the history of internal migration. When the ten departments of northern France were invaded and secured by Germany, France thereby lost a huge chunk of its industrial strength. New factories and new sources of energy supply had to be found. To them a vast labor force migrated, made up of men seconded out of the army or protected from conscription and of women who migrated from other parts of the labor force, in particular from the clothing and textile industries. To provide them with housing, all governments instituted rent control, without which migration would have ground to a halt.

Within the capital cities, industrial districts grew substantially. The industrial ring around Paris became the Red Belt of the interwar years; Berlin's heavy industrial districts grew substantially too. The Port of London was working to capacity throughout the war. Other provincial cities saw the same concentration in heavy industry.

At the end of the war, many of these war factories reconverted to civilian production. Most of the female labor force made way for demobilized men by returning to their prewar trades, though in the commercial and white-collar sectors, the presence of women was enduring. Economic demobilization did not restore the prewar distribution of the population. The war tended to increase the urbanization of the labor force, a development which brought misery to many cities in Britain when the interwar depression began in May 1920. The same overcapacity and oversupply of labor hit all of Europe at different points over the next decade. Through shutting down the outlet of international migration, and creating overcapacity in industrial sectors that could not compete in the changed international marketplace, the war helped bring about the economic crisis of the interwar years. The economic and social consequences of war-related demographic change are part of the balance sheet we need to draw up about the negative effects of the conflict.

Nuptiality and Family Life

Throughout Europe, total war meant a transformation of the age composition and sex ratio of large parts of the home population. Mobilization feminized the civilian populations of all combatant nations. Since the bulk of recruits were under the age of 30, there was also a distorted age pattern among civilians. The infirm, the old, and the very young among the male population were still there.

This had a particular meaning on the land, where in 1914 a majority of the population of Europe still lived and worked. Agricultural work – backbreaking, unending, and of vital importance both to the nation and to the men in uniform – was carried out by these people and especially by women. Soldiers wrote constantly to their wives with advice about how to care for their farms; the fact that the harvest of 1914 was brought in successfully by the residual family members on farms throughout Europe ensured that the war would go on. Harvest failure would have stopped the war, not because of a shortage of food, but because farmer-soldiers would have deserted by the tens of thousands. It was – so they believed – to defend their families that they had gone off to war. As long as their families were safe and the harvest assured, they could and did go to the war.

The second adjustment necessitated by this massive mobilization of manpower was in the labor market. It is untrue to say that men went off to war and women went off to work. Women had been at work long before the war of 1914. What occurred during the war was a lateral shift across the occupational spectrum. Women changed jobs, and in many cases, they performed tasks denied to them before the war. In virtually every labor market, a skilled job was a job not done by a woman. This ascriptive discrimination was a luxury no combatant country could afford after the outbreak of war. Hence the skill composition of the labor force shifted, and so did the place of women in it. This was especially the case in the engineering trades, transformed into munitions industries in a bare few months. But women workers appeared everywhere in wartime Europe, and in some instances, they were there for good. Whereas heavy industrial employment reverted to its status as a masculine preserve after the war, employment in the service sector – banking, commercial, and allied work – became much more open to women. And since such tertiary-sector work was in the growth sector of every economy, women had access to jobs more stable than those of industrial workers in shipbuilding, house-building, or engineering.

The temporary end of unemployment and the huge expansion of war-related industrial production increased women's wages. This leveling-up reduced (but did not eliminate) the differential between male and female pay. In addition, separation allowances to make up for the loss of male wages were paid directly to women. In poor households, the war appeared, as the British worker Robert Roberts, a resident of working-class Salford, put it, as an entirely unanticipated liberation from primary poverty. Inflation wiped out many of these gains, but it is clear that the people who suffered most from the wartime price spiral were middle-class people on fixed incomes.

Diversified employment for women in wartime multiplied the daily tasks women faced. Full-time employment led to heavy overtime commitments. By 1917, the average working week in Britain was 60 hours long. This activity did not obscure women's tasks in managing the household. And in countries hit by severe shortages, especially in Central and Eastern Europe, there were other jobs which had to be done. Standing in endless lines for rations was one task, called facetiously "dancing the Polonaise." And if that did not exhaust a woman, there was still the need to scavenge for food or fuel in the countryside surrounding the towns and cities where industrial production took place.

These pressures on family life dominated the rhythms of daily existence. Soldiers were well aware of these hardships, and only rarely looked down upon their civilian counterparts who, after all, had a bed to sleep in at night. More frequently, soldiers were painfully conscious of the fact that their loved ones were under severe pressure during the war. This provided all the more reason to make that one final push that would bring the conflict to an end.

Adaptations

Family life was reconfigured in a host of ways in wartime. Much of the tension of daily life constricted freedom of action; there was less food, and less time for leisure for most people. But for some, the war relaxed family constraints. This contrast can be seen clearly in the recollections of two Belgian children. One of them, Marie Lacante, grew up in Ypres, a town held by the British army in the autumn of 1914. Marie and her family fled the fighting and moved south. They boarded a train, which took 14 days to get to Normandy. There, the family was

> unloaded … and brought to a market square … where people looked us over as though we were for sale. My father and mother were taken away to work on a farm. My father was told to drive the horses though he had never handled a horse in his life. I was twelve and a half years old and my sister was ten. We had to work in a bakery, two small children alone in a foreign country, not knowing any French!

After two days, they ran away to Paris, where they found jobs in a battery factory. Every day they commuted in to work from lodgings in Villeneuve. "I don't know how we survived it," wrote Marie Lacante years later, but they did. So did millions of other refugee families, some holding together, others, like the Lacantes, fragmented and lonely.

Not all children knew the war as a family disaster. André Houwen was also born in Flemish Belgium, near Ypres, but he remembers the war differently.

> We children had a wonderful time while the English were in Reningelst. We almost never went to school …. They had also converted a barn to a cinema. Every Thursday afternoon we got to go to the movies, from two to four …. All the children were given an orange, a chocolate bar, chewing gum, and sometimes a banana.

In that cinema André encountered his screen hero, Charlie Chaplin, but – as he recalled many years later – "We still went there chiefly for the oranges."[2]

These two reflections on war in one corner of the western front show how difficult it is to generalize about adaptations to war conditions. Some individuals and some families were broken into fragments never assembled again; others continued to stick together, and even at times to piece together a vision of war that was as much comic as tragic. They were the lucky ones.

There was a three-part trajectory of marriage patterns in wartime. The first period – lasting a few months in 1914 – described an upward inflection in the marriage rate. This is an understandable reaction to the uncertainties of the war crisis and a reflection of the tendency of some young people to make a commitment to the future, even when it was most uncertain. After this initial moment, marriage rates plummeted. And only after hostilities were over did the marriage rate return to its prewar level.

The same movement, albeit separated by about a year, described fertility movements. There is some upward movement in the birth rate of a number of countries nine months after the outbreak of war, and some indication – again, nine months later – of the fruits of sexual relations in the period of leave before the major battles of 1916, Verdun and the Somme. But for the bulk of the war, European fertility rates reached all-time lows.

Aftermaths

When the war was over, the primary aim of every social group was a restoration of family life. This was a vexed and fragile enterprise, given the presence of millions of wounded and broken men who returned home from military service. Even though statistics are incomplete, there appear to have been a number of clear means by which family life was stabilized in the aftermath of war.

The first was a shift in patterns of nuptiality. It is one of the myths of the war that it produced a generation of spinsters. Nothing of the kind happened. Despite the fact that perhaps one-quarter of those who died in combat were married, and thus approximately two million women were widowed because of the war, the proportion of those who were married ten years after the war is not much different from the same statistic in the pre-1914 period.

How was this possible? Two phenomena appear to have operated powerfully in stabilizing marriage patterns after 1918. The first was the end of the wave of out-migration so salient before 1914. The war, and its repercussions, trapped in Europe a large population of young, marriageable males. Without the war, these young men would have left Europe. The war kept them there.

The second phenomenon relates to women's choice of a spouse. In some cases, notably that of France, the war reduced the age difference between marriage partners. In 1900, the average age difference between husband and wife was about four years. After the war, these older potential husbands were dead. What women did was to adjust their definitions of an appropriate partner and to begin to marry men the same age or younger. In Britain the same phenomenon may have operated not over age cohorts but over social and geographical boundaries. In the pre-1914 period, the age difference·between British spouses was relatively small – perhaps two years at most. But after 1918 there is evidence of women marrying men in "lower" social classes or from different social regions. Avoiding spinsterhood was the rule, even in those countries where spinsterhood was a recognized part of the "Western European marriage pattern" described above.

Another facet of the adaptation of family forms to the upheaval of war is their expansion to include people whose bonds were experiential rather than biological. The men who had served in uniform frequently formed associations to perpetuate the personal ties they had forged under the most adverse of circumstances. These groups also served to defend the interests of veterans, whose entitlements to pensions were always contested and whose reintegration into civil society was never untroubled. Many of these societies of *anciens combattants* also took it upon themselves to help the widows and orphans of their dead comrades. Some even believed it was their moral obligation to speak out on social and political issues in the name of their dead brethren.

And "brethren" is not too strong a word here. Whether on the extreme right in the groups that coalesced to form the Nazi movement, or on the left in pacifist veterans' organizations in France, fictive kinship operated openly and with deep dedication. After all, these men, the generation of fire, formed a family of survivors whose language and whose dedication to each other was forged in the trenches.

These masculine societies were very visible in interwar Europe. Their rhetoric and their beliefs helped deepen conventional gender roles. Here we come across one of the paradoxes of World War I. By destroying so many families, the war set in motion forces which led to a restoration of family life in conventional patriarchal forms. This restoration of the role of the masculine required a return to a subordinate position for women in domestic and in extra-domestic life.

In this sense, a war that had created millions of jobs and new opportunities for women closed those vistas as soon as hostilities were over. Restoration of the family meant the over-feminization of women. Their reproductive function was what mattered. Everything else – votes for women, increased educational opportunities, continuing employment in clerical jobs – came second. First came nurturing the new generation.

It is important to note that these ideological currents were not uncontested. In its early years, the Bolsheviks provided women with abortion on demand. In contrast, in 1920 in France, legislation was passed to suppress the dissemination of information about contraception. In addition, most men and women continued to use contraception, whatever the ideologues insisted was their patriotic duty. The decline in fertility in motion well before 1914 continued unabated until the eve of World War II.

In one sense, however, the pro-natalist drive of World War I and its aftermath coincided with a more sinister development. Reproduction as a political policy to enhance what we term "strategic demography" was an old theme in European history. What the 1914–18 war added to biological warfare was extermination as a political strategy. That this occurred on the fringes of the European war – in Turkish Armenia in 1915 – did not diminish its significance. Total war entailed the mobilization of hatred, and the cultivation of a bellicose wartime culture preparing the way for atrocities and war crimes. If the enemy was the embodiment of evil – as propaganda on both sides proclaimed time and again – then the enemy population was just as much a target as the enemy army. This was the logic of blockade and of aerial bombardment. It was also the logic of the removal of subversives, of the enemy within. The Turkish genocide of Armenian civilians in 1915 was a precedent for the future, one which showed that it was possible to destroy the collective life of an entire people in an area they had occupied for millennia. The demographic consequences of genocide are no less significant than their moral consequences; both form central parts of the legacy of World War I.

Notes

1   Sigmund Freud, "Thoughts for the Times on War and Death" (1915), in *The Penguin Freud Library*, vol. 12, London, Penguin, 1991, pp. 79–80.
2   As cited in Marilyn Shevin-Coetzee and Frans Coetzee (eds.), *World War I and European Society: a Sourcebook*, Lexington, MA, D. C. Heath, 1995, pp. 151–2.

References and Further Reading

Chickering, Roger, *The Great War and Urban Life in Germany. Freiburg 1914–1918*, Cambridge, Cambridge University Press, 2007.

Davis, Belinda, *Home Fires Burning. Food, Politics and Everyday Life in World War I Berlin*, Chapel Hill, University of North Carolina Press, 2001.

Faron, Olivier, *Les Enfants du deuil. Orphelins et pupilles de la nation de la Première Guerre mondiale (1914–1918)*, Paris, La Découverte, 2001.

Faron, Olivier (ed.), "La Population dans la Grande Guerre," theme issue of *Annales de démographie historique*, 1, 2002.

Feldman, Gerald D., *The Great Disorder. Politics, Economics and Society in the German Inflation, 1914–24*, Oxford, Oxford University Press, 1993.

Gatrell, Peter, *Russia's First World War. A Social and Economic History*, London, Longman, 1989. Ch. 11.

Grebler, Leo, and Winkler, Wilhelm, *The Cost of the World War to Germany and Austria-Hungary*, New Haven, Yale University Press, 1940.

Handelsmann, Marcel, et al., *La Pologne: sa vie économique et sociale pendant la Grande Guerre*, New Haven, Yale University Press, 1930.

Healey, Maureen, *Vienna and the Fall of the Hapsburg Empire: Total War and Everyday Life in World War I*, Cambridge, Cambridge University Press, 2004.

Huber, Michel, *La Population de France pendant la guerre*, Paris, Presses Universitaires de France, 1931.

Kohn, Stanislas, and Meyendorff, Alexander F., *The Cost of the War to Russia*, New Haven, Yale University Press, 1932.

Longworth, Philip, *The Unending Vigil. The History of the Commonwealth War Graves Commission*, 1967; new ed., Barnsley, Leo Cooper, 2003.

Mitchell, T. J., and Smith, G. M., *Medical Services: Casualties and Medical Statistics of the Great War*, London, HMSO, 1931.

Mortara, Giorgio, *La Salute pubblica in Italia durante e dopo la Guerra*, Bari, Laterza, 1925.

Offer, Avner, *The First World War. An Agrarian Interpretation*, Oxford, Oxford University Press, 1989.

Osborne, Eric W., *Britain's Economic Blockade of Germany 1914–1919*, London and New York: Frank Cass, 2004.

Pozzi, Lucia, "La Population italienne pendant la Grande Guerre," in *Annales de démographie historique*, 1, 2002, pp. 121–41.

Prost, Antoine, "Compter les vivants et les morts: l'évaluation des pertes françaises de 1914–1918," *Le Mouvement social*, 222, January–March 2008, pp. 41–60.

Robert, Jean-Louis, and Winter, Jay, "Un Aspect ignoré de la démographie urbaine de la Grande Guerre: le drame des vieux à Berlin, Londres et Paris," *Annales de démographie historique*, 1993, pp. 303–29.

Roerkohl, Anne, *Hungerblockade und Heimatfront: Die kommunale Lebensmittelversorgung in Westfalen während des Ersten Weltkrieges*, Stuttgart, Franz Steiner, 1991.

Sanitätsbericht über das deutsche Heer im Weltkriege 1914–1918, vol. 3, Berlin, Mittler, 1934.

Urlanis, Boris, *Wars and Population*, Moscow, Progress, 1971; new ed., Seattle, University Press of the Pacific, 2003.

Vincent, Paul, *The Politics of Hunger: The Allied Blockade of Germany 1915–1919*, Athens, Ohio University Press, 1985.

Waites, Bernard, *A Class Society at War: England, 1914–18*, Leamington Spa, Berg, 1987.

Wall, Richard, and Winter, Jay (eds.), *The Upheaval of War. Family, Work and Welfare in Europe, 1914–1918*, Cambridge, Cambridge University Press, 1988.

War Office, *Statistics of the Military Effort of the British Empire during the Great War, 1914–1920*, London, HMSO, 1922; new ed., Uckfield (East Sussex), Naval and Military Press, 2000.

Whalen, Robert, *Bitter Wounds. German Victims of the Great War, 1914–1939*, Ithaca, Cornell University Press, 1984.

Winter, Jay, *The Great War and the British People*, London, Macmillan, 1985.

Winter, Jay, "Migration, War and Empire: the British Case," in *Annales de démographie historique*, 1, 2002, pp. 143–59.

Winter, Jay, and Robert, Jean-Louis (eds.), *Capital Cities at War. London, Paris, Berlin, 1914–1919*, Cambridge, Cambridge University Press, 1997.

Winter, Jay and Robert, Jean-Louis (eds.), *Capital Cities at War. Paris, London, Berlin, 1914–1919*, vol. 2, *A Cultural History*, Cambridge, Cambridge University Press, 2007.

Ziemann, Benjamin, *War Experiences in Rural Germany, 1914–1923*, 1997; translation from the German, New York and Oxford, Berg, 2007.

CHAPTER EIGHTEEN

Women and Men

Susan R. Grayzel

> You love us when we're heroes, home on leave,
> Or wounded in a mentionable place.
> You worship decorations; you believe
> That chivalry redeems the war's disgrace.
> You make us shells. You listen with delight,
> By tales of dirt and danger fondly thrilled.
> You crown our distant ardours while we fight,
> And mourn our laurelled memories when we're killed.[1]

In these searing words from British poet Siegfried Sassoon's "The Glory of Women," the gap between men (combatants) and women (noncombatants) during World War I is clearly defined. Sassoon gives voice to one vision of the complex interaction between the roles assigned to men and women during the war. Until quite recently views such as his went largely unquestioned. Was not the masculine experience of this war that of carnage on the front lines and the feminine experience that of cheering men on, binding their wounds, waiting anxiously for their return, and mourning their deaths? Yet new approaches that underscore the importance of gender in understanding the war(s) of both men and women have broadened out these categories, forcing us to recognize differences and to consider female pacifists and female soldiers, as well as male warriors and male war-resisters, worthy of attention.[2]

What follows will examine some of the myriad war experiences and understandings of men and women in the participant nations in roughly chronological order. Limited space means that it cannot do justice to all of them and thus regrettably ensures a bias toward the experiences of those in the major powers (Austria-Hungary, Britain, France, Germany, Russia, and the United States). Overall, the aim is to shed light on how states deployed gender as a mechanism for mobilizing support and maintaining morale, to explore what contributions men and women made to various war efforts (and efforts to resist the war), and to uncover how such experiences were incorporated into understandings of the war.

One of the issues raised by the newer studies concerns the experiences or spaces that can readily be separated out by gender. When was gender more or less important than other forms of affiliation and identification, such as class, age, ethnicity, or nation? For instance, the general acceptance of war by Europeans in the summer of 1914 is seen as a general phenomenon. Yet on closer examination, it exhibits distinctive differences in terms of class, age, nation – and gender.[3] If women were shown cheering on their men, more men than women still took to the streets. If in places such as Britain, men were photographed lining up to volunteer for the army, such images masked the voices of dissidence and resistance that also greeted the war's arrival.[4] Leading members of the British women's suffrage campaign split over whether or not to support the war and thus reject the internationalist strands of what was a transnational movement.[5] Some socialist men and women spoke out vigorously against the war even as, in most left-wing European political parties, nationalism – and a particularly gendered version of this – trumped pacifism. For instance, the German socialist press could print the message that "we do not want our wives and children to be sacrificed to the bestialities of Cossacks."[6] In the end, most socialists, women and men, supported their national cause.

Meanwhile, many among the elites saw the war as providing an opportunity to demonstrate the quintessence of manhood, as a test of virility offering opportunities for glory and heroism. War called on young men to be "men" – physically fit and active, armed and ready for danger and excitement, unfettered by sentimental ties to home or even self-preservation. Male artists and writers across Europe, from Thomas Mann to Rupert Brooke, spoke of the purging and cleansing aspects of war. Of course, men in the colonizing powers of Europe had possessed outlets for the violent expression of nationalism in the imperial wars of the late nineteenth and early twentieth centuries, but the full-scale mobilization of 1914 provoked new and more widespread calls for the rejuvenation that would accompany the leap away from "a world grown old and cold and weary."[7] Masculinity and militarism were intimately linked, whether in prewar avant-garde movements like Italian futurism, whose 1909 manifesto celebrated violence, or in conservative youth organizations such as the Boy Scouts, whose leader, Robert Baden-Powell, stressed the preparation of male bodies for potential fighting as vital to national safety. This was not just propaganda; wartime letters and postwar memoirs suggest the power that this conception of manhood possessed and how tormented those who believed that they might not live up to it felt.[8]

Some men, by virtue of age or disability, found themselves removed from this omnipresent image of the warrior heeding the call to arms. Early recruiting posters in Britain tried to enlist men by highlighting the virility of those who could respond to the summons and the dependency or emasculation of those too old to fight. One poster featured an older gentleman patting a younger man on the back and claiming that he only wished he could go to war as well.[9] To be out of uniform was to reveal one's inability to take part in the national defense and became a badge of dishonor; so much so that along with stories of younger men lying about their age in order to volunteer came accounts of older men determined to find their way to the firing line or otherwise contribute to the war effort.

Ideas about the manliness of those willing or able to fight, and hence their heterosexual desirability, also appeared in popular culture. As the refrain of one music-hall ditty, sung presumably by a voluptuous woman, put it: "[O]n Saturday I'm willing, if you'll only take the shilling [i.e. enlist], To make a man of any one of you."[10] Other types of propaganda made use of direct appeals to women to encourage them to send their men cheerfully to battle and to do their best to persuade them to enlist. British posters featured a little girl asking her father, "Daddy, what did you do in the Great War?" and more sexualized images showed ethereal women beckoning men to action.[11] Thus recruitment techniques varied from stressing the need for fathers to protect their daughters to demonstrating to young men that if they wanted to attract young women, they had to become the military defenders of their homeland.

One of the most controversial recruiting techniques in Britain involved women who took the messages of the posters a step further and handed out white feathers, an emblem of cowardice, to men who were not in uniform. This sort of public shaming used women to suggest that those who had not joined up were lacking in the basic qualities of manhood and thus that no woman would find them desirable, sexually or otherwise. Even as the government itself had encouraged women to ask their men if they "were not worth fighting for," the white-feather campaign seemed to many a disgraceful female usurpation of their appropriate, unquestioningly supportive role.[12] As the main British feminist newspaper commented: "if there really are imbeciles of this type going about, we would ask them to consider what a man may feel towards a woman who practically says to him: 'I cannot go to the front and have no intention of doing so, but please go yourself and protect me!' "[13]

The initial war of movement brought armies into contact with civilians on both the western and eastern fronts. German armies in both cases, and the Russian armies that advanced into East Prussia and especially Galicia, confronted enemy populations that had a high proportion of women, children, and the elderly. With invasions, particularly that of Belgium, came tales of atrocities in the Allied media accompanied by images of brutal masculine beasts subduing a hapless and feminized civilian population.[14] Atrocity propaganda began in 1914 but reached its intensity in 1915 as horrific accounts of rape and sadistic violence began to spread more widely.

Some of this imagery took especially graphic form; posters depicted a simian-faced beast in a German helmet swinging a bloody club labeled *Kultur* while carrying the prostrate body of a bare-breasted woman. The phrase "Remember Belgium" became shorthand for the desecration of innocence; in one poster it appears at the top in stark, red letters above an image of a German soldier crushing a half-clothed woman underneath his boot.[15] The implied threat of violence to seemingly safe American or British women was designed to make the stakes of this war clear: it was the duty of decent, heroic men to defend innocent women from the depravity of a rapacious, brutal enemy. It was also the duty of women who lived in safety to encourage their "best boy" to protect them from such assaults.

In an effort both to record the situation faced by those under occupation and to bolster support for the war against a "barbaric" German enemy, Allied states such as France and Britain created special commissions to investigate the abuses suffered by civilians in occupied Belgium and France. The French government issued its first report in January 1915, and the British followed in May with the publication of the report of the Bryce Committee on Alleged German Outrages in Belgium. Both provided detailed accounts of women who had been sexually assaulted and even mutilated by members of the German military. Such documents, which were broadly circulated, helped to shore up other propaganda that transformed the invasion of Belgium into the "Rape of Belgium" and the German enemy into the "Hun."[16]

In France, a debate ensued in 1915 about the so-called "children of rape" and whether or not laws concerning abortion should be changed to allow those French women raped and impregnated by the enemy to abort these pregnancies. Once such a proposal had been introduced in the French legislature, politicians and social commentators filled the national news media with opinions as to whether or not French maternal lineage could eradicate the stain of such a brutal and awful paternity. In the end, the laws were not changed, although official measures were put into place to aid any woman who became pregnant through rape either to put the child up for adoption or to care for it herself. Despite the violence of the imagery surrounding the tales of "Boche rape," these public accounts were also quick to send the message to French men that their duty remained to embrace any such children as their own, and to fight even more fiercely against those who had attacked their homes and families.[17]

Along with such accounts of deviant masculinity run amok came countervailing stories of the close bonds and love that existed among men in arms. Critics such as Paul Fussell have analyzed the homoerotic quality of British soldier-authors, but combatant men of all nations – from Henri Barbusse in France to Erich Maria Remarque in Germany – produced war narratives that highlighted the intense feelings of loyalty and affection that bound often diverse groups of men together.[18]

The year 1915 also witnessed the first modern genocide, perpetrated by the Ottoman Empire against its Armenian population, including women and men of all ages (see chapter 13). As in the case of German conduct in Belgium, the Allies made official efforts to determine whether the reports were true or not.[19] Here, too, the sexual and gendered dimension of the destruction of the Armenians was highlighted, including the rape of women and girls. In late April, the Committee Union and Progress executed Armenian male community, intellectual, and religious leaders and began the deportation of the remaining population. Firsthand testimony described not only murder and rape, but also deaths during the deportation marches caused by starvation and illness, abandonment, and even suicide.[20] Despite the similarity with accounts of the atrocities on the eastern and western fronts, the massacre of Armenians had much less international resonance than the "rape of Belgium." More concern was expressed in Allied media over that year's political and military stasis.

One response to this sense of paralysis came from the organized feminist movement. Some of the leading members of the international women's movement decided to call for a woman-only gathering to discuss a peaceful resolution of the war. The first women's peace conference was organized by socialist women, notably the German activist Clara Zetkin. Representatives from Britain, France, Germany, and Russia met in Berne in neutral Switzerland in March 1915 and emerged determined to call for an end to the war. In late April of that year and with American activist Jane Addams in the chair, women from nearly all the belligerent states (with the notable exception of France), as well as from many neutral ones, gathered in The Hague to discuss what they could do to end the war. Speaking on behalf of all mothers who suffered the loss of their children through war, the participants passed resolutions that urged world leaders to embark upon continuous mediation until peace could be brokered. After the conclusion of the meeting, delegates from the Women's Peace Congress approached the leaders of both belligerent and neutral states and tried to persuade them to agree to mediation and a negotiated peace settlement as soon as possible.[21]

From 1915 onward, the voices of this determined feminist minority became part of the wartime political landscape. Each nation had its own responses to antimilitarist and antiwar activity, and such women usually faced hostility from the international news media and their own governments. Some of the most vocal activists, such as Louise Saumoneau in France and Clara Zetkin and Rosa Luxemburg in Germany, were jailed for their antiwar work; others, such as Britain's Sylvia Pankhurst, combined opposition to the war more generally, with protests about costs that had shifted to working-class families as a result of the war. Pankhurst organized working-class women in the East End of London to protest against the wartime increases in rents, and the similar movement in Glasgow in 1915 was also led by women (see chapter 27).

Thus by the end of the first year of the war, the mobilization of women had become increasingly visible, both in the waged workforce and as a political force to be reckoned with in terms of economic issues. In contrast to the international gathering of women to protest the war in April 1915, a mass demonstration organized by the pro-war faction of the British feminist movement under the leadership of Emmeline Pankhurst took place in London in July. Marchers demanded women's right to serve the nation and support the war effort. Whatever the impact of the march itself, the number of British women in the labor force expanded by some 400,000 during the war's first year.[22] In other nations, the recruitment of women to positions that had hitherto been closed to them, and thus their visible presence in these "new" occupations, began in 1915 and accelerated throughout the war years.[23] In Russia, it is estimated that women made up 43.2 percent of the industrial workforce by 1917 while in France they were nearly a third of the munitions workforce by spring 1918.[24] What such statistics mask is the shift of working-class women from domestic service to work in wartime factories or wartime occupations, often in roles hitherto reserved to men. The novelty lay not in the entrance of women to the world of waged work but in the types of work performed and the repercussions of these changes. For example, in the United States, white domestic servants turned to factory work, and African American women began to transfer from agricultural labor to replace them as a mainstay of domestic labor.[25]

Whether or not there was overt public support for women's factory work or resistance to it, the female worker, especially in the munitions industry, became emblematic of the wartime mobilization of women and of the alleged transformation of gender roles and even identities. Not only did the sheer numbers of women involved expand greatly in all participant nations, but women's role in manufacturing weapons challenged a powerful gendered taboo, as women now seemed to be participating in the culture of death instead of performing their "natural" roles as givers of life. Women were at one and the same time declared to be essential for the war effort yet patronized, feared, and condemned for infringing upon male roles.

As crucial sectors of the wartime workforce became feminized, states tried to ensure on a more practical level that factory work and motherhood would not prove incompatible. The contradiction between waged labor and familial labor – given the amount of time and work required to feed a family in wartime Austria, Germany, or Russia – was one with which every government had to grapple. While women's wartime wages never matched those of men, they often represented an improvement on prewar standards. But states also came under pressure to compensate for the loss of earnings of mobilized husbands and fathers, a measure demanded by the men themselves in recognition of their continued status as family breadwinners. The most widespread method adopted was an allowance paid directly to the dependents of those serving in the military, in some cases after means testing and in others to all such families.[26] By the end of 1915, financial support – available only to "warrior families" – was being paid to millions in Germany.[27] This policy would change as wartime conditions worsened, and ultimately such monies became means-tested.[28] Once provided, the funds could also be manipulated in efforts to affect the recipients' behavior. In Austria, the government cut funds for soldiers' wives who did not have young children when it needed to increase the number of married women in the waged labor force, and it also removed allowances if a soldier broke military law or deserted.[29] In nations like Britain, "separation allowances" were meant both to encourage enlistment in the war's early years and to allow the state to perform the task of an absent husband or son. Such funds came with increased government intervention as the state attached the receipt of allowances to women's "good" behavior. Separation allowances, while granted to unmarried women and illegitimate dependents, could be removed if a woman were caught engaging in sexual misconduct or abusing alcohol. Thus the British government took on the obligation of policing the actions of the female dependents of male soldiers.[30]

Industrial labor was far from the only way in which women participated directly in the war. The year 1915 also witnessed the expansion of women's medical services. Most participant nations relied on a female nursing staff, starting with a professional corps that grew rapidly to include younger and more inexperienced women recruited under the auspices of the Red Cross in nearly every nation or, in Britain, as part of the Voluntary Aid Detachments (VAD).[31] Nursing appealed to women who wanted to help the war effort in a direct way, and many younger women who joined up did so because of close connections with men in arms. They provided vital support but were seen as pure, selfless, and heroic caregivers, as wartime participants whose wartime work did not challenge gender norms. Most were not supposed to be directly in the line of fire, but in practice, nurses from every nationality serving in or near the battle zones frequently came close to battlefields wherever they served. One British nurse, Edith Cavell, went beyond her prescribed roles and aided Allied soldiers to escape via her clinic in Belgium. Her execution by the Germans in 1915 for aiding the enemy made her an international martyr in part because her gender and her occupation were seen as rendering her "innocent," whatever her actions.[32]

Since nurses had direct contact with injured male bodies, authorities set up strict rules to govern their relations with the men for whom they cared. Nurses from places such as Australia and the United States, who were required to be single and thus presumed to be sexually innocent, were given ranks above those of enlisted men and thus were subject to regulations against "fraternizing" with the majority of the men with whom they interacted.[33] Such encounters were especially fraught when they involved colonial troops and European women. Assumptions based on race and gender intersected when colonial troops, from India or Africa, and later, African American soldiers, became involved in the conflict. British officials, for example, tried to prevent nurses from caring directly for Indian troops for fear that this would compromise their "honor."[34]

In contrast to the welcome that women nurses received, the few women doctors who existed and wanted to serve were initially greeted with hostility. Often thwarted by the military, such women set off on their own, as was the case with several American women physicians, and most famously, Dr. Elsie Inglis, who raised funds through the leading British suffragist organization, the National Union of Women Suffrage Societies, to set up the Scottish Women's Hospitals in France and later in Serbia and Russia. In 1915, Britain's War Office permitted Dr. Louisa Garrett Anderson and Dr. Flora Murray to establish what became the Endell Street Military Hospital in London. By the war's end, women physicians served the British army in places ranging from Malta to India to East Africa.[35] Women also worked in the midst of the carnage as ambulance drivers and stretcher-bearers.

Contacts of a much more intimate kind between men and women also preoccupied wartime governments. The sheer human upheaval of the conflict multiplied opportunities for sexual relations outside legitimate channels, including prostitution. As already noted in relation to separation allowances, belligerent states sought to control women's behavior, especially their sexuality, both as a means of halting the spread of venereal diseases and of maintaining morale and order. Yet the same governments were often eager to find, and indeed to provide, outlets for male heterosexuality. In France and Germany, for instance, the provision of legalized brothels continued, but as was the case throughout war-torn Europe, the bulk of sexual encounters occurred not between prostitutes and soldiers but between soldiers and so-called amateur girls, motivated variously by love, desire, infatuation with men in uniform, sympathy, and the exchange of sex for material support. In fear of this unregulated sexuality, states such as Germany also instituted stricter penalties against any woman that a soldier identified as the source of his venereal disease.[36]

Legalized prostitution contradicted Anglo-American norms and expectations, and such establishments were allegedly off limits to British, Dominion, and Imperial troops. Soldiers in the British army had a message from Lord Kitchener himself emblazoned on their pay-packet envelope warning them to resist entirely the "temptation in both wine and women."[37] If this were not sufficient, the British government passed a series of measures under the Defence of the Realm Act that ultimately made any woman suspected of infecting a member of His Majesty's Forces with a venereal disease subject to medical examination, arrest, and punishment. The danger of sexually transmitted diseases also caused anxiety about the behavior of women in places like London where men found themselves on furlough. Women, too, were concerned about the damage that might be inflicted by the irresponsible behavior of some members of their sex, and tried to establish alternative places of entertainment and relaxation for unattached soldiers.[38]

It is also apparent that men's views of what governments deemed sexual misconduct varied. Some expressed shock or discomfort about interactions with sexually available women, going so far as to describe the women concerned as taking advantage of soldiers.[39] Others depicted such encounters as moments of escape and release from the widespread traumas of the war. Here, the novelist Erich Maria Remarque contrasts a German soldier's reaction to officially sanctioned sex with that to a clandestine encounter with a young Frenchwoman:

> How different all this is from the business in the other ranks' brothels, the ones we have permission to visit ... I feel the lips of the slim, dark girl, and push myself against them, close my eyes and try as I do so to wipe it all out, the war and the horror and the pettiness, so that I can wake up young and happy.[40]

If wartime culture implied that men in uniform epitomized masculinity and deserved sexual rewards for this, the exchange of sex for food or of sex across enemy lines, as in Remarque's scenario, remains open to a range of interpretations.

Military men themselves received mixed messages about sex. On the one hand, popular culture in places such as France was filled with imagery suggesting that heterosexual sex, particularly of the procreative variety, was precisely what soldiers should be doing when not actively fighting. In some of the most disturbing of such images, a bayonet and a penis become equated with one another, as an image shows three children hanging off a blade with the words "a good thrust" written above, suggesting that a true man knew how to wield each one for the national good.[41] On the other hand, even in France, soldiers were warned of the "dangers in a kiss" and told to beware of women as carriers of disease and immorality. The love of comrades for one another could also express itself sexually as well as emotionally, against prevailing military and civilian expectations.

Despite levels of venereal disease that did affect the fitness of the military, what overwhelmed contemporaries was the scale of death, wounding, and permanent disability that soldiers faced in battle. From 1915, the brutally injured male body had become an icon of the war. Subjected to the more widespread use of new weapons such as chemical-gas shells and machine guns, soldier-authors depicted gruesome and senseless deaths and the agony of those suffering terrible wounds. A newly recognized ailment had also cropped up: shell shock. Some interpretations of shell shock – the exhibition of symptoms associated prior to the war with "hysteria" – have insisted that the ailment itself had everything to do with gender, that "shell shock was the body language of masculine complaint."[42] Not only was masculinity associated with stoicism and lack of visible signs of fear but the immobility of men in the trenches of the western front surely further eroded their sense of manliness. Such readings fit in with arguments that World War I induced a so-called crisis of masculinity.[43] However, this does little to help us understand shell shock in troops that did not experience entrenchment and belies the evidence that even those at "home," including women, could suffer war-induced psychological ailments.[44] New interpretations of the phenomenon emphasize that shell shock was first and foremost seen as an illness, not a sign of masculine failure, and that theories and treatments as well as individual disabilities varied widely.[45]

In 1916 the United Kingdom introduced conscription, with the exception of Ireland, and with it arose the possibility for an alternative and complex masculine role: that of the "conscientious objector," whose status would be determined by a local tribunal. Those who objected to war on religious or moral grounds could serve as ambulance drivers or in other support roles. However, a minority of conscientious objectors refused to do anything that could be construed as supporting the war and went to prison. Here, they engaged in hunger strikes and tried to raise awareness of their ill treatment (becoming another kind of body in pain) to a largely unsympathetic public. Some feminists opposed to war, such as Catherine Marshall, saw themselves as having an especial responsibility to such men, since their gender alone protected them from having to face conscription.[46]

In the meantime, by the end of 1916, the importance of women as war workers gained more widespread recognition and gave rise to debates at fairly high levels of government in both Germany and Britain about whether or not to conscript women as well as men. The National Register created in Britain in 1915 as a prelude to the introduction of conscription collected data on women as well as men from age 16 to 65.[47] In Germany, some military leaders had urged that women be included in the Auxiliary Service Law of 1916 that compelled the labor of all men from ages 17 to 60 not already performing military service.[48] The fact that politicians and social commentators in both Germany and Britain even raised this possibility suggests that women's ability to aid the war effort was being taken quite seriously. That the measure was never introduced says as much about the desire not to destabilize gender roles as it does about the effectiveness of efforts to secure women's labor by voluntary measures.

The crisis year of 1917 saw both men and women challenging the circumstances and consequences of the war, and on occasions the conflict itself, as they engaged in mutinies, strikes, and revolution (see chapter 19). Countervailing attempts to remobilize the war efforts for the "final push" led to harsher attacks on those seen as betraying the national cause, and the "enemy within" could be painted in terms of gender as well as class and ethnicity. The French executed the alleged double-agent Mata Hari in the late fall of 1917, using her as an example of the dangers inherent in feminine licentiousness.[49]

But gender shaped the growing tensions of the war effort in other ways as well. For instance, what occurred among French troops in May–June 1917 has been characterized in a variety of ways (see chapter 28). But a strong underlying feature of the "mutinies" was the soldiers' concern for their families, fueled in part by false rumors that Indo-Chinese troops had repressed women strikers in Paris. It was a protest from those at the bottom over the conditions of their lives: soldiers wanted more leave, better food, and better treatment of their families, and their families in turn wanted assurances that their beloved sons and husbands would be better treated and that they themselves would have adequate supplies.[50] Some 30,000 women munitions factory workers also struck in May 1917 over economic conditions, but linked these to cries for "peace" and for the government to send shirkers to the front and their men home.[51] Still, if both combatant and noncombatant voices spoke of "peace" and the government feared what this might mean, there is little indication that French protesters of either sex would have supported peace at any cost, particularly that of a German victory.

If the provisioning of civilians was becoming difficult in Allied nations like France, where bread was rationed from 1917, it was worse in the nations affected by the Allied blockade such as Germany and Austria-Hungary. By 1917, civilians in Berlin had become direct participants in an economic war, and riots increased due to the scarcity of basic foodstuffs and the failure of government rationing schemes to distribute them. The failure of the potato crop meant that Germans had to rely on turnips as their basic source of food in 1917, hence the appellation "Turnip Winter," and the caloric intake of all civilians dropped markedly. Basic questions about the fairness of food and fuel distribution became increasingly politicized and women were active in bread riots, strikes, and protests against the regime. As one woman observed: "Why should we work, starve, send our men out to fight? … The state which called upon us to fight cannot even give us decent food."[52] Conditions in wartime Austria were even worse. In Vienna, lower-class and middle-class women and children took part in sustained rioting to demand that the state guarantee an equitable distribution of the food supply.[53]

One of the most hotly contested changes in gender roles came with the removal of the combat exclusion for women. Indeed, even before recruitment lagged in Britain, women had formed themselves into the "Woman's Volunteer Reserve" to prepare themselves should England be invaded. Exceptional individuals like Flora Sandes or Ecaterina Teodoroiu fought on the eastern front for the Serbian and Romanian armies, respectively, and these are only the most well-known women taking up arms. Meantime, in recognition of the noncombatant tasks that could be performed by women and thus free men for "the fighting line," the British government created an official auxiliary to the armed forces in 1917, the Women's Army Auxiliary Corps (later the Queen Mary's Army Auxiliary Corps); it later added women's branches of the Naval and Air Forces. By 1918, women had taken over a variety of tasks for the military in Germany, and the French government employed "civilian" women to carry out similar military support though it refused to allow them to don uniforms. In contrast, the US army, which needed to mobilize far less of its population, only employed women in its nursing corps.[54]

The most widespread challenge to the combat exclusion for women came in revolutionary Russia. Russia itself had experienced the food riots and strikes that characterized economic protests elsewhere, and such actions were often dismissed by contemporaries as "women's riots."[55] But, as was the case in Germany, the protests took a political turn, with strikes on International Women's Day sparking the overthrow of the Tsar in March 1917.[56] After the collapse of the Romanov dynasty and under the authority of the Provisional Government, which was trying desperately to maintain Russia's participation in the war, a Women's "Battalion of Death" came into being in June 1917. This represented a radical move on account of the numbers of women involved and the public nature of raising such a volunteer battalion explicitly to shame men who refused to fight. In the climate of widespread mutinies, a battalion of women was supposed to serve as a heroic example to men refusing to do their duty. Led by Maria Bochkareva, approximately 300 women members of the Women's Battalion of Death marched toward the battle zones in the summer of 1917. The total number of women enlisting in combat units during the summer rose to between 5,500 and 6,500. There was remarkable parity in terms of pay and access to veterans' benefits for Russian women soldiers, at least in theory. Their actual military contributions are harder to gauge, as the Women's Battalions of Death fought only in the summer offensive of 1917 that was doomed to failure from the outset. Popular reaction varied from praise for their heroism to claims that the women soldiers had been unable to overcome a feminine tendency to hysterics. Their last known act came as they helped defend the Winter Palace against the Bolsheviks during the November Revolution. As an example of the extent of total war, the creation of officially recognized female combatant units shows the willingness of at least one government to harness women's patriotism and to move beyond the exclusion of women from performing this most basic wartime task.[57]

By the end of 1917, the war had changed again. With the German Spring Offensive of 1918, the western front once again witnessed a war of movement and one that would increasingly impinge on the home front. While naval and aerial attacks had targeted homes, and thus women and children far removed from zones of occupation, ever since the war began, renewed active warfare on the western front exposed French civilians to artillery fire and then to occupation on a scale unknown since 1914. Paris faced the long-range gun, "Big Bertha," and several devastating air raids during that spring and summer. One of the worst attacks on the city took place on Good Friday, March 29, 1918, when a shell from Big Bertha struck the church of Saint-Gervais, killing 72 women ranging in age from 81 to 11, along with 19 men, and injuring 36 women and 30 men. Of the dead, 11 were under age 18.[58] In contrast to public discussion about "aces" – the fighter pilots who represented a modern heroic warrior (see chapter 11) – air raids renewed emphasis on the "innocence" of their feminine victims and the depravity of their male attackers.

By 1918, the war had provided many female victims, from the celebrated, such as Edith Cavell, to the unnamed, and public discussion began in a number of states about the appropriate way to recognize the sacrifices and services of women. Recognition of women's wartime roles quickly became caught up in debates over women's enfranchisement, as virtually none of the participant states had truly universal suffrage. In Europe, only Finnish and Norwegian women possessed the vote before the war. The first participant nation to give women the vote during the conflict was Russia's Provisional Government in the summer of 1917, a right that proved extremely short-lived. As was the case in Russia, it was a revolutionary regime – the Council of People's Representatives – that first gave German women a vote, a right that would be enshrined in the Weimar Constitution.

After the United States had entered the war, some leading feminists, notably Alice Paul's National Woman's Party, picketed the White House. Most controversially, they marched with signs asking "Kaiser Wilson" to prove that the democracy that the Allies were fighting to preserve actually existed at home by supporting the participation of women in American political life. In January 1918, President Wilson's support of the Constitutional Amendment granting women's suffrage helped secure its passage by the House of Representatives. The final ratification of the Amendment would not take place until 1920.

Like the United States, the British prewar women's suffrage movement had actively campaigned with little concrete effect to obtain the political rights that women in Dominions such as New Zealand and Australia already possessed. What is striking about the Representation of the People Act that finally passed both Houses of Parliament in 1918 is that it only partially enfranchised women, and with a different age qualification from that of men (women had to be over 30), so that it failed to reward the bulk of women who had performed some sort of war service with the vote. In this case, service did not equal suffrage. Yet the same legislation disenfranchised conscientious objectors, suggesting that their lack of war service could be penalized.[59]

The idea of rewarding women's sacrifices by granting them political rights emerged in wartime France when members of the legislature debated giving women "suffrage for the dead," that is, the right to vote on behalf of a dead male relative, or a "familial" vote for those women who now found themselves head of their families. Both measures failed. So too did any effort to grant women's suffrage in the immediate postwar period, even though supporters argued that French women deserved such a right in part because of their contributions to the war effort. In contrast to the successor nations of the Austro-Hungarian Empire and to nearly all other belligerent states, France stood out for its continued failure to enfranchise its female population.[60]

In addition to the strains of demobilizing the entire population – both men in arms and women in the waged wartime labor force – states also had to determine how to achieve stability after the traumas of war. Local and national war memorials and accompanying rituals were elaborated in order to celebrate victory (in some cases), honor the dead (in all cases), and impart retrospective political meaning to the devastation caused by the war (see chapter 38). This meant recognizing the gendered segregation of wartime roles and sacrifice in the no less gendered postwar process of mourning in which the commemorated dead were almost entirely male and the bereaved substantially (though by no means exclusively) female. Tensions emerged in a number of ways, not least in the conflict between the (feminized) family and the (masculine) state as to who had "ownership" of the fallen dead, which turned on the issues of the repatriation of bodies and the design and construction of memorials. In France, families – usually represented by mothers and wives – lobbied for the right to return their sons and husbands for burial in local cemeteries, which the government eventually allowed. Of course, not all bodies could be identified and not all were reclaimed. Countries such as Australia, Britain, and Canada allowed no such repatriation. Britain, France, Italy, and the United States all produced national ceremonies to honor the war dead that involved a version of burying the "unknown soldier," a single male body that could stand in for all the bodies killed in the war.

***

How does gender affect our understanding of World War I and vice versa? A good starting-point is to compare and contrast the overall situation of men and women in 1914 with that of 1918. Across participant nations, both women and men had *waged* war in new ways during these years. Not all men had fought nor had all women worked for the war effort; yet few men or women were completely unaffected by the war. If femininity had been modified to include women in uniforms and even trousers, such changes had been made "for the duration," and were not seen as altering women's fundamental nature. Expectations for appropriate gendered behavior had changed relatively little during the war years: working-class women were still likely to spend some portion of their lives in the waged labor force, and women of all classes were supposed to marry. Postwar societies continued to emphasize motherhood as a national duty and the source of feminine fulfillment, whether or not women could realistically fulfill this task given the numbers of missing men.

The two roles most subversive of gender – female soldiers and male war-resisters – remained anomalous and suspect. Maleness was still caught up if not always in the overt emblems of military service then with exhibiting physical fitness – hence the difficulty for disabled veterans in being breadwinners and exercising authority within the home.[61] The very scale of wartime casualties made maternity and more babies vital for many governments, although women seem to have been reluctant to compromise the growing modern understanding of marriage by returning to the large families of earlier generations. The forms of nationalism that emerged in postwar Europe were tied ever more closely to masculine privilege – this being especially clear in the case of fascism.[62] Yet the war had accorded recognition in at least some democratic states to the idea of full female citizenship. And it had helped confirm women's traditional concerns – the family, education, and children's welfare – as matters of vital importance, giving greater public visibility to both women and these issues. Experiences during the war varied by nationality, age, class, and race – but gender remains among the most important of these factors in shaping both wartime lives and the legacy of the conflict.

Notes

1   Siegfried Sassoon, "The Glory of Women," in *Counter-Attack and Other Poems*, London, Dutton, 1918, p. 32.
2   Braybon, "Winners or Losers," "Introduction"; Melman, "Introduction." For masculinity, see Horne, "Masculinity in Politics and War."
3   Hew Strachan, *The First World War*, vol. 1, *To Arms*, Oxford, Oxford University Press, 2001, ch. 2.
4   Adrian Gregory, "British 'War Enthusiasm' in 1914: a Reassessment," in Braybon (ed.), *Evidence, History and the Great War*, pp. 67–85.
5   Jill Liddington, *The Long Road to Greenham: Feminism and Anti-Militarism in Britain since 1820*, London, Virago, 1989.
6   Friedrich Stampfer, quoted in Strachan, *First World War*, vol. 1, *To Arms*, pp. 121–2.
7   Rupert Brooke, "Peace," in Ian Parsons (ed.), *Men Who March Away: Poems of the First World War*, London, Chatto and Windus, 1965, p. 40.
8   Strachan, *First World War*, vol. 1., pp. 133–42.
9   Parliamentary Recruiting Committee (PRC) poster, in the Imperial War Museum.
10 Cited in Trevor Wilson, *The Myriad Faces of War. Britain and the Great War*, Cambridge, Polity Press, 1986, p. 706.
11 PRC poster no. 79, Imperial War Museum.
12 Gullace, "*Blood of Our Sons.*"
13 *The Common Cause*, March 5, 1915.
14 John Horne and Alan Kramer, *German Atrocities, 1914. A History of Denial*, London and New Haven, Yale University Press, 2001, pp. 175–225.

15 Grayzel, *Women's Identities*, p. 65.

16 Gullace, "*Blood of Our Sons*"; Walton Rawls, *Wake Up, America! World War I and the American Poster*, New York, Abbeville Press, 1998. See the summary of atrocity propaganda in Grayzel, *Women and the First World War*, pp. 16–19.

17 Audoin-Rouzeau, *L'Enfant de l'ennemi*; Harris, "'The Child of the Barbarian'"; Grayzel, *Women's Identities*, ch. 2.

18 Paul Fussell, *The Great War and Modern Memory*, London, Oxford University Press, 1975; Henri Barbusse, *Under Fire*, 1916; trans. from French by Robin Buss, London, Penguin, 2003; Erich Maria Remarque, *All Quiet on the Western Front*, 1929; trans. from German, 1929; new trans. by Brian Murdoch, London, Cape, 1994.

19 Ara Sarafian, "The Archival Trail: Authentication of the Treatment of Armenians in the Ottoman Empire, 1915–1916," in Richard G. Hovannisian (ed.), *Remembrance and Denial: the Case of the Armenian Genocide*, Detroit, Wayne State University Press, 1998, pp. 51–65; Donald E. Miller and Lorna Touryan Miller, *Survivors: An Oral History of the Armenian Genocide*, Berkeley and Los Angeles, University of California Press, 1993.

20 Miller and Miller, *Survivors*; testimony in Higonnet, *Lines of Fire*, pp. 167–71, 280–1.

21 Jane Addams et al., *Women at The Hague: The International Congress of Women and its Results*, Urbana, University of Illinois Press, 2003; Rupp, *Worlds of Women*, pp. 26–30.

22 Gerard De Groot, *Blighty: British Society in the Era of the Great War*, London, Longman, 1996, p. 49.

23 Braybon, "Women, War, and Work"; Daniel, *War From Within*; Maureen Healy, *Vienna and the Fall of the Hapsburg Empire: Total War and Everyday Life in World War I*, Cambridge, Cambridge University Press, 2004.

24 Braybon, "Women, War, and Work," p. 152.

25 Braybon, "Women, War, and Work," p. 153; Greenwald, *Women, War, and Work*.

26 Bock, "Poverty and Mothers' Rights."

27 Daniel, *War from Within*, p. 283.

28 Davis, *Home Fires Burning*.

29 Sieder, "Behind the Lines," p. 119; Healy, *Vienna*, p. 196.

30 Pedersen, *Family, Dependence and the Origins of the Welfare State*, ch. 2; Braybon, "Women, War, and Work"; Woollacott, *On Her Their Lives Depend*; Thom, *Rude Girls*; Downs, *Manufacturing Inequality*; Daniel, *War From Within*; Davis, *Home Fires Burning*; Healy, *Vienna*.

31 On VADs, see Donner, "Under the Cross."

32 Darrow, "French Volunteer Nursing"; Schulte, "The Sick Warrior's Sister"; on Cavell, see Gullace, "*Blood of Our Sons*," pp. 99–100, and Wheelwright, *Fatal Lover*, pp. 119–25.

33 Zeiger, *In Uncle Sam's Service*; Holmes, "Day Mothers."

34 Philippa Levine, "Battle Colors: Race, Sex and Colonial Soldiery in World War I," *Journal of Women's History*, 9/4, 1998, pp. 104–30.

35 Leneman, *In the Service of Life*.

36 Daniel, *War From Within*; Usborne, "Pregnancy."

37 Copies of this document can be found at the Imperial War Museum, London.

38 Grayzel, *Women and the First World War*, ch. 5.

39 Bourke, *Dismembering the Male*, ch. 3.

40 Remarque, *All Quiet*, p. 104.

41 See the image in Huss, "Pronatalism," p. 342.

42 Showalter, "Rivers and Sassoon," p. 64.

43 Summation of Showalter and Leeds in Stryker, "Mental Cases," p. 157.

44 Trudi Tate, *Modernism, History and the First World War*, Manchester, Manchester University Press, 1998, ch. 1; Grayzel, *Women's Identities*, ch. 1.

45 Stryker, "Mental Cases."

46 Thomas C. Kennedy, *The Hound of Conscience: A History of the No-Conscription Fellowship, 1914–1919*, Fayetteville, University of Arkansas Press, 1981; Vellacott, *From Liberal to Labour*.

47   Wilson, *Myriad Faces*, p. 167.
48   Daniel, *War From Within*, pp. 65–71.
49   Wheelwright, *Fatal Lover*.
50   John Keegan, *The First World War*, London, Hutchinson, 1998, pp. 329–30.
51   Downs, "Women's Strikes."
52   Davis, *Home Fires Burning*; Daniel, *War from Within*. Quote is from Blücher von Wahlstatt, in Thierry Bonzon and Belinda Davis, "Feeding the Cities," in Jay Winter and Jean-Louis Robert (eds.), *Capital Cities at War: London, Paris, Berlin 1914–1919*, Cambridge, Cambridge University Press, 1997, p. 338.
53   Healy, *Vienna*, p. 35.
54   See Grayzel, *Women and the First World War*, ch. 4.
55   Barbara Engel, "Not by Bread Alone: Subsistence Riots in Russia during World War I," *Journal of Modern History*, 69/4, 1997, pp. 696–721; Gatrell, "The Epic and the Domestic."
56   McDermid and Hillyar, *Midwives*.
57   Abraham, "Bochkareva and the Russian Amazons"; Stockdale, "My Death for the Motherland" (figures in ibid., p. 95).
58   Jules Poirier, Les *Bombardements de Paris (1914–1918)*, Paris, Payot, 1930, pp. 225–30.
59   Gullace, *"Blood of Our Sons."*
60   Bard, *Les Filles de Marianne*; Smith, *Feminism and the Third Republic*; Grayzel, *Women's Identities*, ch. 6.
61   Bourke, *Dismembering the Male*; Cohen, *War Come Home*.
62   Sluga, "Masculinities, Nations."

References and Further Reading

Abraham, Richard, "Maria L. Bochkareva and the Russian Amazons of 1917," in Linda Edmondson (ed.), *Women and Society in Russia and the Soviet Union*, Cambridge, Cambridge University Press, 1992, pp. 124–44.

Audoin-Rouzeau, Stéphane, *L'Enfant de l'ennemi, 1914–1918*, Paris, Armand Colin, 1995.

Bard, Christine, *Les Filles de Marianne: Histoire des féminismes, 1914–1940*, Paris, Fayard, 1995.

Bock, Gisela, "Poverty and Mothers' Rights in the Emerging Welfare States," in Thébaud (ed.), *History of Women in the West*, vol. 5, pp. 402–32.

Braybon, Gail, "Women, War, and Work," in Hew Strachan (ed.), *The Oxford Illustrated History of the First World War*, Oxford, Oxford University Press, 1998, pp. 149–62.

Braybon, Gail, "Introduction," in Gail Braybon (ed.), *Evidence, History and the Great War: Historians and the Impact of 1914–18*, New York and Oxford, Berghahn, 2003, pp. 1–29.

Braybon, Gail, "Winners or Losers: Women's Symbolic Role in the War Story," in Braybon (ed.), *Evidence, History and the Great War*, pp. 86–122.

Bourke, Joanna, *Dismembering the Male: Men's Bodies, Britain and the Great War*, London, Reaktion Books, 1996.

Cohen, Deborah, *The War Come Home: Disabled Veterans in Britain and Germany, 1914–1939*, Berkeley and Los Angeles, University of California Press, 2001.

Daniel, Ute, *The War From Within: German Working-class Women in the First World War*, translation from German, Oxford, Berg, 1997.

Darrow, Margaret H., "French Volunteer Nursing and the Myth of War Experience in World War I," *American Historical Review* 101/1, 1996, pp. 89–106.

Darrow, Margaret H., *French Women and the First World War: War Stories of the Home Front*, Oxford, Berg, 2000.

Davis, Belinda J., *Home Fires Burning: Food, Politics, and Everyday Life in World War I Berlin*, Chapel Hill, University of North Carolina Press, 2000.

Donner, Henriette, "Under the Cross: Why VADs Performed the Filthiest Task in the Dirtiest War," *Journal of Social History*, 30/3, 1997, pp. 687–704.

Downs, Laura Lee, "Women's Strikes and the Politics of Popular Egalitarianism in France, 1916–1918," in Leonard Berlanstein (ed.), *Rethinking Labor History: Essays on Discourse and Class Analysis*, Urbana, University of Illinois Press, 1993, pp. 114–37.

Downs, Laura Lee, *Manufacturing Inequality: Gender Division in the French and British Metalworking Industries, 1914–1939*, Ithaca, Cornell University Press, 1995.

Gatrell, Peter, "The Epic and the Domestic: Women and War in Russia, 1914–1917," in Braybon (ed.), *Evidence, History and the Great War*, pp. 198–215.

Grayzel, Susan R., *Women's Identities At War: Gender, Motherhood, and Politics in Britain and France during the First World War*, Chapel Hill, University of North Carolina Press, 1999.

Grayzel, Susan R, *Women and the First World War*, Harlow, Longman, 2002.

Greenwald, Maurine Weiner, *Women, War and Work: The Impact of World War I on Women Workers in the United States*, Ithaca, Cornell University Press, 1980.

Gullace, Nicoletta F., *"The Blood of Our Sons": Men, Women, and the Renegotiation of British Citizenship During the Great War*, Basingstoke, Palgrave Macmillan, 2002.

Harris, Ruth, "'The Child of the Barbarian': Rape, Race and Nationalism in France during the First World War," *Past and Present*, 141, 1993, pp. 170–206.

Healy, Maureen. *Vienna and the Fall of the Habsburg Empire: Total War and Everyday Life in World War I*, Cambridge, Cambridge University Press, 2004.

Higonnet, Margaret R. (ed.), *Lines of Fire: Women Writers of World War I*, New York, Plume, 1999.

Higonnet, Margaret R., et al. (eds.), *Behind the Lines: Gender and the Two World Wars*, New Haven and London, Yale University Press, 1987.

Holmes, Katie, "Day Mothers and Night Sisters: World War I Nurses and Sexuality," in Joy Damousi and Marilyn Lake (eds.), *Gender and War: Australians at War in the Twentieth Century*, Cambridge, Cambridge University Press, 1995, pp. 60–80.

Horne, John, "Masculinity in Politics and War in the Age of Nation-States and World Wars, 1850–1950," in Stefan Dudink et al. (eds.) *Masculinities in Politics and War: Gendering Modern History*, Manchester, Manchester University Press, 2004, pp. 22–40.

Huss, Marie-Monique, "Pronatalism and the Popular Ideology of the Child in Wartime France: the Evidence of the Picture Postcard," in Richard Wall and Jay Winter (eds.), *The Upheaval of War: Family, Work and Welfare in Europe 1914–1918*, Cambridge, Cambridge University Press, 1988, pp. 329–67.

Leneman, Leah, *In the Service of Life: The Story of Elsie Inglis and the Scottish Women's Hospitals*, Edinburgh, Mercat Press, 1994.

McDermid, Jane, and Hillyar, Anna, *Midwives of the Revolution: Female Bolsheviks and Women Workers in 1917*, London, UCL Press, 1999.

Melman, Billie, "Introduction," in Melman (ed.), *Borderlines: Genders and Identities in War and Peace, 1870–1930*, London and New York, Routledge, 1998.

Offen, Karen, *European Feminisms, 1700–1950: A Political History*, Stanford, Stanford University Press, 2000.

Pedersen, Susan, *Family, Dependence and the Origins of the Welfare State: Britain and France, 1914–1945*, Cambridge, Cambridge University Press, 1993.

Rupp, Leila, *Worlds of Women: The Making of an International Women's Movement*, Princeton, Princeton University Press, 1997.

Schulte, Regina, "The Sick Warrior's Sister: Nursing during the First World War," in Lynn Abrams and Elizabeth Harvey (eds.), *Gender Relations in German History: Power, Agency and Experience from the Sixteenth to the Twentieth Century*, Durham, NC, Duke University Press, 1997, pp. 121–41.

Showalter, Elaine, "Rivers and Sassoon: The Inscription of Male Gender Anxieties," in Higonnet (ed.), *Behind the Lines*, pp. 61–9.

Sieder, Reinhard, "Behind the Lines: Working-Class Family Life in Wartime Vienna," in Richard Wall and Jay Winter (eds.), *The Upheaval of War: Family, Work and Welfare in Europe 1914–1918*, Cambridge, Cambridge University Press, 1988, pp. 109–38.

Sluga, Glenda, "Masculinities, Nations, and the New World Order: Peacemaking and Nationality in Britain, France, and the United States after the First World War," in Dudink et al. (eds.) *Masculinities in Politics and War*, pp. 238–54.

Smith, Paul, *Feminism and the Third Republic: Women's Civil and Political Rights in France, 1918–1945*, Oxford, Oxford University Press, 1996.

Stockdale, Melissa K., "'My Death for the Motherland is Happiness': Women, Patriotism, and Soldiering in Russia's Great War, 1914–1917," *American Historical Review*, 109/1, 2004, pp. 78–116.

Stryker, Laurinda, "Mental Cases: British Shellshock and the Politics of Interpretation," in Braybon (ed.), *Evidence, History and the Great War*, pp. 154–71.

Thébaud, Françoise, "The Great War and the Triumph of Sexual Division," in Thébaud (ed.), *History of Women in the West*, vol. 5, pp. 21–75.

Thébaud, Françoise (ed.), *A History of Women in the West*, vol. 5, *Toward a Cultural Identity in the Twentieth Century*, Cambridge, MA, Harvard University Press, 1994.

Thom, Deborah, *Nice Girls and Rude Girls: Women Workers in World War I*, London, I. B. Tauris, 2000.

Usborne, Cornelie, "'Pregnancy is the Woman's Active Service': Pronatalism in Germany during the First World War," in Richard Wall and Jay Winter (eds.), *The Upheaval of War: Family, Work and Welfare in Europe 1914–1918*, Cambridge, Cambridge University Press, 1988, pp. 389–416.

Vellacott, Jo, *From Liberal to Labour with Women's Suffrage: the Story of Catherine Marshall*, Montreal, McGill-Queen's Press, 1993.

Wheelwright, Julie, *The Fatal Lover: Mata Hari and the Myth of Women in Espionage*, London, Collins and Brown, 1992.

Woollacott, Angela, *On Her Their Lives Depend: Munitions Workers in the Great War*, Berkeley and Los Angeles, University of California Press, 1994.

Zeiger, Susan, *In Uncle Sam's Service: Women Workers with the American Expeditionary Force, 1917–1919*, Ithaca, Cornell University Press, 1999.

CHAPTER NINETEEN

Public Opinion and Politics

John Horne

Although World War I was long thought of mainly in military terms, deep changes in society shaped its nature. Foremost among these were the growth of nation-states, the emergence of mass politics, and the expansion of the market economy. Participation in each was determined by hierarchies of ethnicity, gender, class and, in the colonial setting, "race." The nation was by no means universally accepted, for it challenged the multinational basis of dynastic empires in Europe and held an ambivalent place in overseas colonialism. Women and many lower-class men were excluded from formal politics. The culture of the market was strongest in cities, yet much of Europe still lived in the countryside. Nonetheless, the nation, politics, and the market intersected in what we might think of as a "public sphere," though contemporaries used the term "public opinion."[1] In more developed parts of the world, this amounted to a space in which opinion and choice were exercised with some autonomy. Public opinion was expressed in various ways, from the press and elections to political activism and consumer choice.

In the eyes of liberals and democrats, the modern nation was inseparable from an active and informed public opinion. Yet in parts of Europe, especially in the east and south, tradition and deference prevailed. The modern state also disposed of levels of force unknown to more traditional states and deployed greater bureaucratic control over its subjects than had its predecessors. Still, societies with a public sphere could not be based on constraint alone but required choice and consent. The legitimacy of regimes (even autocracies) turned on their ability to accommodate public opinion, at least in some degree.

Before 1914, it was imagined that normal life would be suspended in time of war while mass armies sought a decisive victory. Legal provision for a state of exception (the Prussian state-of-siege law of 1851, the French equivalent of 1878) allowed military control in the interest of national security once war came, but little thought had been given to managing the public sphere in a protracted conflict.[2] It was soon evident, however, that public opinion and its wartime offshoot, morale, would be vital in a new type of war seemingly without end.

The Outbreak of War

Wartime powers immediately strengthened the capacity of governments to control public opinion. In addition to the state of exception already mentioned, parliament was marginalized in countries with a weak constitutional system, such as Russia, Austria-Hungary, and later Italy. Yet in the opening weeks, governments were surprised by the popular support shown for the regime in the face of the international crisis. Subsequently, especially in the interwar years, the mood of unity was turned into the myth of mindless crowds thronging the boulevards of Europe's capitals and cheering their nations on to catastrophe. Careful research has shown that in reality there was little euphoria outside limited circles. The response in France, Germany, and Britain was one of resolve at the news of war followed by demonstrations of patriotic solidarity with the soldiers once they left for the front.[3] Even in Russia, where Tsar Nicholas II feared that war might bring revolution as in 1905, the initial mood was one of unity. The protests that many had feared (or threatened) would meet the outbreak of a European war failed to occur.

In part, this is explained by the nature of the July Crisis. Had war broken out over Franco-German rivalry in Morocco, the result might have been different. As it was, the war was seen on all sides as one of legitimate self-defense; the German Chancellor Bethmann Hollweg refused to allow Germany to mobilize before Russia precisely so as to secure the support of the German Social Democratic Party (SPD). Nations and empires seemed threatened in their essence, an impression confirmed as one invasion followed another – Austria-Hungary against Serbia, Russia against Germany and Austria, Germany against Belgium and France, menacing Britain.

But the deeper processes already mentioned were also at work. The war galvanized the sense of national community and involvement in politics that had been growing in the previous half-century. Political parties, intellectuals, clergy, newspapers, pressure groups, and labor organizations were the actors in a powerful reflex of unity that found expression in a political truce – the *Union Sacrée* in France; the *Burgfrieden*, or fortress truce, in Germany. In fact politics were less suspended than focused on defining the national or imperial cause and stigmatizing the enemy. On all sides the groups most opposed to war or the regime were neutralized. Socialists in particular had declared their principled hostility to war. But a majority of socialists and trade unionists had long since made the nation-state their frame of action, and the gains they had won reinforced their national logic. This reality was cruelly driven home by the Second International's inability to prevent war and by the assassination of the French socialist and peace advocate, Jean Jaurès.[4]

War Cultures

Wartime states used their powers to shape opinion in two ways – by censorship and propaganda. Yet neither was as powerful as was made out by a second interwar myth, according to which governments and the press deliberately manipulated opinion with mendacious tales. Indeed, "propaganda" first took on its current pejorative meaning in this postwar literature.[5] For a long time, historians subscribed to this view of propaganda and confined themselves to describing how the effort was organized.[6] More recently, it has been accepted that many in power believed the views purveyed by the propaganda. This has refocused attention on the ideas and languages of wartime, which some have argued amounted to a "self-mobilization" of societies behind the war or to distinctive "war cultures" in the belligerent states.[7] Other historians continue to view the war as based on constraint, not consent.[8] There was a balance between the two, varying with country and over time. But it has become vital to understand not just who tried to shape opinion, and how, but also the meanings that contemporaries gave to the war.

Censorship was a negative means of safeguarding security and promoting consensus. The wartime powers of the state greatly reinforced its control over publications, this being most notable in liberal countries that normally enjoyed a high degree of press freedom, such as Britain, France, and, to some extent, Germany. Yet tensions arose between the military authorities, who wished to curtail news, and editors and press magnates, who needed to keep their readers informed. There was logic on both sides. Irresponsible journalism could compromise military security as well as stoking the panics that swept societies as they entered the war and faced invasion. Ordinary people translated their heightened emotions into spy mania, fears of subversion, and legends of enemy brutality. "News" of poisoned reservoirs surfaced in Berlin, Brussels, and London in August 1914, while tales circulated in the Entente countries of Belgian babies with hands supposedly severed by German soldiers. Such stories were the mythic currency of wartime. They were rarely deliberate fabrications, despite later accusations, but uncritical journalists embellished and circulated them and the state wished to censor such excesses.[9]

Yet it was also true that in societies accustomed to information and public opinion, nothing fed rumor more than the absence or inadequacy of news. The French awoke on August 29, 1914 to the communiqué announcing that the front extended from "the Somme to the Vosges," revealing that the Germans had actually invested national territory rather than being held at bay in Belgium. Along with the flood of refugees, this bland announcement stoked a panic that was only halted by the victory on the Marne 10 days later. The importance of news for the stabilization of opinion led the press in Britain and France to accept a form of self-censorship on the basis of instructions issued by the military authorities, with government reserving the right to penalize or close down papers that persistently infringed these.[10] The arrangement was subject to perpetual tension, however, because the press was a major political player and resented undue restrictions. It intervened in the conduct of the war, as when Clemenceau exposed the chaos of French military medical services in his newspaper in 1914 or the *Times* reported the "shell scandal" (or shortage) in the British Expeditionary Force (BEF) in May 1915.[11] Even in Germany, where the military's role was stronger than in Britain or France, the same logic meant that the Central Office of Censorship established in Berlin after the failure at the Marne could not fully control an active press with wide-ranging views.[12] The centrality of newspapers to opinion limited censorship, and the harder the war became the truer this proved to be.

Propaganda was the positive tool used to shape public understanding of the war. Yet the state engaged in surprisingly little of this on its own account in the first half of the conflict, and what it did undertake was directed above all to the strategically important neutral countries. The Entente powers sought to bring the United States and Italy into the war on their own side, while the Central Powers tried to ensure that both countries stayed out. Neutral opinion also mattered because, in a conflict that contemporaries believed to be about values, it served as an international public sphere in which moral self-justification could be achieved. So governments founded information agencies, such as Wellington House, under the Liberal writer, Charles Masterman, which was answerable to the Foreign Office, or the Maison de la Presse, established by the French Ministry of Foreign Affairs in 1916.

The interaction between events, belief, self-delusion, and manipulation in this international propaganda can briefly be illustrated by reference to the issue of German atrocities in 1914. Fueled by a collective myth that guerrillas (or *francs-tireurs*) were rising up against the German invasion and also by a deep hostility to civilian involvement in warfare, the German army engaged in savage behavior toward Belgian and French civilians, of whom some 6,500 were killed in a matter of weeks. In reality there was no such civilian opposition, and with some justification the press and governments of the Entente accused the Germans of atrocities (see chapter 13). The Belgian, French, and British governments (the first from exile) all investigated the German war crimes. While making some uncritical claims and drawing some exaggerated conclusions, their reports proved broadly accurate.

Realizing the *franc-tireur* uprising was a myth, but faced with a public relations disaster, the German Navy Ministry organized the ringing rejection of Allied atrocity charges by 93 intellectuals in October 1914. Aimed at neutral opinion, this triggered furious responses from Allied intellectuals (see chapter 22). The German army also produced a "White Book" rebutting the Allied accusations, although to do so it suppressed evidence from disbelieving German soldiers and Belgian civilians. In the charged atmosphere of the war, German barbarism for one side and Belgian ferocity and Allied mendacity for the other defined what was at stake, generating exaggeration and hyperbole. But bedrock reality in this instance favored the Allies, and Germany's reputation suffered accordingly.[13]

The state did engage in some propaganda at home. Materials such as atrocity reports were widely publicized. In Russia, where the autocracy feared letting propaganda out of government control, the semi-official Skobelev Committee (which had been set up during the Russo-Japanese War) operated under the patronage of the Tsar, producing newsreels and films, including one on German atrocities in Belgium, as well as postcards.[14] In Britain, the recruitment drive to raise a volunteer army comparable in size to the conscript forces of the Continent generated a major propaganda campaign, in which the Parliamentary Recruiting Committee (PRC) took a lead role, drawing on the traditions and resources of the political parties.

But the PRC highlights the essential point, which is that "self-mobilization" of the public sphere provided the real force behind the war effort in the first two years of the conflict. Society organized itself in terms of the war – whether through advertising that drew on wartime themes (in France it seemed that everything could be marketed using the image of the mythic "seventy-five," or 75-mm field-gun) or war-loan campaigns to mobilize small-scale savings. Intellectuals and artists offered their services (see chapters 22 and 23). Schoolteachers enrolled children in the patriotic effort. Middle-class women took the lead in a vast outpouring of charitable solidarity with wartime causes, from the soldiers and prisoners of war to victims of enemy brutality – Belgians and Serbs in the case of the Entente.

The cultures of wartime not only organized essential functions but also expressed the central issues and key emotions raised by the conflict. The national or imperial cause was imagined in terms culled from history and folklore, which had characterized popular literature and school textbooks before the war, and was contrasted with the enemy who was portrayed in brutish or diabolical form, frequently according to crude racial stereotypes. Invasion was presented in terms of "violation," often in highly sexualized imagery, and "hatred" became a legitimate public emotion.[15] At the heart of the phenomenon lay the distinction between soldiers and civilians. Never before had the bulk of adult men been required to serve in the armed forces, many risking death at the front. With couples and families separated and women cast into the double role of home support and wartime substitute for male labor, recognition of the soldier's sacrifice became the organizing ideal of social relations. It was underscored by its opposite, the "shirker" who avoided his wartime duty (*embusqué* in French, *Drückeberger* in German).[16]

National community, mass politics, and the market thus intersected with the requirements of an extended conflict. The resulting "propaganda" was largely a matter of conviction and permeated many of the institutions of society. Within the constraints of its functions, it varied in content. For example, Catholics and socialists in France or Germany rallied to very different senses of the nation. The resultant sense of wartime community was powerful, especially during the first half of the conflict. The exclusion of dissidents was in part the work of the repressive agencies of the state – but it owed at least as much, if not more, to public opinion.

Endurance and Protest

Yet the war had a dynamic that disrupted expectations and challenged the very cultures that it developed. This dynamic sprang from the predominance that industrialized firepower gave to the defensive in 1914–18, confounding both command doctrines and the soldiers' expectations. How to win in such conditions became the key problem. Trying to solve it resulted in failed offensives, unimagined casualties, huge numbers of prisoners, and a prolongation of the war beyond all expectations. But it also transformed military technology, produced new ways of fighting, and imposed a reorganization of the economy in order to deliver the armaments and food on which victory came to depend.

From the point of view of governments the "morale" of both soldiers and civilians became increasingly vital for the capacity to sustain such a war effort. It was this psychological quality that Clemenceau referred to with his aphorism that the winning side would be the one that *believed* in victory a quarter of an hour longer than its opponent. As the war went on, armies developed an elaborate apparatus to monitor the feelings of soldiers and their fighting spirit, which included sampling the vast exchange of correspondence with the home front. Likewise, in regimes that were used to keeping an eye on domestic opinion, the state surveyed civilian responses to the conflict via the reports of police spies, prefects, and military commanders of the interior (the latter being the key intelligence agency within Germany). Even liberal Britain now concerned itself with domestic dissent as well as foreign subversion, notably through MI5 (or Section Five of Military Intelligence).[17] The transition from the Tsarist to the Bolshevik regime was marked by a shift in focus on the part of the security apparatus from threats to authority to a broader monitoring of opinion.[18]

Yet what the state read as "morale" and "loyalty" was in fact a public opinion that grew in complexity as the war turned into a test of endurance. Though pervasive in societies with more developed public spheres, "war cultures" were biased toward the elites. More subordinate elements of society were less actively involved, including the peasantry, which in many countries supplied much of the infantry. Indeed, in states such as Italy, Russia, or Turkey, the peasants belonged to a traditional order, faithful (at best) to throne and altar but without much sense of the "nation." The conditional inclusion in the state felt by many working-class communities became a source of fragility, as did the limited loyalty felt by some ethnic minorities. Self-mobilization for the war was a differentiated, uneven process.

Several developments actively weakened support for the war from 1916. Foremost was the toll of the dead, wounded, and prisoners of war (POWs), which rose inexorably without bringing victory appreciably closer. The soldiers' morale turned on military issues – small-group cohesion, officer–man relations, adequate food and arms, and the quality of leadership (see chapter 12). But it was also related to the purpose of the war and to the communities (real or imagined) for which the men risked their lives. The idea that the home population ignored the men at the front is another postwar myth, which spoke to the veterans' subsequent concern that their sacrifice might be diminished or forgotten. During the war soldiers generally remained close to their families, whose anxiety and grief at the death of their loved ones were among the most widespread emotions.

Of course, there were aspects of the "home front" that soldiers felt to be morally repugnant during the conflict. As well as "shirkers" these included the "profiteers" who benefited from the misfortune of others and flouted the ideal of collective sacrifice.[19] But "morale" was a two-way relationship. Along with home leave, letters formed a bond between front and rear, especially since only a fraction could be read by the authorities, and they counteracted official silence on matters such as failed offensives or mutinies. French prefects during the mutinies in 1917 noted that the soldiers' news depressed civilians, yet the generals held that it was the rear that had "contaminated" the front. When Hindenburg and the nationalist right insisted in a further postwar myth that the German army had been "stabbed in the back" by civilians, they ignored the links between the two. The war of attrition imposed a huge sacrifice on civilians as well as soldiers. If the legitimacy of the regime and the mobilizing ideal were weak, the sacrifice called both of these into question.

The industrial mobilization was a second development that strained support for the war. This was because the munitions effort was based not on a presumed equality of sacrifice but on the opposite principle of the division of labor.[20] An entire social group, the skilled workers, was removed from risk and put to work (along with women and unskilled men) manufacturing the weapons of war. In effect, the industrial working class was reconstituted on a new base. Inflation, crowded accommodation, and the feeling that living standards were falling provoked widespread strikes in the second half of the war, despite legal restrictions. Everywhere, 1917–20 witnessed the worst industrial unrest yet seen.[21] But the sense of working-class grievance conflicted with the perception by others (not least the soldiers at the front and their families, especially in the countryside) that workers were now the "shirkers" in relation to the ultimate sacrifice.

The globalization of the struggle in 1917 also strained support for the war, since feeding the population while maintaining the fighting capacity of the army now became the main task. It was one that the Entente powers (except Russia) were better equipped than the Central Powers to fulfill by virtue of their maritime supremacy and more effective organization of food and fuel supplies. Their governments were also more attuned to civilian opinion. Declining calorific intake directly affected the physical capacity to prosecute the war. But it also translated into food protests where supplies were most wanting (Russia, Austria, and eventually Germany) and it further distorted the social relations of sacrifice. Urban dwellers accused peasants of hoarding. Middle- and lower-middle-class people struggling to make ends meet on a fixed income condemned working-class wage increases, though often these were below inflation. And the *nouveaux riches* who profited from the war (the "speculators" and "profiteers") became figures of hate.

Each of these developments was a potential source of opposition to the war. Whether it became so, and how, depended on the variable participation of different groups in the public sphere according to nationality, class, gender, and race. "Race" was the most peripheral. Recruitment of indigenous populations in both Russian Central Asia and French Algeria and West Africa provoked revolts that were summarily repressed, though with some mediation in the case of West Africa (see chapters 35 and 37). While this brought the war home to the Empire, the areas concerned were too remote to disrupt the Russian or French military efforts. The British by and large kept nonwhite troops out of the European theater after 1915, while French colonial troops on the western front proved immune to the mutinies of 1917. Colonial workers in France, including the Chinese labor recruited for work behind the lines, engaged in occasional internecine riots or were the object of racial hostility from French workers threatened with the front. But they were not overtly hostile to the war. Rather, the war affected indigenous opinion at one remove, when Wilsonian notions of democracy and self-determination were used by nationalist movements in 1919–20 to demand progress toward emancipation in Egypt, India, and elsewhere – at the cost of violent clashes with the colonial powers.[22]

Gender, by contrast, was central to the war in Europe, given how men and women's roles were both polarized and transformed by the conflict. In comparison with the pre-war period, women gained new prominence in social protest but they combined this with a heightened sense of their traditional role in protecting the family. This latter point was underlined by the provision of separation allowances for the wives of mobilized men in virtually all the belligerent societies, including Tsarist Russia, creating a compact between the state and the family over military service. Women workers played an important part in strikes in France, Germany, Italy, and Russia in 1917–18, partly because they were exempt from the military sanctions applied to male mobilized workers. In Paris in mid-1917 they demanded the return of their husbands and the dispatch of profiteering *patrons* (bosses) to the front.[23] In Italy, working-class women protested against the departure of their menfolk by lying in front of troop trains. In the countries worst affected by food shortages (Russia, Germany, Austria, and Italy), women took the lead in consumer protests, forcing price reductions, seizing scarce goods, and (in some parts of Italy) occupying the land.[24]

Such protests might amount to outright opposition to the war, as when women workers demonstrated in Petrograd on International Women's Day in March 1917, triggering the downfall of Tsarism. Yet they might also renegotiate the terms on which women would support the conflict, as with the French women's strikes of summer 1917, which were settled by increased wages and improvements for home workers. Indeed, the very centrality of gender and the family to the war meant that outright opposition ran the risk of undermining the position of the men at the front, which made it unlikely that gender alone would provide a basis for revolt. The problem was evident in the fragmentation of the feminist and suffragette movements. Many feminists argued that women should oppose the war on the grounds of their sex – the French primary-school teacher, Hélène Brion, who was tried for her antiwar stance in 1918, declared: "War represents the triumph of brute strength, while feminism can only triumph through moral strength and intellectual values." But just as many embraced the chance to show that wartime service provided a path to civic and political rights for women. Meanwhile, feminist socialists opposed the war on grounds of class, not gender.[25]

Class proved a more focused source of opposition since it was doubly concentrated – in the working-class militancy created by the munitions effort and in the revolutionary socialism that offered a language of resistance to the continuation of the war. Across Europe and eventually the United States the munitions effort placed a premium on the role of the skilled male engineering worker, who, in common with other skilled workers, had been at the heart of the prewar political cultures of labor and socialism. But it also eroded his position by accelerating mechanization and mass manufacturing, with the attendant growth of the semi-skilled worker who was often a rural immigrant, a foreigner, or a woman. The result was a volatile labor militancy whose core concern was "worker control" of power relations in the factory. This militancy was driven by skilled workers but extended to the semi-skilled, who often imbibed the political culture of the skilled in the process. Organizationally, it centered on local delegates (or "shop stewards"). Militancy spread to other sectors of wartime labor. But in arsenals and munitions factories from Birmingham to Turin, Paris, Berlin, Vienna, Petrograd, and beyond, shop stewards' movements challenged the perceived class iniquities of the war economy, and even the war itself.[26]

Socialism provided a language and symbolism for antiwar protest (the *Internationale*, the red flag) that went beyond industrial militancy, since its class terminology encompassed all workers and, in some countries, appealed to the urban middle classes and peasantry. When, in the crisis of August 1914, the revolutionary rhetoric espoused by the Second International collided with the pragmatism of much socialist activity, it destroyed the unity of the International. Many socialists and trade unionists, including the majority of the SPD, saw themselves as critical supporters of the war effort and went on to become overtly reformist.[27] But as the war became bogged down, the dream of proletarian unity resurfaced as a means of ending it. Dissident socialists and trade unionists from both sides met in two Swiss villages, Zimmerwald (September 1915) and Kienthal (April 1916), in order to hammer out an accord. Along with denunciations ("Europe has become a gigantic human slaughterhouse," wrote Trotsky, author of the Zimmerwald Manifesto), they resurrected the class unity of prewar Marxism in order to denounce the "imperialism" of all the warring nations.[28]

Turning this into action to end the war was another matter. Despite symbolic acts, such as the refusal by the leading SPD deputy, Karl Liebknecht, to vote war credits in the Reichstag, opponents of the war remained a minority in the French and German socialist parties for most of the conflict, in the latter case forming an Independent German Social Democratic Party (USPD) in April 1917. Moreover, the revulsion of "minority" socialists against the war was tempered by an unwillingness to envisage peace at the price of defeat. Much pacifism remained heavily qualified, as became apparent when socialist delegations from the warring nations prepared for a major conference in 1917 in Stockholm, again under neutral sponsorship. The meeting was constantly postponed and in the end never held. But it had become apparent that no common view would prevail on who was responsible for the war, how it should end, or on what terms.[29]

Socialists, then, remained divided. Only a minority within the minority was prepared to urge revolution over peace, and to use violence to achieve it. This was the strategy hammered out by the Bolsheviks in exile as they abandoned the dream of socialist unity in favor of a tightly centralized movement, internationally as well as in Russia. The revolution that broke out in Russia in March 1917 gave them the chance to seize power in November. But this confirmed the international split between reformist and revolutionary socialism while turning some revolutionaries in more "advanced" movements, such as Rosa Luxemburg in Germany, against the Bolshevik project.[30] Elsewhere in Europe, despite the international symbolism of the March revolution, which was widely understood as the triumph of local workers' movements in self-governing Soviets against an "imperialist" war, labor militancy and socialist opposition were neither strong enough by themselves, nor overlapped sufficiently, to produce mass rejection of the conflict on the grounds of class alone.

Nationality was even more central than class to the dynamic of societies at war and hence to opposition to the conflict. After all, the war arose from a clash between a dynastic Austria-Hungary and a Serb nation whose aspirations were felt to threaten the Dual Monarchy. The war assumed the scope that it did because the alliance system extended it to the major nation-states that had emerged or been reshaped since the mid-nineteenth century (Britain, France, Germany, and Italy), as well as to the multinational empires. Nations were becoming the dominant form of political community in Europe and this gave them a substance beyond any particular nationalism.[31] Because they were organic rather than ideological in character, they might be reordered in the light of wartime sacrifice, reversing existing hierarchies and including new elements. But the dynastic empires were deprived of the affective resources of the nation in waging war and, worse, might have to confront nationalism as a form of opposition. Since the state's wartime legitimacy turned on its ability to raise and sustain a mass army despite unprecedented losses, nationality became important above all in connection with issues of recruitment, casualties, and the military goals of the war.

Nations were not exempt from ethnic dissent. Republican France experienced little resistance by soldiers from its national subgroups (only later did Breton nationalists wrongly claim that Brittany had been a source of cannon fodder), but a federated German Reich was more exposed to this type of pressure. The Supreme Command singled out Alsace-Lorrainers as particularly "unreliable" (some sang the *Marseillaise*, and in May 1918 they were responsible for one of the most serious German mutinies, at Beverloo in Belgium).[32] By 1918 many Bavarian soldiers blamed the perpetuation of the war on the Prussians.[33] But the most serious such opposition was that faced by the British in Ireland when military recruitment (which Irish nationalists had endorsed in return for securing Home Rule) provoked the Easter Rising in 1916 on the part of a minority. This led to the nationalist project being redefined by opposition to the war, not by its acceptance, reinforcing "unionists" in the converse logic. The result was widespread resistance to the attempt to extend conscription to Ireland in 1918 followed by the War of Independence of 1919–21. Whether this amounted to a failure of British nation-building, nationalist opposition to a political union, or a colonial-style revolt (or all three) is a moot point (see chapter 27).

Far more typical of nation-states during the war, however, was the way in which military sacrifice and the wartime moral economy resulted not in rejection of the nation but in competing versions of what it stood for. By 1917, the war of attrition had strained if not fractured the political truces of 1914. But nation more than class provided the touchstone for arguing how the war should be waged and to what end. When some 50,000 French soldiers mutinied in May–June 1917 in incidents that affected the bulk of units on the western front, the protest was against the war in the most general sense of a heartfelt desire that the fighting should end. This did not mean defeat, however, for the mutinies took place behind the lines, not at the front, and never entailed mass surrender. Specifically, the soldiers protested against the renewal of pointless offensives, such as that on the Chemin des Dames in April–May 1917, and invoked their moral entitlement to rest and home leave. As Leonard Smith has shown, they were acting as citizen-soldiers who took it on themselves to renegotiate the terms on which the war should be prosecuted. By and large, despite the horror of the conflict, they did not question the logic of national self-defense (chapter 28). The related slump in civilian morale was marked by a loss of confidence in France's ability to win but not by any serious acceptance of French defeat.[34]

The general perception by the French that they were fighting a war of self-defense against an enemy occupying home territory meant that a core sense of nationality could be drawn on to overcome the crisis of 1917, despite a failure to restore the *Union sacrée*. What a defensive war meant for Germany was more ambivalent. As we have seen, the military and political leadership took great care in 1914 to ensure that their insistence on backing Austria-Hungary in what would almost certainly be a European war should, for public purposes, be presented as self-defense against Russia. Initial successes prompted industrialists, the military, and the political right to propose that victory should take the form of German hegemony in Europe. This was opposed by a popular vision of the war as truly defensive – with the Battle of the Somme being the German Verdun. As the political system polarized in 1916–17 between a virtual military dictatorship under Hindenburg and Ludendorff and a Reichstag majority composed of the SPD, the Catholic Centre Party and the Progressives, the clash over war aims became a conflict between opposed visions of the nation. Whereas the right urged an all-out war of conquest in the name of a radical, anti-Semitic nationalism, the left favored a negotiated, non-expansionist peace and the creation of a constitutional monarchy.[35] Each vision in turn would shape Germany's fate over the final year of the war and in military defeat.

The very potency of the nation thus made it a source of contention and division as well as unity in wartime. Multiethnic dynastic empires, however, faced the problem of how to mobilize less developed societies for the same war without the resources of the nation. True, we should not underestimate the resilience of the dynastic bond. The Austro-Hungarian army (fighting on three fronts against Russia, Serbia, and Italy) performed "surprisingly well" in the first half of the war.[36] The vast number of prisoners taken on the eastern front (70 percent of the total for World War I, or some six million men) was due less to the weak loyalty of subordinate nationalities (Poles, Czechs, South Slavs, and Italians in the case of Austria-Hungary) than to a more mobile warfare in which sudden advances overwhelmed the enemy.[37]

But the Austro-Hungarian and Russian armies were drained by the campaigns of 1914–15, and it proved more difficult to replenish the cadres of junior officers and NCOs from societies that were less educated and politically less integrated than in more developed nation-states. Also, the experience of captivity was crucial for the legitimacy of the regimes concerned. POWs of the Dual Monarchy became deeply critical of what they perceived as their neglect by a government that viewed them as disloyal. The critical interrogation they underwent on their return home in 1918, after the Bolsheviks had taken Russia out of the war, confirmed a rejection of the Empire that had been born or fostered in the camps.

In both Russia and Austria-Hungary the war reinforced the pressure on the regimes to "nationalize" the Empire, which only heightened the internal contradictions of their war efforts. Privileging the key national groups (Austrians and Magyars in the case of the Dual Monarchy, Russians in that of the Tsarist Empire) reinforced the devolution of political authority to the detriment of the autocratic principle while alienating the excluded nationalities. In the Russian case this led to a negative mobilization against the minority groups, which were cast as the "enemy within" during the great retreat from Galicia in spring and summer 1915. In a wave of xenophobia, the High Command deported millions of Germans, Poles, and Jews from the borderlands into the interior, creating a humanitarian crisis, until the liberals and the Duma ended the persecution.[38] Yet if the Tsar made too many concessions to Russian patriotism, whose spirit animated the self-mobilization for the war by the industrialists and the local assemblies (*zemstva*), this undermined his authority.[39] The result was paralysis, and by late 1916 Nicholas II was seen as the main obstacle to a successful national effort, paving the way for the March Revolution.

In the Dual Monarchy, suspicion of the subordinate by the dominant groups was matched by the feeling of the former (notably the Czechs and South Slavs) that home rule was now the minimum due to them for supporting the war. The young Emperor Karl, who succeeded Franz-Josef in late 1916, sought to endorse these aspirations and relegitimize the war effort by holding out the hope of a federation of nationalities – the dream his uncle Franz Ferdinand had nurtured before his assassination at Sarajevo in 1914. While this initially garnered the approval of both the Czechs and the Croats, it aroused the hostility of the dominant Austrians and Magyars and was in any event vitiated by Karl's failure to enforce his federal project. With the Western Allies beginning to favor the breakup of Austria-Hungary into successor nation-states, political legitimacy in the subordinate nationalities refocused on leaders in exile. The recriminations of the moral economy began to assume a national form, with the Austrians or Hungarians blamed for profiteering and shortages. But military allegiance was the defining issue in 1918 as volunteers (Czechs, Poles, Slovaks, even Croats) fought with the Allies while units from the same countries in the imperial army disintegrated as the dynastic bond dissolved.[40]

Of course, the most radical "nationalization" of a multi-ethnic society at war was that launched by the Committee Union and Progress in 1915–16 with the genocide of the Ottoman Armenians, who were accused of supporting the Russians and thus of being "the enemy within."

Remobilization or Revolution

By 1917 opposition to how the war was fought and organized, and criticism of its aims, compounded a general weariness. Even in Britain and France, the self-mobilization of the beginning no longer sufficed. Consequently, states strove to remobilize support in the quest for Clemenceau's "final quarter of an hour." The outcome turned on military events and on living conditions in the countries concerned, both of which favored the Western powers, though Germany's defeat did not seem inevitable until the summer of 1918 – and not even then for German civilians. But public opinion mattered more, not less, in the last half of the war.

This might seem surprising. Coercion had always been used by the wartime state and it might logically have expanded in the face of multiple challenges to the war effort. But, paradoxically, an erosion of state legitimacy made it harder to use force while a renewal of legitimacy meant that a measure of endorsement had been secured, thus reducing the need to do so. Hence Bethmann Hollweg eased press censorship in early 1917 in order to facilitate the discussion of war aims and Karl I allowed nationalist opinion greater expression in the Dual Monarchy in the same period. The March Revolution triggered an explosion of freedom in Russia. In Britain and France, where the state remained unshaken, the targeting of antiwar opinion was selective, with Clemenceau in power declining to use the crackdown he had earlier threatened.[41] Also, the scale of executions in response to the 1917 mutinies (less than 50) was far below that of 1914–15. Perhaps in a modern state, truly harsh repression requires a dictatorship rooted in popular legitimacy. Certainly there was no equivalent of the social protest of 1917–18 in World War II, nor any parallel for the state repression by Soviet Russia or Nazi Germany in World War I.

Persuasion was only the more important. In Britain and France, the state discreetly backed the social and political elites as they sought to remobilize support for the war from the spring of 1917. In France this took the form of an umbrella body, the Union des Grandes Associations contre la Propagande Ennemie (UGACPE), which was launched in March 1917 with a "national oath" at the Sorbonne. Under its aegis numerous patriotic organizations reminded the French of the justice of their cause and the importance of victory. The state primary-school teachers played an important role in disseminating these messages. The British equivalent was the National War Aims Committee. Like the UGACPE, it was inaugurated with a public rededication to the war on August 4, 1917 at Queen's Hall, London and, like the PRC earlier in the war, it used the constituency organizations of the Liberal and Conservative Parties to reach a mass audience. Measuring the impact of this effort independently of the amelioration of living conditions (notably by rationing) and the dawn of victory from July 1918 is impossible. Yet there is little doubt that opinion more broadly was remobilized behind the war in the two countries in 1918.[42]

Elsewhere, the same impulse had contrary results. The German army's introduction of "patriotic instruction" for the troops in 1917–18 forbade any mention of constitutional reform or limited war aims (both anathema to the Supreme Command), thus removing the chance to relaunch the war with a new national compact.[43] The same measure introduced by the Austro-Hungarian army was not allowed to address the nationalities question.[44] Deep discord precluded political remobilization (or in the case of the Dual Monarchy channeled it into the breakaway nationalist movements), and in each case supplied the agenda of the revolutions that accompanied defeat. In Russia, the Provisional Government sought to remobilize the nation by a democratic war effort. Kerensky saw himself as a new Danton and imagined that the March Revolution would unleash the martial energy of the people. In fact, profound weariness and socialist opposition to the war, conveyed by the countervailing power of the Soviets, demobilized Russian opinion – to the benefit of Lenin and a further, very different revolution.

Italy was an intermediary case. While radical and democratic interventionists had wanted the war to complete the Risorgimento, the government of Salandra (and its successors) sought to use the conflict to restore social authority and curtail democracy. They were supported by General Cadorna, the commander in chief, and by the fact that the army (like those of Eastern Europe) was in part composed of peasant conscripts with little sense of the nation. However, the reversal of Caporetto in October 1917 turned what many Italians had seen as an opportunistic war of expansion into a struggle to defend the national territory, which, in the Veneto, now lay under Austro-German occupation. While this did not produce total unity, it sufficed to galvanize a more truly national effort, including political education in the army and the civilian population and a moderation of military discipline. This transformed the basis of postwar politics (see chapter 31).

***

These attempts to remobilize nations and empires meant that in the second half of the war the focus of state propaganda was no longer neutral countries, which had less importance once Italy and the United States entered the fray, but rather domestic opinion (civilian and military) and also the enemy. The Western Allies, in particular, targeted German troops by underlining the virtues of democracy and the discrepancy between living standards on the two sides, and also sought to woo the soldiers of the minority nationalities in the Austro-Hungarian armies.[45] The language of Wilsonian democracy and national self-determination helped recast the Allied effort as a liberal crusade, while the Bolsheviks, as they left the war, launched an ideological offensive against the "imperialism" of those that continued it. Despite the disparate opposition to the conflict, or perhaps because of it, the war had become not only a struggle over nationality and the balance of power but also a battle of ideologies.

Notes

1 Habermas, *Structural Transformation*.
2 Renouvin, *Forms of War Government*, pp. 11–14.
3 Becker, *1914*, pp. 259–363; Verhey, *Spirit of 1914*, pp. 72–114; Gregory, *Last Great War*, pp. 9–39.
4 Haupt, *Socialism and the Great War*, pp. 216–49.
5 Horne, "'Propagande' et 'Vérité'".
6 E.g., Michael Sanders and Philip Taylor, *British Propaganda during the First World War*, London, Macmillan; Gary Messinger, *British Propaganda and the State in the First World War*, Manchester, Manchester University Press, 1992.
7 John Horne, "Introduction," to Horne (ed.), *State, Society and Mobilization*, pp. 1–18 (for self-mobilization); Audoin-Rouzeau and Becker, *Understanding the Great War*, pp. 102–3 (for war cultures).
8 The debate has been especially sharp in France; cf. Frédéric Rousseau, *La Guerre censurée. Une histoire des combattants européens de 14–18*, Paris, Seuil, 1999, pp. 307–10.
9 Horne and Kramer, *German Atrocities*, pp. 175–225; Troy Paddock (ed.), *A Call to Arms*, for the press in different countries at the start of the war.
10 Sir Edward Cook, *The Press in Wartime*, London, Macmillan, 1920 (by the former director of the Press Bureau); Claude Bellanger et al. (eds.), *Histoire générale de la presse française*, vol. 3, *De 1870 à 1940*, Paris Presses Universitaires de France, 1972, pp. 412–20.
11 Jean-Baptiste Duroselle, *Clemenceau*, Paris, Fayard, 1988, pp. 587–9; Steven Koss, *The Rise and Fall of the Political Press in Britain*, Vol. 2, *The Twentieth Century*, London, Hamilton, 1984, pp. 238–47.
12 Koszyk, *Deusche Presse*, pp. 68–83.
13 Horne and Kramer, *German Atrocities*, pp. 229–61.
14 Jahn, *Patriotic Culture*, pp. 40–1, 155–7, 165.
15 Stibbe, *German Anglophobia*.
16 Ridel, *Les Embusqués*.
17 Wrigley, "Labour in Britain 1917–20," in Wrigley (ed.), *Challenges of Labour*, p. 265.
18 Peter Holquist, "'Information is the Alpha and Omega of our Work': Bolshevik Surveillance in its Pan-European Context," *Journal of Modern History*, 69/3, 1997, pp. 415–50 (esp. 422–4).
19 Bouloc, *Profiteurs*, Robert, "Image of the Profiteer."
20 Horne, "'L'Impôt du sang'."
21 Leopold Haimson, "General Introduction," in Haimson and Sapelli (eds.), *Strikes, Social Conflict and the First World War*, pp. 17–18.
22 Erez Manela, *The Wilsonian Moment: Self-Determination and the International Origins of Anticolonial Nationalism*, Oxford, Oxford University Press, 2007.
23 Mathilde Dubesset, Françoise Thébaud, and Cathérine Vincent, "The Female Munition Workers of the Seine," in Fridenson (ed.), *French Home Front*, pp. 183–218.
24 Barbara Engel, "Not by Bread Alone: Subsistence Riots in Russia during World War I," *Journal of Modern History*, 69/4, 1997, pp. 696–721; Daniel, *The War from Within*, pp. 244–50; Giovanna Procacci, "La Protesta delle donne delle campagne," in Procacci, *Dalla Rassegnzione alla rivolta*, pp. 207–50.

25 Karen Offen, *European Feminisms, 1700–1950*, Stanford, Stanford University Press, 2000, pp. 257–61 (here p. 261).

26 Hinton, *First Shop Stewards' Movement* (Britain); Robert, *Les Ouvriers, la patrie et la révolution* (France); Kocka, *Facing Total War* (Germany); Mandel, *Petrograd Workers*; and Paolo Spriano, *Storia di Torino operaio et socialista*, Turin, Einaudi, 1958, pp. 318–480.

27 Horne, *Labour at War*, for Britain and France; Carl Schorske, *German Social Democracy, 1905–1917. The Development of the Great Schism*, Cambridge, MA, Harvard University Press, 1955; new ed., 1983, pp. 285–330.

28 Leon Trotsky, "The Zimmerwald Manifesto," in Isaac Deutscher (ed.), *The Age of Permanent Revolution: A Trotsky Anthology*, New York, Dell, 1964, pp. 80–3.

29 Kirby, *War, Peace and Revolution*, pp. 155–6.

30 Rosa Luxemburg, "The Russian Revolution," 1918, trans. from German in Bertram Wolfe (ed.), *Leninism or Marxism? The Russian Revolution*, Ann Arbor, Ann Arbor Paperbacks for the Study of Communism and Marxism, 1961.

31 Anderson, *Imagined Communities*, pp. 9–12.

32 Alan Kramer, "'*Wackes*' at War: Alsace-Lorraine and the Failure of German National Mobilization, 1914–1918," in Horne (ed.), *State, Society and Mobilization*, pp. 105–21 (116–20).

33 Ziemann, *War Experiences*, pp. 142–3.

34 Becker, *Great War and the French People*, pp. 217–35.

35 Chickering, *Imperial Germany*, pp. 160–7.

36 Roshwald, *Ethnic Nationalism*, p. 74.

37 Rachamimov, *POWs and the Great War*, pp. 39–42.

38 Lohr, *Nationalizing the Russian Empire*; Peter Gatrell, *A Whole Empire Walking: Refugees in Russia during World War I*, Bloomington, Indiana University Press, 1984, pp. 49–72.

39 Lewis Siegelbaum, *The Politics of Industrial Mobilization in Russia, 1914–17. A Study of the War Industries Committee*, London, Macmillan, 1984.

40 Cornwall, "Disintegration and Defeat. The Austro-Hungarian Revolution," in Cornwall (ed.), *Last Years of Austria-Hungary*, pp. 167–96.

41 John Horne, "Remobilizing for 'Total War': France and Britain, 1917–1918," in Horne (ed.), *State, Society and Mobilization*, pp. 195–211.

42 Cabanes, *Victoire endeuillée*, pp. 23–95.

43 Wilhelm Deist, "The German Army, the Authoritarian Nation-State and Total War," in Horne (ed.), *State, Society and Mobilization*, pp. 160–72 (171).

44 Mark Cornwall, "Morale and Patriotism in the Austro-Hungarian Army, 1914–1918," in Horne (ed.), *State, Society and Mobilization*, pp. 173–91 (184–8).

45 Cornwall, *Undermining of Austria-Hungary*.

References and Further Reading

Anderson, Benedict, *Imagined Communities: Reflections on the Origins and Spread of Nationalism*, 1983; new ed., London, Verso, 1991.

Audoin-Rouzeau, Stéphane, and Becker, Annette, *1914–1918: Understanding the Great War*, 2000; trans. from French, London, Profile Books, 2002.

Becker, Jean-Jacques, *1914: Comment les Français sont entrés dans la guerre*, Paris, Editions de la Fondation Nationale des Sciences Politiques, 1977.

Becker, Jean-Jacques, *The Great War and the French People, 1980*; trans. from French, Leamington Spa, Berg, 1986.

Bouloc, François, *Les Profiteurs de guerre*, Brussels, Editions Complexe, 2008.

Chickering, Roger, *Imperial Germany and the Great War 1914–1918*, Cambridge, Cambridge University Press, 1998.

Cornwall, Mark, *The Undermining of Austria-Hungary: The Battle for Hearts and Minds*, London, Macmillan, 2000.

Cornwall, Mark (ed.), *The Last Years of Austria-Hungary. A Multi-National Experiment in Early Twentieth Century Europe*, Exeter, University of Exeter Press, 2002.

Daniel, Ute, *The War from Within. German Working Class Women in the First World War*, 1989; trans. from German, Oxford, Berg, 1997.

Fridenson, Patrick (ed.), *The French Home Front, 1914–1918*, 1989; 2nd ed., trans. from French, Oxford, Berg, 1992.

Gregory, Adrian, *The Last Great War. British Society and the First World War*, Cambridge, Cambridge University Press, 2008.

Habermas, Jürgen, *The Structural Transformation of the Public Sphere: An Inquiry into a Category of Bourgeois Society*, 1962; trans. from German, Cambridge, MA, MIT Press, 1989.

Haimson, Leopold, and Sapelli, Giulio (eds.), *Strikes, Social Conflict and the First World War*, Milan, Feltrinelli, 1992.

Haupt, Georges, *Socialism and the Great War: The Collapse of the Second International*, Oxford, Clarendon Press, 1972.

Hinton, James, *The First Shop Stewards' Movement*, London, Allen and Unwin, 1973.

Horne, John, "'L'Impôt du sang': Republican Rhetoric and Industrial Warfare in France, 1914–1918," *Social History*, 14/2, 1989, pp. 201–23.

Horne, John, *Labour at War: France and Britain, 1914–1918*, Oxford, Clarendon Press, 1991.

Horne, John (ed.), *State, Society and Mobilization in Europe during the First World War*, Cambridge, Cambridge University Press, 1997.

Horne, John, "Labor and Labor Movements in World War I," in Jay Winter, Geoffrey Parker, and Mary Habeck (eds.), *The Great War and the Twentieth Century*, New Haven, Yale University Press, 2000, pp. 187–227.

Horne, John, "'Propagande' et 'vérité' dans la Grande Guerre," in Prochasson and Rasmussen (eds.), *Vrai et Faux dans la Grande Guerre*, pp. 76–95.

Horne, John, and Kramer, Alan, *German Atrocities 1914. A History of Denial*, New Haven, Yale University Press, 2001.

Jahn, Hubertus, *Patriotic Culture in Russia during World War I*, Ithaca, Cornell University Press, 1995.

Kirby, David, *War, Peace and Revolution: International Socialism at the Crossroads, 1914–1918*, London, Gower, 1986.

Kocka, Jürgen, *Facing Total War: German Society, 1914–1918*, 1973; trans. from German, Leamington Spa, Berg, 1984.

Koszyk, Kurt, *Deutsche Pressepolitik im Ersten Weltkrieg*, Düsseldorf, Droste, 1968.

Lasswell, Harold, *Propaganda Technique in World War I*, 1927; new ed., Cambridge, MA, MIT Press, 1971.

Lohr, Eric, *Nationalizing the Russian Empire: The Campaign Against Enemy Aliens during World War I*, Cambridge, MA, Harvard University Press, 2003.

Mandel, David, *The Petrograd Workers and the Fall of the Old Regime*, London, Macmillan, 1983.

Paddock, Troy (ed.), *A Call to Arms. Propaganda, Public Opinion, and Newspapers in the Great War*, Westport, CT and London, Praeger, 2004.

Prochasson, Christophe, and Rasmussen, Anne (eds.), *Vrai et faux dans la Grande Guerre*, Paris, Editions la Découverte, 2004.

Rachamimov, Alon, *The POWs and the Great War. Captivity on the Eastern Front*, Oxford, Berg, 2002.

Renouvin, Pierre, *The Forms of War Government in France*, New Haven, Yale University Press, 1927.

Ridel, Charles, *Les Embusqués*, Paris, Colin, 2007.

Robert, Jean-Louis, *Les Ouvriers, la patrie et la revolution: Paris, 1914–1919*, Besançon, Annales Littéraires de l'Université de Besançon, no. 592, 1995.

Robert, Jean-Louis, "The Image of the Profiteer," in Jay Winter and Jean-Louis Robert (eds.), *Capital Cities at War. London, Paris, Berlin 1914–1919*, Cambridge, Cambridge University Press, 1997, pp. 104–32.

Roshwald, Aviel, *Ethnic Nationalism and the Fall of Empires: Central Europe, Russia and the Middle East, 1914–1923*, London, Routledge, 2001.

Stibbe, Matthew, *German Anglophobia and the Great War, 1914–1918*, Cambridge, Cambridge University Press, 2001.

Verhey, Jeffrey, *The Spirit of 1914: Militarism, Myth and Mobilization in Germany*, Cambridge, Cambridge University Press, 2000.

Wildman, Allan, *The End of the Russian Imperial Army*, Vol. 1, *The Old Army and the Soldiers' Revolt (March–April 1917)*, Princeton, Princeton University Press, 1980.

Wrigley, Chris (ed.), *Challenges of Labour. Central and Western Europe 1917–1920*, London, Routledge, 1993.

Ziemann, Benjamin, *War Experiences in Rural Germany 1914–1923*, 1997; trans. from German, Oxford, Berg, 2007.

CHAPTER TWENTY

Military Medicine

SOPHIE DELAPORTE
(translated by John Horne)

World War I had a paradoxical impact on the bodies and minds of the men who fought in it. As has already been noted (chapter 17), the time-honored link between war and disease was broken in Western Europe thanks to advances in public health (inoculation, sanitation) in the half-century before the war. These advances benefited the vast armies that took to the field and prevented the epidemics that had often devastated previous military campaigns, the exception being the flu pandemic of 1918. The same was less true in Eastern Europe, where contagious diseases such as cholera, typhoid fever, and typhus continued to ravage soldiers and civilians, and was even less so in Africa and the Middle East. On the other hand, industrialized warfare resulted in a high incidence of death and wounds in the concentrated conditions of combat on the western and Italian fronts. While it is impossible to say what proportion of the total nine or ten million military dead of the war succumbed to combat as opposed to noncombat-related disease, it was much higher than in earlier conflicts. The "brutalization" that the historian George Mosse saw as a legacy of the war was direct and physical as far as the soldiers' bodies were concerned.[1]

One consequence of this paradox was a rapid evolution of military medicine. As with other aspects of the conflict, much work remains to be done on the situation in other theaters before broader conclusions can be drawn, and for that reason this chapter will focus on the armies of the western front, taking the French army as the principal example. In this theater, the unprecedented casualties during the war of movement in 1914 caused chaos in the systems of evacuation and hospitalization for wounded men. Not the least important part of the medical revolution wrought by the war in the French and other armies was the emergence of a complex system for the care of the wounded, extending from battlefield triage and field hospitals behind the lines to centers of specialization and convalescence in the interior. Military nursing also grew as never before. However, in what follows the focus will be less on the infrastructure of the medical services than on how military doctors dealt with the impact of trauma, both physical and psychological, on the combatants.

The scale of the challenge was immense. Projectiles ruptured protective barriers such as the peritoneum, which lines the abdominal cavity, the mater dura, or outermost protective layer around the brain and spinal cord, and the pleura, a thin covering of the lungs. Limbs were crushed and faces destroyed. Psychological damage was unprecedented. Never had bodies been annihilated, mutilated, and made ill on such a scale. In the French case alone, some 2.8 million soldiers were wounded. Half of all men who took part in combat were wounded twice and a further 300,000 were wounded three or four times. Seven million war invalids left a visible trace of the conflict in Europe for a long time, 350,000 of them totally incapacitated.

The war called into question some of the dominant principles of medical care and challenged medicine in basic ways. The resultant conflicts over both theory and practice will be examined in three key fields. The first is that of stomach wounds, which, along with head and chest wounds, show particularly clearly the move from abstinence from surgery to intervention. The second area is that of wounds to the limbs. Together with facial wounds these demonstrate the converse move from intervention (amputation in the case of limbs) to conservation, a tendency crystallized by the debate over the radical procedure known as "guillotine" amputation. The third field is that of the treatment of soldiers who suffered psychological trauma.

Surgical Intervention: Stomach Wounds

In the case of the French army, our knowledge of medical practices and attitudes during the war comes largely from the publications of the Société de chirurgie (Society of Surgery).[2] Here, the views of frontline doctors, who were usually young and had been thrown into battle without preparation or experience, came up against those of more senior doctors on the home front, who only saw the war at a distance but who had the major say in the surgical procedures to be used.

During the early months of the war, the tendency to abstain from intervening in stomach wounds accorded with the principles laid down by the most eminent surgeons of the Société de chirurgie. These principles were set out in a speech by Edmond Delorme on August 10, 1914 giving his "Advice to Surgeons" on wounds to the abdomen, advice whose value and authority were recognized by the entire scientific community. For Delorme, "immediate laparotomies (or incisions through the cavity wall of the abdomen) must be rejected."[3] The essence of the text was repeated in a circular addressed to military surgeons at the front in October 1914, thus reinforcing the principle that operations on stomach wounds should be avoided. This orthodoxy was taught in the Army Medical Service's schools and confirmed more generally by military medicine in the early part of the war. Its predominance is explained by the poor outcome of stomach operations under military conditions in earlier wars.

Would the new war confirm this "failure" of surgery? While the surgeons who first wrote on the subject reflected the prevailing orthodoxy, they denounced the consequences of abstention in some cases. But members of the Société de chirurgie were hesitant to endorse requests from the front for a more actively interventionist approach. They, like many others, found it hard to grasp the change in the nature of combat and its effects on the human body, and anyway they lacked precise reports on surgery at the front. Nonetheless, an interventionist fringe reacted with incomprehension to the prevalent wait-and-see attitude toward stomach operations, especially when the latter had become the norm in peacetime conditions.

A turning point came in June 1915 when a leading authority, Edouard Quénu, made a comprehensive report on the treatment of stomach wounds to the Société de chirurgie. Quénu recognized that the nature of battle now made it vital to conduct laparotomies as soon as feasible, while the stabilization of the front and the reorganization and improvement of the Service de Santé (Military Medical Service) also made this more possible. In four reports from June 1915 to January 1916, Quénu succeeded in reorienting the debate on doctrine. The flow of detailed notes and observations from surgeons at the front to the members of the Society also put the latter in closer touch with actual conditions there and reduced the distance between those determining policy at home and those enacting it behind the lines.

Quénu had initially shown restraint in the discussion, but in June he broke with a caution that had been due partly to inadequate information and launched into a "hymn to laparotomy."[4] He sought nothing less than to convert medical opinion as a whole to the new practice in order to win over the surgeons at the front. After a detailed elaboration of the observations by those working in combat conditions, Quénu provided a meticulous analysis. Both the increase in favorable reports on operations as well as the rise in the number of laparotomies performed suggested that circumstances had forced military surgeons to change their minds. The rapid standardization of the new procedure shows how effectively professional information was diffused at the front, a process in which the Society was helped by a variety of medical reviews, especially in *La Presse médicale* and *Lyon chirurgical*.

Quénu, however, was not an unreserved interventionist, for he also sought to fix limits to operations, limits that were imposed by the nature of battle on the western front. In his view, early evacuation was the precondition for successful intervention, showing that the success of operations was dependent on the conditions in which they were carried out. Early evacuation, how it was carried out, and bottlenecks of the wounded in field hospitals were all factors that impinged on the practice of laparotomy. The conditions in which the patient could be treated outweighed the kind of wound and its seriousness in the decision on whether to operate. Two sorts of situation emerged, depending on whether the front was quiet or convulsed by offensives and counteroffensives. For the stabilization of the front gave surgeons the chance to carry out operations close to the lines, whereas intense fighting made it much harder to create the conditions necessary for rapid laparotomies.

The Army Medical Service responded at an organizational level by specialization. It tried to deal with the problem of bottlenecks by organizing mobile units for stomach wounds and, in emergency cases, by the use of triage and dedicated surgical units in order to reduce the number of stomach wounds that were left untreated. Trench warfare also allowed specialized units to work close to the front, thus countering the principal argument of the abstentionists that adequate facilities could only be made available in the rear or the interior. Casualty clearing stations, where the wounded were assessed and categorized, worked alongside mobile surgical units, allowing rapid surgical intervention.

The practice of laparotomy was thus inextricably bound up with the conditions that determined whether an operation could take place – speedy evacuation, transport of the wounded, and the congestion or otherwise of field hospitals in the forward areas. Surgeons, for their part, understood the critical importance of the environment in which they worked, and it was often on the personal initiative of surgeons performing stomach and abdominal wounds that overcrowding in hospitals at the front was reduced. Other experienced surgeons endorsed Quénu's beliefs, and those who favored refraining from laparotomies found themselves an isolated minority. Nonetheless, if the evidence supported the interventionists, the results remained very uneven owing to the highly variable conditions in which the surgery was carried out. On average, from the end of 1914 to mid-1916, there was 70 percent mortality in stomach operations, a level that came down to between 50 and 60 percent in the last two years of the war. Despite these figures, the Société de chirurgie decided in May 1916 to adopt the principle of surgical intervention in the case of stomach wounds, thus overturning the official doctrine of abstention and ending the debate that had raged since the start of the war. But the new doctrine depended on the provision of the material and organizational resources that were essential if such lengthy and complex operations were to stand a chance of success in combat conditions. Wartime practice thus came into line with that which had prevailed in peacetime surgery since the end of the nineteenth century, and despite a high death rate, operating on stomach wounds remained standard procedure in the wars of the twentieth century.

However, medical discourse had nothing to say about the long-term consequences of such wounds, on whether, for example, the victims would use internal prostheses for the intestine or an artificial rectum. Here the historian encounters the silence of the sources. Little is known about the later lives of those who came through their operations, their pain, and the nature of their handicaps. The survivors of stomach and intestinal wounds in World War I apparently remained silent for the rest of their lives.

Surgical Intervention: Amputations

The seminal event as far as the treatment of arm and leg wounds are concerned occurred when a report from the front by two military doctors, Victor Pauchet (1869–1936) and Alain Sourdat, was read out to the Société de chirurgie on November 18, 1914. The report, entitled "L'Amputation en saucisson" (literally, amputation like a sliced sausage), was quickly published, and triggered a major debate down to the end of 1915 not just on how to treat wounded limbs but also on surgical practice on the battlefield.[5] The same issues arose in other armies, the procedure being known by the British and Americans as the "guillotine amputation." In the French case the debate struck the august Société de chirurgie like a thunderbolt and prompted reactions of a rare violence. It was, if anything, an even sharper example than that of stomach wounds of the gap between how the war had been imagined by medics beforehand, and was still imagined at home, and how it was experienced at the front.

Guillotine amputations called into question the classic practices of amputation in wartime and in particular the principle of conservation that had been enunciated at the outset to the conflict. When Pauchet and Sourdat's paper was read out to the Société de chirurgie, it was the first text written on the question by doctors at the front.[6] Whereas the question of stomach wounds above all concerned the conditions of surgery, that of amputations was a matter of techniques. The very term "like a sliced sausage" immediately caused a stir, notwithstanding the inverted commas. In their first publication the authors made no attempt to justify it, any more than they sought to indicate the optimal timing of intervention or the necessary medical organization of the front. Their paper seemed disconnected from the nature of the war, and the significance of the latter only emerged in a new paper written in 1915.

On this occasion, the authors related their observations to the fighting that took place from the retreat from Belgium in August to the battle of the Marne in early September and which saw some of the worst casualty levels of the war (chapters 4 and 12). A new technique such at that advocated by Pauchet and Sourdat was presented to the Society explicitly as a contribution to wartime medicine. But the implicit aim was to emphasize its general applicability and win professional endorsement so as to secure its legitimacy at the front. In order to do this, Pauchet and Sourdat described their procedure in terms of an apparent polarity between amputating and conserving a limb, the latter being more in line with the advice given by the military medical authorities at the beginning of the war, and argued that their method represented both a break with prevailing practice and a continuation of it. They described the operation as consisting of "sectioning" the affected member straight across, of "cutting [it] as with a cleaver below the affected site so as to be able to use the fragments of flesh." If they talked of preferring to "scrape away the bone" and of "drawing back" the member that was to be amputated, this was clearly because they wanted to conserve the flesh, rather than leaving a protruding stump. The absence of extensive stitching was supposed to promote a rapid healing of the wound. The required surgical movements were seen as "simple" and "short," even if they needed patience on the part of the person performing them. Pauchet insisted that the "knife should steadily follow the line of the existing wound" and "patiently detach the splinters of bone stuck to the usable skin tissue."[7] According to the authors themselves, the procedure was akin to cooks preparing meat.

Pauchet and Sourdat insisted on the speed, safety, and above all the economy of their procedure. But they also pointed out that it did not constitute a "definitive method but rather an emergency method," requiring a second intervention. It was an "amputation in two phases" which, after the first and most radical intervention in which the limb was severed, would need "tidying up." The express intent of the authors was to respond to the extreme overcrowding of field hospitals during the first weeks of the war – of whose conditions and consequent changes in practice the home front still seemed to be largely ignorant.

The members of the Society were not long in reacting. At an extraordinary meeting on December 9, 1914, following a communication on amputations *en saucisson*, their indignation knew no bounds. In this it reflected medical opinion more generally. Those who spoke expressed the views of surgeons who worked in hospitals far from the front but who had seen some of the amputees who had undergone the new procedure and who had been able to study its consequences: "I absolutely condemn the use of the so-called procedure 'en saucisson'"; "profound stupefaction on the part of the doctors treating these patients," who had seen stumps from which "the bone was protruding by between 7 and 10 centimeters." One member proclaimed that the "amputation 'en saucisson' has put us back a hundred years, to the time when limbs were amputated with an instrument in the form of a pruning knife," another that the method "appears brutal, anti-surgical, and monstrous," and yet another stating: "I find it difficult to grasp the need for the procedure of amputations 'en saucisson.'" The operation was even likened to the mutilation practiced by Indo-Chinese pirates on captured French colonial soldiers. In short, the technique was seen as barbarous and the term itself was unanimously rejected.

In condemning the "defective results" of guillotine amputations, the Society adhered to strictly medical criteria. The main charge related to the stump, which was said to be left in a very poor state, although it was the basis for applying a prosthesis and thus for reintegrating the amputee into civilian life. There was also the question of nerve irritation provoked by the amputation, a long-recognized phenomenon. Here the surgeons showed that they were familiar with the publications of Weir Mitchell on American Civil War amputees. In this sense, amputees were a well-established category in military medicine, with a rich literature, unlike most types of invalids from World War I.

The surgeons contested each of the advantages described by Pauchet and Sourdat, and notably the supposedly more "economical" and "certain" character of their procedure. They equally objected to the supposed rapidity with which it could be carried out, which the two military surgeons had claimed as a particular advantage. Members of the Society turned to well-established operations such as the classic procedure associated with Celse and Desault, which had proved themselves in former wars as well as in civil surgery.

The Society thus considered the break with established practice to be a deliberate provocation and found unanimously that guillotine amputations had no justification. Nor was it content just to object to the relevance and value of the procedure, for it also sought to ensure that the latter did not gain currency at the front. The standing of the Society within the medical community as a whole emerged clearly at the end of the debate when its criticisms led the Ministry of War (which was responsible for the Service de Santé) to order a "surgical inquiry" into the work of the two men and, in a highly unusual step for wartime, to forbid Pauchet to perform guillotine amputations.

The controversy – over the frightening name, the method used, and the consequences observed – in effect turned the Société de chirurgie into the wartime watchdog of safe medical practice on behalf of the combatants. The fact that neither Pauchet nor Sourdat could present their communication in person doubtless widened the gulf of incomprehension between established practitioners on the home front and those at the fighting front whose task it was to perform emergency surgery. The whole affair also shows the power of the medical establishment when it came to determining practice on the western front.

The sequel to the debate occurred in April 1915 and was marked by a change in tone. Surgeons at the front had reported in communications to the Society that they saw guillotine amputations as a minimalist approach and one that was much less traumatic for patients than the classical procedures. Victor Pauchet confronted his opponents when he addressed the Société de chirurgie in person.[8] From the outset he claimed that the controversy had been caused by a "misunderstanding" that arose from the fact that his and Sourdat's initial communication had not been made orally to the Society but rather by "a hasty and short report that was read out to you." He emphasized that the members of the Society were simply not familiar with the "conditions [under which] his field hospital had operated during the initial phase of the campaign." Above all he sought to explain the circumstances that had led him to privilege this type of amputation. As with the issue of stomach and abdominal wounds, Pauchet tried to bridge the gap between the "reality" of the battlefield and the difficulty of those at home in imagining it. He also provided the details that had been lacking in his November report when he described the experience of his medical unit as it retreated from Montmédy in the Meuse to Sainte-Menehould in the Marne before and during the battle in early September. His tale, like that of many eyewitness accounts by army doctors, struggled to describe the experience accurately, and especially the carnage and chaos of the first post-combat surgery in August and September 1914.

In the first part of his speech, Pauchet insisted on the sheer intensity of operating in such conditions. He described the rhythm of "work" in his unit as "formidable" and in trying to convey some idea of it he cited statistics for the period of September 7, 1914 to February 7, 1915. In those five months his field hospital had cared for 9,670 wounded soldiers, of whom 1,590 had undergone an operation, including 170 trepanations (operations on the skull) and 203 amputations. Of the latter, 31 (15 percent) had died – 8 percent for those affected in their arms, 22 percent for those who lost lower limbs. These figures indicate the intensity of military surgery on the western front in the first phase of the war and there is no reason to suppose it was different in the British or German armies. Yet Pauchet's figures also even out the spikes that were noted in the opening weeks of the conflict, and especially during the battle of the Marne. Amputations were the most important category of operation, with a relatively low mortality. However, a preliminary triage had already been carried out by stretcher-bearers on the battlefield and a further selection had been made by the medics in the casualty clearing stations. Pauchet's field hospital thus received wounded men who had already passed through a double filter.

Pauchet noted that the conditions of battle necessitated rapid evacuation of the wounded to unknown destinations. Along with overcrowded medical facilities, this meant that follow-up treatment by the frontline surgeon was impossible. There was, in addition, the constant fear of the enemy, a factor undreamed of by medics on the home front. As for the nature of the procedure, Pauchet underlined the fact that the surgeons had to "work" without any home "comforts," and that this was just as true for the patients, whose skin he described as "covered in a crust composed of filth, earth, blood, and excrement: this crust was extremely septic and had to be removed with a cloth soaked in liquid petroleum before iodine could be applied." It was only when the Service de Santé set up a new field hospital in Pauchet's sector on the Marne that conditions improved to the point where they bore some comparison with those behind the lines. But this was only as the front stabilized in November 1914.

In the last part of his speech, Pauchet sought to answer objections and defend his procedure. One by one he defended the points made in his initial report, reinforcing his position rather than making any concessions. If home-front medical opinion had restricted the use of guillotine amputations, Pauchet argued that what had been designated an exceptional method was precisely a response to the "exceptionally serious and difficult" conditions of modern warfare. In the end, the only concession he made (but it was not unimportant) was to give up the term that he had initially coined – "like a sliced sausage" – which he referred to as a "sin of youth." He recounted:

> Twenty years ago, when I was an intern, a railway employee came to see me bleeding and in a state of shock with a crushed foot. I sawed it off at the point where the flesh was still healthy; several days later, I trimmed the bone ... and the patient made a very good recovery. One of my comrades, who was present at the operation, cried: "You cut that like a sausage." The word stayed with me and I served it up to you.

At the end of a long address, guillotine amputations seemed to have won the approval of the majority of the Society's members, who went so far as to acknowledge their economic and conservative virtues. Once more, the reality of the war imposed an intellectual and professional reorientation on those at home when faced with the need for new methods imposed by experience at the front, methods which they had initially criticized – the more so because, in this case, they had only seen patients at one remove, after they had already undergone an amputation in the improvised circumstances of the front. This was true elsewhere, besides France, and field amputations increasingly used the guillotine method.

As the war progressed, there was no major debate in France on whether conservation was preferable to intervention, as happened with the change of doctrine over abdominal wounds. Rather there was a steady movement in the direction of conservation that was determined by military factors, just as the original case for guillotine amputations had been. The need for amputations was, of course, not eliminated. But the stability of the front, medical units operating close to the lines and thus able to combat infection (notably from gas gangrene) and give first aid in the most urgent cases, and also the development of splints for fractured limbs were among the factors that reduced the need for amputation. Conservation was simply a practice that became more widespread because conditions allowed it.

Psychological Trauma

The main pathology encountered by psychiatry during World War I arose from the impact of explosive shells and mines on the human organism. The British term "shellshock" conveyed the phenomenon graphically. The French had no real equivalent for the English term but used a variety of expressions in an effort to capture the traumas provoked by explosions – amongst others, "cerebral commotion," "cerebral congestion," "nervous accidents," "medullary commotion," "emotional shock," *obusite* ("shellitis"), "commotional shock," or even the "psychic lame." For the most part, however, French psychiatrists agreed on the term *commotion*.

The variety of appellations adopted by French psychiatrists was also a function of the spectrum of psychic injuries provoked by explosions, which included physical wounds to the central nervous system, with a consequent reduction of functions, as well as neuroses and psychoses that had no visible wounds but which impaired physical as well as psychological functions. The essential point is that shell explosions could suddenly produce a variety of neurological and psychic troubles despite the absence of any apparent physical wound.

Here, too, the French case shows how differently these traumas could be classified and interpreted. There were strictly mental disturbances, such as confusion, "confusional accidents," "hysterical psychosis," "emotive psychosis," "obnubilation" (clouding over), "depression," "amnesia," and "delirium." But explosions also caused various "nervous disturbances" that affected hearing (deafness or semi-deafness), sight (blindness), speech (mutism, stammering) and motor control – with trembling, "astasia-abasia" (the inability to stand or walk normally), "paraplegia," "paralyses," and different sorts of convulsion. In Britain and the English-speaking world more generally, "shellshock" initially referred to all these posttraumatic conditions. The term appeared for the first time in 1915 in relation to the symptom produced by the explosion of a large shell whether or not there was a visible wound, and medical literature of the period devoted much space to the subject. However, the experience gained by the British army in the first three years of the war resulted in a more "mature" range of diagnosis that distinguished between the different conditions that had unfortunately been lumped together as "shellshock." The term had gained a wide popular currency that it has never entirely lost, and was blamed for spreading false and dangerous ideas among the troops. But its use in medical circles was proscribed.[9]

The level of mental and nervous disturbance noted among combatants made it essential to organize facilities for the treatment of individual cases. As in other fields of medicine and surgery, this process was characterized by a lack of preparation and foresight, despite the experience of past conflicts. Individual doctors took the initiative in improvising centers of "neuropsychiatry" in the war zone and neurological or psychiatric centers in the interior. It should be noted, however, that in contrast to other medical disciplines, psychiatry and neurology benefited from the presence of specialists on the home and fighting fronts, which helps explain the speed with which such centers were set up.

In the French case, doctors organized military neuro-psychiatric units several kilometers behind the front that allowed for the earliest possible treatment of the affected soldier after diagnosis. The first results from these units encouraged the Army Medical Service to extend the experiment. One of the purposes of the units at the front was to avoid the hasty and often unwarranted evacuation of the traumatized soldiers that had occurred in the early months of the war. But they were also part of the broader reorganization of combat medicine according to the principles of diagnosis, triage, treatment at the front, and eventual evacuation to more specialized facilities in the interior. The centers at the front enjoyed the approval of the medical world, which agreed on their therapeutic value. In particular they were held to be a "barrage" erected against the hasty evacuation of patients, which was often seen as a failure from the point of view of therapy. Specialist centers also made their appearance in the French interior. Although they were, for the most part, set up in the big mental hospitals of the main towns and cities, they were run separately. However, the task appeared harder here than at the front. The posttraumatic condition was usually more advanced and the results seemed to favor the earliest possible intervention.

From the outset, doctors understood the desirability of treating victims of psychic and neurological conditions virtually immediately. They attached great importance to the "setting" in which this kind of patient was treated, which meant keeping the soldier in the "atmosphere" of combat. Firmer military discipline than in the interior, the proximity of the front, and the remoteness of the family were all felt to contribute to successful treatment. The link with the "primary group" remained stronger. Psychiatrists also considered mental disturbances to be relatively benign, which helps explain the fairly short periods of hospitalization in the army's neuro-psychiatric centers, lasting on average two to three weeks. According to the statistics, 34 percent of patients returned directly to the front, while the rest benefited from a period of convalescence, were sent back to the regimental depots, or went on leave. "Curability" seemed directly related both to how quickly the malady was treated after diagnosis and to the setting in which this occurred.

In many ways, therefore, military psychiatry treated trauma to the mind in much the same way that it did trauma to the body. The sooner treatment began, the quicker the patient recovered, whereas once complications set in, the therapy required became more arduous. In Italy, according to a study by Bruna Bianchi, the level of return to active service decreased as the war went on.

> Whereas in 1915–16 60 percent of soldiers who had been hospitalized in the forward services of the Third Army returned to the front, in 1917 the percentage was no more than 40 percent. Those who were transferred from the forward services of the First Army to psychiatric hospitals rose from 8.3 percent in 1916 to 21 percent in 1917. Seventy per cent of soldiers who left the psychiatric hospital of Vicenza (First Army) returned to the front in 1916, against 52 percent in 1917 and 21 percent in 1918. In the psychiatric hospitals of Treviso and Padua, which served the Second and Fourth Armies, only 20 percent of patients were hospitalized for more than three months at the beginning of the war compared to 50 percent in 1917.[10]

In one British case, concerning a hospital in Renfrewshire, of 500 cases presenting between January 1916 and January 1917, 31 percent "returned to duty," 22 percent were sent to stay with "their friends," and 27 percent were "sent to asylums."[11]

In the interior, doctors found that the difficulties increased significantly and recovery was slower for those who had been disturbed for some time. The evacuation of the "shellshocked" patient marked a break with his military setting to which he would have to readapt after his recovery. As one specialist wrote:

> In evacuating the patient to the interior, contact [with the front] is broken and the capacity to adapt is suppressed. Once cured, the patient will have to readjust to life in the trenches. One can well imagine that such a readaptation, which would be hard for many, might seem impossible notably to the emotionally disturbed whose pathological imagination will obsessively go over the tragic spectacles of the war while getting them out of all proportion, make him relive past anguish, and project onto the future the terrors that he has already gone through. In the light of this it is easy to understand the advantages of maintaining disturbed men at the front.[12]

Overall, however, there was considerable uniformity in the therapeutic practices in the case of traumatized soldiers whether these were administered at the front or in the interior. Nor was there a marked difference in the content of the treatments depending on the nature of the trauma. So, for example, there was widespread use of hydrotherapy (dubbed *balnéothérapie* or *balnéation* by the French). Psychiatrists believed that this type of treatment calmed excitement and anxiety, which was often acute after trauma. Its sedative quality was particularly applicable to the mentally disturbed but was relevant for most convalescing patients. But with the use of the cold douche, hydrotherapy could also become a means of coercion. Sleep and rest appeared to be essential and beneficial since most combat soldiers suffered acute fatigue, even if this might appear simplistic as a form of therapy. Rest seemed above all the most humane and least medical treatment.

Medical opinion also considered the diet of the mentally disturbed patient to be a matter of some significance, and one of the elements that favored a return to "normality," or at least to the state of mind that had preceded the trauma. If the loss of appetite was a symptom of the condition, it might be that the recovery of a normal diet could become both a form of treatment and the sign of a return to normality more generally. Gymnastics were a means of rehabilitating mentally disturbed soldiers by reconnecting them with their own bodies. A number of experiments were conducted in this regard, and gymnastics occupied an important place in psychotherapy. In particular, it aimed in the simplest possible way to reestablish particular functions that the trauma had partially blocked. In effect, the same approach was taken as with physiotherapy for the reeducation of soldiers with amputated limbs.

Other therapies used in the case of soldiers with nervous or mental conditions included hypnosis, which was especially widespread in treatment centers in the interior. Also called "reeducation by suggestion," the doctor tried to help the patient recover his lost faculties by inducing a deep sleep. Chloroform was equally used for therapeutic purposes, the idea being that anaesthetizing a patient excited his faculties and helped the return of speech or hearing. In fact, it seemed to many doctors that those afflicted by deafness only recovered the use of one ear, with the restoration of hearing taking far longer in the other.

There were also coercive therapies. Electricity had been used to treat mentally traumatized patients since the end of the nineteenth century and was in no sense a wartime innovation. It was brutal in its effects and often deliberately so, being delivered with a certain theatricality because it worked by persuasion as much as coercion. This was particularly the case with the method known as *torpillage* (from the *torpille*, or electric eel), used by an influential psychiatrist, Clovis Vincent, who ran a neurological center for the army at Tours. Vincent administered a sharp galvanic current (100 to 120 milliamps) to the patient's body so that the latter would distinguish between the physical reality of pain and his traumatized state of mind. The level of pain was hard to bear and the fear of its renewed application undoubtedly played a part in the procedure. Doctors favoring the coercive approach all used one form or another of electro-shock treatment in order to "provoke" or "trigger" a reaction that would alter the patient's state of mind.

It remains difficult to measure the suffering endured by the patients who underwent this type of treatment, the more so since the doctors themselves were divided over its impact. It is no less difficult to judge the results obtained. Few failures were reported and those doctors using the method declared themselves very satisfied with it. As we have seen, the procedures used to treat soldiers afflicted with psychic or neurological traumas during World War I did not display any real breakthroughs. For the most part they were "classic" measures in widespread use before the war that underwent no major modification or innovation during the conflict. The impact of the war is more evident in the growing conviction by the end of 1914 that it was vital to treat the mentally disturbed as early as possible rather than in the nature of the treatments that they underwent.

***

In all, World War I helped modify medical practice by a continuous exchange between the front and the interior, and especially between doctors and surgeons at the front, who were thrown into combat on an unprecedented scale and had to deal with a new range of wounds or at least a new balance between them, and those medics who remained at home, far removed from the violence of battle and the wounds it caused, but who held the professional power to decide which therapies would be applied. Changes in practice and doctrine came about because those at the front succeeded in breaking the imagined war of those in the rear in order to secure the professional endorsement of the latter for new orthodoxies. It also turned on the readiness of the greatly expanded military medical services to incorporate the new or modified approaches into what became a vast medical effort involving services at the front and throughout the nation.

Notes

1 George Mosse, *Fallen Soldiers: Reshaping the Memory of the World War*, Oxford, Oxford University Press, 1990, pp. 159–81.

2 In 1935 the Société de chirurgie (Society of Surgery) reassumed its title of Académie de chirurgie (Academy of Surgery). Its principal goal was to keep its members abreast of the latest developments in surgery and to debate the issues that arose from them. It also proclaimed itself the guarantor of medical ethics. It was composed of titular or honorary members, associates, and foreign members.

3 Edmond Delorme, "Conseils aux chirurgiens," *La Presse médicale*, August 1914, p. 599.

4 Jules Abadie, *Les Blessures de l'abdomen*, Paris, Masson, 1916.

5 *Bulletins et Mémoires de la Société de Chirurgie*, November 24, 1914.

6 The sessions of the Société de chirurgie were interrupted by the looming war on July 29, 1914 and only resumed on October 14, 1914.

7 Victor Pauchet and Alain Sourdat, "L'Amputation en saucisson" and accompanying debate, *Bulletins et Mémoires de la Société de Chirurgie*, November 1914, pp. 1216–19.

8   Victor Pauchet and Alain Sourdat, "L'Amputation en saucisson" and accompanying debate, *Bulletins et Mémoires de la Société de Chirurgie*, April 1915, pp. 861–76.

9   Lerner, "Historiographie de la psychiatrie de guerre," pp. 217–30.

10 Bianchi, "La Psychiatrie italienne et la guerre," *Vingtième siècle*, 41, March 1994, pp. 74–85.

11 R. D. Hotchkis, "Renfrew District Asylum as War Hospital for Mental Invalids; Some Contrasts in Administration; with an Analysis of Cases admitted during the First Year," *Journal of Mental Science*, 1917, pp. 243–9.

12 Gilbert Ballet and Joseph Rogues de Fursac, "Les psychoses commotionnelles," *Paris médical*, 1916, p. 2.

Further Reading

Bianchi, Bruna, "La Psychiatrie italienne et la guerre," *Vingtième siècle*, 41, March 1994, pp. 74–85.

Bianchi, Bruna, *La Follia e la fuga: nevrosi di guerra, diserzione e disobbedienza nell'esercito italiano (1915–1918)*, Rome, Bulzoni, 2001.

"Le Choc traumatique et l'histoire culturelle de la Grande Guerre" (ed. Jay Winter), *14–18 Aujourd'hui–Today–Heute*, 3, 2000 (theme issue).

Delaporte, Sophie, *Les Médecins dans la Grande Guerre*, Paris, Bayard, 2003.

Delaporte, Sophie, *Gueules cassées de la Grande Guerre*, Paris, Editions Agnès Vienot, 2004.

Leese, Peter, *Shell Shock: Traumatic Neurosis and the British Soldiers of the First World War*, Basingstoke, Palgrave Macmillan, 2002.

Lerner, Paul, *Hysterical Men. War, Psychiatry and the Politics of Trauma in Germany, 1890–1930*, Ithaca, NY, Cornell University Press, 2003.

Lerner, Paul, and Micale, Mark (eds.), *Traumatic Pasts: History, Psychiatry and Trauma in the Modern Age, 1870–1930*, Cambridge, Cambridge University Press, 2001 (esp. part 4, on World War I).

"Shell Shock and the Cultural History of the Great War" (ed. Jay Winter), *Journal of Contemporary History*, 35(1), January 2000 (theme issue, with a significant but not complete overlap of articles with the special issue of *14–18 Aujourd'hui*, above).

Ulrich, Bernd, " '… als wenn nichts geschehen wäre.' Anmerkung zur Behandlung der Kriegsopfer während des Ersten Weltkriegs," in Gerhard Hirschfeld, Gerd Krumeich, and Irina Renz (eds.), *Keiner fühlt sich hier mehr als Mensch … Erlebnis und Wirkung des Ersten Weltkriegs*, Essen, Klartext, 1993, pp. 115–29.

van Bergen, Leo, *Before My Helpless Sight: Suffering, Dying and Military Medicine on the Western Front, 1914–1918*, Farnham, Ashgate, 2009.

Weindling, Paul, *Epidemics and Genocide in Eastern Europe 1890–1945*, Oxford, Oxford University Press, 2000.

Whitehead, Ian, *Doctors in the Great War*, London, Leo Cooper, 1999.

CHAPTER TWENTY-ONE

Science and Technology

ANNE RASMUSSEN
(translated by Heather Jones)

World War I is often depicted as a war of machines in which technology and science played a pivotal role and humans were turned into helpless, impotent puppets confronted with the artillery's "storm of steel," chlorine gas clouds, and explosive poison-gas shells. The French mathematician Paul Painlevé stated in November 1915 that the war was "a battle of science and machines," while in December 1917, an advocate for the opposing German scientific camp, the Berlin academic Emil Fischer, one of the first winners of the Nobel prize for chemistry, declared that, "in short, modern warfare is in every respect so horrifying, that sensible people can only regret that it draws its means from the progress of the sciences."[1]

Until recently, historians emphasized the subordination of science and technology to the needs of the war effort. They focused upon the strategic role science and technology played in the outcome of the conflict and the impact of new inventions developed for use on the battlefield. However, more recently the emphasis has shifted. The production of pure scientific knowledge and its applications is no longer the only valid subject of research and the history of science has expanded to incorporate scientific activity in its broadest sense. It looks at how science governs action; how it allows humans to influence the physical and social world around them; how it engenders norms and ideals; and how it promotes particular discourses and authoritative positions. Seen from this perspective, the range of ways that science was involved in the war appears as diverse as the many new forms of technology that the conflict produced.

Engineers and Scientists at War

By the end of the long war it was evident that the technical environment, which included tanks, planes, submarines, high explosives, and gas, was very different to that which had existed at the outset.[2] New armaments had a major effect on operational practices on the battlefield: artillery killed at long range, inaugurating the anonymous death that would typify twentieth-century conflicts. Better communication systems meant that for the first time commanders could operate at a considerable distance from their soldiers – and this was even truer of naval communications. Science and technology also became important in other ways. Naval warfare and resultant food shortages made it essential to replace previously imported raw materials with synthetic substitutes. There was also a strong sense shared by all the belligerents that their investment in science and technology really mattered. The Allies, for example, believed that since the late nineteenth century they had fallen behind in the scientific field, especially chemistry, while Germany had developed the capacity to industrially organize its scientific output. This heightened the importance the Allies placed upon science. In Italy, where, since unification, scientific development had depended upon foreign assistance, the slogan *Fare come in Germania* (Do as in Germany) became the mantra that expressed a new faith in science, illustrating how it was seen as the driving force behind production and national emancipation during the war. It was clear that technology shaped the nature of combat – and the "sciences" were directly associated with this process, according to a linear interpretation that connected the basic sciences and the laboratory to the engineer and operational practices on the battlefield. The war thus seemed to mark a moment of major scientific change.

In fact, while World War I did produce real technological changes, it did not result in any scientific revolution. As Lloyd George concluded, it was basically an "engineer's war." In this regard, the two world wars differed dramatically. During World War I, the use of science on the battlefield was part of a longer tradition of "the science of warfare" – chemistry, physics, mechanics – that had been the task of army engineers for centuries. During World War II, by contrast, major scientific breakthroughs occurred, such as the atomic bomb, the development of radar technology, and the invention of short-range rockets. These stemmed from radically new forms of knowledge that gave rise to previously unknown weapons and ways of fighting.

The major changes during World War I related above all to how science and technology were organized. It rapidly became clear that to win the war a country would have to master industrial mass production, a task that required scientists as well as engineers. World War I thus came to be perceived in the popular imagination as a "chemists' war," a description linked to the totally unprecedented scale on which explosives were needed during the conflict – causing the majority of deaths recorded in all theaters of operations. The phrase also referred to the massive demand for synthetic products, particularly nitrates, which were used to make fertilizers and explosives. Germany had pioneered this process following Haber's discovery of nitrogen fixation, developed using the Haber–Bosch procedure of 1908. Overall, however, the strategic effects of gas warfare were minimal. In military terms, the use of toxic gases as a weapon did not produce the decisive breakthrough and a return to mobile combat that would end the deadlock of the trenches. Yet during the two final years of the war the use of gas intensified. This occurred in conjunction with the development of ever more toxic emissions, as well as better means of transmission and dissemination of poison gases, a task carried out by the artillery during this period. Overall, 4.6 percent of shells fired in the war were chemical shells, a figure that rose to 15 percent in the final 11 months. Due to their devastating psychological effect, these shells became a weapon in the war of attrition, rather than a weapon that marked a significant technological breakthrough. However, they were part of the process of totalization that the warfare of attrition unleashed, aimed at the annihilation of the enemy.[3] According to this interpretation, the technical changes that occurred before the war and during the conflict were not decisive in bringing about victory. Their potential was not fully exploited because the military system was unable to adapt to such innovations and because production levels were too low. Thus the outcome of the war was largely determined by weapons that were already in use at the outbreak of the conflict.

However, new forms of interdisciplinary collaboration emerged between engineers and scientists, which enabled engineers to respond more effectively to the demands of modern warfare. This is illustrated by the sheer number of different disciplines that were involved in any one military domain. For example, to identify enemy artillery emplacements a wide variety of types of science, not normally associated with each other, were required. Trigonometry was used to determine the location points of enemy guns and to construct extremely detailed maps. This task involved mathematics, geography, geodesy, cartography, meteorology, astronomy, and aerial photography, as well as optics or even telegraphy. Scientists whose peacetime research had been purely theoretical now had to overcome the gap between theory and practice to apply their work to the war effort. A group in France organized by Pierre Weiss and Aimé Cotton, which included mathematicians such as Emile Borel and Jacques Hadamard, focused upon just this problem. They combined laboratory work with experiments at the front and their work proved particularly fruitful in 1915. University teaching also experienced this shift away from theory to a focus upon the practical applications of science and technology. The emphasis on applied science produced advanced techniques for submarine detection, targeting fire, aeronautical instrumentation, optics in range finders (telemeters) and gun sights, aerial photography, and wireless radio transmission. As a result, a whole culture of precision developed which had to be applied to the alien environment of the battlefield, rather than the usual controlled peacetime world of the laboratory.[4] This is why historians of science, such as Daniel Kevles, accord such particular importance to the strategic development of the submarine which made the conflict also a "physicists' war" because of the new practical research required.

Mobilizing Science and Technology

As hopes for a short war faded, it became clear in scientific circles that science would be crucial for national defense. Mobilizing scientific resources became vitally important. "When Syracuse was under siege, Archimedes applied the rigorous rules of geometry in order to construct giant catapults: what kind of scientist can remain deaf to the call of his country when it is in danger?," Painlevé stated, nurturing a mythology of scientific patriotism that also drew upon the *levée en masse* of the French revolutionaries in 1793.[5] Closely involved in the development of military aviation, Painlevé blurred the boundaries between scientific and political mobilization, becoming Minister for Education in November 1915, and, later, Minister for War in March 1917, before finally being appointed head of government. In this way, the perception grew that nations not only used armies in modern warfare but also "fought above all through the minds of their elites. Victory would show that intellectual superiority and scientific prowess were every bit as crucial, perhaps even more so, than material superiority."[6] Success depended upon achieving the correct balance between effectively using scientific personnel and organizing production to cater for the needs of a total war – which was increasingly seen as a "scientific and industrial" conflict.

There was a widespread debate as to how best to mobilize scientists. Scientists wanted their skills to be used appropriately, requesting that they be mobilized in a way that took their abilities into account, such as assignment to state research institutions. Marie Curie and Jean Perrin told the physicist Paul Langevin: "You could be of greater service than a thousand sergeants ... despite the great esteem that we have for this honorable rank."[7]

The press echoed this public debate; notably, *The Times*, in which H. G. Wells wrote accusingly in June 1915: "we are to this day being conservative, imitative and amateurish when victory can fall only to the most vigorous employment of the best scientific knowledge."[8] For scientists on both sides scientific talent was being wantonly wasted fighting at the front. This came to be symbolized by the death in the Dardanelles at age 28 of the young Oxford physicist, Harry Moseley, the discoverer of atomic numbers. Given the existing shortage of scientists, it appeared inconceivable that a group, whose skills were so important to the national interest, should be sacrificed on the battlefield. Despite military resistance, the different armies gradually made special arrangements for scientists: for example, from the beginning of 1918 the American War Department reassigned scientists from the infantry to military or civil technical bureaus.

During the war, adequately mobilizing scientific personnel was not the only problem: integrating scientists into the military system also gave rise to difficulties. Scientists, such as the psychologist Henri Piéron, highlighted the caution of the general staffs and their failure to exploit the new intellectual resources available to them. He frequently condemned them for their "noble principle of failing to use skills which have always formed the basis of our military organization."[9] For example, he deplored the fact that the French army did not use psycho-physiology, which had advanced greatly in America, where it was used to examine recruits and to assess their aptitudes, particularly in the air force. Piéron's complaints echoed those of the professional scientific community in general, for whom the misuse of scientific knowledge and expertise by the military authorities and conservative politicians had become a discursive leitmotif. For scientists, the military and politicians were unable to incorporate civilian skills into their existing operating structures, partly because they were unwilling to make the necessary strategic and intellectual effort this entailed, and partly because they were reluctant to use science to develop wartime military and industrial innovation.

Thus a contemporary cultural discourse that was highly critical of the military's attitude toward science emerged in academic circles during the war and until recently, the vast majority of historians of science generally accepted it. Yet thanks to the work of David Edgerton, there is now a much more nuanced understanding of the situation during the war. As Edgerton shows, there was actually considerable military funding for scientific research before the war: then this funding went on to surpass civilian investment.[10] In Great Britain, for example, "service departments" were developed before 1914, in conjunction with the Admiralty, the War Office, and, from 1918, the Air Ministry. Investment was provided by "special supply ministries" which were created during the conflict, particularly the Ministry of Munitions. These agencies financed research in their own laboratories, as well as in private companies involved in military production. They formed the basis for the direct involvement of scientists in military research. Employed on temporary contracts, these scientists provided advice regarding the development of new weapons or operational research. In other cases, they worked for large research laboratories attached to universities, financed by military institutions – this was the norm in America in particular where, in 1916, the eminent astronomer, George Ellery Hale, succeeded in establishing the National Research Council (NRC) after convincing President Wilson of the need for "national preparedness" based upon promoting essential research. This was seen as crucial if the United States was to overcome German military and industrial competition. The NRC, a private, elitist organization, was the principal agent for scientific engagement with the military, following Hale's belief that "war should mean research."[11] The war encouraged collaboration between government, military, and university institutions – a collaboration that would go on to characterize the twentieth century.

Given the premium placed upon innovation during the conflict, the role of the inventor became particularly important. Innovation was also necessary at an institutional level. Lloyd George repeatedly stated that the war required the permanent adaptation of defensive and offensive armed systems. To this end, new institutional and material facilities were created, to carry out purely military research. The British Admiralty established a Board of Invention and Research in July 1915, directed by the most eminent scientists in the country such as J. J. Thomson, W. H. Bragg, Charles Parsons, and E. Rutherford. However, as Roy Macleod has shown, tensions developed inside the Royal Navy between the military and this scientific group. The experiment came to an end in September 1917. The most significant British institution was the Department of Scientific and Industrial Research which dated from December 1916; it worked in conjunction with its equivalents in Australia, Canada, and New Zealand.[12] The armaments' administration also exercised direct authority over a certain number of laboratories such as Imperial College, London, Birmingham, and Cambridge.

These institutional structures for promoting innovation involved professionals from the technical and engineering corps. The system also incorporated a whole range of small-scale inventors involved in creating new defensive technologies, showing that scientific mobilization was not limited to leading scientific figures but that a form of technical democracy also emerged. In France, the onus was placed upon the state, which responded by establishing institutions to promote inventions that would assist national defense. Organizations that had existed before the war were reorganized more effectively: a *Direction des inventions* was established at the Ministry for Education, and later, attached to the Ministry of Munitions under Albert Thomas. Its task was to examine and coordinate propositions put forward by inventors and to reply to research requests made by the Naval and War Ministries. Thus the scientists appointed by Painlevé (five members of the Institute, nine university professors and ten civil engineers), under Emile Borel's technical leadership, gained influence particularly as they had access to the resources of the military such as armament facilities and the technical corps. In Italy, Vito Volterra and Giuseppe Belluzzo established state bodies, some of which carried out general research such as *l'Ufficio di invenzioni e ricerche*, and others that focused upon specific specializations, such as the *Laboratorio di ottica e meccanica di precisione*. The emerging aeronautical industry was one sector that received considerable institutional support: in 1918 in Japan, for example, the government founded the Aeronautics Research Institute which was placed under the aegis of the University of Tokyo.[13] In America, the military hoped that a dual system that combined engineers and scientists would develop new weaponry. This system was partly based upon national agencies, such as the National Advisory Committee for Aeronautics, which were supported by the leading "statesmen of science," the most militant of whom were the academics Robert A. Millikan and Georges Ellery Hale. It also relied upon initiatives taken by civilian inventors and industrial firms such as the Sperry Gyroscope Company, belonging to the inventor Elmer Sperry, which developed devices for stabilizing ships that were tested at naval experimental facilities. In order to emphasize the crucial importance of innovation, the US Secretary of the Navy recruited the American national hero of invention, Thomas Edison, to the war effort, shortly after the torpedoing of the *Lusitania* in 1915. Edison was given the task of bringing together "practical men who are accustomed to doing things, and not talking about it," rather than those who were experts in theoretical research. The men selected were to form a Naval Consulting Board which would call upon "the natural inventive genius of Americans to meet the new conditions of warfare."[14] The Board received some 100,000 suggestions from the public, ranging from how to improve the daily life of soldiers, to procedures to deal with food-supply problems or protective measures to be taken in response to new weapons. However, few of these proposals had any real potential, leading to some strong criticism of inventors by scientists. There was a tension between the two groups: scientists had little respect for inventors, even believing sometimes that they were using the war to make profits. The wartime institutional landscape, with its new structures and organizations, was riven by competitive rivalries as well as conflicts with authority that divided civilian advisers from military technical units, and engineers from the culture of scientific research.[15]

Organization, Production, and Command

The idea that World War I marked the beginning of modern Western "technological-scientific systems" was a common illusion in contemporary discourse. However, it is important to be wary of such claims. In fact, Germany had pioneered this kind of systematic cooperation between science and technological development since the late nineteenth century. An imperial institute for physics, the *Physikalisch-Technische Reichanstalt*, was founded in 1887 which was intended to combine basic scientific research with the development of technology for industry. Over the following two decades, other major national laboratories, engaged in research and standardization, followed suit, such as the National Bureau of Standards in the United States, the national centre for experimental trials at the *Conservatoire national des arts et métiers* in France, and the National Physical Laboratory near London. In addition, Imperial Germany explicitly linked national economic growth with scientific development, establishing its own new structures to facilitate advances in research. This culminated with the establishment of the *Kaiser-Wilhelm Gesellschaft* in 1911 which financed the *Kaiser-Wilhelm* Institutes (KWI). These were partly autonomous institutions that specialized in the different natural sciences. Thus, in Germany, the framework for scientific and industrial cooperation was already in place before the war. This meant that during the conflict, German military, industry, and academia were able to effectively coordinate their efforts.

However, the new use of science and technology on the battlefield required new forms of organization that went beyond prewar developments: to work effectively outside the laboratory and university, wartime innovations had to be integrated into a system of production that delivered them from the conceptual blueprint to the battle zone. This was one of the fundamental changes that occurred during the conflict at an operational level: science, industry, and the military worked together to an unprecedented extent, within an integrated system that was managed through the complex wartime command system. Few European industries had implemented Taylorization in 1914; nevertheless, the ability to effectively organize mass production along scientific lines became a crucial aspect of efficient war production in all industrial sectors, not just in the manufacture of explosives and chemicals. In most of the specialist industries that increased in importance because of the conflict, such as optic glass, poison gas, machine guns, or airplanes, no manufacturer had mastered assembly-line production at the start of the war. Yet for much of the war (and in the Allied case, until the end), factories were able to meet the enormous needs of armies. For example, helium, needed for balloons and zeppelins which were used in bombing operations and naval reconnaissance, developed in America from a laboratory curiosity to a mass-produced war gas.

The boom in war production particularly affected those involved in manufacturing substitute products which were used to replace strategic resources that could no longer be imported, or which were prohibited owing to the hostilities. Before the war, Germany had supplied numerous chemical products and specialist instruments throughout Europe and worldwide. The market for these German goods even extended to Japan which, in return, had sent students to train in Germany. Certain countries, such as Russia, were so dependent on foreign manufacturing for some items that they had enormous problems adapting to "modern warfare" as they lacked indigenous substitutes, particularly the necessary components for producing munitions.

Great Britain also had to replace German-manufactured goods and it turned to its universities for assistance: for example, the chemists working at King's College London were employed to produce the national supply of optic glass. Britain also looked to universities in its dominions, such as McGill in Québec, where the science departments supervised the production of thousands of tons of acetone. It was also necessary to adapt the scientific and industrial network within Britain to deal with the war effort, which required multiple, different initiatives. The Board of Trade established the Chemical Products Supply Committee, headed by the Lord Chancellor, Haldane, "to consider and advise as to the best means of obtaining for the use of British industries sufficient supplies of chemical products, colours, dyestuffs of kinds hitherto largely imported from countries with which we are at present at war." This led to the foundation of the British Dyestuffs Corporation in December 1914, which was partly financed by the Treasury. A more ambitious program resulted in the creation of the Committee for the Promotion of Industrial and Scientific Research in August 1915. Led by the Fellows of the Royal Society, including Lord Rayleigh and the chemist, Raphaël Mendola, it was responsible for organizing scientific research and training for industry and responding to the immediate needs of the war effort.

The novel, systematized, complex role of chemistry during the war epitomizes the organization of wartime sciences into an integrated war effort – a process which was also dependent upon laboratory research.[16] In Germany, chemistry was structured on the basis of a bilateral scientific and industrial system of organization. At the beginning of 1915, the Minister for War had made the KWI in Berlin, which specialized in physical chemistry and electrochemistry, its official research centre and placed it in charge of research programs under the direction of Fritz Haber. Famous researchers such as Willstätter, Neuberg, Bickel, and Epstein joined the KWI, which had 1,500 employees and 10 research departments by the end of the war. It was mainly focused upon developing the Haber–Bosch procedure to allow for the production of nitric acid on a massive scale. In January 1916, Haber estimated that the production of synthetic saltpeter, which was unknown in Germany before the war, had reached 25 million tons per month. This, he claimed, had "made possible the conduct of the war in the last few months."[17] Particular KWI units specialized in chemical warfare, working closely with the chemical firm I. G. Farben: its laboratories at Leverkusen and the 3,000-plus researchers it employed by 1916 provided the German command with considerable resources for researching, producing, and developing toxic products. In contrast to the policy adopted by the Allies, the entire resources of the Ruhr chemical industry were adapted and redirected toward this mass production for the war effort. All the major firms in the German chemical industry participated in this program: Bayer, BASF (Badische Anilin-und-Soda

Fabrik), and Farbwerke Hoechst combined their efforts to manufacture chlorine, phosgene, and dichlorethylsulfide (mustard gas). Haber, who was given a military rank by the German high command, controlled this organization. The complete integration of military and scientific functions was clear when Haber personally supervised the first gas attacks in spring 1915 on the western and eastern fronts, wearing his military uniform.

In contrast, on the Allied side, there were numerous, complex governmental agencies. Production structures were split: the main division was between the chemical poison-gas program and the manufacture of shells, which was under different leadership. In France, research into chemical warfare was carried out by the *Laboratoire municipal de Paris* (Kling), the Sorbonne (Grignard), the *Ecole supérieure de pharmacie* (Lebeau), the *Faculté de médicine* (Degrez, Achard), and the *Collège de France* (Mayer). In addition to these teams of scientists, the worlds of medicine and pharmaceuticals also worked for the war effort, developing measures to protect soldiers, studying the physiological impact of gas on the body and therapeutic methods to help combatants. Responsible for the research and development of chemical weapons, the *Commission des études chimiques de guerre* predated the establishment of the *Direction du matériel chimique de guerre* in June 1915. The *Direction* had its own units which implemented its policies and it was completely dedicated to chemical warfare. It was attached to the *Sous-secrétariat d'Etat de l'Artillerie et des munitions* (the French Ministry of Munitions), because artillery shells became the main way of attacking enemy positions with gas following attempts to gas the enemy using indiscriminate chlorine gas clouds in 1915. If the entire organization was under the control of a military figure, Colonel Ozil, all of its departments also relied upon scientific expertise. Charles Moureu and Gabriel Bertrand from the biochemistry laboratory at the Institut Pasteur were among those scientists who assisted this institution. Moureu and Bertrand were the masterminds behind the chemical warfare research program while Grignard, Job, Lebeau, Maquenne, and Urbain, all leading chemistry academics, were in charge of its implementation. Sixteen laboratories in total were used for this work. Thirteen of these were reserved for research into aggressive substances, providing the theoretical basis for a system which planned, tested, and produced chemical-warfare materials that were then loaded into specially designed shells by officer-chemists attached to the Artillery General Staff.

In Great Britain, chemical warfare was based upon close collaboration between the army services and the Royal Society Chemistry Committee. At the Ministry of Munitions, which was set up on the orders of Lord Kitchener in 1915, the Chemical Sub-Committee was given charge of a research division made up of renowned chemists from the Royal Society, such as Crossley, Baker, Thorpe, and Bailey. The British system distinguished between those involved in the unit for researching offensive weapons, which was based at the Trench Warfare Department attached to the Ministry of Munitions, and those engaged in the defensive research organization, under the control of the War Office. As the war continued, a new department was created that centralized the whole British chemical warfare effort: the Chemical Warfare Department at the Ministry of Munitions.[18] For all the belligerent countries involved, the pressures of waging chemical warfare led to the establishment of integrated systems: the war's own totalizing logic necessitated greater coordination and centralization of services and functions.

The rationalization of production was the main consequence of the new involvement of science and technology in war. Other, less obvious changes were also important. These gave rise to new relationships between science and the military – such as long-term planning and collaborative structures – which would have great significance for later conflicts.

Paradoxically, it was the need to respond to the demands of a long war that meant that states had to rapidly adapt their research systems, making them more efficient and capable of producing immediate, concrete results. This marked a significant shift in the traditional time scale by which scientists worked. It encouraged the idea that science should develop new methods that would allow for long-term planning and management, as well as preparation for war. The permanent restructuring of administrative practices reveals this shift. Lloyd George's cabinet, as well as that of Albert Thomas, with its team of experts in the social sciences led by François Simiand, began to investigate what kinds of new state structures were needed, arguing that rationalization would encourage new ideas. At the same time, the first efforts were also made to make the most effective use of human resources. For example, psychology was used in the treatment of shell shock, in order to return traumatized soldiers to the battlefield as quickly as possible; psychological selection tests were also introduced for pilots which assessed a candidate's aptitude for the role. The American psychologist, Robert Yerkes from the NRC, who promoted such developments, emphasized that the use of "pure science" went beyond simply achieving victory; it would also result in a new world as suggested by the title of his 1920 book, *New World of Science*. For many such commentators, science had a mission to establish particular values, and in this way science was an integral part of the wartime discourse that portrayed the conflict as a battle for civilization.

Science and the Legitimization of the War

Once hostilities were declared, each side rapidly claimed that it had right on its side and was waging the conflict in accordance with the laws of war. Such ideological claims required the constant mobilization of cultural discourses to legitimize the enormous and rapidly evolving war effort in the eyes of civilian populations. In a war defined by propaganda battles over what was true or false, "science" played a crucial role: it was seen as objective, authoritative, and based upon academic knowledge and verifiable evidence.[19] Investigations into the causes of the war and who was responsible for it, as well as the collection of evidence for atrocities committed by troops, were all driven by the need to establish the "truth" about what had happened. Censorship and state propaganda were also considered justified in the interests of "truth." Given this context, science was rapidly recruited to support a multitude of "truth" claims.

Of all authority figures, those working within the experimental sciences played a particularly important role. As Max Planck, rector of the Berlin Academy, stated at the end of 1914: "One thing only we know, that we members of our university ... will stand together as one man and hold fast until – despite the slander of our enemies – the entire world comes to recognize the truth and German honour."[20] This may appear paradoxical: while experts in the social sciences were associated with ideology, traditionally scientific discourse was seen as neutral, focused on proof, immune to being swayed by external public opinion. German elite intellectuals, the *Gebildeten*, had also traditionally often avoided becoming involved in politics in order to retain a kind of public neutrality that they felt was the best way to fulfill their elite role of preserving certain values. In addition, wartime mobilization had assigned scientists to tasks directly connected to their professional skills to assist the war effort; in principle, no wider role was envisaged for them. However, scientists were no less susceptible than the rest of the population to wartime ideologies and for some, their practical engagement with the war also led to a propaganda role as they sought to explain the principles at stake in the conflict. For many "organic" scientists, particularly those who were too old to fight and whose sons were at the front, assisting the war effort through their writing was one way of overcoming the sense of guilt they felt at being part of a generation that was protected from the worst of the war's horrors.

During the first weeks of the war, one text above all others came to symbolize this kind of scientific role in propaganda: the "Appeal to the World of Culture," *An die Kulturwelt*, signed by 93 leading German intellectuals, including many scientists, which was published in October 1914 and translated into over ten languages. The fact that it became emblematic is somewhat misleading; it was neither the first, nor the most remarkable, of a long series of protest declarations by European intellectuals about the war.[21] However, the text of the "Appeal to the World of Culture," which refuted accusations that Germany was responsible for causing the war, as well as rejecting charges that Germany was to blame for the invasion of Belgium and the atrocities committed there, marked the moment when European intellectuals joined the war effort (see chapter 22). During the course of the following four years, it was used by Allied intellectuals to justify their own contribution to the war against Germany. The "Appeal" was seen as representing the collective views of "German science," perceived as a unitary bloc. In part this was due to the sheer range of diverse disciplines and points of view represented among its signatories, which included figures such as Paul Ehrlich, Emil Fischer, Ernst Haeckel, Walther Nernst, Wilhelm Ostwald, Wilhelm Röntgen, and Adolf von Beyer. The "Appeal" led to the fragmentation of a shared European intellectual sphere into separate national entities. In France, academic and intellectual groups published a response to the German "Appeal," lampooning its arguments; at the same time they withdrew membership from Germans. On October 21, 1914, some 150 British intellectuals signed a "reasoned statement," which was published in *The Times* where they pledged support for "a defensive war, fought for liberty and peace," and William Ramsay published inflammatory patriotic diatribes on behalf of the Royal Society.

From this point on, the intellectual reaction to the war was essentially a moral debate that invoked the name of science in order to denounce the enemy for crimes, savagery, and a quasi-anthropological moral inferiority. The term "educated barbarians" was used to describe those who were to blame for what was seen as calculated and systematic "civilized destruction." The era of what *The Times* described as the "professor-made war" had arrived.[22] For intellectuals in the Entente countries, the German "Appeal" signified that German science was subservient to the German military and state. This belief continued to influence relations after the war: their involvement in the "Appeal" remained a "stigma upon the intellectual and moral integrity of German scientists," according to the President of Columbia University, Nicholas M. Butler, while the *Académie des sciences* in France considered that German science had been "an enormous operation whereby a whole people worked together in patient servility to develop the most formidable killing machine that has ever existed." In the scientific world, the role of German scientists during the war was seen as an act of betrayal. Articles 228–230 of the Treaty of Versailles even allowed for the possible trial of scientists as war criminals.

Perhaps the most significant and long-lasting result of this discourse was the consolidation of the idea of "national science." The French mathematician Pierre Duhem, who was also a historian of science, had pioneered this concept at the turn of the century, claiming that science had a national character: French science was thus determined by different national traits than British science, for example. The war reactivated these stereotypes, creating a system of rigid binary oppositions that defined how German science was described: in a reference to German formalist tendencies, German science was seen as geometric in contrast to the spirit of finesse that characterized French science – *Scientia germanica ancilla scientiae gallicae*.[23] Numerous pamphlets, often written by renowned scientific figures, reinforced these stereotypes which were intended to discredit enemy science by depicting it as sterile or mere imitation or even plagiarism. Another approach was to rewrite national histories of scientific development, removing all reference to the enemy's contribution to scientific advances. Examples of this kind of literature included the *Oxford Pamphlets* published in 1914–15 and the 1916 German anthology *Deutschland und der Weltkrieg*, as well as the French book *Les Allemands et la science*, which contained contributions from 22 renowned French scientists.

At the other extreme, some scientists also opposed the war. However, such "dissidence" was rare; the "spirit of 1914" generally dominated in scientific circles. Only a small number of strong personalities declared their opposition to the conflict. In November 1914, along with nine other German intellectuals, Albert Einstein, at that time professor at the University of Berlin and Director of the *Kaiser Wilhelm Institut* for theoretical physics, established the *Bund Neues Vaterland*, a small group that sought democratic reforms. Einstein had refused to sign the "Appeal to the World of Culture," instead co-signing the counter-manifesto produced by the Berlin physiologist G. F. Nicolaï, the "Appeal to Europeans." The *Bund Neues Vaterland* tried to make contact with pacifists in neutral countries. In September 1915, Einstein also visited the French pacifist Romain Rolland in Switzerland, who a year earlier had published his famous appeal "*Au-dessus de la mêlée*" (see chapter 22). However, in 1916, the *Bund* was dissolved by the German government. For other scientists, continuing to pursue the kind of international collaboration between institutions that had developed since the late nineteenth century became a point of honor during the war. This particularly applied to scientists from neutral countries: one example was the Dutch scientist Hendrik Lorentz, a passionate internationalist who played an important liaison role between scientists who now found themselves on opposing sides in the conflict. Certain scientific disciplines also tried to maintain international links – those involved in research into radioactivity, for example, tried to preserve structural and personal contacts, as advocated by the British scientist Frederick Soddy.

It is also important to note that opinions shifted over the course of the war. As the nature of the conflict changed, a few leading German intellectuals among the 93 who had signed the "Appeal to the World of Culture" began to distance themselves from their initial patriotic fervor. At the start of 1916, Max Planck wrote an open letter, intended for physicists in Allied countries, in which he stated that he could no longer unconditionally support the German army: for Planck this letter was a means of unburdening himself of a heavy "mental scruple."[24] As John Horne has shown, the war experience was constantly changing throughout the conflict and was marked by different phases of cultural demobilization and remobilization. Such chronological shifts, as well as national and individual differences and the diverse nature of the various scientific disciplines, also influenced how scientists experienced the conflict: there was no one uniform scientific war.[25]

Epilogue: the War and Changes in Scientific Practices

During the immediate postwar period, the priority was to rebuild the network of international scientific collaboration that had existed before the war, which had imploded in August 1914. This reconstruction, however, took place along political lines. The former allies replaced the prewar *Association internationale des Académies*, with a new International Research Council (IRC) which had a policy of long-term ostracization of Germany. Although international science was theoretically a collaborative effort, the IRC prohibited scientists from the former Central Powers from taking part in international meetings. By barring Germans, Austrians, Hungarians, and Bulgarians in this way, the organizers of the IRC were acting in accordance with the articles of the Treaty of Versailles that had annulled all prewar agreements that had been made with Germany. They were also complying with the clauses regarding the control, regulation, and prohibition of certain scientific research activities in Germany. Thus the "cold war in science" supported the science of the victors over that of the defeated. However, national differences emerged in this regard, with some leading lights in the IRC encouraging French and Belgian scientists to refuse all interaction with the former Central Powers whereas others, such as the American George Ellery Hale or the British secretary of the Royal Society in London, Arthur Schuster, favored contacts with German scientists, believing they could not be held responsible for military and political events – a view that gained support throughout the 1920s.[26] In Germany itself, there was a long-running debate within the scientific community as to how the 93 signatories who put their name to the "Appeal to the World of Culture" could distance themselves from the declaration, as they were invited to do in 1919 by the Swedish physicist Arrhenius, who was at the center of the international system of Nobel prizes. Although Haber, Nernst, and Planck, as a sign of détente, were prepared to acknowledge an error of judgment, they would not go so far as to make a retraction. This contrasted with Einstein's position. Although the "spirit of Locarno" progressively eased tensions, the scientific world remained haunted by the shadow of the war. The issues at stake in the debate, however, changed. Science professionals often claimed that they wished to move on from the war, adopting the traditional internationalist rhetoric that science was about the universal sharing of knowledge. Yet at the same time, many also hoped for further public recognition of the new role and status that science had gained during the conflict in Western societies.

The war brought about major changes in scientific practices during the interwar period and it also had an ongoing impact upon scientific communities and the way that science was perceived. During the four years of conflict, a "scientific war culture" had subordinated scientific investigation to the logic of pursuing victory and participating in the clash between national scientific and technical systems. However, wartime science also operated within the existing parameters of the scientific sphere and was often seen by scientists as an opportunity to implement reforms which had first been suggested in the late nineteenth century. It also enabled the relationship between science and industry to be restructured, along the lines of the German prewar model which had so fascinated the Allies. This wartime restructuring had an ongoing impact. Several of the institutions established during the war were made permanent, such as the Department of Scientific and Industrial Research in Britain or the Chemical Warfare Service in the United States. Others survived by being incorporated into the peacetime restructuring of institutions that took place in the 1920s, while sometimes retaining their links with the military. This was particularly the case in France where the *Direction des inventions* was replaced by the *Office national des recherches scientifiques et industrielles et des inventions* in 1922. Perhaps the most significant legacy of the war, however, was to reinforce the idea of a national science in all countries. In Germany, a new organization, the *Notgemeinschaft der deutschen Wissenschaft*, was created by leading members of the Berlin Academy in 1920. Its aim was to rebuild the German scientific network to deal with what was seen as a national science crisis. In Italy, the mathematician Vito Volterra, the most internationally renowned Italian scientist of his generation, established the *Consiglio Nazionale delle Richerche* in 1919 under the aegis of his affiliation with the IRC. In the East, the Bolshevik revolution prolonged the war effort, leading Russian scientists to hope for greater state support than in the past.

The role that science played during the war was also used to enhance its status during the postwar period. From as early as 1916, the majority of scientific journals focused their attention upon how science would be reorganized after the anticipated victory. In many cases the wartime discourse encouraging mobilization for the nation gave way to a postwar discourse that emphasized mobilization for science. This campaign was able to raise significant financial support, despite the return to peace and financial retrenchment, with most of the funding coming from international philanthropic sources, such as the Rockefeller institution. However, state funding for research was also crucial: even countries with the most liberal economic cultures now recognized the importance of state intervention owing to the development during the war of an ideology of a "national science." The war had thus raised the status of scientists within society and had legitimized their role.

The end of the war also revealed that the image of science that emerged from the conflict was highly ambiguous. During the 1920s, the British scientist J. B. S. Haldane, one of the founders of the modern biology of evolution, defended the practice of chemical warfare in a number of publications aimed at the general public. Haldane, who had served in the war and been wounded twice, had experimented on chemical warfare agents. According to Haldane chemical warfare was no more reprehensible than heavy artillery fire. In the future, he argued, poison gas would be more strategically important than traditional weapons and its use was justified on "humanitarian grounds" because it temporarily incapacitated an individual and caused relatively few deaths.[27] Ultimately, many scientists believed, science would civilize war and only the rare commentator, such as the French historian, Jules Isaac, accused science of complicity in mass murder or "science homicide."

The general assumption was that scientists worked on the basis of a real intellectual autonomy which had not been particularly affected by the war. In this way, the conflict revived the old idealist discourse of a pure science dedicated to seeking the truth, independent of all external demands, existing within a neutral intellectual space. Yet such assertions of scientific independence did not stop a number of scientists from continuing the collaboration begun during the war by working with military agencies during the interwar period. The French physicist and militant socialist, Jean Perrin, writing in the early 1930s, saw nothing incongruous in praising the progressive virtues of science as the foundation of modern civilization and asserting that it was up to politicians to stop "human power that has been acquired beyond measure turning into a cause of ruin, war, and death."[28]

Notes

1 Johnson, *The Kaiser's Chemists*, p. 180.
2 Van Creveld, *Technology and War*; Hartcup, *The War of Invention*.
3 Lepick, *La Grande Guerre chimique* (p. 312 for the figures).
4 David Aubin and Patrice Bret, "Introduction," in *Le Sabre et l'éprouvette*, pp. 43–7.
5 Paul Painlevé, 1918, Discours à l'Academie des sciences, séance du 7 janvier, *Comptes rendus de l'Académie des sciences*, vol. 166, 1, p.17.

6   Albert Mathiez, *Revue de Paris*, December 1, 1917, pp. 542–65.

7   Bensaude-Vincent, *Langevin. Science et vigilance*, p. 86.

8   H. G. Wells, *The Times*, June 11, 1915.

9   Piéron, "Psychology in Relation to the War," p. 479.

10   Edgerton, "British Scientific Intellectuals," p. 3; Soubiran, "De l'utilisation contingente des scientifiques."

11   Kevles, *The Physicists*, p. 116; Kevles, "George Ellery Hale, The First World War…"; Schroeder-Gudehus, *Les Scientifiques et la paix*.

12   MacLeod and Andrews, "Scientific Advice in the War at Sea"; Pattison, "Scientists, Inventors and the Military in Britain."

13   On France see: Galvez-Behar, "Le Savant, l'inventeur et le politique"; Roussel, "L'Histoire d'une politique des inventions"; on Italy: Tomassini, "Le Origini"; on Japan: Bartholomew, *The Formation of Science in Japan*.

14   Kevles, *The Physicists*, p. 106.

15   Cf. Macleod and Andrews, "Scientific Advice in the War at Sea"; Pattison, "Scientists, Inventors and the Military in Britain"; Roussel, "L'Histoire d'une politique des inventions"; Soubiran, "De l'Utilisation contingente des scientifiques."

16   The following paragraph draws upon the information in Lepick, *La Grande Guerre chimique* and Johnson, *The Kaiser's Chemists*.

17   January 2, 1916 in Stern, *Einstein's German World*, p. 119.

18   MacLeod, "The Chemists go to War."

19   Rasmussen, "Mobiliser, remobiliser, démobiliser"; Prochasson and Rasmussen, *Au nom de la patrie*, pp. 203–20.

20   Heilbron, *The Dilemmas of an Upright Man*, p. 71.

21   Vom Brocke, "Wissenschaft und Militarismus"; Ungern-Sternberg, "*Der Aufruf, 'An die Kulturwelt!*'"

22   *Times*, January 5, 1915.

23   Duhem, *La Science allemande*, p. 143.

24   Heilbron, *The Dilemmas of an Upright Man*, p. 78.

25   John Horne, "Introduction," in Horne (ed.), *State, Society and Mobilization in Europe during the First World War*, Cambridge, Cambridge University Press, 1997, pp. 1–17; Rasmussen, "Mobiliser, remobiliser, démobiliser."

26   Schroeder-Gudehus, *Les Scientifiques et la paix*.

27   Haldane, *Callinicus: A Defence of Chemical Warfare*.

28   Aubin and Bret, "Introduction," in *Le Sabre et l'éprouvette*, pp. 43–7.

References and Further Reading

Bartholomew, James R., *The Formation of Science in Japan. Building a Research Tradition*, New Haven, London, Yale University Press, 1989.

Bensaude-Vincent, Bernadette, *Langevin. Science et vigilance*, Paris, Belin, 1987.

Crawford, Elisabeth, *Nationalism and Internationalism in science. 1880–1939. Four Studies of the Nobel Population*, Cambridge, Cambridge University Press, 1992.

Dahan, Amy, and Pestre, Dominique (eds.), *Les Sciences pour la guerre, 1940–1960*, Paris, Editions de l'Ecole des Hautes Etudes en Sciences Sociales, 2004.

Duhem, Pierre, *La Science allemande*, Paris, A. Hermann, 1915.

Edgerton, David, "Science and War," In R. C. Olby et al. (eds.), *Companion to the History of Modern Science*, London, Routledge, 1990, pp. 934–45.

Edgerton, David, "British Scientific Intellectuals and the Relations of Science, Technology and War," in Paul Forman and J. M. Sánchez-Ron (eds.), *National Military Establishments and the Advancement of Science and Technology. Studies in the 20th Century History*, Dordrecht, Kluwer Academic, 1996.

Galvez-Behar, Gabriel, "Le Savant, l'inventeur et le politique. Le rôle du sous-secrétariat d'Etat aux Inventions durant la Première Guerre mondiale," *Vingtième siècle. Revue d'histoire*, January–March 2005, pp. 103–17.

Haber, Ludwig F., *The Poisonous Cloud: Chemical Warfare in the First World War*, Oxford, Clarendon Press, 1986.

Haldane, John Burdon Sanderson, *Callinicus : A Defence of Chemical Warfare*, London, Kegan Paul, 1925.

Hartcup, Guy, *The War of Invention. Scientific Developments, 1914–18*, London, Brassey's, 1988.

Heilbron, John L., *The Dilemmas of an Upright Man: Max Planck as Spokesman for German Science*, Berkeley and London, University of California Press, 1986.

Isaac, Jules, *Paradoxe sur la science homicide*, 1922; new ed. in *Alliage*, 52, 2002, pp. 79–87.

Jessen, Ralph, and Vogel, Jakob (eds.), *Wissenschaft und Nation in der europäische Geschichte*, Frankfurt am Main and New York, Campus, 2002.

Johnson, Jeffrey Allan, *The Kaiser's Chemists. Science and Modernization in Imperial Germany*, Chapel Hill and London, University of North Carolina Press, 1990.

Kevles, Daniel J., "George Ellery Hale, the First World War, and the Advancement of Science in America," *Isis*, 59, 1968, pp. 427–37.

Kevles, Daniel J., *The Physicists: The History of a Scientific Community in Modern America*, New York, Knopf, 1978.

Krige, John, and Pestre, Dominique (eds.), *Science in the Twentieth Century*, Amsterdam, Harwood Academic, 1997.

Lepick, Olivier, *La Grande Guerre chimique 1914–1918*, Paris, Presses Universitaires de France, 1998.

MacLeod, Roy, and Andrews, Kay E., "Scientific Advice in the War at Sea, 1915–1917: The Board of Invention and Research," *Journal of Contemporary History*, 6/2, 1971, pp. 3–40.

Mommsen, Wolfgang J., "Wissenschaft, Krieg und die Berliner Akademie der Wissenschaften," in W. Fischer (ed.), *Die Preussische Akademie der Wissenschaften zu Berlin 1914–1945*, Berlin, Akademie Verlag, 2000, pp. 4–23.

Morrell, Jack, *Science at Oxford 1914–1939*, Oxford, Clarendon Press, 1997.

Painlevé, Paul, *De la Science à la défense nationale: discours et fragments*, Paris, Calmann-Lévy, 1931.

Pattison, Mark, "Scientists, Inventors and the Military in Britain, 1915–1919: the Munitions Inventions Department," *Social Studies of Science*, 12/4, 1983, pp. 521–68.

Piéron, Henri, "Psychology in Relation to the War," *L'Année psychologique*, 21, pp. 479–81.

Prochasson, Christophe, and Rasmussen, Anne, *Au nom de la patrie. Les intellectuels et la Première Guerre mondiale, 1910–1919*, Paris, La Découverte, 1996.

Prochasson, Christophe, and Rasmussen, Anne, *Vrai et faux dans la Grande Guerre*, Paris, La Découverte, 2004.

Rasmussen, Anne, "Mobiliser, remobiliser, démobiliser: les formes d'investissement scientifique en France dans la Grande Guerre," in Le Sabre et l'éprouvette: l'invention d'une science de guerre, 1914–1939," *14–18 Aujourd'hui–Today–Heute*, 6, Paris, Noêsis, 2003, pp. 49–59.

Roussel, Yves, "L'Histoire d'une politique des inventions 1887–1918," *Cahiers pour l'histoire du CNRS 1939–1989*, 3, 1989, pp. 19–57.

"Le Sabre et l'éprouvette. L'invention d'une science de guerre 1914–1939," *14–18 Aujourd'hui–Today–Heute*, 6, Paris, Noêsis, 2003.

Schroeder-Gudehus, Brigitte, *Les Scientifiques et la paix. La communauté scientifique internationale au cours des années 20*, Montréal, Les Presses de l'Université de Montréal, 1978.

Soubiran, Sébastien, "De l'utilisation contingente des scientifiques dans les systèmes d'innovation dans les marines française et britannique entre les deux guerres mondiales. Deux exemples, la conduite du tir des navires et la télémécanique," unpublished doctoral thesis, University of Paris 7, 2002.

Stern, Fritz, *Einstein's German World : Historical Reflections*, Princeton, Princeton University Press, 1999.

Szöllösi-Janze, Margit, *Fritz Haber 1868–1934. Eine Biographie*, Munich, C. H. Beck, 1998.

Tomassini, Luigi, "Le Origini," in Raffaella Simili and Giovanni Paoloni (eds.), *Per una storia del Consiglio Nazionale delle Ricerche*, Rome and Bari, Laterza, 2001, vol. 1, pp. 5–71.

Ungern-Sternberg, Jürgen, and von Ungern-Sternberg, Wolfgang *Der Aufruf "An die Kulturwelt!" : Das Manifest der 93 und die Anfänge der Kriegspropaganda im ersten Weltkrieg*, Stuttgart, F. Steiner, 1986.

Van Creveld, Martin, *Technology and War: from 2000 B.C. to the Present*, London, Collier Macmillan, 1989.

Vom Brocke, Bernhard, "Wissenschaft und Militarismus. Der Aufruf der 93 'An die Kulturwelt' und der Zusammenbruch der internationalen Gelehrtenrepublik im ersten Weltkrieg," in William M. Calder III, Hellmut Flashar, and Theodor Lindken (eds.), *Wilamowitz nach 50 Jahren*, Darmstadt, Wissenschaftliche Buchgesellschaft, 1985, pp. 647–719.

CHAPTER TWENTY-TWO

Intellectuals and Writers

CHRISTOPHE PROCHASSON
(translated by Heather Jones)

European intellectuals mobilized as rapidly as the troops. Almost to a man, younger intellectuals enlisted to fight, despite the fact that they were often assigned to duties that did not match their professional abilities or their perceived special social status. Older intellectuals needed no encouragement to join the propaganda war, swiftly entering into a battle of words that frequently predated military hostilities and, in many countries, continued long after the war on the battlefield had ended. The zeal, with which many older male intellectuals produced propaganda to defend their countries, probably arose from their desire as fathers to use their intellectual skills to support the sacrifices their sons were making. It was an attempt to compensate morally for their position as non-combatants.[1]

After the conflict, the militant patriotism of many intellectuals and the role they played in the propaganda war were perceived negatively, particularly in the 1920s. The idea that intellectuals had betrayed society in the so-called "treason of the clerks" was popularized in France in 1927 in a book of the same name by Julien Benda.[2] However, this sense of intellectual "betrayal" had already developed during the war in occupied countries such as Romania and Belgium, where there was considerable debate over whether intellectuals should remain silent in response to the occupation of their countries. Here the question of intellectual collaboration with the enemy was a major issue. The majority of Belgian writers opted for silence in the face of occupation or decided to limit their writing to private personal diaries.[3] British writers did not face such constraints: on September 18, 1914 *The Times* published a manifesto calling upon people to support the war being waged to defend "civilization," signed by 52 British writers, including some of the most prestigious literary names of the day such as Chesterton, Doyle, Galsworthy, Kipling, and Wells.

German academics were the first intellectuals to rally en masse in support of their state. The intensive mobilization of scientists was remarkable in Germany, but artists were also involved in the war effort. During the first month of hostilities 100 patriotic poems were published daily in the German press. The obscure poet, Ernst Lissauer, suddenly became famous owing to the mass reproduction of one of his poems, *Hassgesang gegen England*, known in English as the hymn of hate against England. The poem attacked Britain, which was perceived as Germany's greatest enemy.[4] The reopening of the theaters in October 1914 resulted in a slew of plays defending the German cause and justifying the invasion of Belgium.

However, it was the mobilization of German academia in support of the war effort that was the dominant feature of this period. The stance it adopted during the first weeks of the war would impact heavily for many years to come upon Germany's relations with intellectuals in enemy states and, in particular, upon its links with French academics and scientists. Part of a national modernization process that began in 1890, German universities had become closely associated with state policy.[5] Few academics had escaped the influence of the rampant Pan-German attitudes that existed within the university system. The frequent denunciations of the prewar militarist culture of German universities appeared to be justified by events following the outbreak of war in 1914. The German press was inundated with patriotic articles or letters by renowned German academics: for example on August 18, 1914 a triumphalist Anglophobe text, entitled "England's blood guilt for the war" (*Englands Blutschuld am Weltkrieg*), was published by the zoologist Ernst Haeckel and the philosopher Rudolf Eucken.

However, one particular initiative by German intellectuals had a much greater impact, provoking a series of reactions across the world. On October 4, 1914 a group of German intellectuals published a declaration entitled an "Appeal to the World of Culture" (*Aufruf an die Kulturwelt!*). Planned and written by three writers, Ludwig Fulda, Hermann Sudermann, and George Reicke, the 93 signatories to this declaration provided a veritable who's who of the arts and sciences in Germany, including 58 university professors, 43 of whom were members of the Prussian Academy of Sciences.[6] Some of the greatest German minds of the day signed, such as Walther Nernst, Wilhelm Ostwald, Max Planck, Wilhelm Roentgen, and Fritz Haber. Every confessional outlook and political opinion was represented among the signatories, with the sole exception of social democracy. However, it is important to note that ten of the so-called "'93" withdrew their signature following publication of the declaration, claiming that they had not been informed as to the whole content of the text which they had been asked to support. The astronomer Wilhelm Foerster and the economist Lujo Brentano were among those who withdrew their consent in this way.

The declaration was skillfully written, repeating throughout in relation to Allied charges the refrain: "It is not true." The text staunchly refuted a series of accusations made against Germany, ranging from its responsibility for the outbreak of the war, to the rape of Belgium and German breaches of international law. It also asserted Germany's right to act in legitimate self-defense. This petition by German intellectuals was not the only such declaration published in Germany during the war. A subsequent notable example was the "Declaration by the Second and Third-Level Teachers of the German Reich," produced by the Berlin philologist Ulrich von Wilamowitz-Moellendorf and the historian Dietrich Schäfer on October 16, 1914. Similarly, in July 1915, another petition, signed by 1,347 German professors, artists, and writers, called for Germany to annex territories conquered east and west of its borders. However, translated into 14 languages, it was the "Appeal to the World of Culture" that had the greatest long-term impact.

Intellectuals in other countries adopted similar tactics.[7] On October 11, 1914 the Russian intelligentsia assumed a unified front, publishing a declaration entitled, "To Our Country and to the Whole of the Civilised World," which was signed by 1,100 Russian intellectuals. On November 3, French academics published a "Declaration by French Academics to the Universities of Neutral Countries. A Reply to the Statement by German Universities," which was their response to the German declaration issued on October 16.

In December, Professor Nikolaj Zverev issued a statement denouncing the violation of the laws of war by Germany that was signed by 250 Russian intellectuals. The latter were quick to remobilize in support of a new declaration, "To the World of Culture: A Protest by Russian Professors and Intellectuals," published in January 1915. It denounced all forms of militarization of culture. Even in Portugal, neutral until 1916, intellectuals rallied around the former President of the Republic, Théophile Braga, also a philosopher and a poet, who published a declaration on October 23, 1914 that from now on it was necessary "to avoid all contact with the German scientific and cultural communities." However, in certain other neutral countries such as Denmark, Norway, Sweden, Greece, and Spain there were some favorable reactions to the German "Appeal to the Civilized World." Despite this, in 1915 Spanish intellectuals published a declaration in support of the Allied cause signed by numerous artists such as Manuel de Falla and Miguel de Unamuno.

Many centuries of shared intellectual endeavor had provided Europe and the West with a common intellectual heritage and shared cultural references that proved to be a problem for competing intelligentsias on opposing sides following the outbreak of war. Each national culture had contributed to the creation of a shared concept of "civilization," which all the different wartime declarations now sought to defend against the perceived barbarity of the enemy. Those intellectuals living in Allied countries adopted the theory of the two Germanys, one good and one bad, in order to explain Germany's previous cultural achievements. The idea that German intellectuals had somehow betrayed their cultural heritage appeared in many of the declarations published by their Russian, French, and British counterparts who believed that German intellectuals had abandoned their great cultural traditions in favor of a militarist state and the privileges it offered them. The Russian declaration, published in December 1914, depicted a Germany where Prussian influences had usurped an earlier German culture that had produced Kant, Fichte, Goethe, and Schiller. The same interpretation appeared in the declaration by 52 British writers in September 1914 and the French academics' text on November 3, which expressed a real admiration for the achievements of German science.

In France, the war provoked new attitudes toward Germany that resulted in multiple intellectual realignments. German philosophy had long been a staple of French philosophers' work and they were hit particularly hard by what they viewed as their German colleagues' betrayal of civilization. As a result French philosophers adopted several intellectual strategies in order to redefine their relationship with Germany. The controversy surrounding Kant, which involved Victor Basch, Victor Delbos, Emile Boutroux, Alphonse Aulard, and Georges Fonsegrive, illustrated this process of reinterpretation which the most virulent French protagonists used to settle old scores with Germany and to deny it any sort of intellectual greatness. These debates often became a way to engage with wider issues. Thus, French intellectuals argued over whether science was responsible for a process of dehumanization. Many believed that this was true in the case of German science. This debate was seen as an opportunity to question the pro-science ideology upon which the French Republic was, in part, founded. Science and progress had already been subject to very harsh attacks in the reactionary intellectual climate that had characterized the years after 1910.[8]

German intellectuals faced the same problems caused by the collapse of a shared European culture as their French counterparts but did not adopt the same solutions. For example, Ludwig Fulda had translated the French writers Beaumarchais, Rostand, and Molière. One of the most famous signatories of the "Appeal to the Civilized World,"

Karl Lamprecht, had introduced Germans to the work of the Belgian Walloon historian
Henri Pirenne. This was a prior intellectual bond now at odds with the wartime German
idea that only the Flemish part of Belgian culture was worth preserving. The majority of
German intellectuals promoted the "ideas of 1914," a vaguely defined set of cultural
assertions about German wartime identity, which emphasized the values of strength and
virility. These characteristics were perceived as the defining traits of "German science,"
and as part of a German *Kultur* that was the opposite of the superficial refinement represented by the values of *civilisation* promoted by French intellectuals. German intellectuals felt threatened by what they perceived as the Allies' double barbarism: their use
of the "Slav" and the "Negro" as soldiers in the European theater while claiming to be
the guarantors of Western Christian civilization.[9] This led some Russian intellectuals,
such as Nikolaj Berdjaev, Vasilij Rozanov, Vladimir Ern, and Sergej Bulgakov, as well as
symbolist poets, to respond in similarly polarized terms, depicting a German culture
dominated by the body, matter, and the machine, in conflict with a Russian culture
rooted in the spiritual values of the soul and mind of the human being.

European intellectuals were heavily criticized for their extreme wartime positions,
particularly because there was an assumption that their "professional experience" should
have led them to adopt more measured attitudes and more independent ways of thinking. Julien Benda's *Treason of the Intellectuals* was one example of this barrage of criticism, which, although largely justified, failed to explain the context in which the
intellectuals' trenchant mobilization occurred. The culture of war allowed little room for
maneuver and it was practically impossible to avoid being caught up in it. Almost by
default, intellectuals were involved in attempting to justify their nation's wartime actions
due to their social role. However, it is striking how the successive breach of wartime
thresholds of violence pushed many intellectuals to go beyond merely justifying their
own side's actions. In Austria-Hungary, many German-speaking intellectuals regarded
war itself as beneficial, although there were several notable exceptions, such as Gustav
Klimt, Arthur Schnitzler, and the pacifists Karl Kraus and Stefan Zweig. The majority of
Austro-Hungarian intellectuals, including academics, supported the wartime dictatorship of Prime Minister Karl Stürgkh. Men such as Robert Musil, Stefan George, Hugo
von Hoffmannsthal, and Hermann Bahr even believed that the conflict would have a
positive effect, ending a prewar period that they perceived as suffering from a serious
spiritual malaise. Others saw the war as a unique opportunity to establish the complete
domination of the German people over the Magyar and Slav nations. Even the "betrayal
of Italy" was seen as favoring the unification of the state. However, following the military
setbacks experienced by the *dual monarchy*, the enthusiasm of the opening months of
the war appeared to decline.[10]

Clearly some intellectuals and writers interpreted the war as a divine surprise and
believed that it would enable the realization of earlier prewar plans and destroy cultural
apathy.[11] In Russia, there was a large symbolist, mystic, and Slavophil cultural grouping
that saw the conflict as an opportunity to heal the divisions in Russian culture, unify the
country, and close the gap which existed between the culture of the elites and that of the
people. The war's reactivation of the ancient clash between Slavs and Germans, with
their opposing definitions of human existence, would bring about a regeneration of the
Russian soul.[12] The Italian Futurists and some intellectuals such as Gabriele d'Annunzio
also expected Italy's entry into the war to inspire similar redeeming national virtues.[13] In
some respects the attitudes of revolutionary intellectuals also reflected the same preoccupations: for example, those who followed Lenin's lead were delighted by the war,

seeing it as an occasion for social revolution, while Grigorij Plekhanov feared a German victory would halt the onward march of progress in Russia. In Bulgaria and in Romania, cultural elites also saw the war as an opportunity to be seized. Bulgarian intellectuals were keen to use the conflict to gain influence in the West, while their Romanian counterparts used the war to accelerate a process of national unification in which cultural issues played a major role, placing intellectuals in a foremost position in society.

However, although the overwhelming majority of European intellectuals backed their state and supported the war, there is a danger in reducing the entire spectrum of intellectual debate and opinion to these two positions, however variously they were expressed. It was precisely because these attitudes enjoyed hegemonic status and were generally seen as the only viable viewpoint that they gave rise to a new feature in the history of intellectuals: dissent. Several tiny isolated groups energetically opposed the war, denouncing its disastrous consequences and calling for it to end immediately. Such groups were thin on the ground; in some areas it was merely several individuals who adopted an antiwar stance. The opposition never involved more than a minority and certain countries experienced no antiwar activity at all. The progress of the conflict over time influenced this process. However, although attitudes did change during the course of the war, German and Austrian intellectuals were not affected by pacifism to the same degree as their French, Russian, and British counterparts, who were faced with several significant antiwar voices and organized, if weak, antiwar networks. In Germany, only three dissenters, the Berlin historian Hans Delbrück, the Göttingen mathematician David Hilbert, and the physicist Albert Einstein, resisted the total domination of the "ideas of 1914." In October 1914, a counter-declaration, "An Appeal to Europeans" (*Aufruf an die Europaër*), was published by the professor of medicine, Georg Friedrich, together with Albert Einstein, Otto Buck, and Wilhelm Foerster. However, only 100 copies could be secretly distributed in Germany, although it was also translated into Swedish, Danish, Finnish, and English. Intellectual pacifism was rare in Germany and operated within a very restricted milieu – there were only a handful of intellectual pacifists linked to the avant-garde journal *Die Aktion*.

In France, pacifist intellectuals also faced state repression and surveillance. The French writer Romain Rolland remained in Switzerland during the war, from where he made his pacifist views known in a series of articles published between August and December 1914 in the Swiss newspaper, *Le Journal de Genève*. These articles were later published in 1915 as a book called *Au-dessus de la mêlée* (Above the Fray).[14] This work became a rallying point for a handful of young pacifist intellectuals who from 1915 on regularly visited Rolland. These visits were more or less carried out in secret and represented a certain amount of danger for those involved. They illustrate an additional new dimension to the wartime mobilization of intellectuals. In *Au-dessus de la mêlée*, Rolland attacked intellectuals for their blind wartime servility, castigating Germany and France equally.

Despite wartime censorship, Rolland was able to correspond with Gorky, who was the principal opponent of the war in Russia. Several Russian disciples of Tolstoy, such as his former secretary Valentin Bulgakov, also waged a pacifist campaign, believing that all wars of liberation were simply a delusion. In September 1914, 42 of these intellectuals signed a declaration denouncing the war as a massacre of peoples. However, it had no effect. In Britain, a minority of intellectuals mobilized against the war, including George Bernard Shaw, Bertrand Russell, Arthur Graeme-West, and the members of the Bloomsbury group, who were later joined by Siegfried Sassoon. Sassoon had epitomized the exemplary soldier-poet. However, after being wounded at the battle of Arras in April 1917, he began to denounce what he termed the delusion of a defensive war. Russell, who helped found the pacifist Union of Democratic Control, was a model intellectual dissident, particularly in his opposition to his colleagues at Cambridge. He was an admirer of Romain Rolland, whose actions he sought to emulate. In 1916, Russell published a collection of his articles in a book entitled *Justice in Wartime*. This collection included his article, "An Appeal to the Intellectuals in War-Time," which left an enduring mark upon British public memory.

The aesthetic avant-garde also refused to support the war at times, although the reasons for their stance often defied explanation (see chapter 23). From Bulgarian modernists who rejected all war poetry, to Dadaists, and Surrealists, the war inspired a whole range of literature that encouraged people to resist the conflict. Among those who produced such antiwar writing were those connected with *Die Aktion*, which was influenced by expressionism from 1915. This avant-garde engagement with the war played an important role in the rejuvenation of European culture in the postwar period, although it was not the only factor. A wide range of different forms of cultural demobilization thrived on the disillusion and suffering the war produced. This led to many prominent patriotic writers becoming disenchanted with patriotism. Skepticism and irony were the result, as exemplified by H. G. Wells's novel, *Mr Britling Sees It Through* (1916), and *The Saint's Progress* (1919) by John Galsworthy. In Britain, young writers who had fought in the trenches used their work to reproach their elders for the war, employing old literary forms in new ways or inventing new styles that were ironic, laconic, or understated.[15] In this way, writers sought to reassert their autonomy within society. The idea that the war was fundamentally changing literature was so pervasive that the relationship between war and writing began to be studied even before the conflict had ended. In France in 1916, Paul Adam published one of the first books on the subject, *La Littérature et la guerre* (Literature and the War).

However, writing propaganda in support of the war effort remained by far the most common way that writers became involved in the conflict. On September 2, 1914 the head of the British propaganda office, Charles Masterman, a minister who was close to Lloyd George, organized a meeting to recruit writers to support Britain's cause. The event, held at the British propaganda headquarters at Wellington House in London, was attended by many of the leading lights of the literary establishment, including William Archer, Robert Bridges, Hall Caine, Sir Arthur Conan Doyle, John Galsworthy, Thomas Hardy, H. G. Wells, Israël Zangwill, and Arnold Bennett. Rudyard Kipling, who was unable to be present, sent a letter offering his services. The majority of the other writers also agreed to assist, with the exception of Thomas Hardy, the only person who refused. In this way Britain recruited a large group of writers who supplied war propaganda, much of it directed at America. The United States was inundated with hundreds of thousands of books and brochures produced by the writers mobilized by Wellington House.[16]

This war literature was far from insignificant. It included accounts of wartime experiences by several writers in uniform, such as those written by John Buchan, the author of a famous account of the battle of the Somme, and John Masefield, who became known for his turbulent narrative of the Gallipoli disaster.[17] However, this war literature also drew upon writing by those who had visited the front-line areas. Bennett, Kipling, and Doyle were among this group. Doyle, whose attempts to volunteer were unsuccessful because of his advanced age, became involved in organizing a private defense force.

In addition, propaganda writing also included short stories and novels about the war that were full of local color. These glorified the Allies' exploits and lambasted the villainy of the Germans, who were blamed for the outbreak of the conflict. British propaganda also tended to emphasize the defense of France and to echo French war culture with its calls for all-out war. American writers who had migrated to Europe before the conflict, such as Henry James (who died in 1916) and Edith Wharton, were extremely active in sending propaganda for the Allies back to the United States.[18] Their example was followed by a number of their American and Canadian colleagues.[19]

The war placed far greater demands on intellectuals than the prewar period. The most extreme was the experience of combat, which was a seminal event in the life of many young intellectuals. These men paid a terrible price, equal to that of the rest of the population. In fact, the casualty rate among intellectuals may even have been higher than the average. In France, whole college cohorts were decimated, with those who matriculated after 1910 particularly badly affected. The *Ecole Normale Supérieure* lost 239 students or former students, and 50.7 percent of the class of 1914 were killed. The *Ecole Polytechnique* lost 260 students or former students and 23.7 percent of the year of 1913 died in the war. These high death rates are partially explained by the fact that young intellectuals often served as subaltern officers who had to lead the men of their section or company into battle – a particularly risky combat role. In addition, some of these young men had a very strong sense of patriotic duty that led them to take greater risks out of a desire to act heroically. They were eager to go beyond simply doing their duty. Charles Péguy is a case in point. A celebrated poet and intellectual, Péguy volunteered for front-line service and was killed at Villeroy on September 5, 1914 – a classic example of the extreme support for the war that was shared by many intellectuals.

It is important to remember that fighting on the battlefield was the principal way that intellectuals, artists, and writers engaged with the war. This explains why the experience of the writer lies at the heart of the war literature the conflict produced. The idea of the combatant-writer or the soldier-poet took on a particularly powerful meaning. Between 1924 and 1926 in France an Association of Combatant Writers published an anthology of writers who had died in the war, consisting of five volumes covering 525 deaths.[20] Whether a writer had lived through the wartime experiences he wrote about mattered greatly to a readership that included numerous veterans. Every country had key literary figures who fought or died in the war and many writers experienced combat in the front line. The Italian, Gabriele d'Annunzio; the German, Ernst Jünger; the Frenchman, Jean Giono; the American, John Dos Passos; Dimcho Debelianov, who was Bulgarian; and Britain's Ford Madox Hueffer were among those who took part in the fighting.

Not all shared the same combat experience. D'Annunzio joined the air force at age 52. His plane crashed in January 1916 in dunes on the gulf of Trieste. Ernst Jünger served in the infantry, where he fought continuously on the western front from 1915 to the final retreat in 1918. Giono experienced the war as a soldier in an alpine infantry regiment and had his eyes burned by mustard gas in May 1918. Dos Passos was accepted into Norton-Harjes Ambulance Corps in January 1917 but did not arrive in France until June 1917. Debelianov was killed at the front in 1916, while Hueffer became a junior officer in the 9th Battalion of the Welsh Regiment in July 1916 and fought in the battle of the Somme. Regardless of whether the war was experienced up close or at a distance, in the artillery or in the infantry, as an officer or as an ordinary soldier, its impact upon writers was the same: a new, unprecedented level of intense confusion due to the disjunction between the biographical self and its literary counterpart.

During and immediately after the war, national literatures were dominated by the need to bear witness to the war experience.[21] In France, Henri Barbusse began a whole new genre with his novel *Le Feu* (1916).[22] This inspired a wide range of works such as *Les Croix de Bois* by Roland Dorgelès (1919), *Vie des Martyrs* (1917) and *Civilisations* (1918) by Georges Duhamel, and Léon Werth's novel *Clavel soldat*, published in 1919.[23] The situation was similar across Europe, the United States, and Canada. When Ernst Jünger stated in the preface to the 1920 edition of *In Stahlgewittern (Storm of Steel)* that he was writing for his front-line comrades, he did so out of a need to remember, to memorialize the experience of the war, and in order to convey the reality of the conflict to those who had escaped it.[24] He was not the only German writer to respond in this way: Werner Beumelburg, one of the most prolific writers on the war experience, published *Die Gruppe Bosemüller* in 1930; Walter Flex's work *Der Wanderer zwischen beiden Welten* (The Wanderer between Two Worlds) was written in 1916–17 and published in 1925; Ernst Johannsen published *Vier von der Infanterie* (Four Infantryman on the Western Front) in 1929.[25] All of these writers saw their books as a way of bearing witness to the conflict. In Germany, books about the war were more overtly political than their French or German counterparts. The enormous success of some more pacifist war writers alarmed both politicians and the authorities: by April 1931, Erich Maria Remarque had sold 3 million copies of *All Quiet on the Western Front* (*Im Westen Nichts Neues*), which had been published for the first time in 1929, while Theodor Plievier's novel about the navy, *Des Kaisers Kulis* (The Kaiser's Coolies), published in 1930, had been translated into 18 languages within a year.[26]

European women writers were excluded from the canon of war literature as war writing became associated with the act of bearing witness to the male war experience, with military experience privileged above all else.[27] Women's war writing came to be seen as inauthentic and unrealistic, and the reality of how the war had impinged on women's lives was forgotten. This occurred despite the fact that during the war women experienced deportation and endured bombardment when civilian targets were attacked. They also worked in the resistance networks set up in occupied territories, cared for the wounded, and even took part in combat in the case of those women soldiers who volunteered to fight on the eastern front. Two of these women soldiers, the Anglo-Irish Flora Sandes, who served in the Serbian army, and Marina Yurlova, who enlisted with the Cossacks in the Caucasus and then on the eastern front, wrote memoirs.[28] Women, including Emmeline Pankhurst, Rebecca West, Edith Wharton, Margit Kaffka, Marianne Moore, Edith Södergran, and Colette, produced a considerable amount of war literature, but much of it did not focus on pacifist themes or fit easily within any "feminine" literary canon.[29]

Although the war influenced all literary genres, it did so in different ways and impacted on some more than others. Literary output was not restricted to those works that defended the interests of the belligerent states, and even those writers who were most involved in producing state propaganda continued to produce creative work. For example, Bennett was able to publish two novels that barely touched on the war, *The Lion's Share* (1916) and *The Roll Call* (1918), in between writing two propaganda articles. The limits of a writer's autonomy were continually being renegotiated, and thus it is important to examine how the war modified prewar literary practices.

Perhaps above all other genres, poetry experienced a wartime mobilization, especially by the "soldier-poets." The image of the "fallen poet" became one of the most powerful symbols of the loss of talent during the war, epitomized by the deaths of Charles Péguy and Alan Seeger, the young American poet who joined the foreign legion at the beginning of the war and was killed on July 4, 1916 during the battle of the Somme. Established prewar poets continued to write during the conflict. However, it was the soldier-poets, who turned to poetry as a secret way to express their feelings, who really made poetry the chosen mode of writing about the war. Poetry was seen as the literary form that could express experiences that prose seemed unable to fully capture. While much war poetry continued to be written in a traditional patriotic style, using high diction, a new poetic language gradually emerged that was halfway between lyricism and realism. This allowed for the development of one of the main themes of war poetry: the return of the dead. German examples of this kind of writing include the work of Heinrich Lersch and of Anton Schnack, a former combatant at Verdun and a veteran of the battles of 1918. Ivor Gurney in Britain, Giuseppe Ungaretti in Italy, and Guillaume Apollinaire in France also evoked the theme of the rising of the dead.

Without doubt war poetry was the principal aesthetic conduit for the revival of religious feeling during the war.[30] Images of the passion of Christ appeared in poems in multiple different forms. The experience of the trenches was often depicted as sanctifying, as in the neoclassical poems of Jean-Marc Bernard, who was killed in 1915. A similar theme is evident in the work of Siegfried Sassoon (*War Poems*, 1919), notably in the poem "The Redeemer" drafted in November 1915, in which Christ appears in the trenches. The same religious themes emerged, deeply influenced by a strong romantic sensibility, in the work of Wilfred Owen. This romantic style was also to be found among other British writers such as Kipling, whose 17-year-old son was killed in 1915 fighting with the Irish Guards at the battle of Loos only three weeks after he had enlisted. A recurring motif in the work of these war writers was the "sacrifice of Abraham," which was used to depict the guilt that fathers bore for the deaths of their sons.

This type of war poetry was far removed from the word play or the use of irony that came to characterize modernist writing. In fact it could be read as a brief moment when poets experienced a "return to traditional order." The aesthetic divide between the traditional and the modern was particularly pronounced in certain national contexts. For example, in Bulgaria, war poetry had a major impact. There was a clash between those such as Ivan Vazov, who wished to use their poetry to justify the war, and those modernist poets such as the symbolist Debelianov, who refused to refer to the war at all in their work. Vazov was one of the most famous Bulgarian poets of the day and used his poetry to attack the Serbs, the British, and the French. The poet Kiril Hristov adopted a similar stance in his work *Pobedni Pesni* (Songs of Victory), published in 1916. Such divisions also emerged within the literary community in France. Within the milieu of small artistic journals that published prose and poetry, there was considerable debate about how writers should respond to the war. Often this debate took on political overtones. Those in favor of an art based upon "relevance" to contemporary issues opposed those who supported maintaining an artistic "distance." The debate polarized those who believed that poetry should focus upon the purely aesthetic and avoid social issues and those who favored pacifist poetry to condemn the war. This was partially a continuation of a debate that had begun before the conflict that had pitted artistic engagement with social issues against "art for art's sake," although it took on new meaning in the context of war.

However, it was the novel that had the greatest long-term impact on war literature.[31] The novel was without doubt the literary form that was best suited to capture the reality of the lived experience in a narrative form, attracting a large reading public both during and after the war. For this reason it met the public demand for texts that bore witness to the war experience. War novels often blurred the boundaries between pure fiction and the act of witnessing to authorial experience. It was not always easy to distinguish between autobiographical novels and first-person memoirs. "Truth" and fiction merged in the novel form in variable proportions that were often difficult to discern. Some novelists deliberately played upon these ambiguities. One example of this was the novel *Nach Paris!* which appeared in *Le Mercure de France* in 1919 before its publication as a book in 1920. Its author, the Swiss writer Louis Dumur, constructed its narrative around the fictional journal of a young German student. Dumur stated in the foreword: "I do not attempt to reproduce or to copy word for word the account given by my narrator. I limited myself to taking notes. Afterwards by placing myself in the position of my Boche, I was able to write his story in my own way." It was this shift in the relationship between truth and fiction within the text that was the main literary innovation of the new war literature.

During the nineteenth century the novel had become *the* leading literary genre, gaining a mass popular following. Therefore, it was the natural choice for those writers who wished to convey their extraordinary wartime experiences to the general public. As a result of the democratization of warfare and the advent of the mass citizen army, war was no longer the sole preserve of a small number of male fighters. The novel had to adapt to this new cultural environment. This process was not always straightforward. How was it possible to reconcile the freedom of the writer, epitomized by the fictional adventure, with the demand for truth inherent in the testimonial function required of war novels?

The war novel was constructed around a standard series of narrative devices that rapidly became fixed features of the genre. Those who read such works included war veterans and those who had experienced the war on the home front. Within the war novel they encountered a series of familiar war topics, either real or imagined. By 1916–18 the war novel was developing its own characteristics and narrative conventions, which largely revolved around particular set-pieces. It was through disrupting or subverting the stereotypical war narrative that authors were able to show their originality. The acclaimed French war novel, *Gaspard* by René Benjamin, published in 1915, provided a detailed account of each of the phases in the odyssey of the *poilu*. It described the mobilization period, the joyful departure of the soldiers for the front, their baptism under fire, life in billets, being wounded, treatment in hospital, and the return to the front line, and so on. Great emphasis was placed on describing each situation in detail in keeping with the new role of the novel as a kind of witness-fiction. However, characterization suffered as a result. Developing strong characters had been a key feature of the nineteenth-century novel, but the new war-novel narrative focused upon ethnology, rather than psychological depth.

This writing had an immense impact upon how society perceived the war. Often this was due to the film adaptations of war novels. For example, Georg Wilhelm Pabst adapted Johannsen's novel *Four Infantrymen on the Western Front* for the screen in 1930, Raymond Bernard turned Roland Dorgelès's book *Wooden Crosses* into a film in 1932 and, most famously of all, Lewis Milestone made Remarque's *All Quiet on the Western Front* into the biggest war film worldwide between the wars (see chapter 24). Such films made the books they were based upon into iconic versions of the war that were seen as "representative" of the individual experience. This led to the development of clichés that soon came to be taken as established "truths" about the war. In this way war novels came to be understood as eyewitness "testimonies." Historians working on the war were not always able to detach themselves from these established war narratives or to reject the particular socio-historical "truths" they promoted. The attempt by Jean Norton Cru in his work *Témoins* (Witnesses) to select what he perceived as the most accurate witness accounts of the conflict was heavily criticized. The works he chose as accurately bearing witness to the war, such as *Ma pièce* by Paul Lintier, and those he rejected, such as *Le Feu* by Barbusse, did not match public expectations at the end of the 1920s. Thus war literature, including that written during the conflict, played a key social role which must be taken into account in any examination of war culture. It was particularly important in the constitution and diffusion of myths and legends that were central to the history of the war.[32]

Intellectuals engaged with the war in a wide variety of ways. Their role was not confined to literature or to the paroxysm of combat experience. British writers, who had a long-established tradition of civic opposition to the state, immediately offered their services to the press or to propaganda agencies. They became reporters, translators, and censors. Similarly, in France, the writer Apollinaire famously worked as a press-office censor during the war. These intellectuals experienced what S. K. Ratcliffe described as a "spiritual conversion" in an article entitled "The English Intellectuals in Wartime" which appeared in *Century Magazine* in October 1917. In Austria, a special service responsible for collecting heroic accounts of the war recruited many writers such as Rainer Maria Rilke and Stefan Zweig. It operated as part of the war archive, the *Kriegsarchiv*. Theater companies were also involved in visiting soldiers in order to help troops cope with the boredom they regularly faced. In France, Emile Fabre, the administrator of the *Comédie française*, created the *Théâtre aux Armées* (Theater for the Troops) in 1915. Theater played an enormous role as a leisure activity in the Bulgarian army. In Russia, Fëdor Chalyapin, who financed two military hospitals, also sang for the wounded.

The remarkable mobilization of German academics in support of the war effort has already been discussed. They viewed the war as defensive and therefore justified. However, French academics also staunchly supported their nation's cause. A large number devoted a considerable amount of their working hours to producing propaganda. As in Germany, historians and philosophers were the most sought after for this work. Prewar international professional friendships between individuals who now found themselves on opposing sides of the war came under enormous strain and many did not survive the conflict. However, academics also began to be concerned about this breakdown of international university links. Plans were developed during the war for the creation of new forms of postwar academic cooperation, from which, however, German science was to be excluded, at least initially. On March 25, 1917 at the Palais d'Orsay in Paris, 180 academics from countries allied with or friendly toward France gathered for lunch. This meeting between Belgian, Italian, Russian, Serbian, Portuguese, American, Brazilian, and Czech colleagues led to the creation in May 1917 of the *Comité pour le rapprochement universitaire* (Committee for Academic Cooperation).

Several important academic figures paid a heavy personal price for their role during the war. The president of the *Académie des sciences morales et politiques*, the philosopher Henri Bergson, launched the first academic attack on Germany in a speech made to a gathering of members of the academy on August 8, 1914 in which he stated: "The fight against Germany is the fight of civilization against barbarism." Bergson thus provided French academics with the justification for waging an unlimited war against their German colleagues. At the request of Aristide Briand, he traveled to America four times to carry out speaking tours intended to win over American public opinion to support the Allied cause. Other famous French academics followed Bergson's example, taking part in numerous conferences and writing on subjects far removed from their original area of expertise. As academics became more militant they began to work for numerous propaganda agencies and institutions involved in national defense. They also worked on their own initiative. For example, the historian Ernest Lavisse and the sociologist Emile Durkheim founded a *Comité d'études et documents* to study the war which brought together the elite of French academia, including figures such as Charles Andler, Joseph Bédier, Gustave Lanson, Charles Seignobos, Jacques Hadamard, Henri Bergson, and Emile Boutroux.[33] In Oxford, a group of historians of modern history also joined forces to publish propaganda brochures with the support of Oxford University Press.

The wartime experiences of the renowned Belgian historian Henri Pirenne summarize the extent of the mobilization of European academics in support of their national war effort.[34] Pirenne, an economic historian, had enjoyed excellent relations with his German colleagues before the war. He was greatly shocked by their mobilization in support of Germany: the publication of the "Appeal to the World of Culture" particularly surprised him. This initial intellectual and emotional trauma was exacerbated by the death of his son, Pierre Pirenne, at age 18, at the battle of the Yser. Pierre was one of three Pirenne sons fighting in the conflict. In March 1915, the Germans, irritated by the ongoing resistance to their occupation of Belgium by academics at the University of Ghent, secretly arrested Henri Pirenne and his colleague Paul Frédéricq. Following his arrest in 1915, Pirenne was held at Crefeld officer camp and later at Holzminden camp where 10,000 Belgians were interned. While incarcerated he taught the history of Belgium to other inmates. A spell in Jena followed, before Pirenne was finally moved to Creuzburg an der Werra where he worked on his *Histoire de l'Europe*. The imprisonment of one of Europe's best-known intellectual figures aroused a flurry of fruitless protests in neutral states. After the war Ghent University dedicated memorials to those students who had died in the conflict, including a plaque that honored Pierre Pirenne. At the dedication ceremony, Henri Pirenne paid tribute to the solidarity between professors and students during the war: "if it [the university] resolutely refused to open its doors during the enemy occupation, despite the threats and orders of the occupier, it was because its staff did not wish to lecture from the podium while their students were fighting under shellfire in battles that echoed distantly to us on the wind from the west." Pirenne went on in the interwar years to greatly influence the groundbreaking *Annales* movement started by Marc Bloch and Lucien Febvre, both historians who had been wartime soldiers.

Academics were not only seen as useful propaganda agents. Their professional skills were also valuable to countries at war. They worked for the military as translators employed by the general staff, as geographers producing maps for the cartography service and as inventors. The laboratories of the universities and the *grandes écoles* were placed at the disposal of the military. Chemists were not the only group who were involved in military inventions: physiologists, doctors, and physicists all contributed to the mobilization of science in support of the national war effort. In addition, many intellectuals worked in the state civil service during the war. In France, the Ministry for Armaments was full of academics, particularly Durkheimian social scientists. Even the Minister, Albert Thomas, a renowned socialist, was a former student of the *Ecole Normale Supérieure* and a trained historian. He surrounded himself with a veritable think tank of social experts that included the sociologists Maurice Halbwachs, Henri Hubert, and Hubert Bourgin; the economist François Simiand; the geographer Fernand Maurette; the celebrated historian of Britain, Paul Mantoux; and the philologist Mario Roques. It was the political involvement of these men with the socialist and radical left during the prewar period that had forced the state to obtain the support of the trade unions in its management of social issues. These academics provided the state with skilled sociological and statistical analysis during the war. This development, together with the new forms of government adopted during the conflict, led to the emergence of a system of political advisors in France, which had lagged behind Germany in this area. Political analysts made great capital out of this new advisory system during the interwar years.

Once the war ended intellectuals rapidly became the focus for criticism. Their support for the war effort came under sharp scrutiny and they were also accused of playing a role in the outbreak of the conflict. In France, intellectuals were particularly severely criticized as, since the Dreyfus affair, they were considered to occupy a special position of social authority. Without denying the extent of the role played by intellectuals across Europe in mobilizing societies for war, it is necessary to point out that these cultural elites were largely participating in a system that extended far beyond any one social grouping. In all the belligerent countries every individual was involved in the war effort. All were implicated and each member of society placed their skills and resources at the service of the nation. In this regard intellectuals acted similarly to the rest of the population. Very few were able to resist the tremendous pull exercised by wartime nationalism. The prewar period had been marked by efforts to universalize the intellectual sphere in the face of centrifugal forces that aimed at nationalizing it. The war put an end to this idealistic dream. The international intellectual landscape of Europe was in ruins by the end of the conflict and had to be reconstructed gradually with painstaking care. In 1929, in a preface to Henri Pirenne's volume on Belgium at war produced for the Carnegie Foundation, the director of the series, James Shotwell, wrote: "The history of the war will continue long after the end of the conflict." History has undoubtedly proven him right.

Notes

1 Hanna, *Mobilization of Intellect*.
2 Julien Benda, *La Trahison des clercs*, Paris, Grasset, 1927; translated as *The Treason of the Intellectuals*, 1928; new edition, London and New York, Norton, 1982.
3 Sophie de Schaepdrijver, "Occupation, Propaganda and the Idea of Belgium," in Roshwald and Stites (eds.), *European Culture in the Great War*, pp. 274–5.
4 Marsand, *The Nation's Cause*, pp. 61–3.
5 Ringer, *Decline of the German Mandarins*, pp. 113–27.
6 Jürgen and Wolfgang Ungern-Sternberg, *Der Aufruf "An die Kulturwelt!"* For the English translation of the text, see "The Appeal to the World of Culture," in P. Van Houtte, *The Pan-Germanic Crime: Impressions and Investigations in Belgium during the German Occupation*, London, Hodder and Stoughton, 1915, pp. 155–61.
7 Prochasson and Rasmussen, *Au Nom de la patrie*, pp. 126–42.
8 Hanna, *Mobilization of Intellect*, pp. 105–208.
9 Ringer, *Decline of the German Mandarins*, pp. 180–99; Mommsen, "German Artists, Writers and Intellectuals," pp. 29–31.
10 Steven Beller, "The Tragic Carnival: Austrian Culture in the Great War," in Roshwald and Stites, *European Culture in the Great War*, pp. 127–61.
11 Stromberg, *Redemption by War*, pp. 39–60.
12 Richard Stites, "Days and Nights in Wartime Russia: Cultural Life, 1914–1917," in Roshwald and Stites, *European Culture in the Great War*, pp. 8–31.
13 Cali, Corni and Ferrandi (eds.), *Gli intellettuali e la Grande Guerra*.
14 Romain Rolland, *Au-dessus de la mêlée*, Paris, Paul Ollendorff, 1915; translated as *Above the Battlefield*, Cambridge, Bowes and Bowes, 1914; new translation, London, Allen and Unwin, 1916.

15 Fussell, *Great War and Modern Memory*, pp. 75–113; Hynes, *A War Imagined*, pp. 203–15.
16 Michael Sanders and Philip Taylor, *British Propaganda during the First World War*, London, Macmillan, 1982, pp. 38–51.
17 John Buchan, *The Battle of the Somme. First Phase*, London, Nelson, 1917; John Masefield, *Gallipoli*, London, William Heinemann, 1916.
18 Hermione Lee, *Edith Wharton*, London, Vintage, 2007, pp. 440–515.
19 Buitenhuis, *Great War of Words*.
20 Association des Ecrivains Combattants, *Anthologie des écrivains morts à la guerre*, Paris, Edgar Malfère, 1924–6, 5 vols; Beaupré, *Ecrire en guerre*, pp. 47–72.
21 Boucher, *Le Roman allemand*; Riegel, *Guerre et Littérature*; Smith, *The Embattled Self*.
22 Henri Barbusse, *Under Fire. The Story of a Squad*, translated from French by W. Fitzwater Wray, New York, E. P. Dutton, 1917; new translation by Robin Buss, London, Penguin, 2003.
23 Roland Dorgelès, *Wooden Crosses*, London, Heinemann, 1920; Georges Duhamel, *Civilization*, New York, The Century Co., 1919; new translation (E. S. Brooks), Gloucester, Dodo Press, 2008; Duhamel, *The New Book of Martyrs*, New York, G. H. Doran, 1918; Léon Werth was not translated into English.
24 Ernst Jünger, *Storm of Steel*, new translation (Michael Hofmann), London, Allen Lane, 2003, from the 1961 German text that was close to the 1920 original. The earlier English translation by Basil Creighton, *The Storm of Steel: From the Diary of a German Storm Troop Officer on the Western Front*, London, Chatto and Windus, 1929, used the more nationalist revised German edition of 1924.
25 Of these works, only Johannsen's was translated into English, as *Four Infantry Men on the Western Front*, London, Methuen, 1930.
26 Theodor Plievier, *The Kaiser's Coolies*, London, Faber, 1932.
27 Higonnet (ed.), *Lines of Fire*.
28 Flora Sandes, *An English Woman-Sergeant in the Serbian Army*, London, Hodder and Stoughton, 1916; Marina Yurlova, *Cossack Girl*, London, Cassell, 1934.
29 Sharon Oudit, *Fighting Forces, Writing Women. Identity and Ideology in the First World War*, Routledge, London, 1994.
30 See chapter 16 above.
31 Rieuneau, *Guerre et revolution dans le roman français*.
32 Smith, *The Embattled Self*, on the French case.
33 Eric Thiers, "Le Comité d'études et de documents sur la guerre," *Mil neuf cent. Revue d'histoire intellectuelle*, 23, 2005, pp. 23–48.
34 Lyon, *Henri Pirenne*, pp. 197–276.

References and Further Reading

Beaupré, Nicolas, *Ecrire en guerre, écrire la guerre. France, Allemagne 1914–1920*, Paris, Editions CNRS, 2006.
Boucher, Maurice, *Le Roman allemand (1914–1933) et la crise de l'Esprit*, Paris, Presses Universitaires de France, 1961.
Buitenhuis, Peter, *The Great War of Words. British, American, and Canadian Propaganda and Fiction, 1914–1933*, Vancouver, University of British Columbia Press, 1987.
Cali, Vincenzo, Corni, Gustavo, and Ferrandi, Giuseppe (eds.), *Gli intellettuali e la Grande Guerra*, Bologna, Il Mulino, 2000.
Cork, Richard, *A Bitter Truth : Avant-Garde Art and the Great War*, New Haven, Yale University Press, 1994.
Cross, Tim (ed.), *The Lost Voices of World War I. An International Anthology of Writers, Poets and Playwrights*, 1988; 2nd ed., London, Bloomsbury, 1998.

Field, Frank, *British and French Writers of the First World War. Comparative Studies in Cultural History*, Cambridge, Cambridge University Press, 1991.

Fussell, Paul, *The Great War and Modern Memory*, Oxford, Oxford University Press, 1975.

Goldberg, Nancy Sloan, *En l'honneur de la juste parole. La poésie française contre la grande guerre*, New York, Peter Lang, 1993.

Hanna, Martha, *The Mobilization of Intellect. French Scholars and Writers during the Great War*, Cambridge, MA, Harvard University Press, 1996.

Higonnet, Margaret R. (ed.), *Lines of Fire. Women Writers of World War I*, New York, Plume, 1999.

Hoeres, Peter, *Krieg der Philosophen. Die deutsche und die britische Philosophie im Ersten Weltkrieg*, Paderborn, Ferdinand Schöningh, 2004.

Hynes, Samuel, *A War Imagined. The First World War and English Culture*, London, Bodley Head, 1990.

Lyon, Bryce, *Henri Pirenne. A Biographical and Intellectual Study*, Ghent, E. Story-Scientia, 1974.

Marsand, Elizabeth A., *The Nation's Cause: French, English and German Poetry of the First World War*, London, Routledge, 1991.

Mommsen, Wolfgang, "German Artists, Writers and Intellectuals and the Meaning of War, 1914–1918," in John Horne (ed.), *State, Society and Mobilization in Europe during the First World War*, Cambridge, Cambridge University Press, 1997, pp. 21–38.

Mommsen, Wolfgang M. (ed.), *Kultur und Krieg. Die Rolle der Intellektuellen, Künstler und Schriftsteller im Ersten Weltkrieg*, Munich, Oldenburg, 1996.

Pomeau, René, "Guerre et roman dans l'entre-deux-guerres," *Revue des Sciences Humaines*, January–March, 1963, p. 77–95.

Prochasson, Christophe, and Rasmussen, Anne, *Au nom de la patrie. Les intellectuels et la première guerre mondiale*, Paris, La Découverte, 1996.

Riegel, Léon, *Guerre et littérature. Le bouleversement des consciences dans la littérature romanesque inspirée par la Grande Guerre (littératures française, anglo-saxonne et allemande), 1910–1930*, Paris, Klincksieck, 1978.

Rieuneau, Maurice, *Guerre et révolution dans le roman français, 1919–1939*, Paris, Klincksieck, 1974.

Ringer, Fritz K., *The Decline of the German Mandarins: The German Academic Community, 1890–1933*, Cambridge, MA, Harvard University Press, 1969.

Roshwald, Aviel, and Stites, Richard (eds.), *European Culture in the Great War. The Arts, Entertainment and Propaganda, 1914–1918*, Cambridge, Cambridge University Press, 1998.

Smith, Leonard V., *The Embattled Self. French Soldiers' Testimony of the Great War*, Ithaca, Cornell University Press, 2007.

Soulez, Philippe (ed.), *Les Philosophes et la Guerre de 14*, Saint-Denis, Presses Universitaires de Vincennes, 1988.

Stromberg, Roland, N., *Redemption by War. The Intellectuals and 1914*, Lawrence, The Regents Press of Kansas, 1982.

Winter, Jay M., *Sites of Memory, Sites of Mourning. The Great War in European Cultural History*, Cambridge, Cambridge University Press, 1995.

CHAPTER TWENTY-THREE

The Visual Arts

ANNETTE BECKER
(translated by Helen McPhail)

Between 1914 and 1918, visual artists were part of the European "front generation" – or at times declined to belong to it. We can therefore legitimately take their artistic expressions as a form of historical evidence. As the world was precipitated into a war in which millions died – artists, whether or not of the avant-garde, tried like all their contemporaries to hold out against everything that was destructive in the conflict. The overwhelming presence of death, the heartbreak of separations, the wounds and the trauma, and an existence that hovered between the banal and the supernatural charged every element of life with unaccustomed energy. The resulting artistic works enable us to follow the flux of the war, from the front to the home front, from faith to grief, from suffering to mourning.

As Philippe Dagen and Richard Cork have shown, some artists retreated into a refusal to represent the war, but most, whether working in the plastic arts, film, or music, participated fully in the culture of wartime, from premonitory enthusiasms to cruel disillusionment.[1] Together they created a body of work that gave the war its deepest meaning. This "war culture" or, better, these war cultures, were inseparable from hatred, suffering, patriotism, grief, and mourning, all of which are expressed in works showing a certain aesthetic disorder, even kitsch. But this was a way of denying the death of art, and thus death itself. It is surely proof of a vital aesthetic that they sought to make this heart of violence visible: death, and the modernity of death, with shattered bodies and hundreds of thousands of men simply missing were their subject. Moreover, the war shaped the work of many of the artists who survived well into the future. The dismemberment of the body, a theme dear to the avant-garde, probably had its physical as well as symbolic origin in the "great slaughter." The poet Guillaume Apollinaire invented the term "surrealism" in 1916 when he was recovering from a head wound, and as André Breton later declared: "Surrealism cannot be understood historically except in relation to war – I mean from 1918 to 1938 – in relation both to that from which it sprang and of that to which it returns."[2]

1913–14: Artists Join the War

In the decade before World War I was born one of the most significant movements in modern art. It assumed different forms among the cosmopolitan avant-garde of different centers (Cubism with Picasso in Paris, the Vorticism of Wyndham Lewis in London,

Expressionism and Abstraction with Kandinsky, Franz Marc and the Blaue Reiter in Munich, and Marcel Duchamp's own form of deconstruction in New York from 1913). But what might loosely be termed Modernism was founded on a common rejection of aesthetic conventions (such as perspective) that had been predominant since the Renaissance, as well as on a clash of values with official and bourgeois art.[3] In their numerous international visits and exchanges, a certain number of these avant-garde artists deliberately evoked a purely imaginary war that they hoped would lead humanity toward a purer and more modern world. But the vision of the apocalypse also generated its own fears, and such works would soon be seen as horribly premonitory. In the Italian Futurists' manifesto Filippo Marinetti famously declared: "We will glorify war – the world's only hygiene – militarism, patriotism, the destructive gesture of freedom-bringers, beautiful ideas worth dying for," while certain Expressionists, such as Ludwig Meidner with his cities under bombardment, believed in violence of, and within, art.[4] These artists were already "bombarding" the world with their urgent and ill-omened enthusiasm.

In August 1914, the majority of avant-garde artists therefore welcomed the declaration of war with a certain excitement. Apollinaire, recognized as the chief critic defending the Cubists, recorded his premonition of a radical rupture: it would be easy enough, he thought, to mourn the old world – for it would at the same time be the birth of a new world:

> … we said farewell to a whole world
> Furious giants reared up over Europe …
> I felt within me new beings full of the skill
> To build and fit out a whole new universe …

I shall never forget that nighttime drive with never a word between us

O			
de	ô		
parture	night		s t
sombre	so tender	ô	a e
In which	of before	vil	h n
Our **3** headlights died	the war	lages where d e	

FARRIERS RECALLED TO THE COLOURS   g

                     n

                     i

                     n

                     r

                     o

BETWEEN MIDNIGHT AND ONE O'CLOCK IN THE   m

To			
wards	or perhaps	to	golden
LISIEUX			
all		ver	
blue		sailles	

and 3 times we stopped to change a punctured tyre

> … we arrived in Paris
> Just as the draft was posted

We understood my friend and I
That our little car had taken us into a new
        Epoch
And that though we were both already full-grown men
We had just been born.[5]

This poem contains a calligramme, a form with which Apollinaire had experimented since the end of 1912 in his passionate enthusiasm for using the actual shape of the phrase to show something of the action that it described. In this poem written from the front, the broken form recounts the background, the front, while the writing becomes drawing. The art-critic-turned-soldier metamorphoses into a visual artist, using drawings amongst and within his words – just as his friends the Futurists or Cubists had incorporated verbal elements in their works of art.

Thus the artists, like so many others, actively consented to this just and cleansing war, at least at first. Engagement in the conflict was, then, experienced as a struggle between life and death, between good and evil. Patriotism became mystical, with loyalties that functioned along clear-cut national lines. In many cases this led to a syncretism between religious sentiment and patriotic feelings. The Russian artist Natalia Gontcharova expressed this powerfully in her 1914 series of wood engravings, *Images mystiques de la guerre* (Mystical images of the war).[6] Music, such as Debussy's final work, *Ode à la France*, or Max Reger's *Ein Vaterlandische Ouverture* (Patriotic Overture) in which he incorporated quotations from *Deutschland über Alles*, were as typical of this engagement as the patriotic designs for postcards by the Russians Vladimir Lebedev or Lavrov. From this starting point, Chagall, Dix, Steinlen, Nash, and many others were to offer an extraordinary descent into Hell. The "holy war" imagined by Malevitch and so many artists determined to break with "this old world" of which they "were weary" (as Apollinaire had put it before the war) would soon reveal itself as a time of death, rupture, and mourning.[7]

Yet whether conscripts or volunteers, these artists initially found a genuine inspiration in the spectacle of war that can often be followed in their correspondence. Fernand Léger, for example, wrote that "there was at the front this super-poetic atmosphere that excited me profoundly. Good God! What faces! ... I was dazzled by the breech of a 75 [field-gun] open in full sunshine ... It taught me more about my development in plasticity than all the museums in the world." Otto Dix similarly felt that "I *had* to have this experience: how someone beside me might suddenly fall, be finished ... I am a man of reality. I must see everything. I must experience life in all its depths. That is why I volunteered."[8] The letters of Max Beckmann, a hospital medical orderly, follow the personal ruptures experienced by the artist, between his stated wish to take part in the fighting, seeing the front at last, and the shell shock which he suffered at the end of 1915:

I came out through crowds of wounded men and limping soldiers, returning from the battlefield, and I heard this strange music, on a scale so great as to make one tremble. When a salvo came echoing past, it was as if the gates of eternity were being violently thrown open. Everything suggests space, distance, infinity. I would love [it if] I could paint this turmoil. Oh! This immense gulf, enough to make me shiver. (October 1914, from the Russian front)

I waver constantly between the great joy of everything that I see afresh, depression for the loss of my individuality, and a sense of the deepest irony for myself and sometimes for the world. After all this can only lead to admiration: its variety is beyond description and its inventiveness is immeasurable. (March 2, 1915)

It was so marvellous here that even the savagery of the mass killing, of its insistent rhythms continually ringing in my ears, cannot spoil my pleasure. (March 28, 1915)[9]
For me the war is a miracle even if it is somewhat disagreeable.[10]

Beckmann, no less than Léger, Duchamp-Villon, Nevinson, or Schmitt-Rotluff – to mention only painters who were combatants – was incapable, at least at first, of shedding either his fascination with the war or his horror at its tragedy – hence the ambiguity of the words and pictorial representation. In the 1920s or 1930s many artists would go back over what they had thought they felt in the war, ranging between beauty and violence, despair and fascination. This was the case, for example, with the surrealist painter André Masson, who at the end of his life recalled that

For me, violence was part of existence, and one had to get used to it. Indeed, that is why I returned from Switzerland to become a soldier and I wanted to be a soldier from below, to see the violence – not to inflict it, to see it – but, fundamentally, I took part in it, and I had to apply myself to it too. I fired shots and I was shot at … there were moments of true happiness, even in the firing line … There were things that were damned fantastic to see, sometimes, even if it was only the evening fire-works … The flares, the smell of the battlefield, so intoxicating … It is the war, in fact, that has brought me close to others. Before I lived completely apart. The war threw me into the human loam, made me human. It is terrible to say, but it is through this that I had the feeling of coming back into the community of my own kind.[11]

In Germany and Great Britain (and therefore in Canada and Australia) – among other countries – designated official artists were commissioned to show the war by following their units.[12] The fact that they were officially war artists does not mean that they were conformist or without talent. The choice of artists who were mobilized shows that they were young, in general open to modernity, and that their knowledge of the front would prevent them from painting images taken from historical stereotypes, particularly as they were generally left to choose their own subjects. They therefore sought to express in their own representational style the history of the engagement in all of its destructiveness, even though some of them had already been fighting for some time or had been wounded or suffered from shell shock.

The new military artifice of camouflage enabled the artists, many of whom were engaged in this activity, to move beyond the contradiction between aesthetics and destruction. In France, the camouflage service was actually created by a painter, Guirand de Scevola, and Fernand Léger and André Mare were illustrious members of it.[13] Since the fragmentation of Cubism, Futurism, and Expressionism appeared highly appropriate to soldiers charged with concealing guns or ships, the avant-garde plunged into the modernity of the war through this technique – and vice versa. The presence of the avant-garde in camouflage, at the very heart of the effectiveness of the war, is one of World War I's many hidden paradoxes.[14] Another arose from the activity in the service of Cubism of the German-born art dealer Daniel-Henry Kahnweiler, who had to take refuge in Switzerland, which resulted in the artistic revolution of Braque (French) and Picasso (a Spanish "neutral" living in Paris) being attacked in France as *boche* art, Kubism with a K.[15] Hence Léger's sharp reply:

To all those idiots who wonder if I am or will still be a Cubist when I return, you can tell them that, yes, far more than ever. There is nothing more Cubist than a war like this one, which splits a chap up more or less cleanly into several bits and flings him out to the four points of the compass.[16]

The armored trains, the "guns in action" of the Futurists Gino Severini and Giacomo Balla, Christopher Nevinson's soldiers returning to the trenches or the symbolic portraits mourning the death of a Prussian officer by the American Marsden Hartley, the victorious cavalry of the Russian Aristarkh Lentulov – all remind us that color and fragmentation, the wellsprings of modernity, were also mobilized to represent industrial war and industrial death. Sometimes the works tend toward abstraction, finding an outlet in the hyperreality of the destruction created by war.[17] Did the radical modernity of these "war artists" push noncombatants such as Picasso or Juan Gris to a "return to order," or did that evolution have little to do with the war?[18]

Artists between Consent and Sacrifice

Artists thus revealed clearly the visions of the war that were current more generally. This was true not only of the avant-garde but also of more conventional artists, since there was a vast production of frequently secondary quality but which perhaps expressed even more clearly the cultural tendencies of societies at war.

Initially, the artists concentrated primarily on atrocities; French, British, and Russians competed in anti-Germanism.[19] On the western front, the invasion of Belgium and then of northern France and the sad accompanying parade of atrocities, mixing reality and myth, confirmed the representations of the enemy. Kazimir Malevitch, in his popular-style woodcuts, and Maïakovski, in written captions, let fly against the Germans and Austrians. There was a good reason for this. If it is always difficult to represent death, even when accusing the murderer, surely the recognition of one's own share of guilt in trivialization of violence makes such representation virtually impossible? Hence the infinite number of representations of enemy atrocities: far from being works of propaganda or suppressing the reality of death, they were almost the only way in which the intensification of the conflict could be shown, in terms of enemy "barbarity." The pointed helmet carried like a trophy by a British soldier in the painting by the soldier-artist Eric Kennington of his own regiment, the Kensingtons, is typical of this attitude. Everything in the painting expresses the extreme exhaustion of the soldiers. They gaze with blank eyes, and one man is asleep on the floor of the barn where they are billeted; the artist shows himself in the middle of this scene of deep weariness, which might appear devoid of purpose; but, inexorably, the pointed helmet recalls the enemy.[20]

Portrayals of the ruins of thousands of shattered churches symbolized both the willingness to accept sacrifices for the sake of the country and the hatred of the "other." Prime amongst them was the omnipresent image of the cathedral of Reims, which it was even recommended should be left in ruins as public proof of German shame. It seems logical that innocent children and defenseless women should be targeted by the Germans in reality and also exploited by the Allies in counter-propaganda because the conflict was at some level a war of religion, a crusade against a barbarous enemy, seen as devoid of all moral conscience and a repudiation of "civilization."[21]

In a vast canvas of 1915 showing the triumph of death German-style, with the devil/kaiser orchestrating tortures, the Danish artist and long-time resident in France, Otto Friez, portrays God, Right, and Truth engaged in a struggle against the Devil, Death, and lies. This was no mere "war propaganda" designed to convince "one's own" side to fight against an enemy lacking conscience and soul: it was a vision inspired by real suffering, that of seeing one's country or region violated by an enemy capable of any barbarity. This same faith was evident in all the countries that joined in the war. In Italy, Mario Sironi presented the Austrians as "inhuman assassins." It was probably the American George Bellows who went furthest in the depiction of atrocities against civilians, with vast, almost "hyperrealist" paintings in which sadistic Germans are violently illuminated by the naked bodies of their victims, human shields designated for death.

However, wartime painters did not show the horrors endured by civilians in their own right, but only as a means of denouncing enemy barbarity. The remarkable exception is the very fine work of Christopher Nevinson, showing a dead child lying face down on the pavement, with no trace of her assailants. The title, *A Taube*, refers to the name of a German bomber, but is also a word-play on death and peace, since *Taube* means "dove" in German.

In Paris the great artistic exhibitions of the war period consisted, logically, of two kinds of work: those that denounced the Germans, particularly in the Panthéon, showing classical, medieval, or modern works of art sheltered there because they were "under attack" by the *Boche*; and those that heroized the French and the Allies fighting back, like the *Pantheon of the War*, which was visited by hundreds of thousands of Parisians. This war panorama was a vast fresco that depicted civilian and military personalities who were working for the Allied cause.[22] The other belligerent nations followed suit, for all the capital cities held substantial art exhibitions on the theme of military sacrifices, generally representing works by the most traditional artists. The huge statue of Hindenburg, inaugurated in September 1915 in Berlin to commemorate the victory of Tannenberg, is typical of this patriotic art that linked the war, national greatness, and the embellishment of the capitals.

Suffering, Mourning, and Disillusionment

Artists quite naturally shared the changing perceptions of the war and, after the illusions of the opening period, discovered its suffering, drama, and tragedy. Like their comrades in the trenches they endured, but disillusionment, division, and dislocation were increasingly woven into their imagery. Whether at the front or in the rear, the artists changed because the war turned out to be different from what they had expected. Romanticism and exaltation gave way to brutality, violence, death, and mourning. This was well expressed by Félix Vallotton, the Swiss artist who wished to represent the "true" war: "From now on I do not believe in blood-stained sketches, in detailed painting, in things seen, or even experienced directly. It is through meditation alone that the essential synthesis of such evocations can emerge."[23] Edouard Vuillard depicted a German soldier being interrogated by French soldiers. Everything in his painting is dreary, gray, and immensely sad. Each person is playing his part, nothing more. The soldiers of Dunoyer de Segonzac, Otto Dix, Wyndham Lewis, Théophile-Alexandre Steinlein, Christopher Nevinson, and the Australian Will Dyson are ever more lost, plunged into a hell of mud.[24] Mathurin Méheut goes so far as to paint a watercolor of the execution of a deserter, while Adrien Ouvrier – like many others – stuck to depicting daily life in the trenches. This rehumanization of the soldiers through their individual portraits and their "normal" activities as men who eat, drink, and read or write letters, who sleep or laugh, was also effected through photography, as instanced by the images that Marc Bloch brought back from the front line.[25] While such photographs were not seen as works of art at the time, they are increasingly so today, and to put them alongside paintings thus appears appropriate.[26]

For in the photographs, as in the paintings, the truncated trees and stumps of branches gradually became the metaphor for wounding and death, men without heads, missing or lying on the ground, impotent and almost invisible. The artists increasingly painted the consequences of the war, the wounded in particular, such as the aid posts of Ossip Zadkine or John Singer Sargent's line of gassed men, while Grosz and Beckmann showed them in hospital or the morgue, and Ernst Barlach depicted them lying in a common grave. If casualty stations and hospitals became the subject of choice, it is because they made it possible to show suffering far removed from the heroization of combat. In a letter written in 1918 the British artist Paul Nash summarized what he had seen and tried to show in his pictures, in which nothing appeared except shell holes and shattered trees:

> It is unspeakable, godless, hopeless. I am no longer an artist interested and curious, I am a messenger who will bring back word from the men who are fighting to those who want the war to go on for ever. Feeble, inarticulate, will be my message, but it will have a bitter truth.[27]

Thus it was that the central contradiction experienced by the combatants and in particular by those who were artists, painters, musicians, and intellectuals in the broadest sense, was located at the heart of the "war culture" and in the moral disaster that it would provoke during and above all after the war. Art is highly revelatory of this "confusion of feelings." From the works of warrior exaltation and patriotic denial to those of resignation, anguish, grief, rage, protest, and rejection – everything was spoken, sung, mourned, drawn, painted, and sculpted, often by the same hands. Like composers and librettists, practitioners of the plastic arts – whether regarded as popular or avant-garde – were definitely not victims but rather consenting actors in the conflict. More acutely than most, they were led to show its unbearable results – death, devastation, and disillusionment with the ideal of the possibility of peace and happiness.

For a certain realism enabled them to put aside the painting of heroic history, a style which could no longer decently illustrate the killing fields. The sufferings of the front are finally truly visible if we approach the artists from this angle, and the works of Luc-Albert Moreau, William Orpen, or André Devambez are good examples. Just like soldiers who were writers and poets, the soldier-painters were praised by many combatants for their ability to portray the unspeakable experiences of the front. Robert Graves said of the artist Eric Kennington: "Mr. Kennington is not the embarrassed visitor in an odd kind of salon … He is a soldier, he is at home in the trench and the shell-hole, he knows what is happening, knows what to see in it, where and how to see it."[28]

For the artists too, the truth of the first-hand witness became the gold-standard for knowledge of the war. Only those who had suffered in the trenches were judged worthy of portraying them. This explains why the plight of civilians, and of women in particular, was rarely visible in contemporary war art, apart from the occasional depiction of war factories, and munitionnettes. Australians passing through England in transit to the front or returning home were struck by the civilian population of the "old country," hence George Lambert's portraits of soldiers that include civilians, and pub interiors with barmaids. Civilians reappear in the paintings of postwar mourning, in particular in the work of some artists who were women, such as the Australians Dora Meeson and Hilda Rix Nicholas, in the terrible *Desolation*.[29] But these were the exception, not the rule.

Turning to Religious Art

Artists caught up in the war, whether combatants or not, attempted to represent the conflict with the aesthetic arms of the past, whether recent or remote. But the war was their present, and it posed the question of how to represent the impossibility of the future, how to portray the sky, the landscapes, and the ruined towns when these were empty, and might remain so forever. It was very frequently through images of religious style that the artists sought to respond to the challenge of expressing the atrocities and killings, while never forgetting grief and compassion.

Messianism, hope, despair, apocalypse, redemption, suffering, sacrifice, crusade, punishment – all were depicted, carved, or sculpted by artists in two registers – that of popular or propaganda imagery, and that of the avant-gardes. Four themes from Europe's shared religious traditions dominated: the Massacre of the Innocents, the Apocalypse of St. John, the Passion and Resurrection of Christ, and the grief of the Virgin. In part this Christian imagery respected the minority or majority position of Catholicism and Protestantism, depending on the nation, acquiring a universal meaning which included Jews and those who practiced no religion.[30] Religious subjects and formats (triptychs, wood-carvings) expressed the war as consent became "sacrifice" and rejection was renamed ordeal or despair.

As for the absence or eclipse of God, surely that too was a form of spiritual anguish? Christopher Nevinson illustrates this in his painting *The Paths of Glory*, in which he shows two soldiers face down on the ground, crushed by death. They were crushed a second time when the censors of the War Office refused permission for the work to be shown. Nevinson then covered the canvas with a strip bearing the word "censored," leaving nothing else visible but a corner of a battlefield, full of the detritus of war where only a boot-sole and a helmet are identifiable, simultaneously very close and very far from humanity.[31] Georges Rouault undertook his *Miserere* series while Schmitt-Rotluff asked – in defense of his carved Christ whose forehead was branded with the date "1918" – "Has not Christ appeared to you?" Beckmann's works of this period exemplify a spirit of crushed exaltation, as a critic observed in 1919:

> Such forms surge up from a bitterness that is almost mystical: the ecstasy of grief ... A Grünewald stripped of his flesh – of his flesh but not his soul. The details are imposed by the painful fervour of our machine age. ... A whole nation has admitted to a sense of superiority; it has sinned in a way beyond calculation and must expiate the sin in a manner beyond calculation. Rotten flesh is burned slowly with monstrous instruments of torture, and the Spirit can reflect on it.[32]

It is surely in his *Resurrection*, a vast painting in gray, black, and white, that Beckmann went furthest in depicting this sense of dereliction. The treatment could not be further from the artist's earlier approach to the subject in 1909, when he adopted the style of Rubens. In the painting of 1918 Beckmann has moved from the vertical lines of hope to the crushing horizontal. The work is hardly a Resurrection at all, but simply a Last Judgment in which only the dead or suffering bodies present the drama that pins them down in the vast emptiness of their agony. The great legs of one figure seem to turn into a scythe dripping with blood as black as the star shining above a catastrophe that it can no longer illuminate. To drive the point home, Beckmann deliberately left the painting unfinished.[33]

Mourning and despair have replaced the chimera of a world reborn in the purity of a spiritualized war. The utopian landscapes of the Apocalypse painted by Ludwig Meidner in the years 1910–13 have become unbearable reality. Only derision, cynicism, and sometimes compassion could survive in the new world. Hence Otto Dix's portrayals of the sick with their crucified bodies and George Grosz's Christ wearing a gas-mask who cries out: "Be silent and do your duty."[34] As Günther Anders rightly remarks, contemporaries could not have mistaken the meaning of the engraving: Christ was outraged by the war, the gas-mask echoed the crown of thorns. But it created a scandal, because it was easier to accuse the artist than the war.[35]

Creativity on behalf of peace and against the barbarity of the war was the only way in which disillusioned artists could survive in the conflict. In 1914 Franz Marc wrote about the death of his friend August Macke: "The insatiable war has enriched itself with one more heroic death, but German art has lost another artist."[36] Marc himself was to be killed at Verdun in 1916. The Futurist Boccioni died from a fall from his horse; the very distinctive and promising Vorticist sculptor from Britain, Henri Gaudier-Brzeska, died in the Artois offensive in 1915; his German equivalent Lehmbruck, in a state of shock and unable to recover from the war, committed suicide with gas in 1919; and Apollinaire and the Austrian painter Egon Schiele died as a result of the flu pandemic.

Demobilization within Wartime Mobilization; Mobilization within Postwar Demobilization: from Dada to the New Objectivity

Some, if they were not subject to call-up or if they refused to respond to it, chose exile as soon as the war broke out. A number of artists went to Switzerland; in Geneva, the Belgian artist Frans Masereel met Romain Rolland who, like him, was a volunteer with the International Red Cross. Masereel founded a newspaper, *Les Tablettes*, in which he published black-and-white drawings and caricatures against the war. The remarkable series of ten woodcuts, *Debout les morts* (The Dead Arise) appeared in 1917. The most spectacular image shows two decapitated nurses bearing their own heads on a stretcher: one head wears a pointed German helmet, the other a French *képi*.[37]

The Dada movement was founded in 1915 around the Cabaret Voltaire in Zurich.[38] To some extent the Dadaists needed the war in order to come into existence, to prosper, and to die; but they could not admit this, and so their mobilization was also their way of demobilizing themselves in relation to the war. Their wartime grief was expressed by denunciation and disorder at an international level. As Hugo Ball wrote in 1917: "The spirit of Europe is dying, and is fighting to exist. Schools are not teaching how it should be asserted. We must find it."[39] And the German poet and Dadaist, Richard Huelsenbeck, added in 1918:

> We had to find a common point between the Russians, the Romanians, the Swiss and the Germans? That set up such a witches' sabbath that you can scarcely imagine it: rows from morning to night, a sort of tremendous dizziness with trombones and African drums, a sort of ecstasy with tap-dancing and Cuban dances.[40]

The Dadaists' international dimension was an intolerable provocation for their detractors. Many of them came from the fringes of Europe: Romania – such as Tristan Tzara and Marcel Janco – Bohemia, Hungary, eastern Germany, Russia, Poland.[41] A major consequence of the war was to dismantle these territories and re-form them, to eliminate ancient centers and to create new ones. Having reconvened in Berlin and Paris during the latter part of the war and after the end of hostilities, the Dadaists demobilized themselves by celebrating links between the Germans and the French, and by maintaining their "neutrality" as in Zurich or New York in 1916. Yet the cosmopolitan tradition of the avant-garde meant they were never far from the war, as Hugo Ball remarked in 1917: "If our abstract pictures were hung in a church, it would not be necessary to cover them on Good Friday. Desolation itself has become an image."[42] Without crusading, but with determination, Dadaism sought to save art, even the whole of European civilization, from its own suicide. Their rupture spoke to the nothingness of the war by refusing to represent it.[43]

Those who had fought, those who had escaped the front, through illness (Grosz), wounds (Beckmann), or faking (Jean/Hans Arp, whose double first name indicates the problems of being from Alsace), shared the same games, the same "practical jokes" of demobilization with those who had from the beginning stood apart from the war. "No pity. After the carnage we still have the hope of a purified humanity," as the Dadaist manifesto proclaimed.[44] Dadaists preached the new suicide of a world barely emerging from its warmongering suicide. Their nihilism was so well adapted to the disaster of postwar Europe that they ended by being mobilized in a new form of war, seen as a destructive agent which turned in on itself. They turned themselves into artistic terrorists whose weapons were derision, humor, slander, scatology, gratuitous scandal – a form of art for art's sake – and, above all, antimilitarism. In some respects their "total art" took over from "total war."

As free spirits in a world corseted by powerful national attachments, the Dadaists denied the concept of nationality. The *Dada Almanach* cited humorously those who inveighed against their contaminated foreign origins and attempted to subvert the dominant values of the years 1914–20 – to fight, to believe in the nation, to be in mourning, to commemorate. They exploded such values by means of words, painting, cabaret evenings, dramatized parodies of parliamentary debates, fake trials – even using the real ones that were inflicted on them as new *happenings*. Those who had been able to witness the catastrophe of a world at war from their wartime observation posts in neutral Switzerland could see the total failure of former belief systems above all in defeated Germany. For this reason, the movement became more violently politicized there than elsewhere, contesting the Republic, which they could only see as the continuation of the Empire. In 1918, Baader and Hausmann put types of news item such as these into the press: "Dadaists demand the Nobel Peace Prize," or "Minister Scheidemann takes part in Dadaism." At the same time André Breton sent this collage in a letter to Boris Frankel, his wartime comrade and, like himself, a doctor, a few days after the death of their mutual friend Jacques Vaché:

31 July 1914: JEAN JAURES
? January 1919: Jacques Vaché
16 January 1919: KARL LIEBKNECHT[45]

Whereas the French Dadaists remained highly intellectualized, those in Germany really believed in the Revolution. In July and August 1920 the first Dada International Fair in Berlin was a libertarian street demonstration – a substitute for political mobilization – in which a Dada republic was founded at Nikolasee, one of Berlin's lakes, and the National Assembly was leafleted with tracts declaring "Oberdada against Weimar." These artists mocked the mass production of colored photographs during the war, which they considered to be fake, ugly, and a form of kitsch, and more generally they made humor and derision criteria of good taste in the face of all solemn, serious, and industrial production. Paradoxically, however, they valued the byproducts of wartime art once they had been able to subvert them, rather than having to take them at face value. Innocent kitsch proved the aesthetic superiority of Dadaists, hence the Berlin pig. This "ceiling sculpture, Prussian archangel," a model of a soldier with a pig's head, was attached to the ceiling with the following inscription round its neck: "To understand this work of art, you must wear country clothing and carry a heavy rucksack, while you do exercises for twelve hours every day on the Tempelhof training ground. ... Hung by the Revolution." Another model displayed an iron cross instead of genitals and a gas-mask, "protecting" them absurdly from chemical attacks, which had been the war's spectacular novelty. Antimilitarist caricatures and photomontages were fixed to all the walls; *Butchery*, painted by Otto Dix, showed butchers with pigs' heads just back from the battlefields, their regimental marks clearly visible. In Grosz's forcefully expressive drawings, Germany herself was shown bleeding through the soldiers' belt-buckles bearing the official motto *Gott mit uns* (God with Us).[46]

Dadaist responses to the murderous onslaughts of the war and the repression of the Spartakists in January 1919 during the German Revolution drew to some extent on both graffiti in public toilets and the incisions left by soldiers in disused quarries used as shelters during the war. In a letter that Jacques Vaché wrote to André Breton in November 1918, not long before his suicide, he expressed the agonizing contradictions of a tragic period in which both continued mobilization and demobilization both seemed equally impossible. The war was over, but Vaché still wore his uniform and rolled out his metaphors like a cinema reel:

> I will emerge from the war slightly lame, perhaps in good health; like these splendid village idiots (that's what I hope) ... or perhaps ... or perhaps ... what a film I'll make! ... – How am I going to manage, my poor friend, to get through these final months in uniform? – (They told me that the war was over).[47]

The works of Otto Dix and George Grosz, as the stylistic trend of the "new objectivity" developed, also express traumatic shock, or "shell shock," which had become the metaphor for the rupture of the whole war.[48] They rejected all sanitization, all demobilization of the war experience. Their invalids were in a state of endless war, not only as a metaphor for violence and brutal instincts, but as the reality of bodies and souls condemned in perpetuity by the spirit of the conflict. One of the most impressive works on display at the Berlin Dadaist fair was a painting by Otto Dix whose title, *The War Cripples (With Self-Portrait)*, and even more whose subtitle, *45% employable*, was highly revealing. Although Otto Dix was not genuinely part of the group, he had agreed to contribute a certain number of works to the exhibition, which belonged to his first postwar phase, confronting the consequences of the war, notably in the form of mutilated bodies in the streets of large German cities. Dix created four similar works in 1920: *Prague Street, The Matchseller, Skat Players,* and *The Barricade*. Each painting depicts permanently disabled men and others back from the war, surrounded by the detritus of war and "civilization," with derisory religious relics, beaux-arts, and kitsch that have been massacred and torn apart by war and then civil war; monstrous prostitutes recall the monstrosity of the front, Eros and Thanatos juxtaposed. Dix combined all tactics in order to make his contemporaries confront the brutality of the war and the brutalization of the postwar world. In *Prague Street*, depicting the most elegant thoroughfare in prewar Dresden, two disabled veterans pass by without seeing each other, as they would have done before the war, but now the *bourgeois* and the beggar are no more than disjointed puppets in a two-dimensional space, echoing the plaster busts in the window of the sex shop, whose sadomasochism is both a complement and a contrast to the horror of the scene. For the two disabled men have lost all possibilities of sexuality, while the shop window is bursting with it. The dog beside them carries a newspaper in his jaws bearing the legible message, *Juden Raus* (Jews Out). The world has come a long way since 1914, says the artist, but where is it going?

It was also in Dresden that the Director of the Academy of Beaux-Arts, Oskar Kokoschka, had made a statement against the revolution of 1918–19, asserting that it might lead to the destruction of all culture. The Dadaists derided the sacral aspects of Expressionism and Dix's response to Kokoschka could be seen in *The Matchseller*, where a dog walking past a blind, legless beggar urinates on Kokoschka's text, which is trailing in the gutter. Dix does not show compassion for this artistic "civilization," even though Expressionism had been one of its emanations, but rather for the poor debris of its tragic reign.

It was only during the second half of the 1920s that Dix returned to depicting the front and his own experience of the war, notably with his cycle of engravings, *Der Krieg*. Here he held back nothing in showing the most horrible consequences of the fighting on bodies and souls: skeletons dismembered and re-dismembered by shells, bodies mingled into one with the tumbled earth, suicides, cries of distress, or the murmurings of dying men: "*Maman, Mutter, Mother*."[49]

For after the great massacres of the war, death could not be normalized. It remained unbearable, leaving individuals and societies in a state of shock. This is why the triptych is particularly frequent in the postwar work of Dix, Beckmann, or the French artist André Devambez. Borrowed from the Middle Ages, it presents the symbolic form of the Trinity and at the same time shows the fragmentation of the body that necessarily precedes its resurrection. These detonating visions of horror and grief are in symbiosis with the message of Christianity – dereliction and transformation through suffering in imitation of Christ and the Virgin – or the nation. Form and content are perfectly united, functioning like the memory of the war: fragmented, multiplied, refracted, impossible to reassemble in a single piece, in a single space, in a single moment. They also express the anachronism of religious painting in a time of war.[50] In Rouault's *Miserere* – begun, as we have seen, during the war and continued during the following 20 years to be published only after World War II– grief and despair have replaced the hope of a world re-created in the purity of a spiritualized war. And who can believe that the soldiers of Stanley Spencer in the war memorial-fresco in the Sandham Memorial Chapel at Burghclere (1928–9), will genuinely experience the Resurrection? As a preparatory sketch shows, Spencer had indeed intended to show only invalid bodies, incapable of standing upright, incapable of raising themselves among the dead. Similarly, the mothers in Käthe Kollwitz's work are simply *pietàs*, weeping, without hope for any tomorrow. Their vengeful instinct has dried up – is it possible to yearn for revolution from a state of mourning? All these works show a Good Friday with no Easter Sunday. When the strongly conservative and Catholic artist Georges Desvallières designed the poster for Léon Poirier's film *Verdun, visions d'histoire* (1928), even he showed the return of the dead as terrifying skeletons that could find no rest.

* * *

Walter Benjamin saw clearly that Guillaume Apollinaire had invented the un-inventible, which had already come about. "The chapters 'Persecution' and 'Assassination' in *Poète assassiné* contain the famous description of a pogrom of poets. Publishers were taken by storm, books of poetry burned, poets massacred. The same scenes were occurring at the same moment across the whole world."[51]

In fact World War I coincided with Apollinaire's literary project dating from the turn of the century, to write a novel on the end of the world. The "Assassinated Poet," Apollinaire himself, who would be merely "wounded," was too convinced of the justice of France's cause in the war to denounce it – unlike Benjamin, when he wrote in 1929 about the Surrealists. Many of the latter, like Max Ernst, had since prewar times been aware of certain works that were created out of mental instability and had been highly impressed by them. It is often possible to link their allegiance to Dadaism and then Surrealism, their knowledge of works by mentally unstable artists, and their interest in "primitive" art to World War I. When the Nazis organized their exhibition of degenerate art in Munich in 1937, they used one of the ironic devices that had been written on the walls of the Dadaist fair in 1920: "Take Dada seriously, it's worth it." They took the message literally, showing the works one final time before destroying them as "insults to the heroes of the Great War [... and as] military sabotage."[52] The mobilization of the Nazis against all "degeneration" led them to destroy the art of the 1920s, this "Jewish aesthetic gangrene." Where they still perceived only heroism, these artists had very rap-idly seen misfortune, suffering, and disillusionment. But all sides were in agreement: this art, these artists, in their immense diversity, owed everything or virtually everything to the ruptures of the war.

Notes

1   Dagen, *Silence des peintres*; Cork, *Bitter Truth*.
2   Becker, *Guillaume Apollinaire*.
3   Jane Turner (ed.), Grove Dictionary of Art, *From Expressionism to Post-Modernism. Styles and Movements in 20th Century Western Art*, Grove Art, 2000; L. Brion-Guerry, *L'Année 1913, les formes esthétiques de l'oeuvre d'art à la veille de la Première Guerre mondiale*, 3 vols., Paris, Editions Klinksieck, 1973; Jill Lloyd, *German Expressionism, Primitivism and Modernity*, New Haven, Yale University Press, 1991.
4   Umbro Apollonio (ed.), *Futurist Manifestos*, London, Thames and Hudson, 1973, p. 22.
5   Guillaume Apollinaire, "La petite auto," in *Oeuvres poétiques, Calligrammes, Poèmes de la paix et de la guerre (1913–1916)* (1918), Paris, Gallimard (La Pléiade), pp. 207–8.
6   Album, *Images mystiques de la guerre, 1914*, reproduced in E. Petrovnia and J. C. Marcadé (eds.), *La Russie à l'avant-garde, 1900–1935*, Brussels, Europalia, 2005.
7   Apollinaire, "Zone," *Alcools*, in *Oeuvres poétiques*.
8   Fernand Léger, quoted in the catalog of his retrospective, Fondation Maeght, Editions Maeght, 1988. Otto Dix, quoted by Iain Boyd Whyte, "Otto Dix's Germany: From Wilhelmine Reich to East/West Divide," *Otto Dix*, London, Tate Gallery, 1992, p. 28.
9   Quoted by Carla Schulz-Hoffmann, "War, Apocalypse, and the 'Purification of the World'," *The Romantic Spirit in German Art, 1790–1990*, London, Hayward Gallery, 1992, p. 198.
10 Max Beckmann, letter from the Belgian front, in *Self-Portrait in Words, Collected Writings and Statements, 1903–1950* (ed. Barbara Copeland Buenger), Chicago, University of Chicago Press, 1997, p. 149.
11 André Masson, *Vagabond du surréalisme*, Paris, Editions Saint-Germain-des-Près, 1975.
12 Meirion and Susie Harries, *War Artists*.

13 Cooper, *Fernand Léger*; André Mare, *Carnets de guerre 1914–1918*, Paris, Herscher, 1996.

14 *André Mare, cubisme et camouflage, 1914–1918*, exhibition catalog, Bernay, Musée Municipal des Beaux-Arts, dir. Nicole Zapata-Aubé, 1998; Kahn, *"Les Camoufleurs."*

15 Green, *Cubism and its Enemies.*

16 Fernand Léger, quoted in the catalog of his retrospective, Fondation Maeght.

17 Malvern, *Modern Art.*

18 Silver, *Esprit de Corps*, pp. 27–73.

19 Jahn, *Patriotic Culture in Russia*, pp. 11–83.

20 "The Kensingtons at Laventie, 1915," Imperial War Museum, London.

21 Audoin-Rouzeau and Becker, *Understanding the Great War*, pp. 114–16.

22 Levitch, *Panthéon de la Guerre.*

23 Quoted in Marina Ducrey (with Katia Poletti), *Félix Vallotton (1865–1925): L'œuvre peint*, coédition Fondation Félix Vallotton, l'Institut suisse pour l'étude de l'art, and 5 Continents Editions, 2005.

24 Corbett (ed.), *Wyndham Lewis.*

25 March Bloch, *L'Histoire, la guerre, la résistance* (ed. Annette Becker), Paris, Gallimard (Quarto), 2006.

26 Joëlle Beurier, "Death and Material Culture: The Case of Pictures during the First World War," in Saunders, *Matters of Conflict*, pp. 109–22. For example, the writer and artist Jean Cocteau, *Photographies et dessins de guerre, réunis et présentés par Pierre Caizergues*, Arles, Actes Sud, 2000.

27 Cork, *Bitter Truth*, p. 198.

28 Graves, quoted in ibid.

29 Catherine Speck, "Women Artists and the Representation of the First World War," in *War and Other Catastrophes, Journal of Australian Studies*, 60, Brisbane, University of Queensland Press, 1999.

30 Annette Becker, "Les Artistes, la guerre, le sacré," in Jean-Jacques Becker et al. (eds.), *Histoire Culturelle de la Grande Guerre*, Paris, Armand Colin, 2005, pp. 125–38.

31 "Paths of Glory," Imperial War Museum, London.

32 Julius Meier-Graefe, 1919, quoted in *Romantic Spirit in German Art*, p. 202.

33 Both paintings are in the Staatsgalerie, Stuttgart.

34 Grosz, Portfolio, *Hintergrund*, no. 10, 1918.

35 Günther Anders, *George Grosz*, 1961; trans. from German, Kingston, Australian Capital Territory, Alia, 2005.

36 Quoted by Cork, *Bitter Truth.*

37 Roger Avermaete, *Franz Masereel*, Antwerp, Fonds Mercator, 1975.

38 *Dada, Zurich-Paris, 1916–1922*, Paris, Editions Jean-Michel Place, 1981 (Dada reviews); Marc Dachy, *Archives dada, chronique*, Paris, Hazan, 2005; Dachy, *Dada.*

39 Hugo Ball, *La fuite hors du temps, Journal 1913–1921*, Editions du Rocher, 1993, p. 217.

40 Quoted in Marc Dachy, *Archives Dada, Chronique*, Paris, Hazan, 2005, p.136.

41 Krisztina Passuth, *Les Avant-gardes de l'Europe Centrale*, Paris, Flammarion, 1988.

42 Hugo Ball, *La Fuite hors du temps*, p. 219; Robert Motherwell (ed.), *The Dada Painters and Poets: An Anthology*, Cambridge, Cambridge University Press, 1951 (new ed., 1981).

43 Annette Becker, "The Avant-Garde, Madness and the Great War," *Journal of Contemporary History*, 35/1, 2000, pp. 71–84.

44 Manifeste dada, 1918.

45 30 janvier 1919, quoted in Marguerite Bonnet, *André Breton, naissance de l'aventure surréaliste*, José Corti, 1988, p. 148.

46 Extracts in particular from his portfolio *Gott mitt uns.*

47 Jacques Vaché, *Lettres de guerre*, Paris, Au Sans Pareil, 1919.

48 Exhibition *Allemagne années vingt, la nouvelle objectivité*, Musée de Grenoble, 2003.

49 Dix, *The War*.
50 Apart from Lucien Jonas, who stuck to his anti-German Catholicism in his pictures and war memorials. Annette Becker, "Lucien Jonas, 'Le sauveur'," in *Valentiana. Cent images, cent textes, cent ans à Valenciennes,* 2526, Valenciennes, Cercle Historique et Archéologique de l'Arrondissement de Valenciennes, 2000.
51 Walter Benjamin, "Le Surréalisme, le dernier instantané de l'intelligentsia européenne" (1929), trans. from German in *Oeuvres*, vol. 2, Paris, Gallimard (Folio), 2000, p. 125.
52 Quoted in the catalog of the 1937 exhibition in relation to Dix's "Self portrait of Crippled Soldiers," which was destroyed after the exhibition. Los Angeles County Museum of Art, Exhibition *Entartete Kunst, 1937. Degenerate Art, the Fate of the Avant-Garde in Nazi Germany,* Los Angeles, 1991.

References and Further Reading

Audoin-Rouzeau, Stéphane, and Becker, Annette, *1914–1918. Understanding the Great War,* 2000; translated from French, London, Profile Books, 2002.

Becker, Annette (ed.), "Une Grande Guerre, 1914–années trente," *20–21.siècles. Cahiers du centre d'art et d'histoire Pierre Francastel,* 4, winter 2006–7.

Becker, Annette, *Apollinaire, une Biographie de guerre,* Paris, Tallandier, 2009.

Cooper, Douglas, *Fernand Léger, Dessins de guerre 1914–1918,* Paris, Berggruen, 1956.

Corbett, David (ed.), *Wyndham Lewis and the Art of Modern War,* Cambridge, Cambridge University Press, 1998.

Cork, Richard, *A Bitter Truth, Avant-Garde Art and the Great War,* New Haven, Yale University Press, 1994.

"La couleur des Larmes, les peintres et la Première Guerre mondiale," www.art-ww1.com/fr/visite.html

Dachy, Marc, *Dada: The Revolt of Art,* London, Thames and Hudson, 2005.

Dachy, Marc, *Archives Dada, Chronique,* Paris, Hazan, 2005.

Dagen, Philippe, *Le Silence des peintres, les artistes face à la Grande Guerre,* Paris, Fayard, 1996.

Dix, Otto, *The War,* Péronne, Historial de la Grande Guerre/ Milan, 5 Continents Editions, 2003 (cycle of etchings with critical essays by Annette Becker and Philippe Dagen).

Goebel, Stefan, "Exhibitions," in J. Winter and J.-L. Robert (eds.), *Capital Cities at War,* vol. 2, Cambridge, Cambridge University Press, 2007.

Green, Christopher, *Cubism and its Enemies: Modern Movements and Reaction in French Art, 1916–1928,* New Haven, Yale University Press, 1987.

Harries, Meirion, and Harries, Susie, *The War Artists: British Official War Art of the Twentieth Century,* London, Michael Joseph, 1983.

Jahn, Hubertus, *Patriotic Culture in Russia during World War I,* Ithaca, Cornell University Press, 1995.

Kahn, Elizabeth, *The Neglected Majority: "Les Camoufleurs," Art History and World War,* London, University Press of America, 1984.

Levitch, Mark, *Panthéon de la Guerre. Reconfiguring a Panorama of the Great War,* Columbia, University of Missouri Press, 2006.

Malvern, Sue, *Modern Art, Britain and the Great War,* New Haven, Yale University Press, 2004.

Saunders, Nicholas (ed.), *Matters of Conflict. Material Culture, Memory and the First World War,* London, Routledge, 2004.

Silver, Kenneth, *Esprit de Corps: The Art of the Parisian Avant-Garde and the First World War, 1914–1925,* Princeton, Princeton University Press, 1989.

CHAPTER TWENTY-FOUR

Film and the War

PIERRE SORLIN

War seems ideally suited to action movies. It gives spectators what they pay for – thrills, emotion, danger, heroism, and treason. Yet during the first years of the cinema, there was little fighting on the silver screen. If we take the example of an important American company, Biograph, which issued more than two hundred films a year around 1910, war accounted for less than one percent of its production.

Films of War

It was thanks to "factual" films that military conflicts first entered the cinema. The Anglo-Boer War (1899–1902) provided operators with the chance actually to film military operations. Interestingly, the main features of war films and the problems they pose to historians were already apparent during that campaign. Only a few cameramen went to the Transvaal. They were seldom allowed to visit the zone of operations and had to work in the rear. And some films were obvious "fakes" since the pictures were perfectly sharp, the soldiers efficient and everything was under control.

In the movies shot during the first decade of the century the platoon of soldiers was the key operational unit. Was this because contemporary military theory was shaped by the realities of colonial warfare? Whatever the reason, the imaginary warfare of the cinema was represented as the sum of heroic actions carried out by a handful of individuals. An important change took place with the Turkish-Italian conflict of 1911–12 and the Balkan Wars of 1912–13. Now instead of isolated soldiers, entire military units filed by on the screen. Cinematic depiction concentrated on the massive frontal advance of infantry or cavalry, but nothing was shown of firepower, heavy artillery, or logistics, the individual soldiers apparently carrying all they needed with them. Again, should we blame the cult of the offensive that had become fashionable amongst the general staffs or the dominant view that wars in the future would be short and over in a matter of days? Or were military theories less important than contemporary developments in filmmaking?

In 1908 the French Pathé Company, a leading producer that occasionally shot films dealing with recent events, converted these into weekly news magazines. This was the birth of the newsreel. The format met with such success that the company created nationally registered subsidiaries in Britain, Germany, the USA, and many other countries.

Other companies followed suit in France (Gaumont, Éclair), Britain (Gaumont Graphic, Topical Budget), and the USA, but on the eve of the war most European cinemas showed Pathé newsreels. In Austria, Germany, and Russia, local operators shot special issues dedicated to the sovereign, while Pathé covered ordinary events. In August 1914, the first images of German mobilization following the declaration of war were shot by the French company's operators. The newsreel companies did not look for originality; they were content with recording street scenes, public ceremonies, and military parades, which could be filmed for free. Whereas documentaries in the first decade of the cinema had focused mostly on individuals, newsreels introduced "the masses" to the silver screen.

Innovation also took place in fiction filmmaking. As films grew longer, short sketches and comic episodes were no longer enough. The plot had to become more complex and the action sequences extended. In 1912, the American film, *The Battle of Gettysburg*, which reconstructed the main phases of that engagement, was already a 60-minute movie. Meanwhile Italian studios, which could call on hundreds of extras at little cost and take advantage of historical monuments, contrived a new genre, the "colossal," which mingled love stories and epic scenes of combat. The success of these films prompted the Americans to imitate them, and the competition between these two countries resulted in the multiplication of war films precisely on the eve of the European conflagration.

War Cinema

It is unfortunately impossible to know how spectators in 1914 imagined a modern conflict. Did they envisage a war of movement, won by infantrymen? Did they go to the pictures to acquaint themselves with foreign and domestic events? It is unlikely this was the case, since the printed press remained the main source of information, while the cinema was considered mere entertainment. This explains why nobody in August 1914 thought in terms of a war cinema. There were war films, often fanciful and full of picturesque details, but they were ill-suited to an understanding of operations. General staffs had prepared their military campaigns carefully but had done little with regard to public opinion – perhaps because hostilities were expected to be very brief.

Governments quickly realized how important it was to control and monitor information, but their wish to reassure the country with plentiful and optimistic news met the resistance of the military authorities. Obsessed by the fear of espionage, the generals refused to let journalists visit the front line, let alone cameramen hampered by 40 kg of camera, tripod, and film. Hastily organized information services provided the newspapers with press releases but they had no material for films. Furthermore, most movie companies faced a difficult situation because their technicians had been mobilized, their laboratories requisitioned for war production, and all they could do was record what could be freely filmed in the streets during parades or in railway stations when soldiers left for the front. During the first year of the conflict, many newsreels were filled, alongside banal scenes of military reviews, with the usual items about social activities and sport.

In Germany and Austria the Pathé companies were confiscated as enemy property and given to national firms. The most important of these was owned by a camera manufacturer, Oskar Messter, who had already made documentaries. In October 1914, he launched the first regular German newsreels, the *Messter-Woche* (Messter Week). His operators were dispatched to the rear of the combat zone, where they were hampered by transport problems, and when their images were damaged or arrived too late, they had to be replaced by pictures of life on the home front. A Danish company, Nordisk, had long been established in German-speaking countries, where it managed a large chain of movie theaters. As neutrals, its expert operators had not been conscripted and they were allowed to shoot a few *Kriegsbilder* (war pictures), which were technically much better than Messter's films but far removed from the hardships of the conflict. As the German military was extremely wary of espionage and leaks of secret information, it showed no interest in the diffusion of pictures and was content simply to warn that nothing could be revealed about artillery, camouflage, or the organization of the trenches. After a hesitant start, Messter chose a particular point of view, with his pictures emphasizing the good treatment of the ordinary German soldier and the quality of his food, armaments, and living conditions. Owing to restrictions on consumption, German civilians experienced considerable material discomfort, but at least until 1917, the newsreels encouraged them to believe that their hardship was useful and helped their menfolk fight.

In November 1914 Messter launched the *Sascha Messter Woche*, an Austrian version of his *Wochenschau*, but in this he had been anticipated by the Austro-Hungarian government which, as early as September, had created its own official newsreel – the *Kriegs Journal*. Vienna faced two particular problems. First, there were many ethnic groups in the multinational empire whom the military were concerned should serve far from their homelands. Thus Slavs were not sent to the Russian front or Italians to the Alps but were instead deployed in distant provinces, where films showing how well they were treated served to reassure their families and discourage them from helping the enemy. Second, Vienna found it necessary to gather the unreliable populations of Galicia and the Trentino in camps and, again, newsreels were used to prove that they wanted for nothing. Austrian films were unusual in that their political function was clear from the start.

Most French newsreels shot between 1914 and 1917 have unfortunately been lost. The only complete surviving series, that of Gaumont, presents a country where people gaily seek to preserve their peacetime habits. Everyday life, resourceful ways of overcoming wartime difficulties, and patriotic ceremonies intended to mobilize popular enthusiasm alternate with glimpses of the French army. In February 1915, after lengthy negotiations, the newsreel companies agreed with the War Ministry that their operators would be allowed to work in the army zone but under censorship. Contrary to previous practice, the news films seldom lingered over official ceremonies and, when they did, it was always to emphasize the close relationship between France and the British or Russian allies. Not much was shown regarding the soldiers' everyday life, despite the fact that this was probably what civilians really wanted to see. Of course, no bayonet charges, hand-to-hand fighting or shelling of the trenches were ever presented to the public. The soldiers seemed locked in routine – carrying food, mounting guard, installing machine-guns and firing. Nineteen sixteen was marked by the long, bloody defense of Verdun against German attack. The battle lasted from February to December and involved more than a million soldiers on both sides. But little footage of Verdun was shown on the newsreels, possibly because operators had no access to the sector. The only significant treatment came with Eclair's *Around Verdun*, made in November, whose images offer an impressive panorama of the besieged city. At the end of the film a wounded cameraman is shown being evacuated – possibly to demonstrate how dangerous an activity filming could be.

Britain offers a striking contrast with Germany and France. Since there was no conscription until 1916, cameramen were able to cross the Channel with the first contingents of the British Expeditionary Force. While Kitchener's volunteer army was forming in England in 1914–15, cinema audiences could witness the helplessness of Belgian refugees carrying their children and belongings along the roads of their country. Did such distressing pictures lure some British and Irish men into volunteering? Here, as in France, the Pathé documents are not available, but we have Gaumont's and Topical Budget's newsreels.[1] The British newsreels quickly showed that they were less constrained than their French or German counterparts. Of course there were countless ceremonies in the presence of members of the royal family or generals, but the tone was relaxed and the soldiers did not hesitate to greet the cameraman and the audience behind him. In a May 1915 item entitled "Changing Quarters," as a camera mounted on a car passes an infantry unit, the operator and men cheer each other warmly and the film keeps running as long as the men wave their hands. German or French soldiers never looked so relaxed, not because they were more serious, but because the operators had been instructed to select only suitably soldierly scenes. In a *Gaumont British* sequence, nurses were seen seated on the knees of wounded men, stroking their heads and combing their hair – an image inconceivable elsewhere. The soldiers seemed content, and if they were not shown to be as materially well treated as in the German newsreels, they were seen to take life sportingly – indeed, sport was actually paramount in their activities. This relaxed approach extended to revealing military equipment, as in an August 1915 Gaumont film showing how gunners assembled and dismantled a machine gun: there may have been a wealth of useful details for the Germans in such a document.

British films were not merely heartening, they were also frank about some of the realities of war. An agreement between the newsreel companies and the army resulted in permission to film behind the lines so that spectators could see coffins brought home from the continent (*Topical Budget*, September 1, 1915), dead bodies (*Topical Budget*, September 8, 1915) and wounded men (*Gaumont*, August 5, 1915). There were no dreadful images, no smashed faces, and no severely disabled men, and the public were offered more royal visits to hospitals than invalids, but the relative openness of British films contrasted with the discretion of their foreign counterparts and raises an important question: what could be shown in the cinema? Answers diverged. Some found it urgent to disclose the distressing side of war, because people had to be awakened to such realities, and also because it was the only way to mourn the loss of loved ones. *The Times* on September 16, 1916 published a letter that read: "I have lost a son in battle, and I have seen the films [about the battle of the Somme] twice. I am going to see them again. I want to know what was the life, and the life-in-death, that our dear ones endured."[2] Others doubted whether this was the right solution. Are not such pictures "too painful for public exhibition?" questioned *The Star* on August 25, 1916. In some cases, town councils forbade the projection of revealing films in front of young people, and soldiers sometimes wrote from the front to say that civilians should be spared distressing pictures. Oddly enough a few contended that the view of bodies might dissuade the young from enlisting. The debate makes us ask ourselves what is bearable, what can or cannot be displayed on a screen. It is easy today to blame censorship for the emptiness and inaccuracy of war information, but are we certain that people wanted to know? Did spectators or opinion leaders attempt to obtain more serious pictures? If we look at the contemporary voices that criticized newsreels in the press, we find that when demanding more realism what they meant was not mud, rain, rats, shelling, and wounded men but rather action, advance, and all that was likely to cheer civilians up and alleviate the intolerable waiting.

At the outset of the war British and French newsreels no longer reached Russia. Local producers were all too happy to get rid of the foreign competition. With the help of the Ministry of War they set up a cinematic weekly, *The Mirror of War*. In a few weeks the Russian army conquered Galicia and part of Poland and in the wake of the invasion, operators worked at ease and produced sharp, well-framed pictures. Until May 1915 the Russian films, filled with happy privates and long files of prisoners, gave an optimistic view of the conflict. However, the Austrian counter-offensive in the summer of 1915 scattered the film operators and on-screen military information was replaced by tourist images and endless official ceremonies. To what extent did the display of pomp and circumstance at a moment of deep crisis in the Russian war effort alienate public opinion toward the Tsar and his entourage? (See chapter 32.)

By the time their country entered the war in May 1915 the Italians had seen many war films projected by the diplomatic efforts of both camps. The High Command understood that the cinema might help to raise civilian morale and created a cinematographic unit, which worked rather freely for two years. Little has survived of the pictures it took, but the remaining images show the disastrous state of an unprepared army: heavy guns drawn by oxen, ill-dressed soldiers taking up positions in the mud or snow, outdated armaments and even, in some cases, attacks on open ground against a well-entrenched adversary. None of these images was ever screened; effective censorship meant that, beside the usual headings about socialites and sport, celebrations and military gatherings were mostly shown in the newsreels.

The audience for film grew throughout the conflict. In Germany, for instance, about seven hundred new cinema theaters opened between 1914 and 1919. It has sometimes been suggested that people went to the pictures in order to escape their worries. This may be true, but there is no way of proving such a psychological explanation. The reverse could equally be the case – that many were too worried to enjoy going out. Perhaps we should stick to more prosaic motives. Full employment guaranteed relatively high wages, few goods were available, and prices were stable in cinemas whereas they had risen in theaters. The British case seems to confirm this point. From 1913 through 1916 about half of the seats cost less than four pence; meanwhile it is estimated (we do not have exact figures) that the number of tickets increased by 80 percent. In May 1916 the Entertainments Tax, index-linked to inflation, raised prices by 20 and sometimes 30 percent; in the following two years cinemas lost one-quarter of their clientele – although this remained at a higher level than in 1913.

Information films had a very limited place in the programs, fiction making up the bulk of the projections in all countries. Patriotic films flourished in 1914–15. In Britain, 66 flag-waving pictures were shot in 1914 alone. A few titles set the tone: *The German Spy Peril, Your Country Needs You, The War against the Huns, The United Front, Killed in Action*; cowards or indifferent people became aware of their duty, civilians proved vigilant and worked hard, while soldiers were heroic. The spirit was identical on the other side with titles such as *Guarding the Rhine, German Women*, and *German Trust*. The outburst of vociferous patriotism was short-lived. Britain produced only four war pictures in January 1915 while in the following months most nationalist films were a failure with audiences. Serials – adventure stories involving the same group of characters and shown week after week – had been extremely popular before the war. Mobilization made it difficult to shoot them regularly, but the British and the French tried hard with *Ultus* and *Vampires*, respectively, though they were unable to meet the exhibitors' expectations. Pathé preferred to import the serials made by its American branch. *The Perils of*

Pauline, The Exploits of Elaine, and *The Mysteries of Myra* did very well in Europe but threw the door wide open to US pictures. The Central Powers were beyond American reach, and films there were so scarce that British or French movies could still be shown provided they were not patriotic. Little by little a domestic output was established. Germany had its own serials, including the very strange *Homonculus,* in which a manlike artificial creature becomes a cruel dictator and provokes a world war. With a few exceptions, from 1915 onwards, the feature films screened in the fighting countries were amusing or thrilling pictures akin to those projected before 1914.

Film as War Propaganda

In 1915, the belligerents believed that a modern conflict could not go on indefinitely. In 1916, both sides attempted to break the enemy – the Russians in Galicia, the Germans at Verdun, and the French and British on the Somme. All these offensives failed, with high casualties. The Somme was a particular shock for Britain since this was the first mass engagement of the volunteer Kitchener Army, and the casualties on the first day of the battle, July 1, 1916, were the highest in British history. Public opinion was deeply affected. Cameramen had filmed the preparations; they returned home on July 10 and it was decided that their material should be used to inform the public. Editing began on July 13 and a 74-minute film entitled *The Battle of the Somme* was released on August 21, although the battle would last two more months.

Previously the military office for propaganda had issued a few amateurish films, notably *Britain Prepared,* which emphasized the strength of the Royal Navy, but was elusive on terrestrial operations, so that the *Manchester Guardian* and the *Star* found it disappointing. *The Battle of the Somme,* on the other hand, was carefully made and its circulation masterfully organized; one million Londoners formed lines to see it and, in six weeks, it was said to have attracted some twenty million Britons[3]. Contemporary testimonies show that spectators were moved, especially by the sequence during which soldiers get out of the trench and run – some of them falling. The film remains impressive today.[4] There are a few blunders; some men have been artificially put in front of the camera and smile awkwardly, and the famous attack is clearly a fake. The soldiers leave their trench quietly, those who fall are careful not to hurt themselves, and, once on the ground, they lie comfortably. Audiences in 1916 were less critical than we are; nobody noted the mistakes, which do not spoil the picture. Its most striking feature is how it focuses on the life and works of the ordinary soldiers. Officers are mere silhouettes and there is no commentary on the strategic goals of the battle. The captions are short and purely factual, conveying what a soldier in the field could understand. Three main themes are tackled in succession: first, the preparation, with the arrival of troops and munitions and heavy shelling on the German lines; second the attack, which is short, with quick shots taken from various angles; third, the aftermath, which slowly and inexorably explores a battlefield laid waste, with long files of prisoners, the wounded, and the bodies. The devastation caused by war had never been exposed in such a direct, insistent and dramatic way.

Distributed all over the world by the Foreign Office, the film met with a warm response in neutral countries, especially in the USA. Such favorable reaction is worthy of note. We are used to seeing propaganda as brainwashing and propagandist films as emphatic and full of confidence. But there was no patriotic optimism here or trite catchphrases. The uniforms were British, but the last third of the film did not belong to either camp and could have been shot on any part of the western front. The neutrals, fed up with slogans, appreciated the restrained, factual content of the picture. Interestingly, its direct, unembellished character counted in favor of the British.

The Central Powers did not miss the point. Their agents reported that the film was a powerful moral weapon with which the clumsy *Messter Woche* could not compete, and they urged their respective governments to find a reply. Who could rise to the challenge? Many people in Germany were anxious to preserve the industrial markets conquered before the war and were already thinking about the future. In November 1916, with the help of Messter, a group of businessmen and financiers closely connected to the engineering and armaments industries founded the Deutsche Lichtbild-Gesellschaft (German Photography Company, or DEULIG), which was entrusted with advertising German industry abroad. Messter, under the aegis of DEULIG, offered to respond to the British film, but he had sent no operator to France and had little interesting material available. There were endless arguments about the best way of countering *The Battle of the Somme*, and it was only on January 19, 1917, at a time when the campaign was merely a bad memory, that *Bei unseren Helden an der Somme* (*With our Heroes on the Somme*) was released.

The film had been advertised long in advance, and newspapers and spectators were informed that "heroic German operators" had been exposed to enemy fire on the front line in the course of shooting "the greatest cinematic document of this terrible war." Too much had been expected; the public was disappointed. The 33-minute picture was much shorter than its British counterpart. It comprised three sections. At the outset, in line with the dominant style of the *Messter Woche*, soldiers were seen leading their normal lives. Suddenly, the British began to bombard them in such an awkward way that the French civilians who were behind the German lines had to flee. The purpose of the first part was twofold, to prove that the British were the aggressors and to show German audiences what would happen if battles ever took place in their country. But, at the same time, it appeared that the Germans had not been able to detect the British preparations and had not remained on guard. Reinforcements arrived, captions announced a German counter-offensive, which was part two, and part three consisted of a local engagement. Many shots had been borrowed from previous battles, with some men wearing the "spiked helmet" that had been replaced by the steel helmet in 1916. Others had been filmed in the rear, since in reality the operators could not have worked anywhere near exploding shells or run ahead of the attacking troops – but nobody noted such fakes. There were, as usual, cohorts of prisoners, and the film came to a sudden end, with no conclusion or attempt at explaining the importance of the operations and no mention of the fact that the British attack had failed. The press was enthusiastic but nobody was fooled; it was a poor work, which was never sent abroad.

The coverage given to the Somme was especially intense in French newsreels, perhaps because filming at Verdun was almost impossible. Later, most sequences shot during the battle were edited together in a special issue titled *The French Offensive on the Somme, July 1916*. Was it an answer to *The Battle of the Somme*? Their many similarities are obvious. Both stress the fire power and perfect readiness of their respective armies but show almost nothing of the fighting, and neither explains why the offensive did not put an end to the war or, more importantly, even alludes to the part played by the ally. But released only when the battle was over, the French film went almost unnoticed.

The Somme films, especially the British movie, marked a turning point in the use of cinematic material. *The Battle of the Somme* had shown how effective a good picture could be, but the experience could not be repeated. The film had been screened in cinemas, with exhibitors agreeing to free showings, but they refused to do so again and the follow-up productions of the War Office, *The Battle of the Ancre and the Advance of the Tanks* (January 1917) and *The Battle of Arras* (June 1917), met with a lukewarm response. The War Office found it necessary to intervene in the production of filmed news. In May 1917 it took control of *Topical Budget* and produced a twice-weekly newsreel that was compulsorily projected at the end of every film show. A few months earlier, in January 1917, the French Ministry of War had broken its agreement with the private film companies, which it blamed for producing patchy material. A Section Photographique et Cinématographique de l'Armée (Photographic and Cinematographic Section of the Army) was created under the direct authority of the government and given the monopoly of filming and photographing the war. It produced a weekly newsreel, the *War Annals*, which all movie theaters had to show. Meanwhile, the Italians had set up a Cinematic Unit controlled by the High Command and fixed *Rules for the War Correspondents*.

The reorganization of cinematic information in the Entente modified people's view of military operations. Cinema is important here because it unwittingly provides a direct testimony to the climate of the period. Previously, documentary film manifested an absolute lack of concern for what was happening outside the national community. A significant change occurred in the first months of 1917 as pictures began to circulate from country to country and allied forces were introduced in the newsreels. In November 1917 an edition of the *War Annals* celebrated "the conjuncture of the English and French armies in Flanders" with a caption about "brotherhood of arms." Likewise, in March 1918 *Topical Budget* showed two columns of soldiers meeting each other, one British and one French, and lingered on the exchange of smiles and cigarettes, underlining the theme of fraternization. In March 1918, when the Germans attacked part of the British sector, a *War Annals* issue showed French units coming to their aid. In October 1918 a *Topical Budget* operator who was filming British troops entering Lille left them to focus on a French soldier, followed him, and ended on a group of French women. Overall, in 1918, 40 percent of the subjects treated by *Topical Budget* concerned allied countries – Belgium, Italy, Greece, and China but above all France and the USA.

Another innovation was the emphasis placed on modern warfare and on the use of sophisticated weaponry. Until 1917, infantry attacks and life in the trenches or in the rear made up the bulk of military information in the newsreels; the main arms were the rifle and the machine gun. But in 1918, tanks and anti-tank defenses, long-range guns and howitzers took the lead, and audiences saw trains carrying huge piles of shells to the front and leaving with thousands of gigantic, empty cases. Aviation was given a lot of space. Whereas, previously, individuals were neither singled out nor named, now there were portraits of famous pilots with details about their deeds while politicians or generals, instead of attending ceremonies, visited aircraft factories. Was this a way of diverting audiences' attention from the depressing stalemate, or did it just reflect the evolution of the conflict? Whatever the answer, cinema audiences were offered a quite different view of the war.

What part did American intervention in the war play in this transformation of the cinematic representation of the conflict? The landing of US troops, the only good news for the Allies in the difficult year of 1917, was extensively exploited in Britain, France, and Italy. Several newsreel issues were dedicated to the arrival of the "Teddies," and there were also episodes that dealt with "America at war." Cinema screens showed fraternizing between American and other allied soldiers and the perfect equipment of the US army – and paid tribute to the latter's efficiency on the battlefield. The homage to America was also a way of counterbalancing the worst event of 1917, the defection of Russia. There are no images of the 1917 revolution in the *War Annals* or in the issues of *Topical Budget* that we can still consult. Although there is no precise evidence, it is hard to believe that governments did not instruct their cinematic services to emphasize the perfect cohesion of the "Entente" at a time when Russia was treating with Berlin and Vienna – and so edit Russia out of the newsreels.

Of course, American film companies had long been interested in the conflict. The US newsreels were fairly different from their European counterparts in that they paid more attention to foreign problems. In October 1914 operators were sent to Europe, where they filmed the fighting in Belgium. During the following years a score of documentaries shot on both sides were released in America. The troops that disembarked in summer 1917 included a cinematic unit of the Signal Corps that was entrusted with following operations and illustrating the part played by American soldiers in the victory. Initially, emphasis was placed on training, collaboration with other armies, and visits by officials, but after a few months American operators freed themselves from European models and did not hesitate to select a few men and follow them for a short while (necessarily in actions staged in the rear). The editing was quick and lively, and made more alert by swift changes of framing shots. There was also, in captions, an anti-German stance, which could not be found in European films. The American producers did not hesitate to endow their films with political opinions that the Europeans carefully avoided.

The Americans were the first to use the cinema systematically in campaigns for enlistment and public loans. Charlie Chaplin, Mack Sennett, and other stars cooperated in the making of patriotic pictures, and their example spread. Whereas, previously, Europeans had publicized war loans in the most traditional manner, with written exhortations or at best with colored posters, cinema advertising boomed in 1917. The German government, with pressing financial needs, called up actors and cameramen while Henny Porten, a famous female star, crusaded for the national defense and, from September 1917, featured in pictures backing the war effort. Professional rivalries and the conflicts of interest that weakened cinema propaganda marred her attempts. On the one hand film producers, jealous of Nordisk's dominant position, denounced "the struggle of that company to put the entire German market under its control," and did their best to hamper its expansion. On the other hand, the shipping, chemical, and electrical industries and the Reichsbank considered DEULIG's foreign policy too conventional and pitted another agency against it – the Bild- und Film-Amt (BUFA). Backed by the military information services, BUFA produced documentaries and feature films that really challenged Messter. In December 1917 the Supreme Command, which had become politically dominant, gathered all services and agencies, including Messter and Nordisk, into the *Universum Film Aktien-Gesellschaft*, known as UFA. But there was no real collaboration; each department continued carrying out its own projects and only after the war did UFA become a leading film company.

The Legacy of the War on the Cinema

The same questions always arise in discussing the mass media: did they genuinely inform public opinion, and did they exert any influence? The answer depends on one's understanding of information and influence. In 1914, cinema was considered merely a pastime;

newsreels and documentaries were an amusement because, as was often said, they opened a window on the world, but they were not meant to communicate serious information. The press had become important in the nineteenth century, and people who had learnt how to read the papers were used to interpreting their silence or their forced optimism. Cinema, by contrast, had no such importance. Governments and general staffs looked with disapproval on operators who were likely to leak secrets, and film companies did not want to bother their public with unpleasant images, so that, during the first months of the conflict, there was a tacit agreement that operations were to be followed in newspapers while little could be learnt about them from films. It was the passing of time – the endless succession of unchanging days – that gave birth to a war cinema. Ordinary citizens wanted first to learn more about the hardships that were the lot of their friends or relatives, and secondly to know when the war would end, but nobody was in a position to satisfy them; all they could do was try to guess on the basis of the media. Screened week after week, the sight of the front, however unsatisfactory, became a ritual, and many spectators clung to it to gain an insight into life in the trenches, a sense of the reality of the fighting and perhaps a glimpse of a son or husband. There were differences from country to country. The debate that took place in Britain about the limits of what could be shown was unique, and even in that country it seems that civilians did not want to witness the full horrors of war. Most films offered a rather sanitized version of what was happening, but they created a new feeling about it and often provoked a strong emotional response. As some spectators said after attending *The Battle of the Somme*, it gave "a sense of participating." That is why it is difficult to talk about information or influence. Spectators learnt very little, were neither convinced nor revolted by the images, but they gained a different understanding of the conflict – an impression unknown to previous generations.

Miles of raw film had been shot during the hostilities. Britain, France, and Italy did not bother to conserve them, and it is estimated that 60 percent have been lost. Britain and France, locked into the celebration of their victory and the mourning for their heroes, did not use visual documents to look back at the conflict, and there was no time for reflection in an Italy paralyzed by social and political conflicts. It should be added that the war destroyed European filmmaking. In 1914 the main exporters of moving pictures were France, Denmark, and Italy, while American output, quantitatively predominant, was aimed at domestic consumers. French domination did not survive the declaration of war. Pathé's production shrank, the firm lost its markets, and it survived only thanks to its American branch; in the years that followed the peace it was obliged to sell all its subsidiaries. Nordisk, in August 1914, had opted for the Austro-German camp where it had a stake in production and distribution. Its profits were high in 1915 and 1916 but it was then challenged by German firms and, after the war, its alliance with the defeated countries ensured its downfall. The tremendous prewar success of Italian films was fragile. The studios had borrowed much money from the banks and were crippled with debts, while the closing of most outlets resulted in a spate of bankruptcies. It took Italy 20 years to reappear in foreign movie markets. Hollywood, however, benefited from the conflict. Between 1914 and 1917 American film exports had already grown threefold; by the end of the decade, 90 percent of the films released everywhere in Europe were of American origin.

Nevertheless, the hostilities were not the only cause of the disaster. While the Americans rationalized their studios and cared about distribution as well as production, European companies dissipated their efforts and competed with each other instead of sharing the markets between them. They relied too much on bank loans and neglected distribution. They were already losing their Latin American clients in 1914 and even without the conflict their sales to other countries would have decreased in the 1920s. The hostilities had been less damaging for the Americans than for the Europeans. Hollywood, intent on producing thrilling, moving stories, was quick to seize hold of a conflict that had shaken the world. The studios spurned informative films, which provided neither individual heroism nor romance, but shot 11 feature films dealing with the war before the arrival of the talkies.[5]

Germany was a different case. Deprived of foreign pictures during the hostilities, the country developed its own industry. There were over 200 film companies in 1919 compared to 30 in 1913, and the creation of UFA provided Germany with up-to-date equipment, as modern and efficient as Hollywood's. Immediately after the Armistice the harsh debates began about the origins of the war, German responsibilities for the conflict, and the causes of the defeat – and widespread use was made of the cinema to shed light on the past. Communists and socialists made didactic short films, the former to show how capitalism had led to the general conflagration, the latter to display the horrors of war and promote international cooperation. Simultaneously the Stahlhelm used war documentaries to celebrate the bravery of the German army.

From 1926 to 1933 Germany issued 17 war films, more than twice the production of France or Britain. Six fictional films were dedicated to the German navy. This sheds light on a controversial problem. For after the Battle of Jutland in 1916, the German fleet never again sought a full-scale engagement and was taxed at home with pusillanimity. U-boat warfare, by contrast, was severely criticized by the allies. The films aimed to show that the sailors had been as good as any others and that the submariners, who risked their lives in trying conditions, were not pirates. There was pride in these works, but not nationalism or feelings of revenge. Five further films were rather banal war stories with a touch of love interest.[6] Two offered a grim vision of life and death in the trenches without criticizing either the government or the Supreme Command.

There were also four historical documentaries made with stock shots and reenacted scenes. There was no artistic pretension in these movies. Nothing was done to soften the contrast between the faded, clumsy archival shots and the sharp pictures taken in peacetime. The actors who played the part of the Kaiser, the Tsar, or senior officers performed as plainly as possible and the account was clear and didactic. *Douaumont* (1931) and *Tannenberg* (1932) reconstructed two episodes of the conflict. Much more ambitious were *Der Weltkrieg* (*The World War*, 1927) and *1914, Die letzten Tage vor dem Weltbrand* (*1914, The Last Days before the World Conflagration*, 1931), which tried to explain the causes of the conflict. The former, stressing the excessive power of both the British navy and the Russian army, illustrated the classic thesis of the "encirclement" of Imperial Germany. The latter, inspired by the recently published German diplomatic documents, portrayed a weak, pacific Tsar manipulated by his ministers. The most interesting aspect of these films was the limited part reserved for France. In *Der Weltkrieg* the Marne was a secondary episode, emphasis being placed on the eastern front and on Russian attacks. In *The Last Days*, France was reduced to the figure of Jaurès fighting hopelessly for peace. It is significant that, despite the occupation of the Ruhr and the quarrels over reparations, German movies directed at a general public accused Tsarist Russia more than France.

German spectators saw both American and national war films but the contrast between the two styles and plot lines was so obvious that both could be enjoyed in their own way.

German films presented a collective protagonist, a platoon, a crew, or a group of friends. Sometimes the men were anonymous or were named after their origin or their job. Shot at medium range, the films focused on the soldiers, their attitudes, and their gestures. The story unfolded without breaks, the editing avoided all devices such as shot-reverse shot or close-ups likely to interrupt its development, and the audience followed the men closely. American films were centered on a hero – brave, a daredevil – who might be hurt or wounded but who survived and married the pretty girl. There were unexpected camera movements, strange cuts, brutal cut-ins. War was portrayed as dangerous but also as an adventure in which young people discovered both themselves and each other.

It is against this background that the polemic provoked by the Hollywood-made film of Erich Maria Remarque's best-selling novel, *All Quiet on the Western Front* (1930), exploded.[7] The film paints a rather sad picture of the war but it was neither the first nor the last critical view of the conflict. Despite their ultimate optimism – the hero survives – most American movies displayed appalling battle scenes and there were horrors in other contemporary French or German pictures. Furthermore, the sequence of *All Quiet* in which civilians prove totally unaware of the hardships soldiers suffer in the trenches was likely to please veterans. However the film was banned from German screens for eight months and was authorized only after 50 minutes out of 140 had been cut. In France 20 minutes were censored and the ban was total in fascist Italy. As is usually the case with controversial works, it was less the plot than a conjunction of various factors that infuriated spectators in different countries. The protagonist was German, but the winners disliked a German hero, while the Germans hated an American point of view on their war. The film had a cleverly conflated central character who was typical both of American movies and of the group of comrades characteristic of German films. The editing process was original; there were many close-ups, especially on food, which was a permanent concern of the men, and the idea of hunger was made acceptable provided it was not linked to incessant scenes of eating. Some sequences were stunning. The battle scene begins in German fashion, with the Germans' subjective view of the French attack, but then the camera hung over the battlefield on a mobile crane (a tool never used in Europe) makes the combatants look like dwarfs. Most impressive was the sound (another novelty) – not only the hyperrealistic sounds of heavy guns and shells, but also the clever and at times disturbing musical score. In short, this was a creative work that made spectators feel uncomfortable and it triggered endless polemics: fighting for peace versus honoring the war dead.

Fifty Years After

As is generally the case, it was not the film itself that was at stake but rather the contrasting views that it brought to the surface of public debate. Films are not important for what they show but for what they disclose indirectly. In this instance, *All Quiet* helped revive an intense political debate about the meaning of the war. However, only a few more films about World War I were made during the 1930s, since the coming conflict diverted people's attention toward more urgent issues and, from 1940 onward, World War II overwhelmed the screens.

It was only in the middle of the twentieth century that World War I reappeared on the screen. In less than a decade the cinema suddenly produced another view of the conflict. First there was *Paths of Glory* in 1957.[8] Then came *La Grande Illusion*, which was released in 1937, severely cut and then banned on a charge of pacifism, and re-released in its entirety in 1959.[9] Italy, which had always avoided the theme, produced *La Grande Guerra*, while in 1964 *King and Country* came from Britain.[10] Fifty years had elapsed and the survivors were old and ready to reconsider the past. Europe was trying to overcome its divisions and Western Europe had chosen the American camp, helping it to bury old quarrels. There were also the television channels, which needed new, exciting programs. Great evocations of historical events, with archival footage, reconstructions, testimonies, and interviews with historians spread from the USA in the late 1950s and archivists began to hunt for newsreels in the archives of production companies. The films mentioned above were, to a large extent, a reaction against a celebration that otherwise ran the risk of being purely a formality.

La Grande Illusion met with a favorable response, being recognized as a classic, though few people had seen it when it originally came out. The friendship between a French and a German officer, the love story between a German farmer's wife and a French soldier, perfectly suited the mood of the 1950s. The other films met with a strong reaction. In Italy there was a violent campaign to ban *La Grande Guerra,* and if *Paths of Glory* was not prohibited in France its distributor did not dare release it. Both *Paths of Glory* and *King and Country* attacked head-on the theme of "execution as a deterrent" – that is, the judicial murder of soldiers to intimidate their comrades. Yet the impact of *La Grande Illusion* was ultimately stronger, perhaps because it came first, but also because it was stylistically much more interesting. The dialogs are reduced to a minimum, whereas in *King and Country* there is a long protest against capital punishment. *Paths of Glory* achieves a striking contrast between the reserve officer, a barrister, who is the defender of his men, and the generals who, being exclusively interested in promotion and honors, sacrifice lightheartedly the soldiers in hopeless attacks and shoot them if they fail. The Italian film *The Great War* is less sophisticated than *La Grande Illusion*. It relies on an alternation of dramatic and humorous scenes, and is in effect a comedy interspersed – and eventually marred – by the horror of war.

The controversies of the 1960s had nothing in common with the arguments that had surrounded *All Quiet*. They marked the end of an epoch, for in their wake the behavior of generals, the attitudes of officers toward the soldiers, the distress of the infantrymen, and the pathos of military executions could never be seen in the same way again. It is not by chance that numerous historians revisited World War I in the 1970s. Their authors may have begun their work earlier, but the films unlocked the issues and made it possible to rethink the conflict. Subsequently, there were many other films about the war but they were no longer contentious. World War I had entered History.

The films shot between 1914 and 1918 provide the modern viewer with information on the war, but still photographs say as much as the movies. The importance of the cinema lies elsewhere, and that may be why historians seldom use it. For it shows what people saw at the time, forming part of their life and their understanding of the event. The British debate about the "bearable," the impact of *The Battle of the Somme,* and the changes in the conception of newsreels after 1917 all give us glimpses of the reactions of the audiences. But it is only by looking at the pictures themselves that we can imagine the spectators' feelings. In the postwar era, films helped fix the common understanding of the conflict. *All Quiet,* often shown on television and remade for the small screen in 1979, has become a staple view of the reality of trench warfare, and all the more so in that it supports the view of World War I as a tragic catastrophe that is now dominant in Europe.[11] Historians have to take account of this. Their publications will never be as convincing as a good film, however biased the latter may be.

Notes

1   The complete catalog of the war newsreels still available is to be found at bufvc.ac.uk/data-bases/newsreels.

2   This poses a serious problem: what can be inferred from the "letters to the editor"? In a letter published in *Bioscope* (August 1, 1918), another person protested against the screening of "happenings that may even at that very moment be occurring to those we hold most dear." But the two years that had elapsed between these letters may account for the difference in viewpoint.

3   There were only 44 million Britons at the time.

4   It is available, together with *The Battle of the Ancre,* on a video-cassette (DD 702) published by the Imperial War Museum, London.

5   Notably *The Four Horsemen of the Apocalypse, The Big Parade, What Price Glory,* and *Wings.*

6   *Westfront 1918* (*Western Front, 1918*) and *Niemandsland* (*No Man's Land*), both shot in 1931.

7   Production: Universal; directed by Lewis Milestone, starring Lew Ayres.

8   Production: Harris–Kubrick; directed by Stanley Kubrick, starring Kirk Douglas.

9   Production: RAC; directed by Jean Renoir, starring Jean Gabin, Eric von Stroheim, and Pierre Fresnay.

10 *La Grande Guerra*, production: De Laurentiis, directed by Mario Monicelli, starring Vittorio Gassman, Alberto Sordi; *King and Country*, production BHE/Warner; directed by Joseph Losey, starring Dirk Bogarde and Tom Courtenay.

11 Directed by Delbert Mann, starring Richard Thomas.

References and Further Reading

Barkhausen, Hans, *Filmpropaganda für Deutschland im Ersten und Zweiten Weltkrieg,* Hildesheim and Zurich, Olms, 1992.

Britain and the Cinema in the First World War, special issue of *The Historical Journal of Film, Radio and Television,* 13, 2, 1993.

Brownlow, Kevin, *The War, the West and the Wilderness,* London, Secker and Warburg, 1979.

Dibbets, Karel, and Hogenkamp, Bert (eds.), *Film and the First World War,* Amsterdam, Amsterdam University Press, 1995.

Fielding, Raymond, *The American Newsreels, 1911–1967,* Norman, University of Oklahoma Press, 1972.

Kelly, Andrew, *Cinema and the Great War,* London and New York, Routledge, 1997.

Kester, Bernadette, *Film Front Weimar. Representations of the First World War in German Films of the Weimar Period (1919–1933),* Amsterdam, Amsterdam University Press, 2003.

Lemaire, Françoise, *Les Films militaires français de la première guerre mondiale,* Paris, ECPA, 1997.

Lemaire, Françoise, *World War and Popular Cinema, 1914 to the Present,* Edinburgh, Edinburgh University Press, 2000.

Martinelli, Vittorio, "Il Cinema italiano in armi," in Reno Renzi (ed.), *Sperduto nel buio. Il cinema italiano e il suo tempo, 1905–1930,* Bologna, Capelli, 1991.

Mould, David, H., *American News Film, 1914–1919: The Underexposed War,* New York, Garland, 1983.

Oppelt, Ulrike, *Film und Propaganda im ersten Weltkrieg. Propaganda als Medienrealitat im Aktualitäten- und Dokumentarfilm,* Stuttgart, Steiner, 2002.

Paris, Michael (ed.), *The First World War and Popular Cinema, 1914 to the Present,* Edinburgh, Edinburgh University Press, 2000.

Reeves, Nicholas, *Official British Film Propaganda during the First World War,* London, Croom Helm, 1986.

Reeves, Nicholas, "Through the Eye of the Camera: Contemporary Cinema Audiences and their 'Experience' of War in the Film *Battle of the Somme*," in Hugh Cecil and Peter H. Liddle (eds.), *Facing Armageddon. The First World War Experienced*, London, Leo Cooper, 1996, pp. 780–98.

Rother, Rainer (ed.), *Die letzten Tage der Menschheit. Bilder der ersten Weltkrieges*, Berlin, Ars Nicolai, 1994.

Sanders, Michael L., and Taylor, Philip M., *British Propaganda during the First World War, 1914–1918*, London, Macmillan, 1982.

Véray, Laurent, *Les Films d'actualité français de la Grande Guerre*, Paris, SIRPA, 1995.

Ward, Larry Wayne, *The Motion Picture Goes to War: The U.S. Government Film Effort during World War I*, Ann Arbor, Michigan University Research Press, 1985.

Wood, Richard (ed.), *Film and Propaganda in America. A Documentary History*, vol. 1, *World War I*, New York, Greenwood Press, 1991.

Select Filmography of World War I

1916 *The Battle of the Somme* (Britain, filmed by Geoffrey Malins & John McDowell)
1917 *The Battle of the Ancre and the First Tanks* (Britain, dir. Geoffrey Malins)
– *Bei unseren Helden an der Somme* (Germany)
1919 *J'Accuse!* (France, dir. Abel Gance)
1927 *Der Weltkrieg* (Germany, dir. Léo Lasko)
– *Wings* (USA, dir. William A. Wellman)
1928 *Verdun. Visions d'histoire* (France, dir. Léon Poirier)
1930 *All Quiet on the Western Front* (USA, dir. Lewis Milestone)
– *Hell's Angels* (USA, dir. Edmund Goulding & Howard Hughes)
– *Journey's End* (Britain, dir. James Whale)
– *Westfront 1918* (Germany, dir. G. W. Pabst)
1931 *Douaumont. Die Hölle von Verdun* (Germany, dir. Heinz Paul)
– *1914: Die letzten Tage vor dem Weltbrand* (Germany, dir. Richard Oswald)
– *Niemandsland* (Germany, dir. Victor Trivias)
1932 *Les Croix de bois* (France, dir. Raymond Bernard)
– *Tannenberg* (Germany, dir. Heinz Paul)
1937 *La Grande Illusion* (France, dir., Jean Renoir)
1938 *J'Accuse!* (France, dir. Abel Gance)
1941 *Sergent York* (USA, dir. Howard Hawks)
1957 *Paths of Glory* (USA, dir. Stanley Kubrick)
1959 *La Grande Guerra* (Italy, dir. Mario Monicelli)
1964 *King and Country* (Britain, dir. Joseph Losey)
1969 *Oh! What a Lovely War* (Britain, dir. Richard Attenborough)
1979 *All Quiet on the Western Front* (Britain/USA, dir. Delbert Mann)
1981 *Gallipoli* (Australia, dir. Peter Weir)
1989 *La Vie et rien d'autre* (France, dir. Bertrand Tavernier)
1996 *Capitaine Conan* (France, dir. Bertrand Tavernier)
2001 *La Chambre des officiers* (France, dir. François Dupeyron)
2004 *Un long dimanche de fiancailles* (France, dir. Jean-Pierre Jeunet)
2005 *Joyeux Noël* (France, dir. Christian Carion)

PART IV

States, Nations, and Empires

CHAPTER TWENTY-FIVE

Austria-Hungary and "Yugoslavia"

MARK CORNWALL

When Henry Wickham Steed, the *Times* correspondent in the Austro-Hungarian Empire, left Vienna for the last time in the summer of 1913, he felt a sense of impending catastrophe due to the Empire's unresolved South Slav problem.[1] A year later, the Austro-Hungarian elite went to war in order to crush the kingdom of Serbia, which they perceived as the key source of a poisonous agitation for an independent state of the south Slav peoples – or "Yugoslavia." Four years later, it was the Habsburg Empire that lay crushed with over a million men sacrificed in its defense. The monarchy, which for 400 years had dominated East–Central Europe, splintered in October 1918 into a myriad of theoretically "national" states. One of the successors founded on the Habsburg ruins was a South Slav or Yugoslav entity, clustered around a rejuvenated Serbia. Despite appalling casualties, Serbia could emerge from the war claiming that, as the victor "David," it had finally slain the Habsburg "Goliath."

Neither of these processes, the dissolution of Austria-Hungary and the creation of Yugoslavia (or the "Kingdom of Serbs, Croats, and Slovenes" as it was known for its first decade), could have occurred without World War I. Few in 1914 envisaged or even desired such a radical transformation of Eastern Europe. Historians have long wrestled with the question of how far the victorious Allied Powers were really responsible without reaching a consensus. In the interwar period, those in the region who felt either satisfied or aggrieved at the Paris peace settlement were quite ready to hold the Western countries responsible. Certainly, Austria-Hungary's collapse had been accelerated by its military defeats on three fronts and its basic inability to win a long war against superior enemy forces. But no less important was the encouragement that the Allies increasingly gave to disaffected national émigrés (Czechs, Poles, Serbs/Yugoslavs) to form new states, which, by 1918, was widely publicized within the Habsburg lands.[2]

Yet despite these external pressures, the war years also constituted a fundamental domestic crisis of legitimacy for the Habsburg monarchy. Recent scholarship has confirmed that a crumbling belief in the Habsburg state framework was crucial to the monarchy's disintegration. From 1917 in particular, alongside the masses that had been mobilized to fight the war since 1914, counter-mobilizations against the Empire took place on the basis of regional socioeconomic and nationalist grievances. This shift of allegiance, often propelled forward by regional nationalist activists, was a widespread phenomenon, especially in the South Slav lands of the Empire.

The crisis of legitimacy underlay Austria-Hungary's tragedy in World War I. While we will pay due attention to hopes and fears in various regions of the Empire, the dialectic between the monarchy's demise and Yugoslavia's rise is a useful focus and one surprisingly understated and unexplored by historians. It amply points up key processes at work, particularly the dilemmas facing the authorities in terms of civilian loyalty, state legitimacy, and the management of "total war." Moreover, if the South Slav problem effectively started Austria-Hungary's war, it remained for the monarchy a Gordian knot which most of the ruling elite seemed unable to cut throughout the war.[3] One reason was that any radical reshaping of the South Slav lands, to bring Serbs, Croats, and Slovenes together in a new national unit, was incompatible with the prevailing "dualist structure" of the Empire, by which the Habsburg monarchy had been sharply divided since 1867 into two self-governing states, Cisleithania ("Austria") and Hungary, with Bosnia-Herzegovina annexed as a separate entity in 1908. In contrast, Serbia's program of war aims offered a dream of Yugoslav unity that presupposed the demise of the Empire. For much of the war this seemed wildly utopian. But from mid-1917, not only was the Serbian government-in-exile again acting as the main Yugoslav vanguard but the Yugoslav message now began to find a greater resonance in the South Slav lands of the Empire itself. When combined with a similar process occurring in Czech and Polish regions, this national fermentation inside and outside the monarchy's borders sucked legitimacy from the Empire and led to its disintegration.

States of Emergency

On July 31, 1914, when Emperor Franz Josef issued a proclamation for general mobilization, about three million men from 11 different nationalities were called to the colors and began to entrain for either the Balkan or eastern fronts. Many would later recall the "whirl of enthusiasm" around them: the excitement, particularly among German-Austrians, Magyars, and Croats, that a short war was imminent against the Serbian/Russian menace, and a sense that at this critical point the monarchy was presenting an image of surprising solidarity in view of its prewar domestic crises.[4] The Hungarian Prime Minister, Count István Tisza, wrote to his brother that the general atmosphere was "very good." Wine and champagne seemed to be flowing at Hungarian railway stations. Certainly for many adolescents, the war offered unknown adventures and the chance for some personal or even national fulfillment. The emotion was captured well in the words of one German Bohemian youth leader: "I curse the war because it brings discord into my calm beautiful world, stirs up my peaceful heart. I must however bless it as the cleansing storm which may usher in a more vigorous era."[5]

Yet parallel to such optimism was anxiety, even in official circles. Russia's entry into the war suggested that, like the "sorcerer's apprentice," Austria-Hungary might be losing control of events.[6] A strong mood of resignation or passive acceptance seems also to have prevailed in many quarters in the face of officially manipulated pro-war demonstrations. At the start of the war, this more than hinted at some underlying national divisions. These were quite obvious in the Serb-Croat regions, where Serbs were viewed as sympathetic to the enemy and their property vandalized in Zagreb and Sarajevo in the wake of Archduke Franz Ferdinand's murder. But also in the Bohemian lands Czech and German views immediately clashed on the purpose and legitimacy of this sudden Habsburg war. Indeed, one individual who on the day of mobilization traveled from Dresden to Prague, crossing German and Czech Bohemia, could contrast the joyous war fever in Dresden in imperial Germany with the seriousness that accompanied flower-decked troop carriages in German Bohemia. In the Czech communities he then saw only tears and silent dejection, and at the Prague railway station, amidst the swarming crowds, he heard no singing and sensed anxiety rather than ecstasy.[7] While for many Germans a sense of serious duty prevailed, for many Czechs the idea of an anti-Russian crusade or even a pan-German mission suggested a problematic Czech future should the monarchy win.

The ruling Habsburg clique that launched the war in July 1914 was single-mindedly committed to its prosecution. For the two governments, Austrian and Hungarian, it was fortuitous that both their parliaments were not sitting and could voice no criticism. The Hungarian assembly might indeed have been obliging, for when it reconvened in November 1914 it quietly approved Tisza's course of action. However, the Austrian parliament, or Reichsrat, elected by universal male suffrage, had proved an increasingly difficult forum to manage. In March 1914, faced with Czech obstruction, the wily Austrian Prime Minister, Count Karl Stürgkh, had simply prorogued parliament and turned to rule by emergency decree under paragraph 14 of the constitution.

On the outbreak of war, he declined to recall the legislature (the building became a military hospital), judging that "every political debate will damage Austria more than a lost battle." The result was that for two-thirds of the war years in Cisleithania ("Austria" as it was termed from late 1915), there was no forum where public opinion might indirectly find an outlet, or where a common Austrian patriotism might be negotiated or at least "managed." In a perceptive study, written soon after the war, Josef Redlich argued that a major gap developed between government and governed in Austria as in no other belligerent country.[8] The political truce of 1914 in Hungary, termed by Tisza a "splendid manifestation of unity," was always deceptive. Although the national parliament sat in Budapest for most of the war, it was anything but representative. Non-Magyars such as Slovaks, Romanians, and Serbs constituted 40 percent of the electorate but still secured a minute fraction of parliamentary deputies; and the Social Democratic party, with its strong trade-union base, had no deputies at all. In Hungary, therefore, Tisza's regime was gradually challenged by extra-parliamentary socialists and nationalists.

The regimes in Hungary and Austria immediately bolstered their wartime strength by enacting emergency legislation, negotiated by the governments and military elite a few years earlier. Across the Empire, these arbitrary powers were used to monitor and quell dissent, suspending "subversive" meetings and associations, censoring the press and mail, and introducing widespread internment without trial. In Hungary, where the regime closely guarded its independence, it was the civilian authorities that were invested with these special powers, and the political regime remained largely intact. Austria, however, was run as a bureaucratic-military dictatorship. A political-military struggle developed there as the Army High Command (AOK) persistently tried, in defense of "war interests," to extend its authority into the civilian sphere. In the shape of a new *Kriegsüberwachungsamt* (War Supervisory Office) in Vienna, the AOK had its own instrument for coordinating defense and sending directives to the provinces. But military control was naturally tightest in those regions designated as *Armee im Felde* (war zone) to the south and northeast of the monarchy – Bosnia-Herzegovina, Galicia, much of Moravia and, from May 1915, most crownlands near to Italy. There, martial law reigned, but the military authorities were still forced to work parallel to an existing civilian administration.[9] The real political–military clash came outside the war zone, particularly in Bohemia, where the AOK was constantly vigilant to Czech subversive behavior, but where Stürgkh was largely successful in retaining the Emperor's ear and rejecting calls for greater military control.

The Czech situation shows how hard it was to mobilize the whole Empire behind the war effort. For the historian it also exemplifies the problems involved in evaluating civilian morale without succumbing too easily to the stereotype of "nationalist wartime resistance" that became the official line in the postwar Czech state. Although Czech mobilization had passed off without incident, it was widely accepted by the authorities (with some justification) that many Czechs did not see Russia as the enemy. The military stereotype of Czech unreliability was reinforced by mounting "evidence" of treachery at the front, rumors about Czech volunteer units in Russia and a general tendency to exaggerate Czech insubordination, most notably an entirely mythic "mass desertion" from Infantry Regiment 28.[10] Most Czech politicians, in contrast to their German neighbors, did decline to make firm statements of loyalty to the Habsburg war and their behavior was clearly ambivalent. When in mid-1915 two of their number, Karel Kramář and Alois Rašín, were tried by the military and condemned to death (though the sentences were later commuted), they became national martyrs.

However, the Czech historian Ivan Šedivý has recently qualified this stereotype of Czech national resistance. From the start Czechs were more disaffected than Germans, constituting 74 percent of those 4,600 arrested in Bohemia for political reasons by the end of 1916. Yet aside from many incidents provoked by alcohol and reminiscent of scenes from the *Good Soldier Švejk*, there was no overt resistance to the war in this period. Moreover, under the impact of Austria-Hungary's military advances of 1915–16, as well as uncertainty over the fate of their arrested colleagues, most of the Czech parties began to cooperate with the Austrian regime. There were hundreds of displays of Czech loyalty to the Emperor and Austria by local authorities, schools, clergy, and some politicians. Even if, according to Šedivý, about half of these statements were "written to order," many were undoubtedly sincere, sometimes coupled with the renaming of local streets in honor of the imperial family (today's Jan Palach square in Prague was from 1916 to 1918 named after the Empress Zita, while the town of České Budějovice even professed a Hindenburg Square). The evidence suggests some opportunism on the part of Czech politicians, but also some real Czech commitment to Austria which later accounts tried to conceal.[11]

This pattern was mirrored in the southern provinces, for example in the pure-Slovene crownland of Carniola, where the Catholic leader Ivan Šušteršič pledged his full allegiance, or across the dualist border in autonomous Croatia. In Croatia, as in Bohemia, a military-political tussle for power developed, but there too the politicians finally prevailed. In June 1915, Hungary permitted the Croatian assembly, or Sabor, to reopen, providing some Croatian legitimization of the war, especially the new war against Italy, where the enemy coveted Croatian territory. Yet in a Sabor statement, Croatian leaders immediately indicated that their support for the Habsburg cause was conditional. Loyalty was now juxtaposed with an open demand for greater Croatian unity in a postwar restructured monarchy.[12] In this way the ruling Croat-Serb Coalition in Zagreb sent a clear warning to Budapest, while retaining an opportunistic stance until the final month of the war.

For all those who professed loyalty, however, there were many who did not, and who quickly fell victim to the authorities' vigilance against subversion. By 1915, in the Slovene lands and Dalmatia for instance, hundreds of suspect community leaders had been interned. Due to the lifting of parliamentary immunity, this included prominent politicians such as the Slovene Franc Grafenauer (in German-controlled Carinthia) or the Croat Ante Tresić-Pavičić (in Dalmatia). As with Karel Kramář, these men soon personified a defiant and disloyal side to the national perspective, and their later release from prison (1917) did not heal the wounds. In regions of the monarchy close to the front, vigilance was even more brutal, particularly for ethnic Ruthenes (Ukrainians), Serbs, or Italians.

In Galicia, a "spy psychosis" permeated the army and all civilians became suspect: the hanging-out of washing was a clear sign of links to the Russians. In late 1914 thousands of "treacherous" Ruthenes were transported to the hinterland, joining an enormous wave of refugees from the east, including many orthodox Jews who would be fuel for anti-semitic agitation in Bohemia or Vienna. From southern Tyrol, in May 1915, over 100,000 Italians were evacuated northward, many to be interned because of sympathy with "perfidious Italy." Subsequent policy in this war zone was uncompromising. Irredentists were rooted out, martyrs created such as Cesare Battisti (executed) and Bishop Endrici of Trento (imprisoned until the end of the war), and the military tended to view all aspects of Italian culture as suspicious.

In the South Slav lands, the hysteria over Serb traitors was even more predictable. While thousands of Serbs in southern Hungary had been arrested at the start of the war, the "moveable front" of 1914 provides some explanation at least for the atrocities that Austro-Hungarian soldiers committed against Bosnian Serbs, later publicized to the world in an international enquiry.[13] In January 1915, the Croat General Stjepan Sarkotić became governor of Bosnia-Herzegovina and Dalmatia. Owing to political interference his writ in Dalmatia was always weak, but in Bosnia he was able to impose tight military control. Far from being lulled by the semblance of calm, he noted on his arrival that he was "sitting on a volcano" and hoped "with God's help to prevent any outbreak of lava."[14] His solution was to ban all political activity, closing the Bosnian *Sabor* and the Sarajevo city council, and particularly targeting the Serb population. National or confessional equality, he argued, could not apply to Serbs because of the war; their professed "loyalty" he judged to be simply a mask. In Bosnia their confessional schools were put under state control, their cultural associations were closed down, and even the Cyrillic alphabet was banned. The climax came in early 1916, in the wake of Austria's conquest of Serbia, when 156 Serbs were put on trial in Banjaluka for connivance with the enemy and 16 were given the death penalty. It was the kind of regime that the AOK desired elsewhere, but which the monarchy's political structure worked against. Sarkotić's own wish, that the imperial authorities should adopt a consistent policy toward Serbs to stamp out all political activity, would never be fulfilled.[15]

Economic Boom and Bust

In June 1915, the governor of the monarchy's central bank reported to the Austro-Hungarian Council of Ministers that economically the war was a mixed blessing, stimulating some sectors but bringing "enormous interference with the normal run of economic life."[16] Ultimately, it was a battle for the Empire's survival as the economy experienced more than four years of "an almost uninterrupted contraction."[17]

Not least was the issue of how to fund a conflict that by November 1918 had cost the monarchy a total of 90,000 million crowns. The finance ministers had made no contingency plans for a lengthy war and were forced early on to arrange a huge loan of 950 million crowns from a consortium of Austro-Hungarian banks. It was spent immediately and the governments, reluctant to dampen patriotism by raising taxes, resorted like

Germany to public loans. The first was launched in November 1914, in Austria and Hungary, respectively, accompanied by major propaganda campaigns. These were strikingly successful, the Creditanstalt bank alone receiving 190 million crowns, while leading personalities such as Archduke Friedrich, the commander in chief, boasted of their personal contribution. In the following years a further series of "war bonds" were issued, all publicized in dramatic, colorful posters. Yet public involvement diminished as the cost of living mounted and the banks shouldered a greater part of the burden. Austria's eighth loan secured only a quarter of the amount in real terms subscribed in either of the first two loans. Public subscription was also uneven across the Empire, testimony most strikingly to weaker commitment amongst Czechs, who by 1918 preferred to invest in their own future with special Czech banknotes.[18]

A major alternative was simply to print money. By the end of 1914 the amount of currency circulating had doubled, and by the end of the war it had multiplied tenfold. Austria's wartime inflation was worse than in most other major belligerent countries (including Italy) because the government continued to draw so heavily on the central bank and failed, until 1917, to impose rigid price controls.[19] As prices spiraled far beyond wages, the cost of living in Austria doubled in a year (summer 1915–16) and the black market flourished. The years 1917–18 saw galloping inflation in both halves of the Empire and the crown by the end of the war had one-fifteenth of its prewar value.

If the monarchy's financial management left much to be desired, its material crisis was, arguably, largely beyond its control as it was forced into autarky. From September 1914, Austria-Hungary had moved swiftly toward a centrally controlled economy, most notably by setting up "agencies" on the German model, which had a monopoly on procurement and management of raw materials. One historian has assessed this gigantic war-economy infrastructure (91 such agencies by 1918) as ingenious; the metal agency alone contributed "substantially to the Empire's astonishing military staying-power."[20] By early 1915, after a sharp dip in industrial production and many radical readjustments, the economy seemed to have stabilized and entered something of a "new normality." Arms manufacturers such as Škoda naturally benefited. Other firms, if imaginative, managed to adapt despite the dramatic losses in manpower due to conscription. Thus the Bat'a shoe company, through securing state orders, increased its daily production from 350 pairs of shoes in 1914 to 10,000 by 1917.

Whether we can term this early boom phase (1915–16) one of "war prosperity" seems more questionable.[21] Alongside any short-term rise in iron or coal production there were many long-term anxieties, as the oil wells were destroyed in war-torn Galicia, the transport infrastructure proved clumsy and inflexible, and the Allied blockade intensified and the monarchy began to resemble in macrocosm its own besieged eastern fortress of Przemyśl. From 1916, iron, steel, and coal production began to decline; by at least late 1917 the munitions factories could not secure the necessary raw materials to sustain output. Not surprisingly, the Austro-Hungarian common ministerial council, meeting alternatively in Vienna and Budapest, spent a large proportion of its time trying to resolve insuperable supply problems.

The real catastrophe from start to finish, however, was the food supply. The crisis was caused by the Allied blockade, poor harvests, and weak management, and it eroded morale on the home and fighting fronts. It poisoned the legitimacy of the Habsburg regime and not simply in terms of how civilians came to view their "incompetent" authorities. Fueled by propaganda and rumor, it increasingly set regions of the monarchy against each other, looking to their own interests first, and undermined a dualist system that supposedly was built on Austrian-Hungarian cooperation. By March 1915 flour was rationed across the Empire; by the end of the year, over half the bakeries in Prague had gone out of business. Recent research has highlighted the degree to which food was the key to wartime politics in the imperial capital, Vienna.[22] There, women, fighting a daily battle for survival against profiteers, "dirty refugees," and their own neighbors, perceived their own sacrifice in the food lines as paralleling that of their men in the trenches. By May 1916 there were the first hunger riots; thereafter, from 1917, the legitimacy of the Viennese authorities sharply deteriorated as starvation encroached.

Well might the mayor of Vienna try to deflect the blame, lambasting the Hungarians for being "more interested than the English in seeing us starve." For it was the case that Hungary, relatively rich in agricultural resources compared to Cisleithania (whose "bread-basket" Galicia was under Russian occupation until July 1917), balked at any coordinated "food office" and saw to its own needs first before bailing out either Austria or the army. Economic dualism in wartime meant duplication of effort.[23] Only in February 1917 did the emperor set up a "Joint Food Committee" under General Ottokar Landwehr to advise the Austrian and Hungarian governments on better food coordination. It was a thankless task, for Landwehr had no executive power; when not having to petition Berlin for grain supplies from Romania, he continued to be thwarted in Budapest. In this way, and with the press publicity that it evoked, the food issue seemed to show only too well that dualism had become dysfunctional. As one Slovene politician remarked at the end of 1917, "because of their economic exploitation the Magyars are the most hated people among all Austrians irrespective of nationality."[24]

In the South Slav regions, this inequality of rationing encouraged a migration of population across domestic borders in search of food, and produced a range of tensions that could easily turn in a nationalist direction. For example, when Landwehr visited Croatia in May 1917, he observed good bread on sale at the railway stations but found the governor in Zagreb opposed to any extra requisitioning in the Croatian countryside to bail out the misery in neighboring Bosnia. In Bosnia, treacherous transport links and a bad harvest in 1916 had only compounded an ongoing demographic crisis; a province that in peacetime had covered only two-thirds of its food needs had, through the war in the Balkans, been flooded with 100,000 refugees and occupied by an army of 40,000.[25] Urban centers such as Sarajevo and Mostar were especially badly hit. Indeed, a map produced by the Vienna censor office at this time, based on censored correspondence, highlighted cases of famine in southwest Bosnia, as well as along the Dalmatian coast and to the north in Istria and Styria. As in Vienna, the food crisis by 1917–18 had become the most serious test of Habsburg legitimacy. Its impact was summed up by a chemist's wife in Rovinj (Istria) when she wrote: "the land looks as if the enemy has destroyed everything, dried up and contaminated ... People wander around like ghosts, dead from hunger ... [but] one minister has said, 'the people down there should get used to starving and dying'."[26] The seeds that the authorities could not sow were now being planted by local politicians and activists who were commuting across the dualist divide bearing a Yugoslav agenda.

Serbia's Golgotha

By late 1917, as we will see, the cause of South Slav unity was acquiring a life of its own within the monarchy in terms of Slovene–Croat–Serb connections. Serbia's wartime role, however, was crucial for keeping the Yugoslav idea alive in a specifically anti-Habsburg way, since the government of Nikola Pašić was agitating for unification outside or on the ruins of the Empire, and injected into that mission a myth of bloody self-sacrifice.[27]

The picture of national martyrdom could be painted in striking colors from the start. In the early months of hostilities Serbia (with quirky Montenegro at its side) had stood alone against Austria-Hungary in the Balkans and had achieved the first complete victory over the Central Powers, shattering Vienna's confidence and even managing by December 1914 to retake Belgrade. At that time, Serbia's war aims declaration at Niš transformed at a stroke a small defensive war into a magnanimous struggle for South Slav "national liberation," sending out a regenerative message that the monarchy's rulers would always find difficult to match. While Niš confirmed that the war aims of Serbia and Austria-Hungary were irreconcilable, the monarchy's mission to crush Serbia still seemed more realistic than the latter's "Yugoslav" utopia. Because of this, the later legend of a Serbian wartime "Golgotha" followed by "resurrection" was a potent one, surviving to be evoked during subsequent episodes of Serbian national insecurity.[28]

The Serbian Golgotha had several stages. It began in early 1915 when, during a long respite from hostilities, a devastating typhus epidemic killed 100,000 Serbian civilians. Ten months later, Serbia was again deserted by its allies and left with Montenegro to fend for itself against a fresh German–Austrian offensive. It was a notorious Allied "betrayal," particularly since the British Foreign Secretary in May 1915 had intimated some support for Pašić's ambitions. It finally set Serbophiles like the historian R. W. Seton-Watson on a crusade to publicize the Serb (and Yugoslav) cause in the west, lending their weight to South Slav émigrés from the Habsburg Empire who from mid-1915 had clustered in London as a Yugoslav Committee. Meanwhile, the Serbian army had undergone an epic winter retreat across the Albanian mountains to reach Allied sanctuary on the island of Corfu. They lost 70,000 men on the way, some deserting, some picked off by Albanian snipers, many succumbing to the atrocious elements. In the words of one British participant:

> It is terrible to have lived through days such as these. To us the privations that we endured, the discomforts, the frequent lack of food, were as nothing to the sense of participation in so hideous a tragedy, the knowledge of one's utter inability to stem, in the smallest degree, the inexorable tide of disaster ... The tears of Serbia are as the bloody sweat that fell at Gethsemane.[29]

"Serbia in exile," the story of the heroic retreat and reconstruction of a nation politically (on Corfu) and militarily (at Salonika), is one with few parallels in the history of World War I. But it is only half the "Golgotha": a mirror image of sacrifice and resurrection might be identified in occupied Serbia and Montenegro from 1916 to 1918. Recent research has been uncovering strategies for Serbian survival under the Austrian and Bulgarian regimes of occupation. The Austrian authorities encouraged escapism in the form of cinema, theater, and other entertainments, and to some extent the native population collaborated with the occupiers. While the latter were certainly ransacking the region economically, the degree to which the occupation was a "reign of terror and plunder," seeking to crush the Serbian intelligentsia at every turn perhaps needs revision (although Conrad von Hötzendorf was certainly a hawk in this regard).[30]

Life in the Bulgarian zone of occupation was much harsher. The occupiers, bent on reversing their defeat in the Second Balkan War of 1913, began a concerted campaign to turn the natives into Bulgarians; those who resisted were often "sent to Sofia," a euphemism for execution, and the upshot was a dramatic reaction. In February 1917 a revolt erupted – the only mass uprising against occupation during World War I – resulting in the death of perhaps 20,000 Serbs.[31] It reinforced a combative Serbian legend of active resistance to any foreigners who dared to invade the national soil. Despite the repression, thereafter the phenomenon of guerrilla bands *(chetniks)* took shape in the mountain regions of Montenegro, Bosnia, and Serbia, becoming by 1918 an increasing security headache for Sarkotić and the regimes of occupation.

Alongside this resistance, Serbia's epic retreat of 1915–16 had substantially shaped the myth of the nation's populist democratic struggle. King, cabinet, and generals were seen to be participating in the national tragedy alongside Serbian youth. Behind the myth the picture was rather less edifying. The dominant figure in Serbian politics, Pašić always refused a more representative national coalition to determine Serbia's future. As in other belligerent regimes across Europe (Hungary being a typical example), an initial *union sacrée* gave way to a radicalization of prewar political animosities and exposed political-military tensions. In Serbia's case, it produced a major showdown in 1916–17 between two factions. Regent Alexander and Pašić moved to eliminate the military clique who had earlier encouraged terrorism in Bosnia and who had a radical nationalist vision (with links to Pašić's political opponents); the clique's removal would also cast Serbia in a better light with Austria-Hungary if the latter managed to conclude a separate peace with the Allies in 1917. Through a rigged trial and the execution of the *éminence grise* of the radicals, Colonel Dimitrijević ("Apis"), Alexander, and Pašić were able to destroy a dangerous rival but they also exposed the factional undercurrents in Serbia's wartime leadership.[32]

The same obsession with control was clear in Pašić's dealings with the Yugoslav Committee. This émigré body, led by Ante Trumbić, was largely run by Dalmatian Croats who, together with Slovene delegates like Bogumil Vošnjak, agitated from London to establish a Yugoslav federal state with ample security on the Adriatic against any Italian and German threats. The Committee's main success was in propaganda which familiarized Allied countries with the Yugoslav agenda and, with Italian help in 1918, publicized the cause in the Habsburg Empire itself, encouraging some subjects there to rethink their allegiances. The Committee's main failure was in securing formal Allied recognition, which was blocked by both Serbia and Italy.[33] This stands in marked contrast to the Czech émigré machine, which had no real rivals, established a Czechoslovak Legion, and used this as leverage to secure Allied recognition for the new state in 1918.

Pašić, having encouraged the creation of the Committee, viewed it simply as a propaganda tool, an adjunct to Serbian designs, and thwarted any further recognition that might make it a competitor. Only in July 1917, and for tactical reasons, was he prepared to issue the Corfu Declaration, a joint statement with the Yugoslav Committee, which announced the goal of a kingdom of Serbs, Croats, and Slovenes, based on equal rights and under the (Serbian) Karadjordjević dynasty. In fact, this was no concession on Pašić's part, for Serbia still dominated the agenda. Similarly, in relations with Italy, Trumbić faced a major obstacle to any Allied recognition since Yugoslav aspirations on the Adriatic clashed with Italy's own territorial ambitions. In 1918, the Committee took heart when official Italy seemed to be following a "nationality policy" in support of the Slavs of Austria-Hungary, hosting in April a Rome Congress of Oppressed Nationalities. But, as with Serbian behavior, it was something of an illusion. The Committee was used by Orlando in Italy's tactical propaganda campaign against the Habsburg Empire; by the end of the war its political weakness was very clear. Pašić also finally ensured that in Allied eyes Serbia was in control of the Yugoslav mission. Not least, the Serbian army was the main "Yugoslav" military force that fought the monarchy, shed blood for the Allied cause, and participated fully in the victorious advance into South Slav territory in September 1918.

Shifts of Allegiance

At the time, and in retrospect, many felt that the winter of 1916–17 was a watershed for the Habsburg Empire, months when the prospect of change was in the air. Emperor-king Franz Josef had died; Stürgkh had been murdered in a Viennese restaurant in a singular protest against his unrepresentative regime; and with Romania's entry into the war and invasion of Transylvania (albeit short-lived), István Tisza's claim to embody the security of Hungary looked much weaker. In a climate of increasing war-weariness and serious food privation, the notion that old forces challenged the new was highlighted on December 30, 1916 when King Karl was crowned in Budapest. One journalist present in the Matthias church in Buda observed that "the king's unforgettably youthful bearing seemed destined to mark him to appear forever young in the doom of history, already looming in the wings." It was a contrast to "the gaunt bony figure" of Tisza, clad in black and "solemnly peering through his eye-glasses like a Calvinist churchwarden."[34]

Within a few months, Karl would dismiss Tisza, just as he sidelined other obstinate veterans of the Habsburg elite such as Burián and Conrad. Yet the speedy coronation in Budapest was a sign that the "new regime" itself was wedded to the dualist system, or at least found it very difficult to think outside that domestic order. The vibrancy of the system was already suspect even to former supporters. It had been weakened on the one hand by Hungary's tendency to economic autarky, and on the other (from Hungary's viewpoint) by the non-parliamentary regime in Austria which had severely curtailed the normal dualist political channels between Vienna and Budapest. In November 1916, the Central Powers' public announcement of support for a future united Polish state also implied that the postwar monarchy would need restructuring outside the dualist framework.

In this secondary stage of hostilities from 1916, the Habsburg war urgently required fresh legitimacy in order to justify its continuation into a third or fourth year, all the more so as many of the monarchy's war objectives (against Serbia and Montenegro, Romania, and even Russia in 1917) seemed now to be completed. Earlier in the war there had been a degree of public consensus behind the empire's "defensive mission," with many examples of self-mobilization on behalf of the patriotic cause (and not only in German and Hungarian regions). Alongside that, the authorities had exercised consider-able coercion under the emergency laws, not least by tightly censoring the press and trying to ensure an Empire-wide coordination. Through bodies such as the War Press Office they also tried to manage the flow of information in newspapers, cinemas, and public exhibitions. Yet recent research has emphasized that the battle to control informa-tion was one that the monarchy gradually lost, especially after 1916, when Austrian censorship was relaxed.[35] Despite an awareness of initiatives in enemy countries, there was never any civilian propaganda organization set up to promote a supranational Austrian patriotism (the idea was only dreamily pursued at the very end of the war). Whether such an ideal was realistic anyway is another question, for a similar patriotic campaign in the army in 1918 was a dismal failure.[36] The fact was that the Austrian and

Hungarian regimes by 1917 did not possess enough legitimacy amongst their populations to manage effectively a course of patriotic instruction. Indeed, their own behavior in 1917–18 further undermined their status, just as their obstinate continuation of the war at Germany's side seemed to be leading the monarchy toward the abyss.

In Hungary, late 1916 witnessed the public dissolution of the *union sacrée* of 1914–16. With Hungarian integrity threatened as Romania invaded Transylvania and Tisza still adamant against any "national coalition," his dictatorship was publicly condemned by Andrássy, Apponyi, and the rest of the opposition. Some, like Mihály Károlyi, had already burnt their bridges in announcing that the priority was peace and a foreign policy separate from Berlin. The key political debate in the final years was to be over the franchise and its extension to match the sacrifice that Hungarian soldiers were making. Although members of a "Suffrage bloc" managed slowly to maneuver a bill through parliament, it was watered down into insignificance by September 1918 for, despite his fall from power, Tisza's view of political representation (that "Hungary has always absorbed western trends only to the extent that they correspond with the country's interest")[37] was largely upheld in the sloth-like government of Sándor Wekerle. Hungary's regime therefore stayed elitist and alien to many, including the extra-parliamentary Social Democrats and the massively expanding trade-union movement. Moreover, for all leading Magyar politicians, Károlyi included, security of the Hungarian/Magyar nation was the priority: other nationalities only had cultural significance. While Slovak aspirations had long been suppressed, Romanian political and intellectual life in Transylvania was decimated from late 1916 when 3,000 "traitors" were dispatched to an internment camp at Sopron.

Just as the regime in Budapest pursued an elitist Magyar course, wholly committed to dualism and therefore blocking any Yugoslav unity, so in 1917 the government in Vienna followed a comparable German course. In their notorious Easter program of 1916 the German nationalist parties had moved to solidify German control of Austria. Galicia was to be given special autonomy to exclude Poles and Ruthenes from the Reichsrat, ensuring a German majority; German would be made Austria's state language; and the administration of Bohemia would be split on ethnic lines so that the Czech majority could never again outvote the Germans. This radical blueprint was taken up by Karl's new Austrian government under Clam-Martinic, who spent his first months negotiating with German and Polish politicians to try to pass a new constitution (a "German solution") by emergency decree.[38] When Karl dropped the idea and sought to reconvene the Reichsrat in May 1917, the Czech and South Slav (largely Slovene) political clubs were, not surprisingly, already highly suspicious of the regime's direction. They presented their own declarations to parliament, demanding Czech-Slovak and South Slav national entities within a new federal state structure. While still envisaged under the Habsburg scepter, these plans were radical in encroaching on Hungarian territory and requiring the dismantling of dualism. They were a parallel Slav stance against any "German course." When Clam and his successor Ernst von Seidler made clear their opposition, the way was prepared for that national polarization which would mount steadily in Austria over the last 18 months of the war.

The shift in allegiance of thousands of South Slavs away from the Habsburg regime was most clearly expressed in the so-called "declaration movement" which took off in late 1917 and spread southward from the Slovene lands into Croat and Serb regions of Dalmatia and Bosnia. Under the guidance of Catholic clergy and Reichsrat deputies led by Anton Korošec, a grassroots agitation developed in support of the May Declaration with mass petitions and rallies. The motives of participants were complex. For some the declaration for Yugoslav unity seemed to offer economic or "national" security in the face of rising threats from inside the monarchy (German Austrians) or outside (Italy). But this did not necessarily mean that most signatories envisaged an independent Yugoslav state. Many long retained a dual loyalty to the Habsburgs and to Yugoslav unity; thus at one rally in March 1918 a cry went up: "We want to be free in a great Habsburg Yugoslavia." In other words, adherence to the declaration was not simply a "legal cloak" to protect agitators who had already abandoned the Empire.[39]

As in the Czech provinces and always with one eye on the course of nationalist agitation abroad, the home-grown South Slav movement took a more radical turn from April 1918, when it was clear that the Austro-Hungarian governments were banking on victory at the side of Germany and that this in turn would mean an uncompromising German–Magyar future. Korošec and the Slovene radicals moved in August to host a Slav festival in Ljubljana which launched a National Council for Austria's South Slavs, a deliberate forerunner for a broader council to include representatives from Croatia and Bosnia (where politicians were, respectively, still opportunistic or closely monitored by the Sarkotić regime). The Habsburg authorities certainly tried to ban such agitation, but as with the food crisis, paper regulations were largely ignored by local officials. Another course would have been to tell opportunistic Slovene or Croat leaders, as a counterweight to Serbian and Allied propaganda, that the postwar monarchy would offer its own South Slav solution. However, until the bitter end the Habsburg elite could not agree on a solution. They not only tended to view the homegrown agitation as "artificial" and emanating from outside the monarchy, but also could rarely see beyond the dualist system, with the unresolved fate of Bosnia being a major bone of contention.[40]

In October 1918, defeat and Allied occupation from the south meant that the Empire could no longer control its centrifugal forces. National leaders in all regions of the monarchy drew the logical conclusion. Their new councils, which had slowly been forming in Prague, Ljubljana, and elsewhere, waited for the right moment to assume control, judging that for their nation's future it was vital to sever the discredited Habsburg connection and find security in a different territorial framework with other "co-nationals" (Czechs with Slovaks, and Galician Poles with brethren to the north, but also German-Austrians with Germany, and Magyars in an independent Greater Hungary). Moves in these directions fed off each other, while any tactics by the Habsburg elite, such as Emperor Karl's belated conversion to national self-determination in his manifesto in October 1918, were rightly seen as disingenuous or just too late.

In late October, as a national council took power in Zagreb to the strains of the Serbian national anthem and the *Marseillaise*, one Croat captured the mood:

> Everybody, even the poorest individual, senses that the old world is disintegrating, the loud clash of its collapse whips up our nerves into a new expectation which appears like a great light, like some new golden era that will bring happiness to all. And that future is all the more fascinating when it is compared with reality, with the immediate wartime past of grief, poverty, the whole nightmare of war.[41]

A Yugoslav framework for this "golden era" now emerged ever more clearly as the Serbian army advanced through Serbia up to the Bosnian border, and as the internal and external Yugoslav political movements were able to come face to face for the first time (Pašić, Trumbić, and Korošec meeting in Geneva in early November). In the region itself, a mass of confused loyalties existed, and more research is needed on how aware the various strands of the population were of a common ethnicity.[42] What is apparent is that at the end of the war most of the South Slav leaders were keen to play down differences and stress the uniform character and purpose of Slovenes, Croats, and Serbs as one "three-titled nation." For many, as we have seen, the shift in allegiance had occurred gradually over four years. But in 1918 it accelerated. It seemed clear that the Habsburg monarchy, whether victorious or defeated, offered no security for its Southern Slavs in postwar Europe, and that the risk of subscribing to a fully Yugoslav future was one worth taking.

Notes

1   Henry Wickham Steed, *Through Thirty Years 1892–1922*, 2 vols., London, Heinemann, 1924, vol. 1, p. 366.

2   Cornwall, *The Undermining of Austria-Hungary*.

3   A metaphor used by General Stjepan Sarkotić, wartime governor of Bosnia, in his diary of 1918 (Sarkotić papers, Croatian State Archives, Zagreb). For a new analysis, see Cornwall, "Habsburg Elite."

4   Typical is Edmund Glaise-Horstenau, *Die Katastrophe: Die Zertrümmerung Österreich-Ungarns und das Werden der Nachfolgestaaten*, Zurich, Leipzig, and Vienna, Amalthea, 1929, p. 29.

5   Quoted in Johannes Stauda, *Der Wandervogel in Böhmen 1911–1920*, 2 vols., Reutlingen, Harwalik, 1978, vol. 2, p. 64.

6   Constantin Schneider, *Die Kriegserinnerungen 1914–1919*, ed. Oskar Dohle, Vienna, Böhlau, 2003, p. 30.

7   Gustav Peters, *Erinnerungen* [unpublished memoirs], p. 19, in Sudetendeutsches Archiv, Munich.

8   Josef Redlich, *Österreichische Regierung und Verwaltung im Weltkriege*, Vienna, Hölder-Pichler-Tempsky, 1925, p. 141.

9   Führ, *Das k.u.k. Armeeoberkommando und die Innenpolitik in Österreich 1914–1917*, p. 21, n. 49.

10 See the evaluation in Ivan Šedivý, *Češi, české země a velká válka 1914–1918*, Prague, NLN, 2001, pp. 83–4. Even so, poor discipline in this Czech regiment has been well-documented by Richard Plaschka: "Zur Überganges von Einheiten des Infanterieregimentes Nr 28 an der russischen Front 1915," in *Österreich und Europa. Festgabe für Hugo Hantsch zum 70. Geburtstag*, Graz and Vienna, Styria, 1965, pp. 455–64.

11 Šedivý, *Češi, české země*, pp. 195–213.

12 Josip Horvat, *Politička povijest Hrvatske*, 2 vols., Zagreb, August Cesazrec, 1990, vol. 1, pp. 333–4.

13 R. A. Reiss: *Report upon the Atrocities committed by the Austro-Hungarian Army during the First Invasion of Serbia*, London, Simpkin, Marshall, Hamilton, Kent, 1916.

14 Sarkotić diary, 1 January 1915: quoted in Signe Klein, "Freiherr Sarkotić von Lovćen. Die Zeit seiner Verwaltung in Bosnien-Herzegovina von 1914 bis 1919," Ph.D. thesis, University of Vienna 1969, p. 38.

15 See Hamdija Kapidžić, *Bosna i Hercegovina pod austrougarskom upravom*, Sarajevo, Svjetlost, 1962, pp. 205–13.

16 März, *Austrian Banking and Financial Policy*, p.168. Much of the following draws on März's very full analysis.

17 Max-Stephan Schulze, "Austria-Hungary's Economy in World War I," in Stephen Broadberry and Mark Harrison, eds., *The Economics of World War I*, Cambridge, Cambridge University Press, 2005, p. 82.

18 Šedivý, *Češi, české země*, pp. 239–42.

19 März, *Austrian Banking*, p. 208.

20 Ibid., pp. 119–20.

21 Cf. Šedivý, *Češi, české země*, p. 222.

22 Healy, *Vienna and the Fall of the Habsburg Empire*, ch. 1. She suggests that Vienna's streets became an alternative political forum when the Reichsrat was closed (p. 302).

23 Schulze, "Austria-Hungary's Economy," p. 90.

24 Karel Verstovšek, quoted in Cornwall, "Experience of Yugoslav Agitation," p. 660.

25 Ottokar Landwehr, *Hunger. Die Erschöpfungsjahre der Mittelmächte 1917/18*, Zurich, Leipzig and Vienna, Amalthea, 1931, pp. 56–60.

26 Cornwall, "Experience of Yugoslav Agitation," p. 661.

27 The best discussion is Mitrović, *Serbia's Great War.*

28 See for example the public history about Serbia's "Golgotha and Easter": Silvija Curić and Vidosav Stevanović (eds.), *Golgota i vaskrs Srbije 1915–1918*, Belgrade, Beogradski izdavačko-grafički zavod – Partizanska knjiga, 1986.

29 Alice and Claude Askew, *The Stricken Land. Serbia as We Saw It*, London, E. Nash, 1916, pp. 247, 358.

30 Cf. Michael B. Petrovich, *A History of Modern Serbia 1804–1918*, 2 vols., New York and London, Harcourt, Brace Jovanovich, 1976, vol. 2, pp. 625–6. For a revisionist view, see Gumz, *Resurrection and Collapse of Empire* (which appeared too late for this chapter).

31 See Andrej Mitrović, *Ustaničke borbe u Srbiji 1915–1918*, Belgrade, 1987.

32 For a full analysis, see David MacKenzie, *The "Black Hand" on Trial: Salonika 1917*, New York, Columbia University Press, 1985.

33 For a succinct evaluation see Gale Stokes, "The Role of the Yugoslav Committee in the Formation of Yugoslavia," in Djordjević (ed.), *Creation of Yugoslavia*, pp. 51–71. For more detail on the propaganda campaigns, see Cornwall, *The Undermining of Austria-Hungary*, and Dragovan Šepić, *Italija, saveznici i jugoslavensko pitanje 1914–1918*, Zagreb, Skolska knjiga, 1970.

34 John Bátki, ed., *Krúdy's Chronicles: Turn-of-the-Century Hungary in Gyula Krúdy's Journalism*, Budapest, Central European University Press, 2000, p.183.

35 See Healy, *Vienna and the Fall of the Habsburg Empire*, ch. 3; Cornwall, *The Undermining of Austria-Hungary*, pp. 24–9, 284–6.

36 Cornwall, *The Undermining*, pp. 268–87, 405–15.

37 Vermes, *István Tisza*, p. 400.

38 The best discussion is in Felix Höglinger, *Ministerpräsident Heinrich Graf Clam-Martinic*, Graz and Cologne, Böhlau,1964, pp. 132–57. Austria's Polish leaders were now more intractable, bargaining for a "greater Poland" and offering only conditional loyalty. In early 1918, after Vienna rashly publicized a partition of Galicia, most turned against the regime.

39 Cornwall, "Experience of Yugoslav Agitation," and Vlasta Stavbar, "Izjave v podporo Majniško Deklaracije," *Zgodovinski časopis*, 46/3, 1992–3, pp. 357–81; 46/4, pp. 497–507; 47/1, pp. 99–106.

40 See the illuminating Common Ministerial Council debate of May 30, 1918: Miklós Komjáthy (ed.), *Protokolle des Gemeinsamen Minsterrates der Österreichisch-Ungarischen Monarchie (1914–1918)*, Budapest, 1966, pp. 661–9.

41 Horvat, *Politička povijest Hrvatske*, vol. 2, p. 77.

42 Stevan K. Pavlowitch, *Serbia: The History behind the Name*, London, C. Hurst, 2002, p. 109.

References and Further Reading

Banac, Ivo, *The National Question in Yugoslavia: Origins, History, Politics*, Ithaca and London, Cornell University Press,1984.

Cornwall, Mark, "The Experience of Yugoslav Agitation in Austria-Hungary, 1917–18," in H. Cecil and P. Liddle (eds.), *Facing Armageddon: The First World War Experienced*, London, Leo Cooper, 1996, pp. 656–76.

Cornwall, Mark, *The Undermining of Austria-Hungary: The Battle for Hearts and Minds*, Basingstoke, Macmillan, 2000.

Cornwall, Mark, "The Habsburg Elite and the Southern Slav Question," in L. Höbelt and T.G. Otte (eds.), *A Living Anachronism? European Diplomacy and the Habsburg Monarchy*, Vienna, Böhlan, 2010.

Cornwall, Mark (ed.), *The Last Years of Austria-Hungary: A Multi-National Experiment in Early Twentieth Century Europe*, Exeter, Exeter University Press, 2002.

Djordjević, Dimitrije (ed.), *The Creation of Yugoslavia 1914–1918*, Santa Barbara and Oxford, Clio, 1980.

Führ, Christoph, *Das k.u.k. Armeeoberkommando und die Innenpolitik in Österreich 1914–17*, Graz and Vienna, Böhlau, 1968.

Galántai, József, *Hungary in the First World War*, Budapest, Akadémiai Klado, 1989.

Graz, Gusztáv, and Schüller, Richard, *The Economic Policy of Austria-Hungary*, New Haven, Yale University Press, 1928.

Gumz, Jonathan, *The Resurrection and the Collapse of Empire in Habsburg Serbia, 1914–1918*, Cambridge, Cambridge University Press, 2009.

Healy, Maureen, *Vienna and the Fall of the Habsburg Empire. Total War and Everyday Life in World War 1*, Cambridge, Cambridge University Press, 2004.

Herwig, Holger, *The First World War: Germany and Austria-Hungary 1914–1918*, London, Edward Arnold, 1997.

Kann, R., Király, B., and Fichtner, P. (eds.), *The Habsburg Empire in World War I*, New York, Columbia University Press, 1977.

Király, Béla, and Dreisziger, Nándor (eds.), *East Central European Society in World War I*, Boulder, CO, Boulder Social Science Monographs, 1985.

März, Eduard, *Austrian Banking and Financial Policy: Creditanstalt at a Turning Point 1913–1923*, New York, St Martin's Press, 1984.

May, Arthur J., *The Passing of the Hapsburg Monarchy 1914–1918*, 2 vols, Philadelphia, University of Pennsylvania Press, 1968.

Mitrović, Andrej, *Serbia's Great War 1914–1918*, London, Hurst, 2007.

Rauchensteiner, Manfred, *Der Tod des Doppeladlers. Österreich-Ungarn und der Erste Weltkrieg*, Graz and Vienna, Styria Verlag, 1993.

Roshwald, Aviel, *Ethnic Nationalism and the Fall of Empires: Central Europe, Russia and the Middle East, 1914–1923*, London and New York, Routledge, 2001.

Rozenblit, Marsha, *Reconstructing a National Identity: The Jews of Habsburg Austria during World War I*, Oxford, Oxford University Press, 2001.

Vermes, Gabor, *István Tisza: The Liberal Vision and Conservative Statecraft of a Magyar Nationalist*, New York, Columbia University Press, 1985.

CHAPTER TWENTY-SIX

Belgium

SOPHIE DE SCHAEPDRIJVER

At 8:00 a.m. in the morning of August 4, 1914, the largest invasion army ever mobilized entered Belgian territory. The German Empire's attack on a neutral state was an instant *casus belli*, and "Belgium" became shorthand for the moral issues of the war. As an emblem, Belgium was central, but its experience was particular, even marginal. The Belgians waged a war in which most of their country was in enemy hands, civilians had to face the invader directly, and the military front was cut off from society. This war, conducted not only at the front but also in exile or under occupation, prefigured the conditions imposed on much of Europe in World War II; but it diverged from the dominant experience of war in the West in World War I.

The visibility of Belgium in World War I studies leaves much to be desired. Belgium remains "missing in action" even from recent reference works.[1] One reason is the shortage of syntheses, owing to the dispersion of sources and the fragmentation of the national self-image.[2] Another pertains to methods of history teaching and writing in Belgium: much primary research is done by students and remains unpublished. There is, however, a recent resurgence in scholarship, which this contribution seeks to highlight.[3]

"Brave Little Belgium," 1914

On August 2, the Belgian government received an ultimatum demanding the German armies' right of passage in their campaign against France. Acceptance would jeopardize national autonomy (breaching Belgium's obligations as a neutral meant forgoing international protection), but rejection meant facing a superior enemy. Appalled, the government and King placed their trust in the inviolability of conventions and chose to defend Belgium's neutrality, a stance that soon garnered high praise in Entente and neutral opinion.[4]

On August 3, an unsuspecting nation woke up to a war for which little had prepared it. The 1913 campaign of preparedness notwithstanding, Belgium possessed little martial tradition, a robust mistrust of the nation-in-arms concept (general military service was not introduced until 1913), an army whose dog-drawn guns, lottery-drawn conscripts, and shako headgear suggested 1830 rather than 1914, and a solid faith in the neutral status that had shielded the country from war for three generations. Yet the government's resolve met with widespread approval. Abhorrence of war merged with fury at those who forced the country into the conflict. "Those German swine are going to mow down our young men because we have remained loyal to the preservation of our inviolable, neutral territory," wrote the historian Paul Fredericq. In the absence of official surveys, Belgium's public mood in early August cannot be studied systematically, but available testimonies tend to corroborate what Henri Pirenne, historian and eyewitness, wrote of August 3: "a day passed in a kind of delirium of anger, worry, and resolve." In other words, there was the same mixture of apprehension and determination as elsewhere, complete with some patriotic effervescence in the capital and some anti-German disturbances, especially in the large cities, though none leading to casualties.[5]

There was no organized or collective form of protest. Even political cultures in opposition to the bourgeois and Francophone Belgian state – Socialists and members of the Flemish Movement – rallied to the nation's defense, adding to the early volunteer movement that brought together some 20,000 men, corresponding to 50 percent of a conscription levy – an impressive turnout by Belgian standards.[6] The army had been mobilized already, without incident; it numbered 234,000 troops. In Brussels, on August 4, amidst great public displays of resolve, King Albert I appeared before Parliament to announce Belgium's entry into the war, on the day that the German army crossed the border near Liège.

Liège, an industrial city on the Meuse River surrounded by concrete fortresses sunk in steeply hilly terrain, was the first target of the revised Schlieffen Plan; and it was there that military violence erupted on Belgian soil for the first time since 1831. The invaders suffered an initial setback with heavy casualties. But the city was taken on August 7, after the first aerial bombardment of civilians in history. Austrian Škoda 305-mm howitzers destroyed the last fortress on August 16. Despite chivalric flourishes – the Belgian commander Leman, when taken prisoner, was handed back his sword – the siege of Liège was an industrial clash: *lüttichieren*, "to liègify," a short-lived German verb coined for the occasion, meant the taking of a modern fortress with overwhelming force.

Outnumbered and outgunned, the Belgian army retreated north to fortified Antwerp, the "national redoubt." Brussels was taken without a fight on August 20. In the southeast, British and French forces had to retreat after clashes in Mons and Charleroi. Both before and after the battle of the Marne, the Belgian army made sorties from Antwerp; though ill-coordinated and costly, these actions immobilized part of the German forces. On October 6, orders were given to evacuate the city and four days later, Antwerp fell. About 4,000 men were captured by the Germans and Belgian prisoners of war now numbered 30,000. Another 30,000 escaped to Holland, where they were interned for the duration of the war. The main body of the Belgian army retreated to the westernmost part of Flanders to rejoin the northern section of the Allied armies. Its final defensive stand on the Yser River – coinciding, further south, with the first battle of Ypres – began badly for the exhausted Belgians, but the inundation of the front lines (using the region's centuries-old system of canals and sluices) helped turn the tide. The battle of the Yser was over on November 2, "First Ypres" 10 days later. Mobile warfare, in Belgium as elsewhere on the western front, had turned into stalemate. As with other armies, the opening months of the war were the most lethal; half of the 26,000 Belgian war dead were killed between August 4 and November 2, 1914.

Belgian civilians, too, had experienced violence. A total of 5,500 men, women, and children were killed – stabbed, drowned, beaten to death with rifle butts, or shot in mass executions – by the invading armies between August 4 and late October. These massacres occurred wherever the attackers suffered inexplicable setbacks and were driven by an army culture suffused with fear of *francs-tireurs* (civilian snipers). On the Entente side, accurate reports were dramatized with fictitious and lurid details, which, after the war, brought the entire massacres issue into undeserved disrepute.[7]

Myth aside, outrage over the brutal invasion of a small neutral country was genuine and widespread in Entente (and neutral) opinion. Belgium became a symbol – first of heroic resistance (Liège was awarded the medal of the French Legion of Honor, while the *New York Times* ran verse comparing "the lads of Liège" to "the lads of old Thermopylae/Who stayed the storming Persians"), then of heroic victimization. Among the traumatized Belgians themselves, the praise lavished on "Brave Little Belgium" reinforced a sense of the outbreak of war as a moment of national elevation.

The Routine of War, 1915–16

When the war's first winter began, Belgium was a badly battered belligerent. The field army had been reduced from 117,500 men to 52,000. Entrenched with sandbags on 30 km of waterlogged Yser front, the army lacked men, cadres, weapons, munitions, supplies, and finances. As commander of the army, King Albert resided close behind the front with Queen Elisabeth, and the royal couple helped sustain morale in an army cut off from its home base (as a sign of affection, the troops took to calling the beloved round loaves of Belgian army-issue bread "Alberts," the detested French ones "Joffres"). The government of national unity created in August 1914 resided in the Norman coastal town of Le Havre, cut off from its administrative staff – and from the population. Almost one and a half million Belgians (out of a total population of 7.6 million) fled the invaders, the most massive exodus in Low Countries history. Most sought refuge in the neutral Netherlands; others crossed into France, and a third group fled to Britain in whatever vessel was available. Belgium was largely overrun: of its 2,636 communes, 2,598 were occupied. The civilian massacres had caused massive internal flight, especially from the worst-hit cities such as Dinant (where one in ten inhabitants had been killed) and Leuven (Louvain). Hundreds of thousands of houses, farms, and livelihoods had been destroyed, thousands of civilians deported to German prison camps as *francs-tireurs*. Warfare had caused great damage to populous and productive regions. Communication and transportation lines were smashed. Material shortages were acute; starvation threatened in the cities.

From November 1914 onward, a form of war routine was reestablished at the Yser, in exile, and in occupied Belgium. The Belgian army recovered a kind of equilibrium. Supply lines were established, largely on credit. In March 1915, the conscripts and volunteers of August joined the ranks after training in France, followed by conscripts and volunteers from exile and from unoccupied West Flanders; in addition, an estimated 30,000 volunteers escaped the occupied country via the Netherlands. In this way, over 130,000 troops were added. Little is known regarding the integration of these newcomers or, indeed, Belgium's military mobilization generally: a recent work has charted soldiers' settling into a war routine through their private writings,[8] but there is no comprehensive study of how the army on the Yser fought the war, of the role of junior officers, chaplains, or of military and private welfare.

No large operations happened on the Belgian front. The terrain was unpropitious, and King Albert kept his troops out of allied offensives, considered wasteful impositions on a neutral power.[9] The government-in-exile, wedged between a monarch still concerned with Belgian neutrality and demanding allies, could do little else but establish a cramped routine of channeling what resources it could muster – loans, international aid, Belgian assets abroad – toward the Belgian war effort and uphold international solidarity by constant reminders of Belgium's plight. The under-funded Belgian Documentary Bureau published solid rebuttals of German accusations on *francs-tireurs* and other issues. Secret surveys and clandestine correspondence enabled Belgium's ministers and their small staffs to chart attitudes in the occupied country, but not to influence them. Their authority over Belgians in exile remained limited, but it increased over time, especially as regards labor placement.[10]

Among the refugees, too, a certain routine emerged. An array of charitable organizations and government services (foreign and Belgian) helped devise more long-term arrangements. The Netherlands housed destitute refugees in camps; Britain controlled Belgian munitions workers strictly to avoid labor and draft disputes; in France, Belgian refugees were integrated into the wartime labor market (munitions, agriculture) more informally.[11] Many refugees returned to Belgium after Germany had issued guarantees for personal safety – and made threats of confiscation of property. Still, some 600,000 Belgians remained abroad until the Armistice, a heterogeneous group in terms of background, circumstances, and willingness to contribute further to the Belgian war effort.

The mass flight of 1914 did not indicate the collapse of an entire system, as would happen in 1940. "In 1914, even in the thick of the exodus, the willingness to uphold the structures of the [Belgian] state prevailed over fear and despondency." Holders of public office considered it their obligation to stay and face the invader.[12] Order was reestablished and the now-occupied country settled into an uneasy routine. Occupied Belgium was administered by a Governor-General, a kind of vice-regal position occupied successively by three elderly Prussian aristocrats, the generals Colmar von der Goltz, Moritz von Bissing, and Ludwig von Falkenhausen. The Governor-General, appointed directly by the Emperor on the colonial model, oversaw a military and a civilian administration functioning from the central to the local level.[13] Although the Belgian national bureaucracy was not, as yet, dismantled, national public life shriveled; the commune became the real locus of "native" administrative continuity. Municipal governments functioned throughout the war, albeit under heavy German control. Always relatively autonomous, they increased their prerogatives and obligations, levying taxes, issuing emergency money, providing work on public projects, and devising welfare measures. Proctor correctly concludes that the precise dynamics of Belgium's occupation are most fruitfully studied at the local level, all the more so as the regime was not the same across Belgium.[14] The Governor-General administered two-thirds of the occupied country only; the area behind the front – all of West Flanders, most of East Flanders, and a large part of Hainaut, comprising some 22 percent of the occupied population – formed the *Etappe*, a district under the command of the German Fourth Army, which had a more repressive and exploitative regime than the Government-General. The line between *Etappe* and Government-General was a military frontier, closed to civilians.[15]

As the most densely populated country in the world and also one of the most highly industrialized, Belgium had not been self-sufficient in generations. Between the British blockade and overstretched Germany's refusal to provide for the occupied territories, starvation threatened. Private initiative broke the stalemate; a conglomerate of Brussels charities aided by industry magnate Ernest Solvay formed the nationwide *Comité Central de Secours et d'Alimentation* (Central Committee of Food and Aid, hereafter *Comité*). Presided by entrepreneur Emile Francqui, the *Comité* sought international aid through

Herbert Hoover, the later US President, then a 40-year-old businessman in London. Hoover's Commission for Relief in Belgium (hereafter Commission), a neutral organization, centralized funds, purchased and shipped food, and guaranteed its safety from German confiscation.

The German authorities, wary of famine and revolt, tolerated the relief effort. In Belgium, the *Comité*, through its regional and local branches – which became more autonomous as the war dragged on – sold the imported foodstuffs in special stores, granted aid, tapped domestic resources, coordinated charitable efforts, charted needs, and administered welfare. To escape German control, the *Comité* remained an ad hoc organization lacking formal ties to the Belgian state; yet it was a kind of proto-welfare state with 125,000 agents and the prestige of US protection. There is no recent monograph on the *Comité* (or, indeed, on the wartime feeding of Belgium, then the largest food-aid effort in history). But the growing body of scholarship on Belgium's wartime welfare arrangements demonstrates how these informal, paternalistic efforts effected some real benefits in national health (infant mortality actually declined), ensured a (relative) check on dearth and profiteering that maintained a minimal level of public confidence, and provided a channel for political energies in a silenced public culture.[16] These political energies were in the main masculine. With relatively few men drafted because of occupation, women did not take men's places, and, with rewarding pursuits in short supply and food a grave matter, men took over the domain of victualing responsibilities.[17] This underscores the cramped nature of life in occupied Belgium. Travel was very severely restricted by German rules, the confiscation of private vehicles, and the dearth of public transportation. For the first time in decades, distances were expressed in walking hours. Public space was unrecognizable: the country was bristling with borders and many areas were off limits (beaches, railway embankments, parks). Information was scarce. Activities slowed down in all domains.

Still, many Belgians supported the national war effort as best they could, forming a kind of "home front" in which familiar space and routine activities became loci of confrontation with, or at least passive resistance to, the invader. Communes disputed German taxation, seizures and, from 1916, forced labor, as best they could. Hundreds of local dignitaries were deported to German prison camps. The *Comité*'s agents, again at personal risk, worked to keep Belgian resources such as domestic foodstuffs from the occupier, and actively discouraged Belgians from working in Germany. The attitude of Belgian labor needs further study, but what we do know suggests a widespread refusal to contribute to the German war effort; examples are the massive strikes in the railway workshops of Mechelen and Luttre in 1915.

A multifarious patriotic culture rejected the occupiers' authority; in the words of Cardinal Mercier, Catholic primate of Belgium: "This Power is not a legitimate power. In your heart of hearts you owe it neither esteem, nor loyalty, nor obedience." His pastoral letter for New Year 1915, read to crowded churches, became a rallying-cry; promptly confiscated, it circulated underground at considerable risk.[18] Clandestine press networks offered Entente news, circulated reports on the 1914 massacres, reminded readers of the circumstances of Belgium's entry into the war, and sharply denied any legitimacy to the occupier. The best-known underground paper is the *Libre Belgique*, launched by Brussels Catholics in early 1915, and fiercely persecuted. The underground press testifies to what Horne has called the "self-mobilization" of informal networks of fellow-townspeople; the best represented milieu is that of the Catholic middle classes, traumatized by the invasion because they had long considered Germany the epitome of trustworthiness. Patriotic culture found further expression in rituals, jokes, tricolor knickknacks, buttons, and head-gear.[19] The ban on these emblems was eluded inventively; at the first anniversary of the invasion, ivy leaves were worn on lapels as a sign of fidelity. But the massive fines imposed on municipalities for even symbolic infractions further impoverished the country.

Other networks engaged in more material forms of resistance, such as smuggling Entente soldiers and Belgian volunteers out of the country. In October 1915, an Englishwoman, Edith Cavell, head of the Brussels school for nursing, was executed for this reason; hers became an instant *cause célèbre*.[20] Intelligence work provided further support for the front. Occupied Belgium was a privileged area for Entente intelligence. Belgium's railway network, the densest in the world, now under total German control, was the object of intense clandestine scrutiny: entire households observed train move-ments from rented rooms with views of the tracks, taking turns to jot down details – familiar space becoming front-line space. Allied intelligence agents recruited Belgian leaders of spy networks in the Netherlands: the Germans' high-voltage electric fence along the Belgian–Dutch border did not deter movement back and forth, though it killed hundreds. Most Belgian networks worked for British intelligence, more discreet and efficient than its Belgian and French counterparts, and offering military rank, a "major recruiting tool" for civilians wishing to emulate the military front.[21]

The complex drama of Belgium's occupation has long been overshadowed by the violent morality tale of the invasion.[22] Recent scholarship aims to recover this complexity by placing the "home front" in the context of the entire occupation experience. "Home front" attitudes necessarily alternated with those of coexistence – a fact that Belgians abroad (and interwar historians) often failed to grasp. When the Germans attempted to channel Belgian resources toward their war effort, the "home front" emerged; but as regards the occupiers' other priority, that of public order, their wishes largely met those of the Belgian authorities. The logic of policing, as Majerus has demonstrated, made for improvised if tense partnerships at odds with the image of an entire society risen against the invader.[23]

Germany's Belgium

Once stalemate had set in on the western front, Germany's leaders sought to make the most of the capture of Belgium. Designs on Belgium shifted and changed with the for-tunes of war, and no consensus existed among imperial decision-makers – or even within the occupation administration, an improvised civilian–military hybrid rife with clashes over competences and encroached upon by other German interests.[24] But two condi-tions dominated until late in the war: Belgium had to be subordinated to the German war effort, and, after the war, kept within the German orbit as much as feasible – or, that failing, weakened permanently.[25]

Subordination to the German war effort was, first and foremost, material. The occu-pied country was expected to finance its own occupation and even part of Germany's war in the west. Taxation bit deeply into reserves, as did the massive requisitioning of indus-trial raw materials, livestock and domestic goods such as copper utensils and wool mat-tresses (entailing irksome searches of private homes). Domestic foodstuffs and coal were not requisitioned wholesale so as not to jeopardize international relief; but they were produced and sold under tight German control.

This policy intensified from August 1916: under the auspices of the Third Supreme Command, rational gave way to extreme exploitation. Governor-General von Bissing, who died in April 1917, condemned this policy as short-sighted, but his successor von Falkenhausen tended to concur with Ludendorff's priorities. Belgium's ailing industries were placed under complete German control; firms reluctant to accept the occupiers' interference had to close down and see their equipment seized. Machines, factory buildings, furnaces, and narrow-gauge railway tracks were demolished or dismantled and shipped to Germany. Unlike other belligerents, Belgium's industries did not benefit from the war economy; they were condemned to paralysis by the British blockade and by German interference. Forms of coexistence in the first half of the war – arrangements allowing Belgian business to survive without serving the occupier – were closed off from 1916, leaving no option except accommodating German needs. How many Belgian businesses took this lucrative path has not been determined, but the occupation undoubtedly left most of them worse off.[26]

Another resource was Belgian labor, plentiful because of low mobilization and unemployment.[27] The occupying authorities attempted to attract Belgian men to German industry, such as the Ruhr coal mines. Given meager results (some 12,000 men), the policy was enforced in May 1916 by a ban on Belgian job-creation schemes. The next step was deportation and forced labor, imposed by the Supreme Command and industrial lobbies. From October 1916, laborers (whether jobless or employed) were deported in cattle-cars to German "distribution centers" and "industrial lodgings" – camps in all but name. Others were deported for front-line labor. Of the 120,000 men taken, 2,500 died during deportation, a large number shortly thereafter, and many remained invalids. Brutal and messy, the deportations were more an expression of Supreme Command hubris than the implementation of a considered policy.[28] They were useless for Germany's industry, catastrophic for its international standing, and hotly contested by Socialists and Catholics in the *Reichstag*. They were halted in February 1917 for the Government-General, but continued until war's end in the *Etappe*.

In terms of putting Belgium to work for Germany, forced labor was a ham-fisted measure of last resort. Civilian occupation officials held on to the fond if unrealistic notion of a thriving Belgian economy under German control. The larger aim was to dismantle the "home front" and create a basis of common interest, perhaps even legitimacy, for the occupation regime. A Political Department, answerable to the Governor-General directly, channeled the legitimation effort in policies toward the Catholic Church, the *Comité*, and the press. Recently published, the Department's reports highlight another legitimizing endeavor – *Flamenpolitik* (pro-Flemish policy), which sought to engender pro-German feelings by addressing Flemish linguistic grievances.[29] Flemish was given pride of place in the public domain (street names, military posters) and school curricula. The strategy became more radical in October 1916 with the forcible Flemishization of the University of Ghent (the largest city in the *Etappe*). In March 1917, Belgium was divided into Flemish and Walloon regions, with Brussels the capital of Flanders. In Berlin, Chancellor von Bethmann Hollweg received representatives of a "Council of Flanders," a self-appointed body with no legislative or executive power. Belgian assets were diverted to subsidize "Flemish" cultural and social life. *Flamenpolitik* mobilized much German cultural expertise. Its discourse redefined the invasion of Belgium as the liberation of a "brother" people from an artificial state guilty of suffocating German-ness – just as happened on the wider European stage. As Bethmann told the *Reichstag* in April 1916, Germany pledged never again to abandon its Flemish brethren to "Gallicization." *Flamenpolitik* was more than a divide-and-conquer expedient of occupation policies; in adding to the definition of Germany's war as a crusade against encirclement, it was an element of Wilhelmine war culture.[30]

Flamenpolitik created a milieu of sympathetic Flemings that developed its own beleaguered outlook on the war. Occupation officials had hoped to gain the sympathies of the Flemish population at large, or, at least, of the leading intellectuals and politicians engaged in the Flemish Movement. This proved a miscalculation. Pro-Flemish spokesmen publicly rejected the acceptance of even long-overdue rights from the hands of the invader. Paul Fredericq, professor of history and lifelong pro-Fleming, was deported to Germany – together with his colleague Henri Pirenne – for resisting the creation of a "Flemish" university at Ghent. But others within the rank and file of the Flemish Movement proved more receptive. Calling themselves "activists" in order to convey a vigorous pro-Flemish stance, they numbered an estimated 20,000.[31] Caught between military control and compatriots' hostility, hampered by internal strife and an incapacity to see beyond language issues, "activism" enjoyed little public authority, Council of Flanders and Flemish ministries notwithstanding; its representatives were by and large unable to enter the crucial terrain of municipal power or *Comité* authority. Activist endeavors consisted of brokering favors (administrative positions, non-*Comité* welfare arrangements), supporting the persecution of hostile Flemings, and producing a vast body of anti-Belgian rhetoric (periodicals, pamphlets, "catechisms," poetry, songs, drama, posters, and cartoons). Activism was a major discursive presence in an otherwise silenced public culture; but its irrelevance as a governing power underscored the occupiers' inability to enroll "native" institutions in the German war effort.

Crisis and Remobilization, 1917–18

Throughout the war, Belgium's fighting front and "home front" kept up a kind of symbolic dialogue. Trench periodicals spoke of little else but conditions in the soldiers' inaccessible hometowns and villages; patriotic behavior under occupation was held to mirror the troops' "sacrifice." But direct communication was completely severed. Yet, in the spring of 1918, two Belgian soldiers fresh from the front made a spectacular appearance at a theater in heavily-occupied Ghent.

Staged by the Germans, the event was meant to undermine Belgian legitimacy and strengthen *Flamenpolitik*. The two soldiers had belonged to a pro-Flemish group within the Belgian Army (the so-called Front Movement); having crossed into occupied Belgium with ill-defined aims of liaising with activism, they were promptly coopted to portray the Belgian Army as brutally discriminatory vis-à-vis Flemish soldiers. Their arrival provided activism with a measure of front prestige.

It also demonstrated a fissure along the Flemish issue in the military as well as on the home front. The Front Movement condemned the predominance of the French language in an army where Flemings were overrepresented (an estimated 65 percent, as against 55 percent of the Belgian population). Grown out of student associations and Catholic prayer groups, it became more radical in 1917, staging nocturnal demonstrations and issuing protestations addressed to King Albert ("You, Sire, are the only one we trust"). Though the Front Movement has been the object of much research, scholars have tended to place it within the narrow context of Belgian linguistic grievances, not the wider crisis of "the impossible year" 1917 – a crisis that seems to have hit the Belgian army as it did others, and by no means its Flemish troops only.[32] Discontent was expressed in diaries, correspondence, and action. Throughout 1917, military tribunals tallied 5,630 cases of soldiers going absent without leave as against 1,203 in 1916 – 1,007 of them in December 1917 alone. The rise continued through the spring of 1918. Of the Belgian army's 359 deserters, 324 crossed the lines (or tried to do so) in the last year of the war.[33] Belgian refugees protested against the draft, and discontent rose among Belgian munitions workers in France and Britain.

The crisis of war legitimacy hit occupied Belgium as well. After the war, patriotic accounts would single out activists for opprobrium. But recent scholarship on post-occupation trials – for war profiteering, the dissemination of "defeatist" messages, informing, and other infractions – has thrown light on a far wider range of "unpatriotic" behavior.[34] As the occupation wore on and material and intellectual impoverishment took their toll, the "home front" fractured in different ways. The German-controlled press stepped up its campaign against the *Comité*, middlemen helped siphon off Belgian resources for German ends, and police spies assisted in the dismantling of resistance networks. Less dramatic forms of "uncivic" behavior increased. Recipients of relief devised fraudulent arrangements, the crime rate went up considerably and war profits were made in the countryside, as the postwar savings accounts of the Peasant League would show.

All this took place against the backdrop of a general weariness regarding the pieties of patriotism. Brussels barely celebrated the national holiday of July 21, 1917. "Last year," an observer wrote, "we believed [July 21] to be the last national holiday under the yoke. This year, we do not know any longer; we do not believe in anything anymore."[35] Fearing deportation and famine, Belgian laborers went to work in Germany (in all an estimated 160,000, up from 22,000 in October 1916).[36] As Rawe has pointed out, these were reluctant workers, and their performance in the Ruhr was substandard.[37] Still, many felt alienated from Belgium's patriotic elites. Another line of tension was generational. Cruel patriotic taunts against "idle youth" seeking amusement instead of trying to join the army on the Yser prompted young literati to defy convention and befriend Germans.[38] Public pacifist pleas – manifestations, pamphlets – abounded from December 1916, coinciding with German peace overtures. And even where the "home front" did not crack, it was hardly monolithic. A mid-1917 report by Governor-General von Falkenhausen noted that the occupied Belgians hated the Germans as much as ever, but detested one another, too. The working classes resented the propertied, town and country were at loggerheads, the Belgians in exile came in for much venom, and activism bitterly divided Flemings. Private diaries noted a general atmosphere of suspicion, rancor, irritability and pessimism.[39]

Yet neither fighting nor home front collapsed. The nature of this endurance needs further study. But it seems as if, like most other belligerent societies, Belgium re-rallied around the basic notion of national defense. At the front, efforts to ensure soldiers' material and moral welfare were stepped up. The crisis in troop morale never seriously shook the basic consensus over the necessity to hold out. Even the Front Movement never advocated defeatism, and would disavow its self-appointed "emissaries" after the war. Nor should its importance be overestimated: an underground, inchoate movement, it never reached more than some 5,000 men, occasional supporters included. Even the suspicious French military attaché thought Belgian morale all in all excellent. The German offensive of spring 1918 hardened defensive resolve. The imperative of liberating the occupied country and the King's prestige counted for much.[40] This was borne out by the liberation offensive from September 28, in which the Belgian army (finally placed under Allied command) played a significant role, reaching the Scheldt River by November 11.

Under occupation, too, a form of "remobilization" seems to have occurred in spite of the absence of the state. More research is needed, but a few elements can be highlighted. Patriots launched new underground papers such as, in Antwerp, from January 1917, the *Vlaamsche Wachter* (The Flemish Guardian), a highbrow anti-activist periodical; and, in Brussels, from April 1918, *Le Flambeau* (The Torch), founded by liberal academics. Other clandestine papers gained a new lease of life, such as the stalwart *Libre Belgique*, which, laid low by a series of raids in 1916, reemerged with new editors and distributors, and appeared continuously until the liberation. Espionage networks, though fewer in number, became more efficient.[41] Public protestations against the occupation measures – deportations, *Flamenpolitik* – galvanized a sense of resistance. In February 1918, the judiciary went on strike. The *Comité*, in spite of its much heavier burden (food scarcity and German appropriations had worsened since 1916, and American protection disappeared with the United States' entry into the war) remained an alert and trusted presence, operating under Spanish and Dutch guarantee, and doubling its efforts to limit, specifically, the malnutrition of children. Belgians' basic refusal of German authority endured. One occupation official – a Socialist academic – publicly acknowledged as much in 1919:

> The systematic destruction of the Belgian state's economic and administrative infrastructure, the extreme disruption of all of public life, culminating in the general paralysis of the judiciary – those were the political fruits of the German administration in Belgium. And all this without even remotely breaking the stubborn resistance of this people [and] its obstinate expectation of delivery.[42]

Belgium's War Legacy

On November 22, 1918, King Albert, at the head of the Yser army, solemnly rode past the cheering crowds of flag-festooned Brussels. Behind this classic image of a victory parade in a national capital lay some significant differences with other victors of World War I.

First, the army that marched past represented a relatively small portion of society: 20 percent of Belgian men of military age had served, as against 54 percent in Britain and 89 percent in France. Second, the military pageant marked the awkward reunion, after four years of complete separation, of different segments of Belgium at war – army and civilians, government and society, the exiled and the occupied. Third, the cheering crowds had lived under foreign occupation for four years: a civilian war experience as unique as the postwar issues it generated.

How, and how much, did the particularities of Belgium's war experience influence its postwar history – its position in the world, societal reconstruction, and memory of the conflict? The question cannot be answered comprehensively: many aspects, such as the place of veterans in postwar society, or the changing nature of Belgium's colonial policy, require further study. But a few elements stand out.

The country's past status as symbol of the Entente war discourse proved an awkward legacy. During the Paris Peace Conference, Belgian spokesmen attempted to use the moral credit of 1914 to obtain territorial advantage, but in vain. The four-year hecatomb had diminished the stature of Belgium's sacrifice of 1914 and the indignation over its civilian dead, especially given its lower military losses, with one death for fifty men of military age compared to one in six for France. Among Belgians, the sudden demotion to supplicant status after four years of Entente eulogies made for a bewildered and even "self-pitying" vision of world affairs.[43] The country to be sure had been hit very hard by the war materially. Maynard Keynes's assertion to the contrary was incorrect: the conflict left the Belgian economy severely weakened, its population malnourished, its finances depleted, and its infrastructure in tatters.[44] Five years after the Armistice, the shacks of the homeless still dotted the landscape in the front zone and around the ruined cities of 1914, a sign of the painstaking transition to postwar normalcy.[45]

Other forms of damage materialized instantly. The liberation occasioned a brief spell of public violence all over Belgium. Civilian crowds, sometimes aided by returned soldiers, exacted popular vengeance on "bad Belgians" (war profiteers, activists, women suspected of intimacy with Germans). Pianos were thrown out of windows, farmhouses burnt, men beaten, and women were stripped and had their hair shorn.[46] This violence disappeared as the criminal justice system started functioning (military courts at first, very quickly replaced by a revived and reinforced civilian jurisdiction). Belgium's judiciary, its prestige much enhanced by an aura of resistance to the invader, was instrumental in relegitimizing public order by adjudicating the fierce, focused rancor among the formerly occupied population – against police informers, activists, and, massively, compatriots accused of war profiteering.[47] Like the judiciary, the fiscal system could not become an agent of public justice until after the war. A special tax on "extraordinary war profits" was levied in 1919. In 1920, succession rights were increased by half to finance a state endowment for veterans. Between 1919 and 1925, the tax burden was redistributed to the (relative) benefit of Belgium's working classes.

Another means of legitimizing public authority was the immediate introduction of simple universal suffrage for all men over 21, a reform imposed by Albert and his advisers without consulting the (former) Le Havre government, and pushed through without a constitutional revision approved by parliament. Conservatives resented the reform as a brutal coup, but their plea to consider the war a mere "parenthesis in the functioning of our national institutions" (in the words of a Catholic senator) was untenable. Universal suffrage for men, an urgent issue even before the war, was an absolute priority in a postwar cultural context that exalted soldiers' sacrifice. That same context made women's suffrage a lost cause from the start (Albert, using his enormous prestige as the "Soldier King," threatened to veto it). Parliamentary voting rights were granted to a very small group of women: former political prisoners as well as widows and mothers of dead soldiers and executed civilians (the former only if they had not remarried, the latter only if widowed). This was a nod to women's wartime sacrifice – though not, significantly, to their war *effort* – that barely registered in the political landscape.

How did war monuments commemorate the different kinds of wartime sacrifice? Recent research paints a picture of dispersion. Nothing came of government plans to erect a national monument to Belgium's military and civilian dead – apparently for financial reasons; and, unlike what happened in France, the Belgian state tended to dismiss local memorials as "extravagant expenses" that did not befit times of hardship, and deny them subsidies.[48] This did not stop municipalities all over Belgium from erecting their own monuments to dead soldiers and civilians. Both groups could be commemorated on the same monument, yet there were differences: soldiers were portrayed as heroes giving their lives for Belgium; civilians as victims of Germany. Belgian national authorities steered clear of accusatory commemorations of civilian victims, ever more so after the fiascos of the Leipzig war-crimes trial of 1921 and the Ruhr occupation of 1923, a normalizing stance that came "at the price of considerable local bitterness."[49] Like that of fallen soldiers, the memory of executed civilian resisters concentrated on the notion of sacrifice, at the price of imprecision regarding the choices made under occupation. A heroine like Gabrielle Petit, an intelligence agent shot in 1916 at age 23, was remembered mainly as a kind of Christian martyr whose voluntary death constituted her main contribution to the nation's cause.[50]

In fact, "sacrifice" was a blunt conceptual instrument in dealing with the issues of the occupation, as shown by the half-hearted remembrance of the sufferings of forced-labor deportees. Only those who had died while being deported were commemorated; the survivors, however damaged, could not shake off suspicions of having worked for the enemy, and they received scant symbolic and material compensation.[51] It was also easy to subvert "sacrifice" in the cause of past collaborationism, since the postwar miseries of former activists could be redefined as a form of disinterested sacrifice in the service of an oppressed nation – Flanders. This points to a particular legacy of Belgium's war – the rise of Flemish counter-nationalism. This was a largely Catholic, small-town, and middle-class phenomenon alienated by what it saw as the excesses and ingratitude of postwar mass society, and entertaining its own militant war memory, in which commemoration of Flemish dead at the Yser incongruously merged with the glorification of activists to deny all legitimacy to the Belgian state. In 1930, it marked the hundredth anniversary of the Belgian revolution by the erection of the Yser Tower, a defiantly anti-Belgian memorial to the dead built on the Yser front, bearing the inscription "All for Flanders – Flanders for Christ," and offering a focal point for the crowds who had been making annual "pilgrimages" to Flemish war graves since 1920. Belgium's least local and most vocal monument to the dead, then, was a counter-nationalist monument which was also an antiwar statement, though one driven more by anti-Belgian feeling than pacifism.[52] It is worthy of note in this context that postwar Belgian cinema's most outspoken antiwar message was couched in the language of Flemish counter-nationalism. The 1928 film *Met Onze Jongens aan den Yzer* (With Our Boys at the Yser front) channels the theme of soldiers' victimization in the trenches into a diatribe against the Belgian state.[53]

If Flemish counter-nationalism developed its own vision of the war, "Belgian patriotic" memorial production was overwhelmingly Francophone.[54] Only Francophone civilian victims of the Germans were commemorated at the national level, with Flemish ones restricted to the local level. Does this indicate the overriding importance of the linguistic dimension in the construction of memory? Exactly how did this differential transmission operate? Answering such questions requires more pan-Belgian scholarship on memorial culture and on its reception and societal context than is presently available. One possible area of investigation is the response to a major work that attempted to make sense of the war as a national experience: Henri Pirenne's *La Belgique et la Guerre Mondiale*, published by the Carnegie Foundation in 1928. Belgium's war, for Pirenne, was that of a profoundly liberal public culture defending itself against the encroachments of an imperial invader. Thus defined, the war formed a kind of vindication of what Pirenne, in his multivolume *Histoire de Belgique*, had defined as the country's *raison d'être*: its status as a heterogeneous yet voluntarily cohesive microcosm of Western Europe. Belgium's victory marked a blow against "that most false and also most pernicious of ideas," to wit, the incipient racism that pervaded German imperial culture.[55]

To what extent did Pirenne's perspective on the past war agree with Belgian national self-definition? It is true that the one attempt to translate a "Pirennesque" vision into popular media, the 1931 film *Le Carillon de la Liberté* (The Chimes of Liberty), written by Armand Wullus, a Flemish war invalid and fierce opponent of Flemish counter-nationalism, was no success, though mainly perhaps because of the agitprop woodenness of the scenario, ridiculed by contemporary critics. A later film does seem to indicate the appeal of a Belgian self-definition not too far removed from Pirenne's vision, the wildly popular 1937 *Gardons notre sourire* (Keep On Smiling), a comedy on the occupation that portrayed Belgian culture as essentially sociable, pragmatic, conciliatory, irreverent, and, as a contemporary reviewer exulted, "impermeable to cruelty." The film was reissued in 1949, to equal popular success, proof of the enduring appeal of this particular image of Belgium at war.[56]

An even more elusive stratum of war memory is that of family dynamics. The pronatalist, patriarchal discourse of the postwar years hides the emergence of an array of household practices – women's paid employment, family planning – that quietly but persistently translated families' memory of wartime vulnerability into arrangements for future protection.[57]

A final noteworthy dimension of Belgium's war legacy is that of indifference. Trapped between exaltation and rejection, the memory of Belgium at war seems enveloped by a widening fog of amnesia from at least the mid-1920s. It is an understatement to say that homegrown war literature did not reach the iconic stature it enjoyed (and still enjoys) in some other Western cultures, for it barely registered. Contemporary Belgian literature on 1914–18 tends not to concentrate on the Belgian war experience.[58] The archival preservation of war documents has long been characterized by baffling carelessness, as all scholars of World War I Belgium can attest.[59] A study of this indifference as a cultural phenomenon in its own right is rendered possible precisely by the fact that, fortunately, it now seems a thing of the past.

Notes

My thanks go to Michaël Amara, Emmanuel Debruyne, John Horne, Tammy Proctor, Xavier Rousseaux, and Reinhold Zilch for their comments, and to Stéphanie Claisse, Aurore François, Christoph Roolf, Christoph Schmidt-Supprian, and Jan Van der Fraenen for allowing me to consult their unpublished work.

 1   Tammy M. Proctor, "Missing in Action: Belgian Civilians and the First World War," *Revue Belge d'Histoire Contemporaine* 35/4, 2005, pp. 547–72; an exception is Gerhard Hirschfeld, Gerd Krumeich, and Irina Renz (with Markus Pöhlmann), *Enzyklopädie Erster Weltkrieg*, Paderborn, Schöningh, 2003: several entries touch on Belgium's war.
 2   No syntheses were attempted between Pirenne, *La Belgique*, 1928, still essential, and De Schaepdrijver, *De Groote Oorlog* 1997/*La Belgique* 2004.
 3   Jaumain et al., *Une guerre totale?*
 4   Sophie De Schaepdrijver, "Champion or Stillbirth: The Symbolic Uses of Belgium in the Great War," in Tony Judt et al., *How Can One Not be Interested in Belgian History? War, Language and Consensus in Belgium since 1830*, Dublin and Ghent, Trinity College and Academia Press, 2005, pp. 55–83.
 5   On the latter, Majerus and Vrints in Jaumain et al., *Une guerre totale?*
 6   Gubin and Stengers, *Grand siècle.*
 7   Horne and Kramer, *German Atrocities.*
 8   Benvindo, *Des hommes.*
 9   Thielemans, *Albert I.*
10   No study of the "Le Havre" government exists, but see Haag, *Broqueville*, and Janet Polasky, *The Democratic Socialism of Emile Vandervelde. Between Reform and Revolution*, Oxford, Berg, 1995.
11   Amara, *Des Belges.*

12 Michaël Amara, "L'exode... de 1914," *Cahiers d'Histoire du Temps Présent*, 1, 2005, pp. 47–64 (here p. 51).

13 Benoît Majerus, "Von von Falkenhausen (Ludwig) zu von Falkenhausen (Alexander). Die deutsche Verwaltung Belgiens in den zwei Weltkriegen – Brüche, Kontinuitäten und Lernprozesse," in Günther Kronenbitter, Markus Pöhlmann, and Dierk Walter (eds.), *Besatzung. Funktion und Gestalt militärischer Fremdherrschaft von der Antike bis zum 20. Jahrhundert*, Paderborn, Schöningh, 2006, pp. 131–45.

14 Proctor, *Missing*. Good recent examples: Detournay, *Grande Guerre*, on Tournai; Jaumain and Piette, *Bruxelles*; Luc Vandeweyer, *Een kleine stad in een "Groote Oorlog": de Eerste Wereldoorlog en het activisme te Tienen en omgeving*, Tienen, Aqua Fortis, 2003, on Tienen (Tirlemont).

15 Entries by Zilch (Generalgouvernement) and Thoss (Etappe) in Hirschfeld et al., *Enzyklopädie*.

16 See the contributions by Piette and Jacques and by Masuy-Stroobant in Jaumain et al., *Une guerre totale?*; different contributions in Jaumain and Piette, *Bruxelles*; Scholliers and Daelemans, *Standards*.

17 Eliane Gubin, "Réflexions sur guerre et genre en Belgique (1914–1918)," in Gubin, *Choisir l'histoire des femmes*, Brussels, Éditions de l'Université de Bruxelles, 2007, pp. 203–16.

18 Meseberg-Haubold, *Widerstand*, remains indispensable.

19 Jaumain and Piette, *L'humour*.

20 Proctor, *Female Intelligence*.

21 Debruyne, in Jaumain et al., *Une guerre totale?*; also Gubin, *Choisir*, pp. 237–58, Proctor, *Female Intelligence*, Van Ypersele and Debruyne, *Ombres*.

22 Zuckerman, *Rape*, pp. 136–41, 195, 263 and passim; John Horne, "L'invasion de 1914 dans la mémoire (France, Grande-Bretagne, Belgique, Allemagne)," in Sylvie Caucanas and Rémy Cazals (eds.), *Traces de 14–18*, Carcassonne, Les Audois, 1997, pp. 115–26.

23 Majerus, *Occupation*.

24 Majerus, *Falkenhausen*; Zilch, *Okkupation*, pp. 107, 129.

25 Wende, *Belgische Frage*, remains essential; see also Zilch, *Okkupation*. On Antwerp, see Schmidt-Supprian in Jaumain et al., *Une guerre totale?* and Schmidt-Supprian, "Antwerp Question."

26 Information in Wende, *Belgische Frage*.

27 For excellent recent scholarship on recruitment and forced labor see Thiel and Rawe in Jaumain et al., *Une guerre totale?*; also Thiel, *Menschenbassin*, Kai Rawe, "".. wir werden sie schon zur Arbeit bringen!" Ausländerbeschäftigung und Zwangsarbeit im Ruhrkohlenbergbau während des Ersten Weltkriegs*, Essen, Klartext, 2005.

28 Thiel, *Menschenbassin*. Cf. Thierry Delplancq, "Une chasse aux 'oisifs.' Les déportations de civils à Bruxelles en 1917," in *Bruxelles et la vie urbaine. Archives – art – histoire*, special issue of *Archives et Bibliothèques de Belgique*, 64, Brussels, 2001, pp. 513–39.

29 Amara and Roland, *Gouverner*.

30 On *Flamenpolitik* and other cultural policies and contacts, different essays in Roland Baumann and Hubert Roland (eds.), *Carl Einstein-Kolloquium 1998: Carl Einstein in Brüssel: Dialoge über Grenzen/ Carl Einstein à Bruxelles: Dialogues par-dessus les frontières*, Frankfurt a.M., Peter Lang, 2001; also De Schaepdrijver, *Occupation*, Roland, *La colonie*, Ulrich Tiedau, "De Duitse cultuurpolitiek in België tijdens de Eerste Wereldoorlog," *Cahiers d'Histoire du Temps Présent*, 11, 2003, pp. 21–43, and the essays by Convents, Hubert, Kott, and Roolf in Jaumain et al., *Une guerre totale?*

31 This figure includes occasional sympathizers, signatories of petitions, and so on. Van Hees in Reginald De Schryver, Bruno De Wever et al. (eds.), *Nieuwe encyclopedie van de Vlaamse Beweging*, Tielt, Lannoo, 1998, 3 vols.; see Antoon Vrints, *Bezette stad. Vlaams-nationalistische collaboratie in Antwerpen tijdens de Eerste Wereldoorlog*, Brussels: Archives Générales du Royaume, 2002, and Vandeweyer, *kleine stad*, on activism in Antwerp, on Tienen; also

Vandeweyer in Jaumain et al., *Une guerre totale?* On the complementary emergence of Walloon activism, see Kesteloot, in the same volume.

32 Daniel Vanacker, *De frontbeweging. De Vlaamse strijd aan de Ijzer*, Koksijde: De Klaproos, 2000.

33 Benvindo, *Des hommes.*

34 Xavier Rousseaux and Laurence Van Ypersele, "Leaving the War: Popular Violence and Judicial Repression of 'Unpatriotic' Behavior in Belgium (1918–1921)," *European Review of History*, 12/1, March 2005, pp. 3–22.; Rousseaux and Van Ypersele, *La Patrie.*

35 De Schaepdrijver, in Baumann and Roland, *Einstein.*

36 Thiel, in Jaumain et al., *Une guerre totale?*

37 Rawe, in Jaumain et al., *Une guerre totale?*

38 On these contacts, see Roland, *La colonie.*

39 De Schaepdrijver, in Jaumain et al., *Une guerre totale?*

40 Benvindo, *Des hommes*; Van Ypersele, *Le Roi Albert.*

41 Debruyne, in Jaumain et al., *Une guerre totale?*; Van Ypersele and Debruyne, *Ombres.*

42 Heinrich Waentig, *Belgien*, Halle, 1919, quoted in De Schaepdrijver, *La Belgique*, p. 245.

43 Van Ypersele, in Hirschfeld et al., *Enzyklopädie*; Marks, *Innocent Abroad*; Sophie De Schaepdrijver, "'A Signal Service': Neutrality and the Limits of Sacrifice in World War One Belgium," in Madelon de Keizer and Ismee Tames (eds.), *Small Nations: Crisis and Confrontation in the 20th Century*, Amsterdam:, Walburg Pers, 2008, pp. 64–82.

44 Scholliers and Daelemans, *Standards.*

45 Carnel, in Jaumain et al., *Une guerre totale?*

46 Benoît Majerus, "Bruxelles, 1918: révolution et sortie de guerre," in Philippe Chassaigne and Jean-Marc Largeaud (eds.), *Villes en guerre (1914–1945)*, Paris: Colin, 2004, pp. 196–207; Van Ypersele, *Sortir*; on sheer looting and destruction, Tallier in Jaumain and Piette, *Bruxelles.*

47 Rousseaux and Van Ypersele, in Jaumain et al., *Une guerre totale?*

48 Claisse, in Jaumain et al., *Une guerre totale?*

49 John Horne, "Locarno et la politique de démobilisation culturelle: 1925–1930," in *Démobilisations culturelles après la Grande Guerre*, theme issue of *14/18. Aujourd'hui–Today–Heute. Revue annuelle d'histoire*, 5, 2002, pp. 72–87. See also Horne and Kramer, *German Atrocities* and Wolfgang Schivelbusch, *Die Bibliothek von Löwen. Eine Episode aus der Zeit der Weltkriege*, Munich, C. Hanser, 1988. On Belgium's occupation of the Ruhr, Laurence Van Ypersele, "Belgien und die Ruhrbesetzung: Wagnisse und Erwartungen," in Gerd Krumeich and Joachim Schröder (eds.), *Der Schatten des Weltkriegs: Die Ruhrbesetzung 1923*, Essen, Klartext, 2004, pp. 99–118.

50 Sophie De Schaepdrijver, "Les dangers de l'idéalisme: souvenirs contestés de l'occupation allemande en Belgique," in *Démobilisations culturelles*, pp. 114–27; Engelen, in Jaumain et al., *Une guerre totale?*; Proctor, *Female Intelligence*; Van Ypersele and Debruyne, *Ombres.*

51 Stéphanie Claisse, "Le déporté de la Grande Guerre: un 'héros' controversé. Le cas de quelques communes du Sud Luxembourg belge," *Cahiers d'Histoire du Temps Présent*, 7, 2000, pp. 127–48.

52 Beck, entry on "IJzerbedevaarten" [Yser Pilgrimages], in De Schryver et al., *Nieuwe Encyclopedie.*

53 Engelen, *Grote Oorlog Verbeeld.* Diverse entries by Bruno De Wever in De Schryver et al., *Nieuwe Encyclopedie*, deal with postwar radicalization. Also Van Everbroeck in Jaumain et al., *Une guerre totale?* and Van Everbroeck, *Borms.*

54 Van Ypersele, in Jaumain et al., *Une guerre totale?*

55 De Schaepdrijver, *La Belgique*, p. 303. See Schöttler, in Jaumain et al., *Une guerre totale?*

56 Engelen, *Grote Oorlog Verbeeld.*

57 Gubin, *Réflexions.*

58 Buelens, in Jaumain et al., *Une guerre totale?*; Sophie De Schaepdrijver, "Death Is Elsewhere: The Shifting Locus of Tragedy in Belgian First World War Literature," in *Belgian Memories,*

theme issue of *Yale French Studies*, ed. Catherine Labio, 102, 2002, pp. 94–114; Sophie De Schaepdrijver, "Grands coeurs et rancoeurs: les fictions d'occupation en Belgique," in Pierre Schoentjes (ed.), *La Grande Guerre, un siècle de fictions romanesques*, Geneva, Droz, 2008, pp. 183–201.

59 Tallier, in Tallier and Boijen, *La Belgique. Note:* The Belgian State Archives are assembling a comprehensive guide to Belgium's World War I sources.

References and Further Reading

Amara, Michaël, *Des Belges à l'épreuve de l'exil. Les réfugiés de la Première Guerre Mondiale*, Brussels, Éditions de l'Université de Bruxelles, 2008.

Amara, Michaël, and Roland, Hubert (eds.), *Gouverner en Belgique occupée. Oscar von der Lancken-Wakenitz – Rapports d'activité 1915–1918. Édition critique*, Brussels and Frankfurt a.M., P.I.E. and Peter Lang, 2004.

Benvindo, Bruno, *Des hommes en guerre: les soldats belges entre ténacité et désillusion 1914–1918*, Brussels, Archives Générales du Royaume, 2005.

Detournay, Céline, *La Grande Guerre sous le regard de l'élite tournaisienne occupée*, Brussels, Archives Générales du Royaume, 2003.

Engelen, Leen, *De Grote Oorlog Verbeeld. De Eerste Wereldoorlog in de Belgische speelfilm, 1918–1940*, Ghent, Academia Press, 2009.

Gubin, Éliane, and Stengers, Jean, *Histoire du sentiment national en Belgique des origines à 1918*, Vol. 2, *Le grand siècle de la nationalité belge, de 1830 à 1918*, Brussels, Racine, 2002.

Haag, Henri, *Le comte Charles de Broqueville, Ministre d'État, et les luttes pour le pouvoir (1910–1940)*, 2 vols., Louvain-la-Neuve and Brussels, Érasme-Nauwelaerts, 1990.

Horne, John, and Kramer, Alan, *German Atrocities 1914: A History of Denial*, New Haven and London, Yale University Press, 2001.

Jaumain, Serge, Amara, Michaël, Majerus, Benoit, and Vrints, Antoon (eds.), *Une guerre totale ? La Belgique dans la Première Guerre mondiale. Nouvelles tendances de la recherche historique. Actes du colloque international organisé à l'ULB du 15 au 17 janvier 2003*, Brussels, Archives Générales du Royaume, 2005.

Jaumain, Serge, and Piette, Valérie (eds.), *Bruxelles en '14–'18: la guerre au quotidien*, Brussels, 2005, theme issue of *Cahiers de la Fonderie: revue d'histoire sociale et industrielle de la Région bruxelloise*, 32.

Jaumain, Serge, and Piette, Valérie (eds.), *L'humour s'en va-t-en guerre. Bruxelles et la caricature en 14–18*, Brussels, Archives de la Ville, series *Fontes Bruxellae*, 2, 2005.

Majerus, Benoit, *Occupation et logiques policières. La police bruxelloise en 1914–1918 et 1940–1945*, Brussels, Académie Royale de Belgique, 2007.

Marks, Sally, *Innocent Abroad: Belgium at the Paris Peace Conference of 1919*, Chapel Hill, University of North Carolina Press, 1981.

Meseberg-Haubold, Ilse, *Die Widerstand Kardinal Merciers gegen die deutsche besetzung Belgiens 1914–1918: ein Beitrag zur politischen Rolle des Katholizismus im ersten Weltkrieg*, Frankfurt a.M., Peter Lang, 1982.

Pirenne, Henri, *La Belgique et la guerre mondiale*, Paris, Presses Universitaires de France, 1928, illustrated reprint in Pirenne, *Histoire de Belgique des origines à nos jours*, Brussels, La Renaissance du Livre, 1975, vol. 5.

Proctor, Tammy M., *Female Intelligence: Women and Espionage in the First World War*, New York and London, New York University Press, 2003.

Roland, Hubert, *La "colonie" littéraire allemande en Belgique*, Brussels, AML/Labor, 2003.

Rousseaux, Xavier, and Van Ypersele, Laurence (eds.), *La Patrie crie vengeance! La répression des "inciviques" belges au sortir de la guerre 1914–1918*, Brussels, Le Cri, 2008.

Schaepdrijver, Sophie de, *La Belgique et la Première Guerre Mondiale*, Brussels and Frankfurt a.M., P.I.E. and Peter Lang, 2004; revised translation of: *De Groote Oorlog. Het koninkrijk België tijdens de Eerste Wereldoorlog*, Amsterdam, Atlas, 1997.

Schaepdrijver, Sophie de, "Occupation, Propaganda, and the Idea of Belgium," in Aviel Roshwald and Richard Stites (eds.), *European Culture in the Great War: the Arts, Entertainment, and Propaganda, 1914–1918*, Cambridge, Cambridge University Press, 1999, pp. 267–94.

Schmidt-Supprian, Christoph, "The Antwerp Question: the Significance of the Port City of Antwerp during the First World War," PhD thesis, Trinity College Dublin, 2005.

Scholliers, Peter, and Daelemans, Frank, "Standards of Living and Standards of Health in Wartime Belgium," in Richard Wall and Jay Winter (eds.), *The Upheaval of War: Family, Work and Welfare in Europe, 1914–1918*, Cambridge, Cambridge University Press, 1988, pp. 139–58.

Tallier, Pierre-Alain, and Boijen, Richard (eds.), *La Belgique et la première Guerre Mondiale. État des sources – État de la recherche*, Brussels, Archives Générales du Royaume, 2002.

Thiel, Jens, *Menschenbassin Belgien. Anwerbung, Deportation und Zwangsarbeit im Ersten Weltkrieg*, Essen, Klartext, 2007.

Thielemans, Marie-Rose (ed.), *Albert I: carnets et correspondance de guerre 1914–1918*, Paris and Louvain-la-Neuve, Duculot, 1991.

Van Everbroeck, Christine, *August Borms. Zijn leven, zijn oorlogen, zijn dood. Een biografie*, Amsterdam and Antwerp, Meulenhoff-Manteau, 2005.

Van Ypersele, Laurence, *Le Roi Albert, Histoire d'un mythe*, Ottignies, Quorum, 1995.

Van Ypersele, Laurence, "Sortir de la guerre, sortir de l'occupation. Les violences populaires en Belgique au lendemain de la Première Guerre Mondiale," *Vingtième Siècle*, 83, July–September 2004, pp. 65–74.

Van Ypersele, Laurence, Debruyne Emmanuel, and Claisse, Stéphanie, *De la guerre de l'ombre aux ombres de la guerre: l'espionnage en Belgique durant la guerre 14–18. Histoire et mémoire*, Brussels, Labor, 2004.

Wende, Frank, *Die belgische Frage in der deutschen Politik des Ersten Weltkrieges*, Hamburg, Böhme, 1969.

Zilch, Reinhold, *Okkupation und Währung im Ersten Weltkrieg. Die Deutsche Besatzungspolitik in Belgien und Russisch-Polen, 1914–1918*, Goldbach, Keip, 1994.

Zuckerman, Larry, *The Rape of Belgium: The Untold Story of World War One*, New York, New York University Press, 2004.

CHAPTER TWENTY-SEVEN

Britain and Ireland

ADRIAN GREGORY

There is no official memorial to either the English or the British dead of World War I. The Cenotaph in Whitehall and the Tomb of the Unknown Warrior in Westminster Abbey are officially memorials to the dead of the British Empire. Scotland, Wales, India, Australia, Canada, and even Ireland all have "national" memorials to the dead of the war. But "Britain" and its largest single component, England, do not. This is more than a semantic point. In studying Britain during World War I it is always vital to bear in mind the potential anachronism of this unit of study. The assumption of an essential continuity of experience in "British" history in the twentieth century, which has informed most histories of the war, masks the more radical aspects of the upheaval it caused. Conversely, the historiography of Ireland has seen the period 1912–23 as the epoch of the "Irish Revolution," but in so doing has until recently portrayed the war as a mere backdrop. The grand narratives of emergent colonial self-rule and independence have also only recently begun to take the war seriously. It is therefore worth remembering that the political unit that declared war on August 4, 1914 was not "Britain," but the United Kingdom of Great Britain and Ireland and the associated Dominions and Colonies of the British Empire.

Britain's road to war was paved with imperial issues. These were due not so much to direct colonial rivalry between the British and German Empires but to the pressure of a more competitive world that made British isolation seem somewhat less than splendid. The result was a set of accommodations that aligned Britain with France and then Russia in the Triple Entente (or "Understanding") from 1904 to 1907. While the "understanding" never amounted to a binding agreement, it nonetheless drew Britain into possible European involvement in the event that its partners became embroiled in a continental war. That possibility was accentuated by the Anglo-German naval race which resulted in an open-ended challenge to British naval supremacy from 1906 to 1911.[1] Britain met the challenge, but was forced to collaborate further with the French. Once German priorities switched from the global and maritime to the European and military in 1912–13, the stage was set for a fundamental upheaval in the European balance of power. Britain would find it hard to stand aside in such a crisis because its security was now linked to France and Russia, which would inevitably be involved, and also because the specter of continental domination by one power had traditionally been seen as against Britain's essential interests.

Nonetheless, all this was implicit logic rather than a foregone conclusion, so that British involvement in a European conflagration seemed anything but inevitable to contemporaries. True, there was an increase in popular hostility to Germany in which the Northcliffe press empire played a prominent role. But such hostility was less marked amongst the governing elites and the working class. In many respects the antagonism had climaxed in 1910–11, and thereafter attention was increasingly distracted from international relations by domestic concerns. An upsurge of labor militancy and the activities of militant suffragettes appeared to threaten the social order, but the greatest preoccupation was the evolving threat over the relationship between Great Britain and Ireland.

With its passage through parliament in 1912, Home Rule for Ireland was set to come into force in 1914. The opposition Conservative Party resolutely opposed the ruling Liberal Party and the Irish Parliamentary Party over the measure. But more seriously still, the Protestant majority in Ulster began organizing for armed resistance in 1912, with the formation of a paramilitary Ulster Volunteer Force (UVF), while in 1914, a group of British officers stationed at the Curragh military camp in Ireland signaled their unwillingness to coerce Ulster Protestants into accepting Home Rule. All this provoked the formation of the Irish Volunteers by nationalists who were determined to defend Home Rule when it was implemented. Thus Ireland in 1914 seemed poised on the brink of civil war, while the United Kingdom as a whole was politically divided on the issue. The potential compromise was an opt-out clause for Protestant Ulster, but it remained an open question as to whether this would be accepted by either Irish nationalists or intransigent Unionists.

It was only toward the end of July 1914, a full month after the assassination of the Archduke Franz Ferdinand at Sarajevo, that the European crisis displaced Irish Home Rule from the centre of attention in the United Kingdom. The instinctive opinion of the majority of the population was that the Bosnian crisis was a Balkan affair of no possible interest to offshore islanders, and it was only when the crisis opposed Germany and Austria to Russia and France that there was any intimation that the United Kingdom might become involved (see chapter 1).

From July 28, however, elements in the Conservative press began implying that the United Kingdom had a moral responsibility to stand by France. To the shock of many of his Liberal Cabinet colleagues, Sir Edward Grey, the Foreign Secretary, who had been working hard to defuse the crisis, admitted that there had been military conversations between the British and French armies and that the French were expecting British military support as well as naval protection of their north coast. The logic of British alignment with a security system based on opposed alliances now came into play. But it was a painful matter for a Liberal government to admit this both to itself and to the country, when the party's historic allegiance lay with continental nonalignment and a high moral tone in international affairs. Failure to do so, however, threatened to court diplomatic disaster while handing political victory to the Conservative Party. The government was rescued by German strategic planning. The violation of Belgian neutrality provided the moral cause that the Liberals required (Britain was a guarantor of Belgian independence) while making it clear that German war aims threatened vital British interests. Even then, not all Liberals were convinced, nor was the left-wing Independent Labour Party (ILP). The government was certainly not forced into war by public opinion. The image of huge crowds demanding war in Whitehall and outside Buckingham Palace is entirely erroneous. Public opinion was deeply divided, and almost to the last minute it is probably the case that neutrality was the more popular course, although there was sympathy with France, and later, Belgium. If there was enthusiasm for war it was quite socially limited, probably most evident amongst young men of the middle classes.

Parliamentary debates revealed an unexpected benefit of the war crisis. John Redmond, the leader of the Irish Parliamentary Party, was a great supporter of the British Empire, which he saw as an Anglo-Irish joint venture, while the Ulster Unionists, led by Sir Edward Carson, had always stressed their loyalty to the imperial ideal. Both men pledged the loyalty of their respective parties and paramilitaries, with the nationalists promising to cooperate in the defense of Ireland to free the British army for duty elsewhere. There was a palpable relief at the lifting of the specter of civil war. Despite the continued opposition of the ILP (an exceptional stance amongst socialists in countries embarking on the war), the bulk of the Parliamentary Labour Party and the trade unions supported the war, as did most of the suffragettes. With resolve if not enthusiasm, the population acquiesced in Britain's declaration of war on Germany on August 4, 1914 when the Germans refused to call off their invasion of Belgium (though even then three Liberal ministers resigned). Actual enthusiasm was strongest amongst intellectuals, particularly the young. Rupert Brooke's poem "August 1914," with the line: "Now God, be thanked who matched us with this hour," was not representative of majority opinion. But as with intellectuals and artists in other countries, it captured the heady sense that war might provide an exciting revolt against the perceived materialistic sterility of contemporary society.

The United Kingdom entered the war without peacetime conscription and was consequently in a position to send only a small British Expeditionary Force (BEF) to France. Composed of career soldiers and reservists, it played a significant but junior role in the retreat to the Marne and subsequent stabilization of the western front (see chapter 4), but could not match the armies based on universal military service that were the norm with continental powers. Hence the most striking feature of the first months of the war in both the United Kingdom and the Dominions was massive voluntary enlistment in the armed forces, predominantly the army. Of the approximate total of 5 million men mobilized during the war in Britain, about half joined in the first two years by volunteering – an achievement unequaled in any state in any war. The other half would eventually be raised by conscription in the second half of the war.[2] The scale of volunteering is often taken as evidence of a latent enthusiasm for war on the part of the young men of the era. Undoubtedly the romance and excitement of war did attract some recruits. But the story is more complex. Mass unemployment at the outbreak of war fulfilled its usual role as a recruiting sergeant, and many men understandably hesitated to join until the issue of separation allowances was resolved at the end of August. Along with moral pressure and peer pressure, the sophisticated recruiting campaign spearheaded by the Parliamentary Recruiting Committee (PRC) also played a role, particularly with the organization of "Pals" battalions from September.

Sometimes the pressure was less subtle. In the countryside in particular, landowners frequently simply ordered their employees to enlist. The timing of the peak of voluntary enlistment is also revealing, not in the first flush of the war but at the end of August and start of September, after somewhat exaggerated reports of the defeat of the BEF had appeared in the press. This suggests that the perceived duty of defense played a much larger role in men's thinking than any abstract enthusiasm for war itself. A second spurt of volunteering was observable after the German navy bombarded the east-coast towns of Scarborough and Hartlepool in December 1914. Although the PRC had made use of

German atrocities in Belgium, it seems clear that atrocities against British civilians had more resonance, and had received more intense and detailed press coverage.[3]

Enlistment rates varied with region and occupation. The lower middle classes were at the forefront everywhere, but there was also substantial working-class enlistment in the early months. By contrast, rural areas were much more backward, with the exception of the Scottish Highlands.[4] This also in large part explains the key variable in Ireland, where John Redmond had urged the nationalists not just to defend Irish soil but to join the British army. The North of Ireland had much higher enlistment rates than the South, but this was less to do with religion or politics than sociology. The same contrasts were apparent as in England and Wales. The industrialized and urban north saw higher enlistment rates of Unionist and nationalist, Catholic and Protestant.[5] Nonetheless, politics could not be entirely banished. The Irish Volunteers split over support for the war. The majority followed Redmond's lead in supporting enlistment and renamed themselves the "National Volunteers." The idea of fighting in defense of "small nations" resonated amongst Irish Nationalists and allegations of atrocities by protestant "Prussians" against Roman-Catholic Belgians had a particular appeal. A small minority of the nationalists opposed the war and continued to style themselves the Irish Volunteers. In the Dominion armies many of the early volunteers were recent migrants from Great Britain. But the rhetoric of the war as a test of "nationhood" had powerful resonance in the Dominions, reinforced by the memory of the prominent role of Australian, New Zealand, and Canadian volunteers in the South African War (see chapter 35).

Volunteer recruiting was stimulated by Lord Kitchener, the hero of imperial campaigns in the Sudan and South Africa, who had been appointed as Secretary of State for War in order to instill confidence in the Liberal Government's capacity to run the war effort. Kitchener's view that the war would last at least two years was less radical than is sometimes suggested; in fact hardly anyone had any clear idea how long the war would last, and the idea that it would be "over by Christmas" is largely absent from contemporary discussion in 1914. However, Kitchener's decision to encourage the building of a huge citizen army would have profound effects on the development of the war for the British Empire.[6]

Prior to war the Committee of Imperial Defence had considered two different possible strategies, an army-led "continental commitment" and a "traditionalist" naval strategy consisting of a blockade and the capture of German trade. The latter was an updated version of the perceived strategy of the Napoleonic period, in which the primary British role would be that of banker and munitions supplier to a continental coalition. The war began with a compromise between the two courses of action, in effect committing the British Empire to both. But where the naval-dominated strategy meant minimum disruption to the civilian economy and even an expansion of the export trade to capture prewar German markets, a massive continental-style army threatened to undermine Britain's financial stability and entailed substantial social reorganization.

The implications of the two approaches surfaced very quickly. On the one hand there was "business as usual," which meant trying to minimize the impact of war on everyday life. On the other hand there was the demand that everyone should make sacrifices and "do their bit." This clash was apparent in the appeals of hoteliers and theater managers in the press that people continue spending money on leisure activities in order to maintain employment, whilst others demanded that professional football should be banned for the duration of the war to stop attracting crowds of "shirkers" who should be performing military service. Volunteering for military service was the paradigmatic sacrifice, but giving time and money was also widely encouraged. There was an early proliferation of war charities, for soldier's comforts, for the wounded, for refugees. The first "flag day" was held in Glasgow in early September 1914 and before long the selling of flags on the streets, predominantly by female volunteers, had become a pervasive feature of British society. In a counterpart to male volunteering, numerous young middle-class women volunteered as nurses in the Voluntary Aid Detachments (VADs). Other women were recruited into a newly formed women's police force, designed to control public morality, particularly amongst the working class.[7]

In effect, mass mobilization of British and imperial manpower for a major military effort on the western front and in secondary theaters such as Gallipoli (see chapter 7) turned the reciprocal effort of civilian society into a home front.[8] Prewar, there had been speculation about the working class in wartime, with fears that unemployment and rising prices could lead to social upheaval. The requirements of the war economy rapidly cured initial unemployment and, indeed, led to new employment opportunities for the poorest, who had been chronically underemployed before the war. But inflation proved to be a real problem, and during the first year of the war the "real wages" of much of the regularly employed working class fell. Overtime and increased family employment went some way to counteracting this, but the strain on industrial workers was real enough.[9]

The initial response was generally patient, but in two specific areas of the United Kingdom there was a clear rise in labor militancy. The strikes in the mining areas of South Wales and the growing militancy in Clydeside both had their roots in long-standing grievances, but were also part of a new language of wartime morality, in which sacrifice for the common good was the yardstick and "profiteering" for personal gain was considered as reprehensible as "shirking" military duty. In Glasgow the initial militancy stemmed from the long-standing housing problem. Women began "rent strikes" against landlords accused of using war conditions, especially the absence of husbands in the forces, to raise rents. Accusations of "Kaiserism" linked the struggle at the front to justice at home. Fearful the protest would spread, the government introduced a Rent Control Act that was the first major state intervention in the private housing market.

The mines of South Wales had a long-standing record of poor labor relations, and the strikes of 1915 were directed against mine owners accused of failing to match increased profits with higher wages. Because the anthracite coal of South Wales still fueled a significant part of the Royal Navy, the strikes represented a potential strategic threat and the government acted quickly to defuse the situation. The "Treasury Agreements" brokered by Lloyd George gave rise to a more comprehensive attempt to settle labor issues for the duration of the war. The government skillfully played off the interests of labor and business. Strikes in war-related industries were deemed illegal and the movement of individual workers was restricted. Trade unionists were persuaded to accept a "dilution" of skilled labor for the duration of the war, allowing the use of unskilled male and female labor. In return, the government agreed to control "profiteering" in industry by the introduction of an "Excess Profits Tax" and to expand the role of government arbitration in labor disputes. The trade union leaders were willing to make sacrifices for the nation, but not for increased private profits. Government was the big winner in this process, which helped restrain the costs of the war, already threatening to spiral out of control.[10]

The acceptance of dilution was helped by an increasingly strident public campaign, led by prominent pro-suffrage agitators, principally Emmeline and Christabel Pankhurst, for "women's right to serve." This was not as spontaneous as it appeared, for behind the scenes the organizers were encouraged by Lloyd George precisely to put pressure on the trade unions. The first impact of the war had been to increase female unemployment, but by 1915 the demand for labor had already seen significant substitution of male labor not only in industry but, perhaps more significantly, in commerce. Most of the women entering the workforce were not doing so for the first time and, indeed, the larger picture is one of change in female employment, particularly from textiles and domestic service, rather than women leaving the home.[11]

The labor situation in 1915 also gave rise to a widespread moral panic about drinking, with Lloyd George (as Minister for Munitions) claiming that drink was a more dangerous enemy than German submarines. A set of increasingly draconian restrictions was put in place, encouraged by the example of prominent figures (including the king) in pledging to abstain from alcohol for the duration of the war. This campaign created something of a populist backlash, with some accusing the government of pandering to the "pump-puritans" of organized nonconformity in the Liberal party, who were using the war as an excuse to drive through their long-standing teetotal agenda.

By the spring of 1915 serious doubts were emerging as to the competence of the Liberal Government to run the war effort. The escalating cost and brutality of the war proved difficult to incorporate within traditional liberal values. The first air raids on Great Britain and the sinking of merchant shipping focused popular hostility on the enemy within. From the start of the war there had been widespread stories that the German population in the United Kingdom was supporting espionage and sabotage. The use of poison gas, the steady drip of atrocity stories from Belgium, and finally the killing of large numbers of civilians in the sinking of the passenger liner the *Lusitania* led to an explosion of violence against the German immigrant population and, indeed, other foreigners who could be mistaken for Germans. The worst ethnic riots in the history of Great Britain ensued, principally in Liverpool, London, and Hull, but including small communities throughout England and Scotland.[12] The right-wing press accused the government of failing to act sufficiently vigorously in the internment of aliens, and this was added to a litany of perceived failures in the management of the war.

Operational failures added to this growing discontent as the failure of the initial landings at Gallipoli coincided with reports of a "shell shortage," handicapping the army in France. Although the latter scandal saw a backlash against the Northcliffe press (which had launched an attack on the immensely popular Lord Kitchener), leading to copies of *The Times* being burnt on the London stock exchange, it added to the feeling that the war needed more vigorous prosecution. The result was the formation in May 1915 of a "war coalition" that incorporated both Conservatives and token Labour representation.

During 1915 it became apparent that volunteering, however impressive, was waning and could not supply the manpower required by the military effort on the Continent. The inclusion of the Conservatives in the coalition introduced strong pressure for the measure into the heart of government. Liberal figures hoped that it could be avoided and, indeed, in 1915 the problems of equipping and arming the "New Armies" were even more pressing. The labor movement, fearing "industrial conscription," was strongly opposed to the measure, or at least without a parallel conscription of wealth. Furthermore, any introduction of conscription within the United Kingdom would raise delicate questions regarding Ireland, where conscription would be unpopular and unworkable. On the other hand the popular sense grew that the voluntary system was itself becoming inequitable, with the patriotically minded, including the fathers of families, being exploited, whilst others shamelessly shirked their duty. The hope that the "Derby

Scheme," whereby men "attested" their willingness to serve if needed, could solve the problem proved misplaced, and conscription was introduced, first for unmarried and then for all adult men, in January and May 1916, respectively.

The effects of the war on Ireland had proved contradictory. Home Rule had been enacted but suspended for the duration of the war, apparently freezing civil strife over the country's future. Hard-line Unionists turned revolt against Home Rule into proof of loyalty as they volunteered for the army, with the UVF providing the core of the 36th (Ulster) Division. Their leader, Sir Edward Carson, joined the coalition government. Yet despite insensitivity by the War Office to Nationalists, they too volunteered, many serving in the 16th (Irish) Division (which, like the 36th Division, fought on the western front), while men from both traditions fought at Gallipoli in the 10th Division.[13] Nationalist opinion remained by and large cautiously supportive in the belief that the war for the freedom of small nations would secure the path to Irish independence. The positive economic effects of the war on Ireland, which benefited from full employment and an agricultural boom, further reduced social tensions.

Yet volunteering waned in Ireland as elsewhere, and the threat of conscription placed a heavy burden on the fragile nationalist consensus (John Redmond, the Irish Parliamentary Party leader, had declined a place in the coalition government). Advanced Nationalists promoted the idea that Britain's war had no legitimacy in Ireland and should be resisted. In 1915, James Connolly, the leader of the socialist and nationalist Irish Citizens Army, had called for armed revolt but been restrained by a group within the Irish Volunteers who had their own revolutionary plans. The prominent figures of this group had been recruited into the long-standing militant organization, the Irish Republican Brotherhood, and held to the view that "England's difficulty is Ireland's opportunity." A splinter group within a splinter group, they were led by the strange and charismatic Padraig Pearse, who advocated the idea of "blood sacrifice" to reinvigorate an Irish nationalism compromised by the professional politicians of the Irish Parliamentary Party. Whether successful or not, a republican rising would reawaken Ireland's dormant desire for immediate and complete independence from Britain.[14]

The rebellion planned for Easter 1916 was to seize Dublin with a full-scale military operation (rather than a guerrilla campaign) and establish a "Sovereign Independent State," as the Proclamation put it. In military terms it was a fiasco. Attempts to enlist German support gained only a half-hearted response and the Royal Navy intercepted the arms shipment intended to supply the uprising. The leaders of the Irish Volunteers therefore failed to endorse the rebellion and in the end it was limited to roughly two thousand Irish Citizen Army and Irish Volunteer members in Dublin, with their headquarters in the General Post Office (GPO). After a week of destructive fighting around the city center (including bombardment of the GPO by a British gunboat in the Liffey River), it was crushed by a relatively small number of British troops, including significant numbers of Irishmen. In political and propaganda terms, however, the Rising was anything but a fiasco. Legally the British government had a perfect right to execute all rebels taken in arms and, indeed, the German and other armies in Europe conducted mass executions under much less provocation. But the particular political sensitivities at play were very different. In the end the British conducted 15 executions, including those of Pearse and Connolly, but by dragging out the process, they allowed popular sympathy to develop on behalf of the condemned men. The cult of nationalist martyrdom took over, while the mass internment of the other rebels created a new and sophisticated republican cadre. Yet Irish soldiers fighting in France (and dying in far greater numbers) were frequently outraged at the Rising, while Ulster Protestants had their stereotype of nationalist disloyalty confirmed. It was only during the second half of the war that nationalist Ireland would displace the old Home Rule Party with a new Sinn Féin movement that drew its legitimacy from 1916.[15]

Conscription in Britain was supported in principle, but in the first year of its operation over a million appeals were lodged by individuals or their employees against being conscripted, a number similar to the number of volunteers in the first year of the war. "Attested" married men in particular were enraged that they were being called up before the unattested unmarried. These figures should not be taken to indicate widespread opposition to the war effort. Despite the publicity such cases received and the widespread hostility they incurred, conscientious objectors made up a tiny fraction of all appeals, perhaps one percent. The majority were on grounds of domestic hardship or indispensability to business. War rhetoric of unlimited sacrifice increasingly conflicted with individual interests.

In human terms the impact of the war became more severe during the summer of 1916 as the "New Armies" raised by mass volunteering went into action on the Somme. July 1, 1916 was an unprecedented military disaster, although this was not widely known at the time, but the human impact was unevenly spread and fell principally on the towns of the industrial north of England, London, and the Protestants of Ulster.[16] The implicit contrast between the loyal sacrifice of the Ulstermen of the 36th (Ulster) Division at Thiepval on July 1–2 and the Dublin rebels further damaged the perception of Irish nationalism, although the nationalist 16th (Irish) Division would soon suffer its own heavy casualties on the Somme.[17] This was indicative of the way that the Somme battles became a series of local martyrdoms for various parts of the Empire: Beaumont Hamel for Newfoundland, Delville Wood for South Africa, Mametz Wood for Wales, and Pozières for Australia. Just as Gallipoli for the Australians and New Zealanders and Ypres for the Canadians had taken on a specific resonance of national pride, these Somme battles had a double effect, on the one hand emphasizing a particular national experience, on the other hand the participation in an imperial effort. This idea was captured in official propaganda, particularly the film *The Battle of the Somme*, which became a box-office hit throughout the Empire (see chapter 24). The film minimized the worst horrors of the battle, for example the vast numbers of unburied bodies and the breakdown of the medical services, but it was perceived at the time as being unprecedented in the realism of its portrayal of the human cost of war, in particular the scene of a British soldier apparently being killed. Although this was staged, it was widely believed to be real.

Amongst the deaths on the Somme was that of the prime minister's son. This personal tragedy added to Asquith's weight of responsibility and by late 1916 it was widely felt that he was no longer up to the task of directing the war effort. David Lloyd George was believed to have done a good job as Minister of Munitions and had been growing increasingly close to the leadership of the Conservative party, who had once demonized him as a dangerous radical. A plot supported by the great press barons, the Canadian Max Aitken (Lord Beaverbrook) and Northcliffe, led to Lloyd George taking the prime-ministership in December 1916 and reconstructing the government with a much stronger Conservative component. Asquith took a substantial section of the Liberal party into "opposition" although the electoral truce of 1914 still held.[18]

The new government faced immediate difficulties. The cost of the war had depleted British holdings of overseas assets and the difficulty of raising new loans in the United States had increased.[19] The Russian Revolution in March added a new level of uncertainty to the progress of the war and the beginnings of unrestricted submarine warfare threatened the UK food supply. Military operations on the Somme had failed to achieve a decisive victory and the new prime minister lacked confidence in the commander of the BEF, Sir Douglas Haig.

These new pressures were somewhat eased by the entry into the war of the United States, which guaranteed the financial situation and allowed a more coordinated response to food supply. But U-boat sinkings quickly reached an alarming level. The answer to the problem was already understood in theoretical terms, the introduction of convoys, but the Admiralty was somewhat reluctant to do so because convoys would require the provision of escort vessels, and convoying would automatically reduce the quantity of imports available compared with the more rapid flow produced by independent sailings. Nevertheless, shipping losses made the move inevitable and convoying quickly reduced losses to a manageable level (see chapter 10).

It is easy to exaggerate the effectiveness of the U-boat blockade. There was never a real food shortage in wartime Britain, and although the composition of "war bread" was altered, Britain never introduced bread rationing. Domestic production of arable crops was encouraged by guaranteed prices and overseas food stocks were bought up as a precaution. Farming in Britain and Ireland became more profitable than it had been for any time for half a century and farmers were exempt from Excess Profit Taxes and Income Tax. Tenant farmers were also largely exempt from military service, an exemption that was informally extended locally, amidst great controversy, to many of their sons.[20]

Labor shortages were dealt with by increased utilization of child and female labor and the employment of prisoners of war. Whilst the countryside prospered, urban discontent increased, and led to a strike wave in 1917. The main focus of attention was on the shop stewards' movement amongst the skilled engineering workers. Rebelling against the official trade union leadership and openly defying the Munitions of War Act, these strikes were perceived to be political, connected with antiwar sentiment that was reinforced by calls for a negotiated peace originating with the Russian soviets.[21] Although some of the leadership did share these sentiments, the principal cause was discontent at a perceived collaboration between the state and the employers in violating trade union custom and practice, particularly over the utilization of "leaving certificates" to control the workers. Industrial discontent was not in fact limited to skilled workers. Perhaps half of all strikes were started by unskilled workers, including women, and although the trade unionization of women increased during the war, at least some of the strikes were begun by non-unionized workers. The underlying reasons for these strikes, which also partly explain the strikes of skilled men, were the steep rise in the cost of living, the long hours (60 and more) that had to be worked to keep pace with this and the generally severe conditions in the workplace. Intermittent shortages, caused not by lack of supply, but difficulties of distribution, added to the problem and saw the emergence of queues in the winter of 1917. Popular discontent was kept on the boil by the perception of widespread profiteering by employers, food retailers, and farmers.

The government response was threefold. The powers of the Defence of the Realm Act (DORA) were used to isolate and even imprison suspected subversives; an intensified domestic propaganda in the form of the National War Aims Committee was utilized to persuade workers of the justice of the war; and most importantly the government began a policy of industrial "appeasement," using arbitration boards to grant significant "war bonuses" in many industries in order to counter the rising cost of living. At the end of 1917 this was joined by the introduction of food subsidies and the first intimations of rationing.[22]

The strike wave should be kept in perspective. It was less severe than pre- or postwar industrial militancy, most workers did not strike and most strikes were short. Even at its height, less than one working day in a thousand was lost. Most reports confirmed the underlying patriotism of the workforce and the figures for war-loan subscriptions in 1917 demonstrate that the most industrialized areas, including those of much apparent militancy, also showed the highest per-capita subscription to war loans, with Glasgow near the top of the table. The major exception was South Wales, where the industrial discontent may have been more linked to a genuinely socialist critique of the war resting on a more entrenched political militancy.

The major lasting effect of the strikes was to increase middle-class discontent. Exaggerated stories of the high wages earned by munitions workers (and an alleged boom in piano sales to their families!), an ever-increasing burden of taxation, greater inconveniences, and an erosion in relative standards of living and therefore status created deep resentment of the "strikers." By early 1918 the wages of even unskilled workers were beginning to equal the salaries of clerks. This was further exacerbated by the greater human burden on the middle classes, who resented the exemption from military service of skilled workers. The commercial and service sectors had disproportionately contributed manpower under both the volunteer system and conscription and had suffered correspondingly heavy casualties. The sense that the ungrateful working class were "shirkers" became widespread. One result was a growing right-wing populism, manifested in support for demagogic politicians calling for more extreme policies of total war, which represented a more immediate political threat in by-elections than any left-wing or pacifist group.

The low point in British morale was reached in the winter of 1917–18. London was the target of intensified air raids by "Gotha" bombers and throughout the country breakdowns in local distribution led to long queues for sugar, margarine and, in January 1918, meat. Reports of shortages at home and worry about their families were the chief causes of low morale among the troops in the field. The Bolshevik revolution in November increased fears that a revolutionary movement could develop although the climax of working-class discontent had already passed. Local action, beginning in Birmingham, set a precedent for the control of distribution and by February 1918 rationing had begun to be implemented throughout Great Britain for sugar, margarine, and meat. The results were nearly instantaneous and were widely approved. This came just in time as the culminating crisis of the war developed.

The German offensive of March 1918 created a manpower crisis for the army. Uniquely amongst the combatants, Britain had already recruited women volunteers to serve in the armed forces in noncombatant roles, releasing men for the front. But in March 1918 the government was forced to extend the age limits of conscription, restrict the tribunals, and call for a widespread "comb out" from industry. The major untapped sources of manpower were India, the Dominions, and Ireland. Australia had twice rejected conscription by referendum, and although Canada introduced it in the face of opposition from the Francophone population, this was too late to really affect the military situation. Indian troops were used only indirectly, to release British troops from the Middle East to serve in France. This left Ireland. While constitutional nationalism had staged a recovery in late 1917 despite the growing strength of Sinn Féin, ongoing talks about the future of Ireland would have no chance of success if the British state imposed a measure for which it had no legitimacy. Yet intensification of conscription in Britain without including the other component of the Union was unthinkable. Not for the first time, a

British government, caught on the horns of an Irish dilemma, took short-term action that utterly compromised its long-term goals. The attempt to impose conscription further undermined the Irish Parliamentary Party and rallied opinion (outside Protestant Ulster) behind Sinn Féin. In practice there was no real effort to enforce Irish conscription, but the damage was done.[23]

The government survived a test in parliament over its alleged failure to provide adequate reinforcements to the BEF. Despite more strikes in summer 1918, public opinion overall rallied to the national cause. Munitions production increased, the comb-out of industrial workers proceeded reasonably smoothly, and war loans campaigns were successful. War-aims rhetoric was increasingly in line with the idealism of "Wilsonian principles," ideas that gained significant support from the labor movement.[24] Although the bloody fighting of the year saw the heaviest casualties of the war, the view that the home front faced the prospect of revolution (Ireland apart) is unsustainable. Although the government still planned for war in 1919, the situation on the battlefield improved visibly from early August, and by September the observant grasped that an early victory might be at hand.

Nevertheless the Armistice of November 11, 1918 burst on the population almost as unexpectedly as the outbreak of war, and unlike the latter, saw a massive demonstration of popular joy in Britain, the Dominions, and even Ireland that was marred only by the absence of the war dead and the shadow of the global pandemic of influenza which indiscriminately killed combatants and civilians alike. Yet, as elsewhere, conflict did not end with the war (see chapter 37). Intervention by British forces in Russia and a series of rebellions in the Middle East both resulted in continuing military action that provoked growing discontent at home. But it was Ireland that caused the biggest postwar problem.

The "khaki election" of December 1918 shook the political landscape of the United Kingdom. The main victors were the Conservative-Unionists and their coupon "Liberal" allies. The war had seen the triumph of previously unpopular Conservative policies, particularly imperial protection and conscription. The party that had taken a strong prewar line against Germany appeared decisive and justified compared with the divided Liberals. The massive new electorate created by the Representation of the People Act of 1918, including female voters over 30, tended to vote either Conservative or Labour, reflecting the wartime polarization of opinion between the working class and the middle class.[25]

As a result the Labour Party emerged as the official opposition within Great Britain. Increased trade union membership had increased the financial power of the party to fight elections and the activity both of the War Emergency Workers' National Committee and of the Labour Party on a local level had reinforced the perception of the Labour Party as the defender of working-class interests. Yet the Party also made an appeal to white-collar workers and intellectuals and in 1918 it adopted both a constitution committing it to collectivist socialism and a program of sweeping reforms, many of which arose from the discontents of wartime.[26]

In lock step with the decline of the Liberals was the destruction of their traditional allies, the Irish Parliamentary Party. Sinn Féin swept the polls in Ireland and implemented their avowed policy of abstention from the Westminster parliament. The precise meaning of the Irish vote remains unclear and it cannot be taken as a pure endorsement of the immediate implementation of an Irish Republic, but rather as a rejection of British rule as implemented in wartime. Nevertheless the elected Sinn Féin representatives immediately formed a "national convention," a shadow parliament of their own which would claim legitimate authority in Ireland. Even before the end of the war the first acts of armed resistance had occurred, and when the British authorities suppressed the convention a full-scale guerrilla war broke out. Eventually widespread revulsion within Britain at the counter-insurrectionary repression forced the government to negotiate. In 1922, a quasi-independent Irish Free State was formed, which gradually acquired virtually full sovereignty between the wars, though not before a vicious civil war had pitted anti-Treaty republican militants against the Free State, which was eventually victorious.[27]

Ironically the only part of Ireland which actually received Home Rule was the North, where a devolved government and parliament were given authority over six counties of Ulster with a Protestant majority and proceeded to impose an often brutal hegemony over the Catholic population in the name of public order. Not surprisingly, the official memory of World War I was radically different in the two parts of the Ireland, with Unionist Ulster celebrating the "blood sacrifice" of the 36th (Ulster) Division that had supposedly sealed its birthright on the Somme, whereas the Free State, while not entirely ignoring the war, found its foundation myth in the Easter Rising of 1916.[28]

In a further irony, with the independence of Southern Ireland the UK suffered a greater territorial loss than defeated Germany. Overall, the British Empire was both strengthened and weakened by the war. The participation of the Dominions in the conflict gained them access to the inner circles of political deliberations, as the presence of the Australian and South African prime ministers at the Paris Peace Conference testified. This reinforced the sense of imperial connectedness, yet also strengthened national identity in the Dominions and a growing tendency to independent action. The signs of imperial dissolution were even more apparent elsewhere, and notably in India, where wartime proposals for reform leading to independence were overriden in 1919 by repressive action against the perceived link between colonial nationalism and Bolshevism. The same was true in Egypt and the new Middle Eastern "mandates" that Britain had taken over from Ottoman Turkey.[29] Imperial overstretch, which had contributed to bringing Britain into the war, was if anything even more evident after it.

In Britain itself, the war had wrought fundamental transformations. The basis of political citizenship had been redefined from property ownership and gender toward a citizenship based on "national service." The inevitable granting of the vote to young men on the basis of their military service had also opened the door to female enfranchisement. At the same time "citizenship" was defined in more ethnic terms as "aliens" were increasingly excluded. The partition of Ireland removed the Union from its defining position in prewar politics. Instead the nascent politics of class, already apparent prior to 1914, became firmly embodied in competing political parties under universal suffrage. In 1922, a Conservative government replaced Lloyd George's coalition. But while a conservative cultural and political hegemony was apparent in British, or more accurately English, society between the wars, it was a transformed conservatism, less rooted in elite dominance and deference and more populist in its appeal to the lower middle classes, more modernizing and increasingly dependent on female support. Meanwhile, the Labour Party, combining the language of class with its own variant of a more general appeal, entered government twice. If its program of social reforms was impossible to implement in the climate of financial retrenchment following the war (exacerbated in turn by the 1930s Depression), it provided the template for a new postwar period after 1945.

The shadow of bereavement fell heavily over interwar Britain, so heavily in fact, that the demographic impact of the war has been exaggerated to this day (see chapter 17).

British per-capita casualties were half those of France and less than Germany's. Approximately one in five families lost a close relative, which was bad enough but not the "lost generation" of popular legend.[30] Initially the memory of war concentrated on the idea of a "justified sacrifice" in the "war to end all wars," but this idea was slowly undermined and more or less destroyed by World War II, leaving instead a view of a "futile war." Britain had achieved its primary war aim with the postwar destruction of the German fleet, perhaps the most serious threat to British security of the entire twentieth century. Yet this "negative" success was easily lost sight of as a result of the high-flown rhetoric of the war. The proliferation of rituals of commemoration had begun with the need to overcome wartime divisions and mend the social fabric.[31] But the stress on the pervasiveness of loss created in turn a sense of the war as an ultimately unjustifiable disaster – a perception that remains strong today.[32] Indeed, this peculiarly British memory of the war has become a key component of the very British identity that the war did so much to promote: Britain and England have no specific war memorial and yet the memory is everywhere.

Notes

1   Paul Kennedy, *The Rise of Anglo-German Antagonism, 1860–1914,* London, Allen and Unwin, 1981; Rueger, *Great Naval Game.*

2   Ian Beckett, "The Nation in Arms," in Beckett and Simpson (eds.), *Nation in Arms,* pp. 2–35 (here 12–13).

3   On atrocities, see Gregory, *Last Great War,* pp. 40–69.

4   Ibid., pp. 73–95.

5   David Fitzpatrick, "The Logic of Collective Sacrifice: Ireland and the British Army, 1914–1918," *Historical Journal,* 38/4, 1995, pp. 1017–30.

6   Simkins, *Kitchener's Army.*

7   Gregory, *Last Great War,* pp. 95–108.

8   The term itself was used retrospectively by the satirical magazine *Punch* in relation to April 1915 (*Mr Punch's History of the Great War,* London, Cassell, 1919, p. 32).

9   Hugh A. Clegg, *A History of British Trade Unions since 1889,* vol. 2, *1911–1933,* Oxford, Oxford University Press, 1983, pp. 141–4.

10 Clegg, *British Trade Unions,* pp. 120–35; Adams, *Arms and the Wizard.*

11 Deborah Thom, "Women and Work in Wartime Britain," in Richard Wall and Jay Winter (eds.), *The Upheaval of War. Family, Work and Welfare in Europe, 1914–1918,* Cambridge, Cambridge University Press, 1988, pp. 297–326.

12 Gregory, *Last Great War,* pp. 235–8.

13 Philip Orr, "200,000 Volunteer Soldiers," in Horne (ed.), *Our War,* pp. 63–77.

14 Jeffery, *Ireland and the Great War,* pp. 37–68; Horne (ed.), *Our War,* chs. 1–5.

15 Laffan, *Resurrection of Ireland,* pp. 77–168.

16 Robin Prior and Trevor Wilson, *The Somme,* New Haven and London, Yale University Press, 2005; McCartney, *Citizen Soldiers,* pp. 211–15; Gregory, *Last Great War,* pp. 122–31.

17 Orr, "200,000 Volunteer Soldiers."

18 Wilson, *Myriad Faces,* pp. 408–23.

19 Broadberry and Howlett, "Business as Usual?," pp. 215–22.

20 Horn, *Rural Life,* pp. 47–92.

21 James Hinton, *The First Shop Stewards' Movement,* London, Allen and Unwin, 1973, pp. 196–212.

22 Noel Whiteside, "Concession, Coercion or Cooperation? State Policy and Industrial Unrest in Britain, 1916–1920," in Leopold Haimson and Giulio Sapelli (eds.), *Strikes, Social Conflict and the First World War: An International Perspective,* Milan, Feltrinelli, 1992, pp. 107–22.

23   David Fitzpatrick, *The Two Irelands, 1912–1939*, Oxford, Oxford University Press, 1998, pp. 63–75.
24   French, *Strategy*, pp. 193–206.
25   Waites, *A Class Society at War*, pp. 179–239; Kenneth Morgan, *Consensus and Disunity: the Lloyd George Coalition Government, 1918–1922*, Oxford, Clarendon Press, 1979, pp. 26–45.
26   Winter, *Socialism and the Challenge of War*, pp. 234–69.
27   Hart, *IRA at War*; Fitzpatrick, *Two Irelands*, pp. 75–114.
28   Keith Jeffery, "Echoes of War," in Horne (ed.), *Our War*, pp. 263–75.
29   Erez Manela, *The Wilsonian Moment. Self-Determination and the International Origins of Anti-colonial Nationalism*, Oxford, Oxford University Press, pp. 63–97, 159–75.
30   Winter, *Great War and the British People*, pp. 65–99 ("The Lost Generation").
31   Gregory, *Silence of Memory*.
32   Todman, *Myth and Memory*.

References and Further Reading

Adams, R. J. Q., *Arms and the Wizard: Lloyd George and the Ministry of Munitions, 1915–1916*, London, Cassell, 1978.

Adams, R. J. Q., and Poirier, Philip, *The Conscription Controversy in Great Britain, 1900–1918*, Basingstoke, Macmillan, 1987.

Beckett, Ian, and Simpson, Keith (eds.), *A Nation in Arms. A Social Study of the British Army in the First World War*, Manchester, Manchester University Press, 1985.

Bond, Brian, *The Unquiet Western Front. Britain's Role in Literature and History*, Cambridge, Cambridge University Press, 2002.

Bourne, John M., *Britain and the Great War 1914–1918*, London, Edward Arnold, 1989.

Bowman, Timothy, *The Irish Regiments in the Great War – Discipline and Morale*, Manchester, Manchester University Press, 1999.

Broadberry, Stephen, and Howlett, Peter, "The United Kingdom during World War I: Business as Usual?," in Stephen Broadberry and Mark Harrison (eds.), *The Economics of World War I*, Cambridge, Cambridge University Press, 2005, pp. 206–34.

Bush, Julia, *Behind the Lines. East London Labour, 1914–1919*, London, Merlin, 1984.

Constantine, Stephen, Kirby, Maurice W., and Rose, Mary B. (eds.), *The First World War in British History*, London, Edward Arnold, 1995.

de Groot, Gerard, *Blighty. British Society in the Era of the Great War*, London, Longman, 1998.

Fitzpatrick, David, *Politics and Irish Life, 1913–1921: Provincial Experience of War and Revolution*, 1977; new ed., Cork, Cork University Press, 1998.

French, David, *The Strategy of the Lloyd George Coalition 1916–1918*, Oxford, Oxford University Press, 1992.

Fussell, Paul, *The Great War and Modern Memory*, Oxford, Oxford University Press, 1975.

Gregory, Adrian, *The Silence of Memory. Armistice Day, 1919–1946*, Oxford, Berg, 1994.

Gregory, Adrian, *The Last Great War. British Society and the First World War*, Cambridge, Cambridge University Press, 2008.

Gregory, Adrian, and Paseta, Senia (eds.), *Ireland and the Great War: A War to Unite Us All?*, Manchester, Manchester University Press, 2002.

Grieves, Keith, *The Politics of Manpower, 1914–1918*, Manchester, Manchester University Press, 1988.

Gullace, Nicoletta, *"The Blood of Our Sons": Men, Women, and the Renegotiation of British Citizenship During the Great War*, Basingstoke, Palgrave, 2002.

Hart, Peter, *The IRA at War, 1916–1923*, Oxford, Oxford University Press, 2003.

Horn, Pamela, *Rural Life in England in the First World War*, Dublin, Gill and Macmillan, 1984.

Horne, John (ed.), *Our War. Ireland and the Great War*, Dublin, RTE/ Royal Irish Academy, 2008.

Hynes, Samuel, *A War Imagined. The First World War and English Culture*, London, Bodley Head, 1990.

Jeffery, Keith, *Ireland and the Great War*, Cambridge, Cambridge University Press, 2000.

King, Alex, *Memorials of the War in Great Britain. The Symbolism and Politics of Remembrance*, Oxford, Berg, 1998.

Laffan, Michael, *The Resurrection of Ireland. The Sinn Féin Party, 1916–1923*, Cambridge, Cambridge University Press, 1999.

McCartney, Helen B., *Citizen Soldiers. The Liverpool Territorials in the First World War*, Cambridge, Cambridge University Press, 2005.

Marwick, Arthur, *The Deluge. British Society and the First World War*, 1965; new ed., London, Macmillan, 1991.

Messinger, Gary, *British Propaganda and the State in the First World War*, Manchester, Manchester University Press, 1992.

Millman, Brock, *Managing Domestic Dissent in the First World War*, London, Frank Cass, 2000.

Reznick, Jeffrey S., *Healing the Nation. Soldiers and the Culture of Care-giving in Britain during the Great War*, Manchester, Manchester University Press, 2005.

Robb, George, *British Culture and the First World War*, Basingstoke, Palgrave Macmillan, 2002.

Rueger, Jan, *The Great Naval Game: Britain and Germany in the Age of Empire*, Cambridge, Cambridge University Press, 2007.

Sanders, Michael, and Taylor, Philip, *British Propaganda during the First World War*, London, Macmillan, 1982.

Silbey, David, *The British Working Class and Enthusiasm for War, 1914–1916*, London, Frank Cass, 2005.

Simkins, Peter, *Kitchener's Army. The Raising of the New Armies 1914–1916*, Manchester, Manchester University Press, 1988.

Thom, Deborah, *Nice Girls and Rude Girls: Women Workers in World War I*, London, I. B. Tauris, 1998.

Todman, Dan, *The Great War. Myth and Memory*, London, Hambledon Continuum, 2005.

Waites, Bernard, *A Class Society at War. England 1914–1918*, Leamington Spa, Berg, 1987.

Watson, Janet S. K., *Fighting Different Wars. Experience, Memory and the First World War in Britain*, Cambridge, Cambridge University Press, 2004.

Wilkinson, Alan, *The Church of England and the First World War*, 1978; new ed., London, SCM Press, 1996.

Wilson, Trevor, *The Myriad Faces of War. Britain and the Great War 1914–1918*, Cambridge, Polity Press, 1986.

Winter, Jay M., *Socialism and the Challenge of War. Ideas and Politics in Britain, 1912–1918*, London, Routledge and Kegan Paul, 1974.

Winter, Jay M., *The Great War and the British People*, London, Macmillan, 1986.

CHAPTER TWENTY-EIGHT

France

LEONARD V. SMITH

In the decades before 1914, the French had made various strategic choices that helped pave the way to war. France had been humiliated by Prussia in the war of 1870–1, most notably by the incorporation into the now-united German Empire of the border provinces of Alsace and Lorraine. The guardians of the newborn Third Republic would pursue a policy of creating alliances that would deter Germany in the future. As would be the case in the Cold War, deterrence was not about military parity, but about military superiority. Central to French strategy was an alliance with Imperial Russia. The combination of French capital and Russian manpower, it was hoped, would so intimidate Germany that it would never go to war with France again. A series of treaties, some secret clauses of which remained unknown even to senior officials before war broke out, bound together the unlikely allies – the one republic among the Great Powers to the most authentic autocracy. But the Franco-Russian alliance also encircled Germany, and implicated the French in Russian objectives in the volatile Balkans.

Republican France also sought to restore French greatness, somewhat more doubtfully, through imperial expansion. This led to a rivalry with Britain in Africa and Asia. As late as 1898, this competition nearly led to war, but it was resolved by series of secret diplomatic agreements. Britain, too, was concerned about increasing German power on the Continent. The logical outcome was the Entente Cordiale, or understanding reached in 1904 on respective spheres of influence in North Africa, which was followed by army talks and a naval agreement. All this gave Britain an interest in avoiding French defeat in a war with Germany that had not been there in 1870–1.

When war actually came, the French had few choices. The German Schlieffen Plan called for an immediate invasion of France in the event of a general European war, whatever its cause. On 31 July 1914, the German government cabled the ambassador in Paris to demand the French forts at Toul and Verdun, even if France chose to abandon its Russian ally in the looming confrontation. When German troops poured into Belgium en route to France, the point became moot. Inadvertently, Germany handed France a monumental moral and propaganda advantage. A *Union sacrée* (sacred union) brought together as never before the political regime of the Third Republic and the affective community of France, in order to resist the invader. A minuscule number of draftees refused mobilization, and there was so little opposition on the left that the government felt it unnecessary to round up some 2,500 people on Carnet B, the long-standing list of persons deemed by the authorities likely to cause trouble.[1] The *Union sacrée* succeeded through inclusion – of the Socialists on the left, the Catholic Church in France, and of monarchists and others on the anti-republican Right. Bitter internal quarrels that had poisoned politics for decades were put aside.

At the heart of the *Union sacrée* was national indignation at the invader. France, like Belgium and Serbia, could consider itself a "violated" nation – the overtones of sexual aggression in the term being lost on no one. The Russian alliance and the entente with Britain, which in retrospect had done quite a bit to disrupt the balance of power in Europe, now looked like the most prudent of precautions. The Schlieffen Plan was a military response to the diplomatic and strategic encirclement of Germany, and to a Franco-Russian-British policy of deterrence through military superiority. But none of this mattered once the Germans crossed the Belgian frontier. The time had come, the French concluded, to deal with the enemy across the Rhine once and for all, and to reclaim Alsace and Lorraine in the process. The long-dormant question of the "lost territories" would speedily become a salient French war aim, the symbol of keeping France safe from the enemy across the Rhine.

Quite contrary to the intentions of the elaborate war plans drawn up by both sides, and notwithstanding casualties that made the first months of the war the most lethal of the entire conflict, the military outcome of the first battles proved inconclusive. Following the logic of their prewar alliance, the French and the Russians sought to overwhelm Germany with simultaneous offensives. But French commander, General Joseph Joffre, and most of the French high command completely misread German strategy. The French army embarked on a virtually foredoomed offensive into German Lorraine and failed to see until the eleventh hour the German threat from the north through Belgium. Only the inherent flaws in the Schlieffen Plan and the timely decision by Joffre to recognize and take advantage of a retreat that soldiers had already decided upon themselves spared France a disaster on the scale of 1870 or 1940. The "Battle of the Marne" proper (September 6–8, 1914) indeed drove back the invader (see chapter 4). But by the time the fighting died down in November, and after nearly 330,000 French dead, the Germans still held not only Alsace and Lorraine but most of northeastern France as well, some of the richest and most industrialized areas in the country. Paradoxically, stalemate on the western front provided the framework for the "totalization" of the war.

This outcome had considerable diplomatic as well as military implications. Alsace and Lorraine, after all, had been essentially border regions incorporated into pre-revolutionary France and places where German and the Alsatian dialect were spoken more commonly than French. To a surprising degree, the French had heeded Léon Gambetta's famous advice back in 1871 to think about the "Lost Provinces" always, but to speak about them never. The lands of occupied northeastern France were something else altogether. These lands had been attached to the monarchy since the Middle Ages, and France could not remain France without them. Essentially, the military outcome of 1914 had rendered a negotiated peace unthinkable, simply because France had nothing it could negotiate. National survival became equated with victory at whatever cost.

After massive economic dislocation in the fall of 1914, the French converted their productive capacities to war as efficiently as any people in Europe. The agricultural economy continued to function remarkably well, even though the war began at harvest time. Rural France mobilized impressive numbers of women, older workers, and children, thereby avoiding a grave food crisis in the winter of 1914–15. Wartime agricultural production would never reach its prewar levels, because of shortages in workers, machinery, and fertilizers. But widespread hunger would never become an issue, as it would in blockaded Germany.

As no one had expected a long war, many strategic industries were seriously short-staffed because of workers sent to the front – precisely when stocks at the front had become exhausted following the first battles of the war. Industrial production was also seriously affected by the loss of much of northeastern France, one of the most heavily industrialized parts of the country, to German occupation. Half or more of prewar production of coal and steel had come from areas now in German hands. Yet through an exceptionally effective collaboration among capital, labor, and the government, the French economy retooled for war. A supervised cartel of employers in the strategic metallurgical industries managed the massive increase in imports of raw materials. Other industries organized similarly, with the largest companies collaborating with considerable autonomy. The government established a Ministry of Armaments in December 1916, under the direction of reformist Socialist Albert Thomas, who had been a disciple of Jean Jaurès. Through managing the continuing participation of the unions, Thomas hoped to pioneer permanent collaboration across class lines in a mixed economy that would combine the goals of justice contained in socialism and of private initiative contained in capitalism. The state, thus, would become the instrument of a new corporatism that would lay the foundation for the further development of reformist socialism after the war.

Certainly, French armaments production increased dramatically. By the end of the war, shell production had increased tenfold from its level in the summer of 1915, and the production of powder and explosives sixfold. By 1918, French industry produced 1,000 artillery pieces per month, and 261,000 shells and 6 million cartridges per day. Arguably, France played the role the United States would play in World War II – the "arsenal of democracy." For better or worse, World War I made France one of the world's foremost producers of weaponry, which it remains today.

This is not to say that the mobilization of the wartime economy always proceeded smoothly or to the satisfaction of all of the French. The very success of the mobilization of labor created new fault lines of political division, even within the labor movement. By July 1917, some 1.7 million people were employed in the munitions industry alone. Of these some 1 million comprised essentially new categories of laborers – women (some 400,000) and mobilized workers, men under military discipline but released for industrial labor. Foreign workers (from the French Empire, Europe, and China) comprised another nearly 175,000, including nearly 30,000 prisoners of war.[2] Women, of course, were not new to the paid labor force in France. But the insatiable demand for skilled labor in war industries opened up unprecedented opportunities. Traditional (and male dominated) trade unions were at best ambivalent about an influx of female labor. Men feared that the more women entered the factories, the more men would be culled and sent to the front. Those remaining would see their wage rates threatened by women able to do the same work for less money. A common practice in France as well as in Britain was "dilution," according to which a complex task hitherto performed by one man, who typically belonged to a union, would be broken down into several tasks performed by several women, who typically did not. Employers did not always rise above pitting the genders of the working classes against each other.

Few domestic political questions, at the front or in the interior, proved more vexing than that of the *embusqués*, or "shirkers." By definition, an *embusqué* was a man fit for military service hiding in a job behind the lines for which he was not needed. But how to determine who was "needed"? In the initial labor crisis of late 1914 and early 1915, thousands of men were returned willy-nilly from the front to the factories, without any systematic determination of utility. For the next four years, the political process would try to regulate who would serve in the factory and who at the front, with debatable success. The unions had at best a conflict of interest in the matter, as the need to cooperate in the war effort and to enhance their political status clashed with a reluctance to send union members from the factories to the trenches. Even the mobilized workers released for war work could, theoretically, be sent back to the front at any time. The government likewise faced conflicting demands. The Jacobin logic of male equality required that all serve – a concept that became known as the *impôt du sang* or "blood tax." Rival politicians, women, and soldiers exerted considerable pressure on the government based on this logic. Yet the government and the military had to remain aware of the practicalities of the situation. Some men were simply more valuable to the war effort in the factories, as well as in the technical and medical schools, than in the trenches.

Political pressures would thus lead parliament to pass laws regulating the mobilized workforce that the government would quietly sabotage through limited enforcement. The Loi Dalbiez of August 1915 had the goal of examining the case of every single mobilized worker, and retaining only the minimum needed for war production. But so porous did the boundaries set up by the law prove that the government passed another measure, the Loi Mournier, in August 1917. It targeted particularly men age 24–35, a population that had spent much of the war in the factories and held by the authorities to be a hotbed of labor militants, actual or potential. Yet the same conflict of ideology versus practicality continued. John Horne has calculated that of some 88,000 men returned to combat units as a result of the Loi Mourier, only about 6,000 came from war factories. And indeed, the total figure of 88,000 had to be set against 73,000 older soldiers sent home from the front.[3] The problem of the *embusqué* was never satisfactorily resolved, and he would live on as a figure in postwar, not wartime, memory.

The mobilization of the national community behind the lines produced a complex war culture. The French state had long been keenly interested in the political opinions of the French, never more so than during World War I. The prefects, the eyes and ears of the state in the province, sent back voluminous reports describing civilian morale, though such reports could often reveal as much about the author as about the subject. But the state did far more than observe public opinion. A censorship apparatus ultimately employing some 2,000 persons regulated journalism, publishing, and theatrical performances. The army established its own formidable censorship structure, which endeavored to control the circulation of information between the front and the interior. But the volume of correspondence both ways was simply overwhelming, unless the military wanted to employ half of its personnel reading the mail of the other half. Thousands of reports were generated monitoring correspondence between soldiers and civilians. But even during the mutinies of 1917, letters were rarely seized unless they overtly advocated sedition. Soldiers could write with some measure of impunity of their daily lives, their opinions of the war, and most anything else.[4] The boundaries set up by censorship proved highly permeable. And censorship, by definition, is negative in that it seeks to regulate what may *not* be said. War culture in France depended more significantly on self-mobilization across a broad social spectrum.

No nation takes its intellectuals and artists more seriously than France, and nowhere did these shapers of culture more enthusiastically embrace the war effort. Poet Charles

Péguy was killed in the first days of the war, and became a nationalist martyred hero who never had to face the dirty, bloody, stalemated war of the trenches. But plenty of others did. Two famous postwar pacifists, writer Henri Barbusse and philosopher Émile Chartier (better known as Alain), volunteered for military duty, even though they were above the age of active service. Foreigners resident in France, such as writers Blaise Cendrars and Guillaume Apollinaire, fought for their adopted country. Others clearly above military age put their formidable skills to work mobilizing the home front. The *Comité d'Etudes et de Documents sur la guerre* (Committee of Studies and Documents on the War) comprised some of the most prestigious figures in French social science. Led by historian Ernest Lavisse and sociologist Émile Durkheim, the Committee churned out countless pamphlets explaining the war effort in French and seven foreign languages.

The "objectivity" of the social, human, and natural sciences sought to legitimize a virulent attack not just on present-day Germany, but on German culture itself. Some argued that the real roots of French-ness were Latin, and that France was the true heir of Greek and Roman classicism. The Franks and the Gauls, it turned out, had not really been Germanic tribes, at least not in the same sense as those who had settled on the other side of the Rhine. Consequently, "true" French culture needed to be purified of Germanic influence. Composers Camille Saint-Saëns and Vincent d'Indy wrote diatribes against the influence of Richard Wagner on French music. Erik Satie's *Parade* (1917) brought kitschy tunes, a typewriter, and a pistol into the orchestra pit, as a deliberate reaction to the lush, symphonic German musical tradition. Some intellectuals found German influence literally malodorous. Captain Augustin Cochin was a prominent historian, and the offspring of one of the most distinguished academic families in France. He wrote that the Germans "have a special odor, very strong, and that you can't get rid of," as well as their own species of fleas, much larger than those that afflicted the French. Psychologist Dr. Edgar Bérillon suggested in a lecture in 1917 that the population of Alsace and Lorraine could never really be assimilated into Germany because they would always find the smell of Germans too disagreeable. So effectively had French intellectuals and artists stoked the passions of World War I that one of the few genuine wartime pacifists among them, Romain Rolland, wrote in 1919: "This war has been, to some extent, their war. They have poisoned millions of minds with their murderous ideologies. Sure of *their* truth, prideful and implacable, they have sacrificed to the triumph of the ghosts of their spirit millions of young lives. History will hardly be able to forget it."[5]

But it would be a mistake to believe that the cultural mobilization of France behind the lines was purely the work of elites. Popular culture embraced the conflict at least as fervently as elite culture, and reached many more of the French in doing so. Children, for example, became conscripted soldiers in the culture wars through the efforts of teachers and the producers of toys, games, and children's literature. At first, children seem like puzzling candidates for mobilization, as ineligible either for combat or industrial labor. But who more easily appreciated the moral purity of the French cause, and who could better exemplify it? The war worked its way into every aspect of the primary school curriculum. Quite young students were read bloodthirsty stories of the campaigns, and asked to calculate shell requirements and casualties as part of everyday arithmetic assignments. Learning the alphabet became a form of war work. For example, in a book entitled *L'Alphabet de la Grande Guerre* (1915) children learned that "C" is for "Charge." As the text explained: "The charge of the bayonet is the supreme moment of combat."[6]

A whole genre of ferocious children's literature recounted tales of the *enfant héroïque* (heroic child). Their innocence and selfless devotion would inspire the nation to the victory that adults found so elusive. "Those cursed dog Germans will bite the dust bathed in blood," proclaimed Jean Louis, a 10-year-old boy in *Guerre de 1914: Un coin de province à l'avant, Jean Louis le petit Français* (1916). "I will fight like papa, I will imitate him," he concluded.[7] Children's literature became populated with male and female miniature guerrilla warriors. Girls spied on the enemy, and killed them by stealth. Boys followed and sometimes joined combat regiments. Children gave no quarter, and killed cheerfully. When caught by the enemy, which happened frequently, these tiny literary heroes bravely accepted their own death, by firing squad or the bayonet. Their last words, inevitably, were patriotic cries, commonly "Vive la France!"

But as the war dragged on, cultural mobilization became increasingly difficult because of the continued stalemate at the front. To a great degree, French strategic objectives remained the same from the first days of the war to the last.[8] Joffre and his successors knew that together France, Britain, Russia, and (after 1915) Italy could bring more force to bear than Germany and its two major, but more rickety allies, Austria-Hungary and Turkey. The key lay in coordinated offensives on different fronts that would overwhelm the ability of the Central Powers to use its interior lines of communication to shift forces to where they were most needed. But there remained major impediments to carrying out this strategy. Germany was not the only country with fragile allies, as the Western powers learned from the outset with Italy and much more dramatically with Russia in 1917. Britain would not have a large army on the continent until 1916, and had strategic ambitions elsewhere in the world (notably the Ottoman Empire) that the French would eye with suspicion. Only in the last months of the war would there be anything resembling a unified Allied command structure, and never anything like the authority wielded by General Dwight Eisenhower in World War II.

Nevertheless, through a series of offensives carefully negotiated with the Russians and the British, Joffre promised to complete the "Miracle of the Marne" by achieving a rupture (*percée*) of the German lines, which would enable the Allied forces to pour in reserves, shatter the whole German position on the western front, and end the war. Two major offensives in 1915 failed to achieve this, in the Artois in the spring, and in the Champagne and again in the Artois in the fall. Nevertheless, Joffre insisted that France was still winning the war through *grignotage* or "nibbling" at the enemy. As his popularity began to wane, he pinned his hopes on a joint offensive with the British along the Somme, planned for the summer of 1916. In the meantime, however, the German high command planned its own exercise in *grignotage*, by attacking the series of forts at Verdun in February 1916. The tactical assumption remained that France would contest every inch of national territory, independent of its strategic significance as traditionally calculated. As a result, the French and the Germans fought for nearly nine months with horrendous casualties, with the battle lines at about the same place at the end of 1916 as they had been at the beginning. The offensive along the Somme began in the summer of 1916, with the French contributing about one-third of the Allied troops. Casualties were even greater than those of Verdun, with likewise no gains of strategic significance. To some extent, France's fortunes became tied to whether its ally, Russia, or Germany's ally, Austria-Hungary, would collapse first. In the meantime, as the fateful year of 1917 dawned the French turned to Robert Nivelle to restore the war of movement in the West.

Certainly, French soldiers, like other soldiers in the trenches, did not always and everywhere conform to their literary image of sheep marching uniformly into slaughter. Indeed, had they done so the war could not possibly have lasted as long as it did, because there would not have been enough soldiers left to continue to wage it. Notwithstanding horrendous casualties, which frequently reached 20 percent of effectives per engagement, French soldiers had some ability to determine their own conduct. They left the trenches, in great fear and more or less in good faith, but simply stopped moving forward when they perceived their efforts as no longer likely to result in anything but their complete massacre. The command structure then found itself obligated to accept results essentially determined in the field as adequate, and to construe continued stalemate as victory.

Given the mud, the vermin, the weather, the ever-present danger of death or mutilation, what kept French soldiers, or any soldiers, in the trenches for four long years? Some historians argue for external coercion, pure and simple. Total coercion during the war produced total alienation after it. Others argue that the matter is considerably more complex. The problem, they contend, was not alienation, but the reverse – total and individualized implication, an ideological construct known as consent. There was more to consent than affective patriotism. Rather, the individual in the trenches became intensely identified with his comrades and the collectivity itself, and consequently with the war. He could not surrender that identity without in some sense surrendering himself. This made discipline primarily horizontal rather than vertical. Francique Vial was a member of the Territorial Army, men toward the upper end of the age limit for military service. He considered himself and his comrades mature adults who never really left the civilian society whence they came:

> It thus happened that discipline no longer came from the grip of wills from above on the wills from below. It came from below, spontaneously, from the effect of respect and affection that the soldier felt for conscientious and good leaders, who took care of him and who worked alongside him on the same task. No, one did not come to the territorials at the front in order to talk about class struggle. They are an egalitarian and democratic army, and we cannot say often enough, a fraternal army.[9]

Consent, those who support the notion argue, cannot be explained simply by propaganda, which soldiers themselves dismissed as *bourrage de crâne* (literally, head-stuffing). Rather, it had deep roots in experience at the front itself. In the case of France, consent also had deep roots in the Republic, and in the massive investment of the 40 years before 1914 in creating citizens through schools and soldiers through conscription. For better or worse, the work of the French Revolution in creating civic and military identity came to fruition under the Third Republic. But consent, which in any event existed to one degree or another among all the countries that sent soldiers to the front, was by no means an unambiguously good thing. Because it implicated the individual totally with the collectivity, and with the cause of the collectivity, consent actually deepened as the war continued. Louis Mairet wrote in all seriousness of what he had learned in his time in the trenches: "The warrior prevents the end of the war."[10] By 1917, the war had become a struggle between the irresistible force of total mobilization, sustained by consent, and the immoveable object of the lines of trenches themselves.

Jean Jacques Becker has described 1917 as the "impossible year," here meaning the year in which ends and means in the French war effort became irreconcilable.[11] Multiple crises at the front and in the interior appeared seriously to call into question continued French participation in the war. These crises, most of which had some sort of counterpart in nearly every country that fought World War I, were resolved through what John Horne has argued was a "second mobilization," which took place during the conflict itself.[12] Mutinies in the French army were settled from within, strikes in the interior were resolved, and national politics were stabilized through a reinvigorated wartime government under Georges Clemenceau. Consent was re-engineered by the national community. The French, in short, decided that France could not remain France without victory. Yet the second mobilization would have its own consequences in the years to come. It set up extraordinary expectations of a victory by the French for the French. Such were not, as we will see, the circumstances of the actual end of the war in 1918.

The decision to continue was made first and most fundamentally at the front, by thousands of citizen-soldiers of France. The French army mutinies of 1917, still widely misunderstood in the English-speaking world, began in the wake of the failed offensive along the Chemin des Dames, begun in April 1917. General Robert Nivelle had an exaggerated faith in his ability to break through the German lines thanks to the *barrage roulant*, or "creeping barrage," that lay at the heart of the new tactics. The artillery and the infantry would simply move forward at the same predetermined speed, thereby guaranteeing cover for the men advancing on foot. To some extent, the *barrage roulant* was also a one-time trick. The Germans quickly learned simply to withhold their counter barrage until the creeping barrage ended. And no barrage could creep forward indefinitely, at least not unless the defending artillery had been silenced. The results of the offensive have certainly been no surprise to military historians. Soldiers slogged through near-frozen mud uphill to battered but still strong and very deep German positions. Nivelle himself was dismissed on May 15, and replaced by General Philippe Pétain, the hero of Verdun and the apostle of the defensive.

The point in connecting the Chemin des Dames offensive to the 1917 mutinies is not so much that this particular effort was any more militarily disastrous than the French offensives that preceded it, but that the pattern of expectations falling from *percée* to *grignotage* had become unacceptable to many French soldiers. The most common form of mutiny involved soldiers collectively refusing to take up positions in the front lines when ordered to do so. They would then depart to open areas and hold demonstrations airing their myriad demands. In all, incidents of collective indiscipline occurred in nearly one half of all of the divisions in the French army. The total number of "mutineers" is most reliably estimated at between 25,000 and 50,000. But such estimates are intrinsically misleading and perhaps a bit beside the point, since the French army mutinies comprised hundreds of thousands of individual decisions made and remade over a period of several weeks.

Most senior commanders initially took a passive role, relying on junior officers to restore something resembling order to the troubled units. Pétain lauded the case of one army corps, in which the commander surrounded the would-be demonstrators with cavalry and gendarmes, whereupon he gave them a certain amount of time to rejoin their units. For good measure, he had each company commander identify five "leaders" from each company. The incident fizzled, and the discontented soldiers returned to their duties. "Here is how a leader," Pétain wrote, "worthy of the name, who knows how to join firm words and energetic action, can bring back together a group of men led astray and terrorized by a few leaders."[13] Such observations would play a critical role in controlling the narrative of the mutinies once they were over. But in the short run, the command structure simply lacked the means to resolve the matter in its favor if words passed to deeds. Only the cavalry (particularly from colonial units) were deemed certain to fire on French soldiers if ordered to do so. And they were never numerous enough to prevail over infantry who, after all, were heavily armed themselves. To a great extent, the mutinies for a time displaced the formal authority structure in the French army.

Consequently, understanding the mutinies must focus on the discontented soldiers themselves. Nothing is more surprising about the demands of the discontented soldiers of the spring of 1917 than their diversity. They moved effortlessly from relatively mundane matters such as the quality of their food, to concern for their families behind the lines, to issues as abstract as "injustice." The expressed worry that "blacks" were mistreating soldiers' wives referred to widespread (but apparently untrue) reports that colonial troops had been used to suppress women's strikes. Soldiers sought very traditional male roles as protectors of and providers for their families. Above all, soldiers wanted "peace." But as we will see, when pressed they plainly did not mean peace on any terms, or even on terms inconsistent with the war aims of the national community for the preceding three years. They sought *both* immediate peace and a reformed leave policy, though the former presumably would render the latter irrelevant.

At the heart of drama of the mutinies of 1917, lay the negotiation of the political identity of the French citizen-soldier. The mutinies brought to the surface a tension as old as French democracy itself between direct democracy and representative government. The mutinies had become an exercise in direct democracy. Yet in difficult but essential partnership with direct democracy existed representative government. The state and its army drew their power from representative government. The citizen-soldier served the army as a representation of the state, and the state as a representation of the sovereign people. Discontented soldiers returned again and again to the necessity of transmitting their concerns to their elected representatives in the Chamber of Deputies. A soldier from the 274th Infantry regiment wrote to his deputy: "Do not forget that we hold in our hands the destiny of the country. If by this winter you have not shown your willingness to negotiate [with the Germans], we will give way." A soldier from the 36th Infantry Regiment wrote: "We refused to march not to bring about a revolution, rather to attract the attention of the government in making them understand that we are men, and not beasts to be led to the *abattoir* to be slaughtered, that we want what is due to us and that we demand peace."[14]

Both direct democracy and representative government drew their legitimacy from the same source, the General Will of the sovereign people. Consequently, the soldier obeyed a source of authority originating in himself and his compatriots. Whether in obeying his commanders as the instrument of representative government or disobeying in claiming his right as a citizen to agitate against the war, the soldier remained bound to an authority ultimately emanating from himself and his compatriots. The soldiers did not have the secret to victory that had escaped everyone else up to that time. Consequently, soldiers would eventually have to decide whether to lose the war again or to endorse conventional military authority and their commanders' solutions for winning it.

The repression took place only after soldiers made the essential decision to continue. The discontented soldiers agreed to accept military authority when no external coercion could have compelled them to do so. Repression of the mutinies comprised two elements – courts martial to identify and punish symbolic "leaders" of the mutinies, and a remarkably successful effort on the part of the generals to command the narrative of the mutinies, to cast it in terms favorable to itself. French historian Guy Pedroncini arrived at figures that suggest considerable prudence – 3,427 soldiers tried as a result of the mutinies, with 554 death sentences, and 49 soldiers actually shot.[15]

Yet the numbers told only part of the story. A relatively small population identified as "leaders" could accept blame for the disturbances, though they were no more responsible for the mutinies than matches for forest fires. Dubious and vague criteria were applied capriciously. The command structure proved remarkably effective at regaining command of the historical narrative of the mutinies. Conventional military discipline holds officers at all levels responsible for the conduct of their men. The high command evaded blame by inventing a massive defeatist conspiracy in the interior. No substantial links have ever been established between the mutinies and domestic pacifist movements. But by assigning such a large role to internal subversion, the command structure could make the mutinies yet another battle in civil-military relations – a war right and left have always known how to fight very well. The French have continued sporadically to argue about the mutinies in largely the same terms ever since. Sadly lacking on both sides of such debates has been a nuanced appreciation of the soldiers' agonized and even morally ambiguous decision to continue the war. For in the end, the mutinies of 1917 were more about consenting to the war than rejecting it.

By the middle of 1917, most of the 1.3 million Frenchmen who would die in World War I were already dead and France was in mourning. The collective decision to continue the war had its own dynamic in civilian society. In addition, the mobilization of French society had fostered old and new tensions along fault lines of class, gender, and race. Discontented workers agitated for higher wages in a situation of exploding inflation, as well as better working conditions and a fair sharing of sacrifices. Many were women, trying to cope with unprecedented responsibilities as wage earners and heads of families. The troubles in the interior in 1917 separated women from men, and native French from thousands of foreign workers brought in to support the war effort.

Labor activism divided the French along lines of gender. Sending skilled male laborers from the front back to the factories had always been controversial, and suspicions of corruption abounded both among women and among soldiers. But with the military quite literally looking over their shoulders, men of military age proved reluctant to down tools. In addition, while many union leaders would try to forget this after the war, they had worked hard to keep men producing for the war effort, as a lingering effect of the *Union sacrée*. Most men resented dilution, and its threat to unionized labor. Women, for their part, appreciated the higher pay that came with more skilled labor, yet resented being paid less than men for the same work. They liberally denounced harsh foremen and arrogant supervisors as shirkers.

Women, not men, drove labor activism in the spring and summer of 1917. No woman, after all, stood any risk of being sent to the front. The most significant wave of strikes in 1917 took place, coincidentally, during the mutinies. Strikes began in the clothing industry, among workers called the *midinettes*. In the end, some 10,000 women marched, waving the tricolor flag and calling for a cost-of-living raise and the *semaine anglaise* (Saturday afternoons off) with no loss of pay. The matter became more serious when strikes spread to the metalworking and munitions factories throughout the Paris region. Probably in conscious contrast to the *midinettes*, the metal workers carried the revolutionary red flag. Some women encouraged their colleagues to down tools by arguing that the war would end when they stopped building the means for it. Over 42,000 workers in these industries struck in all, nearly 75 percent of them women. Given that only about 30 percent of all metalworkers were women, this meant that they struck in highly disproportionate numbers.[16]

The striking women wanted "peace," but who in Europe by June 1917 did not? "Down with the war!" striking women would cry, but in virtually the same breath, "Long live our *poilus*! [literally, "hairy ones," the diminutive term for French soldiers]." But only a tiny percentage of the French – female or male, civilian or soldier – wanted peace at any price. The "peace" advocated usually amounted to France regaining Alsace and Lorraine and the Germans accepting financial responsibility for the material damage they had done. Such a peace could (and eventually did) pass for a French victory. Like discontented soldiers at the front, discontented women in the factories declined to abandon the war effort. Women returned to their duties with relatively minor concessions (wage increases, rapidly inflated away) and mild repression (lost wages from the strike, and a few women dismissed or arrested). The claims and expectations of labour were largely deferred to the day of victory.

Some of the frustrations of 1917 vented themselves on non-European foreign workers, over 220,000 people (mostly men) from the French Empire and China brought into France to work for the war effort. France had also mobilized some 600,000 soldiers from its empire, enough to make a good deal of trouble if the colonial relationship went sour. Plenty of French-born men and women viewed colonial labor as a threat to native workers, a tool of the government and the employers used to send more men to the front and to reduce the wages of the women left behind. Race trumped class during the labor unrest of 1917, in a variety of violent episodes in which French nationals attacked foreign workers.[17] The racial politics of the interior in 1917 seemed to unify the French in their desire to rid themselves of non-white workers after the war. Workers of color were repatriated after 1918 by any means necessary, including police round-ups in Paris and Marseilles. But traditions of labor and migration had been established. The empire had come to France on a large scale for the first time. World War I proved an important step in making France a multiracial country.

"High politics," the realm of representatives, ministers, and the head of state, was the last sector of the French public sphere to embark upon a second mobilization in 1917. The rise of "The Tiger," Georges Clemenceau, sent to friend and foe the message that France would prevail in World War I, or die in the attempt. Particularly in the English-speaking world, historians have often described Clemenceau as having flogged his compatriots to victory – the great man who stood taller than the nation he led. But the decision to continue had already been made in French society writ large in several stages over the course of 1917. Clemenceau articulated the desire of the national community to prevail in the conflict. A few "traitors," most famously the alleged spy Mata Hari, were executed on dubious grounds, and several political rivals were imprisoned. But Clemenceau maintained the constitutional framework of the Third Republic. Indeed, most of Clemeneau's enemies would re-emerge by the 1920s, and would help engineer his own marginalization from public life.

Joffre's strategy of overwhelming Germany by pressure on multiple fronts worked in the end, though hardly in the way he had envisaged. Germany, not France, restored the war of movement. A brilliantly executed, tactically innovative German offensive was begun against the British in March 1918, and it pushed back the whole Allied position until by the summer, the Germans were in artillery range of Paris. In near-desperation, the British and Americans permitted the appointment of General Ferdinand Foch as supreme commander. While Foch's authority was more or less limited to the deployment of reserves, this enabled him to impose an unprecedented level of coordination over Allied strategy. Beginning on 18 July 1918, Foch and the Allies staged a succession of counterattacks that created relentless pressure on the western front until the German army felt compelled to ask for an armistice. The Americans, somewhat more in the abstract, played the role envisaged by Joffre for Russia as the supplier of unlimited manpower. Through the fall of 1918, the Allies generalized their attack on the Central Powers in theaters long dormant. The British along with some French advanced through the Arabic-speaking parts of the Ottoman Empire, in part to solidify their claims to imperial expansion once the war was over. The British, French, and Serbians abandoned their self-imposed internment at Salonika, broke through the lines of Germany's tiny and weak ally Bulgaria, and advanced to the borders of Hungary. Certainly, this hastened the disintegration of the Habsburg Monarchy, further assisted by the Italian victory in northern Italy. At tremendous cost in blood, treasure, and upheaval, attrition had worked in the end.

Yet the armistice signed on November 11 foreshadowed the limits of the French victory, which was not entirely a victory, and was assuredly Allied rather than French. The term "armistice" implies a cessation of hostilities, not surrender. Foch did everything he could to make these terms synonymous, and to give France the total victory it had not quite won in the field. France would immediately reoccupy the rest of northeastern France and, above all, Alsace and Lorraine. The Allies would temporarily occupy the Rhineland, with the French taking special care to send in black African colonial troops as a calculated humiliation. Yet just what it all had been for would in a remarkably short time prove less obvious than it seemed to the millions of French civilians who poured into the streets on the evening of November 11 in frenzied celebration. Celebrations at the front proved considerably more muted.[18]

It has always been easy and not altogether unjustified to heap scorn on the French role in the failed quest for peace after the armistice. On 28 June 1919, the apparent victors and the apparent vanquished signed what became known as the Treaty of Versailles. The French made sure the signing took place in the Hall of Mirrors at the palace of Versailles, the site of the proclamation of the German Empire in 1871. Niccolò Machiavelli had said centuries earlier that a defeated enemy should be either rehabilitated or annihilated, and the Versailles Treaty did neither. A vengeful Germany under Adolph Hitler would 20 years later plunge Europe into a conflict far worse even than World War I. In the English-speaking world, a good bit of the blame for the failure of the treaty has been attached to the French, for demanding a vindictive peace that by the 1930s they lacked the means or even the will to enforce.

Whatever the accuracy of these claims, the role of France in creating and executing the Versailles Treaty cannot be understood apart from the ongoing struggle within the national community to figure out what the war had been about and how it could be justified. Peacemaking for the French continued the effort to transform a narrative of national survival into a narrative of national triumph. Central to this effort were the notorious *Kriegschuld* or "war guilt" provisions of the treaty (Articles 231 and 232) and provisions for trying the now-exiled Kaiser and other Germans accused of war crimes (Articles 227–30), although these provisions could not wholly be blamed on the French. The idea that impoverished Germany could somehow pay for the entire cost of World War I was probably known to be absurd at the time. Moreover, Germany would never be able to pay anything unless its economy revived, precisely what the Allies and particularly the French feared. So began the bitter history of the reparations question, which would do so much to poison international politics in Europe between the wars.

A variety of military provisions sought to keep Germany in a permanently weakened state. Germany could have an army of no more than 100,000 men, no military aircraft, and a navy suited only to coastal defense. German territorial concessions amounted to considerably less than the French had wanted. Marshal Foch and General Mangin believed that France could remain safe only through detaching the left bank of the Rhine from Germany, through an "independent" Rhineland which all understood would become a satellite state dependent on France. The other Allies dismissed such a brazen attempt to dismember Germany. In the end, the French had to settle for a demilitarized Rhineland, enforced by a 15-year military occupation.

In part, the vindictiveness of France was driven by an actual deterioration in its strategic position since 1914. France was still a nation of 40 million people facing a Germany of over 60 million people. The French gladly accepted colonial expansion, under the guise of League of Nations "mandates." But few in France deluded themselves that the new colonies would prove of any use against a resurgent Germany. In August 1914, French security based itself on an explicit alliance with Imperial Russia and a de facto alliance with Britain. By 1920, it had neither. The Bolshevik regime, in any event engaged in a desperate civil war to save itself, wished only ruin on capitalist regimes everywhere. The successor states to the Habsburg Monarchy were small, weak, and embroiled in ethnic hatreds. They made unpromising and ultimately hopeless allies. Interwar France was haunted by the idea that it had given up 1.3 million dead and ruined its economy to emerge less safe than before.

The Third Republic became more divided against itself over the course of the interwar period. As elsewhere in Europe, the left split between Socialists and Communists, often marginalizing both. Meanwhile, anti-republican groups flourished on the extreme right. The center remained an unstable mixture of personalities and policies, as had largely been the case before 1914. But the Third Republic was a nineteenth-century liberal regime now facing twentieth-century problems. Muddle in the political center and poisoned opinion at the extremes led to inertia in internal and foreign affairs. The supreme symbol of the failure of the French to capitalize on the "victory" of 1918 became the Maginot Line, a colossally expensive collection of connected forts designed to stop the Germans at the French border. The Maginot Line, quite literally, encased the citizen-soldier in concrete.

Notes

1   Becker, *1914*, p. 379.
2   Horne, *Labour at War*, p. 74.
3   Horne, " 'Impot du Sang.' "
4   See Hanna, *No One is Happy in War*.
5   Quoted in Prochasson and Rasmussen, *Au nom de la patrie*, 124.
6   Quoted in Audoin-Rouzeau, *Guerre des enfants*, illustrations.
7   Quoted in ibid., p. 146.
8   See Doughty, *Pyrrhic Victory*.
9   Vial, *Territoriaux de France*, p. 34.
10   Mairet, *Carnet d'un combatant*, pp. 249–50.
11   Becker, *1917 en Europe: l'année impossible*.
12   See the essays in Horne, *State, Society and Mobilization*.
13   Quoted in Smith, "The French High Command," p. 83.
14   Quoted in Smith, *Between Mutiny and Obedience*, pp. 192–3.
15   Pedroncini, *Les Mutineries de 1917*, pp. 194, 215.
16   See Downs, *Manufacturing Inequality*, ch. 4.

17   See Stovall, "Colour-blind France?"
18   See Cabanes, *Victoire endueillée*.

References and Further Reading

Audoin-Rouzeau, Stéphane, *Men at War. National Sentiment and Trench Journalism in France during the First World War*, 1986; English translation, Oxford and Providence, RI, Berg, 1992.

Audoin-Rouzeau, Stéphane, *La Guerre des enfants, 1914–1918*, Paris, Armand Colin, 1993.

Becker, Annette, *War and Faith. The Religious Imagination in France, 1914–1930*, 1994; English translation, Oxford and Providence, RI, Berg, 1998.

Becker, Jean-Jacques, *1914: Comment les français sont entrés dans la guerre*, Paris, Presses de la Fondation Nationale des Sciences Politiques, 1977.

Becker, Jean-Jacques, *The Great War and the French People*, 1983; English translation, Leamington Spa, Berg, 1986.

Becker, Jean-Jacques, *1917 en Europe: l'année impossible*, Brussels, Éditions Complexe, 1997.

Cabanes, Bruno, *La Victoire endueillé: la sortie de guerre des soldats français, 1918–1930*, Paris, Éditions de Seuil, 2004.

Doughty, Robert, *Pyrrhic Victory: French Strategy and Operations in the Great War*, Cambridge, MA, Belknap Press of Harvard University Press, 2005.

Downs, Laura, *Manufacturing Inequality: Gender Division in the French and British Metalworking Industries, 1914–1939*, Ithaca, Cornell University Press, 1995.

Fridenson, Patrick (ed.), *The French Home Front, 1914–1918*, Oxford and Providence, RI, Berg, 1992.

Godfrey, John, *Capitalism at War. Industrial Policy and Bureaucracy in France 1914–1918*, Leamington Spa, Berg, 1987.

Hanna, Martha, *The Mobilization of Intellect. French Scholars and Writers during the Great War*, Cambridge, MA, Harvard University Press, 1996.

Hanna, Martha, *No One is Happy in War: A Peasant Marriage in World War I France*, Cambridge, MA, Harvard University Press, 2006.

Horne, John, "'L'Impôt du Sang': Republican Rhetoric and Industrial Warfare in France, 1914–1918," *Social History* 14/2, 1989, pp. 201–23.

Horne, John, *Labour at War: France and Britain, 1914–1918*, Oxford, Clarendon Press, 1992.

Horne, John (ed.) *State, Society and Mobilization in Europe during the First World War*, Cambridge, Cambridge University Press, 1997.

Mairet, L., *Carnet d'un combattant (11 février 1915–16 avril 1917)*, Paris, Georges Crès, 1919.

Pedroncini, Guy, *Les Mutineries de 1917*, Paris, Presses Universitaires de France, 1967.

Prochasson, Christophe, and Rasmussen, Anne, *Au nom de la patrie: les intellectuals et la première guerre mondiale (1910–1919)*, Paris, Éditions de la Découverte, 1991.

Ridel, Charles, *Les Embusqués*, Paris, Armand Colin, 2007.

Smith, Leonard, *Between Mutiny and Obedience: The Case of the French Fifth Infantry Division during World War I*, Princeton, Princeton University Press, 1994.

Smith, Leonard, "The French High Command and the Mutinies of Spring 1917," in H. Cecil and P. Liddle (eds.), *Facing Armageddon: The First World War Experienced*, London, Leo Cooper, 1996, pp. 79–92.

Smith, Leonard, *The Embattled Self: French Soldiers' Testimony of the Great War*, Ithaca, Cornell University Press, 2007.

Stovall, Tyler (1993) "Colour-blind France?: Colonial Workers during the First World War," *Race and Class* 35, 33–55.

Vial, F., *Territoriaux de France*, Paris, Berger-Levrault, 1919.

Winter, Jay, and Robert, Jean-Louis, *Capital Cities at War. Paris, London, Berlin, 1914–1919*, Cambridge, Cambridge University Press, 1997 and 2007 (2 vols.).

Chapter Twenty-Nine

Germany

Gerhard Hirschfeld
(translated by Mark Jones)

With the departure of the first Chancellor of the German Empire, Otto von Bismarck, in 1890, the basis of German foreign policy changed considerably, and with it, political relations between the major European powers. Up to that point, Bismarck had declared that Germany was a territorially "satisfied" power, but now the German Empire entered the colonial race with France and Great Britain and built a strong battle fleet in the pursuit of *Weltpolitik* (world power). The German naval program began in 1898 and challenged Great Britain as the foremost world and naval power. The German policy of expansion also created considerable tension between Germany and Tsarist Russia, which had established a military treaty with France in 1892–4, presenting Germany with the potential threat of a war on two fronts.

As Britain aligned itself with France and Russia in the early years of the twentieth century, Europe polarized into two power blocks, each viewing the other as a threat. This left European governments with little room to maneuver for fear of losing honor and prestige and undermining their respective alliances. These dynamics can be seen in a succession of international crises before 1914 – over Morocco in 1905 and 1911 and with the Balkan Wars in 1912–13 (see chapter 1).

In response to the assassination of the heir to the Austro-Hungarian Empire at Sarajevo on June 28, 1914, the German government assured the Austrians of its unconditional support for action designed to destroy Serbia, which was deemed to be behind the Bosnian Serb "terrorists" who had carried out the attack. As Kaiser Wilhelm II scribbled in the margin of the telegram sent by the German ambassador from Vienna after the murder of Sarajevo: "Now or never.... We must make a clean sweep with the Serbs, speedily." Vienna received the "blank check" it had hoped for. The German government was at first troubled by what it thought was Austrians' lack of determination. It was further irritated by the fact that the deliberately harsh terms of the ultimatum sent to Serbia by Austria on June 23 now made Austria-Hungary, not Serbia, appear the aggressor in the eyes of world opinion. Belgrade's conciliatory response two days later then threatened to undermine the entire Austro-German ploy to eliminate Serbia as an independent state, with the Kaiser in particular vacillating.

The Chancellor, Theobald Bethmann Hollweg, also began to urge Austrian restraint. But such attempts to calm the situation were half-hearted and thwarted by the German military, which by then had assumed control of affairs. On June 28, Austria-Hungary opened hostilities against Serbia. As Russia predictably began to mobilize first against Austria alone, and then, when the German government declared this a threat to its own security, against Germany too, the German General Staff as well as the political leadership seized the opportunity to present Germany as the victim of aggression and launch a war that would maximize domestic support, and notably that of the Social Democratic Party (SPD). When Russia failed to respond to the German ultimatum of July 31 by suspending its mobilization, Germany mobilized and on August 1, declared war against Russia. Since Germany faced a two-front war against France as well as Russia, the German war plan (defined in 1905 by the chief of the General Staff Count von Schlieffen, later modified by his successor Helmuth von Moltke the Younger) determined that France would be invaded and defeated first, leaving a more sluggish Russian mobilization to be met by the combined forces of the Central Powers subsequently. Consequently, Germany declared war against France on August 3. The next day, a German strike force stormed across the border of neutral Belgium to attack Liège and clear the way to Paris, making a British declaration of war against Germany inevitable – to the outrage of Bethmann Hollweg and much of German opinion. Taking on the world's major naval power, whose fleet Germany had failed to outbuild, had fateful consequences for the kind of war World War I turned out to be.

The response of the German population to the events surrounding the outbreak of war has been shown by recent research to be more complex than the portrayal of national unity and patriotic euphoria conventionally summed up by the notion of the "spirit of 1914." The latter is really a myth constructed at the time by the conservative press and perpetuated long afterwards (including by the Nazis) for political reasons. It is true that the conservative bourgeoisie responded to the ultimatum to Serbia with a good deal of enthusiasm. However, this quickly gave way to nervous tension at the news of the Russian mobilization. Historians now agree, however, that "Germans experienced the outbreak of war differently according to their class, gender, age, location and disposition [with feelings of] pride, enthusiasm, panic, disgust, curiosity, exuberance, confidence, anger, bluff, fear, laughter and desperation."[1] One can speak as little about a *general* "war enthusiasm" as of a refusal of peasants and workers to support the war.

As in other belligerent countries a united political front was formed, including the SPD, which up to then had been in opposition, organizing demonstrations against the prospect of war as late as July 29. "We will not desert the Fatherland in the hour of danger," was now the credo of the Social Democrats, all of whose deputies approved war credits and emergency wartime legislation with the rest of the Reichstag on August 4, 1914. A "fortress truce" (*Burgfrieden*) was declared (in reference to the unity that traditionally reigned in a besieged medieval city) and the Kaiser proclaimed: "I no longer recognize parties, only Germans!" At a stroke there appeared to be no limit to consensus and the attainment of social harmony.

In the first months of the war, German intellectuals and artists propagated a new national spirit that met with considerable approval not only amongst the bourgeoisie but also across society. Some saw the outbreak of the war as the dawn of a new era. Many artists volunteered – some such as the painters August Macke, Franz Marc, Otto Dix, and Max Beckmann because they expected new artistic impulses as a result of the war. Even after the war, Otto Dix confirmed that the experience of war at the front had a radical aesthetic quality that had been previously unknown: "the war was a terrible thing, but nevertheless it was something powerful. I cannot in any way deny that. One has to have seen humans in this unleashed condition to really know something about humanity."[2] The famous sociologist Max Weber, who later became an ardent opponent of the German war leadership, responded to the outbreak of the war in August 1914 by exclaiming: "Whether or not it will be successful, this war is truly great and wonderful."[3]

War enthusiasm intensified following the apparently successful advances of the German armies and their first victories in Alsace and Belgium. Even in some of the "red" working-class districts of Berlin and Hamburg, the national flag occasionally appeared. Above all, it was widely believed that Germany was fighting a "just war" in self-defense. In 1914, sizeable numbers of men who not been conscripted before the war now volunteered, along with others who were still below the call-up age. The latter in particular became the object of a patriotic cult, which echoed the myth of the volunteers who had rallied to the Prussian monarchy in the War of Liberation against Napoleon in 1813. Some 260,000 men volunteered in Prussia alone in the first 10 days of the war, of whom 143,000 were then officially drafted. But the upper and middle classes were overrepresented and the numbers were far lower than the impression given by newspaper propaganda, which portrayed German youth as overwhelmed by the spirit of sacrifice. The great majority of the 13 million Germans who fought in the war between 1914 and 1918 did so as conscripts, the bulk of them as reservists who had already performed their military service before the war.

From the beginning there was a "war of words" as well as deeds. Newspapers were filled with patriotic declarations and lyrical outpourings. It was not only the state religion, Lutheranism, which gave the war its theological legitimacy as "the will of God." Catholic associations and organizations placed themselves entirely at the service of the national cause as well. After decades of alienation from the Prussian-German Empire during Bismarck's religious campaign against Catholicism, they saw support of the war as an opportunity to prove their loyalty to the state. In numerous sermons clergy of both major confessions portrayed the death of the soldier for the nation and the sacrificial death of Christ as having a remarkable similarity.

Chauvinistic voices and statements arose from a variety of other sources. At the beginning of October 1914, 93 scholars, writers, and artists signed a declaration entitled the "Appeal to the World of Culture," which sought to both influence public opinion in Germany and in neutral countries and refute the accusations of enemy propaganda "against the lies and slander with which our enemies seek to blacken the pure cause of Germany in this terrible struggle for our existence which has been forced upon us."[4] But the breaches of international law committed by German soldiers as they advanced into Belgium and the north of France could not be denied. These included the shooting of hostages and the destruction of the famous university library of Louvain. The "Appeal of the 93" was seen in a very negative light in the academic world outside of Germany, especially in neutral countries. International scholars were particularly outraged by the claim that militarism and culture were closely connected: "Without German militarism, German culture would have long ago been wiped from the face of the earth."

The manifesto of German scientists, academics, and artists was to have considerable consequences for the "war of the minds," which divided intellectuals and academics internationally and which would still be felt long after hostilities were over (see chapter 22). For many intellectuals, the "good of the nation" had to take priority over all other interests in order to create a "national war society."[5] The result of this intellectual discourse was the romantic construction of "German culture" (*Kultur*), characterized by inner contemplation (*Innerlichkeit*), spirit (*Geist*), and morality. Western "civilization" was its crassly constructed opposite. The intellectuals especially rejected ideas of democracy, materialism, and commercialism, which they attributed to the Western nations. These so-called "ideas of 1914" won considerable approval from the educated bourgeoisie.

The nature of World War I demanded that meaning was constantly attributed to events and that the origins of the war and national war aims were continuously reinterpreted. Controlling this process was the most important task of propaganda, which was quickly used by all sides and became extremely effective. Inside Germany the highest military authority lay with the Deputy Commanding Generals of the country's 25 Army Corps districts (*Stellvertretende Generalkommandos*), who ordered constant surveillance and control of the press. Additionally, at the beginning of 1915, the German Supreme Command (*Oberste Heeresleitung*, OHL) established a General Censorship Office, which eventually became the official Press Office. However, censorship had clear limits. These limits applied to the field post delivered daily between the home and fighting fronts (of which German military censors could only examine a fraction), as well as to the press from neutral countries, which remained available throughout the war. The ability to control information brought back from the war by soldiers on leave was also limited. The longer the war lasted, the less state propaganda could convince the population that their sacrifices were worthwhile. After three years of war and millions dead, even Walter Rathenau, the outstanding organizer of the German war economy, observed: "We still don't know today, what we are fighting for."[6]

Initially, the war in the west went more or less in accordance with the German war plan. Despite unexpected resistance by the Belgian army and militias, Belgium was finally defeated and most of the country occupied, though in the process large numbers of towns and villages were destroyed and thousands of civilians were executed (see chapter 13). However, insufficient soldiers and overstretched supply lines meant that the German war plan failed at the Battle of the Marne. The ensuing stabilization of the western front was by no means an outright defeat for Germany. But it represented a major setback, since the Germans now faced precisely the two-front war that they had sought to avoid.

In the east, underestimation of the speed of Russian mobilization resulted in the invasion, however brief, of national territory, as two Russian armies occupied a large part of East Prussia. Moltke the Younger, since 1906 chief of the OHL, summoned Paul von Hindenburg out of retirement and placed Erich Ludendorff alongside him as his chief of staff to command German forces in the east. The First (East Prussian) Army Corps, under Hindenburg, succeeded in encircling and subsequently destroying the Second Russian Army between August 26 and 30, 1914, with 140,000 Russian soldiers either killed or taken prisoner.

The "Battle of Tannenberg" was the most spectacular German victory of the entire war and was rapidly mythologized, as it contrasted with the battles on the western front where heavy losses were incurred. The name was taken from the spot some miles distant where in the late Middle Ages Teutonic Knights had been defeated by the pagan Lithuanians, with the implication that this time history had been reversed and the barbarians thrown back by modern Germany. Hindenburg gained a legendary reputation as the "Savior of the Nation," and as General Headquarters announced the expulsion of the last Russian soldiers from East Prussia on September 12, Tannenberg also served as a counterweight to the sobering defeat on the Marne. Over the course of the war both Hindenburg and Ludendorff gained increasingly more political power and influence. Still, there were no grounds for thinking that there would be a quick victory in the east.

In all belligerent countries after the war's outbreak, the public began to debate the political and territorial aims that would follow victory. The debate in Germany was initiated by a radical memorandum from the director of the nationalist Pan-German League, Heinrich Class, which demanded far-reaching annexations in Belgium and northern France as well as other territorial gains in Western and Eastern Europe. Numerous further "programs" and "peace-planning" were added, culminating in spring 1915 with the memorandum from five (later six) large German economic associations. Parallel to the industrialists' demands, nationalist professors published the so-called "intellectuals' petition," the war aims of which were also marked by a considerable lack of moderation.

The "September Program" of the German government, first discovered in the 1960s and passionately discussed by German historians at the time, also belongs to these catalogs of German war aims.[7] It comprised the "provisional guidelines for German policy at the peace treaty" that the German Chancellor Bethmann Hollweg signed on September 9, 1914 before he knew the outcome of the Battle of the Marne. Among other aims, he demanded the downgrading of Belgium to the status of a German "vassal state," the reduction of France to a middle-ranking power, the establishment of a mid-European economic association under German leadership, and a territorially integrated colonial empire in Africa. Historians have debated whether this program is a key document in the history of German imperialism or was merely a "formal compromise" between several different opinions at government level.[8] Whatever the answer, explaining why, even in the last year of the war, a "victorious peace" based on German hegemony in Europe was demanded at any cost by those in power remains a fundamental question about German policy.

The debate on war aims became increasingly radical during the period of the Third OHL, directed by Hindenburg and Ludendorff from August 1916. By this stage hardly a government politician risked opposing the uninhibited longing for annexations that drove the OHL, especially in the east. The demands, which were also shared by wide sections of the conservative bourgeoisie, aimed at the extensive "ethnic reallocation of land," meaning, amongst other things, the establishment of an area of German settlement, free of Poles, either side of the provinces of Posen and West Prussia. There was also a range of liberal varieties of war aims, none of which, however, could be realized as a result of the war's outcome. The underlying "philosophy" regarding German rule in Central Eastern Europe during World War I was based upon a policy of enlargement through "ethnic cleansing." This later became a key component of the radical racist programs and, infused with a biological determinism, would prepare the way for Nazi ideas on "living space" and settlement in the east.

Following the failure in the west, Erich von Falkenhayn replaced a badly shaken Von Moltke as head of the OHL, and redefined the German war plan. Highest priority was now given to Russia. The aim was, if not to defeat Russia entirely, to weaken Russia to such a degree that afterwards the German armies could again concentrate on fighting the enemy in the west. The result was the combined German and Austro-Hungarian offensive in the summer of 1915 that drove the Russians out of Galicia and later, out of much Russian Poland, although the Germans failed to eliminate Russian military strength (see chapter 5). The new front ran 300 km further east, from Riga in the north to Romania in the south.

In the west the German armies had extended their defensive lines and made the optimum use of the terrain and prevailing conditions. They dug deep trenches and constructed numerous well-fortified concrete bunkers along the front for protection against enemy shelling. Unlike the German military, the Allied armies could not afford to wait in protected positions. Thus, the German armies in the west faced a series of major enemy offensives in 1915 (see chapter 4). The German defensive positions, however, were strong enough to repel these attacks. On April 22, 1915 the Germans used chemical warfare (chlorine gas) at Ypres, although its use had been banned by the Hague Convention on Land Warfare, which Germany had signed. Faced with the need to break the two-front war, any means seemed legitimate. But gas failed to achieve the breakthrough the Germans had envisaged, and it bore an unexpected cost in the public outrage that it caused in Allied and neutral countries. Of course, the Allies too used poisonous gas, justifying it as a necessary reprisal. Another taboo was lifted on the unrestrained use of force.

German naval strategy failed almost entirely at the start of the war. The Imperial Navy was not only outnumbered in all classes by the British Grand Fleet, but the British Admiralty's decision not to mount a narrow blockade of the German coast also rendered the German Navy's war plan, which aimed at a decisive battle in German waters, ineffective. In autumn 1914 German submarines successfully sank a number of Allied cruisers. This surprising success – the officer responsible, Captain Otto Weddingen, became an early war hero – opened the door for a submarine offensive against the Grand Fleet and also against all shipping (including that of neutral countries) approaching the United Kingdom (see chapter 10). But this failed to paralyze the British economy, and after the disaster of the *Lusitania* in May 1915, when the Cunard liner was sunk off the southern coast of Ireland, with the loss of 1,198 lives, 127 of them American, Germany was forced to suspend unrestricted U-boat warfare for fear of bringing the United States into the war as part of the Allied camp.

At the outbreak of the conflict, very few politicians thought in terms of a long war. They were convinced that economic regulations that accompanied mobilization, such as restrictions on the export of goods important to the war economy and greater facilitation of food and fertilizer imports, were sufficient to meet the immediate demands created by a short campaign. Given that the total population and national product of the Central Powers amounted to only 46 percent and 61 percent, respectively, of the corresponding figures for the Entente, Germany and especially Austria-Hungary could not afford the long war into which they had stumbled. However, it was a crisis in munitions supplies, felt by late October 1914, that resulted in soldiers and politicians having to face up to the need to reshape the economy for a long war.

One of the major problems for German wartime economic planning was the decentralization of a federal system. The entire production of armaments and military substitutes was subordinated to the Prussian War Ministry. But the War Ministry had to share responsibility with the internal military administration that exercised power in Germany's 25 Army Corps districts. The more than 200 so-called war economy corporations (*Kriegsgesellschaften*), which coordinated private enterprises at the national level, were controlled by the newly founded War Raw Materials Office (*Kriegsrohstoffamt*). It was directed by Walter Rathenau, the influential industrialist who later became Foreign Minister in the Weimar Republic. In 1916, the Third OHL gave authority over a still divided economic planning to the new Supreme War Office, but even this institution was unable to gain complete control of munitions production. Industrial mobilization for the production of war materials in Germany had at best a mixed success.

As shown in chapter 15 above, Germany devoted a higher percentage of aggregate supply to war production than any other major belligerent (46 percent in 1917).[9] As a consequence Germany's GDP fell in 1917 to 76 percent of its 1913 level (68 percent in 1919), indicating the cost to the German economy of diverting manpower and resources to the fighting.[10] Agriculture was especially hard hit, with output at 60 percent of its pre-war levels in 1917–18.[11] This was caused by decreases in the numbers of horses and machines available to farmers and shortages of fertilizer and feed, as well as fewer farm laborers. The German economy responded to import shortages by producing materials that had previously been imported. *Ersatz* (replacement) became a common term and was accompanied by a flourishing literature on how to make do with alternative foods and materials (war cookery books). But the British naval blockade made it hard to compensate for reduced food production by imports, and the occupation of large tracts of Eastern Europe proved disappointing in this regard. The situation was made worse by the government's over-bureaucratic, and therefore inefficient, control of the economic system. The attempt to impose maximum prices for food began as early as 1914 and was intended to secure the food supply. But it could not meet absolute shortfalls and finally resulted in the "dead end of the state controlled economy."[12] Consequently, Germans experienced considerable reductions in levels of consumption during the war.

The year of Verdun and the Somme, 1916, intensified the pressures of the two-front war on Germany without resolving them. By concentrating a major offensive on the fortified zone around Verdun, Falkenhayn took the initiative in the west, hoping to destroy the French army and split the French from their British allies. Yet after a battle that dragged on from February to December, and which cost Germany as many dead and wounded as the French, the decisive psychological blow had not been dealt to the French army, which turned the battle into an epic of national defense and ended up retaking all the ground it had initially lost. The Somme, by contrast, was a defensive battle for Germany. The most costly encounter of the war in human and material terms, it was most obviously a failure for the French and especially the British, who had hoped to achieve a decisive breakthrough. Yet Germany suffered some 400,000 casualties, compared to over 600,000 by the allies, in a dreadful bloodletting from which the army in the west never recovered.

Meanwhile, with Germany under pressure in the west, in June the Russians timed an offensive under Brusilov on the Carpathian front, which, without achieving a decisive reversal of positions in the east, reclaimed some of the territory lost to the Austro-German forces in 1915. Only the swift elimination of Romania after its entry into the war on the Allied side in the autumn of 1916 relieved this tightening pressure. In the face of dramatically shrinking army reserves, serious shortages of munitions and the growing dependence of an enfeebled Austria-Hungary, Germany found it increasingly hard to undertake large-scale operations.

The pressure was reflected in a peculiarly defensive discourse that emerged during the Battle of the Somme, which blamed the destructive violence of the war on the attacking allies. This allegation was endlessly repeated in soldiers' letters as well as in official propaganda. It led to the strong conviction that the only way to protect the fatherland was through a "forward defensive position" in enemy territory – defending Germany on the Somme rather than the Rhine. The same logic suggested that the war must continue until security was permanent – in other words, until Germany had achieved a complete victory.

For the Germans the Somme was remarkable for another reason. As enormous losses were incurred, especially as a result of allied artillery attacks, a new concept of tactical warfare, already introduced at Verdun, was confirmed: the "storm trooper." This consisted of the deployment of smaller groups led by officers with front-line experience. The writer Ernst Jünger later created a heroic monument in his war memoirs, *Storm of Steel*, to this new figure on the battlefield, whom Jünger depicted as a stoical fighter hardly troubled by the horrors of industrialized warfare.[13] This ultra-militaristic and anti-bourgeois soldier entered the literature of nationalism in the Weimar Republic and left its mark on the image of the political or paramilitary "fighter" (*Kämpfer*) celebrated by the Nazis.

On May 31, 1916 the German High Seas Fleet sailed out on a reconnaissance probe. However, the British were aware of the maneuver and took up the pursuit. In the waters between the Norwegian coast and Jutland, a series of running engagements between the two navies resulted in heavy losses. At the end of the Battle of Jutland, the only large sea battle of the war, British losses amounted to 115,000 tonnes and 6,945 men. The German fleet lost approximately 60,000 tonnes and 3,058 men. Despite this initial success, the German fleet remained outnumbered and withdrew to harbor. The Royal Navy continued to cancel out the threat of Germany's battleships, leaving U-boat warfare as the only alternative.

The failure of the German army to break the encircling allies at Verdun and the heavy losses incurred during the battles of 1916 led to the replacement of Erich von Falkenhayn as the head of the OHL by the dual leadership of Hindenburg and Ludendorff. For Ludendorff, the "silent dictator," the title of First Quartermaster General was created. The Kaiser and the Chancellor had appointed the duumvirate not just because of their value as military commanders but also because they believed that the popularity of the "victors of Tannenberg" would help to ensure continued public support for the war. During their leadership as the Third OHL, which lasted from August 1916 until the end of October 1918, they took fundamental military and diplomatic decisions that changed the course of the war: unlimited submarine warfare, the "dictated" peace treaties in the east in 1918, the military occupation of Eastern Europe from Finland to the Caucasus (see chapter 30) and, finally, the massive spring offensive in 1918.

The Third OHL also initiated a series of measures within the Reich, which were intended to intensify the mobilization of the population and adapt the economy to the requirements of an all-embracing war. The megalomaniac Hindenburg Program entailed countless guidelines on the expansion and intensification of weapons and armaments production, the creation of new plants, and much tighter controls on labor, including the deportation of workers from occupied Europe. In many areas, however, it remained hollow. Worse, decisions such as those to extend military service for men from the ages of 16 to 60 and to introduce general compulsory service for women aroused the ire of the powerful trade union movement and forced the military bureaucracy to come to terms with organized labor and the SPD.[14] Yet the attempt to aggrandize power in the hands of the military reached dimensions that approached those of a "political military dictatorship" (Max Weber). The ascendancy of the military forced the resignations of the Chancellor Bethmann Hollweg in 1917 and Foreign Minister Richard von Kühlmann in 1918.

Soon after the establishment of the Third OHL, a further fatal decision was taken. On November 1, 1916 the Prussian War Ministry instigated a census of all Jewish soldiers (*Judenzählung*). Politicians and the military had given in to the demands of antisemitic groups, which had repeatedly attempted to prove that German Jews were avoiding their military service and national responsibility. Over the course of the war they campaigned against Jewish "shirkers" and agitated against an allegedly decisive role of Jews in the organization of the war economy. The completion of the Jewish census was accompanied by riots and attacks. Many German Jews rightly felt that they had been humiliated and discriminated against. The exact results of the census were never made public and as a result antisemitic suspicions further increased.

In reality, however, as proven by reliable postwar studies and statistics, Jews proportionately served, and incidentally were killed, in the same numbers as the non-Jewish soldiers. About 12 percent had volunteered, well above one-third had been decorated, three-quarters of all Jewish soldiers had fought at the front (something that the antisemites had constantly disputed) and the level of Jewish losses (at around 12 percent) corresponded with those of other confessions. In February 1917 the *Judenzählung* was abandoned, but long-lasting damage had already been done. The Jewish census of 1916 not only violated the state's promise of equality but it also shook the trust of many Jews in the neutrality of the state and in the protection offered them by German society. It also gave a new impetus to radical antisemitic organizations. For many Germans, Jews were guilty of the military defeat of Germany to which was added, after 1917, responsibility for "Jewish" Bolshevism. Thus, for some historians, the Jewish census of 1916 represents a caesura in modern antisemitism, from which there is a direct line to the murder of the German and European Jewish populations during World War II.[15]

In 1917, Ludendorff and Hindenburg responded to the pressure surrounding the German military effort not by seeking a compromise peace but, on the contrary, by demanding a victorious peace that would make German hegemony in Europe permanent and by adopting an increasingly radical conduct of the war in order to achieve it. The idea of a permanent informal empire in Eastern Europe, including areas of German settlement, was advocated at a political level by a plethora of nationalist movements which found expression in the new Fatherland Party (*Vaterlandspartei*). This nationalistic and chauvinistic party backed the Third OHL and was able to recruit a paper membership of some three-quarters of a million in the last year of the war.

In military terms, the Third OHL sought to end the two-front war once and for all and to achieve a decisive result in the west before the balance of material advantage swung irreversibly behind the Allies. In January 1917 the German Navy command announced the resumption of "unrestricted submarine warfare." Ludendorff and Hindenburg had been convinced that the deployment of submarines could quickly end the war. There were now 10 times more submarines available to the Germans than in 1915. The naval command believed that the strategy of restricting imports available to Britain by sinking merchant shipping entering British waters would force the British to capitulate before American intervention – the predictable result of unrestricted submarine warfare. Despite some initial success, however, the intended turning point of the war failed to materialize as the British countered the new Germany strategy with the convoy system (see chapter 10). The consequences of the miscalculation for Germany were devastating, as military success remained beyond their grasp while the USA entered the war.

Prizing open the two-front pincer meant refocusing on Russia as the weaker ally, especially after the February Revolution. However, this in turn led to strengthening defensive operations in the west. The result was the Third OHL's carefully prepared withdrawal from February 9 to March 15, 1917 to the Siegfried Line, a heavily fortified set of concrete and steel defenses that eliminated the broad exposed salient between Arras and Saint-Quentin, including the battlefield of the Somme. Operation Alberich turned out as one of the most successful German operations of the entire war. The abandoned area was comprehensively destroyed in a scorched-earth policy, and the population deported to the German rear. Consequently Allied planners were forced to modify their plans. While the German press praised the precision of the operation and justified it as a military necessity, it was taken by Allied propaganda as one further example of the Germans' barbaric conduct of the war.

That the German army on the western front succeeded, despite numerical inferiority of two to three, in resisting the attacks of the Allies, was due in large measure to their practice of the doctrine of "deep elastic defense." This was illustrated at the Third Battle of Flanders (the German name for Third Ypres, or Passchendaele). Here, from July to December 1917, the Fourth Army, under General Sixt von Arnim, with the help of concrete machine-gun and artillery positions, repelled the massive attacks of the Second and Fifth British armies. While the Germans lost 217,000 men, British and Allied casualties were more than 320,000. Once again, the defensive demonstrated its advantage.

In all belligerent countries, but especially in Germany, there was widespread exhaustion and war-weariness after three years of war. Despite the deployment of new military technologies, neither side had succeeded in making a decisive breakthrough. The effects on the morale of those directing the war were considerable. At the end of 1916, Ludendorff had unsuccessfully attempted to generate a new fighting spirit by introducing patriotic instruction into the armed forces, delivered by specially trained officers. But it proved impossible to recreate the *furor teutonicus* of the first months of the war. In the face of the massive casualties and widespread privation, the ideas propagated by the nationalist rhetoric at the start of the war, including those of individual courage and selfless effort for the fatherland, became obsolete. Instead propaganda focused on the capacity for suffering and further endurance under extreme wartime conditions. Many soldiers and their families in the homeland no longer wanted to hear of "positive" war aims or Christian justifications for battlefield losses. Instead, the soldier's death was increasingly seen as an individual loss.

For "war-families," as the families of soldiers were called, and above all for women and children, whose husbands and fathers were at the front, the war represented a special challenge. Despite military allowances and other social measures to reduce the economic impact of the war, there was a fall in real family incomes generally, and this was especially the case for war widows. During the final year of the war there was a remarkable increase in offenses against property. Male urban youths, who had often escaped the supervision of their parents, were particularly responsible for growing levels of criminality. People were forced to steal food, clothes, and other vital items. During the course of the war there was a rising curve of public breaches of the peace, resistance to state authority, and other forms of civil disobedience, which eventually developed into riots and revolutionary unrest.

The contribution made by women was decisive for the functioning of wartime society in Germany. At first, the conventional division of labor along gender lines worked reasonably well. The more traditional roles of many women – in the household, in nursing and care professions, as agricultural workers – were seen as part of their patriotic duty and as a feminine contribution to the war, complementing but not challenging masculine roles. Those women who broke the mold of gender by doing formerly masculine work were at first considered as nothing more than replacements for conscripted men. This applied especially to women munitions workers, many of whom had transferred to this sector following initial wartime unemployment. As in pre-war times, they were paid less than their male colleagues. The supposedly emancipating effect of the war has been considerably overrated; in Germany, as in other European countries, what occurred may be best described as an "emancipation on loan."[16] Admittedly, women obtained the right to vote as a result of defeat and revolution, which was a real achievement in comparison with many other Western countries. However, the social reality of the factories and work-places was sobering, and at the end of the war many women were expelled from the "men's jobs" they had temporarily occupied.

As a result of the British naval blockade, as well as of constant bureaucratic mismanage-ment of food provisions, the increasingly meager food supply in the second half of the war placed a particular burden on women. Economic and consumer shortages reached their high point in the notorious "turnip winter" of 1916–17. Consumption was reduced to about 50 percent of its normal level through the introduction of a system of food ration-ing, and illness and death due to food shortages occurred every day in the final two years of the war. The two groups most affected were the young and the old, and wartime mor-tality related directly or indirectly to malnutrition totaled about 700,000.[17]

As early as April 1917, and then again in January 1918, there were hunger protests and finally general strikes in Berlin, Leipzig, Hamburg, and numerous other cities. By the end of January, over half a million workers had joined the protests. This strike action affected the armaments industry in Berlin more than any other sector. As they grew in strength the demonstrations became increasingly political. In response, the government introduced a state of emergency and arrested the strike leaders. In addition, 50,000 armaments workers in Berlin, who until then had been held back from the front, were conscripted. In the face of this repression the strike was broken. Nonetheless, the revolu-tion that determined the last phase of the war and the transition to peace grew from hunger, general hopelessness, and the collapse of the traditional social and political con-tract between rulers and ruled.

Although the German government, under numerous chancellors, persevered with the concept of a victorious peace until late summer 1918, a different course for German politics began to emerge in the Reichstag as an increasing number of deputies demanded an end to hostilities and significant domestic reforms. Such voices were most outspoken on the far left. In December 1914, Karl Liebknecht was the only deputy who objected to the policy of *Burgfrieden*. A year later, as many as 20 deputies refused to approve new war credits and in April 1917, the opposition within the SPD founded a new party, the Independent Social Democratic Party of Germany (USPD), which demanded an imme-diate end to the war.

More moderate in its approach was an emerging majority of the Reichstag that opposed the open-ended continuation of the war and which, in July 1917, voted the famous Peace Resolution calling for a negotiated end to the war and major constitutional reforms. The parties concerned, the Social Democrats, the Catholic Centre Party, the Progressives, and (more hesitantly) the National Liberals, formed an Inter-Party Committee of the Reichstag, and although they were powerless against the Third OHL until defeat loomed, they provided the basis for the emergence of parliamentary democracy in the post-war German Republic, in which they formed the "Weimar Coalition." Nonetheless, the frag-ile nature of the minimal consensus practiced by the Inter-Party Committee was to be seen by the Reichstag's ratification of the Treaty of Brest-Litovsk in March 1918, by which the German military imposed extremely harsh conditions on Bolshevik Russia. Only the USPD rejected the treaty. The SPD abstained while all the other parties sup-ported it. Once again, the Reichstag had given the military the freedom to pursue its political and economic expansion in the east, something that was to have long-term fatal consequences.

The last year of the war began promisingly for Germany. The fighting spirit of the Russian army had finally been broken with the defeat of Kerensky's offensive in June 1917. In December, the Bolsheviks sought an armistice. In order to force the Bolshevik government to sign an official peace treaty, German troops began to occupy large parts of the Ukraine and White Russia and to establish friendly governments in these territories. The Treaty of Brest-Litovsk, signed in March 1918, brought Russian Poland as well as the Baltic states under German rule and effectively gave the Germans military control of the Ukraine and Finland. Russia had lost the ethnically non-Russian borderlands of the Tsarist Empire, along with a third of its population. In nationalist circles in Germany, the "victory peace" unleashed euphoria and restored confidence in the ultimate outcome of the war.

Prospects on the western front, however, were less promising. Ludendorff viewed the continued arrival of American soldiers and material with great concern and decided to gamble everything on a decisive offensive in the west before the American Expeditionary Force was in a position to determine the outcome of the war. The aim of the spring offensive, which began in March 1918, was to split the British and French armies in the hope of forcing each power to capitulate quickly. New tactics were planned, including the use of storm troopers to penetrate the front and cause chaos in the enemy's rear, and the exact coordination of infantry and artillery.

Initially, the spring offensive was successful and the German troops advanced up to 60 km between March 21 and April 5. However, German losses of about 230,000 were so immense that the offensive finally had to be suspended. Ludendorff, who once again had placed "tactics above strategy," could now only undertake wild attacks against the enemy at different points along the front, none of which could achieve his aim of isolating the Allies from each other.[18] The Allied counteroffensive began in June and a carefully prepared assault by French units at Soissons, on July 18, accompanied by 400 tanks, took all the initiative from the Germans. A British attack supported by tanks on August 8 at Amiens was the final turning point of the war on the western front. Although the allies only advanced 10 km, the actual gains were much greater than this might indicate since, for the first time, German soldiers capitulated in large numbers. For Ludendorff, August 8 was the "black day of the German Army."[19] By now, the Americans were also present in large numbers on the western front and had achieved the capability for military action independently of the other Allies. German forces were under constant pressure to retreat. Following years of disappointment, German soldiers who had initially greeted the March offensive with enthusiasm now felt deeply disillusioned and demoralized. In several sectors, they sought opportunities to escape a war they saw as senseless. Historians have identified a figure of up to one million German soldiers who in the last months of the war left their units without permission, and in this context some even speak of a "concealed military strike."[20]

These developments induced a state of panic in Ludendorff by the end of September. Fearing the total collapse of the western front, he sought an immediate armistice. For the Allies this came as a complete shock. The German army remained capable of military operations, with its divisions still far inside enemy territory, and the Allies were planning a new offensive to push into Germany itself in the winter of 1918–19. For the German public the shock was even greater. Until the end they had been fed with idealized reports from the front and exhorted to hold out. Already, Ludendorff excused his military failures by blaming others. The German army and especially its military leadership, he claimed, had not failed. Rather the home front, "poisoned with Marxism," had let the nation down and in effect stabbed the army in the back. The "stab-in-the-back" myth had many creators, but Ludendorff and Hindenburg were the most prominent ones, especially when the latter testified before the Reichstag committee established in 1919 to investigate the causes of German defeat.

The newly formed government under the liberal politician and last Chancellor of Imperial Germany, Prince Max of Baden, requested an armistice from the American President Woodrow Wilson on October 4 and offered to commence peace negotiations. In his reply Wilson demanded – to the horror of conservative politicians and officers – that the traditional ruling elites of Germany be deprived of their power, and implicitly that the Kaiser must abdicate. Ludendorff attempted in vain to change course once again and now argued for the continuation of the war. But it was too late. The desire for peace among the majority of the population was too great, and revolution, which had first began among the sailors of the Home Fleet, spread throughout the Reich. On October 26, Prince Max of Baden forced Ludendorff to resign. On November 9 he announced the abdication of the Kaiser and simultaneously handed over the position of Chancellor to the Social Democrat Friedrich Ebert.

The terms of the armistice that took effect on November 11 at 11:00 a.m., had been stipulated by the Allies in such a way that it was impossible for Germany to recommence the war. A day earlier, Wilhelm II had fled into exile in the Netherlands, but it was not until November 28 that he formally declared that he had relinquished the crown of Prussia (and with it the "associated rights of the crown of the German Empire"). By this time, however, the *Kaiserreich* had already collapsed like a house of cards.

Notes

1　Verhey, *Spirit of 1914*, p. 232.
2　Interview with H. Kinkel (1961), quoted in Dietrich Schubert, "Otto Dix zeichnet den Ersten Weltkrieg," in Wolfgang J. Mommsen, ed., *Kultur und Krieg. Die Rolle der Intellektuellen, Künstler und Schriftsteller im Ersten Weltkrieg*, Munich, R. Oldenbourg, 1996, p. 184.
3　Quoted in Wolfgang J. Mommsen, *Max Weber und die deutsche Politik*, Tübingen, Siebeck, 2nd ed., 1974, p. 206.
4　Jürgen von Ungern-Sternberg and Wolfgang von Ungern-Sternberg, *Der Aufruf "An die Kulturwelt!": das Manifest der 93 und die Anfänge der Kriegspropaganda im ersten Weltkrieg*, Stuttgart, F. Steiner, 1996, p. 156.
5　Stephen Bruendel, *Volksgemeinschaft oder Volksstaat? Die "Ideen von 1914" und die Neuordnung Deutschlands im Ersten Weltkrieg*, Berlin, Akademie Verlag, 2003, pp. 29–48.
6　Letter to Leopold Ziegler, July 28, 1917, in Walther Rathenau, *Briefe. Neue endgültige Ausgabe in drei Bänden*, Dresden, Reissner, 1930, vol. 1, p. 303.
7　Fischer, *Germany's Aims in the First World War*, pp. 103–6.
8　For the former viewpoint, see Fischer, op. cit; for the latter, see Wolfgang J. Mommsen, "Die Mitteleuropaidee und die Mitteleuropapläne im Deutschen Reich," in Mommsen, ed., *Der Erste Weltkrieg*, pp. 104–6.
9　Chapter 15 above, Table 15.3.
10　Chapter 15 above, Table 15.1.
11　Albrecht Ritschl, "The Pity of Peace: Germany's Economy at War, 1914–1918 and Beyond," in Stephen Broadberry and Mark Harrison, *The Economics of World War I*, Cambridge, Cambridge University Press, 2005, p. 46 (Table 2:2).
12　Hans-Peter Ullmann, "Kriegswirtschaft," in Hirschfeld, Krumeich, and Renz (eds.), *Enzyklopädie Erster Weltkrieg*, p. 227.

13 Ernst Jünger, *Storm of Steel*, 1920; trans. Michael Hoffmann, London, Allen Lane, 2003.

14 Feldman, *Army, Industry and Labor*, pp. 197–249.

15 E.g. Christhard Hoffmann, "Between Integration and Rejection: the Jewish Community in Germany, 1914–1918," in John Horne (ed.), *State, Society and Mobilization in Europe during the First World War*, Cambridge, Cambridge University Press, 1997, pp. 89–104.

16 Daniel, *War from Within*, pp. 276–83.

17 Rüdiger Overmans, "Kriegsverluste," in Hirschfeld, Krumeich, and Renz (eds.), *Enzyklopädie Erster Weltkrieg*, p. 665.

18 E.g. Dieter Storz, "'Aber was hätte anders geschehen sollen?' Die deutschen Offensiven an der Westfront 1918," in Jörg Duppler and Gerhard P. Groß (eds), *Kriegsende 1918: Ereignis, Wirkung, Nachwirkung*, Munich, Oldenbourg, 1999, pp. 51–98.

19 Erich Ludendorff, *Meine Kriegserinnerungen 1914–1918*, Berlin, E. S. Mittler, 1919, p. 547.

20 Wilhelm Deist, "The Military Collapse of the German Empire: the Reality behind the Stab-in-the-Back Myth," *War in History*, 3/2, 1996, pp. 186–207.

References and Further Reading

Chickering, Roger, *Imperial Germany and the Great War, 1914–1918*, Cambridge, Cambridge University Press, 1998.

Chickering, Roger, *The Great War and Urban Life in Germany. Freiburg, 1914–1918*, Cambridge, Cambridge University Press, 2007.

Daniel, Ute, *The War from Within. German Working Class Women in the First World War*, 1989; translated from German, Oxford and Washington, DC, Berg, 1996.

Davis, Belinda, *Home Fires Burning. Food, Politics, and Everyday Life in World War I Berlin*, Chapel Hill, North Carolina University Press, 2001.

Deist, Wilhelm, *Militär und Innenpolitik im Weltkrieg 1914–1918*, 2 vols., Düsseldorf, Droste, 1970.

Deist, Wilhelm, "The German Army, the Authoritarian Nation State and Total War," in John Horne (ed.), *State, Society and Mobilization in Europe during the First World War*, Cambridge, Cambridge University Press, 1997, pp. 160–72.

Feldman, Gerald, *Army, Industry and Labor in Gemany 1914–1918*, 1966; new ed., Providence and Oxford, Berg, 1992.

Feldman, Gerald, *The Great Disorder: Politics, Economics and Society in the German Inflation, 1914–1924*, New York and Oxford, Oxford University Press, 1993.

Fischer, Fritz, *Germany's Aims in the First World War*, 1961; translation from German, London, Chatto and Windus, 1967.

Foley, Robert T., *German Strategy and the Path to Verdun. Erich von Falkenhayn and the Development of Attrition, 1870–1916*, Cambridge, Cambridge University Press, 2005.

Geinitz, Christian, *Kriegsfurcht und Kampfbereitschaft. Das Augusterlebnis im Freiburg. Eine Studie zum Kriegsbeginn, 1914*, Essen, Klartext, 1998.

Herwig, Holger, *The First World War. Germany and Austria-Hungary 1914–1918*, London, Arnold, 1997.

Hirschfeld, Gerhard, Krumeich, Gerd, Langewiesche, Dieter, and Ullmann, Hans-Peter (eds.), *Kriegserfahrungen. Studien zur Sozial und Mentalitätsgeschichte des Ersten Weltkriegs*, Essen, Klartext, 1997.

Hirschfeld, Gerhard, Krumeich, Gerd, and Renz, Irina (eds.), *Enzyklopädie Erster Weltkrieg*, Paderborn, Schöningh, 2nd ed., 2004.

Hirschfeld, Gerd, Krumeich, Gerd, and Renz, Irina, eds., *Die Deutschen an der Somme 1914–18. Krieg, Besatzung, Verbrannte Erde*, Essen, Klartext, 2006.

Hirschfeld, Gerhard, Krumeich, Gerd, and Renz, Irina (eds.), *Keiner fühlt sich hier mehr als Mensch… Erlebnis und Wirkung des Ersten Weltkriegs*, Essen, Klartext, 1993.

Hull, Isabel V., *Absolute Destruction. Military Culture and the Practices of War in Imperial Germany*, Ithaca, Cornell University Press, 2005.

Kitchen, Martin, *The Silent Dictatorship. The Politics of the German High Command under Hindenburg and Ludendorff*, London, Croom Helm, 1976.

Kocka, Jürgen, *Facing Total War: German Society 1914–1918*, 1973; translation from German, Leamington Spa, Berg, 1984.

Kruse, Wolfgang, *Krieg und nationale Integration. Eine Neuinterpretation des sozialdemokratischen Burgfriedensschlusses 1914–15*, Essen, Klartext, 1993.

Miller, Susanne, *Burgfrieden und Klassenkampf: Die deutsche Sozialdemokratie im Ersten Weltkrieg*, Düsseldorf, Droste, 1974.

Mombauer, Annika, *Helmuth von Moltke and the Origins of the First World War*, Cambridge, Cambridge University Press, 2001.

Mommsen, Wolfgang J., "German artists, writers and intellectuals and the meaning of war, 1914–1918," in J. Horne (ed.), *State, Society and Mobilization in Europe during the First World War*, Cambridge, Cambridge University Press, 1997, pp. 21–38.

Mommsen, Wolfgang J. (ed.), *Der Erste Weltkrieg. Anfang vom Ende des bürgerlichen Zeitalters*, Frankfurt a.M., Fischer Taschenbuch Verlag, 2004.

Schorske, Carl, *German Social Democracy, 1905–1917: The Development of the Great Schism*, Cambridge, MA, Harvard University Press, 1955.

Ulrich, Bernd, *Die Augenzeugen: deutsche Feldpostbriefe in Kriegs- und Nachkriegszeit, 1914–1933*, Essen, Klartext, 1997.

Verhey, Jeffrey, *The Spirit of 1914: Militarism, Myth and Mobilization in Germany*, Cambridge, Cambridge University Press, 2000.

Winter, Jay, and Robert, Jean-Louis (eds.), *Capital Cities at War: Paris, London, Berlin*, 2 vols., Cambridge, Cambridge University Press, 1997, 2007.

Ziemann, Benjamin, *War Experiences in Rural Germany 1914–1923*, 1999; abridged translation from German, Oxford and New York, Berg, 2006.

CHAPTER THIRTY

German-Occupied Eastern Europe

Vejas Gabriel Liulevicius

During World War I, German military occupation of conquered lands in Eastern Europe was marked both by initial improvisation as well as a sense of expanding possibilities. From the initial aim of establishing "ordered conditions," planners moved to greater horizons of ambition. On a human level, the experience of military occupation had immediate effects on both the conquerors and the subject populations.[1] The eastern front's vast expanse meant that participating in occupation became a hallmark of military service for German soldiers in Eastern Europe. Some two to three million German soldiers shared in this experience over the course of the war. On average, 1.3 million served in the East yearly (half as many as on the western front). The effects on them of the things they saw and did were on a mass scale and would have a lasting impact. The subject populations experienced the occupation as one of inordinate severity and were suspicious of long-term German motives. In historiography, the period of German occupation during 1914–18 in Eastern Europe is less familiar than the period during World War II, marked by the vast tragedy and atrocity of the Nazis' genocide against the Jews and deadly policies of subjugation of non-German peoples. Nonetheless, this prior experience during World War I of the brief realization of a "German Eastern Imperium" had important connections to later treatment of many of the same territories. It was a starting point or baseline for more radical visions of domination in Eastern Europe.[2]

Earlier German Views of Eastern Europe

From the outset, the experience of occupation was conditioned by earlier views of the region and its peoples. Some of these views could be seemingly confirmed; others were fundamentally revised as a result of the experiences of war. An older pattern of German relations with Eastern Europe had been based on a common conservative solidarity of the dynastic and aristocratic elites of the empires (Prussia, Russia, and Austria) that had divided Poland in the partitions of the late eighteenth century. Their shared interest involved the continued subjection of the Poles (in Prussia's ethnically mixed eastern marches, this led to increasingly bitter struggle between Poles and German officialdom). During the course of the nineteenth century, an opposite tradition evolved in German

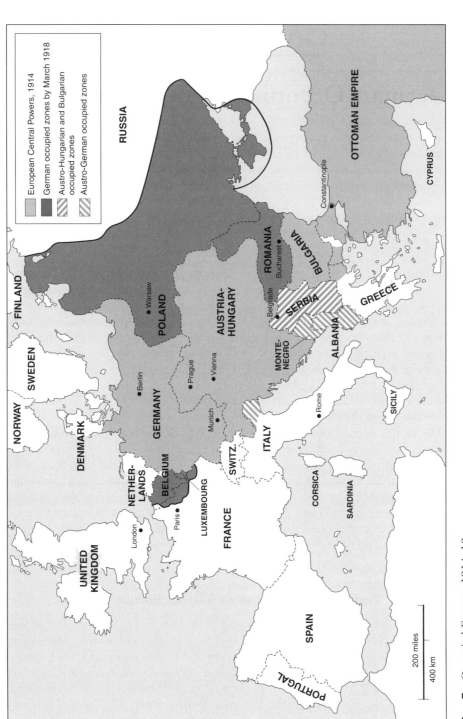

Map 7 Occupied Europe, 1914–18

Legend:
- European Central Powers, 1914
- German occupied zones by March 1918
- Austro-Hungarian and Bulgarian occupied zones
- Austro-German occupied zones

RUSSIA

OTTOMAN EMPIRE

CYPRUS

Constantinople

FINLAND

ROMANIA
Bucharest

BULGARIA

POLAND
Warsaw

AUSTRIA-
HUNGARY

SERBIA
Belgrade

GREECE

NORWAY

SWEDEN

DENMARK

GERMANY
Berlin

Prague

Vienna

Munich

MONTE-
NEGRO

ALBANIA

SWITZ.

ITALY
Rome

SICILY

NETHER-
LANDS

BELGIUM

LUXEMBOURG

FRANCE
Paris

UNITED
KINGDOM
London

CORSICA

SARDINIA

SPAIN

PORTUGAL

200 miles

400 km

radical and socialist circles, which denounced Russia as the "Gendarme of Europe" and saw in Tsarist despotism the embodiment of conservative reaction.

In the later nineteenth century, mutual fears grew between Germany and Russia. German nationalists and political elites expressed anxieties, strongly colored by common Social Darwinist assumptions, about a looming fatal showdown between "Germandom" and "Slavdom." The growing population of the Russian Empire, already 180 million-strong against Germany's 67 million, conjured up nightmares of a "Slavic flood" or "Russian steamroller" bearing down on Germany. Another set of prejudices focused on Eastern Europe was antisemitic, demonizing those *Ostjuden* (Eastern Jews) who arrived in Germany escaping pogroms and persecution in Russia. Antisemites called for an immediate closure of Germany's eastern borders to Jews. Most generally, Russian-ruled Eastern Europe was seen as economically backward, culturally primitive, and politically locked into unitary Tsarist control. Since the partitions, the German term *polnische Wirtschaft* (Polish economy) had been used as a synonym for the chaos and disorganization allegedly characteristic of the region. Similarly, a supposed *Kulturgefälle* (cultural gradient) sloped down the further east one went from Germany. These earlier views conditioned German soldiers' experience of occupation and how its daily realities were perceived.

Conquest and First Impressions

At the most basic level, the fact that the military occupiers first saw these Eastern European lands in a state of devastation wrought by the war set the terms of the initial encounter, with significant consequences. The lasting impressions began with the extreme swings of fortune of the eastern front in the first two years of the war. In August 1914, as Germany invaded France, Russia, mobilizing more quickly than expected to aid its ally, invaded Germany in turn from the east. The result was a traumatic Russian incursion into East Prussia, before German forces under Generals Paul von Hindenburg and Erich Ludendorff expelled the invaders after the battle of Tannenberg. In the following year, these eastern commanders moved into the lands of the Russian Empire in a vast offensive that afterwards was remembered by Germans as the Great Advance of 1915 (and by Russians as the Great Retreat). In short order, as its frontier fortresses fell, Russia lost Congress Poland, Lithuania, and Kurland (southern Latvia), in sum, an area the size of France. Warsaw was taken on August 5, 1915. By the end of the offensive in the fall of 1915, German lines ran deep in enemy territory, from just outside Riga along the Baltic Sea southward to Tarnopol. The front line here was twice as long as that of the west and retained more of the character and alluring promise of a war of movement than the conflict in the trenches of northern France. Germany's war effort was also strengthened by Bulgaria's entry into the war on the side of the Central Powers, which finally overran Serbia by the end of 1915 (Serbia was henceforth under Austrian and Bulgarian occupation, but German economic influence).[3] The successes of the eastern front catapulted Hindenburg and Ludendorff to the Supreme Command in August 1916. They would come to exercise a "silent dictatorship" over wartime Germany.

The occupiers' immediate first impressions were of territories that had been severely damaged, both by the front as it passed through, as well as by a Russian approach harking back to the "scorched-earth policy" of 1812 used against Napoleon: an attempt to leave the territories given up to the enemy in a state of disorder, stripped of population, economic resources, and administration. Warehouses were destroyed, fields put to the torch, bridges dynamited, factories shipped into the interior, and railways sabotaged. Masses of civilians had also either fled on their own or had been dragooned into retreating with the Russian troops (Russian forces subjected Jews and ethnic Germans in particular to brutal deportations). Over one and a half million people fled the territories, leaving some areas apparently depopulated. The remaining population often appeared impoverished and was especially vulnerable to disease, including typhus, malaria, and cholera. The specter of epidemics in the occupied territories continued as an abiding fear for the German command throughout the war.[4]

Other durable impressions had less to do with the wartime suffering of the region and instead were everyday revelations of difference. The ethnic variety of the region was striking to many among the occupiers, as they professed to have earlier thought of the entire region as vaguely Russian, since it was under the Tsar. Now they surveyed enormously complex ethnic diversity: Poles, Lithuanians, Jews, Latvians, Russians, Belarusians, Tatars, Baltic Germans, and after later conquests, Estonians, Ukrainians, and others. Nature itself, the physical geography of the region, often appeared to the occupiers to be primal, untamed, underutilized, and threatening, in the form of dirt and disease. Germans traveling to the region often remarked that the contrast between orderly East Prussia and the occupied territories just over the border showed a division of two worlds. The supposedly endemic disorganization of these lands was seen as *Unkultur*, a chaotic essence which could be redeemed by a German cultural mission of organization and order.

Establishing Administrations

After the Great Advance of 1915, occupation administrations were established in Poland and in "Ober Ost," the region including Lithuania and Kurland. The most immediate priority was the reconstruction of order behind the eastern front, to the rear of the fighting armies. After this had been established, the second priority would be the economic exploitation of these areas in the context of total war. Finally, in the long term, plans were advanced for securing German influence in these lands for the future.

Russian Poland had seen fierce fighting from the start of the war. In August 1914, German troops destroyed the towns of Kalisz and Czestochowa, suspecting sniper fire. In the Great Advance of 1915, the Central Powers conquered Russian Poland. On August 24, 1915, Poland was divided into two governments under the Germans and the Austro-Hungarians. The northern portion became the Imperial German Government General of Warsaw under General Hans von Beseler. In the south, the Austro-Hungarian regime was named the Military Government General in Lublin under General Baron Diller.

The German occupation regime involved the establishment of a civilian administration in Warsaw.[5] Administrators sought to gain the sympathy of the Poles, with greater or lesser success. A school system was set up with Polish instruction, and November 1915 saw the reopening of Warsaw University with instruction in Polish. What remained unclear, however, was the political future of Poland. This has been called "the most delicate of all the questions in the east" or even "perhaps the most complicated political question of World War I."[6] The Central Powers weighed whether Poland should become part of the Habsburg realm (the so-called "Austro-Polish solution"), annexed by Germany in whole or in part, set up as a German-dominated puppet state, or even returned to Russia as the price of a separate peace in the East. This problem was never definitively settled during the war and produced friction between Germany and Austria-Hungary as well as ever worsening alienation among nationally minded Poles. In the interim, the German high command placed its priority on gaining manpower reserves from Poland.

As a result, on November 5, 1916, the administrators of the German and Austro-Hungarian occupied areas jointly declared the establishment of a Polish kingdom. The details were hopelessly vague, with no king and no borders specified. A Provisional Council of State with limited powers was established, made up of appointed Polish representatives. The German high command had wistfully hoped to muster a Polish army to fight for the Central Powers, but the recruiting results were farcically disappointing. Polish political leaders were themselves divided on which side to favor in the war. The socialist leader, Józef Pilsudski, at first cooperated with the Austro-Hungarians in creating Polish legions, but resisted growing German control and was imprisoned in July 1917. Roman Dmowski, leader of the National Democratic Party, favored the Allies and, with the famous pianist Ignacy Paderewski, promoted the Polish cause in the west, with growing success.

In the civil administration, development of native institutional control remained slow. However, in 1917, German authorities began to allow more autonomy in the hope of gaining Polish support. On October 15, 1917, the Central Powers created a Regency Council made up of conservative Polish notables, to form a government. They also allowed the autonomous operation of parts of the judicial and educational systems, but still retained overall control. In the course of the following year, however, potential sympathies eroded still more as Poles observed the further evolution of German war aims in the east.

Further north, in the territory of Lithuania, southern Latvia, and parts of northeastern Poland and Belarus, a German military colony called Ober Ost was established.[7] As opposed to the regime in Poland, it had an exclusively and jealously guarded military character. It took its name from the post of *Oberbefehlshaber Ost*, the Supreme Commander in the East, General Paul von Hindenburg. When Poland was placed under a civil administration, Hindenburg's aide, Erich Ludendorff, announced his determination to build "another kingdom" in this area, with a monopoly of control by the German army. The administrative center was located in Kaunas, Lithuania. As opposed to Poland, here local people were generally considered too backward to be drawn into administrative work, with the notable exception of the Baltic Germans in Kurland, who were often favored. In this veritable military utopia, ambitions for control of populations and cultural and ethnic manipulation took on vast proportions.

The area's population numbered three million, after about a third of the peacetime population had fled or been dragooned away. The army undertook policies that aimed to secure the region economically and politically for the future.[8] Rigorous control of the movement of native populations and economic resources took place (in many ways resembling the colonial policies of European powers overseas), using passes, censuses, the establishment of strict and often arbitrary administrative borders that could not be crossed, and forced labor duties. At the same time, to an extent truly surprising at a time of total war, the Ober Ost administration also undertook cultural work, to create client ethnic groups: supervising schools, publishing newspapers in local languages, sponsoring museum exhibits, archaeological and archival investigations, and encouraging theater. In terms of its political future, the area was to be bound to Germany economically and politically (whether through outright annexation, personal union with a German dynasty, or the establishment of a dependent buffer state). German colonization was planned, especially in Kurland. In 1917, Ober Ost allowed the formation of a Lithuanian "land council" to ratify German plans, but the council proved more independent and less pliable than had been intended (contrary to German wishes, it declared full independence on February 16, 1918, and offered the throne to a minor German prince who was to assume the name Mindaugas II).

In Poland and Ober Ost, intensive economic exploitation was the order of the day, motivated by the impact of the blockade under which Germany itself was suffering.[9] The guidelines of the Ober Ost state itself declared openly that the interests of the army and the German empire always came before those of the occupied territory. In Ober Ost, extensive requisitions of livestock, harvests, and raw materials achieved autarky for the army and exports back to Germany's war effort. Ironically, the regime's own policies undercut hopes for economic recovery of the region: especially the confiscation of horses hampered agriculture. The forests of the region were intensively used for the war. In Poland, agriculture as well as industry was exploited. Machines and factories were broken apart for scrap metal. Seeking complete exploitation of the occupied territories, here, as in Belgium, forced labor was used. In the area of Lodz, Poland, around 5,000 workers (mostly Jewish) were pressed into labor.[10] Polish workers were also pressured to "volunteer" for labor in Germany. In Lithuania, forced labor gangs were shuttled around the country.[11]

German War Aims

From the outset of the conflict, war aims were articulated which foresaw a fundamental reordering of Eastern Europe.[12] A memorandum completed on September 9, 1914 in Chancellor Bethmann Hollweg's office, the so-called September Program, argued for assuring the "security for the German Empire in the west and east for the foreseeable future" and that "as much as possible, Russia must be pushed back from the German border and its domination of the non-Russian vassal peoples must be broken." A reorganized Central Europe under German control, including Poland, would ensure stability. In the first years of the war, despite an official proscription on open war-aims discussion, Pan-German nationalists and representatives of heavy industry unleashed waves of memoranda calling for extensive annexations in Western and Eastern Europe. By contrast, the camp of "liberal imperialists" looked forward to German influence being brought to bear on an enlightened reordering of states on the Continent. The book by Progressive party leader Friedrich Naumann, *Mitteleuropa*, published in fall of 1915 to great interest and resonance, argued for a close union of Germany with Austria-Hungary and other Central European nations in economic and political terms, with respect for the cultural development of all the peoples of the region.[13]

Interest in Naumann's plan reached its highpoint in 1916 and then evaporated, as the popular buzzword of *Mitteleuropa* lost its original generous meaning and became a point of departure for ever-more extensive territorial claims. From an early date, the traumatic Russian invasion of Prussia led nationalists and government officials to argue for territorial revisions on Germany's eastern borders as a "purely military necessity." An abiding project was the plan for a so-called "Polish Border Strip," carved from occupied territory, to offer a frontier buffer zone for Germany.[14] Throughout the war, many variations of this plan were produced (including ones that called for the mass expulsion of Poles and Jews inhabiting the areas, foreshadowing the ethnic cleansings of later decades).

From 1916, Hindenburg and Ludendorff in the Supreme Command took an active role in encouraging large annexations and removed the ban on discussion of war aims. Differences arose among German political leaders concerning how to reorganize the East and the ways by which this should be done. The German government and military agreed in the Kreuznach Program of April 23, 1917 on an extensive shopping list of gains in the West and East, validating the vision of the Supreme Command. Challenging such appetites, the July 17, 1917 Reichstag Peace Resolution called instead for a peace "without annexations or reparations," but success on the battlefield soon trumped this statement of principle. Even as a tremendous revolutionizing of the world political scene unfolded in 1917–18 (the Russian March Revolution, the Bolshevik coup, and American entry into the war), official German war aims in the East were poised to grow radically, with additional conquests. In the process, these demands caused increasing strain with Germany's allies in the Central Powers, Austria-Hungary, Turkey, and Bulgaria, over the division of spoils.

The Experience of Occupation

Obviously, even as they interacted on a daily basis, the experience of occupation took on very different contours for the occupiers and the occupied populations. Neither were the sets of mutual reactions monolithic, but rather they evolved over time.

German soldiers and officers stationed in the territories experienced a varied range of reactions. Relations with the native peoples over whom they exercised armed authority ran from sympathy, respect, and recognition all the way to "compassion fatigue," antipathy, repulsion, and ridicule. The most striking initial reaction was astonishment at the ethnic diversity of many of these areas. Soldiers' newspapers at the front offer testimony to these reactions. A recent study of these newspapers concludes that using "a colonial and at times racist discourse, the newspapers sought to explain why this occupation was justified, and why some eastern peoples were more highly valued than others."[15] While Slavic peoples were generally devalued, those ethnic groups intended for client status in the future were more often praised or presented in a positive light. Also striking was the fact that the "newspapers were surprisingly neutral, and sometimes even positive, in their portrayal of Eastern European Jews."[16] The *Ostjuden* had made up roughly 10 percent of the area's prewar population and between 30 and 50 percent of the urban populations.[17]

This meeting of Germans and Eastern European Jews (often able to communicate with the Germans through their cognate Yiddish) was a tremendously important cultural encounter, as the Central Powers were "now in control of the bulk of European Jewry."[18] At first, "the Germans were often welcomed by the Jews in the Congress Kingdom," in view of the discrimination and violence Jews had suffered under Tsarist rule.[19] There was clearly a special quality to this encounter for German Jews in uniform who found themselves needing to mediate between different identities. Antisemites in the army's ranks claimed that their prejudices had been validated by seeing the miserable conditions of Jewish communities. In addition, despite the image of a united front that the occupying forces sought to project, divisions in the German ranks certainly existed. Resentment against a privileged officer class could be keen. As the occupation dragged on, the makeup of the occupying forces also changed, with repeated reassignment of some troops to the western front. Left behind were older soldiers and Alsatians, who resented the assumption that they could not be trusted in the West. Finally, while officers and officials might indulge fantasies of staying on in the occupied lands after the war as owners of lordly estates, ordinary soldiers were most often motivated by the emotion of keen homesickness.

For the occupied populations, under German rule, the experience began with stark contrasts. Especially in the Great Advance of 1915, terrifying rumors circulated of how the Germans would act upon their arrival. When these worst fears did not materialize, the promise of order made by the occupiers was welcomed, given the chaos of Russian retreat. Although this could have been the basis for reasonably successful occupation policies, the economic demands made by the stressed Central Powers soon undercut potential receptiveness. With a dose of black humor, Lithuanian farmers called the harsh requisitions "inquisitions" instead. Polish Jews joked that "the Germans had indeed brought order to Poland. Whereas before there was corn ... now there was order; whereas before there were oxen ... now there is order."[20] Most of all, forced labor sparked great fear. Resentment at intense and detailed economic exactions was also soon combined with suspicions of sinister long-term motives, going beyond immediate wartime needs to prepare future economic domination.[21] German cultural initiatives in Ober Ost likewise were seen as a portent of future complete Germanization. At the same time, the experience of military occupation could accentuate divisions within the populations themselves. In a classic case of divide and rule, German policies foresaw being able to play different ethnic groups off of one another in the region, with Lithuanians, Ukrainians, and Belarusians set against the Poles. Ethnic Germans in the area suddenly often enjoyed a privileged position. They, along with non-Germans who cooperated with the occupiers, were denounced by local Eastern European nationalists. Sporadic resistance took place in the countryside, and bandit groups grew in the swamps and forests, an increasing challenge to the German claim of control.

Seeming German Triumph in 1918

The year 1918 brought seeming success in furthering war aims that had already been articulated and the opening of yet wider vistas. [22] As German troops advanced eastward into a crumbling Russian Empire, it became increasingly plausible to envision creating a chain of German-dependent states from the White Sea to the Black Sea. Rhetorically, these states were to be "autonomous," but in fact closely bound to the German Empire by political, military, and economic conventions.[23] In the process of cementing these German plans, however, growing strains became evident with the Austro-Hungarian ally, often a partner in military occupation, as well as with Turkey and Bulgaria.

A key earlier event was the outbreak of the March 1917 Revolution in Russia, the overthrow of the Tsar, and the establishment of dual revolutionary authority in a Provisional Government and the Petrograd Soviet. While the government pledged to remain in the war, in March 1917 the Petrograd Soviet called for peace without annexations, a formula of tremendous appeal worldwide. To speed the process of disintegration of the Russian state by "revolutionizing" it from within, the German government and Supreme Command arranged for the Russian Bolshevik leader Vladimir I. Lenin to be sent back from Swiss exile to Russia in April 1917. The growing weakness of the Russian war effort allowed German armies to press forward again in the fall of 1917, as they captured the important port and factory city Riga, as well as the islands of Ösel, Dagö, and Moon off the Estonian coast in September 1917.

A decisive turn came with the Bolshevik coup in Petrograd, on November 7, 1917, overthrowing the Provisional Government. Seeking to consolidate their rule and win over a war-weary populace, the Bolsheviks sent out a worldwide appeal for peace and began negotiations with the Central Powers. An armistice was signed on December 5, 1917, and talks took place in Brest-Litovsk between the Bolsheviks and representatives of Germany, Austria-Hungary, Turkey, and Bulgaria.[24] After inconclusive debates in which both sides sought to capitalize on the new slogan of self-determination which neither believed in, the Bolshevik spokesman Lev Trotsky declared that Russia would leave the conflict without a treaty, and that now a state of "neither peace nor war" existed. After the Bolshevik delegation departed, German commanders recovered from their surprise and simply renewed their attack. Diplomatic cover for the advance was also sought. On February 13, 1918, the Crown Council at Bad Homburg decided to present the advance as a mission of saving imperiled peoples, who would have to present pleas for help "which mention the existing anarchy and continual danger of life and property and appeal to us to intervene to establish order."[25] From February 18, 1918, a million German soldiers moved eastward at astonishing speed, often by train, capturing the rest of Latvia, Estonia, Belarus, and Ukraine, taking Odessa, the Crimea, and moving up to the Don River.

In a panic, Bolshevik negotiators signed the Treaty of Brest-Litovsk on March 3, 1918, determined to save their revolution in spite of the cost. The terms of the dictated peace were vast in scale. Russia gave up control of Finland, Estonia, Latvia, Lithuania, Belarus, Poland, and Ukraine. At a stroke, the former Empire lost a third of its population, a million square miles of territory, and the bulk of its industry and mines. The treaty was passed overwhelmingly in the Reichstag, notwithstanding the latter's earlier Peace Resolution. Only the Independent Social Democrats voted against it, while the majority SPD abstained. Later in the year, on August 27, 1918, a supplementary treaty was signed, with further requirements of reparations from Russia. Brest-Litovsk made clear the expansiveness of German war aims and the kind of terms it would impose on the Allies if it won the war (as a result, Allied public opinion hardened and later exacted strict terms at Versailles). The negotiations also had ripple effects in the occupied areas, especially in Poland, where news of the cession of the Chelm district to Ukraine led to public demonstrations, protests by the Regency Council, and the resignation of the government (replaced by a new government under conservative estate-owner Jan Kanty Steczkowski).

Romania

In the spring of 1918 Germany also imposed a harsh peace on defeated Romania. In 1916, most of Romania had been conquered. It had entered the war in August 1916, and experienced a disaster by the end of the year: two-thirds of its territory fell to the Central Powers, with Bucharest captured by December.[26] The Romanian government retreated to Iasi in Moldavia. A military government of the Central Powers ruled the land, dominated by German officials (while Austrian bureaucrats regretted that their alleged imperial experience with the region and its peoples' psychology was under-utilized). The military government sought to extract as much in the way of resources as it could, and requisitioned food was transported to the Central Powers by railway or up the Danube.[27]

Romania was at long last forced to sue for peace when Russia began negotiations with the Central Powers, leaving it geographically exposed. An armistice with the Central

Powers was agreed on December 9, 1917 in Focsani. After Romanian attempts at delay in negotiations and German ultimatums, the Peace Treaty of Bucharest was signed on May 7, 1918. It reduced Romania "to the position of a vassal state of Germany, with its sovereignty a mere shadow."[28] Although Romania had initially been slated to come under Austro-Hungarian influence, the German Kaiser and Supreme Command edged out their ally. The terms of the treaty were severe. Romania was forced to give up the Dobruja region, part of which was assigned to Bulgaria, while the rest was made a condominium of the four Central Powers, to be administered jointly. Bulgaria was upset with this result, as it had been promised the entire region. Romania remained occupied until some future unspecified date and was to pay reparations covering the costs of military occupation and the holding of prisoners of war. Strategic passes in the Carpathians were ceded to Austria-Hungary. In return, Romania was allowed to occupy Bessarabia, neighboring territory in the former Russian Empire. The port of Constanta was not made a German possession, as Ludendorff had hoped, but still was to be German-dominated economically. The most pressing demands focused on oil and food. A 90-year Austro-Hungarian–German monopoly was to run the oil industry, with the shares divided 56 percent for Germany, 24 percent for Austria-Hungary, and 20 percent retained by Romania.[29] British agents had sabotaged the oil fields by setting them alight before the occupiers took over, but now refineries and drill towers were reconstructed (eventually matching almost half of prewar production, according to a postwar study).[30] Deliveries of Romania's "surplus" food were demanded by the Central Powers. Germany's Reichstag ratified the treaty in June 1918, with the Social Democrats voting in favor this time. While Field Marshal Mackensen, who had helped conquer Romania, observed with satisfaction that: "This time the pen has secured what the sword has won," the German Supreme Command was still not sated.[31]

Ukraine

Viewed as a potential "bread-basket" for the Central Powers amid the privations of the blockade, Ukraine took on special significance in expanding German war aims in Eastern Europe.[32] As Ukraine split off from the disintegrating structure of the Russian Empire, a contest for control ensued. After the February Revolution, a Ukrainian Central Rada (council) was formed on March 17, 1917, taking on the role of a national parliament. After the Bolshevik coup, on November 22, 1917 the Rada declared Ukraine an autonomous republic. In short order, Bolshevik forces invaded in the winter of 1917–18, and seized Kiev. The embattled Rada declared an independent Ukraine on January 25, 1918. Even as the negotiations at Brest-Litovsk unfolded, the Central Rada signed a separate peace treaty on February 9, 1918 with the Central Powers, in which it won support in exchange for the promise of vast shipments of food: a million tons of supplies. The German invasion (which began from February 18, 1918 when the talks at Brest-Litovsk broke down) was presented as a liberation, followed by slower Austro-Hungarian advance from February 28, 1918. By March 1, 1918, the Germans had occupied Kiev, and the Rada returned. On March 12, 1918, the port of Odessa was taken. By early May 1918, German forces occupied the Donetz basin, with its coal and iron fields and mines, and the Crimea. On May 1, Germans captured Taganrog, and on May 6, Rostov. Their forces took up cooperation with the Don Cossacks (with some groups under the leadership of Hetman Krasnov), who spearheaded an uprising against Bolshevik forces from April 1918.[33]

The conquerors now divided up Ukraine into zones of occupation, with Austria-Hungary holding southwestern districts, the rest under German administration.[34] In the chaotic circumstances of the vast occupied territory, however, requisitioning of promised food shipments ran into significant problems. The peasantry (often armed) was hostile to the occupying troops, unwilling to give up seized land or to surrender food. Friction also grew between the Central Powers in requisitions and dividing the loot, as Austria-Hungary's provisioning situation at home became critical.

As Ukraine under the Rada's nominal leadership was unable to meet the economic demands, German forces encouraged an internal political reorientation.[35] On April 28, 1918, German troops disbanded the Rada.[36] It was replaced with the self-appointed government of Hetman Pavlo Skoropadsky, a former Tsarist general. The League of Landowners, meeting in Kiev, acclaimed him as leader on April 29. With Skoropadsky at the helm, a more ordered exploitation of Ukrainian resources followed, but also produced increasing alienation as punitive expeditions to rural areas reasserted large landowners' claims.[37] Large-scale peasant revolts against the Germans broke out in the countryside, so that the demands on troops increased. In Kiev, on July 30, a Socialist Revolutionary assassinated Field Marshal Hermann von Eichhorn in a terrorist act intended to touch off a larger revolt. In the final analysis, the much hoped for wealth of food to be won by occupation of Ukraine did not materialize: grain exports turned out to be only one-tenth of the expected sum.[38]

The Caucasus

A further arena for the growing frictions and conflicts within the Central Powers was the Caucasus, as Germany and Turkey pursued rival claims for influence in the area. By February 1918, Turkish forces were advancing on the Transcaucasus, the area south of the Caucasus Mountains, between the Black Sea and the Caspian Sea. At Brest-Litovsk, the Bolsheviks gave up the Kars, Ardahan, and Batumi districts to Turkey. On April 22, 1918, the Transcaucasian Assembly (encompassing Georgia, Armenia, and Azerbaijan) voted, under Turkish pressure, to separate from Russia, and declared independence.[39] The resulting "Democratic Federative Republic of Transcaucasia" lasted only one month before breaking apart.[40] At the same time, Turkish forces continued their advance toward oil-rich Baku, on the Caspian Sea.

To forestall Turkish domination, on May 26, 1918 Georgian political leaders declared independence, with promises of German aid. A new government was formed under moderate socialist leadership. For the Georgians, "alliance with Germany was more than an expediency," as Georgian intellectuals had long respected German culture, socialists admired the German socialist movement, and nationalists had ties with German revolutionizing efforts from the start of the war.[41] On May 28, 1918, a Georgian–German agreement was signed in Poti, a port on the Black Sea.[42] As Ludendorff explained, military help to Georgia "offered us a means by which, independent of Turkey, we could get at the raw materials of the Caucasus."[43] Beyond this, German influence in the Transcaucasus would open a bridge to Central Asia. Germany offered Georgia military assistance and a restraining influence on Turkey in exchange for use of railroads, shipping, and ports, and monopolies on mining and raw material exports, especially manganese. German troops arrived in Tbilisi on June 10, 1918.[44] A study reports: "They accomplished their task of exploiting Georgia with remarkable skill. The discipline of the troops, the friendly attitude of the officers, and the efficiency of the administrators made the German occupation quite popular."[45] The fragmenting region now saw a multisided contest for influence. Armenia and Azerbaijan had also declared independence, two days after Georgia. British forces probed northward from Persia. Among the provisions of the August 1918 supplemental treaty to Brest-Litovsk, Germany acknowledged Soviet Russian rights to the Caucasus without Georgia, thus ceding any claim to Baku (and promising to restrain the Turks advancing on the city); in return, the Germans were promised a quarter of Baku's annual oil production. Nonetheless, on September 15, 1918, Baku (which briefly had been reinforced with a British unit) fell to the Turks and their Azerbaijani allies.[46]

Finland

As a part of the larger policy of exploiting and expediting the disintegration of the Russian state's structure, Germany also intervened in Finland, which became the "cornerstone of German policy in the Baltic."[47] By early 1918, Finland was caught in a civil war between nationalist Whites and socialist Reds. The nationalists appealed for German help. The cost was a Finnish-German Treaty, signed on March 7, 1918, which established political, economic, and military ties of dependence with Germany. German expeditionary forces, including the Baltic Division under General Count Rüdiger von der Goltz, were landed, and by mid-April had taken Helsinki, as the civil war was brought to a close.[48] It was proposed that a German prince become king of Finland, but the war ended before one was crowned.

Euphoric Vistas

German victory in Eastern Europe appeared obvious when one consulted a map, showing the vast territories occupied by German forces. Ludendorff marveled at the result: "We had broken the blockade in the East, and it seemed that our life could be strengthened by this."[49] He, along with other annexationists, continued to contemplate what Ludendorff called his "favorite idea of settling [ethnic] Germans strewn throughout Russia alongside our soldiers in the eastern territories."[50] The idea of gathering in the two million ethnic Germans living in the lands of the Russian Empire beckoned as a source of manpower in further conflicts.

In terms of the spread of German cultural influence, the crowning act was to be the symbolically rich opening of a German university in the East, as an outpost. After the February 1918 occupation of Estonia, the German army directed the reopening of an old university in Dorpat (Tartu). The ceremony took place on September 15, 1918.[51] The leadership of the university was awarded to a Berlin professor of history, Dr. Theodor Schiemann, an annexationist and friend of the Kaiser. In his post, he was an ardent proponent of Germanization policies, to an extent that worried even Ludendorff.[52] German was the university's exclusive language of instruction, and the faculty entirely German, with the exception of one lonely Estonian scholar. Its character as a military creation was underlined by the sight of faculty lecturing in uniform. A boycott of the university was declared by Estonian and Latvian student organizations in protest.

At the same time, the reality of the eastern conquests on the ground (as opposed to the often misleading outlines of the map) was a more disappointing and perilous one for Germany's strategic situation. A million troops remained stationed in the East, on guard duty and to enforce requisitions, when they might otherwise have been of use in reinforcing the Supreme Command's Spring Offensive on the western front. Among the subject populations, moreover, a darkening mood was to be observed, as alienation from the occupation regimes grew. Yet these realities were ignored, in favor of expanding ambitions.

Indicative of the vast scope of possibilities in Eastern Europe, Ludendorff also weighed an additional plan, *Schlusssteinoperation* (Operation Capstone). This was to be an attack, in unison with the Finns, against Petrograd to crush the Bolshevik regime. Though dissuaded by German diplomats who stressed the advantages of dealing with a weakened revolutionary regime, Ludendorff was still considering the operation as late as September 27, 1918, when it was at last cancelled.[53]

Final Collapse and Consequences

All plans for Eastern Europe, where the Central Powers seemed to have won a decisive victory, came crashing down with German defeat on the western front. The initially promising spring offensive in 1918 stalled and by August had turned into German retreat. In Eastern Europe, Germany's allies began to fall away. Bulgaria was the first, signing an armistice with the Allies on September 30, 1918. Ottoman Turkey followed on October 30 and Austria-Hungary on November 3. The collapse of German authority in the occupied territories was also swift. Soon after revolution broke out in Germany itself on November 9, 1918, German soldiers in the occupation forces began organizing their own councils in imitation of the Russian Soviets. Though cloaked with revolutionary rhetoric, their overriding concern was an orderly return home. They were keenly aware of the dangers of being cut off and isolated among hostile populations. On November 11, 1918, the day of the Armistice on the western front, German troops in Warsaw were disarmed by Polish forces, and Polish leaders, accepting the primacy of Pilsudski (soon released from German captivity), took control. That date has since been celebrated as Poland's Independence Day. In the Baltic region, the recently inaugurated German University of Dorpat closed again and political responsibility passed to local leaders. In Ukraine, revolts against Skoropadsky grew, and rebel forces massed against Kiev. German forces abandoned the city on December 14, 1918. The Hetmanate had lasted less than eight months. Along the eastern front, which had marked the furthest advance of German power, the Bolsheviks' Red Army now moved forward. The Bolsheviks denounced the Treaty of Brest-Litovsk and were fired by the vision of linking up with revolutionary forces in Central Europe.

Even as the guns fell silent in the west, World War I continued in aftershocks in Eastern Europe in the wake of German collapse (see chapter 37). The Allied powers, fearful of Bolshevik expansion, insisted at the armistice that German forces remain in the East to hold off the Red Army. As the disintegration of the withdrawing army was too far advanced, German officers established new paramilitary forces, the *Freikorps*. Some 20,000–40,000 *Freikorps* fighters trekked to the Baltic region, on an alleged crusade against Bolshevism. Called *Baltikumer*, these adventurers rampaged for a year in the region, fighting the Red Army and the young Baltic Republics in turn before being expelled back to Germany in December 1919.

In the aftermath of war, the experience of German occupation had important consequences in the collective memory of both the occupiers and occupied. Among Eastern European peoples who had lived under occupation, its remembered harshness was integrated into nationalist mythologies of an ordeal preceding the salvation of independence.[54] From the German perspective, the memory of seeming triumph in the east and the sense that half the war had been won, followed by complete collapse and national humiliation, retained a sense of the inexplicable. For many, the conviction gained hold that the collapse of German-imposed order in Eastern Europe indicated that something was essentially wrong with the region itself, making it incapable of reform. German nationalists loudly proclaimed the newly independent states of Eastern Europe, chief among them Poland, to be merely "seasonal states" that would soon be extinguished again. Especially radical "lessons" were drawn from the experience of World War I by the Nazis for whom the conquest of "living space" in Eastern Europe became a racial imperative, commanding not the cultivation of non-German peoples but their enslavement and genocide. Hitler stressed repeatedly that his soldiers came not as teachers or to cherish native peoples, but to build a racial empire, as they returned to lands already occupied once before, in the earlier war. Here too World War I showed its long-term brutalizing potential.

Notes

1　Liulevicius, *War Land on the Eastern Front*.
2　Hillgruber, *Germany and the Two World Wars*, p. 47.
3　Roshwald, *Ethnic Nationalism and the Fall of Empires*, p. 126.
4　Weindling, *Epidemics and Genocide in Eastern Europe, 1890–1945*.
5　Polonsky, "The German Occupation of Poland"; Conze, *Polnische Nation und deutsche Politik*.
6　Ritter, *The Sword and the Scepter: The Problem of Militarism in Germany*, vol. 3, p. 100; Geiss, *Der polnische Grenzstreifen 1914–1918*, p. 29.
7　Liulevicius, *War Land on the Eastern Front*; Strazhas, *Deutsche Ostpolitik im Ersten Weltkrieg*.
8　Basler, *Deutschlands Annexionspolitik in Polen und im Baltikum*.
9　Conze, *Polnische Nation und deutsche Politik*, pp. 125–37.
10　Conze, *Polnische Nation und deutsche Politik*, p. 135.
11　Liulevicius, *War Land on the Eastern Front*, pp. 73–4.
12　On war aims in general, see Fischer, *Germany's Aims in the First World War*.
13　Meyer, *Mitteleuropa in German Thought and Action, 1815–1945*.
14　Geiss, *Der polnische Grenzstreifen 1914–1918*.
15　Nelson, "'Unsere Frage ist der Osten': Representations of the Occupied East in German Soldier Newspapers, 1914–1918," p. 500.
16　Ibid., p. 501.
17　Roshwald, *Ethnic Nationalism and the Fall of Empires*, p. 122.
18　Polonsky, "The German Occupation of Poland," p. 119; Aschheim, *Brothers and Strangers*, pp.139–41.
19　Polonsky, "The German Occupation of Poland," p. 116.
20　Quoted in Aschheim, *Brothers and Strangers*, p. 181.
21　Conze, *Polnische Nation und deutsche Politik*, p. 133; Geiss, *Der polnische Grenzstreifen 1914–1918*, p. 40.
22　Baumgart, *Deutsche Ostpolitik 1918*.
23　Fischer, *Germany's Aims in the First World War*, p. 457.
24　Wheeler-Bennett, *Brest-Litovsk: The Forgotten Peace, March 1918*.
25　Quoted in Kitchen, *The Silent Dictatorship*, p. 219.
26　Torrey, *Romania and World War I*.
27　Kerchnawe, *Die Militärverwaltung*, pp. 312–13.
28　Kitchen, *The Silent Dictatorship*, p. 197; Bornemann, *Der Frieden von Bukarest 1918*.
29　Hitchens, *Rumania*, p. 274; Herwig, *The First World War: Germany and Austria-Hungary 1914–1918*, p. 384; Kitchen, *The Silent Dictatorship*, p. 199; Bornemann, *Der Frieden von Bukarest 1918*, p. 166.

30 Kerchnawe, *Die Militärverwaltung*, p. 316; Stone, *The Eastern Front*, p. 280.
31 Quoted in Kitchen, *The Silent Dictatorship*, p. 199.
32 Remer, *Die Ukraine*; Borowsky, *Deutsche Ukrainepolitik*; Fedyshyn, *Germany's Drive to the East*.
33 Holquist, *Making War, Forging Revolution*, p. 146.
34 Allen, *The Ukraine*, pp. 287–306; Eudin, "The German Occupation of the Ukraine in 1918: A Documentary Account"; Meyer, "Germans in the Ukraine, 1918: Excerpts from Unpublished Letters"; *Die deutsche Okkupation der Ukraine. Geheimdokumente*.
35 Subtelny, *Ukraine*, p. 354.
36 Ibid., p. 353.
37 Ibid., p. 357.
38 Herwig, *The First World War: Germany and Austria-Hungary 1914–1918*, p. 386.
39 Pipes, *Formation of the Soviet Union*, p. 107; the date is given as April 25, 1918 in D'Encausse, *The Great Challenge*, p. 88.
40 Suny, *The Making of the Georgian Nation*, p. 191.
41 Ibid., p. 193.
42 Kazemzadeh, *The Struggle for Transcaucasia*, pp.122–4; D'Encausse, *The Great Challenge*, p. 88.
43 Ludendorff, *Meine Kriegserinnerungen*, p. 500.
44 Suny, *The Making of the Georgian Nation*, pp. 192–3.
45 Kazemzadeh, *The Struggle for Transcaucasia*, p. 148.
46 Suny, *The Making of the Georgian Nation*, p. 193.
47 Kitchen, *The Silent Dictatorship*, p. 216.
48 Ibid., pp. 216–21.
49 Ludendorff, *Meine Kriegserinnerungen*, p. 506.
50 Ibid., p. 532.
51 Hans von Rimscha, "Adolf von Harnack, Theodor Schiemann und Karl Dehio in ihren Bemühungen um eine deutsche Universität Dorpat," in *Reval und die baltischen Länder. Festschrift für Hellmuth Weiss zum 80. Geburtstag*, ed. Jürgen von Hehn and Csaba János Kenéz, Marburg, J. G. Herder Institut, 1980, pp. 55–74.
52 Ibid., p. 63.
53 Kitchen, *The Silent Dictatorship*, p. 226.
54 Roshwald, *Ethnic Nationalism and the Fall of Empires*.

References and Further Reading

Allen, W. E. D., *The Ukraine: A History*, New York, Russell and Russell, 1963.

Aschheim, Steven E., *Brothers and Strangers: The East European Jew in German and German Jewish Consciousness, 1800–1923*, Madison, University of Wisconsin Press, 1982.

Basler, Werner, *Deutschlands Annexionspolitik in Polen und im Baltikum 1914–1918*, Berlin, Rütten und Loening, 1962.

Baumgart, Winfried, *Deutsche Ostpolitik 1918. Von Brest-Litowsk bis zum Ende des Ersten Weltkrieges*, Vienna, R. Oldenbourg, 1966.

Bornemann, Elke, *Der Frieden von Bukarest 1918*, Frankfurt a.M., Peter Lang, 1978.

Borowsky, Peter, *Deutsche Ukrainepolitik 1918 unter besonderer Berücksichtigung der Wirtschaftsfragen*. Historische Studien Heft 416, Lübeck, Matthiesen, 1970.

Conze, Werner, *Polnische Nation und deutsche Politik im ersten Weltkrieg*, Cologne, Böhlau, 1958.

D'Encausse, Hélène Carrère, *The Great Challenge: Nationalities and the Bolshevik State 1917–1930*, 1987; translation from French, New York, Holmes and Meier, 1992.

Die deutsche Okkupation der Ukraine. Geheimdokumente, Strasbourg, Éditions Prométhée, 1937.

Eudin, Xenia Joukoff, "The German Occupation of the Ukraine in 1918: A Documentary Account," *Russian Review*, 1/1, November 1941, pp. 90–105.

Fedyshyn, Oleg S., *Germany's Drive to the East and the Ukrainian Revolution, 1917–1918*, New Brunswick, Rutgers University Press, 1971.

Fischer, Fritz, *Germany's Aims in the First World War*, 1961, translation from German, New York, W. W. Norton, 1967.

Geiss, Imanuel, *Der polnische Grenzstreifen 1914–1918. Ein Beitrag zur deutschen Kriegszielpolitik im Ersten Weltkrieg*, Lübeck, Matthiesen, 1960.

Herwig, Holger, *The First World War: Germany and Austria-Hungary, 1914–1918*, London, Arnold, 1997.

Hillgruber, Andreas, *Germany and the Two World Wars*, trans. William C. Kirby, Cambridge, MA, Harvard University Press, 1981.

Hitchens, Keith, *Rumania 1866–1947*, Oxford, Clarendon Press, 1994.

Holquist, Peter. *Making War, Forging Revolution: Russia's Continuum of Crisis, 1914–1921*, Cambridge, MA, Harvard University Press, 2002.

Kazemzadeh, Firuz. *The Struggle for Transcaucasia (1917–1921)*, New York, Philosophical Library, 1951.

Kerchnawe, Hugo, et al., *Die Militärverwaltung in den von den österreichisch-ungarischen Truppen besetzten Gebieten*, Vienna, Hölder-Pichler-Tempsky AG, 1928.

Kitchen, Martin, *The Silent Dictatorship: The Politics of the German High Command under Hindenburg and Ludendorff, 1916–1918*, London, Croom Helm, 1976.

Liulevicius, Vejas, *War Land on the Eastern Front: Culture, National Identity and German Occupation in World War I*, Cambridge, Cambridge University Press, 2000.

Ludendorff, Erich, *Meine Kriegserinnerungen, 1914–1918*, Berlin, E. S. Mittler und Sohn, 1919; abridged translation, *Concise Ludendorff Memoirs 1914–1918*, London, Hutchinson, 1933.

Meyer, Henry Cord, "Germans in the Ukraine, 1918: Excerpts from Unpublished Letters," *American Slavic and East European Review*, 9, 1950, pp. 105–15.

Meyer, Henry Cord, *Mitteleuropa in German Thought and Action, 1815–1945*, The Hague, Martinus Nijhoff, 1955.

Nelson, Robert L., "'Unsere Frage ist der Osten': Representations of the Occupied East in German Soldier Newspapers, 1914–1918," *Zeitschrift für Ostmitteleuropa-Forschung* 51, 4, 2002, pp. 500–28.

Pipes, Richard, *The Formation of the Soviet Union: Communism and Nationalism 1917–1923*, rev. ed., Cambridge, MA, Harvard University Press, 1964.

Polonsky, Antony, "The German Occupation of Poland During the First and Second World Wars: A Comparison," in Roy A. Prete and A. Hamish Ion (eds.), *Armies of Occupation*, Waterloo, Wilfrid Laurier University Press, 1984, pp. 97–142.

Remer, Claus, *Die Ukraine im Blickfeld deutscher Interessen. Ende des 19. Jahrhunderts bis 1917/18*, Frankfurt a.M., Peter Lang, 1997.

Ritter, Gerhard, *The Sword and the Sceptre: The Problem of Militarism in Germany*, vols. 3 and 4, London, Allen Lane, 1973.

Roshwald, Aviel, *Ethnic Nationalism and the Fall of Empires: Central Europe, Russia, and the Middle East, 1914–1923*, London, Routledge, 2001.

Stone, Norman, *The Eastern Front, 1914–1917*, London, Hodder and Stoughton, 1975.

Strazhas, Aba, *Deutsche Ostpolitik im Ersten Weltkrieg. Der Fall Ober Ost, 1915–1917*, Wiesbaden, Harrassowitz, 1993.

Subtelny, Orest, *Ukraine: A History*, 3rd ed., Toronto, University of Toronto Press, 2000.

Suny, Ronald Grigor, *The Making of the Georgian Nation*, 2nd ed., Bloomington, Indiana University Press, 1994.

Torrey, Glenn E., *Romania and World War I*, Iasi, Portland, Center for Romanian Studies, 1995.

Weindling, Paul, *Epidemics and Genocide in Eastern Europe, 1890–1945*, Oxford, Oxford University Press, 2000.

Wheeler-Bennett, John W., *Brest-Litovsk: The Forgotten Peace, March 1918*, London, Macmillan, 1938; new ed., 1963.

Zweig, Arnold, *The Case of Sergeant Grischa*, 1927; translation from the German, New York, Viking Penguin, 1986.

CHAPTER THIRTY-ONE

Italy

ANTONIO GIBELLI
(translated by Paul O'Brien)

Italy's war is generally considered marginal to the history of World War I because it was shorter and less strategically relevant than those on other fronts and because Italy was a power of only secondary importance.[1] Italy entered the war on May 24, 1915, 10 months after it began, and fought in an area that was far smaller than either the western or eastern fronts, whereas the concentration in France of Europe's three main industrial and military powers made that battle zone decisive. Nor could Italy claim comparable status as a great power. Its industrial base was limited and it had fewer demographic resources than Russia or even Austria-Hungary. Italy's eventual allies in the Entente paid little heed to the country's role in the war, a point on which they were at one with Italy's former partners in the Triple Alliance, which had always looked down on their junior ally. Italians themselves, with the exception of the nationalists, saw the war as limited in its aims. Initially Italy declared war only on the Habsburg Dual Monarchy, not Germany, and before calling it the "Great War" or the "World War," Italians referred to it simply as the "Italo-Austrian war."

Yet downplaying Italian intervention would be a mistake for the historiography of the war, since Italy inflicted considerable military and political damage on Austria-Hungary and helped tilt the overall balance of forces against the Central Powers. The victorious German offensive on the eastern front in the spring of 1915 left the Austrians free to face down the ambitious offensive with which Italy opened the war and stabilize the new front in the Alps. But in the long run the presence of a new enemy in the south forced the Austrians to commit significant forces to that area (see chapter 6). While Italy's expansionist aims in the Balkans blurred the question of the rights of nationalities, Italian irredentist claims to Italian-speaking areas of Austria-Hungary added decisively to the pressures that eventually led to the breakup of the Dual Monarchy (see chapter 25).[2]

Although smaller in absolute size than those of other major belligerents, the Italian war effort was not negligible in relative terms. As indicated in chapter 6 above, almost six million men were mobilized, of whom 4,200,000 were sent to the front. While the army was relatively unprepared at the outset, it had become a solid organization by 1917 capable of overcoming the disaster of Caporetto in that year and winning eventual victory. Given a somewhat shorter period of fighting, Italian losses were comparable to those of Britain. Over six hundred thousand Italian soldiers died, or 10.3 percent of the men mobilized, compared to 750,000 dead in the United Kingdom, or 11.8 percent of those mobilized. The Italian death rate was the equivalent of 7.5 percent of all males between 15 and 49 years, compared to 6.3 percent in Britain. Around a million men were wounded, with half a million recognized as permanent invalids, and at a rough estimate, the war resulted in some 200,000 widows and 400,000 orphans. Hence Italian participation in the war was close in scale to that of the other main European powers.

The war was even more important for Italy's internal history, although with the postwar crisis that led to fascism, this of course had a European significance. Italian historiography has always seen the conflict as a watershed in the history of the country since unification, not just because of how Italy entered the war and fought it, but above all because of how it emerged from it. For nationalist and fascist historians, such as Gioacchino Volpe, World War I was the basis for national greatness and a political class that would finally be equal to the tasks that faced it.[3] In this interpretation, the logical outcome of the war was the fascist seizure of power. When Mussolini went to King Vittorio Emmanuele III to receive the prime ministership after the march on Rome, he was supposed to have declared: "Sire, I bring you the Italy of Vittorio Veneto."[4]

Likewise, anti-fascist historiography, which has enjoyed a much better press, saw the war as equally important, although in an opposite sense. According to this view, the later crisis and collapse of the liberal state were foreshadowed by the way in which one sector of the ruling class took the country by a bold and calculated risk into the conflict.[5] Unlike the majority of European countries, including those with reactionary and autocratic regimes (such as Russia), Italy was deeply divided as it entered the war, not only between the broad masses and the political and intellectual elites but also internally within the latter. Somewhat incongruously, the myth of a "great Italy" had taken root in a country that was only partially modernized, and this pushed Italy to intervene in the war not because it was an established great power but because it hoped to become one. Italy's economic, political, and intellectual leaders were hungry for war in the name of ambitions that were intense but often vague. The result was the opposite of what had been intended, for the war exposed the nation's weakness and precipitated the fall of the leaders who had urged it.

Italy's weaknesses can be summed up as inadequate social cohesion and a lack of popular identification with the nation and its institutions. The peculiarities of the process that had led to the territorial and political unification of the country meant that broad sectors of society, such as the workers and peasants, and for different reasons the Catholic Church, felt little confidence in the state or sense of obligation toward it. The state harbored a reciprocal distrust of its citizens, and these contradictory feelings exploded when faced with the test of the war. Fear of disloyalty – and hence of desertion – resulted in a harsh disciplinary regime toward the soldiers (see chapter 6 above). But it also resulted in the persecution of suspected dissidents on the home front. The scale of wartime sacrifice provoked a degree of resentment against those who had wanted the war and who had profited from it that proved impossible to repress. The paucity of the gains in return for the sacrifices provoked a countervailing belief that the country had been betrayed by the "enemy within" – imagined as "saboteurs" and "defeatists." These unsustainable contradictions meant that rather than being reinforced by participation in the war as the ruling elites had intended, the liberal-parliamentary system imploded, leading to Europe's first mass reactionary regime – fascism. The "totalitarian" temptation inherent in the war was in many respects common to all the combatant nations, but in Italy it found fertile ground that brought it to fruition.[6] This also makes the Italian case worthy of attention in a transnational, European perspective.

From Neutrality to Intervention

The first particularity of the Italian case concerns the timing and manner of intervention. Scholars tend to emphasize the precipitate character of the outbreak of war in 1914. Even though it had long been forecast and incorporated into the calculated risks of international power politics, the war still happened suddenly and seemed to result from a chain of unstoppable events rather than premeditated decisions. Whatever the truth of such a perception, it had the effect of reinforcing the defensive character of the war on all sides and underpinning the creation of governments of national unity. Not so in Italy. The absence of clear aggression against one of the member states (which was a condition of the activation of the Triple Alliance), not to mention the lack of prior consultation by Berlin and above all Vienna, showed once again how little Italy's allies trusted her. Added to this was Austria's reluctance to take seriously Italian requests for territorial compensation. All this gave Italy a legitimate pretext to stand aside as Europe slid into war in August 1914.[7]

Yet the resultant situation raised deep divisions in the Italian ruling class over whether or not the country should remain neutral. For nearly ten months it provoked a tense and at times violent debate in leading political, intellectual, and economic circles. The slow elaboration of the decision to intervene (including extended negotiations with both alliances over potential territorial gains) only aggravated the divisions and reinforced the cleavage between the political class, the state, and society. The fact that intervention was not forced on the country but decided by cold calculation removed all justification in terms of self-defense and cast a long shadow over the events that followed. It poisoned later debate over responsibility for a decision with such serious consequences and made it vital to reap enough benefit from the war to justify the sacrifices made in fighting it. The gap between expectations and outcome widened still further.

The positions for and against Italian intervention can be outlined as follows. The bulk of socialists were against the war, and their initial neutrality (*né aderire, né sabotare* – neither support nor sabotage) allowed them to stick to the pacifist tradition of international socialism without actively opposing patriotic sentiments. Also opposed to entry were the Catholics (from the hierarchy and clergy to ordinary lay opinion), as well as the liberals, led by the Piedmontese politician and recent prime minister, Giovanni Giolitti, who formed the parliamentary majority. Giolitti had been the undisputed leader of Italian parliamentary life in the first 15 years of the century, but he was temperamentally reluctant to make hard choices and so opted for a pragmatic approach to neutrality. Although these three currents rejected the war for very different reasons, they represented the bulk of the country as well as the majority in parliament. Strictly speaking, this should have been enough to guarantee Italian neutrality.

On the other side, however, were ranged a number of aggressive advocates of war who, although in a minority, were able to use their economic connections to influence public opinion. Some of them were stirred by a cultural radicalism that was fully in tune with the advanced tendencies of the time. Politically, the most significant were the nationalists, who drew on wider European currents of thought to which they gave an original twist (even for an Italian context) by insisting on themes such as the will to power, the rights of social elites, disdain for the leveling effects of modern democracy, and a consequent dismissal of parliamentarianism. Some nationalists wanted to intervene on the side of the Central Powers who, it was believed, would support Italian colonial aspirations at the cost of Anglo-French interests. Others urged the opposite course, since they considered Italian expansion in the Balkans incompatible with Austrian imperial interests. Those who backed entry on economic grounds were connected with heavy industry and hoped for an expansionary boom following a fairly long period of industrial stagnation in Italy. As elsewhere, intellectuals were attracted to the war by its promise of transformation. In the Italian case they included an array of charismatic figures and veritable myth-builders who unleashed an emotional energy on behalf of intervention. They ranged from Filippo Tommaso Marinetti, the founder of futurism and expounder of an aesthetic of modernity (which expected much from the dynamics of a technological war), to the poet Gabriele D'Annunzio, who proclaimed that existence consisted of endless challenges which made it the very opposite of humdrum mediocrity and who felt that the war would generate vital new energies.

Also prominent in the pro-war line-up were forces with a completely different ideological makeup, even if they were just as insistent that the opportunities offered by the conflict should be seized. First and foremost among them were the "democratic interventionists" and irredentists. They called for war against Austria-Hungary in order to complete the project of the Risorgimento by "liberating" (or "redeeming") the regions still held by Austria (and known collectively as Trento-Trieste), which by geography and partly by language were felt to belong to the Italian nation. This program went hand in glove with a belief that the democratic Entente powers, Britain and France, were arrayed against the reactionary Central Powers in the name of the freedom of European peoples and national self-determination. Also part of this current were some revolutionary syndicalists, headed by such figures as Filippo Corridoni and Alceste De Ambris, who had come to emphasize nation over class but who still saw the chaos generated by the conflict as an opportunity to overturn the balance of power and transform the world through violence.[8]

At the heart of the interventionist line-up, owing to its dominance of the print media, was the *Corriere della Sera*, the Milan newspaper directed by Luigi Albertini. As for the crown, Vittorio Emmanuele III was initially hesitant but soon became convinced that the war would consolidate the social elites, redefine his own bond with the nation, and counteract the growing influence of organized labor, which seemed to be undermining the cohesion of society. Equally in favor of intervention was the government, led by Giolitti's opponent, the Apulian lawyer Antonio Salandra. The Foreign Minister, Sidney Sonnino, was a one-time supporter of the Triple Alliance who had increasingly become convinced that war against Austria was inevitable.

A case all to itself was that of Benito Mussolini, an exponent of the revolutionary wing of the Socialist Party and chief editor of the party daily, *Avanti!*. In October 1914 Mussolini passed suddenly from a position of intransigent support of neutrality to even more strident interventionism. His choice, while partly opportunistic, was substantially determined by his conviction that the war was an event of such magnitude that whoever remained outside it would be irremediably cut off from the course of history. This was the first step along the path toward his becoming the leader of the extreme right and postwar dictator. During the war he was both a soldier and journalist and remained a prominent agitator for the interventionist cause.[9]

The government policy of intervention, endorsed by the royal house, led to the signing on April 26, 1915 of a secret agreement between Italy and the Entente powers. The so-called Pact of London committed Italy to join the war within a month and, in the event of an allied victory, promised a series of territorial compensations in which irredentist aspirations to complete the Risorgimento in the name of national self-determination vied incongruously with expansionist ambitions. Thus despite the mood of the vast majority of the population, Italian intervention seemed a foregone conclusion by the spring of 1915. Manifestations of anti-war sentiment both in the nation at large and also by members of the majority outside the forum of parliament provoked a grave political crisis in which the major institutions of state – crown and government on one side, parliament on the other – were at odds with each other. Violent interventionist demonstrations took place throughout Italy in May 1915, a month that went down in patriotic and nationalist history as "Radiant May."

Much of this might seem a re-run of the febrile "August days" elsewhere in Europe 10 months earlier. Yet there was one significant difference. The fact that interventionism in Italy was a minority current meant that the Italian *Union sacrée* lacked the foundation of a defensive patriotism. Interventionism was in many respects the covert version of a coercive project that aimed to overturn the existing order as the condition for forging a "greater Italy." Under pressure from the interventionist street demonstrations, the King, rather than following the constitutionally proper course of accepting Salandra's resignation once the latter had lost his majority, reconfirmed him as prime minister and thus allowed his own will to prevail over that of the legislature. Parliament subsequently yielded to the *fait accompli*, voting extraordinary powers to the government in the sitting of May 20–21, 1915. It is a moot question whether Italian intervention was the result of a virtual *coup d'état*, as those favoring neutrality maintained. Formal legality was in fact observed, but the manner in which intervention was brought about marked a major defeat for the parliamentary system and was proof of its fragility.

The Military Effort

Prepared only slowly and still incomplete when war was declared, mobilization plans were not finalized until the end of July 1915. But when applied, they enabled Italy to field a mass army. As shown in chapter 6 above, one and a half million soldiers and 31,000 officers were mobilized initially (of whom a million were at the front), rising to a peak of two million men at the front in late 1917–18. Despite inadequacies of command and moments of severe crisis, such as Caporetto, the Italian army withstood the test of a punishing war and sustained casualty rates that were fully the equivalent of the other major armies. While dissent was present, and on occasions took the form of refusal and even isolated cases of rebellion, this was not so different to what occurred in other armies faced with the prolonged warfare of attrition. Rather, it was for the lack of trust by the ruling class and officer corps in the loyalty and patriotism of the ordinary soldier that the Italian case stood out. One consequence was a harsh and indiscriminate system of military discipline. Another was the lack of consideration shown to the 600,000 Italian prisoners of war, who were largely abandoned to their fate by an unsympathetic high command and government, with 100,000 of them dying in captivity.[10] We shall return to the consequences of this attitude for the home front below.

As in other states, the military effort was only one aspect of mobilization for a war that appeared to many contemporaries to be increasingly "total" in the way it applied to society and the economy. On the financial and industrial level, Italy mounted a significant effort that, all things considered, was sufficient to meet its requirements. Here, too, however, mobilization accentuated social inequalities and tensions. The overall cost of the war has been calculated at some 40 million lire (1913–14 value), whereas annual state expenditure on the eve of the war amounted to 2.5 million lire. This means that the three and a half years of war cost 16 normal peacetime budgets. This exorbitant cost was offset by the emission of government loans (backed by intense publicity drives), which proved effective in tapping into private savings, and by the printing of banknotes.[11] This last measure, however, reduced the value of the currency, increased the cost of living, and lowered the buying power of fixed incomes, and thus contributed to the social upheavals that marked the last part of the war and the postwar period.

As in almost all belligerent countries, the coordination of the industrial mobilization was entrusted to one central organism – the Committee for Industrial Mobilization. This supervised the distribution of resources, beginning with raw materials and manpower, and gave priority to the army.[12] The Committee was answerable to the Under-Secretariat for Arms and Munitions that was set up in 1915 and which in 1917 became a full ministry. As a consequence of the war, the entire state apparatus was reinforced and modernized. Public servants grew from about 340,000 in 1915 to approximately 530,000 in 1921. The staff of the Committee for Industrial Mobilization alone reached almost 5,700 between military and civilians, with almost 2,000 industrial firms under its control employing about a million workers.[13] Despite its inadequate industrial base (in 1914 Italy produced less than one million tons of steel in comparison to 17.6 million in Germany, 7.8 million in Britain, 4.8 in Russia, and 4.6 in France), the country achieved a remarkable increase in its war-related productive capacity, though this was also thanks to Allied support in the form of loans and raw materials. It has been estimated that in the course of the war Italian industry produced over 16,000 pieces of artillery (compared to 21,000 for Great Britain), some 37,000 machine guns (against 240,000 for Britain), and over three million rifles (four million for Britain).[14] The companies involved in this sector, such as FIAT in Turin and Ansaldo in Genoa, saw staggering increases in their capital value, employees, and volume of production.

Propaganda and the Organization of Consent

As the country rallied its energies behind the national effort, the polemics that had dogged the run-up to war seemed to abate. The socialists, who had been among the most fervent defenders of neutrality, adopted a position of cautious patriotic and civil solidarity in an unconvincing attempt to protect both flanks – as committed pacifists and as members of a nation facing the most difficult test of its history.[15] As for the Catholics, having made every effort to avoid the war, including diplomatic initiatives, and having deplored in advance the likelihood that it would further de-Christianize the world, they adopted their habitual rule of obedience toward the constituted secular authority. For this reason, they remained silent about their sympathies for Austria-Hungary as the bulwark of traditionalist Catholicism and allowed an open display of the patriotic and nationalistic sentiments that were present in their own ranks. Catholic patriotic ardor portended an imminent reconciliation between the Church and the Italian state, a reconciliation that was personified in such fiery preachers as the Genoese Father Giovanni Semeria or in clerics involved in the study of behavioral psychology, such as Father Agostino Gemelli, who would go on to found the Catholic University of Milan.[16]

Conflict also seemed to have declined within the political elites. Although the narrowly-based Salandra cabinet faced a crisis in 1916 provoked by the relative success of the Austrian *Strafexpedition* (see chapter 6), this was resolved by the cautious broadening of the base for a new ministry that was presided over by an old-style liberal, Paolo Boselli, but included a Catholic, Filippo Meda, as Minister of Finance, and a group of reformist socialists whose nationalism had long since distanced them from the Socialist Party. Foremost among the latter was Leonida Bissolati, minister without portfolio for government relations with the Supreme Command.[17] Yet in reality, the country was anything but pacified, and tensions which for the moment remained latent were destined to explode once again as the war revealed the degree of sacrifice and mourning that it brought in its train. The conflict between interventionists and non-interventionists had not been overcome but would remain at the core of Italian politics.

Even though the Italian political system was characterized by an oligarchic political class with a decidedly narrow base, this had begun to be undermined by the concession of universal male suffrage following the Libyan war (1912). Moreover, efforts were also made in Italy to mobilize public opinion and forge patriotic solidarity using modern means of mass communication and the organization of consent. True, historians have noted that owing to the belief of General Cadorna, the commander-in-chief, that the only thing required of soldiers was their obedience, the Italian army was slow to organize effective propaganda among the troops (see chapter 6). But a number of initiatives were undertaken on the home front during the war not only by state bodies but also by private concerns stimulated by the sudden and un-hoped for opening of a market for products of mass communication and for the "consumption of emotions." Typical in this regard was the picture postcard, which was an efficient form of mass communication that helped shape the popular imagination of wartime by supplying a set of common readings of the conflict. With couples and families separated *en masse*, the production and consumption of this item increased significantly. Some publishers were long-time specialists in the genre but others produced postcards for the first time. Numerous illustrators who had learnt their trade in children's literature jumped on the bandwagon while others (often young and not infrequently women) seized the chance to try out their skills and display their patriotism.[18]

Equally significant were wall posters, whose use during the war marked a change in the urban landscape. In streets and squares, walls became a medium of intense social communication that sought to incorporate all Italians in the national effort, including the illiterate and those not used to reading newspapers. The campaigns for war loans were particularly important. From 1916 onwards, they were entrusted to talented illustrators who it was hoped could manufacture messages with real emotional impact, combining material self-interest with noble patriotic ideals. One of the best known war-loan posters is that by Achille Mauzan, a French artist who lived in Italy, in which a soldier leaping out of the trenches points his finger at the onlooker to ask him or her to subscribe. The poster appeared in various forms in 1917 – from giant billboards to postcards – and symbolized the Italian war effort. The soldier's intense gaze and stark gesture aimed to create a personal response to the moral imperative that bound the home front to the fighting front. In fact, it was based on a tried and trusted icon that the British artist, Alfred Leete, had first used in his famous poster of Lord Kitchener (1915), and which mutated into Uncle Sam in the USA and in Germany into the steel-helmeted soldier with his metallic stare – though its more distant origin lay in the world of prewar advertising.[19] All this shows how the modernity of the market, propaganda, and politics overlapped and reinforced each other. It also suggests that despite being relatively underdeveloped and lacking a strong democratic tradition, Italy shared in the wider process that accentuated the internal uniformity of national communities.

With the imagination thus mobilized (a process, it should be noted, that included children), Italians, like other belligerent peoples, waged what one patriotic publication called "a war without blood," that is to say, a war that mobilized consciences, emotions, feelings, and everyday activities.[20] As the same book noted, this meant that articles of daily consumption, such as toothpaste or toys, should not be produced by the foe. Nothing said or done, or even thought or dreamed of, should have anything to do with the enemy or aid him in any way. This provides the clearest definition of what was entailed by the "total war" that took shape in Italy as elsewhere in Europe. However, caution needs to be employed when adopting such terminology. The public discourse of patriotic nationalism and the variety of means used to promote it certainly suggest new tendencies in political communications and in the life of society, but they do not prove that "total war" was fought with "totalitarian" efficiency. The message of the wartime mobilization was most effective among the urban middle classes.[21] Workers and peasants remained resistant to the notions it transmitted and were more extraneous to the whole process. Indeed, increases in the cost of living, the intensification of work in the factories and difficulties in procuring food increased social tensions during the war, though these never seriously endangered domestic peace.[22] The most serious episode of unrest was the popular uprising in Turin in August 1917, which was occasioned by bread shortages and which was repressed by the army with 60 lives lost (about 50 protesters and 10 law-enforcement agents).[23]

This explains why large parts of the country – not only military strong points but also industrial areas and eventually the whole of northern Italy – were progressively declared to be "war zones" under a significant degree of military control.[24] Civil liberties were restricted and many offences normally dealt with by civil magistrates came under military law. Suspicion attached not just to those who overtly dissented from the war but also to those who seemed lukewarm in their adherence to the patriotic cause. Denunciations were frequent and more than 60,000 civilians were convicted by military tribunals, many of them to penal sentences. Censorship and repression were as important as the organization of consent in the prosecution of the war. This was especially true in a country like Italy that had been so resistant to the prospect of the war and where the unity brought by intervention, outside state institutions and the political elites, was a matter of appearance rather than popular conviction.

Caporetto and the "Enemy within"

The contradictions that were latent in the Italian war effort exploded in the autumn of 1917 with the defeat at Caporetto.[25] Starting on October 24, an Austro-German offensive transformed the character of the war from attrition to movement in the space of a week. The enemy advance forced the Italian army into a major retreat that resulted in the capture of half the total Italian prisoners of war for the entire conflict and led to a flood of refugees out of the extensive and agriculturally wealthy region of Friuli and part of the Veneto plain, which were now occupied by the invader.[26] The emotion and controversy once surrounding this event are long since gone, and historians now agree that in military terms the rout was due to the nature of the attack itself and to serious errors in the organization of the Italian defense. However, we are more concerned here with the consequences of the defeat, which sent a shock wave through Italian society. For the sudden collapse, the disordered withdrawal and occasional signs of rebellion (in the form of mutinies that seemed to some inspired by events in Russia) all combined to unleash a wave of recrimination. As noted in chapter 6, General Cadorna's initial reaction was to use official communiqués to accuse his men of cowardice and voluntary surrender.

His bulletins were censored by the government precisely because of their inappropriate and counterproductive character, but they nonetheless indicated the desire to find a scapegoat for the collapse in terms of an alleged lack of patriotism and fighting spirit on the part of the ordinary soldiers.

Paradoxically, the invasion of a sizeable area of Italian territory and the threat of total defeat gave the war for the first time the defensive character that it had lacked up till then, and made sense of a renewal of the national effort. Yet enraged and fanatical sectors of the "war party" interpreted the defeat not just as the product of weaknesses that needed to be overcome but also as part of a betrayal by "defeatists" – a veritable "stab in the back." Despite appearances, it was held, "defeatists" remained at heart opposed to the war and hence to Italy's redemption and greatness, thus justifying their elimination or marginalization. The notion of the "enemy within" had already surfaced during the debate over intervention but now it emerged in a far more concrete and dramatic form. What had earlier been mainly verbal accusation was now a prominent feature of public life. Simply to hope for peace, whether as a socialist or Catholic (including the Pope, who in August 1917 referred to the war as a "useless massacre"), was to risk being attacked as a traitor and instigator of revolt. The authoritarian temptation to outlaw opposition became ever stronger and more explicit. The remobilization of the home front after Caporetto saw the formation of committees of civil mobilization. Significantly, their work combined a common commitment to the defense of the threatened homeland with a campaign against the "traitors" hidden in civil society, who were to be denounced, monitored and punished. Even moderate opinion believed that all means justified the supreme goal of national defense and renewal, even if it meant riding roughshod over the norms of constitutional liberalism. As the Minister of Colonies, Ferdinando Martini, had noted in his diary the year before: "In Italy, war and [rule by] parliament are ... irreconcilable terms."[27]

Victory and the Postwar Crisis

While everything at the end of 1917 pointed to the worst (including the exit of Bolshevik Russia from the war, which took enormous pressure off the Central Powers), Caporetto was in fact not the beginning of the end for Italy. A series of measures shored up the situation, including the replacement of Cadorna as commander-in-chief by the more prudent and temperate Armando Diaz, the restructuring of the Supreme Command and the army as a whole, a greater commitment to the organization of consent among the soldiers, increased concern for the needs of the men and, finally, a strong campaign to rally opinion within the country as well as the army. All this helped consolidate the new front established on the Piave River. The degree to which things had changed was seen in June 1918, when the Austrians unleashed their final offensive and once again, during Italy's victorious counteroffensive in what has come to be known as the Battle of Vittorio Veneto in late October–early November 1918 (see chapter 6). This ended with the Armistice of November 4 and the complete surrender of the Austro-Hungarian army. To be sure, much of the final success was due to the disarray of the enemy (see chapter 5). Nonetheless, General Diaz could be forgiven for exaggerating the scale of the Italian triumph in his celebrated victory communiqué of November 4. For apart from certain military episodes during Unification, Vittorio Veneto would remain the only authentic victory of any significance in the entire national history of Italy. Its symbolic and psychological significance was consequently greater than its strictly military import. If the fears, contradictions, and internal divisions that beset wartime Italy culminated at Caporetto, Vittorio Veneto was the opposite, for it fed the illusions held by the "war party" about the rewards due to Italy for its part in the allied victory.

Such misapprehensions would soon clash with the reality of the negotiations taking place in Paris over the peace treaties. Crushed by the dominant interests of the British and French delegations, and further hindered by Woodrow Wilson's hostility to anything smacking of "imperialism," Italy obtained Trento and Trieste but had most of its other claims ignored.[28] These included the expansion of its eastern frontiers and its claims to Dalmatian territories and the Adriatic city of Fiume. The latter had not in fact been mentioned in the Pact of London but had long been a symbolically important objective for nationalists. All this generated a sense of frustration summarized by the slogan of the "mutilated victory." Frustration radicalized internal tensions even further and once more led to those who had opposed intervention being pilloried and accused of dishonoring the war dead by their pacifism. Successive Italian governments were condemned for not having been able to win the appropriate price for the enormous cost of the war.

On the left, the political forces with a mass popular base, especially the socialists and the Catholic democrats organized in the new Popular Party, were too divided to form a common democratic front, despite winning an overall majority in the November 1919 general election. Instead, worsening living conditions that were in large part due to the war fed growing dissent, and prompted a bitter industrial conflict in fall 1920 that led to a widespread employer lockout of engineering workers and a consequent wave of factory occupations.[29] The Socialist Party and the trade union movement were deeply split between reformist and revolutionary programs, and in a climate of international extremism the traditional liberals (led by Giolitti) found it impossible to reconstitute the old constitutional project on the new basis of mass electoral politics. Amid rising fear of revolution on the part of the middle classes, especially in central and northern Italy, the field was left wide open to subversion of a new kind, directly inspired by the war, and the liberal system plunged into crisis.

The issue of Fiume, which symbolized nationalist humiliation at the outcome of the war, provided the initial focus for the authoritarian solution to the crisis. In September 1919 D'Annunzio occupied the city illegally with a motley band of mutinous soldiers and nationalist volunteers and ruled it with a provisional government for more than a year.[30] The Fiume affair echoed the direct democracy and improvised revolutionary action that marked the immediate postwar period elsewhere in Europe, and indeed was conducted as something of an experiment in a new-style "corporatist" government that would later exert some influence on fascism. But in the last analysis, it glorified armed action and underlined the fragility of the liberal state. In an extreme nationalist form, it illustrated a broader lesson taught by the war and its prolongation – that when vital questions such as the survival and greatness of the nation were at stake, force was more important than legality, authoritarian power worked, and the end justified the means.

The way the crisis came to a head brings us back to the issues with which we began, namely the weak national identity and sense of citizenship in Italy before the war, both of which the conflict highlighted. The war undoubtedly changed something. Never before had so many inhabitants from every region been involved in such a dramatic national undertaking, whether by coercion or choice. If national identity is forged by a shared sense of achievement and suffering, Italians achieved and suffered more during World War I than in any previous episode in their history. The lists of the fallen that soon appeared in every town and village with the biggest campaign of monument building ever undertaken in the country showed that nearly everyone had participated and paid a price.[31] The cemeteries and battlefield memorials that soon adorned the former front made the same point.[32]

Furthermore, the scale of the social and cultural upheaval brought about by the war had also made the Italians more similar to each other and closer to other Europeans. Southern peasants, many of whom had never set foot in the north (though they may well have spent time in America), found themselves for the first time in the Alps of the Trentino. Soldiers from remote mountain regions marveled at technology and industrial organization in the shape of the artillery, military engineering works, artificial limbs for the mutilated, and the military applications of electricity. Shell-bursts and stabbing searchlights turned night into day and nature into artifice. As soldiers, ordinary Italians became familiar with the gramophone and the cinema.[33] Before the war they had lived in local communities where the spoken word prevailed, but wartime separation meant they had to write in order to maintain precious contact with home. Today, their letters are an enormous and remarkable testimony to their collective experience. Having left for the front as semiliterates, they had learnt to read newspapers and communiqués that contained vital information for their survival – on exemptions from service or home leave. Where previously they had spoken only their local dialect, now they constructed a common language in order to be understood, which linguists have called "popular Italian."[34] In short, the population as a whole had undergone a process of forced Italianization that was destined to leave a lasting imprint, if only because it was the product of a quite exceptional emotional experience that left a deep legacy of mourning.

But none of this was sufficient to modify the fundamental features of the Italian case. The breadth of the mobilization process and the depth of the anthropological and cultural transformations produced by the war did not increase national cohesion, nor did they heal the divisions that the conflict had in fact deepened. Postwar tensions confirmed that the decision to intervene in the war against majority opinion had truly been a gamble – less for the military and economic challenge, which the nation had met, than in terms of its civil and political institutions, whose solidity had been found sadly wanting. This is why the "totalitarianism" toward which the war beckoned and the brutalization that it unleashed could not be contained and reabsorbed once the conflict was over, but fed into the crisis of the liberal state. The Italian case was unlike that of Germany, which was traumatized by a defeat that remained inexplicable to many Germans, or that of Russia, whose exit from the war destroyed the old regime and produced a new dictatorship before the conflict was over. Italy had emerged victorious from the war. Yet what amounted to a covert civil war destroyed the fragile framework of the existing regime and transformed both state and society as dramatically as in the German and Russian cases. The proof lay in the surprising ease with which the fascist movement emerged in 1919 in response to the difficulties of liberalism and the polarization of social conflict, and quickly supplied a solution to both.

Weapons were easily available to men who had fought in the war and who, having acquired a taste for adventure and even command, were ready to use them. A cult of violence fascinated an envious younger generation that had been too young for military service but was now more than ready to follow its elders. The symbols, language, and political practices of the paramilitary forces that characterized fascism, and which became particularly virulent in 1921–2, owed much to the experience and culture of the war.[35] For example, the *squadristi* (or squad members), as they became known, appropriated the dagger and death's-head symbol of the Arditi, the special assault corps formed in

1917, which went into action after Caporetto (see chapter 6). The same was true of the warlike slogans, aggressive youth cult, and constant references to manliness and death that were also the hallmarks of the fascist paramilitaries. Fascists saw the struggle against the "enemies of the nation" as a direct extension of World War I. Routine violence, from the bodily humiliation of opponents with castor oil to political murder, marked Mussolini's path to power. In October 1922, the attacks of the *squadristi* culminated in the March on Rome, a sort of insurrection following which the king charged Mussolini with forming a new government incorporating the older forces of liberal Italy. In the summer of 1924 came the last open denunciation of fascist violence and illegality in parliament, by the reformist socialist, Giacomo Matteotti, who paid with his life and the desecration of his body. The ease with which Mussolini rode out the ensuing wave of indignation provided him with further proof of his own strength, or rather the weakness of his opponents. On January 3, 1925 he announced the inauguration of the dictatorship and moved rapidly to the construction of the regime that silenced all opposition definitively. Only then, perhaps, was World War I finally over – though preparations for new wars were already under way.

Notes

1   For the relationship between the Italian case and the European context, see the Italian edition of Stéphane Audoin-Rouzeau and Jean-Jacques Becker (eds.), *Encyclopédie de la Grande Guerre, 1914–1918*, Paris, Bayard, 2004, published as *La Prima Guerra Mondiale*, ed. Antonio Gibelli, Turin, Einaudi, 2007, and in particular Antonio Gibelli, "Introduzione all'edizione italiana. Storia transnazionale della Grande Guerra e caso italiano," pp. xvii–xxv.

2   Mark Cornwall, *The Undermining of Austria-Hungary: the Battle for Hearts and Minds*, Basingstoke, Macmillan, 2000, pp. 320–404.

3   Gioacchino Volpe, *History of the Fascist Movement*, 1927; trans. from the Italian, Rome, Soc. An. Poligrafica Italiana, n.d. but 1934, pp. 154–9.

4   Richard J. Bosworth, *Mussolini*, London, Arnold, 2002, p. 170.

5   Corner and Procacci, "The Italian Experience of 'Total' Mobilization." For recent surveys, see Gibelli, *Grande Guerra degli italiani*, and Isnenghi and Rochat, *La Grande Guerra*.

6   Angelo Ventrone, *La Seduzione totalitaria. Guerra, modernità, violenza politica (1914–1918)*, Rome, Donzelli, 2003.

7   Rusconi, *L'azzardo del 1915*, pp. 17–21; Bosworth, *Italy*, pp. 377–417.

8   Pieri, *L'Italia nella prima guerra mondiale*, pp. 48–62; Isnenghi, *Mito della Grande Guerra*, pp. 77–178; Renzi, *Shadow of the Sword*; Gibelli, *Grande Guerra degli italiani*, pp. 15–80.

9   De Felice, *Mussolini*, pp. 221–418; O'Brien, *Mussolini in the First World War*.

10 Procacci, *Soldati e prigioneri*.

11 Galassi and Harrison, "Italy at War," pp. 295–8.

12 Ibid., pp. 283–7; Tomassini, *Lavoro e guerra*.

13 Isnenghi and Rochat, *Grande Guerra*, pp. 292–3.

14 Ibid., p. 299 (Italian figures); Gerd Hardach, *The First World War, 1914–1918*, 1973; trans. from the German, London, Allen Lane, 1977, p. 87 (British figures); also Galassi and Harrison, "Italy at War," pp. 293–5.

15 Gaetano Arfé, *Storia del socialismo italiano, 1892–1926*, Turin, Einaudi, 1965, pp. 212–23; Vigezzi, "Italian Socialism and the First World War."

16 For the most recent synthesis on this theme, see C. Stiaccini, "La Chiesa, l'Italia e la guerra," in Gibelli (ed.), *La Prima Guerra Mondiale*, pp. 125–35.

17 Pieri, *L'Italia nella prima guerra mondiale*, pp. 98–110; Melograni, *Storia politica*, pp. 184–96.

18   Gibelli, *Popolo bambino*, pp. 118–33.
19   Gibelli, *Nefaste meraviglie*, pp. 358–62.
20   Mario Calò, *Guerra senza sangue*, Florence, Bemporad, 1915. See also Gibelli, *Popolo bambino*, pp. 1–176; Andrea Fava, "War, National Education and the Italian Primary School, 1915–1918," in John Horne (ed.), *State, Society and Mobilization in Europe during the First World War*, Cambridge, Cambridge University Press, pp. 53–69.
21   Gibelli, *Grande Guerra degli italiani*, pp. 308–13.
22   Procacci, *Dalla Rassegnazione alla rivolta*, pp. 43–145.
23   Paolo Spriano, *Torino operaia nella grande guerra (1914–1918)*, Turin, Einaudi, 1960, pp. 235–54.
24   Procacci, *Dalla Rassegnazione alla rivolta*, pp. 153–64.
25   Labanca, *Caporetto*.
26   Ceschin, *Esuli di Caporetto*; Gibelli, *Grande Guerra degli italiani*, pp. 282–302.
27   Ferdinando Martini, *Diario 1914–1918*, Milan, Mondadori, 1966, p. 819.
28   For the particular significance of Wilson for Italy, see Daniela Rossini, *Woodrow Wilson and the American Myth in Italy. Culture, Diplomacy and War Propaganda*, 2000; trans. from the Italian, Cambridge, MA, Harvard University Press, 2008.
29   Paolo Spriano, *The Occupation of the Factories: Italy, 1920*, 1964; trans. from the Italian, London, Pluto Press, 1975.
30   John Woodhouse, *Gabriele D'Annunzio: Defiant Archangel*, Oxford, Clarendon Press, 1998.
31   Renato Monteleone and Pino Sarasini, "I Monumenti italiani ai caduti della grande guerra," in Leoni and Zadra (eds.), *La Grande Guerra. Esperienza, memoria, immagini*, pp. 631–2.
32   Livio Vanzetto, "Monte Grappa," in Mario Isnenghi (ed.), *I Luoghi della memoria. Simboli e miti dell'Italia unita*, Bari and Rome, Laterza, 1996, new ed., 1998, pp. 361–74, and Patrizia Dogliani, "Redipuglia," in ibid., pp. 377–89. On the commemoration of the fallen soldiers the most recent contributions are in Janz and Klinkhammer (eds.), *La Morte per la patria* (in particular Bruno Tobia, "Monumenti ai caduti. Dall'Italia liberale all'Italia fascista," pp. 45–62, and Oliver Janz, "Lutto, famiglia e nazione nel culto dei caduti della prima guerra mondiale in Italia," pp. 63–79).
33   Gibelli, *L'Officina della guerra*, pp. 164–83.
34   Ibid., pp. 211–18; Gibelli, *Grande Guerra degli italiani*, pp. 136–61; Caffarena, *Lettere della Grande Guerra*.
35   Gentile, *Origins of Fascist Ideology*, pp. 39–103.

References and Further Reading

Audoin-Rouzeau, Stéphane, and Becker, Jean-Jacques (eds.), *Encyclopédie de la Grande Guerre 1914–1918*, Paris, Bayard, 2004; Italian edition ed. Antonio Gibelli, *La Prima Guerra mondiale*, Turin, Einaudi, 2007.

Bianchi, Bruna, *Crescere in tempo di guerra. Il lavoro e la protesta dei ragazzi in Italia, 1915–1918*, Venice, Cafoscarina, 1995.

Bosworth, Richard, *Italy, the Least of the Great Powers. Italian Foreign Policy before the First World War*, Cambridge, Cambridge University Press, 1979.

Caffarena, Fabio, *Lettere della Grande Guerra. Scritture del quotidiano, monumenti della memoria, fonti per la storia. Il caso italiano*, Milan, Unicopli, 2005.

Ceschin, Daniele, *Gli Esuli di Caporetto. I profughi in Italia durante la Grande Guerra*, Bari, Laterza, 2006.

Corner, Paul, and Procacci, Giovanna, "The Italian Experience of 'Total' Mobilization, 1915–1920," in John Horne (ed.), *State, Society and Mobilization in Europe during the First World War*, Cambridge, Cambridge University Press, 1997, pp. 223–40.

Curli, Barbara, *Italiane e lavoro, 1914–1920*, Venice, Marsilio, 1998.

De Felice, Renzo, *Mussolini il rivoluzionario 1883–1920*, Turin, Einaudi, 1965.

Dentoni, Maria, *Annona e consenso in Italia, 1914–1919*, Milan, Franco Angeli, 1995.

Ermacora, Matteo, *Cantieri di guerra. Il lavoro dei civili nelle retrovie del fronte italiano (1915–1918)*, Bologna, Il Mulino, 2005.

Fiori, Antonio, *Il Filtro deformante. La censura sulla stampa durante la prima guerra mondiale*, Rome, Istituto per l'Età Moderna e Contemporanea, 2001.

Forsyth, Douglas J., *The Crisis of Liberal Italy. Monetary and Financial Policy, 1914–1922*, Cambridge, Cambridge University Press, 1993.

Galassi, Francesco, and Harrison, Mark, "Italy at War, 1915–1918," in Stephen Broadberry and Mark Harrison (eds.), *The Economics of World War I*, Cambridge, Cambridge University Press, 2005, pp. 276–309.

Gentile, Emilio, *The Origins of Fascist Ideology, 1918–1925*, 1996; trans. from Italian, New York, Enigma, 2005.

Gibelli, Antonio, *La Grande Guerra degli italiani 1915–1918*, Milan, Sansoni, 1998; new ed., Milan, BUR, 2007.

Gibelli, Antonio, *L'Officina della guerra. La grande guerra e le transformazioni del mondo mentale*, Turin, Bollati-Boringhieri, 1991, new ed. 2007.

Gibelli, Antonio, *Il Popolo bambino. Infanzia e nazione dalla Grande Guerra a Salò*, Turin, Einaudi, 2005.

Gibelli, Antonio, "Nefaste meraviglie. Grande guerra e apoteosi della modernità," in Barberis, Walter (ed.), *Storia d'Italia. Annali 18. Pace e guerra*, Turin, Einaudi, 2002.

Isnenghi, Mario, *Il Mito della grande Guerra*, 1970, new ed., Bologna, Il Mulino, 2007.

Isnenghi, Mario, and Rochat, Giorgio, *La Grande guerra. 1914–1918*, Milan, La Nuova Italia, 2000.

Janz, Oliver, and Klinkhammer, Lutz (eds.), *La Morte per la patria*, Rome, Donzelli, 2008.

Labanca, Nicola, *Caporetto. Storia di una disfatta*, Florence, Giunti, 1997.

Leoni, Diego, and Zadra, Camillo (eds.), *La Grande Guerra. Esperienza, memoria, immagini*, Bologna, Il Mulino, 1986.

Melograni, Piero, *Storia politica della grande guerra, 1915–1918*, Bari, Laterza, 1969; new ed., 1972.

Mortara, Giorgio, *La Salute pubblica in Italia durante e dopo la guerra*, Bari, Laterza, 1925.

O'Brien, Paul, *Mussolini in the First World War: The Journalist, the Soldier, the Fascist*, Oxford and Providence, RI, Berg, 2005.

Ortaggi, Simonetta, "Italian Women during the Great War," in Gail Braybon (ed.), *Evidence, History and the Great War. Historians and the Impact of 1914–1918*, New York and Oxford, Berghahn, 2003, pp. 216–38.

Pieri, Piero, *L'Italia nella prima guerra mondiale*, Turin, Einaudi, 1965.

Procacci, Giovanna (ed.), *Stato e classe operaia in Italia durante la prima guerra mondiale*, Milan, Franco Angeli, 1983.

Procacci, Giovanna, "Popular Protest and Labour Conflict in Italy, 1915–1918," *Social History*, 14/1, 1989, pp. 31–58.

Procacci, Giovanna, "State Coercion and Worker Solidarity in Italy (1915–1919): the Moral and Political Content of Social Unrest," in Leopold Haimson and Giulio Sapelli (eds.), *Strikes, Social Conflict and the First World War*, Annali della Fondazione Giangiacomo Feltrinelli, 1991, pp. 145–77.

Procacci, Giovanna, *Dalla rassegnazione alla rivolta. Mentalità e comportamenti popolari nella Grande Guerra*, Rome, Bulzoni Editore, 1999.

Procacci, Giovanna, *Soldati e prigionieri italiani nella grande guerra*, Rome, Editori Riuniti, 1993; new ed., Turin, Bollati Boringhieri, 2000.

Renzi, William A., *In the Shadow of the Sword. Italy's Neutrality and Entry into the Great War, 1914–1915*, New York, Bern, Frankfurt, Paris, Peter Lang, 1987.

Rusconi, Gian Enrico, *L'Azzardo del 1915*, Bologna, Il Mulino, 2005.

Serpieri, Arrigo, *La Guerra e le classi rurali italiane*, Bari, Laterza, 1930.

Tomassini, Luigi, "Industrial Mobilization and the Labour Market in Italy during the First World War," *Social History*, 16/1, 1991, pp. 59–87.

Tomassini, Luigi, *Lavoro e guerra. La mobilitazione industriale italiana 1915–1918*, Naples, Edizioni scientifiche italiane, 1997.

Tranfaglia, Nicola, *La Prima guerra mondiale e il fascismo*, Turin, Utet, 1995.

Vigezzi, Brunello, "Italian Socialism and the First World War: Mussolini, Lazzari and Turati," *Journal of Italian History*, 2/2, 1979, pp. 232–57.

Vivarelli, Roberto, *Storia delle origini del fascismo. L'Italia dalla grande guerra alla marcia su Roma*, Bologna, Il Mulino, 1991.

CHAPTER THIRTY-TWO

Russia

ERIC LOHR

The experience of total war changes the meanings and practices of the nation, both during the war and in the acts of memory that follow. The search to understand this complex and multilayered process has been a rich theme in most national histories of World War I. Until very recently, Russia was a marked exception.

World War I and Russian Memory

For over seven decades after World War I, Soviet and Western historiography – when it dealt with the war at all – focused on its relationship to the great revolutionary watershed of 1917. Perhaps because the Soviet Union was able to reconstitute most of the prewar imperial territory into a renewed state and empire, and because the Russian nation remained ambiguously subsumed within this larger entity for the 70 years that followed, there was not the same impetus to delve more deeply into the state–nation–empire nexus that inescapably drove analyses of the Habsburg and Ottoman wartime experiences. Likewise, the powerful links between commemoration and contested meanings of the nation and the war in France, Germany, and Britain simply did not exist for Russia. In 1994, a meeting of the newly formed Association of Scholars of World War I at the Russian Academy of Sciences discussed a study by one of its members that found only one small monument to the war in all of Russia – and this was in a small town far from Moscow. The handful of monuments constructed during World War I had already been destroyed by the end of the 1920s.[1]

Official censure of the commemoration of World War I began during the civil war, when such acts came to be associated with the White opposition to the Bolsheviks. The restrictions on commemoration eased slightly in the late 1930s and during World War II, a time when propaganda rehabilitated Russian military heroes from the Russian past. However, other than General Brusilov – the hero of the 1916 offensive who later served the Bolsheviks in the civil war – the regime found it difficult to find themes or heroes it could support. World War II provided an unambiguous, completely Soviet national war upon which the regime could build its new legitimating myth.[2] It is likely that further research will reveal that officially sanctioned civil war and World War II veterans' associations quietly supported limited acts of memory of World War I.[3] But on the whole World War I remained deep in the shadows of the two great defining moments of Soviet history: the civil war and the Great Fatherland War.

In sharp contrast, the war was explicitly and extensively commemorated by communities of Russian émigrés abroad. Veterans' associations were central to this world, and they organized commemorations, provided material aid to members, and in a particularly active organization in San Francisco, even established a library and published a journal.[4] Remembering the war was especially important for those who hoped to return once Bolshevism fell.

Former officers and civilian officials contributed sources and studies of the war, the most important being several superb monographs published by the Carnegie Endowment project on the social and economic history of the war in the late 1920s and early 1930s. The Hoover Institution at Stanford University and the Bakhmetieff Archive at Columbia University, New York, gathered extensive materials on the war. These materials provided the source base for Alexander Solzhenitsyn's massive and underrated literary-historical exploration of the conflict. The hero of his story is the Russian nation and the common people whose lives were wasted by incompetent generals and politicians.[5] But Solzhenitsyn's two war volumes have not received the attention of his other writings, and have spurred little historical or public debate.

In general, the level of interest, commemoration, and discussion of the war in Russia remains far below the remarkably persistent interest elsewhere. In fact, the yearly festivities at the Russian cemetery in Saint-Hilaire-le-Grand near Mourmelo, France, to commemorate the two Russian divisions that fought on French soil in 1916–18, remain bigger than any commemorative events in Russia.[6] Public opinion polls show little awareness of World War I in contemporary Russia.[7] There are few if any battlefield markers, and since the breakup of the Soviet Union, most battle sites have ended up in foreign countries. As a result, scholarship on the war has evolved with less connection to public debates and concerns, and perhaps thus with less attention to national questions than in many other countries.

However, there are strong signs that this is changing. Since the fall of communism, there has been a renewed academic interest in the war, and to a degree it has come into the broader public consciousness as well. The glossy large-circulation journal *Rodina* regularly publishes articles and photographs from World War I and served as an important conduit between scholars conducting fresh work in newly available archival collections and the broader public throughout the 1990s. This nationalistic journal also exemplifies the powerful ways in which contemporary Russian nationalism can drive a new academic and popular interest in the subject. Given the recent surge of Russian nationalism and projects to ground contemporary identity in recovered strands of pre-Soviet national history that can be traced through emigration, it seems likely that new forces will foster a growing public and academic interest in Russia's World War I. The narrative that follows pays particular attention to the issue that will likely be at the center of this process: the various meanings of the Russian nation at war.

Russia and the Outbreak of War

As in all belligerent countries, mobilization is the key word for the war. Initially, nearly all war planners thought the speed, effectiveness, and totality of the mobilization of the standing army, and more importantly, the reserves, would determine the outcome of what most presumed would be a short campaign. The literature on the outbreak of the war is large and assigns different weights to the various contributing factors. But there is wide agreement on the central importance of Russian military modernization to convincing German authorities that their window of opportunity to launch a war was closing fast. After recovering from the turmoil of the 1905 revolution, Russia embarked on a period of rapid industrial growth. Spending on defense and transport rose rapidly, culminating in the declaration of the "Great Military Program" in 1912. This program, scheduled for completion in 1917, was partly funded by French loans and focused on bringing down the number of days required to mobilize the Russian army and launch an offensive. The program's central goal was to cut the period required for full mobilization by half, to 18 days. This would render Germany's Schlieffen Plan hopeless, as it required at least six weeks with the bulk of the German army in Belgium and France before troops could be brought back to the Russian front. When the diplomatic crisis broke out in the Balkans, this purely strategic consideration played a significant role in German decisions to take such a provocative, high-risk approach.

Historians have found it less easy to explain why Russia also took a risky and belligerent approach during the crisis. The tsar followed the Habsburg declaration of war on Serbia on July 28, 1914 with an order for partial mobilization on July 29, then an order for full mobilization two days later – both against the advice of his military leaders. The tsar took the fateful decision to embark upon full mobilization without even informing the minister of war. It appears that the key figures encouraging this approach were the Grand Duke Nikolai Nikolaevich (named commander in chief of the Russian armies when war was declared) and the Foreign Minister Sergei Sazonov. The latter is particularly interesting and important, for he was closely affiliated with an influential group of liberal and moderate conservative politicians and publicists who had been critical of Russian concessions in the Balkans in previous crises. Their "neo-Slav" ideology was a curious mix of liberal constitutionalism and great power nationalism focused on the aim of influence or conquest in the Balkans.

This small but influential group shows that democratization in the Russian Empire after 1905 had greatly altered the backdrop for foreign policy decision-making. In many ways, the tsar felt pressure to present himself as the embodiment of the Russian nation, and felt that he needed popular nationalist opinion on his side in order to maintain legitimacy. After backing down in the 1908 Balkan crisis because Russia had still not recovered from the domestic turmoil and military debacles of 1905, many felt that Russia could not be humiliated again in the Balkans. So in the critical days of the July crisis, the tsar may have felt that he could not ignore popular opinion and thus was more willing to follow Sazonov's advice to make the "gesture" of support for Serbia in the form of a partial mobilization. The issue was not simply the technical and strategic aspects of mobilization schedules, but also the new inseparability of mobilizing the military from mobilizing the nation and public opinion. This made it much more difficult for Russia's rulers to conceive of bold strategic reversals or of backing down on public statements.[8] On July 31, Germany sent Russia an ultimatum demanding that it stop mobilizing troops. France and Germany began to mobilize, and Germany declared war the following day when it received no response from Russia.

The Russian War Effort

Russia mobilized efficiently and soberly (a prohibition on alcohol was declared primarily to avoid the time-consuming traditional village drinking bouts accompanying conscription). Still, Russia was not able to put overwhelming numbers into the field quickly enough to meet the army's strategic goals. One of the key problems was a division of opinion that was never resolved between focusing the initial offensive in Galicia against the Habsburg army, or in East Prussia against the Germans. Russia's ally France pressed hard for a major attack against Germany, while Russian public opinion and several key military figures favored an all-out drive to knock Austria out of the war and pursue Russian interests in the Balkans. Rather than choose, the Russian command divided forces and attacked in both directions. The strategically crucial attack on East Prussia was launched on the fourteenth day of mobilization with two armies. The Russian armies outnumbered the Germans in East Prussia by three to two, but Iakov Zhilinskii, the Russian general who ordered the offensive, was well aware that this did not give Russia overwhelming force, commenting that "History will condemn me … but I have given the order to march."[9]

After a successful opening phase, in which the Russian armies defeated the Germans at Gumbinnen, the German commander was replaced by Hindenburg and his chief-of-staff, Ludendorff, who together took an offensive approach. With superior military intelligence and communications, the duumvirate split the two Russian armies, nullifying their numerical advantage, and scored separate victories against each of them (see chapter 5). First, on August 28, Germany attacked Samsonov's army in the south, gambling that Rennenkampf would not come to his aid. The gamble paid off spectacularly, with a victory at the Masurian Lakes that destroyed one of the Russian armies. On September 9, with fresh reinforcements from the western front, this victory was followed up with a rout of Rennenkampf at the battle later named after the medieval conflict at Tannenberg, leading to the withdrawal of Russia from East Prussia.[10]

However, at the same time, the larger force of four Russian armies made rapid progress against Austria, capturing Lwów (Lemberg/Lviv/Lvov) by September 3 and raising the specter of either the collapse of the Austrian army under a continuing Russian offensive, or a Russian turn against Germany's flank. Germany was forced to reinforce Austrian troops with its own newly formed Ninth Army in order to hold the line.

By the end of 1914, the strategic stalemate was in place both on the eastern and western fronts. Among all the belligerent powers, the dominance of artillery and the unanticipated rate of consumption of shells now required the mobilization of the economy, as well as the army. Compared to others, Russia responded slowly in scaling up industrial production to the required levels. Nor did successes against the relatively undersupplied Austrian and Ottoman armies in Galicia and then in Eastern Anatolia toward the end of 1914 prepare the Russian army command for the onslaught of the German counter-offensive in western and southwestern Poland in spring 1915. By September 1915, two-thirds of all German combat units were in the east, fighting in a desperate drive to knock Russia out of the war. The offensive was bloody and successful, leading to what is known in Russia simply as the "Great Retreat." The German advance between April and September 1915 pushed the front lines deep to the interior of the prewar boundaries of the Russian Empire, with Galicia, Russian Poland, and parts of Ukraine, Belarus, and Lithuania all falling to the Central Powers.

All these gains came at a great cost in men, material, and time to Germany and its allies, while failing to force Russia out of the war. Britain and France were able to mobilize their economies and prepare for another round of fighting in the west. When the Germans gave up on the Russian offensive and turned back to a focus on the western front, they faced a more formidable, better-supplied enemy. In this sense, Russia's survival aided the Entente. But it came at horrific cost. Over 20 million of Russia's population, and some of its best industrial centers and farmland, fell under enemy occupation.

Over a million soldiers were taken prisoner, and many were forced to work in German and Austrian agriculture and industry. The old Russian army was decimated, with most of the trained prewar officer corps dead or imprisoned. A serious manpower shortage emerged and led to desperate moves such as the imposition of conscription on poorly trained and less reliable groups that had previously been exempt: primary family bread-winners, men over 40, and Muslim groups in Central Asia. The conscription of Muslims led to a massive violent rebellion against Russian rule in 1916 that took a major military deployment and brutal measures to subdue.

Moreover, during the retreat, the army used its extensive powers over civilian affairs to conduct a violent and disruptive set of policies toward civilians near and well to the interior of the front lines. Most dramatically, the army singled out and forcibly expelled roughly a million foreign subjects, Russian-subject Germans, and Jews to the interior of the country and to Siberia. The army command rarely intervened to punish Cossack military units in particular for conducting a wave of looting and abuse of local civilians, including extensive pogroms against Jews. Such policies added to the streams of refugees who chose to move to the interior rather than fall under German occupation. By early 1917, an estimated six million refugees had moved to the interior of the country.[11] All this occurred while the army whipped up hysteria about treason and traitors, accusing Jews, Germans, Polish Catholics, and others of disloyalty. Violence and anger spread throughout the country, boiling over in a massive pogrom against foreigners and anyone with Germanic names in Moscow in May 1915.[12]

Yet, Russia not only survived the German offensive of 1915, but increased its pro-duction of shells and improved its battle performance. One key to averting defeat was the effective series of measures to bring society into the war effort that the tsar reluc-tantly accepted in the spring and summer 1915, at the peak of the German attack. A series of mixed government–private boards, councils, and organizations were created with prominent participation of industrialists and elected officials from the municipal to the national level. These organizations took on many different tasks in coordinating the expansion of production of shells and other supplies for the war. At the same time, the tsar allowed the formation of a national organization of representatives from elected county and municipal councils. This organization, the *Zemgor*, took on many functions that the government administration simply had been incapable of fulfilling – including provision for the masses of refugees flooding into the interior, beds and hospitals for the wounded, the organization of charity, and the coordination of industrial produc-tion. Not coincidentally, the reactionary government ministers who embodied the long-standing hostility of the regime toward any such empowerment of society were sacked and replaced in June 1915 by relative moderates who enjoyed a degree of pub-lic support.

These measures came in the context not only of the Great Retreat, but also the for-mation of the "Progressive Bloc," a grand opposition coalition of unprecedented breadth that was formed by the leaders of all but the most extreme fringe parties in the national *Duma* (parliament). By summer 1915, evacuation plans were being made for the historic cities of Kiev and Riga, and a sense of severe crisis swept through all of Russia. But society came together and the government made some concessions to allow elected local officials and private entrepreneurs and professionals to mobilize for war on a new level.

The results were striking. Although shortages of shells and other military material were in part met through imports from abroad, just as important were rapidly increased levels of domestic production. The country survived the German offensive and emerged with an expanding industrial supply system. By autumn 1915, Germany gave up its drive to force Russia to sue for peace and turned the bulk of its forces back against France. Russia's shell production doubled from 1915 to 1916. Although military historians stress his tactical innovations, the quality and quantity of weapons and shells at General Brusilov's disposal certainly helped in his successful offensive against Austria in the summer of 1916.[13]

Thus, far from collapsing under the strains of war, the Russian Empire was able to ramp up shell production and win battles in 1916. But, rather than consolidate politically the new spirit of cooperation that had proven so effective in helping to shift the Russian mobilization effort into another gear during the darkest months of 1915, the tsar inexplicably chose a path of confrontation. Perhaps sensing that the crisis had passed as the German offensive came to an end in fall 1915, he began to replace relatively popular ministers with reactionaries who had no support at all in society.

One of the most important of these moves was the appointment of Aleksei Khvostov in October 1915 to the post of Minister of the Interior. Khvostov was the leader of the notorious proto-fascist "Right" faction in the Duma – one of the only groups that had not joined the "Progressive Bloc." One of his favorite topics was the international conspiracy of Jews, Germans, and foreigners to exploit the simple Russian people, and his faction was affiliated with the Union of Russian People, a group with a history of agitating for pogroms. In March 1916, the tsar fired the last widely respected member of the government, Minister of War Aleksei Polivanov. As one of the key architects of the system of state–private cooperation in military production, Polivanov garnered much praise for Russia's improved military supplies and performance.[14] Incredibly, the tsar's letter of dismissal identified Polivanov's close cooperation with the military-industrial committees as the reason he was sacked.

Why the tsar launched this reactionary offensive on the home front in the wake of the German offensive remains difficult to understand. In some measure, the tsar saw himself as the embodiment of the nation, an image and theme that he and his handlers had been promoting long before the war. Among several symbolic gestures during the war, the tsar changed the national and state tricolor flag, adding the emperor's standard of the black double-headed eagle to signify his fusion with the nation.[15] Against the vehement objections of his entire cabinet, he left the capital for the front to take personal charge of the war effort in August 1915, at the worst point of the Great Retreat. His concept of the nation had no place for law, elected officials, and industrialists between himself, the people, and God. Just as importantly, his decision to embark for the front left a political vacuum in the capital, which the empress Alexandra filled in ways that were much exaggerated by rumor and press, but significant nonetheless. By most accounts, her long-time confidante Rasputin played a role in the disastrous ministerial appointments that followed.

But the more important impacts of Rasputin and Alexandra were in the symbolic realm, where they contributed greatly to the desacralization of the monarchy in popular culture.[16] In effect, the monarchy was decoupled from the nation, facilitated by rumors that the "German" empress and a cabal of traitors and highly placed courtiers and generals of German descent were undermining the war effort. The turning point came when Paul Miliukov, the left-leaning leader of the main liberal party (the Constitutional Democrats) and of the Progressive Bloc, gave a speech in November 1916 asking if the actions of the government were "stupidity or treason." The speech was censored but spread like wildfire throughout the country in hand-copied versions. The Progressive

Bloc, the leaders of the war-industry committees, and even leading generals in the army began to see the tsar and his intransigence as a barrier to a successful war effort.

While the tsar pursued his archaic vision of an organic fusion of monarch and people, liberals believed ever more strongly that only the extension of equal rights and obligations before the law to all individual citizens of the Russian Empire could create the effect that the concept of the "nation in arms" had exerted in the French Revolution. The hope was that the revolution would turn an unwilling army of conscripts into a national army fighting for republican ideals.

On the outbreak of the war, the liberals had declared their full support for the tsar and the war effort, vowing to put the political struggle against the monarchy aside until victory.[17] But they were infuriated by the fact that the regime responded not only by failing to extend rights as the counterpart of wartime obligations, but by severely repressing "suspect" minorities – even though they were full Russian citizens.[18] Liberals and many conservatives came to agree that the tsar's opposition to the involvement of society undermined the war effort and his refusal to expand a sense of modern citizenship sapped the will of the nation to fight and contribute to the war.

Revolution

In many ways, the tsar accomplished a remarkable feat. Although support for the war remained high if not universal among the ruling elites in Russia by the beginning of 1917, he managed to lose the confidence of everyone. By the end of 1916, conspiracies to overthrow the tsar were rife, not only among the active opposition, but also among some highly placed officials in the court and military.

The February revolution (March by the Western Calendar) had a very significant popular element to be sure, but it was the heavy-handed overreaction of the tsar that was the key to turning three days of demonstrations in the capital into a full-scale crisis. The immediate cause of the demonstrations was a temporary severe shortage of flour and fuel in Petrograd due to heavy February snows and resulting transport difficulties. On February 19, the government announced that bread rationing would be introduced on March 1, leading to panic buying and long lines in the streets. The disruption of fuel deliveries led several major factories to temporarily close, meaning that even without going on strike thousands of workers were available for the street protests against bread shortages that began on February 23. The next day, 200,000 workers left the factories to join the demonstrations. While it was already the largest demonstration of the war, the commander of the Petrograd garrison, General Sergei Khabalov, thought that the correct course of action would be to avoid confrontation with the crowds and allow the demonstrations to run their course according to the general wartime pattern of strikes, which tended to be of short duration in order to avoid undermining troops at the front. However, the tsar overruled Khabalov and ordered him to fire into the crowds if necessary.

Consequently, early on February 26 – only three days into the demonstrations – several units from the garrison were sent in the streets, where they killed hundreds of protesters. Later that day, mutiny broke out both among troops already deployed in the city and among those remaining in the garrison, with widespread disobedience of orders to fire into crowds. Socialist activists formed a council (the Petrograd Soviet), two-thirds of which was composed of soldiers who had abandoned the army. The Petrograd Soviet organized the mutineers into a Red Guard that became an important force for order in a city that descended rapidly into an orgy of violence and chaos, and its leaders claimed to speak for the workers and peasants of the entire country. But the Soviet did not want to claim power itself, instead working out a program with the leaders of the Progressive Bloc for a government that was to be formed essentially out of the leadership of the Bloc and by members of the Duma.

Meanwhile, the tsar, isolated in Pskov, remained obstinately opposed to concessions and made plans to escalate the repression by sending battle-hardened troops from the front to Petrograd. Only the intervention of the top-ranking commander in the army (after the tsar), Chief of Staff Mikhail Alekseev changed his mind. Alekseev conducted something close to a coup d'état, sending a circular to the leading army commanders making the case for abdication and requesting each to send separate telegrams to the tsar. When Nicholas received the generals' telegrams, he acquiesced early in the morning of March 2, declaring his abdication in favor of the Grand Duke Michael. The Grand Duke in turn refused to accept the crown the following day, himself abdicating and leaving authority solely in the hands of the new "Provisional Government."

The old regime had fallen in stunningly rapid fashion, just a week after protests against bread shortages began in Petrograd. What did the regime change mean for the war effort? The new regime faced the daunting prospect of implementing major domestic reforms while continuing to fight total war. But so many had framed their opposition to the tsar in patriotic terms for so long that faith in the notion that freedom would bring new energy to the war effort ran deep. The new regime immediately declared full equality before the law for all citizens, abolishing all legal differentiation on the basis of religious, ethnic, or social origins. Russia's new leaders believed that with freedom, the army could mobilize more effectively around an inspiring new definition of the nation and citizenship.

The Petrograd Soviet quickly sought to bring these ideals directly to the soldiers in the form of a "declaration of soldiers' rights." The Minister of War, Alexander Guchkov, had been the leader of the Octobrist Party, the main moderate liberal/conservative force in Russia between 1905 and 1917, and a strong proponent of the Duma and society taking an active role in defense. Still, for him, the regulations went too far, and he resigned on May 1 rather than sign them, predicting they would lead to the collapse of all authority in the army. His replacement, Alexander Kerensky, leader of the socialist "Trudovik" faction in the Duma, issued the declaration 10 days later. Except for cases of direct insubordination, it transferred all power to punish soldiers to "elected army organizations, committees, and courts," and gave full political freedom to soldiers while on duty. It was a risky bet that "the freest Army and Navy in the World [would] prove that there is strength and not weakness in Liberty."[19]

Kerensky continued to pursue his strategy of creating a new nation-in-arms by preparing for an even greater gamble – a major new offensive in Galicia. He spent much of the weeks preceding the offensive at the front trying to spread his vision of fighting harder and better now that there was something inspiring for which to fight. Knowing the result, historians have been very dismissive of his approach. But at the time, Kerensky was not regarded as crazy at home or abroad. Mobilization of men continued apace and the army reached its largest size of the war on the eve of the offensive. It is often forgotten that by early 1917, on paper the Entente had gained a great advantage of at least 60 percent in men and guns on all its fronts with Germany and Austria-Hungary.[20] While there was an immediate, sharp drop in industrial and military production in the months following the February revolution, allied support and accumulated supplies meant there was no shortage of shell and weaponry for the offensive. Not least, Russian troops had a numerical advantage of nearly three to one in most areas of the offensive, and Russian heavy artillery outnumbered the enemy by five to one. The United States had just announced its entry into the war, and promised an influx of supplies, and eventually, troops. The hero of the successful 1916 campaign, Brusilov, was in charge of the offensive, which began on June 16.

For the first time in the war, the Russians had an overwhelming preponderance of artillery along a broad front, and used it to devastating effect, clearing the way for rapid and easy advance over 30 km into Austrian Galicia through sustained bombardments that obliterated enemy defenses. For nearly three weeks, the Russian army advanced with little opposition other than from its own ranks, where the soldier councils debated orders to attack, often delaying or even rejecting them. Few in the army foresaw the effect when the German forces launched their first counterattacks on July 6. Still enjoying great numerical and artillery advantage, the Russian army should have been able to easily thwart the counteroffensive. However, this was remarkably effective, in large part because hundreds of thousands of Russian soldiers refused to fight or deserted the army. Officers who dared to block or threaten the deserters were often shot. Within days, the offensive became a rout. Only the thin numbers on the enemy side saved Russia from an unstoppable invasion, as Germany and Austria decided not to push deep into Russia immediately. The problems at the front nearly led to collapse in the capital as well. Reacting to a government decision to send units from the Petrograd garrison to the front to help thwart the enemy counteroffensive, machine gunners from the garrison joined sailors from the Kronstadt naval base and Bolshevik Red Guards from the factories in a violent coup attempt in Petrograd on July 3–5, that was defeated in part by the government's publication of documents alleging that Lenin was a German agent. Lenin went into hiding and other leading Bolsheviks were arrested.

Kerensky's and the Allies' gamble was one of the greatest strategic errors of the entire war. It contributed directly to the collapse of the liberal-democratic provisional government in Russia, paving the way for the Bolsheviks to seize control of the entire country a few months later. While on paper, the numbers favored the Russians, the logic of Kerensky and everyone else involved contained a number of serious flaws. First among these was the failure of the notion held so strongly by Kerensky and others that liberty would bring greater willingness to die. Had Kerensky enjoyed the benefit of twenty-first-century scholarship on the French revolutionary armies, he might have known that the notion of the voluntaristic "nation in arms" itself was greatly exaggerated, and that order, forced conscription, and discipline were at least as important to French victory as the much-celebrated instances of volunteer heroism.[21]

But it was by no means only Kerensky who chose liberty over order in the army. One of the first acts of the Petrograd Soviet during the February revolution had been the issuance of the infamous "Order No. 1," which called for the election of soldier committees in all army units and their subjection to the authority of the Soviet rather than the army. This parallel structure and democratization of life in the army suited the ideal of the newly emerging "citizen-soldier." But the new regime so privileged soldier rights over order that the soldiers lost the fear of military discipline and court martial that is more significant to the operation of armies than many people would like to think. In retrospect, Guchkov had been right, and Kerensky wrong about the need for old-fashioned discipline in the army.

The Failure of National Mobilization

Did the mass desertion mean that Russian soldiers (most of whom were peasants) lacked the capacity for democracy, or that it revealed their utter lack of a sense of national identity? This is a standard interpretation in the historiography, and there is something to it.[22] By far the most important meaning of revolution for Russian peasants was the notion of the "great repartition," the dream of the expropriation of noble and individually owned land and its fair distribution through communes throughout the country. This understanding of revolution meant several things. First, peasants did not share the focus of Kerensky and the liberal elites on equality of rights and obligations before the law. They saw the revolution as a chance for equality of land distribution. But when it became clear that the new government was going to postpone land reform until the end of the war, peasants began to take matters into their own hands. One reason peasant soldiers were increasingly eager to get home was to ensure that they were able to participate in the coming land redistribution to the communes. While it is understandable that the Provisional Government did not want to embark on a major land reform in wartime, peasants did not accept this policy. When Victor Chernov, the leader of the party that had promoted agrarian revolution for decades (the Social Revolutionary Party), joined the government in May 1917 as Minister of Agriculture and counseled patience, the main result was that peasants began to switch their support to the only party that called immediately for peace and full-scale agrarian revolution – the Bolsheviks.

More broadly, notions of the Russian nation had been closely linked in the popular mind with the tsar for all of the country's existence. To ask an entire nation to switch its allegiance and loyalty to an abstract set of ideals, to a government that called itself "provisional," and only promised the reforms that most of the country cared about at some undefined later date, was a lot to ask. Some leaders were aware of this, like the liberal leader Paul Miliukov, himself passionately opposed to the monarchy and a proponent of a constitutional republic. Nonetheless, he argued in spring 1917 for the retention of at minimum a figurehead monarch to facilitate a gradual shift of loyalties and political conceptions of the nation.

But was the Russian soldier really lacking a sense of patriotism and of fighting for the Russian nation? This question has not received enough attention.[23] Scholarship on the French mutinies has stressed that the soldiers protested against mindless, endless, bloody offensives – not necessarily against the war or their country (see chapter 28). Likewise, in the Russian case, there were plenty of signs that Russian soldiers may have supported a defensive war to protect the country, but strongly opposed a war of foreign conquest pursued through bloody offensives in foreign lands. The government had a chance to foresee this in the successive March and April 1917 public controversies and street protests over Foreign Minister Miliukov's revelation of Russia's previously secret war aims of conquest of Austrian Galicia, Constantinople, and the Straits. The June offensive itself was not directed toward the defense or reconquest of Russian lands, but rather, toward the conquest of the Galician province of Austria. It is often forgotten that throughout the entire war – even after the Great Retreat pushed the front deep into the territory of the Russian Empire – the Russian army was deployed in Ukrainian, Polish, Belarusian, Armenian, Azeri, Georgian, Moldovan, Latvian, and Jewish areas where few Russians lived. Soldiers' memoirs often remarked on the sense of leaving "Russia" long before arriving at the front. This too made it more difficult to conceive of the war as crucial to the defense of the Russian people.

Even for those who supported a defensive war, by 1917 the accumulation of losses was enough to question the logic of continuing the fight. Between August 1914 and October 1917, 15 million soldiers served in the Russian army. Estimates range from 1.3 to two million killed in action or later of wounds incurred in battle.[24] Almost five million prisoners were taken.

The great mutiny of 1917 began with tens of thousands of deserters leaving the ranks each month after the February revolution, expanding to a quarter-million in August.[25] But the army was enormous, and by no means did it completely melt away. In October 1917, five million soldiers remained at the front. Still, the German counteroffensive led to the fall of Riga and cleared a short path to the capital, Petrograd.

Kerensky now learned his lesson, perhaps too well. He saw the need for discipline in the army, and on July 16, appointed the charismatic proponent of harsh measures, Lavr Kornilov, commander in chief. Rather than bring new discipline and organization, a confusing series of separate but interrelated events in July and August exacerbated the disintegration of the army and state authority. The key event was a misunderstanding between Kerensky and Kornilov. Convinced that the government lacked the fortitude to suppress another rumored Bolshevik coup attempt, Kornilov stationed reliable front-line troops well behind the front with quick railroad access to either Petrograd or Moscow. A series of misunderstandings through the telegraph and the intrigues of an intermediary who intentionally provoked a conflict between the two men led Kornilov to send troops to Petrograd to prevent the coup and to help establish a military dictatorship with Kerensky's participation. Kerensky either willfully or intentionally misread this act as an attempt to overthrow him in a military coup from the right. He ordered the arrest of Kornilov and expanded his own claims to near-dictatorial power.[26]

Kornilov was very popular among the army elite and parts of society that favored a turn toward discipline and order to stop the rapid disintegration of both military and civil authority. Kerensky's primary motive in arresting him probably lay in his political sense that he needed to maintain a close alliance with the left. Bringing Kornilov into a joint military dictatorship would have meant an irrevocable break with the left, and Kerensky always felt that the history of revolutions showed that the greatest danger was from the right.

However, by arresting Kornilov, Kerensky lost credibility and support from the army, police, and proponents of order from the liberals to the right. Thus, when the Bolsheviks launched their next coup attempt in October (November by the Western Calendar), he found little to no support in the army or elsewhere. Moreover, the entire affair further discredited the army command and undermined discipline at the front.

The Bolshevik Revolution and Russian Withdrawal from the War

The most important immediate events leading to the Bolshevik coup on October 25 were related to the war and the idea of defending the Russian nation in ways that are often overlooked. The immediate crisis was the German capture of Riga and three key islands defending the way to Petrograd on October 21. The Russian general staff assumed these were preparations for a German attack on Petrograd. It ordered the evacuation of Revel, and began preparations to move the government to Moscow. The socialist party leaders and press reacted angrily to this attempt to abandon "Red Petrograd" and formed a "military-revolutionary committee" to arm and organize workers to defend the city against the Germans and counterrevolutionaries. A key aspect of the coup was the

Bolshevik success in gaining control over this committee. Presenting themselves as defenders of the revolution and the city against the Germans and the Provisional Government probably helped the Bolsheviks avoid more strenuous resistance from many quarters.

The coup began on October 25 and took less than two days to succeed in the capital. Already on the 26th, the Bolsheviks issued two decrees that assured Russian withdrawal from the war and incapacity for further fighting. The Decree on Land declared the immediate nationalization and redistribution of land belonging to landlords, clergy, and the crown to peasants – essentially a declaration of the Great Repartition many peasants had long awaited. The Decree on Peace was essentially an appeal to the other powers to enter negotiations to end the war and a declaration to the country that Russia had no intention to continue fighting. Together, the decrees brought another round of mass departures from the army as peasants rushed home to be on hand when the expropriated lands in their home region were redistributed.

The Central Powers at first welcomed the idea of an armistice and a negotiated peace on the eastern front. Ludendorff immediately began to plan for a major offensive on the western front. Austria, thoroughly exhausted by the war and facing a serious economic crisis, needed peace badly. Armistice talks began on December 3 and led to the declaration of a formal ceasefire on December 6. Long before 1914, German war aims had focused on gaining territory from the Russian Empire, and the Germans began negotiations by demanding the cession of Poland and Russia's Baltic provinces (which they already occupied). When the Bolsheviks used delaying tactics while trying to stimulate revolution in Europe, Germany responded in December by recognizing the Ukrainian Rada's declaration of independence. The Bolshevik regime responded by sending troops to prevent Ukrainian secession. With the Bolsheviks marching toward Kiev, the desperate Ukrainian government signed a separate peace agreement with the Central Powers on February 9 that brought German and Austrian troops into the country. They drove out the Bolsheviks and made Ukraine a German dependency. On February 17, the Central Powers attacked and advanced quickly, meeting practically no resistance. Facing the real prospect that the Germans would march to Petrograd and depose the Bolsheviks as they had just done in Kiev, the regime finally accepted Germany's peace terms. But the German, Austrian, and Hungarian armies just kept advancing until the Bolsheviks finally accepted the dictated terms of their punitive peace on March 1.

The Treaty of Brest-Litovsk forced the Bolsheviks to give up Poland, Finland, Ukraine, Estonia, Latvia, Lithuania, Transcaucasia, and Bessarabia. This comprised roughly one-third of its urban population, three-quarters of its coal and iron deposits, and a territory nearly twice the size of prewar Germany. In short, it transferred most of the non-Russian Romanov lands to the German Empire. Another clause gave German and Austrian citizens extraterritorial privileges throughout the Bolshevik state that more closely resembled the rights of foreigners in the Ottoman and Chinese empires than anything in the Russian past. When the central powers lost the war eight months later, the Bolsheviks were already embroiled in a full-scale civil war that lasted three more years. By the end of that war, of all the territories lost at Brest-Litovsk, only Ukraine and the Caucasus had been reconquered.

One of the more palpable results of the war was thus that the Soviet Union became a revanchist state that ultimately joined with Nazi Germany in 1939 to regain some of its lost lands. But the war also is linked to the origins of the contemporary Russian nation. The Treaty of Brest-Litovsk reduced the Soviet state to a Russian core not much larger than the size of the current Russian Federation. The first official recognition of the Russians as a distinct nationality within the Empire was created by the Bolsheviks when they created the Soviet Union as a union of distinct republics.[27]

These consequences of the war are difficult to celebrate or incorporate into contemporary Russian national narratives. The horrific death toll and destructive impact of both the civil war and World War II make it unlikely that Russia's World War I will ever compete as a focus of mourning and commemoration. But both scholars and the Russian public are increasingly exploring these issues and coming to a greater realization of the interlinked nature of the entire disastrous period of Russian history from 1914 to 1945. For decades, most assumed the watershed of the century was 1917; but more now recognize that it all began in 1914.

Notes

1   Cohen, "Oh, That! Myth, Memory, and World War I."
2   Brandenberger, *National Bolshevism*; Weiner, *Making Sense of War*.
3   Interview, Aleksandr Kavtaradze (World War II veteran and leading scholar of Russia in World War I and the civil war), Moscow, June 20, 1996. Kavtaradze's work on the role of World War I officers in the Red Army and other writings are revealing in this regard.
4   Cohen, "Oh That! Myth, Memory and World War I", pp. 69–82; V. Ershov, "Emigrantskie organizatsii veteranov voiny v 1920–1930–e gody (po materialam GARF)," in A. Kruchinin (ed.), *Pervaia mirovaia voina i uchastie v nei Rossii (1914–1918)*, pt. 2, Moscow, 1997.
5   Solzhenitsyn, *August 1914.*
6   The 90th anniversary celebration in June 2006 was attended by the Russian ambassador, at least 1,000 people, and was televised in Russia. On the cemetery, see: http://crdp.ac-reims.fr/ressources/dossiers/memoire/LIEUX/1GM_CA/cimetieres/russes/saint_hilaire.htm
7   For analysis of recent public opinion about the war, see Cohen, "Oh that! Myth, Memory and World War I," p. 84.
8   Lieven, *Russia and the Origins of the First World War.*
9   Lincoln, *Passage Through Armageddon*, p. 63.
10 Showalter, *Tannenberg.*
11 Gatrell, *A Whole Empire Walking.*
12 Lohr, *Nationalizing the Russian Empire.*
13 On this point, most historians agree that Norman Stone goes too far in his argument against the common wisdom that Russia's shell shortage was the defining factor in its military failures and successes (Stone, *Eastern Front*).
14 For a dissenting view on this evaluation of Polivanov and the significance of state–private cooperation in military production, see Fuller, *Foe Within.*
15 Wortman, *Scenarios of Power*, vol. 2, p. 511.
16 Figes and Kolonitskii, *Interpreting the Russian Revolution.*
17 Lohr, "The Russian Press," pp. 91–114.
18 Lohr, *Nationalizing the Russian Empire.*
19 Lincoln, *A Passage Through Armageddon*, p. 404.
20 Stone, *The Eastern Front, 1914–1917*, London, Penguin, 1975, p. 282.
21 Moran and Waldron (eds.), *The People in Arms*, esp. chs. 2, 6, 8.
22 For one example among many, see Lincoln, *Passage Through Armageddon*, pp. 380–4.
23 For a discussion of this problem, see: Sanborn, *Drafting the Russian Nation*, and Sanborn, "The Mobilization of 1914"; Seregny, "Zemstvos, Peasants and Citizenship"; Smith, "Citizenship and the Russian Nation," and responses by Sanborn and Seregny, *Slavic Review* 59/2, Summer 2000, pp. 267–342.

24   Gatrell estimates 2 million dead (including victims of infectious disease). Pipes estimates 1.3
      million dead by July 1917, including 900,000 battlefield deaths and 400,000 from combat
      wounds. See Gatrell, *Russia's First World War*, 1; *Rossiia v Mirovoi Voine 1914–1918 goda
      (vtsifrakh)* (Moscow, 1925), p. 4, cited in Richard Pipes, *The Russian Revolution, 1899–1919*,
      London, Harvill, 1997, p. 418.
25   Wildman, *End of the Russian Imperial Army*, vol. 2, p. 232.
26   Pipes, *The Russian Revolution*, pp. 448–64. For the older interpretation that Kornilov inten-
      ded a coup, see Wildman, *End of the Russian Imperial Army*, pp. 184–223.
27   Martin, *Affirmative Action Empire*.

References and Further Reading

Brandenberger, David, *National Bolshevism: Stalinist Mass Culture and the Formation of Modern
    Russian National Identity, 1931–1956*, Cambridge, MA, Harvard University Press, 2002.
Cohen, Aaron J., "Oh, That! Myth, Memory, and World War I in the Russian Emigration and the
    Soviet Union," *Slavic Review*, 62/1, 2003, pp. 69–82.
Figes, Orlando, *A People's Tragedy: The Russian Revolution, 1891–1924*, New York, Penguin, 1996.
Figes, Orlando, and Kolonitskii, Boris, *Interpreting the Russian Revolution: The Language and
    Symbols of 1917*, New Haven, Yale University Press, 1999.
Florinsky, Michael T., *The End of the Russian Empire*, New Haven, Yale University Press, 1931.
Fuller, William C., Jr., *The Foe Within: Fantasies of Treason in Late Imperial Russia*, Ithaca, Cornell
    University Press, 2006.
Gatrell, Peter, *Russia's First World War: A Social and Economic History*, Harlow, Pearson Longman,
    2005.
Gatrell, Peter, *A Whole Empire Walking: Refugees in Russia During World War I*, Bloomington,
    Indiana University Press, 1999.
Golder, Frank (ed.), *Documents of Russian History, 1914–1917*, New York, The Century Co., 1927.
Kruchinin, A. (ed.), *Pervaia mirovaia voina i uchastie v nei Rossii (1914–1918)*, pt. 2, Moscow,
    1997.
Lieven, Dominic, *Russia and the Origins of the First World War*, New York, St. Martin's Press,
    1983.
Lincoln, W. Bruce, *A Passage Through Armageddon: The Russians in War and Revolution*, New
    York, Oxford, Oxford University Press, 1994.
Lohr, Eric, *Nationalizing the Russian Empire: The Campaign Against Enemy Aliens during World
    War I*, Cambridge, Harvard University Press, 2003.
Lohr, Eric, "The Russian Press and the 'Internal Peace' at the Beginning of World War I," in Troy
    R. E. Paddock (ed.), *A Call to Arms: Propaganda, Public Opinion, and Newspapers in the Great
    War*, Westport, CT, Praeger, 2004, pp. 91–114.
Martin, Terry, *The Affirmative Action Empire: Nations and Nationalism in the Soviet Union,
    1923–1939*, Ithaca: Cornell University Press, 2001.
Moran, Daniel, and Waldron, Arthur (eds.), *The People in Arms. Military Myth and National
    Mobilization since the French Revolution*, Cambridge, Cambridge University Press, 2003.
Nolde, Boris, *Russia in the Economic War*, New Haven, Yale University Press, 1928.
Sanborn, Joshua, *Drafting the Russian Nation: Military Conscription, Total War, and Mass Politics,
    1905–1925*, DeKalb, Northern Illinois University Press, 2003.
Sanborn, Joshua, "The Mobilization of 1914 and the Question of the Russian Nation:
    A Reexamination"; Seregny, Scott J., "Zemstvos, Peasants and Citizenship: The Russian Adult
    Education Movement and World War I"; Smith, S. A., "Citizenship and the Russian Nation
    during World War I: A Comment"; and responses by Sanborn and Seregny, *Slavic Review*, 59/2,
    2000, pp. 267–342.
Showalter, Dennis, *Tannenberg: Clash of Empires*. Hamden, CT, Archon Books, 1991.

Solzhenitsyn, Aleksandr Isaevich, *August 1914*, trans. H. T. Willetts, London and New York, Penguin, 1990.

Solzhenitsyn, Aleksandr Isaevich, *November 1916*, trans. H.T. Willetts, New York, Farrar, Straus and Giroux, 1999.

Stone, Norman, *The Eastern Front, 1914–1917*, London, Penguin, 1998.

Weiner, Amir, *Making Sense of War: The Second World War and the Fate of the Bolshevik Revolution*, Princeton, Princeton University Press, 2002.

Wildman, Allan, *The End of the Russian Imperial Army*. 2 vols., Princeton, Princeton University Press, 1980–7.

Wortman, Richard S., *Scenarios of Power: Myth and Ceremony in Russian Monarchy*, vol. 2, Princeton, Princeton University Press, 2000.

CHAPTER THIRTY-THREE

The Ottoman Empire

HAMIT BOZARSLAN

Historians and social scientists in Turkey pay little attention to World War I as such. Nor have foreign scholars been much drawn to study the impact on the Ottoman Empire of its participation in the sequence of international wars that began and ended in Turkey, from the two Balkan Wars (1912–13) to the Greco-Turkish War of 1921–2.[1] Yet Ottoman Turkey was deeply involved in the broader cycle of violence of which World War I was the epicenter, and that same cycle of violence led to the final breakup of the multiethnic empire after 600 years and to the emergence of the modern Turkish nation-state.

The "Young Turk" Revolution and proclamation of the Second Constitutional Monarchy in July 1908 was followed by Bulgaria's formal independence and the outright annexation by Austria-Hungary of the former Ottoman provinces of Bosnia and Herzegovina. While these events did not provoke an armed conflict, they produced new tensions in the Balkans. Three years later, the new Ottoman regime faced an insurrection in Albania, followed by that country's independence, as well as the Italian invasion of its remaining North African provinces, in contemporary Libya. Immediately afterward, in 1912 and 1913, the two Balkan Wars amputated Macedonia and much of Thrace, the Empire's last major territories in Europe, including the symbolically important city of Thessalonica. Only sharp antagonisms between the aggressors of the Balkan League, with Greece, Serbia, and Montenegro turning on Bulgaria to seize the latter's portion of Macedonia, allowed the Ottoman army to reestablish a European bridgehead beyond Constantinople by retaking Edirne (Adrianopolis), another symbolically important city, in the Second Balkan War.

In October 1914, the Ottoman Empire declared war on Russia, France, and Britain. Ottoman forces were engaged on at least four fronts during the conflict, and in 1915 Gallipoli became an important theater of battle for the Western Allies (see chapter 7). The end of World War I marked the dissolution of the Ottoman Empire, but also the beginning of the war that led to the foundation of modern Turkey. The Treaty of Lausanne, signed on July 23, 1923, recognized the independence of the new state and put an end to the famous "Eastern question." Months later the population exchanges between Turkey and Greece became the most important example of the forced realignment of people with borders in the postwar world.

Official history in Turkey considered the only significant part of this long sequence of events to be the War of Independence. The rest, including World War I, was dismissed as either the result of Western aggression, the betrayal of the Balkan and Arab provinces, or the simple backdrop to Turkish independence. In the 1920s and 1930s, Turkish nationalist historiography, which glorified Mustafa Kemal for his role as a commander at Gallipoli, was even less sympathetic toward the late Ottomans. They were blamed for being unable to defend the Empire or even numbered among the enemies of the Turks, guilty of trying to annihilate them as a nation. The radical republic of Mustafa Kemal, now known as Ataturk, did not see itself as the continuation of the Ottoman Empire but rather as the liberator of the Turks from the Ottoman yoke. The Empire's history, language, and even alphabet were repudiated.[2] No wonder, then, that the Turkish Republic was unwilling to commemorate wars waged by predecessors who were thought of as its enemy.

Yet as modern Turkish and Western historiography insists, there were strong continuities between the Ottoman Empire and the Turkish Republic.[3] The Kemalist elite was an ideological and organic offspring of the Committee Union and Progress, which exercised power for the last decade of the Empire, from 1908 to 1918. However, this is not to deny the tremendous interstate and internal conflicts that took place from 1908 to 1923–4, which produced massive demographic, social, and political changes that went well beyond the establishment of new states and new borders.

The main objective of this chapter is to explore some of the deep effects of this decade of war on both the Ottoman Empire and Turkey. We shall deal, first, with the demographic effects of the wars, mainly within the territorial framework of the current Turkey. We shall then analyze the Pan-Turkist and Pan-Islamist policies of the Committee Union and Progress, and their failure, before going on to describe the intellectual and political universe of the Committee's leaders. After looking briefly at the militarism of the Ottoman Empire between 1914 and 1918, and the militarization of its economy, we shall discuss the new forms of mass violence that arose during the war, of which the Armenian genocide was the most radical manifestation. Finally, we shall look briefly at another consequence of World War I – the end of "Ottomanism." But before dealing with these different aspects of the conflict, it is important to understand why the Ottoman Empire entered the war nearly three months after it started, on October 29, 1914.

The Ottoman Decision to Go to War

The Italo-Turkish War and the Balkan Wars were "imposed" on the Ottoman Empire by external aggression. The last Turkish war, the War of Independence, was also in large part a defensive response by notables, the religious *ulema* (Muslim legal scholars), and some of the officer corps to the invasion of what remained of the Ottoman Empire by British, French, Italian, and Greek forces. In World War I, however, the Ottoman Empire was not attacked, or even provoked, by any belligerent power. On the contrary, the Allies underwrote Ottoman territorial integrity and promised to respect its neutrality in return for an undertaking not to intervene. In response to these demands, the "Triumvirate" composed of the Interior Minister Tal'at Pasha, the War Minister Enver Pasha, and the Minister of Naval Forces, Cemal Pasha, decided to enter the war on the side of the Central Powers. They informed the country's official government only after bombardment of the Russian coast had already begun.[4]

Nearly a century later, the reasons for this rapid decision are still not clear. According to the Committee Union and Progress's own argument, the Empire would inevitably be drawn into the world conflict, so that it was better to enter it as soon as possible and on its own terms in order to maximize the benefits.[5] Obviously, Enver and Cemal, as well as many German-trained officers in the Ottoman forces, were confident that Germany's military skill and might would secure a swift and decisive victory.[6] It is also possible that the three Unionist leaders saw the war as an historic opportunity to end European control of Ottoman finances, for they immediately abolished the unequal commercial treaties that the Ottoman Empire had been forced to sign, known as capitulations. The war may have seemed to present another chance for revenge on Russia, and it was also supposed that a possible Russian defeat would open the gates to Central Asia, thus allowing the construction of the Turan Empire, or a political entity encompassing all Turkic peoples that would replace the disintegrating Ottoman Empire. Finally the war provided an unexpected window of internal opportunity, since Russia and France would no longer be in a position to demand administrative and political reforms in the Eastern provinces and an improvement in the position of the Armenian minority. The expected patriotic mobilization would enable the already defeated liberal opposition within the nationalist movement to be decisively marginalized.

The Demographic Effects of the 1912–24 Wars and Population Exchanges

No reliable data exist on the exact size of the Ottoman population on the eve of World War I. Estimates vary from 20 to 26 million, with a low population growth of around 1 percent per annum. Some 40–45 percent of this population were supposedly Turkish, some 35–40 percent Arab, and the remainder Kurdish, Armenian, Greek, and Jewish.[7] As far as the territory of the current Republic of Turkey is concerned (principally Anatolia), Ottoman sources estimated its population to be just over 14 million in 1912. In 1922, this had decreased to 11.6 million, whereas in 1927, with 13.64 million inhabitants, Turkey had nearly recovered its prewar demographic weight. Finally, 25 percent of the population within the borders of current Turkey was urban in 1914, whereas by 1923 this had shrunk to 18 percent.[8]

By themselves, these figures do not reveal much about the dramatic changes that took place in the composition of the Anatolian population. According to the Ottoman figures, which probably overestimated the percentage of Muslims, Christians (mainly Armenians and Greeks) constituted almost 20 percent of the population of current-day Turkey.[9] After the Armenian genocide of 1915–16, with approximately one million victims, and the population exchange with Greece in 1924, which led to the expulsion of nearly a million Greek Orthodox from Anatolia and half a million Muslims from Greece, the Christian population in Turkey dropped to only 2 percent (together with Jews they constitute less than 1 percent today).[10] Furthermore, the makeup of urban Turkey changed especially sharply during and after the world war and the War of Independence.[11] Many cities lost most of their artisans, who were traditionally Christians, and entire districts and villages remained empty for years.

There is no reliable number for Turkish Muslim victims of World War I. The figure of 3 or 3.5 million deaths advanced by some Turkish nationalist historians, eager to minimize the scale of Armenian victims, makes little sense. Mortality on such a scale, along with the established death or departure of almost 3 million Armenians and Greeks, would simply have made it impossible for Turkey to reach 13.5 million inhabitants in 1927. The reverse movement of Muslims from Greece and other migrations from the Balkans and the Caucasus, which can be reckoned at just over a million, could not have made up a shortfall of 6 million.[12] Nonetheless, it is undeniable that the wars had a terrible effect on young Turkish Muslim males. According to Erik-Jan Zürcher, the peacetime establishment of the Ottoman army in 1914 was around 100,000, with a projected expansion to double that in time of war. World War I forced the Ottoman government to mobilize men far in excess of this, with correspondingly high casualty rates. About 325,000 soldiers died as a result of battle, mainly on the Caucasian front and at Gallipoli, while some 60,000 others died of various illnesses. Between 400,000 and 700,000 men were wounded, and the cumulative number of deserters amounted to almost 500,000 at the end of the war.[13] Compared to World War I, the War of Independence which opposed two rather weak armies, one Greek, the other Turkish, was much less deadly, with the Turkish army losing only 5,241 soldiers and 14,152 wounded.

The New Political Elite: Turkish Nationalism and Pan-Islamism

The prewar Ottoman Empire had many paradoxes. This was especially true of its cities, Istanbul, Izmir (Smyrna), and Aleppo. These urban centers had a flourishing intellectual and commercial life and were open to the outside world, the Ottoman Empire having experienced the modernization that marked all European states in the nineteenth and early twentieth centuries.[14] Although it was much less powerful than the two other aging multiethnic European Empires, Austria-Hungary and Russia, it disposed of quite efficient networks of communication, though railways were still sparse, especially in the east. Almost all the Ottoman cities were connected with Istanbul by telegraph and many seaports had regular connections with Europe. From the second half of the nineteenth century, there was high geographical mobility within the Empire and significant emigration toward North and South America.[15]

Yet in spite of considerable efforts undertaken since the 1839 *Tanzimat* reforms, the state bureaucracy and army were corrupt and above all disorganized. Indeed, in some respects the situation had deteriorated. The long reign of Abdulhamid II (1876–1909) saw bureaucrats and the military recruited mainly on the basis of loyalty to the sultan, so that by end of this period, the army was officered either by loyalists or dissidents. The divorce between the westernized civil and military intelligentsia and the Palace, between the "Young" and the "Old" Turks, led to the 1908 Revolution, which brought the Young Turks to power and, after a period of upheaval, saw the more compliant Mehmed V replace his brother as sultan. The instability continued down to the eve of the war as liberal and nationalist currents vied for control of the Young Turks' Committee Union and Progress, while fending off conservative attempts to use the army to revert to a more authoritarian monarchy. In the process the civil service was destabilized and distrust of the state grew. In the provinces, the Committee could only establish its rule at the cost of a series of mini-coups d'état.[16] True, the Revolution had been welcomed by city-dwellers, the intelligentsia, and the Christian communities. But fears inspired by what increasingly amounted to a single-party regime gradually replaced the initial revolutionary fervor.

In July 1912, a secret committee of self-styled officer liberators *(Halaskar Zabitan)* forced the pro-Unionist government of Said Pasha to resign, prompting a counter-putsch in January 1913 organized by Enver Pasha, one of the main figures of Unionism. The head of the new pro-Unionist government, Mahmut Chevket Pasha, was assassinated in July of the same year, and although the responsibility of the liberals as well as other opposition groups was never proved, the liberal party (*Hürriyet ve Itilaf Firkasi*) was banned and its leaders either executed or exiled. The now hard-line Committee Union and Progress became undisputed master of the country. It included officers (Enver and Cemal), bureaucrats (Talat), intellectuals (Ziya Gökalp), and "men of the shadow" (such as the committee's two gunmen, Dr. Bahaeddin Sakir and Dr. Nazim). These men not only had a radically different profile from the "Old Turks," they were also distinct from a more sophisticated current of Young Turks who were either liberals or constitutional nationalists. Henceforth, such men were marginalized (e.g., Ahmed Riza, a former head of the Committee Union and Progress) or forced into exile.

The most important figures of the new elite were "children of the borderlands."[17] Many of the leading officers originated from the Balkans, while a number of the ideologues close to the Committee who turned "Turkishness" into an ideology and a nationalist utopia were either from the Russian Empire (such as Ahmed Agaoglu, Yusuf Akçuraoglu, and Hüzeyinzade Ali (Turan)) or were not Turks at all (Ziya Gökalp and Tekin Alp (Moïse Cohen)). For these men, the loss of the Balkans in 1912–13 meant the loss of Ottoman identity, prompting them to evolve rapidly toward a profoundly anti-Christian Turkish nationalism.[18] They no longer believed in the fraternity of the Ottoman ethnic communities but, as Ziya Gökalp put it, rather in Turkey's destiny to "grow up and become Turan," that is, an empire including all the Turkic regions of the Russian Empire.

Turkish and Pan-Turanist nationalism were not new in the history of the Unionist movement. Many of the key actors of the Committee Union and Progress had adhered to them as early as 1905–6.[19] But they only gained real momentum after the Revolution of 1908, with the foundation that year of a *Türk Dernegi* (Turkish Association) and an associated paramilitary organization called *Türk Gücü* (or Turkish force), whose motto was: "Türkün gücü herseye yeter" (The force of the Turk suffices for everything). In 1912, yet another association, *Türk Ocagi* (Turkish Heart), was founded with open Unionist support, its aim being to "bring the Turkish race and language to perfection."[20] At its 1913 Congress, the Committee Union and Progress officially adopted Turkish nationalism as its ideology.

Many of these nationalists, including those coming from the Caucasus and Crimea, were unaware of the realities of the Muslim communities in the Russian Empire, which, though supportive of the Ottoman Turks, did not identify with Pan-Turanian projects.[21] But Pan-Turanism, which inspired the disastrous Caucasian campaign against Russia in 1914–15, was not only a fatal utopia. It was also a source of tension within the Empire's Muslim majority. The nationalist policies of the Unionist government, which aimed at the "Turkification" of the non-Turkish Muslim groups, also deepened divisions within the Muslim population.[22] Already in the aftermath of the revolution, Turkish nationalism provoked massive reactions among the Albanians, pushing them first to dissidence and then to open rebellion against Istanbul. The Arabs, including those most favorable to the Ottoman Empire, also vehemently rejected the idea of "Turkishness" along with the official designation "Young Turk Government" used by the Unionists in their documents. While a radical minority of Arab subjects aimed at outright independence, the majority claimed either a large measure of autonomy or the transformation of the Empire into a dual Turkish-Arab entity. A nascent movement of Kurd nationalists also formulated distinct claims, and only the anti-Armenian hostility of the Unionist government convinced Kurdish dignitaries to remain loyal to it during World War I. Even many Turks defined themselves in religious terms, as Muslims, rather than as nationalists.[23]

The Unionists tried to calm the opposition of the non-Turkish Muslim communities by recalling the duty of Islamic fraternity. Pan-Islamism became inseparable from Pan-Turkism. By using this sacred register of discourse, the Unionists also hoped to muster hostility to British, French, and Russian colonialism. The *jihad*, which was declared at the start of the war against the Entente powers, called on Muslims around the world to support the Ottoman war effort.[24] While promoting Turkish nationalism and Pan-Turanism, the Unionist government switched constantly between religion and secular nationalism or tried to combine them without provoking further tensions.

Yet these tensions emerged into the open in the last two years of the conflict for several reasons. First, despite the Russian Revolution and Civil War, it proved impossible to conquer Turkic Central Asia. Even when Russian forces were at their weakest, the Ottoman army could only manage to occupy parts of the Caucasus. But the sources of the failure were not just military. The conferences of Russian Muslims organized in the aftermath of the February Revolution formulated collective demands on behalf of Muslims but in the context of the new regime in Russia, and refused to adhere to any extra-Russian, Pan-Islamist, or Pan-Turanist program.[25] Second, with the Arab revolt of 1916 and the loss of Mesopotamia in 1918, the Empire was reduced to Anatolia. Third, the *jihad* had little impact on the rest of the Muslim world. Indian, Egyptian, and North African Muslims by and large stayed loyal to the British and French Empires, hoping for reforms at the war's end (see chapter 35).

The Unionist regime had to abandon its imperial, Pan-Turan, or Pan-Ottoman ambitions and develop instead an Anatolian-based populist nationalism.[26] This switch from utopia to reality made it all the more important for the Turks to secure their Anatolian heartland and to reinforce the anti-Christian aspects of Turkish nationalism. None of this excluded a more limited "closer Turan," uniting Anatolian and Azeri Turks, but for the moment even this remained a vision for the future.

The Unionist Worldview

The contradictions and tensions that marked Unionist nationalism were perceptible in the power structures that the Committee Union and Progress elaborated during the war. A sizeable gap existed between the Committee's claim to represent both nation and state (it was, according to its motto, "the soul of the state") and political practicalities. In fact, the official unionist government, led by Said Halim Pasha from 1913 to 1916, had restricted powers.[27] As we have seen, the decision to go to war was not taken by the government. Although the Committee decided at the 1913 congress to abolish its protective secrecy, the main structures of the movement remained underground or functioned without government control throughout the war years. In fact, the Committee behaved as "a secret society working in the daylight" (Hannah Arendt). The hard core of the Committee, or "Triumvirate," consisted of "three Pashas": Enver, Cemal, and Tal'at. Each of these leaders had his own secret network, and together they controlled another underground body called the *Techkilat-i Mahsusa*, or "Special Organization," which played a key role in exterminating the Armenians and in clandestine operations in the Caucasus. These bodies coexisted with a police organization that was "autonomous from the state" but shared the Unionists' "militarist" outlook and structure.[28]

The Unionist worldview was dominated by cults of secrecy and enmity. As the titles of its internal papers suggest ("Bomb," "Bayonet," "Weapon"), the Committee drew no distinction between external war and operations against its domestic foes. To some extent, it had reproduced the culture of the Ottoman state since it continued to conceive of those who held power as being above society, not part of it. But whereas the traditional Ottoman state was an end in itself, imbued with a paternalist duty to balance different elements of society (the bureaucracy, religious communities, local elites, etc.), the new regime believed that the state held the destiny of the nation in its hands. If it remained above society and enjoyed judicial immunity, this was to secure the historic goals of the nation and ensure its survival. Such a state could brook no societal divisions; as the agent of history it needed nothing less than total unity and homogeneity.

Ziya Gökalp (1876–1924), who became the Committee's main ideologue after the 1911 Congress, played a decisive role in the formulation of these concepts. Of Kurdish descent, he was much more than the bard who sang the glories of the Triumvirate. He was the architect of an almost sacred "synthesis" of Unionist beliefs.[29] This synthesis, widely shared by Turkish nationalists, both responded to liberal criticism and also solved the turmoil that periodically beset Turkish intellectuals. For Gökalp vehemently rejected decentralization, anti-nationalism, and the autonomy of the civil sphere, all of which were defended by the liberals. Instead, he proclaimed the holiness of the "collectivity" incarnated by the "state" and magnified the role of the "geniuses and heroes" who held power and who were the only ones worthy to represent the nation.[30] According to him, individuals had no rights, but only obligations – notably to "listen to the voice coming from the nation" and "execute their duty."[31]

After the defeat of the liberals following the 1913 military coup, Gökalp appealed to Turkists, Islamists, and westernizers by combining their programs in a single formula: "Turkification, Islamicization, Secularization." "Turkification" was to be the main aim of the Unionist regime, but it required Islamicization since no society could exist without a moral code. Gökalp also explained that civilization was different from nation and religion. Throughout history, the Turks had demonstrated their ability to adopt the most advanced civilization, which in the twentieth century meant accepting Western ideas but controlling their undesirable effects through Islam. In line with these precepts, the Unionist regime implemented an astonishing reform program, much of it during the war, including a new family code, the prohibition of forced marriages, and state control over the *medreses*, or Islamic seminaries.

Militarism and the War Economy

Commenting on the disorder that followed the revolution of 1908, Gökalp wrote that "order could be established only thanks to the martial law [of 1913], which adopted the slogan: there are no rights, but only duties."[32] In his poetry, he constantly glorified the army and military discipline.[33] In some respects, power in the prewar Ottoman Empire corresponded to his image of the perfect state. It was not a military regime since the army recognized the supremacy of the single-party state. But the Unionist officers – the "heroes and geniuses" who monopolized the key military posts – were key members of the political regime.

The centrality of the army after 1908 marked an important shift in Ottoman history. Military prestige had long been undermined by defeats such as those of 1877 and 1893, which brought humiliation and the loss of Ottoman territory. Also Abdulhamid II was so fearful of a coup d'état that he was reluctant even to allow military parades. In one sense, this mistrust continued during the Unionist decade. Although many revolutionary and patriotic students volunteered during the Balkan Wars and the reconquest of Edirne (Adrianopolis) in 1913 created euphoria amongst Muslim nationalists, political intervention by the army bred fear and increased mistrust in the population at large. This ambivalence, along with the feeling that World War I was not a question of self-defense for Turkey, explains the absence of enthusiasm and mass volunteering when the conflict broke out.

As the war progressed, the Ottoman capital and many Ottoman cities experienced a vogue for militarism that amounted to a kind of "war culture," although it was an almost exclusively state-sponsored phenomenon. It took many shapes, starting with the nationalist poetry of Ziya Gökalp, who urged the conquest of the "Red Apple," that is, the promised Turan. The state published an illustrated magazine, *Harb Mecmuasi*, which celebrated the "living deaths" of the martyred soldiers.[34] War propaganda assumed multiple forms, ranging from the interpretation of holy men's dreams as premonitions of imminent victory to the use of cigarette papers to endorse the war effort.[35] Unionist activists and intellectuals stimulated the mobilization of charitable solidarity via many organizations, including an Islamic Association of Women's Work. The mobilization of young men for the army occasioned military parades.

As in the case of other belligerent countries, militarization extended to the economy (see chapter 15). The total cost of the war is estimated to have been 398.5 million Turkish gold liras, financed by the massive emission of paper liras (one gold lira, initially worth six paper liras, was worth six times more by the end of the war), and resulting in massive inflation.[36] In fact, the Ottoman government followed the same path as other European belligerents in financing the war, but with two notable differences. First, the Ottoman economy was much less developed and also faced certain structural weaknesses. In particular, the Unionist government had only limited power in the Arab provinces, so that the rural regions of Anatolia bore the brunt of the economic and financial effort. Second, the militarization of the war went hand in hand with its "Turkification" in social and economic as well as political terms. The objective was not new. Since the 1908 boycott of European products and Christian traders, which followed the declaration of independence of Bulgaria and the annexation of Bosnia and Herzegovina, the Unionists had been obsessed with creating a "national" economy. This in turn meant an end to the supposed "stranglehold" of the minorities over trade, manufacturing, and finance and the creation of a "national bourgeoisie."

In reality the ethnic minorities' share of the economy was weak. In 1911, they owned fewer than 5 percent of the 282 firms in the metal industry, compared to more than 20 percent belonging to the "Turks" (i.e., Muslims)[37], the others being owned by foreign companies. But they were the ideal scapegoats and an easy target for economic "Turkification." The war created the conditions for a massive confiscation of the property of the minorities, beginning with Armenian assets in 1915, for which purpose *ad hoc* committees were set up in every major city.[38] The Muslim merchants and notables who profited from this state-organized spoliation became one of the main strata supporting the Committee Union and Progress and, later on, the Kemalist resistance during the War of Independence. Non-Muslim merchants in Istanbul were the target of excessive taxation and confiscation, as well as imprisonment.[39] During its 1916 Congress, the Committee Union and Progress declared itself satisfied with the economic switch "from non-national to national hands."[40] It also made Turkish the compulsory language for economic activities.

The creation of a national bourgeoisie was thus one of the principal aims pursued by the Committee through the war economy. Speculation on cereals, sugar, and particularly horse transport, which was largely controlled by Unionists, was one of the instruments used at a time when the war economy was generating shortages and high prices. State-sponsored institutions such *Heyet-i Mahsusa-i Ticariyye* (the Special Commercial Delegation) or *Esnaf Cemiyeti* (the Society of Tradesmen) became repositories of "war profiteers" and *nouveaux riches*. In his postwar novel, *Zaniyeler*, the writer Selaheddin Enis painted a harsh portrait of these *nouveaux riches*, among whom he described religious men who could not live without ham and the Turkish mistresses of German officers who were used to "champagne baths."[41]

The policy of creating a national bourgeoisie had repercussions in almost all provinces. New banks and credit firms were created in every major town and shared in war profits. The National Economy Bank of Konya, for instance, quadrupled its profits in only three years, from 9,000 Turkish liras in 1914 to 45,493 liras in 1916, yielding a 40 percent dividend for shareholders. Thanks to the increase in grain prices, the profits of the Village Economy Bank of Kayseri soared from 10,000 to 50,000 liras in 1916.[42] Yet in the second half of the war, serious problems of food supply arose, in part driven by economic nationalism, in part arising from the disruption of production due to the war economy. While the cities were particularly hard hit, eastern Anatolia (devastated by the Armenian genocide) and the Arab provinces of Syria and Lebanon were also affected.[43]

More than wartime militarization, it was the policy of forming a national bourgeoisie that undermined the discourse of national unity and created real resentment. For in contrast to the luxurious life of the *nouveaux riches*, the urban population survived in famine-like conditions. The situation was particularly dramatic in Istanbul, by far the largest city with a population of some 710,000 adults (foreigners and the military excluded). The cost-of-living index (base 100 in July 1914) rose to 405 in January 1917, 1645 in January 1918, and 2205 in December the same year.[44] Reactions against this misery become public from 1917, including within the Committee Union and Progress. Intellectuals and activists opened the debate on solidarity and proposed different, more market-oriented programs of solidarity and nationalist populism, which the regime was forced at least in part to adopt.[45]

New Forms of Violence

Throughout the nineteenth century, the Ottoman regime used the army to suppress domestic insurgencies as well as to fight external wars. The letters of von Moltke the Elder, who as a young officer had been sent to Turkey to advise the Ottoman army in its repression of the Kurdish revolts of the 1830s, provide heart-rending testimony to routine brutality used in dealing with the ethnic minorities.[46] As James J. Reid has shown, the Ottoman army became one of the main agents of coercion against its own population. The regular army, which contained many bands of *basibozuks* (irregulars), waged a kind of civil war on the population, provoking reciprocal violence on the part of the anti-Ottoman insurgents in the Balkans.[47] But the massacres of the Armenians from 1894 to 1896 demonstrated that the extermination of Christians was a path that could become tolerated – or even sponsored – by the state.[48]

Once the short honeymoon between the different Ottoman communities after the revolution of 1908 came to an end, the dynamic of ethnic and religious enmity resumed with new intensity, as the Unionist regime began to pursue its reductively nationalist ideology. The "boycott" of 1908 against the non-Muslim merchants, organized by local Unionist committees, mobilized both workers and Turkish Muslim merchants along the Aegean coast, while the anti-Armenian pogroms of 1909 in Adana were followed by an explicitly anti-Christian campaign on the part of the main Unionist ideologues.[49] Muslims were seen as the Ottoman equivalent of the Third Estate in pre-revolutionary France, that is, as the sovereign people oppressed by an elite of "usurpers" in the form of the ethnic minorities, which sought to deprive the "people" of its own country.[50] On the eve of the war, Unionist discourse defined Christians as "microbes" that threatened the biological existence of the Muslim Turks.[51] Ziya Gökalp dismissed human rights as "a perpetual revolutionary microbe," and as we have seen, the "war culture" of 1914–15 further facilitated ideological mobilization against the minorities, with Gökalp calling for revenge against our "former slaves."[52]

In the Unionist imagination, the war turned the ethnic minorities into the "enemy within" and the stalking horse for the external enemies that all too obviously ringed the Empire. The scope for domestic violence rose to a new level. By the same token, the war removed any possibility of intervention other than by force on the part of Britain, France, and Russia to protect the Christian minorities, thus reinforcing the stereotype of the enemy within. Germany, on the other hand, which had undoubted influence on the Unionist regime, was reluctant to criticize the internal affairs of a vital ally. In fact the initial victims were Greeks, 200,000 of whom were expelled before and during the first month of World War I, despite Greek neutrality in the conflict.[53] But the imaginary conflation of the external and internal enemy converged on the Armenians, in Istanbul and throughout the Empire, but especially in the Armenian heartland of eastern Anatolia, which was also the hinterland of the Caucausus campaign where invasion ebbed and flowed across the frontier with Russia (see chapter 7).

The genocide of the Armenians at the hands of the Committee Union and Progress and its "Special Organization" has been discussed in chapter 13, and is the subject of a vast literature.[54] Following Stéphane Audoin-Rouzeau and Annette Becker, the point here is to underline the specific role of World War I in creating new forms, and a new intensity of violence against what was by and large an unarmed civilian population.[55] Rather than being linked to security concerns, however illusory, as the Unionist discourse pretended at the time and official literature has maintained ever since, the destruction of the Armenians was driven by a well-developed Social Darwinism that the war allowed the Unionists to put into practice.[56]

War was the dominant metaphor in the beliefs of Unionist leaders and intellectuals, with society a struggle for survival between antagonistic "racial" groups.[57] This perception explains how the marginal revolutionary activities of the Armenian committees, the participation of some (Russian) Armenians in the Russian army, and the Armenians' self-defense against Ottoman military violence following defeat by the Russians at Sarikamish in January 1915 were seen as a betrayal on the part of the entire Armenian population. Many Unionists considered the Armenians to be both an upper class and an ethnic group, whose mission in both cases was to exploit and exterminate the Turkish nation.[58] Dr. Resid, the Unionist governor of Diyarbakir and self-declared Social Darwinist, explained in his memoirs that he believed the war had set the two nations against each other and could only end with the elimination of one of them: "I couldn't remain undecided in the face of these two alternatives. My Turkishness took precedent over my calling as medical doctor. I told myself: 'we must eliminate them (*ortadan kaldirmak*) instead of being eliminated by them.'"[59]

In the light of such beliefs, and given the invasions of Ottoman territory in the Caucasus and at Gallipoli, it is not surprising that the orders for massacres and for deportation to the Syrian desert should have targeted the entire Ottoman Armenian population, including communities over 1,000 km from the war zones. Nor is it surprising that deportation should have been conducted in conditions that made death by mistreatment and starvation (where it had not occurred by slaughter) a deliberate act, amounting to what a later generation would call "genocide." For within a few months, a large proportion of the Armenian population was dead and the historic territory in Eastern Anatolia was eerily empty. By 1916 somewhere in the region of one million of the 1.8 million Armenians of the Ottoman Empire had perished.[60] Nor did the extermination stop there, for it extended to other Christian groups, notably the Assyrians and Chaldeans.[61]

The End of the Ottoman Empire

World War I resulted in the dismantling of the Ottoman Empire and the constitution of new states in its former Arab provinces.[62] It also signaled the end of "Ottomanism" as an important current of political life between 1908 and 1918, and one defended by some liberal Young Turks, such as Prince Sabahaddin. Sabahaddin wished to reform the Empire by radical decentralization and the reinvigoration of civil society. He was opposed to military dominance (and had urged neutrality in the war) and also rejected any attempt to turn the state and nation into sacred entities. Not surprisingly, perhaps, the Unionists condemned him to death, though he managed to survive.[63] But many Turks shared his views, as did Armenians, Greeks, Jews, Kurds, and Arabs, who constituted the main forces of Ottoman liberalism. In the wake of the war, such perspectives were no longer viable and erstwhile liberals such as the Arab, Sati al-Husrî, or the Kurd, Cheriff Pasha, opted to become nationalists within their own communities instead.

The end of World War I was also the starting point of a new conflict, the Turkish War of Independence, which took the shape of an internal struggle between Muslims and non-Muslims. In particular, the surviving Armenians tried to return with Allied backing and the Greeks of the Aegean and Black Sea coastal regions tried to restore a kind of multiethnicity by carving out autonomous zones.[64] Following the defeat of the Greek army in 1922, almost all the Anatolian Greeks left Turkey under duress or were deported in 1924 in one of the largest population exchanges in the first half of the twentieth century (see chapter 37). As a result the new Republic of Turkey was 99 percent Muslim.

***

The new Turkish state was thus born of a further episode of division and ethnic expulsion. Yet violence between the nation and its minorities has continued to characterize its history, especially regarding the Kurds and Alevis. The difficulties inherent in making the project of a homogeneous society fit the complexities of a diverse region have produced structural tension. It is precisely because of this that the memory of the Armenian genocide has proved so unpalatable and remains the ghost at the feast of official commemoration of World War I in the Turkish Republic.

Notes

1 Zürcher, "Between Death and Desertion"; Feroz Ahmad, *Ittihatçiliktan Kemalizme*, Istanbul, Kaynak, 1985; François Georgeon, *Des Ottomans aux Turcs. Naissance d'une nation*, Istanbul ISIS, 1995; and Vincent Duclert's three articles ("La destruction des Arméniens," "L'Empire ottoman et la conduite de la guerre," and "La paix et la Turquie kémaliste") in Stéphane Audoin-Rouzeau and Jean-Jacques Becker (eds.), *L'Encyclopédie de la Grande Guerre*, Paris, Bayard, 2004.

2 Kemal Karpat, "Introduction," in Karpat (ed.), *Ottoman Past and Today's Turkey*, Leiden, Brill, 2000, pp. vii–xxii.

3 Zürcher, *Unionist Factor*.

4 Aksakal, *Ottoman Road to War*.

5 See the documents published by Mete Tunçay, *1915–1916, Yazilari*, Istanbul, Afa, 1991.

6 Mustafa Gencer, *Jön-Türk Modernizmi ve "Alman Ruhu." 1908–1918 Dönemi Türk-Alman Iliskileri ve Egitim*, Istanbul, Iletisim, 2003.

7 Erol Köroglu, *Türk Edebiyati ve Birinci Dünya Savasi (1914–1918), Propagandadan Milli Kimlik Insasina*, Istanbul, Iletisim, 2004, p. 69.

8 Zürcher, *Turkey*, p. 164.

9 Youssef Courbage and Philippe Fargues, *Chrétiens et juifs dans l'islam arabe et turc*, Paris, Payot, 1992; new ed. 2005, p. 223.

10 Kemal Ari, *Büyük Mübadele. Türkiye'ye Zorunlu Göç (1923–1925)*, Istanbul, Tarih Vakfi, 2000. To the figures for Christian expellees should be added 200,000 Greeks who were forced to leave in 1914, tens of thousands of Eastern Christians who fled to Iran and the current Iraq, and tens more thousands of Greeks who fled to Greece between 1921 and 1922.

11 Understanding the deep significance of these changes requires urban studies that for the moment remain largely unrealised. Two exceptions are: Hervé Georgelin, *La Fin de Smyrne. Du cosmopolitisme aux nationalisme*, Paris, Editions CNRS, 2005, and Ugur Ü. Üngör, "'A Reign of Terror.' CUP Rule in Diyarbakir Province, 1913–1918," MA thesis, University of Amsterdam, 2005.

12 Gülten Kazgan, "Milli Türk Devletinin Kurulusu ve Göçler," *Cumhuriyet Dönemi Türkiye Ansiklopedisi* (Istanbul), 6, 1986, p. 1557.

13 Zürcher adds that the number of total mobilised soldiers was 400,000 in March 1917, 200,000 in March 1918, and 100,000 at the end of the war (Zürcher, "Between Death and Desertion").

14 Ilber Ortayli, *Osmanli Imparatorlugu'nda Iktisadî ve Sosyal Degisim*, Ankara, Turhan, 2000.

15 Christopher Clay "Labour Migration and Economic Conditions in Nineteenth Century Anatolia," in Sylvia Kedouri (ed.), *Turkey before and After Atatürk. Internal and External Affairs*, London, Frank Cass, 1999, pp. 1–32.

16 Elie Kedouri, *Arabic Political Memoirs and Other Studies*, London, Frank Cass 1974, p. 9.

17 Erik-Jan Zürcher, "The Young Turks – Children of the Borderlands," *International Journal of Turkish Studies*, 9/1–2, 2003, pp. 275–86.

18 Zafer Toprak, "Cihan Harbi'nin Provasi: Balkan Harbi," *Toplumsal Tarih*, 104, 2002, p. 46. Dadrian, *Armenian Genocide*, also links the Armenian genocide to the Balkan Wars.

19 M. Sükrü Hanioglu, *Preparation for a Revolution. The Young Turks, 1902–1908*, Oxford, Oxford University Press, 2001.

20 Füsun Üstel, *Imparatorluktan Ulus-Devlete Geçiste Türk Milliyetçiligi. Türk Ocaklari 1912–1913*, Istanbul, Iletisim, 1997, p. 100.

21 Jacob M. Landau, *Pan Turkism in Turkey. A study in Irredentism*, London, Hurst, 1981.

22 Fuat Dündar, *Ittihat ve Terakki'nin Müsülmanlari Iskân Politikasi, 1913–1918*, Istanbul, Iletisim, 2001.

23 E.g., the memoirs of Sevket Süreyya Aydemir, *Suyu Arayan Adam*, Istanbul, Remzi, 1971.

24 Jacob M. Landau, *The Politics of Pan-Islam. Ideology and Organization*, Oxford, Clarendon Press, 1994.

25 Ihsan Ilgar (ed.), *Rusya'da Birinci Müsülman Kongresi*, Ankara, Kültür Bakanligi, 1990.

26 Köroglu, *Türk Edebiyati*, p. 29.

27 The Arab-Egyptian origins of Said Halim and his Islamist inclinations seem to have been decisive factors leading to his selection as prime minister.

28 Ferdan Ergut, *Modern Devlet ve Polis. Osmanli'da Toplumsal Deneltimin Diyalektigi*, Istanbul, Iletisim, 2004, p. 275.

29 Uriel Heyd, *Foundations of Turkish Nationalism. The Life and Teachings of Ziya Gökalp*, London, Lusac, 1950.

30 Ziya Gökalp, *Makaleler V*, ed. Riza Kardas, Istanbul, Kültür Bakanligi, 1981, p. 36.

31 Ziya Gökalp, *Yeni Hayat, Dogru Yol*, Ankara, M. E. B. Yayinlari, 1976, pp. 13–14.

32 Ziya Gökalp, *Makaleler*, vol. 1, ed. Sevket Beysanoglu, Ankara, Kültür Bakanligi, 1976, p. 156.

33 Gökalp, *Yeni Hayat*, p. 48.

34 A new edition of this journal, edited by Ali Fuat Bilkan and Ömer Cakir (*Harp Mecmuasi*, Istanbul, Kaynak Kitapligi, 2004), was published in the wake of the celebrations of the 90th anniversary of World War I.

35 Köroglu, *Türk Edebiyati*, p. 177; Zafer Toprak, *Ittihat-Terakki ve Devletçilik*, Istanbul, Tarih Vakfi, 1995, p. 24.

36 Toprak, "Cihan Harbi'nin Provasi," p. 61; Pamuk, "Ottoman Economy," pp. 130–1.

37 Tevfik Cavdar, "Devralinan Iktisadi Miras," *Cumhuriyet Dönemi Türkiye Ansiklopedisi* (Istanbul), 4, 1986, p. 1055.

38 Hilmar Kaiser, "1915–1916 Ermeni Soykirimi Sirasinda Ermeni Mülkleri, Osmanli Hukuku ve Milliyet Politikalari," in Erik-Jan Zürcher (ed.), *Imparatorluktan Cumhuriyete Türkiye'de Etnik Catisma*, Istanbul, Iletisim, 2005, pp. 123–56.

39 Toprak, "Cihan Harbi'nin Provasi," p. 120.

40 Ibid., p. 100.

41 Selaheddin Enis, *Zaniyeler*, 1923; new ed., Istanbul, İletişim, 1989.

42 Toprak, "Cihan Harbi'nin Provasi," pp. 77–80.

43 Pamuk, "Ottoman Economy," pp. 124–6.

44 Georgeon, *Des Ottomans aux Turcs*, pp. 253–73.

45 Zeki Arikan, *Tarihimiz ve Cumhuriyet. Muhittin Birgen (1885–1951)*, Istanbul, Tarih Vakfi, 1997; Pamuk, "Ottoman Economy," p. 125.

46 Helmuth von Moltke, *Briefe über Zustände und Begebenheiten in der Türkei aus den Jahren 1835–1838*, Nordtestedt, BoD Verlag, 2000.

47 James J. Reid, *Crisis of the Ottoman Empire. Prelude to Collapse 1838–1878*, Stuttgart, Franz Steiner, 2000. For insurgent violence, see Fikret Adanir, *Die Makedonische Frage*, Stuttgart, Franz Steiner, 1979.

48 Jelle Verheij, J. " 'Les Frères de terre et d'eau': sur le rôle des Kurdes dans les massacres arméniens de 1894–1896," *Les Annales de l'autre islam*, 5, 1998, pp. 225–76; Gustave Meyrier, *Les Massacres de Diarbekir. Correspondance diplomatique du Vice-Consul de France 1894–1896*, Paris, Editions L'Inventaire, 2000.

49 An official association was created in order to better organize the boycott (Y. Dogan Cetinkaya, *1908 Osmanli Boykotu. Bir Toplumsal Hareketin Analizi*, Istanbul, Iletisim, 2004).

50 Mehmed Asaf, *1909 Adana Ermeni Olayari ve Anilarim*, Ankara, TTK, 1986; Hamit Bozarslan, "Allemagne ou France: dualités ottomanes et problème des modèles," *CEMOTI*, 12, 1991, pp. 71–98.

51 Hans-Lukas Kieser, "Dr. Mehmed Reshid (1873–1919): A Political Doctor," in Kieser and Schaller (eds.), *Völkermord*, pp. 245–80.

52 Ziya Gökalp, *Makaleler 5*, ed. R. Kardas, Ankara, Kültür Bakanligi Yayinlari, 1981, p. 156; Gökalp, *Külliyati, Siirleri ve Halk Masallari*, ed. Fevziye A. Tansel, Ankara, TTK, 1977, p. 67.

53 Erik-Jan Zürcher, *Savas,Devrim ve Ulusallasma. Türkiye Tarihinde Geçis Dönemi (1908–1928)*, Istanbul, Bilgi Üniversitesi, 2005, p. 78.

54 Akçam, *Empire to Republic*; Dadrian, *Armenian Genocide*; Bloxham, *Great Game of Genocide*.

55 Stéphane Audoin-Rouzeau and Annette Becker, *14–18, Understanding the Great War,* 2000; trans. from French, New York, Hill and Wang, 2002, pp. 64–8.

56 For contemporary Unionist views, Tunçay, *1915–1916, Yazilari;* for the current official view, Institut de politique étrangère, *Le Problème arménien: neuf questions, neuf réponses,* Ankara, Institut de politique étrangère, 1982.

57 Hamit Bozarslan, "L'Extermination des Arméniens et des Juifs: quelques éléments de comparaison," in Kieser and Schaller (eds.), *Völkermord,* pp. 317–45.

58 M. R. Mehmed Resid Sahingiray, *Hayati ve Hâtiralari,* Izmir, Akademi Kitabevi, 1997, p. 98, and Talat Pacha, *Talat Pasa'nin Anilari,* Istanbul, Say Yayinlari, p. 75.

59 Quoted in Taner Akçam, *Türk Ulusal Kimligi ve Ermeni Sorunu,* Istanbul, Iletisim Yayinlari, 1992, pp. 175–6.

60 T. C. Basbakanlik Devlet Arsivleri Genel Müdürlügü, Osmanli Arsivi Daire Baskanligi, *Osmanli Belgelerinde Ermeniler (1915–1920),* Ankara, T. C. Devlet Arsivleri Genel Müdürlügü, 1994, pp. 93–6.

61 Üngör, "Reign of Terror."

62 Nadine Méochy and Peter Sluglett (eds.), *The British and French Mandates in Comparative Perspectives/ Les Mandats français et anglais dans une perspective comparative,* Leiden, Brill, 2004.

63 Hamit Bozarslan, "Le Prince Sabahaddin (1878–1948)," *Revue suisse d'Histoire,* 53/3, 2002, pp. 287–301.

64 Gün Zileli, "Tarih Yapicilar ve Gerçek Yapicilar," in Emrah Cilasun, *"Baki Ilk Selâm," Cerkes Ethem,* Istanbul, Belge, 2004, pp. 13–15. On the massacres of Armenians during the War of Independence, see Vahé Tachjian, *La France en Cilicie et en Haute- Mésopotamie. Aux confins de la Turquie, de la Syrie et de l'Irak (1918–1933),* Paris, Karthala, 2004.

References and Further Reading

Akçam, Taner, *Empire to Republic: Turkish Nationalism and the Armenian Genocide,* London, Zed Books, 2004.

Aksakal, Mustafa, *The Ottoman Road to War in 1914: the Ottoman Empire and the First World War,* Cambridge, Cambridge University Press, 2008.

Bloxham, Donald, *The Great Game of Genocide: Imperialism, Nationalism and the Destruction of the Ottoman Armenians,* Oxford, Oxford University Press, 2005.

Dadrian, Vahakn N., *The History of the Armenian Genocide: Ethnic Conflict From the Balkans to Anatolia and the Caucasus,* Oxford and New York, Berghahn, 2003.

Emin, Ahmet, *Turkey in the World War,* New Haven, Yale University Press, 1930.

Kieser, Hans-Lukas, and Schaller, Dominik J. (eds.), *Der Völkermord an den Armeniern und die Shoah,* Basle, Chronos Verlag, 2002.

Pamuk, Sevket, "The Ottoman Economy in World War I," in Stephen Broadberry and Mark Harrison (eds.), *The Economics of World War I,* Cambridge, Cambridge University Press, 2005, pp. 112–36.

Roshwald, Aviel, *Ethnic Nationalism and the Fall of Empires: Central Europe, Russia and the Middle East,* London, Routledge, 2001.

Shaw, Stanford, J., *The Ottoman Empire in World War One,* Ankara, Turkish Historical Society, 2006, 2 vols.

Trumpener, Ulrich, *Germany and the Ottoman Empire 1914–1918,* Princeton, Princeton University Press, 1968.

Zürcher, Erik-Jan, "Between Death and Desertion: the Experience of the Ottoman Soldier in World War I, *Turcica,* 28, 1996, pp. 235–58.

Zürcher, Erik-Jan, *The Unionist Factor. The Role of the Committee Union and Progress in the Turkish National Movement (1905–1926),* Leiden, Brill, 1984.

Zürcher, Erik-Jan, *Turkey. A Modern History,* London, I. B. Tauris, 2004.

CHAPTER THIRTY-FOUR

The United States

JENNIFER D. KEENE

Unlike Europe's rush to war in 1914, the United States took two and a half years to enter the conflict. Even before the nation officially joined the Allied side, the country found itself caught up in the opportunities and dangers presented by this worldwide conflagration. Once the United States declared war on Germany in 1917, the need to raise, supply, and transport an army overseas quickly reshaped American society. The government assumed new powers to direct the economy, control dissent, and conscript men. Emboldened by their sudden economic importance, workers, women, and blacks all demanded recognition of their rights as citizens. Meanwhile, the American military struggled to overcome its lack of preparation and field an army that could contribute enough to the eventual victory to win the United States a significant say in the final peace settlement. From farm to factory, training camp to battlefield, the White House to town hall, marshaling the nation's resources to fight America's first total war accomplished more than victory against Germany; it transformed American society and the role that the nation played in the world.

The Path to War

"It would be the irony of fate if my administration had to deal chiefly with foreign affairs," the newly elected president Woodrow Wilson noted before his inauguration in 1912.[1] During his campaign, Wilson had focused on the domestic reform issues that most interested Americans. Four years later, the United States faced a myriad of foreign policy crises and Wilson won reelection with the slogan "he kept us out of war." The nation's official policy of neutrality in World War I was becoming increasingly difficult to maintain, however, in the face of the trade war that erupted between Britain and Germany.

By 1915, both Britain and Germany were using their navies to disrupt the trade of their enemy, thereby hoping to gain an advantage that would propel their armies to victory along the western front. The British established a blockade that included mining the North Sea, while Germany turned to its new weapon, the U-Boat or submarine, to launch surprise attacks against merchant and military vessels. Both tactics met with protest from neutral nations. Norway and Sweden complained that Britain had violated international law by disrupting their use of the North Sea. The American government also officially denounced British interference in shipments between neutral countries. Yet as long as the Americans' traditional route through the English Channel remained open, the effective closure of the North Sea did little to disrupt normal American trading patterns. To maintain good relations with its most important prewar trading partner, the Americans grudgingly accepted the limitations that Britain placed on its trade with Germany, such as the illegal ban on food shipments, with little fanfare. The United States reacted more negatively when Britain added cotton to the contraband list and demanded that the British buy excess American cotton to stabilize the price. Overall, Britain maintained an effective blockade because few neutral ships dared enter the North Sea. By 1916, American trade with Germany was less than 1 percent of what it had been in 1914, but had tripled with Britain and France.

By contrast, Wilson immediately protested when Germany declared a submarine blockade around British waters and warned all ships, belligerent or neutral, to stay out of the war zone. International law required that passengers be given time to vacate a ship carrying contraband before its cargo was sunk, a rule that negated the very element of surprise that made the U-boat a valuable weapon. Once spotted, armed merchant and passenger ships could easily attack and sink the fragile submarines. Wilson denied that it was a double standard to hold Germany strictly accountable to the rules of international law, but accept illegal British blockade policies.[2] The difference, he claimed, was that British violations did not directly threaten American lives. Secretary of State William Jennings Bryan argued to no avail that if Americans and American ships stayed out of British waters, there was little chance that German U-boats would threaten their lives or property.

The real crisis in American–German relations began in May 1915 when Germany sank the *Lusitania*, a British passenger ship that also carried munitions. The attack killed 1,198 passengers, including 127 Americans. When the *Lusitania* went down, Wilson's trusted advisor Colonel Edward House was in Europe trying to negotiate a peace settlement. Rather than convincing the belligerents to negotiate, this visit persuaded House that an Allied victory was desirable. In the wake of the sinking, Wilson also hardened his stand. He demanded that Germany pay reparations and accept the right of Americans to travel on any ship they wished. Bryan resigned in protest, convinced that Wilson cared more about protecting the rights of neutrals than keeping the nation out of the war.

Bryan represented a significant segment of American opinion in 1915, especially within Midwestern and Southern farming communities, where strong ethnic and class loyalties sustained support for neutrality. German American farmers refused to accept Wilson's one-sided application of international law. Millions of other rural folk worried that northeastern banks and businesses were forcing the country to choose sides simply to continue their profitable war trade with Great Britain. Leading female reformers and suffragists also joined the chorus urging neutrality, and formed the Women's Peace Party to seek a diplomatic solution to the war. Urban elites, however, strongly endorsed Wilson's efforts to protect the nation's honor and economy by bringing Germany into line. At this point, the dividing line within the American population was over how vigorously to pursue economic opportunities created by a bottomless war trade, not direct intervention, a step that few Americans considered either possible or desirable.[3]

With the United States and Germany still in dispute over who was responsible for the *Lusitania* disaster, two other controversial sinkings pushed German–American relations to the breaking point. In August 1915, the Germans sank another British passenger ship, the *Arabic*, and two Americans were among the victims. Seven months later, German torpedoes hit the *Sussex*, an unarmed English Channel steamer, in an attack that killed 80 passengers and injured several Americans on board. Faced with Wilson's ultimatum to stop threatening American lives and property or face a break in diplomatic relations, Germany yielded. In the *Arabic* Pledge on September 1, 1915, Germany agreed to refrain from sinking passengers ships without warning and in the *Sussex* Pledge on May 4, 1916 halted surprise attacks on merchant ships.

Despite these pledges, the war continued to creep ever closer to American shores. Throughout the period of neutrality, internal sabotage effected by German agents destroyed factories, ships, and goods. The largest terrorist act occurred in July 1916, when German spies within the United States engineered a huge explosion along the Hudson River in Black Tom, New Jersey that destroyed munitions awaiting shipment to the Allies. Shrapnel from the blast poked holes in the Statue of Liberty and shattered windows in lower Manhattan.

As Germany continued to build U-boats at a frenzied pace, American businessmen formalized their close trading ties with Britain. On January 15, 1915, the financial behemoth J. P. Morgan became the purchasing and contracting agent for the British government within the United States. Over the next two years, the House of Morgan worked closely with British military and financial officials to award more than 4,000 contracts worth over $3 billion to American businesses. In addition, American bankers extended commercial credit to the Allies that averaged nearly $10 million a day.[4] By 1917, the British were overwhelmingly dependent on American credit and supplies to continue the war (see chapter 15). Almost overnight, the United States transformed itself from a debtor to a creditor nation and made inroads into world and domestic markets traditionally dominated by British capital. The jobs and steady income provided by these war contracts spread the benefits of wartime trade throughout the American economy. These financial and economic ties helped to build strong support for the Allied cause, especially within urban areas. British propagandists also provided an emotional reason for Americans to turn against Germany. A massive advertising campaign within the United States highlighted German atrocities in Belgium and cast German submarine attacks as contrary to the laws of civilized warfare.

Strong financial ties did not guarantee a tension-free relationship between Britain and the United States. In the summer of 1916, as controversial German sinkings ceased, relations with Britain became strained over the British decision to blacklist American firms that traded with Germany. The violent suppression of the Irish Easter Rebellion also fueled already strong anti-British feelings within the Irish-American community. In addition, Wilson became increasingly frustrated by the Allies' unwillingness to consider a negotiated settlement. A second visit by Colonel House to Europe in 1916 found the British intransigent on the issue of freedom of the seas, the Germans unmovable on the issue of submarine warfare, and the French unwilling to consider negotiations until they were closer to victory along the western front.

While momentarily calming the crisis on the high seas, Wilson faced a more immediate problem in Mexico. In the spring of 1916 Mexican rebel Francisco "Pancho" Villa launched a series of murderous raids against American border towns. In pursuit of Villa and his forces, 12,000 American troops marched nearly 300 miles into Mexico. The Mexican government regarded the incursion as an invasion and American troops clashed with the Mexican army in Carrizal on June 21, 1916. Wilson prepared an address requesting permission from Congress to occupy northern Mexico, but upon learning that

American troops had attacked first at Carrizal, he abandoned his plan to fight Mexico. Wilson told his personal secretary:

> Someday, the people of America will know why I hesitated to intervene in Mexico ... Germany is anxious to have us at war with Mexico, so that our minds and our energies will be taken off the great war across the sea .... It begins to look as if war with Germany is inevitable. If it should come, I pray God it may not, I do not wish America's energies and forces divided for we will need every ounce of reserve we have to lick Germany.[5]

The two governments talked throughout the fall, and in January 1917 American troops withdrew.

That same month, Germany made the fateful decision to resume unconditional submarine warfare. German officials reasoned that their now substantial fleet of U-boats could sink enough Allied shipping fast enough to win the war before the Americans could arrive in force along the western front. It is easy to see why Germany dismissed the immediate military potential of the United States. During the period of neutrality, the nation had made few preparations for war. There were no fully organized divisions, corps, or armies, and available active duty and reserve troops numbered fewer than 350,000. The nation had 55 planes in questionable condition, enough artillery and ammunition to support approximately 220,000 men, and no tanks.[6] The Americans were somewhat more prepared with rifles, possessing enough to arm 890,000 troops.

Unaware of Germany's decision, Wilson made one final effort to suggest "a peace without victory." In a speech before Congress on January 22, 1917, Wilson outlined principles that he felt would end both this war and prevent futures ones. In this address, Wilson based his plan for a just peace on "American principles, American policies," which he defined as democracy, freedom of the seas, no entangling alliances, and equality of rights among nations. These were, Wilson asserted, "the principles and policies of forward-looking men and women everywhere, of every modern nation, of every enlightened community. They are the principles of mankind and must prevail."[7] Little did Wilson realize that within three months of uttering these words the nation would be at war.

In preparation for the announcement on January 31, 1917 that Germany would resume unconditional submarine warfare, German Foreign Minister Arthur Zimmermann attempted to take advantage of the Americans' recent trouble with Mexico. On January 16 Zimmermann sent a telegram to the German ambassador in Mexico instructing him to "make Mexico a proposal of alliance on the following basis: make war together, make peace together, generous financial support and an understanding on our part that Mexico is to re-conquer the lost territory in Texas, New Mexico and Arizona" ceded to the United States in the nineteenth century.[8] Zimmermann also suggested encouraging Japan to join the alliance to threaten America's Pacific island possessions. British intelligence cryptographers scored a major triumph when they both intercepted and deciphered the telegram. Britain presented the telegram to the Wilson administration at the end of February and its contents were released to the public in March. That month, German U-boats sank three American merchant ships. The tangible physical danger that Germany now posed to the nation's territorial and economic security convinced Wilson to ask Congress for a declaration of war.

Yet in his war address, Wilson did not dwell on these threats to the nation's borders or economy. Instead, he quickly summarized Germany's crimes on the high seas, then went on to cast the war in broader, idealistic terms. The United States, he declared, had "no quarrel with the German people." Instead, the United States was fighting against the "little groups of ambitious men" who used the German people as pawns to aggrandize their power. Wilson succinctly framed the war's purpose in a phrase that has resonated in American foreign policy ever since: the world, he declared "must be made safe for democracy."[9]

Congress overwhelmingly supported Wilson's request for a declaration of war against Germany, but approval was not unanimous. "I shall always believe we could and ought to have kept out of this war," House majority leader Claude Kitchin, a Democrat from North Carolina, remarked during the Congressional debate over the war resolution.[10] The United States officially declared war against Germany on April 6, 1917. The nation did not enter the war against Austria-Hungary until December 7, 1917, mostly to prevent Italy from leaving the war after its defeat at Caporetto, and never declared war against the Ottoman Empire or Bulgaria.

The Home Front

The war quickly changed the role that the federal government and its designated officials played in the lives of ordinary Americans. Within days of declaring war, Wilson decided to send troops rather than just financial or material aid to the western front. For men of fighting age, the immediate introduction of conscription took the decision to enter the army away from the individual and placed it in the hands of one of the 4,647 local draft boards formed to implement draft regulations.[11] The fear that too many volunteers from essential manufacturing and agricultural sectors might hamper the nation's ability to perform its vital function of feeding and supplying the Allied side heavily influenced the decision to rely primarily on conscription to raise the wartime force. Traditionally, however, the United States had only used conscription to spur enlistments once initial enthusiasm for war waned. The government worked hard to counter the popular view, well expressed by one congressman, that "there is precious little difference between a conscript and a convict."[12] Selective service, the government repeatedly told the American public, was a modern management technique designed to place men where they could best serve the war effort. Far from forcing the unwilling into uniform, the government contended that the draft selected men "from a Nation which volunteers in mass."[13]

American men exhibited less than overwhelming enthusiasm for going to war. During the short window available for enlistment, men did not flock to the colors and the army had to fill many spaces reserved for volunteers with conscripts. Although 24 million men registered for the draft without incident, millions then took advantage of their right to request a deferment because of their occupation or support of dependents. Overall, nearly three million of the draft-eligible male population refused to register or report to induction centers once called into service. In some isolated instances, draft evaders even engaged in armed confrontation with authorities. Yet the manpower pool was large enough for the draft to operate successfully in spite of these problems. In the end, over 72 percent of the wartime army was conscripted.

The government organized the selective service system without delay. It took more time for federal agencies to exert their full authority to manage the economy. In the winter of 1917–18, gridlock paralyzed railroads and ports, while an unusually cold winter created fuel shortages. To sort out this mess, a newly empowered War Industries Board ranked industries to ensure those most critical to the war effort received raw materials ahead of nonessential wartime businesses. The agency also established industrial committees to set price and production codes, and became the purchasing agent for Allied governments. By far the strongest step the government took was nationalizing the privately owned railroad system. Railroad companies eased their objections once the government offered generous financial compensation for use of their trains and track. In 1920, the government returned the railroads to their owners over the objections of labor unions lobbying for permanent nationalization.

Nationalizing industries was one approach to managing the wartime economy. At the other end of the spectrum lay the policies pursued by Food Administration director Herbert Hoover. The President possessed extensive powers to regulate the food and fuel industries. Hoover, however, opted to use high prices and patriotic appeals to control the nation's food supply. To stimulate production, he forced the American and Allied governments to pay high prices for agricultural goods. To curb civilian demand, he organized a propaganda campaign around the slogan "food will win the war" to encourage wheat-less Mondays, meatless Tuesdays, and pork-less Saturdays.

Patriotism helped the nation conserve sugar, but it did not blind businessmen and workers to the new economic opportunities that war made available to them.[14] The steel, copper, petroleum, and meat-packing industries enjoyed a healthy increase in profits once they began selling their products to the government. The government built high wages and union protection into its wartime contracts in exchange for a no-strike pledge from labor. Through the National War Labor Board, the federal government began maintaining fair and decent work standards for the first time in American history. The government took a hard line against industrialists who opposed collective bargaining, yet it also used sedition laws to harass antiwar radical labor groups. Both measures helped conservative trade unions like the American Federation of Labor increase their membership by 70 percent between 1917 and 1920.

In the end, however, business profited more than workers from the war. Workers received high wartime wages, but after adjusting for the considerable inflation, real wages only increased 4 percent. When the war ended and the government canceled its contracts, workers lost governmental support for their right to organize unions. Without the government stopping them, many manufacturers quickly returned to their old union-busting ways. The strong partnership that business created with the government during the war lasted longer. The prewar emphasis on punishing and regulating corporations gave way to new faith that the government could build a cooperative, friendly alliance with business to protect the common good.

The war initiated a major demographic shift within the United States as Southern blacks began to migrate north to fill vacancies generated by booming wartime production, conscription, and the interrupted flow of immigrants from Europe. African American migrants hoping to find the "promised land" in the North were often disappointed, however. Stuck in unskilled or semiskilled factory jobs and denied membership in white-only unions, black workers often jumped at the chance to work as strikebreakers. The explosive combination of economic competition and racial hostility triggered a series of racial riots in northern cities during the war. At the war's conclusion, the desire of whites to maintain the racial status quo collided with demands for change from African Americans, resulting in widespread racial violence and an upsurge in lynching in 1919.[15]

Women also assumed multiple new roles in factories and offices. Suffragists demanded that the nation thank women for their wartime contributions by giving them the right to vote. For months, members of the militant National Women's Party stood outside the White House with banners asking, "How long must women wait for liberty?"[16] The more conservative National American Woman Suffrage Association followed a different tack, presenting the right to vote as a way for women to protect their families and nation. "Every slacker has a vote ... Every pro-German who can not be trusted with any kind of military or war service will have a vote," Carrie Chapman Catt proclaimed. "It is a risk, a danger to a country like ours to send 1,000,000 men out of the country who are loyal and not replace those men by the loyal votes of the women they have left at home."[17] At the end of the war, the 19th Amendment to the American constitution finally granted women the right to vote. Their wartime work, however, failed to create any permanent opportunities for women in higher-paying or skilled industrial occupations.

Besides female suffrage, the war provided an opportunity for temperance reformers to add another amendment to the Constitution that permanently banned the manufacture and distribution of alcohol. The desire to protect the innocent young men heading to the training camps from the evils of drink and the need to conserve the nation's grain resources led to strict regulations concerning alcohol consumption and production during the war. Temperance advocates seized the moment to win crucial congressional and state support for prohibition and the nation officially went dry on January 16, 1920.

While various groups on the home front took advantage of the wartime environment to enact long desired changes in American society, the government tried to keep Americans focused on winning the war effort through a massive propaganda campaign headed by the Committee on Public Information. This agency plastered the nation with posters urging Americans to buy liberty bonds, organized a civilian army of public speakers known as "four-minute men" to address movie audiences on the causes and progress of the war, and offered translations of its pamphlets in multiple languages to spread its message throughout the nation's polyglot population.

Over There

"I hope you have not arrived too late." This was the greeting that General John J. Pershing received from the American Ambassador to France upon his arrival in Paris two months after the American declaration of war.[18] When the war ended on November 11, 1918, the Americans looked back over the previous 19 months and marveled that they had managed to raise an army of over 4 million men, transport 2 million to France, and command a field army of 1.2 million in major offensive operations along the western front. Despite these significant achievements, the Americans paid a price for their inexperience and lack of preparedness. American-commanded operations in the last four months of the war (when the United States took over its own sector of the western front) were hampered by disorganization in the rear, high casualty rates, and constantly changing leadership, problems all symptomatic of an army forced by circumstances to fight before it was fully trained and formed.

From 1914 to 1917, the professional military establishment in the United States did not completely ignore the war in Europe. With Congress only willing to authorize a small increase in the size of the army, however, there were few preparations defense officials could make to enter the fray at a moment's notice. As late as 1916, war plans prepared by the General Staff focused on protecting the United States from invasion. Given the distance that most Americans felt from events in Europe, it was perhaps fitting that it took an American military attaché in Greece to envision actually sending American troops overseas. In 1916, Captain Edward Davis took the initiative and developed a plan to land 500,000 American troops in Salonika to force Bulgaria out of the war.[19] Once the United States actually entered the war, the military quickly discarded this idea. The War College concluded:

> The Western Front is nearest to us; it can be most readily reached and with the least danger; we there fight with England and France with whom we have the greatest natural interests; and we can make our power felt on that front quicker and stronger than anywhere else; and we are there opposed by Germany, who is our only real enemy.[20]

Although nothing came of it, the exercise of considering another point of entry into the war revealed the misgivings that many Americans felt about sending troops into the bloody morass that had produced cataclysmic casualties at the Somme and Verdun. This sentiment was expressed best by Senator Thomas S. Martin, who when he heard of the War Department's initial request for $3 billion to equip the wartime force, exclaimed, "Good Lord! You're not going to send soldiers over there, are you?"[21]

The feeling that the Allies had squandered millions of men, coupled with Wilson's desire to use a strong showing on the battlefield to enhance his position at the peace table, led to an early American decision to create an independent army that controlled its own sector of the western front. When the American Expeditionary Forces (AEF) Commander, John J. Pershing, sailed for France, he left with these instructions from Secretary of War Newton Baker:

> In military operations against the Imperial German Government, you are directed to coop-erate with the forces of the other countries employed against the enemy; but in so doing the underlying idea must be kept in view that the forces of the United States are a separate and distinct component of the combined forces, the identity of which must be preserved.[22]

Except for outlining these general principles, Baker later liked to recall that he gave Pershing only two orders, one to go to France and the other to come home. No American commander before or since has had greater latitude in directing overall military operations.

In the summer of 1917, Pershing traveled to France and selected the Lorraine sector as the eventual site for an independent American presence along the western front. He also devised an overall strategic plan that settled on taking Metz as the key to defeating Germany. Controlling the key German railroad lines and iron mines above the city and the coal mines in the Saar, Pershing contended, would give the AEF a definitive victory in 1919.[23] In retrospect, the selection of Metz as a decisive target appears less convincing because the railroad line that Pershing expected to cut at Metz actually turned west much further north at Thionville, while the coal and iron reserves in the Saar region only accounted for 10 percent of Germany's available resources. Nonetheless, the goal of tak-ing Metz strongly influenced American training and operational planning.

To fight in the open terrain of the Moselle Valley, Pershing developed an open warfare strategy that served his dual purposes of training his army to fight in this region while also establishing a unique American combat doctrine that clearly separated American fighting technique from that of the French or British. Open warfare became Pershing's mantra throughout the war, a concept defined as much by the failings he saw in the Allied approach to war as by his eagerness to champion American initiative and individualism.

Trench warfare, the AEF commander concluded, had weakened the aggressive spirit of the Allied forces, and now their troops fought ineffectively when forced out of the trenches and into the open battlefield. By contrast, Pershing contended:

> open warfare is marked by scouts who precede the first wave, irregularity of formation, comparatively little regulations of space and time by the higher command, the greatest possible use of the infantry's own fire power to enable it to get forward, variable distances and intervals between units and individuals, use of every form of cover and accident of the ground during the advance, brief orders, and the greatest possible use of individual initiative by all troops engaged in the actions.[24]

To further his goal of open warfare, Pershing decided to form divisions of 28,000 men. Twice the size of their Allied counterparts, Pershing expected these larger divisions to have greater staying power in the field as the American Army surged forward toward Metz. Open warfare also privileged the firepower of the infantry over the artillery, a preference apparent when Pershing rejected an early suggestion that he double the size of both the infantry and artillery. As a result, American divisions went into combat with the same artillery as European divisions half their size.

Pershing's steadfast commitment to creating an independent army caused much conflict with the French and British. Pershing's reliance on his Allies to train, transport, and equip his troops did force some compromises in how and where the Americans fought. Despite Pershing's insistence on developing a distinct training regime, over the course of the war 25 American divisions spent time training with the French while nine divisions encamped with the British. In addition, hundreds of French and British instructors traveled to the United States to help train American troops. The reliance and influence that Allied trainers exerted on American troops were a constant source of concern for AEF commanders, who regarded their Allies with a mix of respect and disdain.

Reports of incremental success in building an independent American army failed to impress the Allies. For them, the only measure of progress that mattered was the American presence on the battlefield. The defeat of Russia meant that German divisions from the east would soon be making their way to the western front, where Allied commanders expected the German manpower advantage to increase by as much as 60 percent. French Commander in Chief Philippe Pétain worried that "the American army, if it wished to retain its autonomy, would be of no use to the Allies in 1918, except, perhaps, along some quiet section of the front."[25]

As Pétain suggested, to be an effective fighting force in 1918 required some alterations in Pershing's grand strategic plan. Although Pershing repeatedly resisted Allied demands to amalgamate American troops permanently into their armies, American units did a significant amount of fighting under British and French command. In a heralded moment at the height of the German spring offensives, Pershing went to Marshal Ferdinand Foch, the newly appointed Supreme Commander of the Allied Armies on the western front, to tell him that in light of the seriousness of the situation, "all that we have is yours; use them as you wish."[26] Subsequently, American infantry units fought alongside the British and French throughout the spring and summer. Some units even stayed with Allied forces after the Americans finally took over their own sector of the western front in August.

Many American soldiers initially looked forward to fighting. One soldier later recalled that he and his friends "were simply fascinated by the prospect of adventure and heroism… . Here was our one great chance for excitement and risk. We could not afford to pass it up."[27] Once on the front lines, however, American soldiers soon realized that real war bore little resemblance to their romantic fantasies. On the western front, Americans experienced both the horrors of trench warfare and the difficulties of conducting a war of movement during the sweeping counteroffensives and attacks that slowly pushed the Germans back toward their own border in the summer and fall of 1918. As one soldier succinctly noted, "those that weren't scared, weren't there."[28]

The war ended before Pershing had time to demonstrate either the wisdom or folly of attacking Metz, although in September 1918 the AEF successfully executed part of Pershing's initial plan by straightening out the Saint-Mihiel salient. Pershing had expected this battle to put the Americans in a better position to launch their planned 1919 attack on Metz. Instead, it proved a costly diversion that left the Americans with only two weeks to get into position 60 miles away to begin the Meuse–Argonne offensive, the American component of the final coordinated Allied attack along the western front. Contrary to American expectations, their larger divisions often proved unwieldy and difficult to maneuver during this final 47-day battle. With a lack of confidence in his troops' training, Pershing and his staff tended to give units carefully constrained instructions that undermined rather than encouraged the individual initiative that open warfare depended on for its success. In the end, critics charged, bigger divisions simply led to increased numbers of casualties.[29]

The final campaign did produce one genuine war hero on the American side, Sergeant Alvin York. York entered the military as a conscientious objector, but training-camp officials persuaded him to put aside his religious doubts and fight. York was an expert marksman who grew up hunting wild turkeys in the Tennessee Appalachian Mountains. He catapulted to fame within the United States when he singlehandedly rescued his ambushed patrol by killing 20 Germans, silencing 35 German machine guns, and taking 132 prisoners. In previous American wars, individual acts of heroism often turned the tide of battle. In the mechanized slaughter along the western front, York's extraordinary actions were still not enough to make a decisive difference in the Meuse–Argonne campaign.

When the guns fell silent along the western front, nearly 53,500 American men had died in combat as compared to 1.3 million Frenchmen and 900,000 from Britain and the Empire. Fully engaged from the opening days of the war, France and Britain lost an average of 900 and 457 men a day, respectively. For the Americans, the bulk of the fighting came in the last six months of the war, with their first year at war primarily given over to training and transporting troops overseas. The overall American average of 195 deaths a day reflects this lag between the American declaration of war and heavy involvement on the western front. Yet once American troops began fighting in earnest, their losses mirrored those of their Allied counterparts. In the summer and fall of 1918, deaths averaged 820 a day, not too far off the French figure and almost twice as many as the British.[30] These figures reflect the ferocious fighting that American troops encountered, as well as their overall lack of preparation for combat on the western front.

The Americans had reasons to be proud of the part they played in the final military victory. In the immediate aftermath of the conflict, enthusiasts wildly claimed that the United States had singlehandedly won the war, while detractors contended that the Americans accomplished little more than convincing Germany it was hopeless to continue. The truth lay somewhere in between. The Americans may not have won the war for the Allies, but they certainly kept them from losing it. At key moments in the German spring offensives in 1918, American troops helped stop the Germans from taking Paris. Newly arrived American divisions provided key strength to French-led counteroffensives over the summer, and in the fall American-commanded assaults pinned down large numbers of German troops, helping make possible British and French advances to the north.

Why Americans had fought and died became an open question once peace negotiations began. The challenge of fashioning a lasting peace proved as difficult as mobilizing the nation for war. For the first time, an American president traveled to Europe to oversee the peace process personally. How well Wilson succeeded in his quest to reshape the world became the measuring stick Americans used to decide if their sons and husbands had sacrificed their lives in vain.

Negotiating the Peace

In 1917, Wilson's "peace without victory" speech and his war address outlined his definition of a just peace. In January 1918 he refined his message even more with a speech that became known as the Fourteen Points. This address outlined a prescription for peace that both reflected Wilson's idealistic view of a future without war and also served the interests of the United States. Provisions to guarantee freedom of the seas and free trade now linked the spreading of democracy to the expansion of laissez-faire capitalism, a measure likely to advance American trading interests at the expense of imperialist powers such as Britain and France. Wilson's suggestion that the world disarm would certainly improve the security of the United States, which had traditionally maintained a small peacetime military. The promises to redraw the map of Europe along ethnic lines and consult colonial populations before determining their futures established the principle of "self-determination," an idea likely to cause conflict with the Allies over their own territorial ambitions in Europe and Africa. Finally, Wilson's proposal for a League of Nations envisioned collective security replacing the balance of power in order to maintain world peace.

Overall, the Fourteen Points were an ambitious proposal that reflected a desire to remake the world in the American mold and create a future without war. Wilson understood the challenges ahead. "England and France have not the same views with regard to peace that we have … [but after the war] we can force them to our way of thinking, because by that time they will […] be financially in our hands," Wilson told an aide.[31] While the last part of Wilson's prediction came to pass, at the Paris Peace Conference the Allies proved resolute in rejecting most of Wilson's plan.[32] Hinting at the trouble to come, French Prime Minister Georges Clemenceau did not even bother to read the Fourteen Points until Germany requested an armistice based on them in October 1918. Only the threat of a separate American peace settlement with Germany encouraged France and Britain to accept the Fourteen Points (minus the provision for freedom of the seas) as the basis for the armistice on November 11, 1918. On the eve of peace negotiations, Clemenceau quipped, "God gave us his Ten Commandments and we broke them. Wilson gave us his 14 points – well, we shall see."[33]

Once in Paris, Wilson came face to face with France's strong desire for a punitive peace and the guarantee of traditional defense pacts to contain any future German threat. Wilson was not opposed to dealing strongly with Germany, having moderated his initial view that the war was only against the German government and not its people. The harsh peace settlement that Germany inflicted on Russia in 1918 angered Wilson and he now agreed with the importance of depriving Germany of her navy and colonies. He parted company with the French, however, over their insistence that Germany be completely eviscerated.

Wilson also had problems at home where skeptics in Congress chafed at the president's plan to dramatically alter the nation's approach to foreign affairs by joining the League of Nations. Having eschewed any formal alliances since the eighteenth century, isolationists and traditionalists in Congress feared ceding too much power to the League of Nations. Critics chafed over the pledge member nations made to defend each other if attacked. "Are you ready to put your soldiers and your sailors at the disposition of other nations?," Senator Henry Cabot Lodge, the leading Republican opponent of the treaty, asked the American people.[34] Lodge was not an isolationist, but instead preferred the traditional balance-of-power approach to foreign policy. Overall, Lodge proposed adding 14 American reservations to the treaty, including one explicitly stating that "the United States assumes no obligation to preserve the territorial integrity or political independence of any other country or to interfere in controversies between nations," unless Congress gave explicit approval to send American troops overseas.[35]

Wilson refused to accept any alterations to the treaty, arguing that modifications would require renegotiation with all its signatories. He ignored hints from the other side of the Atlantic that Europe might accept American reservations if they were required to secure ratification. It was entirely possible Wilson intended to use this unyielding position as a negotiating strategy. Once the Senate vote was near, and Wilson was sure Lodge would not formulate other objections, perhaps he intended to bend. For the moment, however, Wilson stood firm and instead resolved to take his case directly to the people.

In just three weeks Wilson traveled 10,000 miles and made 40 speeches to hundreds of thousands of people. He offered a powerful defense of the League, and the momentum of public support began swinging his way as he crisscrossed the country proclaiming the virtues of becoming a member nation. Wilson mocked opponents' concerns about sending American troops throughout the world. "If you want to stamp out the smoldering flames in some part of Central Europe, you don't send to the United States for troops," Wilson contended. Besides, he noted, no nation could be forced to send troops against its will. The League would only select "them at their own consent, so the United States would in no such circumstances conceivable be drawn in unless the flames spread to the world," he assured his listeners.[36]

Wilson never acknowledged that joining the League of Nations represented a dramatic departure from the traditional American insistence on avoiding entangling alliances. Instead, Wilson used his extraordinary oratory skills to reduce audiences to tears by recalling those who fell on the battlefield to spread peace and democracy throughout the world. "What of our pledges to the men that lie dead in France?," he asked in the last public speech he gave in Pueblo, Colorado. "Nothing less depends upon this decision, nothing less than the liberation and salvation of the world."[37] Within hours after delivering this speech, his doctor rushed a twitching and nauseated Wilson back to Washington, DC, where two days later he suffered a stroke. His life in the balance and permanently paralyzed on his left side, Wilson spent the rest of his presidency hidden in the White House. Wilson was "as much a victim of the war as any soldier who died in the trenches," observed British Prime Minister David Lloyd George.[38]

Instead of using Wilson's collapse to win sympathetic support for the treaty, the president's inner circle kept the seriousness of his illness a secret. Wilson's secretary issued a statement attributing his collapse to exhaustion and assured the public he was resting comfortably. For weeks, however, Wilson only spent three hours a day out of bed and saw no one except his wife and physician. Wilson rejected all private suggestions that he resign, and still refused to accept any reservations to the treaty. It remains unclear whether this stubbornness was due to his convictions or symptomatic of a stroke-induced mental impairment. Regardless of the real reason, Wilson's refusal to compromise doomed the treaty to defeat. The Senate never ratified the Versailles Treaty and the United States never joined the League of Nations. Instead, the United States signed its own separate peace treaties with Germany, Austria, and Hungary in October 1921. Not all of Wilson's dreams died when the Senate rejected the treaty. Despite the nation's refusal to join the League of Nations, the United States continued to pursue the ideals of disarmament and collective security through a series of multinational agreements in the 1920s.

Postwar America

The crusade to make the world safe for democracy fared poorly within the United States both during and after the war. To control the antiwar movement and German propagandists, the government enacted a series of restrictive laws that severely curtailed Americans' right to free speech. The Trading with the Enemies Act in 1917 required all foreign-language publications to submit English-language translations of articles about the war to the Postmaster General. The Espionage Act of 1917 made it a crime to obstruct military recruitment, encourage mutiny, or aid the enemy by spreading lies. In 1918, the Sedition Act went even further by prohibiting anyone from uttering, writing, or publishing "any abusive or disloyal language" concerning the flag, constitution, government, or armed forces.

With the war won, the German threat evaporated. The menace of Bolshevism quickly took its place as the focus of government concern. Anxiety over disloyal immigrants continued, but federal investigators now centered their attention on Eastern Europeans, whom they suspected of importing radical communist ideas into the United States in the wake of the Russian Revolution. The war and subsequent Red Scare provided the momentum needed by anti-immigration groups to dramatically restrict immigration in the postwar period. A nation that had annually absorbed nearly a million immigrants from Europe now begrudgingly welcomed fewer than 200,000 a year.

The war had another marked effect on American society by establishing World War I veterans as a distinct political force.[39] Thousands returned home with war wounds that they grappled with for the rest of their lives. By 1921, most veterans were convinced that the war had permanently changed their lives, even if they were not suffering directly from mental or physical injuries. Unable to find jobs in the postwar recession, veterans believed they had missed their chance to get ahead in life. During the war, workers received the highest wages in American history, while soldiers collected $30 a month. Even worse, wartime contracts guaranteed industrialists generous profits. Veterans believed the federal government had failed to balance the financial burden of the war equally between civilians and soldiers. To rectify this past injustice, they agitated for adjusted compensation. In 1924, veterans settled for a bond certificate that matured in 1945, rather than an immediate cash settlement. With the economy improving, veterans accepted this compromise, satisfied the country had acknowledged its monetary debt to them.

At the time, this appeared to settle the issue once and for all. But in 1932, three years into the Great Depression, 30,000 World War I veterans organized a two-month march on Washington, DC to demand early payment of their wartime bonus. The government's decision to use the army to violently evict these veterans resulted in a backlash against President Herbert Hoover that contributed to the election of Franklin D. Roosevelt. The hope of avoiding a similar clash with veterans at the end of World War II induced the government to create the most comprehensive social welfare program in American history for these returning servicemen. The nation, therefore, felt the aftershocks of its first experience with mass conscription long after the last American soldier came home in 1920.

* * *

The United States took a long time to decide that military engagement in World War I was in its national interest. Once it entered the conflict the demands of total war quickly reconfigured American society. The war touched all segments of the American population, many of whom realized that the crisis presented an opportunity to achieve long-coveted changes, including female suffrage, immigration reform, market consolidation, or simply a new job and address. Mobilizing the manufacturing and agricultural sectors, selecting men for the military, and regulating transportation and media networks required an exertion of unparalleled state power. The precedent set by the government's wartime management of the economy created the foundations for a managerial state that would evolve dramatically over subsequent decades. The state's surveillance of the American population created an atmosphere in which dissent became practically impossible and established a police-state apparatus that never disbanded. Overall, the measures taken to marshal the nation's resources for war established the modern American state.

The impact of the war on American foreign policy was equally significant. Seeking to provide a broader purpose for the conflict, Woodrow Wilson articulated ideological principles that became the basis for future American overseas adventures. Spreading democracy through the principle of self-determination emerged as the cornerstone of American foreign policy, as did the expectation that progress depended on the rest of the world adopting the American form of capitalism. For this reason, the Fourteen Points stand alongside the Declaration of Independence and Emancipation Proclamation as one of the most important documents in American history.

In the broadest and narrowest sense, American involvement in the war tipped the balance in favor of the Allies on the western front. American material and financial support proved crucial even before the United States formally entered the war, while American troops contributed significantly to the final victory in 1918. Over 15 percent of the American male population served in the military during the war and over one million saw combat along the western front. They were part of the unlucky generation that came together from throughout the world to fight the bloodiest war to date.

Notes

1   Knock, *To End All Wars: Woodrow Wilson and the Quest for a New World Order*, p. 19.
2   Zieger, *America's Great War*, pp. 41–2.
3   Keith, *Rich Man's War, Poor Man's Fight*, pp. 24–54.
4   Zieger, *America's Great War*, pp. 30–1.
5   Levin, *Woodrow Wilson and World Politics*, p. 311.
6   Weigley, *History of the United States Army*, p. 362.

7   Graham, *The Great Campaigns: Reform and War in America*, p. 326.
8   Zimmermann Telegram, reproduced at http://www.archives.gov/digital_classroom/lessons/
    zimmermann_telegram/zimmermann_telegram.html.
9   Graham, *The Great Campaigns: Reform and War in America*, pp. 330–2.
10 Keith, *Rich Man's War, Poor Man's Fight*, p. 14.
11 Keene, *Doughboys, the Great War and the Remaking of America*, pp. 18–19.
12 Chambers, *To Raise an Army: The Draft Comes to Modern America*, p. 165.
13 Rawls, *World War I and the American Poster*, p. 112.
14 Kennedy, *Over Here*, pp. 93–143.
15 Barbeau and Henri, *The Unknown Soldiers: African-American Troops in World War I*,
    pp. 175–89.
16 Schaffer, *America in the Great War*, p. 93.
17 Ibid., pp. 91–2.
18 Pershing, *My Experiences in the World War*, vol. I, p. 60.
19 Spector, "'You're Not Going to Send Soldiers Over There, Are You!'," pp. 1–4.
20 Trask, *The AEF and Coalition Warmaking, 1917–1918*, p. 7.
21 Keith, *Rich Man's War, Poor Man's Fight*, p. 42.
22 *United States Army in the World War, 1917–1919*, vol. 1, p. 3.
23 Millett, "Over Where? The AEF and the American Strategy for Victory, 1917–1918,"
    p. 239.
24 *United States Army in the World War, 1917–1919*, vol. 2, p. 491.
25 Ibid., pp. 186–7.
26 Bruce, *A Fraternity of Arms*, p. 195.
27 Langer, *Gas and Flame in World War I*, p. xviii.
28 Coffman, *The War to End All Wars*, p. 289.
29 Nenninger, "American Military Effectiveness in the First World War," pp. 42–153.
30 Audoin-Rouzeau and Becker, *14–18, Understanding the Great War*, p. 22.
31 Zieger, *America's Great War*, p. 163.
32 Harries and Harries, *The Last Days of Innocence*, pp. 409–14.
33 Widenor, "The United States and the Versailles Peace Settlement," p. 40.
34 Ibid., p. 49.
35 Keene, *The United States and the First World War*, p. 75.
36 Ibid., p. 75.
37 Ibid., p. 110.
38 Kennedy, *Over Here*, p. 361.
39 Keene, *Doughboys, the Great War and the Remaking of America*, pp. 179–214.

References and Further Reading

Audoin-Rouzeau, Stéphane, and Becker, Annette, *14–18, Understanding the Great War*, New
    York, Hill and Wang, 2002.
Barbeau, Arthur E., and Florette, Henri, *The Unknown Soldiers: African-American Troops in World
    War I*, New York, Da Capo Press, 1996.
Braim, Paul, *The Test of Battle: The American Expeditionary Forces in the Meuse–Argonne Campaign*,
    Shippensburg, PA, White Mane Publishing, 1987; new ed., 1998.
Bruce, Robert, *A Fraternity of Arms: America & France in the Great War*, Lawrence, University
    Press of Kansas, 2003.
Chambers, II, John Whiteclay, *To Raise an Army: The Draft Comes to Modern America*, New York,
    The Free Press, 1987.
Coffman, Edward, *The War to End All Wars: The American Military Experience in World War I*,
    New York, Oxford University Press, 1968.
Ferrell, Robert J., *Woodrow Wilson and World War I, 1917–1921*, New York, Harper and Row, 1985.

Ford, Nancy Gentile, *American All! Foreign-Born Soldiers in World War I*, College Station, Texas A&M University Press, 2001.

Graham, Otis L., Jr., *The Great Campaigns: Reform and War in America, 1900–1928*, Englewood Cliffs, NJ, Prentice-Hall, 1971.

Harries, Meirion, and Harries, Susie, *The Last Days of Innocence: America at War, 1917–1918*, New York, Vintage Books, 1997.

Keene, Jennifer D., *The United States and the First World War*, New York, Longman, 2000.

Keene, Jennifer D., *Doughboys, the Great War and the Remaking of America*, Baltimore, Johns Hopkins University Press, 2001.

Keith, Jeanette, *Rich Man's War, Poor Man's Fight: Race, Class and Power in the Rural South during the First World War*, Chapel Hill, University of North Carolina Press, 2004.

Kennedy, David, *Over Here: The First World War and American Society*, New York, Oxford University Press, 1980.

Knock, Thomas J., *To End All Wars: Woodrow Wilson and the Quest for a New World Order*, New York, Oxford University Press, 1992.

Langer, W. L., *Gas and Flame in World War I*, New York, Knopf, 1965.

Levin, N. G., *Woodrow Wilson and World Politics: America's Response to War and Revolution*, New York, Oxford University Press, 1968.

Millet, Allan R., "Over Where? The AEF and the American Strategy for Victory, 1917–1918," in Kenneth J. Hagan and William R. Roberts (eds.), *Against All Enemies: Interpretations of American Military History from Colonial Times to the Present*, Westport, CT, Greenwood Press, 1986, pp. 235–56.

Nenninger, Timothy K., "American Military Effectiveness in the First World War," in Allan R. Millet and Williamson Murray (eds.), *Military Effectiveness: The First World War*, vol. 1, Boston, Allen and Unwin, 1988, pp. 142–53.

Pershing, John J., *My Experiences in the World War*, vol. 1, New York, Frederick A. Stokes, 1931.

Rawls, Walton, *World War I and the American Poster*, New York, Cross River Press, 1988.

Schaffer, Ronald, *America in the Great War: The Rise of the War Welfare State*, New York, Oxford University Press, 1991.

Smythe, Donald, *Pershing. General of the Armies*, Bloomington, Indiana University Press, 1986.

Spector, Ronald, "'You're Not Going to Send Soldiers Over There, Are You!': The American Search for an Alternative to the Western Front 1916–1917," *Military Affairs*, 36/1, February 1972, pp. 1–4.

Trask, David F., *The AEF and Coalition Warmaking, 1917–1918*, Lawrence, University of Kansas Press, 1993.

United States Army in the World War, 1917–1919, 18 vols., Washington, DC, Center for Military History, 1988.

Weigley, Russell F., *History of the United States Army*, New York, Macmillan, 1967.

Widenor, W. C., "The United States and the Versailles Peace Settlement," in J. M. Carroll and G. C. Herring (eds.), *Modern American Diplomacy*, Wilmington, DE, Scholarly Resources, 1996, pp. 41–60.

Zieger, Robert H., *America's Great War: World War I and the American Experience*, Oxford, Rowman and Littlefield, 2000.

CHAPTER THIRTY-FIVE

The French and British Empires

ROBERT ALDRICH AND CHRISTOPHER HILLIARD

World War I was a world war partly because of the involvement of European colonies scattered around the globe. Many of the belligerent powers claimed overseas possessions. Britain's Empire covered 32 million sq km and counted 400 million inhabitants in 1914, while France's empire encompassed 10.5 million sq km and a population of 44 million. Their allies, including Belgium, Italy, Portugal, and the United States, boasted overseas colonies. On the other side of the battle lines, Germany's relatively newly acquired colonies formed the fifth largest overseas empire in geographical size, and the Near Eastern provinces of Ottoman Turkey represented an object of expansionist desires among the allies. When war was declared, Britain's settler colonies ("dominions") – Canada, Australia, New Zealand, Newfoundland, and South Africa – had achieved self-government, but were seen by both colonials and Britons as indefectibly tied to the Crown, and the Union Flag flew over huge territories from western Africa to eastern Asia and the South Pacific. France governed much of northern, western, and equatorial Africa, Madagascar, and Indochina and, like Britain, possessed islands spread across the world's oceans.

The British and French colonies were drawn into the war in various ways. Some colonies represented great strategic stakes. French Morocco, for example, the scene of confrontations with Germany in 1905 and 1911, guarded the sea-lanes between the Atlantic and the Mediterranean, as did Britain's Gibraltar across the straits. Fighting also took place in colonial territory. Just hours after the declaration of war between France and Germany, a German warship shelled the Algerian coast; the first German territory occupied in the name of King George V was the Samoan island of Upolu, seized by New Zealand forces. Most British and French colonies avoided conflict on their soil; however, the British and French, and their colonial allies, mounted successful campaigns to take Germany's colonies in Africa and Oceania (see chapter 8) and the Turkish Middle East (see chapter 7).

The colonies were important above all for their manpower and material resources. In what the French called the *appel à l'empire*, settlers and indigenous people were enrolled by their hundreds of thousands and dispatched to virtually every front. In Europe they were joined by "natives" brought to work in war industries, agriculture, and construction work behind the lines. The war took a cruel toll on men shipped from far away to battle on behalf of a country to which they pledged their loyalties with varying degrees of willingness. The reciprocal effects on the colonial world – the establishment of national myths, demands for greater political autonomy and representation, the personal experience of those who had served, the redrawing of colonial boundaries – were dramatic and long-lasting. Colonial concerns did not lie at the heart of the conflict, but the shock of the fighting and its aftermath reverberated throughout the domains conquered by Europeans.

Colonial Participation in the War

The most striking difference in the role played by the French and British colonies in World War I was the contrast in the burden borne by settlers as opposed to colonized peoples. The French Empire was by and large not one of settlement, with the largest population of European inhabitants, in Algeria and Tunisia, numbering little more than a million in 1914. Hence the French had no option but to mobilize the indigenous peoples of the Empire. Britain, by contrast, could draw on the white populations of the dominions, though indigenous Africans were used in the campaigns against Germany in South-West Africa and above all in Tanganyika (see chapter 8). Additionally, it could use India, which, as always, was in a category of its own.

India stood at the center of Britain's strategic thinking about the Empire. Yet India was not just a possession to be defended at great cost, but also an offensive asset. The armies of continental Europe dwarfed the British army, and at the start of the war, Britain was the only belligerent country without a system of conscription, which it would not introduce until 1916. In these circumstances, India provided much-needed troops. Numbering 155,000 at the beginning of the war, the Indian army was, as David Omissi observes, " 'Indian' only in a nominal sense": the great majority of its recruits came from the north and northwest of the Subcontinent (defending the North-West Frontier was one of its primary purposes).[1] Recruits from the cities were shunned as effete, as were men from the south and the east. In the years after 1857, the Bengal regiments that had mutinied were disbanded and the Bengalis, who were supposedly insufficiently warlike, were now replaced in the ranks of the Indian army by Sikhs from the Punjab and other members of the "martial races," a more or less formal category in the Raj's taxonomy of its subjects. Many of the Indians who served in France were Punjabi Muslims and Sikhs.

The Indian infantry was light infantry, trained and equipped for a colonial rather than a European war. The first Indian units to fight in France and Belgium suffered heavy casualties. For much of 1915, the Indian Corps, with two infantry divisions and two cavalry divisions (a total of 28,500 Indian troops and 16,000 from British army units brought into the corps), held the front in the Neuve Chapelle–Givenchy sector. After continued losses – of British officers as well as Indian men – and with concern about morale, the infantry divisions were removed at the end of 1915.[2] From this point onward, Mesopotamia became the main theater of the Indian troops. By the end of hostilities, India had provided the British war effort with over 1,270,000 men, 827,000 of them combatants. India also supplied money and resources worth more than £146 million.

Before the outbreak of war, many of Britain's leaders had been skeptical of the military value of the settler colonies. In 1909, New Zealand had given Britain the money to build a Dreadnought battleship (it saw action in the war's North Sea battles), but the dominion still depended on the Royal Navy for its own defense. Sir Wilfrid Laurier's

prewar plans for an independent Canadian navy that could be lent to Britain in emergen-
cies were scuttled by opposition from Anglophone Canadians who wanted direct dona-
tions to the Royal Navy and French Canadians who wanted no such offering to Britain.
Though Canada could not provide Britain with a naval force, Canadian industry nevertheless supplied British forces in France with munitions. Canada also committed troops,
quickly and in large numbers, about 458,000 all told. If the other dominions did not
contribute arms and machinery, they too made extraordinary if not profligate contributions of manpower. New Zealand sent a tenth of its entire population overseas to fight,
some 112,000. Australia sent 332,000; 136,000 white South Africans went to war,
mostly against German forces in Africa and only belatedly on the western front. Black
South Africans were barred from military service, but 44,000 were sent to France in the
South African Native Labour Contingent.[3] Newfoundland, still a dominion separate
from Canada, contributed a regiment that was all but destroyed at Beaumont-Hamel
at the Somme on July 1, 1916: of 790 officers and men, 272 were killed and 438
wounded.[4]

The "expeditionary forces" sent by the dominions were not discrete colonial armies.
They acted as corps within the British armies fighting on the western front, or were
combined with other colonies' troops; when depleted by casualties, some regiments
merged with British units. Nevertheless, colonial forces were by no means dissolved into
a homogenized "imperial" military force. Shut out of the upper levels of strategy and
command, colonial political and military leaders took pains to assert as much control as
they could over "their" forces. The Australian Imperial Force and the Canadian
Expeditionary Force remained intact to the end of the war. Until 1917 British generals
led both, in part because of shortages of experienced colonial officers at the outset. The
second British general to lead the Canadian forces, Sir Julian Byng, deliberately promoted Canadian officers, one of whom, Sir Arthur Currie, eventually replaced him. The
Australian forces, too, came under the control of one of their own, Sir John Monash.
Both Currie and Monash continued the process of turning their forces into a relatively
autonomous national force, especially during the response to the Ludendorff offensive
in 1918.

The much smaller pool of French citizens living in the colonies was composed of
those with European ancestry (and naturalized Jews in Algeria), the inhabitants of
France's old colonies in the Antilles and La Réunion, and a small number of évolués –
"advanced" natives, or indigenous people who were considered to be assimilated into
French culture. Overall, some 134,210 overseas French citizens were mobilized, 92,000
of them in Algeria, and they left for Europe almost as soon as fighting began in 1914.
The French also mobilized 545,240 indigenous soldiers, 437,653 of whom served in
Europe or the Near East.[5] The French thereby continued a long tradition of using
"native" troops, especially the *tirailleurs sénégalais*, light infantry recruited from throughout western Africa (despite their always being referred to as Senegalese). The *tirailleurs*,
as Myron Echenberg points out, basically formed a mercenary army that had already
played a large role in the acquisition and defense of France's Empire.[6] The colonized, in
general, were not obliged to do military service until 1917, but campaigns of recruitment offered pecuniary inducements to sign up and became increasingly coercive (and
more contested) during the course of the war. Men of all backgrounds responded: the
mobilized included 269,950 Muslims from Algeria, Tunisia, and Morocco, 181,512
black Africans, 48,922 from Indochina, 41,355 from Madagascar, 2,434 from French
Somalia, and 1,067 from the French Pacific.[7] The overseas forces, with their colorful

names, traditions, and uniforms – the *zouaves* and *turcos* (Algerian infantry), *spahis* (North African light cavalry), *goumiers marocains* (Moroccan levies), and *tirailleurs* – thus became incorporated into the effort to win the war for "greater France."

Some in France had expressed concerns about use of colonial troops, such as the cost of transport (and the bounty paid to volunteers), the ability of soldiers from tropical or Mediterranean regions to adapt effectively to conditions in Europe, the fact that most indigenous soldiers did not understand French, the possible dangers of leaving colonies insecurely guarded against rebellion, and the uncertain results on "natives" of life in the metropole. The metropolitan army traditionally held the colonial forces (and many of the French commanders assigned to them) in low esteem. Others objected to the use of colonial soldiers for different reasons – the socialist Jean Jaurès, assassinated on the eve of the war, had argued that the Republic ought to be defended by citizens, not colonized mercenaries. However, the war demanded all resources, and the use of nonwhite soldiers had been promoted for several years before 1914, especially given France's chronically low birth rate and festering resentment at a Germany that had dealt France a humiliating defeat in 1870–1. General Charles Mangin's book, *La Force noire* (1910), articulated the rationale, arguing that "warrior instincts ... remain extremely powerful in primitive races": Africans could live in harsher climates than other races, centuries of porterage had developed their ability to shoulder heavy loads, the black nervous system made them resistant to pain, and endemic warfare in Africa prepared men for the battlefield.

Indigenous colonial troops from North Africa arrived immediately war broke out in 1914 and in force in 1915 and 1916. However, the belief persisted in some quarters that the Indochinese were not physically up to battle and that Africans were primitive in their fighting behavior. This latter view was reciprocated by the Germans, who had already condemned the use of colonial troops in the Franco-Prussian War in 1870 as "barbaric," and who now formally protested to the French government at the employment of racially "primitive" soldiers in the European theater. Nonetheless, African and Asian men came to play a significant role in the French army on the western front. By 1917 even the anticolonial Georges Clemenceau strongly advocated their employment, and the government commissioned Blaise Diagne – a Senegalese notable recently elected the first African member of the French parliament – to lead a recruitment campaign in West and Equatorial Africa.

Conditions of service, however, were far from easy. Although not segregated, the non-Europeans encountered racial discrimination and violence. The military hierarchy awarded promotions to "natives" with the greatest parsimony; in 1917, there were only six black African officers, the highest-ranking four lieutenants, and a couple of hundred Muslim officers.[8] Distance from home deprived colonial men of the consolations of family, though various support organizations ministered to their needs, provided rest and recuperation in hostels, and encouraged their *esprit de corps*. Daily life for colonial soldiers, especially during cold winters, proved even harder than for ordinary *poilus*. Military authorities had to concede sending colonial units to the Midi for the winter, although bad conditions in Fréjus – with the mistral wind howling – led soldiers to call the base "Camp Misery," and many suffered respiratory infections.

Some historians have argued that the French military command used soldiers from the colonies, particularly non-Europeans, as "cannon fodder," sending them to the most dangerous engagements. Strategists had certainly thought that Africans would be most useful as shock troops. Joe Lunn points out the difficulty of relying on statistical evidence to determine if this was the case – whether to compare figures for the mobilized, those actually sent to France, those who saw action, and those who served in different units. He argues that during the last 30 months of the war, when colonial soldiers fought in greatest numbers, Senegalese losses were approximately twice as high as those suffered by French infantrymen. Jacques Frémeaux, however, concludes that though the military brass made no effort to save "native" blood, they by no means sacrificed colonial soldiers indiscriminately.[9]

The colonial troops, generally combined with metropolitan units, served along the western front, including at Ypres and Verdun, in the opening stages of the war. Primarily colonial battalions were used at the Chemin des Dames (the second battle of the Aisne) in 1917, where the death rate reached 45 percent, leading the commander, none other than General Mangin, to be branded the "butcher of the blacks" by his detractors. Colonial soldiers played a particularly noteworthy part in the battles of the Somme and at Verdun in retaking the fort of Douaumont. The Armée de l'Orient, which fought in the Dardanelles and Balkans, also included many colonial units. In both northern France and at Gallipoli, where the French sent 80,000 colonials, the men fought alongside soldiers from the British Empire, including Anzacs (members of the Australian and New Zealand Army Corps).[10] A total of 87,000 soldiers from the colonies died in the war, including 16,000 French citizens and 70,000 "natives." This represented 13 percent of those mobilized, though not all of the latter saw action, since many continued to garrison the colonies. Around 240,000 colonial soldiers, including 200,000 indigenous troopers, were wounded.[11]

The French also brought 220,668 "natives" – in addition to Europeans, including 230,000 Spaniards – to staff essential industries, especially armaments and munitions factories, and to work on farms and in vineyards replacing laborers serving on the front. Labor unions were hardly enthusiastic about the presence of foreign workers, but the war economy demanded manpower that was increasingly scarce on the home front. The largest number of colonial migrant workers, a total of 75,864, came from Algeria, with 48,981 from Indochina, as well as 36,740 recruited outside the French colonial sphere in China. The migrants were supposed to be paid the same wages, and provided equivalent working conditions, as French workers, although the cost of their transport to France, food, and lodging was generally deducted from their pay, and not all employers provided the minimum wage. The workers were spread around France, but with large numbers in Paris and Marseille and other ports. Civilian and military authorities made some efforts to provide for colonial soldiers' and migrants' needs. A mosque was set up in the colonial military hospital in Paris, "Moorish" cafés opened, and couscous appeared on mess-hall tables. The military also required that Muslim soldiers killed in battle be interred according to Islamic rites, and the government quashed a Catholic bishop's plan to evangelize among the Muslims.

French authorities and indigenous officials, such as Indochinese mandarins hired for the purpose, kept close surveillance over the migrants, keen to detect any possible subversion. John Horne has shown, through examination of reports of the Tunisian censors, that many colonial workers complained about low wages, overwork, high prices, and the shock of living in France; others, however, seemed content with their conditions and enjoyed the metropolitan life which they had glimpsed in colonial propaganda, but which most had never experienced. Migrants' assignations with prostitutes, and even more so, sexual and romantic liaisons with French women, particularly worried officials, and censors even fretted about "dirty postcards."[12] Altercations between colonial men and Europeans almost inevitably occurred. Tyler Stovall characterizes several incidents as race riots, especially during 1917 and 1918, when labor unrest spread. The most serious occurred in Le Havre, where an exchange of insults between a Frenchman and a Moroccan degenerated into a protracted street brawl. Most confrontations involved hooligan attacks by small groups of Frenchmen reacting against what they perceived as colonials taking away their jobs and women; false rumors that colonials were used as strike-breakers during industrial action in 1917 also inflamed tensions. The police made few arrests, but occasionally colonial workers countered with violence of their own. For French and colonial society in general, the experience of migrant labor, and the questions it provoked, foreshadowed issues that have endured to today.[13]

Soldiers from the British Empire, too, felt the strangeness of what was, for them, a new world. "I have used nothing of this country up to date, except water and fruit," wrote a Punjabi Muslim serving in France, "… but now my inner man begins to prompt me and I am afraid of falling. Many distinguished people here have given up making any distinction between clean and unclean things, and I suppose there is not one percent of them who refuse to eat with the French."[14] The experiences of travel and combat focused attention on the defining characteristics of peoples from different parts of the British Empire, especially for soldiers from the dominions. Encounters with troops from other colonies and from Britain prompted much discussion of the "distinctive" characteristics of particular dominions. Were colonials less deferential to officers? Were they in some way tougher, or more resourceful? Often the characteristics identified were not really very distinctive: Australasians were struck by the singular practicality of the Anzacs, but Canadians detected a distinctively Canadian practicality in their soldiers' approach to things. Nor, inevitably, were the war's "lessons" about colonial characteristics always coherent. The New Zealanders described themselves as less formal and more irreverent than the Tommies, but their reputation as "the silent division" (because they did not sing) points to another possible interpretation of the "national character." Whatever the veracity of these perceptions, military service on the western front, in Turkey, and in the Middle East created situations where colonials felt that their emerging national types were laid bare; the consistency of the stereotypes mattered less than the assumption of genuine colonial characteristics to detect.

The Impact of the War on the Colonies

The experience of colonial men who fought and worked abroad in the service of the imperial war effort had long-lasting effects on colonial societies, which will be discussed below. But the home societies were also directly affected by the war while it lasted, not least through the growing manpower crisis and the question of whether conscription should be applied in the Empire. In the British settler dominions, after the first burst of enlistment, the numbers of new recruits fell, partly because of the high casualty lists, and partly because (at least in Australia and Canada) many eager early volunteers were colonists born in Britain. Colonial-born Europeans were more reluctant. After Britain itself introduced conscription in 1916, the settler colonies took steps toward following suit. New Zealand did so in July the same year, but in Australia and Canada, conscription was fiercely contested. French Canadians, resentful of alienating actions taken by Protestant-dominated national and provincial governments since the beginning of the war, resisted conscription; so did organized labor and farmers (the categories overlapped, many Québécois living in rural areas). Robert Borden's Union government pushed through the conscription legislation after winning the fiercely fought general election at the end of 1917. A number of Liberals left their leader, Laurier, who supported the war but opposed conscription, and joined Borden's government. Laurier lost his now impossible position as Quebec's leader to the separatist Henri Bourassa. The old party system was in tatters, and the divisions the war had exacerbated were demonstrated again in labor and farm protests, and anti-recruitment riots in Quebec City the following year.

Determinedly opposed by trade unions, conscription was twice defeated when put to a referendum in Australia. Though the 1916 Easter Uprising in Ireland was a nagging presence in both sides' polemics about commitment to the imperial war effort, the voting divided largely along class lines. That military service had remained a matter of choice meant that veterans' contributions to Australia would be all the more contested a political property. The Returned Servicemen's League enjoyed direct access to the cabinet, and in the 1920s and 1930s often weighed into politics in support of a conservative version of the nationhood that they claimed to represent. In New Zealand, the absence of bitter conscription disputes and the extent of the sacrifice – observers remarked that there was scarcely a family not represented at the front – meant that military service divided that dominion less. In New Zealand, too, Anzac and Gallipoli loomed large in the liturgy of national pride and national grief (from 1916, commercial uses of the word "Anzac" were outlawed), but there, in contrast to Australia, the Anzac mystique was not the preserve of white colonists only. Maori too had volunteered for the war effort; for them, the rewards of service were collective political bargaining chips, rather than the individuated rewards of citizenship for which indigenous soldiers in the French Empire could strive. Maori leaders who operated within colonial institutions, especially parliamentarians, laid claim to the Anzac legend, seeking to embed in it a story of racial partnership forged through shared sacrifice in negotiations with New Zealand's powerbrokers during the 1920s.

In the French case, too, the investment of the colonies in the war, at home and in Europe, had a profound impact that centered both on continued recruitment and on the wartime levy on the local economy. The departure of many administrators for war service – in 1918, only about a quarter of the administrative posts in the colonies remained filled – left a lack of bureaucratic infrastructure, and siphoning-off of funds brought many colonial projects to a standstill. At the beginning of the war, French authorities had confiscated the assets of enemy nationals, including the numerous Germans in Morocco, and business ties between the colonies and Germany, such as German trading in Tahiti, were cut. Local production became geared to the war economy, as the state established a virtual monopoly over purchase of vital commodities – requisitions that ironically caused scarcities in the colonies. Taxes, which fell most heavily on "natives," were increased to fund the war. Officials, however, secured strongly worded endorsements of France's war aims from the Sultan of Morocco, the King of Cambodia, and other leaders. Censorship and surveillance of dissidents increased, and a French propaganda campaign drummed up support for the war and counteracted enemy propaganda, especially that directed at Islamic countries, which portrayed the Germans and Turks as liberators of colonized Muslims.

Though pro-German and pro-Turkish overtures enjoyed little success, colonial revolts punctuated the war years, with rebellions in French West Africa the most serious. In the Grande Rivière uprising in 1915–16, 160,000 insurgents in 500 villages maintained staunch resistance over nine months; several thousand were killed by French soldiers, and in the repression the French confiscated all weapons, including ones used for hunting.[15]

Rebellions also broke out in Algeria, Morocco, New Caledonia, and Indochina – for throwing his support behind a rebellion, the Annamese emperor Duy Thanh was forced to abdicate and was sent into exile.

Generally revolts were precipitated by coercive recruitment strategies; campaigns to recruit soldiers, especially in black Africa, turned into military roundups of men virtually forced to join the army, especially after extension of mandatory military service to all the African colonies in November 1917. Diagne's recruitment drive, which ultimately yielded 77,000 soldiers, sparked such opposition that many African men fled to British or Portuguese territories to avoid conscription – Lord Lugard, Governor of British Nigeria, remarked that the French were practicing a "coercion not possible under our system."[16] Joost Van Vollenhoven, former Governor-General of Indochina, having served at the front line for two years before being appointed Governor-General of French West Africa, was so angered at the recruitment campaign (and Diagne's incursions on his own authority) that he resigned and asked to return to the front, where he died in battle. One French official wrote of the recruitment drive as "trafficking in human flesh by the sergeant recruiter."[17]

Although revolts clearly touched on various general grievances of colonized peoples – the Grande Rivière insurrection began with the killing of a Frenchman renowned for brutality – they did not immediately endanger the survival of the Empire. Nevertheless, the genesis of later nationalist groups, such as the VVS in Madagascar and Destour in Tunisia, can be traced to the colonial rebellions; Abd el-Krim's rebellion in the Rif mountains soon after the war escalated into a major conflagration in French Morocco, and even a 1930 revolt in Indochina may be judged a riposte to destabilization produced by the war.

The Legacy of the War for Empire

With service came expectations. That the sacrifice of "blood and treasure" for the British Empire's war effort would lead to political demands for increasing self-government (in India's case) or to a more powerful voice in international affairs (in the case of the settler colonies) had not been unpredicted. For this reason, those most committed to the Empire – British officials in the colonies as well as metropolitan politicians – were sometimes the least enthusiastic about extensive colonial participation in the war effort. As Robert Holland writes, "the most conservative elements in Indian administration tended to be wary of bidding up India's role in Imperial belligerency while those *least* committed to the status quo supported a thoroughgoing exploitation of Indian manpower and resources."[18] Conversely, the British politician who made the British war effort into a genuinely imperial one, David Lloyd George, enjoyed a questionable pedigree as an imperialist, having been a leading "pro-Boer" or "Little Englander" during the Anglo-Boer war. The battery of imperial institutions that Lloyd George set up in 1917 – the Imperial War Cabinet, the Imperial Development Board, the Imperial War Conferences – did not reflect a conversion to the kind of faith in the Empire held by Lord Milner, the imperial grandee whom he appointed to the War Cabinet. Rather, it reflected Lloyd George's determination to use all of Britain's political and economic resources to the fullest – for the sake of winning Britain's war, not for the greater glory of its overseas possessions.

While the Imperial War Conference met in London in April–May 1917, the British War Cabinet invited dominion prime ministers to several special meetings. Lloyd George extended to the dominions a level of consultation that buttressed the legitimacy of his demands on their populations and economies, but without drawing representatives of the settler colonies into the inner circle of British decision-making. Both the 1917 and the 1918 Imperial War Conferences provided a forum for the articulation of postwar colonial ambitions as well as for coordinating imperial war policy. At the 1917 conference, dominion leaders went well beyond the constitutional changes envisaged by Milner and other British proponents of "imperial federation," demanding recognition of the settler colonies as "autonomous nations of an Imperial Commonwealth." The conference resolved that the dominions should have an "adequate voice in foreign policy." One consequence of the rumblings toward a more clearly autonomous status was that the settler colonies were not subsumed under Britain at the Paris peace conference. The 1918 Imperial War Conference turned into the empire's delegation in Paris, but the individual dominions' leaders signed the peace treaties as representatives of distinct though not discrete nations.

In the 1920s, official British recognition of the dominions' right to their own foreign policy and freedom from legislative interference from Westminster had been important to the maintenance of the legitimacy of imperial ties in South Africa and the Irish Free State, but in the other parts of the Empire demand for the further reform of dominion status was less pressing. After securing British recognition of Canada's powers to make treaties for itself, Canadian concerns about control from London slackened. Australia and New Zealand showed still less political self-assertion, waiting until the 1940s before ratifying the Statute of Westminster. This was the 1931 British act, which had begun to take shape during the war, that formalized the redefinition of dominion status and abolished the British parliament's power to legislate for the dominions without their consent. The dominions remained culturally and demographically tied to Britain. Even with competition from Hollywood, the British culture industry remained a powerful presence, while metropole and colony remained components of an "imperial press system," albeit one left to private enterprise rather than one shaped by an official "inter-imperial" news service.[19] Ordinary Britons, meanwhile, continued to migrate to the colonies. Between 1920 and 1929, 1,319,206 people left Britain for new homes elsewhere in the Empire, and British and colonial governments alike encouraged imperial migration. Between 1919 and 1924, the British government's Overseas Settlement Committee provided free passages to the dominions for over 86,000 demobilized servicemen and their families. Further settlement schemes and child migration programs organized by governments and charities in Britain as well as the dominions also supported continued migration throughout the interwar period.[20]

For India, the imperial politics of the war involved more substantial questions of power than did the clarification and refinement of the extent of the practical sovereignty of the dominions. The size of the Subcontinent's human and material contribution raised Indian expectations of political reform, as did references to national self-determination as a war aim. There was also, from 1916, a reenergized nationalist presence, as the Muslim League and the (primarily Hindu) Congress together called for "home rule" in India. Nationalist demands and the strain that the war placed on the Raj forced a certain rethinking of British assumptions about government of the Subcontinent. As Thomas R. Metcalf argues, British rule in India had long relied on an assumption of abiding "difference" between British and Indian cultures and their respective political institutions and capacities; the settler colonies' nineteenth-century progression from dependency to responsible government was premised on the fundamental compatibility of the settler and metropolitan populations.[21] Now, on August 20, 1917, the British minister responsible for India, Edwin Montagu, declared that the government's objective was "the gradual development of self-governing institutions, with a view to the progressive realization of responsible government in India as an integral part of the Empire." The reforms that Montagu and the viceroy, Lord Chelmsford, outlined in March 1918 gave substance to the declaration, enlarging the Indian electorate and creating representative institutions at the provincial level. The vision of a self-governing India that would remain "an integral part of the Empire" was contested – not just by Conservative elder statesmen like Lord Curzon and Arthur Balfour but also by "sub-imperialists" such as General Reginald Dyer. With the subsequent support of the Punjab's governor, Dyer ordered troops to fire on unarmed protestors at Amritsar in April 1919, killing nearly 400 and wounding over 1,200. Montagu, as Metcalf writes, "saw embodied in [the massacre] a larger concept of empire that marked India out as a place apart," a vision of empire that his reforms sought to dismantle.[22] In the three decades after the Montagu–Chelmsford reforms, opponents of dominion status for India scored many successes in delaying realization of Indian self-government; but the 1919 reforms' induction of so many Indians into provincial politics and administration initiated a process that could not be resisted forever.

While Britain's war undermined the Raj's foundations, it also dramatically increased the territory under British control in the Middle East. When Turkey entered the war, Britain formalized its occupation of Egypt (still technically part of the Ottoman Empire), declaring a protectorate. After the Armistice, the British administration refused permission for a delegation of Egyptian nationalists to attend the Paris peace conference, and used martial law to arrest the delegates; Woodrow Wilson's eventual acquiescence to Britain's claim to Egypt dealt a disillusioning blow to Egyptians who had seen in Wilson's rhetoric of self-determination a liberal solution to British rule.[23] The Egyptian protectorate shored up Britain's existing strategic assets in the region, in particular the Suez Canal; using colonial forces (especially the Indian Army), Britain extended its territorial holdings, and oil interests, in Mesopotamia and Palestine. Together with Britain's support of the Arab revolt, these conquests and acquisitions would generate further imperial complications for many years to come. They reflected Lloyd George's concern to reorient Britain's war aims after 1916. Haig was overwhelmingly concerned with the western front; Lloyd George wanted the war to yield imperial gains. Just as the British war *effort* was not fully "imperial" until Lloyd George became prime minister, so too did Britain pursue positively imperial war *aims* only after 1916.

As Christopher M. Andrew and A. S. Kanya-Forstner show, France never clearly articulated its colonial war aims.[24] Except for the use of colonial resources, imperial discussions – never a priority in Paris – were left mostly to the colonial "lobby." Indeed, they argue, France largely lost control of colonial policy-making during the war, with such serious mistakes as an underestimation of the Arab revolt in the Middle East. At the end of the war, France did claim the spoils of victory, and enriched its colonial portfolio with the addition of two former German colonies, Togo and Kamerun (though having to divide both with Britain). Thanks to the 1916 Sykes–Picot Agreement between London and Paris, France also won a League of Nations mandate to govern Syria and Lebanon. Britain, of course, gained the increasingly vexing Palestine mandate.

As in the British case, the French colonial lobby and some indigenous leaders in the colonies themselves considered that the war had transformed the political bonds of empire. Blaise Diagne, for example, hoped that the settlement would see the extension of greater rights and benefits to the colonized countries that had contributed to victory.

As in Britain, leaders gathered to consider postwar policy. A colonial conference convened in Paris by General André Maginot in 1917 nevertheless failed to deliver substantial gains. Access to French citizenship became easier for soldiers, though they still were required to renounce their customary status in *statut personnel* (civil law) to do so, a renunciation unacceptable, in particular, to most Muslims. The French doled out naturalizations meagrely – in the five years after the war, for instance, only five Malagasy veterans became citizens. Former soldiers were henceforth exempted from required labor service on public works and from the *code de l'indigénat* (or native labor code), which allowed administrators rather than judges to impose fines and various punishments, but exemptions were not always enforced. The state accorded pensions to ex-servicemen, in theory if not in practice equivalent to those for returned French servicemen. Veterans, in the colonies as in France, received preferential hiring for certain jobs, such as museum guards and café licensees. Remaining true to hallowed Republican centralization, the government did not even consider devolution of administration to the colonies, a refusal to concede self-government largely maintained until the end of the Empire.

Yet the war, at least indirectly, had sparked increased opposition to colonialism. Wilson's Fourteen Points held out the possibility for democratic self-determination for colonized peoples.[25] The Bolshevik Revolution also mandated a more overt anticolonialism that gained adherence in the new French Communist Party and the branches it established in the colonies. In February 1919, the first Pan-African Congress meeting in Paris (chaired by Diagne and the American W. E. B. Du Bois) provided a symbolic beginning to the movement for cultural valorization, international cooperation, and political emancipation for those of African heritage. Ten days before the signing of the Versailles treaty, a young Vietnamese activist in Paris, Nguyen Ai Quoc, published a moderately worded pamphlet calling for the extension of democratic liberties in Indochina and representation of the colony in the French parliament – one of the first public manifestos of the leader who later took the name of Ho Chi Minh.

The psychological impact of the war on individual French and colonized people is undoubted, though difficult to measure with precision. Certainly *métropolitains* had grown more aware of an empire that had stubbornly failed to inspire great enthusiasm among the general public. Many who may have never seen an African or a Vietnamese came into contact with soldiers and workers from afar; as Lucie Cousturier's 1920 memoir *Des Inconnus chez moi* (Strangers in My House) recounts, after initial reticence, empathetic links often developed. A *journée de l'Armée d'Afrique et des troupes coloniales* in 1917 and similar fund-raising days aimed to inform the public of the contribution to the war effort made by colonial troops. The image of Africans as primitive – a stereotype dear to the colonial imaginary – was now complemented by the paternalistic image of the brave and loyal *tirailleur sénégalais*, personified in the smiling African pictured on cartons of the Banania breakfast drink.

For the colonized, the discovery of France was an eye-opener, but one that held ambiguous meaning, as the testimonies collected by Joe Lunn record.[26] Tens of thousands of veterans and migrant workers then returned home, many soldiers decorated with medals, but many also physically incapacitated or psychologically traumatized by battlefield experiences. Some nursed resentment at colonialist exploitation. Others safeguarded memories of bravery, camaraderie, and sacrifice. Babary Diallo's 1926 novel *Force Bonté* recounted pride in service to the French, and a compatriot, returning from the front, remarked poignantly: "Before, I was a nigger (*nègre*), but now I am a Frenchman." Colonial soldiers, though facing discrimination in France, found the French at home less arrogant and racially exclusivist than settlers – soldiers and migrant workers were astounded, for instance, to see white women laboring in factories or working as prostitutes. They often judged the discipline of the military less arbitrary than the colonial order imposed at home. The bravery and endurance of the French people at war impressed colonials, but they also became aware of the tensions and fragilities in metropolitan life not visible from the colonies. Amadou Hampaté Bâ, a soldier who became a distinguished African public servant and writer, summed up the mixed feelings:

> We were proud of the part played by African soldiers in the victory. When the survivors returned home in 1918 and 1919, they faced a new social phenomenon: … the end of the myth of the invincible and faultless white man.… [N]ow, the black soldiers had experienced trench warfare alongside their white comrades. They had seen heroes and courageous men, but they had also seen those men cry and scream with terror. In the cities, they had seen white thieves, poor whites, and even white beggars …. And it was then, in 1919, that the spirit of emancipation and the voicing of demands began to appear.[27]

In the interwar years, French links with the Empire nevertheless increased, though as Martin Thomas has shown, cracks in the colonial armor began to widen.[28] "Let us resolutely turn towards the Empire," Albert Sarraut, former Governor-General of Indochina, summoned the French.[29] Policy-makers led by Sarraut articulated plans for the development of colonial domains, the creation of productive infrastructures, and increased provisions for education and medical care, accompanied by continued endeavors to "pacify" rebellions. Trade with the Empire increased, though by the early 1930s, only 13 percent of imports into France came from the colonies, while 17 percent of France's exports were destined for the *outre-mer*, the totals up from 10 percent in 1914. In 1931, a grand colonial exhibition in Paris organized by Marshal Lyautey, France's colonial elder statesman, offered a consecration of French imperialism to eager spectators and potential colonials. However, as Frémeaux remarks, the Empire was more of a "refuge" than a new frontier as France struggled with economic crisis, political disharmony, challenges from resurgent international rivals, and growing colonial nationalism.[30] The French general staff, meanwhile, convinced of the value of the *force noire*, examined possibilities for future use of colonial soldiers.

* * *

Imagining his death, Rupert Brooke, a cherished poet in the colonies as well as in Britain, had envisaged "some corner of a foreign field" as "forever England." The Somme, Passchendaele, Ypres, and what would become "Anzac Cove" after the Gallipoli campaign became part of the imaginative and emotional geography of the British dominions; a Canadian medical officer's poem about poppies blowing between crosses "in Flanders fields" became part of the Empire's repertoire of commemoration. The war-scarred landscape of northern France was dotted with cemeteries where men from the British and French Empires were buried, as well as grandiose memorials raised to the Anzac, Canadian, Indian, and South African soldiers who died on French soil. In the colonial botanical garden in Paris, monuments to the colonial war dead were also raised – a bas-relief stele showing an African woman looking forlornly at a grave dedicated *Aux Soldats coloniaux* (To the Colonial Soldiers), monuments ornamented with Malagasy and Cambodian motifs to commemorate their war dead, and an ornate ritual communal building set amidst a bamboo grove for Vietnamese Buddhists. In Paris, a large mosque was built in the 1920s in honor of Muslims' war service. Memorials were also erected throughout the empires – statues to Anzacs in every Australian and New Zealand town, and great shrines of remembrance in their major cities. Throughout the French Empire, war memorials were erected to those who had died, from simple obelisks to grandiose monuments, such as the statue of a French and a Senegalese soldier ("Demba and Dupont") in Dakar. The sites of commemoration lasted through the colonial age. Many indeed survived decolonization, and veterans of the world wars still gather at shrines in places such as Pondicherry, a former French enclave in India. The memorial in Casablanca, however, was "repatriated" to France when Morocco became independent, and the victorious Algerian nationalists covered the monument in Algiers with a block of concrete. "Demba and Dupont" were removed from outside government house in Dakar after Senegal's independence in 1960, but the statue has recently been re-erected with fanfare in a newly named Place du Tirailleur Sénégalais.[31]

Back in France, the work of the colonial soldiers and wartime workers gradually seemed to fade from memory. Yet in 1994, the city of Fréjus recreated a monument to black soldiers modeled on a memorial in Reims (inspired by the successful defense of that city by black troops against the German offensive in 1918), which the Germans destroyed in 1940. The inscription by Léopold Sedar Senghor, poet of *négritude* and first president of independent Senegal, reads: "Passer-by, they fell fraternally united so that you may remain French." In 2006, President Jacques Chirac unveiled a memorial to Muslim soldiers of World War I at Verdun. The rector of the Paris mosque commented: "Here it was that the Islam of France was born. It took root in the fields of Verdun, Douaumont, and Fleury where Algerian, Tunisian, and Senegalese *tirailleurs* and the Moroccan *tabors* defended an anguished France."[32]

British commemorations cast victory as an imperial achievement. The "million dead" they spoke of referred to the whole Empire's sacrifice, not just the losses of the British Isles (see chapter 27). Sometimes the dominions spoke in the idiom of empire when they honored their dead; other times, they nationalized the war, making its achievements and sacrifices part of a national story, rather than an Australian or Canadian chapter of an imperial one. Throughout the twentieth century, celebrations of Australians' conduct at Gallipoli proved compatible with denunciations of the campaign's British architects; republicans and monarchists alike now make "pilgrimages" to Gallipoli. Since the early 1990s, Australia, Canada, and New Zealand have all built tombs of Unknown Soldiers killed in World War I; the values for which those soldiers are taken to stand are not closely associated with the Empire. Other soldiers' bodies were not repatriated from France. One of the institutions chartered as a result of the 1917 Imperial War Conference was the Imperial War Graves Commission, which today (as the Commonwealth War Graves Commission) continues to maintain cemeteries and memorials for the Empire's war dead around the world. The commission's charter prescribed that every fallen soldier would be commemorated individually; that the graves would be uniform, without distinction of rank; and that the men would be buried as close as possible to where they had died – not returned to Britain or the colonies. As sacrifice had been common, it was said, so would the memorial be. The hundreds of thousands of uniform graves at once testify to the imperial nature of the war and suggest that death surpasses other bonds. But the distinctiveness of the sacrifice in each dominion and colony also ensured that in the long run the war experience helped dissolve the bonds of empire on which it had so powerfully drawn.

Notes

1 David Omissi, introduction to Omissi (ed.), *Indian Voices*, p. 2.
2 Omissi, *Indian Voices*, p. 3, appendix A; Jeffrey Greenhut, "The Imperial Reserve: The Indian Troops on the Western Front, 1914–15," *Journal of Imperial and Commonwealth History*, 12/1, 1983, pp. 55–73.
3 Figures from Robert Holland, "The British Empire and the Great War, 1914–1918," in Brown and Louis, *British Empire, Twentieth Century*, p. 117.
4 Robin Prior and Trevor Wilson, *The Somme*, New Haven, Yale University Press, 2005, p. 78.
5 Frémaux, *Les Colonies*, p. 63.
6 Echenberg, *Colonial Conscripts*.
7 Frémeaux, *Les Colonies*, p. 63.
8 Ibid., p. 158.
9 Joe Lunn, " "Les Races Guerrières"," pp. 531–4; Frémeaux, *Les Colonies*, p. 207.
10 Frémeaux, *Les Colonies*, p. 180.
11 Ibid., pp. 202–6.
12 Horne, "Immigrant Workers."
13 Stovall, "Racial Violence in France during the Great War."
14 Omissi (ed.), *Indian Voices*, p. 278.
15 Michel, *Les Africains et la Grande Guerre*, ch. 3.
16 Quoted in Michel, *Les Africains*, p. 52.
17 Quoted in ibid., p. 51.
18 Holland, "British Empire and the Great War," p. 123.
19 See Simon J. Potter, *News and the British World: The Emergence of an Imperial Press System, 1876–1922*, Oxford, Clarendon Press, 2003, esp. ch. 8.
20 Stephen Constantine, "Migrants and Settlers," in Louis, *Oxford History*, vol. 4.
21 Metcalf, *Ideologies of the Raj*, esp. p. 225.
22 Ibid., p. 230.
23 Manela, *Wilsonian Moment*, pp. 56–75.
24 Andrew and Kanya-Forstner, *France Overseas*, pp. 164–5.
25 Manela, *Wilsonian Moment*.
26 Lunn, *Memoirs of the Maelstrom*.
27 Quoted in *Mémoires d'outre-mer*, p. 64.
28 Martin Thomas, *The French Empire between the Wars: Imperialism, Politics and Society*, Manchester, Manchester University Press, 2005.
29 *Mémoires d'outre-mer*, p. 98.
30 Frémeaux, *Les Colonies*, p. 294.
31 Ruth Ginio, "African Colonial Soldiers between Memory and Forgetfulness: The Case of Post-colonial Senegal," *Outre-Mers*, nos. 350–1, 2006, pp. 141–56.
32 *Le Monde*, February 21, 2006.

References and Further Reading

Ageron, Charles-Robert, *Les Algériens musulmans et la France, 1871–1919*, Paris, Presses Universitaires de France, 1968, 2 vols.; vol. 2, pt. 4 on war.
Aldrich, Robert, *Vestiges of the Colonial Empire: Monuments, Museums and Cultural Memories*, New York, Palgrave Macmillan, 2005.
Andrew, Christopher, and Kanya-Forstner, A. S., *France Overseas: The Great War and the Climax of French Imperial Expansion*, London, Thames and Hudson, 1981.
Balesi, Charles, *From Adversaries to Comrades-in-Arms: West Africa and the French Military, 1885–1919*, Waltham, MA, Crossroads Press, 1999.

Barcellini, Serge, "Les Monuments en hommage aux combattants de la 'Grande France' (Armée d'Afrique et Armée coloniale)," Institut de Stratégie Comparée, Commission Française d'Histoire Militaire, Institut d'Histoire des Conflits Contemporains, www.stratisc.org/TC_8.htm.

Bernard, Augustin, *L'Afrique du Nord pendant la guerre*, Paris, Presses Universitaires de France, 1926.

Brown, Judith M., and Louis, William Roger (eds.), *The Twentieth Century*, vol. 4, William Roger Louis (ed.), *The Oxford History of the British Empire*, 5 vols, Oxford, Oxford University Press, 1998–9. Especially chapters by Robert Holland, John Darwin, and Judith M. Brown.

Carlier, Claude, and Pedroncini, Guy (eds.), *Les Troupes coloniales dans la Grande Guerre*, Paris, Economica, 1997.

Compère-Morel, Thomas (ed.), *Mémoires d'outre-mer. Les colonies et la première guerre mondiale*, exhibition catalog, Péronne, Historial de la Grande Guerre, 1996.

Conklin, Alice, *A Mission to Civilize: The Republican Idea of Empire in France and West Africa, 1895–1930*, Stanford, CA, Stanford University Press, 1997.

Echenberg, Myron, *Colonial Conscripts: The Tirailleurs Sénégalais in French West Africa, 1857–1960*, London, James Currey, 1991.

Frémeaux, Jacques, *Les Colonies dans la Grande Guerre. Combats et épreuves des peuples d'outre-mer*, Paris, Soteca, 14–18 Editions, 2006.

Gammage, Bill, *The Broken Years: Australian Soldiers in the Great War*, 1974; new ed., Melbourne, Penguin, 1975.

Grey, Jeffrey, *A Military History of Australia*, rev. ed., New York, Cambridge University Press, 1999.

Horne, John, "Immigrant Workers in France during World War I," *French Historical Studies*, 14/1, 1985, pp. 57–88.

Inglis, Ken S., *Sacred Places: War Memorials in the Australian Landscape*, Melbourne, Melbourne University Press, 1998.

Lunn, Joe, *Memoirs of the Maelstrom: A Senegalese Oral History of the First World War*, Oxford, James Currey, 1999.

Lunn, Joe, "'Les Races Guerrières': Racial Preconceptions in the French Military about West African Soldiers during the First World War," *Journal of Contemporary History*, 34/4, 1999, pp. 517–36.

Manela, Erez, *The Wilsonian Moment: Self-Determination and the International Origins of Anticolonial Nationalism*, Oxford, Oxford University Press, 2007.

McKernan, Michael, *The Australian People and the Great War*, Sydney, Collins, 1980; new ed., 1984.

Metcalf, Thomas R., *Ideologies of the Raj*, Cambridge, Cambridge University Press, 1994.

Michel, Marc, *Les Africans et la Grande Guerre. L'Appel à l'Afrique (1914–1918)*, 1982; new ed., Paris, Karthala, 2003.

Morton, Desmond, "'Junior but Sovereign Allies': The Transformation of the Canadian Expeditionary Force, 1914–1918," *Journal of Imperial and Commonwealth History*, 8/1, October 1979, pp. 56–67.

Morton, Desmond, and Granatstein, J. L., *Marching to Armageddon: Canadians and the Great War, 1914–19*, Toronto, Lester and Orpen Dennys, 1989.

Nasson, Bill, *Springboks on the Somme: South Africa in the Great War, 1914–1918*, Johannesburg, Penguin, 2007.

Omissi, David (ed.), *Indian Voices of the Great War: Soldiers' Letters, 1914–1918*, Basingstoke, Macmillan, 1999.

Perry, Frederick W., *The Commonwealth Armies: Manpower and Organisation in Two World Wars*, Manchester, Manchester University Press, 1988.

Phillips, Jock, Boyack, Nicholas, and Malone, E. P. (eds.), *The Great Adventure: New Zealand Soldiers Describe the First World War*, Wellington, Allen and Unwin, 1988.

Pugsley, Christopher, *Gallipoli: The New Zealand Story*, Auckland, Hodder and Stoughton, 1984.

Scates, Bruce, *Return to Gallipoli: Walking the Battlefields of the Great War*, Cambridge, Cambridge University Press, 2006.

Serle, Geoffrey, *John Monash: A Biography*, Melbourne, Melbourne University Press, 1982.

Sinclair, Keith, *A Destiny Apart: New Zealand's Search for National Identity*, Wellington, Allen and Unwin, 1986.

Stovall, Tyler, "The Color Line behind the Lines: Racial Violence in France during the Great War," *American Historical Review*, 103/3, June 1998, pp. 737–69.

Thobie, Jacques, and Meynier, Gilbert, *Histoire de la France coloniale*, vol. 2, *L'Apogée (1871–1931)*, Paris, Armand Colin, 1991.

Thomson, Alistair, *Anzac Memories: Living with the Legend*, Melbourne, Oxford University Press, 1994.

Vance, Jonathan, *Death So Noble: Memory, Meaning and the First World War*, Vancouver, University of British Columbia Press, 1997.

White, Richard, *Inventing Australia: Images and Identity 1688–1980*, Sydney, Allen and Unwin, 1981.

PART V

Legacies

CHAPTER THIRTY-SIX

The Peace Settlement, 1919–39

CAROLE FINK

> The treaty ... has in practice settled nothing.[1]
> This complex treaty ... will be what you make of it.[2]

The peace settlement after World War I has a dreadful reputation in the public mind. Unlike the treaties in 1814–15, which only gradually unraveled, after 1919 both the victors and vanquished alike almost immediately contested the peacemakers' decisions. Even before the delegations left Paris, both sides attacked the wisdom and probity of the treaties, which were presciently dubbed by Marshal Foch a 20-year armistice.[3]

Why was the peace settlement after World War I so controversial and, ultimately, so unsuccessful? This chapter will examine the major elements of the treaties, and discuss the subsequent debate, aftermath, modifications, and collapse. It will show the uniqueness of the peacemaking moment after World War I and also place the occasion within a larger historical context. It will explore why the Paris Peace settlement fell short of public expectations, was neglected by its creators, and was manipulated by its opponents. It will also address the debate over how a faulty and abandoned structure may or may not have contributed to the outbreak of World War II.

The Treaties, 1919–23

Three imperial democracies, France, Great Britain, and the United States, shaped the major elements of the Paris Peace settlement. For obvious political reasons, they were determined to secure the fruits of their victory.[4] Yet, even among this limited coterie, there were clashing interests and an unequal power balance. The Franco-British Entente had fought for four long years and expended huge human and material resources but had suffered unequally. France, one of the war's main battlefields, aimed at permanently reducing German power and creating substitutes in Eastern Europe for its lost Russian ally; Britain, with its principal naval and colonial goals already achieved, now sought to guard its economic interests, revive the European balance of power, and protect its shaken empire. The United States, which had entered the fighting in the last year, had the most grandiose design of all, to create a stable world of democratic governments, limited armaments, and open markets.[5]

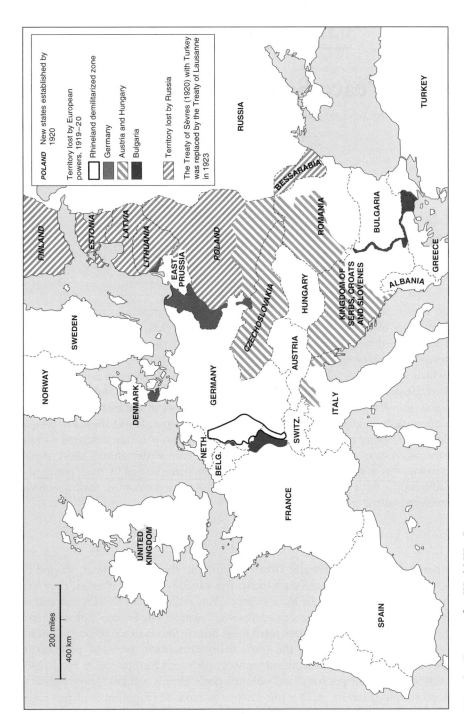

Map 8 Europe after World War I

POLARD New states established by
1920

Territory lost by European
powers, 1919–20

Rhineland demilitarized zone

Germany

Austria and Hungary

Bulgaria

Territory lost by Russia

The Treaty of Sèvres (1920) with Turkey
was replaced by the Treaty of Lausanne
in 1923

Unlike earlier peace conferences, there were significant exclusions at Paris. Among these was a key Entente member, Russia, which had fallen under Soviet control and civil war. Former enemies, Germany, Austria, Hungary, Bulgaria, and Turkey, were, until the last moment, barred from the proceedings. Germany, which at war's end still occupied huge swaths of territory, had sued for an armistice on the basis of Wilson's seemingly liberal Fourteen Points. Its new and fragile republican government and its militant public were unprepared for a punitive peace.

Another problematic aspect of peacemaking from a structural, political, and moral standpoint was the behavior of partner governments and peoples. Japan and Italy, which were included in the council of victors, focused almost exclusively on their national and territorial goals and exited dissatisfied. Czechoslovakia, Greece, Poland, Romania, and Serbia bolstered their expansive territorial claims against the Central Powers and each other with military faits-accomplis. Britain's Middle Eastern clients, the Jews and the Arabs, arrived in Paris with competing claims to Palestine. Other claimants, less influential and persuasive – Black Africans, Vietnamese, Chinese, Ukrainians, Albanians, and the Baltic peoples – flocked to the French capital but were given short shrift by the victors.[6]

After the grand public opening in January 1919, US President Woodrow Wilson, who had made an unprecedented trip to Europe, virtually dominated the proceedings. For two full months his vision of a League of Nations took precedence over all other issues. Indeed, in the only outwardly democratic deliberations of the Paris Peace Conference, the League Commission proceeded to draft a revolutionary covenant, creating a Council, Assembly, and Secretariat and including clauses on the arbitration of international disputes and collective security as well as colonial mandates, disarmament, and humanitarian functions.[7]

There were glaring incongruities in the covenant. The Anglo-American draft assumed the continuation of the old diplomatic order, including the maintenance of European colonial empires and US predominance in Latin America. By establishing the League Council and insisting on unanimity in all decisions, the Great Powers intended to dominate world affairs, leaving no voice for the others. Germany and Soviet Russia were each to undergo a probationary period before applying for League membership; and Article 19 provided only a vague formula for peaceful treaty revision. Undoubtedly, a robust League required active American participation; but above all, effective global cooperation and governance would require major reductions in its members' sovereignty, which was an unlikely prospect at the time. Not unexpectedly, London and Washington resisted France's efforts to set up a military arm to collective security.[8]

Amid growing signs of public impatience, in late March 1919 the "Big Three," Georges Clemenceau, David Lloyd George, and Woodrow Wilson, turned their full attention to the treaty with Germany. Their deliberations, held in secret, were punctuated by bleak reports from Eastern Europe of famine, disease, pogroms, Bolshevik incursions, and inter-allied fighting, and they were colored by their often-conflicting experts' advice. Among the three there was frequently fierce disagreement over the treatment of the principal foe, Germany, which now threatened to withhold its signature.[9]

The draft treaty presented to the German delegation on May 7 was shocking indeed. The Reich was stripped of all its colonies and forced to disarm, cede substantial territories (mostly without plebiscites) and population, acknowledge its responsibility for the outbreak of hostilities in 1914, accept an unnamed amount of reparations, turn over the Kaiser and other war criminals to judicial proceedings, and allow numerous incursions on its sovereignty, including the internationalization of its waterways. Faced with the Germans' protests, the three altered a few clauses, notably allowing a plebiscite in Upper Silesia, and the Germans ultimately signed on June 28, 1919, the fifth anniversary of the shots fired at Sarajevo.

Long ago, A. J. P. Taylor labeled the Versailles treaty too harsh for German acceptance but also lacking the moral or practical means to survive.[10] To reduce Germany's power and strengthen their clients, the Big Three had strayed from their professed principles. Specifically, in separating East Prussia from the Reich by a corridor, removing Danzig and Memel, and prohibiting union between Germany and Austria, they violated the principle of self-determination.

On the other hand, Versailles was far milder than the Treaty of Brest-Litovsk, in which Imperial Germany in March 1918 had stripped Russia of almost all its European possessions, one-third of its agricultural production, and three-quarters of its coal and ore, and had created a chain of puppet states from Finland to Georgia.[11] Indeed, the Reich that signed the treaty in 1919 was as strong, if not stronger than five years earlier. It had not been partitioned, and its industrial and agricultural heartland and its cities remained intact. Despite substantial losses, its total population exceeded France's by 20 million; and the new states on its eastern borders, Lithuania, Poland, and Czechoslovakia, were far less menacing than Tsarist Russia.[12]

Nonetheless, 'Versailles' immediately became an emblem for 'victors' justice' and a failed Wilsonianism. A vigorous German propaganda machine took aim at the treaty, particularly at the 'war guilt' and war crimes clauses. Vociferous critics such as John Maynard Keynes as well as a bevy of English, American, and neutral opponents of the treaty joined the critical chorus.[13]

Similar objections were applied to the treaties with Austria (St. Germain, September 10, 1919), Bulgaria (Neuilly, November 27, 1919) and Hungary (Trianon, June 4, 1920), which severely punished these three small states with major territorial losses, reparations, and restrictions on their sovereignty. Critics opposed the "Balkanization" of Eastern Europe and feared the rise of petty nationalist rivalries, economic anarchy, and persecution of minorities, which would become a breeding ground for bolshevism.[14]

At war's end, with the collapse of three European empires and the establishment and expansion of several states, the number of subject peoples had been reduced from some 100 to about 30 million souls. Among these, however, particularly in Poland, Czechoslovakia, and Romania, were former dominant groups of Germans and Hungarians. In addition, almost four million Jews fell under new governments and were vulnerable to spoliation, violence, and expulsion.[15]

Wilson had originally hoped to insert a clause guaranteeing religious freedom and equality into the League of Nations Covenant; but he was stopped cold by Japan's proposal to establish global protection for racial minorities, which posed serious complications for the United States and the British Empire. Instead, the international protection of minority rights came into being as a result of a series of individual treaties imposed by the victors on the new and expanded states in Eastern Europe, specifying rights of citizenship, schools, language, and religious practice, which were placed under the guarantee of the as yet unborn League of Nations.[16]

Although the minorities, and especially Jewish groups, hailed this innovation, other observers were less sanguine. The new rulers of Eastern Europe, resenting this major incursion on their sovereignty, demanded a *universal* system of minority protection, which the Western powers of course refused. Except for those with a powerful outside patron, most minorities were too frightened to appeal for international protection, and neither Britain nor France was inclined to police the peace settlement in Eastern Europe.[17]

Aftermath, 1920–4

By January 1920, the major peace delegations had left Paris, and the new League of Nations was born. However, there was a vacuum at the heart of the new world system. The United States had withdrawn from the settlement it had helped to create; France had lost an Anglo–American guarantee of its security; Soviet Russia, which had formed the Communist International to counter the capitalist world order, was at war with Poland; the new German republic, facing domestic anarchy, proved obstreperous over reparations; and the former Entente was fragmented over managing the burdens of victory.[18]

The fate of the Middle East lay in Franco-British hands; and without US or Russian participation, Britain was the clearly dominant partner. At the San Remo Conference in April–May 1920, the two squabbling Allies patched together an agreement over the Arab lands of the former Ottoman Empire. Smoothing out their differences and ignoring local populations, they assigned mandates over Palestine and Mesopotamia (Iraq) to Great Britain and over Syria and Lebanon to France. Although the Zionists rejoiced at achieving international recognition, disgruntled Arab nationalists seethed over Anglo-French perfidy.[19]

The Allied victory over the Ottoman Empire had initially appeared incontrovertible and irreversible. However, the extremely harsh Treaty of Sèvres, signed under protest by the Sultan on August 10, 1920, was a dead letter almost from the start. Mustafa Kemal, the hero of the Gallipoli campaign, formed a rival government in Ankara, stopped a Greek invasion, and forced the Entente to negotiate. The Treaty of Lausanne, signed on July 23, 1923, was a stunning reversal of the Sèvres document. Turkey retained all of Anatolia as well as Istanbul and the Straits, was relieved of reparations and the hated capitulations, and accepted far weaker minority clauses than were imposed on Eastern Europe. With French support, Kemal achieved another stunning victory: the obligatory exchange of populations based on religious faith. Some one million Christians were forcibly expelled from Asia Minor and some 350,000 Muslims from Greece, though the figures for the entire period of the Greco-Turkish War may have been considerably higher.[20]

This surgical removal procedure, supervised by the League of Nations, sent a chilling message to other minorities. Indeed, all over the new Eastern Europe, in the wake of the Bolshevik and Turkish revolutions, refugee and statelessness problems had swelled to ominous proportions. Through expropriation, physical threats, and the denial of the rights of citizenship to religious, ethnic, or political groups, the new states threatened tens of thousands of Armenians, Greeks, Jews, White Russians, and others, leaving the League and private welfare organizations reeling over their immense humanitarian tasks.[21] The closing of traditional emigration routes to the United States, Latin America, and the British Empire exacerbated the problem.

Revisionist clamor against the Paris treaties pervaded the European and world environment. Among the allies there was widespread disappointment over the results of their triumph, and among the losers an almost unanimous rejection of the consequences of defeat. Buffeted by the shocks of postwar inflation, unemployment, and social unrest, many blamed the peace settlement for their political and economic misery. Visual artists depicted ruined lives and landscapes, composers produced sounds of bitterness and despair; poets lamented the postwar 'Waste Land'; and combat veterans contrasted the empty present with an idyllic prewar world.[22]

Things did not settle down in the volatile region between Germany and Russia. At the Porto Rosa Conference in 1921, Eduard Beneš, Czechoslovakia's foreign minister, succeeded in blocking any form of Danubian Federation, thus sustaining all the financial, trade, and communication barriers that divided the new Eastern Europe. Territorial disputes abounded, particularly between Poland and all its neighbors. The military blocs between France and its East European clients, as well as among the Little Entente, only hid the nationalist rivalries in the region.[23]

The apogee of revisionist striving occurred at the 34-nation summit meeting held in Genoa in April–May 1922. This conference was the brainchild of British premier David Lloyd George, who strove to create a new form of peace between victors and vanquished and revive investment, trade, and political ties between Western and Eastern Europe. The Genoa Conference failed, not only because of its hasty, improvised design but also because of America's absence, France's obstruction, and the separate Soviet–German treaty at Rapallo, which sent a frightening signal of the dangers of irredentism. Europe slid into chaos, with a wave of assassinations, the Fascist seizure of power in Italy, and the Franco-Belgian invasion of the Ruhr in January 1923 to collect unpaid reparations.[24]

By the end of that year, however, the balance had shifted dramatically. France's leader, Raymond Poincaré, lacked adequate resources to back up his militancy, and he had no long-term plan to enforce Versailles. Moreover, Britain and the United States demanded a new reparations settlement. Into the breach arrived a skilled German leader, Gustav Stresemann, a former wartime annexationist and monarchist transformed into a pragmatic republican, who rescued the Reich through accommodation instead of defiance. Deploying his considerable diplomatic skills, Stresemann collaborated with London and Washington on the Dawes Plan, which scaled down German payments and effectively ended France's bid to force compliance with the Paris Peace Treaties.[25] With Soviet Russia excluded, the United States in a limited role, and the East European actors now abject bystanders, Germany had once more become a key player in the international order.

Treaty Revision, 1925–9

The Locarno treaties of 1925, long the subject of historical controversy, opened the gates of treaty revision. In the pleasant lakeside town in Switzerland, France, Germany, Great Britain, and Italy renegotiated the peace treaties and church bells tolled over their accomplishment. In return for acknowledging the inviolability of the Reich's western border, Stresemann obtained the withdrawal of the Allied Disarmament Commission, the evacuation of the Cologne zone, and Germany's entry into the League without any obligation to loosen its ties to Moscow. More important, despite French pressure, Stresemann evaded an "eastern" Locarno. The Reich's borders with Poland and Czechoslovakia were subject merely to non-binding arbitration treaties.[26]

How had this happened? Britain, consumed by its global interests, insisted on the restoration of the European balance of power. France, in increasingly desperate economic straits and rebuffed in its efforts for a British or US commitment, bowed to the inevitable, even at the cost of sacrificing its East European clients. Mussolini, the opportunist partner, welcomed the weakening of France, even at Germany's expense.[27]

The period between 1926 and 1929 has been represented as a golden age for Europe. As US funds poured into the continent in the form of short-term loans, Germany paid reparations and reentered the international system. In September 1926, Stresemann made his triumphant entry into the League of Nations, was seated as a permanent council member, and joined the Locarno triumvirate that met regularly in various Geneva hotel rooms. In 1928, Germany signed the Kellogg–Briand Pact outlawing war.[28]

Nonetheless, the Weimar Republic remained Europe's foremost revisionist power. Under Stresemann's deft leadership, Berlin maintained its ties with Moscow, secretly rearmed, and covertly subsidized German minority groups throughout Eastern Europe. Stresemann not only kept pressure on his Western partners to scale down reparations and evacuate the entire Rhineland ahead of schedule but also maintained a threatening stance against Poland over the corridor and German minority rights.[29] On October 3, 1929, following his great diplomatic victory with the Young Plan, Stresemann died suddenly of a stroke at age 51, on the eve of the Wall Street crash and the onset of the World Depression.

Scholars contest the Stresemann legacy. Some have regarded this Nobel peace-prize winner as simply a tough, cunning nationalist, who was biding his time until the Reich was free to strike forcefully against Germany's neighbors in the East.[30] Others perceive a genuinely conciliatory Reich leader, committed to economic over military might, and more akin to Adenauer than to Hitler.[31]

Whichever interpretation one selects, it is nonetheless certain that Gustav Stresemann's achievements in a short period were spectacular: Germany's rehabilitation, the liberation of German soil, and the balancing act between East and West. On the other hand, the negatives were also obvious: his failure to bolster German democracy, restrain German irredentism, and inspire trust among Germany's Eastern neighbors.

Historians also question the Allies' behavior in the 1920s. Could the United States have worked more generously in the postwar period to stabilize the peace settlement?[32] Could Great Britain have overcome its antipathy towards Marianne and bolstered France's strength and confidence?[33] Could East European statesmen have shown less belligerency towards their minorities and a more conciliatory stance towards their neighbors?[34] Could the Soviet Union have been integrated into the Versailles system?[35]

The larger debate continues over the era itself. Could Western Europe have overcome its imperial proclivity and salvaged the heartland? Were the 1920s a time of lost opportunities and "illusions," or was European peace doomed by a flawed construction? Could collective security have been established among the victors? Could peaceful revision have been implemented and former enemies reconciled with the peace settlement? Could the League of Nations have become a more robust instrument?[36]

This much was evident in 1929. Even one of the severest critics of the Paris Peace settlement recognized that "no solution could have been free from hardship and anomaly";[37] and, despite all its imperfections, the system was still in place.[38] It took two cataclysmic events – the radicalization of German politics and the world depression – to change everything.

Breakdown, 1930–9

In September 1930, scarcely three months after the last Allied forces evacuated the Rhineland, Germany's national elections sent shockwaves throughout Europe and the world. A total of 107 members of the National Socialist party won seats in the parliament, making the followers of Adolf Hitler the second largest party in the Reichstag. The beleaguered government of Heinrich Brüning, pursuing an unpopular deflationary policy and fending off Nazi taunts, grew increasingly belligerent on the world stage, call-ing for League sanctions against Poland for its violations of minority rights, forging an abortive customs union with Austria, and demanding an end to reparations and German parity in armaments.[39]

Neither the League nor the Allies were prepared to curb Germany's bombast and threats. The waves of fear and anxiety that permeated the international atmosphere were not conducive to demonstrations of militancy in the name of collective security. Indeed, the popular mind had become convinced that that was the "mistake of 1914," when the nations had rushed headlong into a devastating war. The most famous novel and film in the early 1930s, Erich Maria Remarque's *All Quiet on the Western Front*, conveyed a poignant antiwar message. A great wave of pacifism spread through the capitals of Western Europe. In 1933, the Oxford Union Society voted never to fight for King and Country, and the Labour Party threatened a general strike if war broke out.[40]

By 1931, the depression had engulfed the entire globe. Because the world had become linked by a precarious economic structure, local troubles created international repercus-sions. Thus Central Europe's banking crises shook the world's financial system. Trade patterns were also disrupted. In response, politicians devised stopgap recovery programs – import quotas, foreign exchange controls, and other restrictive measures – that frag-mented the world further into "national sub-markets" and deeply damaged poor nations. Great Britain, the home of free trade, emulated the United States by introducing high tariffs, devaluing sterling, tending its imperial interests, and distancing itself from the economic problems of Europe and Asia.[41]

Within this moral and political vacuum, a major Asian crisis erupted in September 1931. Exploiting the assassination of a Japanese intelligence officer, the local Japanese army in Manchuria took military action to conquer the entire province. The Chinese government, mired in civil war, did not defend itself but instead appealed for support from the League of Nations under Article 11 of the Covenant and from Washington under the Nine-Power Pact of 1922 and the Kellogg–Briand Pact of 1928. The League Council, called reluctantly into action, responded by dispatching a five-member investi-gating commission to the Far East.[42]

In retrospect, the invasion of Manchuria has been considered the first major breach in the peace settlement and a prelude to World War II, when a belligerent power preyed on its weak neighbor before a divided world community. At the time, however, the issues were less clear. To the Eurocentric League, Manchuria seemed exceedingly far away. Many influential League members, including France, Italy, and the Netherlands, regarded Japan's behavior in Manchuria as falling well within the standard imperialist practice of bringing order to a chaotic region; and Great Britain had neither the financial nor mili-tary power to halt Japan on its own. The two most interested outsiders, the United States and the Soviet Union, withheld meaningful collaboration with Geneva and refused to intervene on their own.[43]

Stymied by the threat of a Japanese veto, the League took an extremely cautious stance. The Lytton Commission, which arrived after the Japanese conquest of Manchuria, issued a report October 1932 with an evenhanded description of the events, assigning blame to both sides. When the small powers insisted on League action, a special Assembly voted to boycott the Japanese puppet state of Manchukuo. On March 27, 1933, Japan made its dramatic exit from Geneva.[44]

The damage to the League was immediate and overwhelming. A great power had flaunted the treaties and its League obligations, and there was no collective response.

Governments threatened by larger, belligerent neighbors now recognized that local incidents might well endanger their survival.[45]

Hitler's appointment as chancellor of Germany two months earlier had also disrupted the international community. The Nazi leader, who had continually voiced his grievances against Versailles, now seemed poised to topple the treaty. Again, the reality was more complex than perceived at the time. As witnessed by his first acts – Germany's exit from the League, the bilateral pacts with his neighbors, and the onset of rearmament – Hitler sought not only to dismantle the Paris Peace settlement but also to resurrect and expand the vast German empire of March 1918. Moreover, persecuting and spoliating the German Jews and driving them penniless into exile signaled a new element, the vicious racist program of the Third Reich.[46]

Indeed, the peace settlement was quickly unraveling at the hands of world statesmen. Reparations had been cancelled in 1932. The Economic and Disarmament conferences had failed miserably. Poland, in the wake of its treaty with Berlin, renounced its Minority Treaty in September 1934, and its neighbors threatened to follow suit. Soviet Russia's entry into the League of Nations in 1934 did little to revive the moribund organization.

On October 3, 1935, fascist Italy flexed its muscles. After issuing a series of threats Rome launched an invasion of Ethiopia, and another weak League member appealed to Geneva. The crisis was again a baffling one, not only because of Ethiopia's remoteness and questionable domestic order, but particularly because of the international stakes involved. Britain and France, requiring Rome's help against Nazi Germany, were slow to condemn an act of aggression once more framed in the standard terms of an imperial civilizing mission. This time the League, remorseful over Manchuria, voted mild sanctions against Italy; but it also shrank before an arms embargo or breaking off diplomatic relations.

Fearing another damaging withdrawal from the League, Britain and France acted independently to control the crisis. Foreign Secretary Sir Samuel Hoare and Foreign Minister Pierre Laval privately patched up a solution that gave Italy control over two-thirds of Ethiopia. When the proposal was exposed, it raised a public uproar but it also undermined Geneva's efforts to halt the fighting. Faced with Italy's triumph in May 1936, the League dropped its sanctions and failed to contest Mussolini's conquest or to stop the Duce's eventual exit.[47] Ethiopia simply confirmed the League's helplessness to protect its members.

By the spring of 1936, when the League Secretariat took possession of the beautiful Palais des Nations on the shores of Lake Geneva, the organization had lost its place as the guardian of the peace settlement. Its leadership was feeble, and the membership was divided between a minority seeking to strengthen and a majority intent on drastically reducing their peacekeeping obligations. Following two years of bitter negotiations, the Assembly in September 1938, led by the British Commonwealth, voted to abandon Article 16, the duty of all governments to take action against an aggressor and support the victim.[48]

Great Britain, the major guarantor of the Paris Peace settlement, was now dominated by a strong belief in appeasement.[49] Confronted by the belligerency of the fascist powers and the disarray all over Eastern Europe, by America's stiff neutrality and the ominous events inside the Soviet Union, Britain was prepared to sacrifice the treaties. Before a helpless League council in March 1936, Britain and France had passively acquiesced in violations of Versailles *and* the Locarno Pact after Hitler's troops reentered the demilitarized zone of the Rhineland.[50]

Britain's goal was to stave off another world war, whose potential destructiveness was exposed during the fighting in Ethiopia, China, and Spain. British Prime Minister, Neville Chamberlain, was the prime advocate of a new realism toward the Third Reich. Distrusting the old tenets of collective security and considering himself unbound by obligations to France and its allies, Chamberlain set out to win Hitler's participation in a new European order by acknowledging Germany's role as a great power in Central Europe and satisfying its grievances against the alleged injustices of Versailles.[51]

Although subject to heavy criticism then and now, Chamberlain's was neither a naïve nor unrealistic strategy for an overextended government. From Palestine to India, Britain faced restive forces in its far-flung empire, along with a looming Japanese threat to its naval bastion in Singapore. It could expect scant support from the Dominions, which had made clear their unwillingness to shed blood to protect the Paris Peace settlement. Under Chamberlain, Britain launched a substantial program of rearmament in 1937, but one that was never designed for intervention in a continental conflict.[52]

There were nonetheless two weaknesses in Chamberlain's strategy, treating the peace treaties as dispensable and considering Hitler as an aggrieved German patriot who could be separated from his more fanatic followers by judicious territorial concessions. The Allies' acceptance of Austria's destruction in March 1938 and their sacrifice of Czechoslovakia at the Munich conference in September of that year only whetted Hitler's appetite, weakened the potential forces of opposition, and made war inevitable, especially when Nazi Germany's next victim, Poland, refused to bow to London's counsel or Hitler and Stalin's threats.

Whether or not Britain, one year later, was better equipped to resist the Nazi onslaught, Neville Chamberlain had undoubtedly sacrificed considerable moral and material resources to his appeasement policy. There was a good answer to Lloyd George's taunting query in 1919 – "Are you prepared to die for Danzig?" – which was echoed by the appeasers 20 years later. When force trumps treaties, even the most imperfect ones, there is no safety for any state, large or small.

Chamberlain also shared responsibility for the destruction of the international minorities system, which Britain had helped to create. Hitler's persecution of the Jews from 1933 onward had already unleashed a wave of anti-semitism all over Eastern Europe as well as a horrendous refugee problem, which the West and the League were unprepared to solve. By drastically reducing Jewish immigration to Palestine in 1939, Britain closed a major place of refuge at the same time as the United States and the British Empire and Dominions all refused a place to fleeing, impecunious Jewish refugees. The war that erupted in 1939 gave Germany an almost unfettered power to strike at its racial enemies, to persecute, despoil, and commit genocide; and its enemies were unable or unwilling to protect the millions of victims.

Conclusions

Will the public ever change its mind about the Paris Peace Treaties? Probably not. Television documentaries, high-school and university texts, and the popular literature all continue to portray a defective handiwork created by benighted and ill-informed Allied diplomats, which made the Depression, Hitler, and World War II inevitable. The post-Cold War violence in the Balkans and Africa, and the ongoing struggle in the Middle East, provide bleak reminders of the peacemakers' blunders in 1919.[53]

The peace treaties after World War I were undoubtedly faulty in their conception. America's pretension to remold Europe and the world, Britain's unyielding imperialist stance, and France's narrow economic and territorial aims dominated the proceedings. Unlike earlier diplomatic gatherings, however, each disagreement and each decision were exposed to the harsh glare of public scrutiny and the complaints by the defeated, making the three all the more anxious and determined to speed their work to completion.

Moreover, the peacemakers fell victim to a rigid nineteenth-century mindset that impelled them to codify and legitimize their state of affairs. Ignoring the sudden and surprising turn of world events in 1918, they considered themselves full-scale victors in a position to dictate terms to Europe and the world. Their treaties, a mélange of major and minor provisions, were unclear, contradictory, and undoubtedly shortsighted. Ignoring Bismarck's wise maxim that treaties were not eternal, the three attempted to create unassailable norms without provision either for enforcement or modification.

The authors themselves were vulnerable to criticism. A rigid, politically vulnerable Woodrow Wilson became an easy target of derision; a wily, supple Lloyd George soared between hardliner and revisionist; and the caustic Clemenceau, wedged between the hardliner Foch and his two powerful colleagues, was an easy object of opprobrium.[54] In six hectic, dangerous months these three politicians brought order to a stricken world; but it was an order based on a transitory moment of unity that almost immediately dissolved.

Yet despite its deficiencies, the Paris settlement did not make World War II inevitable.[55] Whatever the hardships and anomalies, if the next generation of statesmen had taken responsibility for building a law-abiding international community, both flexible and peaceful, Europe and the world might well have been spared another brutal conflict.

Notes

1 John Maynard Keynes, 'The Peace of Versailles,' *Everybody's Magazine,* 43 (Sept. 1920), pp. 37–8.
2 George Clemenceau's remarks to the French Chamber, Sept. 25, 1919, quoted in Jean-Baptiste Duroselle, *Clemenceau,* Paris, Fayard, 1988, p. 773.
3 Sharp, *The Versailles Settlement,* p. 189.
4 See Becker, chapter 14 above.
5 Thomas J. Knock, *To End all Wars: Woodrow Wilson and the Quest for a New World Order,* Princeton, Princeton University Press, 1992.
6 Stephen Bonsal, *Suitors and Suppliants: The Little Nations at Versailles,* 2nd ed., New York, Prentice Hall, 1946.
7 David Hunter Miller, *The Drafting of the Covenant,* 2 vols., New York, Putnam, 1928.
8 Zara Steiner, "The League of Nations and the Quest for Security," in R. Ahmann, A. M. Birke, and M. Howards (eds.), *The Quest for Stability: Problems of West European Security, 1918–1957,* Oxford and New York, Oxford University Press, 1993, pp. 35–70.
9 Arthur S. Link (ed.), *The Deliberations of the Council of Four, March 24–June 29, 1919. Notes of the Official Interpreter Paul Mantoux.* 2 vols., Princeton, Princeton University Press, 1992.
10 A. J. P. Taylor, *The Origins of the Second World War,* 2nd ed., New York, Random House, 1969, p. 32.
11 Fritz Fischer, *World Power or Decline: The Controversy over Germany's Aims in the First World War,* 1965; translation from German, London, W. W. Norton, 1974, pp. 90–1.
12 "The framers of the Versailles settlement achieved the precise opposite of what they had set out to do. They had tried to weaken Germany physically but instead strengthened it geopolitically. From a long-term point of view Germany was in a far better position to dominate Europe after Versailles than it had been before the war. As soon as Germany threw off the

shackles of disarmament, which was just a matter of time, it was bound to emerge more powerful than ever." Henry Kissinger, *Diplomacy*, New York, Knopf, 1944, pp. 242, 245. Important details in Gerhard Weinberg, "The Defeat of Germany in 1918 and the European Balance of Power," *Central European History*, 2, 1969, pp. 248–60.

13 Herman J. Wittgens, "War Guilt Propaganda Conducted by the German Foreign Ministry during the 1920s," *Canadian Historical Association, Historical Papers/Communications Historiques*, Montréal, 1980, pp. 228–47, and, esp., John Maynard Keynes, *The Economic Consequences of the Peace*, London, Macmillan, 1919, and *A Revision of the Treaty*, London, Macmillan, 1922.

14 Steiner, *The Lights that Failed*, p. 99.

15 Alan Sharp, "Britain and the Protection of Minorities at the Paris Peace Conference," in A. C. Hepburn (ed.), *Minorities in History*, London, Arnold, 1978, pp. 170–88.

16 Details in Carole Fink, *Defending the Rights of Others: The Great Powers, the Jews, and International Minority Protection, 1878–1938*, Cambridge, Cambridge University Press, 2004, pp. 133–264.

17 Ibid., pp. 267–74.

18 See, esp., Arnold Wolfers, *Britain and France between Two Wars: Conflicting Strategies of Peace from Versailles to World War II*, New York, W. W. Norton, 1966.

19 Ann Williams, *Britain and France in the Middle East and North Africa*, London, Macmillan, 1968, pp. 23–37; also Norman Rose, *Chaim Weizmann: A Biography*, New York, Viking, 1986, pp. 202–5.

20 Allied and Associated Powers, *Treaty of Peace with Turkey*, London, Carnegie Endowment for International Peace, 1923; Renée Hirschon, *Heirs of the Greek Catastrophe: The Social Life of Asia Minor Refugees in Piraeus*, Oxford, Berghahn, 1988, p.xvi.

21 See chapter 27 above; also Claudena M. Skran, *Refugees in Inter-War Europe: The Emergence of a Regime*, Oxford, Oxford University Press, 1995, and Michael Marrus, *The Unwanted: European Refugees in the Twentieth Century*, New York, Oxford University Press, 1985.

22 See esp. C. E. Montague, *Disenchantment*, London, Chatto and Windus, 1922.

23 Eduard Beneš, "The Little Entente," *Foreign Affairs* 1 (Sept. 1922), pp. 66–72; also Joseph Rothschild, *East Central Europe between the Two World Wars*, Seattle, University of Washington Press, 1974, pp. 4–11, 33–4, 76–86.

24 Carole Fink, *The Genoa Conference: European Diplomacy, 1921–1922*, rev. ed., Syracuse, NY, Syracuse University Press, 1993.

25 Stephen A. Schuker, *The End of French Predominance in Europe: The Financial Crisis of 1924 and the Adoption of the Dawes Plan*, Chapel Hill, University of North Carolina Press, 1976.

26 Patrick Cohrs, "The First 'Real' Peace Settlements after the First World War. Britain, the United States, and the Accords of London and Locarno, 1923–1925," *Contemporary European History* 12/1, 2003, pp. 1–31.

27 Clemens A. Wurm, *Die franzöische Sicherheitspolitik in der Phase der Umorientierung, 1924–1926*, Frankfurt a.M., Peter Lang, 1979; Alan Cassels, "Repairing the *Entente Cordiale* and the New Diplomacy," *Historical Journal* 23/1, 1980, pp. 133–53; and, esp., Gaynor Johnson (ed.), *Locarno Revisited: European Diplomacy, 1920–1929*, London and New York, Frank Cass, 2004.

28 Jacobson, *Locarno Diplomacy*.

29 See, esp., Christian Höltje, *Die Weimarer Republik und das Ostlocarno-Problem. Revision oder Garantie der deutschen Ostgrenze von 1919*, Würzburg, Holzner-Verlag, 1958.

30 The foremost proponents were Hans. W. Gatzke, *Stresemann and the Rearmament of Germany*, Baltimore, Johns Hopkins University Press, 1954, and Annelise Thimme, *Gustav Stresemann: Eine politische Biographie zur Geschichte der Weimarer Republik*, Hanover, O. Goedel, 1957, but see also C. M. Kimmich, *Germany and the League of Nations*, Chicago, University of

Chicago Press, 1976, and Wolfgang Michalka and Marshall Lee (eds.), *Gustav Stresemann*, Darmstadt, Wissenschaftliche Buchgesellschaft, 1982.

31   Jonathan Wright, *Gustav Stresemann: Weimar's Greatest Statesman*, Oxford, Oxford University Press, 2002; Christian Baechler, *Gustave Stresemann (1878–1929): De l'impérialisme à la sécurité collective*, Strasbourg, Presses Universitaires de Strasbourg, 1996; Manfred Berg, *Gustav Stresemann und die Vereinigten Staaten von Amerika: Weltwirschaftliche Verflectung und Revisionspolitik, 1907–1929*, Baden Baden, Nomos, 1990.

32   See, esp., Kathleen Burk, "The Lineaments of Foreign Policy: The United States and a 'New World Order' 1919–1939," *Journal of American Studies* 26, 1992, pp. 377–91; also Frank Costigliola, *Awkward Dominion: American Political, Economic, and Cultural Relations with Europe, 1919–1933*, Ithaca and London, Cornell University Press, 1984, and Melvyn Leffler, *The Elusive Quest: America's Pursuit of European Stability and French Security*, Chapel Hill, NC, University of North Carolina Press, 1979.

33   John Cairns, "A Nation of Shopkeepers in Search of a Suitable France," *American Historical Review* 79, 1974, pp. 710–43.

34   Ádám, *The Versailles System and Central Europe*.

35   Jacobson, *When the Soviet Union entered World Politics*.

36   For discussions of these questions, see Charles Maier, "The Two Postwar Eras and the Conditions for Stability in 20th-Century Western Europe," *American Historical Review* 86, 1981, pp. 327–52; Carole Fink, "The Great Powers and the New International System, 1919–1923," in Paul Kennedy and William I. Hitchcock (eds.), *From War to Peace: Altered Strategic Landscapes in the Twentieth Century*, New Haven, CT and London, Yale University Press, 2000, pp. 17–35, 257–65; and, esp. Sally Marks, *The Illusion of Peace: International Relations in Europe, 1918–1933*, 2nd ed., New York, Palgrave Macmillan, 2003, and Marks, *The Ebbing of European Ascendancy: An International History of the World, 1914–1945*, London, Arnold, 2002. See also Jon Jacobson, "Is There a New History of the 1920s?" *American Historical Review*, 88, 1983, pp. 617–45.

37   Winston S. Churchill, *The World Crisis: The Aftermath*, New York, Charles Scribner's Sons, 1929, p. 239.

38   Cohrs, *The Unfinished Peace*, pp. 608–20.

39   Herbert Hömig, *Brüning: Kanzler in der Krise der Republik*, Paderborn, F. Schöningh, 2000.

40   David Stevenson, *Cataclysm: The First World War as Political Tragedy*, New York, Basic Books, 2004, pp. 468–72; also Martin Ceadel, *Pacifism in Britain, 1914–1945: The Defining of a Faith*, Oxford, Oxford University Press, 1980.

41   Gilbert Ziebura, *World Economy and World Politics, 1924–1931: From Reconstruction to Collapse*, Oxford, Oxford University Press, 1990, pp. 139–48; see also Patricia Clavin, *The Failure of Economic Diplomacy: Britain, Germany, France, and the United States, 1931–1936*, New York, St Martin's Press, 1996.

42   Justus D. Doenecke, *The Diplomacy of Frustration: The Manchurian Crisis of 1931–1933*, Stanford, CT, Stanford University Press, 1981; also Christopher Thorne, *The Limits of Foreign Policy: The West, the League and the Far-Eastern Crisis, 1931–1933*, New York, Putnam, 1972.

43   Steiner, *The Lights that Failed*, pp. 722–6.

44   Walters, *A History of the League of Nations*, pp. 463–99.

45   Poland, in particular, perceived the risk of a border issue with Germany and the League's manifest weakness to intervene. See unsigned memorandum [Nov. 1931?], Archiwum Akt Nowych, Warsaw, MSZ 2259.

46   Weinberg, *Hitler's Foreign Policy*.

47   James Burgwyn, *Italian Foreign Policy in the Interwar Period, 1918–1940*, Westport, CT and London, Praeger, 1997, pp. 100–44.

48   Walters, *League of Nations*, pp. 687–8, 709–20, 777–82.
49   Gottfried Niedhart, "Appeasement. Die britische Antwort auf die Krise des Weltreichs und das internationale System der Zwischenkriegszeit," *Historische Zeitschrift* 221, 1978, pp. 52–76.
50   Stephen A. Schuker, "France and the Remilitarization of the Rhineland, 1936," in Patrick Finney, *The Origins of the Second World War*, London and New York, Arnold, 1997, pp. 222–44.
51   R. A. C. Parker, *Chamberlain and Appeasement: The Coming of the Second World War*, New York, St Martin's Press, 1993.
52   Peter Neville, *Neville Chamberlain: A Study in Failure?*, London, Hodder, 1992. Review of the debate in Frank McDonough, *Neville Chamberlain, Appeasement, and the British Road to War*, Manchester, Manchester University Press, 1998, pp. 1–12.
53   For example: Margaret Macmillan, *Six Months that Changed the World: The Treaty of Versailles and the Road to World War II*, sound recording, 14 lectures, New York, 2004; *The Great War and the Shaping of the Twentieth Century*, Alexandria, Virginia: PBS Home Video, 1996; Niall Ferguson, *The Pity of War*, London, Allen Lane, 1998.
54   See esp., Georges Clemenceau, *Grandeur and Misery of Victory*, 1930; translation from French, London, Harrap, 1930.
55   Stevenson, *Cataclysm*, p. 430.

References and Further Reading

Ádám, Magda, *The Versailles System and Central Europe*, Aldershot, Ashgate/Variom, 2004.

Adamthwaite, Anthony, *Grandeur and Misery: France's Bid for Power in Europe, 1914–1940*, London, Arnold, 1995.

Artaud, Denise, *La question des dettes interalliées et la reconstruction de l'Europe (1917–1929)*, 2 vols., Lille, Université de Lille, 1978.

Boemeke, Manfred F., Feldman, Gerald D., and Glaser, Elisabeth (eds.), *The Treaty of Versailles: A Reassessment after 75 Years*, Cambridge, Cambridge University Press, 1998.

Cohrs, Patrick O., *The Unfinished Peace after World War I*, Cambridge, Cambridge University Press, 2006.

Craig, Gordon A., and Gilbert, Felix (eds.), *The Diplomats, 1919–1939*, Princeton, Princeton University Press, 1994.

Fromkin, David, *A Peace to End all Peace: The Fall of the Ottoman Empire and the Creation of the Modern Middle East*, New York, Holt, 2001.

Jacobson, Jon, *Locarno Diplomacy: Germany and the West 1925–1929*, Princeton, Princeton University Press, 1972.

Jacobson, Jon, *When the Soviet Union entered World Politics*, Berkeley, University of California Press, 1994.

Kent, Bruce, *The Spoils of War: The Politics, Economics, and Diplomacy of Reparations, 1918–1932*, Oxford, Oxford University Press, 1989.

Keylor, William (ed.), *The Legacy of the Great War: Peacemaking 1919*, Boston, Houghton Mifflin, 1998.

Krüger, Peter, *Die Aussenpolitik der Republik von Weimar*, Darmstadt, Wissenschaftliche Buchgesellschaft, 1985.

Macmillan, Margaret, *Peacemakers: The Paris Peace Conference of 1919 and its Attempt to End War*, London, John Murray, 2001.

Mayer, Arno J., *Politics and Diplomacy of Peacemaking: Containment and Counterrevolution at Versailles, 1918–1919*, London, Weidenfeld and Nicolson, 1968.

Schwabe, Klaus, *Woodrow Wilson, Revolutionary Germany, and Peacemaking, 1918–1919: Missionary Diplomacy and the Realities of Power*, 1971; translation from German, Chapel Hill and London, University of North Carolina Press, 1985.

Sharp, Alan, *The Versailles Settlement: Peacemaking in Paris, 1919*, New York, St. Martin's Press, 1991.

Steiner, Zara, *The Lights that Failed*, Oxford, Oxford University Press, 2005.

Walters, F. P., *A History of the League of Nations*, London, Oxford University Press, 1965.

Watt, D. C., *How War Came: The Immediate Origins of the Second World War, 1938–1939*, New York, Pantheon, 1989.

Weinberg, Gerhard, *Hitler's Foreign Policy: The Road to World War II, 1933–1939*, New York, Enigma, 2005.

CHAPTER THIRTY-SEVEN

War after the War: Conflicts, 1919–23

PETER GATRELL

Four uninterrupted years of mass bloodshed in the chief theaters of war did not make the postwar world a more peaceful place. Revolutions, civil wars, wars of independence, ethnic conflicts, and anticolonial uprisings occurred around the globe. Churchill observed that "the war of the giants has ended; the quarrels of the pygmies have begun," but this contemptuous remark overlooked the close connection between these "quarrels" and the recent "European" war.[1] Two decisive shifts in geopolitics make sense of these conflicts. The first new element was the Bolshevik revolution in November 1917, which had repercussions far beyond Russia. A second, related element was the struggle for the legacy of the disintegrating empires of Austria-Hungary, Germany, Russia, and Ottoman Turkey, a process entailing the creation of new nation-states, often with the kind of friction such as border disputes, territorial claims, and population movements that encouraged armed conflict.

The Russian Revolution had far-reaching significance. Workers' control and economic nationalization transformed the balance of power, while peasants seized and redistributed land with the blessing of the state. Terror, in the form of the Cheka, became a legitimate weapon in pursuit of revolutionary ideology.[2] And a new Red Army was mobilized in order to defend the new state.

Bolshevism injected fierce new energies into the complex interplay of radical, liberal, and reactionary tendencies in postwar Europe. Lenin's uncompromising declaration that there would be "no more landlords" held a genuine appeal for those impoverished peasants throughout Central and Eastern Europe. Ethnic differentiation, as in Ukraine, the Baltic States, Hungary, Czechoslovakia, and parts of the Balkans, added a powerful extra ingredient. The task for propertied elites outside Russia was to retain what power they could, and their answer was to embark on programs of land reform. European workers, too, were captivated by the news from Russia of factory committees and urban soviets, while bourgeois fears of expropriation were no less real than proletarian hopes of a better world.

The Entente powers feared that world revolution emanating from Soviet Russia would destroy not only the status quo in Europe, but also the global imperial order, which they had just expended so much energy to maintain. For these reasons, too, counter-revolutionary wars were launched in European and Asiatic Russia as well as in Russia's western borderlands. In addition to military intervention in Russia, the international powers sought through diplomatic, political, and economic interference to dictate the territorial and social form of the new polities emerging from the Russian, Habsburg, and Ottoman empires.

The political, military, social, and economic challenges that beset the world's empires during World War I have been discussed elsewhere in this volume.[3] The outcome was the establishment of successor states out of the wreckage of imperial polities. In the Baltic region three new states, Estonia, Latvia, and Lithuania, came into being. Independent Poland emerged with territory ceded from Austria-Hungary, Germany, and Russia. The old Habsburg Empire splintered into multiple new states, including Czechoslovakia and Yugoslavia. A new nation-state, Turkey, replaced the Ottoman Empire. Even Armenia, caught between Russia and Turkey, could now claim to have a state in the shape of the new titular socialist republic with its capital in Erevan. These states faced enormous problems of reconstruction. Serbia, for example, now part of the new Yugoslavia, had to rebuild the fabric of society and economy following the devastation brought about by six years of uninterrupted war.

The process of territorial redivision and the doctrine of self-determination multiplied rather than lessened the chances of conflict. Territorial claims and counterclaims abounded. Italy and Yugoslavia were at loggerheads over their rival claims to the former Austro-Hungarian port of Fiume, while Poland demanded Upper Silesia from Germany. Defeated states, notably Hungary and Bulgaria, did badly, Hungary being dismembered and Bulgaria being obliged to give up territory in Macedonia and western Thrace that it appropriated during the war. "Self-determination" too raised difficult questions. What did the doctrine mean for Ireland, India, and Egypt? What about "national minorities" in the newly independent states, who threatened (so it was thought) to mount irredentist claims, such as Hungarians in Romania? What decisions would be reached about Jews who lacked a state of their own?

One other preliminary point is worth emphasizing. New states, whether revolutionary or conservative in complexion, quickly established a defense capability, and existing states soon rebuilt their armies on orthodox lines. However, many of the conflicts described in this chapter involved irregular forces. Whereas regular armies were expected to adhere to an agreed code of conduct (which is not to say that they invariably did), no such precepts constrained irregular armies. Some veterans believed they had a duty to "beat the world into new shapes," even if this meant trampling over noncombatants.[4] For this reason, as well as the high stakes created by the virulent ideologies of revolutionary socialism and nationalism, conflict frequently assumed a particularly brutal form, with civilians often numbered among the casualties.

Revolutionary Challenges and Civil Wars

The outbreak of civil war in Russia was entirely predictable. The Bolshevik leadership knew that to unleash "class war" was also to invite civil war, since propertied elites would not give up without a fight and could mobilize political forces in support of their own cause. Widespread conflict took place between November 1917 and May 1918, well before foreign forces intervened on behalf of the "White" armies. Lenin wrote (in January 1918) that the revolution had provoked "frantic resistance of the propertied classes, who are fully aware that they face the final and decisive fight for the preservation of private landholding." The Cheka unleashed terror at the Bolsheviks' political opponents, real or perceived. Landowners, merchants, priests, and many intellectuals were also caught up in the maelstrom. The handbook issued to soldiers who enlisted in the Red Army explained that "our army is so called because it spills blood under the red flag ... and therefore the color of our banner is the color of blood."[5]

The first phase of the internationalization of the Russian Civil War was marked in May and June 1918 by the uprising of Czech prisoners of war in Siberia who wished to take part in the war against Germany in order to achieve Czech independence. Taking up arms against the Soviet regime, whose troops stood in their way, they joined forces with the Bolsheviks' Socialist Revolutionary opponents. Other groups – conservative and monarchist, as well as liberal in complexion – also began to organize opposition to the Bolsheviks. Admiral Aleksandr Kolchak (1874–1920) imposed his own authoritarian rule on anti-Bolshevik forces by the end of 1918, providing refuge in the major Siberian towns for the desperate civilians who threw in their lot with the Whites. But the opposition never crystallized into a coherent movement, nor did it develop a unified military command. In November 1919 refugees fled even further eastward in the company of Kolchak's bedraggled army. One eyewitness depicted them as "men moving like living dead through the taiga."[6]

On the southern front, the White "Volunteer army" under General Anton Denikin (1872–1947) enjoyed greater success during 1918, only to be driven from the North Caucasus and the Don region by the Red Army in the spring of 1919. Cossack troops, who endured a tempestuous relationship with Denikin, were now exposed to Bolshevik wrath. The Bolsheviks expelled Cossacks irrespective of age or gender from the Don Territory, with the intention of replacing them with a more reliable and "healthy element." In the Crimea, Chekists executed several thousand counterrevolutionaries who had served under General Piotr Wrangel (1878–1928). Further west, in Ukraine, the frequent changes of regime prompted further violence and population displacement. Thus when Kiev came under the control of the fiercely anti-Bolshevik Hetman Skoropadskii (1873–1945) in March 1918, White Russian refugees from Soviet-controlled territory quickly entered the city in order to take shelter from Bolshevik terror. But their refuge proved to be short-lived: Skoropadskii was driven out along with his German masters in December, to be replaced by a short-lived nationalist Directory under Semen Petliura (1879–1926).[7]

In northern Russia the Allied intervention began in earnest when British and Dominion troops landed at Archangel in the autumn of 1918, initially to keep Russia in the war but thereafter to support anti-Bolshevik forces. They stayed throughout 1919, reaching a peak of 20,000 men. It is worth noting that some of the British military personnel involved in the intervention also helped preserve the British imperial presence in the Middle East. Edmund Ironside (1880–1959) moved from Archangel to take command of British forces in Persia, where he was instrumental in putting Reza Khan in power.[8]

Complicating the picture further was the parallel conflict launched by peasant armies against Bolshevik rule. At issue was the procurement of food. The large estates, with potential surpluses, had been dismantled, so any grain necessarily lay with the peasantry. In the absence of sufficient manufactured goods to exchange for grain the Bolsheviks were obliged to obtain it by force. Initially they affirmed the importance of class division in the countryside, forming "committees of poor peasants" whose role was to compel rich "kulaks" to sell their surplus grain. In 1919 the government resorted instead to using detachments of troops and party activists who descended upon villages to appropriate grain from all and sundry, in accordance with nationally and regionally determined quotas. Peasants reacted by reducing sowings and taking up arms against the Bolsheviks. This movement gathered particular momentum once it became apparent to the peasantry that the White armies had been defeated and the large landowners would never return. The radical anarchist Nester Makhno (1889–1934) dominated large swathes of Ukraine between 1919 and 1920. In Tambov, the veteran revolutionary Aleksandr Antonov (1881–1922) led a band of 20,000 peasants who kept the Red Army at bay from August 1920 until the middle of the following year. These "Greens" shared a profound dislike of the communist monopoly of power and its impact on peasant self-government of the kind that had flourished in 1917. Hence the slogan, "down with the communists, long live the soviets."[9]

A similar ideology found favor with some workers and above all with sailors on the naval base at Kronstadt, where support for the Bolsheviks had been at its strongest in the first phase of the 1917 revolution. Kronstadt sailors took up arms at the beginning of 1921, complaining about the abandonment of "soviet democracy." Their uprising was suppressed with murderous determination. Kronstadt became a byword for Bolshevik resolve or terror, depending on one's point of view. Meanwhile, the Cheka pursued its battle against political opponents of the fledgling Soviet state, justifying its bloodshed on the grounds that "there can be no half measures."[10]

Russia continued to be beset by armed struggles, including the so-called Basmachi revolt in Central Asia. Informed by recent memories of the uprising in Turkestan in 1916, the Basmachi opposed the new regime's attempt to reorganize land tenure and schooling along secular lines. Around 20,000 Muslim warriors confronted the Bolsheviks, who struggled to retain control of Tashkent and who abandoned the countryside to the rebels. Desperate to retain control of this cotton-rich region, the Bolsheviks reached an accommodation with local landlords and merchants, restoring free trade and backtracking on the antireligious campaign. However, the conflict erupted again as Enver Pasha (1881–1922) tried to realize his dream of a Pan-Turkish polity embracing Central Asia, Turkey, and Afghanistan. He called upon irregular troops, who relied in turn upon local support. Failing to defeat the peasantry militarily, Lenin railroaded the Tenth Party Congress into accepting the New Economic Policy in March 1921, allowing peasants to engage in private trade. In Central Asia he promised the local population the right to Sharia courts and Koranic schools. However, these concessions did not erase the memory of repression, particularly the Red Army's bombing campaigns against the insurgents.[11]

In newly independent Finland, civil war took a brutal form. The Finnish radicals enjoyed widespread popular support, but unlike the Bolsheviks they were wedded to social democracy, not proletarian revolution. What sealed their fate, however, was their tactical alliance with the revolutionaries in Petrograd. Their White opponents, soldiers under the command of General Carl Mannerheim (1867–1948), were motivated "by the hope … of getting free of Russian oppression." They included the famous *Jäger* troops who had been trained in Germany. The Finnish Civil War thus began as a struggle between competing visions of national liberation and civil liberty, respectively. When the Red Guards evacuated Helsinki in April 1918 they were accompanied by columns of starving civilian refugees, who hoped to make their way to Petrograd or even Siberia. The desperate German soldiers stripped the soldiers and civilians of clothing and other belongings. The capture of Viipuri by the Whites was accompanied by summary executions.[12]

Hungary came closest to emulating the Soviet example. Workers' councils emerged in Budapest at the end of 1917 but the state survived intact until the military collapse in

November 1918. The revolution was led by the youthful Emil Sebestyén, better known as Béla Kun (1886–1939), who was released from a Russian prisoner-of-war camp into the arms of Bolshevik comrades. Other contemporaries and associates, such as Tibor Szamuely, Mátyás Rákosi, and Ferenc Münnich, followed the same course. In Hungary, to which Kun returned late in 1918, he found a defeated and dismembered country and an enthusiasm for radical social change among unemployed workers, peasants, middle-class refugees, and veterans. A coalition of socialists and communists soon collapsed, leaving the path clear for Béla Kun to take power in March 1919. Adopting Lenin as his model, and believing in an imminent Pan-European revolution ("we shall pursue this goal through all hell"), Kun promptly announced the formation of a soviet republic. He nationalized industrial enterprises and farms, deployed a Hungarian version of the Cheka and, as in Russia, soon antagonized farmers, who not only lost food but also their land. Perhaps Kun's greatest tactical mistake was to seek to export revolution to Slovakia and Romania, a move that prompted his neighbors, accompanied by French troops, to inter-vene and unseat him in August after 133 days in power. The Red Army, pinned down by Denikin in south Russia, was powerless to act, even if Lenin had so wished.

Thus where the Entente had failed in Russia, it succeeded in Hungary. Béla Kun fled to Austria and thence to Russia, arguing that "it would not have served the interests of international world revolution to make another Finland in Hungary." A vicious counter-revolution ensued, orchestrated by the future dictator Admiral Miklós Horthy (1868–1957), who was given a free hand by the Entente. Unlike Kun, he had no qualms about turning Hungary into another Finland and combined antisemitism with the ruthless pursuit of revolutionaries. The politician turned historian Oscar Jászi memorably wrote that "the Whites worked out a cold and refined system of vengeance and reprisal, which they applied with the cruelty of scoundrels masquerading as gentlemen."[13]

The "land question" provoked unease throughout Europe. It ran like a thread through the Russian Revolution and Civil War. Successor states grappled with the problem in broadly similar ways, namely by redistributing land to the peasantry. The aim here was to forestall peasant militancy rather than to wait for peasant anger to explode. The Yugoslav government went some way toward meeting their demands by expropriating the land of the largest Hungarian, Austrian, German, Turkish, and other landowners, in order to strengthen the position of the South Slav peasantry. This was a long drawn-out process. In Bulgaria, where land was more equally distributed to begin with, the peasant leader and Prime Minster Aleksandar Stamboliiski (1879–1923) nevertheless confiscated pri-vate estates.[14] Elsewhere, social tension, although marked, did not result in armed con-frontation on a large scale. This is not to minimize the political significance of labor militancy or the fierce reaction it provoked. The German army was re-created in order to crush labor protest in the Ruhr and elsewhere. Class conflict in 1919–20 became the breeding ground for fascism in Italy, where local elites responded to the triumph of municipal socialism by rallying to the fascist cry for "action."[15]

Empires as Battleground

Woodrow Wilson's Fourteen Points (January 8, 1918) dramatically transformed the geopolitics of continental Europe, partly by legitimizing the claim to "self-determination" and partly by naming specific sites of potential transformation. The Bolsheviks' stance at Brest-Litovsk raised the stakes further.[16] Successor states launched rival claims to the territory that had hitherto been under the jurisdiction of imperial powers or (as in

Poland and the Baltic) subject to German wartime occupation and administration. The victorious Entente powers sometimes encouraged the resulting conflicts by taking sides.

The end of the Russian Empire had profound consequences in the Caucasus, in the Baltic region, and in the western borderlands. In 1918 nationalist parties took power in Armenia and Azerbaijan, which almost immediately came to blows over the assertion of rival claims to territory. Georgia's declaration of independence in May 1918 brought an end to a short-lived Transcaucasian Federation. Georgia and Armenia only narrowly averted war in December 1918, thanks to British mediation, a reminder that the rival European powers all had commercial, economic, and political ambitions in the Caucasus.[17]

In the winter of 1918 the German withdrawal from the Baltic region and Ukraine allowed Soviet troops and Bolshevik commissars to attempt to influence the political future of the region. They were rebuffed in Estonia. Lithuanian patriots, having appropriated the arms and equipment left behind by the retreating German army, drove out the Red Army and declared an independent state.[18] The result was a bewildering military situation in the western borderlands of the former Russian empire. Polish and Ukrainian military units came to blows in eastern Galicia, where the victorious Poles incarcerated Ukrainians in camps and prisons in 1918–19. A final settlement of the territorial dispute did not take place until March 1923.

Meanwhile, Lithuania and Poland were at loggerheads over their respective claims to Vilno, a cosmopolitan city where Jews, Poles, and Lithuanians lived side by side. In Poland, a new republic had come into being in November 1918, led by Józef Piłsudski (1867–1935), who was wedded to the restoration of Poland's "historic" (that is, pre-1772) borders. The conflict dragged on until an irregular force of 20,000 men under the command of the Polish general Lucjan Żeligowski (1865–1947) seized the city in October 1920, claiming that Lithuania had taken Russia's side in the Polish–Soviet War. Żeligowski also bombed the Lithuanian city of Kaunas (Kovno). Following a plebiscite, Lithuania was obliged to accept a fait accompli, but this dramatic action remained a source of anger in Lithuania throughout the interwar period. Another trouble spot was the hitherto German port of Memel, which the Treaty of Versailles placed in the hands of an Allied Commission. Again Lithuania and Poland each had designs on the city. In a now familiar pattern, irregular troops, acting this time on behalf of Lithuania, seized Memel in January 1923. The Allies eventually recognized its status as an autonomous region of Lithuania, small recompense, however, for the loss of Vilno.[19]

Poland also secured control of the western part of Belarus in February 1919, a measure that seemed at first to many of its inhabitants preferable to rule by Moscow, or indeed by Germany, whose forces remained there until November 1918. However, the Belarusians' attitude rapidly changed as a result of the iron grip of Polish administration, which promoted the Polonization of economic, cultural, and religious life. Polish rule was challenged by an alliance between Russia and Lithuania, but this alliance proved short-lived. Poland and the Soviet leaders eventually agreed to partition Belarus. The persistent Polish repression impoverished the Belarusian population, around 100,000 of whom emigrated.

These internal hostilities and external conflicts were given added momentum by the war that broke out between Soviet Russia and Poland in early 1919 following the German retreat from the "Land Ober Ost."[20] In 1920 Polish troops quickly captured territory in Belarus and Ukraine, Piłsudski having reached an understanding with Petliura, according to which Ukraine would forfeit its western borderlands of Eastern Galicia in exchange for Poland's help in driving the Bolsheviks from the rest of Ukraine. In May 1920 the Poles took Kiev and drove out the Soviet regime. But the Polish occupation lasted barely a month, and Soviet troops under the command of Mikhail Tukhachevskii (1893–1937) chased the Poles back to the edge of Warsaw, encouraging peasants and workers in Galicia, Lithuania, and Belarus to adopt Bolshevism. Following a sustained Polish counteroffensive, the Red Army was driven back; Polish patriots spoke of the "miracle on the Vistula."[21]

The Treaty of Riga finally brought the war to an end in March 1921. The Soviet Union remained isolated and impoverished. War also imposed considerable costs on Poland which, more than any other state with the exception of Armenia, was faced with an enormous problem of economic reconstruction and refugee relief. The Polish–Soviet War demonstrated several important features of postwar European conflict. One was that a new state had to improvise in order to create an army from scratch. Another was that "peace" brought with it a settling of accounts, specifically one in which Jews were equated with Bolshevism. Finally, conflict had important international repercussions. In the Polish–Soviet war, British and German dockers, adopting the slogan "Hands Off Russia," refused to load goods destined for Poland. Lenin renounced international revolution. The American Relief Administration intervened to avert famine in Poland and to mitigate its impact in Russia.[22]

Other flashpoints in Europe included Fiume, the Burgenland, Teschen, and Upper Silesia. In contravention of the Treaty of Versailles, irregulars under the command of Gabriele D'Annunzio (1863–1938) claimed Fiume on Italy's behalf in September 1919 and remained there for 15 months. The dispute was not settled until 1924, which gave the city to Italy and the surrounding territory to Yugoslavia. In Central Europe, Hungary was left smarting over the decision by the Allies to award the Burgenland to Austria. In 1921 Hungarian paramilitaries seized control. They withdrew only after a plebiscite persuaded the Allies to hand the town of Sopron back to Hungary. Poles and Czechs fought over Teschen (Cieszyn), which was eventually awarded to Czechoslovakia in 1920. Upper Silesia, the location of substantial coalfields and a largely Polish workforce, had originally been assigned to Poland during discussions at Versailles, but Lloyd George agreed to a plebiscite following German protests that the loss of the region would make it difficult to meet reparations payments. Poles objected to the results of the plebiscite, held in March 1921, which upheld German claims. A group of Polish nationalists, with France's tacit blessing, crossed the frontier. Germany protested at this breach of the peace treaty, but before a diplomatic solution could be found German Freikorps troops stormed the convent at St. Annaberg. After months of diplomacy the Allies eventually divided Upper Silesia between Poland and Germany, leaving Poland with most of the industrial assets.[23]

The Ottoman Empire was also the site of fresh conflict as great powers and emerging states alike sought to capitalize on its perceived vulnerability. British and French troops occupied Istanbul between November 1918 and October 1923, where they faced a determined underground resistance movement.[24] Armenian patriots looked to revenge the genocide of 1915 by acquiring territory in eastern Anatolia. Armenian armed forces initially made headway in northeastern Anatolia and actually received territorial recompense under the Treaty of Sèvres in August 1920. Greek patriots hoped to conclude unfinished business from the Balkan Wars of 1912–13 by incorporating western Anatolia with its substantial Greek communities into "Greater Greece." Encouraged by Britain,

Greek forces captured Izmir (Smyrna) in May 1919; as they moved further east they struggled to maintain lines of communication and soon ran short of food and munitions. The hero of Canakkale (Gallipoli), Mustafa Kemal (1880–1938), moved the capital to Ankara and reorganized the Ottoman army, astutely concluding a peace agreement with the Soviet Union. Kemal's efforts paid dividends, in the shape of victory over the exhausted Greeks. When he retook Smyrna in 1922, around 30,000 mainly Greek residents were massacred in full view of British marines, who had instructions not to intervene. Allied fears that Kemal would press home his advantage and claim control of the Dardanelles brought Britain and Turkey to the brink of war. The revival of the Turkish army also stemmed the Armenian tide in eastern Anatolia. A revolutionary junta in Athens overthrew the monarchy and executed the royalist generals, whom it blamed for the debacle.[25]

The Treaty of Lausanne in July 1923 aimed "to bring to a final close the state of war which has existed in the East since 1914." It confirmed Turkey's territorial integrity and obliged the government in Erevan to renounce its claims to a "Greater Armenia." The Treaty also provided for a compulsory exchange of population between Greece and Turkey, although plans for this had already been drawn up in 1914. Around 350,000 Muslims were uprooted from Greece and moved to Turkey. Up to a million individuals – Turkish nationals of the Greek Orthodox faith – fled for Greece, either immediately following Turkey's recapture of Smyrna or after the Treaty. Estimates also suggest that up to half a million displaced persons remained unaccounted for following this exchange. The League of Nations established a Refugee Settlement Commission in Greece, but resources were badly stretched and many urban refugees lived in makeshift barracks for years to come. In Turkey itself, Kemal captured the popular imagination and paved the way for a national state, the constitution of 1921 having consigned the Ottoman imperial tradition to history.[26]

Far from being dismembered, the British Empire was effectively enlarged as a result of acquiring mandates in the Middle East. Here too, empire constituted a site of violence and international rivalry. In Egypt, leading nationalists in the Wafd party demanded independence. The peremptory negative response of the British authorities led to a wave of strikes and student demonstrations in support of the Wafd that peaked in the spring and summer of 1919. Close on a thousand Egyptians and Europeans lost their lives as a result of the British military intervention to crush the "fanatics." A political settlement took many more months to achieve.[27] Further east, the British and French sought to capitalize upon the faltering grip of Ottoman rule over the lands of the Hijaz, Mesopotamia and Syria. Britain supported the military campaign launched by Sharif Hussein, who used the holy city of Mecca as a base from which to sustain the so-called "Arab Revolt." Hussein enlisted the support of disaffected officers who had served during the war in the Ottoman army. His army was made up of irregular troops; many ordinary soldiers simply went home. When local tribesmen protested that Hussein was a British puppet, the Royal Air Force duly confirmed their view by bombing them into submission. In what was explicitly regarded as "a novel experiment," the British also deployed the RAF as a means of maintaining control over their extensive mandate in Iraq, where they backed the local Sunni minority. The Iraq revolt in the autumn of 1920 claimed the lives of perhaps 8,500 Iraqis and 2,000 British.[28] Stability of a sort came to the region when the British abandoned direct rule in Iraq and allowed Hussein to take power in Baghdad where, as King Faisal, he too marginalized the Shia majority. In the Hijaz the neighboring British-backed house of Saud paved the way for the subsequent creation of "Saudi Arabia." Yet further east, the Red Army invaded Persia in 1920 and remained there for 18 months, lending their support for a time to the Jangali revolutionaries who established the short-lived Socialist Republic of Iran.[29]

In India, where 70,000 British troops were stationed, the end of the war helped to inflame nationalist sentiment against the British occupation. The authorities passed the "Black Acts," suppressing freedom of speech and detaining political activists without trial. A peaceful demonstration of 20,000 people who gathered to celebrate a Hindu festival at Jallianwala Bagh in Amritsar in April 1919, led to the death of around 400 unarmed Indian civilians at the hands of men under the command of General Reginald Dyer. Degrading treatment of the local residents became the order of the day. Although rebuked by an official inquiry, Dyer earned from his British supporters the epithet of "savior of the Punjab"; by contrast, the Secretary of State for India, Edwin Montagu (1879–1924) – a Jew – was regarded in some circles as "suspect." In India itself the Congress Party rallied additional support among the lower middle class, hardly an omen of enhanced British control. Indian members of the inquiry likened Dyer's action to German atrocities in Belgium and France. What is more, the loyalty of India's Muslim population could not be taken for granted if Britain pursued, as it seemed, a vendetta against Turkey. The Khilafat movement – backed by 10,000 guerrillas – was a beneficiary of this perception. In Madras the British commander, Major General John Burnett–Stuart, spoke of "extermination or arrest" as the appropriate response, and expressed satisfaction at the death of 2,330 rebels. In adjacent parts of the Empire, too, such as Afghanistan and Burma, the British faced determined armed resistance.[30]

However, the most brutal fighting within the British imperial orbit took place much closer to home, across the Irish Sea, involving nationalist politicians, the Irish Republican Army (IRA), Unionists (Sir Edward Carson gave Dyer his wholehearted support), the British army, and British paramilitaries. Irish republican volunteers who comprised the IRA were opposed to negotiations with Britain and thus also to nationalists who were ready to embrace it. Michael Collins (1890–1922) called the volunteers a "rabble." Others regarded them as "scum" or at best "raw" individuals. They enjoyed considerable license; by 1919 the British state had more or less ceased to function in Cork. The regular police were powerless to act (they were vastly understaffed) and trials of IRA suspects were aborted owing to lack of witnesses. This explains the controversial employment of the Black and Tans, auxiliaries who arrived at the beginning of 1920, and the British government's recourse to martial law. The Irish War of Independence had some elements of class war; for example, the IRA opposed foxhunting and large landownership. But the volunteers, drawn from the ranks of shop assistants, craftsmen, and farming families, were not social revolutionaries, and prized "respectability" rather than radicalism. "National liberation," not class enmity, provided the driving force.[31]

The British failed to defeat the IRA militarily; the writing was on the wall when the Chief of the Imperial General Staff, Sir Henry Wilson, demanded an army of 200,000 men. In the end the solution was political, with Ireland partitioned in December 1921 between a self-governing Free State and a Protestant-dominated Northern Ireland that remained part of the United Kingdom. One of the military leaders that the British government sent to Ireland was the 31-year-old Bernard (later Field Marshal Lord) Montgomery (1887–1976). He concluded that Lloyd George "was right – the only way was to give [the Irish] some form of self-government and let them squash the rebellion themselves" – and indeed, a bitter civil war broke out for a further 18 months between supporters and opponents of the settlement with Britain.[32] Still, the war against the

British had a wider resonance within the Empire. Nationalists in Egypt, India, and elsewhere followed events in Ireland very closely, and even if Gandhi was troubled by Sinn Fein violence, others were inspired. For their part, imperialists anguished about their inability to control their far-flung possessions.[33]

Forms and Instruments of Violence

Many of the conflicts described above took on the character of "dirty wars" fought by irregular troops and distinguished by the use of force against civilians. Irregular troops seized food, fodder, and horses. They held civilians hostage and summarily tortured and executed their prisoners. Paramilitary groups, notably in Ireland but also in Bulgaria, Yugoslavia, and Hungary, meted out summary "justice" – in Hungary with the implicit approval of Horthy. Organized armies were also imbued with a sense of mission, which contributed to unrestrained violence against civilians and military foes. The Red Army, like the British army overseas, deployed new weapons of war against civilian populations. States had recourse to forced migration, either as a weapon of war – as in the Soviet deportation of all Cossacks – or as an instrument of politics – as in the reciprocal expulsion of Greeks and Turks to create more ethnically homogeneous states in both cases after 1923.

The widespread militarization of civilian life and the efflorescence of irregular warfare after 1918 suggest connections with World War I. Those participating in irregular warfare and radical right-wing movements were often army veterans. In Italy, fascists turned thoughts of war into a program for action against the "enemy within." According to Adrian Lyttleton, "the war accustomed men to killing, and made them more likely to seek violent solutions to their problems in peacetime." Fascism appealed to the *arditi*, or crack troops, who survived World War I, as well as to ex-officers and militant nationalist students.[34] The Hungarian revolution depended upon militant ex-prisoners of war who returned from captivity in Russia, while the counterrevolution drew upon proto-fascist youths who espoused violence as a means of "purifying" society. In Ireland the despised Black and Tans were army veterans, but so were some of their IRA opponents, even if the latter looked for political symbolism and legitimacy to the Dublin rising of Easter 1916, and not the Somme. These arguments should not be pushed too far. Many more veterans, including prisoners, returned with relief to civilian life rather than sought fresh killing fields.

Further connections with the war stemmed from the way the latter had created new fault-lines, both territorial and ideological, which fueled reciprocal violence on both sides. Thus in Ireland, the brutality of the War of Independence came in part from the readiness of youthful radical nationalists to volunteer for the IRA, and to target the British, members of the Protestant elite, and any Irish politician prepared to contemplate a deal with Britain. In turn, the British responded to the IRA campaign with raids, revenge killings, arson, and sabotage. The Black and Tans inspired fear among the local population, with people often being killed for being in the wrong place at the wrong time. The culture of masculine "toughness" contributed to the widespread violence and much "tit-for-tat" killing. The IRA also prided itself on sobriety and a new national purity, while the Black and Tans frequently regarded the local population as inferior. The web of violence was thus spun in an extensive fashion.[35]

In Germany, meanwhile, some junior officers who enlisted during the war stayed on to rescue the "honor" of the army, defend German communities on either side of the new national frontiers, and fight the Spartacists. To be sure, many more than the 400,000 men who joined the Freikorps enlisted instead in the antiwar Reichsbund. But the issue is not just about numbers. One Freikorps volunteer encapsulated the militancy of his comrades as follows: "People told us that the war was over. That made us laugh. We ourselves are the war." It was these men who rallied to the call to "restore order" in Berlin and Munich, which they did with great enthusiasm in the early months of 1919, adopting a "shoot-to-kill" policy toward citizens who were found in possession of weapons. In Munich, it was a matter of pride that "Reds will be executed free of charge."[36]

The Russian Civil War was similarly characterized by a self-reinforcing spiral of organized and random violence alike. Ordinary citizens were caught up in the crossfire between Reds and Whites, often in a haphazard fashion. The peasant wars of 1918–21 were vicious affairs, in which often poorly equipped "Green" armies tortured, maimed, and murdered Bolshevik officials and burned party documents and tax records. Young peasant men – bound by codes of comradeship and keen to denounce excessive drinking and gambling – played a dominant role. The "Greens" accused the Bolsheviks of being "vampires." In Central Asia the Basmachi recruited young unemployed farmers who were tempted by the offer of food and horses, but whose chief motivation appears to have been a firm adherence to Islam and a readiness to offer themselves as martyrs. In each instance the Bolsheviks attempted to reassert their authority by superior force and repression (including surrounding villages and starving members into submission). Only the compromise of the NEP prevented further bloodshed.[37] Irregular counterrevolutionary troops amounting to private armies also rampaged – there is no other word – across eastern Siberia and the Far East, backed by the Japanese in Manchuria, and responded with atrocities to civilian resistance.

The zone of Eastern Europe comprising the former frontier territories of the Russian Empire was particularly prone to violence in the years after World War I, as ethnic rivalries fed ideological and territorial animosities. Civil war exacted a heavy toll on the Jewish population concentrated in eastern Ukraine who had suffered from pogroms in the past. Jews were widely associated with Bolshevism and fell victim in 1919 to the forces of the Ukrainian Directory, headed by Petliura, or to local warlords, who obeyed no law but their own. Those Jews who refused to pay "protection money" were tortured, raped, forced from their homes, or killed. The victims numbered tens of thousands. In Galicia, Poland, and Belarus too, there were widespread reports of pogroms against the Jewish population. We should also bear in mind the longer-term significance of the German presence in Poland and the Baltic in shaping perceptions of the radical right toward the *Ostjuden* (Jews from the east), whom they encountered and reviled.[38]

In Finland, in May 1918 close on 10,000 rebels were executed either semi-legally or by means of extrajudicial killings. The bloodletting of the civil war was an opportunity to settle old scores. Similar numbers died in prison from malnutrition and disease in just a few months. The struggle ended as class war with a vengeance.[39] Of paramount importance in the Baltic states that emerged from the collapse of Tsarist power was the continued presence of ethnic German Freikorps under the control of General von der Goltz. Goltz spoke of "salvaging what was salvageable" by restoring the power of the Baltic German nobility and promising land to his volunteers. His troops sacked the towns along the Baltic coast before entering Riga and launching a terror campaign. As late as October 1919, German irregulars were still trying to dominate Latvia.

As in Germany, so in Hungary the revolution yielded bloodthirsty results. The secret police, along with the unpleasant "Lenin boys," were given a license to prey on the bourgeoisie, landlords, and Kun's political opponents. Tőkés describes them as gangs of sailors, criminals, and hooligans, who robbed at will; what Lenin thought of them is not recorded. Béla Kun's terror campaign was followed by an equally determined "White" terror. Some 5,000 people may have lost their lives in the bloodbath of 1919–20 at the hands of the paramilitaries under Pál Prónay and others who went unpunished. A further 75,000 individuals were imprisoned, and 100,000 went into exile, many of them to Soviet Russia, where Stalin eventually killed those who had managed to escape Horthy's death squads. Remarkably, Bulgaria avoided civil war, although Stamboliiski fought a running battle with the Bulgarian communists and gave free rein to his "Orange Guard," which broke strikes and suppressed middle-class dissent.

Yet it would be misleading to focus entirely on irregular warfare and paramilitary forces, and to miss the important developments in conventional armies. In Soviet Russia, the Red Army originated as a volunteer army but it rapidly gave way to a professional conscript force. Ex-Tsarist officers were recruited as military specialists; there were some 70,000 by 1920, one-third of the total officer corps. At the end of the Civil War the Red Army totaled five million men, although it faced problems of low morale and desertion, before giving conscripts and their families greater material security.[40] Other new states, as in the Baltic, capitalized upon the national units that emerged in Tsarist Russia during the war. Latvia's army rested upon combination of volunteers and British aid. The Polish army, only 6,000 strong in November 1918, grew to 300,000 within six months, as Poles returned from France, Germany, Austria, and Russia. Conscription during the Polish–Soviet War brought the numbers up to one million. The supply of arms, equipment, and uniforms was hastily improvised.[41]

Defeated states, such as Hungary and Germany, faced a considerable challenge. In Germany General von Seeckt (1866–1936) disdained the Freikorps as he re-created a 100,000-strong conventional army. Turkey and Greece, like Poland, raised an army in order to fight wars. Kemal's forces were supplied by the underground in occupied Istanbul. Both armies, we should note, took a terrible revenge on unarmed civilians in 1920–21. One great power, Britain, revised its assumptions about the conduct of war, acknowledging that it could never deploy sufficient numbers of men to police its empire. It hit upon the Royal Air Force as an instrument of control; aircraft had the potential to operate over difficult terrain in India and the Middle East, with the added attraction of being relatively cheap.[42]

***

This chapter has indicated the most important sites of violence in post-1918 Europe and beyond and has related mass violence to revolutionary upheavals and the reconfiguration of territory that followed the war. Account has also been taken of the nature of postwar conflicts. In his study of Germany, Richard Bessel argues that it was a "postwar society" rather than a "peacetime" society.[43] Much the same applies to countries such as Hungary, Czechoslovakia, and the Baltic States. The population of Soviet Russia, Poland, and Turkey, as well as Ireland, did not begin to live anything approaching a normal life until the mid-1920s. The Middle East and India continued to be crucibles of conflict.

The heaviest loss of life took place in Russia. Battlefield casualties in the Russian Civil War and the Polish–Soviet War amounted to 125,000 Red Army deaths and 175,000 among the opposing White and Polish forces. To these figures should be added a further 500,000 military and civilian deaths from epidemic disease. The war between

Greece and Turkey may have cost the lives of around 68,000 troops and at least 30,000 civilians.[44] To be sure, excess mortality was not always directly related to mass violence. The flu pandemic in 1918 killed at least 20 million people, although these losses may have been inflated by the diversion of resources to the final stages of the European war. Other conflicts, although bitter, yielded smaller casualties. In Ireland, for example, deaths certainly did not exceed 1,000, and the French occupation of Syria caused the deaths of 5,000 on either side.[45]

Numbers alone do not convey the significance that these conflicts acquired or their key characteristics. Many of these dirty wars involved undisciplined freebooters and imperial adventurers. One explanatory element was the absence of organized supplies of food, fodder, and munitions, which encouraged irregular troops (and deserters) to pillage. This improvised extraction of resources invited confrontation with the local population. Another feature was the indiscriminate mass murder committed in support of a Manichaean vision of good against evil. The Russian Civil War, like the Hungarian revolution and counterrevolution, promoted a doctrine of annihilating one's opponents. Identifying one's enemy was not always easy. Civilians were frequently caught up in indiscriminate killing perpetrated by young men. The Italian fascist Blackshirts (*squadristi*) were overwhelmingly youths whose comradeship manifested itself in beating and humiliating their opponents, notably by forcing them to drink large quantities of castor oil. Hungarians, Reds and Whites alike, described the torture and killing of their opponents as "English" – "half-English" referred to torture that stopped short of death.[46] Minorities, including Jews who lacked the unambiguous protection of the state, were an easy target in Urga, Lake Balaton in Hungary, and for Ukrainian extremists in Kiev and Volhynia. So too were the ordinary middle-class citizens who fell victim to the "Lenin boys" on the streets of Budapest in 1919 or to the Orange Guard in Sofia in 1920.

The search for political stability had mixed results. The Anglo-Irish settlement created a viable new state, albeit with painful memories of civil war. British troops remained in Ulster and India, but left Silesia, Russia, the Caucasus, Turkey, and Persia. Stability of a kind returned to these regions. The Bolshevik Party cemented its rule in Russia. The political solution in Finland entailed the formation of a moderate Social Democratic Party and the exile of Finnish communists to Soviet Russia, although many workers threw in their lot with the illegal Communist Party.[47] Elsewhere, victors and vanquished were configured in ethnic as well as class terms. In Yugoslavia, political stability was achieved by suppressing first the Croat Peasant Party and then the Communist Party in 1921, following the assassination of the Minister of the Interior, for which the Communists disclaimed responsibility. A large part of the nation "was excluded from political life."[48]

To be sure, the dogs of war did not always bark. Some states, like Czechoslovakia, Yugoslavia, and Estonia, were relatively stable and successful. Britain (notwithstanding "race" riots and police strikes in 1919), France, the Netherlands, and Belgium remained fundamentally undisturbed, although the same cannot be said of their imperial possessions, and France provoked an international outcry when with Belgium it occupied the Ruhr in 1923. Steady economic recovery helped restore a degree of normalcy at least until the Great Depression. The Genoa Conference (1922) contributed to a reduction in tension by beginning the complex process of reintegrating Russia into the international economy. At the same time, it would be wrong to overlook the scope for further havoc in the theaters of conflict mentioned above. Potential dangers included the widespread espousal of violence as an instrument with which to destroy one's political opponent or "class enemy," the thirst for revenge on the part of "victim" states, and the persistence of rural poverty and inequality. Beyond Europe, the maintenance of imperial rule, combined with mass impoverishment, helped to fan the flames of discord. No great insight was needed to see that large portions of the world in 1923 offered precious few signs of stability and security.

Notes

1   Quoted in Davies, *White Eagle*, p. 21.
2   The Cheka was the abbreviated form in Russian of "The All-Russian Extraordinary Commission to Combat Counter-Revolution and Sabotage."
3   See chs. 14, 19, 25, 30, 32, 33, 35.
4   Ernst Jünger, quoted in Waite, *Vanguard of Nazism*, p. 28.
5   V. I. Lenin, "Theses on the question of the immediate conclusion of a separate and annexationist peace," in Lenin, *Collected Works*, vol. 26, Moscow, Progress Publishers, 1972; Sanborn, *Drafting the Russian Nation*, p. 175.
6   Smele, *Civil War in Siberia*, pp. 369–71, 593.
7   Acton (ed.), *Critical Companion*, pp. 319, 735–8; Reshetar, *Ukrainian Revolution*, pp. 158–9.
8   Chaqueri, *Soviet Socialist Republic*, pp. 298–308.
9   Figes, *Peasant Russia*, p. 330; Acton (ed.), *Critical Companion*, pp. 370–80; Erik Landis, "Waiting for Makhno: legitimacy and context in a Russian peasant war," *Past and Present*, 183, 2004, pp. 199–238.
10 Sanborn, *Drafting the Russian Nation*, p. 175.
11 Olcott, "Basmachi," points out that this term, derived from the Turkish word for "plunder," was given the resistance movement by Russian officials. The rebels called themselves "freedom fighters."
12 Upton, *Finnish Revolution*.
13 Details in Tökés, *Béla Kun*, pp. 99, 203 (quotations), p. 214; Jászi, *Revolution*, pp. 160–1. See also Bodó, "Paramilitary violence."
14 Rothschild, *East-Central Europe*, pp. 210, 268–9; Bell, *Peasants in Power*; Tomasevich, *Peasants*, pp. 344–82.
15 Lyttelton, "Fascism and violence," p. 259; Bessel, *Germany*, p. 261.
16 Mayer, *Political Origins*, pp. 296–312, 329–93.
17 Suny, *Looking Toward Ararat*, p. 125.
18 This is the spelling used by British observers at the time. The Poles preferred Wilno (or Vilno), the Lithuanians Vilnius, which is how it is known today.
19 Senn, *Great Powers*, p. 57.
20 See ch. 30.
21 Davies, *White Eagle*, pp. 102–4, 223.
22 Latawski, *Reconstruction*; Baron and Gatrell, *Homelands*, pp. 23–9; Davies, *White Eagle*, pp. 253–63.
23 Mayer, *Politics and Diplomacy*, pp. 673–715; Waite, *Vanguard of Nazism*, p. 232; Campbell, "Struggle."
24 Criss, *Istanbul*, pp. 115–39.
25 Smith, *Ionian Vision*. On the Chanak crisis see Ferris, "Far too dangerous."
26 Hirschon, *Crossing the Aegean*, pp. 3–20, 39–52; Renée Hirschon, *Heirs of the Greek Catastrophe: The Social Life of Asia Minor Refugees in Piraeus*, Oxford, Berghahn, 1998, p.xvi.
27 Townshend, *Britain's Civil Wars*, pp. 191–2.
28 Sluglett, *Iraq*, pp. 61, 91, quoting Leo Amery, May 1925.
29 Chaqueri, *Soviet Socialist Republic*.
30 Derek Sayer, "British reaction to the Amritsar massacre, 1919–1920," *Past and Present*, 131, 1991, pp. 130–64; Lawrence, "Forging a peaceable kingdom," pp. 574–6; Townshend,

Britain's Civil Wars, pp. 132–44; Gallagher, "Nationalisms," p. 363. The reference is to the "Third Afghan War" (May–August 1919) and the Kuki-Chin rebellion in 1917–19.

31 Hart, *The IRA and its Enemies*, p. 135; Townshend, *Britain's Civil Wars*, pp. 57–67; Lawrence, "Forging a peaceable kingdom," pp. 576–81.

32 Hamilton, "Montgomery." Montgomery's first cousin had been assassinated by the IRA.

33 Hart, *The IRA and its Enemies*, p. 22; Davis, "Influence"; Gallagher, "Nationalisms," p. 365; Jeffery, *The British Army*.

34 Lyttleton, "Fascism and violence," pp. 262–3.

35 Hart, *The IRA and its Enemies*, pp. 14, 17, 83.

36 Tőkés, *Béla Kun*, p.159; Waite, *Vanguard of Nazism*, pp. 42, 88–91. The Freikorps numbers are in dispute.

37 Figes, *Peasant Russia*; Raleigh, *Experiencing Russia's Civil War*; Olcott, "Basmachi," p. 364.

38 Salo Baron, *The Russian Jew under Tsars and Soviets*, 2nd ed., New York: Macmillan, 1976, pp. 179–86; Bessel, *Germany*, p. 258; Eley, "Remapping the nation," p. 221; Prusin, *Nationalizing a Borderland*.

39 Upton, *Finnish Revolution*, pp. 486–7, 492–6, 502–3, 512, 519–20.

40 Acton (ed.), *Critical Companion*, pp. 403–15; Sanborn, *Drafting*, pp. 46–55.

41 Latawski, *Reconstruction*, p. 169; Davies, *White Star*, pp. 37, 41–6, 83–4.

42 Omissi, *Air Power*. On the role played by the infant Polish air force in the war against Soviet Russia see Davies, *White Star*, pp. 127–9.

43 Bessel, *Germany*, p. 283.

44 Urlanis, *Wars and Population*, pp. 85–96, 216.

45 See http://www.correlatesofwar.org/Datasets.htm

46 Bodó, "Paramilitary violence."

47 Upton, *Finnish Revolution*, p. 519.

48 Seton-Watson, *Eastern Europe*, pp. 220–1; Rothschild, *East-Central Europe*.

References and Further Reading

General and Comparative Works

Barkey, Karen, and von Hagen, Mark, *After Empire: Multiethnic Societies and Nation-Building. The Soviet Union and the Russian, Ottoman and Habsburg Empires*, Boulder, CO, Westview Press, 1997.

Baron, Nick, and Gatrell, Peter (eds.), *Homelands: War, Population, and Statehood in Eastern Europe and Russia, 1918–1924*, London, Anthem Press, 2004.

Eley, Geoff, "Remapping the nation: war, revolutionary upheaval and state formation in Eastern Europe, 1914–1923," in Peter Potichnyj and Howard Aster (eds.), *Ukrainian-Jewish Relations in Historical Perspective*, Edmonton, Canadian Institute of Ukrainian Studies, 1988, pp. 205–46.

Gallagher, Jack, "Nationalisms and the crisis of Empire, 1919–1922," *Modern Asian Studies*, 15, 1981, pp. 355–68.

Jackson, George D., *Comintern and Peasant in East Europe, 1919–1930*, New York, Columbia University Press, 1966.

Mayer, Arno, *The Politics and Diplomacy of Peacemaking: Containment and Counterrevolution at Versailles, 1918–1919*, New York, Vintage, 1967.

Mayer, Arno, *Political Origins of the New Diplomacy, 1917–1918*, New York, Vintage, 1970.

Omissi, David, *Air Power and Colonial Control: The Royal Air Force, 1919–1939*, Manchester, Manchester University Press, 1990.

Roshwald, Aviel, *Ethnic Nationalism and the Fall of Empires: Central Europe, Russia and the Middle East, 1914–1923*, London, Routledge, 2001.

Rothschild, Joseph, *East-Central Europe between the Two World Wars*, Seattle, University of Washington Press, 1974.

Urlanis, Boris Z., *Wars and Population*, Moscow, Progress Publishers, 1971.

Armenia

Nassibian, Akaby, *Britain and the Armenian Question, 1915–1923*, London, Croom Helm, 1984.

Suny, Ronald G., *Looking Toward Ararat: Armenia in Modern History*, Bloomington, Indiana University Press, 1993.

Austria

Leidinger, Hannes, and Moritz, Verena, *Gefangenschaft, Revolution, Heimkehr: Die Bedeutung der Kriegsgefangenenproblematik für die Geschichte des Kommunismus in Mittel- und Osteuropa 1917–1920*, Vienna, Böhlau Wien, 2003.

The Baltic States

Eidintas, Alfonsas, and Zalys, Vytautas, *Lithuania in European Politics: The Years of the First Republic, 1918–1940*, Basingstoke, Macmillan, 1997.

Senn, Alfred E., *The Great Powers: Lithuania and the Vilna Question, 1920–1928*, Leiden, Brill, 1966.

Britain

Jeffery, Keith, *The British Army and the Crisis of Empire, 1918–1922*, Manchester, Manchester University Press, 1984.

Lawrence, Jon, "Forging a peaceable kingdom: war, violence and fear of brutalization in post-First World War Britain," *Journal of Modern History*, 75, 2003, pp. 557–89.

Townshend, Charles, *Britain's Civil Wars: Counterinsurgency in the Twentieth Century*, London, Faber and Faber, 1986.

Bulgaria

Bell, John Douglas, *Peasants in Power: Alexander Stamboliski and the Bulgarian Agrarian National Union, 1899–1923*, Princeton, Princeton University Press, 1977.

Central Asia

Buttino, Marco (ed.), *In a Collapsing Empire: Underdevelopment, Ethnic Conflicts, and Nationalisms in the Soviet Union*, Milan, Feltrinelli, 1993.

Olcott, Martha Brill, "The Basmachi or Freemen's Revolt in Turkestan 1918–1924," *Soviet Studies*, 33/3, 1981, pp. 352–69.

Finland

Arosalo, Sirkka, "Social conditions for political violence: Red and White terror in the Finnish Civil War of 1918," *Journal of Peace Research*, 35, 1998, pp. 147–66.

Upton, Anthony E., *The Finnish Revolution*, Minneapolis, University of Minnesota Press, 1980.

France

Prost, Antoine, *In the Wake of War: Les Anciens Combattants and French Society*, Oxford, Berg, 1992.

Germany

Bessel, Richard, *Germany after the First World War*, Oxford, Clarendon Press, 1993.
Waite, Robert G. L., *Vanguard of Nazism, The Free Corps Movement in Postwar Germany, 1918–1923*, Cambridge, MA, Harvard University Press, 1952.

Greece/Macedonia

Hirschon, Renée, *Crossing the Aegean: An Appraisal of the 1923 Compulsory Population Exchange between Greece and Turkey*, London, Berghahn, 2003.
Smith, Michael Llewellyn, *Ionian Vision: Greece in Asia Minor 1919–1922*, London, Allen Lane, 1973.

Hungary

Bodó, Béla, "Paramilitary violence in Hungary after the First World War," *East European Quarterly*, 38, 2004, pp. 129–72.
Jaszi, Oscar, *Revolution and Counter-Revolution in Hungary*, London, P. S. King, 1924.
Tökés, Rudolf L., *Béla Kun and the Hungarian Soviet Republic: The Origins and Role of the Communist Party of Hungary in the Revolutions of 1918–1919*, New York, Praeger, 1967.

Ireland

Hamilton, Nigel, "Montgomery, Bernard Law [Monty], first Viscount Montgomery of Alamein (1887–1976)," *Oxford Dictionary of National Biography*, Oxford, Oxford University Press, 2004, http://www.oxforddnb.com/view/article/31460, accessed 18 Aug. 2005.
Hart, Peter, *The I.R.A. and Its Enemies: Violence and Community in Cork, 1916–1923*, Oxford, Oxford University Press, 1998.
Hart, Peter, *The I.R.A. at War, 1916–1923*, Oxford, Oxford University Press, 2003.
Jeffery, Keith, *Ireland and the Great War*, Cambridge, Cambridge University Press, 2000.
Townshend, Charles, "The Irish Republican Army and the development of guerrilla warfare, 1916–1921," *English Historical Review*, 47, 1979, pp. 425–37.

Italy

Lyttleton, Adrian, "Fascism and violence in post-war Italy: political strategy and social conflict," in Wolfgang Mommsen and Gerald Hirschfeld (eds.), *Violence and Terror in Nineteenth- and Twentieth-Century Europe*, New York, St. Martin's Press, 1982, pp. 257–74.
Sonnesso, Antonio, "Working class defence organization, anti-fascist resistance and the *arditi del popolo* in Turin, 1919–1922," *European History Quarterly*, 33, 2003, pp. 183–218.

The Middle East

Chaqueri, Cosroe, *The Soviet Socialist Republic of Iran, 1920–1921: Birth of the Trauma*, Pittsburgh, University of Pittsburgh Press, 1995.
Kedourie, Elie, *England and the Middle East: The Destruction of the Ottoman Empire, 1914–1921*, new ed., London, Mansell, 1987.
Sluglett, Peter, *Britain in Iraq, 1914–1932*, Ithaca, NY, Cornell University Press, 1976.

Poland

Davies, Norman, *White Eagle, Red Star: The Polish-Soviet War, 1919–1920*, London, Macdonald, 1972.

Latawski, Paul (ed.), *The Reconstruction of Poland, 1914–1923*, London, Macmillan, 1992.

Motyl, Alexander, "Ukrainian nationalist political violence in inter-war Poland," *East European Quarterly*, 19, 1985, pp. 45–55.

Romania

Livezeanu, Irina, *Cultural Politics in Greater Romania: Regionalism, Nation Building and Ethnic Struggle, 1918–1930*, Ithaca, NY, Cornell University Press, 1995.

Mitrany, David, *The Land and the Peasant in Rumania: The War and the Agrarian Problem, 1917–1921*, New Haven, Yale University Press, 1930.

European Russia

Acton, Edward, Cherniaev, Vladimir, and Rosenberg, William (eds.), *Critical Companion to the Russian Revolution*, London, Edward Arnold, 1997.

Figes, Orlando, *Peasant Russia, Civil War: The Volga Countryside in Revolution, 1917–1921*, Clarendon Press, Oxford, 1989.

Mawdsley, Evan, *The Russian Civil War*, 2nd ed., Edinburgh, Birlinn, 2000.

Raleigh, Don, *Experiencing Russia's Civil War: Politics, Society, and Revolutionary Culture in Saratov, 1917–22*, Princeton, Princeton University Press, 2002.

Sanborn, Joshua, *Drafting the Russian Nation: Military Conscription, Total War, and Mass Politics 1905–1925*, DeKalb, Northern Illinois University Press, 2003.

Swain, Geoffrey, *The Origins of the Russian Civil War*, London, Longman, 1996.

Siberia and the Far East

Smele, Jonathan D., *Civil War in Siberia: The Anti-Bolshevik Government of Admiral Kolchak, 1918–1920*, Cambridge, Cambridge University Press, 1996.

Upper Silesia

Campbell, F. G., "The struggle for Upper Silesia, 1919–1920," *Journal of Modern History*, 42/3, 1970, pp. 361–85.

Lesniewski, Peter, "The 1919 insurrection in Upper Silesia," *Civil Wars*, 4, 2001, pp. 22–48.

Turkey

Criss, Nur Bilge, *Istanbul under Allied Occupation, 1918–1924*, Leiden, Brill, 1999.

Ferris, John R., " 'Far too dangerous a gamble?' British intelligence and policy during the Chanak crisis, September–October 1922," *Diplomacy and Statecraft*, 14, 2003, pp. 139–84.

Ukraine

Abramson, Henry, *A Prayer for the Government: Ukrainians and Jews in Revolutionary Times, 1917–1920*, Cambridge, MA: Harvard University Press, 1999.

Prusin, Alexander, *Nationalizing a Borderland: War, Ethnicity, and Anti-Jewish Violence in East Galicia, 1914–1920*, Tuscaloosa, University of Alabama Press, 2005.

Reshetar, John, *The Ukrainian Revolution, 1917–1920: A Study in Nationalism*, Princeton, Princeton University Press, 1952.

Yugoslavia

Tomasevich, Jozo, *Peasants, Politics, and Economic Change in Yugoslavia*, Stanford, Stanford University Press, 1955.

CHAPTER THIRTY-EIGHT

Mourning and Memory, 1919–45

LAURENCE VAN YPERSELE
(translated by Helen McPhail)

The unprecedented shock of World War I meant the end of nineteenth-century optimism. The large-scale mobilization of civilians as well as soldiers was vital in sustaining the war effort of most belligerent powers to the end. Yet mass death on an unprecedented scale was omnipresent. Accommodating these two dimensions of the war was central to the experience of soldiers and civilians during the conflict. Doing so once the war was over and the outcome known presented a new challenge. It became the very essence of how the war-dead were mourned and the war was remembered throughout the interwar years and even beyond.

Collective Memory

It is impossible to retrace this process without a brief discussion of memory itself, a subject that the history of World War I has helped place firmly on the agenda of historical analysis.[1] Memory is composed of collective representations by groups and the direct experiences of individuals. It operates as a reconstruction of past reality in order to understand both the self and the world. It confirms shared values and behavior and guarantees self-esteem – though at the price of distortion, inversion, and screening-out. It thus involves selective forgetting. To the extent that it is shared, it is consensual and homogenizes recollections. At its core lies not the event but the meaning the event holds for the cohesion and identity of a group.

Also pertinent is the distinction between "living" memory and "official" memory.[2] "Living" memory consists of recollections of personal experience by individuals and communities. "Official" memory is the representation of the past through public commemoration for particular goals by those in power. War memorials, official ceremonies, school textbooks are all part of this "official" memory. These two types of memory may overlap and confirm each other or do the opposite.[3]

How is it possible to move from one form of memory to the other? And what processes are involved? How do groups and societies emerge from a war, in terms of mourning and self-esteem? Is reconciliation between former enemies compatible with fidelity to the war dead? Such questions, which are now recognized as vital in the resolution of conflicts more generally, were central to the memories generated by World War I.

Patterns of Memory in the Interwar Years

The war experiences to which memory gave retrospective meaning differed from state to state, and not least in relation to victory and defeat. While Germany lost over two million dead and the nation was undoubtedly defeated, the troops who returned home were hailed as victors. Moreover, none of the fighting had taken place on German territory. It was thus difficult to accept defeat unconditionally.

Great Britain also mounted a considerable war effort (with virtually a million military dead, including the Empire), but suffered no military operations on its own soil. On the other hand, the British were on the winning side. Similarly "victorious," France was one of the countries most severely affected by the war. Nine *départements* were occupied for four years, the north of the country was devastated, and the losses were proportionately the highest of any of the great powers, with little short of one and a half million military dead. It was through the figure of the *poilu*, the ordinary soldier, that the French both mourned and commemorated their painful victory. By contrast, the experience of the occupied civilians of the north was marginalized.

Belgium, on the other hand, exalted both the martyrdom of its civilians and the glory of its armies. True, this small country was only marginally affected by the fighting and suffered proportionately fewer deaths at the front than other belligerent nations (some 40,000). Yet almost wholly occupied by Germany, Belgium saw its national wealth systematically destroyed and a number of its workers deported, as well as suffering more than 20,000 civilian deaths at the hands of the German military. The dominant experience was thus one of invasion and occupation.

In Italy, the cult of the military dead was used to justify the state's decision to participate in a war, despite widespread reluctance as well as the loss of over 600,000 military dead. It was essential to move beyond this destabilizing experience by establishing a consensual and apolitical memory. Commemorating the dead with war memorials emerged as "the first patriotic cult of united Italy," helping construct a national identity before being appropriated by fascism.[4]

The situation in countries whose soldiers had been primarily engaged on the eastern front was even more complex. As has been explained in previous chapters, the Bolshevik Revolution and subsequent civil war in Russia, though resulting in lower military losses than the world war, served to efface the latter from "official memory" and from acts of public mourning, despite the omnipresence of a "living memory" of the conflict.[5] Yet fighting continued not just in Russia but in zones of ethnic tension, contested borders, and attempted revolution across Central and Eastern Europe, making it difficult to establish consensual memories of World War I while adding new subjects of commemoration in the future.[6]

The situation in the east was further complicated by the conflicting war experiences within the societies concerned. The Austro-Hungarian Empire was dismantled and its constituent nations either claimed their independence or had it forced upon them. Whereas the Hungarians and Austrians had to accept defeat and territorial loss, with sizeable minorities now in neighboring states, the new Czechoslovakia claimed victor status. It turned the mythic tale of the volunteer "Legionaries" who had fought in Russia and with the Allies into a symbol of the national democratic struggle. But this failed to accommodate the mass of Czech and Slovak soldiers who fought in the ranks of the Austro-Hungarian armies, and excluded the new state's German and Hungarian minorities from national memory.[7] Comparable difficulties attended the creation of an official memory of the war in the new Yugoslavia, where Serbia's appalling military losses and the country's occupation by Austro-Hungarian and Bulgarian forces overshadowed the very different experiences of Croats and Slovenes – fellow South Slavs in the new state – who had served in the Habsburg military.

In Poland, it was impossible to construct a homogeneous official memory of a war that in the east had largely been fought on the territory of the new state, but in which Poles themselves had been split between the Austrian and German armies on one side and Tsarist Russia on the other. The inclusion of Ukrainian and Belarusian minorities in the new state and a large Jewish population only compounded the memory problems, with the result that the foundation myth of sacrifice and redemption (including the Unknown Soldier) was sought as much in the border wars of Ukraine and Lithuania and in the Polish–Soviet War of 1919–20 as in the insuperable complexities of World War I.

For all the distinctiveness of national cases, the official memory of World War I can be divided into three periods. The first, from 1918 to 1924, was dominated by the cult of the dead in a direct extension of the "cultures of wartime." The Locarno Pact of 1925 marked the opening of a second period based on a measure of reconciliation between former enemies and an emphasis on peace. Finally, the reemergence of international tensions in the 1930s led to a slow remobilization of minds that gathered speed after the Munich crisis. Yet this periodization does not apply uniformly to all countries or to the relationship between official and living memory, since the latter was often at variance with the former.

Mourning and Hatred, 1918–24

The memory of the war that prevailed after the Armistice was rooted directly in the cultures of wartime. It was impossible to awake from four years of warfare as from an ordinary nightmare. To deal with mourning and suffering, social dislocation, and the work of physical reconstruction or building a new regime or nation, it was vital in most cases to sustain the meaning of the war. Since the soldiers had fallen in the name of the nation, the nation must keep their memories alive, and the former enemy must pay for the damage inflicted. Sacrifice demanded reparation. In this sense, the clash between the opposing war cultures culminated in the peace settlement.[8]

This paroxysm of wartime culture was the result of popular as well as official opinion. French soldiers, for example, greeted the end of the war with patriotic fervor and fantasies of violence toward the enemy population.[9] They were opposed to any hasty peace and determined to crush the enemy on his home ground. Yet the violence remained verbal, and when French troops arrived in Alsace-Lorraine and the Rhineland, there were no atrocities or acts of brutality. In contrast, the liberation of Belgium provoked considerable violence by Belgians against traitors and women who had slept with Germans.[10] These different reactions were rooted in the contrasting experiences of the war already referred to, with Belgium's wartime plight continuing to be symbolized by the civilian martyrs.[11] Any civilians who betrayed this view, such as adulterous women or "profiteers," were not true Belgians and were rapidly punished, with popular support.[12]

Despite the inevitable delays before the Allied armies were fully demobilized, the end of the war was signaled most clearly by the return of the soldiers. In most cases, they received enthusiastic acclaim. There were exceptions, such as the return of the Irish nationalists who had volunteered for the British army, following the voting of Home Rule. The Easter Rising in 1916 created its own martyrs, and by the end of the war the returning soldiers stood outside the symbolic politics that legitimized the Irish Free State, created in December 1921.[13] But the majority of belligerent nations celebrated the return of their soldiers, whether in France (where they were welcomed as liberators in the north), Belgium or, despite the outcome of the war, in Germany, where the returning men were told by Hindenburg on November 12, 1918 that they were seen as heroes in every sense by the nation.[14] Although most German soldiers demobilized peacefully, extreme nationalist groups argued that with Germany threatened by annihilation, the war was not over.[15] From 1919 to 1921 paramilitary Freikorps units embodied the will to continue the struggle against national, class, and ethnic enemies, and exalted violence for its own sake.[16] No less than the victors, therefore, the defeated acknowledged the heroism and sacrifice of their soldiers, even if different conclusions were drawn.

All this made the absence of the dead cruelly felt. Some proclaimed victory and others denied defeat, but mourning was the most widely shared process of this immediate postwar period. Allied celebrations were balanced between joy and grief. When King Albert returned to Belgium on November 22, 1918, the crowds acclaimed the parade by Belgian and Allied troops and there were scenes of delirium around the royal family. But in his famous speech from the throne the king equally honored the living and the dead, and included among the latter not only those who had perished in battle but those who had suffered or died for their country at the hands of the Germans as civilian martyrs.

In July 1919, in Paris and London, the victory parades that followed the signing of the Treaty of Versailles were also about mourning. In Paris, a vast cenotaph (or empty tomb) was set up at the foot of the Arc de Triomphe before the parade on July 14, and the latter was led by a thousand disabled veterans. In the equivalent parade in London on July 19, another Cenotaph, initially designed as a temporary structure by Sir Edwin Lutyens, attracted the greatest fervor from the crowds. In both cases the glory of the living existed in the shadow of the dead.[17]

In fact in all the nations that had gone to war, the undisputed hero was a dead combatant incarnated in the form of an unknown soldier. As a funerary and commemorative practice, this was a genuine innovation of World War I. It sought to acknowledge in a tangible and individualized form both the vast numbers of the war dead and the fact that, owing to industrialized violence, many of them had left no physical trace but had become "the Missing." The very anonymity of the ordinary soldier who symbolized the loss of an entire nation guaranteed equality for all heroes and allowed for the mourning of each individual. The ceremony took place in all the capital cities, with the exception of Berlin and Moscow.[18] The first were Paris and London in 1920. Rome and Washington followed in 1921, Brussels, Prague, and Belgrade in 1922, Bucharest and Vienna in 1923, and so on. The ceremonies followed a somewhat similar ritual, with the participation of leading civil and military dignitaries as well as veterans and huge crowds of ordinary citizens, while the burial site was powerfully symbolic (the Arc de Triomphe, Westminster Abbey, etc.).[19]

Yet the cult of the dead did not stop there, for there were also the military cemeteries on the battlefields and above all the innumerable memorials set up in the soldiers' home villages or urban communities, where they belonged as individuals and members of society. The scale of the commemorative movement that swept through Europe, and beyond, demonstrates how hard it was to assuage the grief of these societies in mourning. And those who took the initiative in it at the local and institutional level were less often officials than self-motivated activists and community leaders, the creators and embodiments of "living memory."[20]

On the battlefields, from Belgium to Turkey, areas of ground were nationalized and set aside to remember the defeated as well as the victors, in line with Article 225 of the Treaty of Versailles. To this day, these form large, landscaped military cemeteries where death is tamed by the beauties of nature and its horror concealed. Despite the resemblance of all these cemeteries, the plots of ground accorded to the defeated were much smaller than those of the victors, as with the German cemeteries in France or Austrian cemeteries in Italy; and the graves of soldiers of the Allied armies had the benefit of a stone or a cross, white and pure as the cause they defended, while the crosses of the vanquished were an equally symbolical black. The United Kingdom and Dominions decided not to repatriate the bodies of their soldiers, whereas France and the United States ceded to family pressures and allowed this (some twenty percent of French bodies were thus reburied in the interior). But in the vast majority of cases, soldiers who died at the front remained buried there.

The missing – the dead who had left no remains – posed a problem, since no individual grave marked their resting place for grieving relatives. The result was monuments especially dedicated to their memory, such as the Menin Gate at Ypres and the arch to the British and French missing of the Somme, designed by Lutyens, which soars over the ridge of Thiepval in the centre of the battlefield.[21] No less significant were the bodies without names – the physical fragments that strewed the battlefields and which, on the western front, were brought together in great *ossuaires* (or monumental charnel houses), such as those of Douaumont at Verdun and Notre-Dame de Lorette in the Pas-de-Calais.

Local memorials addressed the reality that the bulk of the dead remained at the front by transporting the memory of each man in the absence of his body back to his family and home community. This brought the war deep into landscapes that had escaped the realities of war, such as Australia or Canada – and in record time, since the majority of such memorials, approved by local communities and frequently funded by them, date from the first half of the 1920s.[22] In fact, more than the military cemeteries, these innumerable war memorials still bear witness to the presence of the dead in every society that took part in the war, expressing the mourning, gratitude, and patriotic faith that ran through local communities. They also convey the fear of oblivion – of forgetting – and occupy highly visible settings in public squares or near important buildings such as town halls, churches, or schools. In the United Kingdom, memorials took the form of useful public buildings such as halls and libraries, while in Germany "heroes' woods" evoked romantic nature to express everlasting remembrance. For these memorials were only rarely cries of pacifist outrage. Rather they sought to make mass death meaningful and to legitimate suffering and sacrifice. The lists of names, usually carved in alphabetical order, perpetuated the equality encountered on the battlefield. The survivors and the dead were transformed into courageous heroes, fixed in stone or bronze without visible wounds, in the arms of the Nation or Christ.

The monuments thus evoked the obligation of the postwar nation to remember and live up to the sacrifice made by its combatants. In some cases, the civilians at the rear were similarly honored by being represented on the memorials. This is true in France, but also in Germany, Italy, or Bohemia.[23] For the recognition of the living was the unavoidable corollary of the heroic dead; hence the carved children laying stone wreaths on the monuments themselves and the solemn annual parade of local schools in front of their war memorial. However, the atypical war experience of Belgium resulted once again in a distinctive dual emphasis as far as monuments are concerned. For the soldier usually shares the commemorative space with the civilian victim deported or executed by a German firing squad. As early as 1919, martyred Belgian patriots were given full national funerals, while the Unknown Soldier had to wait until 1922. Unlike in France, there was no denial of memory in respect of the sufferings endured by civilians under enemy occupation.

In Eastern Europe, the difficulties already alluded to in achieving a consensual "official" memory of the war found an echo in the construction of national monuments and rituals. The volunteer legionaries of Czechoslovakia supplied not only a legitimating myth for the state but a national memorial on Vítkov Hill in Prague, inaugurated in 1928, in which a "temple of the political and cultural renaissance" of the nation consisted both of a museum to the Legionaries and a mausoleum containing the remains of those who perished in the struggle for independence.[24] By contrast, the preexisting Heroes' Square in Budapest was adapted to contain the tomb of the Hungarian unknown warrior. But a monument to the territories lost at the Treaty of Trianon was also erected outside the capital, perhaps unique in postwar Europe as a monument to defeat and the irredentist fantasies that it fostered.

In Germany and Austria, however, it proved impossible to achieve any homogenized "official memory" of the war, despite the plethora of local memorials, as elsewhere. In Germany, right-wing nationalist associations erected a monument to the victory of Tannenberg in 1914, when the Russian invasion of East Prussia had been repulsed, which was opened by the former victor, Hindenburg, now President of the Republic, in 1927. Twenty unknown soldiers were interred in the memorial, which was built on the plan of a medieval crusader fortress. Only belatedly did the Republic seek to install a national war memorial in an eighteenth-century guard-house in central Berlin. But it achieved no consensus and failed to become a focus of national ritual.[25]

National monuments and rituals were preeminently sites of "official memory." Yet the various groups that generated their own living memory of the war through local and institutional memorials did so in other ways as well. Veterans, widows, and orphans demanded recognition and gratitude for their sacrifice for the Nation, and the heroism that is part of such sacrifice, while at the same time presenting a host of specific demands (including the pensions that loomed so large in interwar social security spending). The various associations to which they belonged thus played a fundamental role in shaping the memory of the war.[26] They included the war disabled, who did not present themselves as victims but energetically rejected pity and demanded the respect due to heroes. Nonetheless, at the more intimate level of couples and families, we may wonder how much any of these collective practices genuinely provided the support needed in working through a grief that was ultimately singular and private, no matter how widely shared.[27]

In this regard, the commemorative messages of the war memorials were ambiguous. On the one hand, they spoke of the eternal glory of the departed and so rejected grief, yet on the other hand they demanded grief without end, since only the tears of the living guaranteed that the memory of the dead would survive. And among the tragic aspects of death in war which the memorials and rituals could not overcome were the impossibility of being with the loved one in his final moments, the absence of bodies, and the inversion of the normal passage of the generations, with the young dying before the old. It is understandable that mourning remained problematic for many families throughout the interwar years and even later – a theme taken up by certain modern writers. [28]

Still, on all sides the nation was invoked to give meaning to mass death, including for the defeated. Everywhere, too, patriotism and hatred of the enemy were synonymous.

And the active participation of national authorities and local associations, the presence of crowds, and the scale of newspaper accounts show how the official will and the needs of the population converged in the memory of the war, though not always with agreement on what it had signified. The proximity of the date of the Armistice (November 4 in Italy, November 11 for the western front powers) to All Saints, the Day of the Dead in Catholic countries, further strengthened the funerary aspect of the ceremonies. The observance of two minutes' silence on that date by all citizens of the United Kingdom and Dominions was surely the most impressive expression of universal participation in the memory of World War I. But other dates were also selected to underline the national basis of memory. Belgium initially designated August 4, the date of the German invasion in 1914, before finally settling on November 11. Participation in the war was especially significant for young nations such as Australia, New Zealand, or Canada and successor states in Eastern Europe such as Czechoslovakia, Romania, and Yugoslavia. The Australians chose to commemorate the arrival of the ANZACs at Gallipoli on April 25, 1915, while Unionist Northern Ireland marked the heroic exploits of the 36th Ulster Division at the battle of the Somme in 1916, on July 1, as a title-deed to the province's distinct status as part of the United Kingdom following the partition of Ireland.

Yet so recent and unresolved was the impact of the war that memory could on occasion revert to the experience of wartime culture. This was notably the case with the occupation of the Ruhr in 1923–5 in order to restore the halted flow of German reparations.[29] The support of French and Belgian public opinion for their respective governments was clearly rooted in the passions and memory of the war. Even more clearly, as collective resistance indicated, many Germans experienced the occupation as a resumption of the war, though this time with Germany being invaded. The violence on both sides was more symbolic than physical, but World War I was played out again in the Ruhr, and while in the end German resistance was broken, France and Belgium lost some of the moral capital they had gained in 1914–18.

Demobilizing Minds, 1925 to the Later 1930s

The years that followed the evacuation of the Ruhr were marked by a shift in mood. The desire to calm the memories of war was actively promoted by politicians such as Aristide Briand and Gustav Stresemann, respectively French and German Foreign Ministers in the second half of the 1920s, and came to fruition in the signing of the Locarno Pact in 1925. "Cultural demobilization" developed faster in Britain than France and proved more difficult in Germany.[30] Everywhere, there were those who refused to dismantle wartime attitudes. Nonetheless, over time, passions cooled, the vision of the war was transformed, and especially in the western half of Europe, as well as in the Dominions and the United States, an essentially pacific mood developed.

Officially, the men of Locarno sought to reconstruct the retrospective meaning of the war by reversing the terms of the war cultures and redirecting the moral capital of sacrifice into peacemaking. Thus, Briand emphasized the horror of the war and spoke of the soldiers in terms of heroic victims, while Stresemann emphasized the disastrous consequences of the conflict for all, defeated and victors. Both presented the war as a global catastrophe. From this point of view, the ultimate meaning of World War I and its sacrifices was end to all war. Henceforward, a nation was civilized to the extent that it opposed any renewal of armed conflict. The enemy was now war itself, against which the former

enemies combined. A vivid expression of this new vision was Germany's diplomatic rehabilitation. Excluded from the peace negotiations in 1919, it now took its place as a full
partner first in the negotiations leading to Locarno and then entry into the League of
Nations, with Briand, Stresemann, and the British Foreign Secretary, Austen Chamberlain,
winning the Nobel Peace Prize, the latter in 1925, the former two in 1926.[31] This pacific
ambition was directed at the younger generations, with school textbooks rewritten in
France and Belgium. The ideal of peace and the League of Nations relegated responsibility for the war and the memory of German war crimes to second place.[32]

The reversal of the meaning of the war was championed in various pacifist and democratic *milieux*. Examples can be seen in the eyewitness accounts written by veterans in
the form of memoirs and of historical novels, which increasingly insisted on the horror
of war. Incidents of cowardice, self-mutilation, or fraternization with the enemy were
transformed into a rejection of the war. The soldier became the heroic martyr of a disgraceful butchery – often with the corollary that these eyewitness accounts suppressed
(or continued to be unable to express) the deliberate violence and killing in which the
soldiers had also engaged.[33] Such accounts – of which several were turned into films –
met with considerable success and helped to extend this new image of the war in favor of
peace.[34] In France soldiers who had been summarily executed "as an example" and who
had hitherto been excluded from general memory were rehabilitated after a campaign in
parliament, and could now be inserted into narratives of the war.[35] Other aspects of the
war also had to be altered retrospectively if memory was to be squared with the changes
in meaning. In liberal and left-wing circles, the cultural mobilization was now explained
as manipulation by propaganda. Influential works were published on the subject, amongst
others by the American political scientist Harold Lasswell and the pacifist Labour MP in
Britain, Sir Arthur Ponsonby.[36] They did not distinguish between the different sides and
made propaganda responsible for the collective madness of the war. In particular, the
German atrocities of 1914 (see chapter 13 above) were now dismissed as an Allied invention. Ironically, this view coincided with the "innocentist" campaign conducted by
German diplomacy and the views of German nationalists, which were vigorously endorsed
by the Nazis when they came to power. The result was a general discrediting of statements by the press and government in Western democracies just as the dictatorships that
emerged in Italy and Germany (and for rather different reasons in Soviet Russia) engaged
in unprecedented campaigns of state propaganda.[37]

The pacific aims of the men of Locarno encountered three major barriers: the difficulty for defeated states in turning the soldier into a victim without implying acceptance
of the peace settlement; the marginalization of the memory of German invasion and
occupation, symbolized by the "German atrocities" of 1914; and the reluctance of the
victor states to relativize or even renounce the thesis of German "war guilt," on which
reparations were founded.[38]

The transformation of the soldier into heroic victim was not self-evident. Victory gave
the veterans of the Allied states the right to reinvest their capital of heroism in the preservation of peace, although this did not automatically mean reconciliation with Germany.
While those veterans' organizations that formed an international body linked to the
League of Nations welcomed dialog and partnership with their enemies, other Allied
veterans were reluctant to embrace the former foe.[39] But the proportion of German veterans who refused such contact (notably the right-wing Stahlhelm) was much higher, for
the weight of the defeat made it harder to accept this new vision of the war. Field Marshal
von Hindenburg's speech at the inauguration of the Tannenberg memorial in 1927,

exalting precisely the warrior heroism of German soldiers defending their nation against Russian invasion, made any such cultural demobilization difficult.

Although less vital to international relations, the marginalization of invasion, occupation, and civilian suffering in the changing official memories of the war created tensions in the countries concerned. This is particularly true of Belgium. In order to sustain the spirit of Locarno, the national authorities increasingly refrained from associating themselves with the inauguration of memorials recalling the massacre of civilians in 1914. School textbooks were rewritten to the same end, and in 1930, after German protests, the Minister for Defense went so far as to remove a symbolic painting of the German atrocities by an Italian artist, Luigi Brignoli, entitled "The Severed Hands," from the walls of the Army Museum.[40] This official attitude did not prevent the inhabitants of the "martyred cities" from keeping up their local memory. For example, in 1936, the year in which Belgium reestablished diplomatic neutrality, a national memorial in memory of the "Teutonic fury" of 1914 was erected in Dinant, site of the largest massacre. But this took place in the absence of representatives of the government and royal family. Cultural demobilization and the official silence that it required were widely seen as a serious threat to the memory of the war, especially in French-speaking Belgium, which had borne the brunt of the invasion.[41]

Finally, the issue of German responsibility for the war remained a sensitive question for both sides. If wholehearted French and British pacifists were prepared to reject German guilt and call for the revision of the Treaty of Versailles, continued reparations as well as questions of national security made this difficult to contemplate for many in France and Britain. In any event, active denial of war guilt in Germany and German resentment at both reparations and continued Allied occupation of the Rhineland made widespread revision of the meaning and memory of the war problematic. The legend of the "stab in the back," the wish to revise the "Versailles diktat," and the belief in an international threat aimed at the elimination of the German nation persisted at the heart of German politics. Even a man of peace such as Stresemann publicly rejected German guilt. As for the Nazis, they waved the banners of domestic treason and international conspiracy in an attempt to galvanize the German nation into a spirit of revenge. Like fascist Italy, Nazi Germany sought to redirect the memory of the war to the benefit of its own policies.[42]

To these difficulties in dismantling the violence and passions of the war must be added the development of fascist movements more or less everywhere in Europe throughout the 1930s and the continued ethnic tensions within and between the new states in the eastern half of the continent that fostered them. Such movements fed on the fervors born of the war and used an idealized version of the comradeship of the trenches as one source of their propaganda. Persuaded by the fantasy of total mobilization to defend a nation deemed to be under permanent threat, the Nazis tried to transform German society into a warrior community in which violence became a symbol of virility and a mark of blind loyalty to the leader. Even where such movements never came to power, they disturbed minds and opposed pacification.

Overall, therefore, the process of cultural demobilization after World War I, of which the "Locarno spirit" was the most public expression, achieved only limited results. The dismantling of wartime attitudes and a pacifist reaction to the conflict remained restricted developments despite the pervasive experience of mourning, even in democratic societies. In Germany, the refusal to accept fully the realities of defeat prevented any possibility of symbolically reinvesting wartime sacrifice in a peaceful view of the future. Pacifism as a formal movement remained weak everywhere, even if it was more widespread in Britain and France as a mood and aspiration. In Belgium, there was a clear gap between the official memory of the war as expressed in the politics of coexistence with Germany and the living memory of invasion and occupation. Still, the memory of the war had evolved since the immediate postwar period, and by the early 1930s in the Western democracies the belief was widespread that war on such a scale should never occur again.

Cultural Remobilization and Engagement in World War II

The international situation deteriorated markedly during the second half of the 1930s. Peace appeared ever more fragile and the impotence of the League of Nations was increasingly obvious. From 1933 to 1936, pacifist fears were confirmed by the rise of fascism in general and Hitler's accession to power in particular. Hastened by civil war in Spain in 1936 and the Nazi annexation of Austria and then of the Czech Sudetenland in 1938, a growing sense of crisis plunged the democracies into deep disarray. The memory of World War I as a catastrophe (updated through fears of gas bombardment from the air directly onto civilian targets) seemed more relevant than ever.[43] Yet growing determination to resist foreign expansion by the fascist states pointed to rather different conclusions – the need for cultural and political remobilization for war (as well as military rearmament). However, remobilization was no simple return to the spirit of 1914–18. Its stated purpose was far more complex, with memories of World War I, defense of democracy, and ideological antifascism blending in varying degrees according to country and milieu.

In France and Great Britain, a number of pacifist and socialist movements faced an insoluble challenge: how to struggle simultaneously both for peace and against German and Italian aggression.[44] Elsewhere, many democrats who were opposed both to communism and all forms of fascism sought to maintain the meaning of 1914–18 as it had become accepted since the end of the 1920s. The Munich Conference of 1938 was simply a final attempt, among others, to save the peace so that World War I would genuinely remain the "Last of the Last." It needed the setback of Munich and Hitler's total destruction of the Czechoslovak state before the great democracies could make up their minds to another war, while anti-fascist communists were muzzled by the Russo-German Non-Aggression Pact of August 1939. In short, it was against this particularly complex background that cultural remobilizations for war occurred.

Although this process is still wide open to research, it is clear that the memory of World War I affected the evolution of international relations and the way in which the coming war was imagined. Similarly, memories of 1914–18 played an ambiguous or even contradictory role once World War II broke out. The massive exodus of the Belgian and French populations in May 1940 came in part from the memory of the massacres of August 1914; but it should be noted that in 1914 this had fanned hatred of the enemy and stiffened the will to resist, while in 1940 it reinforced a paralyzing fear. It is equally clear that the exaggerated denunciation of wartime propaganda in the interwar years helped sow doubt in the minds of populations during World War II. Furthermore, the collaborationist movements used the memory of World War I as an absurd and pointless conflict to justify their quiescence toward the occupier.[45] Pétain, for example, acted as if the war was over in 1940 and did his utmost to avoid further suffering, thus finally creating the new world dreamed of by the veterans of 1914–18 (many of whose organizations supported the Vichy regime). Conversely, many World War II resisters drew on the memory of the heroes of World War I, seeing themselves as their true heirs. This was a significant theme in the underground press and the motivation of resistance networks in both France and Belgium. It seemed once more to be a case of defending the nation as it was trampled underfoot by an irredeemably wicked enemy.[46] Ironically, in this context, it was the figure of General de Gaulle, a prisoner of war in the earlier conflict, who confronted Pétain, the erstwhile hero of the battle of Verdun.

In the aftermath of the war, the resisters in Western European nations and the soldiers who fought in the opening and closing campaigns were commemorated as heroes in the steps of their glorious predecessors, their names being added to the war memorials of 1914–19 in each locality – though separate Resistance monuments were also established.[47] In the USSR, by contrast, World War II became the "Great Patriotic War" in which the ordinary soldiers were the heroes, filling the void made by the exclusion of the veterans and the military dead of World War I from public and official memory.[48] In Germany, from 1946 onwards, the Allies ordered the destruction of both Nazi memorials and of earlier war memorials that were seen as aggressively militaristic. Although at the local level these orders were not always carried out, nationalistic or vengeful inscriptions carved on many war memorials were effaced.[49] The remaking of official German memory – in different variants in the two postwar states – started in each case from a decisive rupture of historical and cultural continuity. New meanings – and monuments – were gradually elaborated to take account of the Nazi period and a second world war that was for the Germans a far greater catastrophe than its predecessor.

World War I thus offered sharply different commemorative frameworks to the various societies concerned, with the continuities most evident in the Western democracies. Yet here, too, the actual experiences of World War II, which differed in so many ways from those of World War I, struggled at first to find their own commemorative forms of expression. Abstract memorials to the Resistance and the victims of the war bore witness as much to the difficulty of expressing the inexpressible as to a determination to sustain their memory. In time, almost everywhere the memory of World War II came to overshadow the memory and significance of its predecessor as the truly pivotal event of the twentieth century. Henceforward, no one could ignore the fact that 1914–18 had not been the "Last of the last."

Looked at in the longer-term, the commemorative traditions of World War I turned on the soldiers' sacrifice in the unprecedented mass killings of industrialized battle, even when fought in remote and primitive locations in the Carpathian mountains, Gallipoli, or the Italian alps. It was the heroism of the war dead and of the veterans that gave both mourning and commemoration their "official" meaning in what was perceived as a war for the survival (or creation) of the nation. And while the status of victor or vanquished shaped the political uses to which the sacrifice was retrospectively put, the fact that the common soldier (rather than leaders and commanders) was the hero of the war, whatever the conflict's outcome, was the fundamental originality of the war's commemorative legacy. The distorting effects of the process are clear. Leaving aside the neglect of the soldiers' memory in the new Soviet state, elsewhere other groups (such as civilians, the inhabitants of invaded and occupied regions, and above all the circa one million victims of the Armenian genocide) were relegated to the sidelines, if not ignored completely. Of course in the regions and among the groups concerned (such as the Armenian Diaspora), memories and commemorations subsisted. But they tended to be at odds with the language and imagery of heroic sacrifice that remained the crux of national memories. While there were those who saw the soldiers as victims whose sacrifice had no point, even for peace, they were even more marginal – confined to artistic avant-gardes such as the Surrealists and to more extreme pacifists.

The victorious combatants of World War II used the commemorative heritage of the earlier conflict to claim meaning and status for their conflict, and to the extent that, unlike World War I, this did prove to be the pivotal war of the twentieth century, it allowed World War II by contrast to express the futility of war and conflict more powerfully at a popular level than had been the case between the wars. Yet the complexities of World War II for countries that had been invaded and occupied, as well as for those that were finally defeated, meant that heroic myth-histories (such as those of the Resistance in its different manifestations) broke down over time in the face of memories of collaboration and compromise and, above all, the reality of the Holocaust. The mental framework of heroic memory proved impotent in the face of the gas chambers, calling for a different kind of commemoration.

It was not until the end of the 1960s (also the moment when the generation of 1914 began to disappear) that a different commemorative framework emerged, without necessarily displacing heroic memory, which dwelt on the absolute nature of victimhood. This victim memory is no longer linked to the concept of sacrifice but to the memory of an indefeasible offence against humanity, culminating in genocide. It does not claim civic recognition through community ceremonies but proclaims universal human rights through the media and before the courts. These two forms of memory are intrinsically different and have different purposes. Rather than competing, they coexist and complement each other. In recent years historians have denounced abuses of memory, but have paid little attention to the particular nature of these different forms of memory: on the one hand, the affirmation of identity through the concept of sacrifice and, on the other, the recognition of universal values through the concept of crimes (war crimes, "crimes against humanity," "genocide") that distinguish above all between perpetrator and victim. Taken together, they encompass the relationships between memory, meaning, and commemoration that the two world wars have bequeathed to the present.

Notes

1   Halbwachs, *Les cadres sociaux*.
2   Marie-Claude Lavabre, "La mémoire fragmentée. Peut-on agir sur la mémoire?," in *Cahiers français*, 303, July–August 2001, p. 9; Jay Winter, "Guerre et mémoire au XXe siècle. Une interprétation des monuments aux morts fondée sur l'interaction sociale," in Stéphane Audoin-Rouzeau et al (eds.), *La politique et la guerre. Pour comprendre le XXe siècle européen. Hommage à J.-J. Becker*, Paris, Editions Agnès Viénot-Noesis, 2002, pp. 138–53.
3   Serge Barcellini, "Les Politiques de la mémoire: du droit au souvenir au devoir de mémoire," *Cahiers français*, 303, July-August 2001, p. 24; Luc Boltanski and Laurent Thévenot, *On Justification. Economies of Worth*, 1991; translation from French, Princeton, Princeton University Press, 2007.
4   Oliver Janz, "Entre deuil et triomphe: le culte politique des morts en Italie après la Première Guerre mondiale," in A. Duménil, N. Beaupré, and Christian Ingrao (eds.), *L'ère de la guerre. Violence, mobilisation, deuil 1914–1945*, vol.1, Paris, Agnès Viénot Editions, 2004, p. 273.
5   Merridale, *Night of Stone*, pp. 125–7.
6   See chs. 32 (Russia) and 37 (postwar conflicts) above.

7   Mark Cornwall, "Mémoire de la Grande Guerre dans les pays tchèques, 1918–1928," in John Horne (ed.), *Démobilisations culturelles après la Grande Guerre: 14–18, Aujourd'hui– Today– Heute*, 5, May 2002, pp. 89–101.

8   John Horne, "Introduction," in Horne (ed.), "*Démobilisations culturelles …*,". p. 47.

9   Cabanes, *Victoire endeuillée*.

10   Van Ypersele, "Sortir de la guerre."

11   Becker, *Oubliés de la Grande Guerre*; J.-Y. Le Naour, "Les désillusions de la libération d'après le contrôle postal civil de Lille: octobre 1918-mars 1919," *Revue du Nord*, 80/325, 1998, pp. 393–404.

12   Rousseau and Van Ypersele (eds.), *La Patrie crie vengeance*, pp. 195–200.

13   Jeffery, *Ireland and the Great War*, pp. 107–43.

14   Bessel, *Germany after the First World War*, pp. 69–90.

15   Christian Ingrao, "Etudiants allemands, mémoire de guerre et militantisme nazi: étude de cas," in Horne (ed.), *Démobilisations culturelles*, pp. 55–71; W. Struve, *Élites against Democracy. Leadership Ideals in Bourgeois Political Thought in Germany 1890–1933*, Princeton, Princeton University Press, 1973.

16   R. Thoms, *Bibliographie zur Geschichte des deutschen Freikorps*, Berlin, Project + Verlag Erwin Meissler, 1997; R. Thoms and S. Pochanke, *Handbuch zur Geschichte der deutschen Freikorps*, Bad Soden and Salmünster, MTM, 2001.

17   Winter, *Sites of Memory*.

18   Germany, however, has sites where unknown soldiers have been interred, such as the Tannenberg memorial inaugurated in 1927 or the Neue Wache in Berlin, inaugurated in 1931.

19   Mosse, *Fallen Soldiers*, pp. 80–93.

20   Becker, *Monuments aux morts*; Winter, *Sites of Memory*; Winter, "Forms of Kinship and Remembrance in the Aftermath of the Great War," in Winter and Sivan (eds.), *War and Remembrance in the Twentieth Century*, pp. 40–60.

21   Stamp, *Memorial to the Missing*, pp. 129–85.

22   Inglis, *Sacred Places*; Vance, *Death So Noble*.

23   Annette Becker, "Le Culte des morts, entre mémoire et oubli," in Stéphane Audoin-Rouzeau and Jean-Jacques Becker (eds.), *Encyclopédie de la Grande Guerre 1914–1918*, Paris, Bayard, 2004, p. 1105.

24   Mark Cornwall, "Mémoires de la Grande Guerre dans les pays tchèques, 1918–1928," in Horne (ed.), *Démobilisations culturelles*, pp. 89–101.

25   Mosse, *Fallen Soldiers*, pp. 94–8.

26   Winter, "Guerre et mémoire au XXe siècle."

27   Audoin-Rouzeau and Becker, *Understanding the Great War*, pp. 182–225.

28   Trevisan, *Les Fables du deuil*, p. 199.

29   Krumeich and Schröder (eds.), *Der Schatten des Weltkriegs*.

30   Horne "Introduction," in Home (ed.), *Démobilisation culturelles*, pp. 45–53.

31   John Horne, "Locarno et la politique de démobilisation culturelle: 1925–1930," in Horne (ed.), *Démobilisations culturelles*, p. 77, for the formulation of the term.

32   Olivier Loubès, *L'Ecole et la patrie. Histoire d'un désenchantement.1914–1940*, Paris, Editions Belin, 2001.

33   Stéphane Audoin-Rouzeau, *Men at War, 1914–1918. National Sentiment and Trench Journalism in France during the First World War*, 1986; translation from French, Providence, RI and Oxford, Berg, 1992, Conclusion; Smith, *The Embattled Self*, pp. 148–94.

34   E.g., *All Quiet on the Western Front* (1930, from the novel by Erich Maria Remarque) and *Les Croix de bois* (1932, from the novel by Roland Dorgelès). See ch. 24 above.

35   Offenstadt, *Les Fusillés de la Grande Guerre*.

36   Lasswell, *Propaganda Technique*; Arthur Ponsonby, *Falsehood in Wartime*, London, George Allen and Unwin, 1928.

37 John Horne, "'Propagande' et 'Vérité' dans la Grande Guerre," in Christophe Prochasson and Anne Rasmussen (eds.), *Vrai et faux dans la Grande Guerre*, Paris, Editions La Fabrique, 2004, pp. 76–95.

38 Horne, "Locarno et la politique de démobilisation culturelle," pp. 78–80.

39 Prost, *In the Wake of War*, pp. 36–8.

40 F. Frédéric, "Les 'mains coupées': le tableau, la légende et l'histoire," *Cahiers belges d'Histoire militaire*, 3, March 2005, pp. 35–61.

41 Laurence Van Ypersele and Emmanuel Debruyne, *De la guerre de l'ombre aux ombres de la guerre. L'espionnage en Belgique durant la guerre 1914–1918. Histoire et mémoire*, Brussels, Labor, 2004, pp. 151–66.

42 Mosse, *Fallen Soldiers*, pp. 182–200.

43 Dennis Showalter, "'Plus jamais': du moins pas comme cela: imaginer la guerre après 1918," in Horne (ed.), *Démobilisations culturelles*, pp. 145–57.

44 Vaisse (ed.), *Le pacifisme en Europe*.

45 Pierre Laborie, "La mémoire de 1914–1918 et Vichy," in Sylvie Caucanas and Rémy Cazals (eds.), *Traces de 14–18. Actes du Colloque de Carcassonne*, Carcassonne, Les Audois, 1997, pp. 219–32.

46 Jean-Marie Guillon and Pierre Laborie (eds.), *Mémoire et Histoire: la Résistance*, Toulouse, Privat, 1995; Fabrice Maerten, "L'impact du souvenir de la Grande Guerre sur la Résistance en Belgique durant le second conflit mondial," in Ypersele (ed.), *Imaginaires de guerres*, pp. 303–36.

47 Pieter Lagrou, *The Legacy of Nazi Occupation: Patriotic Memory and National Recovery in Western Europe, 1945–1965*, Cambridge, Cambridge University Press, 2000, pp. 38–58.

48 Merridale, *Night of Stone*, pp. 346–9.

49 Mosse, *Fallen Soldiers*, pp. 211–20.

References and Further Reading

Audoin-Rouzeau, Stéphane, and Becker, Annette, *1914–1918. Understanding the Great War*, 2000; translation from French, London, Profile Books, 2002.

Audoin-Rouzeau, Stéphane, and Prochasson, Christophe (eds.), *Sortir de la Grande Guerre. Le Monde et l'après-1918*, Paris, Tallandier, 2008.

Becker, Annette, *Les Monuments aux morts. Mémoire de la Grande Guerre*, Paris, Editions Errance, 1988.

Becker, Annette, *Oubliés de la Grande Guerre. Humanitaire et culture de guerre. Populations occupées, déportés civils, prisonniers de guerre*, Paris, Editions Noêsis, 1998.

Bessel, Richard, *Germany after the First World War*, Oxford, Oxford, University Press, 1993.

Cabanes, Bruno, *La Victoire endeuillée. La sortie de guerre des soldats français (1918–1920)*, Paris, Seuil, 2004.

Fussell, Paul, *The Great War and Modern Memory*, Oxford, Oxford University Press, 1977.

Gregory, Adrian, *The Silence of Memory. Armistice Day 1919–1946*, Oxford, Berg, 1994.

Halbwachs, Maurice, *Les Cadres sociaux de la mémoire*, Paris, 1926, new edition, Editions du Champ urbain,1956.

Horne, John (ed.), *Démobilisations culturelles après la Grande Guerre: 14–18, Aujourd'hui–Today–Heute*, 5, May 2002.

Horne, John, and Kramer, Alan, *German Atrocities, 1914. A History of Denial*, New Haven and London, Yale University Press, 2001, pt. 4.

Inglis, K. S., *Sacred Places. War Memorials in the Australian Landscape*, Melbourne, Melbourne University Press, 1998.

Jeffery, Keith, *Ireland and the Great War*, Cambridge, Cambridge University Press, 2000.

King, Alex, *Memorials of the Great War in Britain: the Symbolism and Politics of Remembrance*, Oxford, Oxford University Press, 1996.

Kruemeich, Gerd, and Schröder, Joachim, *Der Schatten des Weltkriegs. Die Ruhrbesetzung 1923,* Düsseldorf, Klartext, 2004.

Lasswell, Harold, *Propaganda Technique in World War I,* 1927; new edition, Cambridge, MA, MIT Press, 1971.

Merridale, Catherine, *Night of Stone. Death and Memory in Russia,* London, Granta, 2000.

Mosse, George, *Fallen Soldiers. Reshaping the Memory of the World Wars,* New York, Oxford University Press, 1990.

Norton Cru, Jean, *Témoins,* 1929; new edition (with preface by Frédéric Rousseau), Nancy, Presses Universitaires de Nancy, 2006.

Offenstadt, Nicolas, *Les Fusillés de la Grande Guerre et la mémoire collective (1914–1999),* Paris, Editions Odile Jacob, 1999.

Prost, Antoine, *In the Wake of War. "Les Anciens Combattants" and French Society 1914–1939,* Providence, RI and Oxford, Berg, 1992.

Rousseau, Xavier, and Van Ypersele, Laurence (eds.), *La Patrie crie vengeance. La répression des "inciviques" en Belgique après la première guerre mondiale,* Brussels, Le Cri, 2006.

Smith, Leonard V., *The Embattled Self. French Soldiers' Testimony of the Great War,* Ithaca and London, Cornell University Press, 2007.

Stamp, Gavin, *The Memorial to the Missing of the Somme,* London, Profile Books, 2006.

Todman, Dan, *The Great War. Myth and Memory,* London, Hambledon Continuum, 2005.

Trevisan, Carine, *Les Fables du deuil: la Grande Guerre, mort et écriture,* Paris, Presses Universitaires de France, 2001.

Vaisse, Maurice, *Le Pacifisme en Europe des années 1920 aux années 1950,* Brussels, Bruylant, 1993.

Van Ypersele, Laurence (ed.), *Imaginaires de guerres. L'histoire entre mythe et réalité,* Louvain-la-Neuve, Academia-Bruylant/Presses Universitaires de Louvain, 2003.

Van Ypersele, Laurence, "Sortir de la guerre, sortir de l'occupation: les violences populaires en Belgique au lendemain de la Première guerre mondiale," *Le Vingtième Siècle. Revue d'Histoire,* Paris, 83, July–September 2004, pp. 65–74.

Vance, Jonathan, *Death So Noble. Memory, Meaning and the First World War,* Vancouver, University of British Columbia Press, 1997.

Winter, Jay, *Sites of Memory, Sites of Mourning. The Great War in European Cultural History,* Cambridge, Cambridge University Press, 1995.

Winter, Jay, and Sivan, Emmanuel (eds.), *War and Remembrance in the Twentieth Century,* Cambridge, Cambridge University Press, 1999.

Select Primary Sources

A substantial amount of primary source material was published in English, often in translation from the languages of the main belligerent powers, during and after the war, especially in the interwar period. What follows is merely a selection. While the tendency in the early publications was to favor generals and political leaders, there is also much relating to the experience of ordinary women and men in various places and situations. Categorization is by role and perspective in relation to the war, but since these were often multiple, this can be arbitrary.

1. Document Collections

– *The Treatment of Armenians in the Ottoman Empire, 1915–1916: Documents presented to Viscount Grey of Fallodon by Viscount Bryce and Arnold Toynbee*, London, HMSO, 1916; new ed. (presented by Ara Sarafian), Princeton, Gomidas Institute, 2000. *Evidence of the Armenian genocide by two of the most trenchant critics in the Entente powers.*

Bell, Julian (ed.), *We Did Not Fight.1914–1918: Experiences of War Resisters*, London, Cobden-Sanderson, 1935.

Browder, Robert, and Kerensky, Alexander (eds.), *The Russian Provisional Government, 1917: Documents selected by Robert Paul Browder and Alexander Kerensky*, 3 vols., Stanford, University of Stanford Press, 1961.

Cardinal, Agnes, Goldman, Dorothy, and Hattaway, Judith (eds.), *Women's Writing on the First World War*, Oxford, Oxford University Press, 2000.

Cross, Timothy, *The Lost Voices of World War One: An International Anthology of Writers, Poets and Playwrights*, 1988; 2nd ed., London, Bloomsbury, 1998.

Geiss, Immanuel, *July 1914: Outbreak of the First World War – Selected Documents*, 1965; trans. from German, London, Batsford, 1967.

Golder, Frank (ed.), *Documents of Russian History, 1914–1917*, New York, The Century Co., 1927.

Higonnet, Margaret (ed.), *Lines of Fire: Women Writers on World War I*, New York, Plume, 1999.

Higonnet, Margaret (ed.), *Nurses at the Front: Writing the Wounds of the Great War*, Boston, Northeastern University Press, 2001.

Hirschfeld, Gerhard, Krumeich, Gerd, and Renz, Irina (eds.), *Scorched Earth. The Germans on the Somme 1914–18*, 2006; trans. from German, Barnsley, Pen and Sword, 2009. *Documents, with introductory essays.*

Horne, Charles, *Source Records of the Great War*, 7 vols., n. pl. (USA), National Alumni, 1923; reprinted as *Source Records of World War I*, Lewiston, NY and Lampeter, Edwin Mellen Press, 1998.

Kautsky, Karl, *Outbreak of the World War: German Documents Collected by Karl Kautsky*, ed. Max Montgelas and Walther Schücking, 1919; trans. from German, London, Oxford University Press, 1924.

Lutz, Ralph Haswell (ed.), *Fall of the German Empire, 1914–1918. Documents of the German Revolution*, 2 vols., Stanford, Stanford University Press, 1932.

Neiberg, Michael, *The World War I Reader*, New York, New York University Press, 2006.

Panichas, George (ed.), *Promise of Greatness. The War of 1914–1918*, London, Cassell, 1968. *Retrospective views by the war "generation" from the perspective of the 1960s.*

Silkin, Jon (ed.), *The Penguin Book of First World War Poetry*, London, Penguin, 1979; new ed., 1996.

2. Politicians and Diplomats

Albert I, *The War Diaries of Albert I, King of the Belgians*, ed. R. Van Overstraeten, 1953; trans. from French, London, Kimber, 1954.

Bauer, Otto, *The Austrian Revolution*, 1923; trans. from German, London, Parsons, 1925. *Account of the collapse of the Dual Monarchy by a leading "Austro-Marxist."*

Bethmann-Hollweg, Theodor von, *Reflections on the World War,* 1919–1921, London, Thorn and Butterworth, 1920. *German Chancellor 1909–1917. Only the first of two volumes (covering the outbreak of war) were translated into English.*

Burián von Rajecz, Stephan, *Austria in Dissolution: being the Personal Recollections of Stephan, Count Burián*, 1923; trans. from German, London, Ernest Benn, 1925.

Clemenceau, Georges, *France Facing Germany. Speeches and Articles*, trans. from French, New York, Dutton, 1919. *French Prime Minister, 1917–19.*

Clemenceau, Georges, *Grandeur and Misery of Victory*, 1930; trans. from French, London, Harrap, 1930. *Ruminations on the outcome of the war.*

Czernin, Count Ottokar, *In the World War*, 1919; trans. from German, London, Cassell, 1919. *Aristocrat from Bohemia and Foreign Minister of Austria-Hungary 1916–18, whose conflicting policies reflected the growing desperation and disintegration of the Dual Monarchy.*

Djemal, Ahmed Pasha, *Memories of a Turkish Statesman, 1913–1919*, London, Hutchinson, 1922. *One of the triumvirate of the Committee Union and Progress directing the Turkish war effort.*

[Dutton, David (ed.)], *Paris 1918: The War Diary of the British Ambassador, the 17th Earl of Derby*, Liverpool, Liverpool University Press, 2001.

Grey of Fallodon, Edward, *Twenty-Five Years, 1892–1916*, London, Hodder and Stoughton, 1928. *British Foreign Secretary on the outbreak of war in 1914.*

Hindenburg, Paul von, *Out of My Life*, 1920; trans. from German, London, Cassell, 1920; new abr. ed., *The Great War*, London, Greenhill, 2006. *Victor (with Erich Ludendorff) over the Russian armies invading East Prussia in 1914, Supreme Commander and virtual head of government, 1916–18, formulator of the "stab-in-the-back" myth in 1919 and President of the Weimar Republic 1925–34.*

House, Edward M., *The Intimate Papers of Colonel House*, Boston, Houghton Mifflin, 1926–28, 4 vols. *Adviser to Woodrow Wilson at the Paris Peace Conference.*

Károlyi, Michael, *Memoirs of Michael Károlyi. Faith without Illusion*, trans. from Hungarian, London, Jonathan Cape, 1956.

Kautsky, Karl, *The Dictatorship of the Proletariat*, 1918; trans. from German, London, National Labour Press, 1919; new ed., Ann Arbor, University of Michigan Press, 1964. *Reformist critique of the Bolshevik Revolution (cf. Luxemburg, op. cit.).*

Kerensky, Alexander, *The Kerensky Memoirs: Russia and History's Turning Point*, London, Cassell, 1965. *Second Prime Minister of the Provisional Government, March–November 1917 and architect of Russia's failed remobilization for a democratic war effort.*

Lenin, Vladimir, *Imperialism, the Highest Stage of Capitalism*, 1917; new trans. from Russian, Moscow, Foreign Languages Publishing House, 1952 (*Selected Works of V. I. Lenin*, vol. 1, pt. 2). *Written in Swiss exile in 1916, an influential theoretical reflection on the imperialist nature of capitalism and why imperialism favored war, allowing the "advanced" workers to be bribed into national, not class, allegiances.*

Lenin, Vladimir, *The State and Revolution*, 1917; new trans. from Russian, Moscow, Foreign Languages Publishing House, 1952 (*Selected Works of V. I. Lenin*, vol. 2, pt. 1). *Lenin uses Trotsky's idea of "permanent revolution" to explain how the overthrow of tsardom may lead directly to the proletarian revolution, whose internationalization is the condition of its survival.*

Lloyd George, David, *War Memoirs of David Lloyd George*, London, Odhams, 1934–6, 2 vols.

Luxemburg, Rosa, "The Russian Revolution," 1918, trans. from German in Bertram Wolfe (ed.), *Leninism or Marxism? The Russian Revolution*, Ann Arbor, Ann Arbor Paperbacks for the Study of Communism and Marxism, 1961. *Revolutionary Marxist critique of a "proletarian" revolution conducted by a minority party in the circumstances of Russia in 1917.*

Mantoux, Paul, *The Deliberations of the Council of Four (March 24–June 28 1919)* (ed. Arthur S. Link and Manfred Boehmke), trans. from French, Princeton, Princeton University Press, 1992, 2 vols.

Masaryk, Tomas, *The Making of a State: Memories and Observations, 1914–1918*, trans. from Czech, London, Allen and Unwin, 1927. *Postwar president of Czechoslovakia.*

Mercier, Désiré (Cardinal), *Cardinal Mercier's Own Story*, trans. from French, London, Hodder and Stoughton, 1920. *Catholic Primate of Belgium and leader of the resistance to the German occupation.*

Miliukov, Paul, *Political Memoirs 1905–1917*, trans. from Russian, Ann Arbor, University of Michigan Press, 1967. *Leader of the Constitutional Democratic (Cadet) Party whose demands for reform for a more effective war effort contributed to the downfall of the Tsarist regime. First Foreign Minister in the Provisional Government of 1917.*

Morgenthau, Henry, *Ambassador Morgenthau's Story*, New York, Doubleday Page, 1918; repr., Ann Arbor, Gomidas Institute, 2000. *US ambassdor to the Ottoman Empire.*

Naumann, Friedrich, *Central Europe*, 1915; trans. from German, London, King, 1916. *Liberal imperialist and wartime advocate of permanent German Hegemony over Central Europe.*

Nicolson, Harold, *Peacemaking, 1919*, London, Constable, 1937; new ed., Methuen, 1964. *Junior British diplomat at the Paris peace conference and subsequent political and literary figure. Includes a diary of the conference.*

Pilsudski, Józef, *The Memories of a Polish Revolutionary and Soldier*, London, Faber, 1931. *Created the Polish Legions, which fought from 1914 to 1917 with the Central Powers to gain Polish independence, but withdrew support for Germany and Austria-Hungary with the Russian Revolution. Chief of State of newly independent Poland, 1918–22, and commander-in-chief in the Polish–Soviet War of 1920.*

Poincaré, Raymond, *The Memoirs of Raymond Poincaré*, 4 vols., abr. trans. from French, London, Heinemann, 1926–30. *President of France throughout the war.*

Rathenau, Walther, *Walther Rathenau: Industrialist, Banker, Intellectual and Politician: Notes and Diaries, 1907–1922* (ed. Harmut Pogge von Strandmann), Oxford, Clarendon Press, 1985. *Leader of German industrial mobilization and postwar Foreign Minister; assassinated by nationalists in 1922.*

Redmond, John, *The Irish Nation and the War: Extracts from Speeches made in the House of Commons and in Ireland since the Outbreak of the War*, Dublin, Sealy, Bryers and Walker, 1915. *Leader of the Irish Parliamentary Party who advocated support of the war effort in return for securing Irish Home Rule.*

Sazonov, Sergei, *Fateful Years, 1909–1916: the Reminiscences*, London, Cape, 1928. *Russian Foreign Minister 1910–June 1916.*

Scheidemann, Philip, *Memoirs of a Social Democrat*, 1928; trans. from German, London, Hodder and Stoughton, 1929. *Wartime leader of German socialists and head of the first, provisional government of the postwar republic.*

Trotsky, Leon, *The Age of Permanent Revolution: A Trotsky Anthology* (ed. Isaac Deutscher), New York, Dell, 1964. *Esp.* "The Zimmerwald Manifesto" (1915), *the first, major antiwar statement by international socialists (pp. 79–83) and* "Terrorism in War and Revolution" (1920), *a justification of revolutionary terror (pp. 110–16).*

Whitlock, Brand, *Belgium under German Occupation. A Personal Narrative*, London, Heinemann, 1920. *US ambassador to Belgium, 1914–17.*

Wilson, Woodrow, *The Papers of Woodrow Wilson* (ed. Arthur S. Link), Princeton, Princeton University Press, 1979–91 (vols. 30–64).

3. Military Leaders

Brusilov, Aleksei, *A Soldier's Notebook*, London, Macmillan, 1930; repr., Westwood, CT, Greenwood, 1971. *Most successful Russian commander of the war.*

Denikin, Anton, *The Russian Turmoil. Memoirs, Military, Social and Political by General A. I. Denikin*, London, Hutchinson, 1922. *Successful wartime commander who led the White Army in southern Russia during the Civil War before exile in 1920.*

Falkenhayn, Erich von, *General Headquarters, 1914–1916 and its Critical Decisions*, trans. from German, 1919; new ed., Nashville, Battery Press, 2000. *German supreme commander from after the Marne to Verdun.*

Foch, Ferdinand, *The Memoirs of Marshal Foch* 1931; trans. from French, London, Heinemann, 1931. *Leading French commander and Allied commander-in-chief 1918.*

Haig, Douglas, *War Diaries and Letters* (ed. Gary Sheffield and John Bourne), London, Weidenfeld and Nicolson, 2005. *Commander of the British Expeditionary Force, 1915 to the end of the war.*

Hoffmann, Max, *War Diaries and Other Papers*, 1928; trans. from German, London, Martin Secker, 1929, 2 vols. *Brilliant German general on the eastern front.*

Jellicoe, John, *The Jellicoe Papers. Selections from the Private and Official Correspondence of Admiral of the Fleet Earl Jellicoe of Scapa* (ed. A. Temple Patterson), Shortlands (Kent), Navy Records Society, 1966, 2 vols.

Joffre, Joseph, *The Memoirs of Marshal Joffre*, 1932; trans. from French, London, Geoffrey Bles, 1932, 2 vols. *French commander-in-chief down to December 1916.*

Knox, Alfred, *With the Russian Army 1914–1921*, London, Hutchinson, 1921, 2 vols. *British military attaché.*

Lawrence, T. E., *Seven Pillars of Wisdom. The Complete 1922 "Oxford" Text* (ed. Jeremy Wilson), Woodgreen Common, J. and N. Wilson, 2004. *The original version of the celebrated account of the British sponsored Arab campaign against Ottoman Turkey. See also the truncated* Revolt in the Desert, *London, Jonathan Cape, 1927.*

Lettow-Vorbeck, Paul von, *My Reminiscences of East Africa*, London, Hurst and Blackett, 1920. *Commander of German forces in the East African campaign, 1914–18.*

Liman von Sanders, Otto, *Five Years in Turkey*, 1920; trans. from German, Annapolis, United States Naval Institute, 1927; repr. Nashville, Battery Press, 2000. *German military adviser to Ottoman Turkey and commander of the Turkish forces at Gallipoli.*

Ludendorff, Erich, *My War Memories* 1919; trans. from German, London, Hutchinson, 1919. *Victor (with Hindenburg) over the Russian invading armies in 1914. The real power behind the Third Supreme Command, under Hindenburg, 1916–18.*

Pershing, John, *My Experiences in the World War*, London, Hodder and Stoughton, 1931. *Commander of the American Expeditionary Force to Europe.*

Pétain, Philippe, *Verdun*, London, 1929; trans. from French, Elkin Mathews, 1930. *Pétain's account of the vital 1916 battle for much of which he commanded the French armies.*

Pierrefeu, Jean de, *French Headquarters, 1915–1918*, 1920; trans. from French, London, G. Bles, 1924. *Author of the daily communiqué and observer of High Command politics.*

Spears, Edward, *Liaison 1914: A Narrative of the Great Retreat*, 1968; new ed., London, Cassell, 2000. *Liaison officer for the British Expeditionary Force with the French army during the opening campaign of the war.*

4. Soldiers

Aitken, Alexander, *Gallipoli to the Somme: Recollections of a New Zealand Infantryman*, London, Oxford University Press, 1963. *Fought as a corporal and junior officer.*

Belmont, Ferdinand, *A Crusader of France: Lettres d'un officier de chasseurs alpins*, 1916; trans. from French, London, Melrose, 1917. *French Catholic officer killed in 1916.*

Bloch, Marc, *Memoirs of War, 1914–1915*, 1969; trans. from French with introduction by Carole Fink, Ithaca, Cornell University Press, 1980. *The celebrated medieval historian and co-founder of the* Annales *(1929), who fought as a junior officer on the western front.*

Bloem, Walter, *The Advance from Mons, 1914*, 1916; trans. from German, London, Peter Davies, 1930. *Account by a reserve officer of the invasion campaign 1914.*

Breen, Dan, *My Fight for Irish Freedom*, Dublin, Talbot Press, 1924; new ed., Dublin, Anvil Books, 1981. *Nationalist from Tipperary who took the first action against British forces in Ireland, January 1919, sparking the Irish War of Independence.*

Carrington, Charles (pseud., Charles Edmonds), *A Subaltern's War: Being a Memoir of the Great War from the Point of View of a Romantic Young Man [...]*, London, P. Davies, 1929. *Served as a lieutenant in the Royal Warwickshire Regiment throughout the war on the western front. A deliberate counterpoint to the "literature of disenchantment."*

De Man, Hendrik, *The Remaking of a Mind: A Soldier's Thoughts on War and Reconstruction*, London, Allen and Unwin, 1919. *Young Marxist in the Belgian Workers' Party who was transformed by combat experience on the western front.*

Desagneux, Henri, *A French Soldier's War Diary, 1914–1918*, 1971; trans. from French, Morley, Elmfield Press, 1975. *Soldier rising to captain who fought in the principal battles on the western front.*

Dwinger, Edwin, *The Army behind Barbed Wire: a Siberian Diary*, 1929; trans. from German, London, Allen and Unwin, 1930. *Experience of being a prisoner of war in Russia.*

Heinz, Max, *Loretto. Sketches of a German Volunteer*, New York, Liveright, 1930. *Private and NCO who fought on the western front in 1915 and 1917–18.*

Kettle, Tom, *The Ways of War*, London, Constable, 1917. *Wartime journalism of the Irish nationalist intellectual and activist who volunteered service in the British army with a view to securing Home Rule.*

Lemercier, E. E., *Letters of a Soldier*, 1916; trans. from French, London, Constable, 1917, and with the title *Soldier of France to his Mother*, New York, McClure, 1917. *A bestseller, remarkable for the horrors of the western front conveyed in a spirit of patriotic self-sacrifice and filial love.*

Lewis, Cecil, Saggittarius Rising, 1936; new ed., London, Greenhill, 2003. *British fighter pilot who flew with the elite 56 Squadron of the Royal Flying Corps in France.*

Lucy, John, *There's a Devil in the Drum*, London, Faber, 1938. *Vivid memoir of the campaigns in 1914 by a young Irishman in the prewar Regular Army.*

Lussu, Emilio, *Sardinian Brigade*, 1938; trans. from Italian, New York, 1939; new ed., London, Prion Books, 2000. *Classic account of the Austro-Italian front, written in anti-fascist exile.*

(Moynihan) *The Moynihan Brothers in Peace and War, 1909–1918* (ed. Deirdre McMahon), Dublin, Irish Academic Press, 2004. *Nationalist family from Co. Kerry with one brother on the western front.*

Mussolini Benito, *My Diary, 1915–1917*, 1923; trans. from Italian, Boston, Small, Maynard, 1925. *The self-construction of a fascist using front-line experience.*

Richards, Frank, *Old Soldiers Never Die*, London, Faber, 1933. *Fought as a private throughout the war in the Royal Welch Fusiliers.*

Richthofen, Manfred von, *The Red Air Fighter*, 1917; trans. from German, 1918; new ed., Barnsley, Pen and Sword, 2005. *Highest scoring ace of World War I and a national hero in Germany.*

Riou, Gaston, *The Diary of a French Private. War-Imprisonment 1914–15*, 1916; trans. from French, London, Allen and Unwin, 1916.

Tawney, Richard, *The Attack and Other Papers*, London, Allen and Unwin, 1953. *Remarkable account of combat experience in the battle of the Somme first published in 1916 by the Christian Socialist intellectual and historian.*

Teilhard de Chardin, Pierre, *The Making of a Mind: Letters from a Soldier-Priest, 1914–1919*, 1961; trans. from French, London, Collins, 1965. *Formative experience of a leading Catholic theologian.*

Witkop, Philipp (ed.), *German Students' War Letters*, trans. from German, London, Methuen, 1929; new ed., Philadelphia, Pine Street Books, 2002, with foreword by Jay Winter. *Immensely influential volume that went through multiple editions in Germany, with varying degrees of nationalist emphasis.*

York, Alvin, *Sergeant York: His Own Life Story and War Diary*, Garden City, NJ, Doubleday, Doran, 1928. *Classic account of York's fighting with the American Expeditionary Force and the mass capture of enemy soldiers that made him a hero and legend in the United States.*

5. Women

Bluecher, Evelyn, *An English Wife in Berlin. A Private Memoir of Events, Politics and Daily Life in Germany throughout the War and the Social Revolution of 1918*, London, Constable, 1920. *Wife of a German aristocrat.*

Botchkareva, Maria, *My Life as Peasant, Exile and Soldier*, New York, F.A. Stokes, 1919. *Russian woman who fought as a soldier.*

Brändström, Elsa, *Among Prisoners of War in Russia and Siberia, 1920*; trans. from German, London, Hutchinson, 1929. *Daughter of Swedish ambassador in Petrograd; coordinated prisoner-of-war relief throughout the war for the Swedish Red Cross.*

Brittain, Vera, *Chronicle of Youth: Great War Diary, 1913–1917*, London, Gollancz, 1981. *English student and volunteer nurse; to be compared with her classic postwar* Testament of Youth.

Brittain, Vera, *Testament of Youth*, London, Gollancz, 1933.

Cooper, Caroline, *Behind the Lines: One Woman's War, 1914–1918*, Sydney, Collins, 1982. *The letters home from a woman from Adelaide who spent the entire war in Leipzig, her correspondence being smuggled out through Switzerland.*

Eisenmenger, Anna, *Blockade: the Diary of an Austrian Middle Class Woman, 1914–1924*, London, Constable,1932.

(Graeffe, Constance), *"We Who are so Cosmopolitan": The War Diary of Constance Graeffe, 1914–1915* (ed. Sophie de Schaepdrijver), Brussels, Archives Générales du Royaume, 2008. *Life in German-occupied Belgium.*

King, Olive, *One Woman at War: Letters of Olive King, 1915–1920*, Melbourne, Melbourne University Press, 1986. *Remarkable account of a woman who joined the Scottish Women's Hospital Unit and went with it to Serbia.*

Mihaly, Jo, *There We'll Meet Again: a Young German Girl's Diary of the First World War by Piete Kuhr, later known as Jo Mihaly*, Great Britain, n. pl., W. Wright, 1998. *Account by a girl who was 12 when the war began of life in East Prussia.*

Pankhurst, Sylvia, *The Home Front. A Mirror to Life in England during World War I*, London, Hutchinson, 1932. *A suffragette leader who broke with her mother, Emmeline, by opposing the war on grounds of class and pacifism.*

Sandes, Flora, *An English Woman-Sergeant in the Serbian Army*, London, Hodder and Stoughton, 1916. *Anglo-Irish woman who fought in the Serbian army.*

Wharton, Edith, *Fighting France. From Dunkerque to Belfort*, New York, Scribners, 1919. *Travels in wartime France by the American novelist.*

6. Noncombatant Men

Catchpool, Corder, *On Two Fronts. Letters of a Conscientious Objector*, n. pl., Headley Bros., 1918; new ed. London, Allen and Unwin, 1940. *Quaker who served in the Friends' Ambulance Unit but refused to accept conscription in 1916 and was imprisoned until 1919.*

Clark, Andrew, *Echoes of the Great War: the Diary of the Reverend Andrew Clark, 1914–1918* (ed. James Munson), Oxford, Oxford University Press, 1985. *Remarkable portrait of the war's impact on rural English life.*

Corday, Michel, *The Paris Front: An Unpublished Diary, 1914–1918*, 1932, trans. from French, London, Gollancz, 1933. *Sceptical, mildly pacifist viewpoint.*

Hanssen, Peter, *Diary of a Dying Empire*, 1925; trans. from Danish, 1955; new ed., London, Kennikat, 1973. *Viewpoint of Danish minority representative (North Schleswig) in the Reichstag, 1906–18.*

Hoover, Herbert, *An American Epic*, vol. 1, *The Relief of Belgium and Northern France, 1914–1930*, Chicago, Henry Regnery Co., 1959. *Mining engineer and businessman (later President of the United States) who organized international food relief for occupied Belgium and France.*

Massart, Jean, *Belgians under the German Eagle*, trans. from French, London, Fisher Unwin, 1916. *Belgian biologist and resistance leader who escaped midwar.*

Mendelssohn-Bartholdy, Albrecht, *The War and German Society. The Testament of a Liberal*, New Haven, Yale University Press, 1937.

Ussher, Clarence, *An American Physician in Turkey. A Narrative of Adventures in Peace and in War*, Boston, Houghton Mifflin, 1917; new ed., London, Sterndale Classics, 2002. *Eyewitness to the destruction of the Armenians of Van in 1915.*

7. Intellectuals

— "The Appeal to the World of Culture," in P. van Houtte, *The Pan-Germanic Crime: Impressions and Investigations in Belgium during the German Occupation*, London, Hodder and Stoughton, 1915, pp. 155–61. *The influential (and inflammatory) declaration of support by 93 leading German artists, intellectuals, and scientists for Germany's cause and the German army's actions in Belgium.*

— *Why We are at War: Great Britain's Case*, Oxford, Clarendon Press, 1914. *Influential statement by the Oxford Historical Faculty.*

Alain (pseud., Emile Chartier), *Mars, or the Truth about War*, 1921; trans. from French, London, Cape, 1930. *Disillusionment with war of an influential Republican philosopher and leading intellectual who volunteered for military service.*

Barrès, Maurice, *The Soul of France*, 1917; trans. from French, London, n. p., 1917; also as *The Faith of France*, Boston, Houghton and Mifflin, 1918. *A Catholic nationalist celebration of the sacrifice of soldiers from all traditions in France, as expressed through their letters.*

Benda, Julien, *The Treason of the Intellectuals*, 1927; trans. from French, 1928; new ed., London, Morton, 1982. *Critical of support by intellectuals for the war.*

Freud, Sigmund, "Thoughts for the Times on War and Death" (1915), in *The Penguin Freud Library*, vol. 12, London, Pelican, 1985, pp. 61–89. *Musings on mass death and mourning, especially of the young, by the middle-aged and old.*

Halévy, Elie, "The World Crisis of 1914–1918: an Interpretation," in Halévy, *The Era of Tyrannies. Essays on Socialism and War*, 1938; trans. from French, London, Allen Lane, 1967, pp. 161–90. *Reflection on the threat to liberalism engendered by the war.*

Keynes, John Maynard, *The Economic Consequences of the Peace*, London, Macmillan, 1919. *Leading critic of the "harsh" peace terms imposed on Germany.*

Langenhove, Fernand van, *The Growth of a Legend. A Study Based Upon the German Accounts of Francs-Tireurs and "Atrocities" in Belgium*, London, Putnam, 1916. *Classic socio-pyschological analysis of the German illusion of mass civilian resistance to the invasion of Belgium in 1914.*

Lavisse, Ernest, and Andler, Charles, *German Theory and Practice of War*, Paris, n.p., 1915. *Text issued by the semi-official Committee of Studies and Documents on the War, stating the French case against Germany.*

Mann, Thomas, *Reflections of a Nonpolitical Man*, 1922; trans. from German, New York, Ungar, 1983. *Support for the German war effort, written in 1915–17 by the novelist who after the war accepted democracy and opposed Nazism (see 9. Writers).*

Rolland, Romain, *Above the Battlefield*, Bowes and Bowes, Cambridge, 1914; new translation, London, Allen and Unwin, 1916. *Key French pacifist text.*

Russell, Bertrand, *Why Men Fight. A Method of Abolishing the International Duel*, New York, The Century Company, 1917. *Anti-war text by the British philosopher dismissed from Trinity College Cambridge in 1916 for his protest against conscription.*

Zweig, Stefan, *The World of Yesterday*, 1942; trans. from German, London, Cassell, 1943. *Autobiography of the Austrian Jewish pacifist and correspondent of Romain Rolland.*

8. Journalists

Ansky, S., *The Enemy at His Pleasure. A Journey through the Jewish Pale of Settlement during World War I* (ed. Joachim Neugroschel), New York, Holt, 2002. *Maltreatment and pogroms behind the Russian front.*

Bean, C. E. W. (Charles), *Letters from France (Concerning the Australian Force)*, 1917.

Bean, C. E. W. (Charles), Gallipoli Correspondent. The Frontline Diary of C.E.W. Bean, Sydney, George Allen and Unwin, 1983. *Journalist (later official historian) instrumental in forging the image of the Anzacs.*

Cobb, Irvin, *The Red Glutton: With the German Army at the Front*, New York, George H. Doran, 1915. *American journalist skeptical of Allied atrocity charges against Germany (cf. Davis, op. cit.).*

Davis, Richard Harding, *With the Allies*, London, Duckworth, 1915. *Pro-Allied account of the German invasion of Belgium in 1914 by the doyen of American war reporters.*

Dosch-Fleurot, Arno, *Through War to Revolution: Being the Experiences of a Newspaper Correspondent in War and Revolution, 1914–1920*, London, J. Lane, 1931. *On Russia.*

Gibbs, Philip, *Realities of War*, London, Hutchinson, 1929. *Disenchanted vision, to be compared with his wartime dispatches in the liberal press.*

Gibbs, Philip, *The War Dispatches of Sir Philip Gibbs*, 1964; new ed., London, Tandem, 1968.

MacDonagh, Michael, *In London during the Great War: the Diary of a Journalist*, London, Eyre and Spottiswoode, 1935.

Reed, John, *Ten Days that Shook the World*, 1919; new ed., London, Folio Society, 2006. *Classic account of the November 1917 Revolution in Russia by American war reporter.*

Reed, John, *The War in Eastern Europe: Travels through the Balkans*, 1916; new ed., London, Phoenix, 1994. *Eyewitness accounts of both sides of the eastern front.*

Wolff, Theodor, *The Eve of 1914*, 1934; trans. from German, London, Gollancz, 1935. *Wolff was the Liberal editor of the* Berliner Tageblatt.

9. Writers

Barbusse, Henri, *Under Fire*, 1916; trans. from French 1917; new trans. by Robin Buss, London, Allen Lane, 2003. *Winner of 1916 Prix Goncourt and a bestseller on the basis of its realistic portrayal of the horrors of trench warfare.*

Blunden, Edmund, *Undertones of War*, London, Cobden-Sanderson, 1928; new ed., Penguin, 2000. *Blunden served with the Royal Sussex Regiment 1915–19. One of the most celebrated contributions to the so-called "literature of disenchantment" of the later 1920s.*

Cummings, E. E. (Edward Estlin) *The Enormous Room*, 1922; new ed., London, Penguin, 1999. *Withering account of the poet's wrongful imprisonment for sedition in France, where he had volunteered for ambulance service.*

Dorgelès, Roland, *Wooden Crosses*, 1919; trans. from French, London, Heinemann, 1920. *One of the most influential postwar novels by a former soldier, made into a film in 1932.*

Duhamel, Georges, *The New Book of Martyrs*, 1918; trans. from French, London, William Heinemann, 1918.

Duhamel, Georges, *Civilisation 1914–1918*, 1918; trans. from French, London, Swarthmore Press, 1919. *Duhamel was a prewar doctor and novelist who served as a surgeon on the western front. Conveys not only the horror of war but also how it undermined prewar beliefs in science and progress.*

Genevoix, Maurice, *'Neath Verdun, August–October 1914*, trans. from French, London, Hutchinson, 1916. *Preface by Ernest Lavisse, doyen of French historians and leading educator of the Third Republic. First part of Genevoix's larger work,* Ceux de Verdun [Those of Verdun]. *A deeply realistic, barely fictional account based on the combat experience of one who voiced veteran memory down to the 1960s.*

Graves, Robert, *Goodbye to All That*, 1929; new ed. (ed. Richard Perceval Graves), Oxford, Berghahn Books, 1995. *Autobiography and key text of the so-called "literature of disenchantment." Heavily revised in 1957 edition. This edition restores the original version.*

Hasek, Jaroslav, *The Good Soldier Svejk*, 1923; trans. from Czech, 1920; new trans. by Cecil Parrot, London, Penguin, 1973. *A parody of the war culture of Austria-Hungary in the first year of the war through the eyes of an inadvertent Czech subversive. Hasek was made a prisoner of war on the eastern front.*

Hemingway, Ernest, *A Farewell to Arms*, London, Jonathan Cape, 1929. *Trauma, love, and disillusionment, drawn from Hemingway's service as an ambulance driver on the Italian front in 1918, where he was wounded and had a doomed love affair with an American nurse, Agnes von Kurowsky.*

Jünger, Ernst, *Storm of Steel*, 1920; trans. from German by Basil Creighton, London, Chatto and Windus, 1929 (based on the more nationalist German edition of 1924); new ed., trans. Michael Hofmann, London, Allen Lane, 2003 (based on 1961 German text, closer to the 1920 original). *Classic text celebrating the new warrior forged by industrialized warfare.*

Kraus, Karl, *The Last Days of Mankind: a Tragedy in Five Acts (abridged and edited by Frederick Ungar [...] trans. by Alexander Gode and Sue Ellen Wright)*, New York, Ungar, 1974. *Satirical vision of World War I written by the Viennese author and journalist 1915–19 and first published in the latter year.*

Mann, Thomas, *The Magic Mountain. A Novel*, 1924; trans. from German by John Woods, New York, Knopf, 1995. *Written during and after the war by a noncombatant, about the forces that made the war and shaped Germany's destiny in particular. Though set in a prewar Swiss sanatorium, it ends with the protagonist, Hans Castorp, entering combat on the western front.*

Manning, Frederic, *The Middle Parts of Fortune: Somme and Ancre 1916*, London, Piazza Press, 1929; new ed., London, Peter Davies, 1977, intro. by Michael Howard. *Australian writer from an upper middle-class background who enlisted as an ordinary soldier.*

Martin du Gard, Roger, *The Thibaults (Summer 1914)*, 1936; trans. from French, London, John Lane, 1939. *First part of the novel cycle of the same name charting the disintegration of a world through the war, in which the author served in a transport unit.*

Maurois, André, *The Silence of Colonel Bramble*, 1918, trans. from French, London, John Lane, 1919. *Affectionate portrait by a French novelist assigned as interpreter to the British Expeditionary Force in France.*

O'Flaherty, Liam, *Return of the Brute*, London, Mandrake, 1929; new ed., Dublin, Wolfhound, 1998. *Minor classic by a later Irish Republican about brutality and shell shock on the western front.*

Owen, Wilfred, *The Collected Poems of Wilfred Owen* (ed. C. Day Lewis with a memoir by Edmund Blunden), London, Chatto and Windus, 1963. *Owen, killed in November 1918, wrote what have become the canonical poems of World War I in English.*

Remarque, Erich Maria, *All Quiet on the Western Front*, 1929; trans. from German, 1929; new trans. by Brian Murdoch, London, Cape, 1994. *Bestselling pacifist account, made into a box-office success by Hollywood in 1930.*

Renn, Ludwig, *War*, 1929; trans. from German, 1929; new ed., London, Mott, 1984. *Pacifist-inclined account by an aristocratic wartime officer who joined the German Communist Party in 1928.*

Romains, Jules, *Verdun*, 1938; trans. from French, London, 1939; new ed., London, Prion, 2000. *Part of Romain's novel cycle of French collective psychological experience, with the war at its center.*

Salomon, Ernst von, *The Outlaws*, 1930; trans. from German, London, Jonathan Cape, 1931. *Fictionalized account of experiences of a postwar Freikorps fighter in the Baltic and Silesia.*

Sassoon, Siegfried, *Memoirs of an Infantry Officer*, 1930, new ed., London, Faber, 1973. *The second of a three part semi-fictional autobiography,* The Complete Memoirs of George Sherston, 1928–1936, *dealing with Sassoon's wartime service, heroism, protest, and "breakdown".*

Sherriff, R. C. (Robert Cedric), *Journey's End*, London, 1929; new ed., Harmondsworth, Penguin, 1983. *Influential first portrayal of combat (and breakdown) in the war on the mainstream London stage. Sherriff fought from 1915 to 1918 on the western front and was wounded at the third battle of Ypres (Passchendaele) in 1917.*

Wells, Herbert G., *Mr Britling Sees it Through*, London, Cassell, 1916. *Semi-autobiographical novel on the need to see the war through despite the evaporation of initial enthusiasm for the liberal crusade.*

Zweig, Arnold, *The Case of Sergeant Grischa*, 1927; trans. from German, London, Secker, 1928. *Picaresque novel about captivity, escape, changed identities, and the conflict of elemental humanity with (Prussian) military discipline.*

Extended Bibliography

The Further Reading sections following each chapter indicate secondary literature in French, German, and Italian as well as English. What follows is an extended (but not exhaustive) indication of secondary works available in English, organized by category. Where works are mentioned more than once, the category containing the full details is shown in brackets.

1. Reference and Bibliography

Beckett, Ian, *The First World War: The Essential Guide to Sources in the UK National Archives*, Richmond, Public Record Office, 2002.

Bourne, John, *Who's Who in World War One*, London, Routledge, 2001.

Falls, Cyril, *War Books: A Critical Guide*, London, P. Davies, 1930.

Gilbert, Martin, *The Routledge Atlas of the First World War*, 1970; new ed., London, Routledge, 1994.

Herman, Gerald, *The Pivotal Conflict: A Comprehensive Chronology of the First World War, 1914–1919*, Westport, Greenwood Press, 1992.

Herwig, Holger, and Heyman, Neil M. (eds.), *Biographical Dictionary of World War I*, Westport, CT, 1982.

Higham, Robin, and Showalter, Dennis (eds.), *Researching World War One: A Handbook*, Santa Barbara, CA, Greenwood, 2003.

Hughes, Matthew, and Philpott, William, *The Palgrave Concise Historical Atlas of the First World War*, London, Palgrave Macmillan, 2005.

Lengel, Edward, *World War I Memories: An Annotated Bibliography of Personal Accounts Published in English since 1919*, Oxford, Scarecrow Press, 2004.

Prost, Antoine, and Winter, Jay, *The Great War in History. Debates and Controversies 1914 to the Present*, 2004; trans. from French, Cambridge, Cambridge University Press, 2005.

Pope, Stephen, and Wheal, Elizabeth-Anne (eds.), *The Macmillan Dictionary of the First World War*, London, Macmillan, 1995.

Tucker, Spencer C., *The European Powers in the First World War. An Encyclopedia*, New York, Garland, 1996.

2. General

Albrecht-Carrié, René, *The Meaning of the First World War*, Englewood Cliffs, NJ, Prentice Hall, 1965.

Audoin-Rouzeau, Stéphane, and Becker, Annette, *1914–1918. Understanding the Great War*, 2000; trans. from French, London, Profile Books, 2002.

Beckett, Ian, *The Great War 1914–1918*, Harlow, Pearson, 2001.

Best, Geoffrey, *Humanity in Warfare. The Modern History of the International Law of Armed Conflict*, London, Weidenfeld and Nicolson, 1980.

Braybon, Gail, *Evidence, History and the Great War. Historians and the Impact of 1914–1918*, Oxford, Berghahn, 2003.

Cecil, Hugh, and Liddle, Peter (eds.), *Facing Armageddon: The First World War Experienced*, London, Leo Cooper, 1996.

Chickering, Roger, and Förster, Stig (eds.), *Great War, Total War. Combat and Mobilization on the Western Front, 1914–1918*, Cambridge, Cambridge University Press, 2000.

Cruttwell, Charles, *A History of the Great War, 1914–1918*, 1934; new ed., London, Granta, 1982.

Ferguson, Niall, *The Pity of War*, London, Allen Lane, 1998.

Ferro, Marc, *The Great War, 1914–1918*, 1969; trans. from French, London, Routledge and Kegan Paul, 1973.

Geyer, Michael, "The Militarization of Europe, 1914–1945," in John Gillis (ed.), *The Militarization of the Western World: 1870 to the Present*, Rutgers, NJ, Rutgers University Press, 1989, pp. 65–102.

Gilbert, Martin, *The First World War: A Complete History*, New York, Henry Holt, 1996.

Horne, John (ed.), *State, Society and Mobilization in Europe during the First World War*, Cambridge, Cambridge University Press, 1997.

Howard, Michael, *The First World War*, Oxford, Oxford University Press, 2000.

Jones, Heather, Schmidt-Supprian, Christoph, and O' Brien, Jennifer (eds.), *Untold War. New Interpretations of the First World War*, Leiden, Brill, 2008.

Keegan, John, *The First World War*, London, Hutchinson, 1998.

Kramer, Alan, *Dynamic of Destruction. Culture and Mass Killing in the First World War*, Oxford, Oxford University Press, 2007.

Macleod, Jenny, and Purseigle, Pierre, *Uncovered Fields. Perspectives in First World War Studies*, Leiden and Boston, Brill, 2004.

Moran, Daniel, and Waldron, Arthur (eds.), *People in Arms: Military Myth and National Mobilization since the French Revolution*, Cambridge, Cambridge University Press, 2002.

Morrow, John, *The Great War. An Imperial History*, Abingdon, Routledge, 2004.

Neiberg, Michael, *Fighting the Great War: A Global History*, Cambridge, MA, Harvard University Press, 2005.

Neiberg, Michael (ed.), *World War I*, Aldershot, Ashgate, 2005.

Pick, Daniel, *The War Machine. The Rationalisation of Slaughter in the Modern Age*, New Haven, Yale University Press, 1993.

Prior, Robin, and Wilson, Trevor, *The First World War*, London, Cassell, 1999.

Purseigle, Pierre (ed.), *Warfare and Belligerence. Perspectives in First World War Studies*, Leiden and Boston, Brill, 2005.

Robbins, Keith, *The First World War*, 1984; new ed., Oxford, Oxford, University Press, 2002.

Saunders, Nicholas, *Killing Time: Archaeology and The First World War*, Stroud, Sutton, 2007.

Sheffield, Gary, *Forgotten Victory. The First World War: Myth and Realities*, 2001; new ed., London, Review, 2002.

Stevenson, David, *Cataclysm. The First World War as Political Tragedy*, New York, Basic Books, 2004.

Stone, Norman, *World War One: A Short History*, London, AllenLane, 2007.

Strachan, Hew, *The First World War*, vol. 1, *To Arms*, Oxford, Oxford University Press, 2001.

Strachan, Hew, *The First World War: A New Illustrated History*, London, Simon and Schuster, 2003.

Strachan, Hew (ed.), *The Oxford Illustrated History of the First World War*, Oxford, Oxford University Press, 1998.

Taylor, Alan (A.J.P.), *The First World War: An Illustrated History*, London, Hamilton, 1963.

Williamson, Samuel, and Pastor, Peter (eds.), *Essays on World War I. Origins and Prisoners of War*, New York, Columbia University Press, 1983.

Winter, Jay, *The Experience of World War I*, London, Macmillan, 1988.

Winter, Jay (ed.), *The Legacy of the Great War: Ninety Years On*, Columbia, University of Missouri Press, 2009.

Winter, Jay, and Baggett, Blaine, *1914–18, the Great War and the Shaping of the Twentieth Century*, London, BBC Books, 1996.

Winter, Jay, Parker, Geoffrey, and Habeck, Mary R. (eds.), *The Great War and the Twentieth Century*, New Haven, Yale University Press, 2000.

3.   Origins

Afflerbach, Holger, and Stevenson, David (eds.), *An Improbable War? The Outbreak of World War I and European Political Culture before 1914*, Oxford and New York, Berghahn, 2007.

Albertini, Luigi, *The Origins of the War of 1914*, 1952; trans. from Italian, 1952–5, 3 vols.; new ed., New York, Enigma, 2005.

Andrew, Christopher M., *Théophile Delcassé and the Making of the Entente Cordiale. A Reappraisal of French Foreign Policy 1898–1905*, London, Macmillan, 1968.

Barraclough, Geoffrey, *From Agadir to Armageddon. Anatomy of a Crisis*, London, Weidenfeld and Nicolson, 1982.

Berghahn, Volker, *Germany and the Approach of War in 1914*, 1973; 2nd ed., London, Macmillan, 1993.

Boehmeke, Manfred, Chickering, Roger, and Förster, Stig (eds.), *Anticipating Total War: the German and American Experiences, 1871–1914*, Cambridge, Cambridge University Press, 1999.

Bosworth, Richard, *Italy, the Least of the Great Powers. Italian Foreign Policy before the First World War*, Cambridge, Cambridge University Press, 1979.

Bosworth, Richard, *Italy and the Approach of the First World War*, London, Macmillan, 1983.

Bulcholz, Arden, *Moltke, Schlieffen and Prussian War Planning*, Oxford, Berg, 1991.

Carroll, Malcolm, *French Public Opinion and Foreign Affairs 1870–1914*, 1931; reprint, Hamden, CT, Archon Books, 1964.

Chickering, Roger, *We Men Who Feel Most German. A Cultural Study of the Pan-German League, 1886–1914*, London, Allen and Unwin, 1984.

Clarke, Ignatius, *The Great War with Germany, 1890–1914: Fictions and Fantasies of War-to-Come*, Liverpool, Liverpool University Press, 1997.

Coogan, John, *The End of Neutrality. The United States, Britain and Maritime Rights, 1899–1915*, Ithaca, NY, Cornell University Press, 1981.

Cooper, Sandi, *Patriotic Pacifism. Waging War on War in Europe 1815–1914*, New York, Oxford University Press, 1992.

Dedijer, Vladimir, *The Road to Sarajevo*, London, MacGibbon and Kee, 1967.

Echevarria, Antulio, *Imagining Future War: the West's Technological Revolution and Visions of War to Come, 1880–1914*, Westport, CT, Praeger, 2007.

Erickson, Edward, *Defeat in Detail. The Ottoman Army in the Balkans, 1912–1913*, Westport, CT, Praeger, 2003.

Evans, Robert, and Pogge von Strandmann, Hartmut (eds.), *The Origins of the First World War*, Oxford, Clarendon Press, 1990.

Farrar, Lancelot, *The Short War Illusion* (5. Military).

Fay, Sidney, *The Origins of the World War*, 1928; 2nd rev. ed., New York, Macmillan, 1939.

Fischer, Fritz, *War of Illusions: German Policies from 1911 to 1914*, 1969; trans. from German, London, Chatto and Windus, 1975.

French, David, *British Economic and Strategic Planning, 1905–1915*, London, Allen and Unwin, 1982.

Gatrell, Peter, *Government, Industry and Rearmament in Russia, 1900–1914: the Last Argument of Tsarism*, Cambridge, Cambridge University Press, 1994.

Geiss, Immanuel, *German Foreign Policy 1871–1914*, London, Routledge and Kegan Paul, 1976.

Geyer, Dietrich, *Russian Imperialism: the Interaction of Domestic and Foreign Policy, 1860–1914*, Leamington Spa, Berg, 1987.

Gooch, John, *The Plans of War: The General Staff and British Military Strategy c. 1900–1916*, London, Routledge and Kegan Paul, 1974.

Hall, Richard, *The Balkan Wars 1912–1913. Prelude to the First World War*, London, Routledge, 2000.

Hall, Richard, *Bulgaria's Road to the First World War*, Boulder, Eastern European Monographs, 1996.

Hamilton, Richard, and Herwig, Holger, *Decisions for War 1914–1917*, Cambridge, Cambridge University Press, 2005.

Hamilton, Richard and Herwig, Holger (eds.), *The Origins of World War I*, Cambridge, Cambridge University Press, 2003.

Hamilton, Richard, and Herwig, Holger (eds.), *War Planning, 1914*, Cambridge, Cambridge University Press, 2009.

Haupt, Georges, *Socialism and the Great War: the Collapse of the Second International*, 1965; trans. from French, Oxford: Clarendon Press, 1972.

Hayne, M. B., *The French Foreign Office and the Origins of the First World War*, Oxford, Clarendon Press, 1993.

Herrmann, David G., *The Arming of Europe and the Making of the First World War*, Princeton, Princeton University Press, 1996.

Herwig, Holger (ed.), *The Outbreak of World War I: Causes and Responsibilities*, Boston, Houghton Mifflin 1997.

Hewitson, Mark, *Germany and the Causes of the First World War*, Oxford, Berg, 2004.

Hull, Isabel, *Absolute Destruction. Military Culture and the Practices of War in Imperial Germany*, Ithaca, NY, Cornell University Press, 2005.

Joll, James, *1914: The Unspoken Assumptions*, London, Weidenfeld and Nicolson, 1968 (inaugural lecture), republished in H. W. Koch (ed.), *The Origins of the First World War*, pp. 307–28.

Joll, James, *The Second International, 1889–1914*, 1955; new ed., London, Routledge and Kegan Paul, 1974.

Joll, James, *The Origins of the First World War*, 1984; 2nd ed., London, Longman, 1992.

Keiger, John, *France and the Origins of the First World War*, London, Macmillan, 1983.

Kennan, George, *The Fateful Alliance: France, Russia and the Coming of the First World War*, New York, Pantheon, 1984.

Kennedy, Paul, *The War Plans of the Great Powers, 1880–1914*, London, Allen and Unwin, 1979.

Kennedy, Paul, *The Rise of Anglo-German Antagonism 1860–1914*, London, Allen and Unwin, 1981.

Kennedy, Paul, *The Rise and Fall of the Great Powers*, London, Unwin Hyman, 1988.

Koch, H. W. (ed.), *The Origins of the First World War*, London, Macmillan, 1972.

Krumeich, Gerd, *Armaments and Politics in France on the Eve of the First World War: The Introduction of Three-Year Conscription 1913–1914*, 1980; trans. from German, Leamington Spa, Berg, 1984.

Langhorne, Richard, *The Collapse of the Concert of Europe: International Politics, 1890–1914*, London, Macmillan, 1981.

Lieven, Dominic, *Russia and the Origins of the First World War*, London, Macmillan, 1983.

Massie, Robert, *Dreadnought: Britain, Germany and the Coming of the Great War*, London, Cape, 1992.

Miller, Steven, Lynn-Jones, Sean, and Van Evera, Stephen (eds.), *Military Strategy and the Origins of the First World War*, Princeton, Princeton University Press, 1991.

Mombauer, Annika, *Helmuth von Moltke and the Origins of the First World War*, Cambridge, Cambridge University Press, 2001.

Mombauer, Annika, *The Origins of the First World War: Controversies and Consensus*, London, Longman, 2002.

Mommsen, Wolfgang J., "The Topos of Inevitable War in Germany in the Decade before 1914," in Volker Berghahn and Martin Kitchen (eds.), *Germany in the Age of Total War*, London, Croom Helm, 1981, pp. 23–45.

Nolan, Michael, *The Inverted Mirror. Mythologizing the Enemy in France and Germany, 1898–1914*, New York and Oxford, Berghahn, 2005.

Porch, Douglas, *The March to the Marne. The French Army 1870–1914*, Cambridge, Cambridge University Press, 1981.

Ritter, Gerhard, *The Schlieffen Plan. Critique of a Myth*, 1956; trans. from German, London, Wolff, 1958.

Ritter, Gerhard, *Sword and the Sceptre. The Problem of Militarism in Germany*, 1963–68; trans. from German, London, Allen Lane, 1972–1973; vol. 1, *The Prussian Tradition 1740–1890* (1972); vol. 2, *The European Powers and the Wilhelminian Empire, 1890–1914* (1972); *The Tragedy of Statesmanship – Bethmann Hollweg as War Chancellor, 1914–1917* (1973); *The Reign of German Militarism and the Disaster of 1918* (1973).

Röhl, John, *1914: Delusion or Design?* 1971; trans. from German, London, Elek, 1973.

Rueger, Jan, *The Great Naval Game: Britain and Germany in the Age of Empire*, Cambridge, Cambridge University Press, 2007.

Schöllgen, Gregor (ed.), *Escape into War? The Foreign Policy of Imperial Germany*, New York and Oxford, Berg, 1990.

Seligmann, Matthew, *Spies in Uniform: British Naval and Military Intelligence on the Eve of the First World War*, Oxford, Oxford University Press, 2006.

Snyder, Jack, *The Ideology of the Offensive. Military Decision Making and the Disasters of 1914*, Ithaca, NY, Cornell University Press, 1984.

Steiner, Zara, and Neilson, Keith, *Britain and the Origins of the First World War*, 1977; 2nd ed., London, Macmillan, 2003.

Stevenson, David, *Armaments and the Coming of War, Europe 1904–1914*, Oxford, Clarendon Press, 1996.

Stevenson, David, *The Outbreak of the First World War: 1914 in Perspective*, Basingstoke, Macmillan, 1997.

Strachan, Hew, *European Armies and the Conduct of War*, London, Allen and Unwin, 1983.

Tombs, Robert (ed.), *Nationhood and Nationalism in France. From Boulangism to the First World War, 1889–1918*, London, HarperCollins, 1991.

Tuchman, Barbara, *The Proud Tower. A Portrait of the World before the War: 1890–1914*, 1966; new ed., New York, Ballantine, 1997.

Turner, Leonard, *The Origins of the First World War*, London, Edward Arnold, 1970.

Weber, Eugen, *The Nationalist Revival in France, 1905–1914*, Berkeley and Los Angeles, University of California Press, 1968.

Williamson, Samuel, *The Politics of Grand Strategy: Britain and France Prepare for War, 1904–1914*, Cambridge, MA, Harvard University Press, 1969.

Williamson, Samuel, *Austria-Hungary and the Origins of the First World War*, London, Macmillan, 1991.

Williamson, Samuel, *July 1914: Soldiers, Statesmen and the Coming of the Great War: A Brief Documentary History*, Boston, Bedford and St. Martin's Press, 2003.

Wilson, Keith (ed.), *Decisions for War*, London, UCL Press, 1995.

Wilson, Keith, *The Policy of the Entente: Essays on the Determinants of British Foreign Policy 1904–1914*, Cambridge, Cambridge University Press, 2009.

Zuber, Terence, *Inventing the Schlieffen Plan: German Military Planning 1871–1914*, Oxford, Oxford University Press, 2002.

4. International Relations during the War

Burk, Kathleen, *Britain, America, and the Sinews of War, 1914–18*, Boston and London, Allen and Unwin, 1985.

Farrar, Marjorie, *Conflict and Compromise: the Strategy, Politics and Diplomacy of the French Blockade, 1914–1918*, The Hague, Nijhoff, 1974.

Fischer, Fritz, *Germany's War Aims in the First World War*, 1961; trans. from German, London, Chatto and Windus, 1967.

French, David, *British Strategy and War Aims 1914–16*, London, Allen and Unwin, 1986.

French, David, *The Strategy of the Lloyd George Coalition 1916–1918*, Oxford, Oxford University Press, 1992.

Gatzke, Hans, *Germany's Drive to the West (Drang nach Westen): A Study of Germany's Western War Aims during the First World War*, 1950; new ed., Oxford, Oxford University Press, 1966.

Kirby, David, *War, Peace and Revolution: International Socialism at the Crossroads, 1914–1918*, London, Gower, 1986.

Lloyd, Ambrosius, *Wilsonian Statecraft: Theory and Practice of Liberal Internationalism during World War*, Wilmington, S. R. Books, 1991.

Mayer, Arno, *Political Origins of the New Diplomacy, 1917–1918*, New Haven, Yale University Press, 1959.

Philpott, William, *Anglo-French Relations and Strategy on the Western Front 1914–18*, London, Macmillan, 1996.

Renzi, William, *In the Shadow of the Sword. Italy's Neutrality and Entry into the Great War* (26. Italy).

Rossini, Daniele, *Woodrow Wilson and the American Myth in Italy* (26. Italy).

Rothwell, Victor, *British War Aims and Peace Diplomacy, 1914–1918*, Oxford, Oxford University Press, 1971.

Schulz, Gerhard, *Revolutions and Peace Treaties, 1917–1920*, 1967; trans. from German, London, Methuen, 1972.

Shanafelt, Gary, *The Secret Enemy: Austria-Hungary and the German Alliance, 1914–1918*, Boulder, CO, Eastern European Monographs, 1985.

Speed, Richard, *Prisoners, Diplomats and the Great War: A Study in the Diplomacy of Captivity*, New York and London, Greenwood, 1990.

Stevenson, David, *French War Aims against Germany, 1914–1919*, Oxford, Clarendon Press, 1982.

Stevenson, David, *The First World War and International Politics*, Oxford, Oxford University Press, 1988.

Trachtenberg, Marc, *Reparation in World Politics: France and European Economic Diplomacy, 1916–1923*, New York, Columbia University Press, 1980.

Trumpener, Ulrich, *Germany and the Ottoman Empire, 1914–1918*, Princeton, Princeton University Press, 1968.

Wade, Rex, *The Russian Search for Peace, February to October 1917*, Stanford, Stanford University Press, 1969.

Weber, Frank, *Eagles on the Crescent: Germany, Austria-Hungary and the Turkish Alliance, 1914–1918*, Ithaca, NY, Cornell University Press, 1970.

Wheeler-Bennett, John W., *Brest-Litovsk: The Forgotten Peace, March 1918*, London, Macmillan, 1938; new ed., 1963.

Zeman, Zbynek, *A Diplomatic History of the First World War*, London, Weidenfeld and Nicolson, 1971.

5. The Military and Naval War

Anderson, Ross, *The Forgotten Front: the East African campaign 1914–1918*, Stroud, Tempus, 2004.

Asprey, Robert, *The First Battle of the Marne*, London, Weidenfeld and Nicolson, 1962.

Asprey, Robert, *The German High Command at War: Hindenburg and Ludendorff and the First World War*, New York, Morrow, 1991.

Babington, Anthony, *For the Sake of Example. Capital Courts-Martial, 1914–1920*, London, 1983; new ed., Penguin, 2002.

Badsey, Stephen, *Doctrine and Reform in the British Cavalry 1880–1918*, Farnham, Ashgate, 2008.

Barnett, Correlli, *The Sword-Bearers: Studies in Supreme Command in the First World War*, London, 1963; new ed., Cassell, 2000.

Beckett, Ian (ed.), *1917: Beyond the Western Front*, Leiden, Brill, 2009.

Bidwell, Shelford, and Dominick, Graham, *Fire-Power: British Army Weapons and Theories of War 1904–1945*, London, Allen and Unwin, 1982.

Bond, Brian (ed.), *The First World War and British Military History*, Oxford, Clarendon Press, 1991.

Bruce, Robert B., *A Fraternity of Arms: America and France in the Great War*, Lawrence, University of Kansas Press, 2003.

Cassar, George, *The French and the Dardanelles. A Study of the Failure in the Conduct of War*, London, Allen and Unwin, 1971.

Cassar, George, *The Forgotten Front. The British Campaign in Italy, 1917–1918*, London, Hambledon, 1998.

Clayton, Anthony, *Paths of Glory. The French Army 1914–1918*, London, Cassell, 2003.

Collyer, J. J., *The Campaign in German South West Africa 1914–1915*, 1937; repr. London and Nashville, The Battery Press, 1997.

Cooper, Malcolm, *The Birth of Independent Airpower: British Air Policy in the First World War*, London, Unwin Hyman, 1986.

Deist, Wilhelm (ed.), *The German Military in the Age of Total War*, Leamington Spa, Berg, 1985.

Doughty, Robert, *Pyrrhic Victory. French Strategy and Operations in the Great War*, Cambridge, MA, Harvard University Press, 2005.

Dowling, Timothy, *The Brusilov Offensive*, Bloomington, Indiana University Press, 2008.

Ellis, John, *The Social History of the Machine Gun*, London, 1976; new ed., Pimlico, 1993.

Erickson, Edward, *Ordered to Die: A History of the Ottoman Army in the First World War*, Westport, CT, Greenwood, 2000.

Erickson, Edward, *Ottoman Army Effectiveness in World War One: A Comparative Study*, London, Routledge, 2007.

Farrar, Lancelot, *The Short-War Illusion: German Policy, Strategy and Domestic Affairs. August–December 1914*, Santa Barbara, CA, ABC–Clio, 1973.

Fewster, Kevin, Basarin, Vecihi, and Basarin, Hatice, *Gallipoli: the Turkish Story*, London, Allen and Unwin, 2003.

Foley, Robert, *German Strategy and the Path to Verdun. Erich von Falkenhayn and the Development of the War of Attrition, 1870–1916*, Cambridge, Cambridge University Press, 2005.

Geyer, Michael, "Insurrectionary Warfare: the German Debate about a Levée en Masse in October 1918," *Journal of Modern History*, 73, 2001, pp. 459–527.

Golovnin, Nicholas, *The Russian Army in the World War*, New Haven, Yale University Press, 1931.

Gooch, John, *The Plans of War: The General Staff and British Military Strategy* (3.Origins).

Greenhalgh, Elizabeth, *Victory through Coalition. Politics, Command and Supply in Britain and France, 1914–1918*, Cambridge, Cambridge University Press, 2005.

Griffith, Paddy, *Battle Tactics on the Western Front: the British Army's Art of Attack, 1916–1918*, London and New Haven, Yale University Press, 1994.

Gudmundsson, Bruce, *Stormtroop Tactics: Innovation in the German Army, 1914–1918*, London, Praeger, 1989.

Haber, L. F., *The Poisonous Cloud. Chemical Warfare in the First World War*, Oxford, Clarendon Press, 1986.

Halpern, Paul, *The Naval War in the Mediterranean, 1914–1918*, London, Allen and Unwin, 1987.

Halpern, Paul, *A Naval History of World War I*, London, UCL Press, 1994.

Hankey, Maurice, *The Supreme Command 1914–1918*, 2 vols., London, Allen and Unwin, 1961.

Harris, J. P., *Douglas Haig and the First World War*, Cambridge, Cambridge University Press, 2008.

Herwig, Holger, *"Luxury Fleet": The Imperial German Navy 1888–1918*, London and Atlantic Highlands, NJ, Ashfield Press, 1987.

Herwig, Holger, *The First World War. Germany and Austria-Hungary, 1914–1918*, London, Arnold, 1997.

Herwig, Holger, *The Marne, 1914. The Opening of World War I and the Battle that Changed the World*, New York, Random House, 2009.

Hirschfeld, Gerhard, Krumeich, Gerd, and Renz, Irina (eds.), *Scorched Earth. The Germans on the Somme 1914–18*, 2006; translation from German, Barnsley, Pen and Sword, 2009.

Horne, Alistair, *The Price of Glory. Verdun 1916*, London, Penguin, 1962.

Hough, Richard, *The Great War at Sea: 1914–1918*, Oxford, Oxford University Press, 1983.

Hull, Isabel, *Absolute Destruction* (3. Origins).

Jeffery, Keith, *Field Marshal Sir Henry Wilson. A Political Soldier*, Oxford, Oxford University Press, 2008.

Keegan, John, *Opening Moves: August 1914*, London, Pan, 1971.

Kennett, Lee, *The First Air War, 1914–1918*, New York, Free Press, 1991.

King, Jere Clemens, *Generals and Politicians. Conflict between France's High Command, Parliament and Government* (22. France).

Kitchen, Martin, *The German Offensives 1918*, Stroud, Tempus, 2001.

Kitchen, Martin, *The Silent Dictatorship* (23. Germany).

Liddell Hart, Basil, *History of the First World War*, London, Pan, 1972. Originally *The Real War 1914–1918* (1930); enlarged as *A History of the World War* (1934).

Lupfer, Timothy, *The Dynamics of Doctrine: the Changes in German Tactical Doctrine during the First World War*, Fort Leavenworth, KA, Paper no. 4, 1981.

Macleod, Jenny, *Reconsidering Gallipoli*, Manchester, Manchester University Press, 2004.

Marder, Arthur, *From the Dreadnought to Scapa Flow: The Royal Navy in the Fisher Era, 1904–1919*, 5 vols., London, Oxford University Press, 1961–1970.

Middlebrook, Martin, *The First Day of the Somme, 1 July 1916*, London, Allen Lane, 1971.

Middlebrook, Martin, *The Kaiser's Battle*, London, Allen Lane, 1978.

Neiberg, Michael, *The Second Battle of the Marne*, Bloomington, Indiana University Press, 2008.

Millet, Allan, and Williamson, Murray, *Military Effectiveness*, vol. 1, *The First World War*, London, Unwin Hyman, 1988.

Morrow, John, *German Airpower in World War I*, Lincoln, Nebraska, University of Nebraska Press, 1982.

Morrow, John, *The Great War in the Air: Military Aviation from 1909 to 1921*, Washington DC, Smithsonian Institution Press, 1993.

Morselli, Mario, *Caporetto 1917: Victory or Defeat?*, London, Cassell, 2001.

Neilson, Keith, *Strategy and Supply: the Anglo-Russian Alliance, 1914–1917*, London, Allen and Unwin, 1984.

Paice, Edward, *Tip and Run: The Untold Tragedy of the Great War in Africa*, London, Weidenfeld and Nicolson, 2007.

Palazzo, Alberto, *Seeking Victory on the Western Front. The British Army and Chemical Warfare in World War I*, Lincoln, Nebraska, University of Nebraska Press, 2000.

Philpott, William, *Bloody Victory: The Sacrifice on the Somme and the Making of the Twentieth Century*, New York, Little John, 2009.

Porch, Douglas, *The March to the Marne: The French Army 1871–1914* (3. Origins).

Prior, Robin, and Wilson, Trevor, *Command on the Western Front. The Military Career of Sir Henry Rawlinson 1914–18*, Oxford, Blackwell, 1992.

Prior, Robin, and Wilson, Trevor, *Passchendaele. The Untold Story*, New Haven, Yale University Press, 1996.

Prior, Robin, and Wilson, Trevor, *The Somme*, New Haven, Yale University Press, 2005.

Ritter, Gerhard, *The Schlieffen Plan* (3. Origins).

Rothenberg, Gunther, "The Austro-Hungarian Campaign Against Serbia in 1914," *Journal of Military History*, 53, 1989, pp. 127–46.

Rudenno, Victor, *Gallipoli. Attack from the Sea*, New Haven, Yale University Press, 2008.

Sheffield, Gary, *The Somme*, 2001; new ed., London, Cassell, 2003.

Sheffield, Gary, and Todman, Dan (eds.), *Command and Control on the Western Front: the British Army's Experience 1914–1918*, Stroud, History Press, 2007.

Showalter, Dennis, *Tannenberg. Clash of Empires*, Hamden, CT, Archon Books, 1991.

Smythe, Donald, *Pershing: General of the Armies*, Bloomington, Indiana University Press, 1986.

Snyder, Jack, *The Ideology of the Offensive: Military Decision Making and the Disasters of 1914*, Ithaca, NY, Cornell University Press, 1984.

Stone, Norman, *The Eastern Front 1914–17*, London, Hodder and Stoughton, 1975; new ed., Penguin, 1998.

Strachan, Hew, *European Armies and the Conduct of War*, London, Allen and Unwin, 1983.

Terraine, John, *The Road to Passchendaele: The Flanders Offensive of 1917: A Study in Inevitability*, 1977; new ed., London, Secker and Warburg, 1984.

Terraine, John, *Douglas Haig: The Educated Soldier*, 1963; new ed., London, Leo Cooper, 1990.

Thompson, Mark, *The White War. Life and Death on the Italian Front, 1915–1919*, London, Faber, 2008.

Townshend, Charles, *The British Campaign in Ireland, 1919–1921* (25. Ireland).

Trask, David, *Captains and Cabinets: Anglo-American Naval Relations, 1917–1918*, Columbia, MO, University of Missouri Press, 1972.

Trask, David, *The AEF and Coalition Warmaking, 1917–1918*, Lawrence, University Press of Kansas, 1993.

Travers, Tim, *The Killing Ground. The British Army, the Western Front and the Emergence of Modern Warfare, 1900–1918*, London, Unwin Hyman, 1987.

Travers, Tim, *How the War was Won: Command and Technology in the British Army on the Western Front 1917–18*, London, Routledge, 1992.

Travers, Tim, *Gallipoli, 1915*, Stroud, Tempus, 2001.

Tuchman, Barbara, *The Guns of August*, 1962; new ed., New York, Ballantine, 2004.

Whittam, John, *The Politics of the Italian Army, 1861–1918*, London, Croom Helm, 1977.

Wildman, Allan, *The End of the Russian Imperial Army*, 2 vols. (31. Russia).

Woodward, David, *Lloyd George and the Generals*, East Brunswick, NJ, Associated Press, 1983.

6. Soldiers

—— *Journal of Contemporary History*, 35/1, January 2000. Issue on "shell-shock."

Ashworth, Tony, *Trench Warfare, 1914–1918: The Live and Let Live System*, London, Macmillan, 1980.

Audoin-Rouzeau, Stéphane, *Men at War 1914–1918. National Sentiment and Trench Journalism in France during the First World War*, 1986; trans. from French, Leamington Spa: Berg, 1992.

Barham, Peter, *Forgotten Lunatics of the Great War*, New Haven and London, Yale University Press, 2004.

Beckett, Ian, and Simpson, Keith (eds.), *A Nation in Arms* (19. Britain).

Bourke, Joanna, *Dismembering the Male* (8. Gender).

Bourke, Joanna, *An Intimate History of Killing. Face-to-Face Killing in Twentieth Century Warfare*, London, Granta Books, 1999.

Cook, Tim, *At the Sharp End* (21. Canada).

Cook, Tim, *Shock Troops* (21. Canada).

Corrigan, Gordon, *Sepoys in the Trenches* (24. India).

Dallas, Golden, and Gill, Douglas, *The Unknown Army*, London, Verso, 1985.

Fogarty, Richard, *Race and War in France* (22. France).

Fuller, John G., *Troop Morale and Popular Culture in the British and Dominion Armies 1914–1918*, Oxford: Oxford University Press, 1990.

Gammage, Bill, *The Broken Years. Australian Soldiers in the Great War* (15. Australia).

Hanák, Péter, "Vox Populi: Intercepted Letters in the First World War," in Hanák, *The Garden and the Workshop. Essays on the Cultural History of Vienna and Budapest*, Princeton, Princeton University Press, 1998, pp. 179–212.

Hayes, Geoffrey et al. (eds.), *Vimy Ridge: A Canadian Reassessment* (21. Canada).

Holmes, Richard, *Tommy. The British Soldier on the Western Front*, London, HarperCollins, 2004.

Keegan, John, *The Face of Battle: A Study of Agincourt, Waterloo and the Somme*, London, Cape, 1976.

Leed, Eric, *No Man's Land: Combat and Identity in World War I*, Cambridge, Cambridge University Press, 1979.

Leese, Peter, *Shell Shock* (11. Science, technology, and medicine).

Lunn, Joe, *Memoirs of the Maelstrom. A Senegalese Oral History of the First World War* (13. Africa).

McCartney, Helen, *Citizen Soldiers* (19. Britain).

Macdonald, Lynn, *They Called it Passchendaele*, London, Macmillan, 1978.

Nasson, Bill, *Springboks on the Somme* (13. Africa).

Omissi, David (ed.), *Indian Voices of the Great War* (24. India).

Oram, Gerard, *Worthless Men: Race, Eugenics and the Death Penalty in the British Army during the First World War*, London, Francis Boutle, 1998.

Philips, Jock et al. (eds.), *The Great Adventure* (28. New Zealand).

Rachamimov, Alon, *POWs and the Great War. Captivity on the Eastern Front*, Oxford and New York, Berg, 2002.

Rothstein, Andrew, *The Soldiers' Strikes of 1919*, London, Macmillan, 1980.

Saunders, Nicholas, *Trench Art. Materialities and Memories of War*, Oxford and Providence, RI, Berg, 2003.

Sheffield, Gary, *Leadership in the Trenches: Officer-Man Relations, Morale and Discipline in the British Army in the Era of the First World War*, London, Macmillan, 2000.

Shephard, Ben, *A War of Nerves. Soldiers and Psychiatrists, 1914–1994*, London, Cape, 2001.

Smith, Leonard, *Between Mutiny and Obedience: The Case of the French Fifth Infantry Division* (22. France).

Stanley, Peter, *Men of Mont St-Quentin: Between Victory and Death*, Melbourne, Scribe, 2009.

Stephenson, Scott, *The Final Battle. Soldiers of the Western Front and the German Revolution of 1918*, Cambridge, Cambridge University Press, 2009.

Watson, Alex, *Enduring the Great War. Combat, Morale and Collapse in the German and British Armies, 1914–1918*, Cambridge, Cambridge University Press, 2008.

Wilcox, Vanda, "Discipline in the Italian Army 1915–1918," in Pierre Purseigle (ed.), *Warfare and Belligerence*, pp. 73–100 (2. General).

Winter, Denis, *Death's Men: Soldiers of the Great War*, London, Allen Lane, 1978.

7.   Gender

Abraham, Richard, "Maria L. Bochkareva and the Russian Amazons of 1917," in Linda Edmondson (ed.), *Women and Society in Russia and the Soviet Union*, Cambridge, Cambridge University Press, 1992, pp. 124–44.

Braybon, Gail, *Women Workers in the First World War* (19. Britain).

Braybon, Gail, "Winners or Losers: Women's Symbolic Role in the War Story," in Braybon (ed.), *Evidence, History and the Great War*, pp. 86–122 (2. General).

Bourke, Joanna, *Dismembering the Male: Men's Bodies, Britain and the Great War*, London, Reaktion Books, 1996.

Daniel, Ute, *The War From Within: German Working-class Women* (23. Germany).

Darrow, Margaret, *French Women and the First World War: War Stories of the Home Front*, Oxford, Berg, 2000.

Downs, Laura Lee, *Manufacturing Inequality: Gender Division in the French and British Metalworking Industries, 1914–1939*, Ithaca, NY, Cornell University Press, 1995.

Gatrell, Peter, "The Epic and the Domestic: Women and War in Russia, 1914–1917," in Braybon (ed.), *Evidence, History and the Great War*, pp. 198–215 (2. General).

Grayzel, Susan, *Women's Identities At War: Gender, Motherhood, and Politics in Britain and France during the First World War*, Chapel Hill, University of North Carolina Press, 1999.

Grayzel, Susan, *Women and the First World War*, Harlow, Longman, 2002.

Greenwald, Maurine Weiner, *Women, War and Work: The Impact of World War I on Women Workers in the United States*, Ithaca, NY, Cornell University Press, 1980.

Gullace, Nicoletta, *"The Blood of Our Sons": Men, Women, and the Renegotiation of British Citizenship During the Great War*, Basingstoke, Palgrave, 2002.

Harris, Ruth, "'The Child of the Barbarian': Rape, Race and Nationalism in France during the First World War," *Past and Present*, 141, 1993, pp. 170–206.

Hause, Steven C., and Kenney, Anne R., *Women's Suffrage and Social Politics in the Third French Republic*, Princeton, Princeton University Press, 1984.

Higonnet, Margaret et al. (eds.), *Behind the Lines: Gender and the Two World Wars*, New Haven and London, Yale University Press, 1987.

Holmes, Katie, "Day Mothers and Night Sisters: World War I Nurses and Sexuality," in Damousi and Lake (eds.), *Gender and War*, pp. 60–80 (15. Australia).

Horne, John, "Masculinity in Politics and War in the Age of Nation-States and World Wars, 1850–1950," in Stefan Dudink and Karen Hagemann (eds.), *Masculinities in Politics and War. Gendering Modern History*, London, Macmillan, 2004, pp. 22–40.

Huss, Marie-Monique, "Pronatalism and the Popular Ideology of the Child in Wartime France: the Evidence of the Picture Postcard," in Wall and Winter (eds.), *The Upheaval of War*, pp. 329–67 (8. Society).

Jensen, Kimberley, *Mobilizing Minerva: American Women and the First World War*, Urbana, University of Illinois Press, 2008.

Leneman, Leah, *In the Service of Life: The Story of Elsie Inglis and the Scottish Women's Hospitals*, Edinburgh, Mercat Press, 1994.

McDermid, Jane and Hillyar, Anna, *Midwives of the Revolution: Female Bolsheviks and Women Workers in 1917*, London, UCL Press, 1999.

McMillan, James, "The Great War and Gender Relations. The Case of French Women and the First World War Revisited," in Braybon (ed.), *Evidence, History and the Great War*, pp. 135–53 (2. General).

McMillan, James, *Housewife or Harlot. The Place of Women in French Society, 1870–1940*, Brighton, Harvester Press, 1981.

Melman, Billie (ed.), *Borderlines: Genders and Identities in War and Peace, 1870–1930*, London and New York, Routledge, 1998.

Offen, Karen, *European Feminisms, 1700–1950: A Political History*, Stanford, Stanford University Press, 2000, pp. 213–310.

Ouditt, Sharon, *Fighting Forces, Writing Women. Identity and Ideology in the First World War*, London, Routledge, 1994.

Pedersen, Susan, *Family, Dependence and the Origins of the Welfare State: Britain and France, 1914–1945*, Cambridge, Cambridge University Press, 1993.

Potter, Jane, *Boys in Khaki, Girls in Print. Women's Literary Responses to the Great War 1914–1918*, Oxford, Oxford University Press, 2008.

Robert, Jean-Louis, "Women and Work in France during the First World War," in Wall and Winter (eds.), *The Upheaval of War*, pp. 251–66 (8. Society).

Roberts, Marie-Louise, *Civilisation without Sexes: Reconstructing Gender in Postwar France, 1917–1927*, Chicago and London, University of Chicago Press, 1994.

Rupp, Leila, *Worlds of Women: The Making of an International Women's Movement*, Princeton, NJ, Princeton University Press, 1997.

Scates, Bruce, and Frances, Raelene, *Women and the Great War*, Cambridge, Cambridge University Press, 1997.

Schulte, Regina, "The Sick Warrior's Sister: Nursing during the First World War," in Lynn Abrams and Elizabeth Harvey (eds.), *Gender Relations in German History: Power, Agency and Experience from the Sixteenth to the Twentieth Century*, Durham, NC, Duke University Press, 1997, pp.121–41.

Showalter, Elaine, "Rivers and Sassoon: The Inscription of Male Gender Anxieties," in Higonnet (ed.), *Behind the Lines*, pp. 61–9.

Sluga, Glenda, "Masculinities, Nations, and the New World Order: Peacemaking and Nationality in Britain, France, and the United States after the First World War," in Dudink and Hagemann, *Masculinities in Politics and War*, pp. 238–56.

Smith, Angela, *Suffrage Discourse in Britain during the First World War*, Aldershot, Ashgate, 2005.

Smith, Paul, *Feminism and the Third Republic: Women's Civil and Political Rights in France, 1918–1945*, Oxford, Oxford University Press, 1996.

Stockdale, Melissa K. "'My Death for the Motherland Is Happiness': Women, Patriotism, and Soldiering in Russia's Great War" (31. Russia).

Thébaud, Françoise, "The Great War and the Triumph of Sexual Division," in Thébaud (ed.), *A History of Women in the West*, vol. 5, *Toward a Cultural Identity in the Twentieth Century*, 1991; trans. from French, Cambridge, MA, Harvard University Press, 1994, pp. 21–75.

Theweleit, Klaus, *Male Fantasies* (35. Legacy).

Thom, Deborah, *Nice Girls and Rude Girls: Women Workers in World War I*, London, I. B. Tauris, 2000.

Vellacott, Jo, *Pacifists, Patriots and the Vote. The Erosion of Democratic Suffragism in Britain during the First World War* (19. Britain).

Wheelwright, Julie, *The Fatal Lover: Mata Hari and the Myth of Women in Espionage*, London, Collins and Brown, 1992.

Woollacott, Angela, *On Her Their Lives Depend: Munitions Workers in the Great War*, Berkeley and Los Angeles, University of California Press, 1994.

Zeiger, Susan, *In Uncle Sam's Service: Women Workers with the American Expeditionary Force, 1917–1919*, Ithaca, NY, Cornell University Press, 1999.

8. Society

Coetzee, Frans, and Shevin-Coetzee, Marilyn (eds.), *Authority, Identity and the Social History of the Great War*, Oxford, Berghahn, 1995.

Dunn, Seamus, and Fraser, Thomas, G. (eds.), *Europe and Ethnicity. World War I and Contemporary Ethnic Conflict*, London, Routledge, 1996.

Grayzel, Susan, *Women's Identities at War* (7.Gender).

Haimson, Leopold, and Sapelli, Giulio (eds.), *Strikes, Social Conflict and the First World War*, Milan, Feltrinelli, 1992.

Horne, John, *Labour at War. France and Britain, 1914–1918*, Oxford, Clarendon Press, 1991.

Horne, John, "Social Identity in War: France, 1914–1918," in Thomas G. Fraser and Keith Jeffery (eds.), *Men, Women and War*, Dublin, Lilliput Press, 1992, pp. 119–35.

Offer, Avner, *The First World War. An Agrarian Interpretation* (9. Economy).

Panayi, Panikos (ed.), *Minorities in Wartime. National and Racial Groupings in Europe, North America and Australia in the Two World Wars*, Oxford, Berg, 1992.

Stibbe, Matthew, and Oltmer, Jochen (eds.), *Captivity, Forced Labour and Forced Migration in Europe during the First World War*, London, Routledge, 2009.

Wall, Richard, and Winter, Jay (eds.), *The Upheaval of War. Family, Work and Welfare in Europe, 1914–1918*, Cambridge, Cambridge University Press, 1988.

Winter, Jay, and Robert, Jean-Louis (eds.), *Capital Cities at War. Paris, London, Berlin 1914–1919*, Cambridge, Cambridge University Press, 1997.

Winter, Jay, and Robert, Jean-Louis (eds.), *Capital Cities at War*, vol. 2 (10. Culture).

Wrigley, Chris (ed.), *Challenges of Labour: Central and Western Europe, 1917–1920*, London, Routledge, 1993.

9. Economy

Bell, Archibald, *A History of the Blockade of Germany and of the Countries Associated with her in the Great War, Austria, Bulgaria and Turkey, 1914–1918*, London, HMSO, 1937.

Beveridge, William, *British Food Control*, London, Oxford University Press, 1928.

Broadberry, Stephen, and Mark Harrison (eds.), *The Economics of World War I*, Cambridge, Cambridge University Press, 2005.

Burk, Kathleen, *Britain, America and the Sinews of War* (4. International Relations).

Feldman, Gerald, *Army, Industry and Labor in Germany* (23. Germany).

Feldman, Gerald, *The Great Disorder: Economics, Politics and Society in the German Inflation* (23. Germany).

Feldman, Gerald, "Mobilizing Economies for War," in Winter et al. (eds.), *The Great War and the Twentieth Century*, pp. 166–86 (2. General).

Ferguson, Niall, *The Pity of War*, (2. General). Chs. 5, 9, 11, and 14.

Fridenson, Patrick (ed.), *The French Home Front* (22.France). Chs. 3, 4, 5 and 6.

Gide, Charles (ed.), *Effects of the War upon French Economic Life* (22. France).

Godfrey, John, *Capitalism at War* (22. France).

Hardach, Gerd, *The First World War 1914–1918*, 1973; trans. from German, London, Allen Lane, 1977.

Holtfrerich, Carl-Ludwig, *The German Inflation 1914–1923. Causes and Effects in International Perspective*, 1980; trans. from German, Berlin, De Gruyter, 1986.

Horn, Martin, *Britain, France and the Financing of the First World War*, Montreal, McGill-Queen's University Press, 2002.

Lloyd, E.M.H., *Experiments in State Control at the War Office and the Ministry of Food*, Oxford, Clarendon Press, 1924.

Mouré, Kenneth, *The Gold Standard Illusion: France, the Bank of France and the International Gold Standard, 1914–1939*, Oxford, Oxford University Press, 1939.

Offer, Avner, *The First World War: An Agrarian Interpretation*, Oxford, Clarendon Press, 1989.

Osborne, Eric, *Britain's Economic Blockade of Germany 1914–1919*, London and New York, Frank Cass, 2004.

Redmayne, R. A. S., *The British Coal-Mining Industry During the War*, Oxford, Clarendon Press, 1923.

Siegelbaum, Lewis, *The Politics of Industrial Mobilization in Russia* (31. Russia).

Strachan, Hew, *Financing the First World War*, Oxford, Oxford University Press, 2004.

Trachtenberg, Marc, *Reparations in World Politics: France and European Economic Diplomacy, 1916–1923*, New York, Columbia University Press, 1980.

Vincent, Paul, *The Politics of Hunger: The Allied Blockade of Germany 1915–1919*, Athens, Ohio University Press, 1985.

Winter, Jay (ed.), *War and Economic Development*, Cambridge, Cambridge University Press, 1975.

Winter, Jay and Jean-Louis Robert, (eds.), *Capital Cities at War. Paris* (1997– 8. Society).

Wrigley, Chris (ed.), *The First World War and the International Economy*, Cheltenham, Edward Elgar, 2000.

10. Culture

Audoin-Rouzeau, Stéphane, and Becker, Annette, *14–18: Understanding the Great War* (2.General).

Becker, Annette, *War and Faith* (22. France).

Bergonzi, Bernard, *Heroes' Twilight: A Study of the Literature of the Great War*, 1965; 2nd ed., Basingstoke, Macmillan, 1980.

Bracco, Rosa Maria, *Merchants of Hope. British Middlebrow Writers and the First World War, 1919–1929*, Oxford, Berg, 1993.

Bridgewater, Patrick, *The German Poets of the First World War*, London, Croom Helm, 1985.

Buitenhuis, Peter, *The Great War of Words. British, American, and Canadian Propaganda and Fiction, 1914–1933*, Vancouver, University of British Columbia Press, 1987.

Capdevila, Luc, and Voldman, Danièle, *War Dead. Western Societies and the Casualties of War, 2002;* trans. from French, Edinburgh, Edinburgh University Press, 2006.

Cork, Richard, *A Bitter Truth. Avant-Garde Art and the Great War*, New Haven and London, Yale University Press, 1994.

Crook, Paul, *Darwinism, War and History. The Debate over the Biology of War from the "Origins of Species" to the First World War*, Cambridge, Cambridge University Press, 1994.

Das, Santanu, *Touch and Intimacy in First World War Literature*, Cambridge, Cambridge University Press, 2005.

Debauche, Leslie, *Reel Patriotism. The Movies and World War I*, Madison, University of Wisconsin Press, 1997.

Deer, Patrick, *Culture in Camouflage. War, Empire and Modern British Literature*, Oxford, Oxford University Press, 2009.

Dibbets, Karl, and Hogenkamp, Bert (eds.), *Film and the First World War*, Amsterdam, Amsterdam University Press, 1995.

Eksteins, Modris, *Rites of Spring: The Great War and the Birth of the Modern Age*, London, Bantam Press, 1989.

Field, Frank, *British and French Writers of the First World War. Comparative Studies in Cultural History*, Cambridge, Cambridge University Press, 1991.

Frantzen, Allen, *Bloody Good: Chivalry, Sacrifice and the Great War*, Chicago, University of Chicago Press, 2004.

Fussell, Paul, *The Great War and Modern Memory*, Oxford, Oxford University Press, 1975.

Goebel, Stefan, *The Great War and Medieval Memory. War, Remembrance and Medievalism in Britain and Germany, 1914–1940*, Cambridge, Cambridge University Press, 2006.

Hanna, Martha, *The Mobilization of Intellect* (22.France).

Harries, Meirion and Harries, Susie, *The War Artists: British Official War Art of the Twentieth Century*, London, Michael Joseph, 1983.

Hoover, Arlie, *God, Germany, and Britain in the Great War. A Study in Clerical Nationalism*, Westport, CT, Praeger, 1989.

Horne, John, and Kramer, Alan, *German Atrocities, 1914. A History of Denial*, London and New Haven, Yale University Press, 2001.

Hynes, Samuel, *A War Imagined. The First World War and English Culture*, London, Bodley Head, 1990.

Kahn, Elizabeth, *The Neglected Majority: "Les Camoufleurs," Art History and World War*, London, University Press of America, 1984.

Kelly, Andrew, *Cinema and the Great War*, London, Routledge, 1997.

Kern, Stephen, *The Culture of Time and Space, 1880–1918*, Cambridge, MA, Harvard University Press, 1983.

Lasswell, Harold, *Propaganda Technique in World War I*, 1927; new ed., Cambridge, MA, MIT Press, 1971.

Levitch, Mark, *Panthéon de la Grande Guerre: Reconfiguring a Panorama of the Great War*, Columbia, University of Missouri Press, 2006.

Malvern, Sue, *Modern Art, Britain and the Great War*, New Haven, Yale University Press, 2004.

Marsland, Elizabeth, *The Nation's Cause: French, English and German Poetry of the First World War*, London, Routledge, 1991.

Mommsen, Wolfgang, "German Artists, Writers and Intellectuals and the Meaning of War, 1914–1918," in Horne (ed.), *State, Society and Mobilization in Europe*, pp. 21–38 (2. General).

Mosse, George, *Fallen Soldiers* (34. Legacy).

Paddock, Troy R. E., *A Call to Arms. Propaganda, Public Opinion and Newspapers in the Great War*, London and Westport, CT, Praeger, 2004.

Paris, Michael, *Over the Top: The Great War and Juvenile Literature in Britain* (19. Britain).

Paris, Michael (ed.), *The First World War and Popular Cinema: 1914 to the Present*, Edinburgh, Edinburgh University Press, 1999.

Pogge von Strandmann, Hartmut, "The Role of British and German Historians in Mobilizing Public Opinion in 1914," in Benedikt Stuchtey and Peter Wende (eds.), *British and German Historiography, 1750–1950. Trends, Perceptions, Transfers*, Oxford, Oxford University Press, 2000, pp. 335–71.

Prior, Robin, *Churchill's "World Crisis" as History*, London, Croom Helm, 1983.

Roshwald, Aviel, and Stites, Richard (eds.), *European Culture in the Great War. The Arts, Entertainment, and Propaganda, 1914–1918*, Cambridge, Cambridge University Press, 1999.

Saunders, Nicholas (ed.), *Matters of Conflict. Material Culture, Memory and the First World War*, London, Routledge, 2004.

Schweitzer, Richard, *The Cross and the Trenches. Religious Faith and Doubt among the British and American Great War Soldiers*, Westport, CT, Praeger, 2003.

Sherry, Vincent, *The Cambridge Companion to the Literature of the First World War*, Cambridge, Cambridge University Press, 2005.

Sherry, Vincent, *The Great War and the Language of Modernism*, Oxford, Oxford University Press, 2003.

Silver, Kenneth, *Esprit de Corps. The Art of the Parisian Avant-Garde and the First World War, 1914–1925*, Princeton, Princeton University Press, 1989.

Stromberg, Roland, *Redemption by War. The Intellectuals and 1914*, Lawrence, Regents' Press of Kansas, 1982.

Tate, Trudi, *Modernism, Literature and the First World War*, Manchester, Manchester University Press, 1998.

Wallace, Stuart, *War and the Image of Germany: British Academics* (19. Britain).

Watkins, Glenn, *Proof through the Night: Music and the Great War*, Berkeley, University of California Press, 2003.

Weber, Thomas, *Our Friend "The Enemy": Elite Education in Britain and Germany before World War I*, Stanford, Stanford University Press, 2007.

Wilson, Keith (ed.), *Forging the Collective Memory. Government and International Historians through Two World Wars*, Providence, Berghahn, 1996.

Winter, Jay, "Propaganda and the Mobilization of Consent" in Hew Strachan (ed.), *The Illustrated History of the First World War*, Oxford, Oxford University Press, 1998, pp. 216–26.

Winter, Jay, *Sites of Memory, Sites of Mourning. The Great War in European Cultural History*, Cambridge, Cambridge University Press, 1995.

Winter, Jay, *Remembering War* (34. Legacy).

Winter, Jay and Robert, Jean-Louis (eds.), *Capital Cities at War. Paris, London, Berlin, 1914–1919*, vol. 2, *A Cultural History*, Cambridge University Press, 2007.

Wohl, Robert, *The Generation of 1914*, London, Weidenfeld and Nicolson, 1980.

11. Science, Technology, and Medicine

Bergen, Leo van, *Before My Helpless Sight: Suffering, Dying and Military Medicine on the Western Front, 1914–1918*, Farnham, Ashgate, 2009.

Haber, Ludwig, *The Poisonous Cloud: Chemical Warfare in the First World War* (5. Military).

Hartcup, Guy, *The War of Invention. Scientific Developments, 1914–18*, London, Brassey's, 1988.

Johnson, Jeffrey Allan, *The Kaiser's Chemists. Science and Modernization in Imperial Germany*, Chapel Hill and London, University of North Carolina Press, 1990.

Leese, Peter, *Shell Shock: Traumatic Neurosis and the British Soldiers of the First World War*, Basingstoke, Palgrave Macmillan, 2002.

Lerner, Paul, *Hysterical Men. War, Psychiatry and the Politics of Trauma in Germany, 1890–1930*, Ithaca, NY, Cornell University Press, 2003.

MacLeod, Roy, "The Chemists go to War: The Mobilization of Civilian Chemists and the British War Effort, 1914–1918," *Annals of Science*, 50, 1983, pp. 455–81.

Morrell, Jack, *Science at Oxford 1914–1939*, Oxford, Clarendon Press, 1997.

Pattison, Mark, "Scientists, Inventors and the Military in Britain, 1915–1919: the Munitions Inventions Department," *Social Studies of Science*, 12/4, 1983, pp. 521–68.

Whitehead, Ian, *Doctors in the Great War*, London, Leo Cooper, 1999.

Weindling, Paul, *Epidemics and Genocide in Eastern Europe 1890–1945*, Oxford, Oxford University Press, 2000.

12.   Politics (see also individual states, below)

Carsten, Francis, *War against War: British and German Radical Movements in the First World War*, London, Batsford, 1982.

Deutscher, Isaac, *The Prophet Armed: Trotsky, 1879–1921*, London, Oxford University Press, 1954; new ed., London, Verso, 2003.

Fainsod, Merle, *International Socialism and the World War*, Cambridge, MA, Harvard University Press, 1935.

Haupt, Georges, *Socialism and the Great War* (3. Origins).

Horne, John, "Labor and Labor Movements in World War I," in Winter et al. (eds.), *The Great War and the Twentieth Century*, pp. 187–227 (2. General).

Kitchen, Martin, *The Silent Dictatorship. The Politics of the German High Command* (23. Germany).

Kirby, David, *War, Peace and Revolution: International Socialism at the Crossroads, 1914–1918*, Aldershot, Gower, 1986.

Nettl, Peter, *Rosa Luxemburg*, London, Oxford University Press, 1966.

Roshwald, Aviel, *Ethnic Nationalism and the Fall of Empires: Central Europe, Russia and the Middle East, 1914–1923*, London, Routledge, 2001.

Schulz, Gerhard, *Revolutions and Peace Treaties* (4. International Relations).

Wrigley, Chris (ed.), *Challenges of Labour* (8. Society).

13.   Africa

Anderson, Ross, *The Forgotten Front: the East African campaign 1914–1918*, Stroud, Tempus, 2004.

Balesi, Charles, *From Adversaries to Comrades-in-Arms: West Africa and the French Military, 1885–1919*, Waltham, MA, Crossroads Press, 1999.

Conklin, Alice, *A Mission to Civilize: the Republican Idea of Empire in France and West Africa, 1895–1930*, Stanford, Stanford University Press, 1997.

Echenberg, Myron, *Colonial Conscripts. The Tirailleurs Sénégalais in French West Africa, 1857–1960*, London, Currey, 1991.

Fogarty, Richard S, *Race and War in France* (22. France).

Hodges, Geoffrey, *The Carrier Corps. Military Labor in the East African Campaign, 1914–1918*, Westport, CT, Greenwood Press, 1986.

Lunn, Joe, *Memoirs of the Maelstrom: A Senegalese Oral History of the First World War*, Oxford, James Currey, 1999.

Miller, Charles, *Battle for the Bundu. The First World War in East Africa*, London, Macdonald and James, 1974.

Nasson, Bill, *Springboks on the Somme. South Africa in the Great War*, Johannesburg, Penguin, 2007.

Page, Melvin (ed.), *Africa and the First World War*, Basingstoke, Macmillan, 1987.

Page, Melvin, *The Chiwaya War: Malawians and the First World War*, Boulder, Westview Press, 2000.

Paice, Edward, *Tip and Run. The Untold Tragedy of the Great War in Africa*, London, Weidenfeld and Nicolson, 2007.

Samson, Anne, Britain, *South Africa and the East African Campaign: The Union Comes of Age, 1914–1918*, London, I.B. Tauris, 2005.

Stapleton, Timothy, *No Insignificant Part. The Rhodesia Native Regiment and the East African Campaign of the First World War*, Waterloo, Ont., Wilfrid Laurier University Press, 2006.

Strachan, Hew, *The First World War in Africa*, Oxford, Oxford University Press, 2004.

14.   Asia (see also India)

Dickinson, Frederick, *War and National Reinvention. Japan in the Great War, 1914–1919*, Cambridge, MA, Harvard University Press, 1999.

Dijk, Kees van, *The Netherlands Indies and the Great War, 1914–1918*, Leiden, KITLV Press, 2007.

Guoqui, Xu, *China and the Great War. China's Pursuit of a New National Identity and Internationalization*, Cambridge, Cambridge University Press, 2005.

15.   Australia

Andrews, Eric, *The Anzac Illusion: Anglo-Australian Relations during World War I*, Cambridge, Cambridge University Press, 1993.

Bean, Charles E. W., *The Official History of Australia in the War of 1914–1918*, 5 vols., Sydney, Angus and Robertson, 1921–1942.

Bean, Charles E. W., *The Story of Anzac*, Sydney, Angus and Robertson, 1934.

Damousi, Joy, and Lake, Marilyn (eds.), *Gender and War: Australians at War in the Twentieth Century*, Cambridge, Cambridge University Press, 1995.

Gammage, Bill, *The Broken Years: Australian Soldiers in the Great War*, 1974; new ed., Melbourne: Penguin, 1975.

Inglis, Ken S., *Sacred Places* (34. Legacy).

Lake, Marilyn, *A Divided Society. Tasmania during World War I*, Melbourne, Melbourne University Press, 1975.

Macleod, Jenny, *Reconsidering Gallipoli* (5. Military).

McKernan, Michael, *The Australian People and the Great War*, Sydney, Collins, 1980; new ed., 1984.

Serle, Geoffrey, *John Monash. A Biography*, Melbourne, Melbourne University Press, 1982.

Stanley, Peter, *Men of Mont Quentin: Between Victory and Death* (6. Soldiers).

Thomson, Alistair, *Anzac Memories. Living with the Legend*, Melbourne, Oxford University Press, 1994.

16.   Austria-Hungary

Beller, Steven, "The Tragic Carnival: Austrian Culture in the First World War," in Aviel Roshwald and Richard Stites (eds.), *European Culture in the Great War* (10. Culture).

Cornwall, Mark (ed.), *The Last Years of Austria-Hungary: A Multi-national Experiment in Early Twentieth Century Europe*, Exeter, University of Exeter Press, 2002 (expanded version of 1992 original ed.).

Cornwall, Mark, *The Undermining of Austria-Hungary: the Battle for Hearts and Minds*, Basingstoke, Macmillan, 2000.

Deák, István, *Beyond Nationalism: A Social and Political History of the Habsburg Officer Corps, 1848–1918*, New York, Oxford University Press, 1992.

Galántai, József, *Hungary in the First World War*, 1974; trans. from Hungarian, Budapest, Akadémiai Kiadó, 1989.

Glaise-Horstenau, Edmund, *The Collapse of the Austro-Hungarian Empire*, 1929, London, Dent, 1930.

Gratz, Gustáv, and Schüller, Richard, *The Economic Policy of Austria-Hungary during the War*, New Haven, Yale University Press, 1928.

Hanák, Péter, "Vox Populi: Intercepted Letters" (6. Soldiers).

Healy, Maureen, *Vienna and the Fall of the Habsburg Empire: Total War and Everyday Life in World War I*, Cambridge, Cambridge University Press, 2004.

Herwig, Holger, *The First World War. Germany and Austria-Hungary* (5. Military).

Kann, Robert (ed.), *The Habsburg Empire in World War I: Essays on the Intellectual, Military, Political and Economic Aspects of the Habsburg War Effort*, Boulder, Eastern European Monographs, 1977.

Király, Béla, and Dreisziger, Nandor (eds.), *East Central European Society in World War I*, Boulder, Eastern European Monographs, 1985.

Pastor, Peter, *Hungary between Wilson and Lenin: the Hungarian Revolution of 1918–1919 and the Big Three*, Boulder, Colorado, Eastern European Quarterly, 1976.

Redlich, Joseph, *Austrian War Government*, New Haven, Yale University Press, 1929.

Rees, H. Louis, *The Czechs during World War I*, Boulder, Colorado, East European Monographs, 1992.

Rozenblit, Marsha, *Reconstructing a National Identity: The Jews of Habsburg Austria during World War I*, Oxford, Oxford University Press, 2001.

Roshwald, Aviel, *Ethnic Nationalism and the Fall of Empires* (12. Politics).

Rothenberg, Gunther, *The Army of Francis-Joseph*, West Lafayette, Indiana, Purdue University Press, 1976.

Shanafelt, Gary, *The Secret Enemy: Austria-Hungary and the German Alliance* (4. International Relations).

Valiani, Leo, *The End of Austria-Hungary*, 1966: trans. from Italian, London, Secker and Warburg, 1973.

Zeman, Zbynek, *The Break-Up of the Habsburg Empire 1914–1918. A Study in National and Social Revolution*, London, Oxford University Press, 1961.

17.   The Balkans and Eastern Europe

Banac, Ivo, *The National Question in Yugoslavia. Origins, History, Politics*, Ithaca, NY and London, Cornell University Press, 1984.

Bucur, Maria, "Romania: War, Occupation, Liberation," in Roshwald and Stites (eds.), *European Culture in the Great War*, pp. 243–66 (10. Culture).

Eglezou, Georgia, *The Greek Media in World War I and its Aftermath: The Athenian Press and the Asia Minor Crisis*, London, I.B. Tauris, 2009.

Hall, Richard C., *The Balkan Wars, 1912–1913* (3. Origins).

Held, Joseph, "Culture in Hungary during World War I," in Roshwald and Stites (eds.), *European Culture in the Great War*, pp. 176–92 (10. Culture).

Kelbetcheva, Evelina, "Between Apology and Denial: Bulgarian Culture during World War I," in Roshwald and Stites (eds.), *European Culture in the Great War*, pp. 215–42 (10. Culture).

Király, Bela and Dreisziger, Nandor (eds.), *East Central European Society* (16. Austria-Hungary).

Leontaritis, George, *Greece and the First World War: From Neutrality to Intervention, 1917–1918*, Boulder, Eastern European Monographs, 1990.

Levene, Mark, "Frontiers of Genocide: Jews in the Eastern War Zones, 1914–1920 and 1941," in Panayi (ed.), *Minorities in Wartime*, pp. 83–117 (8. Society).

Liulevicius, Vejas, *War Land on the Eastern Front. Culture, National Identity and German Occupation in World War I*, Cambridge, Cambridge University Press, 2000.

Mitrovic, Andrej, *Serbia's Great War, 1914–1918*, London, Hurst, 2007.

Nolte, Claire, "Ambivalent Patriots: Czech Culture in the Great War," in Roshwald and Stites, (eds.), *European Culture in the Great War*, pp. 162–75 (10. Culture).

Rechter, David, *The Jews of Vienna and the First World War*, London, Littman Library of Jewish Civilization, 2001.

Roshwald, Aviel, *Ethnic Nationalism and the Fall of Empires* (12. Politics).

Roshwald, Aviel, "Jewish Cultural Identity in Eastern and Central Europe during the Great War," in Roshwald and Stites (eds.), *European Culture in the Great War*, pp. 89–126 (10. Culture).

Siegel, Harold, "Culture in Poland during World War I," in Roshwald and Stites (eds.), *European Culture in the Great War*, pp. 58–88 (10. Culture).

Stone, Norman, *The Eastern Front, 1914–1917* (5. Military).

Sukiennicki, Wiktor, *East Central Europe during World War I: From Foreign Domination to National Independence*, Boulder, Colorado, Eastern European Monographs, 1984.

Torrey, Glen, *Romania and World War I*, Portland, Center for Romanian Studies, 1995.

Wachtel, Andrew, "Culture in the South Slavic Lands, 1914–1918," in Roshwald and Stites (eds.), *European Culture in the Great War*, pp. 193–214 (10. Culture).

18. Belgium

De Schaepdrijver, Sophie, "Occupation, Propaganda, and the Idea of Belgium," in Roshwald and Stites (eds.), *European Culture in the Great War,* pp. 267–94 (10. Culture).

Horne, John and Kramer, Alan, *German Atrocities, 1914* (10. Culture).

Marks, Sally, *Innocent Abroad. Belgium at the Paris Peace Conference of 1919*, Chapel Hill, University of North Carolina Press, 1981.

Proctor, Tammy, *Female Intelligence: Women and Espionage in the First World War*, New York, New York University Press, 2003.

Scholliers, Peter, and Daelemans, Frank, "Standards of Living and Standards of Health in Wartime Belgium" in Richard Wall and Jay Winter (eds.), *The Upheaval of War* (8. Society).

Zuckerman, Larry, *The Rape of Belgium. The Untold Story of World War I*, New York and London, New York University Press, 2004.

19. Britain

Adams, R. J. Q., *Arms and the Wizard. Lloyd George and the Ministry of Munitions, 1915–1916*, London, Cassell, 1978.

Adams, R.J.Q., and Poirier, Philip, *The Conscription Controversy in Great Britain, 1900–1918*, Basingstoke, Macmillan, 1987.

Beckett, Ian and Simpson, Keith (eds.), *A Nation in Arms. A Social Study of the British Army in the First World War*, Manchester, Manchester University Press, 1985.

Bond, Brian, *The Unquiet Western Front. Britain's Role in Literature and History*, Cambridge, Cambridge University Press, 2002.

Bourne, John, *Britain and the Great War 1914–1918*, London, Edward Arnold, 1989.

Braybon, Gail, *Women Workers in the First World War: the British Experience*, London, Croom Helm, 1981.

Burk, Kathleen (ed.), *War and the State: The Transformation of British Government, 1914–1919*, London, Allen and Unwin, 1982.

Bush, Julia, *Behind the Lines. East London Labour, 1914–1919*, London, Merlin, 1984.

Ceadel, Martin, *Pacifism in Britain: 1914–1945. The Defining of a Faith*, Oxford, Clarendon Press, 1980.

Constantine, Stephen, Kirby, Maurice W., and Rose, Mary B. (eds.), *The First World War in British History*, London, Edward Arnold, 1995.

Deer, Patrick, *Culture in Camouflage. War, Empire and Modern British Literature* (10. Culture).

Fuller, John, *Troop Morale and Popular Culture* (6. Soldiers).

French, David, *The Strategy of the Lloyd George Coalition* (4. International Relations).

Gaffney, Angela, *Aftermath: Remembering the Great War in Wales*, Cardiff, Cardiff University Press, 1998.

Gregory, Adrian, *The Last Great War. British Society and the First World War*, Cambridge, Cambridge University Press, 2008.

Gregory, Adrian, *The Silence of Memory. Armistice Day, 1919–1946*, Oxford, Berg, 1994.

Grieves, Keith, *The Politics of Manpower, 1914–1918*, Manchester, Manchester University Press, 1988.

Groot, Gerard de, *Blighty. British Society in the Era of the Great War*, London, Longman, 1998.

Gullace, Nicoletta, *"The Blood of Our Sons'* (7. Gender).

Haste, Cate, *Keep the Home Fires Burning: Propaganda in the First World War* (10. Culture).

Hinton, James, *The First Shop Stewards' Movement*, London, Allen and Unwin, 1973.

Horn, Pamela, *Rural Life in England in the First World War*, Dublin, Gill and Macmillan, 1984.

Howard, Michael et al, *A Part of History. Aspects of the British Experience of the First World War*, London, Continuum, 2008.

Hynes, Samuel, *A War Imagined. The First World War and English Culture*, London, Bodley Head, 1990.

Kennedy, Thomas, *The Hound of Conscience: A History of the No-Conscription Fellowship 1914–1919*, Fayetteville, AK, University of Arkansas Press, 1981.

Liddle, Peter, (ed.), *Home Fires and Foreign Fields: British Social and Military Experience in the First World War*, London, Brassey's, 1985.

McCartney, Helen, *Citizen Soldiers. The Liverpool Territorials in the First World War*, Cambridge, Cambridge University Press, 2005.

MacDonald, Catriona and McFarland, E. W., *Scotland and the Great War*, East Linton, Tuckwell Press, 1999.

McKibbin, Ross, *The Evolution of the Labour Party, 1910–1924*, Oxford, Oxford University Press, 1974.

Marwick, Arthur, *The Deluge. British Society and the First World War*, 1965; new ed., London, Macmillan, 1991.

Messinger, Gary, *British Propaganda and the State in the First World War*, Manchester, Manchester University Press, 1992.

Millman, Brock, *Managing Domestic Dissent in the First World War*, London, Frank Cass, 2000.

Morgan, Kenneth, *Consensus and Disunity: The Lloyd George Coalition Government 1918–1922*, Oxford, Clarendon Press, 1979.

Panayi, Panikos, *The Enemy in our Midst: Germans in Britain during the First World War*, Providence and Oxford, Berg, 1991.

Pugh, Martin, *Electoral Reform in War and Peace, 1906–18*, London, Routledge and Kegan Paul. 1978.

Reeve, Nicholas, *Official British Film Propaganda during the First World War*, Croom Helm, 1986.

Reznick, Jeffrey S., *Healing the Nation. Soldiers and the Culture of Care-giving in Britain during the Great War*, Manchester, Manchester University Press, 2005.

Robb, George, *British Culture and the First World War*, Basingstoke, Palgrave, 2002.

Robbins, Keith, *The Abolition of War: The Peace Movement in Britain, 1914–1919*, Cardiff, University of Wales Press, 1976.

Sanders, Michael, and Taylor, Philip, *British Propaganda during the First World War*, London, Macmillan, 1982.

Silbey, David, *The British Working Class and Enthusiasm for War, 1914–1916*, London, Frank Cass, 2005.

Simkins, Peter, *Kitchener's Army. The Raising of the New Armies 1914–1916*, Manchester, Manchester University Press, 1988.

Suttie, Andrew, *Rewriting the First World War: Lloyd George, Politics and Strategy, 1914–1918*, Basingstoke, Palgrave Macmillan, 2005.

Swartz, Marvin, *The Union of Democratic Control in British Politics during the First World War*, Oxford, Clarendon Press, 1971.

Terraine, John, *Impacts of War 1914–1918*, London, Cooper, 1993.

Thom, Deborah, *Nice Girls and Rude Girls* (7. Gender).

Thompson, J. Lee, *Politicians, Propaganda and the Press: Lord Northcliffe and the Great War*, Kent, OH, Kent State University Press, 1999.

Todman, Dan, *The Great War. Myth and Memory*, London, Hambledon Continuum, 2005.

Turner, John (ed.), *Britain and the First World War*, London, Unwin Hyman, 1988.

Vellacott, Jo, *Pacifists, Patriots and the Vote. The Erosion of Democratic Suffragism in Britain during the First World War*, Basingstoke, Macmillan, 2007.

Waites, Bernard, *A Class Society at War. England 1914–1918*, Leamington Spa, Berg, 1987.

Wallace, Stuart, *War and the Image of Germany: British Academics 1914–1918*, Edinburgh, Donald, 1988.

Watson, Janet, *Fighting Different Wars. Experience, Memory and the First World War in Britain*, Cambridge, Cambridge University Press, 2004.

Wilkinson, Alan, *The Church of England and the First World War*, 1978; new ed., London, SCM Press, 1996.

Wilson, Trevor, *The Myriad Faces of War. Britain and the Great War 1914–1918*, Cambridge, Polity Press, 1986.

Winkler, Henry, *The League of Nations Movement in Great Britain, 1914–1918*, New Brunswick, Rutgers University Press, 1952.

Winter, Jay, *The Great War and the British People*, London, Macmillan, 1986.

Winter, Jay, *Socialism and the Challenge of War. Ideas and Politics in Britain, 1912–1918*, London, Routledge and Kegan Paul, 1974.

Woollacott, Angela, *On Her Their Lives Depend. Munitions Workers* (7. Gender).

20. The British Empire (see also Australia, Canada, India, and New Zealand)

Brown, Judith, and Louis, William Roger (eds.), *The Twentieth Century*, vol. 5 of William Roger Louis (ed.), *The Oxford History of the British Empire*, 5 vols., Oxford, Oxford University Press, 1998–1999. Esp. chs. by Robert Holland, John Darwin, and Judith Brown.

Darwin, John, *Britain, Egypt and the Middle East: Imperial Policy in the Aftermath of War, 1918–1922*, London, Macmillan, 1981.

Fromkin, David, *A Peace to End All Peace. Creating the Modern Middle East* (29. Ottoman Empire).

Jeffery, Keith, *The British Army and the Crisis of Empire, 1918–1922*, Manchester, Manchester University Press, 1984.

Manela, Erez, *The Wilsonian Moment. Self-Determination and the International Origins of Anti-Colonialism* (34. Peacemaking).

Perry, F. W., *The Commonwealth Armies. Manpower and Organization in Two World Wars*, Manchester, Manchester University Press, 1988.

21. Canada

Cook, Tim, *At the Sharp End: Canadians Fighting the Great War, 1914 to 1916*, Toronto, Viking, 2007.

Cook, Tim, *Shock Troops: Canadians Fighting the Great War, 1917–1918*, Toronto, Viking, 2008.

Hayes, Geoffrey, Iarocci, Andrew, and Bechthold, Mike (eds.), *Vimy Ridge: A Canadian Reassessment*, Waterloo, Ont., Wilfrid Laurier University Press, 2007.

Morton, Desmond, and Granatstein, J. L., *Marching to Armageddon: Canadians and the Great War, 1914–19*, Toronto, Lester and Orpen Dennys, 1989.

Morton, Desmond, and Wright, Glenn, *Winning the Second Battle: Canadian Veterans and the Return to Civilian Life, 1915–1930*, Toronto, University of Toronto Press, 1987.

Vance, Jonathan, *Death So Noble: Memory, Meaning and the First World War*, Vancouver, University of British Columbia Press, 1997.

22.   France

Andrew, Christopher, and Kanya-Forstner, A. S., *France Overseas: The Great War and the Climax of French Imperial Expansion*, London, Thames and Hudson, 1981.

Audoin-Rouzeau, Stéphane. *Men at War* (6. Soldiers).

Augé-Laribé, M., and Pinot, P., *Agriculture and Food Supply in France during the War*, New Haven, Yale University Press, 1927.

Becker, Annette, *War and Faith: The Religious Imagination in France, 1914–1930*, 1994; trans. from French, Oxford, Berg, 1998.

Becker, Jean-Jacques, *The Great War and the French People*, 1980; trans. from French, Berg, Leamington Spa, 1986.

Challener, Richard, *The French Theory of the Nation in Arms, 1866–1939*, New York, Columbia University Press, 1955.

Clayton, Anthony, *Paths of Glory* (5. Military).

Cruickshank, John, *Variations on Catastrophe: Some French Responses to the Great War*, Oxford, Clarendon Press, 1982.

Darrow, Margaret, *French Women and the First World War* (7. Gender).

Doughty, Robert, *Pyrrhic Victory* (5. Military).

Douglas, Allen, *War, Memory and the Politics of Humor. The Canard Enchaîné and World War I*, Berkeley, University of California Press, 2002.

Downs, Laura, *Manufacturing Inequality* (7. Gender).

Fine, Martin, "Albert Thomas: A Reformer's Vision of Modernization, 1914–1932," *Journal of Contemporary History*, 12, 1977, pp. 545–64.

Flood, P. J., *France, 1914–1918: Public Opinion and the War Effort*, Basingstoke, Macmillan, 1990.

Fogarty, Richard, *Race and War in France: Colonial Subjects in the French Army, 1914–1918*, Baltimore, Johns Hopkins University Press, 2008.

Fridenson, Patrick (ed.), *The French Home Front, 1914–1918*, trans. from French, Oxford, Berg, 1992.

Gide, Charles (ed.), *Effects of the War upon French Economic Life*, Oxford, Oxford University Press, 1923.

Godfrey, John, *Capitalism at War. Industrial Policy and Bureaucracy in France, 1914–1918*, Leamington Spa, Berg, 1987.

Goldberg, Nancy, *Women, Your Hour is Sounding: Continuity and Change in French Women's Great War Fiction, 1914–1919*, New York, St. Martin's Press, 1995.

Hanna, Martha, *The Mobilization of Intellect. French Scholars and Writers during the Great War*, Cambridge, MA, Harvard University Press, 1996.

Hanna, Martha, *No One is Happy in War: A Peasant Marriage in World War I France*, Cambridge, MA, Harvard University Press, 2006.

Horne, John, "Immigrant Workers in France during World War I," *French Historical Studies*, 14/1, 1985, pp. 57–88.

Horne, John, "'L'Impôt du Sang': Republican Rhetoric and Industrial Warfare in France, 1914–1918," *Social History* 14/2, 1989, pp. 201–23.

Horne, John, *Labour at War* (8. Society).

Horne, John, "Remobilizing for 'total war': France and Britain, 1917–1918," in Horne (ed.), *State, Society and Mobilization*, pp. 195–211 (2. General).

Keiger, John, *Raymond Poincaré*, Cambridge, Cambridge University Press, 1997.

King, Jere, *Generals and Politicians. Conflict between France's High Command, Parliament and Government, 1914–1918*, Berkeley, CA., University of California Press, 1951.

King, Jere, *Foch versus Clemenceau: France and German Dismemberment, 1918–1919*, Cambridge, MA, Harvard University Press, 1960.

Krumeich, Gerd, *Armaments and Politics in France* (3. Origins).

McMillan, James, *Housewife or Harlot?* (7. Gender).

McPhail, Helen, *The Long Silence. Civilian Life under the German Occupation of Northern France, 1914–1918*, London, I. B. Tauris, 1999.

Papayanis, Nicholas, *Alphonse Merrheim: the Emergence of Reformism in Revolutionary Syndicalism, 1871–1925*, Dordrecht, Nijhoff, 1985.

Prost, Antoine, *Republican Identities in War and Peace. Representations of France in the Nineteenth and Twentieth Centuries*, Oxford, Berg, 2002.

Rearick, Charles, *The French in Love and War: Popular Culture in the Era of the World Wars*, New Haven, Yale University Press, 1997.

Renouvin, Pierre, *The Forms of War Government in France*, 1925; trans. from French, New Haven, Yale University Press, 1927.

Robert, Jean-Louis, "Women and Work in France" (7. Gender).

Smith, Leonard, *Between Mutiny and Obedience: The Case of the French Fifth Infantry Division during World War I*, Princeton, Princeton University Press, 1994.

Smith, Leonard, *The Embattled Self. French Soldiers' Testimony of the Great War*, Ithaca, NY, Cornell University Press, 2007.

Smith, Leonard, Audoin-Rouzeau, Stéphane, and Becker, Annette, *France and the Great War 1914–1918*, Cambridge, Cambridge University Press, 2003.

Stovall, Tyler, "Colour-blind France?: Colonial Workers during the First World War," *Race and Class*, 35, pp. 33–55.

Sweeney, Regina, *Singing Our Way to Victory. French Cultural Politics and Music during the Great War*, Middletown, CT, Wesleyan University Press, 2001.

Watson, David, *Georges Clemenceau: A Political Biography*, London, Methuen, 1974.

Weber, Eugen, *Action Française: Royalism and Reaction in Twentieth Century France*, Stanford, Stanford University Press, 1962.

Wohl, Robert, *French Communism in the Making, 1914–1924*, Stanford, Stanford University Press, 1966.

Young, Robert (ed.), *Under Siege. Portraits of Civilian Life in France during World War I*, Oxford, Berghahn, 2000.

23. Germany

Armeson, Robert, *Total Warfare and Compulsory Labor: A Study of the Military-Industrial Complex in Germany during World War I*, The Hague, Nijhoff, 1964.

Bessel, Richard, *Gemany after the First World War*, Oxford, Oxford University Press, 1993.

Broué, Pierre, *The German Revolution, 1917–1923*, 1971; trans. from French, Leiden, Brill, 2005.

Chickering, Roger, *Imperial Germany and the Great War, 1914–1918*, Cambridge, Cambridge University Press, 1998.

Chickering, Roger, *The Great War and Urban Life in Germany. Freiburg, 1914–1918*, Cambridge, Cambridge University Press, 2007.

Daniel, Ute, *The War from Within. German Working Class Women in the First World War*, 1989: trans. from German, Oxford, Berg, 1996.

Davis, Belinda, *Home Fires Burning. Food, Politics, and Everyday Life in World War I Berlin*, Chapel Hill, North Carolina University Press, 2001.

Deist, Wilhelm, "The German Army, the Authoritarian Nation State and Total War," in Horne (ed.), *State, Society and Mobilization in Europe during the First World War*, pp. 160–72 (2. General).

Epstein, Klaus, *Matthias Erzberger and the Dilemma of German Democracy*, Princeton, Princeton University Press, 1959.

Feldman, Gerald, *Army, Industry and Labor in Germany 1914–1918*, 1966; new ed., Providence, RI and Oxford, Berg, 1992.

Feldman, Gerald, *The Great Disorder: Politics, Economics and Society in the German Inflation, 1914–1924*, New York, Oxford University Press, 1993.

Fischer, Fritz, *Germany's Aims in the First World War* (4. International Relations).

Foley, Robert T., *German Strategy and the Path to Verdun* (5. Military).

Herwig, Holger, *The First World War. Germany and Austria-Hungary* (5. Military).

Herwig, Holger, *"Luxury Fleet"* (5. Military).

Hoffmann, Christhard, "Between Integration and Rejection: the Jewish Community in Germany, 1914–1918," in Horne (ed.), *State, Society and Mobilization*, pp. 89–104 (2. General).

Horn, Daniel, *The German Naval Mutinies of World War I*, New Brunswick, NJ, Rutgers University Press, 1969.

Hull, Isabel, *Absolute Destruction. Military Culture in Imperial Germany* (3. Origins).

Jarausch, Konrad, *The Enigmatic Chancellor: Bethmann Hollweg and the Hubris of Imperial Germany*, New Haven, Yale University Press, 1973.

Jelavich, Peter, "German Culture in the Great War," in Roshwald and Stites (eds.), *European Culture in the Great War*, pp. 32–57 (10. Culture).

Kitchen, Martin, *The Silent Dictatorship. The Politics of the German High Command under Hindenburg and Ludendorff*, London, Croom Helm, 1976.

Kocka, Jürgen, *Facing Total War: German Society 1914–1918*, 1973; trans. from German, Leamington Spa, Berg, 1984.

McKibbin, David, *War and Revolution in Leipzig 1914–1918: the German Independent Socialist Party in the Revolution of 1918*, New York, Peter Lang, 2001.

Moeller, Robert, *German Peasants and Agrarian Politics 1914–1924. The Rhineland and Westphalia*, Chapel Hill, University of North Carolina Press, 1986.

Mombauer, Annika, *Helmuth von Moltke* (3. Origins).

Mommsen, Wolfgang, "German Artists, Writers and Intellectuals and the Meaning of War, 1914–1918," in Horne (ed.), *State, Society and Mobilization in Europe*, pp. 21–38 (2. General).

Mommsen, Wolfgang, "The Spirit of 1914 and the Ideology of a German 'Sonderweg'," in Wolfgang Mommsen, *Imperial Germany 1867–1918. Politics, Culture and Society in an Authoritarian State*, London, Edward Arnold, 1995, pp. 205–16.

Morgan, David, *The Socialist Left and the German Revolution: A History of the German Independent Social Democratic Party, 1917–1922*, Ithaca, NY, Cornell University Press, 1975.

Moyer, Laurence, *Victory Must Be Ours: Germany in the Great War, 1914–1918*, London, Leo Cooper, 1995.

Natter, Wolfgang, *Literature at War, 1914–1940. Representing the "Time of Greatness" in Germany*, New Haven, Yale University Press, 1999.

Nolan, Molly, *Social Democracy and Society: Working Class Radicalism in Düsseldorf, 1890–1920*, Cambridge, Cambridge University Press, 1981.

Ringer, Fritz, *The Decline of the German Mandarins. The German Academic Community, 1890–1933*, Cambridge, MA, Harvard University Press, 1969.

Rosenberg, Arthur, *Imperial Germany. The Birth of the German Republic 1871–1918*, 1928; trans. from German, 1931; Oxford, Oxford University Press, 1970.

Ryder, Arthur, *The German Revolution of 1918: A Study of German Socialism in War and Revolt*, Cambridge, Cambridge University Press, 1967.

Schorske, Carl, *German Social Democracy, 1905–1917: The Development of the Great Schism, 1905–1917*, Cambridge, MA, Harvard University Press, 1955.

Stephenson, Scott, *The Final Battle. Soldiers of the Western Front and the German Revolution* (6. Soldiers).

Stibbe, Matthew, *British Civilian Internees in Germany: the Ruhleben Camp, 1914–1918*, Manchester, Manchester University Press, 2008.

Stibbe, Matthew, *German Anglophobia and the Great War, 1914–1918*, Cambridge, Cambridge University Press, 2001.

Verhey, Jeffrey, *The Spirit of 1914. Militarism, Myth and Mobilization in Germany*, Cambridge, Cambridge University Press, 2000.

Welch, David, *Germany, Propaganda and Total War 1914–1918*, London, Athlone Press, 2000.

Whalen, Robert, *Bitter Wounds: German Victims of the Great War 1914–1939*, Ithaca, NY, Cornell University Press, 1984.

Wheeler-Bennett, John, *Hindenburg: The Wooden Titan*, London, Macmillan, 1936, new ed., 1967.

Yaney, George, *The World of the Manager. Food Administration in Berlin during World War I*, New York, Peter Lang, 1994.

Ziemann, Benjamin, *War Experiences in Rural Germany 1914–1923*, 1999; trans. from German, Oxford and New York, Berg, 2006.

24. India

Authority of the Government of India, *India's Contribution to the Great War*, Calcutta, Superintendent of Government Printing, 1923.

Collett, Nigel, *The Butcher of Amritsar. General Reginald Dyer*, London, Hambledon, 2007.

Corrigan, Gordon, *Sepoys in the Trenches: the Indian Corps on the Western Front, 1914–15*, Staplehurst, Spellmount, 2006.

Ellinwood De Witt, C., and Pradhan, S. D. (eds.), *India and World War I*, New Delhi, Manohar, 1978.

Omissi, David (ed.), *Indian Voices of the Great War: Soldiers' Letters, 1914–1918*, Basingstoke, Macmillan, 1999.

25. Ireland

Bowman, Timothy, *The Irish Regiments in the Great War – Discipline and Morale*, Manchester, Manchester University Press, 1999.

De Wiel, Jérôme aan, *The Catholic Church in Ireland 1914–1918: War and Politics*, Dublin, Four Courts Press, 2003.

Denman, Terence, *Ireland's Unknown Soldiers: the 16th (Irish) Division in the Great War*, Dublin, Irish Academic Press, 1992.

Dudley Edwards, Ruth, *Patrick Pearse: the Triumph of Failure*, 1977; new ed., Dublin, Irish Academic Press, 2006.

Dungan, Myles, *They Shall Grow Not Old. Irish Soldiers and the Great War*, Dublin, Four Courts Press, 1997.

Fitzpatrick, David, *Politics and Irish Life 1913–1921: Provincial Experience of War and Revolution*, 1977; new ed., Cork, Cork University Press, 1998.

Fitzpatrick, David (ed.), *Ireland and the First World War*, Dublin, Lilliput Press and Trinity History Workshop, 1986.

Gregory, Adrian, and Paseta, Senia (eds.), *Ireland and the Great War: "A War to Unite Us All?,"* Manchester, Manchester University Press, 2002.

Hart, Peter, *The I.R.A. at War, 1916–1923*, Oxford, Oxford University Press, 2003.

Hennessy, Thomas, *Dividing Ireland. World War I and Partition*, London and New York, Routledge, 1998.

Horne, John (ed.), *Our War. Ireland and the Great War*, Dublin, RTE/Royal Irish Academy, 2008.

Jeffery, Keith, *Ireland and the Great War*, Cambridge, Cambridge University Press, 2000.

Johnson, Nuala, *Ireland, the Great War and the Geography of Remembrance,* Cambridge, Cambridge University Press, 2003.

Laffan, Michael, *The Resurrection of Ireland. The Sinn Féin Party, 1916–1923,* Cambridge, Cambridge University Press, 1999.

Orr, Philip, *The Road to the Somme: Men of the Ulster Division tell their Story,* 1987; new ed., Belfast, Blackstaff Press, 2008.

Orr, Philip, *Field of Bones. An Irish Division at Gallipoli,* Dublin, Lilliput Press, 2006.

Townshend, Charles, *The British Campaign in Ireland, 1919–1921: the Development of Political and Military Policies,* London, Oxford University Press, 1975.

26. Italy

Bosworth, Richard, *Italy and the Approach of the First World War* (3. Origins).

Bosworth, Richard, *Italy, the Least of the Great Powers* (3. Origins).

Corner, Paul, and Procacci, Giovanna, "The Italian Experience of 'Total' War, 1915–1920," in John Horne (ed.), *State, Society and Mobilization in Europe during the First World War,* Cambridge, Cambridge University Press, 1997, pp. 223–40.

Forsyth, Douglas, *The Crisis of Liberal Italy. Monetary and Financial Policy, 1914–1922,* Cambridge, Cambridge University Press, 1994.

Galassi, Francesco, and Harrison, Mark, "Italy at War, 1915–1918," in Stephen Broadberry and Mark Harrison (eds.), *The Economics of World War I,* pp. 276–309 (9. Economy).

Gentile, Emilio, *The Origins of Fascist Ideology, 1918–1925,* 1996; trans. from Italian, New York, Enigma, 2005.

Morselli, Mario, *Caporetto 1917: Victory or Defeat?,* London, Frank Cass, 2000.

O'Brien, Paul, *Mussolini in the First World War: The Journalist, the Soldier, the Fascist,* Oxford and Providence, Berg, 2005.

Ortaggi, Simonetta, "Italian Women during the Great War," in Braybon (ed.), *Evidence, History and the Great War,* pp. 216–38 (2. General).

Procacci, Giovanna, "Popular Protest and Labour Conflict in Italy, 1915–1918," *Social History,* 14/1, 1989, pp. 31–58.

Procacci, Giovanna, "State Coercion and Worker Solidarity in Italy (1915–1919): the Moral and Political Content of Social Unrest," in Leopold Haimson and Giulio Sapelli (eds.), *Strikes, Social Conflict and the First World War,* pp. 145–77 (8. Society).

Renzi, William, *In the Shadow of the Sword. Italy's Neutrality and Entry into the Great War, 1914–1915,* Berne, Peter Lang, 1987.

Rossini, Daniele, *Woodrow Wilson and the American Myth in Italy. Culture, Diplomacy and War Propaganda,* 2000; trans. from Italian, Cambridge, MA, Harvard University Press, 2008.

Schindler, John, *Isonzo. The Forgotten Sacrifice of the Great War,* London and Westport, CT, Praeger, 2001.

Thompson, Mark, *The White War. Life and Death on the Italian Front, 1915–1919,* London, Faber, 2008.

Tomassini, Luigi, "Industrial Mobilization and the Labour Market in Italy during the First World War," *Social History,* 16/1, 1991, pp. 59–87.

Viegezzi, Bruno, "Italian Socialism and the First World War: Mussolini, Lazari and Turati," *Journal of Italian History,* 2/2, 1979, pp. 232–57.

Webster, R. A., *Industrial Imperialism in Italy, 1908–1915,* Berkeley, University of California Press, 1974.

Wilcox, Vanda, "Discipline in the Italian Army 1915–1918," in Pierre Purseigle (ed.), *Warfare and Belligerence. Perspectives in First World War Studies,* Boston and Leiden, Brill, 2005, pp. 73–100.

27. Neutral States

Abbenhuis, Maartje, *The Art of Staying Neutral. The Netherlands in the First World War, 1914–1918*, Amsterdam, Amsterdam University Press, 2006.

Albert, Bill, *South America and the First World War. The Impact of the War on Brazil, Argentina, Peru and Chile*, Cambridge, Cambridge University Press, 1988.

Dehne, Phillip, *On the Far Western Front: Britain's First World War in South America*, Manchester, Manchester University Press, 2009.

Due-Nielsen, Carsten, "Denmark and the First World War," *Scandinavian Journal of History*, 10/1, 1985, pp. 1–18.

Romero Salvadó, Francisco J., *Spain, 1914–1918. Between War and Revolution*, London, Routledge, 1999.

28. New Zealand

Phillips, Jock, Boyack, Nicholas, and Malone, E. P. (eds.), *The Great Adventure: New Zealand Soldiers Describe the First World War*, Wellington, Allen and Unwin, 1988.

Pugsley, Christopher, *Gallipoli: the New Zealand Story*, Auckland, Hodder and Stoughton, 1984.

Pugsley, Christopher, *On the Fringe of Hell: New Zealanders and Military Discipline in the First World War*, Auckland, Hodder and Stoughton, 1991.

29. The Ottoman Empire and the Middle East

Akçam, Taner, *A Shameful Act: the Armenian Genocide and the Question of Turkish Responsibility*, New York, Metropolitan Books, 2006.

Aksakal, Mustafa, *The Ottoman Road to War in 1914: the Ottoman Empire and the First World War*, Cambridge, Cambridge University Press, 2008.

Bloxham, Donald, *The Great Game of Genocide: Imperialism, Nationalism and the Destruction of the Ottoman Armenians*, Oxford, Oxford University Press, 2005.

Dadrian, Vahakn, *The History of the Armenian Genocide: Ethnic Conflict from the Balkans to Anatolia and the Caucasus*, Oxford and New York, Berghahn, 2003.

Darwin, John, *Britain, Egypt and the Middle East* (20. British Empire).

Emin, Ahmed, *Turkey in the World War*, New Haven, Yale University Press, 1930.

Erikson, Edward, *Defeat in Detail. The Ottoman Army in the Balkans, 1912–1913* (3. Origins).

Erikson, Edward, *Ordered to Die: A History of the Ottoman Empire in the First World War* (5. Military).

Fromkin, David, *A Peace to End All Peace. Creating the Modern Middle East 1914–1922*, London, André Deutsch, 1989.

Hovannissian, Richard, *The Armenian Genocide: Wartime Radicalization or Premeditated Continuum?*, Somerset, NJ, Transaction, 2006.

Laycock, Jo, *Imagining Armenia: Orientalism, Ambiguity and Intervention 1878–1925*, Manchester, Manchester University Press, 2009.

Nassibian, Akaby, *Britain and the Armenian Question, 1915–1923*, London, Croom Helm, 1984.

Roshwald, Aviel, *Ethnic Nationalism and the Fall of Empires* (12. Politics).

Trumpener, Ulrich, *Germany and the Ottoman Empire* (4. International Relations).

Winter, Jay (ed.), *America and the Armenian Genocide of 1915*, Cambridge, Cambridge University Press, 2003.

Zürcher, Erik Jan, *The Unionist Factor. The Role of the Committee of Union and Progress in the Turkish National Movement 1905–1926*, Leiden, Brill, 1984.

30. Portugal

Ribeiro de Meneses, Filipe, " 'All of Us are Looking Forward to Leaving': The Censored Correspondence of the Portuguese Expeditionary Corps in France, 1917–1918," *European History Quarterly*, 30, 2000, pp. 333–55.

Ribeiro de Meneses, Filipe, *Portugal 1914–1926. From the First World War to Military Dictatorship*, Bristol, HiPLAM, 2004.

Vincent-Smith, John, "Britain, Portugal and the First World War, 1914–1916," *European Studies Review*, 4, 1974, pp. 207–38.

31. Russia

Cohen, Aaron J., "Oh, That! Myth, Memory, and World War I in the Russian Emigration and the Soviet Union," *Slavic Review*, 62/1, 2003, pp. 69–82.

Engel, Barbara, "Not by Bread Alone: Subsistence Rioting in Russia during World War I," *Journal of Modern History*, 69/4, 1997, pp. 696–721.

Figes, Orlando, *A People's Tragedy: The Russian Revolution, 1891–1924*, New York, Penguin, 1996.

Figes, Orlando, and Kolonitskii, Boris, *Interpreting the Russian Revolution: The Language and Symbols of 1917*, New Haven, Yale University Press, 1999.

Florinsky, Michael, *The End of the Russian Empire*, New Haven, Yale University Press, 1931.

Fuller, William C. Jr., *The Foe Within: Fantasies of Treason in Late Imperial Russia*, Ithaca, NY, Cornell University Press, 2006.

Gatrell, Peter, "The Epic and the Domestic: Women and War in Russia, 1914–1917," in Braybon (ed.), *Evidence, History and the Great War*, pp. 198–215 (2. General).

Gatrell, Peter, *A Whole Empire Walking: Refugees in Russia During World War I*, Bloomington, Indiana University Press, 1999.

Gatrell, Peter, *Russia's First World War: A Social and Economic History*, Harlow, Pearson Longman, 2005.

Gleason, William, "The All-Russian Union of Zemstvos and World War I," in Terence Emmons and Wayne Vucinich (eds.), *The Zemstvo in Russia: An Experiment in Local Self-Government*, Cambridge, Cambridge University Press, 1982, pp. 365–82.

Hagen, Mark von, *Soldiers in the Proletarian State: The Red Army and the Soviet Socialist State, 1917–1930*, Ithaca, NY and London, Cornell University Press, 1990.

Hagen, Mark von, "The Great War and the Mobilization of Ethnicity in the Russian Empire," in Barnett Rubin and Jack Snyder (eds.), *The Post-Soviet Political Order: Capitalist and State Building*, London, Routledge, 1998, pp. 34–57.

Holquist, Peter, *Making War. Forging Revolution. Russia's Continuum of Crisis 1914–1921*, Cambridge, MA, Harvard University Press, 2002.

Jahn, Hubertus, *Patriotic Culture in Russia during World War I*, Ithaca, NY, Cornell University Press, 1995.

Kaiser, Daniel, *The Workers Revolution in Russia, 1917. The View from Below*, New York, Cambridge University Press, 1987.

Keep, John, *The Russian Revolution: A Study in Mass Mobilization*, London, Weidenfeld and Nicolson, 1976.

Koenker, Diane, *Moscow Workers and the 1917 Revolution*, Princeton, Princeton University Press, 1981.

Koenker, Diane, and Rosenberg, William, *Strikes and Revolution in Russia, 1917*, Princeton, Princeton University Press, 1989.

Lih, Lars T., *Bread and Authority in Russia 1914–1921*, Berkeley, University of California Press, 1990.

Lincoln, W. Bruce, *A Passage Through Armageddon: The Russians in War and Revolution*, New York, Oxford, Oxford University Press, 1994.

Lohr, Eric, *Nationalizing the Russian Empire: The Campaign against Enemy Aliens during World War I*, Cambridge, Harvard University Press, 2003.

McAuley, Mary, *Bread and Justice. State and Society in Petrograd 1917–1921*, Oxford, Clarendon Press, 1991.

Mandel, David, *The Petrograd Workers and the Fall of the Old Regime*, London, Macmillan, 1983.

Melancon, Michael, *The Socialist Revolutionaries and the Russian Anti-War Movement 1914–1917*, Columbus, Ohio State University Press, 1990.

Nolde, Boris, *Russia in the Economic War*, New Haven, Yale University Press, 1928.

Petrone, Karen, "Family, Masculinity and Heroism in Russian War Posters of the First World War," in Melman (ed.), *Borderlands*, pp. 43–52 (7. Gender).

Robinson, Paul, *The White Russian Army in Exile, 1920–1941*, Oxford, Clarendon Press, 2002.

Roshwald, Aviel, *Ethnic Nationalism and the Fall of Empires* (12. Politics).

Sanborn, Joshua, *Drafting the Russian Nation: Military Conscription, Total War, and Mass Politics, 1905–1925*, DeKalb, Northern Illinois University Press, 2003.

Siegelbaum, Lewis, *The Politics of Industrial Mobilization in Russia, 1914–17. A Study of the War Industries Committee*, London, Macmillan, 1984.

Smith, J. T., "Russian Military Censorship during the First World War," *Revolutionary Russia*, 14/1, 2001, pp. 71–95.

Sokol, Edward, *The Revolt of 1916 in Central Asia*, Baltimore, Johns Hopkins University Press, 1954.

Stockdale, Melissa K., "'My Death for the Motherland is Happiness': Women, Patriotism, and Soldiering in Russia's Great War 1914–1917," *American Historical Review*, 109/1, February 2004, pp. 78–116.

Stone, Norman *The Eastern Front, 1914–1917* (5. Military).

Struve, Peter, *Food Supply in Russia during the World War*, New Haven, Yale University Press, 1930.

Wildman, Allan, *The End of the Russian Imperial Army*. 2 vols., Princeton, Princeton University Press, 1980–7.

Zagorsky, S. O., *State Control of Industry in Russia during the War*, New Haven, Yale University Press, 1928.

Zuckerman, Frederic, "The Political Police, War, and Society in Russia, 1914–1917," in Coetzee and Shevin-Coetzee (eds.), *Authority, Identity and the Social History of the Great War*, pp. 29–56 (8. Society).

32. The United States of America

Barbeau, Arthur, and Florette, Henri, *The Unknown Soldiers: African-American Troops in World War I*, New York, Da Capo Press, 1996.

Bruce, Robert, *A Fraternity of Arms: America and France in the Great War* (5. Military).

Capozzola, Christopher, *Uncle Sam Wants You. World War I and the Making of the Modern American Citizen*, Oxford, Oxford University Press, 2008.

Coffman, Edward, *The War to End all Wars*, 1968; new ed., Lexington, University of Kentucky Press, 1998. *Based inter alii on oral history.*

Harries, Meirion, and Harries, Susie, *The Last Days of Innocence: America at War, 1917–1918*, New York, Vintage, 1992.

Jensen, Kimberley, *Mobilizing Minerva* (7. Gender).

Keene, Jennifer, *Doughboys. The Great War and the Remaking of America*, Baltimore and London, Johns Hopkins University Press, 2001; new ed., 2003.

Keene, Jennifer, *The United States and the First World War*, Harlow, Pearson Education, 2000. *Includes documents.*

Keith, Jeanette, *Rich Man's War, Poor Man's Fight: Race, Class and Power in the Rural South during the First World War*, Chapel Hill, University of North Carolina Press, 2004.

Kennedy, David, *Over There: The First World War and American Society*, Oxford, Oxford University Press, 1980.

Luebke, F. C., *Bonds of Loyalty. German-Americans and World War I*, DeKalb, Northern Illinois University Press, 1974.

Meiggs, Mark, *Optimism at Armageddon. Voices of American Participants in the First World War*, Cambridge, MA, Harvard University Press, 1997.

Mock, J. R., and Larson, C., *Words that Won the War. The Story of the Committee on Public Information*, Princeton, Princeton University Press, 1939.

Rawls, Walton, *World War I and the American Poster*, New York, Cross River Press, 1988.

Schaeffer, Ronald, *America in the Great War: The Rise of the War Welfare State*, Oxford, Oxford University Press, 1991.

Smythe, Donald, *Pershing* (5. Military).

Zieger, *America's Great War. World War I and the American Experience*, Oxford, Rowman and Littlefield, 2000.

33.   Peacemaking and Continued Conflict

Ádám, Magda, *The Versailles System and Central Europe*, Aldershot, Ashgate/Variom, 2004.

Adamthwaite, Anthony, *Grandeur and Misery: France's Bid for Power in Europe, 1914–1940*, London, Arnold, 1995.

Baron, Nick, and Gatrell, Peter (eds.), *Homelands: War, Population, and Statehood in Eastern Europe and Russia, 1918–1924*, London, Anthem Press, 2004.

Boemeke, Manfred, Feldman, Gerald, and Glaser, Elizabeth (eds.), *The Treaty of Versailles: A Reassessment after 75 Years*, Cambridge, Cambridge University Press, 1998.

Burgwyn, James, *The Legend of the Mutilated Victory: Italy, the Great War and the Paris Peace Conference, 1915–1919*, London, Greenwood, 1993.

Cecil, Hugh, and Liddle, Peter (eds.), *At the Eleventh Hour: Reflections, Hopes and Anxieties at the Closing of the Great War, 1918*, Barnsley, Leo Cooper, 1998.

Clements, Jonathan, *Prince Saionji. Japan*, London, Haus Publishing, 2008.

Clements, Jonathan, *Wellington Koo. China*, London, Haus Publishing, 2009.

Cohrs, Patrick, *The Unfinished Peace after World War I*, Cambridge, Cambridge University Press, 2006.

Craig, Gordon, and Gilbert, Felix (eds.), *The Diplomats, 1919–1939*, Princeton, Princeton University Press, 1994.

Dallas, Gregor, *1918. War and Peace*, London, John Murray, 2000.

Davies, Norman, *White Eagle, Red Star: The Polish-Soviet War, 1919–1920*, London, Macdonald, 1992.

Ferrell, Robert J., *Woodrow Wilson and World War I, 1917–1921*, New York, Harper and Row, 1985.

Fromkin, David, *A Peace to End all Peace. Creating the Modern Middle East* (29. The Ottoman Empire).

Gerwarth, Robert, "The Central European Counterrevolution: Paramilitary Violence in Germany, Austria and Hungary after the Great War," *Past and Present*, 200, 2008, pp. 175–209.

Jacobson, Jon, *Locarno Diplomacy: Germany and the West 1925–1929*, Princeton, Princeton University Press, 1972.

Harmer, Harry, *Friedrich Ebert. Germany*, London, Haus Publishing, 2009.

Kent, Bruce, *The Spoils of War: The Politics, Economics, and Diplomacy of Reparations, 1918–1932*, Oxford, Oxford University Press, 1989.

Keylor, William (ed.), *The Legacy of the Great War: Peacemaking 1919*, Boston, Houghton Mifflin, 1998.

King, Jere, *Foch versus Clemenceau* (22. France).

Knock, Thomas J., *To End All Wars: Woodrow Wilson and the Quest for a New World Order*, New York, Oxford University Press, 1992.

Luckau, Alma, *The German Delegation at the Paris Peace Conference*, New York, Columbia University Press, 1941; new ed., New York, H. Fertig, 1971.

Macmillan, Margaret, *Peacemakers. Six Months that Changed the World*, London, John Murray, 2001.

Maier, Charles, *Recasting Bourgeois Europe: Stabilization in France, Germany and Italy in the Decade after World War I*, Princeton, Princeton University Press, 1975.

Manela, Erez, *The Wilsonian Moment. Self-Determination and the International Origins of Anticolonial Nationalism*, Oxford, Oxford University Press, 2007.

Mayer, Arno, *Politics and Diplomacy of Peacemaking: Containment and Counter-Revolution at Versailles, 1918–1919*, London, Weidenfeld and Nicolson, 1968.

Morton, Brian, *Woodrow Wilson. United States*, London, Haus Publishing, 2008.

Nelson, Keith, " 'The Black Horror on the Rhine': Race as a Factor in Post-World War I Diplomacy," *Journal of Modern History*, 42, December 1970, pp. 606–27.

Prusin, Alexander, *Nationalizing a Borderland: War, Ethnicity and Anti-Jewish Violence in East Galicia, 1914–1920*, Tuscaloosa, University of Alabama Press, 2005.

Reshetar, John, *The Ukrainian Revolution, 1917–1920: A Study in Nationalism*, Princeton, Princeton University Press, 1952.

Schwabe, Klaus, *Woodrow Wilson, Revolutionary Germany, and Peacemaking, 1918–1919. Missionary Diplomacy and the Realities of Power*, Chapel Hill and London, University of North Carolina Press, 1985.

Seipp, Adam, *The Ordeal of Peace: Demobilization and the Urban Experience in Britain and Germany, 1917–1921*, Farnham, Ashgate, 2009.

Sharp, Alan, *The Versailles Settlement: Peacemaking in Paris, 1919*, New York, St. Martin's Press, 1991.

Sharp, Alan, *David Lloyd George. Great Britain*, London, Haus Publishing, 2009.

Sharp, Alan and Fischer, Conan (eds.), *After the Versailles Peace Treaty: Enforcement, Compliance, Contested Identities*, London, Routledge, 2008.

Silverman, Daniel, *Reconstructing Europe after the Great War*, Cambridge, MA, Harvard University Press, 1982.

Swain, Geoffrey, *The Origins of the Russian Civil War*, London, Longman, 1996.

Temperley, Harold (ed.), *A History of the Peace Conference of Paris*, 6 vols., London, Oxford University Press, 1920–4.

Upton, Anthony, *The Finnish Revolution*, Minneapolis, University of Minnesota Press, 1980.

Waite, Robert, *Vanguard of Nazism. The Free Corps Movement in Postwar Germany, 1918–1923*, Cambridge, MA, Harvard University Press, 1952.

Walters, Francis, *A History of the League of Nations*, London, Oxford University Press, 1952, new ed., 1965.

Watson, David, *Georges Clemenceau. France*, London, Haus Publishing, 2009.

Weintraub, Stanley, *A Stillness Heard Around the World: the End of the Great War, November 1918*, London, Allen and Unwin, 1986.

Willis, James, *Prologue to Nuremberg: the Politics and Diplomacy of Punishing War Criminals of the First World War*, Westport, CT, Greenwood, 1982.

34. Legacy

Barr, Niall, *The Lion and the Poppy: British Veterans, Politics and Society, 1921–1939*, Westport, CT, Praeger, 2005.

Brandt, Susanna, "The Memory Makers: Museums and Exhibitions of the First World War," *History and Memory*, 1, 1994, pp. 95–122.

Clout, Hugh, *After the Ruins. Restoring the Countryside of Northern France after the Great War*, Exeter, University of Exeter Press 1996.

Cohen, Aaron J., "Oh, That! Myth, Memory and World War I in the Russian Emigration and the Soviet Union," (31. Russia).

Cohen, Deborah, *The War Come Home: Disabled Veterans in Britain and Germany, 1914–1939*, Berkeley, University of California Press, 2001.

Evans, Suzanne, *Mothers of Heroes, Mothers of Martyrs. World War I and the Politics of Grief*, Montreal and Kingston, McGill-Queen's University Press, 2007.

Fritzsche, Peter, *Germans into Nazis*, Cambridge, MA, Harvard University Press, 1998.

Fussell, Paul, *The Great War and Modern Memory* (10. Culture).

Gentile, Emilio, *Origins of Fascist Ideology* (26. Italy).

Gerwarth, Robert, "The Central European Counterrevolution: Paramilitary Violence in Germany, Austria and Hungary after the Great War," *Past and Present*, 200, 2008, pp. 175–209.

Gregory, Adrian, *The Silence of Memory: Armistice Day 1919–1946*, Oxford, Berg, 1994.

Gregory, Adrian, "Peculiarities of the English? War, Violence and Politics: 1900–1939," *Journal of Modern European History*, 1, 2003, pp. 44–59.

Hanson, Neil, *The Unknown Soldier: the Story of the Missing of the Great War*, London, Doubleday, 2005.

Horne, John, and Kramer, Alan, *German Atrocities, 1914*, part 4 (10. Culture).

Inglis, Ken, *Sacred Places. War Memorials in the Australian Landscape*, Melbourne, Melbourne University Press, 1998.

Ingram, Norman, *The Politics of Dissent: Pacifism in France 1919–1939*, Oxford, Clarendon Press, 1991.

Jeffery, Keith, *Ireland and the Great War* (25. Ireland).

Kavanagh, Gaynor, *Museums and the First World War. A Social History*, London, Leicester University Press, 1994.

King, Alex, *Memorials of the War in Great Britain. The Symbolism and Politics of Remembrance*, Oxford, Berg, 1998.

Lawrence, Jon, "Forging a Peaceable Kingdom: War, Violence and the Fear of Brutalization in Post-First World War Britain," *Journal of Modern History*, 75/3, 2003, pp. 557–89.

Levy, Carl, and Roseman, Mark (eds.), *Three Postwar Eras in Comparison. Western Europe, 1918–1945–1989*, Basingstoke, Palgrave Macmillan, 2001.

Lloyd, David, *Battlefield Tourism. Pilgrimage and the Commemoration of the Great War in Britain, Australia and Canada, 1919–1939*, Oxford, Berg, 1998.

Longworth, Philip, *The Unending Vigil: the History of the Commonwealth War Graves Commission*, 1967; new ed., Barnsley, Leo Cooper, 2003.

Martin, Benjamin, *France and the Après-Guerre, 1918–1924. Illusions and Disillusionment*, Baton Rouge, Louisiana State University Press, 2002.

Merridale, Catherine, *Night of Stone. Death and Memory in Russia*, London, Granta, 2000.

Mosse, George, *Fallen Soldiers: Reshaping the Memory of the World Wars*, Oxford and New York, Oxford University Press, 1990.

Pegg, Carl, *Evolution of the European Idea, 1914–1932*, Chapel Hill, University of North Carolina Press, 1983.

Prost, Antoine, *In the Wake of War. "Les Anciens Combattants" and French Society, 1914–1933*, Oxford, Berg, 1992.

Prost, Antoine, "Monuments to the Dead," in Pierre Nora (ed.), *Realms of Memory. The Construction of the French Past*, vol. 2, *Traditions*, New York, Columbia University Press, 1997, pp. 307–30.

Schivelbusch, Wolfgang, *The Culture of Defeat. On National Trauma, Mourning and Recovery*, 2001; trans. from German, London, Granta, 2003 (esp. pp. 189–288, on Germany after 1918).

Sherman, Daniel, *The Construction of Memory in Interwar France*, Chicago, University of Chicago Press, 1999.

Siegel, Mona, *The Moral Disarmament of France. Education, Pacifism and Patriotism, 1914–1940*, Cambridge, Cambridge University Press, 2004.

Smith, Leonard, *The Embattled Self. French Soldiers' Testimony* (22. France).

Spiering, Menno, and Wintle, Michael (eds.), *Ideas of Europe since 1914: the Legacy of the First World War*, Basingstoke, Palgrave Macmillan, 2002.

Stamp, Gavin, *The Memorial to the Missing of the Somme*, London, Profile Books, 2006.

Steiner, Zara, *The Lights that Failed. European International History, 1919–1933*, Oxford, Oxford University Press, 2005.

Theweleit, Klaus, *Male Fantasies. Women, Floods, Bodies, History*, 1977; trans. from German, 2 vols., Cambridge, Polity Press, 1987–9.

Thomson, Alistair, *Anzac Memories* (15. Australia).

Todman, Dan, *The Great War. Myth and Memory* (19. Britain).

Vance, Jonathan, *Death So Noble*. (21. Canada).

Whalen, Robert, W., *Bitter Wounds. German Victims* (23. Germany).

Winter, Jay, *Sites of Memory, Sites of Mourning* (10. Culture).

Winter, Jay, *Remembering War. The Great War Between Memory and History in the Twentieth Century*, New Haven and London, Yale University Press, 2006.

Winter, Jay and Sivan, Emmanuel (eds.), *War and Remembrance in the Twentieth Century*, Cambridge, Cambridge University Press, 1999.

Wirsching, Andreas, "Political Violence in France and Italy after 1918," *Journal of Modern European History*, 1, 2003, pp. 60–79.

Index

Aachen 51
Abd el-Krim 531
Abdulhamid II, Emperor of the
    Ottomans 497, 501
Abdulkerim Pasha, Brig.-Gen. 107
Abercorn (Northern Rhodesia) 120
Abstraction (in art) 339, 342
Académie des sciences 316, 333
Achard, Charles 314
Achi Baba heights 102
activists
    Belgian Flemish 393, 395
    Bolshevik 560
    lay Catholic 243
    popular vengeance on in Belgium 396
    singled out for opprobrium in Belgium
        394
    socialist 485
    unionist (Turkey) 501
    women 266
Adam, Paul 328
Adana (anti-Armenian pograms, 1909) 503
Addams, Jane 266
Aden 103
Adenauer, Konrad 549
Admiralty *see* British Admiralty
Adrianopolis 8, 494, 501
Adriatic Sea 152, 161, 166
    hazards of employing large ships in 151
    seaplanes employed over 160
    Yugoslav aspirations on 379
AEF (American Expeditionary Force) 167,
    218, 443, 515, 516, 517

AEG (Allgemeine Elektrizitäts
    Gesellschaft) 225
Aegean Sea 192, 504
aerial warfare 156
    bombardment 260, 387
    heroes 158
Aeroplane, The 159 (magazine)
Aerschott (Belgium) 238
Afghanistan 561, 566
Africa 12, 112–26, 295
    campaigns to take Germany's colonies
        in 524
    colonial troops from 268
    French rivalry with Britain in 418
    see also Central Africa; East Africa; North
        Africa; South Africa; South West Africa;
        sub-Saharan Africa; West Africa
African-Americans
    domestic servants 267
    migrants 513
    soldiers 268
Africans 115, 526
    Black 545
    part played by soldiers 535
    primitive image 534
Afrikaners
    antagonism toward Britons 118
    rebellion (1914–15) 118–19
Agaoglu, Ahmed 498
agricultural production 75, 112, 217, 227,
    257, 419–20, 546
    arable crops 411
    boom in 409

output hard hit 438
air raids 272, 412
aircraft 163
  bombing capability 157
  British wartime manufacture 160
  coordinated use of tanks and 181, 183
  development of 182
  firms disappeared 167
  lack of hitting power to destroy
    submarines 149
  large/gigantic 160, 161
  light 160, 162
  manufacturers indissolubly tied to
    military 156
  multi-engined 157
  potential to operate over difficult
    terrain 569
  production of 160, 161–2
  reconnaissance 70, 157, 159, 162, 165,
    166, 182, 313
  submarines brought within range of 149
  superior technology 161
  two-seater, that left much to be desired 166
airships 156, 157, 160
  submarines brought within range of 149
Aisne River 42, 52, 53, 134, 183, 528
Akçuraoglu, Yusuf (Young Turk
    intellectual) 498
Alanbrooke, A. F. B., Field-Marshal
    Viscount 37
Albania 14, 84, 378, 545
  insurrection and independence
    (1911–13) 494
  reactions to Turkish nationalism 498
Albatross (German aircraft) 161
Albert I, King of the Belgians 203–4, 212,
    387, 388, 393, 395, 396, 579
Albertini, Luigi 21, 467
alcohol abuse/consumption 268, 514
Alekseev, Gen. Mikhail 486
Aleppo 97, 104, 497
Alevis (minority people in Ottoman
    Turkey) 504
Alexander, Prince Regent of Serbia 379
Alexandra, Empress of Russia 484
Alexandre, Michel 243
Alexandria 114
Alfonso XIII, King of Spain 205
Algeciras conference (1906) 10
Algeria 112, 527
  infantry 527
  migrant workers from 528

Muslims mobilized for French army 526
  naturalized Jews in 526
  rebellion 531
  recruitment of indigenous populations 285
  victorious nationalists 536
al-Hashimi, Col. Yasin 104
al-Husrî, Sati (Arab nationalist) 504
aliens, enemy
  excluded 414
  internment of 408
All Quiet on the Western Front (Remarque and
    Milestone) 330, 332, 363, 365, 550
Allenby, Gen. Sir Edmund 60, 104
alliance systems 21, 24
Allied Commission (administering
    Memel) 563
Allied Disarmament Commission 548
Alp, Tekin (Moïse Cohen, Young Turk
    intellectual) 498
alphabet learning 422
Alps 355, 474
  Italian 586
Alsace-Lorraine 12, 26, 49, 51, 52, 77, 194,
    204, 210, 211, 212, 515
  first German victories in 434
  French support/desire for return of 205,
    210, 428
  French troops in 578
  incorporation into German Empire 418
  population never really assimilated into
    Germany 422
  problems of being from 347
  remaining German 210
  singled out by German Supreme Command
    as unreliable 287
  time for the French to reclaim 419
Alsatians 453
  dialect 419
Altipiano di Asiago 86, 90
Altkirch 54
Amanus Mountains 97
Amara (Mesopotamia) 105
ambulance units/drivers 91, 268, 329
American Civil War 299
American Constitution (19th
    Amendment) 514
American Federation of Labor 513
American Relief Administration 564
American War Department 310
Amiens 127
Amiens, battle of (1918) 40, 45, 133, 134,
    135, 138

amputations 58, 298–302, 304
Amritsar (massacre, 1919) 533, 566
Anafarta Group (in Ottoman Army at
    Gallipoli) 102
Anatolia 255, 482, 499, 501, 502, 564
    Armenian eastern heartland 503, 504
    Armenian invasion stemmed in 565
    Greek populations 207, 496, 504
    Muslims expelled 193
    Turkey retains 547
Anderson, Louisa Garrett 268
Anders, Günther 346
Andler, Charles 334
Andrássy, Gyula 381
Andrew, Christopher M. 533
Anglophone Canadians 526
Anglo-Americans 20, 269
*Anglo-French Commission Internationale de
    Ravitaillement (1914)* 226
Anglo-French relations 52
    expeditionary force 101, 117
    naval agreement 12
Anglo-German naval competition/race 141,
    403
Anglo-Indian forces 105, 106
Anglo-Persian Oil Company 105
Angola 112, 118, 119
Ankara 547, 565
annexations 14, 211, 372, 450, 451, 452,
    453, 454, 458, 494, 501
Ansaldo (Italian armaments firm) 469
Antilles 526
anti-aircraft defenses 182
anti-Armenian hostility/pogroms 498, 503
anti-Belgian rhetoric 393
anti-Bolshevists 79, 560
anti-Christian nationalism 498, 499, 503
anti-fascism 465
    ideological 585
anti-Germanism 342, 361, 387
anti-immigration groups 520
anti-imperialism 13
anti-militarism 27
anti-Ottoman insurgents 502
anti-Russian crusade 373
anti-Semitism 193, 288, 439, 449, 453, 562
    fuel for agitation 375
    radical organizations 440
anti-submarine operations 149, 150, 152
anti-tank ditches 183
Antivari 151
Antonov, Aleksandr 561

Antwerp 51, 203, 387, 395
Anzacs (Australian and New Zealand Army
    Corps) 101, 102, 104, 528, 530, 582
    memorials/statues to 535, 536
    singular practicality of 529
Apollinaire, Guillaume 251, 331, 333, 338,
    339–40, 346, 350, 422
Apponyi, Albert 381
Aqaba 103
Arab world 112, 496, 504, 545
    British and French divide territories 206–7
    disgruntled nationalists 547
    favorable to Ottoman Empire 498
    insurgents 103
    revolt 533, 565
    warriors 104
Arabic (British passenger ship) 509–10
Arabistan 105
Aras Valley 99, 100
Arc de Triomphe 579
Archangel 560
Archer, William 328
Archimedes 309
Ardahan (Caucasus) 100, 457
Ardant du Picq, Col. Charles 7
Ardennes 51
Arditi 90, 474–5, 567
Argentina 141
Ari Burnu (Gallipoli) 102
Armée de l'Orient 528
Armee im Felde (Austro-Hungarian war
    zones) 373
Armenia 559
    economic reconstruction and refugee
        relief 564
    independence declared 457
    nationalist power 563
    see also Erevan
Armenians 100, 496, 586
    confiscation of assets 501
    deportation orders for 504
    expelled 192
    extermination of 206, 245, 499
    fighting in Russian forces 254–5
    genocide against 192, 196–7, 289, 496,
        502, 503, 564
    intense persecution of 191–2
    marginal revolutionary activities of 503
    mass murder of 198
    massacre by Ottoman Turkish 191, 504
    members of labor battalions executed 192
    new states threatened 547

perished 504
refugees 193
violence and cruelty against 237
Armistice (November 11, 1918) 46, 78, 100, 124, 243, 255–6, 413, 429, 443, 459, 582
  basis for 518
  terms of 444
Army of Islam 100
Arnim, Gen. Sixt von 441
Arp, Jean/Hans 347
Arras, battle of (1917) 183, 328, 440
Arrhenius, S. A. 318
artists 282, 342, 344, 346, 347, 405, 422, 433, 470, 584
  official 341
Artois offensive (1915) 53, 55, 56, 57, 346, 423
arts 338–52
Asia 78, 524
  French rivalry with Britain in 418
  see also Central Asia
Asia Minor 547
Asian crisis (1931) 550
Asir 103
Askari 120, 121, 122, 123, 124
Askeri Bey, Lt.-Col. Suleyman 105
Asquith, H. H., Lord 37, 55, 62, 410
assassinations 244, 280, 457, 498, 527, 550; Sarajevo (1914) 3, 15, 19, 28, 54, 202, 289, 372, 404, 432
Association internationale des Académies 318
Association of Combatant Writers (France) 329
Assyrians 504
Athens 565
Atlantic waters 114
  sea-lanes guarded between Mediterranean and 524
  unrestricted submarine warfare 196
atrocities 188, 190, 191, 198, 244, 245, 568
  accounts of 266
  allegations of 406
  apocalyptic response to 237
  condemned 189
  cultivation of bellicose wartime culture preparing the way for 260
  explanation for 375
  Germans accused of 282
  intense and detailed press coverage of 406
  invasion followed by news of 189
  pacifist identification of war with 197

representations/depiction of 342, 343
responsibility for 238
tales of 265
attrition 45, 46, 56, 57–62, 87, 88, 137, 161, 287, 308, 429, 468
  aerial 163
  mass 159
  murderous 131
  protracted 88, 130
  toxic gas shells in 308
  unexpectedly high 160
Au-dessus de la mêlée (Romain Rolland) 327
Audoin-Rouzeau, Stéphane 503
Aufruf an die Europaër 327
Aulard, Alphonse 325
Australia 62, 237, 311, 410, 414, 524–40
  conscription 412, 529, 530
  designated official artists 341
  infantry/troops 135, 178
  memorials 403, 580, 582
  numbers sent overseas to fight 526
  nurses from 268
  political rights of women 273
  self-government 524
  Statute of Westminster ratified 532
  tombs of Unknown Soldier 536
  wool clip 226
  see also Anzacs
Australian Imperial Force 252, 526
Austria 288, 289, 404
  abortive German customs union with 550
  Allies' acceptance of destruction of (1938) 552
  barred from international meetings 318, 545
  Brusilov's successful offensive against (1916) 484
  emergency legislation 373
  food coordination 377
  gas production 87
  German control of 381
  inflation 376
  intellectuals 327
  Italian requests for territorial compensation 466
  Kriegsarchiv 333
  land expropriation in 562
  major propaganda campaigns 376
  memorials 581
  mobilization 202
  National Council for South Slavs 382
  Nazi annexation of 585

Austria (*cont'd*)
  newsreels 354
  Pathé companies confiscated as enemy
    property 354
  policy of blackmailing Germany for
    resources 72
  prohibiting union between Germany
    and 546
  prospects of joint offensive with Germany
    against Russia 67
  Prussia's conquest of (1866) 41
  reappearance of Ottoman troops in 108
  serious economic crisis 490
  submarines 151
  threshold of disaster 71
  time to finish off 88
  US peace treaties with (1921) 520
Austrian army 482, 490
  Army High Command 373–4, 375
Austrian navy 151
  battle fleet 152
Austro-German force 71
Austro-Hungarian army 176
  aerial bombing of troops 166
  complete surrender of 473
  Czech and Slovak soldiers in 577
  drained by 1914–15 campaigns 288
  enormous losses inflicted on 107
  gun batteries 104
  minority nationalities in 290
  overextended and demoralized 74
Austro-Hungarian Council of Ministers 375
Austro-Hungarian Dual Monarchy 13, 23,
    46, 71, 73, 141, 207, 209, 371–85, 497
  arguments for "bread peace" 77
  attack on Serbia 15, 25, 43, 66, 68, 69, 84,
    191, 202, 203, 287, 371, 375, 433
  aviation 160
  Bosnia-Herzegovina annexed by (1909) 14,
    494
  casualties and losses 251, 252
  centrally controlled economy 376
  collapse (1918) 459
  crisis of legitimacy 371–2
  demands from Slavic populations 14
  disintegrated 245, 558
  dismantled 577
  dramatic crisis (1915) 86
  end of reserves of strength 212
  enfeebled, growing dependence of 438
  ethnic groups 75, 355
  expelled from Trentino and Veneto 82

food shortages 227
future collaboration between Germany
  and 77
Germany and 218, 288, 451, 452
grain-surplus and grain-deficit regions 228
growing strains evident with 454
hardline approach to emergent states in
  Balkans 14
intellectuals 326
irredentist claims to Italian-speaking
  areas 464
Italian Catholics silent about sympathies
  for 469
killings 191
losing control of events 372
mass death of Italian prisoners in
  captivity 194
mobilization plan 68
munitions crisis 224
nationalist and ethnic rivalries 75
official newsreels 355
predicament in Balkans 82
prisoners 93
Russian violence against civilians 190
schools cultivate notions of duty and
  honor 22
strategic passes ceded to 456
unresolved South Slav problem 371, 372
unstable equilibrium between Balkan states
  and 14
US entry into war against 512
war a disaster for civilian population 254
war effort 223
weak constitutional system 280
weakness of 74
Western Allies favor of breakup of 289
see also Central Powers; Franz Ferdinand;
  Franz-Josef
authoritarianism 39, 497, 560
Aux Soldats coloniaux (memorial) 535
avant-garde 327, 339, 341, 342, 344, 345,
  587
  cosmopolitan tradition of 347
  refusal to support the war 328
Avanti! (Italian Socialist Party daily) 467
Aviatik planes 160
aviation 162–9
  cavalrymen in 183
  cult of aces 157–9
  growth of air forces 159–61
  militarization of 156
  national industries 159–60

rapid development 182
sport 156
see also aircraft
Aymerich, Gen. Joseph 117
Azerbaijan 105, 488
  independence declared 457
  militiamen 100
  nationalist power 563
  uniting Anatolian and Azeri Turks 499
  see also Baku

Baader, Johannes 347
Bad Homburg Crown Council (1918) 77,
  455
Bad Kreuznach 211
Baden-Powell, Lt.-Col. Robert 22, 264
Badoglio, Pietro 90
Baghdad 14, 105, 106, 565
Bahr, Hermann 326
Bailey, George 314
Bainville, Jacques 205
Baker, Newton 515
Baker, Herbert Brereton 314
Baku 100, 457, 458
balance of power 208, 519, 543
  collapsing 14
  collective security replacing 518
  disrupted 419
  fundamental upheaval in 403
  opportunity to overturn 467
  restoration of 548
  transformed 558
Balaton, Lake 570
Balfour, Arthur 533
Balkan crisis (1908) 481
Balkan front 372
  trench warfare techniques 178
Balkan League (Bulgaria, Greece,
  Montenegro, Serbia) 8, 14, 73, 494
Balkan Wars (1912–13) 8, 11, 12, 14, 15, 42,
  69, 73, 141, 174, 175, 189, 206, 207,
  353, 378, 432, 494, 495
  Greek patriots hoped to conclude unfinished
    business 564
  revolutionary and patriotic student
    volunteers 501
  Turkish refugees from 192
Balkanization 546
Balkans 9, 66, 69, 73, 78, 107, 108, 481
  annexations in 211
  anti-Ottoman insurgents 502
  Armée de l'Orient in 528

collapsing balance of power 14
ethnic differentiation 558
French implicated in Russian objectives
  in 418
Italy and 82, 84, 464, 467
leading officers of Committee Union
  from 498
migrations from 497
nationalist politics 13
Ottoman help extended to 107
rape and ethnic cleansing 251
reappearance of Ottoman troops in 108
Ball, Albert 159
Ball, Hugo 346, 347
Balla, Giacomo 342
balloons 182, 321–13
Baltic Sea 150, 449
  German and Turkish blockade 219
Baltic States/region 39, 77, 204, 450, 451,
  459, 490, 545
  consequences of end of Russian Empire 563
  cornerstone of German policy in 458
  ethnic differentiation 558
  German rule/withdrawal 443, 563, 568
  Russian control/loss 210, 212
  terror against civilian populations 245
  see also Estonia; Latvia; Lithuania
Banjaluka 375
Bapaume 62, 135
Bar-le-Duc 59
Baracca, Francesco 159
Baratov, Lt.-Gen. N. N. 106
Barbusse, Henri 62, 236, 266, 330, 333, 422
Barlach, Ernst 344
Barnes, H. 28
Barrès, Maurice 205, 237
Barrett, Lt.-Gen. Sir Arthur 105
Basch, Victor 325
Basel 11, 14
BASF (Badische Anilin-und-Soda Fabrik)
  313
basibozuks (irregulars) 502
Basmachi revolt (1916) 561, 568
Basra 105, 106
Battisti, Cesare 375
battle-cruisers 97, 147, 151, 153
  disastrous results for 148
  scant margin of superiority in 144
Battle of the Frontiers (1914) 9, 49–50
battleships 22, 97, 101, 439
  sunk 102
  see also cruisers; dreadnoughts

Batum 100, 193
  given over to Turkey 212, 457
Bavarian army 51, 53
  cavalry 102
  soldiers blamed perpetuation of war on
    Prussians 287
Bayburt (Anatolia) 100
Bayer (chemicals company) 313
bayonet charges 8, 355
Beatty, Rear-Admiral David 145, 146, 147
Beaumont-Hamel 60, 61, 62, 410
Beaverbrook, Max Aitken, Lord 410
Bebel, August 5–6, 11
Béchereau, Louis 156
Becker, Annette 503
Becker, Jean Jacques 424
Beckmann, Max 340–1, 344, 345, 347, 349,
    433
Bédier, Joseph 334
BEF (British Expeditionary Force) 36, 37, 49,
    52, 62, 117, 411
  deployment to the Continent 145,
    355–6
  failure to provide adequate reinforcements
    to 413
  significant but junior role in retreat to
    Marne 405
Belarus 451, 482, 488
  partition of 563
  pogroms against Jewish population 568
  Russia gives up control of 455
Belarusians 450, 454, 578
Belfort 49, 203
Belgian army 136, 203, 212, 387, 388
  deserters 394
  equilibrium recovered 388
  pro-Flemish group within 393, 394
  unexpected resistance by 435
Belgian Congo 114, 116, 117, 204
  brutality of rule 189
Belgian Documentary Bureau 389
Belgian *Force publique* (in Congo) 114, 121,
    123
Belgium 41, 51, 53, 133, 239, 258, 268,
    360, 386–402, 419
  African colonies 112
  assumed to offer no resistance 6
  atrocities committed in 197, 282, 408, 510,
    566
  atypical war experience 580
  call for return to full independence 209
  casualties and losses 252

cinema audiences witness helplessness of
    refugees 356
  civilians deported to German work
    camps 52
  colonial troops for East Africa supplied
    by 120
  divided into Flemish and Walloon
    regions 392
  electrified fence between Netherlands
    and 191, 391
  first German victories in 434
  Flemish culture 326
  garde civique 52, 190
  intellectuals 334
  intentional killing of/savage behavior
    toward civilians 189, 282
  liberation of 394, 578
  martyred patriots given full national
    funerals 581
  massive exodus of populations (1940) 585
  military losses 395
  mobilized to make a stand at main fortified
    cities 49
  mutinies 287
  occupation of Ruhr (1923) 570
  overseas colonies 524
  ports 130
  "rape" of 265, 266
  refugees 52
  reparations owed by Germany to 27
  resistance networks 586
  retreat from 298
  school textbooks rewritten 583
  submarine bases 130, 149
  violation of neutrality 205
  see also Albert I; Leopold II
Belgium (German invasion/occupation) 54,
    149, 179, 189, 191, 203, 250, 254, 265,
    316, 323, 342, 386, 398, 404, 433, 577,
    582, 584
  administered by Governor-General 389
  attempt to attract Belgian men to German
    industry 392
  breaches of international law 434
  Catholic middle classes traumatized by 390
  divide-and-conquer expedient of
    policies 392–3
  Germans irritated by ongoing
    resistance 334
  hate for Germans 394
  living memory of 585
  outrage over 388

plays justifying 324
privileged area for Entente intelligence 391
redefined by Germans as liberation of "brother" people 392
remobilization 395
unexpected resistance by Belgian army 435
volunteers escape from 388
Belgrade 78, 279, 378
evacuation without a fight 69
Bell, A. C. 195
Bellows, George 343
Belluzzo, Guiseppe 311
Below, Gen. Fritz von 60, 61
Below, Gen. Otto von 88
Benda, Julien 323, 326
Benedict XV, Pope 208–9, 238
Benes, Eduard 548
Benjamin, René 332
Benjamin, Walter 350
Bennett, Arnold 328, 330
Berdjaev, Nikolai 326
Bergson, Henri 333, 334
Bérillion, Edgar 422
Berkhman, Gen. G. E. 99
Berlin 49, 243, 307, 313, 392, 581
call to restore order in 568
Dadaists in 347–8
economic war and riots 271
general strikes 442
heavy industrial districts 256
Hindenburg statue in 343
labor militancy 286
no potatoes in 255
red working-class districts 434
Berlin Academy 315, 318
Berlin Central Office of Censorship 281
Berlin Wall 28
Bernard, Jean-Marc 331
Bernard, Raymond 332
Berne 266
Bernhardi, Gen. Friedrich von 9–10
Berthelot, Philippe 58
Bertrand, Gabriel 314
Beseler, Gen. Hans von 450
Bessarabia 208
Bolsheviks forced to give up 490
Romania allowed to occupy 456
Bessel, Richard 569
Bethmann-Hollweg, Theobald von 10, 21, 39, 57, 62, 72, 189, 211, 280, 289, 392, 432, 433

resignation (1917) 439
September Program (1914) 203, 204, 210, 436, 452
Beumelburg, Werner 330
Beyer, Adolf von 316
Bianchi, Bruna 303
Bickel, Adam 313
Big Bertha (long-range gun) 272
"Big Push"/"Great Fuck-Up" 61, 62
Biograph (American film company) 353
Birdwood, Gen. Sir W. R. 101, 102
Birmingham 286, 412
Birmingham University 311
birth rate 114, 259
chronically low in France 527
Bishop, Billy 159, 166
Bismarck, Otto, Prince von 49, 70, 432, 434, 553
Bissing, Gen. Moritz von 389, 391–2
Bissolati, Leonida 470
bite-and-hold tactics 55
Black Acts 566
Black Africans 429, 545
Black and Tans 566, 567
black market 228, 255
Black Sea 100, 107, 150–1, 454, 457, 504
Armenians drowned in 192
blockade of 219
bombarding of Russian ports 206
coast shelled 97
coastal regions 504
defense/control of the Straits 108, 206
seaplanes employed over 160
Black South Africans 526
Blaue Reiter 339
Bloch, Marc 29, 175, 178, 241, 334, 343
blockades 47, 151, 195–6, 209, 213, 219, 225, 228, 255, 389, 406, 420, 438, 442
broken 458
effective 509
impact of 452
intensified 376
logic of 260
provisioning of civilians affected by 271
U-boat 411
Bloomsbury group 327
Blücher (cruiser) 146
Boccioni, Umberto 346
Bochkareva, Maria 272
Boelcke, Oswald 158, 159, 160, 162, 164
Boer revolt (1914–15) 118–19

Boer War (1899–1902) 55, 61, 173, 353, 531
 British concentration camps 189
 prominent role of Dominion volunteers 406
Bohemia 78, 372
 administration split on ethnic lines 381
 AOK vigilant to Czech subversive behavior 373–4
 Czechs arrested for political reasons 374
 Dadaists from 346
 fuel for anti-Semitic agitation in 375
 memorials 580
Bolshevik Revolution (1917) 27, 38, 39, 46, 27, 76, 77, 79, 128, 131, 150, 211, 213, 236, 245, 361, 412, 430, 453, 455, 456, 577
 abortion on demand 260
 atrocities of 244
 far-reaching significance 558
 fate of counterrevolutionaries 244
 focus of US government concern 520
 harsh conditions imposed by German military 442
 mandated anticolonialism 534
 Russian withdrawal from the war 489–91
 seeking for armistice 443
 slogan of 235
 strongest support for 561
 war effort prolonged by 319
 White opposition to 479
 women soldiers against 272
 Socialist Revolutionary opponents 560
bombing 157, 159, 160, 165, 166, 565
 balloons used in operations 312–13
 campaigns against insurgents 561
 civilian populations 157
 strategic 167, 182
Bonapartism 38, 39
boom and bust 375–7
boots and shoes 227
Bordeaux 38, 52, 58
Borden, Robert 529–30
Borel, Emile 309, 311
Boselli, Paolo 87, 89, 469
Bosnia-Herzegovina 69, 373, 382
 annexation of 14, 372, 494, 501
 crisis (1908–9) 14, 404
 famine 377
 guerrilla bands in mountain regions 379
 Serbs in 375, 381, 432
 treacherous transport links and bad harvest 377

Bosporus 206
 blockade of 151
Botha, Gen. Louis 119, 120
Boulogne 203
Bourassa, Henri 530
bourgeoisie 26, 76, 349, 569
 conservative 433, 436
 damnation of 6
 educated 435
 expropriation fears 558
 intellectual 208
 liberal 204
 national 502
Bourgin, Hubert 334
Bourke, Joanna 194, 197
Boutroux, Emile 325, 334
Bouvet (battleship) 101
Boy Scout movement 22, 264
Braga, Théophile 325
Bragg, W. H. 311
Braque, Georges 341
Bratianu, Ion 208
Brazil 141
bread rationing/shortages 227, 271, 411, 471, 485
Breguet, Louis 156, 162
Breguet aircraft 162, 166
Brémond, Col. Edouard 103
Brenta River 90
Breslau/Midilli (cruiser) 97
Brest-Litovsk Treaty (1918) 66, 77, 151, 212, 442, 443, 455, 456, 457, 546
 Allies' fierce reaction to 79
 Bolshevik stance 562
 denounced by Bolsheviks 459
Brentano, Lujo 324
Breton, André 338, 347, 348
Breton nationalists 287
Briand, Aristide 38, 56, 57, 58, 62, 205, 210, 211, 333, 582
 see also Kellogg-Briand Pact
Bridges, Robert 328
Briey-Longwy 203
Briey-Thionville 211
Brignoli, Luigi 584
Brion, Hélène 285
Britain 16, 68, 129, 130–2, 206, 403–17, 570
 African colonial empire 112
 age difference between marriage partners 259
 aligned with France and Russia 432

average working week 257
aviation 160, 161, 162, 167; *see also* RAF;
  RFC
bombarding of points along eastern
  coast 146
casualties and losses 252, 395, 415, 439,
  441, 464–5, 517, 577
chemical warfare 314, 319
cinema prices 357
civilian health 255
coal-bunkering stations 227
colonial troops for East Africa supplied
  by 120
colonists born in 529
conscription 270, 355, 410, 412, 413, 525,
  529
control of Belgian munitions workers 389
control of the seas 115
cultural demobilization 582
deaths per day 184
declaration of war on Germany (1914)
  405
demand for new reparations settlement
  548
designated official artists 341
dilution practice 420
discontent among Belgian munitions
  workers 394
domestic dissent and foreign
  subversion 283
eminent scientists 311
escape to 388
feminists 266, 267
fertility levels 248
films 362, 363, 365
first air raids on 408
flag-waving pictures 357
food supplies 227, 228
French rivalry in Africa and Asia 418
French steel supply imported from 218
German poem attacking 323
Greek forces encouraged by 564–5
in-depth defense 179
intellectuals 325, 327–8
international credit 46
leading suffragist organization 268
limitations on trade with Germany 509
loan-raising powers in US 219
memorials 580
migration from 532
military strikes and agitation 93
minority faiths in 239

munitions production 225
national ceremonies to honor the war
  dead 273
national interests endangered 203
pacifist and socialist movements 585
press freedom 281
prestige undermined throughout Muslim
  world 105–6
propaganda office 328
rearmament program (1937) 552
recruiting posters 264, 265
recruitment drive to raise a volunteer
  army 282
regarded as Germany's primary enemy 71
resolve at news of war 280
ruthless German attempt to knock out
  (1917) 128
schools cultivate notions of duty and
  honor 22
self-mobilization 289
separation allowances 268
service departments 310
starvation attempted by U boat warfare
  129
state pensions 22
stories about German population in 408
strategic ambitions 423
strategy and policy integration 35
tariffs 550
unambiguous support for France 11
university science departments 313
unyielding imperialist stance 553
US relations strained with 510
war economy 255
war effort 219, 223, 576
war supplies from United States 57
women's suffrage 264, 273
young writers who fought in the
  trenches 328
see also Asquith; Balfour; Chamberlain;
  Chelmsford; Churchill; Curzon; Hoare;
  Lloyd George; Milner; Montagu; *also*
  under following headings prefixed
  "British"
British Admiralty 36, 117, 142, 310, 411,
  437
Board of Invention and Research 311
"Room 40" 146
wireless intercepts 149
British Aero Club 156
British Africa 112–24
British Air Ministry 310

British army 43, 101, 107, 129, 134, 135,
    405, 525
  age spectrum of men serving 251
  armored-vehicle operations 183
  casualties and losses 61, 184, 464, 525
  collapse of 88
  diagnosis of conditions lumped together as
    "shellshock" 302
  divisions in Italy 89, 90
  dwarfed by continental European
    armies 525
  expeditionary forces acting as corps
    within 526
  gone past recall 54
  Great Retreat 52
  Irish nationalists in 406, 578
  Irish rebellion crushed by significant
    numbers of Irishmen 409
  Midland division 136
  military conversations between French
    and 404
  morale of 127, 133
  offensive to split French and 443
  quantities of guns and shells 130
  shell shortage 408
  shortage of munitions 176
  soldiers executed for desertion 92
  soldiers warned to resist "temptation" 269
  tanks 182, 183
  women physicians 268
  see also Alanbrooke; Allenby; BEF; Birdwood;
    British New Armies; Byng; Dyer; Gough;
    Haig; Hamilton; Kitchener; Monro;
    Rawlinson; Stopford
British Board of Trade Chemical Products
    Supply Committee 313
British Colonial Office 117
British Commonwealth 551, 532
  War Graves Commission 536
British Documents on the Origins of the War,
    1898–1914 27
British Dyestuffs Corporation 313
British Empire 46, 47, 62, 226, 524, 528,
    531–3, 535, 537, 547
  Aerial League 156
  airplane viewed as tool to unify 157
  cemeteries in France 535
  deaths in combat 517
  defining characteristics of peoples from
    different parts 529
  global protection for minorities a problem
    for 546

India at center of strategic thinking
    about 525
  Irish loyalty to 405
  Jewish refugees refused 552
  large numbers of men brought to the
    Continent 145
  local martyrdoms for various parts of 410
  mandates in the Middle East 565
  memorials to the war dead 403
  Middle East presence 560
  Muslim loyalty to 499
  naval defense of 143
  nonwhite troops kept out of European
    theater 285
  profound effects on development of war
    for 406
  sacrifice for the war effort 531
  strengthened and weakened by the war 414
  very high numbers of men mobilized 250
British Grand Fleet 148, 153
  American battleships work with 149–50
  anchorage in Orkney 144
  attempt by Germans to lure a portion
    of 146, 147
  convoy policy 128
  German Imperial Navy outnumbered in all
    classes by 437
  scant margin of superiority in battle
    cruisers 144
  submarines against 145
British High Command 88
  critics of 131
British Ministry of Munitions 55, 225, 226,
    310
  Chemical Warfare Department 314
  Trench Warfare Department 314
British Ministry of War 357
British National War Aims Committee 290
British navy 508
  challenge to supremacy 403
  film stressing excessive power of 363
  looming Japanese threat to 552
  rivalry with Germany 3, 403
  submarines 102, 145, 150
  superiority 12
  see also British Grand Fleet; Royal Navy
British New Armies 55, 56, 57, 60, 61
  glory and graveyard of 62
  problems of equipping and arming 408
  raised by mass volunteering 410
British Overseas Settlement Committee 532
British Treasury 313

British War Cabinet 130, 531
British War Office 36, 122, 224, 268, 310, 314
  censors refuse permission for painting to be shown 345
  insensitivity to Irish nationalists 409
  intervention in production of filmed news 360
British West African Frontier Force 116
Brittany 287
Brooke, Rupert 264, 405, 535
Brosch, Col. Alexander 70
brothels 269
Brüning, Heinrich 549–50
Brusilov, Gen. Alexei 39, 74, 86, 107, 438, 479, 484, 487
Brussels 279, 387, 392, 394
  charities 389
  school for nursing 391
  underground press 390
  victory parade 395
Bryan, William Jennings 509
Bryce Committee Report (Britain 1915) 265
Buchan, John 328
Bucharest 107, 455, 279
Bucharest Peace Treaty (1918) 456
Buck, Otto 327
Budapest 373, 380, 570, 581
  workers' councils 561
BUFA (Bild-und Film-Amt) 361
Bukharin, Nikolai 212
Bukoba 12
Bukovina 190
Bulair region 101
Bulgakov, Sergei 326
Bulgakov, Valentin 327
Bulgaria 8, 14, 73, 75, 329, 429, 456, 546
  armistice with Allies 459
  army 107, 333
  Balkan League turning on 494
  barred from international meetings 318, 545
  civil war avoided 569
  decision to join Central Powers 42, 207
  entry into the war 449
  independence 454, 501
  intellectuals 327
  land distribution 562
  modernists who rejected all war poetry 328
  obliged to give up territory 559
  paramilitaries 567
  plan to force out of the war 515
  surrender of 46
  war poetry 331
  zone of occupation 378–9
  see also Balkan League
Bülow, Bernhardt, Prince von 10
Bülow, Gen. Karl von 41, 51, 52, 53
Bund Neues Vaterland 317
Burgenland 564
Burgfrieden 280, 433, 442
Burghclere (Stanley Spencer fresco, Sandham Memorial Chapel), 349
Burma 566
Burnett-Stuart, Maj.-Gen. John 566
bush warfare 120, 121
Butler, Nicholas M. 316
Byng, Gen. Sir Julian 526
Byzantine Empire 207

Cadorna, Gen. Luigi 38, 84–5, 86, 87–9, 90, 92, 93, 290, 470, 471–2
Caine, Hall 328
Cairo 103, 115, 124
Cambodia 530, 535
Cambrai, battle of (1917) 132, 165, 181, 183
Cambridge University 311, 328
Camon, Hubert 40
camouflage 341, 355
Canada 273, 311, 329, 330, 410, 524–40
  air aces 166
  concerns about control from London 532
  conscription 529, 412
  designated official artists 341
  gas used against 56
  memorials 403, 580, 582
  prewar plans for independent navy 525–6
  prominent role of volunteers in South African War 406
  self-government 524
  Unknown Soldier 536
Canadian Corps 134
Canadian Expeditionary Force 526
Canakkale 565
canals 136, 387
Cannae (battle, 216 BC) 40, 71
Cape Town 113
capitalism 11, 420, 521
  laissez-faire 518
  wars inherent in the nature of 23
Caporetto, battle of (1917) 38, 85, 88, 89, 90, 91, 92, 181, 130, 213, 290, 464, 468, 512
  and the "enemy within" 471–2

Caproni, Gianni 157
Caproni planes 160, 166
Carden, Sir Sackville 101
Carinthia 375
Carnegie Foundation 189, 335, 397, 480
Carnet B 419
Carniola 374
Carol I, King of Romania 208
Caroline islands 206
Carpathian Mountains 70, 71, 438, 456, 586
Carrizal (Mexico), battle at (1916) 510–11
Carso River 85, 86, 87, 89
Carson, Sir Edward 405, 409, 566
Caspian Sea 77, 100, 457
Castelnau, Edouard Noël de 59
casualties 250–1, 287, 529
    aim to maximize and minimize 45
    air 166
    army eroded/weakened by 73, 78
    cataclysmic 515
    civilians often numbered among 559
    clearing stations 297, 301
    enormous/high 6, 7, 51
    fragmentary evidence of 163
    "friendly" 56
    gas 182
    heavy 74, 102, 127, 128, 387, 410, 412,
        413, 423–4, 441, 525
    higher among officers 252
    innovations that reduced 181
    intellectuals 329
    most severely affected age cohort 251
    predicted 6
    regiments depleted by 69, 526
    rural bias in 252
    some of the worst levels 298
casualty numbers 51, 53, 54, 55, 56, 58, 59,
    61, 68, 71, 86, 87, 91, 104, 133, 415,
    497, 569–70
    estimated 85
    historically unprecedented 184
    pilots 163
Catholic Church
    France 419
    Italy 465
Catholic democrats 473
Catholic University of Milan 469
Catholicism/Catholics 209, 237, 238, 283,
    374, 396, 406
    accused of disloyalty 483
    associations/organizations at service of
        national cause 434
    bearing the brunt for defeatism 89
    bishop's plan to evangelize Muslims 528
    clergy 381, 466
    converts 239, 240
    German Center Party 288, 442
    influenced by papacy 207
    Irish-American 239
    lay activists 243
    opposed to entry into war 466, 469
    prayer groups 393
    strongly conservative 349
    underground paper in Belgium launched
        by 390
Catt, Carrie Chapman 514
Cattaro, Gulf of 151, 152
Caucasian Corps 99
Caucasian front 206
    peasant army brutalized by fighting 244
    soldiers' deaths 497
Caucasus 77, 100, 330, 439, 457–8, 503,
    560, 570
    consequences of end of Russian Empire 563
    given over to Turkey 212
    invasions of Ottoman territory in 504
    migrations from 497
    Ottoman army occupies parts of 499
    refugees in 192
    terror against civilian populations 245
    Turkish nationalists from 498
causality 19–20
    nationalism's role in 21
    structural or functional explanations
        of 21–4
    systemic explanations focusing on 24–5
cavalry 49, 51, 56, 70, 104, 105, 130, 131
    age-old role lost 183
    dismounted 63
    unreliable units 99
Cavell, Edith 268, 272, 391
Celicia 255
Celse 300
Cemal Pasha, Col. Ahmet 103, 495, 496,
    498, 499
Cemal Pasha, Brig.-Gen. Mersinli 104
cemeteries and memorials 480, 535–6, 579,
    580, 582
Cendrars, Blaise 422
Cenotaphs 579
censorship 280, 281, 315, 327, 345, 355,
    356
    bulletins 472
    effective 357

important in prosecution of the war 471
increased 530
press 289, 380
theatrical performances 421
Central Africa 112
Britain's defense of its colonies 121
porters enlisted or forcibly conscripted 124
sustained suffering to peoples of 120
Central and Eastern Europe 248, 251, 290, 568
annexations program 211
anti-Semitism 193, 552
attempted revolution across 577
banking crises 550
contagious diseases 295
customs union 77
deaths from war-related causes 251
declaration that held genuine appeal for impoverished peasants 558
disarray all over 551
food supplies 227
forced labor and deportations 191
German minority groups covertly subsidized 549
idea of permanent informal German empire in 440
Jews 449, 453, 552
memory of brutalities 245
national monuments and rituals 581
occupation of 438, 439, 447–63
oppressed Jews 239
radical transformation of 371
reports of famine, disease, pogroms, Bolshevik incursions, and inter-allied fighting 545
revolutionary tendencies 137
severe shortages 257
territorial gains in 436
treaties imposed on new and expanded states 546
Central Asia 46, 457
Basmachi revolt 561, 568
Muslim groups exempt from conscription 483
Pan-Turkish polity embracing 561
recruitment of indigenous populations 285
ruthless crushing of revolt (1916) 193
Turks in 206, 496, 499
Central Powers (Germany, Austro-Hungarian Empire, Ottoman Empire, Bulgaria) 26, 66, 74, 75, 78, 107, 205, 208, 209, 210, 219, 281, 359, 433, 437, 482, 490

Allies had reserves unavailable to 254
armed conflict continued within defeated countries of 256
armistice with 455–6
blockade contributed to exhaustion of 47
blockade of Russian exports through Dardanelles 228
Bolshevik negotiations with 455
British or French movies shown in 358
Bulgaria's decision to join 42, 207, 449
casualties 250, 251
controlling trade 227
coordinated attacks against 46, 423
crashing down 459
direct military assistance of great value to 108
division of spoils 453
friction between 457
generalized attack in long dormant theatres 429
Italian government under no obligation to support 84
loans to 219
Ottoman Empire support to 97, 103, 495
principal responsibility for the war 27
Regency Council of Polish notables 451, 455
reparations from 72–3
Russian Poland conquered by 450
scientists prohibited from taking part in international meetings 318
support for future united Polish state 380
territorial claims against 545
Triple Entente powers arrayed against 467
Turkey's entry into war on the side of 143–4
Ukrainian peace agreement with 490
war renewed unilaterally 77
Center for the Study of the Causes of the War (Germany) 26
Century Magazine 333
České Budějovice 374
Cevat Pasha, Brig.-Gen. 101, 104, 107
Chad 117
Chagall, Marc 340
Chaldeans 504
Chalyapin, Fëdor 333
Chamber of Deputies (France) 62, 426
Chamberlain, Austen 583
Chamberlain, Neville 552
Champagne 55, 56, 57, 134, 423
Channel Ports 127, 133
ferries 136
seaborne food supplies to 217

Chantilly conference (1915) 57, 58, 60
chaplains 92, 239, 243
Chaplin, Charlie 76, 258, 361
Charleroi 387
Chartier, Emile (Alain) 422
Cheka 244, 558, 559–60, 561, 562
Chelmsford, Frederic, Lord 533
chemical warfare 313, 314, 319, 437
 gas shells 270
Chemical Warfare Service (US) 318
Chemin des Dames offensive (1917) 127,
 129, 135, 177, 179, 211, 254, 287, 425
 colonial battalions primarily used at 528
chemistry 308, 313
Cheriff Pasha 504
Chernov, Victor 488
Chesterton, G. K. 323
Chetniks 379
Chevket Pasha, Mahmut 498
Chiefs of Imperial General Staff 36, 37, 46,
 566
children's literature 422–3
Chile 141, 143, 144
China 193, 206, 360, 545, 552
 labor force in France 285, 420, 428
 migrant workers from 528
 mired in civil war 550
 rights of foreigners in empire 490
chlorine gas 56, 181, 307, 314, 437
chloroform 304
chocolate 258
cholera 76, 106, 250, 294, 295, 450
Chra River 116
Christianity/Christians 238, 240–1, 242,
 243, 349, 496
 extermination of 502, 504
 forcibly expelled 547
 justifications for battlefield losses 441
 threat to existence of Muslim Turks 503
Christmas truce (1914) 180
Churchill, Winston 36, 142, 161, 558
Cieszyn *see* Teschen
cinema 254–8 *see also* film; newsreels
Cisleithania (Austria) 372, 373, 377
citizen-soldiers 425, 426
citizenship 485, 486
 access easier for soldiers 534
 denial of rights of 547
 identity and 239, 473
 political 414
 rewards of 530
civil aviation 156, 167

civil disobedience 441
civil liberties 471
civil subordination 39
civil war 348, 502, 550, 558, 585
 covert 474
 see also Irish Civil War; Russian Civil War
civilian health 254–6
Clam-Martinic, Count Heinrich von 381
clandestine press/papers 390, 395
Clark, Alan 19
Class, Heinrich 436
class conflict 562
class enemy 570, 579
class struggle 424
class war 559, 566, 568
 see also social classes
Clausewitz, Carl von 5, 7, 16, 35, 45, 52, 59,
 202
Clayton, Anthony 54, 59, 62
Clemenceau, Georges 12, 38, 47, 73, 209,
 238, 281, 283, 289, 425, 428, 518, 527,
 545, 553
Clydeside militancy 407
coal 113, 205, 218, 226, 391, 456, 490, 546
 anthracite 407
 bunkering stations 227
 mines 515
 production of 376, 420
 rationing of 226
Cochin, Capt. Augustin 422
Cocos Islands 143
code de l'indigénat 534
codes of honor and duty 25
Cold War 25, 418
Colette 330
Colin, Jean 40
collective indiscipline 130, 425
collective memory 576
collective security 552
 balance of power replacing 518
 demonstrations of militancy in the name
 of 550
collectivist socialism 413
Collège de France 314
Collins, Michael 566
Cologne 51, 548
Colorado 519
Columbia University 316, 480
combat methods 173–87
 hand-to-hand 58, 177, 355
combatant-writers 329
Comédie française 333

Comité central de secours et d'alimentation (Belgium) 389–90, 392, 393, 395
  German-controlled press campaign against 394
Comité des forges 205, 226
Comité d'études et de documents sur la guerre 334, 422
Comité pour le rapprochement universitaire 333
Commission des études chimiques de guerre 314
Committee for Industrial Mobilization (Italy) 469
Committee for the Promotion of Industrial and Scientific Research (Britain) 313
Committee of Imperial Defence (Britain) 35–6, 406
Committee on Public Information (US) 514
Committee Union and Progress (Young Turks) 495, 496, 497, 498, 499–500, 501, 502
  genocide of Armenians 503
  Pan-Turkist and Pan-Islamist policies 495
communes 11, 389, 390
communications systems 20, 41, 43, 44, 149, 179–80
  efficient networks 497
communism/communists 19, 212, 534, 569
  anti-fascist 585
  dislike of monopoly of power (Kronstadt sailors' revolt) 561
  exile of 570
  fall of 480
  ideological differences between fascism and 245
  illegal parties 570
  importing of radical ideas 520
  marginalizing 430
  origins and decline 5
Compiègne 51, 55
concentration camps 189, 244
Concert of Europe (1815) 13, 14, 15, 25
  gradual erosion of 24
concrete bunkers 436–7
  see also Belgian Congo
Congress Party (India) 566
Connolly, James 409
conscientious objectors 270, 517
conscription 52, 54, 75, 78, 82, 87, 118, 119, 270, 355, 388, 512, 569
  absence of bitter disputes 530
  age limits extended 412
  appeals against 410

attempt to extend 287
avoidance of 531
Britain without until 1916 525
countries without 237
exemption from 483
fiercely contested 529
forcible 124, 487
French colonial army in West Africa 114
industrial 408
Ireland, failed attempt to impose on 412–13
legal status of 248
mass 521
Muslim 97, 483
opposed 530
poorly trained and less reliable groups 483
resisted 529
supported in principle 410
universal 7
Conseil Supérieur de Guerre 38
consent 342–3, 345, 424
  organization of 469–71, 472
  re-engineered 425
Conservative Party (Britain) 37, 290, 404, 408, 413
  Lloyd George growing close to the leadership 410
Conservative-Unionists (UK) 413
Conservatoire national des arts et métiers 312
Consiglio Nazionale delle Richerche 319
Constanta 456
Constantine I, King of Greece 73, 207
Constantinople 47, 72, 78, 101, 103, 104, 206
  conquest of 205, 207
  Russia's secret war aims of conquest 488
Constitutional Democrats (Russia) 484
contraband 509
contraception 260
convalescence 295, 303, 304
convoys 128, 145, 149, 440
  introduction of 411
  success in defeating U-boats 137
Cooper, Gary 163
Copeau, Jacques 235
Corfu 73, 151, 378
Corfu Declaration (1917) 379
Corinthians 240
Cork, Richard 338
Cork (city) 566
Corn Production Act (Britain 1917) 227
Coronel, battle of (1914) 36, 144

Corridoni, Filippo 467
Corriere della Sera 467
Cossacks 190, 264, 330, 456
  expulsion/deportation of 560, 567
  military units punished 483
Côte du Poivre (Verdun) 58
Cotton, Aimé 309
cotton 509, 561
Council of Flanders 393
Council of People's Representatives
  (Russia) 272
Cousturier, Lucie 534
cowardice 93, 471, 583
Cradock, Rear-Admiral Christopher 143, 144
Craonne 55
Creditanstalt bank 376
Crefeld officer camp 334
Creusot factory 182
Creuzburg an der Werra 334
Crimea 61, 77, 151, 455, 456
  counterrevolutionaries executed 560
  Tatars deported 193
  Turkish nationalists from 498
crimes against humanity 192, 196, 197, 587
criminality 441
Croatia 78, 377, 382
  Communist Party 570
  legitimization of the war 374
  military-political tussle for power 374
  Peasant Party 570
Croats 93, 94, 289, 372, 382–3, 578
Cromarty Firth 146
Cross River 117
Crossley, Arthur William 314
Crozier, Lt.-Col. Percy 61
Cru, Jean Norton 333
cruisers 143, 146, 152
  armored 146
  auxiliary 144
  light 145
  Northern Patrol (10th squadron) 153
  scout 145
  sunk 144, 145, 437
  see also battle-cruisers
Ctesiphon 105
Cuban Missile Crisis (1962) 20–1
Cubism 338, 339, 340, 341
cultural demobilization 582, 584
Curie, Marie 309
Curragh military camp 404
Currie, Gen. Sir Arthur 526
Curzon, George N., Lord 533

customs union 77, 204
  abortive 550
Cyrillic alphabet 375
Czech banknotes 376
Czech regions/provinces 372, 382
Czech Sudetenland 585
Czechoslovak Legion 379
Czechoslovakia 546, 548, 559, 564, 569,
  570, 577, 582
  Allies' sacrifice of 552
  ethnic differentiation 558
  Hitler's total destruction of 585
  Reich's border with 548
  territorial claims 545
  volunteers 90, 581; Czechs 288, 289, 381
  communities 373
  disaffected 374
  encouragement to form new state 371
  political clubs 381
  subversive behavior 373–4
  uprising of prisoners of war in Siberia 560
Czestochowa 450

Dadaists 328, 346, 347–8, 349, 350
Dagen, Philippe 338
Dagö (island) 454
Daily Chronicle 159
Daily Mail 22
Daimler 157, 161
Dakar 114, 536
Dalmatia 78, 94, 152, 374, 375
  Croat regions 379, 381
  famine along the coast 377
  governor of 375
  Italian claims to territories 473
  South Slav 84
Damascus 97, 104
D'Annunzio, Gabriele 94, 326, 329, 467,
  473, 564
Danube River 69, 73, 78, 107, 455
Danubian Federation 548
Danzig 546, 552
Dar es Salaam 120, 121, 122, 123
Dardanelles 36, 73, 97, 101–3, 143, 178,
  179, 206, 310, 565
  Allied troops diverted to assist Serbia 208
  Armée de l'Orient in 528
  blockade of Russian exports through 228
  Turkish appeals for help 151
Davis, Capt. Edward 515
Dawes Plan (1924) 548
Daylight Saving Act (Britain 1917) 226

DDF (Documents Diplomatiques Français) 27, 28
De Ambris, Alceste 467
death sentences 196, 426
death squads 569
Debelianov, Dimcho 329, 331
Debussy, Claude 340
decision-making 10, 15, 23–4, 29, 38
    fault-lines in 36
    international 20
    management techniques for 21
    role of social Darwinism in influencing 25
    under crisis, command and control 21
"Declaration by the Second and Third-Level Teachers of the German Reich" 324
Declaration of London (1909) 195
Declaration of Paris (1856) 195
Decree on Peace (Russia 1917) 490
defeatism 89, 394, 472
Defence of the Realm Act (DORA) Britain (1914) 269, 411
deflationary policy 549–50
Degrez, Alexandre 314
De Havilland, Geoffrey 157
Delbos, Victor 325
Delbrück, Hans 45, 62, 327
Delcassé, Théophile 206, 207
Delorme, Edmond 296
Delville Wood 62, 410
demobilization 346–9
    cultural 243–5, 317
    economic 256
democratization 22, 481
demography 181, 248–62, 464, 496–7
    impact of the war exaggerated 414
    major shift 513
    ongoing crisis compounded 377
Denikin, Gen. Anton 560, 562
Denmark 325, 355, 362
denunciations 286, 427, 459, 471, 472, 475, 509
Department of Scientific and Industrial Research (Britain) 311, 318
deportations 52, 192, 193, 196, 197, 244, 255, 288, 392, 395, 440–1
    brutal, during Russian retreat 1915 449–50
    civilians as *francs-tireurs* 388
    Cossack 567
    deaths during marches 266
    dignitaries to German prison camps 390
    fear of 394
    hotly contested by Reichstag 392

orders for 504
    widespread 191
    women 330
Derby Scheme (Britain 1915) 408–9
De Robeck, Vice-Admiral Sir John 101
Desault, P. J. 300
desertion 60, 61, 93, 257, 394, 497, 569
    convictions/executions for 92
    mass 488, 489
Destour 531
destroyers 145, 147–8, 149, 150, 151
    American 149
    large flotillas 143
    sunk 145
Desvallières, Georges 349
deterrence 418, 419
DEULIG (Deutsche Lichtbild-Gesellschaft) 359, 361
Deutsche Revue 7
Deutschland über Alles 340
Deutschland und der Weltkrieg (1916 anthology) 317
Devambez, André 344, 349
Diagne, Blaise 527, 531, 533, 534
Diallo, Babary 534
Diaz, Gen. Armando 89, 90–1, 92, 93, 472
dictatorship 78, 326, 583
    bureaucratic-military 373
    publicly condemned 381
Dictionnaire de théologie catholique 236
Die Aktion (journal) 327, 328
Die Grosse Politik der europaïschen Kabinette, 1871–1914 27
Die Kriegsschuldfrage (journal) 26–7
Diet (Croatia) 78
Dieuze-Château-Salins 49
digestive fever 58
Diller, Gen. Erich, Baron von 450
dilution 420, 427
Dimitrijević, Col. Dragutin T. 379
Dinant 388
    mass killings 190
    order to shoot suspect civilians 197
D'Indy, Vincent 422
Direction des inventions 318
Direction du matériel chimique de guerre 314
dirigibles 156
dirty wars 567, 570
disabled war veterans 184
diseases
    contagious 295
    endemic 254, 255

diseases (*cont'd*)
  epidemic 250, 254, 378, 450, 569
  see also cholera; influenza; typhoid; typhus
dissent 283, 327, 473
  arbitrary powers used to monitor and
    quell 373
  intellectual 328
  middle-class 569
  practically impossible 521
  surveillance of dissidents 530
division of labor 284
  gendered 441
Dix, Otto 185, 340, 343, 346, 348, 349, 433
Diyala River 105
Diyarbakir region 100, 503
Dmowski, Roman 451
Dobell, Brig.-Gen. C. M. 117
Dobruja 107, 456
doctors 298, 302
  frontline 296
documentaries 354, 361, 362, 363
Dodecanese islands 94
Dodoma 123
Doering, Major Kurt von 115, 116
Dogger Bank 146
Dominions 273, 413, 414, 524
  distinctive characteristics of 529
  forces 135, 406
  major untapped sources of manpower 412
  memorials 580, 582
  strengthened national identity 414
  see also Australia; Canada; New Zealand;
    Newfoundland; South Africa
Don River 455, 456, 560
Dorgelès, Roland 240, 330, 332
Dos Passos, John 91, 329
Douaumont 528, 536, 580
Douhet, Giulio 157
Doyle, Arthur Conan 323, 328
dreadnoughts 22, 12, 150, 525
  sunk 144, 152
  super 141–2
Dresden 78, 349, 372–3
Dreyfus affair (1894–1906) 38, 335
drifters (small naval craft) 152, 153
drink(ing)
  excessive 568
  moral panic about 408
Duala 116, 117
Dublin 409, 410, 567
DuBois, W. E. B. 534
Duchamp, Marcel 339

Duchamp-Villon, Raymond 341
Duhamel, Georges 330
Duhem, Pierre 316
Duma (Russian parliament) 288, 483
  proto-fascist faction 484
  socialist faction 486
Dumur, Louis 332
Dunkirk 203
Dunoyer de Segonzac, André 343
Dupouey, Mireille 241–2
Dupouey, Pierre 241
Durkheim, Emile 234, 235, 333, 334, 422
Duroselle, Jean-Baptiste 19, 207
Duy Thanh, Annamese emperor 531
Dyer, Gen. Reginald 533, 566
dysentery 250
Dyson, Will 343
Dzerzhinsky, Feliks 244

East Africa 119, 120–4, 163
  Britain's defense of colonies 121
  German mass murder in suppression of
    indigenous rebellion 189
  porters enlisted or forcibly conscripted 124
  sustained suffering to peoples of 120
  West African troops sent to 123
  women physicians served British army
    in 268
East Asiatic Squadron (Germany) 143
East Prussia 40, 52, 71, 265
  contrast between occupied territories
    and 450
  deportations to Russia 191
  expulsion of last Russian soldiers from 435
  Russian army outnumbered Germans
    in 482
  Russian invasion of (1914) 190, 250, 254,
    581
  separating from the Reich 546
  withdrawal of Russia from 482
Easter Rising (Ireland 1916) 287, 414, 530,
    567, 578
  Irish soldiers frequently outraged at
    409–10
  violent suppression of 510
Eastern Europe *see* Central and Eastern
    Europe
eastern front 39, 40, 66–81, 86, 88, 128,
    372, 447, 490
  accounts of atrocities 266
  bloodbath on 250
  brutal violence against civilians 245

deaths in major military encounters 254
enormous losses inflicted on Austro-
    Hungarian armies 107
extreme swings of fortune of 449
German Commander-in-Chief on 212
Germans totally victorious on 132
massive military engagements 173
mobile warfare 174
peasant army brutalized by fighting on
    244
Russian troops kept on 100
successes of 449
theater of paradoxes 66
value of heavy artillery 176
vast number of prisoners taken on 288
victorious German offensive (1915) 464
war of movement 265, 449
women who fought on 271, 330
Eastern Germany 346
Ebergard, Admiral A. A. 99
Ebermeier, Karl 116
Ebert, Friedrich 444
Echenberg, Myron 526
Eclair 354, 355
Ecole Normale Supérieure 329, 334
Ecole Polytechnique 329
Ecole supérieure de pharmacie 314
Economic and Disarmament Conferences
    (1932) 551
Edgerton, David 310
Edirne (Adrianopolis) 494, 501
Edison, Thomas 311
EEF (Egyptian Expeditionary Force) 104
Egypt 103, 104, 114, 414, 559
    Britain formalized occupation of 533
    demand for progress toward
        emancipation 285
    nationalists 567
    Wafd party nationalists 565
Ehrlich, Paul 316
Eichhorn, Field-Marshal Hermann von 457
Einem, Gen. Karl von 55
Einstein, Albert 317, 318, 327
Eisenhower, Gen. Dwight D. 423
electric-shock treatment 304–5
Elisabeth, Queen of the Belgians 388
embusqués see shirkers
Emden (cruiser) 143
émigrés
    Russian 480
    South Slav 378
Emmich, Gen. Otto von 51

Endrici, Bishop of Trento 375
enemy civilians
    targeting of 255
    violence against 189–93, 237, 244–5
"enemy within" 288, 465, 471–2, 503
    Fascist program for action against 567
enfranchisement 272, 273
    female 414
Engels, Friedrich 5, 6
England
    German communities 408
    towns of the industrial north 410
English Channel 12, 46, 53, 54, 509
    see also Channel Ports
Enis, Selaheddin 502
Entente Cordiale (France/Britain 1904) 10,
    12, 418, 543
    fragmented 547
    see also Triple Entente
Entertainments Tax (Britain) 357
Enver Pasha 99, 100, 103, 105, 107, 206,
    495, 496, 498, 499, 561
    counter-putsch organized by 497
Epstein, Fritz 313
Equatorial Africa 116, 524
    recruitment campaign in 527
Erevan 559, 565
Ermattungsstrategie 45, 62
Ern, Vladimir 326
Ernst, Max 350
ersatz foods/materials 438
Erzincan 100
Erzurum 99, 100
Esat Pasha, Brig.-Gen. Mehmet 102
eschatology 238, 244
Esnaf Cemiyeti (Ottoman Society of
    Tradesmen) 502
espionage 193, 355, 395, 408
    fear of 354
Espionage Act (US 1917) 520
Estonia 146, 450, 454, 455, 490, 559, 570
    Bolsheviks forced to give up 490
    Jews from 245
    occupation of (1918) 458
    Russia gives up control of 455
    Soviet troops and Bolshevik commissars
        rebuffed in 563
Etappe 389, 392
Ethiopia 551, 552
    Italy's humiliating defeat by 82
ethnic cleansing 71, 251, 255, 436
    foreshadowing 452

ethnic groups 355, 375, 450
    denial of rights to 547
    deported 192
    differences 69
    diversity 450, 453
    hatreds 430
    ideological mobilization against 503
    intended for client status 453
    limited loyalty felt by 283
    playing off one another 454
    recruits enlisted from 114
    rivalries 75, 568
    routine brutality used in dealing with
        minorities 502
    settling 458
    stigmatized 193
ethnicity 271, 279, 414
    common 383
    policies to divide local populations by 191
ethno-nationalism 191, 193
Eucken, Rudolf 324
Euphrates River 97, 105
Evan-Thomas, Vice-Admiral Hugh 147
Excess Profits Tax (Britain) 407, 411
executions 196, 266, 268, 271, 375
    counterrevolutionaries 560
    deserters 92
    dubious grounds for 428
    euphemism for 378–9
    formalized 190
    grounds for 197
    mass 387, 409
    response to mutinies (1917) 289
    summary 192, 561, 567, 583
    victims of 189
    women and children forced to watch 198
Expressionism 328, 339, 341, 349
extermination 245, 499, 504
    arrest or 566
    call for 237
    state-sponsored 502
extra-judicial killings 568
extreme right 259
    anti-republican groups 430
extremism 570, 579
    international 473

Fabre, Emile 333
facial injuries 184–5
Faculté de médicine 314
Fahrettin Pasha, Brig.-Gen. 103
Faisal I, King of Iraq 565

faith(s) 235, 237, 240, 241, 242, 243
    messianic 245
    minority 239
    religious-style 236
Falkenhausen, Gen. Ludwig von 389, 392,
        394
Falkenhayn, Gen. Erich von 39, 42, 47, 53–4,
        56, 57–60, 62, 66, 71–3, 86, 104, 128,
        132, 436, 438
    Christmas 1915 memorandum 46, 57
    dismissed/replaced for Verdun failure 75,
        238, 439
Falklands 144
Falla, Manuel de 325
family life 271, 285
    nuptiality and 257–8
    restoration of 259, 260
famine 377, 390, 545
    fear of 394
Far East 568
Farben (I. G.) 313
Farbwerke Hoechst 314
Farman brothers 156, 164
Fasbender, Gen. Karl von 53
fascism/fascists 19, 244, 364, 465, 475, 584
    Arditi a legend to be exploited 90
    belligerency of 551
    Blackshirts 570
    breeding ground for 562
    corporatist government that would exert
        some influence on 473
    ideological differences between communism
        and 245
    pacifist fears confirmed by the rise of 585
    political violence 244
    program for action against "enemy
        within" 567
    seizure of power 548
Fatherland Party (Germany 1917–18) 211,
        440
Fay, Sidney Bradshaw 28
Fayolle, Gen. Marie-Émile 60
Faysal, Amir 103, 104
Febvre, Lucien 334
feminists 265, 266, 285
    leading 272
    opposed to war 270
Ferdinand, King of Bulgaria 73
Ferdinand, King of Romania 208
fertility 248, 259
    decline in 260
fertilizers 227, 437

shortages in 420
Fiat 469
Fichte, J. G. 325
fictive kinship 259
field guns 176, 340
field hospitals 58, 295, 300, 301
 bottlenecks of wounded 297
 extreme overcrowding 299
field telephones 179
fighter pilots 166, 182, 272
fighting spirit 443, 472
film 282, 349, 353–67, 397–8, 410, 583 *see also* cinema; newsreels
Finland 77, 204, 439, 458, 459, 546
 Bolsheviks forced to give up 490
 exile of communists to Soviet Russia 570
 German military control of 443
 rebels executed 568
 rebels executed semi-legally or by extra-judicial killings 568
 Russia gives up control of 455
 Soviet Russia loses 212
 women possessing the vote 272
Finland, Gulf of 150
Finnish Civil War (1918) 561, 568
Finnish-German Treaty (1918) 458
firepower 174–8, 226
 brutal efficiency of 185
 industrialized 283
 infantry privileged over artillery 516
Fischer, Emil 307, 316
Fischer, Fritz 28
Fisher, Admiral Sir John, First Sea Lord 36, 142, 144, 147
Fiume 78, 94, 473, 559, 564
flag days 407
Flamenpolitik 392–3, 395
flamethrowers 58
Flanders 42, 53, 62, 66, 387, 389, 392, 397
 conscripts and volunteers from 388
 see also Flemish issues; Ypres
flares 179–80
Flemish issues 258, 394
 commemoration of Yser dead 397
 culture 326
 linguistic grievances 392, 393, 397
 persecution of hostile Flemings 393
 rise of counter-nationalism 397
Flemish Movement 387, 393
Flers 62
Fleury 536
Flex, Walter 240, 330

Flieger-Abteilung 162
flu *see* influenza
flying boats 156, 160
Foch, Gen. (later Marshal) Ferdinand 7, 37, 38, 45, 51, 53, 60, 61, 89, 137, 429, 430, 543, 553
 appointed Supreme Commander of Allied troops 134, 428, 516
Focsani (Armistice 1917) 456
Foerster, Wilhelm 324, 327
Fokker, Anthony 156, 162
Fokker planes 160, 162, 166
Fonck, René 159, 163
Fonsegrive, Georges 325
food 390, 391
 ban on shipments 509
 basic source of 271
 bureaucratic mismanagement of provisions 442
 declining production 228
 frequent lack of 378
 import of 193
 insufficient 191, 194
 key to wartime politics 377
 mediocre 92
 migration in search of 377
 overseas stocks bought up 411
 procurement of 471, 560
 promise of vast shipments of 456
 reduced production 438
 requisitioned 455, 457
 scarcity of 271, 395
 shortages of 193, 227, 442
food consumption
 mass 226
 per capita 228
food parcels 93
food protests 284
food rationing 116, 442
food riots 271
food subsidies 411
food supply 217, 227–8, 238
 absence of 570
 equitable distribution of 271
 meager 442
 more coordinated response allowed 411
 obtaining as quickly as possible 212
 reduction in 195
 requisitioning of 254
 short 93
 threatened 411
football 406

forced labor 191, 244, 390, 392, 451, 483
  gangs shuttled around 452
  great fear sparked by 454
  half-hearted remembrance of sufferings of
    deportees 397
forced marches 192
Foreign Legion 330–1
Foreign Office (Britain) 117
  film distributed all over the world by 358
  information agencies answerable to 281
foreign policy 9, 432, 481, 512, 521
  anti-Anglo-Saxon 20
  balance-of-power approach to 519
foreign workers 285, 420, 427
  massive pogrom against 483
  police round-ups of 428
France 36, 68, 71, 129–30, 131, 132, 204,
    205, 206, 241, 418–31, 482, 515, 564,
    570
  academic and intellectual groups 316
  academic elite 334
  age difference between marriage
    partners 259
  agriculture 217
  Anglo-American guarantee of security
    lost 547
  atrocities committed on civilians 197, 566
  aviation 156, 157, 158, 160, 161, 162,
    163, 166, 167
  Belgian refugees integrated into wartime
    labor market 389
  birth rate 114, 527
  Britain aligned with 432
  Britain's unambiguous support for 11
  camouflage service 341
  capitulation of 127
  casualties and losses 251, 252, 329, 395,
    415, 517, 577
  civilian health 255
  civilian women carry out military
    support 271
  civilians intentionally killed 189
  coal rationing 226
  colonial workers in 285
  Communist Party 27, 534
  conscription law (1905) 7
  contraception legislation 260
  control of the seas 115
  conversions to Catholicism 240
  cultural demobilization 582
  deaths per day 184
  desperate economic straits 548

discontent among Belgian munitions
    workers 394
escape to 388
extension of military service 13–14
fertility levels 248
films 353–4, 360, 361, 363
food supplies 227, 228
forced to dismantle fortresses 203
gas production 87
Gaullist anti-Anglo-Saxon foreign policy 20
German cemeteries in 580
German offensives halted by arrival of new
    troops 88
horrifically mutilated veterans 185
in-depth defense 179
industrial heartland overrun 41
intellectuals 323, 325, 326, 327, 329, 335
inventions that would assist national
    defense 311
Irish soldiers fighting in 409–10
Jews who died for 240
legalized brothels 269
massive exodus of populations (1940) 585
memorials 580
military agreements with Russia 3, 12
military control in the interest of national
    security 279
minority faiths in 239
mobilization 202, 481
narrow economic and territorial aims 553
national ceremonies to honor the war
    dead 273
number of American soldiers in 91
occupation of Ruhr (1923) 570
occupied 179, 191, 265, 288
pacifist and socialist movements 585
pacifist veterans' organizations 259
political advisors 335
press freedom 281
pre-revolutionary, Muslims in 503
recruiting laws 6
reparations owed by Germany to 27
repatriation of soldiers' bodies 580
repatriation of the fallen 273
resistance networks 586
resolve at the news of war 280
return of soldiers 579
right of passage in campaign against 386
role in origins of the war 20
savage behavior toward civilians 282
Schlieffen's plan to concentrate German
    forces against 6

school textbooks rewritten 583

schools cultivate notions of duty and
    honor 22

science/scientists 309, 314, 316, 317

Scottish Women's Hospitals in 268

seizure of Tunisia as a colony 82

self-mobilization 289

soldiers told to beware of women 269–70

strategic thought 40

strikes 285

substantial numbers of German divisions
    to 77

surface attacks on British lines of
    communication to 149

tension between Germany and 11

troops suffering from mental illness 185

war effort 223, 235, 421

women activists 266

women in munitions workforce 267

women's political rights 273

see also Briand; Clemenceau; Delcassé; Laval;
    Poincaré; Ribot; Thomas; Viviani; also
    under headings below prefixed "French"

France (German invasion/occupation) 38,
    189, 250, 254, 256, 342, 418, 420,
    449

    breaches of international law 434

    fair chunks overrun 128

    sufferings endured by civilians 581

Franchet d'Esperey, Gen. Louis 52, 78

Franco-American offensives 183, 517

Franco-British offensives (1915) 84

Franco-German reconciliation 28

Franco-Prussian War (1870–1) 3, 5, 7, 22,
    59, 82, 173, 418

    France's festering resentment at
        Germany 527

    use of colonial troops condemned 527

Franco-Russian alliance 15, 26

    German challenge to 16

Francqui, Emile 389

francs-tireurs (civilian snipers, myth of in
    1914) 189, 190, 282, 388–9

Frankel, Boris 347

Frankfurt 158

Frankfurter Zeitung 189

Franz Ferdinand, Archduke of Austria 3, 19,
    68, 202, 372, 404

Franz-Josef, Emperor of Austria-
    Hungary 212, 289, 372, 380

fraternization with the enemy 583

fraudulent arrangements 394

Frederick II (the Great), King of Prussia 40,
    45

Frédéricq, Paul 334, 387, 393

free trade 518, 561

freedom of the seas 518

Freetown 114

Freikorps 459, 564, 568, 569, 579

Fréjus 527, 536

Frémeaux, Jacques 528, 535

French, Field-Marshal Sir John 36, 37, 52,
    55, 57

French Africa 112, 114, 115, 116, 117, 118

French army 8, 51, 53, 59, 60, 61, 92, 135,
    162, 250, 438

    aim of bleeding white 128

    black African officers 527

    collective indiscipline 425

    deaths 184

    deplored for not using psycho-
        physiology 310

    divisions in Italy 89, 90

    end of war greeted with patriotic fervor 578

    expansion 15

    failure to undermine prewar certitudes 84

    film glimpses of 355

    formidable censorship structure 421

    Great Retreat 52

    infantry losses 163

    losses suffered 9

    military conversations between British
        and 404

    military medicine 295–306

    morally inferior to Germany 7

    Muslim officers in 527

    mutinies 127, 236, 285, 287, 425–6, 427,
        488

    offensive to split British and 443

    peacetime core decimated 54

    Plan XVII 8, 23, 40, 49, 52

    shortage of munitions 176

    significant role of African and Asian men
        in 527

    slow to adapt military clothing to trench
        warfare 177

    soldiers executed for desertion 92

    tanks 182, 183

    virtually foredoomed offensive into German
        Lorraine 419

    wounded soldiers 296

    see also Ardant du Picq; Fayolle; Foch;
        Franchet; Gaulle; Joffre; Langle de Cary;
        Lyautey; Maginot; Nivelle; Pétain

French Army Medical Service 281, 296, 297, 300, 301, 303
French Canadians 526, 529
French Empire 524, 524, 525, 531, 533–6, 537, 531
  enriched colonial portfolio 533
  Muslim loyalty to 499
  non-European foreign workers from 428
  rewards of citizenship for indigenous soldiers 530
  war memorials 536
French Expeditionary Corps (Gallipoli, 1915) 103
French front 303
  plans to coordinate all-out offensive 210
  systematic defense of every position 179
French General Staff 7, 535
  Bureau of Operations 8
French High Command 88
  German strategy misread by 419
French Ministries
  Armaments 334, 420
  Foreign Affairs 281
  Munitions 311, 314
  War 300, 355, 360
French navy 241
  battleships 97
  margin of superiority over other powers 141
  serious challenge in Mediterranean 151
  submarines 102
French Pacific 526
French Revolution 239, 424, 485, 487
French Somalia 526
French West Africa 114, 524, 531
  rebellions 530
  recruitment campaigns 115, 285, 527
Freud, Sigmund 248
Friedrich, Archduke of Austria 376
Friedrich, Ernst 243
Friedrich, Georg 327
Friuli 88, 471
Front Movement (Belgian Army pro-Flemish group) 393, 394
frostbite 100
frozen imports 228
Fulda, Ludwig 324, 325
Fullard, Philip 158–9
Fuller, J. F. C. 35
Furet, François 5, 19
Fussell, Paul 266
Futurists 326, 339, 340, 341, 342, 346, 467

Gaba Tepe (Gallipoli) 101
Galicia 39, 40, 67, 69, 70, 71, 72, 107, 108, 190, 265, 358, 373, 482
  Great Retreat of Russians (1915) 72, 288, 436
  oil wells destroyed 376
  pogroms against Jewish population 568
  Polish and Ukrainian military units came to blows in 563
  possible exclusion of Poles and Ruthenes from Austrian Reichsrat (1916–17) 381
  preparing for major new Russian offensive in (1917) 486
  Russia and 86, 357, 377, 488
  "spy psychosis" 375
  sustained bombardments 487
  terror against civilian populations 245
  Ukrainian forfeit of western borderlands 564
  unreliable populations gathered in camps 355
Galliéni, Gen. Joseph 57
Gallipoli 36, 57, 73, 103, 104, 105, 163, 254, 410, 530, 535, 586
  celebrations/commemoration of Australians at 536, 582
  colonials at 528
  failure of initial landings 408
  Helles sector 101, 102
  important theater for Western Allies 494
  invasions of Ottoman territory in 504
  Irish 10th Division at 409
  Kemal glorified for his role at 495, 547, 565
  Masefield's narrative of 328
  mass mobilization for major military effort 407
  soldiers' deaths 497
Galsworthy, John 323, 328
Gambetta, Léon 419
Gandhi, M. K. 567
gangrene 58, 184
Garros, Roland 160
Garua (Kamerun) 117
gas 44, 58, 62, 270
  production of 87, 313, 314
  use intensified 308
  see also chlorine gas; mustard gas; poison gas
Gaudier-Brzeska, Henri 346
Gaulle, Lt. (later Gen.) Charles de 51, 586
Gaumont 354, 355, 356
Gaza battles (1917) 104

GCR (Gold Coast Regiment) 116
Gemelli, Fr Agostino 469
gender 263, 264, 266, 268, 270–1, 274, 279
    alleged transformation of roles 267
    assumptions based on 268
    central to the war in Europe 285
    labor activism divided along lines of 427
    pitting the working classes against each
        other 420
    segregation of wartime roles 273
Geneva 346, 382, 549, 550, 551
Geneva conferences (1864/1906) 188
Genoa Summit Conference (1922) 548, 570
genocide 78, 191, 192, 197, 248, 255, 260,
        266, 496, 502, 503, 552, 587
    officially recognized as historical fact 196
    revenge for 564
    targeting of civilians prepared the way
        for 254
George, Stefan 326
George V, King of the United Kingdom of
    Great Britain and Ireland 524
Georgia 457, 546
    declaration of independence (1918) 458,
        563
Georgian-German agreement (1918) 457
German army 40–1, 46, 49, 51, 52, 53, 55,
        70, 72, 88, 162, 177, 196, 436–7, 458,
        490
    best noncommissioned officers lost 60
    "blackest day" of (August 8, 1918) 135,
        443
    chauvinistic notions of cultural
        supremacy 156
    civilizing campaign behind its lines 75
    defeat on western front 38–9
    expansion of 13, 15
    failure to break encircling Allies 439
    failure to undermine prewar certitudes 84
    infiltration tactics developed by 181
    instigating systematic trench network 174
    intentional killing of civilians 189, 282, 409
    losses suffered 9
    medical effort 58
    "patriotic instruction" 290
    peacetime core decimated 54
    public health measures 76
    re-created to crush labor protest in
        Ruhr 562
    Riga captured 454, 489
    sea operation in support of 150
    service regulations (1910) 7

shortage of munitions 176
sick and wounded 66
soldiers executed for desertion 92
supply lines 217
war documentaries used to celebrate bravery
    of 363
war enthusiasm following apparently
    successful advances 434
Weapons and Munitions Procurement
    Agency 224
"White Book" rebutting Allied
    accusations 282
see also Belgium (invasion); Below; Beseler;
    Bissing; Bülow; Eichhorn; Einem;
    Emmich; Falkenhausen; Falkenhayn;
    Fasbender; Goltz; Heerringen;
    Hindenburg; Hoffmann; Kluck; Krafft;
    Ludendorff; Moltke; Rennenkampf;
    Rupprecht; Stenge
German Army League 10
German-Austrians 372, 382
German Baltic Division 458
German Bight 143
German East Africa 115
German East Asiatic Squadron 36
German Empire 76, 386, 403
    assuring security in west and east 452
    departure of first Chancellor 432
    disintegrated 245, 558
    incorporation of Alsace and Lorraine
        into 418
    most non-Russian Romanov lands
        transferred to 490
    relinquished rights of the crown 444
    states closely bound to 454
German encirclement 10–11, 15, 16, 363
    crusade against 393
    diplomatic and strategic 419
    Franco-Russian alliance and 418
German General Staff 13, 53, 57, 72, 175,
        433
    Zeppelin generated unrealistic expectations
        in 157
German High Command 76, 128, 132, 211
    policy of aggression at sea 128
    priority on gaining manpower reserves from
        Poland 451
    reluctance to take risks 145
German High Seas Fleet 46, 144–5, 147,
        148, 150
    decision not to risk in major encounter 146
    reconnaissance probe 439

German Imperial Naval Office 142
German language 419
German navy 102, 141, 149, 196, 206, 432, 508
  airships used successfully as scouts 160
  bombardment of east-coast English towns 405
  British access to substantial portions of codes 146
  exposed to risks in excess of possible gains 150
  fictional films dedicated to 363
  losses 439
  postwar destruction of fleet 415
  resumption of unrestricted submarine warfare 440
  rivalry with Britain 3
  strain on 146
  strategy failed almost entirely at the start 437
  war plan rendered ineffective 437
  see also Ebergard; German High Seas Fleet; German submarines; Haus; Hipper; Hopman; Scheer; Souchon; Spee; Tirpitz; Usedom; Weddingen
German Navy Ministry 282
German Revolution (1919) 348
German South West Africa 112, 114, 115, 124
  campaign to conquer 118
  indigenous peoples used in campaigns 525
German Spring Offensive (1918) 272, 459
German Supreme Command 51, 54, 103, 104, 287, 290, 361, 363, 436, 437, 439, 440, 442, 454, 456, 458
  annexations 453
  deportation and forced labor imposed by 392
  General Censorship Office 435
  Hindenburg and Ludendorff catapulted to (1916) 449
German Supreme Court 197
German Tank Corps 183
German University of Dorpat 458, 459
German war effort 223, 313, 361
  attempt to channel Belgian resources toward 391–3
German Wars of Unification (1864–71) 49
German West Africa 112, 116, 119
Germanization 454, 458
Germans
  accused of disloyalty in Russia 483

assets confiscated in French Empire 530
Baltic 450, 451
barred from taking part in international meetings after the war 318
common identity with Russians, Romanians, Swiss in Dadaist avant-garde 346
deported to Siberia 192
ethnic 192, 450, 454, 458, 568
former dominant groups of in post-war successor states 546
portrayed as liberators of colonized Muslims 530
Germany 73, 128–9, 404, 432–46, 569
  active denial of war guilt 584
  alliance with Ottoman Empire 46, 47
  American bank loans and supplies 210
  "army honor" of 567–8
  Aufruf an die Kulturwelt (Appeal to the World of Culture) 316, 317, 318, 324, 325–6, 334
  aviation 156, 157, 158, 160, 161, 162, 163, 166, 167
  barred from Paris Peace Conference 545
  birth rate 114
  Britain declares war on (1914) 405
  casualties and losses 251, 252, 415, 439, 441, 443, 576
  chemical industry 313–14
  civilian health 255
  colonies 112
  cultural demobilization 582
  deaths per day 184
  defensive posture 128
  loss of navy and colonies (1919) 519
  designated official artists 341
  dictatorship 583
  economic cooperation between Austria-Hungary and 218
  facial wounds 185
  fertility levels 248
  films 358, 359, 363, 364
  final offensive (1918) 132–3
  first academic attack on (1914) 333
  food supplies 227–8
  foreign and military policy 9
  French resentment at 527
  French and British perceptions of 12
  friction between Austria-Hungary and 451
  gas production 87, 313
  harsh peace settlement inflicted on Russia (1918) 518
  hegemony in Europe 288, 440

hunger 420
incoherent and aggressive pre-war foreign policy 10
industrial markets 359
industrial organization of scientific output 308
"innocentist" campaign 583
intellectuals 323–7
League of Nations membership 545, 548, 549, 551, 583
memorials 580, 581
memory of brutalities 245
military strikes and agitation 93
minority faiths in 239
mobilization 481
munitions crisis 224
mutual fears grew between Russia and 449
naval expansion 22
negotiations for future collaboration between Austria-Hungary and 77
new cinema theaters 357
newly-acquired colonies 524
newsreels 354–5
occupations in Eastern Europe, 447–63
occupations in West 391–3
support for Irish Easter Rising (1916) 381
prohibiting union between Austria and 546
promulgation of Prussian law of siege (1851) 38, 279
prospects of joint offensive with Austria against Russia 67
radicalization of politics 549
railway network 70
rearmament 551
recruiting laws 6
reparations 26, 27, 509, 545, 547, 548–9, 551, 582, 584
resolve on outbreak of war 1914 33, 280
responsibility for causing war 15, 26–9, 316
retaliation for allied blockade of 47
returning soldiers 579
revisionism 26, 27, 28
schools cultivate notions of duty and honor 22
science and technology 312, 313, 316–17
radio stations in colonies 114
strikes 285
submarine blockade around British waters 147, 149–50, 509
Sweden sympathetic toward 205
universities closely associated with state policy 324

US peace treaty with (1921) 520
war economy 255, 435, 439
women activists 266
see also Bethmann-Hollweg; Bismarck; Central Powers; Nazi Germany; Stresemann; also headings above prefixed "German"
Geyer, Michael 63
Ghent University 334
   Flemishization of 392, 393
Gibbs, Philip 159
Gibraltar 524
Giolitti, Giovanni 466, 467, 473
Giono, Jean 329
Givenchy 525
Glasgow 267
   labor militancy and rent strike 407
   war-loan subscriptions 412
Glenn Curtiss 156, 161
Gnome (engine firm) 157
Goeben/Yavus Sultan Selim (battle-cruiser) 97, 150–1
Gökalp, Ziya 498, 500, 501, 503
Gold Coast 116, 123
gold standard restoration 224
Goliath (battleship) 102
Goltz, Gen. (later Field-Marshal) Colmar, Baron von der 6, 7, 105, 389, 568
Goltz, Gen. Count Rüdiger von der 458
Gontcharova, Natalia 340
Good Soldier Švejk 374
Gorizia, battle of (1916) 85–7
Gorky, Maksim 327
Gorlice 72
Gotha planes 160, 412
Göttingen 327
Gough, Gen. Sir Hubert 37, 131, 132
goumiers marocains (Moroccan soldiers) 527
Gouraud, Gen. Henri 103, 178
Graeme-West, Arthur 327
Grafenauer, Franc 375
grain 227, 377, 514
   hoarding 228
   increase in prices 502
   surplus 560–1
Grande Rivière uprising (French West Africa 1915–16) 530, 531
grand strategy 35, 46, 47
Grandmaison, Col. Louis de 8
Grappa, Mount 90, 91
Graves, Robert 62, 344
Graziani, Gen. Jean-César 91

Great Advance/Retreat (1915) 52, 288, 449,
    450, 454, 483, 484, 488
Great Depression (1930s) 414, 520, 549,
    550, 552, 570
Great Powers 14, 24, 25, 418
    competition for colonies and investment
        markets 26
    intention to dominate world affairs 545
Greco-Turkish War (1921–2) 494, 569–70
Greece 8, 14, 73, 192, 325, 360
    army raised to fight wars 569
    claim to Smyrna 207
    compulsory exchange of population between
        Turkey and 504, 547, 565
    doomed dream of Greater Greece in
        Asia 78
    League of Nations Refugee Settlement
        Commission 565
    official entry into the war 78, 208
    potentially explosive naval race between
        Turkey and 141
    territorial claims 545
    war between Turkey and 569–70
    see also Balkan League; Constantine I
        (King)
Greek Orthodox faith 565
Greens (peasant anti-Bolshevik forces
    1918–21) 561, 568
grenades 165, 175, 181
Grey, Sir Edward 404
Grignard, F. 314
Gris, Juan 342
Groener, Wilhelm 71
Grosz, George 243, 344, 346, 347, 348
Guchkov, Alexander 486, 487
guerrilla warfare 120, 122, 191, 282, 379
    full-scale 414
    internecine 256
Guillaumat, Louis 78
guillotine amputations 296, 298, 299, 300,
    301, 302
Guirand de Scevola, L.-V. 341
Gulf of Saros 101
Gumbinnen (battle, 1914) 482
Gurney, Ivor 331
Guynemer, Georges 158, 159, 160, 164

Haber, Fritz 56, 308, 313, 314, 318, 324
Haber-Bosch procedure 308, 313
Habsburg Dual Monarchy 68, 69–70, 77,
    108, 152, 371, 373, 450, 482
    army leadership 191

declaration of war on Serbia (1914) 481
disintegration into successor states 71,
    429–30, 559
empire splintered into multiple new
    states 559
Italy and 379, 464
most serious test of legitimacy 377
pressures that eventually led to breakup
    464
shift in allegiance of South Slavs from 381
see also Austria, Hungary, Austria-Hungarian
    Dual Monarchy
Hadamard, Jacques 309, 334
Haeckel, Ernst 316, 324
Hague Conferences/Conventions
    (1899/1907) 188, 194, 244–5, 437
Hahn, Otto 56
Haig, Gen. Sir Douglas 37, 46, 55, 57, 60–1,
    62, 87, 130, 131, 133, 134, 137
    Lloyd George's lack of confidence in 411
    overwhelmingly concerned with western
        front 533
Hainaut 389
Hakki Bey, Col. Hafiz 99
Halbwachs, Jeanne 242
Halbwachs, Maurice 234, 334
Haldane, J. B. S. 319
Haldane, Richard, Lord 12, 313
Hale, George Ellery 310–11, 318
Halil Pasha, Brig.-Gen. 104, 105, 106
Hamadan (Persia) 106
Hamburg 434, 442
Hamilton, Gen. Sir Ian S. 36, 101, 102
Hamilton, Richard 24
Hampaté Bâ, Amadou 535
Handeni (German East Africa) 122
Hankey, Maurice 37
Harb Mecmuasi (magazine) 501
Hardy, Thomas 328
Haritan (Syria) 104
Hartlepool 405
Hartley, Marsden 342
Harwich force (British navy) 145
Haus, Admiral Anton 151
Hausmann, Raoul 347
Hawker, Lanoe 160
Heerringen, Gen. Josias von 51, 52
Heinkel, Ernst 156
Heligoland Bight 143, 145
Helsinki 458, 561
Hemingway, Ernest 91
Hentsch, Richard 52–3

Herero people 189
  rising (1904–5) 118
Herr, Gen. Frédéric Georges 59
Hertz, Robert 235
Herwig, Holger 24
Hetmanate 456, 457, 459, 560
Hilbert, David 327
Hilmi Pasha, Brig.-Gen. Mustafa 107
Hindenburg, Paul von 39, 42, 44, 62, 63, 68,
     70, 71, 72, 75, 77, 128, 132, 134, 211,
     212, 284, 440, 444, 451, 453, 482, 581,
     583–4
  returning soldiers told they were seen as
     heroes 579
  statue to commemorate Tannenberg 343
  summoned out of retirement 435
  virtual military dictatorship under
     Ludendorff and 288, 439, 449
Hindenburg Line 135–6, 179
  see also Siegfried Line
Hindenburg Program (1916) 75, 226, 439
Hindu Congress 532
Hipper, Rear-Admiral Franz von 146, 147
Hispano-Suiza 161
Hit (Mesopotamia) 106
Hitler, Adolf 53, 70, 72, 549, 551–2, 585
Ho Chi Minh (Nguyen Ai Quoc) 534
Hoare, Sir Samuel 551
Hobsbawm, Eric 20
Hoffmann, Gen. Max 212
Hoffmannstahl, Hugo von 326
Hohenzollern royal family 158
Holland, Robert 531
Holland see Netherlands
Hollywood 362, 363, 364, 532
Holocaust 20, 587
Holzminden camp 334
home rule
  Czechs and South Slavs 289
  India 532–3
  Irish see Irish Home Rule
Home Rule for Ireland Act (Britain
     1914) 404, 409
Hoover, Herbert 390, 513, 521
Hopman, Rear-Admiral Albert 150
Horne, John 317, 390, 421, 424–5, 528
horses 58, 218
  battlefield successors of 183
  see also cavalry
Horthy, Admiral Miklós (Nicholas) 152, 562,
     567, 569
Hoskins, Gen. A. R. 123

hostages 244, 434, 567
Hötzendorff, Franz Conrad von 39, 68, 69,
     70, 71, 74–5, 86, 378
House, Col. Edward 509
Houwen, André 258
howitzers 51, 59, 360, 387
  increasingly heavy 176
  mobile units 101
Hristov, Kiril 331
Hubert, Henri 334
Hueffer, Ford (Ford Madox Ford) 329
Huelsenbeck, Richard 346
Hull 408
human rights 503, 546–7, 552, 587
human shields 190
"Hun" barbarism 52, 265
Hungarian revolution (1919) 567, 570
Hungarians 78, 208
  former dominant groups of 546
  irredentist claims of 559
  torture and killing of opponents 570
Hungary 107, 372, 379, 380, 382, 429, 546
  army 490
  autonomous status used to keep food
     supplies from Austrian lands 228
  barred from international postwar
     meetings 318, 545
  Dadaists from 346
  dismembered 559
  emergency legislation 373
  ethnic differentiation 558
  food coordination 377
  major propaganda campaigns 376
  military collapse (1918) 561–2
  paramilitaries 564, 567, 569
  political truce (1914) 373
  public dissolution of *Union sacrée* 381
  revolution bloodthirsty results 568
  Serbs arrested in 375
  US peace treaty with (1921) 520
  see also Horthy; Kun; Rákosi; Tisza
hunger 77, 193, 195, 228, 420
hunger riots 377
hunger strikes 270
Hunter-Weston, Lt.-Gen. A. G. 101
Huntington, Samuel 25
Hürriyet ve Itilaf Firkasi (Turkish Liberal
     Party) 498
Husayn/Hussein ibn-Ali, Sharif of
     Mecca 103, 565
Hüzeyinzade, Ali 498
hydrophones (anti-submarine measure) 152

hygiene regulations 76
hyperrealism 342, 343, 364

Iasi 455
ideological mobilization 244, 503
ideologues/ideologies 78, 260, 498, 500,
    558–61, 567–8
  antifascist 585
  battle of 291
  murderous 422
  neo-Slav 481
Ihsan Bey, Ali 99, 106
illegitimate dependents 268
ILP (British Independent Labour Party) 404,
    405
Immelmann, Max 160, 162, 164
immigration/immigrants
  colonial and Chinese into France, 427,
    528–9
  interrupted flow of to USA 256, 513, 520
  reform of 521
  violence against 408
Imperial War Conferences (1917/1918)
    531–2, 536
Imperial War Graves Commission 536
imperialism 3, 21
  capitalist 11
  denounced 286
  ideological offensive against 291
incendiary ammunition 182
Independent Social Democrats (USPD,
    Germany) 455
India 250, 525, 533, 559, 569
  British troops in 570
  colonial troops 105–6, 120, 268
  cutting Britain's lifeline to (Ottoman,
    German policy) 103
  demand for progress toward
    emancipation 28, 531–33, 552
  former French enclave 536
  loyalty of Muslim population 566
  major untapped sources of manpower 412
  memorials to the war dead 403
  nationalists 566, 567
Indian Army 105, 525, 533
  cavalry 104
  infantry 55, 525
  lancers 104
Indian Corps (Western Front, 1914–15) 525
Indian Expeditionary Force (British East
    Africa) 121
Indian Ocean 120, 143

protecting shipping in 121
Indochina 524, 526, 527, 535
  call for extension of democratic
    liberties 534
  migrant workers from 528
  revolt (1930) 531
industrial mobilization 217–33
inflation 223, 224, 255, 257, 284, 357, 376,
    501, 513
influenza 250, 251, 255
  mutant virus 250
  pandemic 124, 295, 346, 570
  see also Spanish flu
Inglis, Elsie 268
Institut Pasteur 314
intellectuals 237, 280, 317, 323–7, 405, 422,
    433, 457, 498, 500, 502
  academics and 434
  artists taken seriously 421
  atrocity charges by 282
  Catholic 239
  democracy, materialism and commercialism
    rejected by German intellectuals 325–6,
    434–5
  protest declarations by 316
  unionist (Ottoman Turkey) 501
  war the dominant metaphor in beliefs
    of 503
intelligence (military) 90, 391
  agent shot 397
  cryptographers score major triumph 511
  derived from wireless intercepts 146
  key agency 283
  role in naval operations 143
  superior 482
Inter-Allied Control Boards 226
international law 188, 189
  breaches of 194–6, 434
  violated 508–9
international relations 15
  important factors in 141
  prevailing state (before 1914) 21–5
  Social Darwinism and 9, 25
International Women's Day 272, 285
internment 66, 381, 408, 409, 429
iodoform 58
IRA (Irish Republican Army) 566, 567
Iraq 106, 547, 566
  maintaining British control over
    mandate 565
IRC (International Research Council) 318,
    319

Ireland 149, 270, 413, 559
 British attempt to extend conscription 287,
  412–13
 conscription unpopular and
  unworkable 408
 effects of the war on 409
 farming 411
 liner, *Lusitania*, torpedoed off the coast
  of 196, 437
 major untapped sources of manpower 412
 memorials to the war dead 403
 military recruitment/enlistment rates 287,
  406
 normal life 569
 paramilitaries 567
 partition (1921) 414, 566, 582
 temporary anchorages on the north
  coast 144
 threat over relationship between Britain
  and 404
 see also Easter Rising; Ulster; *also under*
  following headings prefixed "Irish"
Iringa (German East Africa) 123
Irish-Americans 510
Irish Citizens Army 409
Irish Civil War (1922–3) 404, 405, 414, 566,
 570
Irish Free State 414, 566, 570
 legitimacy of imperial ties 532
 symbolic politics that legitimized 579
Irish Guards 331
Irish Home Rule 287, 404, 410, 578
 only part which actually received it 414
 revolt against 409
Irish nationalism 404, 405, 410
 cult of martyrdom 409
 urged to join British army 406
Irish Parliamentary Party 404, 405, 409, 413
 undermined 416
Irish Republican Brotherhood 409
 see also IRA
Irish Unionists *see* Ulster Unionists
Irish Volunteers 404, 406, 409
Irish War of Independence (1919–21) 287,
 567
iron and steel 205, 226, 376, 456, 490, 515
 exports/imports 218
 production of 420, 469
Ironside, Edmund Gen. 560
irredentism/irredentists 207, 467
 claims 82, 84, 93, 464, 559
 failure to restrain 549

fantasies fostered by monument to
 defeat 581
frightening signal of dangers of 548
irregular armies 559
Isaac, Jules 319
Islam 47, 100, 528
 firm adherence by Basmachi anti-Bolshevik
  forces to 568
 German propaganda directed at Islamic
  countries 530
 see also Muslims
Islamic Association of Women's Work 501
Islamists/Islamicization 495, 500
Ismaliya 103
Ismet Bey (Ismet Inönü), Col. Mustafa 104
Isonzo River 39, 84
Istanbul 191, 197, 497, 498, 502, 503
 Kemal's forces supplied by
  underground 569
 non-Muslim merchants 501
 occupied 564, 569
 trials held after the war 192, 196
 Turkey retains 547
Istria 84, 93, 377
Italian army
 casualties and losses 85, 88, 89, 464–5,
  468
 cohesiveness 91, 93
 elite Alpine units 82
 execution for desertion 92
 expansion of 86
 failure to reply to roll calls 92
 forced into major retreat 471
 ignominious surrender 89
 number of divisions 90
 propaganda among the troops 470
 soldiers lacked main motivating belief 84
 unity of divisions 90
 see also Cadorna; Diaz
Italian front 39, 42, 82–96
 conditions of combat 178, 295
 infantry attacks supported by biplanes 166
 plans to coordinate all-out offensive on 210
Italian Supreme Command 85, 357, 470
 Cinematic Unit controlled by 360
 prisoners abandoned to their fate by 468
Italians 288, 355
 ethnic 375
Italo-Turkish War (1911–12) *see* Libyan war
Italy 68, 74, 141, 194, 206, 429, 464–78,
 512, 545, 550
 Austro-German occupation 290, 471

Italy (*cont'd*)
aviation 157, 160, 163
betrayal of/defection from Triple
Alliance 86, 151, 207, 326
clash over Fiume and Dalmatian coast 78,
564
control over Ethiopia 551
coveted Croatian territory 374
defeatism 89
dictatorship 583
emerging aeronautical industry 311
entry into the war 151, 207
Fascist 244, 548, 562, 567, 570, 584
fast MAS boats 152
films 354, 357, 360, 361, 364, 365
food supplies 227, 228
gas production 87
invasion of Ethiopia 551, 552
loans 219, 469, 470
memorials 273, 580
memory of brutalities 245
military defeat of Ottoman Turkey 14, 82
overseas colonies 524
regions promised to 207
rural bias in casualties 252
schools cultivate notions of duty and
honor 22
scientific development/scientists 308, 319
strikes 285
territorial ambitions 379
war a disaster for civilian population 254
war effort 470
weak constitutional system 280
see also Boselli; Giolitti; Matteotti;
Mussolini; Nitti; Orlando; Risorgimento;
Salandra; Vittorio Emmanuele
Izmir 192, 497, 565
see also Smyrna
Izzet Pasha, Ahmet, Marshal 100, 101
Izzet Pasha, Gen. Hasan 99

Jaffa 104
Jakalswater-Riet 119
James, Henry 329
Jangali revolutionaries (Persia, post-war) 566
Japan 141, 545
behavior in Manchuria 550
entered war on Entente side 143, 206
looming threat to British naval bastion in
Singapore 552
proposal to establish global protection for
racial minorities 546

small assault groups (Russo-Japanese War) 8
Japan Aeronautics Research Institute 311
Jasin (German East Africa) 121
Jászi, Oscar 562
Jaunde (Yaoundé, Kamerun) 117, 118
Jaurès, Jean 11, 13, 347, 363, 420
assassination of 280, 527
Jean Bart (French flagship) 151
Jeanjean, Marcel 163
Jellicoe, Admiral John 144, 145, 147, 148,
151
Jena 334
Jerabulus 97
Jerusalem 104
Jesuits 238
Jews 75, 240, 241, 245, 349, 449, 454, 488,
496, 504, 545, 546, 559, 563, 566, 578
accused of disloyalty 483
census of all soldiers in German army
439–40
expulsion of 192, 450, 452, 483, 546
naturalized 526
orthodox 375
persecution of 71, 190, 375, 440, 453,
483, 551, 552, 568, 570
role in organization of war economy
(Germany) 439
widely associated with international
conspiracy, Bolshevism 484, 568
Jiddah 103
jihad 499
jingoism 22
Job, André 314
Joffre, Gen. Joseph 8, 38, 41, 42, 45, 49,
51–61, 87, 133, 210, 419, 429
costly offensives 84
joint offensive with British along the
Somme 423
removed from command 62
strategy of overwhelming Germany 428
Johannsen, Ernst 330, 332
Joll, James 21, 24, 29
Jones, David 62
Jordan River 104
journalism 281, 354
Judenzählung (census of Jews in German
Army, 1916) 439, 440
July Crisis (1914) 15–16, 21, 280, 481
Jünger, Ernst 62, 175, 238, 329, 330, 439
Junkers, Hugo 161
just war 23, 434
Jutland, battle of (1916) 46, 147–9, 363, 439

Kaffka, Margit 330
Kahnweiler, Daniel-Henry 341
Kaiser Wilhelm *see* Wilhelm II
Kaiser-Wilhelm Gesellschaft 312
Kalahari Desert 119
Kalisz 450
Kalkfontein (German South-West Africa) 119
Kamerun 112, 114, 115, 116–18, 121, 123, 124, 533
Kamil Pasha, Brig.-Gen. Mahmut 100
Kamina (German wireless station, Togo) 116
Kandinsky, Wassily 339
Kanya-Forstner, A. S. 533
KAR (King's African Rifles) 121, 123
Karabib 120
Karadjordjević dynasty 379
Karas Mountains 119
Karl I, Emperor of Austria 78, 212–13, 289, 380, 381, 382
Károlyi, Mihály 381
Kars 99, 100, 193
  given over to Turkey 212, 457
Kaunas 451, 563
Kavkazskaya Army (Russian army in the Caucasus) 99, 100
Kâzim Bey, Col. 107
Keegan, John 54
Kellogg-Briand Pact (1928) 549, 550
Kemal Pasha (Kemal Atatürk), Lt.-Col. Mustafa 101, 102, 104, 495, 547, 565, 569
Kennan, George 19
Kennedy, John F. 20
Kennington, Eric 342, 344
Kenya 113, 121, 122
Kerensky, Aleksandr 76, 100, 290, 443, 486, 487, 488, 489
Kerr, Admiral Mark 163
Kevles, Daniel 309
Keyes, Commodore Roger 145
Keynes, John Maynard 396, 546
Khabalov, Gen. Sergei 485
"khaki election" (United Kingdom, 1918) 413
Khilafat movement (Muslims in India, 1919–24) 566
Khvostov, Aleksei 484
Kibata (German East Africa, Battle of, December 1916) 123
Kiel Canal 150
Kienthal (socialist anti-war meeting, Switzerland, 1916) 286

Kiev 457, 459, 490, 560
  Bolsheviks seize 456
  evacuation plans for 483
  Soviet regime driven out of 564
  Ukrainian extremists in 570
Kilmer, Joyce 239
Kingdom of Serbs, Croats and Slovenes (Yugoslavia) 371
King's Own Scottish Borderers (1st) 61, 62
Kionga triangle (German East Africa) 123, 124
Kipling, Rudyard 157, 323, 328, 331
Kiresh Tepe (Gallipoli) 102
Kirkuk 106
Kitchener, Field-Marshal Horatio, Lord 36, 37, 55, 102, 269, 314
  famous poster of 470
  press attack on 408
  volunteer army 356, 258, 406
Kitchin, Claude (US, Democratic Congressman) 512
Kleist, Lt.-Gen. Alfred von 119, 120
Klimt, Gustav 326
Kling, A. 314
Kluck, Gen. Alexander von 41, 51, 52, 53
Kobarid *see* Caporetto
Koch, Rudolf 59
Kokoschka, Oskar 349
Kola peninsula 194
Kolchak, Admiral Aleksandr V. 99, 560
Kollwitz, Käthe 349
Kolubra River 69
Komarow, battle of (1914) 70
Kondoa Irangi (German East Africa) 122, 123
Königsberg (cruiser) 120–1
Köprüköy (north-eastern Turkey) 99
Korean War casualties 61
Kornilov, Gen. Lavr 489
Korošec, Anton 381, 382
Kosch, Gen. Robert 107
Krafft von Dellmensingen, Gen. Konrad 88
Kramář, Karel 374, 375
Krasnov, Gen. Pyotr 456
Kraus, Karl 326
Kress von Kressenstein, Lt.-Col. Friedrich, Baron 103
Kreuznach Program (1917) 453
Kriegs Journal 355
Kriegsbilder 355
Kriegsüberwachungsamt (War Supervisory Office, Austria) 373
Kronstadt naval base 487, 561

Krupp 224
 howitzers/field guns 51, 59, 176
Kühlmann, Richard von 10, 439
Kultur 54, 236, 265, 434
Kum Kale (Dardanelles) 101
Kun, Béla 562, 569
Kurds 496, 498–500, 502, 504
 cavalry units 99
Kurland 449, 450, 451, 452
Kusseri (Kamerun) 117
Kut-al-Amara 105, 106
KWI *(Kaiser-Wilhelm Institute)* 312, 313,
 317

La Bassée 55
La force noire (book, General Mangin,
 1910) 114
La Neuville 241
La Presse médicale (journal) 297
La Réunion 526
labor movement 11, 285–6
 France 413, 420
Laboratoire municipal de Paris 314
Labour Party (Britain) 408, 413, 414, 550
 support for war 405
 see also ILP
Lacante, Marie 258
Lafont, Bernard 164
Lambert, Frederick Rudolph, 10th Earl of
 Cavan 91
Lambert, George 344
Lamprecht, Karl 326
Lancken, Oscar, Baron von der 211
land redistribution 490, 558
Landwehr, Gen. Ottokar 377
Langdon, John 29
Langemark (Battle of, Belgium, 1914) 53
Langevin, Paul 309
Langle de Cary, Gen. Fernand de 51
Lanrezac, Gen. Charles 52
Lanson, Gustave 334
laparotomies 296, 297
Lasswell, Harold 583
Latin America 363, 545, 547
Latvia 449, 450, 451, 488, 559
 army rested upon combination of volunteers
  and British aid 569
 Bolsheviks forced to give up 490
 German irregulars still trying to
  dominate 568
 Latvians deported to Russia 192
 Russia gives up control of 455

student organizations 458
Laurier, Sir Wilfrid 525–6, 530
Lausanne Treaty (1923) 494, 547, 565
Laval, Pierre 551
Lavisse, Ernest 334, 422
Lavrov, A. 340
Lawrence, Capt. T. E. 103
Le Cateau 52
Le Flambeau (Belgian paper) 395
Le Havre 52, 529
 Belgian government-in-exile in, 388, 396
Le Journal de Genève 327
Le Mercure de France 332
League of Nations 27, 124, 518, 519, 547,
 549, 585
 Covenant 545, 546, 550
 Germany's membership 545, 548, 549,
  551, 583
 mandates 430, 533
 Refugee Settlement Commission in
  Greece 565
 Soviet Russia's membership 545, 551
 US refusal to join 520
leave periods 92, 426
Lebanon 502, 533, 547
Lebeau, Paul 314
Lebedev, Vladimir 340
L'Echo de Paris 205
Leete, Alfred 470
left-wing groups 26, 27, 89, 259, 288, 419,
 430, 473, 583
 Communist 212
 political parties 264, 404
 press 10
 support for war effort 118
Léger, Fernand 341–2
legitimacy 26, 76, 208, 289, 381, 390, 393,
 409, 410
 civilian participation in resisting
  invasion 189
 crisis of 371–2, 394
 deteriorated 377
 experience of captivity crucial for 288
 food the most serious test of 377
 imperial ties 532
 maintaining 481
 political 289, 567
 theological 434
Lehmbruck, Wilhelm 346
Leicestershire 227
Leipzig 197
 general strikes 442

war-crimes trial (1921) 396
Leman, Gen. Gérard 387
Lemberg 71, 191, 482
    see also Lwow/Lviv
Lenin, Vladimir I. 23, 26, 76, 77, 100, 290,
    326, 454, 487, 558, 559, 561, 562
  international revolution renounced 564
"Lenin boys" 568–9, 570
Lentulov, Aristarkh 342
Leopold II, King of Belgium 112
Lersch, Heinrich 331
Les Allemands et la science (book, 1916) 317
Les Rivages (Dinant, Belgium) 190
Les Tablettes (newspaper) 346
Lettow-Vorbeck, Gen. Paul von 120, 121–4
Lewis, Cecil 158
Lewis, Wyndham 338, 343
Liberal Party/Government (Britain) 37, 290,
    404, 405, 406, 410, 413
  organized nonconformity 408
liberal press 10
liberalism 39, 472, 474, 504
liberals 89, 208, 279, 288, 466, 469, 473,
    485, 498, 500, 504, 530
liberty bonds (USA) 514
Libre Belgique (Belgian underground
    paper) 390, 395
Libya 14, 82, 103, 494
Libyan war (1911–12) 94, 470, 353, 495
Liddell Hart, B. H. 62
Liebknecht, Karl 286, 347, 433, 442
Liège 49, 51, 176, 203, 387, 433
  awarded French Legion of Honor 388
life expectancy 255
Lille 191
lime chloride 58
Limpopo River 115, 124
Lindemann, Thomas 25
Lintier, Paul 333
Lion (battle-cruiser) 146
liquor consumption 164
Lissauer, Ernst 323
Lithuania 449, 451, 482, 490, 546, 559
  farmers 454
  forced labor gangs shuttled around the
    country 452
  Red Army driven out by patriots 563
  Russia gives up control of 455
  terror against civilian populations 245
Lithuanians 192, 450, 563
Liverpool 196, 408
livestock 391

dependence on imported feeds 227
  requisitioning of 254
living standards 284, 290, 412
Ljubljana 84, 382
Lloyd George, David 26, 37, 38, 55, 62, 88,
    89, 29, 131, 225, 226, 308, 311, 315,
    328, 408, 410, 519, 533, 545, 552, 553,
    564, 566
  coalition replaced 414
  Genoa summit the brainchild of 548
  hostility to employing British forces on
    western front 134
  level of consultation extended to
    Dominions 531–2
  misjudgment over Nivelle 130
  Treasury agreements brokered by 407
loans 210, 219, 376, 412, 469, 470, 481,
    548
Locarno Pact (1925) 548, 549, 551, 578,
    582, 583, 584
Lodge, Henry Cabot 519
Lodz 452
logistics 217–18
Loi Dalbiez (1915) 421
Loi Mourier (1917) 421
London 37, 207, 338, 379, 410
  air raids/bombardment 254, 412
  anxiety about behavior of women 269
  ceremonies (1919) 579
  émigré South Slavs in 378
  ethnic riots 408
  exclusive stores 159
  locations: East End 267; Endell Street
    Military Hospital 268; Queen's
    Hall 290; Wellington House 281, 328;
    Westminster Abbey 579
London Treaty (1913) 14
London University
  Imperial College 311
  King's College 313
Loos offensive (1915) 37, 56, 331
looting 483
Lorentz, Hendrik 317
Louvain (Leuven) city 238, 388
Louvain (Leuven) University library 52, 190,
    434
Lovcen, Mount 151
Lowes Dickinson, G. 24, 25
Lublin 70
Lublin Military Government General 450
Ludendorff, Gen. Erich 13, 39, 40, 41, 42,
    44, 45, 46, 51, 62, 63, 68, 70, 71, 72,

Ludendorff, Gen. Erich (*cont'd*)
    75, 77, 128, 132, 134, 137, 135, 137,
    152, 183, 209, 211, 212, 238, 392, 435,
    437, 440, 441, 443, 444, 451, 453, 456,
    457, 458, 459, 482, 490, 526
  virtual military dictatorship under
    Hindenburg and 288, 439, 449
Lüderitz (German South-West Africa) 118,
    119
Lugard, Frederick, Lord 531
Lunn, Joe 527, 534
Lusitania sinking (1915) 147, 195–6, 213,
    238, 311, 408, 437, 509
Lutheranism 236, 434
Lutyens, Sir Edwin 579, 580
Luxembourg 52, 203
  German invasion of 204
Luxemburg, Rosa 266, 286
Lwow/Lviv 70, 107, 482
Lyautey, Gen. (later Marshal) Hubert
    62, 535
Lyon chirurgical (journal) 298
Lyttleton, Adrian 567
Lytton Commission (1932) 550

Maastricht Appendix 51
Macedonia 107, 207, 494
  Balkan League seizure of 8, 14, 73
  Bulgaria obliged to give up territory in 559
machine guns 61, 102, 136, 138
  concrete pillboxes with emplacements 179
  fixed forward-firing 160
  range of 175
Macke, August 346, 433
Mackensen, Field-Marshal August von 39, 72,
    73, 107, 456
Macleod, Roy 311
Madagascar/Malagasy 524, 526, 531, 534,
    535
Magdeburg (cruiser) 146
Maginot, Gen. André 534
Magyars 288, 289, 326, 372, 382
  economic exploitation 377
  leading politicians 381
  prisoners 194
Mahenge (German East Africa) 123
Mahiwa (battle, 1917, German East
    Africa) 124
Maison de la Presse 281
Majestic (battleship) 102
Maji Maji rising (1905–6) 120, 123
Makhno, Nester 561

Makombe revolt (Portuguese East Africa,
    1917) 124
malaria 73, 122, 450
Malevich, Kazimir 340, 342
Malmaison 183
malnutrition 114, 194, 195, 395, 442
  death rates from 255, 568
Malta 268
Mametz Wood 410
Manchester Guardian 189, 358
Manchuria 550, 551, 568
Mangin, Gen. Charles 114, 430, 527, 528
Manhattan 510
Mann, Thomas 77, 264
Mannerheim, Gen. Carl 561
Mannock, Edward (Mick) 159, 164–5
Mantoux, Paul 334
Maori volunteers 530
Maquenne, Léon 314
Marc, Franz 339, 346, 433
March on Rome (1922) 475
Marder, Arthur 195
Mare, André 341
Mariana islands 206
Marinetti, Filippo Tommaso 339, 467
Marne
  first battle (1914) 36, 38, 40, 41, 42, 52,
    53, 57, 162, 174, 127, 182, 203, 254,
    281, 298, 300, 301, 387, 405, 419, 435,
    436
  second battle (1918) 45, 133
marriage patterns 258, 259
Marseillaise 382
Marseilles 428, 528
Marshall, Catherine 270
Marshall, Gen. George C. 37
Marshall, Sir William R. 106
Marshall islands 206
martial law 500, 566
Martin, Thomas S. 515
Martini, Ferdinando 472
Marx, Karl 23
Marxism/Marxists 11, 286, 443–4
masculinity 260
  crisis of 270
  deviant 266
  epitomized 269
  militarism and 264
Masefield, John 328
Masereel, Frans 346
mass armies 248–50
mass communication 470

mass murder 189, 190, 198, 237, 319, 570
massacres 188, 190, 191, 192, 196, 197, 198,
    238, 243, 266, 388, 502, 504, 533, 565
  condemned 189, 192
  memory of (1914) 585
Massis, Henri 239
Masterman, Charles 281, 328
Masurian Lakes, battle of (1914) 68, 71, 482
Mata Hari 271, 428
Materialschlachten (battles of material) 62
Matteotti, Giacomo 475
Maude, Gen. Sir Frederick Stanley 106
Maunoury, Gen. Michel 52
Maurette, Fernand 334
Mauss, Marcel 234
Mauzan, Achille 470
Max, Prince of Baden 444
May Declaration (Czechs/South Slavs
    1917) 381
Mayakovsky, Vladimir 236, 245, 342
Mayer, André 314
McCudden, James 166
McGill University 313
Mecca 103, 565
Mechelen railway workshops 390
Meda, Filippo 469
Medina 99, 103
Mediterranean 99, 112, 206
  access to 14, 15
  eastern, decision-making in 38
  French and British naval bases 114
  French responsibility for security in 21
  Germany's theoretical allies in 141
  naval convention concerning future war
    in 82–4
  sea-lanes guarded between Atlantic and 524
  submarine warfare 151, 152
Meeson, Dora 344
Méheut, Mathurin 343
Mehmed V, Ottoman Sultan 497
Meidner, Ludwig 339, 346
Memel 546, 563
memorials 580, 582, 584
  destruction of 586
Mendola, Raphaël 313
Menin Gate (Ypres) 580
mental illness 185
mentally traumatized patients 302–5
mercenaries 459, 526, 527
merchant shipping 143
  all-out assault on 128
  convoys to guard 149

sinking of 408, 440, 511
submarines used against 147, 195
surface raiders disguised as 144
surprise attacks halted on 510
Mercier, Cardinal, Catholic primate of
    Belgium 390
Mesopotamia 99, 104, 105–6, 108, 533, 547,
    565
  West Africans employed in river work 115
  see also Iraq
Messines, battle of (1917) 136, 165, 183
Messter, Oskar (German newsreel
    maker) 354, 355, 359, 361
metallurgical industries 420
Metcalf, Thomas R. 532, 533
Metz 515, 516, 517
Meuse, River 51, 56, 57, 58, 59, 60, 137,
    300, 387
Meuse-Argonne offensive (1918) 183, 517
Mexico 213, 510–11
MI5 (British Military Intelligence) 283
middle classes 257, 286
  Catholic 390
  discontented 412
  dissent suppressed 569
  enlistment rates 406
  fear of revolution on the part of 473
  lower 414, 566
  polarization of opinion between working
    class and 413
  struggling to make ends meet 284
  victim to "Lenin boys" 570
  women's charitable solidarity with wartime
    causes 282
  young women volunteer nurses 407
Middle East 14, 42, 46, 108, 163, 295, 569
  British mandates/control 414, 565, 533,
    560
  Entente forces in 97
  fate in Franco-British hands 547
  Indian troops used to release British
    from 412
  rebellions/revolts 413, 533, 552, 565
  Turkish 524
Middlebrook, Martin 61
midinettes (Paris women clothing
    workers) 427
migration 77, 256–8, 259, 497, 513
  child 532
  forced 547, 565, 567
  imperial 532
  search of food 377

Milan 467
Milestone, Lewis *see "All Quiet ..."*
militancy 548, 550, 568
  labor/industrial 285, 286, 407, 412, 562
  political 412
militarism 9, 21, 39, 54, 114, 205, 256, 339,
    434, 495
  masculinity and 264
  predominates over pacifism 24
  vogue for 501
  war economy and 500–2
military aviation 156, 158, 162
military medicine 295–306
  rudimentary state of 254
military participation/losses 248–54
military police 92
military service 82, 237, 386
  Black South Africans barred from 526
  colonized not obliged to do 526
  compulsory 22
  exemption from 411, 412
  extension of 13–14, 439, 531
  granting the vote to young men on the basis
    of 414
  high levels amongst established Anglo-
    Jewry 239
  mandatory 531
  matter of choice 530
  shirkers who should be performing 406,
    420–1
  universal 405
  wounded and broken men who returned
    home 259
  see also conscription
military tribunals 471
militias 435
Miliukov, Paul 488
Millerand, Alexandre 56
Millikan, Robert A. 311
Milner, Alfred, Lord 531
minefields 101, 152
  concealed batteries sheltered behind 151
  defense of 150
  laying 99, 153
  made up of buried mortars 183
  maintaining and clearing 153
mines 141, 150, 152, 181
  devastating effects of 142
minesweeping flotillas 153
mining production 112
mining strikes 407
minorities

chilling message to 547
covertly subsidized 549
destruction of the international system 552
easy target for extremists 570
international protection of 546–7
national 290, 559
negative mobilization against 288
persecution of 546
racial 546
religious 239, 345
routine brutality used in dealing with 502
violations of rights 550
Mirror of War, The (cinematic weekly) 357
Mitchell, Col. Billy 167
Mittelafrika 115, 119, 204
Mitteleuropa 204, 452
Mittelmeerdivision (German Mediterranean
    Squadron, 1914) 143
Modernism 339
Moldavia 455
Moltke (the Elder) Count Helmuth von 5, 6,
    7, 41, 502
Moltke (the Younger), Gen. Helmuth von 11,
    13, 15, 16, 39, 52, 53, 71, 433, 435
  replaced by Falkenhayn as head of
    OHL 436
Mombasa 122
Monash, Gen. Sir John 526
Monchy-le-Preux (battle, 1918) 135
Monro, Sir Charles 102
Mons 51, 52, 387
Montagu, Edwin 533, 566
Montenegro 8, 14, 151, 378, 380
  guerrilla bands in mountain regions 379
  occupied 378
Montgomery, Lt.-Col. Bernard (later Field-
    Marshal Lord) 566
Montmédy 300
Moon (island) 454
Moore, Marianne 330
Moorish cafés (for colonial workers,
    France) 528
morale 8, 47, 54, 58–9, 74, 78, 105, 127,
    130, 133, 150, 269, 279, 283, 284, 287,
    388, 412, 569
  cinema might help to raise 357
morality 407, 434
Morane planes 160
Moravia 373
Moreau, Luc-Albert 344
Morgan (J. P.) 219, 226, 510
Morgenthau, Henry 192

Moroccan Crisis
  First (1905) 3, 12, 432, 524
  Second (1911) 3, 8, 9, 10, 11, 12, 116,
    156, 432, 524
Morocco 13, 62, 531
  assets of enemy nationals confiscated 530
  Franco-German rivalry in 280
  independent 536
  Muslims mobilized for French army 526
  rebellion 531
  tabors 536
mortality 192, 193, 248, 442, 496
  amputation 301
  excess 195, 570
  stomach operations 298
mortars 183
Morto Bay 102
Moscow 483, 489
Moseley, Harry 310
Moselle Valley 515
Mosse, George 295
Mostar 377
Mosul 106
Moureu, Charles 314
Mourmelo 480
mourning and hatred 578–82
movies 353–67
Möwe (surface raider) 144
Mozambique 112, 115, 124
  Delagoa Bay 122
Mudros Armistice (1918) 104, 106
Mukden, battle of (1905) 174
Mulhouse 211
multi-ethnicity 13, 14, 70, 494, 497, 504
  dynastic empires 288
Munich 339, 568
  Nazi exhibition of degenerate art
    (1937) 350
Munich Conference (1938) 552, 585
Munitions of War Act (Britain 1915) 225,
  411
Münnich, Ferenc 562
murder 71, 255, 266, 380
  political 475
  see also mass murder
Murmansk railway construction 194
Murray, Flora 268
music 340, 422
Musil, Robert 326
Muslim League 532
Muslims 103, 193, 503, 534, 565, 566
  Britain's prestige undermined 105–6

conscript 97, 483
euphoria amongst nationalists 501
expulsion from Greece 496, 497, 547, 565
interment of soldiers killed in battle 528
internal struggle between non-Muslims
  and 504
jihad had little impact on 499
memorial to soldiers at Verdun 536
mobilized for French army 526
mosque built in Paris in honor of war
  service 536
officers in French army 527
propaganda which portrayed Germans and
  Turks as liberators of 530
Punjabi 525, 529
realities of communities in Russian
  Empire 498
warriors confront Bolsheviks 561
Mussolini, Benito 465, 467, 475, 548, 551
mustard gas 181, 314, 329
mutinies 127, 130, 236, 271, 272, 284, 287,
  425–6, 427, 485, 488, 489, 520, 525
Mwanza (German East Africa) 123
Myshlayevskii, A. Z. 99

Nairobi 122
Namur 49, 51, 176
Nancy 51, 52
Napoleonic conflicts 5, 24, 40, 434
  chances of wounded soldier surviving 184
  convoys to guard merchant shipping 149
  perceived strategy 406
Narangomba (battle, 1917, German East
  Africa) 124
Narew River 69
Narocz, Lake 74
Narva (Ukraine) 77
Nash, Paul 340, 344
Nasiriyah (Mespotamia) 105
nation-in-arms concept 7, 8, 13, 386, 485,
  486, 487
nation-states 280, 287, 288, 289
  creation of 558, 559
National Advisory Committee for Aeronautics
  (US) 311
National American Woman Suffrage
  Association 514
National Aviation Fund (Germany) 156
National Bureau of Standards (US) 312
National Democratic Party (Poland) 451
National Economy Bank of Konya
  (Turkey) 502

National Liberals (Germany) 442
National Physical Laboratory (Britain) 312
National Register (Britain) 270
national security 8, 12, 279, 382
National Socialist Party (Germany) 549–50
    see also Nazi Germany
National Union of Women Suffrage Societies
    (Britain) 268
National War Aims Committee (Britain) 411
National War Labor Board (US) 513
National Women's Party (US) 272, 514
nationalism/nationalists 13, 24, 75, 82, 141,
    191, 197, 206, 237, 264, 373, 381–2,
    436, 452, 457, 469, 470, 480, 494, 497,
    501, 531–3, 536, 546–8, 566, 579
    anti-Christian 498, 499, 503
    anti-Semitic 288
    colonial 414, 535
    constitutional 412
    economic 502
    ethnic 25
    literature of 439
    militant students 567
    militaristic 21
    movements 285
    populist 499, 502
    radical 195, 379, 567
    revolutionary 559
    right-wing 244, 284, 581
    see also Irish Nationalists
nationalities 191, 285, 287–91, 464, 491
    nationalization 513, 558
    land 490
naturalization 534, 546
Naumann, Friedrich 452
Naumann, (Capt.) Heinrich 123
Naval Consulting Board (US) 312
naval war 47, 53, 102, 115, 141–55
    arms race 3, 12–13, 22
    bases 114
    blockade 195–6
    reconnaissance 312–13
Nazi Germany 35, 243, 259, 433, 436, 439,
    490, 551–2, 584
    exhibition of degenerate art (1937) 350
    political violence 244
    reification by ideologues 78
    responsibility for World War II 28
    state repression 289
    violence a symbol of virility 584
Nazim, Mehmed 498
Nazuhi Bey 100

Neiberg, Michael 61
Nernst, Walther 316, 318, 324
Nesle 62
Netherlands 147, 550, 570
    Belgian leaders of spy networks in 391
    destitute refugees housed in camps 389
    electrified fence between Belgium and 191,
        391
    escape to/refuge in 387, 388
    Wilhelm II exiled in 444
Neu Langenburg (German East Africa) 123
Neuberg, C. 313
Neuilly Treaty (1919) 546
neurology 303
    damage/trauma 185, 305
neuroses 302
neutral shipping 509
    all-out assault on 128
    diplomatic complications of sinking 147
    pressure on 227
    rights of 195
neutrality 47, 49, 57, 73, 84, 106, 115, 116,
    117, 118, 121, 203, 219, 266, 355,
    358–9, 386, 389, 405, 466–8, 495, 503,
    509, 510, 511, 551
    abandoned 206, 207
    defended 386, 469
    not respecting laws of 208
    violation of 189, 205, 404
Neuve-Chapelle (battle, 1915) 55, 525
Nevinson, Christopher 341, 342, 343, 345
New Caledonia 531
New York 196, 219, 239, 339, 347
    Bakhmetieff Archive (sources on
        Russia) 480
New York Daily News 19
New York Times 388
New Zealand 178, 311, 410, 524, 582
    Britain given money to build Dreadnought
        battleship 525
    conscription 529, 530
    political rights of women 273
    prominent role of volunteers in South
        African War 406
    self-government 524
    Statute of Westminster ratified 532
    tenth of population sent overseas to
        fight 526
    Unknown Soldier 536
    see also Anzacs
Newfoundland 410, 524, 526
Newfoundland Battalion (1st) 61, 62

newsreels 282, 354–8, 361, 365
  see also Pathé
Ngaundere (Kamerun) 116, 117
Nicholas II, Tsar of Russia 73, 76, 205, 280, 289, 481
  committee operating under patronage of 282
  concessions to patriotism 288–9
  intransigence 484–5
  overthrow (1917) 272, 454
  plans to escalate repression 486
  public opinion toward 357
Nicholas, Hilda Rix 344
Nicolai, Col. August 101
Nicolaï, G. F. 317
Niemen River 68
Nietzsche, Friedrich 22
Nieuport 53, 54
Nieuport planes 160
Nigeria 116, 117, 123, 531
Nikolai Nikolaevich, Gen., Grand Duke of Russia 100, 481
Nikolasee (Dada "republic" founded) 347
Nine-Power Pact (1922) 550
Nis (Serbia) 378
Nitti, Francesco Saverio 90
Nivelle, Gen. Robert 38, 59, 62, 63, 129, 210, 423
  dismissed and replaced by Pétain 425
Nivelle Offensive (1917) 130, 182, 425
Nixon, Gen. Sir John 105
no man's land 60, 61
  capture of prisoners in 177, 180
noncombatants 188, 194, 254, 263, 271, 559
  artist 342
  gap between combatants and 256, 263
  inhumane treatment of 189
  soldiers employing violence against 197
  women in armed forces 412
Nordisk (Danish film company) 355, 361, 362
North Africa 46, 122, 524
  airplanes used in campaigns 157
  colonial compensation conceded 84
  French colonial army in 114
  indigenous colonial troops from 527
  Italian invasion of Ottoman provinces 494
  light cavalry 527
  most valuable colonial possessions 112
  spheres of influence in 418
North Sea 46, 145, 146, 150, 152, 525
  effective closure of 509

extensive minefields 153
fortified zones between Verdun and 179
seaplanes employed over 160
North-West Frontier 525
Northamptonshire 227
Northcliffe press empire 404, 410
Northern Barrage (minefield) 153
Northern Ireland 566, 582
  see also Ulster
Northern Rhodesia 120, 121, 122, 124
Northey, Gen. Sir Edward 122, 123
Norton Harjes Ambulance Corps 329
Norway 147, 325, 439, 508–9
  leans toward Entente 205
  women possessing the vote 272
Notgemeinschaft der deutschen Wissenschaft (German scientific body) 318–19
Notre-Dame de Lorette 580
nouveaux riches 284, 502
November revolution *see* Bolshevik Revolution
Noyon 55, 56
NRC (US National Research Council) 310, 315
Nsamaking (Kamerun) 117
nuptiality 257–8
Nurettin Bey, Col. Yusef 105
Nuri Bey, Major 100
nurses 268, 295
  filmed 356
  voluntary 407
nutrition 228
  intentionally poor 194
Nyasaland 121, 124

Ober Ost (German military colony) 450, 451, 452
Oberlindober, H. 243
Octobrist Party (Russia) 486
Odessa 77, 455, 456
Offer, Avner 25, 195
Office national des recherches scientifiques et industrielles et des inventions 318
OHL (Oberste Heeresleitung) see German Supreme Command
oil industry 456, 458
oilfields 77
Omissi, David 525
Operation Alberich (1917) 440
Operation Albion (1917) 150
Operation Capstone (1918) 459
optic glass 312, 313
Oran 114

Orange Guard (Bulgaria) 569, 570
Orange River 118–19
Orkney 144, 153
Orlando, Vittorio Emanuele 38, 89, 90, 379
Orpen, William 344
Ösel (island) 150, 454
Ostjuden (Jews of Eastern Europe) 449, 453
  perceptions of radical right toward 568
Ostwald, Wilhelm 316, 324
Otavi (German South-West Africa) 120
Ottoman Empire/armed forces 8, 14, 100,
  115, 423, 482, 494–507, 533
  advantages of entering the war 206
  agreement over Arab lands 547
  Allied victory over 547
  anticipated carving up of 213
  Arabic-speaking parts 429
  Armenians in 191, 192, 237, 245, 501,
  504
  collapse (1918) 459
  confirming in German sphere of
  influence 15
  disintegration of 245, 558
  engagement of Entente forces 97
  fresh conflict 564
  General Staff 99
  German alliance with 46, 47
  German officers on service in 99, 496
  High Command 97, 104, 106
  mandates taken over by Britain 414
  military defeat by Italy in Libya (1911)
  14, 82
  nationalist politics eroding remains of power
  in Balkans 13
  Near Eastern provinces 524
  officer corps 99
  rape and ethnic cleansing 251
  rights of foreigners in 490
  Russia declares war on 206
  Turkish nationalism 191, 498
  war effort 223
  see also Central Powers; Turkey
Ottomanism 504
Oughton, Frederick 164–5
Ourcq River 52
Ouvrier, Adrien 343
Ovillers 61
Owen, Wilfred 22, 62, 331
Oxford pamphlets (1914–15) 317
Oxford University 334
Oxford Union Society 550
Ozil, Colonel 314

Pabst, G. W. 332
Pacelli, Mgr *see* Pius XII
Pacific 143, 511
  opportunity to force Germans out of 206
pacifism 27, 186, 235, 264, 317, 326, 422,
  473, 583, 587
  Communist 243
  great wave of, after the war 422, 550
  identification of war with atrocity 197
  intellectuals affected by 327
  militarism predominates over 24
  tradition of international socialism 466
  veterans' organizations 259
Pact of London (1915) 84, 467, 473
Paderewski, Ignacy 451
Painlevé, Paul 307, 309, 311
Palais des Nations (League of Nations
  headquarters) 551
Palestine 99, 103, 104, 106, 108, 130, 131
  competing claims to 545
  drastically reducing Jewish immigration
  to 552
  mandates over 533, 547
  restive forces 552
Pals battalions 405
Pan-African Congress (Paris 1919) 534
Pan-European revolution 562
Pan-German League 10, 436
Pan-Germanism 324, 373, 452
Pan-Islamism 495, 497–9
Pan-Ottoman ambitions 499
Pan-Serbianism 14
Pan-Slav objectives 13, 14
Pan-Turanism 498, 499
Pan-Turkic nationalism 206
Pan-Turkist policies 495, 561
Panama Canal 144
Pangani valley 122
Pankhurst, Christabel 407
Pankhurst, Emmeline 267, 330, 407
Pankhurst, Sylvia 266–7
Panthéon 343
paramilitaries 22, 94, 255, 404, 439, 459,
  498, 564, 566, 567, 569, 579
  fascist 474–5
Paris 6, 41, 49, 51, 93, 127, 258, 272, 338,
  339, 341, 514
  academics friendly to France meet
  (1917) 333
  American troops help stop Germans from
  taking 518
  artistic exhibitions of war period 343

colonial conference (1917) 534
colonial exhibition (1931) 535
Dadaists in 347
demand for return of husbands 285
evacuation of government from 38, 52
Indochinese troops repress women
    strikers 271
industrial suburbs 256
intermittent German bombardment of 254
labor militancy 286
large numbers of migrant workers 528
mosque built in honor of Muslims' war
    service 536
police round-ups of foreign workers 428
strikes 427
victory parades (1919) 579
see also Declaration of Paris
Paris Peace Conference/Treaties 473, 518,
    532
see also Versailles
Parliamentary Labour Party (Britain) 405
Parsons, Charles 311
Parsons, Edwin 164
Pas-de-Calais 580
Pašić, Nikola 378, 379, 380, 382
Passchendaele 37, 62, 254, 441, 535
    Belgian capture of 136
Pathé (film production) 353, 354, 356, 357,
    362
Pathfinder (scout cruiser) 145
Patocka, Jan 238
Patriotic Auxiliary Service Law (Germany
    1916) 225
patriotism 212, 236, 239, 260, 290, 323,
    339, 340, 373, 380, 394–5, 412, 434,
    466, 513
    alleged lack of (Italy) 472
    Catholic (Italy) 469
    children enrolled in the effort 282
    compatibility of Jewishness and 239,
        439–40
    concessions to (Russia) 288–9
    film 357, 361
    prominent writers disenchanted with 328
    scientific 309
    weariness with (Belgium)
    women's 272
    Pau, Gen. Paul-Marie 49
Pauchet, Victor 298–9, 300, 301
Paul, Alice 272
Pearse, Padraig 409
Peasant League (Belgium) 394

Pedroncini, Guy 426
Péguy, Charles 13, 329, 330, 421–2
pensions 22, 534, 581
Péricard, Jacques 238
Péronne 51, 61, 62
Perrin, Jean 309, 319
Pershing, Gen. John J. 137, 514, 515–16,
    514
Persia 105–6, 560, 570
    Red Army invasion (1920) 566
Pétain, Gen. (later Marshal) Philippe 38, 45,
    55, 59, 60, 62, 130, 133, 137, 161,
    166–7, 179, 425, 516, 585–6
Petit, Gabrielle 397
Petliura, Semen (postwar Ukrainian
    leader) 560, 563–4, 568
Petrograd 39, 76, 100, 454, 455, 485–6, 487
    attack against 459
    Finnish radicals' tactical alliance with
        revolutionaries 561
    labor militancy 286
    Liberals incapable of generating military
        activity 128
    quick railroad access to 489
    women workers demonstrate 285
philosophy 325
phosgene 58
Physikalisch-Technische Reichanstalt 312
physiotherapy 304
Piave River 89, 90, 91, 473
Picardy 42, 53, 181, 183
Picasso, Pablo 338, 341, 342
Piedmont 82, 466
Piéron, Henri 310
pillage 251, 255
    brutality and 191
Pilsudski, Józef 451, 459, 563–4
Pinot, Robert 205
Pirenne, Henri 326, 334, 335, 387, 393, 397,
    398
Pirenne, Pierre 334
Pius X, Pope 208–9
Pius XII, Pope 209
Planck, Max 315, 317, 318, 324
Plava 85
plays 324
plebiscites 545, 546, 564
Plekhanov, Grigorii 327
Pless conference (1917) 213
Plezzo 88
Plievier, Theodor 330
Plumer, Gen. Herbert 131, 136

poets/poetry 62, 240, 251, 263, 325,
    328–30, 338, 346, 350, 421–2, 467,
    500, 535, 548
  modernist 331
  nationalist 501
  négritude 536
  neoclassical 331
  patriotic 323, 331
  symbolist 326, 331
pogroms 350, 449, 483, 484, 545, 568
  anti-Armenian (1909) 503
  Poincaré, Raymond 12, 20, 26, 27, 28, 29,
    60, 548
Poirier, Léon 349
poison gas 181, 182, 244, 308, 312, 319,
    408, 437
  explosive shells 307
Pola (Austrian naval base) 151, 152
Poland 39, 41, 77, 204, 209, 372, 449, 482,
    546, 547, 563
  army numbers 569
  Bolsheviks forced to give up 490
  cession of Chelm district to Ukraine 455
  Dadaists from 346
  devastated by scorched-earth policies 70
  divided into two governments 450
  economic reconstruction and refugee
    relief 564
  forced labor 452
  German priority on gaining manpower
    reserves from 451
  Independence Day 459
  independent with ceded territory 559
  loggerheads with Lithuania over
    territory 563
  longer-term significance of German presence
    in 568
  minority rights 549, 550
  new republic (1918) 563
  normal life 569
  pogroms against Jewish population 568
  proposed removal from Russian control 210
  refusal to bow to counsel or threats 552
  sanitary conditions 250
  territorial claims/disputes 545, 548
  terror against civilian populations 245
  see also Pilsudski; Russian Poland; Warsaw;
    Zeligowski
Poland Minority Treaty (1934) 551
Poles 75, 288, 289, 454
  call for mass expulsion of 452
  Catholics accused of disloyalty 483

deported to Russia 192
encouragement to form new state 371
ethnic 450
exclusion from *Reichsrat* 381
Galician 382
nationally-minded 451
population groups 190
seasonal immigrant estate laborers 227
split between armies 578
subjection of 447
worsening alienation among 451
police 570
  round-ups of foreign workers 428
  women (Britain) 407
  see also military police
police-state apparatus 521
  spies 394
Polish-Soviet War (1919–20) 563, 564, 578
  battlefield casualties 569
politics 13, 25, 29, 256, 279–94, 428, 549,
    567, 579 *see also* international politics
Polivanov, Aleksei 484
Ponsonby, Sir Arthur 583
Poona Division 105
popular culture 269, 422
Popular Party (Italy) 473
Port Stanley 144
Porten, Henny 361
porters (African campaigns) 118, 120, 123
  food for 114, 124
  lack of 117, 123
  recruited/conscripted by force 116, 124
Porto Rosa Conference (1921) 548
Portugal 122, 124
  colonial troops for East Africa supplied
    by 120
  intellectuals 325
  last European belligerent to turn to war 208
  overseas colonies 524
Portuguese Africa 12, 112, 118, 119, 123,
    124
  British and German ambitions to take over
    areas of 115
Posen 436
Potiorek, Gen. Oskar 69
Potsdam War Council (1912) 28
Pozières 62, 410
Poznan 70
Prague 279, 372
  Jan Palach square 374
  national councils formed in 382
  railway station 373

Vítkov Hill monument 581
PRC (British Parliamentary Recruiting
    Committee) 282, 290, 405–6
prices 224, 226, 257, 502
    agricultural goods 513
    fixed 227, 228
    guaranteed 411
    stable 357, 509
prisoners 68, 70, 72, 78, 86, 89, 92, 104,
    191, 284, 387, 471, 483
    atrocities/massacres/crimes against 189,
        193–4
    capture in no man's land 177
    death in captivity 93, 468
    difficulty providing sufficient rations to 93
    discontent fueled by hunger 77
    labor shortages and employment of 411,
        420
    lack of consideration shown to 468
    reparations covering the holding of 456
    return to civilian life 567
    submarine 147
    summarily tortured and executed 567
    uprising in Siberia 560
    vast numbers taken 137, 283, 288
    volunteer 90
profiteers 284, 285, 289, 377, 411, 502, 578
    government control of 407
    popular vengeance on 396
    post-occupation trials for 394
Progressive Bloc (Russian opposition
    coalition) 483, 484–5, 486
Progressives (Germany) 288, 442, 452
prohibition (of alcohol US 1920) 514
Prónay, Pál 569
propaganda 22, 47, 90, 114, 189, 190, 207,
    235, 260, 264, 280, 281–3, 290, 323,
    342, 345, 376, 409, 418, 435, 470, 479,
    513, 514, 546, 583
    academics producing 333, 334
    Allied 441
    anti-German hate 9–10
    atrocity 265
    battles over what was true or false 315
    cinema 358–61
    colonial 528
    counterweight to 382
    domestic 411
    multiple forms 501
    official 438
    scientific role in 316
    Soviet 27

support for the war 530
    writers who supplied 328–9, 330
prostitution 269, 528, 535
protectorates 13, 14
Protestantism/Protestants 238, 239, 242
    governments dominated by 529
    minority or majority position 345
    see also Ulster Protestants
protests 407
    endurance and 283–9
    farm 530
    nationalist 197
    troops ordered to fire on unarmed
        protestors 533
    working-class 266–7, 285–6
Provisional Council of State (Poland) 451
Prussia 70, 435
    Bavarian soldiers blamed perpetuation of
        war on 287
    conquest of Austria (1866) 41
    ethnically mixed eastern marches 447
    Russian incursion into 449, 452
    state-of-siege law (1851) 279
    volunteers who rallied to the monarchy 434
    Wilhelm II relinquishes the crown of 444
    see also East Prussia; Franco-Prussian War;
        Frederick II
Prussian Academy of Sciences 324
Prussian Guard 72
Prussian militarism 9, 39, 54, 205
Prussian War Ministry
    census of all Jewish soldiers 439
    production of armaments and military
        substitutes subordinated to 437
    War Raw Materials Section 225
Prussian War of Liberation (1813) 434
Przemyśl 70, 71, 376
Przhevalskii, Gen, M. A. 100
Psichari, Ernest 239, 243
Pskov (Russian military head quarters
    1916–17) 486
psychiatry 185, 302, 303, 304, 305
psychological ailments 270, 296
    see also trauma, "shellshock"
psychology 455, 499
    used in treatment of "shellshock" 315
psychoses 302
public health measures 76
public opinion 9, 11, 12, 21, 22, 24, 189,
    207, 279–94, 333, 354, 404, 413, 455,
    470, 582
    nationalist (Russia) 481

Punjab 525, 529, 533, 566
Putilov (Russian armaments firm) 224
Putnik, Gen. Radomir 69

Q-ships 147
Qingdao (German concession in China) 206
Québec 313, 529, 530
Queen Mary's Army Auxiliary Corps 271
Queenstown (Ireland) 149
Quénu, Edouard 296–7
Qurna (Mesopotamia) 105

R-planes *(Riesenflugzeug)* 161
race 279, 285, 428, 527, 530, 552
  assumptions based on 268
  inferior 22
  Nazi millenarianism founded on 244
  plan to destroy 245
  pseudo-biological concept of 22
  struggle for survival between antagonistic
    groups 503
  widespread violence 513
race riots 285, 428, 513, 529, 570
racism 244, 453
Rada (Ukrainian council/parliament) 456,
  457, 490
Radiant May (Italy 1915) 468
Radical Party (France) 13, 27
RAF (Royal Air Force) 163, 165, 166, 565,
  569
  American squadron attached to 164
  women's branch 271
  see also RFC (Royal Flying Corps), Royal
    Naval Air Service
railway communications 41, 217–18
Rákosi, Mátyás 562
Ramadi (Mesopotamia) 106
Ramsay, William 316
Rand goldmines 112
Rapallo Treaty (1922) 548
rape 251, 568
  horrific accounts of 255, 265
  women who became pregnant through 266
Rasín, Alois 374
Rasputin, Grigori 484
Ratcliffe, S. K. 333
Rathenau, Walther 225, 435, 437
rationing 116, 226, 227, 228, 257, 271, 290,
  377, 411, 412, 442
Rauf Bey, Huseyin 101
raw materials 77, 225, 226, 391, 420, 457,
  469, 512–13

Rawe, Kai 394
Rawlinson, Gen. Henry 45, 55, 60, 133, 134
Rayleigh, J. W. Strutt, Lord 313
rearmament 13, 14
recruitment 264–5, 282, 287, 451, 526, 527
  crime to obstruct (USA) 520
  indigenous populations 285, 531
Red Archive (journal) 27
Red Army 459, 558, 560, 562–4, 569
  bombing campaigns against insurgents 561
  deaths 569
  new weapons of war against civilians 567
  Persia invaded (1920) 566
  torture and killing of opponents 570
Red Cross 93, 268, 346
Red Guards 485, 487
  Helsinki evacuated by 561
Red Scare (USA) 520
Redlich, Josef 373
Redmond, John 405, 406, 409
refugees 52, 76, 89, 191, 192, 193, 228, 258,
  356, 375, 377, 389, 394, 407, 471, 547,
  552, 560
Reger, Max 340
Reich Cereals Agency (Germany) 227
Reich Food Office (Germany) 227
Reichsbund (German veterans'
  movement) 568
Reichsrat (Austrian parliament) 373, 381
Reichstag 5, 10, 211, 225, 286, 288, 433,
  442, 444, 456, 549
  Inter-Party Committee 442
  Peace Resolution (1917) 442, 453, 455
Reicke, Georg 324
Reid, James J. 502
Reims 55, 57, 342, 536
Reiss, Rodolphe A. 191
religion 69, 188, 234, 235, 237, 239
  decline of 22
  freedom of 546
  majority (Catholicism in France) 240
religious art 345–6
religious sociology 234
Remarque, Erich Maria 266, 330, 332, 324,
  363, 550
remobilization 289–90
  crisis and 393–5
  cultural 317, 585–7
Renault 157, 183
Renfrewshire 303
Rennenkampf, Gen. P. K. 482
Renouvin, Pierre 27, 204, 211

rent control 255, 256, 407
reparations 26, 27, 363, 455, 456, 509, 545,
    548–9, 578, 582, 584
    canceled (1932) 551
    German resistance to 547
    peace without annexations or 453
    quarrels over 363
repeating rifles 174–5
Repington, Charles 55, 61
Representation of the People Act (Britain
    1918) 273, 413
repression 244, 289, 327, 348, 379, 428,
    442, 530, 568
    counter-insurrectionary 414
    important in prosecution of the war 471
    persistent 563
    plans to escalate 486
requisitioning 228, 254
Resid Bey, Dr (governor of Diyarbakir) 503–4
respiratory infections 255
Returned Servicemen's League of
    Australia 530
revisionism (causes of the war) 26, 27, 28, 29
revolutionary syndicalists 467
Reza Khan, Shah of Persia 560
RFC (Royal Flying Corps) 156, 157, 159,
    166
    officers recruited from the ranks of public-
    school sportsmen 158
    see also RAF (Royal Air Force), Royal Naval
    Air Service, Trenchard
Rhine River 51, 84
    call for France to seize left bank 205, 210
Rhineland 429, 549
    Allied occupation of 584
    demilitarized zone 430, 551
    French troops in 578
Ribot, Alexander 210
Richthofen, Manfred, Baron von 158, 159,
    162, 164, 183–4
Rif mountains 531
Riga 88, 436, 449
    German capture of 454, 489
    Russian evacuation plans for 483
    terror campaign 568
Riga, Gulf of 150
Riga, Treaty of (1921) 564
right-wing groups 419
    growing populism 412
    nationalist 244, 284, 581
    press 408
    proto-fascist 484

radical 568
Rilke, Rainer Maria 333
Rio Muni (Spanish colony in Africa) 116,
    117, 118
riots 440, 441
    anti-recruitment 530
    ethnic 408
    food 271
    hunger 377
    internecine 285
    racial 285, 428, 513, 529, 570
Ritter, Gerhard 62
Roberts, Robert (wartime childhood) 257
Robertson, Sir William 37, 46
Rockefeller institution 319
Roentgen, Wilhelm 324
Rogers, Capt. Bogart 165
Rohr, Capt. Willy 44
Rolland, Romain 242, 317, 327, 328, 346,
    422
Rolls-Royce 161
Romani, battle of (1916) 103
Romania 39, 66, 73, 74, 75, 108, 129, 380,
    436, 546, 582
    allowed to occupy Bessarabia 456
    army 107, 271
    civilian population 254
    Dadaists from 346
    defeated 211, 455–6
    entry into the war 208, 210, 380, 438
    export of revolution to 562
    grain from 227, 228, 377
    intellectuals 327
    invasion of Transylvania 380, 381
    irredentist claims of Hungarians in 559
    Jews from 245
    Liberals 208
    occupied 323
    prisoner deaths in German captivity 193
    rewarded with Hungarian Transylvania 78
    scores to settle with neighbors 208
    terms imposed on 77, 456
    territorial claims 545
    see also Carol I; Ferdinand
Romanians 373
    ethnic 208
    regarded as traitors by German
    government 194
Romanov dynasty collapse (1917) 272
romanticism (air war) 157–8, 159, 164, 167
Rome Congress of Oppressed Nationalities
    (1917) 379

Röntgen, Wilhelm 316
Roosevelt, Franklin D. 521
Roques, Mario 334
Rosenzweig, Franz 234
Rostand, Edmond 325
Rouault, Georges 345, 349
Rouen 241
Roulers (Belgium) 46
Royal Naval Air Service 158
Royal Navy 46, 52, 101, 118, 146, 148, 195,
    526
    administrative offices/operational
        headquarters 36
    coal for fuel 407
    defeat at battle of Coronel (1914) 144
    first submarines entered service (1902) 142
    interception of German arms shipment
        intended to supply Irish uprising 409
    New Zealand dependent on 525
    propaganda films emphasizing strength
        of 358
    role of intelligence in operations 143
    tensions between military and scientific
        group 311
    threat of German battleships canceled
        out 439
    vital element in East African defense 121
    women's branch 271
    see also Beatty; Cradock; De Robeck;
        Evan-Thomas; Fisher; Jellicoe; Kerr;
        Keyes; Troubridge; Tyrwhitt
Royal Society of London 313, 316, 318
    Chemistry Committee 314
Rozanov, Vasilii 326
Ruanda-Urundi 121, 122, 123, 124
Ruffey, Gen. Pierre-Xavier 51
Ruhr 27, 363, 394
    chemical industry 313
    Franco-Belgian invasion (1923) 548
    labor protest crushed in 562
    occupation of (1923–4) 396, 570, 582
Rumpler biplanes 166
Rupprecht, Gen., Crown Prince of
    Bavaria 50–1, 52, 55
Russell, Bertrand 327, 328
Russia 6, 10, 26, 27, 39, 42, 46, 47, 53,
    66–9, 75, 127, 193, 210, 256, 271, 280,
    327, 380, 404, 413, 479–93, 497, 563,
    578
    Allied intervention in 560
    Allies promise Constantinople to 207
    arms production during war 484

autocracy fears letting propaganda out of
    government control 282
aviation 157, 160
Britain aligned with 432
chance for Ottoman revenge on 496
counterrevolutionary wars 558–9
Dadaists from 346
deaths per day 184
defeats of 128, 516
dependent on foreign manufacturing 313
democratization in 481
deportations to (1915) 192
domination of non-Russian vassal
    peoples 452
East Prussians deported to 191
entry into the war 372, 433
ethnically non-Russian borderlands lost 443
Falkenhayn's aim to secure separate peace
    with 39
fertility levels 248
films 357
food shortages 227
French military agreements with 3, 12
German press campaign against 15
grain reserves/exports/surplus 73, 227,
    228
harsh peace settlement inflicted on
    (1918) 179, 518
important supply route blocked between
    Western allies and 108
intellectuals 324–5, 326, 327
intelligence material passed to Britain
    by 146
military hospitals 333
mobilization 202, 250, 288, 488–9
munitions production 225
Muslims in 498
national units in 569
newsreels 354, 357
pogroms and persecution 449
position as protector of Slav states 14
prisoners harshly treated in 194
rebuilding naval strength 141
refugees in 192
revolt in Central Asia crushed (1916) 193
retreat (1915) 174, 254
rumors about Czech volunteer units in 374
rural bias in casualties 252
Scottish Women's Hospitals in 268
shells imported 218
short-lived occupation of German
    territory 191

strikes 285
stripped of almost all European possessions 546
terror against civilian populations 245
Turks allowed to open new front against 206
vessels destroyed at sea 97
violence channeled into new ideologies 244
war a disaster for civilian population 254
women in industrial workforce 267
see also Bolshevik Revolution; Guchkov; Kerensky; Khvostov; Lenin; Polivanov; Soviet Russia; Stalin; Trotsky; Tsarist Russia; White Russia; *also under following headings prefixed* "Russian"
Russian Academy of Sciences (Association of Scholars of World War I) 479
Russian army 70, 73, 74, 75, 100, 435, 488
acts of violence during invasion 190–1
Armenians in 503
casualties and losses 489
conquering of Galicia and part of Poland 357
decimated 483
devastating offensive against Austrian eastern front 86
drained by 1914–15 campaigns 288
fighting spirit broken 443
film stressing excessive power of 363
Germans outnumbered in East Prussia by 482
great mutiny (1917) 489
major defeat and retreat from Galicia 86
mass departures from 490
number of days required to mobilize 481
opposition from its own ranks 487
seeking to compensate for personnel losses and material shortcomings 72
soldier councils debated orders to attack 487
vulnerable to all-out offensive 71
see also Alekseev; Brusilov; Khabalov; Kornilov; Krasnov; Nikolai; Red Army; Samsonov; Skoropadsky; Tukhachevskii; Wrangel; Zhilinskii
Russian Central Asia 285
Russian Civil War (1918–20) 244, 430, 458, 479–80, 490, 545, 559–62, 577
atrocities of 244
casualties 491, 568–9
doctrine of annihilating opponents 570
Finland caught in 458, 568

see also Kolchak
Russian Empire *see* Tsarist Russia
Russian front 39, 86, 481
German triumphs on 75
plans to coordinate all-out offensive on 210
Russian High Command 70, 74, 288
Russian navy
Baltic fleet 150
Black Sea Fleet 99, 151
see also Kolchak
Russian Poland 68, 69, 212, 357, 436, 450, 455, 482
brought under German rule 443
fierce fighting from start of the war 450
Germans deported to Siberia 192
Russian Provisional Government 272, 290, 454, 488, 490
authority solely in the hands of 486
collapse of 487
coup overthrowing 455
Russian Revolution (1905) 3, 11, 13, 280, 486
Russian Revolution (February/March 1917) 289, 290, 410–11, 440, 453, 454, 485–7
conferences of Russian Muslims organized in aftermath 499
Russian Revolution (November 1917) *see* Bolshevik Revolution
Russian war effort 223, 319, 357, 481–5
regime change and 486
weakened significantly 100
Russians
ethnic 192, 450
first official recognition of as distinct nationality 491
links to 375
Russification 71
Russo-Japanese War (1904–5) 3, 8, 14, 68, 141, 142, 174, 282
care for combatants suffering from psychiatric illnesses 185
first modern grenades employed during 175
Russo-Turkish frontiers/front 99, 254
Ruthenes 375
Rutherford, E. 311

Saar region (Germany) 205, 515
Sabahaddin Bey, Ottoman Prince 504
Sabor
Bosnian assembly 375
Croatian assembly 374

sabotage 408, 510, 567
sacrifice 238–40, 241, 242, 244, 272, 273,
    287, 536, 579, 580
  Australia and New Zealand 530
  Belgium 395–7
  Britain, 406, 407, 410, 415
  collective 284
  consent and 342–3, 345
  Ireland 414
  Germany 435
  Italy 465
  Serbia 378
  ultimate 284
  women's 377
Said Halim Pasha, Ottoman Grand
    Vizier 497, 499
Saint-Germain Treaty (1919) 93, 546
Saint-Gervais church Paris (bombardment
    1918) 272
Saint-Hilaire-le-Grand (Russian
    cemetery) 480
Saint-Jean-de-Maurienne Agreement
    (1917) 207
Saint-Quentin 440
Saint-Saëns, Camille 422
Sainte-Menehould 300
Sakir, Bahaeddin 498
Salandra, Antonio 87, 290, 467, 468, 469
Salford 257
Salonika 38, 42, 57, 66, 73, 75, 78, 102, 429
  Allied troops in 208
  plan to land American troops in 515
Samoa (captured from Germany 1914) 143,
    524
Samsonov, Gen. A. V. 41, 482
San Remo Conference (1920) 547
Sanders, Gen. Otto Liman von 15, 99, 101,
    104, 108
Sandes, Flora 271, 330
Sandfontein (battle in German South-West
    Africa, 1914) 119
Sangnier, Marc 243
sanitary conditions 250
  insufficient at front 191
  military encampments 254
  regulations 76
Sarajevo 375, 377
Sarajevo assassination (1914) 3, 15, 19, 28,
    54, 202, 289, 372, 404, 432
Sargent, John Singer 344
Sarkotić, Gen. Stjepan 375, 379, 382
Sarraut, Albert 535

Sarrebourg (German Lorraine) 49
Sarykamish, battle of (Jan. 1915) 99, 503
Sascha Messter Woche (Austrian newsreel) 355
Sassoon, Siegfried 62, 263, 327–8, 331
Satie, Erik 422
Saudi Arabia 565–6
Saumoneau, Louise 266
Sava River 69
Sazonov, Sergei 481
Scapa Flow 144
Scarborough 405
Scedilveki Bey, Col. Yakup 107
Schäfer, Dietrich 324
Scheer, Admiral Reinhard 147–8
Scheldt River 394
Schiele, Egon 346
Schiemann, Theodor 458
Schlick, Major 190
Schlieffen, Count Alfred von 11, 40, 41, 53,
    433
Schlieffen Plan (1904–5) 6, 7, 8, 15, 23, 49,
    51, 52, 54, 202, 217, 418, 481
  inherent flaws in 419
  revised 387
Schmitt-Rottluff, Karl 341, 345
Schnack, Anton 331
Schnee, Heinrich (Governor German East
    Africa) 121
Schneider (French armaments firm) 182, 224
Schnitzler, Arthur 326
schoolteachers 282, 290
Schroeder, Paul 24–5
Schuster, Arthur 318
Schütztruppen (German colonial paramilitary
    force) 115–16, 117, 118, 120, 121, 122
science and technology 307–22
scorched-earth policy 70, 192, 440, 449–50
Scotland
  German communities 408
  memorials to war dead 403
  temporary anchorages on west coast 144
Scottish Highlands 406
Scottish Women's Hospitals 268
Sea of Marmara 101, 102
seaplanes 156, 160
Sebastopol 151
Sebestyén, Emil see Kun, Béla
Second Socialist International 11, 14
  inability to prevent war 280
  revolutionary rhetoric 286
Section Photographique et Cinématographique
    de l'Armée 360

security
  Austria-Hungary 379
  Britain international 403
  censorship and 281
  European colonies in Africa, internal 114,
    120
  France, 415, 547
  international, pre-war, 23
  USA 511
  see also collective security; national security
sedition 421, 513
Sedition Act (US 1918) 520
Šedivý, Ivan 374
Seeckt, Col. (later Gen.) Hans von 55, 72,
  73, 569
Seeger, Alan 330
Seidler, Ernst von 381
Seignobos, Charles 334
self-determination 285, 291, 382, 467, 518,
  532, 533
  difficult questions raised by 559
  legitimizing the claim to 562
  possibility for 534
  principle violated 546
  spreading democracy through the principle
    of 521
Semeria, Fr Giovanni 469
Senegalese people
  first African member of French
    parliament 527
  losses 528
  tirailleurs 114, 526, 534, 536
Senghor, Léopold Sedar 536
Sennett, Mack 361
separation allowances 268, 269, 285
Serbia 13, 16, 42, 57, 108, 151, 207, 209,
  377–80
  Austria-Hungary attack on 15, 25, 66, 68,
    69, 84, 191, 202, 203, 250, 287, 371,
    433
  casualties and losses 251, 578
  conquest of (1915) 39, 73
  control of the Yugoslav mission 380
  Germany decides to quash in combined
    offensive 207–8
  guerrilla bands in mountain regions 379
  Habsburg declaration of war on (1914) 481
  legend of active resistance to foreigners 379
  national anthem 382
  national insecurity 378
  occupied 378, 449, 578
  policy of national expansion 14

program of war aims 372
rebuilding of 559
Russian support for July 1914 481
Scottish Women's Hospitals 268
territorial claims 545
ultimatum to 432, 433
wartime role 377
see also Balkan League
Serbian army 330, 380
  advance up to the Bosnian border 382
  driven from its homeland 86
  eroded by disease and casualties 73
  purging allegedly disloyal officers 78
  women who fought for 271
Serbs 373, 375, 382–3
  Austro-Hungarian Serbs viewed as enemy
    sympathizers 372
  death of 378
  encouragement to form new state 371
Sereth (Siret) River 107
Service de Santé see French Army Medical
  Service
Servizio P (Italian Propaganda Service) 90
Seton-Watson, R. W. 378
Severini, Gino 342
Sèvres Treaty (1920) 547, 564
sexual relations 259
  immigrant with French women 528
  opportunities outside legitimate
    channels 268–9
sexually transmitted diseases 269
Shantung (Shandong) peninsula China 143
Sharif Hussein see Faisal
Shatt-al-Arab 105
Shaw, George Bernard 327
shell crisis 55, 61, 281
shell production 420, 483, 484
"shellshock" 60, 185, 270, 302, 304, 340,
  341, 348
  psychology used in treatment of 315
  see also psychiatry, psychological ailments,
    psychology, psychoses, trauma
Shia Muslims 565
Shinyanga (German East Africa) 123
shipping 144, 149, 509
  devices for stabilizing 311
  presence in neutral harbors/ports 143, 144
  protecting 121
  raiding 120
  shortage of 47
  see also convoys, merchant shipping; neutral
    shipping

"shirkers" 283, 406, 407, 408, 412, 420–1, 427, 439

shock troops 527 (*see also* stormtroopers)

shop stewards 286, 411

shortages 257, 289, 412, 420
   Belgium 388
   Britain 411
   Germany 422
   food 193, 227, 442, 471, 485
   fuel 485, 512
   munitions 176, 438
   shells and other military material 483

Shotwell, James (Carnegie Foundation) 335

Siberia 100, 191, 483, 561
   Germans deported to 192
   irregular counterrevolutionary troops 568
   uprising of Czech prisoners of war 560

siege warfare 9, 174, 180–1
   grenades used in 175

Siegfried Line 45, 440

Signal Corps 361

Sikhs 525

Sikorsky, Igor 157

Sikorsky planes 160

Silesia 570
   see also Upper Silesia

Simiand, François 315, 334

Simonstown (South-West Africa) 114

Sinai desert 103, 104, 115

Sinn Féin 410, 412, 413–14
   Gandhi troubled by violence of 567

Sironi, Mario 343

Sistovo 107

Sixtus, Prince of Bourbon-Parma 212

skilled workers 286

Skobelev Committee (Russia) 282

Skoda (Czech/Austro-Hungarian armaments firm) 224, 376
   howitzers 51, 59, 387

Skoropadsky, Gen. Pavlo 457, 459, 560

Slavs 68, 69, 326, 355, 379, 453
   see also South Slavs

Slovaks/Slovakia 289, 373, 382, 562

Slovene-Croat-Serb connections 377

Slovene lands 374

Slovenes 93, 94, 377, 379, 381–2, 578

Slovenia 85, 88, 94

Smith-Dorrien, Gen. Sir Horace 122

Smuts, Gen. Jan 119, 122–4

Smyrna 78, 192, 207, 497, 565

snipers 180, 378, 388, 450

social classes 244, 248, 259, 279, 284, 414

focused source of opposition to war 285
perceived iniquities challenged by 286
see also middle classes; working class; upper class

Social Darwinism 9–10, 21, 22, 25, 449, 503

Social Democratic Party (Hungary) 373

Social Revolutionary Party (Russia) 488

social welfare 521

Socialist Party (Italy) 467, 470, 473

Socialist Republic of Iran 566

socialists 6, 13, 89, 93, 225, 237, 264, 283, 286–7, 290, 334, 373, 387, 392, 395, 405, 409, 419, 430, 451, 457, 466, 473, 527
   activists (February/March Revolution, Russia) 485
   feminist 285
   municipal 562
   reformist 420, 470, 475
   revolutionary 285, 286, 559
   views on future war 11
   women 266

Société de chirurgie (Society of Surgery) 296, 298–9, 300

Soddy, Frederick 317

Sodenstern, Col. Georg von 102

Södergran, Edith 330

Sofia 570

Sofsky, Wolfgang 197

Soissons 55, 443

soldier-artists 342, 344

soldier-poets 329, 330–1

solidarity
   charitable 282, 501
   debate on 502
   international proletarian 11
   market-oriented programs of 502
   national 10
   Pan-Slav 13
   patriotic 470
   small group 92

Solvay, Ernest 389

Solzhenitsyn, Alexander 480

Somme, battle of (1916) 37, 43, 45, 46, 60, 128, 133, 134, 135, 175, 176, 179, 181, 182–3, 218, 254, 259, 288, 329, 331, 358, 411, 438, 440, 535
   account by John Buchan 328
   British New Armies 410
   casualties 410, 423, 515
   colonial soldiers' role in 528
   films of (British, French, German) 358–60

commemoration of role of 36th Ulster
Division 582
German resistance 209
German shock at Allied firepower 226
monument to missing British and French,
Thiepval (1932) 580
Newfoundland Regiment destroyed 526
survival rates for injured British soldiers 184
true beginning of aerial warfare 160
Sonnino, Sidney 467
Sophie, Duchess of Hohenberg (assassinated
Sarajevo, June, 1914) 202
Sopron (Hungarian internment camp) 381,
564
Sopwith, T. O. M. 157, 161
Sopwith Camels 165–6
fatal crashes in training 163
Sorbonne 290, 314
Souchon, Rear-Admiral Wilhelm 97
Sourdat, Alain 298–9, 300
South Africa 62, 112, 114, 119, 124, 144,
410, 414
ambitions to extend northward 115
colonial troops for East Africa supplied
by 120, 122
German policy not to attack 118
legitimacy of imperial ties 532
numbers of whites sent overseas to
fight 526
self-government 524
white Defense Force 118
see also Botha; Smuts; Union of South Africa
South African Native Labour Contingent 526
South African War (1899–1902) see Boer War
South America see Argentina; Brazil; Chile
South-eastern Europe 13
South Pacific 524
South Slavs 84, 288, 289, 371, 372, 375, 382
inequality of rationing 377
national liberation 378
political clubs 381
strengthening the peasantry 562
South Tyrol 84, 375
South Wales 407, 412
South-West Africa 112, 113, 114, 115,
118–20, 122, 124
indigenous peoples used in campaigns
against Germany 525
war of annihilation against Herero people
(1904–7) 189
Southern blacks (US) 513
Southern Rhodesia 113

Soviet Russia 20, 27, 35, 78, 212, 289, 479,
485, 486, 545, 547, 548, 560, 586
anti-Bolshevik forces 79
calls for negotiated peace originating
with 411
dictatorship 583
exile of Finnish communists to 570
isolated and impoverished post-1921 564
Kemal's peace agreement with 565
League of Nations membership 545, 551
memory of brutalities 245
nationality institutionalized 491
prison and exile in 569
reduced in size after Brest-Litovsk 490–1
rights to the Caucasus 458
war between Poland and (1919) 563
war guilt debate 26
world revolution and 558
SPAD (Société Pour L'Aviation et ses
Dérivés) 156, 161
spahis (French North African troops) 527
Spain 552
civil war 585
hoped-for role in negotiating peace 205
intellectuals 325
Spaniards 528
Spanish-American War (1898) 141
Spanish flu see influenza
Spartakists 348, 568
SPD (German Social Democratic Party) 5,
280, 286, 433, 439, 442, 455, 456
Spee, Rear-Admiral Maximilian von 143, 144
Spencer, Stanley 349 (see Burghclere)
Sperry Gyroscope Company 311
spirituality 235, 236, 237, 238, 239, 241,
242, 243, 245
Springs, Elliott White 164
spy mania 281
squadristi 474–5, 570
St Cyr Military Academy 49
St Julien (gas attack against Canadians
1915) 56
St Mihiel 167, 517
St Petersburg 212
stab-in-the-back myth 444
Stahlhelm 363
Stalin, Joseph 552, 569
Stamboliiski, Aleksandar 562, 569
Stanford University (Hoover Institution) 480
starvation 124, 129, 266, 377
death from 192, 504
threatened 388, 389

Statute of Westminster (1931) 532
Steczkowski, Jan Kanty 455
Steed, Henry Wickham 371
steel helmets 58, 63, 177, 470
Steinlen, Théophile-Alexandre 340, 343
Stenger, Major-Gen. Karl 194, 197
Stevenson, David 20, 25, 28
Stockholm (planned socialist conference
    1917) 286
Stopford, Lt.-Gen. Sir Frederick 102
stormtroopers 58, 88, 133, 438–9
Stovall, Tyler 528–9
Strachan, Hew 122, 219
Strafexpedition (Austria-Hungary against Italy,
    1916) 85–7, 88. 469
Strait of Otranto 152
Straits region 97, 205, 210
    Turkey's control of 206, 547
    Russia's secret war aims of conquest 488
    see also Bosporus; Dardanelles
strategy and policy 35
Stresemann, Gustav 548, 549, 582, 583, 584
stretcher-bearers 268, 301
strikes 93, 270, 271, 272, 284, 407, 411–13,
    565, 569
    Belgium (on railways under occupation,
        1915) 390
    Britain 407, 570
    France 427–8
    Germany 1917, 1918 442
    Russia (February/March 1917) 485
    women workers' important part in 285
Struma River (Macedonia) 107
Stürgkh, Karl 326, 373, 374
    murdered 380
Styria 377
submarines 102, 142, 148, 150–2, 160, 209,
    254, 408
    aircraft lacking hitting power to destroy 149
    Belgian bases for German submarines 130
    development of 142
    effect of unlimited campaign 128
    inadequate 160
    lethal 254
    occasional prisoners taken by 147
    paths open for 153
    protection from 144
    sinkings by 145, 149, 437
    techniques for detection 309
    telegraph system 114
    unrestricted warfare 147, 196, 213, 411,
        437, 440, 511

used against merchant shipping 147
    see also U-boats
sub-Saharan Africa 42
subversion 283, 332, 347, 348, 373
    fears of 281
    suspected 411
    vigilance against 374
Sudermann, Hermann 324
Suez Canal 103, 112, 113–14, 115, 533
suffrage
    extension of 22
    universal 272, 373, 396, 414, 470
    women's 264, 273, 396, 521
suffragettes/suffragists 285, 405, 513–14
    leading 268, 509
    see also Pankhurst
Sunday, Billy (American preacher) 236
Sunni Muslims 565
Supreme War Office (Germany) 437
surface raiders 144
surgical intervention
    amputations 298–302
    stomach wounds 296–8
Surrealism 338, 350, 587
surrender 46, 89, 471, 473
Sussex (English Channel steamer) 510
Šušteršič, Ivan 374
Suvla Bay (Gallipoli) 102
Swakopmund (German South-West
    Africa) 118, 119, 120
Sweden 325, 508–9
    sympathetic toward Germany 205
    territorial waters 150
Switzerland 41, 93, 211, 212, 242, 266, 286,
    317, 327, 548
    artists in 341, 346, 347
    tensions between German- and French-
        speaking populations 205
Sydney (Australian cruiser) 143
Sykes-Picot Accords (1916) 207, 533
Syria 103, 105, 502, 533, 565
    Armenians deported to 192, 504
    French occupation of 570
    mandates over 547
    Ottoman withdrawal from 104
Szamuely, Tibor 562
Szent István (dreadnought) 152

Tabora (temporary capital, German East
    Africa) 122, 123
Tabriz (Persia, occupied by Ottoman
    troops) 106

Taganrog (Ukraine) 456
Tagliamento River 89
Tahiti 143, 530
Tal'at Pasha 495, 497, 499
Tambov 561
Tanga 120, 121, 123
Tanganyika 124, 525
tanks 136–8, 176, 182–4, 443
  coordinated use of airplanes and 181
  experimental models 62, 182
Tannenberg, battle of (1914) 39, 41, 62, 68,
    75, 240, 254, 435, 439, 449, 482
  commemoration of 343, 581, 583
Taranto (Italian naval base) 151
Tarnopol 449
Tarnow 72
Tartu university (Estonia) 458
Tatars 193, 450
Taurus Mountains 97
Taveta (Kenya, captured by Germans,
    1914) 121, 122
Taylor, A. J. P. 546
Tayyar Bey, Col. Cafer 107
Techkilat-i Mahsusa (Turkish underground
    body) 499
Tehran 1056
Teilhard de Chardin, Pierre 238
Teodoroiu, Ecaterina 271
Territorial Army (France) 424
terror(ism) 457, 510, 558, 568, 569
  against civilian populations 245
  real or perceived opponents 559–60
Teschen 564
Théâtre aux Armées 333
therapeutic procedures/practices 185, 304
Thérèse of Lisieux, St 241
Thessalonica 494
Thiepval (Somme battlefield, monument) 61,
    62, 410, 580
Third Reich 244, 551, 552
Third Republic (France) 424, 428, 430
  creating alliances that would deter
    Germany 418
  tensions between army and 38
Thomas, Albert 225, 311, 315, 334, 420
Thomas, Martin 535
Thomson, J. J. 311
Thorpe, J. F. 314
Thrace 8, 14, 73, 100
  Armenians expelled from 192
  Balkan Wars amputated 494
  Bulgaria obliged to give up territory in 559

Three Year Military Service law (France) 13
Tiflis 100
Tigris River 105
Tikrit 106
Times, The 55, 316, 323, 356, 371
  copies burnt on London stock
    exchange 408
tirailleurs (French light infantry, often raised
    in colonies) 114, 526, 527, 534, 536
Tiroler Kaiserjaeger (elite Austrian mountain
    unit) 70
Tirpitz, Admiral Alfred von 142, 143
Tisza, Count István 372, 373, 380, 381
Togo 112, 117, 124, 533
  conquest of 115–16
Tökés, Rudolf L. 569
Tolmino (Slovenian town on Austro-Italian
    front) 84, 85, 88
Topical Budget (British newsreel
    company) 354, 356, 360, 361
torpedo boats 102, 142, 151, 152
torpedoes 102, 141, 148, 149, 151, 152,
    196, 510
  self-propelled 142
torture 190, 567, 568
total war 47
totalitarian regimes 244, 474
Toul (French fortress) 418
Townshend, Maj.-Gen. Charles 105
toxic gases 308
Trabzon (Trebizond) 100, 151
trade unions 280, 286, 335, 373, 405, 408,
    411, 413, 420, 439, 473, 513
  conscription opposed by (Australia) 530
Trading with the Enemies Act (US 1917) 520
traitors 13, 238, 375, 381, 428, 472, 483,
    484, 572, 578, 584
Transcaucasia 99–101, 107–8, 490, 563
  Bolsheviks forced to give up 490
  Turkish forces advance on (1918) 457
Transvaal 353
Transylvania 78, 208
  Romanian invasion of 380, 381
trauma 177, 184, 338
  emotional 334
  psychological 60, 185, 296, 302–5
Travers, Tim 60
trench fever 58
trench warfare 9, 43, 54, 60–1, 77, 85, 87,
    88, 158, 176, 181, 183, 270, 331, 365,
    424, 436, 516, 517
  attackers stormed/paralyzed 55, 175

trench warfare (*cont'd*)
  best solution to 45
  capture of prisoners in no man's land 177,
    180
  demand for heavy artillery 224
  French slow to adapt military clothing
    to 177
  origins 174
  rudimentary preparation for soldiers and
    junior officers 92
  specialized medical units 297
  strategic significance 42
  supporting wire and concrete strong
    points 136
  tactical purpose 42
  technical expertise 178–80
Trenchard, Gen. Hugh 161
Trentino/Trento 82, 86, 91, 93, 467, 473,
    474
  unreliable populations gathered in
    camps 355
trepanations 300–1
Treviso 303
triage (battlefield medical treatment) 295,
    297, 301, 303
Trianon Treaty (1920) 546, 581
Trieste 82, 84, 91, 93, 329, 467, 473
triplanes 162
Triple Alliance (Germany, Austria-Hungary,
    Italy) 23, 82, 84, 141, 464, 467
  Italy's betrayal of/defection from 86, 151,
    207, 326
Triple Entente (France, Russia, Britain) 23,
    41, 42, 45, 46, 47, 73, 84, 203, 386,
    395–6, 403, 437, 482, 545
  advantage of men and guns on all
    fronts 486
  German proposals unacceptable to (January,
    1917) 210
  Germans accused of atrocities 282
  industrial superiority and engine
    production 161
  intellectuals in 316
  Italian intellectual bourgeoisie generally
    supported 208
  Japan entered war on the side of 143
  jihad declared against 499
  keeping Bulgaria from allying with
    Germany 207
  loans to 219
  maritime supremacy and organization of
    food and fuel supplies 284

Norway leans toward 205
  powers arrayed against Central Powers 467
  shipping available underestimated by
    Germans 149
  success against revolution in Hungary
    (1919) 562
  see also Western Allies
Triumph (battleship) 102
Trotsky, Leon (Lev) 212, 286, 455
Troubridge, Rear-Admiral Sir Ernest 143–4
Trumbić, Ante 379, 382
Tsarist Russia 26, 27, 39, 47, 66, 578
  collapse under pressure of war 128
  crumbling 454
  democratization in 481
  deportations used by 192
  despotism 447
  disintegrating 558
  end of 563
  ethnically non-Russian borderlands lost 443
  final military effort of 75
  French alliance with 418, 430, 432
  German movies accused 363
  growing population 447
  national units that emerged in 569
  realities of Muslim communities in 498
  response to German provocation 97
  ruthless crushing of revolt in Central
    Asia 193
  separation allowances 285
  shell production 484
  states far less menacing than 546
  tension between Germany and 432
  transition to Bolshevik regime 283
  see also Nicholas II; Rasputin
Tsingtau 143
  see also Qingdao
tuberculosis 165, 166
Tuchman, Barbara 20
Tukhachevskii, Mikhail, Marshal 564
Tunisia 82, 531
  Muslims mobilized for French army 526
  reports of censors 528
  tirailleurs (soldiers) 536
Turanism (Pan-Turkic nationalism) 496, 498,
    499, 501
Turin 286, 469
  popular uprising (1917) 471
Türk Dernegi/Türk Gücü/Türk Ocagi (Turkish
    Associations) 498
Turkestan uprising (1916) 561
Turkey 108, 192, 207, 454, 494, 559

barred from Paris Peace Conference 545
casualties Great War 252
casualties Greco-Turkish War 569–70
Christian population 496
compulsory exchange of population between Greece and 504, 547, 565
Dodecanese islands taken by Italy from 94
modern, foundation of 494
polity embracing Central Asia, Afghanistan and 561
territorial integrity confirmed 565
see also Anatolia; Constantinople; Dardanelles; Greco-Turkish War; Kemal; Ottoman Empire; Young Turks
Turkic peoples/regions 496, 498, 499
Turkification 191, 498, 500, 501
Turkish Historical Society 196
Turkish-Italian conflict (1911) *see* Libyan war
Turkish War of Independence (1919) 495, 496, 497, 504
Kemalist resistance 501
Turkish War (1914–18) 97–111
Turkishness 498, 504
Turkists 500
Turks
expropriating the land of 562
expulsion of 567
portrayed as liberators of colonized Muslims 530
Turnip Winter (1916/17) 227–8, 271, 442
typhoid 76, 250, 294, 295
typhus 76, 194, 250, 294, 295, 378, 450
Tyrwhitt, Commodore Reginald 145
Tzara, Tristan 36

U-boats (German submarines) 97, 102, 132, 145, 151, 160, 195, 227, 254, 439, 508, 509, 510
condemned/severely criticized 196, 363
sinkings by 411, 510, 511
success of convoys in defeating 137
unrestricted warfare suspended 437
UFA (Universum Film Aktien-Gesellschaft) 361, 363
UGACPE (Union des Grandes Associations contre la Propagande Ennemie) 290
Uganda 121, 122
Ukraine 77, 78, 204, 456–7, 482, 488
civil war a heavy toll on Jewish population 568
declaration of independence 490
divided up into zones of occupation 456

ethnic differentiation 558
forfeit of western borderlands of Eastern Galicia 564
German control of/withdrawal from 443, 490, 563
Polish troops capture territory in 563
revolts against Skoropadsky 459
Russia loses/gives up control of 212, 455
terror against civilian populations 245
violence and population displacement 560
see also Makhno; Petliura
Ukrainian Directory forces 568
Ukrainians 71, 375, 450, 454, 545, 563, 578
evacuated from war zone 193
Ulster 52
authority over the six counties 414
British troops in 570
Ulster Division (36th) 61, 62, 409, 410, 414, 582
Ulster Protestants 410, 413, 414, 567
enlistment rates 406
majority organizing for armed resistance 404
Ulster Unionists 404, 405, 406, 414, 582
proof of loyalty 409
UN Commission on Human Rights (on Armenian genocide) 196
Unamuno, Miguel de 325
Ungaretti, Giuseppe 331
Union of Democratic Control (British pacifist body) 328
Union of Russian People 484
Union of South Africa 112, 118, 119
Union sacrée (1914–16) 14, 235–8, 280, 418–19, 427
failure to restore 288
public dissolution of 381
United States 28, 46, 147, 508–23, 547, 582
Allied propaganda to 328, 329
anti-British feelings 510
balance of payments with 219
closing of exit routes to 547
conscription 512, 521
construction of powerful warships 141
coordination of allied procurement 226
demand for new reparations settlement 548
development of land planes 156
entry into the war 47, 76, 128, 129, 132, 137, 149, 196, 213, 290, 395, 411, 440, 453, 487, 508, 512, 515
French steel supply imported from 218
German spies within 510

United States (*cont'd*)
  global protection for minorities a problem for 546
  Jewish refugees refused 552
  liberal public opinion 189
  munitions effort 285–6
  national ceremonies to honor war dead 273
  nativist politics 256
  newsreels 360–1
  nurses from 268
  overseas colonies 524
  refusal to ratify Versailles Treaty 26, 520
  repatriation of soldiers' bodies 580
  tariffs 550
  Uncle Sam symbol 470
  numbers of men mobilized 250
  war effort 311, 512–13, 514
  war supplies reaching Britain from 57
  white domestic servants 267
  see also Carter; Eisenhower; Hoover; Kennedy; Reagan; Roosevelt; US military; Wilson, Woodrow
University of Berlin 317
University of Tokyo 311
Unknown Soldier 273, 536, 578, 579, 581
unmarried women 268
Upington (South Africa, Boer rebellion at, 1914) 119
Upper Adige 84, 93
upper class 503
Upper Silesia, post-war conflict over 546, 559, 564
Urbain, Georges 314
US military 514–18, 521
  Air Service 167
  Marines 152
  women in army nursing corps 271
  see also AEF; Pershing
US Secretary of the Navy 311
Usedom, Admiral Guido von 101
USPD (Independent German Social Democratic Party) 286, 442
USSR *see* Soviet Russia
UVF (Ulster Volunteer Force) 404, 409
Uzbek radicals 193

Vaché, Jacques 347, 348
VADs (Voluntary Aid Detachments) 268, 407
Vallotton, Félix 343
Van Deventer, Lt.-Gen. Sir Jacob 122, 123
Van Vollenhoven, Joost 531

Vaterlandspartei (Fatherland Party, Germany 1917–18) 440
Vatican 208–9
Vazov, Ivan 331
Vehip Pasha, Col. Ferit 100, 102
venereal disease 58, 269, 270
Veneto plain 471
Venezia-Julia 93
Venizelos, Eleutherios 73, 207
Verdun, battle of (1916) 38, 41, 43, 44, 46, 47, 51, 52, 56, 57, 58, 61, 62, 63, 86, 128, 130, 240, 288, 331, 346, 358
  aviators attacked during 164
  casualties 59, 423, 515
  colonial soldiers' role 528
  erstwhile hero of 586
  Falkenhayn dismissed/replaced for failure 75, 238, 439
  French look to the British to relieve 60
  German failure to break through 209
  German preoccupation with attack on 74
  little footage shown on newsreels 355, 359
  memorial to Muslim soldiers 536
  tactical warfare introduced at 438
  true beginning of aerial warfare 160
Versailles Treaty (1919) 185, 196, 244, 318, 395, 414, 429, 543–57, 563, 580
  call for revision of 584
  contravention of 564
  possible trial of scientists as war criminals 316
  strict terms exacted 455
  US refusal to ratify 26, 520
  victory parades that followed the signing 579
Verviers (Belgium) 203
Vervoort, André 240
Vesle River 52
Veterans' associations 479–80
Vial, Françque 424
Vichy regime 586
Victor Emanuel III, King of Italy *see* Vittorio
Victoria (W. Africa) 116, 117
Vienna 84, 212, 279, 371, 432
  anti-Semitic agitation in 375
  censor office 377
  food the key to wartime politics in 377
  hunger 228
  militancy 286
  War Supervisory Office 373
Vietnam 534, 545, 536
Viipuri (Finland) 561

Villa, Francisco (Pancho) 510
Village Economy Bank of Kayseri 502
Villain, Raoul (assassin of Jean Jaurès) 13
Villers-Cotterêts 183
Vilna/Vilno 74, 563
Vimy Ridge (battle, 1917) 129
Vincent, Clovis (French psychiatrist) 305
visual arts 338–52
Vittorio Emmanuele III, King of Italy 89, 465, 467, 468
Vittorio Veneto, battle of (1918) 91, 93, 290, 465, 472, 473
Viviani, René 56, 205
Vlaamsche Wachter (underground paper) 395
Voisin, Gabriel (Bébé Grillard) 162
Voisin planes 156, 160, 162
Volhynia (Ukraine) 193, 570
Volpe, Gioacchino (Fascist historian) 465
Volterra, Vito 311, 319
volunteers 90, 237, 258, 270, 289, 328, 356, 387, 388, 410, 512, 529, 581
  artist 433
  Britain 405–9
  Irish republican 566
  myth of (Germany) 434
  nationalist (Italy) 473
  patriotic students (Ottoman Turkey) 501
  women and 330, 407, 412
Vorontsov-Dashkov, Count I. I. 99
Vorticism 338, 346
Vosges mountains 42, 49, 203
Vosnjak, Bogumil 379
Vuillard, Edouard 343
VVS (Malagasy nationalist group) 531

Wagner, Richard 422
Wales 410, 412
  memorials to war dead 403
  mining strikes 407
Wallachia 107
Walvis Bay (South-West Africa) 118, 119
War College (US) 515
war crimes 188, 189, 191, 195, 197, 198, 260, 587
  categories of 196
  Germans attacked at length for 236
  investigated 282
  possible trial of scientists 316
  provisions for trying 429
  responsibility for 583
War Department (US) 515

War Emergency: Workers' National Committee (Britain) 413
war economy 217–33, 435, 439
  disruption of production due to 502
  militarism and 500–2
  perceived class iniquities challenged 286
  unintended consequences of creation of 255
war effort 218–24, 235, 271, 274, 311, 421, 481–5
  attempt to use occupation of Belgium for 390–1
  enthusiastically embraced (France) 421
  focus on winning (USA) 514
  imperial (Britain and France) 529
  industries most critical to 512–13
  large-scale mobilization of civilians 576
  literary propaganda for 390
  mass production for 313
  pictures backing 361
  prolonged by Bolshevik Revolution 319
  regime change and 486
  symbolized (Italy) 470
war guilt question 20, 26–9, 429, 584
War Industries Board (US) 512–13
war neurosis 164, 185
war of movement 265, 272, 449
  difficulties of conducting 517
War Room (Britain) 143
Warsaw 69, 70, 449, 564
  German troops disarmed by Polish forces 459
  Imperial German Government General 450
Warsaw University 450
warships
  construction of 141
  first to be sunk by submarine 145
  operations conducted by ships not initially designed as 153
  see also dreadnoughts
Washington 279, 521
Weber, Col. Erich 102
Weber, Max 10–11, 234, 235, 434, 439
Weddingen, Capt. Otto 437
Wegerer, Alfred von 27
Weimar Republic 235, 437
  basis for emergence of parliamentary democracy 272, 442
  Europe's foremost revisionist power 549
  literature of nationalism in 439
Weir, William, Lord 167
Weiss, Pierre 309

Wekerle, Sándor 381
Wells, H. G. 236, 310, 323, 328
Weltpolitik (Germany policy to become a
    world power) 3, 9, 12–13, 432
Werth, Léon 330
West, Rebecca 330
West Africa 123
    see also French West Africa; German West
    Africa
West Prussia 436
West Riding of Yorkshire 227
Western Allies 35, 72, 76, 78, 84, 102, 116,
    129, 179
  armies 7
  basic purpose 129
  battleships 101
  casualties 250–1
  counter-attack (1918) 133–7
  demographic advantage 181
  favor breakup of Austria-Hungary 289
  fierce reaction to Brest-Litovsk (1918) 79
  Gallipoli an important theater of battle
    for 494
  German troops targeted by 290
  Germans accused of degrading traditional
    forms of combat 174
  High Command 78
  importance placed upon science 308
  important supply route blocked between
    Russia and 108
  intelligence agents 391
  Italy's secret deal with (1915) 207
  moral justification of cause 189
  naval blockade of Germany 195–6
  U-boat warfare severely criticized by 363
  see also Triple Entente
western front 40, 42, 46, 54–6, 57, 66, 90,
    127–38, 173, 190, 209, 258, 423, 429,
    435, 508, 515, 526
  accounts of atrocities 266
  African and Asian men on 115, 527
  air power 160, 161, 162, 163, 166, 182
  alternative to action on 47
  Americans present on 443
  Armistice (1918) 459, 517
  casualties/losses 182, 250, 295
  consolidation of front-line positions 174
  deadlock on 72, 101, 217
  deaths in major military encounters 254
  German defeat on 38–9, 459
  grand strategy 35
  grenades used on 175

Haig overwhelmingly concerned with 533
heavy artillery 176
light railways running the entire length
    of 218
major offensives on 45
Marines diverted to 152
mass mobilization for major military
    effort 407
mutinies 285, 287
prisoner labor under dangerous
    conditions 194
realities of leadership on 44
trench warfare 178, 179, 181, 270, 517
US sector 514
war of movement 265, 272
Wharton, Edith 329, 330
Whippet tank 183
White House 508, 514, 519
White Russia/armies 193, 443, 547, 559,
    561, 562, 568
  battlefield casualties 569
  Bolshevik opposition to 479
  civil war between Reds and 458
  refugees 560
  torture and killing of opponents 570
  see also Denikin; Kolchak; Mannerheim
White Sea 454
Wilamowitz-Moellendorf, Ulrich von 324
Wild von Hohenborn, Adolph 71
Wilhelm, Crown Prince 51, 58, 60
Wilhelm II, Emperor of Germany 10, 12, 38,
    57, 58, 62, 75, 77, 128, 207, 432, 433,
    439, 456
  abdication and exile 39, 40, 429, 444, 486
  Council of War (1912) 14
  demand for Hollweg's resignation 211
  enthusiasm for fleet 142, 144, 146
  Weltpolitik 3
Williamson, Henry 61–2
Willmer, Major Wilhelm 102
Willstätter, R. 313
Wilson, Gen. Sir Henry 566
Wilson, Woodrow 26, 196, 208–10, 213,
    235, 273, 285, 290–1, 310, 413, 444,
    473, 508, 509, 510–12, 515, 519–20,
    533, 546, 553
  Fourteen Points speech (1918) 518, 521,
    534, 545, 562
Windhoek 118, 119, 120
Winnington-Ingram, A. F., Bishop of
    London 237
Winter Palace 272

Wintgens, Capt. Max 123
Wintour, U. F. 224
wireless and cable transmission 36, 43, 143, 309
    intercepts 146, 149
Wochenschau (newsreel) 355
Wolfe (surface raider) 144
women
    adultery and 578
    against profiteers 377
    charitable solidarity with wartime causes 282
    colonials perceived as taking away jobs and 529
    contribution decisive for wartime society 441
    diversified employment for 257
    Eastern Front volunteers 330
    new roles in factories and offices 513
    noncombatant roles in armed forces 412
    over-feminization of 260
    patriotism of 272
    popular vengeance on/violence against 396, 578
    rent strikes against landlords 407
    right to vote 514
    striking 427–8
    trade unionization of 411
    widowed 259
women and men 235, 263–78
    migration from rural to urban areas 255
    roles polarized and transformed 285
Women's Army Auxiliary Corps (Britain) 271
Women's Battalion of Death (Russia) 272
Women's labor 227, 270, 411, 420, 427–8, 535
    police force (Britain) 407
Women's Peace Congress (Hague 1915) 266
Women's Peace Party (US) 509
work camps 52
working class 252, 257, 284
    life expectancy increase 255
    militancy 285
    pitting genders against each other 420
    polarization of opinion between middle class and 413
    protests about costs 266–7
    public morality 407
    red 434
    resentment 394
    substantial enlistment (Britain) 406, 412
    wage increases of condemned 284

World War II 37, 44, 184, 289, 415, 420
    avoiding clash with veterans at end of 521
    conditions imposed on much of Europe 386
    cultural remobilization and engagement 585–7
    French defeat and collaboration 20
    grand strategy 35
    horrific death toll and destructive impact 491
    made inevitable 552
    prelude to 550
    prosecution of war criminals 197
    responsibility of Nazi Germany for 28
    veterans' associations 479–80
    victorious combatants and commemorative heritage 587
wounds
    central nervous system 302
    chest 296
    facial 185, 296
    head 296, 338
    stomach 296–8
Wrangel, Gen. Piotr 560
writers 323–7, 422, 439
    patriotic 328
Wullus, Armand 397
Württemberg, Albrecht, Duke of 51

Xavier, Prince of Bourbon-Parma 212

Yambo (surrender by Ottoman troops to Arabs, 1916) 103
Yeates, V. M. 165–6
Yemen 103
Yerkes, Robert 315
Yiddish 453
Yildirim Army Group 104, 106
Yola, Emir of 117
York, Sgt Alvin 517
Young Plan (1929) 549
Young Turks 206, 494
    liberal 504
    Revolution (1908) 497
    see also Committee Union and Progress
Ypres
    first battle (1914) 42, 53, 258, 387, 437
    second battle (1915) 56, 57, 130, 181, 410
    third battle (1917) 37, 42, 45–6, 127, 131, 133, 136, 181, 183, 254, 441
Yser, battle of (1914) 334, 387, 388, 394
    commemoration of Flemish dead 397
Yudenich, Nikolai N. 100

Yugoslav Committee 378, 379
Yugoslavia 94, 377, 382, 559, 562, 564, 570, 578, 582
 blocking unity 381
 Croat allegiance to 78
 encouragement to form new state 371
 paramilitaries 567
 rise of 372
 see also Croatia, Serbia, Slovenia
Yurlova, Marina 330

Zadkine, Osip 344
Zagreb 78, 372, 374, 377, 382
Zangwill, Israël 328
Zara (Dalmatia) 94
Zayonchkovskii, Lt.-Gen. A. M. 107
Zeligowski, Gen. Lucjan 563

Zemgor (Russian wartime administrative body) 483
Zeppelins 156, 157, 160, 167
 helium for 312–13
Zetkin, Clara 266
Zhilinskii, Gen. Iakov 482
Zimmerman, Arthur 213, 511
Zimmerman, Major Karl 117
Zimmerwald (socialist anti-war meeting, Switzerland, 1915) 286
Zionists 547
Zita, Empress of Austria 212, 374
zouaves (French colonial soldiers) 527
Zürcher, Erik-Jan 497
Zurich 346, 347
Zverev, Nikolaj 325
Zweig, Stefan 326, 333